HOUSING, LAND, AND PROPERTY RESTITUTION RIGHTS OF REFUGEES AND DISPLACED PERSONS

The legal recognition of the housing, land, and property rights of refugees and displaced persons has expanded steadily in recent years as the realization has grown that securing these rights will be beneficial to long-term peace, stability, economic vitality, and justice.

This volume contains more than 240 of the laws, cases, and materials that have been adopted during the past century that accord those unjustly and arbitrarily displaced from their homes and lands with rights: not simply to return to their countries or places of origin, but to return to the original home, land, or property from which they were initially forced to flee.

The breadth of the restitution standards found within this volume, combined with selected examples of case law and other materials, is a clear indication that a right to housing, land, and property restitution for refugees and displaced persons has emerged within the global legal domain.

Scott Leckie is an international human rights lawyer and advocate. He is active in many fields, including economic and social rights, housing rights, forced evictions, housing and property restitution rights for refugees and displaced persons, human rights issues in postconflict and postdisaster situations, and business and human rights.

ALSO BY SCOTT LECKIE

United Nations Peace Operations and Housing, Land and Property Rights: Proposals for Reform (ed., 2007)

Returning Home: Housing and Property Restitution Rights of Refugees and Internally Displaced Persons, Volume 2 (ed., 2007)

Legal Resource Guide on Economic, Social and Cultural Rights (ed., with Anne Gallagher, 2006)

Returning Home: Housing and Property Restitution Rights of Refugees and Internally Displaced Persons (ed., 2003)

National Perspectives on Housing Rights (ed., 2003)

When Push Comes to Shove: Forced Evictions and Human Rights (1995)

Destruction by Design: Housing Rights Violations in Tibet (1994)

From Housing Needs to Housing Rights (1992)

Housing, Land, and Property Restitution Rights of Refugees and Displaced Persons

Laws, Cases, and Materials

Edited by

SCOTT LECKIE

Executive Director
Centre on Housing Rights and Evictions (COHRE)

CAMBRIDGE
UNIVERSITY PRESS

CAMBRIDGE UNIVERSITY PRESS
Cambridge, New York, Melbourne, Madrid, Cape Town, Singapore, São Paulo

Cambridge University Press
32 Avenue of the Americas, New York, NY 10013-2473, USA

www.cambridge.org
Information on this title: www.cambridge.org/9780521858755

First published 2007

Printed in the United States of America

A catalog record for this publication is available from the British Library.

Library of Congress Cataloging in Publication Data
Housing, land, and property restitution rights of refugees and displaced
persons : laws, cases, and materials / edited by Scott Leckie.
     p.   cm.
Includes bibliographical references and index.
ISBN-13: 978-0-521-85875-5 (hardback)
ISBN-10: 0-521-85875-5 (hardback)
1. Restitution.   2. Restitution – Cases.   3. Political refugees – Legal
status, laws, etc.   4. Right of property.   5. Repatriation.   I. Leckie, Scott.
K920.H68   2007
343′.0252 – dc22   2006039212

ISBN   978-0-521-85875-5 hardback

For all of you . . .
Blameless
Yet punished, condemned
To everyone but you . . . nameless
Gazing
Eyes of hope, worn by fear
And yet
Longingly,
The edges of a smile lurks
Dreams of home
Perpetually near

Contents

Acknowledgments

Although the preparation of a book with such sparse narrative as this may seem a quick and easy task, the ultimate completion of this volume – as they somehow always do – took far longer than originally envisaged. As it turned out, accessing, reviewing, selecting, and finally bringing together some of the literally thousands of possible standards on restitution issues was far more complex than initially foreseen at the time of the enthusiastic outset of this process.

Putting together a volume of this size and scope alone would have been truly daunting, and without the generous contribution of considerable time and energy by many friends and colleagues, it surely would have never seen the light of day.

First off, special thanks are due to Jessica Marasovic of the Centre on Housing Rights and Evictions (COHRE), who helped me itemise and access many of the standards found in this volume. Her computer-savvy ways and constantly upbeat spirit greatly assisted throughout the preparation process. Thanks also to Dima Yared for her efforts and to Rhodri Williams, who provided some of the more difficult-to-access texts concerning Bosnia-Herzegovina.

I am very thankful to the Board of Directors of COHRE, most notably our chairperson, John Packer, for approving my request to take a sabbatical leave from my position as executive director of COHRE, without which I may have never found the time to complete this and other works.

And thank you, too, to the many extraordinary people whom I met and who assisted me in so many important ways along the arduous and far too lengthy road that was required to bring this book to fruition. I was fortunate enough to have worked on this volume in a number of my favourite countries – Australia, Cambodia, Canada, Palestine, Switzerland, and Thailand – and offer anonymous thanks to the dozens of friends and other colleagues in these and other places who helped out in important but often unknown ways.

I am especially grateful to John Berger at Cambridge University Press for his support for this project and his extraordinary patience in waiting so calmly for it to come to an end.

And, as always, my deepest thanks go to Kirsten Young – The Harling – inspiration, lifesaver, soulmate, partner, source of my joy, light of my day.

Scott Leckie
Bangkok, 6 August 2006

Preface

This volume contains some 240 of the most important international, regional, and national standards and judicial decisions recognising and addressing the many complexities associated with the housing, land, and property restitution rights of refugees and displaced persons. Many additional laws, cases, and materials on these themes are also in place throughout the world, but the selection found here attempts to provide an accurate and reasonably detailed picture of the current state of affairs with respect to these rights set within their various normative contexts.

The texts included within this book – that can be seen as collectively forming the normative basis for the right of refugees and displaced persons to have restored to them the housing, land, and property rights they held at the time of their displacement – stretch back ten decades to the Hague Conventions of 1907. Throughout the past century, numerous standards have been proposed, discussed, and ultimately approved on restitution, both internationally and at the national level. Over time, these documents have become increasingly specific, in the process refining the precise rights to housing, land, and property restitution enjoyed by those forced by circumstances beyond their control to flee their homes and lands.

In many respects, 2005 was witness to a high point of international standard-setting on these issues, with two vitally important new restitution standards being approved by United Nations (UN) bodies that considerably augment the housing, land, and property restitution rights of refugees and displaced persons. In August 2005, the *'Pinheiro' Principles on Housing and Property Restitution for Refugees and Displaced Persons* (see Section 1.15 for the full text) were approved by the UN Sub-Commission on the Protection and Promotion of Human Rights. The *'Pinheiro' Principles* provide the most comprehensive and consolidated international norm outlining the rights of refugees and displaced persons to have restored to them all of the housing, land, and property rights they held before their displacement.

In December 2005, the UN General Assembly adopted the *Basic Principles and Guidelines on the Right to a Remedy and Reparation for Victims of Violations of International Human Rights and Humanitarian Law* (see Section 1.16 for the full text), which further strengthens the rights of those forced from their homes to achieve a proper remedy for these abuses through the process of restitution. Together, these two new norms exemplify both the level of specificity that has been reached in the international recognition of these rights, as well as indicating the considerable seriousness now accorded these rights by the global community.

While much of the twentieth century was rather unkind to the prospect of housing, land, and property restitution, during the past two decades millions of people throughout the world have been able to formally exercise their housing, land, and property restitution rights and return home, from Tajikistan to Kosovo, from Mozambique to Liberia, and from Bosnia-Herzegovina to South Africa and beyond. Many of the standards contained in this volume were key ingredients in the creation of conditions that led to their eventual return home. These standards have not, alas, been taken seriously in every context they should have been applied, and as a result many tens of millions of refugees and displaced persons with existing, legally recognised, and fully legitimate restitution rights are unable to exercise them because of resistance by States and others responsible for the original displacement, many of which, in fact, are due to arbitrary, discriminatory, and unfair national laws specifically designed to prevent the exercise of housing, land, and property restitution rights.

A Note on the Contents

This volume is intended to be a reference tool and consolidated source of *selected* international, regional, and national legal standards, nonlegal materials, and case law concerning the housing, land, and property restitution rights of refugees and displaced persons. This book is designed to assist those working with people asserting restitution rights – lawyers, refugee and IDP advocates, government officials, UN staff members, fieldworkers, and others – to easily access various types of standards recognising these rights within a single guide.

The volume does not provide analysis of the various standards, nor does it explain their nature, legal standing, or relative normative value. For those readers wishing to explore these issues, they may wish to review Part Five, which provides the citations of a wide range of books, articles, and other analyses of housing and property restitution issues. Most, if not all, of these standards are accessible on the Internet, and readers wishing to reference or otherwise use any of these norms are urged to examine these online to ensure that any updates, amendments, repeals, or other changes are adequately understood.

With one or two notable exceptions, every effort has been made to not include texts that have subsequently been repealed or substantially amended. However, given the frequent changes incorporated into domestic legislation, readers are again urged to confirm the current status of the national laws included in the volume before referencing them in any official manner. In one instance – that of Iraq – even though the standard contained in Section 12.4 resulted in the repeal of one of the regulations preceding it, it was felt important to retain the repealed standard to give readers a sense of the type of restitution regulations occupying powers, in this instance the United States, have proclaimed during their contentious occupation of this sovereign nation.

In the interests of preventing repetition and excessive length, considerable effort was made during the compilation of this volume to limit the number of particular types of standards, most notably relevant General Assembly resolutions and nonrefugee-specific national restitution legislation. The General Assembly, for instance, very rightly adopts essentially the same series of resolutions each year in support of the housing, land, and property restitution rights of Palestinian refugees, but this volume only includes several of the more important pronouncements in this regard, including the most recent such series of resolutions approved in 2005.

In terms of national law, a concerted effort was made to only include a select few examples of domestic legislation regulating restitution efforts in formerly communist countries. Restitution programmes were carried out in many such countries; however, given that the emphasis in this book is on the housing, land, and property restitution rights held explicitly by refugees and displaced persons, it was felt that noting *some* of the restitution laws in Eastern Europe and elsewhere would suffice in revealing the nature of these laws, how they are formulated, and, ultimately, how they differ with and or are similar to restitution laws specifically designed to benefit refugees and the displaced.

A Note on Organisation

Part One includes ten sections, each of which contain *international* texts addressing a wide variety of restitution themes. Section 1 includes sixteen international standards under international humanitarian law, international human rights law, international criminal law, international refugee law, the international law of state responsibility, and specific restitution standards.

Section 2 contains excerpts from fourteen peace agreements concluded since 1991, which explicitly or implicitly recognise housing, land, and property restitution rights for those displaced as a result of the conflict concerned. Peace agreements do not yet systematically address these issues, yet a pattern is emerging whereby constructively addressing housing, land, and property rights concerns within a rights-based peace-building process is increasingly seen as a major component of sustainable peace, reconciliation, economic viability, and overall political stability.

Twenty voluntary repatriation agreements concluded between United Nations High Commissioner for Refugees (UNHCR) and various governments are included in Section 3. Such agreements increasingly include reference to housing, land, and property issues as the international community comes to embrace the notion that successful peace-building can only take place when these issues are properly and justly addressed.

UNHCR's role in strengthening restitution norms for refugees has been a vital one and, in recognition of this, beyond the agreements found in Section 3, five additional UNHCR texts are included in Section 4.

Section 5 includes full texts and excerpts of thirty-nine resolutions adopted by the UN Security Council since 1967 that affirm and reaffirm the crucial nature of protecting the housing, land, and property restitution rights of refugees and others forcibly displaced from their homes and lands.

Similarly, the UN General Assembly has addressed restitution issues since its inception, and as a result, scores of resolutions have been approved by this body, thirty-three of which are included in Section 6 of this volume.

The UN human rights machinery has also become increasingly involved in efforts to promote the housing, land, and property rights of refugees and displaced persons, and various resolutions and other standards approved by the Commission on Human Rights (now "Human Rights Council"), Sub-Commission on the Protection and Promotion of Human Rights, and several human rights treaty bodies are included in Sections 7–9. Section 10 contains two relevant standards approved by expert bodies, which address or are relevant to restitution themes.

Part Two provides several *regional* standards that address housing, land, and property restitution issues in Africa, the Americas, Europe, and the Middle East.

Part Three of the volume contains forty *national* laws and other statements enshrining housing, land, and property restitution rights. Laws from the following sixteen countries are provided: Afghanistan, Albania, Armenia, Azerbaijan, Bosnia-Herzegovina, Bulgaria, Colombia, Estonia, Georgia, Germany, Iraq, Kosovo, Romania, Rwanda, South Africa, and Tajikistan.

Part Four contains selected case law from four adjudicating bodies: the Permanent Court of International Justice, the International Court of Justice, the UN Human Rights Committee, and the European Court on Human Rights. Readers should note that although most of the cases included essentially support the contention that refugees, displaced persons, or other human rights vic-

tims possess housing, land, and property rights, in some instances cases have been included that are more nuanced or even nonsupportive of such perspectives.

Finally, Part Five provides a selected bibliography of various publications addressing different dimensions of the housing, land, and property restitution question.

Readers should note that the various documents found in this book have been organised in descending order, with each section beginning with the oldest documents and ending with the newest.

A Note on What Is Not Included

Although not as numerous as laws in support of restitution rights, many countries have adopted legislation consciously designed to *prevent* the exercise of housing, land, and property rights by refugees and displaced persons. Israel's absentee property laws, Bhutan's nationality laws, housing laws in Croatia, Rwandan legislation on refugee return, and many other pieces of existing law remain in place at the national level in spite of the clear preponderance of normative evidence found in this volume that those displaced from their homes have a right to return to and repossess those homes.

The texts of such laws are not included in the present volume, although the idea of systematically compiling these antirestitution laws into a separate volume may have considerable merit, and anyone wishing to make a positive contribution to the restitution question may well consider undertaking such an exercise.

A Note on Sources

As noted, most of the documents included within this volume are available electronically on the Internet, with the exception of voluntary repatriation agreements and some of the national laws outlined here. Full texts of those available online can best be accessed through the following Web sites:

(1) http://un.org for Part One – Section 1 (International Standards), Section 5 (UN Security Council), Section 6 (UN General Assembly), Section 7 (UN Commission on Human Rights), Section 8

(UN Sub-Commission on the Protection and Promotion of Human Rights), and Section 9 (UN Human Rights Treaty Bodies) and Part Four – Sections 2 and 3;

(2) http://www.usip.org/library/pa.html for Part One – Section 2 (Peace Agreements);

(3) http://www.unhcr.org/cgi-bin/texis/vtx/rsd for Part One – Section 3 (Voluntary Repatriation Agreements) and Section 4 (UN High Commissioner for Refugees);

(4) http://www.worldcourts.com for Part Four – Section 1 (Permanent Court of International Justice); and

(5) http://www.echr.coe.int/ECHR/EN/Header/Case-Law/HUDOC/HUDOC+database for Part Four – Section 4 (European Court of Human Rights).

PART ONE

Housing and Property Restitution Standards – International

1. INTERNATIONAL STANDARDS

INTERNATIONAL HUMANITARIAN LAW

1.1. Hague Convention (IV) Respecting the Laws and Customs of War on Land (1907)[1]

[. . .]

SECTION II – HOSTILITIES – CHAPTER I – MEANS OF INJURING THE ENEMY

[. . .]

Article 23

In addition to the prohibitions provided by special Conventions, it is especially forbidden

[. . .]

(g) To destroy or seize the enemy's property, unless such destruction or seizure be imperatively demanded by the necessities of war;

(h) To declare abolished, suspended, or inadmissible in a court of law the rights and actions of the nationals of the hostile party . . .

[. . .]

Article 25

The attack or bombardment, by whatever means, of towns, villages, dwellings, or buildings which are undefended is prohibited.

[. . .]

Article 28

The pillage of a town or place, even when taken by assault, is prohibited.

[. . .]

1.2. Geneva Convention (IV) Relative to the Protection of Civilian Persons in Time of War (1949)[2]

[. . .]

Article 33

No protected person may be punished for an offence he or she has not personally committed. Collective penalties and likewise all measures of intimidation or of terrorism are prohibited.

Pillage is prohibited.

Reprisals against protected persons and their property are prohibited.

[. . .]

Article 45

Protected persons shall not be transferred to a Power which is not a party to the Convention.

This provision shall in no way constitute an obstacle to the repatriation of protected persons, or to their return to their country of residence after the cessation of hostilities.

Article 46

In so far as they have not been previously withdrawn, restrictive measures taken regarding

---

[1] Adopted on 18 October 1907 and entered into force on 26 January 1910.

[2] Adopted on 12 August 1949 by the Diplomatic Conference for the Establishment of International Conventions for the Protection of Victims of War, held in Geneva from 21 April to 12 August 1949 and entered into force on 21 October 1950.

protected persons shall be cancelled as soon as possible after the close of hostilities.

Restrictive measures affecting their property shall be cancelled, in accordance with the law of the Detaining Power, as soon as possible after the close of hostilities.

[. . .]

Article 49

Individual or mass forcible transfers, as well as deportations of protected persons from occupied territory to the territory of the Occupying Power or that of any other country, occupied or not, are prohibited, regardless of their motive.

Nevertheless, the occupying Power may undertake total or partial evacuation of a given area if the security of the population or imperative military reasons so demand. Such evacuations may not involve the displacement of protected persons outside the bounds of the occupied territory except when for material reasons it is impossible to avoid such displacement. Persons thus evacuated shall be transferred back to their homes as soon as hostilities in the area in question have ceased.

The Occupying Power undertaking such transfers or evacuations shall ensure, to the greatest practicable extent, that proper accommodation is provided to receive the protected persons, that the removals are effected in satisfactory conditions of hygiene, health, safety and nutrition, and that members of the same family are not separated.

The Protecting Power shall be informed of any transfers and evacuations as soon as they have taken place.

The Occupying Power shall not detain protected persons in an area particularly exposed to the dangers of war unless the security of the population or imperative military reasons so demand.

The Occupying Power shall not deport or transfer parts of its own civilian population into the territory it occupies.

[. . .]

Article 53

Any destruction by the Occupying Power of real or personal property belonging individually or collectively to private persons, or to the State, or to other public authorities, or to social or cooperative organizations, is prohibited, except where such destruction is rendered absolutely necessary by military operations.

[. . .]

Article 147

Grave breaches . . . shall be those involving any of the following acts, if committed against persons or property protected by the present Convention: . . . extensive destruction and appropriation of property, not justified by military necessity and carried out unlawfully and wantonly.

[. . .]

1.3. Protocol Additional to the Geneva Conventions of 12 August 1949, and Relating to the Protection of Victims of International Armed Conflicts (Protocol 1) (1977)[3]

[. . .]

Chapter III – Civilian Objectives

Article 52 – General Protection of Civilian Objects

1. Civilian objects shall not be the object of attack or of reprisals. Civilian objects are all objects which are not military objectives as defined in paragraph 2.

2. Attacks shall be limited strictly to military objectives. In so far as objects are concerned, military objectives are limited to those objects which by their nature, location, purpose or use make an effective contribution to military action and whose total or partial destruction, capture or neutralization, in the circumstances ruling at the time, offers a definite military advantage.

3. In case of doubt whether an object which is normally dedicated to civilian purposes, such as a place of worship, a house or other dwelling or a school, is being used to make an effective contribution to military action, it shall be presumed not to be so used.

[. . .]

---

[3] Adopted on 8 June 1977 and entered into force 7 December 1978 in accordance with Article 95.

SECTION III – TREATMENT OF PERSONS IN THE POWER OF A PARTY TO THE CONFLICT

Chapter I – Field of Application and Protection of Persons and Objects

Article 73 – Refugees and Stateless Persons

Persons who, before the beginning of hostilities, were considered as stateless persons or refugees under the relevant international instruments accepted by the Parties concerned or under the national legislation of the State of refuge or State of residence shall be protected persons within the meaning of Parts I and III of the Fourth Convention, in all circumstances and without any adverse distinction.

[. . .]

1.4. Protocol Additional to the Geneva Conventions of 12 August 1949, and Relating to the Protection of Victims of Non-International Armed Conflicts (Protocol II) (1977)[4]

[. . .]

Article 13 – Protection of the Civilian Population

1. The civilian population and individual civilians shall enjoy general protection against the dangers arising from military operations. To give effect to this protection, the following rules shall be observed in all circumstances.

2. The civilian population as such, as well as individual civilians, shall not be the object of attack. Acts or threats of violence the primary purpose of which is to spread terror among the civilian population are prohibited.

3. Civilians shall enjoy the protection afforded by this Part, unless and for such time as they take a direct part in hostilities.

[. . .]

Article 17 – Prohibition of Forced Movement of Civilians

1. The displacement of the civilian population shall not be ordered for reasons related to the conflict

[4] Adopted on 8 June and entered into force on 7 December 1978 in accordance with Article 23.

unless the security of the civilians involved or imperative military reasons so demand. Should such displacements have to be carried out, all possible measures shall be taken in order that the civilian population may be received under satisfactory conditions of shelter, hygiene, health, safety and nutrition.

2. Civilians shall not be compelled to leave their own territory for reasons connected with the conflict.

[. . .]

INTERNATIONAL HUMAN RIGHTS LAW

1.5. Universal Declaration of Human Rights (1948)[5]

[. . .]

Article 8

Everyone has the right to an effective remedy by the competent national tribunals for acts violating the fundamental rights granted him by the constitution or by law.

[. . .]

Article 17

1. Everyone has the right to own property alone as well as in association with others.

2. No one shall be arbitrarily deprived of his property.

[. . .]

Article 25

1. Everyone has the right to a standard of living adequate for the health and well-being of himself and of his family, including food, clothing, housing and medical care and necessary social services, and the right to security in the event of unemployment, sickness, disability, widowhood, old age or other lack of livelihood in circumstances beyond his control.

[. . .]

[5] Adopted on 10 December 1948.

1.6. International Convention on the Elimination of All Forms of Racial Discrimination (1965)[6]

[...]

Article 5(e)(iii)

In compliance with the fundamental obligations laid down in article 2 of this Convention, States Parties undertake to prohibit and eliminate racial discrimination in all of its forms and to guarantee the right of everyone, without distinction as to race, colour, or national or ethnic origin, to equality before the law, notably in the enjoyment of the following rights: ... (e) in particular ... (iii) the right to housing.

[...]

Article 6

States Parties shall assure to everyone within their jurisdiction effective protection and remedies, through the competent national tribunals and other State institutions, against any acts of racial discrimination which violate his human rights and fundamental freedoms contrary to this Convention, as well as the right to seek from such tribunals just and adequate reparation or satisfaction for any damage suffered as a result of such discrimination.

[...]

1.7. International Covenant on Economic, Social and Cultural Rights (1966)[7]

[...]

Article 2

1. Each State Party to the present Covenant undertakes to take steps, individually and through international assistance and co-operation, especially economic and technical, to the maximum of its available resources, with a view to achieving progressively the full realization of the rights recognized in the present Covenant by all appropriate means, including particularly the adoption of legislative measures.

2. The States Parties to the present Covenant undertake to guarantee that the rights enunciated in the present Covenant will be exercised without discrimination of any kind as to race, colour, sex, language, religion, political or other opinion, national or social origin, property, birth or other status.

3. Developing countries, with due regard to human rights and their national economy, may determine to what extent they would guarantee the economic rights recognized in the present Covenant to non-nationals.

[...]

Article 11

1. The States Parties to the present Covenant recognize the right of everyone to an adequate standard of living for himself and his family, including adequate food, clothing and housing, and to the continuous improvement of living conditions. The States Parties will take appropriate steps to ensure the realization of this right, recognizing to this effect the essential importance of international co-operation based on free consent.

[...]

1.8. International Covenant on Civil and Political Rights (1966)[8]

[...]

PART II

Article 2

1. Each State Party to the present Covenant undertakes to respect and to ensure to all individuals within its territory and subject to its jurisdiction the rights recognized in the present Covenant, without distinction of any kind, such as race, colour, sex, language, religion, political or other opinion, national or social origin, property, birth or other status.

---

[6] Adopted on 21 December 1965 and entered into force on 4 January 1969 in accordance with Article 19.

[7] Adopted on 16 December 1966 and entered into force on 23 March 1976 in accordance with Article 27.

[8] Adopted on 16 December 1966 and entered into force on 23 March 1976 in accordance with Article 49.

2. Where not already provided for by existing legislative or other measures, each State Party to the present Covenant undertakes to take the necessary steps, in accordance with its constitutional processes and with the provisions of the present Covenant, to adopt such laws or other measures as may be necessary to give effect to the rights recognized in the present Covenant.

3. Each State Party to the present Covenant undertakes:

(a) To ensure that any person whose rights or freedoms as herein recognized are violated shall have an effective remedy, notwithstanding that the violation has been committed by persons acting in an official capacity;

(b) To ensure that any person claiming such a remedy shall have his right thereto determined by competent judicial, administrative or legislative authorities, or by any other competent authority provided for by the legal system of the State, and to develop the possibilities of judicial remedy;

(c) To ensure that the competent authorities shall enforce such remedies when granted.

[. . .]

Part III

Article 12

1. Everyone lawfully within the territory of a State shall, within that territory, have the right to liberty of movement and freedom to choose his residence.

2. Everyone shall be free to leave any country, including his own.

3. The above-mentioned rights shall not be subject to any restrictions except those which are provided by law, are necessary to protect national security, public order (ordre public), public health or morals or the rights and freedoms of others, and are consistent with the other rights recognized in the present Covenant.

4. No one shall be arbitrarily deprived of the right to enter his own country.

[. . .]

Article 17

1. No one shall be subjected to arbitrary or unlawful interference with his privacy, family, home or correspondence, nor to unlawful attacks on his honour and reputation.

2. Everyone has the right to the protection of the law against such interference or attacks.

[. . .]

1.9. Convention on the Rights of the Child (1989)[9]

[. . .]

Article 16

1. No child shall be subjected to arbitrary or unlawful interference with his or her privacy, family, home or correspondence, nor to unlawful attacks on his or her honour and reputation.

2. The child has the right to the protection of the law against such interference or attacks.

[. . .]

Article 22

1. States Parties shall take appropriate measures to ensure that a child who is seeking refugee status or who is considered a refugee in accordance with applicable international or domestic law and procedures shall, whether unaccompanied or accompanied by his or her parents or by any other person, receive appropriate protection and humanitarian assistance in the enjoyment of applicable rights set forth in the present Convention and in other international human rights or humanitarian instruments to which the said States are Parties.

2. For this purpose, States Parties shall provide, as they consider appropriate, co-operation in any efforts by the United Nations and other competent intergovernmental organizations or non-governmental organizations co-operating with the United Nations to protect and assist such a child and to trace the parents or other members of the family of any refugee child in order to obtain

[9] Adopted on 20 November 1989 and entered into force on 2 September 1990 in accordance with Article 49.

information necessary for reunification with his or her family. In cases where no parents or other members of the family can be found, the child shall be accorded the same protection as any other child permanently or temporarily deprived of his or her family environment for any reason, as set forth in the present Convention.

[...]

1.10. Convention (No. 169) Concerning Indigenous and Tribal Peoples in Independent Countries (1989)[10]

[...]

Article 16

1. Subject to the following paragraphs of this Article, the peoples concerned shall not be removed from the lands which they occupy.

2. Where the relocation of these peoples is considered necessary as an exceptional measure, such relocation shall take place only with their free and informed consent. Where their consent cannot be obtained, such relocation shall take place only following appropriate procedures established by national laws and regulations, including public inquiries where appropriate, which provide the opportunity for effective representation of the peoples concerned.

3. Whenever possible, these peoples shall have the right to return to their traditional lands, as soon as the grounds for relocation cease to exist.

4. When such return is not possible, as determined by agreement or, in the absence of such agreement, through appropriate procedures, these peoples shall be provided in all possible cases with lands of quality and legal status at least equal to that of the lands previously occupied by them, suitable to provide for their present needs and future development. Where the peoples concerned express a preference for compensation in money or in kind, they shall be so compensated under appropriate guarantees.

---

[10] Adopted on 27 June 1989 and entered into force on 5 September 1991 in accordance with Article 38.

5. Persons thus relocated shall be fully compensated for any resulting loss or injury.

[...]

INTERNATIONAL CRIMINAL LAW

1.11. Rome Statute of the International Criminal Court (1998)[11]

[...]

Article 5 – Crimes within the Jurisdiction of the Court

1. The jurisdiction of the Court shall be limited to the most serious crimes of concern to the international community as a whole. The Court has jurisdiction in accordance with this Statute with respect to the following crimes:

(a) The crime of genocide;

(b) Crimes against humanity;

(c) War crimes;

(d) The crime of aggression.

2. The Court shall exercise jurisdiction over the crime of aggression once a provision is adopted in accordance with articles 121 and 123 defining the crime and setting out the conditions under which the Court shall exercise jurisdiction with respect to this crime. Such a provision shall be consistent with the relevant provisions of the Charter of the United Nations.

Article 6 – Genocide

For the purpose of this Statute, "genocide" means any of the following acts committed with intent to destroy, in whole or in part, a national, ethnical, racial or religious group, as such:

(a) Killing members of the group;

(b) Causing serious bodily or mental harm to members of the group;

(c) Deliberately inflicting on the group conditions of life calculated to bring about its physical destruction in whole or in part;

(d) Imposing measures intended to prevent births within the group;

---

[11] Adopted on 17 July 1998 and entered into force on 1 July 2002 in accordance with Article 126.

(e) Forcibly transferring children of the group to another group.

Article 7 – Crimes against Humanity

1. For the purpose of this Statute, "crime against humanity" means any of the following acts when committed as part of a widespread or systematic attack directed against any civilian population, with knowledge of the attack:

(a) Murder;

(b) Extermination;

(c) Enslavement;

(d) Deportation or forcible transfer of population;

(e) Imprisonment or other severe deprivation of physical liberty in violation of fundamental rules of international law;

(f) Torture;

(g) Rape, sexual slavery, enforced prostitution, forced pregnancy, enforced sterilization, or any other form of sexual violence of comparable gravity;

(h) Persecution against any identifiable group or collectivity on political, racial, national, ethnic, cultural, religious, gender as defined in paragraph 3, or other grounds that are universally recognized as impermissible under international law, in connection with any act referred to in this paragraph or any crime within the jurisdiction of the Court;

(i) Enforced disappearance of persons;

(j) The crime of apartheid;

(k) Other inhumane acts of a similar character intentionally causing great suffering, or serious injury to body or to mental or physical health.

2. For the purpose of paragraph 1:

(a) "Attack directed against any civilian population" means a course of conduct involving the multiple commission of acts referred to in paragraph 1 against any civilian population, pursuant to or in furtherance of a State or organizational policy to commit such attack;

(b) "Extermination" includes the intentional infliction of conditions of life, inter alia the deprivation of access to food and medicine, calculated to bring about the destruction of part of a population;

(c) "Enslavement" means the exercise of any or all of the powers attaching to the right of ownership over a person and includes the exercise of such power in the course of trafficking in persons, in particular women and children;

(d) "Deportation or forcible transfer of population" means forced displacement of the persons concerned by expulsion or other coercive acts from the area in which they are lawfully present, without grounds permitted under international law;

(e) "Torture" means the intentional infliction of severe pain or suffering, whether physical or mental, upon a person in the custody or under the control of the accused; except that torture shall not include pain or suffering arising only from, inherent in or incidental to, lawful sanctions;

(f) "Forced pregnancy" means the unlawful confinement of a woman forcibly made pregnant, with the intent of affecting the ethnic composition of any population or carrying out other grave violations of international law. This definition shall not in any way be interpreted as affecting national laws relating to pregnancy;

(g) "Persecution" means the intentional and severe deprivation of fundamental rights contrary to international law by reason of the identity of the group or collectivity;

(h) "The crime of apartheid" means inhumane acts of a character similar to those referred to in paragraph 1, committed in the context of an institutionalized regime of systematic oppression and domination by one racial group over any other racial group or groups and committed with the intention of maintaining that regime;

(i) "Enforced disappearance of persons" means the arrest, detention or abduction of persons by, or with the authorization, support or acquiescence of, a State or a political organization, followed by a refusal to acknowledge that deprivation of freedom or to give information on the fate or whereabouts of those persons, with the intention of removing them from the protection of the law for a prolonged period of time.

3. For the purpose of this Statute, it is understood that the term "gender" refers to the two sexes, male and female, within the context of society. The term "gender" does not indicate any meaning different from the above.

Article 8 – War Crimes

1. The Court shall have jurisdiction in respect of war crimes in particular when committed as part of a plan or policy or as part of a large-scale commission of such crimes.

2. For the purpose of this Statute, "war crimes" means:

(a) Grave breaches of the Geneva Conventions of 12 August 1949, namely, any of the following acts against persons or property protected under the provisions of the relevant Geneva Convention:

(i) Wilful killing;

(ii) Torture or inhuman treatment, including biological experiments;

(iii) Wilfully causing great suffering, or serious injury to body or health;

(iv) Extensive destruction and appropriation of property, not justified by military necessity and carried out unlawfully and wantonly;

(v) Compelling a prisoner of war or other protected person to serve in the forces of a hostile Power;

(vi) Wilfully depriving a prisoner of war or other protected person of the rights of fair and regular trial;

(vii) Unlawful deportation or transfer or unlawful confinement;

(viii) Taking of hostages.

(b) Other serious violations of the laws and customs applicable in international armed conflict, within the established framework of international law, namely, any of the following acts:

(i) Intentionally directing attacks against the civilian population as such or against individual civilians not taking direct part in hostilities;

(ii) Intentionally directing attacks against civilian objects, that is, objects which are not military objectives;

(iii) Intentionally directing attacks against personnel, installations, material, units or vehicles involved in a humanitarian assistance or peacekeeping mission in accordance with the Charter of the United Nations, as long as they are entitled to the protection given to civilians or civilian objects under the international law of armed conflict;

(iv) Intentionally launching an attack in the knowledge that such attack will cause incidental loss of life or injury to civilians or damage to civilian objects or widespread, long-term and severe damage to the natural environment which would be clearly excessive in relation to the concrete and direct overall military advantage anticipated;

(v) Attacking or bombarding, by whatever means, towns, villages, dwellings or buildings which are undefended and which are not military objectives;

(vi) Killing or wounding a combatant who, having laid down his arms or having no longer means of defence, has surrendered at discretion;

(vii) Making improper use of a flag of truce, of the flag or of the military insignia and uniform of the enemy or of the United Nations, as well as of the distinctive emblems of the Geneva Conventions, resulting in death or serious personal injury;

(viii) The transfer, directly or indirectly, by the Occupying Power of parts of its own civilian population into the territory it occupies, or the deportation or transfer of all or parts of the population of the occupied territory within or outside this territory;

(ix) Intentionally directing attacks against buildings dedicated to religion, education, art, science or charitable purposes, historic monuments, hospitals and places where the sick and wounded are collected, provided they are not military objectives;

(x) Subjecting persons who are in the power of an adverse party to physical mutilation or to medical or scientific experiments of any kind which are neither justified by the medical, dental or hospital treatment of the person concerned nor carried out in his or her interest, and which cause death to or seriously endanger the health of such person or persons;

(xi) Killing or wounding treacherously individuals belonging to the hostile nation or army;

(xii) Declaring that no quarter will be given;

(xiii) Destroying or seizing the enemy's property unless such destruction or seizure be imperatively demanded by the necessities of war;

(xiv) Declaring abolished, suspended or inadmissible in a court of law the rights and actions of the nationals of the hostile party;

(xv) Compelling the nationals of the hostile party to take part in the operations of war directed against their own country, even if they were in the belligerent's service before the commencement of the war;

(xvi) Pillaging a town or place, even when taken by assault;

(xvii) Employing poison or poisoned weapons;

(xviii) Employing asphyxiating, poisonous or other gases, and all analogous liquids, materials or devices;

(xix) Employing bullets which expand or flatten easily in the human body, such as bullets with a hard envelope which does not entirely cover the core or is pierced with incisions;

(xx) Employing weapons, projectiles and material and methods of warfare which are of a nature to cause superfluous injury or unnecessary suffering or which are inherently indiscriminate in violation of the international law of armed conflict, provided that such weapons, projectiles and material and methods of warfare are the subject of a comprehensive prohibition and are included in an annex to this Statute, by an amendment in accordance with the relevant provisions set forth in articles 121 and 123;

(xxi) Committing outrages upon personal dignity, in particular humiliating and degrading treatment;

(xxii) Committing rape, sexual slavery, enforced prostitution, forced pregnancy, as defined in article 7, paragraph 2 (f), enforced sterilization, or any other form of sexual violence also constituting a grave breach of the Geneva Conventions;

(xxiii) Utilizing the presence of a civilian or other protected person to render certain points, areas or military forces immune from military operations;

(xxiv) Intentionally directing attacks against buildings, material, medical units and transport, and personnel using the distinctive emblems of the Geneva Conventions in conformity with international law;

(xxv) Intentionally using starvation of civilians as a method of warfare by depriving them of objects indispensable to their survival, including wilfully impeding relief supplies as provided for under the Geneva Conventions;

(xxvi) Conscripting or enlisting children under the age of fifteen years into the national armed forces or using them to participate actively in hostilities.

(c) In the case of an armed conflict not of an international character, serious violations of article 3 common to the four Geneva Conventions of 12 August 1949, namely, any of the following acts committed against persons taking no active part in the hostilities, including members of armed forces who have laid down their arms and those placed hors de combat by sickness, wounds, detention or any other cause:

(i) Violence to life and person, in particular murder of all kinds, mutilation, cruel treatment and torture;

(ii) Committing outrages upon personal dignity, in particular humiliating and degrading treatment;

(iii) Taking of hostages;

(iv) The passing of sentences and the carrying out of executions without previous judgement pronounced by a regularly constituted court, affording all judicial guarantees which are generally recognized as indispensable.

(d) Paragraph 2 (c) applies to armed conflicts not of an international character and thus does not apply to situations of internal disturbances and tensions, such as riots, isolated and sporadic acts of violence or other acts of a similar nature.

(e) Other serious violations of the laws and customs applicable in armed conflicts not of an international character, within the established framework of international law, namely, any of the following acts:

(i) Intentionally directing attacks against the civilian population as such or against individual civilians not taking direct part in hostilities;

(ii) Intentionally directing attacks against buildings, material, medical units and transport, and personnel using the distinctive emblems of the Geneva Conventions in conformity with international law;

(iii) Intentionally directing attacks against personnel, installations, material, units or vehicles involved in a humanitarian assistance or peacekeeping mission in accordance with the Charter of the United Nations, as long as they are entitled to the protection given to civilians or civilian objects under the international law of armed conflict;

(iv) Intentionally directing attacks against buildings dedicated to religion, education, art, science or charitable purposes, historic monuments, hospitals and places where the sick and wounded are collected, provided they are not military objectives;

(v) Pillaging a town or place, even when taken by assault;

(vi) Committing rape, sexual slavery, enforced prostitution, forced pregnancy, as defined in article 7, paragraph 2 (f), enforced sterilization, and any other form of sexual violence also constituting a serious violation of article 3 common to the four Geneva Conventions;

(vii) Conscripting or enlisting children under the age of fifteen years into armed forces or groups or using them to participate actively in hostilities;

(viii) Ordering the displacement of the civilian population for reasons related to the conflict, unless the security of the civilians involved or imperative military reasons so demand;

(ix) Killing or wounding treacherously a combatant adversary;

(x) Declaring that no quarter will be given;

(xi) Subjecting persons who are in the power of another party to the conflict to physical mutilation or to medical or scientific experiments of any kind which are neither justified by the medical, dental or hospital treatment of the person concerned nor carried out in his or her interest, and which cause death to or seriously endanger the health of such person or persons;

(xii) Destroying or seizing the property of an adversary unless such destruction or seizure be imperatively demanded by the necessities of the conflict;

(f) Paragraph 2 (e) applies to armed conflicts not of an international character and thus does not apply to situations of internal disturbances and tensions, such as riots, isolated and sporadic acts of violence or other acts of a similar nature. It applies to armed conflicts that take place in the territory of a State when there is protracted armed conflict between governmental authorities and organized armed groups or between such groups.

3. Nothing in paragraph 2 (c) and (e) shall affect the responsibility of a Government to maintain or re-establish law and order in the State or to defend the unity and territorial integrity of the State, by all legitimate means.

[. . .]

Article 75 – Reparation to Victims

1. The Court shall establish principles relating to reparations to, or in respect of, victims, including restitution, compensation and rehabilitation. On this basis, in its decision the Court may, either upon request or on its own motion in exceptional circumstances, determine the scope and extent of any damage, loss and injury to, or in respect of, victims and will state the principles on which it is acting.

2. The Court may make an order directly against a convicted person specifying appropriate reparations to, or in respect of, victims, including restitution, compensation and rehabilitation.

Where appropriate, the Court may order that the award for reparations be made through the Trust Fund provided for in article 79.

3. Before making an order under this article, the Court may invite and shall take account of representations from or on behalf of the convicted person, victims, other interested persons or interested States.

4. In exercising its power under this article, the Court may, after a person is convicted of a crime within the jurisdiction of the Court, determine whether, in order to give effect to an order which it may make under this article, it is necessary to seek measures under article 93, paragraph 1.

5. A State Party shall give effect to a decision under this article as if the provisions of article 109 were applicable to this article.

6. Nothing in this article shall be interpreted as prejudicing the rights of victims under national or international law.

[. . .]

INTERNATIONAL REFUGEE LAW

1.12. Convention Relating to the Status of Refugees (1951)[12]

[. . .]

Article 21 – Housing

As regards housing, the Contracting States, in so far as the matter is regulated by laws or regulations or is subject to the control of public authorities, shall accord to refugees lawfully staying in their territory treatment as favourable as possible and, in any event, not less favourable than that accorded to aliens generally in the same circumstances.

[. . .]

Article 26 – Freedom of Movement

Each Contracting State shall accord to refugees lawfully in its territory the right to choose their place of residence to move freely within its territory, subject to any regulations applicable to aliens generally in the same circumstances.

[. . .]

1.13. Protocol Relating to the Status of Refugees (1967)[13]

The States Parties to the present Protocol,

Considering that the Convention relating to the Status of Refugees done at Geneva on 28 July 1951 (hereinafter referred to as the Convention) covers only those persons who have become refugees as a result of events occurring before 1 January 1951,

Considering that new refugee situations have arisen since the Convention was adopted and that the refugees concerned may therefore not fall within the scope of the Convention,

Considering that it is desirable that equal status should be enjoyed by all refugees covered by the definition in the Convention irrespective of the dateline 1 January 1951,

---

[12] Adopted on 28 July 1951 and entered into force on 22 April 1954, in accordance with Article 43.
[13] Adopted on 16 December 1966 and entered into force on 4 October 1967 in accordance with Article 8.

Have agreed as follows:

Article 1 – General Provisions

1. The States Parties to the present Protocol undertake to apply articles 2 to 34 inclusive of the Convention to refugees as hereinafter defined.

2. For the purpose of the present Protocol, the term "refugee" shall, except as regards the application of paragraph 3 of this article, mean any person within the definition of article I of the Convention as if the words "As a result of events occurring before 1 January 1951 and . . . " and the words ". . . as a result of such events", in article 1 A (2) were omitted.

3. The present Protocol shall be applied by the States Parties hereto without any geographic limitation, save that existing declarations made by States already Parties to the Convention in accordance with article I B (I) (a) of the Convention, shall, unless extended under article I B (2) thereof, apply also under the present Protocol.

Article 2 – Co-Operation of the National Authorities with the United Nations

1. The States Parties to the present Protocol undertake to co-operate with the Office of the United Nations High Commissioner for Refugees, or any other agency of the United Nations which may succeed it, in the exercise of its functions, and shall in particular facilitate its duty of supervising the application of the provisions of the present Protocol.

2. In order to enable the Office of the High Commissioner or any other agency of the United Nations which may succeed it, to make reports to the competent organs of the United Nations, the States Parties to the present Protocol undertake to provide them with the information and statistical data requested, in the appropriate form, concerning:

(a) The condition of refugees;

(b) The implementation of the present Protocol;

(c) Laws, regulations and decrees which are, or may hereafter be, in force relating to refugees.

Article 3 – Information on National Legislation

The States Parties to the present Protocol shall communicate to the Secretary-General of the United Nations the laws and regulations which they may adopt to ensure the application of the present Protocol.

[. . .]

THE INTERNATIONAL LAW OF STATE RESPONSIBILITY

1.14. International Law Commission's Draft Articles on Responsibility of States for Internationally Wrongful Acts (2001)[14]

[. . .]

Article 3

The characterization of an act of a State as internationally wrongful is governed by international law. Such characterization in not affected by the characterization of the same act lawful by internal law.

[. . .]

Article 14(2)

The breach of an international obligation by an act of a State having a continuing character extends over the entire period during which the act continues and remains not in conformity with the international obligation.

[. . .]

Article 29

The legal consequences of an internationally wrongful act under the Part do not affect the continued duty of the responsible State to perform the obligation breached.

Article 30

The State responsible for the internationally wrongful act is under an obligation: (b) to offer appropriate assurances and guarantees of non-repetition, if circumstances so require.

Article 31

The responsible State may not rely on the provisions of its internal law as justification for failure to comply with its obligations.

---

[14] Fifty-Third Session (2001) Extract from the Report of the International Law Commission on the work of its Fifty-Third Session, Official Records of the General Assembly, Fifty-Sixth Session, Supplement No. 10 (A/56/10), ch.IV.E.1.

[. . .]

Reparation for Injury

Article 34 – Forms of Reparation

Full reparation for the injury caused by the internationally wrongful act shall take the form of restitution, compensation and satisfaction, either singly or in combination, in accordance with the provisions of this chapter.

Article 35 – Restitution

A State responsible for an internationally wrongful act is under an obligation to make restitution, that is, to re-establish the situation which existed before the wrongful act was committed, provided and to the extent that restitution:

(a) Is not materially impossible;

(b) Does not involve a burden out of all proportion to the benefit deriving from restitution instead of compensation.

Article 36 – Compensation

1. The State responsible for an internationally wrongful act is under an obligation to compensate for the damage caused thereby, insofar as such damage is not made good by restitution.

2. The compensation shall cover any financially assessable damage including loss of profits insofar as it is established.

Article 37 – Satisfaction

1. The State responsible for an internationally wrongful act is under an obligation to give satisfaction for the injury caused by that act insofar as it cannot be made good by restitution or compensation.

2. Satisfaction may consist in an acknowledgement of the breach, an expression of regret, a formal apology or another appropriate modality.

3. Satisfaction shall not be out of proportion to the injury and may not take a form humiliating to the responsible State.

Article 38

1. The State responsible for an internationally wrongful act is under an obligation to give satisfaction for the injury caused by that act insofar as

it cannot be made good by restitution or compensation.

2. Satisfaction may consist in an acknowledgement of the breach, an expression of regret, a formal apology or another appropriate modality.

3. Satisfaction shall not be out of proportion to the injury and may not take a form humiliating to the responsible State.

[. . .]

SPECIFIC RESTITUTION STANDARDS

1.15. 'Pinheiro' Principles on Housing and Property Restitution for Refugees and Displaced Persons (2005)[15]

PREAMBLE

Recognizing that millions of refugees and displaced persons worldwide continue to live in precarious and uncertain situations, and that all refugees and displaced persons have a right to voluntary return, in safety and dignity, to their original or former habitual homes and lands;

Underscoring that voluntary return in safety and dignity must be based on a free, informed, individual choice and that refugees and displaced persons should be provided with complete, objective, up to date, and accurate information, including on physical, material and legal safety issues in countries or places of origin;

Reaffirming the rights of refugee and displaced women and girls, and recognizing the need to undertake positive measures to ensure that their rights to housing, land and property restitution are guaranteed;

Welcoming the many national and international institutions that have been established in recent years to ensure the restitution rights of refugees and displaced persons, as well as the many national and international laws, standards, policy statements, agreements and guidelines that have recognized

and reaffirmed the right to housing, land and property restitution;

Convinced that the right to housing, land and property restitution is essential to the resolution of conflict and to post-conflict peace-building, safe and sustainable return and the establishment of the rule of law, and that careful monitoring of restitution Programs, on the part of international organizations and affected states, is indispensable to ensuring their effective implementation;

Convinced also that the implementation of successful housing, land and property restitution Programs, as a key element of restorative justice, contributes to effectively deterring future situations of displacement and building sustainable peace;

SECTION I. SCOPE AND APPLICATION

1. Scope and Application

1.1   The *Principles on Housing and Property Restitution for Refugees and Displaced Persons* articulated herein are designed to assist all relevant actors, national and international, in addressing the legal and technical issues surrounding housing, land and property restitution in situations where displacement has led to persons being arbitrarily or unlawfully deprived of their former homes, lands, properties or places of habitual residence.

1.2   The *Principles on Housing and Property Restitution for Refugees and Displaced Persons* apply equally to all refugees, internally displaced persons and to other similarly situated displaced persons who fled across national borders but who may not meet the legal definition of refugee, (hereinafter 'refugees and displaced persons') who were arbitrarily or unlawfully deprived of their former homes, lands, properties or places of habitual residence, regardless of the nature or circumstances by which displacement originally occurred.

SECTION II. THE RIGHT TO HOUSING AND PROPERTY RESTITUTION

2. The Right to Housing and Property Restitution

2.1   All refugees and displaced persons have the right to have restored to them any housing, land and/or property of which they were arbitrarily or unlawfully deprived, or to be compensated for any housing, land and/or property that is factually

---

[15] Adopted without a vote on 11 August 2005 in Resolution 2005/21 by the UN Sub-Commission on Protection and Promotion of Human Rights, Geneva.

impossible to restore as determined by an independent, impartial tribunal.

2.2   States shall demonstrably prioritize the right to restitution as the preferred remedy to displacement and as a key element of restorative justice. The right to restitution exists as a distinct right, and is prejudiced neither by the actual return nor non-return of refugees and displaced persons entitled to housing, land and property restitution.

Section III. Overarching Principles

3. The Right to Non-Discrimination

3.1   Everyone has the right to non-discrimination on the basis of race, color, sex, language, religion, political or other opinion, national or social origin, property, birth or other status.

3.2   States shall ensure that *de facto* and *de jure* discrimination on the above grounds is prohibited and that all persons, including refugees and displaced persons, are considered equal before the law.

4. The Right to Equality between Men and Women

4.1   States shall ensure the equal right of men and women, and the equal right of boys and girls, to the enjoyment of housing, land and property restitution. In particular, States shall ensure the equal right of men and women, and the equal right of boys and girls, to *inter alia* voluntary return in safety and dignity; legal security of tenure; property ownership; equal access to inheritance; as well as the use, control of and access to housing, land and property.

4.2   States should ensure that housing, land and property restitution Programs, policies and practices recognize the joint ownership rights of both the male and female heads of the household as an explicit component of the restitution process, and that restitution Programs, policies and practices reflect a gender sensitive approach.

4.3   States shall ensure that housing, land and property restitution Programs, policies and practices do not disadvantage women and girls. States should adopt positive measures to ensure gender equality in this regard.

5. The Right to Be Protected from Displacement

5.1   Everyone has the right to be protected against being arbitrarily displaced from his or her home, land or place of habitual residence.

5.2   States should incorporate protections against displacement into domestic legislation, consistent with international human rights and humanitarian law and related standards, and should extend these protections to everyone within their legal jurisdiction or effective control.

5.3   States shall prohibit forced eviction, demolition of houses and destruction of agricultural areas and the arbitrary confiscation or expropriation of land as a punitive measure or as a means or method of war.

5.4   States shall take steps to ensure that no one is subjected to displacement by either State or non-State actors. States shall also ensure that individuals, corporations, and other entities within their legal jurisdiction or effective control refrain from carrying out or otherwise participating in displacement.

6. The Right to Privacy and Respect for the Home

6.1   Everyone has the right to be protected against arbitrary or unlawful interference with his or her privacy and his or her home.

6.2   States shall ensure that everyone is provided with safeguards of due process against such arbitrary or unlawful interference with his or her privacy and his or her home.

7. The Right to Peaceful Enjoyment of Possessions

7.1   Everyone has the right to the peaceful enjoyment of his or her possessions.

7.2   States shall only subordinate the use and enjoyment of possessions in the public interest and subject to the conditions provided for by law and by the general Principles of international law. Whenever possible, the 'interest of society' should be read restrictively, so as to mean only a temporary interference with the right to peaceful enjoyment of possessions.

8. The Right to Adequate Housing

8.1   Everyone has the right to adequate housing.

8.2   States should adopt positive measures aimed at alleviating the situation of refugees and displaced persons living in inadequate housing.

9. The Right to Freedom of Movement

9.1   Everyone has the right to freedom of movement and the right to choose his or her residence. No one shall be arbitrarily or unlawfully forced to remain within a certain territory, area or region. Similarly, no one shall be arbitrarily or unlawfully forced to leave a certain territory, area or region.

9.2   States shall ensure that freedom of movement and the right to choose one's residence are not subject to any restrictions except those which are provided by law, are necessary to protect national security, public order, public health or morals or the rights and freedoms of others, and are consistent with international human rights, refugee and humanitarian law and related standards.

Section IV. The Right to Voluntary Return in Safety and Dignity

10. The Right to Voluntary Return in Safety and Dignity

10.1   All refugees and displaced persons have the right to voluntarily return to their former homes, lands or places of habitual residence, in safety and dignity. Voluntary return in safety and dignity must be based on a free, informed, individual choice. Refugees and displaced persons should be provided with complete, objective, up to date, and accurate information, including on physical, material and legal safety issues in countries or places of origin.

10.2   States shall allow refugees and displaced persons who wish to return voluntarily to their former homes, lands or places of habitual residence to do so. This right cannot be abridged under conditions of state succession, nor can it be subject to arbitrary or unlawful time limitations.

10.3   Refugees and displaced persons shall not be forced, or otherwise coerced, either directly or indirectly, to return to their former homes, lands or places of habitual residence. Refugees and displaced persons should be able to effectively pursue durable solutions to displacement other than return, if they so wish, without prejudicing their right to the restitution of their housing, land and property.

10.3   States should, when necessary, request from other States or international organizations the financial and/or technical assistance required to facilitate the effective voluntary return, in safety and dignity, of refugees and displaced persons.

Section V. Legal, Policy, Procedural and Institutional Implementation Mechanisms

11. Compatibility with International Human Rights, Refugee and Humanitarian Law and Related Standards

11.1   States should ensure that all housing, land and property restitution procedures, institutions, mechanisms and legal frameworks are fully compatible with international human rights, refugee and humanitarian law and related standards, and that the right to voluntary return in safety and dignity is recognized therein.

12. National Procedures, Institutions and Mechanisms

12.1   States should establish and support equitable, timely, independent, transparent and non-discriminatory procedures, institutions and mechanisms to assess and enforce housing, land and property restitution claims. In cases where existing procedures, institutions and mechanisms can effectively address these issues, adequate financial, human and other resources should be made available to facilitate restitution in a just and timely manner.

12.2   States should ensure that housing, land and property restitution procedures, institutions and mechanisms are age and gender sensitive, and recognize the equal rights of men and women, as well as the equal rights of boys and girls, and reflect the overarching principle of the "best interests" of the child.

12.3   States should take all appropriate administrative, legislative and judicial measures to support and facilitate the housing, land and property restitution process. States should provide all relevant agencies with adequate financial, human and other resources to successfully complete their work in a just and timely manner.

12.4   States should establish guidelines which ensure the effectiveness of all relevant housing, land and property restitution procedures, institutions and mechanisms, including guidelines pertaining to institutional organization, staff training and caseloads, investigation and complaints procedures, verification of property ownership or other possessory rights, as well as decision-making, enforcement and appeals mechanisms. States may integrate alternative or informal dispute resolution mechanisms into these processes, insofar as all such mechanisms act in accordance with international human rights, refugee and humanitarian law and related standards, including the right to non-discrimination.

12.5   States should, where there has been a general breakdown in the rule of law, or where States are unable to implement the procedures, institutions and mechanisms necessary to facilitate the housing, land and property restitution process in a just and timely manner, request the technical assistance and cooperation of relevant international agencies in order to establish provisional regimes responsible for providing refugees and displaced persons with the procedures, institutions and mechanisms necessary to ensure effective restitution remedies.

12.6   States should include housing, land and property restitution procedures, institutions and mechanisms in peace agreements and voluntary repatriation agreements. Peace agreements should include specific undertakings by the parties to appropriately address any housing, land and property issues that require remedies under international law or threaten to undermine the peace process if left unaddressed, while demonstrably prioritizing the right to restitution as the preferred remedy in this regard.

13. Accessibility of Restitution Claims Procedures

13.1   Everyone who has been arbitrarily or unlawfully deprived of housing, land and/or property should be able to submit a claim for restitution and/or compensation to an independent and impartial body, and to receive a determination on their claim. States should not establish any preconditions for filing a restitution claim.

13.2   States should ensure that all aspects of the restitution claims process, including appeals procedures, are just, timely, accessible, free of charge, and are age and gender sensitive. States should adopt positive measures to ensure that women are

able to participate on a fully equal basis in this process.

13.3   States should ensure that separated and unaccompanied children are able to participate and are fully represented in the restitution claims process, and that any decision in relation to the restitution claim of separated and unaccompanied children is in compliance with the overarching principle of the "best interests" of the child.

13.4   States should ensure that the restitution claims process is accessible for refugees and other displaced persons regardless of their place of residence during the period of displacement, including in countries of origin, countries of asylum or countries to which they have fled. States should ensure that all affected persons are made aware of the restitution claims process, and that information about this process is made readily available, including in countries of origin, countries of asylum or countries to which they have fled.

13.5   States should seek to establish restitution claims processing centers and offices throughout affected areas where potential claimants currently reside. In order to facilitate the greatest access to those affected, it should be possible to submit restitution claims by post or by proxy, as well as in person. States should also consider establishing mobile units in order to ensure accessibility to all potential claimants.

13.6   States should ensure that users of housing, land and/or property, including tenants, have the right to participate in the restitution claims process, including through the filing of collective restitution claims.

13.7   States should develop restitution claims forms that are simple, easy to understand and use and make them available in the first language or languages of the groups affected. Competent assistance should be made available to help persons in completing and filing any necessary restitution claims forms, and such assistance should be provided in a manner which is age and gender sensitive.

13.8   Where restitution claims forms cannot be sufficiently simplified due to the complexities inherent in the claims process, States should engage qualified persons to interview potential claimants in confidence, and in a manner which is age and gender sensitive, in order to solicit the necessary information and complete the restitution claims forms on their behalf.

13.9   States should establish a clear time period for filing restitution claims. The time period should be widely disseminated and should be sufficiently long to ensure that all those affected have an adequate opportunity to file a restitution claim, bearing in mind the number of potential claimants, potential difficulties of information and access, the spread of displacement, the accessibility of the process for potentially disadvantaged groups and vulnerable individuals, and the political situation in the country or region of origin.

13.10   States should ensure that persons needing special assistance, including illiterate and disabled persons, are provided with such assistance in order to ensure that they are not denied access to the restitution claims process.

13.11   States should ensure that adequate legal aid is provided, if possible free of charge, to those seeking to make a restitution claim. While legal aid may be provided by either governmental or non-governmental sources (be they national or international), such legal aid should meet adequate standards of quality, non-discrimination, fairness and impartiality so as not to prejudice the restitution claims process.

13.12   States should ensure that no one is persecuted or punished for making a restitution claim.

14. Adequate Consultation and Participation in Decision-Making

14.1   States and other involved international and national actors should ensure that voluntary repatriation and housing, land and property restitution Programs are carried out with adequate consultation and participation with the affected persons, groups and communities.

14.2   States and other involved international and national actors should, in particular, ensure that women, indigenous peoples, racial and ethnic minorities, the elderly, the disabled and children are adequately represented and included in restitution decision-making processes, and have the appropriate means and information to participate effectively. The needs of vulnerable individuals including the elderly, single female heads of households,

separated and unaccompanied children, and the disabled should be given particular attention.

15. Housing, Land and Property Records and Documentation

15.1   States should establish or re-establish national multi-purpose cadastre or other appropriate systems for the registration of housing, land and property rights as an integral component of any restitution Programs, respecting the rights of refugees and displaced persons when doing so.

15.2   States should ensure that any judicial, quasi-judicial, administrative or customary pronouncement regarding the rightful ownership of, or rights to, housing, land and/or property is accompanied by measures to ensure registration or demarcation of that housing, land and/or property right as is necessary to ensure legal security of tenure. These determinations shall comply with international human rights, refugee and humanitarian law and related standards, including the right to non-discrimination.

15.3   States should ensure, where appropriate, that registration systems record and/or recognize the possessory rights of traditional and indigenous communities to collective lands.

15.4   States and other responsible authorities or institutions should ensure that existing registration systems are not destroyed in times of conflict or post-conflict. Measures to prevent the destruction of housing, land and property records could include protection *in situ* or, if necessary, short-term removal to a safe location or custody. If removed, the records should be returned as soon as possible after the end of hostilities. States and other responsible authorities may also consider establishing procedures for copying records (including in digital format) transferring them securely, and recognizing the authenticity of said copies.

15.5   States and other responsible authorities or institutions should provide, at the request of a claimant or his or her proxy, copies of any documentary evidence in their possession required to make and/or support a restitution claim. Such documentary evidence should be provided free of charge, or for a minimal fee.

15.6   States and other responsible authorities or institutions conducting the registration of refugees or displaced persons should endeavor to collect information relevant to facilitating the restitution process, for example by including in the registration form questions regarding the location and status of the individual refugee's or displaced person's former home, land, property or place of habitual residence. Such information should be sought whenever information is gathered from refugees and displaced persons, including at the time of flight.

15.7   States may, in situations of mass displacement where little documentary evidence exists as to ownership or possessory rights, adopt the conclusive presumption that persons fleeing their homes during a given period marked by violence or disaster have done so for reasons related to violence or disaster and are therefore entitled to housing, land and property restitution. In such cases, administrative and judicial authorities may independently establish the facts related to undocumented restitution claims.

15.8   States shall not recognize as valid any housing, land and/or property transaction, including any transfer that was made under duress, or which was otherwise coerced or forced, either directly or indirectly, or which was carried out contrary to international human rights standards.

16. The Rights of Tenants and Other Non-Owners

16.1   States should ensure that the rights of tenants, social occupancy rights holders and other legitimate occupants or users of housing, land and property are recognized within restitution Programs. To the maximum extent possible, States should ensure that such persons are able to return to and re-possess and use their housing, land and property in a similar manner to those possessing formal ownership rights.

17. Secondary Occupants

17.1   States should ensure that secondary occupants are protected against arbitrary or unlawful forced eviction. States shall ensure, in cases where evictions of such occupants are deemed justifiable and unavoidable for the purposes of housing, land and property restitution, that evictions are carried out in a manner which is compatible with international human rights law and standards, such that secondary occupants are afforded safeguards of due process, including, *inter alia*, an opportunity for genuine consultation, adequate and reasonable

notice, and the provision of legal remedies, including opportunities for legal redress.

17.2   States should ensure that the safeguards of due process extended to secondary occupants do not prejudice the rights of legitimate owners, tenants and other rights holders to repossess the housing, land and property in question in a just and timely manner.

17.3   States should, in cases where evictions of secondary occupants are justifiable and unavoidable, take positive measures to protect those who do not have the means to access any other adequate housing other than that which they are currently occupying from homelessness and other violations of their right to adequate housing. States should undertake to identify and provide alternative housing and/or land for such occupants, including on a temporary basis, as a means to facilitate the timely restitution of refugee and displaced persons housing, land and property. Lack of such alternatives, however, should not unnecessarily delay the implementation and enforcement of decisions by relevant bodies regarding housing, land and property restitution.

17.4   States may consider, in cases where housing, land and property has been sold by secondary occupants to third parties acting in good faith, establishing mechanisms to provide compensation to injured third parties. The egregiousness of the underlying displacement, however, may arguably give rise to constructive notice of the illegality of purchasing abandoned property, preempting the formation of *bona fide* property interests in such cases.

18. Legislative Measures

18.1   States should ensure the right of refugees and displaced persons to housing, land and property restitution is recognized as an essential component of the rule of law. States should ensure the right to housing, land and property restitution through all necessary legislative means, including through the adoption, amendment, reform, or repeal of relevant laws, regulations and/or practices. States should develop a legal framework for protecting the right to housing, land and property restitution which is clear, consistent and, where necessary, consolidated in a single law.

18.2   States should ensure that all relevant laws clearly delineate every person and/or affected group that is legally entitled to the restitution of their housing, land and property, most notably refugees and displaced persons. Subsidiary claimants should similarly be recognized, including resident family members at the time of displacement, spouses, domestic partners, dependents, legal heirs and others who should be entitled to claim on the same basis as primary claimants.

18.3   States should ensure that national legislation related to housing, land and property restitution is internally consistent, as well as compatible with pre-existing relevant agreements, such as peace agreements and voluntary repatriation agreements, so long as these agreements are themselves compatible with international human rights, refugee and humanitarian law and related standards.

19. Prohibition of Arbitrary and Discriminatory Laws

19.1   States should neither adopt nor apply laws which prejudice the restitution process, in particular through arbitrary, discriminatory, or otherwise unjust abandonment laws or statues of limitations.

9.2   States should take immediate steps to repeal unjust or arbitrary laws, and laws which otherwise have a discriminatory effect on the enjoyment of the right to housing, land and property restitution, and should ensure remedies for those wrongfully harmed by the prior application of such laws.

19.3   States should ensure that all national policies related to the right to housing, land and property restitution fully guarantee the rights of women and girls to non-discrimination and to equality in both law and practice.

20. Enforcement of Restitution Decisions and Judgments

20.1   States should designate specific public agencies to be entrusted with enforcing housing, land and property restitution decisions and judgments.

20.2   States should ensure, through law and other appropriate means, that local and national authorities are legally obligated to respect, implement and enforce decisions and judgments made by relevant bodies regarding housing, land and property restitution.

20.3   States should adopt specific measures to prevent the public obstruction of enforcement of housing, land and property restitution decisions and judgments. Threats or attacks against officials and agencies carrying out restitution Programs should be fully investigated and prosecuted.

20.4   States should adopt specific measures to prevent the destruction or looting of contested or abandoned housing, land and property. In order to minimize destruction and looting, States should develop procedures to inventory the contents of claimed housing, land and property within the context of housing, land and property restitution Programs.

20.5   States should implement public information campaigns aimed at informing secondary occupants and other relevant parties of their rights and of the legal consequences of non-compliance with housing, land and property restitution decisions and judgments, including failing to vacate occupied housing, land and property voluntarily and damaging and/or looting of occupied housing, land and property.

21. Compensation

21.1   All refugees and displaced persons have the right to full and effective compensation as an integral component of the restitution process. Compensation may be monetary or in kind. States shall, in order to comply with the principle of restorative justice, ensure that the remedy of compensation is only be used when the remedy of restitution is not factually possible or when the injured party knowingly and voluntarily accepts compensation in lieu of restitution, or when the terms of a negotiated peace settlement provide for a combination of restitution and compensation.

21.2   States should ensure, as a rule, that restitution is only deemed factually impossible in exceptional circumstances, namely when housing, land and/or property is destroyed or when it no longer exists, as determined by an independent, impartial tribunal. Even under such circumstances the holder of the housing, land and/or property right should have the option to repair or rebuild whenever possible. In some situations, a combination of compensation and restitution may be the most appropriate remedy and form of restorative justice.

SECTION VI. THE ROLE OF THE INTERNATIONAL
COMMUNITY, INCLUDING INTERNATIONAL
ORGANIZATIONS

22. Responsibility of the International Community

22.1 The international community should promote and protect the right to housing, land and property restitution, as well as the right to voluntary return in safety and dignity.

22.2 International financial, trade, development and other related institutions and agencies, including member or donor States that have voting rights within such bodies, should take fully into account the prohibition against unlawful or arbitrary displacement and, in particular, the prohibition under international human rights law and related standards on the practice of forced evictions.

22.3 International organizations should work with national governments and share expertise on the development of national housing, land and property restitution policies and Programs and help ensure their compatibility with international human rights, refugee and humanitarian law and related standards. International organizations should also support the monitoring of their implementation.

22.4 International organizations, including the United Nations, should strive to ensure that peace agreements and voluntary repatriation agreements contain provisions related to housing, land and property restitution, including through *inter alia* the establishment of national procedures, institutions, mechanisms and legal frameworks.

22.5 International peace operations, in pursuing their overall mandate, should help to maintain a secure and stable environment wherein appropriate housing, land and property restitution policies and Programs may be successfully implemented and enforced.

22.6 International peace operations, depending on the mission context, should be requested to support the protection of the right to housing, land and property restitution, including through the enforcement of restitution decisions and judgments. Member States in the Security Council should consider including this role in the mandate of peace operations.

22.7 International organizations and peace operations should avoid occupying, renting or purchasing housing, land and property over which the rights holder does not currently have access or control, and should require that their staff do the same. Similarly, international organizations and peace operations should ensure that bodies or processes under their control or supervision do not obstruct, directly or indirectly, the restitution of housing, land and property.

SECTION VII. INTERPRETATION

23. Interpretation

23.1 The *Principles on Housing and Property Restitution for Refugees and Displaced Persons* shall not be interpreted as limiting, altering or otherwise prejudicing the rights recognized under international human rights, refugee and humanitarian law and related standards, or rights consistent with these laws and standards as recognized under national law.

1.16. Basic Principles and Guidelines on the Right to a Remedy and Reparation for Victims of Violations of International Human Rights and Humanitarian Law (2005)[16]

PREAMBLE

The General Assembly,

Recalling the provisions providing a right to a remedy for victims of violations of international human rights law found in numerous international instruments, in particular article 8 of the Universal Declaration of Human Rights, 1 article 2 of the International Covenant on Civil and Political Rights, 2 article 6 of the International Convention on the Elimination of All Forms of Racial Discrimination, article 14 of the Convention against Torture and Other Cruel, Inhuman or Degrading Treatment or Punishment, and article 39 of the Convention on the Rights of the Child, and of international humanitarian law as found in article 3 of the Hague Convention respecting the Laws and Customs of War on Land of 18 October 1907 (Convention IV), article 91

---

[16] Adopted by UN General Assembly Resolution 60/147 (16 December 2005).

of the Protocol Additional to the Geneva Conventions of 12 August 1949, and relating to the Protection of Victims of International Armed Conflicts (Protocol I) of 8 June 1977, and articles 68 and 75 of the Rome Statute of the International Criminal Court,

Recalling the provisions providing a right to a remedy for victims of violations of international human rights found in regional conventions, in particular article 7 of the African Charter on Human and Peoples' Rights, article 25 of the American Convention on Human Rights, and article 13 of the Convention for the Protection of Human Rights and Fundamental Freedoms,

Recalling the Declaration of Basic Principles of Justice for Victims of Crime and Abuse of Power emanating from the deliberations of the Seventh United Nations Congress on the Prevention of Crime and the Treatment of Offenders and General Assembly resolution 40/34 of 29 November 1985 by which the Assembly adopted the text recommended by the Congress,

Reaffirming the principles enunciated in the Declaration of Basic Principles of Justice for Victims of Crime and Abuse of Power, including that victims should be treated with compassion and respect for their dignity, have their right to access to justice and redress mechanisms fully respected, and that the establishment, strengthening and expansion of national funds for compensation to victims should be encouraged, together with the expeditious development of appropriate rights and remedies for victims,

Noting that the Rome Statute of the International Criminal Court requires the establishment of "principles relating to reparations to, or in respect of, victims, including restitution, compensation and rehabilitation", requires the Assembly of States Parties to establish a trust fund for the benefit of victims of crimes within the jurisdiction of the Court, and of the families of such victims, and mandates the Court "to protect the safety, physical and psychological well-being, dignity and privacy of victims" and to permit the participation of victims at all "stages of the proceedings determined to be appropriate by the Court",

Affirming that the Basic Principles and Guidelines contained herein are directed at gross violations of international human rights law and serious violations of international humanitarian law which, by their very grave nature, constitute an affront to human dignity,

Emphasizing that the Basic Principles and Guidelines contained herein do not entail new international or domestic legal obligations but identify mechanisms, modalities, procedures and methods for the implementation of existing legal obligations under international human rights law and international humanitarian law which are complementary though different as to their norms,

Recalling that international law contains the obligation to prosecute perpetrators of certain international crimes in accordance with international obligations of States and the requirements of national law or as provided for in the applicable statutes of international judicial organs, and that the duty to prosecute reinforces the international legal obligations to be carried out in accordance with national legal requirements and procedures and supports the concept of complementarity,

Noting that contemporary forms of victimization, while essentially directed against persons, may nevertheless also be directed against groups of persons who are targeted collectively,

Recognizing that, in honouring the victims' right to benefit from remedies and reparation, the international community keeps faith with the plight of victims, survivors and future human generations and reaffirms the international legal principles of accountability, justice and the rule of law,

Convinced that, in adopting a victim-oriented perspective, the international community affirms its human solidarity with victims of violations of international law, including violations of international human rights law and international humanitarian law, as well as with humanity at large, in accordance with the following Basic Principles and Guidelines,

Adopts the following Basic Principles and Guidelines:

(i) Obligation to respect, ensure respect for and implement international human rights law and international humanitarian law

1. The obligation to respect, ensure respect for and implement international human rights law

and international humanitarian law as provided for under the respective bodies of law emanates from:

(*a*) Treaties to which a State is a party;

(*b*) Customary international law;

(*c*) The domestic law of each State.

2. If they have not already done so, States shall, as required under international law, ensure that their domestic law is consistent with their international legal obligations by:

(*a*) Incorporating norms of international human rights law and international humanitarian law into their domestic law, or otherwise implementing them in their domestic legal system;

(*b*) Adopting appropriate and effective legislative and administrative procedures and other appropriate measures that provide fair, effective and prompt access to justice;

(*c*) Making available adequate, effective, prompt and appropriate remedies, including reparation, as defined below;

(*d*) Ensuring that their domestic law provides at least the same level of protection for victims as that required by their international obligations.

(ii) Scope of the obligation

3. The obligation to respect, ensure respect for and implement international human rights law and international humanitarian law as provided for under the respective bodies of law, includes, inter alia, the duty to:

(*a*) Take appropriate legislative and administrative and other appropriate measures to prevent violations;

(*b*) Investigate violations effectively, promptly, thoroughly and impartially and, where appropriate, take action against those allegedly responsible in accordance with domestic and international law;

(*c*) Provide those who claim to be victims of a human rights or humanitarian law violation with equal and effective access to justice, as described below, irrespective of who may ultimately be the bearer of responsibility for the violation; and

(*d*) Provide effective remedies to victims, including reparation, as described below.

(iii) Gross violations of international human rights law and serious violations of international humanitarian law that constitute crimes under international law

4. In cases of gross violations of international human rights law and serious violations of international humanitarian law constituting crimes under international law, States have the duty to investigate and, if there is sufficient evidence, the duty to submit to prosecution the person allegedly responsible for the violations and, if found guilty, the duty to punish her or him. Moreover, in these cases, States should, in accordance with international law, cooperate with one another and assist international judicial organs competent in the investigation and prosecution of these violations.

5. To that end, where so provided in an applicable treaty or under other international law obligations, States shall incorporate or otherwise implement within their domestic law appropriate provisions for universal jurisdiction. Moreover, where it is so provided for in an applicable treaty or other international legal obligations, States should facilitate extradition or surrender offenders to other States and to appropriate international judicial bodies and provide judicial assistance and other forms of cooperation in the pursuit of international justice, including assistance to, and protection of, victims and witnesses, consistent with international human rights legal standards and subject to international legal requirements such as those relating to the prohibition of torture and other forms of cruel, inhuman or degrading treatment or punishment.

(iv) Statutes of limitations

6. Where so provided for in an applicable treaty or contained in other international legal obligations, statutes of limitations shall not apply to gross violations of international human rights law and serious violations of international humanitarian law which constitute crimes under international law.

7. Domestic statutes of limitations for other types of violations that do not constitute crimes under international law, including those time limitations applicable to civil claims and other procedures, should not be unduly restrictive.

(v) Victims of gross violations of international human rights law and serious violations of international humanitarian law

8. For purposes of the present document, victims are persons who individually or collectively suffered harm, including physical or mental injury, emotional suffering, economic loss or substantial impairment of their fundamental rights, through acts or omissions that constitute gross violations of international human rights law, or serious violations of international humanitarian law. Where appropriate, and in accordance with domestic law, the term "victim" also includes the immediate family or dependants of the direct victim and persons who have suffered harm in intervening to assist victims in distress or to prevent victimization.

9. A person shall be considered a victim regardless of whether the perpetrator of the violation is identified, apprehended, prosecuted, or convicted and regardless of the familial relationship between the perpetrator and the victim.

(vi) Treatment of victims

10. Victims should be treated with humanity and respect for their dignity and human rights, and appropriate measures should be taken to ensure their safety, physical and psychological well-being and privacy, as well as those of their families. The State should ensure that its domestic laws, to the extent possible, provide that a victim who has suffered violence or trauma should benefit from special consideration and care to avoid his or her re-traumatization in the course of legal and administrative procedures designed to provide justice and reparation.

(vii) Victims' right to remedies

11. Remedies for gross violations of international human rights law and serious violations of international humanitarian law include the victim's right to the following as provided for under international law:

(*a*) Equal and effective access to justice;

(*b*) Adequate, effective and prompt reparation for harm suffered;

(*c*) Access to relevant information concerning violations and reparation mechanisms.

(viii) Access to justice

12. A victim of a gross violation of international human rights law or of a serious violation of international humanitarian law shall have equal access to an effective judicial remedy as provided for under international law. Other remedies available to the victim include access to administrative and other bodies, as well as mechanisms, modalities and proceedings conducted in accordance with domestic law. Obligations arising under international law to secure the right to access justice and fair and impartial proceedings shall be reflected in domestic laws. To that end, States should:

(*a*) Disseminate, through public and private mechanisms, information about all available remedies for gross violations of international human rights law and serious violations of international humanitarian law;

(*b*) Take measures to minimize the inconvenience to victims and their representatives, protect against unlawful interference with their privacy as appropriate and ensure their safety from intimidation and retaliation, as well as that of their families and witnesses, before, during and after judicial, administrative, or other proceedings that affect the interests of victims;

(*c*) Provide proper assistance to victims seeking access to justice;

(*d*) Make available all appropriate legal, diplomatic and consular means to ensure that victims can exercise their rights to remedy for gross violations of international human rights law or serious violations of international humanitarian law.

13. In addition to individual access to justice, States should endeavour to develop procedures to allow groups of victims to present claims for reparation and to receive reparation, as appropriate.

14. An adequate, effective and prompt remedy for gross violations of international human rights law or serious violations of international humanitarian law should include all available and appropriate international processes in which a person may have legal standing and should be without prejudice to any other domestic remedies.

(ix)   Reparation for harm suffered

15. Adequate, effective and prompt reparation is intended to promote justice by redressing gross violations of international human rights law or serious violations of international humanitarian law. Reparation should be proportional to the gravity of the violations and the harm suffered. In accordance with its domestic laws and international legal obligations, a State shall provide reparation to victims for acts or omissions which can be attributed to the State and constitute gross violations of international human rights law or serious violations of international humanitarian law. In cases where a person, a legal person, or other entity is found liable for reparation to a victim, such party should provide reparation to the victim or compensate the State if the State has already provided reparation to the victim.

16. States should endeavour to establish national programmes for reparation and other assistance to victims in the event that the parties liable for the harm suffered are unable or unwilling to meet their obligations.

17. States shall, with respect to claims by victims, enforce domestic judgments for reparation against individuals or entities liable for the harm suffered and endeavour to enforce valid foreign legal judgments for reparation in accordance with domestic law and international legal obligations. To that end, States should provide under their domestic laws effective mechanisms for the enforcement of reparation judgments.

18. In accordance with domestic law and international law, and taking account of individual circumstances, victims of gross violations of international human rights law and serious violations of international humanitarian law should, as appropriate and proportional to the gravity of the violation and the circumstances of each case, be provided with full and effective reparation, as laid out in principles 19 to 23, which include the following forms: restitution, compensation, rehabilitation, satisfaction and guarantees of non-repetition.

19. *Restitution* should, whenever possible, restore the victim to the original situation before the gross violations of international human rights law or serious violations of international humanitarian law occurred. Restitution includes, as appropriate: restoration of liberty, enjoyment of human rights,

identity, family life and citizenship, return to one's place of residence, restoration of employment and return of property.

20. *Compensation* should be provided for any economically assessable damage, as appropriate and proportional to the gravity of the violation and the circumstances of each case, resulting from gross violations of international human rights law and serious violations of international humanitarian law, such as:

(*a*) Physical or mental harm;

(*b*) Lost opportunities, including employment, education and social benefits;

(*c*) Material damages and loss of earnings, including loss of earning potential;

(*d*) Moral damage;

(*e*) Costs required for legal or expert assistance, medicine and medical services, and psychological and social services.

21. *Rehabilitation* should include medical and psychological care as well as legal and social services.

22. *Satisfaction* should include, where applicable, any or all of the following:

(*a*) Effective measures aimed at the cessation of continuing violations;

(*b*) Verification of the facts and full and public disclosure of the truth to the extent that such disclosure does not cause further harm or threaten the safety and interests of the victim, the victim's relatives, witnesses, or persons who have intervened to assist the victim or prevent the occurrence of further violations;

(*c*) The search for the whereabouts of the disappeared, for the identities of the children abducted, and for the bodies of those killed, and assistance in the recovery, identification and reburial of the bodies in accordance with the expressed or presumed wish of the victims, or the cultural practices of the families and communities;

(*d*) An official declaration or a judicial decision restoring the dignity, the reputation and the rights of the victim and of persons closely connected with the victim;

(*e*) Public apology, including acknowledgement of the facts and acceptance of responsibility;

(*f*) Judicial and administrative sanctions against persons liable for the violations;

(*g*) Commemorations and tributes to the victims;

(*h*) Inclusion of an accurate account of the violations that occurred in international human rights law and international humanitarian law training and in educational material at all levels.

23. *Guarantees of non-repetition* should include, where applicable, any or all of the following measures, which will also contribute to prevention:

(*a*) Ensuring effective civilian control of military and security forces;

(*b*) Ensuring that all civilian and military proceedings abide by international standards of due process, fairness and impartiality;

(*c*) Strengthening the independence of the judiciary;

(*d*) Protecting persons in the legal, medical and health-care professions, the media and other related professions, and human rights defenders;

(*e*) Providing, on a priority and continued basis, human rights and international humanitarian law education to all sectors of society and training for law enforcement officials as well as military and security forces;

(*f*) Promoting the observance of codes of conduct and ethical norms, in particular international standards, by public servants, including law enforcement, correctional, media, medical, psychological, social service and military personnel, as well as by economic enterprises;

(*g*) Promoting mechanisms for preventing and monitoring social conflicts and their resolution;

(*h*) Reviewing and reforming laws contributing to or allowing gross violations of international human rights law and serious violations of international humanitarian law.

(x)   Access to relevant information concerning violations and reparation mechanisms

24. States should develop means of informing the general public and, in particular, victims of gross violations of international human rights law and serious violations of international humanitarian law of the rights and remedies addressed by these Basic Principles and Guidelines and of all available legal, medical, psychological, social, administrative and all other services to which victims may have a right of access. Moreover, victims and their representatives should be entitled to seek and obtain information on the causes leading to their victimization and on the causes and conditions pertaining to the gross violations of international human rights law and serious violations of international humanitarian law and to learn the truth in regard to these violations.

(xi)   Non-discrimination

25. The application and interpretation of these Basic Principles and Guidelines must be consistent with international human rights law and international humanitarian law and be without any discrimination of any kind or on any ground, without exception.

(xii)   Non-derogation

26. Nothing in these Basic Principles and Guidelines shall be construed as restricting or derogating from any rights or obligations arising under domestic and international law. In particular, it is understood that the present Basic Principles and Guidelines are without prejudice to the right to a remedy and reparation for victims of all violations of international human rights law and international humanitarian law. It is further understood that these Basic Principles and Guidelines are without prejudice to special rules of international law.

(xiii)   Rights of others

27. Nothing in this document is to be construed as derogating from internationally or nationally protected rights of others, in particular the right of an accused person to benefit from applicable standards of due process.

2. PEACE AGREEMENTS

2.1. Cambodia – Agreement on a Comprehensive Political Settlement on the Cambodia Conflict (1991)

The States participating in the Paris Conference on Cambodia, namely Australia, Brunei Darussalam, Cambodia, Canada, the People's Republic of China, the French Republic, the Republic of India, the Republic of Indonesia, Japan, the Lao People's

Democratic Republic, Malaysia, the Republic of the Philippines, the Republic of Singapore, the Kingdom of Thailand, the Union of Soviet Socialist Republics, the United Kingdom of Great Britain and Northern Ireland, the United States of America, the Socialist Republic of Viet Nam and the Socialist Federal Republic of Yugoslavia,

In the presence of the Secretary-General of the United Nations,

In order to maintain, preserve and defend the sovereignty, independence, territorial integrity and inviolability, neutrality and national unity of Cambodia,

Desiring to restore and maintain peace in Cambodia, to promote national reconciliation and to ensure the exercise of the right to self-determination of the Cambodian people through free and fair elections,

Convinced that only a comprehensive political settlement to the Cambodia conflict will be just and durable and will contribute to regional and international peace and security,

Welcoming the Framework document of 28 August 1990, which was accepted by the Cambodian Parties in its entirety as the basis for settling the Cambodia conflict, and which was subsequently unanimously endorsed by Security Council resolution 668 (1990) of 20 September 1990 and General Assembly resolution 45/3 of 15 October 1990,

Noting the formation in Jakarta on 10 September 1990 of the Supreme National Council of Cambodia as the unique legitimate body and source of authority in Cambodia in which, throughout the transitional period, national sovereignty and unity are enshrined, and which represents Cambodia externally,

Welcoming the unanimous election, in Beijing on 17 July 1991, of H.R.H. Prince Norodom Sihanouk as the President of the Supreme National Council,

Recognising that an enhanced United Nations role requires the establishment of a United Nations Transitional Authority in Cambodia (UNTAC) with civilian and military components, which will act with full respect for the national sovereignty of Cambodia,

Noting the statements made at the conclusion of the meetings held in Jakarta on 9–10 September

1990, in Paris on 21–23 December 1990, in Pattaya on 24–26 June 1991, in Beijing on 16–17 July 1991, in Pattaya on 26–29 August 1991, and also the meetings held in Jakarta on 4–6 June 1991 and in New York on 19 September 1991,

Welcoming United Nations Security Council resolution 717 (1991) of 16 October 1991 on Cambodia,

Recognising that Cambodia's tragic recent history requires special measures to assure protection of human rights, and the non-return to the policies and practices of the past,

Have agreed as follows:

[. . .]

PART V – REFUGEES AND DISPLACED PERSONS

Article 19

Upon entry into force of this Agreement, every effort will be made to create in Cambodia political, economic and social conditions conducive to the voluntary return and harmonious integration of Cambodian refugees and displaced persons.

Article 20

Cambodian refugees and displaced persons, located outside Cambodia, shall have the right to return to Cambodia and to live in safety, security and dignity, free from intimidation or coercion of any kind.

The Signatories request the Secretary-General of the United Nations to facilitate the repatriation in safety and dignity of Cambodian refugees and displaced persons, as an integral part of the comprehensive political settlement and under the overall authority of the Special Representative of the Secretary-General, in accordance with the guidelines and principles on the repatriation of refugees and displaced persons as set forth in annex 4.

[. . .]

ANNEX 4 – REPATRIATION OF CAMBODIAN REFUGEES AND DISPLACED PERSONS

PART I – INTRODUCTION

As part of the comprehensive political settlement, every assistance will need to be given to Cambodian refugees and displaced persons as well as to countries of temporary refuge and the country of origin in order to facilitate the voluntary return of all Cambodian refugees and displaced persons in a peaceful and orderly manner. It must also be ensured that there would be no residual problems for the countries of temporary refuge. The country of origin with responsibility towards its own people will accept their return as conditions become conducive.

PART II – CONDITIONS CONDUCIVE TO THE RETURN OF REFUGEES AND DISPLACED PERSONS

The task of rebuilding the Cambodian nation will require the harnessing of all its human and natural resources. To this end, the return to the place of their choice of Cambodians from their temporary refuge and elsewhere outside their country of origin will make a major contribution.

Every effort should be made to ensure that the conditions which have led to a large number of Cambodian refugees and displaced persons seeking refuge in other countries should not recur. Nevertheless, some Cambodian refugees and displaced persons will wish and be able to return spontaneously to their homeland.

There must be full respect for the human rights and fundamental freedoms of all Cambodians, including those of the repatriated refugees and displaced persons, in recognition of their entitlement to live in peace and security, free from intimidation and coercion of any kind. These rights would include, inter alia, freedom of movement within Cambodia, the choice of domicile and employment, and the right to property.

In accordance with the comprehensive political settlement, every effort should be made to create concurrently in Cambodia political, economic and social conditions conducive to the return and harmonious integration of the Cambodian refugees and displaced persons.

With a view to ensuring that refugees and displaced persons participate in the elections, mass repatriation should commence and be completed as soon as possible, taking into account all the political, humanitarian, logistical, technical and socio-economic factors involved, and with the co-operation of the SNC.

Repatriation of Cambodian refugees and displaced persons should be voluntary and their decision should be taken in full possession of the facts. Choice of destination within Cambodia should be that of the individual. The unity of the family must be preserved.

PART III – OPERATIONAL FACTORS

Consistent with respect for principles of national sovereignty in the countries of temporary refuge and origin, and in close co-operation with the countries of temporary refuge and origin, full access by the Office of the United Nations High Commissioner for Refugees (UNHCR), CRC and other relevant international agencies should be guaranteed to all Cambodian refugees and displaced persons, with a view to the agencies undertaking the census, tracing, medical assistance, food distribution and other activities vital to the discharge of their mandate and operational responsibilities; such access should also be provided in Cambodia to enable the relevant international organisations to carry out their traditional monitoring as well as operational responsibilities.

In the context of the comprehensive political settlement, the Signatories note with satisfaction that the Secretary-General of the United Nations has entrusted UNHCR with the role of leadership and co-ordination among intergovernmental agencies assisting with the repatriation and relief of Cambodian refugees and displaced persons. The Signatories look to all non-governmental organisations to co-ordinate as much as possible their work for the Cambodian refugees and displaced persons with that of UNHCR.

The SNC, the Governments of the countries in which the Cambodian refugees and displaced persons have sought temporary refuge, and the countries which contribute to the repatriation and integration effort will wish to monitor closely and facilitate the repatriation of the returnees. An ad hoc consultative body should be established for a limited term for these purposes. The UNHCR, the ICRC, and other international agencies as appropriate, as well as UNTAC, would be invited to join as full participants.

Adequately monitored short-term repatriation assistance should be provided on an impartial basis to enable the families and individuals returning to

Cambodia to establish their lives and livelihoods harmoniously in their society. These interim measures would be phased out and replaced in the longer term by the reconstruction programme.

Those responsible for organising and supervising the repatriation operation will need to ensure that conditions of security are created for the movement of the refugees and displaced persons. In this respect, it is imperative that appropriate border crossing points and routes be designated and cleared of mines and other hazards.

The international community should contribute generously to the financial requirements of the repatriation operation.

[. . .]

2.2. El Salvador – Peace Agreement between the Government of El Salvador and the Frente Farabundo Martí para la Liberación Nacional (1992)

[. . .]

CHAPTER V

Economic and Social Questions

1 Preamble

One of the prerequisites for the democratic reunification of Salvadorian society is the sustained economic and social development of the country. At the same time, reunification of Salvadorian society and a growing degree of social cohesion are indispensable for fostering development. Hence, the set of agreements required to put a definitive end to the armed conflict in El Salvador must include certain minimum commitments to promote development for the benefit of all sectors of the population.

In accordance with the New York Agreement, the issues covered by this instrument are: the agrarian problem, loans to the agricultural sector, measures required to alleviate the social cost of structural adjustment programmes, appropriate procedures for direct external cooperation designed to encourage community development and assistance projects, establishment of a forum for economic and social consultation and the National Reconstruction Plan. Also, although the general philosophy or orientation of the Government's economic policy, which FMLN does not necessarily share, is not covered by this Agreement, both Parties agree on the need to provide certain basic guidelines so as to ensure the requisite social stability during the transitional period, consolidate peace and make progress towards the reunification of Salvadorian society.

2 The agrarian problem

Lands in excess of the constitutional limit of 245 hectares

The Government of El Salvador shall transfer rural farmland that has not yet been transferred under articles 105 and 267 of the Constitution of the Republic.

It likewise undertakes to ensure that implementation of the relevant constitutional requirements is not evaded by owners of rural holdings in excess of 245 hectares.

State-owned lands which are not currently part of a forestry reserve

The Government of El Salvador shall transfer to beneficiaries of the agrarian reform, as provided in article 104 of the Constitution, State-owned rural farmland which is not part of a forestry reserve.

Under the various land-transfer programmes which the Government of El Salvador is carrying out with State-owned farmland, preference shall be given to former combatants of both Parties who so request voluntarily, are of peasant origin and familiar with farming, and possess no land of any kind. The size of the lots shall be determined by the amount of land available, as mentioned above, and the number of beneficiaries who meet the conditions set out in this section.

Lands offered for sale to the State

Making use of the legal, technical and financial resources available to it, the Government of El Salvador shall seek to acquire and transfer through the Land Bank lands voluntarily offered for sale by their owners. Once the said lands are acquired, they shall be transferred to beneficiaries of the agrarian reform.

Recipients of lands transferred in accordance with the preceding sections

The lands acquired under sections A, B and C of this chapter shall be used to satisfy the need for land of landless peasants and small farmers. Specifically, title to the land shall be transferred legally to the peasants and small farmers designated by law as beneficiaries of the agrarian reform.

Payments for land

The lands referred to in the preceding sections shall be transferred at market prices and on the same credit terms as are granted to beneficiaries of the reformed sector. At the same time, a system of payments may be established on the basis of a fixed price and long-term financing at low, fixed interest rates not subject to interest capitalization. Domestic credit shall be supplemented with financing from international cooperation, for which a special fund, financed from external resources, shall be established for the purchase of land.

New legislation

Since the current agrarian legislation is haphazard, contradictory and incomplete, the Parties agree that it must be harmonized and unified into an agrarian code. To this end, the Government shall submit the relevant draft legislation to the Legislative Assembly no later than 12 months after the signing of this Agreement. If it fails to do so, COPAZ shall take on the task of preparing the corresponding preliminary draft.

3 Lands within conflict zones

The land-tenure system in conflict zones

In accordance with the New York Agreement, the current land-tenure situation in conflict zones shall be respected until a satisfactory legal solution for the definitive land-tenure system is arrived at. Consequently, landholders shall not be evicted pending agreement on such a solution; moreover, they shall be given financial support to increase agricultural production.

In view of the irregularity of the land-tenure system in conflict zones, the Parties agree on the following:

Determination as to who are the "current landholders"

"Landholders" shall mean those currently occupying and/or working the land in conflict zones.

Inventory of cases covered by this part of the Agreement

Within 30 days from the signing of the Agreement, FMLN shall submit an inventory of land or buildings affected by the Agreement. Upon verification that such land or buildings are in fact subject to the provisions of this Agreement, and in accordance with the procedure set forth in the next section, the Government of El Salvador shall seek to provide a satisfactory legal solution for their final disposal through the voluntary sale of such property by the rightful owners to the current holders, on the terms referred to in section 3(F) of this chapter.

Should a rightful owner not wish to sell his property, the Government of El Salvador shall make use of the legal mechanisms at its disposal to try to resettle the peasants or small farmers on such land as may be available for the purpose and shall, as far as possible, seek to ensure that such land is situated in the same zones.

Establishment of a Special Commission

COPAZ shall appoint a special commission whose members shall be of recognized integrity and ability. The special commission, to be formed within 20 days following the signing of this Agreement, shall be entrusted with the following tasks and duties:

To verify the inventory of affected land or buildings within conflict zones. Once the inventory has been verified, the special commission shall submit copies to the Government of El Salvador and to COPAZ;

Should the need arise, to facilitate the settlement of disputes between current holders and rightful owners;

To take any decisions and measures it deems necessary and proper for the prompt and effective fulfilment of the agreements set forth in this chapter.

Legalization of land tenure

Except for particularly complex cases, the Government of El Salvador shall legalize the land-tenure situation in conflict zones definitively within six months from the signing of the cease-fire agreement, granting, as appropriate, individual or collective title to the land.

Payment for lands

Lands shall be purchased from their former owners at market prices. The sale to the current holders shall be subject to the same conditions as those granted to beneficiaries of the reformed sector. However, special conditions may be agreed to in the interests of the peace process.

Verification by COPAZ

COPAZ shall guarantee fulfilment of the agreements set forth in sections 2 and 3.

4   3 July 1991 agreement on occupied lands

The agreement on occupied lands between the Government of El Salvador and peasant organizations shall be respected.

With regard to lands occupied illegally after the date of that agreement, the Government of El Salvador gives notice that it reserves the right to enforce the relevant legal provisions so as to ensure that the rule of law prevails. FMLN holds that the agrarian problem, including land occupations, should be dealt with through consultation and the channels and mechanisms provided by the peace agreements.

[. . .]

2.3. Mozambique – The Rome Process: General Peace Agreement for Mozambique (1992)

[. . .]

Protocol III

(iv)   Return of Mozambican refugees and displaced persons and their social reintegration

(a) The parties undertake to co-operate in the repatriation and reintegration of Mozambican refugees and displaced persons in the national territory and the social integration of war-disabled;

(b) Without prejudice to the liberty of movement of citizens, the Government shall draw up a draft agreement with Renamo to organise the necessary assistance to refugees and displaced persons, preferably in their original places of residence. The parties agree to seek the involvement of the competent United Nations agencies in the drawing up and

implementation of this plan. The International Red Cross and other organisations to be agreed upon shall be invited to participate in the implementation of the plan;

(c) Mozambican refugees and displaced persons shall not forfeit any of the rights and freedoms of citizens for having left their original places of residence;

(d) Mozambican refugees and displaced persons shall be registered and included in the electoral rolls together with other citizens in their places of residence;

(e) Mozambican refugees and displaced persons shall be guaranteed restitution of property owned by them which is still in existence and the right to take legal action to secure the return of such property from individuals in possession of it.

[. . .]

2.4. Liberia – Cotonou Agreement (1993)

[. . .]

Article 18 – Repatriation of Refugees

The Parties hereby commit themselves immediately and permanently to bring to an end any further external or internal displacement of Liberians and to create the conditions that will allow all refugees and displaced persons to, respectively, voluntarily repatriate and return to Liberia to their places of origin or habitual residence under conditions of safety and dignity.

The Parties further call upon Liberian refugees and displaced persons to return to Liberia and to their places of origin or habitual residence and declare that they shall not be jeopardized in any ethnic, political, religious, regional or geographical considerations.

The Parties also call upon the relevant organizations of the United Nations system, particularly the Office of the United Nations High Commissioner for Refugees and the United Nations Development Programme, other intergovernmental and nongovernmental organizations, to implement programmes for the voluntary repatriation, return and reintegration of the Liberian refugees and internally displaced persons.

The Parties proclaim that they shall, jointly or individually, cooperate in all necessary ways with themselves and with the above-mentioned organizations in order to facilitate the repatriation, return and reintegration of the refugees and displaced persons. Amongst others, they agree to:

Establish all necessary mechanisms or arrangements, such as joint repatriation committees, which would facilitate contacts, communications and work with the relevant organizations for purposes of implementing the repatriation, return and reintegration operation and to enable effective decision-making and implementation of the relevant activities;

Facilitate access by the Office of the United Nations High Commissioner for Refugees and other organizations to the refugees and displaced persons who have returned so as to deliver the necessary humanitarian assistance and programmes and monitor their situation;

Guarantee and provide security to the Office of the United Nations High Commissioner for Refugees and the other relevant organizations, their staff, vehicles, equipment and resources necessary to carry out their work;

Provide all other necessary facilities and support that will be necessary to facilitate the implementation of the return, voluntary repatriation and reintegration of refugees and displaced persons.

[. . .]

2.5. Rwanda – Arusha Peace Agreement (1993)

[. . .]

Article 4

The right to property is a fundamental right for all the people of Rwanda. All refugees shall therefore have the right to repossess their property on return.

The two parties recommend, however, that in order to promote social harmony and national reconciliation, refugees who left the country more than 10 years ago should not reclaim their properties, which might have been occupied by other people.

The Government shall compensate them by putting land at their disposal and shall help them to resettle. As for estates which have been occupied by the Government, the returnee shall have the right for an equitable compensation by the Government.

[. . .]

2.6. Bosnia-Herzegovina – General Framework Agreement on Peace in Bosnia-Herzegovina (Dayton Peace Agreement) – Annex 7: Agreement on Refugees and Displaced Persons (1995)

The Republic of Bosnia and Herzegovina, the Federation of Bosnia and Herzegovina, and the Republika Srpska (the "Parties") have agreed as follows:

CHAPTER ONE: PROTECTION

Article I – Rights of Refugees and Displaced Persons

1. All refugees and displaced persons have the right freely to return to their homes of origin. They shall have the right to have restored to them property of which they were deprived in the course of hostilities since 1991 and to be compensated for any property that cannot be restored to them. The early return of refugees and displaced persons is an important objective of the settlement of the conflict in Bosnia and Herzegovina. The Parties confirm that they will accept the return of such persons who have left their territory, including those who have been accorded temporary protection by third countries.

2. The Parties shall ensure that refugees and displaced persons are permitted to return in safety, without risk of harassment, intimidation, persecution, or discrimination, particularly on account of their ethnic origin, religious belief, or political opinion.

3. The Parties shall take all necessary steps to prevent activities within their territories which would hinder or impede the safe and voluntary return of refugees and displaced persons. To demonstrate their commitment to securing full respect for the human rights and fundamental freedoms of all persons within their jurisdiction and creating without delay conditions suitable for return of refugees and

displaced persons, the Parties shall take immediately the following confidence building measures:

(a) the repeal of domestic legislation and administrative practices with discriminatory intent or effect;

(b) the prevention and prompt suppression of any written or verbal incitement, through media or otherwise, of ethnic or religious hostility or hatred;

(c) the dissemination, through the media, of warnings against, and the prompt suppression of, acts of retribution by military, paramilitary, and police services, and by other public officials or private individuals;

(d) the protection of ethnic and/or minority populations wherever they are found and the provision of immediate access to these populations by international humanitarian organizations and monitors;

(e) the prosecution, dismissal or transfer, as appropriate, of persons in military, paramilitary, and police forces, and other public servants, responsible for serious violations of the basic rights of persons belonging to ethnic or minority groups.

4. Choice of destination shall be up to the individual or family, and the principle of the unity of the family shall be preserved. The Parties shall not interfere with the returnees' choice of destination, nor shall they compel them to remain in or move to situations of serious danger or insecurity, or to areas lacking in the basic infrastructure necessary to resume a normal life. The Parties shall facilitate the flow of information necessary for refugees and displaced persons to make informed judgments about local conditions for return.

5. The Parties call upon the United Nations High Commissioner for Refugees ("UNHCR") to develop in close consultation with asylum countries and the Parties a repatriation plan that will allow for an early, peaceful, orderly and phased return of refugees and displaced persons, which may include priorities for certain areas and certain categories of returnees. The Parties agree to implement such a plan and to conform their international agreements and internal laws to it. They accordingly call upon States that have accepted refugees to promote the early return of refugees consistent with international law.

Article II – Creation of Suitable Conditions for Return

1. The Parties undertake to create in their territories the political, economic, and social conditions conducive to the voluntary return and harmonious reintegration of refugees and displaced persons, without preference for any particular group. The Parties shall provide all possible assistance to refugees and displaced persons and work to facilitate their voluntary return in a peaceful, orderly and phased manner, in accordance with the UNHCR repatriation plan.

2. The Parties shall not discriminate against returning refugees and displaced persons with respect to conscription into military service, and shall give positive consideration to requests for exemption from military or other obligatory service based on individual circumstances, so as to enable returnees to rebuild their lives.

Article III – Cooperation with International Organizations and International Monitoring

1. The Parties note with satisfaction the leading humanitarian role of UNHCR, which has been entrusted by the Secretary-General of the United Nations with the role of coordinating among all agencies assisting with the repatriation and relief of refugees and displaced persons.

2. The Parties shall give full and unrestricted access by UNHCR, the International Committee of the Red Cross ("ICRC"), the United Nations Development Programme ("UNDP"), and other relevant international, domestic and nongovernmental organizations to all refugees and displaced persons, with a view to facilitating the work of those organizations in tracing persons, the provision of medical assistance, food distribution, reintegration assistance, the provision of temporary and permanent housing, and other activities vital to the discharge of their mandates and operational responsibilities without administrative impediments. These activities shall include traditional protection functions and the monitoring of basic human rights and humanitarian conditions, as well as the implementation of the provisions of this Chapter.

3. The Parties shall provide for the security of all personnel of such organizations.

Article IV – Repatriation Assistance

The Parties shall facilitate the provision of adequately monitored, short-term repatriation assistance on a non-discriminatory basis to all returning refugees and displaced persons who are in need, in accordance with a plan developed by UNHCR and other relevant organizations, to enable the families and individuals returning to re-establish their lives and livelihoods in local communities.

Article V – Persons Unaccounted For

The Parties shall provide information through the tracing mechanisms of the ICRC on all persons unaccounted for. The Parties shall also cooperate fully with the ICRC in its efforts to determine the identities, whereabouts and fate of the unaccounted for.

Article VI – Amnesty

Any returning refugee or displaced person charged with a crime, other than a serious violation of international humanitarian law as defined in the Statute of the International Tribunal for the Former Yugoslavia since January 1, 1991 or a common crime unrelated to the conflict, shall upon return enjoy an amnesty. In no case shall charges for crimes be imposed for political or other inappropriate reasons or to circumvent the application of the amnesty.

CHAPTER TWO: COMMISSION FOR DISPLACED PERSONS AND REFUGEES

Article VII – Establishment of the Commission

The Parties hereby establish an independent Commission for Displaced Persons and Refugees (the "Commission"). The Commission shall have its headquarters in Sarajevo and may have offices at other locations as it deems appropriate.

Article VIII – Cooperation

The Parties shall cooperate with the work of the Commission, and shall respect and implement its decisions expeditiously and in good faith, in cooperation with relevant international and nongovernmental organizations having responsibility for the return and reintegration of refugees and displaced persons.

Article XI – Mandate

The Commission shall receive and decide any claims for real property in Bosnia and Herzegovina, where the property has not voluntarily been sold or otherwise transferred since April 1, 1992, and where the claimant does not now enjoy possession of that property. Claims may be for return of the property or for just compensation in lieu of return.

Article XII – Proceedings before the Commission

1. Upon receipt of a claim, the Commission shall determine the lawful owner of the property with respect to which the claim is made and the value of that property. The Commission, through its staff or a duly designated international or nongovernmental organization, shall be entitled to have access to any and all property records in Bosnia and Herzegovina, and to any and all real property located in Bosnia and Herzegovina for purposes of inspection, evaluation and assessment related to consideration of a claim.

2. Any person requesting the return of property who is found by the Commission to be the lawful owner of that property shall be awarded its return. Any person requesting compensation in lieu of return who is found by the Commission to be the lawful owner of that property shall be awarded just compensation as determined by the Commission. The Commission shall make decisions by a majority of its members.

3. In determining the lawful owner of any property, the Commission shall not recognize as valid any illegal property transaction, including any transfer that was made under duress, in exchange for exit permission or documents, or that was otherwise in connection with ethnic cleansing. Any person who is awarded return of property may accept a satisfactory lease arrangement rather than retake possession.

4. The Commission shall establish fixed rates that may be applied to determine the value of all real property in Bosnia and Herzegovina that is the subject of a claim before the Commission. The rates shall be based on an assessment or survey of properties in the territory of Bosnia and Herzegovina undertaken prior to April 1, 1992, if available, or may be based on other reasonable criteria as determined by the Commission.

5. The Commission shall have the power to effect any transactions necessary to transfer or assign title, mortgage, lease, or otherwise dispose of property with respect to which a claim is made, or which is determined to be abandoned. In particular, the Commission may lawfully sell, mortgage, or lease real property to any resident or citizen of Bosnia and Herzegovina, or to either Party, where the lawful owner has sought and received compensation in lieu of return, or where the property is determined to be abandoned in accordance with local law. The Commission may also lease property pending consideration and final determination of ownership.

6. In cases in which the claimant is awarded compensation in lieu of return of the property, the Commission may award a monetary grant or a compensation bond for the future purchase of real property. The Parties welcome the willingness of the international community assisting in the construction and financing of housing in Bosnia and Herzegovina to accept compensation bonds awarded by the Commission as payment, and to award persons holding such compensation bonds priority in obtaining that housing.

7. Commission decisions shall be final, and any title, deed, mortgage, or other legal instrument created or awarded by the Commission shall be recognized as lawful throughout Bosnia and Herzegovina.

8. Failure of any Party or individual to cooperate with the Commission shall not prevent the Commission from making its decision.

Article XIII – Use of Vacant Property

The Parties, after notification to the Commission and in coordination with UNHCR and other international and nongovernmental organizations contributing to relief and reconstruction, may temporarily house refugees and displaced persons in vacant property, subject to final determination of ownership by the Commission and to such temporary lease provisions as it may require.

Article XIV – Refugees and Displaced Persons Property Fund

1. A Refugees and Displaced Persons Property Fund (the "Fund") shall be established in the Central Bank of Bosnia and Herzegovina to be administered by the Commission. The Fund shall be replenished through the purchase, sale, lease

and mortgage of real property which is the subject of claims before the Commission. It may also be replenished by direct payments from the Parties, or from contributions by States or international or nongovernmental organizations.

2. Compensation bonds issued pursuant to Article XII(6) shall create future liabilities on the Fund under terms and conditions to be defined by the Commission.

Article XV – Rules and Regulations

The Commission shall promulgate such rules and regulations, consistent with this Agreement, as may be necessary to carry out its functions. In developing these rules and regulations, the Commission shall consider domestic laws on property rights.

Article XVI – Transfer

Five years after this Agreement takes effect, responsibility for the financing and operation of the Commission shall transfer from the Parties to the Government of Bosnia and Herzegovina, unless the Parties otherwise agree. In the latter case, the Commission shall continue to operate as provided above.

Article XVII – Notice

The Parties shall give effective notice of the terms of this Agreement throughout Bosnia and Herzegovina, and in all countries known to have persons who were citizens or residents of Bosnia and Herzegovina.

[. . .]

2.7. Guatemala – Agreement on Identity and Rights of Indigenous Peoples (1995)

[. . .]

F. Rights Relating to Land of the Indigenous Peoples

1. The rights relating to land of the indigenous peoples include both the communal or collective and the individual tenure of land, rights of ownership and possession and other real rights, and the use of natural resources for the benefit of the communities without detriment to their habitat. Legislative and administrative measures must be developed to ensure recognition, the awarding of title,

protection, recovery, restitution and compensation for those rights.

2. The lack of protection of the rights relating to land and natural resources of the indigenous peoples is part of a very wide-ranging set of problems resulting, inter alia, from the fact that both the indigenous and the non-indigenous peasants have had difficulty in having their rights legalized through the acquisition of title and land registration. When, in exceptional cases, they have been able to have their rights legalized, they have not had access to legal mechanisms to defend them. Since this problem is not exclusive to the indigenous population – although the latter has been particularly affected – it should be dealt with in the context of "Social and economic issues and the agrarian question", as one of the considerations to be taken into account in connection with the reform of the land tenure structure.

3. However, the situation with regard to the particular lack of protection and plundering of indigenous communal or collectively held lands merits special attention within the framework of this agreement. The Guatemalan Constitution establishes the obligation of the State to give special protection to cooperative, communal or collectively-held lands; recognizes the right of indigenous and other communities to maintain the system of administration of the lands which they hold and which historically belong to them; and lays down the obligation of the State to provide State lands for the indigenous communities which need them for their development.

4. Recognizing the special importance which their relationship to the land has for the indigenous communities, and in order to strengthen the exercise of their collective rights to the land and its natural resources, the Government undertakes to adopt directly, when that is within its competence, and to promote, when that is within the competence of the legislative organ or the municipal authorities, the following measures, inter alia, which shall be implemented in consultation and coordination with the indigenous communities concerned.

Regularization of the land tenure of indigenous communities

5. The Government shall adopt or promote measures to regularize the legal situation with regard to the communal possession of lands by communities which do not have the title deeds to those lands, including measures to award title to municipal or national lands with a clear communal tradition. To that end, an inventory of the land tenure situation shall be drawn up in each municipality.

Land tenure and use and administration of natural resources

6. The Government shall adopt or promote the following measures:

(a) Recognize and guarantee the right of access to lands and resources which are not occupied exclusively by communities but to which the latter have historically had access for their traditional activities and their subsistence (rights of way, such as passage, wood-cutting, access to springs, etc., and use of natural resources) and for their spiritual activities;

(b) Recognize and guarantee the right of communities to participate in the use, administration and conservation of the natural resources existing in their lands;

(c) Secure the approval of the indigenous communities prior to the implementation of any project for the exploitation of natural resources which might affect the subsistence and way of life of the communities. The communities affected shall receive fair compensation for any loss which they may suffer as a result of these activities; and

(d) Adopt, in cooperation with the communities, the measures necessary for the protection and preservation of the environment.

Restitution of communal lands and compensation for rights

7. Recognizing the particularly vulnerable situation of the indigenous communities, which have historically been the victims of land plundering, the Government undertakes to institute proceedings to settle the claims to communal lands formulated by the communities and to restore or pay compensation for those lands. In particular, the Government shall adopt or promote the following measures:

(a) Suspend the awarding of supplementary titles in respect of property to which the indigenous communities have claimed a right;

(b) Suspend the statute of limitations in respect of any action involving the plundering of the indigenous communities; and

(c) When the statute of limitations has already expired, however, establish procedures to compensate the communities which have been plundered with lands acquired for that purpose.

Acquisition of land for the development of indigenous communities

8. The Government shall take the necessary measures, without detriment to peasant smallholdings, to discharge its constitutional mandate to provide State lands for the indigenous communities which need them for their development.

Legal protection of the rights of indigenous communities

9. In order to facilitate the defence of the aforementioned rights and to protect the communities effectively, the Government undertakes to adopt or promote the following measures:

(a) Develop legal rules recognizing the right of indigenous communities to administer their lands in accordance with their customary norms;

(b) Promote an increase in the number of courts dealing with land cases and expedite procedures for the settlement of those cases;

(c) Urge faculties of law and the social sciences to strengthen the agrarian law component of the curriculum and include a knowledge of the relevant customary norms;

(d) Establish competent legal advisory services to advise on land claims;

(e) Provide the indigenous communities with the services of interpreters, free of charge, in respect of legal matters;

(f) Promote the widest dissemination, within indigenous communities, of information about land rights and the legal recourses available; and

(g) Eliminate any form of discrimination against women, in fact or in law, with regard to facilitating access to land, housing, loans and participation in development projects.

10. The Government undertakes to give the fulfilment of the undertakings set out in this section F the priority which the situation of insecurity and urgency that characterize the land problems of the indigenous communities deserves. To that end, the Government shall, in consultation with the indigenous peoples, establish a joint commission on the rights relating to land of the indigenous peoples to study, devise and propose more appropriate institutional arrangements and procedures. The commission shall be composed of representatives of the Government and of indigenous organizations.

[...]

2.8. Croatia – The Erdut Agreement (1995)

BASIC AGREEMENT ON THE REGION OF EASTERN SLAVONIA, BARANJA, AND WESTERN SIRMIUM

The Parties agree as follows:

1. There shall be a transitional period of 12 months which may be extended at most to another period of the same duration if so requested by one of the parties.

2. The U.N. Security Council is requested to establish a Transitional Administration, which shall govern the Region during the transitional period in the interest of all persons resident in or returning to the Region.

3. The U.N. Security Council is requested to authorize an international force to deploy during the transitional period to maintain peace and security in the Region and otherwise to assist in implementation of this Agreement. The Region shall be demilitarized according to the schedule and procedures determined by the international force. This demilitarization shall be completed not later than 30 days after deployment of the international force and shall include all military forces, weapons, and police, except for the international force and for police operating under the supervision of, or with the consent of, the Transitional Administration.

4. The Transitional Administration shall ensure the possibility for the return of refugees and displaced persons to their homes of origin. All persons who have left the Region or who have come to the Region with previous permanent residence in Croatia shall enjoy the same rights as all other residents of the Region. The Transitional Administration shall also take the steps necessary to re-establish the normal functioning of all public services in the Region without delay.

5. The Transitional Administration shall help to establish and train temporary police forces, to build

professionalism among the police and confidence among all ethnic communities.

6. The highest levels of internationally-recognized human rights and fundamental freedoms shall be respected in the Region.

7. All persons have the right to return freely to their place of residence in the Region and to live there in conditions of security. All persons who have left the Region or who have come to the Region with previous permanent residence in Croatia have the right to live in the Region.

8. All persons shall have the right to have restored to them any property that was taken from them by unlawful acts or that they were forced to abandon and to just compensation for property that cannot be restored to them.

9. The right to recover property, to receive compensation for property that cannot be returned, and to receive assistance in reconstruction of damaged property shall be equally available to all persons without regard to ethnicity.

10. Interested countries and organizations are requested to take appropriate steps to promote the accomplishment of the commitments in this Agreement. After the expiration of the transition period and consistent with established practice, the international community shall monitor and report on respect for human rights in the Region on a long term basis.

11. In addition, interested countries and organizations are requested to establish a commission, which will be authorized to monitor the implementation of this Agreement, particularly its human rights and civil rights provisions, to investigate all allegations of violations of this Agreement, and to make appropriate recommendations.

12. Not later than 30 days before the end of the transitional period, elections for all local government bodies, including for municipalities, districts, and counties, as well as the right of the Serbian community to appoint a joint Council of municipalities, shall be organized by the Transitional Administration. International organizations and institutions (e.g., the Organization for Security and Cooperation in Europe, the United Nations) and interested states are requested to oversee the elections.

13. The Government of the Republic of Croatia shall cooperate fully with the Transitional Adminis-

tration and the international force. During the transitional period, the Croatian Government authorizes the presence of international monitors along the international border of the Region in order to facilitate free movement of persons across existing border crossings.

14. This Agreement shall enter into force upon the adoption by the U.N. Security Council of a resolution responding affirmatively to the requests made in this Agreement.

Done this Twelfth day of November, 1995.

2.9. Tajikistan General Agreement on the Establishment of Peace and National Accord – Protocol on Refugee Issues (1997)

With a view to overcoming the consequences of the civil war and achieving peace and national accord in the country, and in accordance with the protocol on the fundamental principles for establishing peace and national accord in Tajikistan of 17 August 1995, the joint statement on the results of the fourth round of inter-Tajik talks in Almaty and the appeal by the President of the Republic of Tajikistan, Mr. E. Sh. Rakhmonov, and the leader of the United Tajik Opposition, Mr. S. A. Nuri, to their fellow countrymen who had been forced to leave the country, adopted in Moscow on 23 December 1996, the delegations of the Republic of Tajikistan and the United Tajik Opposition (hereinafter referred to as "the Parties"), have agreed as follows:

1. To step up mutual efforts to ensure the voluntary return, in safety and dignity, of all refugees and displaced persons to their homes, and to complete this process within 12 to 18 months from the date of signature of this Protocol. With a view to ensuring their safety, honour and dignity, the Parties also call upon the United Nations, the Organisation for Security and Cooperation in Europe (OSCE) and the Office of the United Nations High Commissioner for Refugees (UNHCR) to provide assistance in order to ensure the safety of returning refugees and displaced persons and to establish and expand their presence at places where such persons are living.

2. The Government of the Republic of Tajikistan assumes the obligation to reintegrate returning refugees and displaced persons into the social and

economic life of the country, which includes the provision to them of humanitarian and financial aid, assistance in finding employment and housing and the restoration of all their rights as citizens of the Republic of Tajikistan (including the return to them of dwellings and property and guaranteed uninterrupted service), and not to institute criminal proceedings against returning refugees or displaced persons for their participation in the political confrontation and the civil war, in accordance with the legislative acts in force in the Republic.

3. The Parties have decided to resume the work of the Joint Commission on problems relating to refugees and, within one month from the date of signature of this Protocol, with the assistance of UNHCR, to draw up a statute of the Commission.

4. The Parties have decided to instruct the Joint Commission, with the participation of representatives of local hukumats (executive committees) and the United Tajik Opposition for the period during which this Protocol is being implemented, to visit on a regular basis, in accordance with a separate timetable, refugee camps in the Islamic Republic of Afghanistan, places in the Commonwealth of Independent States (CIS) where there are concentrations of refugees and districts in the Republic of Tajikistan to which refugees and displaced persons intend to return. Similar visits shall be organised by the Joint Commission to places where displaced persons live in large numbers. The above-mentioned timetable shall be agreed by the Joint Commission within one month from the date of signature of this Protocol.

5. The Parties appeal to the Government of the CIS States to consider issuing temporary identity documents to refugees from Tajikistan and to assist UNHCR in carrying out additional measures to ensure the safety of refugees and to defend their honour and dignity.

6. The Parties express their sincere gratitude to the United Nations, UNHCR, OSCE, donor countries and the Aga Khan Foundation for their assistance and at the same time make an urgent appeal to them and to the International Monetary Fund, the World Bank, the European Development Bank, the Islamic Bank and the Aga Khan Foundation to provide additional and substantial financial and material support to refugees and displaced persons and to the Joint Commission on problems relating to

refugees, and also for the purpose of rehabilitating the national economy destroyed by the war and improving the well-being of the population.

[. . .]

2.10. Sierra Leone – Lomé Peace Agreement (1999)

[. . .]

Article XXII: Refugees and Displaced Persons

The Parties through the National Commission for Resettlement, Rehabilitation and Reconstruction agree to seek funding from and the involvement of the UN and other agencies, including friendly countries, in order to design and implement a plan for voluntary repatriation and reintegration of Sierra Leonean refugees and internally displaced persons, including non-combatants, in conformity with international conventions, norms and practices.

Article XXIII: Guarantee of the Security of Displaced Persons and Refugees

As a reaffirmation of their commitment to the observation of the conventions and principles of human rights and the status of refugees, the Parties shall take effective and appropriate measures to ensure that the right of Sierra Leoneans to asylum is fully respected and that no camps or dwellings of refugees or displaced persons are violated.

[. . .]

2.11. Burundi – Arusha Peace and Reconciliation Agreement for Burundi (2000)

PROTOCOL IV – RECONSTRUCTION AND DEVELOPMENT

PREAMBLE

We, the Parties,

Having considered the issues relating to the overall problem of reconstruction and development, including those associated with rehabilitation and resettlement of the refugees and *sinistrés*, with physical and political reconstruction and with economic and social development,

Having identified the principles, guidelines and activities for the transitional institutions in dealing with these issues,

Having incorporated the essentials of our work, including the analysis of the origin of the specific problems and the principles, guidelines and activities required to remedy this problem, in a report of Committee IV which serves as a reference document for the present Protocol and is reproduced as Annex IV to the Agreement,

Have agreed:

To support the rehabilitation and resettlement of the refugees and *sinistrés* by complying with the provisions of Chapter I of the present Protocol;

To work towards the country's physical and political reconstruction in conformity with the principles and measures set out in Chapter II of the present Protocol;

To strive towards the economic and social development of Burundi by following the guidelines defined in Chapter III of the present Protocol.

Chapter I – Rehabilitation and Resettlement of Refugees and *Sinistres*

Article 1 – Definitions

For the definition of the term "refugee", reference is made to international conventions, including the 1951 Geneva Convention Relative to the Status of Refugees, the 1966 Protocol Relative to the Status of Refugees and the 1969 Organization of African Unity Convention Governing the Specific Aspects of Refugee Problems in Africa.

The term "*sinistrés*" designates all displaced, regrouped and dispersed persons and returnees.

Article 2 – Principles Governing Return, Resettlement and Reintegration

The Government of Burundi shall encourage the return of refugees and *sinistrés* and resettle and reintegrate them. It shall seek the support of other countries and international and non-governmental organizations in carrying out this responsibility.

It shall respect the following principles:

All Burundian refugees must be able to return to their country;

Refugees no longer in their first country of asylum are entitled to the same treatment as other returning Burundian refugees;

Return must be voluntary and must take place in dignity with guaranteed security, and taking into account the particular vulnerability of women and children;

The reception mechanisms must be put in place in advance of the return;

Returnees must have their rights as citizens and their property restored to them in accordance with the laws and regulations in force in Burundi after the entry into force of the Agreement;

All *sinistrés* wishing to do so must be able to return to their homes;

Specific conditions must be provided for *sinistrés* who believe that they can no longer return to their property, so as to enable them to return to normal socio-professional life;

In the return of the refugees and the resettlement and reintegration of the returnees and displaced and regrouped persons, the principle of equity, including gender equity, must be strictly applied in order to avoid any measure or treatment that discriminates against or favours any one among these categories.

Article 3 – Preparatory Activities

The Government shall undertake the following preparatory activities:

Establishing and constituting a National Commission for the Rehabilitation of *Sinistrés* (CNRS), which shall have the mandate of organizing and coordinating, together with international organizations and countries of asylum, the return of refugees and *sinistrés*, assisting in their resettlement and reintegration, and dealing with all the other issues listed in the report of Committee IV. To this end, it shall draw up a plan of priorities. The members of the CNRS shall be drawn *inter alia* from the participating parties and the Government of Burundi, and shall elect the Commission's chairperson;

Establishing and constituting a Sub-Commission of the CNRS with the specific mandate of dealing with issues related to land as set out in article 8 (j) of the present Protocol;

Convening, in collaboration with the countries of asylum and the Office of the United Nations High Commissioner for Refugees, the Tripartite Commissioner, involving in it representatives of the refugees and international observers;

Requesting international organizations and the host countries concerned to conduct a gender and age disaggregated census of the refugees, including the old caseload refugees (1972);

Conducting a multi-dimensional census of the *sinistrés*;

Organizing information and awareness campaigns for refugees and *sinistrés* as well as visits to their places of origin;

Undertaking information and awareness campaigns on the mechanisms for peaceful coexistence and return to *collines* of origin;

Setting up reception committees where they do not yet exist. The role of these committees shall be to receive and provide support services for all the *sinistrés* returning to their homes, ensure their security and assist them in organizing their socio-economic reintegration.

Article 4 – Guidelines Governing Resettlement and Integration

The CNRS shall decide on the activities for the resettlement and integration of refugees and *sinistrés* in accordance with the priority plan taking into account the availability of resources, in order to achieve the following aims and objectives:

To ensure the socio-economic and administrative reintegration of the *sinistrés*;

To give all returning families, including female- and child-headed families, food aid, material support and assistance with health, education, agriculture and reconstruction until they become self-sufficient;

To provide communes, villages and *collines* with assistance in the reconstruction of community infrastructures and with support for income-generating activities, paying special attention to women and enhancing their roles in building and sustaining families and communities;

To settle all those who believe that they cannot yet return on sites close to home, in order to enable them to go and till their fields initially and return to their land later on;

To encourage, to the extent possible, grouped housing in the reconstruction policy in order to free cultivable land;

To ensure equity in the distribution of resources between the ethnic groups on the one hand and the provinces on the other, and to avoid overlap between the various parties involved;

To promote the participation of the population in the resettlement activities;

To help returnees to recover the property and bank accounts left in Burundi before their exile and whose existence has been duly proven;

To offer intensive language courses for returnees to mitigate the language problems;

To assist returnees in other areas such as medical services, psycho-social support, social security and retirement, education of children and the equivalency of diplomas awarded outside Burundi.

Article 5 – Actions with Regard to Returnees in Their Country of Asylum

The Government shall undertake the following actions with regard to returnees in their country of asylum:

Helping returnees settle their disputes in their country of asylum relating notably to immovable property, bank accounts, social security, etc;

In the context of agreements between countries or social security institutions, helping those who were employed in the country of asylum receive social security benefits to which they are entitled in respect of such employment;

Studying ways of indemnifying and compensating returnees for property in the country of asylum they are unable to take with them, profit from or sell;

Assisting pupils and students in their two final years of study in primary, secondary and higher education wishing to complete their studies in the country of asylum.

Article 6 – Other Actions

Any other action decided upon by the CNRS in accordance with the priority plan and in the light of available resources may be taken.

Article 7 – Access and Safety of International Personnel

The Government shall allow international organizations and international and local non-governmental organizations unrestricted access to returnees and other *sinistrés* for purposes of the delivery of humanitarian assistance. It must guarantee the safety of the staff of such organizations and must also facilitate the provision of short-term aid for repatriation, appropriately supervised and without discrimination.

Article 8 – Issues Relating to Land and Other Property

To resolve all issues relating to land and other property, the following principles and mechanisms shall be applied:

Property rights shall be guaranteed for all men, women and children. Compensation which is fair and equitable under the circumstances shall be payable in case of expropriation, which shall be allowed only in the public interest and in accordance with the law, which shall also set out the basis of compensation;

All refugees and/or *sinistrés* must be able to recover their property, especially their land;

If recovery proves impossible, everyone with an entitlement must receive fair compensation and/or indemnification;

Refugees who do not return may receive a just and equitable indemnification if their land had been expropriated without prior indemnification and in contravention of the principle set out in sub-paragraph (a) of the present article;

The policy with respect to distribution of State-owned land shall be reviewed so that priority can be given to the resettlement of *sinistrés*;

An inventory of destroyed urban property shall be drawn up with a view to making it habitable in order to redistribute it or return it as a priority to the original owners;

A series of measures shall be taken in order to avoid subsequent disputes over land, including the establishment of a register of rural land, the promulgation of a law on succession and, in the longer term, the conduct of a cadastral survey of rural land;

The policy of distribution or allocation of new lands shall take account of the need for environmental protection and management of the country's water system through protection of forests;

Burundi's Land Act must be revised in order to adjust it to the current problems with respect to land management;

The Sub-Commission on Land established in accordance with article 3 (b) of the present Protocol shall have the specific mandate of:

Examining all cases of land owned by old caseload refugees and state-owned land;

Examining disputed issues and allegations of abuse in the (re)distribution of land and ruling on each case in accordance with the above principles;

The Sub-Commission on Land must, in the performance of its functions, ensure the equity, transparency and good sense of all its decisions. It must always remain aware of the fact that the objective is not only restoration of their property to returnees, but also reconciliation between the groups as well as peace in the country.

Article 9 – National Fund for *Sinistrés*

A National Fund for *Sinistrés* shall be established, and shall derive its funding from the national budget and from grants by bilateral and multilateral aid agencies or assistance from non-governmental organizations.

Article 10 – Vulnerable Groups

The Government shall ensure, through special assistance, the protection, rehabilitation and advancement of vulnerable groups, namely child heads of families, orphans, street children, unaccompanied minors, traumatized children, widows, women heads of families, juvenile delinquents, the physically and mentally disabled, etc.

[. . .]

2.12. Ethiopia and Eritrea – Agreement between the Government of the Federal Democratic Republic of Ethiopia and the Government of the State of Eritrea (2000)

[. . .]

Article 5

1. Consistent with the Framework Agreement, in which the parties commit themselves to addressing the negative socio-economic impact of the crisis on the civilian population, including the impact on those persons who have been deported, a neutral Claims Commission shall be established. The mandate of the Commission is to decide through binding arbitration all claims for loss, damage or injury by one Government against the other, and by nationals (including both natural and juridical persons) of one party against the Government of the other party or entities owned or controlled by the other party that are (a) related to the conflict that was the subject of the Framework Agreement, the Modalities for its Implementation and the Cessation of Hostilities Agreement, and (b) result from violations of international humanitarian law, including the 1949 Geneva Conventions, or other violations of international law. The Commission shall not hear claims arising from the cost of military operations, preparing for military operations, or the use of force, except to the extent that such claims involve violations of international humanitarian law.

2. The Commission shall consist of five arbitrators. Each party shall, by written notice to the United Nations Secretary General, appoint two members within 45 days from the effective date of this agreement, neither of whom shall be nationals or permanent residents of the party making the appointment. In the event that a party fails to name one or both of its party-appointed arbitrators within the specified time, the Secretary-General of the United Nations shall make the appointment.

3. The president of the Commission shall be selected by the party-appointed arbitrators or failing their agreement within 30 days of the date of appointment of the latest party-appointed arbitrator, by the Secretary-General of the United Nations after consultation with the parties. The president shall be neither a national not permanent resident of either party.

4. In the event of the death or resignation of a member of the Commission in the course of the proceedings, a substitute member shall be appointed or chosen pursuant to the procedure set forth in this paragraph that was applicable to the appointment or choice of the arbitrator being replaced.

5. The Commission shall be located in The Hague. At its discretion it may hold hearings and conduct investigations in the territory of either party, or at such other location as it deems expedient.

6. The Commission shall be empowered to employ such professional, administrative and clerical staff as it deems necessary to accomplish its work, including establishment of a Registry. The Commission may also retain consultants and experts to facilitate the expeditious completion of its work.

7. The Commission shall adopt its own rules of procedure based upon the 1992 Permanent Court of Arbitration Optional Rules for Arbitrating Disputes Between Two States. All decisions of the Commission shall be made by a majority of the commissioners.

8. Claims shall be submitted to the Commission by each of the parties on its own behalf and on behalf of its nationals, including both natural and juridical persons. All claims submitted to the Commission shall be filed no later than one year from the effective date of this agreement. Except for claims submitted to another mutually agreed settlement mechanism in accordance with paragraph 16 or filed in another forum prior to the effective date of this agreement, the Commission shall be the sole forum for adjudicating claims described in paragraph 1 or filed under paragraph 9 of this Article, and any such claims which could have been and were not submitted by that deadline shall be extinguished, in accordance with international law.

9. In appropriate cases, each party may file claims on behalf of persons of Ethiopian or Eritrean origin who may not be its nationals. Such claims shall be considered by the Commission on the same basis as claims submitted on behalf of that party's nationals.

10. In order to facilitate the expeditious resolution of these disputes, the Commission shall be authorized to adopt such methods of efficient case management and mass claims processing as it deems appropriate, such as expedited procedures for processing claims and checking claims on a sample basis for further verification only if circumstances warrant.

11. Upon application of either of the parties, the Commission may decide to consider specific claims, or categories of claims, on a priority basis.

12. The Commission shall commence its work not more than 15 days after it is constituted and shall endeavor to complete its work within three years of the date when the period for filing claims closes pursuant to paragraph 8.

13. In considering claims, the Commission shall apply relevant rules of international law. The Commission shall not have the power to make decisions *ex aequo et bono*.

14. Interest, costs and fees may be awarded.

15. The expenses of the Commission shall be borne equally by the parties. Each party shall pay any invoice form the Commission within 30 days of its receipt.

16. The parties may agree at any time to settle outstanding claims, individually or by categories, through direct negotiation or by reference to another mutually agreed settlement mechanism.

17. Decisions and awards of the commission shall be final and binding. The parties agree to honor all decisions and to pay any monetary awards rendered against them promptly.

18. Each party shall accord to members of the Commission and its employees the privileges and immunities that are accorded to diplomatic agents under the Vienna Convention on Diplomatic Relations.

[. . .]

2.13. Liberia – Comprehensive Peace Agreement between the Government of Liberia and the Liberians United for Reconciliation and Democracy (LURD) and the Movement for Democracy in Liberia (MODEL) and Political Parties (2003)

[. . .]

Article XXX – Refugees and Displaced Persons

1a. The NTGL, with the assistance of the International Community, shall design and implement a plan for the voluntary return and reintegration of Liberian refugees and internally displaced persons, including non-combatants, in accordance with international conventions, norms and practices.

b. Refugees or internally displaced persons, desirous of returning to their original Counties or permanent residences, shall be assisted to do so.

c. The Parties commit themselves to peaceful co-existence amongst returnees and non-returnees in all Counties.

[. . .]

2.14. Sudan – Comprehensive Peace Agreement – Agreement on Wealth Sharing during the Pre-Interim and Interim Period (2004)

WHEREAS the Government of the Republic of the Sudan and the Sudan People's Liberation Movement/Sudan People's Liberation Army (the Parties) have been conducting negotiations in Naivasha, Kenya, since 6th December, 2003, under the auspices of the IGAD Peace mediated Process; and having taken up the division of wealth in pursuit of a comprehensive agreement, that will ensure a just and durable peace in the Sudan;

NOW RECORD THAT they have reached agreement on Wealth Sharing, covering the division of oil and non-oil revenues, the management of the oil sector, the monetary authority and the reconstruction of the South and other war-affected areas during the Pre-Interim and Interim Period;

THE PARTIES AGREE AND CONFIRM THAT they are determined to build on this important Agreement until a comprehensive peace Agreement is reached. It is within this context, that the Parties agree to continue negotiations on the remaining outstanding issues on the Conflict Areas and Power Sharing and subsequently negotiate a comprehensive ceasefire Agreement and Implementation Modalities in order to achieve a final comprehensive Peace Agreement in the Sudan.

[. . .]

2.0 OWNERSHIP OF LAND AND NATURAL RESOURCES

2.1 Without prejudice to the position of the Parties with respect to ownership of land and subterranean natural resources, including in Southern Sudan, this Agreement is not intended to address the ownership of those resources. The Parties agree to establish a process to resolve this issue.

2.2   The Parties agree that the regulation, management, and the process for the sharing of wealth from subterranean natural resources are addressed below.

2.3   The Parties record that the regulation of land tenure, usage and exercise of rights in land is to be a concurrent competency exercised at the appropriate levels of government.

2.4   Rights in land owned by the Government of Sudan shall be exercised through the appropriate or designated levels of Government.

2.5   The Parties agree that a process be instituted to progressively develop and amend the relevant laws to incorporate customary laws and practices, local heritage and international trends and practices.

2.6   Without prejudice to the jurisdiction of courts, there shall be established a National Land Commission that shall have the following functions:

2.6.1   Arbitrate between willing contending Parties on claims over land, and sort out such claims.

2.6.2   The party or group making claims in respect of land may make a claim against the relevant government and/or other Parties interested in the land.

2.6.3   The National Land Commission may at its discretion entertain such claims.

2.6.4   The Parties to the arbitration shall be bound by the decision of the National Land Commission on mutual consent and upon registration of the award in a court of law.

2.6.5   The National Land Commission shall apply the law applicable in the locality where the land is situated or such other law as the Parties to the arbitration agree, including principles of equity.

2.6.6   Accept references on request from the relevant government, or in the process of resolving claims, and make recommendations to the appropriate levels of government concerning:

2.6.6.1   Land reform policies;

2.6.6.2   Recognition of customary land rights and/or law.

2.6.7   Assess appropriate land compensation, which need not be limited to monetary compensation, for applicants in the course of arbitration or in the course of a reference from a court.

2.6.8   Advise different levels of government on how to co-ordinate policies on national projects.

2.6.9   Study and record land use practices in areas where natural resource exploitation occurs.

2.6.10   The National Land Commission shall be representative and independent. The composition of the membership and terms of appointment of the National Land Commission shall be set by the legislation constituting it. The Chairperson of the National Land Commission shall be appointed by the Presidency.

2.6.11   The National Land Commission may conduct hearings and formulate its own rules of procedure.

2.6.12   The National Land Commission will have its budget approved by the Presidency and will be accountable to the Presidency for the due performance of its functions.

2.7   In accordance with this Agreement and without prejudice to the jurisdiction of courts, there shall be established a Southern Sudan Land Commission which shall have the following functions:

2.7.1   Arbitrate between willing contending Parties on claims over land, and sort out such claims.

2.7.2   The party or group making claims in respect of land may make a claim against the relevant government and/or other Parties interested in the land.

2.7.3   The Southern Sudan Land Commission may entertain such claims at its discretion.

2.7.4   The Parties to the arbitration shall be bound by the Southern Sudan Land Commission's decision on mutual consent and upon registration of the award in a court of law.

2.7.5   The Southern Sudan Land Commission shall apply the law applicable in the locality where the land is situated or such other law as the Parties to the arbitration agree, including principles of equity.

2.7.6   Accept references on request from the relevant government, or in the process of resolving claims, and make recommendations to the appropriate levels of government concerning:

2.7.6.1   Land reform policies;

2.7.6.2   Recognition of customary land rights and/or law.

2.7.7   Assess appropriate land compensation, which need not be limited to monetary compensation, for applicants in the course of arbitration or in the course of a reference from a court.

2.7.8   Advise different levels of government on how to co-ordinate policies on GOSS projects.

2.7.9   Study and record land use practices in areas where natural resource exploitation occurs.

2.7.10   The Southern Sudan Land Commission shall be representative and independent. The composition of the membership and terms of appointment of the Southern Sudan Land Commission shall be set by the legislation constituting it. The Chairperson of the Southern Sudan Land Commission shall be appointed by the President of the Government of Southern Sudan.

2.7.11   The Southern Sudan Land Commission may conduct hearings and formulate its own rules of procedure.

2.7.12   The Southern Sudan Land Commission shall have its budget approved by the Government of Southern Sudan and shall be accountable to the President of the Government of Southern Sudan for the due performance of its functions.

2.8   The National Land Commission and the Southern Sudan Land Commission shall co-operate and co-ordinate their activities so as to use their resources efficiently. Without limiting the matters of coordination, the National Land Commission and the Southern Sudan Land Commission may agree:

a) to exchange information and decisions of each Commission;

b) that certain functions of the National Land Commission, including collection of data and research, may be carried out through the Southern Sudan Land Commission;

c) on the way in which any conflict between the findings or recommendations of each Commission may be resolved.

2.9   In the case of conflict between the findings or recommendations of the National Land Commission and the Southern Sudan Land Commission, which cannot be resolved by agreement, the two shall reconcile their positions. Failure to reconcile, the matter shall be referred to the Constitutional Court.

3. VOLUNTARY REPATRIATION AGREEMENTS

3.1. Socialist Republic of Vietnam and UNHCR (1988)[17]

[. . .]

Article 3(b)

The SRV [Socialist Republic of Vietnam] will ensure that such persons would be allowed to return to their place of origin. If return to the place of origin is not feasible, they will be allowed to return to a comparable place of their choice subject to the approval of the local authorities.

[. . .]

Article 12 Annex

The duration of transit [in SRV reception centres] should be kept to a minimum and should not exceed two weeks.

Article 13 Annex

In exceptional cases where the return of an individual or family to the place of origin may prove not to be in the best interest of the returnee, a suitable alternative place will be identified upon consultations between the returnee concerned, the SRV and UNHCR. The ultimate choice of the place of installation will be in accordance with paragraph 3(b) of the Memorandum. However, lack of decision with respect to place of installation of an applicant shall not prevent the authorities from issuing authorisation of return to the country to the applicant concerned.

[. . .]

---

[17] Memorandum of Understanding between the Socialist Republic of Vietnam and UNHCR, 13 December 1988.

3.2. Republic of South Africa and UNHCR (1991)[18]

[. . .]

ANNEXURE

[. . .]

Article 4(a)

The parties hereto shall co-operate on the basis of the following principles and provisions: (b) The returnees will enjoy complete freedom of movement in South Africa and, in this context, will have the right to return to the areas where they lived immediately prior to leaving South Africa or to a comparable area of their choice.

[. . .]

Article 21

The Government, the UNHCR and implementing partner(s) shall consult on the situation of any returning minor or vulnerable person such as the aged and the sick, whose family fails, or is not in a position to take him or her back, with a view to finding an appropriate place of integration, bearing in mind the best interest of the returnee . . .

[. . .]

3.3. Guatemala and UNHCR (1991)[19]

[. . .]

Terms of Reference – Paragraph 2

The Government of Guatemala provides guarantees that, in furtherance of Article 4 of the Constitution of the Republic which guarantees the liberty and equality, as well as the rights of all Guatemalans, returnees shall not suffer any discrimination in the exercise of their social, civil,

political, cultural and economic rights based on the mere fact of having been refugees.

[. . .]

Terms of Reference – Paragraph 6

The Government of the Republic will provide facilities to those returnees without land at the time they abandoned the country, for access to land and registration of the same in conditions similar to that provided to other nationals.

For those returnees who were formerly landowners, had acquired rights to land, or occupied land, in conditions contemplated by the law, the Government will do all in its power to guarantee that they may recover and register the same, or in case an agreement is reached with the owners, legatees, or occupiers, that they may be compensated with land similar in quality and location to those previously owned or occupied, as well as the registration thereof.

[. . .]

3.4. United Republic of Tanzania, Democratic Republic of the Congo and UNHCR (1991)[20]

[. . .]

Article 9 – Access to Returnees for UNCHR

. . . UNCHR shall be allowed to accompany returnees to their home areas and shall enjoy unhindered access to the returnees.

Article 10 – Settlement of Returnees

The Government of the Democratic Republic of the Congo shall take all measures to allow returnees to settle in areas of their origin or choice and assist them recover any property they may have left behind.

Article 11 – Reintegration of Refugees

The Government of the Democratic Republic of the Congo shall ensure the reintegration of Congolese returnees in the socio-economic life of the nation. It shall guarantee to all the returnees, including those

---

[18] Memorandum of Understanding between the Government of the Republic of South Africa and UNHCR on the Voluntary Repatriation and Reintegration of South African Returnees, 16 August 1991 – Annexure to Memorandum of Understanding.

[19] Letter of Understanding between the Government of Guatemala and the Office of the UNHCR Relating to the Voluntary Repatriation of Guatemalan Refugees, 13 November 1991 (Spanish with English translation).

[20] Tripartite Agreement on the Voluntary Repatriation of Congolese Refugees from Tanzania (The Government of the United Republic of Tanzania, the Government of the Democratic Republic of the Congo and the UNHCR), 27 August 1991.

who previously were civil servants or who form part of military units, equal enjoyment of all the socio-economic, civil and political rights recognized in domestic and international law.

[. . .]

Article 20 Role and Function of the Commission

The Commission is responsible for monitoring the implementation of measures to facilitate voluntary repatriation of Congolese refugees and the reintegration of returnees in their communities of origin. It shall ensure the implementation of the provisions of this Agreement, particularly those relating to returnee's security and assistance.

[. . .]

3.5. Islamic State of Afghanistan, Republic of Iran and UNHCR (1992)[21]

[. . .]

Article 7

In its work the Commission shall be guided by respect for the following principles:

[. . .]

(c) repatriants shall, upon return, enjoy freedom of movement and establishment, including the right to return to the areas where they lived prior to leaving Afghanistan or to the area of their choice.

(d) repatriants must be protected from any form of harassment, including unauthorized charges or fees, unlawful arrest or detention, and threats to life or property.

[. . .]

3.6. Republic of Mozambique, Zimbabwe and UNHCR (1993)[22]

[. . .]

---

[21] Agreement between the Government of the Islamic State of Afghanistan, the Government of the Islamic Republic of Iran and the United Nations High Commissioner for Refugees for the Repatriation of Afghan Refugees in Iran, 31 October 1992.

[22] Tripartite Agreement between the Government of the Republic of Mozambique, the Government of Zimbabwe and UNHCR for the Voluntary Repatriation of Mozambican Refugees from Zimbabwe, 22 March 1993.

Article 8 – Treatment of the Returnees

1. Pursuant to the General Peace Accord, as well as other reconciliation initiatives taken by the Mozambican Government and other parties, the returnees shall have the right of return to return their former places of residence or to any other places of their choice within Mozambique. They shall not be subject to any form of legal process, persecution, discrimination or punishment for any reason whatsoever on account of their having been refugees.

2. . . . the Mozambican Government shall issue, together with other relevant parties, a declaration inviting all refugees to return and guaranteeing that no one shall be punished or discriminated against on account of his religion, political affiliation or for having been in exile.

[. . .]

4. The Mozambican Government shall ensure that returnees have access to land for settlement and use, in accordance with Mozambique laws.

5. The Mozambican Government shall, in accordance with the relevant provisions of Protocol III of the General Peace Accord, assist returnees who attempt to recover their lost property.

[. . .]

3.7. Union of Myanmar and UNHCR (1993)[23]

[. . .]

Article 2

The GOUM [Government of the Union of Myanmar] will ensure that the returnees will be allowed to return to their respective places of origin.

[. . .]

Article 13

UNCHR will seek to obtain the necessary funds for appropriate reintegration assistance to returnees under this present understanding which will be aimed at helping those persons to resume their normal life in the shortest possible time. This humanitarian assistance in immediate terms

---

[23] Memorandum of Understanding between the Government of the Union of Myanmar and UNHCR, 5 November 1993.

will cover areas such as . . . initial installation. . . . Assistance in the sectors of . . . water and sanitation will also be provided in the areas of return in coordination with the UNDP's programme in the Rakhine State.

[. . .]

3.8. Abkhazia, Georgia, Russian Federation and UNHCR (1994)[24]

The Abkhaz and Georgian sides, hereinafter referred to as the Parties, the Russian Federation and the United Nations High Commissioner for Refugees,

Recalling Security Council resolutions 849 (1993) of 9 July 1993, 854 (1993) of 6 August 1993, 858 (1993) of 24 August 1993, 876 (1993) of 19 October 1993, 892 (1993) of 22 December 1993, 896 (1994) of 31 January 1994, 901 (1994) of 4 March 1994 and 906 (1994) of 25 March 1994,

Recognizing that the right of all citizens to live in and to return to their country of origin is enshrined in the Universal Declaration of Human Rights and the International Covenant on Civil and Political Rights,

Noting conclusions 18 (XXXI) and 40 (XXXVI) of the Executive Committee of the Programme of the Office of the United Nations High Commissioner for Refugees, which constitute internationally agreed principles governing the repatriation of refugees,

Acting in accordance with the Memorandum of Understanding signed by the Parties on 1 December 1993 and especially paragraph 4, under which Parties expressed their willingness to create conditions for the voluntary, safe and dignified return of displaced persons to their permanent places of residence in all regions of Abkhazia,

Recalling that resolution 428 (V) of 14 December 1950, by which the General Assembly of the United Nations adopted the statute of the Office of the United Nations High Commissioner for Refugees, ascribes to the High Commissioner the function of providing international protection to refugees and of seeking permanent solutions for the problems

of refugees, inter alia, by promoting and facilitating their voluntary repatriation,

Given the responsibility entrusted to the United Nations High Commissioner for Refugees to act, under the Secretary-General's authority, as the international lead agency for the repatriation of displaced persons to Abkhazia,

Noting the desire of the Parties to cooperate with each other to achieve full observance of the principles and safeguards governing voluntary repatriation,

Considering the need, therefore, to establish a framework to define modalities of such cooperation for implementation of the repatriation,

Noting that the Parties agree that a repatriation operation to Abkhazia will imply, prior to its implementation, that the security and living conditions in the areas of return are guaranteed.

Have Agreed on the Following Provisions:

1. The Parties agree to cooperate and to interact in planning and conducting the activities aimed to safeguard and guarantee the safe, secure and dignified return of people who have fled from areas of the conflict zone to the areas of their previous permanent residence.

2. For the purpose of the present agreement, the parties will guarantee the safety of refugees and displaced persons in the course of the voluntary repatriation and rehabilitation operations to be organized.

3. In implementing this voluntary repatriation programme, the Parties undertake to respect the following principles:

    a. Displaced persons/refugees have the right to return voluntarily to their places of origin or residence irrespective of their ethnic, social or political affiliation under conditions of complete safety, freedom and dignity;

    b. The voluntary character of the repatriation shall be ascertained and respected through appropriate arrangements;

    c. Displaced persons/refugees shall have the right to return peacefully without risk of arrest, detention, imprisonment or legal criminal proceedings.

Such immunity shall not apply to persons where there are serious evidences that they

---

[24] Quadripartite Agreement on Voluntary Return of Refugees and Displaced Persons, 4 April 1994 (Abkhazia, Georgia, Russian Federation, UNHCR).

have committed war crimes and crimes against humanity as defined in international instruments and international practice as well as serious non-political crimes committed in the context of the conflict. Such immunity shall also not apply to persons who have previously taken part in the hostilities and are currently serving in armed formations, preparing to fight in Abkhazia. Persons falling into these categories should be informed through appropriate channels of the possible consequences they may face upon return;

d. The Parties shall ensure that returnees, upon return, will enjoy freedom of movement and establishment including the right to return to the areas where they lived prior to leaving the conflict zone or to the area of their choice;

e. The Parties shall ensure that refugees and displaced persons, upon return, will get their expired documents (propiska, passport) extended and validated for their previous place of residence or the elected place of return;

f. The Parties shall ensure that repatriants, upon return, will be protected from harassment, including unauthorized charges or fees and threat to life or property;

g. Returnees shall, upon return, get back movable and immovable properties they left behind and should be helped to do so, or to receive whenever possible an appropriate compensation for their lost properties if return of property appears not feasible.

The Commission mentioned in paragraph 5 below will establish a mechanism for such claims. Such compensation should be worked out in the framework of the reconstruction/rehabilitation programmes to be established with a financial assistance through the United Nations Voluntary Fund;

h. Displaced persons/refugees who choose not to return to Abkhazia shall continue to be assisted and protected until acceptable alternative solutions are found for such cases;

i. In accordance with the fundamental principle of preserving family unity, where it is not possible for families to repatriate as units, a mechanism shall be established for their reunification in Abkhazia. Measures shall also be taken for the identification and extra care/assistance for unaccompanied minors and other vulnerable persons during the repatriation process;

j. The Parties agree that refugees and displaced persons will be guaranteed unimpeded access to all available information on the situation in the areas where repatriation will take place. Such an information should be provided in the framework of a campaign to be launched by the Commission as mentioned in paragraph 9 (b) below.

4. For the purpose of the implementation of voluntary return of displaced persons and refugees to Abkhazia, a quadripartite Commission is hereby established.

5. The principal tasks of the Commission shall be to formulate, discuss and approve plans to implement programmes for the safe, orderly and voluntary repatriation of the refugees and displaced persons to Abkhazia from Georgia, the Russian Federation and within Abkhazia and for their successful reintegration. Such plans should include registration, transport, basic material assistance for a period of up to six months and rehabilitation assistance.

In order to create the conditions for the return of refugees and displaced persons, the Commission will establish a working group of experts to undertake an assessment of the level of damage to the economic and social infrastructure in Abkhazia, the availability of housing and the extent of damage to houses in the areas of return as well as the projected needs in rehabilitation/reconstruction, with financial implications. This survey should be undertaken region by region according to the plan of return to be worked out and accepted by the Parties, bearing in mind that the Parties have agreed to start the repatriation operation with the Gali region.

6. The Commission shall be composed of four members, one being designated by each of the Parties and two representing the Russian Federation and the United Nations High Commissioner for Refugees.

In addition, the Conference on Security and Cooperation in Europe (CSCE) will designate a representative to attend the Commission's meetings in an observer capacity. If circumstances do not allow the designated CSCE representative to attend such meetings, the Commission will keep the CSCE mission in Georgia informed on a regular basis on the progress of the Commission's work.

7. Any member of the Commission may, when attending any meeting of the Commission, be accompanied by such advisers as the Party designating that member may deem necessary. Where a member of the Commission is unable to attend any meeting of the Commission, the Party concerned may designate a substitute.

8. The Commission shall meet as often as required, but no less frequently than once every month. Meetings of the Commission may be convened at the request of any of the members and shall be held on the territory of the Russian Federation, except as the members of the Commission may otherwise agree. The Parties agree to guarantee the personal security of the members of the Commission and personnel involved in the activities agreed.

The first meeting of the Commission shall be scheduled as soon as possible and no later than one week after the adoption by the Security Council of a resolution on a mechanism ensuring the security conditions in the areas of return.

9. During its first meeting, the Commission will set out the modalities of the assessment mentioned in paragraph 5 above and will establish a plan concerning:

a. The areas where repatriation will be primarily conducted according to the level of guaranteed security and preparedness;

b. The implementation of an information campaign among the displaced person/refugee population to encourage voluntary return;

c. The registration process of persons expressing their willingness to return;

d. The activities needed to safeguard the safety of returnees based on the principles set out in paragraph 3 (a) to (j) above;

e. The needs for financial, transport and basic material assistance to displaced persons/refugees as well as projected needs for rehabilitation/reconstruction of the areas of return as mentioned in paragraph 5 above.

10. The Parties agree that representatives of refugees and displaced persons shall be provided with facilities to visit the areas of return and to see for themselves arrangements made for their return.

11. In the event of disagreement within the Commission regarding the application and interpretation of this Agreement, where such disagreement cannot amicably be settled among the members of the Commission, the Commission shall refer such disagreements to the Parties and to the Russian Federation and the United Nations High Commissioner for Refugees.

The Parties, The Russian Federation and The United Nations High Commissioner for Refugees Further Agree as Follows:

a. UNHCR shall have direct and unhindered access to all displaced persons/refugees from Abkhazia in order to undertake activities essential to the discharge of its mandate and operational and monitoring responsibilities;

b. Travel shall be facilitated between and within all areas where refugees and displaced persons are located and areas of return for the personnel of the United Nations and other relevant international and non-governmental agencies cooperating with the United Nations in repatriation, reintegration and rehabilitation programmes. It shall include the free use of airspace and authorized airstrips and airports for relief flights and the exemption from taxes and duties of all goods imported for use in the voluntary repatriation programme of displaced persons/refugees from Abkhazia and for the provision of relief integration and rehabilitation assistance to the Abkhazian region by the United Nations and cooperating agencies, as well as the expeditious clearance and handling of such goods;

c. The Russian Federation will guarantee unimpeded transit of humanitarian supplies through its territory for the purposes of the present Agreement;

d. UNHCR shall establish local offices, as deemed appropriate, at locations to be approved by the Parties concerned, to facilitate voluntary repatriation, reintegration and rehabilitation;

e. The security of the staff and property of the United Nations and the cooperating agencies shall be guaranteed;

f. The allocation and continued use by the Parties, the United Nations and the cooperating agencies of particularly designated radio frequencies for radio communications between their offices, vehicles, and staff, in areas where refugees and displaced persons are located and in areas of return, shall be provided.

This agreement shall enter into force with immediate effect and shall remain in force for the period required for the effective voluntary return of the displaced persons/refugees.

In witness whereof, the authorized representatives of the Abkhaz and Georgian sides, the Russian Federation and the United Nations High Commissioner for Refugees, have signed the present agreement.

Done at Moscow, this fourth day of April 1994 in four originals, three in the Russian language, and one in the English language, the four texts being equally authentic but the English text being authoritative for interpretation purposes.

3.9. United Republic of Tanzania, Republic of Rwanda and UNHCR (1995)[25]

[. . .]

Article 7

To create conditions conducive to the returnees' reintegration, the Government of the Republic of Rwanda shall take all measures to sensitize and prepare local populations residing in areas of return.

[. . .]

Article 10

. . . [T]he Government of the Republic of Rwanda shall take all measures possible to allow returnees to settle in areas of their origin or choice and shall protect their property. It shall also put in place necessary mechanisms to settle all disputes relating to ownership and enjoyment of properties affecting returnees according to due process of law.

[. . .]

Article 12

The Government of the Republic of Rwanda shall ensure the reintegration of Rwandese [*sic*] returnees in the socio-economic life of the nation, benefiting as much as possible from the different national public services available to all citizens. It shall guarantee the returnees equal enjoyment of all the socio-economic, civil and political rights recognized in domestic and international law.

[. . .]

Article 15

To facilitate return in safety and dignity of the refugees and to contribute to the implementation of reintegration measures, the UNHCR shall establish presence in the main areas of the returnee's settlements.

[. . .]

3.10. Republic of Angola and UNHCR (1995)[26]

[. . .]

Article 4(1)

The returnees shall have the right to return to their former places of residence or to any other places of their choice within Angola. They shall not be subject to any form of legal process, persecution, discrimination or punishment on account of their religion, ethnic origin or political affiliation, or for having left the country as refugees.

[. . .]

Article 4(3)

The Government shall ensure that returnees have access to land for settlement and use, in accordance with relevant Angolan laws.

Article 4(4)

The Government shall provide appropriate assistance to returnees who attempt to recover their lost property, in accordance with relevant Angolan laws.

[. . .]

---

[25] Tripartite Agreement on the Voluntary Repatriation of Rwandese Refugees from Tanzania, 12 April 1995.

[26] Memorandum of Understanding between the Government of the Republic of Angola and the UNHCR for the Voluntary Repatriation and Reintegration of Angolan Refugees, 14 June 1995.

3.11. Republic of Liberia and UNHCR (1996)[27]

[. . .]

PREAMBLE (PARA 5)

. . . [A]gree that all Liberian refugees have the right to return to their places of origin or habitual residence under conditions of safety and dignity.

PREAMBLE (PARA 6)

. . . Recognising that special measures and legal arrangements are necessary within Liberia for the safe and orderly repatriation and reintegration of the refugees.

[. . .]

Article 10 – Vulnerable Groups

The Government shall, in cooperation with UNHCR and interested non-governmental organizations, identify vulnerable individuals, in particular unaccompanied minors, single families in need of protected and special attention to assure their fundamental rights.

[. . .]

Government of the Republic of Liberia, Declaration on the Rights and Security of Returnees, *3 January 1996*

The Liberian National Transitional Government:

[. . .]

PREAMBLE (PARA 7)

Underlining the rights and freedoms of all Liberians living outside Liberia as refugees to return home to their place of habitual residence or to establish residence in any part of the country . . .

[. . .]

SECTION A(1)

Declares its commitment to respect the right of all Liberians to return to their places of origin or habitual residence in safety and dignity.

[27] Agreement between the Government of the Republic of Liberia and the UNCHR for Refugees for the Voluntary Repatriation and Reintegration of Liberian Returnees from Asylum Countries, 3 January 1996.

[. . .]

SECTION B(3) DECLARES

. . . No returnees shall suffer any form of harassment, intimidation, discrimination or persecution for reasons of membership of particular social group, ethnic, gender, religious, political opinion, regional or geographical considerations.

SECTION C – RESPECT FOR HUMAN RIGHTS

The basic human rights and fundamental freedoms of returnees will be fully respected and guaranteed. (2) All Liberian citizens are under obligation to respect all national and international instruments relevant to protection of basic human rights.

SECTION D – RETURNEE MONITORING

The United Nations, and in particular UNHCR will be allowed and will receive full cooperation and access to monitor the treatment of returnees in accordance with humanitarian and human rights standards, including the implementation of commitments contained herein.

SECTION E – ACCESS TO LAND

Returnees shall have their rights to their original land restored upon return. In addition, returnees will have access to land for settlement and agricultural use in accordance with Liberian laws.

SECTION F – PROPERTY

All measures will be taken to facilitate, to the extent possible the recovery and restitution to the returnees of their land or immovable and to the extent possible movable property which has been lost or left behind.

[. . .]

3.12. Republic of Burundi, United Republic of Tanzania and UNHCR (2001)[28]

[. . .]

[28] Tripartite Agreement on the Voluntary Repatriation of Burundian Refugees in Tanzania, 8 May 2001.

Article 4 – Responsibilities of the Country of Origin: The Republic of Burundi, Section 5: Settlement of Refugees

In conformity with Protocol IV of the Arusha Peace and Reconciliation Agreement for Burundi, the Government of Burundi shall take all necessary measures to allow returnees to settle in areas of their origin or choice, if possible, and assist them in recovering any property they may have left behind, according to the rules and regulations in force in Burundi.

Article 4 – Section 6: Reintegration of Returnees

The Government of the Republic of Burundi guarantees the reintegration of all returnees into the country's social-economic life. It also guarantees to all returnees equal enjoyment, with all Burundians, of all the socio-economic, civil and political rights of the nation as recognized in domestic and international law.

[. . .]

3.13. The French Republic, the Islamic Transitional State of Afghanistan and UNHCR (2002)[29]

[. . .]

PREAMBLE (PARA 2)

Recognizing that the right of all citizens to leave and to return to their country is a basic Human Rights enshrined, *inter alia*, in Article 13 (2) of the 1948 Universal Declaration of Human Rights and Article 12 of the 1966 International Covenant on Civil and Political Rights.

[. . .]

PREAMBLE (PARA 5)

Resolved to cooperate in order to assist the voluntary, dignified, safe and orderly return to and successful reintegration in Afghanistan of Afghans now in France who also opt to return.

---

[29] Tripartite Agreement between the Government of the French Republic, the Government of the Islamic Transitional State of Afghanistan and the United Nations High Commissioner for Refugees, 28 September 2002.

[. . .]

Article 3 – Voluntary Repatriation

Parties hereby confirm that the repatriation of the Afghans shall take place at their freely expressed wish based on their knowledge of the situation in intended places of return in Afghanistan and any options for continued stay in France.

Afghans who have been granted asylum or any other legal status in France will benefit from the assistance set forth in the present agreement if they express their wish to return voluntarily to their home country.

Afghans illegally staying in France may benefit from said assistance, provided they apply before March 1, 2003.

In compliance of the 1951 Convention relating to the Statues of Refugees and its 1967 Protocol, alternatives to voluntary return recognized as being acceptable under the international law may be examined with regard to Afghans who have no protection or compelling humanitarian needs justifying prolongation of their stay in France, but who nevertheless continue to refuse to avail themselves of the voluntary repatriation programme set forth in this agreement.

The return process of Afghans without protection or compelling humanitarian needs shall be phased, orderly and humane and accomplished in manageable numbers where adequate accommodation is available.

[. . .]

Article 5 – Guarantees upon Return

The government of the Islamic Transitional State of Afghanistan recalls in this respect the guarantees contained in decree No. 297, dated 13.03.1380 (3 June 2002) on the dignified return of Afghan refugees, which fully applies to Afghans returning from France under this agreement. These guarantees also include the right of recovery of movable and immovable properties.

[. . .]

3.14. United Kingdom of Great Britain and Northern Ireland, the Transitional Administration of the Transitional Islamic State of Afghanistan and UNHCR (2002)[30]

The UK Government, the Transitional Islamic Administration of Afghanistan and UNHCR, hereinafter referred to as "the Participants",

(a) Recognizing that the right of all citizens to leave and to return to their country is a basic human right enshrined, *inter alia*, in Article 13(2) of the 1948 Universal Declaration of Human Rights and Article 12 of the 1966 International Covenant on Civil and Political Rights;

[. . .]

(d) Resolved to cooperate in order to assist the voluntary, dignified, safe and orderly repatriation to and successful reintegration in Afghanistan of Afghans now in the United Kingdom who also opt to return;

[. . .]

Paragraph 5 – Commitments upon Repatriation

The Transitional Islamic Administration of Afghanistan will, together with other relevant bodies, carry out the necessary measures to ensure that Afghans abroad can return without any fear of harassment, intimidation, persecution, discrimination, prosecution or any punitive measures whatsoever. These safeguards do not preclude the right of the competent authorities of Afghanistan to prosecute individuals on account of war crimes and crimes against humanity, as defined in international instruments, or very serious common crimes involving death or severe bodily harm. The Transitional Islamic Administration of Afghanistan recalls in this respect the guarantees contained in Decree No. 297, dated 13.03.1380 (3 June 2002) on the dignified return of Afghan refugees, which fully applies to Afghans returning from the United Kingdom under this MoU.

These guarantees also include the right of recovery of movable and immovable properties.

[. . .]

3.15. The Islamic Transitional State of Afghanistan, the Government of the Netherlands and UNHCR (2003)[31]

[. . .]

(a) *Recognizing* that the right of all citizens to leave and to return to their country is a basic human right enshrined, *inter alia*, in Article 13(2) of the 1948 Universal Declaration of Human Rights and Article 12 of the 1966 International Covenant on Civil and Political Rights;

[. . .]

(d) *Resolved* to cooperate in order to assist the voluntary, dignified, safe and orderly repatriation to and successful reintegration in Afghanistan of Afghans now in the Netherlands who also opt to return;

[. . .]

Paragraph 5 – Commitments upon Repatriation

The Transitional Islamic State of Afghanistan will, together with other relevant bodies, carry out the necessary measures to ensure that Afghans abroad can return without any fear of harassment, intimidation, persecution, discrimination, prosecution or any punitive measures in particular on account of their having left, or remained outside of Afghanistan. These safeguards do not preclude the right of the competent authorities of Afghanistan to prosecute individuals on account of war crimes and crimes against humanity, as defined in international instruments, or very serious common crimes involving death or severe bodily harm.

The Transitional Islamic State of Afghanistan recalls in this respect the guarantees contained in Decree No. 297, dated 13.03.1380 (3 June 2002) on the dignified return of Afghan refugees, which fully applies to Afghans returning from the Netherlands under

---

[30] Tripartite Memorandum of Understanding (the MoU) between the Government of the United Kingdom of Great Britain and Northern Ireland (the UK Government), the Transitional Islamic Administration of the Transitional Islamic State of Afghanistan and the United Nations High Commissioner for Refugees (UNHCR), 12 October 2002.

[31] Tripartite Memorandum of Understanding (the MoU) between the Government of the Netherlands, the Transitional Islamic State of Afghanistan, and the United Nations High Commissioner for Refugees (UNHCR), 18 March 2003.

this MoU. These guarantees also include the right of recovery of movable and immovable properties.

Paragraph 6 – Freedom of Choice of Destination

The Transitional Islamic State of Afghanistan accepts that Afghans returning from abroad will be free to settle in their former place of residence or any other place of their choice in Afghanistan.

[. . .]

3.16. Republic of Zambia, Republic of Rwanda and UNHCR (2003)[32]

[. . .]

Article 10

To ensure durable peace and achieve effective national reconciliation, the Government of the Republic of Rwanda shall take all measures possible to allow returnees to settle in their areas of origin or choice and shall protect their property. It shall also utilise existing mechanisms to settle all disputes relating to ownership and enjoyment of property rights by returnees according to due process of law.

[. . .]

3.17. Islamic Republic of Iran, the Islamic Transitional State of Afghanistan and UNHCR (2003)[33]

[. . .]

Article 5 – Voluntary Character of Repatriation

The Parties hereby reaffirm that the repatriation of Afghan refugees and displaced persons in Iran shall take place at their freely expressed wish based on their knowledge of the conditions relating to voluntary repatriation and the situation in intended places of return. Accordingly, the voluntary character of the repatriation shall be fully respected.

[. . .]

[32] Tripartite Agreement on the Voluntary Repatriation of Rwandan Refugees From Zambia, 15 January 2003.

[33] Joint programme between the Government of the Islamic Republic of Iran, the Transitional Islamic State of Afghanistan, and UNHCR for Voluntary Repatriation of Afghan Refugees and Displaced Persons, 16 June 2003.

Article 7 – Freedom of Choice of Destination

The Parties reiterate that the refugees and displaced persons shall be free to return to, and settle in, their former places of residence or any other places of their choice within Afghanistan.

Article 8 – Assurances upon Return

1. The Transitional Islamic State of Afghanistan shall take necessary measures so that refugees and displaced persons can repatriate without any fear of harassment, intimidation, persecution, discrimination, prosecution or any punitive measures whatsoever on account of their having left, or remained outside of Afghanistan.

2. The Transitional Islamic State of Afghanistan recalls in this respect the guarantees contained in Decree No. 297, dated 13.03.1381 (3 June 2002), on Dignified return of Afghan Refugees, which fully applies to Afghan citizens returning from Iran under this Joint Programme.

3. The Transitional Islamic State of Afghanistan shall give assurances that returnees have access to land for settlement and use, in accordance with the relevant national laws.

4. The Transitional Islamic State of Afghanistan shall facilitate, to the extent possible, the recovery and/or restitution to the returnees of land or other immovable or movable property which they may have lost or left behind.

[. . .]

3.18. Republic of Rwanda, Republic of Uganda and UNHCR (2003)[34]

[. . .]

Article 4 – Responsibilities of the Country of Origin: Republic of Rwanda

Clause 5: Settlement of Returnees

To ensure durable peace and achieve effective national reconciliation, the Government of the Republic of Rwanda shall take all measures possible to allow returnees to settle in their areas of origin or choice and shall protect their property. It shall also utilise existing mechanisms to settle all

[34] Tripartite Agreement on the Voluntary Repatriation of Rwandan Refugees in Uganda, 23 July 2003.

disputes relating to ownership and enjoyment of property rights by returnees according to due process of law.

Clause 6: Reintegration of Returnees

The Government of the Republic of Rwanda guarantees the reintegration of all returnees into the country's social-economic life. It also guarantees to all returnees equal enjoyment, with all Rwandans, of all the socio-economic, civil and political rights of the nation as recognized in domestic and international law.

[. . .]

3.19. Republic of Burundi, Republic of Rwanda and UNHCR (2005)[35]

[. . .]

Article 1 – Right to Return

Any Burundian national who is a refugee in Rwanda and who wishes to return to the Republic of Burundi has the right to do so without having to satisfy any pre-condition.

[. . .]

Article 4 – Responsibilities of the Country of Origin: Republic of Burundi

[. . .]

Article 4 – Section 5: Settlement of Returnees

In conformity with Protocol IV of the Arusha Peace and Reconciliation Agreement for Burundi, the Government of Burundi shall take all necessary measures to allow returnees to settle in areas of their origin or choice, if possible, and assist them in recovering any property they may have left behind, according to the rules and regulations in force in Burundi.

[. . .]

3.20. Republic of Sudan, Democratic Republic of Congo and UNHCR (2006)[36]

[. . .]

---

[35] Tripartite Agreement on the Voluntary Repatriation of Burundian Refugees in Rwanda, 18 August 2005.
[36] Tripartite Agreement Sudan-DRC-UNHCR for the Voluntary Repatriation of Refugees from the Democratic Republic of Congo Living in the Republic of Sudan, 30 January 2006.

Article 2 – Right to Return

Any Congolese refugee living in the Republic of Sudan, who wishes to return to the Democratic Republic of Congo, has the right to do so without any pre-conditions.

[. . .]

Article 7 – Responsibilities of the Country of Origin: The Democratic Republic of Congo

[. . .]

Article 7 – Clause 5: Property and Land Rights

In order to achieve sustainable peace and effective national reconciliation, the Democratic Republic of Congo will take appropriate steps to secure refugees rights to access to their properties and justice if required according to established national laws.

[. . .]

---

4. UNITED NATIONS HIGH COMMISSIONER FOR REFUGEES (UNHCR)

4.1. EXCOM Conclusion No. 18 – Voluntary Repatriation (1980)

The Executive Committee,

(a) *Recognized* that voluntary repatriation constitutes generally, and in particular when a country accedes to independence, the most appropriate solution for refugee problems;

(b) *Stressed* that the essentially voluntary character of repatriation should always be respected;

(c) *Recognized* the desirability of appropriate arrangements to establish the voluntary character of repatriation, both as regards the repatriation of individual refugees and in the case of large-scale repatriation movements, and for UNHCR, whenever necessary, to be associated with such arrangements;

(d) *Considered* that when refugees express the wish to repatriate, both the government of their country of origin and the government of their country of asylum should, within the framework of their national legislation and, whenever necessary, in cooperation with UNHCR take all requisite steps to assist them to do so;

(e) *Recognized* the importance of refugees being provided with the necessary information regarding conditions in their country of origin in order to facilitate their decision to repatriate; recognized further that visits by individual refugees or refugee representatives to their country of origin to inform themselves of the situation there – without such visits automatically involving loss of refugee status – could also be of assistance in this regard;

(f) *Called* upon governments of countries of origin to provide formal guarantees for the safety of returning refugees and stressed the importance of such guarantees being fully respected and of returning refugees not being penalized for having left their country of origin for reasons giving rise to refugee situations;

(g) *Recommended* that arrangements be adopted in countries of asylum for ensuring that the terms of guarantees provided by countries of origin and relevant information regarding conditions prevailing there are duly communicated to refugees, that such arrangements could be facilitated by the authorities of countries of asylum and that UNHCR should as appropriate be associated with such arrangements;

(h) *Considered* that UNHCR could appropriately be called upon – with the agreement of the parties concerned – to monitor the situation of returning refugees with particular regard to any guarantees provided by the governments of countries of origin;

(i) *Called* upon the governments concerned to provide repatriating refugees with the necessary travel documents, visas, entry permits and transportation facilities and, if refugees have lost their nationality, to arrange for such nationality to be restored in accordance with national legislation;

(j) *Recognized* that it may be necessary in certain situations to make appropriate arrangements in co-operation with UNHCR for the reception of returning refugees and/or to establish projects for their reintegration in their country of origin.

4.2. EXCOM Conclusion No. 40 – Voluntary Repatriation (1985)

The Executive Committee,

Reaffirming the significance of its 1980 conclusion on voluntary repatriation as reflecting basic principles of international law and practice, adopted the following further conclusions on this matter:

(a) The basic rights of persons to return voluntarily to the country of origin is reaffirmed and it is urged that international co-operation be aimed at achieving this solution and should be further developed;

(b) The repatriation of refugees should only take place at their freely expressed wish; the voluntary and individual character of repatriation of refugees and the need for it to be carried out under conditions of absolute safety, preferably to the place of residence of the refugee in his country of origin, should always be respected;

(c) The aspect of causes is critical to the issue of solution and international efforts should also be directed to the removal of the causes of refugee movements. Further attention should be given to the causes and prevention of such movements, including the co-ordination of efforts currently being pursued by the international community and in particular within the United Nations. An essential condition for the prevention of refugee flows is sufficient political will by the States directly concerned to address the causes which are at the origin of refugee movements;

(d) The responsibilities of States towards their nationals and the obligations of other States to promote voluntary repatriation must be upheld by the international community. International action in favour of voluntary repatriation, whether at the universal or regional level, should receive the full support and co-operation of all States directly concerned. Promotion of voluntary repatriation as a solution to refugee problems similarly requires the political will of States directly concerned to create conditions conducive to this solution. This is the primary responsibility of States;

(e) The existing mandate of the High Commissioner is sufficient to allow him to promote voluntary repatriation by taking initiatives to this end, promoting dialogue between all the main parties, facilitating communication between them, and by acting as an intermediary or channel of communication. It is important that he establishes, whenever possible, contact with all the main parties and acquaints himself with their points of view. From the outset of a refugee situation, the High Commissioner should at all times keep the possibility of voluntary repatriation for all or for part of a group under active review and the High

Commissioner, whenever he deems that the prevailing circumstances are appropriate, should actively pursue the promotion of this solution;

(f) The humanitarian concerns of the High Commissioner should be recognized and respected by all parties and he should receive full support in his efforts to carry out his humanitarian mandate in providing international protection to refugees and in seeking a solution to refugee problems;

(g) On all occasions the High Commissioner should be fully involved from the outset in assessing the feasibility and, thereafter, in both the planning and implementation stages of repatriation;

(h) The importance of spontaneous return to the country of origin is recognized and it is considered that action to promote organized voluntary repatriation should not create obstacles to the spontaneous return of refugees. Interested States should make all efforts, including the provision of assistance in the country of origin, to encourage this movement whenever it is deemed to be in the interests of the refugees concerned;

(i) When, in the opinion of the High Commissioner, a serious problem exists in the promotion of voluntary repatriation of a particular refugee group, he may consider for that particular problem the establishment of an informal ad hoc consultative group which would be appointed by him in consultation with the Chairman and the other members of the Bureau of his Executive Committee. Such a group may, if necessary, include States which are not members of the Executive Committee and should in principle include the countries directly concerned. The High Commissioner may also consider invoking the assistance of other competent United Nations organs;

(j) The practice of establishing tripartite commissions is well adapted to facilitate voluntary repatriation. The tripartite commission, which should consist of the countries of origin and of asylum and UNHCR, could concern itself with both the joint planning and the implementation of a repatriation programme. It is also an effective means of securing consultations between the main parties concerned on any problems that might subsequently arise;

(k) International action to promote voluntary repatriation requires consideration of the situation within the country of origin as well as within the receiving country. Assistance for the reintegration of returnees provided by the international community in the country of origin is recognized as an important factor in promoting repatriation. To this end, UNHCR and other United Nations agencies as appropriate, should have funds readily available to assist returnees in the various stages of their integration and rehabilitation in their country of origin;

(l) The High Commissioner should be recognized as having a legitimate concern for the consequences of return, particularly where such return has been brought about as a result of an amnesty or other form of guarantee. The High Commissioner must be regarded as entitled to insist on his legitimate concern over the outcome of any return that he has assisted. Within the framework of close consultations with the State concerned, he should be given direct and unhindered access to returnees so that he is in a position to monitor fulfilment of the amnesties, guarantees or assurances on the basis of which the refugees have returned. This should be considered as inherent in his mandate;

(m) Consideration should be given to the further elaboration of an instrument reflecting all existing principles and guidelines relating to voluntary repatriation for acceptance by the international community as a whole.

4.3. EXCOM Conclusion No. 101 – Legal Safety Issues in the Context of Voluntary Repatriation of Refugees (2004)[37]

The Executive Committee,

Recalling its Conclusion No. 18 (XXXI) and Conclusion No. 40 (XXXVI) on voluntary repatriation, as well as Conclusion No. 74 (XLV) paragraphs (y), (z) and (aa),

Recalling its Conclusion No. 96 and *noting* that the present Conclusion does not apply to persons found not to be in need of international protection,

Noting the relevance for voluntary repatriation of the Universal Declaration of Human Rights, the International Covenant on Civil and Political Rights, the International Covenant on Economic, Social and Cultural Rights, the International Convention on the Elimination of All Forms of Racial Discrimination, the Convention on the Rights of

[37] Footnotes omitted.

the Child and the Convention on the Elimination of All Forms of Discrimination against Women,

Expressing appreciation for the useful discussions on voluntary repatriation, which took place in the context of the third track of the Global Consultations on International Protection; and *agreeing* with the importance of working towards improved conditions for voluntary repatriation and of strengthening cooperation to make such repatriation sustainable in line with Goal 5, Objectives 2 and 3 of the Agenda for Protection which resulted from those discussions,

Reaffirming that voluntary repatriation, local integration and resettlement are the traditional solutions for refugees, and that all remain viable and important responses to refugee situations; *reiterating* that voluntary repatriation, where and when feasible, remains the preferred solution in the majority of refugee situations; and *noting* that a combination of solutions, taking into account the specific circumstances of each refugee situation, can help achieve lasting solutions,

Reaffirming the voluntary character of refugee repatriation, which involves the individual making a free and informed choice through, inter alia, the availability of complete, accurate and objective information on the situation in the country of origin; and *stressing* the need for voluntary repatriation to occur in and to conditions of safety and dignity,

Recognizing in the context of voluntary repatriation the importance of resolute efforts in the country of origin to create conditions that foster the voluntary and safe return of refugees and to ensure the restoration of national protection,

Recognizing the complexities of large-scale voluntary repatriation and the difficulties which the country of origin may face in seeking to follow the guidance provided in this Conclusion,

Noting the value of countries of origin addressing issues which are of a legal or administrative nature as a means of building confidence, facilitating decisions to return and ensuring sustainable reintegration,

Emphasizing that some legal or administrative issues may only be addressed over time; and *recognizing* that voluntary repatriation can and does

take place without all of the legal and administrative issues addressed in this Conclusion having first been resolved,

Recognizing the usefulness of States, as countries of asylum or countries of origin, and UNHCR concluding, where appropriate, tripartite agreements to facilitate voluntary repatriation efforts, thereby setting out the core elements and modalities of voluntary repatriation, the respective roles and responsibilities of the relevant actors involved, and the obligations of States with respect to returning refugees, while also noting that, under certain circumstances, voluntary repatriation may take place without such agreements,

Recognizing also the importance of spontaneous voluntary repatriation of refugees and that actions to promote organized voluntary repatriation should not create obstacles to the spontaneous return of refugees,

Noting the desirability of incorporating appropriate legal protections for returning refugees in peace agreements, whenever possible, as a measure to build confidence and in support of their promotion in practice,

Acknowledging the importance of promoting an age- and gender-sensitive approach in all aspects of refugee return processes; and, in this regard, *encouraging* UNHCR to develop appropriate standards and indicators that account for such factors in repatriation and reintegration programmes,

Underlining the need for strengthened cooperation among countries of origin, host countries, UNHCR and other international organizations and the international community, to ensure that voluntary repatriation will be sustainable,

Noting that reconciliation in post-conflict situations is a key challenge and that addressing this from the outset, where necessary through transitional justice mechanisms, and involving communities, may contribute to creating conditions conducive to voluntary repatriation and sustainable reintegration,

(a) *Invites* countries of origin, in cooperation with UNHCR, other States and other concerned actors, as necessary and appropriate, to address, at an early stage, issues of a legal and administrative nature which are likely to hinder voluntary repatriation in safety and dignity, by taking into consideration, inter alia, the guidance included in the operative paragraphs that follow;

(b) *Reaffirms* that refugees have the right to return to their own country and that States have the obligation to receive back their own nationals and should facilitate such return; *urges* States to issue necessary travel documents, if required, to facilitate such return; *calls* upon transit countries to assist in the facilitation of return; and also *notes* that refugees may be required to be subject to brief interviews at the relevant border entry point by the authorities of the country of origin for purposes of identification;

(c) *Recognizes* that refugees, in exercising their right to return to their own country, should, in principle, have the possibility to return to their place of origin, or to a place of residence of their choice, subject only to restrictions as permitted by international human rights law;[38] and, in this context, *notes* the importance of efforts that seek to mitigate the likelihood that returning refugees could become internally displaced;

(d) *Emphasizing* that in the context of voluntary repatriation countries of asylum have the responsibility to protect refugees from threats and harassment, including from any groups or individuals who may impede their access to information on the situation in the country of origin or may impede the exercise of their free will regarding the right to return;

(e) *Reaffirms* that voluntary repatriation should not necessarily be conditioned on the accomplishment of political solutions in the country of origin in order not to impede the exercise of the refugees' right to return; and *recognizes* that the voluntary repatriation and reintegration process is normally guided by the conditions in the country of origin;

(f) *Strongly* urges countries of origin to ensure that returning refugees do not face a risk of persecution, discrimination or detention due to their departure from the country or on account of their status as refugees, or their political opinion, race, ethnic origin, religious belief or membership of a particular social group;

(g) *Recognizes* the utility of amnesties in encouraging voluntary repatriation and *recommends* that countries of origin issue amnesty declarations granting returning refugees immunity from prosecution for having left or remaining outside the country of origin; and further *recognizes*, however, that amnesties should not be extended to returning refugees charged with, inter alia, a serious violation of international humanitarian law, or genocide, or a crime against humanity, or a crime constituting a serious violation of human rights, or a serious common crime involving death or serious bodily harm, committed prior to or during exile;

(h) *Recognizes* that, in principle, all returning refugees should have the right to have restored to them or be compensated for any housing, land or property of which they were deprived in an illegal, discriminatory or arbitrary manner before or during exile; *notes*, therefore, the potential need for fair and effective restitution mechanisms, which also take into account the situation of secondary occupants of refugees' property; and also *notes* that where property cannot be restored, returning refugees should be justly and adequately compensated by the country of origin;

(i) *Stresses* the desirability of ensuring that any restitution and compensation framework takes account of the situation of returning refugee women, in particular, where women, especially female heads of households, are prevented from securing property rights in accordance with inheritance laws or where inheritance procedures prevent them from recovering their property within a reasonable period of time;

(j) *Encourages* countries of origin to provide homeless returning refugees, as appropriate, with access to land and/or adequate housing, comparable to local standards;

(k) *Notes* the importance of ensuring nationality; and *urges* countries of origin to ensure that there is no exclusion of returning refugees from nationality and that statelessness is thus avoided; and *recalls* in this context Conclusion No. 78 (XLVI) on the prevention and reduction of statelessness and the protection of stateless persons;

(l) *Notes* also the importance of providing under national law for the recognition of the civil status of returning refugees and changes thereto, including as a result of births, deaths, adoptions, marriage and divorce, as well as of documentation or registration proving that status, issued by the competent bodies in the country of asylum or elsewhere, taking into account the special situation of returning refugee women who may not have documentation

---

[38] See Article 12(3) of International Covenant on Civil and Political Rights.

proving their civil status or who may face difficulties securing recognition of documentation issued by the authorities of the country of asylum;

(m) *Calls on* countries of origin and countries of habitual residence to accept back refugees who are non-nationals but have been habitually resident in that country, including those who were previously stateless there;

(n) *Stresses* the importance of family unity during and following voluntary repatriation; and *calls upon* States, where necessary, to assist spouses and family members of different nationalities to remain together as families;

(o) *Notes* the importance of skills of returning refugees for self-reliance and, in this context, *calls upon* countries of origin to ensure non-discriminatory access for returning refugees to processes, where they exist, to recognize the equivalency of academic, professional and vocational diplomas, certificates and degrees acquired by returning refugees while abroad; and *encourages* countries of origin to recognize the equivalency of primary and secondary education received abroad by returning refugees;

(p) *Recommends* that in consultation with refugee communities consideration be given to addressing the specific needs of returning refugees – including women, children, older people and other persons with special concerns – in order to ensure that they receive adequate protection, assistance and care throughout the repatriation and initial reintegration process; and *stresses* in this context that particular attention needs to be given to ensure that unaccompanied or separated children are not returned prior to successful tracing of family members or without specific and adequate reception and care arrangements having been put in place in the country of origin;

(q) *Reiterates* that UNHCR, in line with its mandate responsibility, be given free and unhindered access to returning refugees, as needed, in particular, so as to monitor the latter's proper treatment in accordance with international standards, including as regards the fulfilment of amnesties, guarantees or assurances on the basis of which refugees have returned;

(r) *Encourages* the country of origin, host countries and UNHCR in cooperation with other relevant actors to provide refugees with complete, objective and accurate information, including on phys-

ical, material and legal safety issues, prior to their voluntary repatriation to and reintegration in the country of origin;

(s) *Encourages* UNHCR to collaborate with other United Nations entities, international and non-governmental organizations, in particular those with mandates and expertise in rule of law, development and peacekeeping as well as peace-building, with a view to removing legal, administrative and other barriers to return in countries of origin, and, in doing so, contributing more generally to promoting the rule of law and respect for human rights and fundamental freedoms;

(t) *Encourages* the international community at large to mobilize adequate and sustained support to countries of origin, particularly those emerging from conflict, to assist them to restore national protection to, including respect for the human rights of, their citizens and former habitual residents, including returning refugees.

4.4. UNHCR Inter-Office Memorandum No. 104/2001, UNHCR Field Office Memorandum No. 101/2001 (2001) – Voluntary Repatriation and the Right to Adequate Housing[39]

1. Recovery of refugees' homes and property in their countries of origin needs to be addressed consistently to ensure that effective solutions to refugee displacement are found. Experience has shown that voluntary repatriation operations are unlikely to be fully successful or sustainable in the longer term if housing and property issues – being an integral part of return in safety and dignity – are left unattended. The purpose of this IOM/FOM is to draw the attention of Bureaux and Field Offices to relevant developments in the area of housing rights in the context of refugee repatriation operations. These developing legal standards should guide and inform UNHCR in the design, implementation and evaluation phases of its work in this important area.

The Need for a Legal Protection Framework Linking the *Right to Return* to the *Right to Adequate Housing*

2. Human rights law in relation to the right to adequate housing has evolved significantly over the past decade. The *right of a refugee to return to her/his country* is now increasingly coupled with

---

[39] Footnotes omitted.

her/his *right to adequate housing*. In this context, the right to adequate housing has developed to extend to the right not to be arbitrarily deprived of housing and property in the first place. As corollary to this, refugees have the right to return not only to their countries of origin but also to recover the homes from which they were previously evicted (restitution). If this is not possible, then the right to adequate compensation for any loss suffered comes into play.

Expert Study on the Relevance of Housing Rights in Refugee Returns/Conclusions

3. In recognition of the importance of these developments both to UNHCR's international protection mandate and to its operational activities, the Department of International Protection undertook a series of Expert Consultations and commissioned a special Study to assess how the right to adequate housing can be better reflected in UNHCR's policy and in the design and implementation of its repatriation operations.

4. The Study makes a number of concrete recommendations to UNHCR, which address issues at the time of flight to safety, as well as during the pre-return and post-return phases. Three overall recommendations can be drawn from the Expert Study and the consultation process:

In most circumstances, conditions of safe and dignified return will not and cannot be met without adequate safeguards designed to protect the rights of returnees to housing and property restitution.

If housing is to be properly treated as an issue of human rights, then all housing-related policies and practices of UNHCR need *per se* to be treated as issues of refugee protection.

Housing issues for refugees should be addressed at an early stage in the cycle of refugee displacement and not only after refugees have returned to their countries of origin.

Restitution Translated into Action

5. The modalities of each repatriation operation will vary, and issues of property and housing restitution will be relevant to a greater or lesser extent, according to the specificity of each situation. Equally, UNHCR may be a major or lesser actor on these issues, depending on the presence or absence of other credible institutions.

Where it is apparent that housing and property issues have to be addressed for voluntary repatriation to be durable and sustainable, Headquarters and Field Offices staff should be aware of the relevant legal standards and need to ensure they are effectively integrated into all relevant aspects of UNHCR's work, including the planning, implementation and evaluation stages of its operation cycle.

In order to facilitate this task, I am pleased to share with you the following two documents, which are herewith attached:

Checklist on the Restitution of Housing and Property (see Annex I): This document is meant to assist offices to deal effectively with restitution matters.

Key excerpts from the Expert Study *Housing and Property Issues for Refugees and Internally Displaced Persons in the Context of Return – Key Considerations for UNHCR Policy and Practice* (see Annex II).

8. Please share this IOM/FOM with all protection and field staff and retain it for future inclusion in the forthcoming *Protection Manual*. Further information and guidance on protection-related aspects of housing and property issues can be obtained from the Protection Policy and Legal Advice Section in DIP.

ANNEX I

Checklist on the Restitution of Housing and Property

A. General Issues

(1) Promoting Housing and Property Rights within Peace Agreements

UNHCR should attempt to play an active role in negotiations leading to peace agreements, with a view to ensuring that the housing and property aspects of voluntary repatriation are fully taken into account. UNHCR should seek to ensure that such agreements explicitly include provisions on the housing and property rights of those choosing to repatriate and that judicial or other mechanisms designed to ensure the implementation of such rights are established. Where refugees voluntarily settle elsewhere, it should be stipulated that this does not affect their right to property restitution or, should this not be possible, compensation or other form of reparation.

(2) Promoting Housing and Property Rights within Repatriation Plans

Assessment missions entrusted with preparing repatriation plans should examine how housing and property restitution will be most effectively integrated in the repatriation plan.

(3) Field Offices Should Develop a Plan of Action on Housing and Property Restitution

Field Offices in countries of origin/return should develop a plan of action on housing and property restitution. This plan will form the first step in developing an effective UNHCR response to these issues. The plan should be based on both the prevailing international and (where consistent with international law) national legal normative frameworks. Guidance can be provided by the Department of International Protection through the Housing and Property Focal Point in the Protection Policy and Legal Advice Section. Every effort should be made to ensure the participation of potential returnees in the development of plans of action.

Plans of action on housing and property restitution should include the promotion of measures that:

Approach housing and property restitution as a human rights and refugee protection issue;

Rectify and provide remedies for any unjust or arbitrary applications of law relating to refugee housing or property;

Protect all persons from homelessness or other housing rights violations;

Ensure consistency between domestic law and relevant international law;

Ensure equal access to impartial and effective judicial and procedural remedies, including any specific mechanism established to promote housing and property restitution;

Ensure that the reconstruction and rehabilitation of damaged housing is seen as an indispensable element of safe and dignified return and that these two processes are seen as forming key elements in the overall restitution process;

Protect housing and property registration records where these still exist and, if necessary, re-establish housing and property registration systems;

Support the establishment of legal aid centres to provide expert legal assistance to returnees seeking to invoke their rights to housing and property restitution;

Ensure that effective systems are created for equitable redress and/or financial or other forms of compensation for returnees unable to exercise their rights to housing and property restitution.

When developing plans of action, Field Offices should also take into account customary (traditional) structures for resolving disputes and addressing issues related to housing, land and property issues, as and where appropriate.

(4) If Necessary, Identify Housing and Property Experts

Field Offices should, if necessary, consider identifying housing and property experts to assist in the development of plans of action and guidelines on housing and property restitution. In addition, national housing and property experts should be utilized to assist in understanding the legal situation and the housing and property issues in the country of return/origin.

(5) Submit Field Office Plans of Action to DIP for Consideration

Once the Field Office has developed s plan of action on housing and property restitution, it should submit it to the Department of International Protection for consideration to ensure overall consistency with refugee, human rights and international law.

B. Flight to Safety, Pre-Return and Return

In addition to the five aforementioned general issues, the different phases of the displacement cycle (from flight to return) potentially involve actions which can be undertaken by UNHCR towards enhancing the prospects of eventual restitution once voluntary repatriation takes place.

(1) Flight to Safety: Preparing for Eventual Restitution – Incorporate Housing and Property Restitution Questions into Refugee Registration Procedures

UNHCR officials engaged in refugee registration should attempt to gather as much information as possible at the time of flight concerning the housing and property situation of the refugee concerned. This information can be invaluable in the return planning process. Attention should be paid to the refugee's address at the time of flight, any legal ownership or tenancy documents they may have in their possession, the name of the owner of the dwelling or land concerned, the names of neighbours and other residents in the same community or any other information which can eventually be used to provide proof of the location of the refugee's original home.

(2) Pre-Return: Setting the Framework for Restitution – Implementation of the Plan of Action on Housing and Property Restitution

UNHCR needs to ensure that issues related to housing and property, as they would, for instance, be reflected in the plan of action, are properly addressed in the planning for and actual implementation of voluntary repatriation operations. Field Offices should pay particular attention to the following elements:

(a) Ensuring Effective Partnership and Inter-Agency Coordination/Cooperation

Identify all relevant international and national institutions, including NGOs and community-based groups, and analyze their relevance to the promotion of housing and property restitution (Who is responsible for what? Where are the gaps? How can they be filled?).

(b) Identify Any Major Housing-Related Obstacles to Return, Including:

The extent of secondary occupation of refugee homes

Whether housing abandonment laws were adopted after flight

Whether inheritance laws discriminate against women or other groups

Whether unjust and arbitrary applications of law occurred after flight

Whether housing and property registration records were destroyed or lost after flight

Whether effective and impartial judicial remedies are in place

In addition, it should be ensured that an analysis of the scope of damaged (but still habit-able)/destroyed (inhabitable) property as well as status of infrastructure are made

(c) Identify All Relevant National Laws Relevant to the Housing and Property Rights of Returnees. Examine, in Particular, Laws Relating to:

The right to adequate housing and property restitution

The right to property and the peaceful enjoyment of possessions

The right to be protected against forced evictions

The right to privacy and respect for the home

The right to freedom of movement and to choose one's residence

The rights of indigenous peoples (as relevant)

(d) Promote Legislative Analysis, Legislative Repeal and Legislative Reform, as Necessary and Appropriate

Legislative Analysis: Collect, translate and analyse housing and property legislation currently in force in countries of origin.

Legislative Repeal: Identify any housing and property legislation which is inconsistent with international human rights standards.

Legislative Reform: Promote the development of a domestic legal system which is consistent with international human rights standards relating to housing and property rights.

Return: Implementation of Housing and Restitution Laws

Besides a fair and efficient property restitution framework, the consideration and promotion of additional measures may be necessary to ensure the full and effective implementation of restitution laws:

Running of public information campaigns to inform claimants about their rights and obligations and to ensure that they receive the necessary guidance and counselling as to the procedures to be followed, including access to fair and effective remedies;

De-mining and reconstruction projects should be tailored to support the implementation of property laws (e.g. priority of shelter projects for those who are currently occupying someone else's home);

Restoration of infrastructure where it is damaged or destroyed;

Establishment of mechanisms to resolve property issues of those who have decided not to return (e.g. creation of a fair and equitable environment for real estate transactions to allow displaced persons and refugees who do not wish to return to integrate into communities or environments of current displacement; such initiatives, however, must not undermine the principle of return);

Creation of sufficient alternative accommodation (interim accommodation) to speed up the restitution process;

Creation of social housing for those who do not have a place to return to;

Establish linkage between property laws and legislation dealing with displaced persons and repatriates;

In case of a flawed national property restitution framework, promote, if possible and as appropriate, proceedings to invoke the right to property before treaty bodies (e.g. European Court of Human Rights; Inter-American Commission on Human Rights).

ANNEX II

5. Implementing a Housing Rights Approach to Housing and Property Restitution

Clarifying, regularising and protecting housing and property rights issues in countries of origin constitute fundamental components of successful repatriation. In the absence of a clear legal and political framework upon which return processes are based, ensuring an enforceable right to housing and property restitution for each returning refugee will be exceedingly difficult. For restitution rights to be protected, housing and property issues must be taken seriously by refugee institutions at all stages of the refugee process: during the flight to safety, during the asylum or pre-return period and within the post-return context.

Given the inseparable linkages between housing and property restitution and the future economic and social stability within countries of origin, there are strong arguments in favour of increasingly viewing, conceiving and executing repatriation programmes not only as tools promoting justice and the return of displaced persons to their homes, but also as part of a larger process of development. Such an approach supports the emergence of the rule of law and the protection and promotion of human rights, and ensures that return programmes do not become simply exercises in moving people between two less than ideal locations. The much discussed 'gap' between return and development finds tangible substance in the search for sustainable solutions to housing and property rights issues arising in the context of restitution. Indeed, an adequate focus on restitution allows the integration of humanitarian, emergency and development considerations into a framework recognising rights, ensuring justice and promoting sustainable, long-term solutions.

In addition to integrating the social and economic rights dimensions of refugee return into larger efforts at reconstruction, repatriation programmes should always explicitly protect the housing and property rights of women, and ensure that discrimination against women is prevented in all areas, in particular in the areas of housing, land and property. Rights to inherit property, rights to participate in the restitution process and equal rights to ownership, use and control of housing, property and land must be guaranteed and securely recognised prior to the involvement of the international community in return processes. Women's rights must pervade all elements of the restitution process, and steps should be taken to use such processes as an opportunity for securing such rights in places where discrimination against women obstructs the enjoyment of housing and property rights.

In addition to the necessity of securing the rights of refugee and IDP women throughout the stages of displacement and return, care must also be taken to ensure that *all* returnees are treated equally with respect to their housing tenure status. In other words, restitution rights should not be restricted to owners of housing, but should be accorded to tenants, housing co-operative residents, those possessing occupancy rights and other tenure groups, as well as owners.

In addition to these generic elements, policymakers and those responsible for implementing these rights at the field level should take a variety of additional factors – legal, social, economic, cultural – into account during the development of plans, mechanisms and policies designed to ensure the enjoyment of restitution rights by returnees. Pro-active steps to promote restitution can be taken during the period of flight, prior to return and subsequent to return to protect the housing and property rights of refugees and IDPs.

Flight to Safety: Preparing for Eventual Restitution

5.1 Incorporating Housing and Property Restitution Issues into First-Line Refugee and IDP Registration Procedures

Systems should be developed by UNHCR and other actors involved with refugee registration procedures to obtain as much detailed information as possible regarding the housing and property situation of the refugee or IDP at the time of flight. All official registration points and relevant forms should include specific questions concerning the address, type of tenure status, ownership records and other personal housing information from the beginning to provide a reasonably objective source of information for use in eventual repatriation. This can act as a powerful tool in ultimately reversing any attempts at ethnic cleansing and maintain housing and property records that may have intentionally been destroyed by refugee and IDP generating States and governments. Above all, this information can be vital in ensuring that restitution finds a key place in repatriation plans.

Pre-Return: Setting the Framework for Restitution

5.2 Creating the Right Mechanisms within Peace Settlements and Country Agreements

As peace settlements and country agreements are almost invariably concluded prior to organised repatriation plans, restitution issues should be considered during the negotiations of these instruments to ensure that restitution rights are firmly included. Specific mention of the legal, judicial and other mechanisms required to protect these rights need explicit inclusion within such texts. If restitution issues are included within peace settlements and country agreements (as they were within the Dayton Accords, for instance), UNHCR and other institutions can be given considerably more lever-age to assert the rights of returnees to housing and property restitution. Equally, if restitution rights are explicitly enshrined within the applicable domestic law in the country of return, the likelihood of refugees and IDPs actually returning home – while by no means guaranteed – is far greater than when such rights are either ignored or treated merely as desired goals or objectives rather than justiciable guarantees.

Although the creation of judicial and other mechanisms to secure housing and property restitution rights to returnees is often indispensable for restitution to occur, practice has shown that given the complexities associated with restitution and the often highly-charged nature of housing and property disputes in many countries of return, establishing procedural remedies alone will not generally be sufficient to guarantee that all persons with rights to restitution will actually be able to exercise these. The restitution process is a broader process than the remedial elements contained within it. Fundamental political decisions concerning the types of claims which can be submitted to a given mechanism, who can present such claims, how far back in time the claims can go, whether a right to appeal decisions made by the mechanism concerned are available, what role, if any, will be played by traditional or non-judicial methods of conflict resolution especially in countries without an independent or functioning judiciary and a range of other considerations will invariably accompany the procedural elements associated with mechanisms designed to promote restitution.

5.3 Effective Institutional Co-Ordination

Refugee and IDP repatriation operations are rarely isolated to UNHCR alone. Many other UN and other inter-governmental agencies, peacekeeping forces, NGO's, national agencies, judicial bodies and other actors are often involved in processes ultimately involving housing and property restitution. To ensure the successful restitution of the original homes of returnees, institutional efforts should be well co-ordinated through the conclusion of memorandums of understanding aimed at promoting co-operative actions prior to, during and subsequent to voluntary return programmes. The appointment of one agency to oversee the co-ordination of restitution may facilitate restitution.

5.4   Refugee Participation in Developing Repatriation Plans

The central role of returnee participation and control of the return process cannot be over-estimated. There is a need to incorporate refugees' own interpretations of what it means to call a place 'home' and an implicit understanding that not all returnees will want to return to their original homes. Repatriation will be more likely to succeed when returnees are involved as equal partners in the consultative process developing policies on return, and when closer attention is paid to 'relations after return, and to recognise that even if repatriation is the end of one cycle, it is also usually the beginning of a new cycle which can challenge and expose some returnees to vulnerability'. Returnee participation will also increase the likelihood of assessing the position of local populations vis-à-vis the returnee population and to ensuring that the local housing law and practice is adequately grasped by the agencies promoting return.

The provision of information conducive to return by potential returnees can also assist in the preparations for repatriation. This is perhaps best illustrated by work now underway in eastern Nepal. A survey of the housing, property and land situation of every Bhutanese refugee at the time of flight is currently under preparation by the refugee communities themselves. This project (which could be surely be replicated elsewhere) seeks to create a comprehensive digital data-base of the lands, homes and properties in Bhutan of each of the 100,000 refugees as a pre-cursor to eventual return and to provide the proper basis for fair and just restitution of those lands, homes and properties. They are also aiming to discern the exact situation of each refugee home and lands today in order to ensure that the original owners get back what is rightfully theirs.

Post-Return: Making Restitution a Reality

5.5   The Human Right to Housing and Property Restitution

The human right to adequate housing and the congruent right to property restitution should guide and be viewed as indispensable elements of any repatriation programme or policy supported by the international community. These rights should be included – explicitly – within peace settlements, repatriation programmes, return plans and any other agreements in which UNHCR is involved. This is true even concerning intractable conflicts. While security guarantees and local conditions will perhaps continue to be the most visible determinant of voluntary repatriation, housing and property concerns should always be taken fully into account from the beginning.

In order to ensure compatibility between international standards on restitution and the domestic laws in the country concerned, legal analysis, repeal and reform should form a cornerstone of programmes designed to ensure the right to housing and property restitution. *Legislative analysis* should involve the collection, translation and thorough analysis of housing and property legislation currently in force in countries of origin (including all international human rights obligations relevant to housing and property rights) to determine the extent to which these laws protect housing and property rights. Measures supporting *legislative repeal* should involve the identification of housing and property laws currently in force in the country of origin, but which are considered to be manifestly incompatible with international standards or which are formulated or applied in a discriminatory manner. *Legislative reform* should involve the promoting the development of a domestic legal system which is compatible between international standards relevant to the restitution of housing and property rights.

The often weak attention accorded economic, social and cultural rights within domestic legal frameworks and the comparative ease with which housing and property rights can be manipulated to prevent return suggests the need for principle-based approaches during all aspects of the return process designed to secure compliance with international housing rights obligations. Devoting attention to housing and property restitution in the context of return provides ample opportunity to UNCHR to assist countries of origin to apply, for instance, the norms of the Covenant on Economic, Social and Cultural Rights to the return and post-return process. Approached in this way, return facilitates the implementation of economic, social and cultural rights, ensures protection within the context of voluntary repatriation, as well as creating conditions favourable for economic development.

5.6 Rectifying Unjust and Arbitrary Applications of the Law

Successful voluntary repatriation may also require steps designed to rectify past unjust and arbitrary applications of the law in order to restore the housing and property rights of returnees. In Bosnia, Croatia, Kosovo, Georgia, Rwanda and elsewhere, the application of discriminatory, biased and unfair laws impinging upon the housing and property rights against members certain groups have contributed to the difficulties surrounding return. Unless such applications of law are reversed and temporarily lost rights restored, repatriation processes will be severely hampered. In cases involving secondary occupation, for instance, it would seem clear that when this has been organised by and is attributable to the State of origin, the same State must be held accountable to reverse these measures. This duty should be included in any repatriation programme developed by or agreed to by UNHCR. In many instances, of course, restitution will be functionally impossible unless past injustices are rectified. While some may argue that reversing the results of past discrimination may only serve to create instability and renewed ethnic conflict, the dangers of allowing these measures to stand are surely larger threats to long-term stability.

5.7 Protection from Homelessness or Other Housing Rights Violations

To succeed and run smoothly, the repatriation process should always ensure that any housing and property restitution component prevents situations of homelessness or other violations of the right to adequate housing. This is relevant in all cases, but particularly in cases involving the secondary occupation of housing and property where evictions of unlawful and illegitimate occupants may need to occur (if voluntary moves are not forthcoming) for restitution rights to be enforced. All programmes of return involving housing and property disputes should contain assurances that even those who have no lawful or other rights to dwell within housing or property registered to returnees, do not become homeless or other rights violations. In this regard, account should be taken of provisions contained in General Comment No. 7 (1997) on Forced Evictions issued by the UN Committee on Economic, Social and Cultural Rights which stipulates that

Evictions should not result in rendering individuals homeless or vulnerable to the violation of other human rights. Where those affected are unable to provide for themselves, the State party must take all appropriate measures, to the maximum of its available resources, to ensure that adequate alternative housing, resettlement or access to productive land, as the case may be, is available.

Restitution will obviously mean that the current occupants of the homes in question will be required to vacate the premises in order to ensure the repatriation of the returnees if and when the original inhabitant makes a successful claim to do so to the appropriate adjudicative body. To the maximum possible extent, such relocation should take place on a voluntary basis, with enforceable legal guarantees in place stipulating that under no circumstances will any secondary occupant become homeless or be forced to reside in intolerable living conditions. The possible social and other ramifications associated with resultant homelessness, instability, poverty, and frustration if the process of relocation is not carried out carefully must not be under-estimated.

5.8 Streamlining Domestic Law with Relevant International Law

The repatriation process will sometimes require the provision of UNHCR assistance to countries of origin to facilitate the streamlining of domestic laws with international obligations held by the country concerned. This can occur through the repeal of domestic laws that are discriminatory in nature or otherwise manifestly incompatible with internationally recognised human rights and refugee law generally. In Kosovo, the relevant UN authorities have repealed a discriminatory housing law, and in Bosnia (much at the request of UNHCR and others), laws on abandoned apartments have been repealed. Undertaking activities designed to promote compatibility between local and international laws, also provides a good opportunity to expand attention to and understanding by municipal authorities and citizens of the manner by which international human rights and refugee addresses issues relating to housing and property rights and how these norms can be incorporated into the national legal framework. This, too, will promote voluntary return and the rule of law.

5.9 Judicial and Procedural Remedies

Given the often-diverse ways by which restitution rights can be obstructed, many housing and property disputes may require remedies developed on a case-by-case basis. Each affected person, including returning refugees, returning IDPs and secondary occupants of housing in which tenancy or ownership rights are in dispute must have the right to effective legal remedies, including the right to a hearing by an independent and impartial tribunal. This accords well with article 8 of the Universal Declaration on Human Rights that ensures that "Everyone has the right to an effective remedy by the competent national tribunals for acts violating the fundamental rights granted him by the constitution or by law".

Because judicial systems are sometimes the actual source of discrimination and other housing and property problems, many repatriation initiatives establish housing and property claims commissions which are immediately accessible to all refugees, IDPs and current occupants in disputed dwellings and through which the right to effective remedies can be exercised. As mentioned above, independent housing and property bodies, such as those in Bosnia, South Africa and planned for Georgia and Kosovo will assist in fairly and equitably solving outstanding housing and property disputes.

5.10 Equitable Redress and Compensation

Post-war reconstruction, repairing the devastation that the war brought in its train, and compensation for losses... constitute a problem common to all these countries. Alongside the reconstruction of material damage a solution had to be found to many social problems arising from changes in citizenship and ownership. The problems of the displaced persons or refugees or expellees have in many countries been among the most difficult. (Heikki Waris and Victor Procope (1953) *The Problem of Compensating Property Losses: Experiences Gained from the Compensation Policy for Displaced Persons in Finland*, in *Economica Internazionale, vol. VI, N. 3, Genova*).

States have sometimes sought to avoid the difficulties often associated with restitution by proposing the provision of compensation to persons for whom restitution is considered to be materially impossible. One UNHCR publication has also supported this approach under certain circumstances. Although rights to compensation are of great importance and recognised for more than half

a century, promises and expectations surrounding the provision of compensation rarely come to fruition. Compensation costs almost invariably reach amounts considerably higher than initially envisaged at the time compensation was agreed. The payment of compensation on a large-scale can also result in the legitimisation of human rights violations, and it can place overwhelming burdens on the economy of States.

While cash compensation is often viewed as a simple means of settling housing and property disputes, cash compensation should be reserved only for exceptional cases involving lost movable assets and human rights violations. Practice has repeatedly shown – particularly in the context of development-based displacement involving the loss of housing – that cash compensation is rarely used to secure an adequate home, and can, in fact, be a reason for a person becoming homeless. The World Bank warns against this form of compensation: "cash compensation alone should generally be avoided, except in well-justified instances, as it typically leads to impoverishment".

There are many alternative means, other than monetary alone, which can satisfy the obligations associated with the provision of compensation. The obvious first alternative to cash compensation would be the construction – by the State or subsidised by the State – of adequate, affordable and accessible housing which could be made available to returnees or displaced secondary occupants. Other housing-based or fair alternative solutions might be made accessible through a range of creative measures, including: the establishment of State housing fund which issues government housing bonds, vouchers or individual subsidies which can only be redeemed in relation to the construction of residences; Government assistance for returnees in finding an empty existing flat or in accessing new housing; tax reductions could be given returnees for a given period; returnees could be placed at the head of the official housing waiting list; state land plots could be allocated to the returnees; government bonds in a substantial sum could be provided to returnees or; returnees could be given favourable housing credits for building materials should they choose to build new housing themselves.

When these limitations are taken into account, the result is often simply that the amounts awarded to recipients is based on an arbitrarily developed limit, which itself may be wholly insufficient as a means of securing justice. Goodwin-Gill has argued in this respect "that the right of refugees to return to one's home "continues to hold primary position in the hierarchy of solutions, but the right of refugees to compensation has still a fairly weak normative base in international law and, like the putative duty to provide solutions, possibly little to recommend it. . . . Although the principle of compensating the victims of violations of human rights has much to commend it, introducing a financial substitute for State and community obligations risks lending respectability to ethnic, religious and ideological cleansing".

When compensation is provided it must be given in a manner which is *reasonable* in terms of its relationship with the value of the damage suffered by the victim. The European Court on Human Rights has stated clearly that compensation for the deprivation of property (as distinct from interference alone) must be given in a prompt, appropriate and effective manner and in "an amount reasonably related to [the value of the property]." However, the Court added in the same judgment that the peaceful enjoyment of possessions clause under the ECHR "does not guarantee a right to full compensation in all circumstances, since legitimate objectives of 'public interest', such as pursued in measures of economic reform or measures designed to achieve greater social justice, may call for less than reimbursement of the full market value". This is relevant when secondary occupants refuse to be re-housed.

It will also be important to ensure that appropriate forms and amounts of compensation are provided to returnees who lost movable property and assets as a result of their flight to safety. In addition to people losing their legal rights to reside in certain homes, many also have lost – through military actions, theft and vandalism – personal affects including household possessions, furniture and other personal goods, agricultural machinery, farm animals and so forth. Returnees should be availed the opportunity to claim such losses before an independent claims body. If it is decided that the returnee has a right to compensation for lost movable property, this should be made at replacement cost or through the substitution of the lost asset with another of comparable productive capacity. Any compensation provided under this rubric must specify regulations for the standard valuation of lost

movable assets. Whatever regulations are developed must ensure that the level of compensation is just and that it provides the affected person(s) with a real substitute for the asset lost.

5.11 Reconstruction and Rehabilitation of Damaged Housing

In recognition of the importance of housing and property to the entire repatriation process, direct UNHCR assistance in the housing/shelter sector has grown markedly in recent years. This has resulted in the reconstruction of tens of thousands of damaged homes in Tajikistan, Bosnia, Kosovo, Rwanda, and elsewhere, and has contributed significantly to the promotion of secure and dignified return. The relationship between the availability of adequate housing resources and return is clear. What is sometimes less evident, however, is the necessity of understanding the often complex legal, policy and political issues surrounding housing and property rights in countries of return and having clarity with respect to ownership and tenants rights *prior to* initiating the reconstruction and rehabilitation process; even if the actual return to the original homes takes place at a later point in the process. For instance, if property disputes are unresolved, the houses occupied by illegitimate occupants may be inadvertently be reconstructed and thus benefit secondary occupants rather than the original owner/tenant. As a result, ethnic cleansing would be cemented rather than reversed.

5.12 Protection or Re-Establishment of Housing and Property Records

Although the protection or re-establishment of housing and property records may seem to have little to do with the mandate of UNHCR, the organisation can play an important role in this respect, and in the process facilitate restitution. In many conflict situations, housing and property cadastres and records are consciously destroyed or confiscated by one of the warring parties with the aim of extinguishing the rights of members of another group. This was the case most recently in Kosovo where more than 50% of these records have disappeared. Without access to such records, determining who is or is not the original owner or inhabitant of a house or property under dispute is made very difficult. Consequently, UNHCR should support efforts aimed at improving housing and property registration systems as a preventative tool against housing rights violations and re-establishing cadastral and housing registration systems where they have been totally or partially destroyed or confiscated.

6. Conclusions

The recognition of the rights of refugees and IDPs not merely to return to their country of origin, but to return to their *original or permanent homes* once they choose to do so has received expanded attention in recent years. The very notion of restitution requires that persons who have suffered violations of their rights, including the loss of the use of their housing or property, should be entitled to the right to 'return to one's place of residence' and the equivalent right to the 'restoration of property'. These two principles should form the fundamental basis for addressing the property and housing issues in the context of return.

Throughout the 1990s, however, UNHCR policy with respect to housing, property and land restitution – while expanding immensely in scope – was irregular and largely *ad hoc* in nature. In some cases, full restitution was pursued, and in others the issue was considerably underplayed. While it is recognised that UNHCR's influence to ensure restitution is limited in situations of spontaneous return, there can be no doubting the fact that in the context of organised return, the role of UNHCR in securing these rights is indispensable. If the larger emphasis on voluntary repatriation is to succeed, heed should be taken of the following perspective concerning on what basis UNHCR is to make policy decisions guiding the work of the organisation:

> *The political aspects of today's refugee problems signal, in particular, the policy dimensions, and the choices that must be made by governments and international organisations. These choices include whether to abide by international obligations; whether to follow established principles, or to respond ad hoc to situations; whether to promote the development of new international instruments or agencies; whether to refine national responses to refugee flows, by changing laws and procedures or introducing obstacles to arrival; whether to go beyond the precedents; whether to support international humanitarian relief; whether to promote solutions, and which ones; whether to try to deal with causes. Each of these political decisions, of course, takes place within a context in which legal rules – human rights*

law, refugee law, international humanitarian law – ought to have their impact. (Guy S. Goodwin-Gill (1998) 'Refugee Identity and Protection's Fading Prospect' in *Refugee Rights and Realties: Evolving International Concepts and Regimes*, Cambridge University Press, Cambridge)

The human right to adequate housing and the right to housing and property restitution for returning refugees and IDPs can be enforced and implemented in a positive and highly effective manner. It will be up to policy-makers within UNHCR to see to it that these rights are kept under constant consideration and that the right to have restored to returnees, housing and property for which they have a right, guides all decisions during the development of programmes of return.

4.5. Global Consultations on International Protection (2002)[40]

Annex I

Activities to Implement Voluntary Repatriation

UNHCR works both with the countries of asylum and origin to create an acceptable framework within which to implement voluntary repatriation. The following sets out activities UNHCR pursues in this regard, both generally and more specifically with regard to the countries of asylum and origin.

In general:

- Facilitate the participation of refugees, including women, in peace-negotiations;

- Include references in peace agreements to the right to return and to other standards relating to voluntary repatriation;

- Work towards agreements on voluntary repatriation, which translate the standards of voluntary repatriation into operational modalities;

- Develop, from the outset, partnerships and close co-operation with other multilateral and bilateral actors, ranging from the local authorities in the countries of asylum and origin, NGOs to development actors;

[40] EC/GC/02/5 25 April 2002, 4th Meeting, footnotes omitted.

- Ensure involvement of the local authorities, as well as use of local capacities and resources;

- Ensure free access of UNHCR to refugees and returnees and vice versa during all stages of the voluntary repatriation process, including a necessary period after return;

- Facilitate fair, expeditious, simple, transparent and non-discriminatory arrangements for the actual return;

- Provide immediate material or financial support, as necessary, to enable return and reestablishment during an initial phase;

In the country of asylum:

- Enable planning for return with other actors by establishing a profile of the refugee population;

- Ensure a free and informed choice by providing accurate and objective information and access to counselling;

- Enable the participation of different age- and gender groups in the decision-making process on return of their families and/or communities by appropriate dissemination of information;

- Negotiate continued protection and assistance for those unwilling and/or unable to return voluntarily;

In the country of origin:

- Undertake an analysis of the obstacles to return;

- Ensure that return is accepted by the country of origin, including the local authorities on the ground;

- Encourage the country of origin to promulgate amnesties and other legal guarantees for returnees;

- Establish substantial UNHCR field presence to promote actions required at the national and local levels to enable actual return in safety; to organise assessment visits; to promote confidence building measures, including dialogue between community leaders and local authorities; to intervene in favour of conditions conducive to return; and to help to prevent the occurrence of security incidents directed against returnees, or at least to enable an appro-priately documented follow up with the authorities;

- Undertake systematic returnee monitoring to identify protection issues and assistance needs; to design appropriate protection and assistance interventions; and to collect relevant country of origin information for potential returnees, host countries and other actors.

- Ensure the inclusion of returnees and areas of return in national recovery and reconstruction plans through the CCA/UNDAF process and other mechanisms.

ANNEX 2

Property-Related Issues in the Context of Voluntary Repatriation

The following paragraphs bring together some recommended standards for addressing property related issues in the context of voluntary repatriation on the basis of relevant international legal standards and best practice.

Broader Principles

(a) The restitution of housing, land and property (hereinafter 'property') is an essential part of the reconstruction, peace-building and national reconciliation processes.

(b) Property restitution rights should be included in peace agreements to facilitate the establishment of the laws, procedures and institutions required to ensure that refugees are able to recover their properties.

(c) Voluntary Repatriation Agreements should include implementing provisions on the modalities of property restitution. Efforts should be made to ensure refugee participation in developing property restitution plans.

Property Restitution Rights

(d) Depending on the circumstances, effective restitution of property rights means the following:

- repeal of any laws and regulations which are inconsistent with international legal standards relating to the rights to adequate housing and property;

- non-application of laws which are designed to, or result in, the loss or removal of tenancy, use, ownership or other rights connected with housing, land or property;
- removal of obstacles preventing the successful recovery of refugees' properties.

(e) Any lack of clarity with respect to nationality and residence should not preclude the recovery by refugees of their properties.

(f) The privatization of refugees' properties during their stay abroad can seriously complicate the exercise of property restitution rights. Efforts should be made to ensure that privatization does not result in the loss of property restitution rights of refugees.

(g) Property restitution rights should extend to their heirs.

(h) The right of refugee women to full equality with respect to housing, property and land restitution, in particular in terms of access, control, ownership and inheritance rights, should be fully respected.

(i) Refugees should be informed about their property restitution rights and, if necessary, receive legal counselling and representation to invoke them.

(j) Although it may take considerable time for refugees to be able to recover heir properties effectively, restitution claims are not rendered void due to the passage of time.

Property Restitution Procedure

(k) The country of origin, where necessary supported by the international community, should establish non-discriminatory, fair and efficient procedures and mechanisms to assess and enforce property restitution claims.

Implementation

(l) The country of origin, as necessary supported by the international community, should run public information campaigns to inform refugees about their property restitution rights and to ensure that they receive the necessary guidance as to the procedures to be followed.

(m) Property records should be freely accessible and available to refugees.

(n) Property restitution processes are only effective if the rights of occupants of refugee homes, who are equally affected by displacement and in need of accommodation, are also protected. The country of origin, where necessary supported by the international community, should assist in finding alternative housing for such occupants as a means to facilitate the recovery of refugee homes and properties.

(o) Reconstruction and rehabilitation projects concerning damaged housing should respect property restitution rights.

5. UN SECURITY COUNCIL

5.1. Resolution 237 – The Situation in the Middle East (1967)[41]

The Security Council,

Considering the urgent need to spare the civil populations and prisoners of war in the area of conflict in the Middle East additional sufferings,

Considering that essential and inalienable human rights should be respected even during the vicissitudes of war,

Considering that all the obligations of the Geneva Convention relative to the Treatment of Prisoners of War of 12 August 1949 should be complied with by the parties involved in the conflict,

1. *Calls upon* the Government of Israel to ensure the safety, welfare and security of the inhabitants of the areas where military operations have taken place and to facilitate the return of those inhabitants who have fled the areas since the outbreak of hostilities;

2. *Recommends* to the Governments concerned the scrupulous respect of the humanitarian principles governing the treatment of prisoners of war and the protection of civilian persons in time of war contained in the Geneva Conventions of 12 August 1949;

3. *Requests* the Secretary-General to follow the effective implementation of this resolution and to report to the Security Council.

[41] 14 June 1967.

5.2. Resolution 242 – Middle East (1967)[42]

The Security Council,

Expressing its continuing concern with the grave situation in the Middle East,

Emphasizing the inadmissibility of the acquisition of territory by war and the need to work for a just and lasting peace in which every State in the area can live in security,

Emphasizing further that all Member States in their acceptance of the Charter of the United Nations have undertaken a commitment to act in accordance with Article 2 of the Charter,

1. *Affirms* that the fulfilment of Charter principles requires the establishment of a just and lasting peace in the Middle East which should include the application of both the following principles:

(i) Withdrawal of Israel armed forces from territories occupied in the recent conflict;

(ii) Termination of all claims or states of belligerency and respect for and acknowledgement of the sovereignty, territorial integrity and political independence of every State in the area and their right to live in peace and within secure and recognized boundaries free from threats or acts of force;

2. Affirms further the necessity

(a) For guaranteeing freedom of navigation through international waterways in the area;

(b) For achieving a just settlement of the refugee problem;

(c) For guaranteeing the territorial inviolability and political independence of every State in the area, through measures including the establishment of de-militarized zones;

3. *Requests* the Secretary-General to designate a Special Representative to proceed to the Middle East to establish and maintain contacts with the States concerned in order to promote agreement and assist efforts to achieve a peaceful and accepted settlement in accordance with the provisions and principles in this resolution.

[. . .]

5.3. Resolution 361 – Cyprus (1974)[43]

The Security Council,

[. . .]

4. *Expresses its grave concern* at the plight of the refugees and other persons displaced as a result of the situation in Cyprus and urges the parties concerned, in conjunction with the Secretary-General, to search for peaceful solutions to the problems of refugees, and take appropriate measures to provide for their relief and welfare and to permit persons who wish to do so to return to their homes in safety;

[. . .]

5.4. Resolution 674 – Kuwait (1990)[44]

The Security Council,

[. . .]

8. *Reminds* Iraq that under international law it is liable for any loss, damage or injury arising in regard to Kuwait and third States, and their nationals and corporations, as a result of the invasion and illegal occupation of Kuwait by Iraq;

9. *Invites* States to collect relevant information regarding their claims, and those of their nationals and corporations, for restitution or financial compensation by Iraq with a view to such arrangements as may be established in accordance with international law;

[. . .]

5.5. Resolution 687 – Kuwait (1991)[45]

The Security Council,

[. . .]

Noting that despite the progress being made in fulfilling the obligations of resolution 686 (1991), many Kuwaiti and third country nationals are still not accounted for and property remains unreturned,

[. . .]

---

[42] 22 November 1967.

[43] 30 August 1974.
[44] 29 October 1990.
[45] 3 April 1991.

D

15. *Requests* the Secretary-General to report to the Security Council on the steps taken to facilitate the return of all Kuwaiti property seized by Iraq, including a list of any property that Kuwait claims has not been returned or which has not been returned intact;

E

16. *Reaffirms* that Iraq, without prejudice to the debts and obligations of Iraq arising prior to 2 August 1990, which will be addressed through the normal mechanisms, is liable under international law for any direct loss, damage, including environmental damage and the depletion of natural resources, or injury to foreign Governments, nationals and corporations, as a result of Iraq's unlawful invasion and occupation of Kuwait;

[. . .]

18. *Decides* also to create a fund to pay compensation for claims that fall within paragraph 16 above and to establish a Commission that will administer the fund;

19. *Directs* the Secretary-General to develop and present to the Security Council for decision, no later than thirty days following the adoption of the present resolution, recommendations for the fund to meet the requirement for the payment of claims established in accordance with paragraph 18 above and for a programme to implement the decisions in paragraphs 16, 17 and 18 above, including: administration of the fund; mechanisms for determining the appropriate level of Iraq's contribution to the fund based on a percentage of the value of the exports of petroleum and petroleum products from Iraq not to exceed a figure to be suggested to the Council by the Secretary-General, taking into account the requirements of the people of Iraq, Iraq's payment capacity as assessed in conjunction with the international financial institutions taking into consideration external debt service, and the needs of the Iraqi economy; arrangements for ensuring that payments are made to the fund; the process by which funds will be allocated and claims paid; appropriate procedures for evaluating losses, listing claims and verifying their validity and resolving disputed claims in respect of Iraq's liability as specified in paragraph 16 above; and

the composition of the Commission designated above;

[. . .]

G

30. *Decides* that, in furtherance of its commitment to facilitate the repatriation of all Kuwaiti and third country nationals, Iraq shall extend all necessary cooperation to the International Committee of the Red Cross, providing lists of such persons, facilitating the access of the International Committee of the Red Cross to all such persons wherever located or detained and facilitating the search by the International Committee of the Red Cross for those Kuwaiti and third country nationals still unaccounted for;

31. *Invites* the International Committee of the Red Cross to keep the Secretary-General apprised as appropriate of all activities undertaken in connection with facilitating the repatriation or return of all Kuwaiti and third country nationals or their remains present in Iraq on or after 2 August 1990.

[. . .]

5.6. Resolution 752 – Yugoslavia (1992)[46]

The Security Council,

[. . .]

6. *Calls upon* all parties and others concerned to ensure that forcible expulsions of persons from the areas where they live and any attempts to change the ethnic composition of the population, anywhere in the former Socialist Federal Republic of Yugoslavia, cease immediately;

7. *Emphasizes* the urgent need for humanitarian assistance, material and financial, taking into account the large number of refugees and displaced persons and fully supports the current efforts to deliver humanitarian aid to all the victims of the conflict and to assist in the voluntary return of displaced persons to their homes.

[. . .]

[46] 15 May 1992.

5.7. Resolution 787 – Bosnia and Herzegovina (1992)[47]

The Security Council,

1. *Reaffirms* that any taking of territory by force or any practice of "ethnic cleansing" is unlawful and unacceptable, and will not be permitted to affect the outcome of the negotiations on constitutional arrangements for the Republic of Bosnia and Herzegovina, and insists that all displaced persons be enabled to return in peace to their former homes.

[. . .]

5.8. Resolution 820 – Yugoslavia (1993)[48]

The Security Council,

1. *Reaffirms* its endorsement of the principles that all statements or commitments made under duress, particularly those relating to land and property, are wholly null and void and that all displaced persons have the right to return in peace to their former homes and should be assisted to do so.

[. . .]

5.9. Resolution 853 – Azerbaijan (1993)[49]

The Security Council,

1. *Requests* the Secretary-General and relevant international agencies to provide urgent humanitarian assistance to the affected civilian population and to assist displaced persons to return to their homes.

[. . .]

5.10. Resolution 876 – Georgia (1993)[50]

The Security Council,

[. . .]

5. *Affirms* the right of refugees and displaced persons to return to their homes, and calls on the parties to facilitate this.

[. . .]

5.11. Resolution 947 – Croatia (1994)[51]

The Security Council,

[. . .]

7. *Affirms* the right of all displaced persons to return voluntarily to their homes of origin in safety and dignity with the assistance of the international community;

8. *Reaffirms* its support for the established principle that all statements or commitments made under duress, particularly those regarding land and ownership, are null and void.

[. . .]

5.12. Resolution 971 – Georgia/Abkhazia (1995)[52]

The Security Council,

[. . .]

Reaffirming also the right of all refugees and displaced persons affected by the conflict to return to their homes in secure conditions in accordance with international law and as set out in the Quadripartite Agreement on voluntary return of refugees and displaced persons (S/1994/397, annex II), signed in Moscow on 4 April 1994,

Deeply concerned about the lack of progress regarding a comprehensive political settlement as well as the slow pace of return of refugees and displaced persons,

[. . .]

5. *Calls upon* the parties to comply with their commitments with regard to the return of refugees and displaced persons, as undertaken in the Quadripartite Agreement and in particular calls upon the Abkhaz side to accelerate the process significantly;

---

[47] 16 November 1992.
[48] 17 April 1993.
[49] 29 July 1993.
[50] 19 October 1993.

[51] 30 September 1994.
[52] 12 January 1995.

6. Decides to undertake, on the basis of a report from the Secretary-General submitted by 4 May 1995 and in the light of any progress achieved towards a political settlement and the return of refugees and displaced persons, a thorough review of the situation in Abkhazia, Republic of Georgia;

[. . .]

5.13. Resolution 999 – Tajikistan (1995)[53]

The Security Council,

[. . .]

8. *Calls upon* the parties to agree to the early convening of a further round of inter-Tajik talks and to implement without delay all confidence building measures agreed at the fourth round of these talks, inter alia, on the exchange of detainees and prisoners of war and on intensification of the efforts by the parties to ensure the voluntary return, in dignity and safety, of all refugees and displaced persons to their homes;

[. . .]

14. *Welcomes* the obligation assumed by the Government of the Republic of Tajikistan to assist the return and the reintegration of refugees as well as the obligations by the parties to cooperate in ensuring the voluntary return, in dignity and safety, of all refugees and displaced persons to their homes, inter alia by stepping up the activities of the Joint Commission on problems relating to refugees and displaced persons from Tajikistan formed by the parties in accordance with the Protocol signed on 19 April 1994 (S/1994/542, annex II), and in this context notes the request by the parties addressed to international organizations and States to provide additional substantial financial and material support to the refugees and internally displaced persons and to the Joint Commission on refugees.

[. . .]

5.14. Resolution 1009 – Croatia (1995)[54]

The Security Council,

[. . .]

---

[53] 16 June 1995.
[54] 10 August 1995.

2. *Demands further* that the Government of the Republic of Croatia, in conformity with internationally recognized standards and in compliance with the agreement of 6 August 1995 between the Republic of Croatia and the United Nations Peace Forces (a) respect fully the rights of the local Serb population including their rights to remain, leave or return in safety, (b) allow access to this population by international humanitarian organizations, and (c) create conditions conducive to the return of those persons who have left their homes.

[. . .]

5.15. Resolution 1019 – Croatia (1995)[55]

The Security Council,

[. . .]

7. Reiterates its demand that the Government of the Republic of Croatia respect fully the rights of the local Serb population including their right to remain or return in safety and reiterates also its call upon the Government of the Republic of Croatia to lift any time-limits placed on the return of refugees to Croatia to reclaim their property.

[. . .]

5.16. Resolution 1036 – Georgia/Abkhazia (1996)[56]

The Security Council,

[. . .]

Reaffirming also the right of all refugees and displaced persons affected by the conflict to return to their homes in secure conditions in accordance with international law and as set out in the Quadripartite Agreement of 14 April 1994 on voluntary return of refugees and displaced persons (S/1994/397, annex II),

[. . .]

Deploring the continued obstruction of such return by the Abkhaz authorities,

[. . .]

---

[55] 9 November 1995.
[56] 12 January 1996.

5. *Demands* that the Abkhaz side accelerate significantly the process of voluntary return of refugees and displaced persons by accepting a timetable on the basis of that proposed by the Office of the United Nations High Commissioner for Refugees, and further demands that it guarantee the safety of spontaneous returnees already in the area and regularize their status in accordance with the Quadripartite Agreement;

6. *Calls* upon the Abkhaz side in that context to promote, as a first step, the return of refugees and displaced persons to the Gali region, in safety and dignity;

[. . .]

8. *Calls* upon the parties to improve their cooperation with UNOMIG and the CIS peace-keeping force in order to provide a secure environment for the return of refugees and displaced persons and also calls upon them to honour their commitments with regard to the security and freedom of movement of all United Nations and CIS personnel and with regard to UNOMIG inspections of heavy weapons storage sites;

[. . .]

5.17. Resolution 1079 – Croatia (1996)[57]

The Security Council,

[. . .]

4. *Urges* furthermore the Republic of Croatia and the local Serb community to avoid actions which could lead to refugee movements and in the context of the right of all refugees and displaced persons to return to their homes of origin, reaffirms the right of all persons originating from the Republic of Croatia to return to their homes of origin throughout the Republic of Croatia.

[. . .]

5.18. Resolution 1088 – Bosnia and Herzegovina (1996)[58]

The Security Council,

[57] 15 November 1996.
[58] 12 December 1996.

[. . .]

11. *Welcomes* the commitment of the parties to the right of all refugees and displaced persons freely to return to their homes of origin or to other places of their choice in Bosnia and Herzegovina in safety, notes the leading humanitarian role which has been given by the Peace Agreement to the United Nations High Commissioner for Refugees, in coordination with other agencies involved and under the authority of the Secretary-General, in assisting with the repatriation and relief of refugees and displaced persons, and stresses the importance of facilitating the return or resettlement of refugees and displaced persons which should be gradual and orderly and carried out through progressive, coordinated programmes that address the need for local security, housing and jobs, while ensuring full compliance with Annex 7 of the Peace Agreement as well as other established procedures.

[. . .]

5.19. Resolution 1120 – Croatia (1997)[59]

The Security Council,

[. . .]

Emphasizing the importance of the obligation of the Government of the Republic of Croatia to allow all refugees and displaced persons to return in safety to their homes throughout the Republic of Croatia, and further emphasizing the importance of the two-way return of all displaced persons in the Republic of Croatia,

[. . .]

Welcoming the Agreement of the Joint Working Group on the Operational Procedures of Return (S/1997/341, annex), but noting with concern that the lack of conditions necessary for the return of displaced persons to the former United Nations Protected Areas from the Region of Eastern Slavonia, Baranja and Western Sirmium prevents the return in any substantial number of those displaced persons seeking to return to Eastern Slavonia,

[59] 14 July 1997.

Baranja and Western Sirmium from other parts of Croatia,

[. . .]

3. *Reaffirms* the right of all refugees and displaced persons originating from the Republic of Croatia to return to their homes of origin throughout the Republic of Croatia;

4. *Strongly urges* the Government of the Republic of Croatia to eliminate promptly the administrative and legal obstacles to the return of refugees and displaced persons, in particular those posed by the Law on Temporary Take Over and Administration of Specified Property; to create the necessary conditions of security, safety, and social and economic opportunity for those returning to their homes in Croatia, including the prompt payment of pensions; and to foster the successful implementation of the Agreement on the Operational Procedures of Return (S/1997/341) treating all returnees equally, regardless of ethnic origin;

[. . .]

17. *Welcomes* the renewed mandate of the Organization for Security and Cooperation in Europe (OSCE) of 26 June 1997 (S/1997/522, annex) providing for a continued and reinforced OSCE presence in the Republic of Croatia, with a particular focus on two-way return of all refugees and displaced persons, protection of their rights, and the protection of persons belonging to national minorities, welcomes also the decision of OSCE for the build-up starting July 1997 of its mission personnel with a view to full deployment by 15 January 1998, and urges the Government of the Republic of Croatia to cooperate fully with the OSCE mission to that end;

18. *Underlines* the observation of the Secretary-General that the essential prerequisite for the successful completion of peaceful reintegration of the Region is the full cooperation of the Government of the Republic of Croatia, which bears the responsibility for convincing the local population that the reintegration of the people of the Region is sustainable and that the process of reconciliation and return is irreversible.

[. . .]

5.20. Resolution 1145 – Croatia (1997)[60]

The Security Council,

[. . .]

Emphasizing the continuing obligation, under the Basic Agreement and international conventions, of the Government of the Republic of Croatia to allow all refugees and displaced persons to return in safety to their homes throughout the Republic of Croatia, and *further emphasizing* the urgency and importance of the two-way return of all displaced persons in the Republic of Croatia,

[. . .]

Recalling the mandate of the Organization for Security and Cooperation in Europe (OSCE) of 26 June 1997 (S/1997/522, annex) providing for a continued and reinforced OSCE presence in the Republic of Croatia, with a focus on the two-way return of all refugees and displaced persons, the protection of their rights, and the protection of persons belonging to national minorities,

[. . .]

7. *Reaffirms* the right of all refugees and displaced persons originating from the Republic of Croatia to return to their homes of origin throughout the Republic of Croatia, *welcomes* the fact that some progress has been made in the peaceful two-way return of displaced persons and the return of refugees in the Region, and *calls upon* the Government of the Republic of Croatia to remove legal obstacles and other impediments to two-way returns, including through the resolution of property issues, the establishment of straightforward procedures for returns, the adequate funding of the Joint Council and all relevant activities of municipalities, the clarification and full implementation of the Amnesty Law, and other measures, as set out in the report of the Secretary-General.

[. . .]

5.21. Resolution 1199 – Kosovo (1998)[61]

The Security Council,

[. . .]

---

[60] 19 December 1997.
[61] 23 September 1998.

Deeply concerned by the flow of refugees into northern Albania, Bosnia and Herzegovina and other European countries as a result of the use of force in Kosovo, as well as by the increasing numbers of displaced persons within Kosovo, and other parts of the Federal Republic of Yugoslavia, up to 50,000 of whom the United Nations High Commissioner for Refugees has estimated are without shelter and other basic necessities,

[. . .]

Reaffirming the right of all refugees and displaced persons to return to their homes in safety, and *underlining* the responsibility of the Federal Republic of Yugoslavia for creating the conditions which allow them to do so,

[. . .]

3. (c) facilitate, in agreement with the UNHCR and the International Committee of the Red Cross (ICRC), the safe return of refugees and displaced persons to their homes and allow free and unimpeded access for humanitarian organizations and supplies to Kosovo;

[. . .]

(e) to facilitate the unimpeded return of refugees and displaced persons under programmes agreed with the UNHCR and the ICRC, providing State aid for the reconstruction of destroyed homes,

[. . .]

5.22. Resolution 1244 – Kosovo (1999)[62]

The Security Council,

[. . .]

Determined to resolve the grave humanitarian situation in Kosovo, Federal Republic of Yugoslavia, and to provide for the safe and free return of all refugees and displaced persons to their homes,

[. . .]

Reaffirming the right of all refugees and displaced persons to return to their homes in safety,

[. . .]

9. *Decides* that the responsibilities of the international security presence to be deployed and acting in Kosovo will include:

[. . .]

(c) Establishing a secure environment in which refugees and displaced persons can return home in safety, the international civil presence can operate, a transitional administration can be established, and humanitarian aid can be delivered;

[. . .]

11. *Decides* that the main responsibilities of the international civil presence will include:

[. . .]

(k) Assuring the safe and unimpeded return of all refugees and displaced persons to their homes in Kosovo;

[. . .]

13. *Encourages* all Member States and international organizations to contribute to economic and social reconstruction as well as to the safe return of refugees and displaced persons, and *emphasizes* in this context the importance of convening an international donors' conference, at the earliest possible date.

[. . .]

5.23. Resolution 1287 – Abkhazia and the Republic of Georgia (2000)[63]

The Security Council,

[. . .]

8. *Reaffirms* the unacceptability of the demographic changes resulting from the conflict and the imprescriptible right of all refugees and displaced persons affected by the conflict to return to their homes in secure conditions, in accordance with international law and as set out in the Quadripartite Agreement of 4 April 1994 (S/1994/397, annex II), and calls upon the parties to address this issue urgently by agreeing and implementing effective measures to guarantee the security of those who

---

[62] 10 June 1999.

[63] 31 January 2000.

exercise their unconditional right to return, including those who have already returned;

[...]

5.24. Resolution 1339 – Georgia (2001)[64]

The Security Council,

[...]

4. *Stresses* the need to accelerate work on the draft protocol on the return of the refugees to the Gali region and measures for economic rehabilitation, as well as on the draft agreement on peace and guarantees for the prevention and for the nonresumption of hostilities;

[...]

7. *Reaffirms* the unacceptability of the demographic changes resulting from the conflict, and *reaffirms also* the inalienable right of all refugees and displaced persons affected by the conflict to return to their homes in secure and dignified conditions, in accordance with international law and as set out in the Quadripartite Agreement of 4 April 1994 (S/1994/397, annex II);

[...]

5.25. Resolution 1357 – Bosnia and Herzegovina (2001)[65]

The Security Council,

[...]

Emphasizing that a comprehensive and coordinated return of refugees and displaced persons throughout the region continues to be crucial to lasting peace,

[...]

2. *Reiterates* that the primary responsibility for the further successful implementation of the Peace Agreement lies with the authorities in Bosnia and Herzegovina themselves and that the continued willingness of the international community and major donors to assume the political, military and economic burden of implementation and

reconstruction efforts will be determined by the compliance and active participation by all the authorities in Bosnia and Herzegovina in implementing the Peace Agreement and rebuilding a civil society, in particular in full cooperation with the International Tribunal for the Former Yugoslavia, in strengthening joint institutions and in facilitating returns of refugees and displaced persons;

[...]

5.26. Resolution 1364 – Georgia (2001)[66]

The Security Council,

[...]

6. *Stresses also* the need to accelerate work on the draft protocol on the return of the refugees to the Gali region and measures for economic rehabilitation, as well as on the draft agreement on peace and guarantees for the prevention and for the nonresumption of hostilities;

[...]

11. *Reaffirms* the unacceptability of the demographic changes resulting from the conflict, and *reaffirms* also the inalienable right of all refugees and internally displaced persons affected by the conflict to return to their homes in secure and dignified conditions, in accordance with international law and as set out in the Quadripartite Agreement of 4 April 1994 (S/1994/397, annex II);

[...]

13. *Welcomes* measures undertaken by the Government of Georgia, the United Nations Development Programme, the Office of the United Nations High Commissioner for Refugees, the Office for the Coordinator of Humanitarian Affairs and the World Bank to improve the situation of refugees and internally displaced persons to develop their skills and to increase their self-reliance with full respect for their inalienable right to return to their homes in secure and dignified conditions;

[...]

[64] 31 January 2001.
[65] 21 June 2001.

[66] 31 July 2001.

5.27. Resolution 1393 – Georgia (2002)[67]

The Security Council,

[. . .]

11. *Expresses* its deep dismay at the lack of progress on the question of the refugees and internally displaced persons, *reaffirms* the unacceptability of the demographic changes resulting from the conflict, *reaffirms* also the inalienable right of all refugees and internally displaced persons affected by the conflict to return to their homes in secure and dignified conditions, in accordance with international law and as set out in the Quadripartite Agreement of 4 April 1994 (S/1994/397, annex II), *recalls* that the Abkhaz side bears a particular responsibility to protect the returnees and to facilitate the return of the remaining displaced population, and *welcomes* the measures undertaken by the United Nations Development Programme, the Office of the United Nations High Commissioner for Refugees and the Office for the Coordinator of Humanitarian Affairs to improve the situation of refugees and internally displaced persons, to develop their skills and to increase their self-reliance, with full respect for their inalienable right to return to their homes in secure and dignified conditions;

[. . .]

5.28. Resolution 1427 – Georgia (2002)[68]

The Security Council,

[. . .]

12. *Stresses* the urgent need for progress on the question of the refugees and internally displaced persons, *calls on* both sides to display a genuine commitment to make returns the focus of special attention and to undertake this task in close coordination with UNOMIG, *reaffirms* the unacceptability of the demographic changes resulting from the conflict, *reaffirms* also the inalienable right of all refugees and internally displaced persons affected by the conflict to return to their homes in secure and dignified conditions, in accordance with international law and as set out in the Quadripartite Agreement of 4 April 1994 (S/1994/397, annex II) and the

Yalta Declaration, *recalls* that the Abkhaz side bears a particular responsibility to protect the returnees and to facilitate the return of the remaining displaced population, and *requests* further measures to be undertaken inter alia by the United Nations Development Programme, the Office of the United Nations High Commissioner for Refugees and the Office for the Coordination of Humanitarian Affairs to create conditions conducive to the return of refugees and internally displaced persons, including through quick-impact projects, to develop their skills and to increase their self-reliance, with full respect for their inalienable right to return to their homes in secure and dignified conditions;

[. . .]

5.29. Resolution 1462 – Georgia (2003)[69]

The Security Council,

[. . .]

14. *Stresses* the urgent need for progress on the question of the refugees and internally displaced persons, *calls* on both sides to display a genuine commitment to make returns the focus of special attention and to undertake this task in close coordination with UNOMIG, *reaffirms* the unacceptability of the demographic changes resulting from the conflict, *reaffirms* also the inalienable right of all refugees and internally displaced persons affected by the conflict to return to their homes in secure and dignified conditions, in accordance with international law and as set out in the Quadripartite Agreement of 4 April 1994 (S/1994/397, annex II) and the Yalta Declaration, *recalls* that the Abkhaz side bears a particular responsibility to protect the returnees and to facilitate the return of the remaining displaced population, and *requests* further measures to be undertaken inter alia by the United Nations Development Programme, the Office of the United Nations High Commissioner for Refugees and the Office for the Coordination of Humanitarian Affairs to create conditions conducive to the return of refugees and internally displaced persons, including through quick-impact projects, to develop their skills and to increase their self-reliance, with full

[67] 31 January 2002.
[68] 29 July 2002.

[69] 30 January 2003.

respect for their inalienable right to return to their homes in secure and dignified conditions;

[. . .]

5.30. Resolution 1491 – Bosnia and Herzegovina (2003)[70]

The Security Council,

[. . .]

Emphasizing that a comprehensive and coordinated return of refugees and displaced persons throughout the region continues to be crucial to lasting peace,

[. . .]

2. *Reiterates* that the primary responsibility for the further successful implementation of the Peace Agreement lies with the authorities in Bosnia and Herzegovina themselves and that the continued willingness of the international community and major donors to assume the political, military and economic burden of implementation and reconstruction efforts will be determined by the compliance and active participation by all the authorities in Bosnia and Herzegovina in implementing the Peace Agreement and rebuilding a civil society, in particular in full cooperation with the International Tribunal for the Former Yugoslavia, in strengthening joint institutions, which foster the building of a fully functioning self-sustaining state, able to integrate itself into the European structures and in facilitating returns of refugees and displaced persons;

[. . .]

5.31. Resolution 1494 – Georgia (2003)[71]

The Security Council,

[. . .]

9. *Welcomes also* the identification in the first Geneva meeting of three sets of issues as key to advancing the peace process (economic cooperation, the return of internally displaced persons and refugees, political and security matters) and the following work on the substance of those issues, including in bilateral working groups by Russia and Georgia as agreed by the two Presidents in their meeting in Sochi in March 2003, and also in the initial high-level meeting of the parties on 15 July 2003, chaired by the Special Representative of the Secretary-General and with the participation of the Group of Friends;

10. *Further welcomes* the commitment of the parties to continue their dialogue on economic cooperation, refugee returns as well as political and security matters regularly and in a structured manner and their agreement to join the Group of Friends again towards the end of the year to review progress and explore future steps and *encourages* them to act upon that commitment;

[. . .]

14. *Stresses* the urgent need for progress on the question of the refugees and internally displaced persons, *calls on* both sides to display a genuine commitment to make returns the focus of special attention and to undertake this task in close coordination with UNOMIG and consultations with UNHCR and the Group of Friends and recalls the understanding in Sochi by Georgia and the Russian Federation that the reopening of the Sochi-Tbilisi railway will be undertaken in parallel with the return of refugees and displaced persons, starting in the Gali district, *reaffirms* the unacceptability of the demographic changes resulting from the conflict, *reaffirms also* the inalienable right of all refugees and IDPs affected by the conflict to return to their homes in secure and dignified conditions, in accordance with international law and as set out in the Quadripartite Agreement of 4 April 1994 (S/1994/397, annex II) and the Yalta Declaration;

15. *Recalls* that the Abkhaz side bears a particular responsibility to protect the returnees and to facilitate the return of the remaining displaced population, and *requests* further measures to be undertaken inter alia by the United Nations Development Programme, the Office of the United Nations High Commissioner for Refugees and the Office for the Coordination of Humanitarian Affairs to create conditions conducive to the return of refugees and internally displaced persons, including through quick-impact projects, to develop their skills and to increase their self-reliance, with full respect for

[70] 11 July 2003.
[71] 30 July 2003.

their inalienable right to return to their homes in secure and dignified conditions;

[. . .]

17. *Endorses* the recommendations by the Secretary-General in his report of 21 July 2003 (S/2003/751, para. 30) that a civilian police component of 20 officers be added to UNOMIG, to strengthen its capacity to carry out its mandate and in particular contribute to the creation of conditions conducive to the safe and dignified return of internally displaced persons and refugees, and *welcomes* the commitment of the parties to implement the recommendations by the security assessment mission of October to December 2002.

[. . .]

5.32. Resolution 1524 – Georgia (2004)[72]

The Security Council,

[. . .]

9. *Urges* the parties to participate in a more active, regular and structured manner in the task forces established in the first Geneva meeting (to address issues in the priority areas of economic cooperation, the return of internally displaced persons and refugees, and political and security matters) and complemented by the working groups established in Sochi, and stresses that results oriented activities in these three priority areas remain key to building common ground between the Georgian and Abkhaz sides and ultimately for concluding meaningful negotiations on a comprehensive political settlement based on the paper entitled "Basic Principles for the Distribution of Competences between Tbilisi and Sukhumi" and its transmittal letter;

[. . .]

14. *Stresses* the urgent need for progress on the question of the refugees and internally displaced persons, *calls on* both sides to display a genuine commitment to make returns the focus of special attention and to undertake this task in close coordination with UNOMIG and consultations with UNHCR and the Group of Friends and *recalls* the understanding in the Sochi summit that the

reopening of the Sochi-Tbilisi railway will be undertaken in parallel with the return of refugees and displaced persons, starting in the Gali district;

15. *Reaffirms* the unacceptability of the demographic changes resulting from the conflict, *reaffirms* also the inalienable right of all refugees and IDPs affected by the conflict to return to their homes in secure and dignified conditions, in accordance with international law and as set out in the Quadripartite Agreement of 4 April 1994 (S/1994/397, annex II) and the Yalta Declaration.

[. . .]

5.33. Resolution 1545 – Burundi (2004)[73]

The Security Council,

[. . .]

Considering that the voluntary and sustainable return of refugees and internally displaced persons will be a critical factor for the consolidation of the peace process, and will require a just solution of the issue of land ownership,

[. . .]

5. *Authorizes* ONUB to use all necessary means to carry out the following mandate, within its capacity and in the areas where its armed units are deployed, and in coordination with humanitarian and development communities:

– to contribute to the creation of the necessary security conditions for the provision of humanitarian assistance, and facilitate the voluntary return of refugees and internally displaced persons,

[. . .]

13. *Requests* all parties and concerned States to facilitate the voluntary, safe and sustainable return of refugees and internally displaced persons, and to cooperate fully to this end with ONUB and the relevant international organizations.

[. . .]

---

[72] 30 January 2004.

[73] 21 May 2004.

5.34. Resolution 1551 – Bosnia and Herzegovina (2004)[74]

The Security Council,

[...]

Emphasizing that a comprehensive and coordinated return of refugees and displaced persons throughout the region continues to be crucial to lasting peace,

[...]

2. *Reiterates* that the primary responsibility for the further successful implementation of the Peace Agreement lies with the authorities in Bosnia and Herzegovina themselves and that the continued willingness of the international community and major donors to assume the political, military and economic burden of implementation and reconstruction efforts will be determined by the compliance and active participation by all the authorities in Bosnia and Herzegovina in implementing the Peace Agreement and rebuilding a civil society, in particular in full cooperation with the International Tribunal for the Former Yugoslavia, in strengthening joint institutions, which foster the building of a fully functioning self-sustaining state, able to integrate itself into the European structures and in facilitating returns of refugees and displaced persons.

[...]

5.35. Resolution 1556 – Sudan (2004)[75]

The Security Council,

[...]

Condemning all acts of violence and violations of human rights and international humanitarian law by all parties to the crisis, in particular by the Janjaweed, including indiscriminate attacks on civilians, rapes, forced displacements, and acts of violence especially those with an ethnic dimension, and expressing its utmost concern at the consequences of the conflict in Darfur on the civilian population, including women, children, internally displaced persons, and refugees,

[...]

Stressing that any return of refugees and displaced persons to their homes must take place voluntarily with adequate assistance and with sufficient security.

[...]

5.36. Resolution 1575 – Bosnia and Herzegovina (2004)[76]

The Security Council,

[...]

Emphasizing that a comprehensive and coordinated return of refugees and displaced persons throughout the region continues to be crucial to lasting peace,

[...]

2. *Reiterates* that the primary responsibility for the further successful implementation of the Peace Agreement lies with the authorities in Bosnia and Herzegovina themselves and that the continued willingness of the international community and major donors to assume the political, military and economic burden of implementation and reconstruction efforts will be determined by the compliance and active participation by all the authorities in Bosnia and Herzegovina in implementing the Peace Agreement and rebuilding a civil society, in particular in full cooperation with the International Tribunal for the Former Yugoslavia, in strengthening joint institutions, which foster the building of a fully functioning self-sustaining state, able to integrate itself into the European structures and in facilitating returns of refugees and displaced persons.

[...]

5.37. Resolution 1582 – Georgia (2005)[77]

The Security Council,

[...]

11. *Urges* the parties to participate in a more active, regular and structured manner in the task forces established in the first Geneva meeting (to address issues in the priority areas of economic

[74] 9 July 2004.
[75] 30 July 2004.

[76] 22 November 2004.
[77] 28 January 2005.

cooperation, the return of internally displaced persons and refugees, and political and security matters) and complemented by the working groups established in Sochi in March 2003, and *reiterates* that results oriented activities in these three priority areas remain key to building common ground between the Georgian and Abkhaz sides and ultimately for concluding meaningful negotiations on a comprehensive political settlement based on the paper entitled "Basic Principles for the Distribution of Competences between Tbilisi and Sukhumi" and its transmittal letter;

[. . .]

15. *Stresses* the urgent need for progress on the question of the refugees and internally displaced persons, *calls on* both sides to display a genuine commitment to make returns the focus of special attention and to undertake this task in close coordination with UNOMIG and consultations with UNHCR and the Group of Friends;

16. *Calls* for the rapid finalization and signature of the letter of intent on returns proposed by the Special Representative of the Secretary-General and *welcomes* the meetings with the participation of the SRSG and UNHCR of the Sochi working group on refugees and internally displaced persons;

17. *Reaffirms* the unacceptability of the demographic changes resulting from the conflict, *reaffirms also* the inalienable right of all refugees and internally displaced persons affected by the conflict to return to their homes in secure and dignified conditions, in accordance with international law and as set out in the Quadripartite Agreement of 4 April 1994 (S/1994/397, annex II) and the Yalta Declaration;

18. *Recalls* that the Abkhaz side bears a particular responsibility to protect the returnees and to facilitate the return of the remaining displaced population;

[. . .]

5.38. Resolution 1615 – Georgia (2005)[78]

The Security Council,

[. . .]

[78] 29 July 2005.

10. *Urges* the parties to participate in a more active, regular and structured manner in the task forces established in the first Geneva meeting (to address issues in the priority areas of economic cooperation, the return of internally displaced persons and refugees, and political and security matters) and complemented by the working groups established in Sochi in March 2003, and *reiterates* that results oriented activities in these three priority areas remain key to building common ground between the Georgian and Abkhaz sides and ultimately for concluding meaningful negotiations on a comprehensive political settlement based on the paper entitled "Basic Principles for the Distribution of Competences between Tbilisi and Sukhumi" and its transmittal letter;

[. . .]

14. *Welcomes* the positive developments towards the reopening of the railways between Sochi and Tbilisi and towards the return of refugees and internally displaced persons;

[. . .]

16. *Stresses* the urgent need for progress on the question of the refugees and internally displaced persons, *calls on* both sides to display a genuine commitment to make returns the focus of special attention and to undertake this task in close coordination with UNOMIG and consultations with UNHCR and the Group of Friends;

[. . .]

18. *Reaffirms* the unacceptability of the demographic changes resulting from the conflict, *reaffirms also* the inalienable rights of all refugees and internally displaced persons affected by the conflict, and *stresses* that they have the right to return to their homes in secure and dignified conditions, in accordance with international law and as set out in the Quadripartite Agreement of 4 April 1994 (S/1994/397, annex II) and the Yalta Declaration;

19. *Recalls* that the Abkhaz side bears a particular responsibility to protect the returnees and to facilitate the return of the remaining displaced population;

[. . .]

6. UN GENERAL ASSEMBLY

6.1. Resolution 8 – Question of Refugees (1946)[79]

The General Assembly,

[. . .]

(c) (iii) the main task concerning displaced persons is to encourage and assist in every way possible their early return to their countries of origin. Such assistance may take the form of promoting bilateral arrangements for mutual assistance in the repatriation of such persons having regard to the principles laid down in paragraph (c) (ii) above.

[. . .]

6.2. Resolution 194 – United Nations Conciliation Commission for Palestine, Protection and a Durable Solution for Palestinian Refugees (1948)[80]

The General Assembly,

Having considered further the situation in Palestine,

1. *Expresses* its deep appreciation of the progress achieved through the good offices of the late United Nations Mediator in promoting a peaceful adjustment of the future situation of Palestine, for which cause he sacrificed his life; and

Extends its thanks to the Acting Mediator and his staff for their continued efforts and devotion to duty in Palestine;

2. *Establishes* a Conciliation Commission consisting of three States Members of the United Nations which shall have the following functions:

(a) To assume, in so far as it considers necessary in existing circumstances, the functions given to the United Nations Mediator on Palestine by the resolution of the General Assembly of 14 May 1948;

(b) To carry out the specific functions and directives given to it by the present resolution and such additional functions and directives as may be given

to it by the General Assembly or by the Security Council;

(c) To undertake, upon the request of the Security Council, any of the functions now assigned to the United Nations Mediator on Palestine or to the United Nations Truce Commission by resolutions of the Security Council; upon such request to the Conciliation Commission by the Security Council with respect to all the remaining functions of the United Nations Mediator on Palestine under Security Council resolutions, the office of the Mediator shall be terminated;

3. *Decides* that a Committee of the Assembly consisting of China, France, the Union of Soviet Socialist Republics, the United Kingdom and the United States of America, shall present, before the end of the first part of the present session of the General Assembly, a proposal concerning the names of the three States which will constitute the Conciliation Commission;

4. *Requests* the Commission to begin its functions at once, with a view to the establishment of contact between the parties themselves and the Commission at the earliest possible date;

5. *Calls Upon* the Governments and authorities concerned to extend the scope of the negotiations provided for in the Security Council's resolution of 16 November 1948 and to seek agreement by negotiations conducted either with the Conciliation Commission or directly, with a view to the final settlement of all questions outstanding between them;

6. *Instructs* the Conciliation Commission to take steps to assist the Governments and authorities concerned to achieve a final settlement of all questions outstanding between them;

7. *Resolves* that the Holy Places – including Nazereth – religious buildings and sites in Palestine should be protected and free access to them assured, in accordance with existing rights and historical practice; that arrangements to this end should be under effective United Nations supervision; that the United Nations Conciliation Commission, in presenting to the fourth regular session of the General Assembly its detailed proposals for a permanent international regime for the territory of Jerusalem, should include recommendations concerning the Holy Places in that territory; that with regard to the Holy Places in the rest of Palestine the

---

[79] 12 February 1946.
[80] 27 November 1948.

Commission should call upon the political authorities of the areas concerned to give appropriate formal guarantees as to the protection of the Holy Places and access to them; and that these undertakings should be presented to the General Assembly for approval;

8. *Resolves* that, in view of its association with three world religions, the Jerusalem area, including the present municipality of Jerusalem *plus* the surrounding villages and towns, the most eastern of which shall be Abu Dis; the most southern, Bethlehem; the most western, Ein Karim (including also the built-up area of Motsa); and the most northern, Shu'fat, should be accorded special and separate treatment from the rest of Palestine and should be placed under effective United Nations control;

Requests the Security Council to take further steps to ensure the demilitarization of Jerusalem at the earliest possible date;

Instructs the Conciliation Commission to present to the fourth regular session of the General Assembly detailed proposals for a permanent international regime for the Jerusalem area which will provide for the maximum local autonomy for distinctive groups consistent with the special international status of the Jerusalem area;

The Conciliation Commission is authorized to appoint a United Nations representative, who shall co-operate with the local authorities with respect to the interim administration of the Jerusalem area;

9. *Resolves* that, pending agreement on more detailed arrangements among the Governments and authorities concerned, the freest possible access to Jerusalem by road, rail or air should be accorded to all inhabitants of Palestine;

Instructs the Conciliation Commission to report immediately to the Security Council, for appropriate action by that organ, any attempt by any party to impede such access;

10. *Instructs* the Conciliation Commission to seek arrangements among the Governments and authorities concerned which shall facilitate the economic development of the area, including arrangements for access to ports and airfields and the use of transportation and communication facilities.

11. *Resolves* that the refugees wishing to return to their homes and live at peace with their neighbours should be permitted to do so at the earliest practicable date, and that compensation should be paid for the property of those choosing not to return and for loss of or damage to property which, under principles of international law or in equity, should be made good by the Governments or authorities responsible;

Instructs the Conciliation Commission to facilitate the repatriation, resettlement and economic and social rehabilitation of the refugees and the payment of compensation, and to maintain close relations with the Director of the United Nations Relief for Palestine Refugees and, through him, with the appropriate organs and agencies of the United Nations;

12. *Authorizes* the Conciliation Commission to appoint such subsidiary bodies and to employ such technical experts, acting under its authority, as it may find necessary for the effective discharge of its functions and responsibilities under the present resolution;

The Conciliation Commission will have it official headquarters at Jerusalem. The authorities responsible for maintaining order in Jerusalem will be responsible for taking all measures necessary to ensure the security of the Commission. The Secretary-General will provide a limited number of guards for the protection of the staff and premises of the Commission;

13. *Instructs* the Conciliation Commission to render progress reports periodically to the Secretary-General for transmission to the Security Council and to the Members of the United Nations;

14. *Calls upon* all Governments and authorities concerned to co-operate with the Conciliation Commission and to take all possible steps to assist in the implementation of the present resolution;

15. *Requests* the Secretary-General to provide the necessary staff and facilities and to make appropriate arrangements to provide the necessary funds required in carrying out the terms of the present resolution.

6.3. Resolution 394 – Palestine: Progress Report of the United Nations Conciliation Commission for Palestine; Repatriation or Resettlement of Palestine Refugees and Payment of Compensation Due to Them (1950)[81]

The General Assembly,

Recalling its resolution 194 (III) of 11 December 1948,

Having examined with appreciation the general progress report dated 2 September 1950, and the supplementary report dated 23 October 1950, of the United Nations Conciliation Commission for Palestine,

Noting with concern:

(a) That agreement has not been reached between the parties on the final settlement of the questions outstanding between them,

(b) The repatriation, resettlement, economic and social rehabilitation of the refugees and the payment of compensation have not been effected,

Recognizing that, in the interests of the peace and stability of the Near East, the refugee question should be dealt with as a matter of urgency,

1. *Urges* the governments and authorities concerned to seek agreement by negotiations conducted either with the Conciliation Commission or directly, with a view to the final settlement of all questions outstanding between them;

2. *Directs* the United Nations Conciliation Commission for Palestine to establish an office which, under the direction of the Commission, shall:

(a) Make such arrangements as it may consider necessary for the assessment and payment of compensation in pursuance of paragraph 11 of General Assembly resolution 194 (III);

(b) Work out such arrangements as may be practicable for the implementation of the other objectives of paragraph 11 of the said resolution;

(c) Continue consultations with the parties concerned regarding measures for the protection of the rights, property and interests of the refugees;

3. Calls upon the governments concerned to undertake measures to ensure that refugees, whether repatriated or resettled, will be treated without any discrimination either in law or in fact.

6.4. Resolution 428 – Statute of the Office of the United Nations High Commissioner for Refugees (1950)[82]

[. . .]

2. *Calls upon* governments to co-operate with the United Nations High Commissioner for Refugees in the performance of his functions concerning refugees falling under the competence of his Office, especially by:

(d) Assisting the High Commissioner in his efforts to promote the voluntary repatriation of refugees.

[. . .]

6.5. Addendum to Definition of a "Refugee" under Paragraph 11 of the General Assembly Resolution (11 December 1948) (1951)[83]

During the meeting at which the definition of a "refugee" was discussed, the members of the commission expressed a desire for certain points relating to that definition of be clarified. In this connection, the question of a Palestine refugee was based, and of the protection of the interests of a category of people who would not be considered as refugees in the event of that criterion being accepted.

In connection with the first point, it is widely known that the overwhelming majority of those who took refuge in the Arab countries are of Arab origin and possessed Palestinian citizenship on 29 November 1947. In practice, therefore, the question is to determine the status of a small non-Arab minority which in the 1931 census was placed in the category of "Others", as opposed to the category of "Arabs", in which all Arabs belonging to the Palestine Arab community, or who considered themselves as belonging to that community, were placed.

---

[81] 14 December 1950.

[82] 14 December 1950.
[83] Prepared by the Legal Advisor, W/61/Add.1, 29 May 1951.

This minority can be divided into two distinct categories:

1. Those who have retained their Palestinian citizenship.

2. Those who acquired another nationality after 29 November 1947, either by resuming their former nationality or by becoming naturalized citizens of a country in which they have racial ties with the majority of the population.

These two categories of persons have one thing in common, that is, that they were not included in the Palestine Arab Community as a result of the statements which they made to the census officials in the 1931 census, thus showing that they possessed a national consciousness other than an Arab national consciousness.

This national consciousness, on which the determination of ethnical origin is based, might have been Greek, Turkish, Armenian or other. Furthermore, a manifestation of this national consciousness has been the resumption of previous nationality, or the acquisition of a new nationality by reason of racial ties with the majority of the population of another country. Those who have been able to change their personal status in this way have become foreigners from the point of view of the State of Israel and must be considered as such by that State and therefore be treated there as foreigners according to the principles of international law.

As regards those who have not acquired, or who have not been able to acquire, a foreign nationality or whose foreign nationality thus acquired is questioned by the Israel authorities, they would continue to belong to minorities in Israel, minorities for whom certain fundamental rights have been recognized by the General Assembly. In particular, they would enjoy the right to return and to dispose freely of their property, as belonging to a non-Arab minority in Israel. The property which they might possess in Israel could not be disposed of, as in the case of the property of Arab refugees who do not wish to return to their homes.

The foregoing considerations would appear to take into account the concern expressed by the members of the Commission regarding the protection of the interests of a small minority of non-Arab Palestinians. The rights of these persons will be guaranteed respectively by the principles of international law and by the relevant provisions of the appropriate General Assembly resolutions.

However, with a view to expanding the ethnical criterion on which the suggested definition is based, a text interpreting the term "of Arab origin" might be considered useful. It would enable non-Arabs who have not acquired a foreign nationality to express an Arab national consciousness and thus to be included in the definition of refugees, in the event, however, of the parties concerned begin prepared to accept the consequences of such an expression of their wishes.

This Article might be drafted as follows:

The term "of Arab origin" appearing in the foregoing Articles relates to persons belonging to the Palestine Arab community and to those who are considered or who consider themselves as belonging to that community.

[. . .]

In the light of the foregoing considerations, the amended definition of a refugee might read as follows:

Article 1

Are to be considered as refugees under paragraph 11 of the General Assembly resolution of 11 December 1948 persons of Arab origin who, after 29 November 1947, left territory at present under the control of the Israel authorities and who were Palestinian citizens at that date.

Are also to be considered as refugees under the said paragraph stateless persons of Arab origin who after 29 November 1947 left the aforementioned territory, where they had been settled up to that date.

Persons who have resumed their original nationality or who have acquired the nationality of a country in which they have racial ties with majority of the population are not covered by the provisions of the above paragraphs of this Article. It is understood that the majority of the said population should not be an Arab majority.

Article 2

The following shall be considered as covered by the provisions of Article 1 above:

1. Persons of Arab origin who left the said territory after 6 August 1924 and before 29 November 1947 and who at that later date were Palestinian citizens:

2. Persons of Arab origin who left the territory in question before 6 August 1924 and who, having opted for Palestinian citizenship, retained that citizenship up to 29 November 1947.

Article 3

The term "of Arab origin" appearing in the foregoing Articles related to persons belonging to the Palestine Arab community and to those who are considered or who considered themselves as belonging to that community.

6.6. Resolution 1388 – Report of the United Nations High Commissioner for Refugees (1959)[84]

The General Assembly,

[. . .]

Expressing the hope that no additional efforts will be spared for the repatriation of refugees who wish to return to their country of origin,

Expressing the hope also that every effort will be made for the resettlement or integration of refugees,

1. *Invites* States Members of the United Nations and members of the specialized agencies to devote, on the occasion of the World Refugee Year, special attention to the problems of refugees coming within the competence of the United Nations High Commissioner for Refugees, and in particular to consider the possibility of:

(a) Improving the legal status of refugees living on, or to be admitted to, their territory by, inter alia, acceding to the Convention relating to the Status of Refugees,

(b) Increasing the facilities for permanent refugee solutions through voluntary repatriation and, for resettlement of refugees, providing further opportunities through the liberalization of immigration laws and regulations and through the inclusion of refugees in resettlement schemes;

(c) Enabling the High Commissioner, through additional voluntary financial contributions, to implement the programmes of international assistance to refugees approved by the Executive Committee of the High Commissioner's Programme for 1959 and 1960;

2. *Authorizes* the High Commissioner, in respect of refugees who do not come within the competence of the United Nations, to use his good offices in the transmission of contributions designed to provide assistance to these refugees.

6.7. Resolution 1390 – World Refugee Year (1959)[85]

The General Assembly,

[. . .]

c) To encourage additional opportunities for permanent refugee solutions through voluntary repatriation, resettlement, or integration, on a purely humanitarian basis and in accordance with the freely expressed wishes of the refugees themselves;

[. . .]

6.8. Resolution 1672 – Refugees from Algeria in Morocco and Tunisia (1961)[86]

The General Assembly,

[. . .]

Requests the United Nations High Commissioner for Refugees to:

(a) Continue his present action jointly with the league of Red Cross Societies until those refugees return to their homes;

(b) Use the means at his disposal to assist in the orderly return of those refugees to their homes and consider the possibility, when necessary, of facilitating their resettlement in their homeland as soon as circumstances permit;

(c) Persist in his efforts to secure the resources which will enable him to complete this task.

[. . .]

---

[84] 20 November 1959.

[85] 20 November 1959.
[86] 18 December 1961.

6.9. Resolution 3212 – Question of Cyprus (1974)[87]

The General Assembly,

[. . .]

5. *Considers* that all the refugees should return to their homes in safety and calls upon the parties concerned to undertake urgent measures to that end:

[. . .]

6.10. Resolution 3236 – Question of Palestine (1974)[88]

The General Assembly,

[. . .]

1. *Reaffirms* the inalienable rights of the Palestinian people in Palestine, including:

(a) The right to self-determination without external interference;

(b) The right to national independence and sovereignty;

2. *Reaffirms also* the inalienable right of the Palestinians to return to their homes and property from which they have been displaced and uprooted, and calls for their return;

3. *Emphasizes* that full respect for and the realization of these inalienable rights of the Palestinian people are indispensable for the solution of the question of Palestine.

6.11. Resolution 35/124 – International Cooperation to Avert New Flows of Refugees (1980)[89]

The General Assembly,

[. . .]

Gravely concerned over the increasing flows of refugees in many parts of the world,

[. . .]

Deeply disturbed by the human suffering affecting millions of men, women and children who flee or are forcibly expelled from their homelands and seek refuge in other countries,

[. . .]

Reaffirming the right of refugees to return to their homes in their homelands,

[. . .]

2. *Invites* all Member States to convey to the Secretary-General their comments and suggestions on international co-operation to avert new flows of refugees and to facilitate the return of those refugees who wish to return.

[. . .]

6.12. Resolution 36/146 – United Nations Relief and Works Agency for Palestine Refugees in the Near East (1981)[90]

[. . .]

B – POPULATION AND REFUGEES DISPLACED SINCE 1967

The General Assembly,

Recalling Security Council resolution 237 (1967) of 14 June 1967,

[. . .]

1. *Reaffirms* the inalienable right of all displaced inhabitants to return to their homes or former places of residence in the territories occupied by Israel since 1967 and declares once more that any attempt to restrict, or to attach conditions to, the free exercise of the right of return by any displaced person is inconsistent with that inalienable right and inadmissible;

2. *Considers* any and all agreements embodying any restriction on or condition for the return of the displaced inhabitants as null and void;

3. *Deplores* the continued refusal of the Israeli authorities to take steps for the return of the displaced inhabitants;

4. Calls once more upon Israel:

[87] 1 November 1974.
[88] 22 November 1974.
[89] 11 December 1980.

[90] 16 December 1981.

(a) To take immediate steps for the return of all displaced inhabitants;

(b) To desist from all measures that obstruct the return of the displaced inhabitants, including measures affecting the physical and demographic structure of the occupied territories.

[. . .]

C – REVENUES DERIVED FROM PALESTINE REFUGEE PROPERTIES

The General Assembly,

Recalling its resolutions 35/13 A to F of 3 November 1980 and all its previous resolutions on the question, including resolution 194 (III) of 11 December 1948,

Taking note of the report of the United Nations Conciliation Commission for Palestine, covering the period from 1 October to 30 September 1981,

Recalling that the Universal Declaration of Human Rights and the principles of international law uphold the principle that no one shall be arbitrarily deprived of private property,

Considering that the Palestinian Arab refugees are entitled to their property and to the income derived from their property, in conformity with the principles of justice and equity,

Recalling, in particular, its resolution 394 (V) of 14 December 1950, in which it directed the United Nations Conciliation Commission for Palestine, in consultation with the parties concerned, to prescribe measure for the protection of the rights, property and interests of the Palestinian Arab refugees,

Taking note of the completion of the programme of identification and evaluation of Arab property, as announced by the United Nations Conciliation Commission for Palestine in its twenty-second progress report, of 11 May 1964, and of the fact that the Land Office has a schedule of Arab owners and file of documents defining the location, area and other particulars of Arab property,

1. *Requests* the Secretary-General to take all appropriate steps, in consultation with the United Nations Conciliation Commission for Palestine, for the protection and administration of Arab property, assets and property rights in Israel, and to establish a fund for the receipt of income derived therefrom, on behalf of their rightful owners;

2. *Calls upon* the Governments concerned to render all facilities and assistance to the Secretary-General on the implementation of the present resolution;

3. *Requests* the Secretary-General to report to the General Assembly at its thirty-seventh session on the implementation of the present resolution.

[. . .]

6.13. Resolution 36/148 – International Co-Operation to Avert New Flows of Refugees (1981)[91]

The General Assembly,

Recalling its resolution 35/124 of 11 December 1980 on international co-operation to avert new massive flows of refugees,

Having examined the report of the Secretary-General,

Noting the comments and suggestions made by Member States, United Nations organs, organizations and specialized agencies submitted in response to General Assembly resolution 35/124,

Gravely concerned over the continuing massive flows of refugees in many parts of the world and the human suffering affecting millions of men, women and children who flee or are forcibly expelled from their homelands,

Reaffirming the strong condemnation of policies and practices of oppressive and racist regimes, as well as aggression, colonialism, apartheid, alien domination, foreign intervention and occupation which are among the root causes of new and massive flows of refugees throughout the world resulting in great human suffering,

Taking into account the importance of socio-economic factors for the creation of refugee situations,

Reaffirming the inviolability of the provisions of the Charter of the United Nations and the Universal Declaration of Human Rights and of other existing international instruments, norms and principles

[91] 16 December 1981.

relevant, inter alia, to responsibilities of States with regard to averting new massive flows of refugees, as well as to the status and the protection of refugees, and also reaffirming the framework of competences of existing international organizations and institutions,

Stressing that massive flows of refugees may not only affect the domestic order and stability of receiving States but also jeopardize the political and social stability and the economic development of entire regions and thus endanger international peace and security,

Noting that, in addition to creating individual human misery, massive flows of refugees can impose great political, economic and social burdens upon the international community as a whole, with dire effects on developing countries, particularly those with limited resources of their own,

Convinced that averting new massive flows of refugees is, therefore, a matter of urgent concern for the international community as a whole,

Reaffirming its resolution 2625 (XXV) of 24 October 1970, by which it approved the Declaration on Principles of International Law concerning Friendly Relations and Co-operation among States in accordance with the Charter of the United Nations,

Commending the United Nations High Commissioner for Refugees and his staff for their untiring humanitarian and social efforts, for which the Office of the High Commissioner has twice been awarded the Nobel Peace Prize,

Commending also, for their contributions, all Governments, United Nations organs, the specialized agencies and intergovernmental and non-governmental organizations which have provided aid and stressing the importance of their efforts in this field,

Conscious of the importance of developing, in order to avert new massive flows of refugees, appropriate means of international co-operation in accordance with the principles of the Charter of the United Nations and, in particular, with the principle of non-intervention in the internal affairs of sovereign States and also of the principle that nothing in the Charter shall authorize the United Nations Organization to intervene in matters that are essentially within the domestic jurisdiction of any State,

1. *Takes note* of the report of the Secretary-General;

2. *Welcomes* the submission of comments and suggestions made in response to General Assembly resolution 35/124 by Member States as well as United Nations organs, organizations and specialized agencies on international co-operation to avert new massive flows of refugees and on facilitating the return of those refugees who wish to return;

3. *Emphasizes* the right of refugees to return to their homes in their homelands and reaffirms the right, as contained in its previous resolutions, of those who do not wish to return to receive adequate compensation;

4. *Decides* to establish a group of governmental experts of seventeen members whose expenses, as a rule, shall be borne by each nominating State for its expert to be appointed, upon nomination by the Member State, by the Secretary-General after appropriate consultation with the regional groups and with due regard to equitable geographical distribution;

5. *Requests* the Group of Governmental Experts on International Co-operation to Avert New Flows of Refugees, in the light of the existing relevant international instruments, norms and principles and with due regard to the rights mentioned in paragraph 3 above to undertake as soon as possible, in order to improve international co-operation to avert new massive flows of refugees, a comprehensive review of the problem in all its aspects, with a view to developing recommendations on appropriate means of international co-operation in this field, having due regard to the principle of non-intervention in the internal affairs of sovereign States;

6. *Requests* the Group of Governmental Experts to be mindful of the importance of reaching general agreement whenever it has significance for the outcome of its work;

7. *Calls* on the Group of Governmental Experts to take into account the comments and suggestions communicated to the Secretary-General in accordance with resolution 35/124 and any further comments and suggestions from Member States and United Nations organs, organizations and specialized agencies as well as the views expressed during the debate on this item at the thirty-sixth session of the General Assembly and also the study to be submitted to the Commission on Human Rights at its

thirty-eighth session by the special rapporteur, pursuant to its resolution 29 (XXXVII) of 11 March 1981, and furthermore the deliberations on this study by the Commission;

8. *Calls upon* Member States who have not yet conveyed to the Secretary-General their comments and suggestions on this item to do so as soon as possible;

9. *Requests* the Secretary-General to prepare a further compilation of the replies received in accordance with paragraph 8 above and to provide the group of governmental experts with all necessary assistance and facilities for the completion of its task;

10. *Calls upon* the Group of Governmental Experts to submit a report to the Secretary-General in time for deliberation by the General Assembly at its thirty-seventh session;

11. *Decides* to include in the provisional agenda of its thirty-seventh session the item entitled "International co-operation to avert new flows of refugees".

6.14. Resolution 37/120 – United Nations Relief and Works Agency for Palestine Refugees in the Near East (1982)[92]

The General Assembly,

[. . .]

G – Population and Refugees Displaced since 1967

1. *Reaffirms* the inalienable right of all displaced inhabitants to return to their homes or former places of residence in the territories occupied by Israel since 1967 and declares once more that any attempt to restrict, or to attach conditions to, the free exercise of the right of return by any displaced person is inconsistent with their inalienable right and inadmissible;

2. *Considers* any and all agreements embodying any restriction on or condition for the return of the displaced inhabitants as null and void;

3. *Strongly deplores* the continued refusal of the Israeli authorities to take steps for the return of the displaced inhabitants;

4. *Calls once more* upon Israel:

(a) To take immediate steps for the return of all displaced inhabitants;

(b) To desist from all measures that obstruct the return of the displaced inhabitants, including measures affecting the physical and demographic structure of the occupied territories.

[. . .]

6.15. Resolution 40/165 – United Nations Relief and Works Agency for Palestine Refugees in the Near East (1985)[93]

The General Assembly,

[. . .]

G – Population and Refugees Displaced since 1967

1. *Reaffirms* the inalienable right of all displaced inhabitants to return to their homes or former places of residence in the territories occupied by Israel since 1967, and declares once more that any attempt to restrict, or to attach conditions to, the free exercise of the right to return by any displaced person is inconsistent with that inalienable right and inadmissible;

2. *Considers* any and all agreements embodying any restriction on, or condition for, the return of the displaced inhabitants as null and void;

3. *Strongly deplores* the continued refusal of the Israeli authorities to take steps for the return of the displaced inhabitants;

4. *Calls once more* upon Israel:

(a) To take immediate steps for the return of all displaced inhabitants;

(b) To desist from all measures that obstruct the return of the displaced inhabitants, including measures affecting the physical and demographic structure of the occupied territories.

[. . .]

[92] 16 December 1982.

[93] 16 December 1985.

6.16. Resolution 48/117 – International Conference on Central American Refugees (1993)[94]

The General Assembly,

[. . .]

Welcoming with satisfaction the progress made in El Salvador in achieving the consolidation of peace in that country, in accordance with the peace agreements and the National Reconstruction Plan, the efforts to achieve peace and reconciliation in Guatemala, and the efforts made in Nicaragua to achieve the objectives of national reconciliation and to assist the uprooted populations, all of which continue to encourage movements of voluntary repatriation and settlement of internally displaced persons,

[. . .]

3. *Urges* the Central American countries, Belize and Mexico to continue to implement and follow up the programmes benefiting refugees, returnees and displaced persons in accordance with their national development plans;

4. *Reaffirms* its conviction that the voluntary repatriation of refugees and the return of displaced persons to their countries or communities of origin continues to be a positive sign of the progress of peace in the region;

5. *Also reaffirms* its conviction that the processes of return to and reintegration in the countries and communities of origin should continue to take place in conditions of dignity and security and with the necessary guarantees to ensure that the affected populations are included in the respective national development plans;

6. *Supports* the special attention that the Central American countries, Belize and Mexico are giving to the particular needs of refugee, repatriated and displaced women and children and to the measures being adopted to protect and improve the environment and to preserve ethnic and cultural values;

[. . .]

8. *Emphasizes* the importance of ensuring, upon the conclusion of the Conference process in May

[94] 20 December 1993.

1994, that the needs of refugees, returnees and displaced persons are specifically reflected in a comprehensive and sustained concept of human development, and that the United Nations Development Programme, with the collaboration of the High Commissioner, continues to support this approach in the post-Conference strategy;

[. . .]

6.17. Resolution 48/118 – Assistance to Refugees, Returnees and Displaced Persons in Africa (1993)[95]

The General Assembly,

[. . .]

Welcoming the prospects for voluntary repatriation and durable solutions across the continent,

Recognizing the need for States to create conditions conducive to the prevention of flows of refugees and displaced persons and to voluntary repatriation,

[. . .]

Recognizing the massive task facing Eritrea of repatriating over half a million refugees, particularly from the Sudan, through its Programme for Refugee reintegration and Rehabilitation of Resettlement Areas in Eritrea, and resettling voluntary returnees already in the country, internally displaced persons and demobilized former combatants, and the enormous burden that this has placed on the Government of Eritrea,

[. . .]

Aware that the voluntary repatriation of large numbers of Somali refugees in neighbouring countries and elsewhere, as well as the return of internally displaced persons to their original homes, will still require a planned and integrated international assistance programme designed to cover their basic needs, ensure adequate reception arrangements and facilitate their smooth integration into their respective communities,

[. . .]

Appealing to the Somalis to implement the Addis Ababa Agreement concerning national reconciliation which the Somali leaders signed on 27 March

[95] 20 December 1993.

1993 in order to create an environment conducive to the repatriation of Somali refugees from the neighbouring countries,

[...]

Encouraging the Government of the Sudan and the Office of the United Nations High Commissioner for Refugees for the efforts they have undertaken for the voluntary repatriation of the large numbers of refugees to their homelands,

[...]

Considering that the repatriation and reintegration of returnees and the relocation of displaced persons are aggravated by natural disasters and that the process poses serious humanitarian, social and economic problems for the Government of Chad,

Cognizant of the appeal to Member States and intergovernmental and non-governmental organizations to continue to provide the necessary assistance to the Government of Chad to alleviate its problems and improve its abilities to implement the programme of repatriation, reintegration and relocation of voluntary returnees and displaced persons,

[...]

Welcoming with appreciation the ongoing activities of the High Commissioner for the voluntary repatriation and reintegration of South African returnees, and hoping that the obstacles to the return of all refugees and exiles in conditions of safety and dignity will be removed without delay,

Recognizing the need to integrate refugee-related development projects in local and national development plans,

[...]

2. *Commends* the Governments concerned for their sacrifices, for providing assistance to refugees, returnees and displaced persons and for their efforts to promote voluntary repatriation and other measures taken in order to find appropriate and lasting solutions;

[...]

6. *Appeals* to Member States, international organizations and non-governmental organizations to provide adequate and sufficient financial, material and technical assistance for relief and rehabilitation programmes for the large number of refugees,

voluntary returnees and displaced persons and victims of natural disasters and to the affected countries;

7. *Requests* all Governments and intergovernmental and non-governmental organizations to pay particular attention to the protection of special needs of refugee women and children;

8. *Calls upon* the Secretary-General, the High Commissioner, the Department of Humanitarian Affairs of the Secretariat and United Nations humanitarian agencies to continue their efforts to mobilize humanitarian assistance for the relief, repatriation, rehabilitation and resettlement of refugees, returnees and displaced persons, including those refugees in urban areas;

[...]

6.18. Resolution 48/152 – Situation of Human Rights in Afghanistan (1993)[96]

The General Assembly,

[...]

Deeply concerned that the repatriation of Afghan refugees has dramatically declined in 1993, owing to the prevailing situation in Afghanistan, and expressing the hope that conditions in the country will allow those still in exile to return as soon as possible,

Aware that peace and security in Afghanistan are prerequisites for the successful repatriation of about four million refugees, in particular the achievement of a comprehensive political solution and the establishment of a freely and democratically elected government, the end of armed confrontation in Kabul and in some provinces, the clearance of the minefields that have been laid in many parts of the country, the restoration of an effective authority in the whole country and the reconstruction of the economy,

[...]

3. *Urges* all the Afghan parties to undertake, where appropriate under the auspices of the United Nations, all possible efforts in order to achieve a comprehensive political solution, which is the only way to bring about peace and the full restoration

[96] 20 December 1993.

of human rights in Afghanistan, based on the free exercise of the right to self-determination by the people, including free and genuine elections, the cessation of armed confrontation and the creation of conditions that will permit the free return, as soon as possible, of about four million refugees to their homeland in safety and dignity, whenever they wish, and the full enjoyment of human rights and fundamental freedoms by all Afghans;

[. . .]

14. *Urgently* appeals to all Member States and humanitarian organizations to continue to promote the implementation of the projects envisaged by the Coordinator for Humanitarian and Economic Assistance Programmes Relating to Afghanistan and the programmes of the United Nations High Commissioner for Refugees, especially the pilot projects for the repatriation of refugees;

15. *Reiterates* its appeal to all Member States, humanitarian organizations and all parties concerned to cooperate fully on the question of mine detection and clearance, in order to facilitate the return of refugees and displaced persons to their homes in safety and dignity.

[. . .]

6.19. Resolution 49/23 – Emergency International Assistance for a Solution to the Problem of Refugees, the Restoration of Total Peace, Reconstruction and Socio-Economic Development in War-Stricken Rwanda (1994)[97]

The General Assembly,

[. . .]

1. *Encourages* the Government of Rwanda to pursue its efforts with a view to creating conditions which would be conducive to the return of the refugees to their country and their resettlement and to the recovery by displaced persons of their property in peace, security and dignity;

[. . .]

3. *Urges* all States, United Nations organizations, specialized agencies and other intergovernmen-

tal and non-governmental organizations and the international financial and development institutions to provide all possible financial, technical and material assistance with a view to facilitating the restoration of basic services, rehabilitating the economy and ensuring the reconstruction of the social and economic infrastructure of Rwanda and the return and resettlement of refugees and internally displaced persons in Rwanda.

[. . .]

6.20. Resolution 49/43 – The Situation in the Occupied Territories of Croatia (1994)[98]

The General Assembly,

[. . .]

6. *Reaffirms* the right of all refugees and displaced persons from the area of the former Yugoslavia to return voluntarily to their homes safely and with dignity, with the assistance of the international community, and in this regard notes that the 1991 census is the basis for defining the population structure of the Republic of Croatia.

[. . .]

6.21. Resolution 49/196 – Situation of Human Rights in the Republic of Bosnia and Herzegovina, the Republic of Croatia and the Federal Republic of Yugoslavia (Serbia and Montenegro) (1995)[99]

The General Assembly,

[. . .]

13. *Expresses* its complete support for the victims of those violations, reaffirms the right of all persons to return to their homes in safety and dignity, considers invalid all acts made under duress affecting ownership of property and other related questions, recognizes the right of victims of ethnic cleansing to receive just reparation for their losses, and urges all parties to fulfil their agreements to this end.

[. . .]

---

[97] 2 December 1994.

[98] 9 December 1994.
[99] 23 December 1994.

6.22. Resolution 50/182 – Human Rights and Mass Exoduses (1995)[100]

The General Assembly,

[. . .]

7. *Invites* the special rapporteurs, special representatives and working groups of the Commission on Human Rights and the United Nations human rights treaty bodies, acting within their mandates, to continue seeking information, where appropriate, on problems resulting in mass exoduses of populations or impeding their voluntary return home and, where appropriate, to include such information, together with recommendations thereon, in their reports and to bring such information to the attention of the United Nations High Commissioner for Human Rights, for appropriate action within his mandate, in consultation with the United Nations High Commissioner for Refugees.

[. . .]

6.23. Resolution 51/114 – Situation of Human Rights in Rwanda (1996)[101]

The General Assembly,

[. . .]

Welcoming the fact that considerable numbers of refugees have recently returned to Rwanda, and affirming the readiness of the international community to assist the Government of Rwanda in reintegrating these returnees,

[. . .]

Welcoming also the commitment of the Government of Rwanda to protect and promote respect for human rights and fundamental freedoms, to eliminate impunity and to facilitate the process of the voluntary and safe return, resettlement and reintegration of refugees, as reaffirmed in the agreements reached at Nairobi, Bujumbura and Cairo in 1995 and at Tunis and Arusha in 1996, and urging Governments in the region to work, in cooperation with the international community, to find durable solutions to the refugee crisis,

Stressing its concern that the United Nations should continue to play an active role in assisting the Government of Rwanda in facilitating the voluntary and orderly return of refugees and the reintegration of returnees, in promoting reconciliation, in consolidating a climate of confidence and stability, and in promoting the rehabilitation and reconstruction of Rwanda,

Reaffirming the link between the voluntary return of refugees to their homes and the normalization of the situation in Rwanda, and concerned that acts of intimidation and violence directed against refugees, particularly by the former Rwandan authorities, have prevented refugees from returning to their homes,

II

[. . .]

7. *Invites* all States, the organizations and bodies of the United Nations system and intergovernmental and non-governmental organizations to continue and to intensify their contributions of financial and technical support to accelerate the efforts of the Government of Rwanda to, inter alia, restore the judicial system, promote reconciliation through the recently established Commission for National Reconciliation and safely reintegrate returning refugees in conditions of safety and dignity, including addressing competing claims to housing and property.

[. . .]

6.24. Resolution 51/126 – Persons Displaced as a Result of the June 1967 and Subsequent Hostilities (1996)[102]

The General Assembly,

[. . .]

1. *Reaffirms* the right of all persons displaced as a result of the June 1967 and subsequent hostilities to return to their homes or former places of residence in the territories occupied by Israel since 1967;

2. *Expresses* the hope for an accelerated return of displaced persons through the mechanism agreed upon by the parties in article XII of the Declaration

---

[100] 22 December 1995.
[101] 12 December 1996.

[102] 13 December 1996.

of Principles on Interim Self-Government Arrangements.

[. . .]

6.25. Resolution 55/153 – Nationality of Natural Persons in Relation to the Succession of States (2000)[103]

The General Assembly,

[. . .]

ANNEX – PART 1

[. . .]

Article 14 – Status of Habitual Residents

1. The status of persons concerned as habitual residents shall not be affected by the succession of States.

2. A State concerned shall take all necessary measures to allow persons concerned who, because of events connected with the succession of States, were forced to leave their habitual residence on its territory to return thereto.

[. . .]

6.26. Resolution 59/117 – Assistance to Palestine Refugees (2004)[104]

The General Assembly,

[. . .]

1. *Notes with regret* that repatriation or compensation of the refugees, as provided for in paragraph 11 of General Assembly resolution 194 (III), has not yet been effected and that, therefore, the situation of the Palestine refugees continues to be a matter of grave concern;

2. *Also notes with regret* that the United Nations Conciliation Commission for Palestine has been unable to find a means of achieving progress in the implementation of paragraph 11 of General Assembly resolution 194 (III), and requests the Concilia-

---

[103] 12 December 2000.
[104] 10 December 2004.

tion Commission to exert continued efforts towards the implementation of that paragraph and to report to the Assembly as appropriate, but no later than 1 September 2005.

[. . .]

6.27. Resolution 59/170 – Office of the United Nations High Commissioner for Refugees (2004)[105]

The General Assembly,

[. . .]

10. *Recalls* the important role of effective partnerships and coordination in meeting the needs of refugees and other displaced persons and in finding durable solutions to their situations, welcomes the efforts under way, in cooperation with refugee-hosting countries and countries of origin, including their respective local communities, United Nations agencies and other development actors, to promote a framework for durable solutions, particularly in protracted refugee situations, which includes the "4Rs" approach (repatriation, reintegration, rehabilitation and reconstruction) to sustainable return, and encourages States, in cooperation with United Nations agencies and other development actors, to support, inter alia, through the allocation of funds, the development and implementation of the 4Rs and of other programming tools to facilitate the transition from relief to development;

11. *Strongly reaffirms* the fundamental importance and the purely humanitarian and non-political character of the function of the Office of the High Commissioner of providing international protection to refugees and seeking permanent solutions to refugee problems, and recalls that these solutions include voluntary repatriation and, where appropriate and feasible, local integration and resettlement in a third country, while reaffirming that voluntary repatriation, supported by necessary rehabilitation and development assistance to facilitate sustainable reintegration, remains the preferred solution;

12. *Recognizes* the desirability of countries of origin, in cooperation with the Office of the High

---

[105] 20 December 2004.

Commissioner, other States and other concerned actors, as necessary and appropriate, addressing, at an early stage, issues of a legal and administrative nature which are likely to hinder voluntary repatriation in safety and dignity, bearing in mind that some legal safety or administrative issues may be addressed only over time and that voluntary repatriation can and does take place without all legal and administrative issues having first been resolved;

13. *Emphasizes* the obligation of all States to accept the return of their nationals, calls upon States to facilitate the return of their nationals who have been determined not to be in need of international protection, and affirms the need for the return of persons to be undertaken in a safe and humane manner and with full respect for their human rights and dignity, irrespective of the status of the persons concerned.

[. . .]

6.28. Resolution 59/172 – Assistance to Refugees, Returnees and Displaced Persons in Africa (2004)[106]

The General Assembly,

[. . .]

17. *Reaffirms* the right of return and the principle of voluntary repatriation, appeals to countries of origin and countries of asylum to create conditions that are conducive to voluntary repatriation, and recognizes that, while voluntary repatriation remains the pre-eminent solution, local integration and third-country resettlement, where appropriate and feasible, are also viable options for dealing with the situation of African refugees who, owing to prevailing circumstances in their respective countries of origin, are unable to return home;

18. *Notes with satisfaction* the voluntary return of thousands of refugees to their countries of origin, and welcomes in this regard the conclusion on legal safety issues in the context of voluntary repatriation of refugees adopted by the Executive Committee of the Programme of the United Nations High Commissioner for Refugees at its fifty-fifth session;

19. *Reaffirms* that voluntary repatriation should not necessarily be conditioned on the accomplishment of political solutions in the country of origin in order not to impede the exercise of the refugees' right to return, and recognizes that the voluntary repatriation and reintegration process is normally guided by the conditions in the country of origin, in particular that voluntary repatriation can be accomplished in conditions of safety and dignity;

20. *Welcomes* the development by the High Commissioner, in cooperation with other United Nations agencies and development actors, of the framework for durable solutions, aimed at promoting lasting solutions, particularly in protracted refugee situations, including the "4Rs" approach (repatriation, reintegration, rehabilitation and reconstruction) to sustainable return.

[. . .]

6.29. Resolution 60/100 – Assistance to Palestinian Refugees (2005)[107]

The General Assembly,

Recalling its resolution 194 (III) of 11 December 1948 and all its subsequent resolutions on the question, including resolution 59/117 of 10 December 2004,

Recalling also its resolution 302 (IV) of 8 December 1949, by which, inter alia, it established the United Nations Relief and Works Agency for Palestine Refugees in the Near East,

Recalling further relevant Security Council resolutions,

Aware of the fact that, for more than five decades, the Palestine refugees have suffered from the loss of their homes, lands and means of livelihood,

Affirming the imperative of resolving the problem of the Palestine refugees for the achievement of justice and for the achievement of lasting peace in the region,

Acknowledging the essential role that the United Nations Relief and Works Agency for Palestine Refugees in the Near East has played for more than

---

[106] 20 December 2004.

[107] 8 December 2005.

fifty-five years since its establishment in ameliorating the plight of the Palestine refugees in the fields of education, health and relief and social services,

Taking note of the report of the Commissioner-General of the United Nations Relief and Works Agency for Palestine Refugees in the Near East covering the period from 1 July 2004 to 30 June 2005,

Aware of the continuing needs of the Palestine refugees throughout all the fields of operation, namely Jordan, Lebanon, the Syrian Arab Republic and the Occupied Palestinian Territory,

Expressing grave concern at the especially difficult situation of the Palestine refugees under occupation, including with regard to their safety, well-being and living conditions,

Noting the signing of the Declaration of Principles on Interim Self-Government Arrangements on 13 September 1993 by the Government of Israel and the Palestine Liberation Organization and the subsequent implementation agreements,

Aware of the important role to be played in the peace process by the Multilateral Working Group on Refugees of the Middle East peace process,

1. *Notes with regret* that repatriation or compensation of the refugees, as provided for in paragraph 11 of General Assembly resolution 194 (III), has not yet been effected and that, therefore, the situation of the Palestine refugees continues to be a matter of grave concern;

2. *Also notes with regret* that the United Nations Conciliation Commission for Palestine has been unable to find a means of achieving progress in the implementation of paragraph 11 of General Assembly resolution 194 (III), and reiterates its request to the Conciliation Commission to exert continued efforts towards the implementation of that paragraph and to report to the Assembly as appropriate, but no later than 1 September 2006;

3. *Affirms* the necessity for the continuation of the work of the United Nations Relief and Works Agency for Palestine Refugees in the Near East and the importance of its operation and its services for the well-being of the Palestine refugees and for the stability of the region, pending the resolution of the question of the Palestine refugees;

4. *Calls upon* all donors to continue to make the most generous efforts possible to meet the antic-ipated needs of the Agency, including those mentioned in recent emergency appeals.

6.30. Resolution 60/101 – Persons Displaced as a Result of the June 1967 and Subsequent Hostilities (2005)[108]

The General Assembly,

[. . .]

1. *Reaffirms* the right of all persons displaced as a result of the June 1967 and subsequent hostilities to return to their homes or former places of residence in the territories occupied by Israel since 1967;

2. *Expresses deep concern* that the mechanism agreed upon by the parties in article XII of the Declaration of Principles on Interim Self-Government Arrangements of 1993 on the return of displaced persons has not been complied with, and stresses the necessity for an accelerated return of displaced persons.

[. . .]

6.31. Resolution 60/103 – Palestine Refugees' Properties and Their Revenues (2005)[109]

The General Assembly,

Recalling its resolutions 194 (III) of 11 December 1948, 36/146 C of 16 December 1981 and all its subsequent resolutions on the question,

Taking note of the report of the Secretary-General submitted in pursuance of resolution 59/120 of 10 December 2004,

Taking note also of the report of the United Nations Conciliation Commission for Palestine for the period from 1 September 2004 to 31 August 2005,

Recalling that the Universal Declaration of Human Rights and the principles of international law uphold the principle that no one shall be arbitrarily deprived of his or her property,

Recalling in particular its resolution 394 (V) of 14 December 1950, in which it directed the Conciliation Commission, in consultation with the parties concerned, to prescribe measures for the

---

[108] 8 December 2005.
[109] 8 December 2005.

protection of the rights, property and interests of the Palestine refugees,

Noting the completion of the programme of identification and evaluation of Arab property, as announced by the Conciliation Commission in its twenty-second progress report, and the fact that the Land Office had a schedule of Arab owners and file of documents defining the location, area and other particulars of Arab property,

Expressing its appreciation for the work done to preserve and modernize the existing records, including land records, of the Conciliation Commission and the importance of such records for a just resolution of the plight of the Palestine refugees in conformity with resolution 194 (III),

Recalling that, in the framework of the Middle East peace process, the Palestine Liberation Organization and the Government of Israel agreed, in the Declaration of Principles on Interim Self-Government Arrangements of 13 September 1993 to commence negotiations on permanent status issues, including the important issue of the refugees.

1. *Reaffirms* that the Palestine refugees are entitled to their property and to the income derived therefrom, in conformity with the principles of equity and justice;

2. *Requests* the Secretary-General to take all appropriate steps, in consultation with the United Nations Conciliation Commission for Palestine, for the protection of Arab property, assets and property rights in Israel;

3. *Calls once again upon* Israel to render all facilities and assistance to the Secretary-General in the implementation of the present resolution;

4. *Calls upon* all the parties concerned to provided the Secretary-General with any pertinent information in their possession concerning Arab property, assets and property rights in Israel that would assist him in the implementation of the present resolution;

5. *Urges* the Palestinian and Israeli sides, as agreed between them, to deal with the important issue of Palestine refugees' properties and their revenues within the framework of the final status negotiations of the Middle East peace process.

[. . .]

6.32. Resolution 60/147 – Basic Principles and Guidelines on the Right to a Remedy and Reparation for Victims of Gross Violations of International Human Rights Law and Serious Violations of International Humanitarian Law (2005)[110]

The General Assembly,

Guided by the Charter of the United Nations, the Universal Declaration of Human Rights, the International Covenants on Human Rights, other relevant human rights instruments and the Vienna Declaration and Plan of Action,

Affirming the importance of addressing the question of remedies and reparation for victims of gross violations of international human rights law and serious violations of international humanitarian law in a systematic and thorough way at the national and international levels,

Recognizing that, in honouring the victims' right to benefit from remedies and reparation, the international community keeps faith with the plight of victims, survivors and future human generations and reaffirms international law in the field,

Recalling the adoption of the Basic Principles and Guidelines on the Right to a Remedy and Reparation for Victims of Gross Violations of International Human Rights Law and Serious Violations of International Humanitarian Law by the Commission on Human Rights in its resolution 2005/35 of 19 April 2005 and by the Economic and Social Council in its resolution 2005/30 of 25 July 2005, in which the Council recommended to the General Assembly that it adopt the Basic Principles and Guidelines,

1. *Adopts* the Basic Principles and Guidelines on the Right to a Remedy and Reparation for Victims of Gross Violations of International Human Rights Law and Serious Violations of International Humanitarian Law annexed to the present resolution;

2. *Recommends* that States take the Basic Principles and Guidelines into account, promote respect thereof and bring them to the attention of members of the executive bodies of government, in particular law enforcement officials and military and security forces, legislative bodies, the judiciary,

---

[110] 16 December 2005. Note: The full text of the Basic Principles and Guidelines is contained in section 1.16 above.

victims and their representatives, human rights defenders and lawyers, the media and the public in general;

3. *Requests* the Secretary-General to take steps to ensure the widest possible dissemination of the Basic Principles and Guidelines in all the official languages of the United Nations, including by transmitting them to Governments and intergovernmental and non-governmental organizations and by including the Basic Principles and Guidelines in the United Nations publication entitled *Human Rights: A Compilation of International Standards.*

6.33. Resolution 60/183 – Permanent Sovereignty of the Palestinian People in the Occupied Palestinian Territory, Including East Jerusalem, and of the Arab Population in the Occupied Syrian Golan over Their Natural Resources (2005)[111]

The General Assembly,

Recalling its resolution 59/251 of 22 December 2004, and taking note of Economic and Social Council resolution 2005/51 of 27 July 2005,

Recalling also its resolution 58/292 of 6 May 2004,

Reaffirming the principle of the permanent sovereignty of peoples under foreign occupation over their natural resources,

Guided by the principles of the Charter of the United Nations, affirming the inadmissibility of the acquisition of territory by force, and recalling relevant Security Council resolutions, including resolutions 242 (1967) of 22 November 1967, 465 (1980) of 1 March 1980 and 497 (1981) of 17 December 1981,

Recalling its resolution 2625 (XXV) of 24 October 1970,

Reaffirming the applicability of the Geneva Convention relative to the Protection of Civilian Persons in Time of War, of 12 August 1949, to the Occupied Palestinian Territory, including East Jerusalem, and other Arab territories occupied by Israel since 1967,

[111] 22 December 2005.

Recalling, in this regard, the International Covenant on Civil and Political Rights and the International Covenant on Economic, Social and Cultural Rights, and affirming that these human rights instruments must be respected in the Occupied Palestinian Territory, including East Jerusalem, as well as in the occupied Syrian Golan,

Recalling also the advisory opinion rendered on 9 July 2004 by the International Court of Justice on the *Legal Consequences of the Construction of a Wall in the Occupied Palestinian Territory*, and recalling further its resolution ES-10/15 of 20 July 2004,

Expressing its concern at the exploitation by Israel, the occupying Power, of the natural resources of the Occupied Palestinian Territory, including East Jerusalem, and other Arab territories occupied by Israel since 1967,

Expressing its concern also at the extensive destruction by Israel, the occupying Power, of agricultural land and orchards in the Occupied Palestinian Territory, including the uprooting of a vast number of fruit-bearing trees,

Aware of the detrimental impact of the Israeli settlements on Palestinian and other Arab natural resources, especially as a result of the confiscation of land and the forced diversion of water resources, and of the dire economic and social consequences in this regard,

Aware also of the detrimental impact on Palestinian natural resources being caused by the unlawful construction of the wall by Israel, the occupying Power, in the Occupied Palestinian Territory, including in and around East Jerusalem, and of its grave effect on the natural resources and economic and social conditions of the Palestinian people,

Reaffirming the need for the immediate resumption of negotiations within the Middle East peace process, on the basis of Security Council resolutions 242 (1967), 338 (1973) of 22 October 1973, 425 (1978) of 19 March 1978 and 1397 (2002) of 12 March 2002, the principle of land for peace and the Quartet performance-based road map to a permanent two-State solution to the Israeli-Palestinian conflict, as endorsed by the Security Council in its resolution 1515 (2003) of 19 November 2003, and for the achievement of a final settlement on all tracks,

Acknowledging the importance of the Israeli withdrawal from within the Gaza Strip and parts of the northern West Bank and of the dismantlement of settlements therein as a step towards the implementation of the road map,

Recalling the need to end all acts of violence, including acts of terror, provocation, incitement and destruction,

Taking note with appreciation of the note by the Secretary-General transmitting the report prepared by the Economic and Social Commission for Western Asia on the economic and social repercussions of the Israeli occupation on the living conditions of the Palestinian people in the Occupied Palestinian Territory, including Jerusalem, and of the Arab population in the occupied Syrian Golan,

1. *Reaffirms* the inalienable rights of the Palestinian people and the population of the occupied Syrian Golan over their natural resources, including land and water;

2. *Calls upon* Israel, the occupying Power, not to exploit, damage, cause loss or depletion of, or endanger the natural resources in the Occupied Palestinian Territory, including East Jerusalem, and in the occupied Syrian Golan;

3. *Recognizes* the right of the Palestinian people to claim restitution as a result of any exploitation, damage, loss or depletion, or endangerment of their natural resources resulting from illegal measures taken by Israel, the occupying Power, in the Occupied Palestinian Territory, including East Jerusalem, and expresses the hope that this issue will be dealt with in the framework of the final status negotiations between the Palestinian and Israeli sides;

4. *Stresses* that the wall being constructed by Israel in the Occupied Palestinian Territory, including in and around East Jerusalem, is contrary to international law and is seriously depriving the Palestinian people of their natural resources, and calls in this regard for full compliance with the legal obligations mentioned in the 9 July 2004 advisory opinion of the International Court of Justice3 and in resolution ES-10/15;

5. *Welcomes* the Israeli withdrawal from within the Gaza Strip and parts of the northern West Bank and the dismantlement of the settlements therein as a step towards the implementation of the road map;

6. *Calls upon* Israel, the occupying Power, in this regard, to comply strictly with its obligations under international law, including international humanitarian law, with respect to the alteration of the character and status of the Occupied Palestinian Territory, including East Jerusalem;

7. *Also calls upon* Israel, the occupying Power, to cease the dumping of all kinds of waste materials in the Occupied Palestinian Territory, including East Jerusalem, and in the occupied Syrian Golan, which gravely threaten their natural resources, namely the water and land resources, and pose an environmental hazard and health threat to the civilian populations;

8. *Requests* the Secretary-General to report to it at its sixty-first session on the implementation of the present resolution, and decides to include in the provisional agenda of its sixty-first session the item entitled "Permanent sovereignty of the Palestinian people in the Occupied Palestinian Territory, including East Jerusalem, and of the Arab population in the occupied Syrian Golan over their natural resources".

7. UN COMMISSION ON HUMAN RIGHTS

7.1. Resolution 1993/77 – Forced Evictions (1993)[112]

The Commission on Human Rights,

Recalling Sub-Commission on Prevention of Discrimination and Protection of Minorities resolution 1991/12 of 26 August 1991,

Also recalling its own resolution 1992/10 of 21 February 1992, in which it took note with particular interest of General Comment No. 4 (1991) on the right to adequate housing (E/1992/23, annex III), adopted on 12 December 1991 by the Committee on Economic, Social and Cultural Rights at its sixth session, and the reaffirmed importance attached in this framework to respect for human dignity and the principle of non-discrimination,

[112] 10 March 1993.

Reaffirming that every woman, man and child has the right to a secure place to live in peace and dignity,

Concerned that, according to United Nations statistics, in excess of one billion persons throughout the world are homeless or inadequately housed, and that this number is growing,

Recognizing that the practice of forced eviction involves the involuntary removal of persons, families and groups from their homes and communities, resulting in increased levels of homelessness and in inadequate housing and living conditions,

Disturbed that forced evictions and homelessness intensify social conflict and inequality and invariably affect the poorest, most socially, economically, environmentally and politically disadvantaged and vulnerable sectors of society,

Aware that forced evictions can be carried out, sanctioned, demanded, proposed, initiated or tolerated by a range of actors,

Emphasizing that the ultimate legal responsibility for preventing forced evictions rests with Governments,

Recalling that General Comment No. 2 (1990) on international technical assistance measures, adopted by the Committee on Economic, Social and Cultural Rights at its fourth session, states, *inter alia*, that international agencies should scrupulously avoid involvement in projects which involve, among other things, large-scale evictions or displacement of persons without the provision of all appropriate protection and compensation (E/1990/23, annex III, para. 6),

Mindful of the questions concerning forced evictions included in the guidelines for States' reports submitted in conformity with articles 16 and 17 of the International Covenant on Economic, Social and Cultural Rights (E/1991/23, annex IV),

Noting with appreciation that the Committee on Economic, Social and Cultural Rights, in its General Comment No. 4, considered that instances of forced eviction were, prima facie, incompatible with the requirements of the International Covenant on Economic, Social and Cultural Rights and could only be justified in the most exceptional circumstances, and in accordance with the relevant principles of international law (E/1992/23, annex III, para. 18),

Taking note of the observations of the Committee on Economic, Social and Cultural Rights at its fifth and sixth sessions concerning forced evictions,

Taking note also of the inclusion of forced evictions as one of the primary causes of the international housing crisis in the working paper on the right to adequate housing, prepared by the expert, Mr. Rajindar Sachar (E/CN.4/Sub.2/1992/15),

Taking note further of Sub-Commission resolution 1992/14 of 27 August 1992,

1. *Affirms* that the practice of forced eviction constitutes a gross violation of human rights, in particular the right to adequate housing;

2. *Urges* Governments to undertake immediate measures, at all levels, aimed at eliminating the practice of forced eviction;

3. *Also urges* Governments to confer legal security of tenure on all persons currently threatened with forced eviction and to adopt all necessary measures giving full protection against forced eviction, based upon effective participation, consultation and negotiation with affected persons or groups;

4. *Recommends* that all Governments provide immediate restitution, compensation and/or appropriate and sufficient alternative accommodation or land, consistent with their wishes and needs, to persons and communities that have been forcibly evicted, following mutually satisfactory negotiations with the affected persons or groups;

5. *Requests* the Secretary-General to transmit the present resolution to Governments, relevant United Nations bodies, including the United Nations Centre on Human Settlements, the specialized agencies, regional, intergovernmental and non-governmental organizations and community-based organizations, soliciting their views and comments;

6. *Also requests* the Secretary-General to compile an analytical report on the practice of forced evictions, based on an analysis of international law and jurisprudence and information submitted in accordance with paragraph 5 of the present resolution, and to submit his report to the Commission at its fiftieth session.

[. . .]

7.2. Resolution 1997/29 – The Right to Restitution, Compensation and Rehabilitation for Victims of Grave Violations of Human Rights and Fundamental Freedoms (1997)[113]

The Commission on Human Rights,

Guided by the Charter of the United Nations, the Universal Declaration of Human Rights, the International Covenants on Human Rights, other relevant human rights instruments and the Vienna Declaration and Programme of Action,

Reaffirming that, pursuant to internationally proclaimed human rights principles, victims of grave violations of human rights should receive, in appropriate cases, restitution, compensation and rehabilitation,

Considering that the question of restitution, compensation and rehabilitation of victims of grave violations of human rights and fundamental freedoms has received insufficient attention and should continue to be addressed in a more systematic and thorough way at the national and international levels,

Noting with interest the positive experience of countries that have established policies and adopted legislation for the reparation of victims of grave violations of human rights,

Reiterating its appreciation of the study on the subject prepared by the former Special Rapporteur of the Sub-Commission on Prevention of Discrimination and Protection of Minorities, Mr. Theo van Boven, contained in his final report (E/CN.4/Sub.2/1993/8),

Recalling its resolution 1994/35 of 4 March 1994, in which it expressed the hope that priority attention would be given to this question, in particular in the specific field of violations of human rights and fundamental freedoms, and regarded the proposed basic principles and guidelines contained in the study of the Special Rapporteur as a useful basis for that purpose,

Recalling also its resolution 1996/35 of 19 April 1996, in which it requested States to provide information to the Secretary-General about legislation already adopted, as well as that in the process of

being adopted, relating to the right to restitution, compensation and rehabilitation,

Taking note of the report of the Secretary-General submitted to the Commission in compliance with its resolution 1996/35 (E/CN.4/1997/29 and Add.1),

Also taking note of resolution 1996/28 of 29 August 1996 of the Sub-Commission on Prevention of Discrimination and Protection of Minorities, in which the Sub-Commission decided to bring to the attention of the Commission on Human Rights the revised draft basic principles and guidelines on the right to reparation for victims of [gross] violations of human rights and international humanitarian law prepared by the former Special Rapporteur, Mr. Theo van Boven,

1. *Calls once more* upon the international community to give due attention to the right to restitution, compensation and rehabilitation for victims of grave violations of human rights;

2. *Expresses* its appreciation to States that provided information on the matter to the Secretary-General, in compliance with Commission resolution 1996/35, for their valuable contribution in this field and requests those that have not yet done so to provide information to the Secretary-General as soon as possible on the legislation already adopted, as well as that in the process of being adopted, relating to the right to restitution, compensation and rehabilitation for victims of grave violations of human rights and fundamental freedoms.

[. . .]

7.3. The Guiding Principles on Internal Displacement (1998)[114]

Introduction – Scope and Purpose

1. These Guiding Principles address the specific needs of internally displaced persons worldwide. They identify rights and guarantees relevant to the protection of persons from forced displacement and to their protection and assistance during displacement as well as during return or resettlement and reintegration.

[113] 11 April 1997.

[114] E/CN.4/1998/53/Add.2.

2. For the purposes of these Principles, internally displaced persons are persons or groups of persons who have been forced or obliged to flee or to leave their homes or places of habitual residence, in particular as a result of or in order to avoid the effects of armed conflict, situations of generalized violence, violations of human rights or natural or human-made disasters, and who have not crossed an internationally recognized State border.

[. . .]

SECTION V – PRINCIPLES RELATING TO RETURN, RESETTLEMENT AND REINTEGRATION

Principle 28

1. Competent authorities have the primary duty and responsibility to establish conditions, as well as provide the means, which allow internally displaced persons to return voluntarily, in safety and with dignity, to their homes or places of habitual residence, or to resettle voluntarily in another part of the country. Such authorities shall endeavour to facilitate the reintegration of returned or resettled internally displaced persons.

2. Special efforts should be made to ensure the full participation of internally displaced persons in the planning and management of their return or resettlement and reintegration.

Principle 29

1. Internally displaced persons who have returned to their homes or places of habitual residence or who have resettled in another part of the country shall not be discriminated against as a result of their having been displaced. They shall have the right to participate fully and equally in public affairs at all levels and have equal access to public services.

2. Competent authorities have the duty and responsibility to assist returned and/or resettled internally displaced persons to recover, to the extent possible, their property and possessions which they left behind or were dispossessed of upon their displacement. When recovery of such property and possessions is not possible, competent authorities shall provide or assist these persons in obtaining appropriate compensation or another form of just reparation.

Principle 30

All authorities concerned shall grant and facilitate for international humanitarian organizations and other appropriate actors, in the exercise of their respective mandates, rapid and unimpeded access to internally displaced persons to assist in their return or resettlement and reintegration.

7.4. Resolution 1999/33 – The Right to Restitution, Compensation and Rehabilitation for Victims of Grave Violations of Human Rights and Fundamental Freedoms (1999)[115]

The Commission on Human Rights,

Guided by the Charter of the United Nations, the Universal Declaration of Human Rights, the International Covenants on Human Rights, other relevant human rights instruments and the Vienna Declaration and Programme of Action,

Reaffirming that, pursuant to internationally proclaimed human rights principles, victims of grave violations of human rights should receive, in appropriate cases, restitution, compensation and rehabilitation,

Reiterating the importance of addressing the question of restitution, compensation and rehabilitation for victims of grave violations of human rights and fundamental freedoms in a systematic and thorough way at the national and international levels,

Recalling its resolution 1996/35 of 19 April 1996, in which it regarded the basic principles and guidelines on the right to redress of victims of grave violations of human rights and international humanitarian law, proposed by Mr. Theo van Boven, as a useful basis for giving priority attention to the question of restitution, compensation and rehabilitation,

Taking note with appreciation of the Secretary-General's note (E/CN.4/1999/53) submitted in compliance with Commission resolution 1998/43 of 17 April 1998,

[115] 6 April 1999.

Also taking note with appreciation of the report of the independent expert appointed by the Commission (E/CN.4/1999/65),

1. *Notes* with satisfaction the positive experience of countries that have established policies and adopted legislation on restitution, compensation and rehabilitation for victims of grave violations of human rights;

2. *Calls upon* the international community to give due attention to the right to restitution, compensation and rehabilitation for victims of grave violations of human rights.

[. . .]

7.5. Report of the Independent Expert on the Right to Restitution, Compensation and Rehabilitation for Victims of Grave Violations of Human Rights and Fundamental Freedoms, Mr. M. Cherif Bassiouni, Submitted Pursuant to Commission on Human Rights Resolution 1998/43 (1999) (Excerpts)[116]

[. . .]

4. The issue of reparations

21. The sections of both versions that define and discuss the forms of reparation available to victims are virtually identical, although with variations. For example, the 1993 version states that reparations shall include: "restitution, compensation, rehabilitation, and satisfaction and guarantees of non-repetition". While the 1996 version also contains that language, it begins the section by stating that "reparations may take any one or more of the forms mentioned below (restitution, compensation, rehabilitation, satisfaction and guarantees of non repetition), which are not exhaustive". While the 1993 version seems to mandate all four forms, this change in the 1996 version perhaps demonstrates a greater flexibility for the State in determining reparations. Thus, under the 1996 version a victim might receive any combination of the enumerated forms of reparation or other types that are not yet formulated.

22. With respect to the definition of "restitution", the 1996 version adds the restoration of "family life"

and "return to one's place of residence" to the other requirements: restoration of liberty, citizenship and employment of property. It is perhaps important to note that the language "return to one's place of residence" replaced restoration of "citizenship or residence". "Restoration of citizenship" remains in the 1996 version. While the language seems similar, the connotation is quite different between "place of residence", which seemingly invokes a return to one's previous home, and restoration of "residence", which invokes a return to the country of residence, such as for a person who is a permanent resident. This is especially true when the word is used alternatively with "citizenship".

23. With respect to the enumeration of damage for which compensation shall be provided, the 1996 version eliminates "harm to property or business, including lost profits", and replaces this language with "material damages and loss of earnings, including loss of earning potential". The sections concerning satisfaction and guarantees of non-repetition contain the changes referred to in the previous section of the present report. In addition to those changes, the 1996 version replaces the language calling for "a declaratory judgment in favour of the victim" with "an official declaration or a judicial decision restoring the dignity, reputation and legal rights of the victim and/or of persons connected with the victim". This expanded language clearly articulates the contents of the decree and, most importantly, calls for the restoration of legal rights.

24. It may also be important to distinguish the traditional question of State to State reparations from the question of State reparations owed to aliens, particularly in the light of distinct norms of customary international law on these matters. Both of these questions relate to but are distinct from the issue of the scope of a right in international law to reparation as a form of redress in the claims of a national or nationals of a given State, proceeding under national law, in respect of human rights violations. Neither are aspects of national procedures covered. Thus, the question remains as to how these guidelines can be implemented under national law. Similarly, it is unclear what remedies may be available under international law to the individual claimant.

[116] Footnotes omitted.

[. . .]

A. Elements of Reparation for Victims: Comparison of the Van Boven Guidelines and the Joinet Guidelines

33. The van Boven and Joinet Guidelines are in agreement with respect to the vital elements of victim reparation: restitution, compensation, rehabilitation and guarantees of non-repetition. Notwithstanding, variances are apparent within each element.

1. Restitution

34. The measure of restitution under each set of guidelines is virtually identical; however, there are some slight differences. Specifically, the van Boven Guidelines call for a "return to one's place of residence", whereas the Joinet Guidelines refer to a "return to one's country". While these two phrases could be read as being synonymous, the van Boven Guidelines could also be interpreted to mean a return to one's original home. This second interpretation goes quite a bit further than the language in the Joinet Guidelines.

35. In addition, the van Boven Guidelines call for a restoration of liberty, while the Joinet Guidelines call for a restoration of the exercise of personal freedoms. Notwithstanding this, both are in complete agreement with respect to the remaining requirements of restitution: family life, citizenship, employment and property.

2. Compensation

36. The types of compensation available under both sets of guidelines are also quite similar, with slight variances. One difference in the proposed revisions to the van Boven Guidelines is the inclusion of the costs of medicines and medical services in the assessment of damages. Additionally, the Joinet Guidelines state that the compensation "*must equal* the financially assessable value of all damage suffered". In contrast, van Boven states that compensation "shall be provided for any economically assessable damage". The Joinet Guidelines seem to be mandating a certain level of compensation (equal to the damage), while the van Boven Guidelines merely require that some amount of compensation be provided, which may or may not be equal to the damage. However, several other provisions in the van Boven Guidelines seem to assure that the damages awarded will not be nominal. For example, van Boven states that "reparations shall be *proportionate* to the gravity of the violations" and "every State shall ensure that *adequate* legal or other *appropriate* remedies are available".

[...]

D. The Right to Reparation

46. The van Boven and Joinet Guidelines take varying approaches to enunciating the right to reparation and the corresponding duties of the State. The van Boven Guidelines begin by imposing a duty under international law to respect and to ensure respect for human rights and international humanitarian law. They define the obligation as including the duty: to prevent violations, to investigate violations, to take appropriate action against the violators, and to afford remedies and reparation to victims.

47. In contrast, the Joinet Guidelines state that: "Any human rights violation gives rise to a right to reparation on the part of the victim or his beneficiaries, implying duty on the part of the State to make reparation and the possibility of seeking redress from the perpetrator".

48. Another key difference is the van Boven Guidelines' reliance on the norms of international law. They clearly state the applicable norms and even specify that, in the event that norms of national and international law conflict, the norm providing the highest degree of protection shall apply.

49. The Joinet Guidelines, however, never state the law that is to be applied to define the violations that give rise to a right to reparation. In addition, the Joinet Guidelines invoke the right to reparation only in the event of a violation of human rights law. In contrast, the van Boven Guidelines add violations of international humanitarian law to the actions that will give rise to the right to reparation. This leads to the conclusion that either the Joinet Guidelines do not differentiate between violations of human rights law and international humanitarian law, or those guidelines do not contemplate a remedy for violations of international humanitarian law.

[...]

B. The Elements of Reparation

60. The elements of reparation enunciated in the Declaration of Basic Principles of Justice for victims of crimes are quite different than those in the van Boven and Joinet Guidelines. The differences concern the various elements of reparation and the allocation of responsibility for reparation.

1. Defining the elements of reparation

61. The Declaration of Basic Principles of Justice does not distinguish between restitution, compensation, and assistance in the same manner that the van Boven and Joinet Guidelines differentiate between restitution, compensation and rehabilitation. In the van Boven and Joinet Guidelines, restitution is concerned with restoring to victims their liberty, citizenship and employment; compensation is concerned with any economically assessable damages such as pain and suffering, lost opportunities and harm to reputation; and rehabilitation is concerned with providing medical, psychological, legal and social services.

62. In contrast, the Declaration of Basic Principles of Justice is not this extensive or elaborate. The restitution section calls for the return of property or payment for the harm suffered and reimbursement of expenses incurred as a result of the victimization. This provision seems to fulfil the function of both the restitution and compensation sections of the van Boven and Joinet Guidelines, albeit in a significantly less specific manner. Instead of providing additional measures for the recovery of damages, the compensation section of the Declaration suggests an alternate source of funds to make the reparation called for in the restitution section. The assistance section parallels the rehabilitation section of the Joinet and van Boven Guidelines in providing for medical, psychological and social services.

63. In addition, the Declaration of Basic Principles of Justice provides for restitution in the form of restoration of the environment in cases of crime causing substantial harm to it. Also, one final significant difference is the omission in the Declaration of collective measures of satisfaction and guarantees of non-repetition, which are both discussed in the van Boven and Joinet Guidelines.

2. The allocation of responsibility

64. The allocation of responsibility for making reparations to victims is approached differently in the van Boven and Joinet Guidelines and in the Declaration of Basic Principles of Justice. While the van Boven and Joinet Guidelines are specific as to the various elements of reparation, they do not articulate clearly who is responsible for providing them to the victim. With respect to certain elements such as collective measures of satisfaction or guarantees of non-repetition, it is clear that the duty to provide them will fall on the State, since these types of measures fall within traditional State functions. However, the matter of paying compensatory damages is quite different. The van Boven and Joinet Guidelines do not articulate clearly whether the State or the individual offender will provide the remedy in such cases nor what the ultimate position of the State is relation to the victim who cannot secure compensation. In this context, it would be important to specify what legal consequences exist where the State fails: (a) to provide a legal basis for redress; (b) to provide access to means of adjudication; and (c) to provide an enforceable remedy. Furthermore, it is necessary to make clear what consequences at the international level exist in connection with the State's non-observance of the claimant's rights vis-à-vis a wrongful act and whether this gives rise to a legal cause for action.

65. In contrast, the Declaration of Basic Principles of Justice plainly sets forth the allocation of responsibility for making restitution to the victim. The primary onus to make restitution to victims and their families is on the offender. However, where the offence was committed by a public official acting in an official or quasi-official capacity responsibility shifts to the State, even if it is a successor State. In cases where the offender or other sources are unable to compensate a victim, the State is urged to provide a remedy. Nonetheless, the Declaration urges only that the burden shift from the offender to the State in cases where the victim has suffered serious physical or mental injury or in instances where claims are brought by the dependants of persons who have been killed or incapacitated.

C. Procedural Issues

66. The Declaration of Basic Principles of Justice and the van Boven and Joinet Guidelines show

consistency on a number of procedural issues. The Declaration states that victims are entitled to redress and recommends that States should establish judicial and administrative mechanisms for victims to obtain prompt redress. In addition, the Declaration encourages the process to be responsive and sensitive to the victims by including them in any proceedings that affect their interests and by ensuring their safety. These concerns are also fully addressed by the van Boven and Joinet Guidelines. On the other hand, the van Boven and Joinet guidelines specifically add the right of access to international procedures to supplement domestic mechanisms for redress. In addition, the Declaration remains silent with respect to jurisdiction, perhaps because the Basic Principles are focussed more on domestic law.

V. An Assessment of the Provisions on Reparations for Victims in the Statute of the International Criminal Court

67. The portion of the Statute of the International Criminal Court (ICC) dealing with compensation for victims is significantly less extensive than either the Declaration of Basic Principles of Justice or the van Boven or Joinet Guidelines on this issue, primarily because, as the article dealing with reparations to victims states, the "Court shall establish principles relating to reparations". Nevertheless, several facets of the Statute should be taken into consideration.

68. First, the Statute defines reparations slightly differently from either the van Boven or Joinet Guidelines. The Statute defines reparations as restitution, compensation and rehabilitation. However, both sets of guidelines add collective measures of satisfaction and guarantees of non-repetition to the Statute's definition.

69. Second, the Statute contemplates a trust fund out of which reparations to victims may be made. This idea of an international fund seems similar to the concept of trust funds enunciated in the Declaration of Basic Principles of Justice. However, it is not mentioned in either set of guidelines. In addition, the Statute also provides for protection of victims and witnesses during Court proceedings – which accords with all three sets of principles.

70. Finally, it should be noted that the ICC Statute does not provide for a definition of a victim or

the exact damages recoverable under the various measures of reparations (medical expenses, loss of earning, etc.). These types of concerns are important especially since a comparison of the Basic Principles of Justice and the van Boven and Joinet Guidelines reveals a lack of uniform terminology in this area. On the other hand, the establishment of these principles on reparations to victims could perhaps be left to the International Criminal Court.

[. . .]

7.6. Resolution 2000/62 – Basic Principles and Guidelines on the Right to a Remedy and Reparation for Victims of Violations of International Human Rights and Humanitarian Law (2000)[117]

The Commission on Human Rights,

Pursuant to Commission on Human Rights resolution 1999/33 of 26 April 1999, entitled "The right to restitution, compensation and rehabilitation for victims of grave violations of human rights and fundamental freedoms", in which the Commission took note with appreciation of the note of the Secretary-General (E/CN.4/1999/53) submitted in compliance with resolution 1998/43 of 17 April 1998 and the report of the independent expert (E/CN.4/1999/65),

Recalling resolution 1989/13 of 31 August 1989 of the Sub-Commission on Prevention of Discrimination and Protection of Minorities in which the Sub-Commission decided to entrust Mr. Theo van Boven with the task of undertaking a study concerning the right to restitution, compensation and rehabilitation for victims of gross violations of human rights and fundamental freedoms, which was contained in Mr. Van Boven's final report (E/CN.4/Sub.2/1993/8) and which resulted in draft basic principles and guidelines (E/CN.4/1997/104, annex), and resolution 1994/35 of 4 March 1994 of the Commission on Human Rights in which the Commission regarded the proposed basic principles and guidelines contained in the study of the Special Rapporteur as a useful basis for giving priority to the question of restitution, compensation and rehabilitation,

[117] 18 January 2000.

Recalling the provisions providing a right to a remedy for victims of violations of international human rights and humanitarian law found in numerous international instruments, in particular the Universal Declaration of Human Rights at article 8, the International Covenant on Civil and Political Rights at article 2, the International Convention on the Elimination of All Forms of Racial Discrimination at article 6, the Convention against Torture and Other Cruel, Inhuman or Degrading Treatment or Punishment at article 11, and the Convention on the Rights of the Child at article 39,

Recalling the provisions providing a right to a remedy for victims of violations of international human rights found in regional conventions, in particular the African Charter on Human and Peoples' Rights at article 7, the American Convention on Human Rights at article 25, and the European Convention for the Protection of Human Rights and Fundamental Freedoms at article 13,

Recalling the Declaration of Basic Principles of Justice for Victims of Crime and Abuse of Power emanating from the deliberations of the Seventh Congress on the Prevention of Crime and the Treatment of Offenders, and resolution 40/34 of 29 November 1985 by which the General Assembly adopted the text recommended by the Congress,

Reaffirming the principles enunciated in the Declaration of Basic Principles of Justice for Victims of Crime and Abuse of Power, including that victims should be treated with compassion and respect for their dignity, have their right to access to justice and redress mechanisms fully respected, and that the establishment, strengthening and expansion of national funds for compensation to victims should be encouraged, together with the expeditious development of appropriate rights and remedies for victims,

Recalling resolution 1989/57 of 24 May 1989 of the Economic and Social Council, entitled "Implementation of the Declaration of Basic Principles of Justice for Victims of Crime and Abuse of Power", as well as Council resolution 1990/22 of 24 May 1990, entitled "Victims of crime and abuse of power",

Noting that in resolution 827 (1993) of 25 May 1993 in which it adopted the Statute of the International Criminal Tribunal for the Former Yugoslavia, the Security Council decided that "the work of the International Tribunal shall be carried out without prejudice to the right of the victims to seek, through appropriate means, compensation for damages incurred as a result of violations of international humanitarian law",

Noting with satisfaction the adoption of the Rome Statute of the International Criminal Court on 17 July 1998 which obliges the Court to "establish principles relating to reparation to, or in respect of, victims, including restitution, compensation and rehabilitation" and obliges the Assembly of States Parties to establish a trust fund for the benefit of victims of crimes within the jurisdiction of the Court and of the families of such victims, and mandates the Court "to protect the safety, physical and psychological well-being, dignity and privacy of victims" and to permit the participation of victims at all "stages of the proceedings determined to be appropriate by the Court",

Recognizing that, in honouring the victims' right to benefit from remedies and reparation, the international community keeps faith and human solidarity with victims, survivors and future human generations, and reaffirms the international legal principles of accountability, justice and the rule of law,

Convinced that, in adopting a victim-oriented point of departure, the community, at local, national and international levels, affirms its human solidarity and compassion with victims of violations of international human rights and humanitarian law as well as with humanity at large,

Decides to adopt the Basic Principles and Guidelines on the Right to a Remedy and Reparation for Victims of Violations of International Human Rights and Humanitarian Law.

[. . .]

7.7. Resolution 2003/34 – The Right to Restitution, Compensation and Rehabilitation for Victims of Grave Violations of Human Rights and Fundamental Freedoms (2003)[118]

The Commission on Human Rights,

Guided by the Charter of the United Nations, the Universal Declaration of Human Rights, the

[118] 23 April 2003.

International Covenants on Human Rights, other relevant human rights instruments and the Vienna Declaration and Programme of Action (A/CONF.157/23),

Reaffirming that, pursuant to internationally proclaimed human rights principles, victims of grave violations of human rights should receive, in appropriate cases, restitution, compensation and rehabilitation,

Reiterating the importance of addressing the question of restitution, compensation and rehabilitation for victims of grave violations of human rights and fundamental freedoms in a systematic and thorough way at the national and international levels,

Recalling its resolutions 1996/35 of 19 April 1996, 1998/43 of 17 April 1998, 1999/33 of 26 April 1999, 2000/41 of 20 April 2000 and 2002/44 of 23 April 2002, as well as its decision 2001/105 of 23 April 2001,

Recalling also the report of the independent expert, Mr. Cherif Bassiouni, appointed by the Commission (E/CN.4/2000/62), and, in particular, the draft of the "Basic principles and guidelines on the right to a remedy and reparation for victims of violations of international human rights and humanitarian law", annexed to his report, and the note by the Secretariat (E/CN.4/2002/70),

Welcoming with satisfaction the positive experience of countries that have established policies and adopted legislation on restitution, compensation and rehabilitation for victims of grave violations of human rights,

1. *Calls upon* the international community to give due attention to the right to a remedy and, in particular, in appropriate cases, to receive restitution, compensation and rehabilitation, for victims of grave violations of international human rights law and humanitarian international law.

[. . .]

7.8. Resolution 2004/28 – Prohibition of Forced Evictions (2004)[119]

The Commission on Human Rights,

[119] 16 April 2004.

Recalling its resolution 1993/77 of 10 March 1993 and the analytical report on forced evictions submitted by the Secretary-General to the Commission at its fiftieth session (E/CN.4/1994/20),

Recalling also Sub-Commission on the Promotion and Protection of Human Rights resolutions 1991/12 of 26 August 1991, 1992/14 of 27 August 1992, 1993/41 of 26 August 1993, 1994/39 of 26 August 1994, 1995/29 of 24 August 1995, 1996/27 of 29 August 1996, 1997/6 of 22 August 1997 and 1998/9 of 20 August 1998,

Reaffirming that every woman, man and child has the right to a secure place to live in peace and dignity, which includes the right not to be evicted unlawfully, arbitrarily or on a discriminatory basis from their home, land or community,

Recognizing that the often violent practice of forced eviction involves the coerced and involuntary removal of persons, families and groups from their homes, lands and communities, whether or not deemed legal under prevailing systems of law, resulting in greater homelessness and inadequate housing and living conditions,

Emphasizing that ultimate legal and political responsibility for preventing forced evictions rests with Governments,

Recalling, however, that general comment No. 2 (1990) on international technical assistance measures (art. 22 of the International Covenant on Economic, Social and Cultural Rights), adopted by the Committee on Economic, Social and Cultural Rights at its fourth session, states, inter alia, that international agencies should scrupulously avoid involvement in projects which involve, among other things, large-scale evictions or displacement of persons without the provision of all appropriate protection and compensation, and general comment No. 4 (1991) on the right to adequate housing (art. 11, para. 1, of the Covenant) in which the Committee considered that instances of forced eviction were, prima facie, incompatible with the requirements of the Covenant and could only be justified in the most exceptional circumstances, and in accordance with the relevant principles of international law,

Noting with interest the recent case law of the European Court of Human Rights, the Inter-American Commission on Human Rights and the African

Commission on Human and Peoples' Rights regarding the prohibition of forced eviction,

Recalling the adoption of general comment No. 7 (1997) on the right to adequate housing (art. 11, para. 1, of the Covenant): forced evictions by the Committee on Economic, Social and Cultural Rights, in which the Committee recognized, inter alia, that women, children, youth, older persons, indigenous people, ethnic and other minorities, and other marginalized or vulnerable groups all suffer disproportionately from the practice of forced eviction, and that women in all groups are disproportionately affected, given the extent of statutory and other forms of discrimination which often apply in relation to the property rights of women, including homeownership and rights of access to property of accommodation, and given the particular vulnerability of women to acts of gender-based violence and sexual abuse when they are rendered homeless,

Noting the provisions on forced evictions contained in the Habitat Agenda, adopted by the second United Nations Conference on Human Settlements (Habitat II) (A/CONF.165/14) convened in June 1996,

1. *Reaffirms* that the practice of forced eviction that is contrary to laws that are in conformity with international human rights standards constitutes a gross violation of a broad range of human rights, in particular the right to adequate housing;

2. *Strongly urges* Governments to undertake immediately measures, at all levels, aimed at eliminating the practice of forced eviction by, inter alia, repealing existing plans involving forced evictions as well as any legislation allowing for forced evictions, and by adopting and implementing legislation ensuring the right to security of tenure for all residents;

3. *Also strongly urges* Governments to protect all persons who are currently threatened with forced eviction and to adopt all necessary measures giving full protection against forced eviction, based upon effective participation, consultation and negotiation with affected persons or groups;

4. *Recommends* that all Governments provide immediate restitution, compensation and/or appropriate and sufficient alternative accommodation or land to persons and communities that have been forcibly evicted, following mutually satisfactory negotiations with the affected persons or groups and consistent with their wishes, rights and needs, and recognizing the obligation to ensure such provision in the event of any forced eviction;

5. *Also recommends* that all Governments ensure that any eviction that is otherwise deemed lawful is carried out in a manner that does not violate any of the human rights of those evicted;

6. *Reminds* all international financial, trade, development and other related institutions and agencies, including member or donor States that have voting rights within such bodies, to take fully into account the views contained in the present resolution and the obligations under international human rights and humanitarian law on the practice of forced eviction;

7. *Requests* the United Nations High Commissioner for Human Rights to give due attention to the practice of forced eviction in discharging her responsibilities and to undertake measures, whenever possible, to persuade Governments to comply with relevant international standards, to prevent planned forced evictions from taking place and to ensure the provision of restitution or just and fair compensation, as the case may warrant, when forced evictions have already occurred;

8. *Welcomes* the report of the expert seminar on the practice of forced evictions convened in Geneva from 11 to 13 June 1997 and the Comprehensive Human Rights Guidelines on Development-Based Displacement adopted by the expert seminar (E/CN.4/Sub.2/1997/7, annex);

9. *Invites* all States to study the Comprehensive Human Rights Guidelines, with a view to considering further appropriate action.

[...]

7.9. Resolution 2004/34 – The Right to Restitution, Compensation and Rehabilitation for Victims of Grave Violations of Human Rights and Fundamental Freedoms (2004)[120]

The Commission on Human Rights,

[120] 19 April 2004.

Guided by the Charter of the United Nations, the Universal Declaration of Human Rights, the International Covenants on Human Rights, other relevant human rights instruments and the Vienna Declaration and Programme of Action,

Reaffirming that, pursuant to internationally proclaimed human rights principles, victims of grave violations of human rights should receive, in appropriate cases, restitution, compensation and rehabilitation,

Reiterating the importance of addressing the question of restitution, compensation and rehabilitation for victims of grave violations of human rights and fundamental freedoms in a systematic and thorough way at the national and international levels,

Recalling its resolutions 1996/35 of 19 April 1996, 1998/43 of 17 April 1998, 1999/33 of 26 April 1999, 2000/41 of 20 April 2000, 2002/44 of 23 April 2002 and 2003/34 of 23 April 2003, as well as its decision 2001/105 of 23 April 2001,

Recalling also the report of the independent expert appointed by the Commission, Mr. Cherif Bassiouni (E/CN.4/2000/62) and, in particular, the draft of the "Basic principles and guidelines on the right to a remedy and reparation for victims of violations of international human rights and humanitarian law", annexed to his report, and the note by the Secretariat (E/CN.4/2002/70),

Welcoming with satisfaction the positive experience of countries that have established policies and adopted legislation on restitution, compensation and rehabilitation for victims of grave violations of human rights,

1. *Calls upon* the international community to give due attention to the right to a remedy and, in particular, in appropriate cases, to receive restitution, compensation and rehabilitation, for victims of grave violations of international human rights law and humanitarian international law;

2. *Takes note* of the report of the Chairperson-Rapporteur of the second consultative meeting on basic principles and guidelines on the right to a remedy and reparation for victims of violations of international human rights and humanitarian law (E/CN.4/2004/57, annex), held in Geneva on 20, 21 and 23 October 2003;

3. *Requests* the Chairperson-Rapporteur of the consultative meetings, in consultation with the independent experts, Mr. Theo van Boven and Mr. Cherif Bassiouni, to prepare a revised version of the "Basic principles and guidelines on the right to a remedy and reparation for victims of violations of international human rights and humanitarian law", taking into account the opinions and commentaries of States and of intergovernmental and non-governmental organizations and the results of the previous consultative meetings (see E/CN.4/2003/63 and E/CN.4/2004/57);

4. *Requests* the United Nations High Commissioner for Human Rights to hold, with the cooperation of interested Governments, a third consultative meeting for all interested Member States, intergovernmental organizations and non-governmental organizations in consultative status with the Economic and Social Council, using available resources, with a view to finalizing the "Basic principles and guidelines on the right to a remedy and reparation for victims of violations of international human rights and humanitarian law", and if appropriate, to consider all options for the adoption of these principles and guidelines; this meeting should have, as a basis for its work, inter alia, the comments received, the revised version of the principles and guidelines to be prepared by the Chairperson-Rapporteur pursuant to paragraph 3 of the present resolution, and the reports of the Chairperson-Rapporteur of the two previous consultative meetings;

[. . .]

7.10. Resolution 2004/55 – Internally Displaced Persons (2004)[121]

The Commission on Human Rights,

[. . .]

Noting the resolve of the international community to find durable solutions for all internally displaced persons and to strengthen international cooperation in order to help them return voluntarily to their homes in safety and with dignity or, based on their free choice, to resettle in another part of their country, and to be smoothly reintegrated into their societies,

[121] 20 April 2004.

[. . .]

2. *Expresses concern* at the persistent problems of large numbers of internally displaced persons worldwide, in particular the risk of extreme poverty and socio-economic exclusion, their limited access to humanitarian assistance, vulnerability to human rights violations, as well as difficulties resulting from their specific situation, such as lack of food, medication or shelter and issues pertinent during their reintegration, including, in appropriate cases, the need for the restitution of or compensation for property;

[. . .]

7.11. Resolution 2005/46 – Internally Displaced Persons (2005)[122]

The Commission on Human Rights,

[. . .]

Emphasizing the primary responsibility of national authorities to provide protection and assistance to internally displaced persons within their jurisdiction during all stages of the displacement cycle, as well as to address the root causes of their displacement in appropriate cooperation with the international community,

Noting the resolve of the international community to find durable solutions for all internally displaced persons and to strengthen international cooperation in order to help them return voluntarily to their homes in safety and with dignity or, based on their free choice, to resettle in another part of their country, and to be smoothly reintegrated into their societies,

[. . .]

Noting that the Rome Statute of the International Criminal Court defines the deportation or forcible transfer of population as a crime against humanity and the unlawful deportation or transfer of the civilian population as well as ordering the displacement of the civilian population as war crimes,

[. . .]

3. *Expresses concern* at the persistent problems of large numbers of internally displaced persons

worldwide, in particular the risk of extreme poverty and socio-economic exclusion, their limited access to humanitarian assistance, vulnerability to human rights violations, as well as difficulties resulting from their specific situation, such as lack of food, medication or shelter and issues pertinent during their reintegration, including, in appropriate cases, the need for the restitution of or compensation for property;

[. . .]

5. *Notes* the importance of taking the human rights and the specific protection and assistance needs of internally displaced persons into consideration, when appropriate, in peace processes and in reintegration and rehabilitation processes;

[. . .]

8. UN SUB-COMMISSION ON THE PROTECTION AND PROMOTION OF HUMAN RIGHTS

8.1. Study Concerning the Right to Restitution, Compensation and Rehabilitation for Victims of Gross Violations of Human Rights and Fundamental Freedoms – Final Report Submitted by Mr. Theo van Boven, Special Rapporteur (1993) (Excerpts)[123]

[. . .]

IX. PROPOSED BASIC PRINCIPLES AND GUIDELINES

137. The Special Rapporteur hereby submits the following proposals concerning reparation to victims of gross violations of human rights.

GENERAL PRINCIPLES

1. Under international law, the violation of any human right gives rise to a right of reparation for the victim. Particular attention must be paid to gross violations of human rights and fundamental freedoms, which include at least the following: genocide; slavery and slavery-like practices; summary or arbitrary executions; torture and cruel, inhuman

---

[122] 19 April 2005.

[123] UN Doc. E/CN.4/Sub.2/1993/8.

or degrading treatment or punishment; enforced disappearance; arbitrary and prolonged detention; deportation or forcible transfer of population; and systematic discrimination, in particular based on race or gender.

2. Every State has a duty to make reparation in case of a breach of the obligation under international law to respect and to ensure respect for human rights and fundamental freedoms. The obligation to ensure respect for human rights includes the duty to prevent violations, the duty to investigate violations, the duty to take appropriate action against the violators, and the duty to afford remedies to victims. States shall ensure that no person who may be responsible for gross violations of human rights shall have immunity from liability for their actions.

3. Reparation for human rights violations has the purpose of relieving the suffering of and affording justice to victims by removing or redressing to the extent possible the consequences of the wrongful acts and by preventing and deterring violations.

4. Reparation should respond to the needs and wishes of the victims. It shall be proportionate to the gravity of the violations and the resulting harm and shall include: restitution, compensation, rehabilitation, satisfaction and guarantees of non-repetition.

5. Reparation for certain gross violations of human rights that amount to crimes under international law includes a duty to prosecute and punish perpetrators. Impunity is in conflict with this principle.

6. Reparation may be claimed by the direct victims and, where appropriate, the immediate family, dependants or other persons having a special relationship to the direct victims.

7. In addition to providing reparation to individuals, States shall make adequate provision for groups of victims to bring collective claims and to obtain collective reparation. Special measures should be taken for the purpose of affording opportunities for self-development and advancement to groups who, as a result of human rights violations, were denied such opportunities.

* Where these principles refer to States, they also apply, as appropriate to other entities exercising effective power.

FORMS OF REPARATIONS

8. Restitution shall be provided to re-establish, to the extent possible, the situation that existed for the victim prior to the violations of human rights. Restitution requires, inter alia, restoration of liberty, citizenship or residence, employment or property.

9. Compensation shall be provided for any economically assessable damage resulting from human rights violations, such as:

(a) Physical or mental harm;

(b) Pain, suffering and emotional distress;

(c) Lost opportunities, including education;

(d) Loss of earnings and earning capacity;

(e) Reasonable medical and other expenses of rehabilitation;

(f) Harm to property or business, including lost profits;

(g) Harm to reputation or dignity;

(h) Reasonable costs and fees of legal or expert assistance to obtain a remedy.

10. Rehabilitation shall be provided, to include legal, medical, psychological and other care and services, as well as measures to restore the dignity and reputation of the victims.

11. Satisfaction and guarantees of non-repetition shall be provided, including:

(a) Cessation of continuing violations;

(b) Verification of the facts and full and public disclosure of the truth;

(c) A declaratory judgment in favour of the victim;

(d) Apology, including public acknowledgment of the facts and acceptance of responsibility;

(e) Bringing to justice the persons responsible for the violations;

(f) Commemorations and paying tribute to the victims;

(g) Inclusion of an accurate record of human rights violations in educational curricula and materials;

(h) Preventing the recurrence of violations by such means as:

(i) Ensuring effective civilian control of military and security forces;

(ii) Restricting the jurisdiction of military tribunals;

(iii) Strengthening the independence of the judiciary;

(iv) Protecting the legal profession and human rights workers;

(v) Providing human rights training to all sectors of society, in particular to military and security forces and to law enforcement officials.

PROCEDURES AND MECHANISMS

12. Every State shall maintain prompt and effective disciplinary, administrative, civil and criminal procedures, with universal jurisdiction for human rights violations that constitute crimes under international law.

13. The legal system, especially in civil, administrative and procedural matters, must be adapted so as to ensure that the right to reparation is readily accessible, not unreasonably impaired and takes into account the potential vulnerability of the victims.

14. Every State shall make known, through the media and other appropriate mechanisms, the available procedures for reparations.

15. Statutes of limitations shall not apply in respect to periods during which no effective remedies exist for human rights violations. Claims relating to reparations for gross violations of human rights shall not be subject to a statute of limitations.

16. No one may be coerced to waive claims for reparations.

17. Every State shall make readily available all evidence in its possession concerning human rights violations.

18. Administrative or judicial tribunals responsible for affording reparations should take into account that records or other tangible evidence may be limited or unavailable. In the absence of other evidence, reparations should be based on the testimony of victims, family members, medical and mental health professionals.

19. Every State shall protect victims, their relatives and friends, and witnesses from intimidation and reprisals.

20. Decisions relating to reparations for victims of violations of human rights shall be implemented in a diligent and prompt manner. In this respect follow-up, appeal or review procedures should be devised.

8.2. Resolution 1994/24 – The Right to Freedom of Movement (1994)[124]

The Sub-Commission on Prevention of Discrimination and Protection of Minorities,

Reaffirming the right of everyone lawfully within the territory of a State to liberty of movement and freedom to choose his residence, and the prohibition of arbitrary deprivation of the right to enter one's own country as set out in article 12 of the International Covenant on Civil and Political Rights and article 13 of the Universal Declaration of Human Rights,

Recognizing that practices of forcible exile, mass expulsions and deportations, population transfer, "ethnic cleansing" and other forms of forcible displacement of populations within a country or across borders deprive the affected populations of their right to freedom of movement,

Noting that policies of forcible displacement are one of the major causes of flows of refugees and internally displaced persons,

Concerned that more than 20 million refugees and even larger and growing numbers of internally displaced persons exist worldwide,

1. *Affirms* the right of persons to remain in peace in their own homes, on their own lands and in their own countries;

2. *Also affirms* the right of refugees and displaced persons to return, in safety and dignity, to their country of origin and/or within it, to their place of origin or choice;

3. *Urges* Governments and other actors involved to do everything possible in order to cease at once all practices of forced displacement, population transfer and "ethnic cleansing" in violation of international legal standards;

4. *Decides* to include under the agenda item entitled "Freedom of movement" a sub-item relating to questions of displacement entitled "Population

[124] 26 August 1994.

displacement" and to keep under constant review respect for the right to freedom of movement, including the right to remain and to return.

8.3. Resolution 1995/13 – The Right to Freedom of Movement (1995)[125]

The Sub-Commission on Prevention of Discrimination and Protection of Minorities,

[. . .]

2. *Also affirms* the right of refugees and displaced persons to return, in safety and dignity, to their country of origin and/or within it to their place of origin or choice;

[. . .]

8.4. Resolution 1997/31 – The Right to Return (1997)[126]

The Sub-Commission on Prevention of Discrimination and Protection of Minorities,

Reaffirming the right of every person to return to his or her own country, as enshrined in article 13, paragraph 2, of the Universal Declaration of Human Rights and article 5 (d) (ii) of the International Convention on the Elimination of All Forms of Racial Discrimination, and the prohibition of arbitrary deprivation of the right to enter one's own country contained in article 12, paragraph 4, of the International Covenant on Civil and Political Rights,

Recalling its resolution 1996/9 of 23 August 1996 in which it affirmed the right of refugees and internally displaced persons to return voluntarily, in safety and dignity, to their country of origin and/or within it to their place of origin or choice, and in which it decided to continue to study the question of the freedom of movement, including the right to return,

Recognizing the fundamental significance of the observance and promotion of the right to return voluntarily to one's country or place of origin as a principal means of resolving the problems and suffering of refugees and internally displaced persons,

Conscious that the arbitrary deprivation of nationality, prohibited by article 15, paragraph 2, of the

Universal Declaration of Human Rights, constitutes a violation of a fundamental and inalienable human right and an impediment to the right to return to one's country,

Concerned that the plight of many refugees in certain parts of the world may represent a serious denial of their right to return and of their right to a nationality, and is likely to result in a serious increase in the phenomenon of statelessness,

1. *Reaffirms* the fundamental right of refugees and internally displaced persons to return voluntarily, in safety and dignity, to their country of origin and/or within it to their place of origin or choice;

2. *Emphasizes* the crucial importance of the right to return voluntarily to one's country or place of origin as a principal means of long-term resolution of the plight of refugees and internally displaced persons;

[. . .]

5. *Urges* all States to respect and promote the right to return and the right to a nationality;

[. . .]

8.5. Resolution 1998/9 – Forced Evictions (1998)[127]

The Sub-Commission on Prevention of Discrimination and Protection of Minorities,

Recalling Commission on Human Rights resolution 1993/77 of 10 March 1993 and the analytical report on forced evictions submitted by the Secretary-General (E/CN.4/1994/20) to the Commission at its fiftieth session,

Recalling also its resolution 1991/12 of 26 August 1991, 1992/14 of 27 August 1992, 1993/41 of 26 August 1993, 1994/39 of 26 August 1994, 1995/29 of 24 August 1995, 1996/27 of 29 August 1996 and 1997/6 of 22 August 1997,

Reaffirming that every woman, man and child has the right to a secure place to live in peace and dignity, which includes the right not to be evicted arbitrarily or on a discriminatory basis from one's home, land or community,

---

[125] 18 August 1995.
[126] 28 August 1997.

[127] 20 August 1998.

Recognizing that the often violent practice of forced eviction involves the coerced and involuntary removal of persons, families and groups from their homes, lands and communities, whether or not deemed legal under prevailing systems of law, resulting in greater homelessness and inadequate housing and living conditions,

Emphasizing that ultimate legal and political responsibility for preventing forced evictions rests with Governments,

Recalling that general comment No. 2 (1990) on international technical assistance measures, adopted by the Committee on Economic, Social and Cultural Rights at its fourth session, states, *inter alia*, that international agencies should scrupulously avoid involvement in projects which involve, among other things, large-scale evictions or displacement of persons without the provision of all appropriate protection and compensation (E/1990/23, annex III, para. 6), and general comment No. 4 (1991) in which the Committee considered that instances of forced eviction were, prima facie, incompatible with the requirements of the International Covenant on Economic, Social and Cultural Rights and could only be justified in the most exceptional circumstances, and in accordance with the relevant principles of international law (E/1992/23, annex III, para. 18),

Noting with interest the recent case law of the European Court of Human Rights and the Inter-American Commission on Human Rights,

Noting with appreciation the adoption of general comment No. 7 (1997) on forced evictions by the Committee on Economic, Social and Cultural Rights (E/1998/22, annex IV), in which the Committee recognized, *inter alia*, that women, children, youth, older persons, indigenous people, ethnic and other minorities, and other vulnerable groups all suffer disproportionately from the practice of force eviction, and that women in all groups are especially vulnerable, given the extent of statutory and other forms of discrimination which often apply in relation to the property rights of women, including home ownership and rights of access to property of accommodation, and given the particular vulnerability of women to acts of violence and sexual abuse when they are rendered homeless,

Noting also the provisions on forced evictions contained in the Habitat Agenda (A/CONF.165/14),

adopted by the United Nations Conference on Human Settlements (Habitat II) convened in June 1996,

1. *Reaffirms* that the practice of forced eviction constitutes a gross violation of a broad range of human rights, in particular the right to adequate housing, the right to remain, the right to freedom of movement, the right to privacy, the right to property, the right to an adequate standard of living, the right to security of the home, the right to security of the person, the right to security of tenure and the right to equality of treatment;

2. *Strongly urges* Governments to undertake immediately measures, at all levels, aimed at eliminating the practice of forced evictions by, *inter alia*, repealing existing plans involving arbitrary forced evictions and legislation allowing arbitrary forced evictions and ensuring the right to security of tenure for all residents;

3. *Also strongly urges* Governments to protect all persons who are currently threatened with forced evictions, and to adopt all necessary measures giving full protection against arbitrary or unreasonable forced eviction, based upon effective participation, consultation and negotiation with affected persons or groups;

4. *Recommends* that all Governments provide immediate restitution, compensation and/or appropriate and sufficient alternative accommodation or land, consistent with their wishes, rights and needs, to persons and communities that have been forcibly evicted, following mutually satisfactory negotiations with the affected persons or groups, and recognizing the obligation to ensure such provision in the event of any forced eviction;

5. *Recommends* that all Governments ensure that any eviction, whether forced or not, is carried out in a manner which does not violate any of the human rights of those evicted;

6. *Invites* all international financial, trade, development and other related institutions and agencies, including member or donor States that have voting rights within such bodies, to take fully into account the views contained in the present resolution and other pronouncements under international human rights and humanitarian law on the practice of forced eviction;

7. *Requests* the United Nations High Commissioner on Human Rights to give due attention to the practice of forced eviction in discharging her responsibilities and to undertake measures, whenever possible, to persuade Governments to comply with relevant international standards, to repeal planned forced evictions from taking place and to ensure the provision of adequate compensation when forced evictions have already occurred;

8. *Welcomes* the report of the expert seminar on the practice of forced evictions convened from 11 to 13 June 1997 and the comprehensive human rights guidelines on development-based displacement adopted by the expert seminar (E/CN.4/Sub.2/1997/7);

9. *Urges* the Commission to invite all States to consider the comprehensive human rights guidelines on development-based displacement as contained in document E/CN.4/Sub.2/1997/7, with a view to approving the guidelines in their present form at its fifty-sixth session;

[. . .]

8.6. Resolution 1998/26 – Housing and Property Restitution in the Context of the Return of Refugees and Internally Displaced Persons (1998)[128]

The Sub-Commission on Prevention of Discrimination and Protection of Minorities,

Conscious that human rights violations and breaches of international humanitarian law are among the reasons why refugees, as defined in relevant international legal instruments, and internally displaced persons flee their homes and places of habitual residence,

Recognizing that the right of refugees and internally displaced persons to return freely to their homes and places of habitual residence in safety and security forms an indispensable element of national reconciliation and reconstruction and that the recognition of such rights should be included within peace agreements ending armed conflicts,

Recognizing also the right of all returnees to the free exercise of their right to freedom of movement and to choose one's residence, including the right to

be officially registered in their homes and places of habitual residence, their right to privacy and respect for the home, their right to reside peacefully in the security of their own home and their right to enjoy access to all necessary social and economic services, in an environment free of any form of discrimination,

Conscious of the widespread constraint imposed on refugees and internally displaced persons in the exercise of their right to return to their homes and places of habitual residence,

Also conscious that the right to freedom of movement and the right to adequate housing include the right of protection for returning refugees and internally displaced persons against being compelled to return to their homes and places of habitual residence and that the right to return to their homes and places of habitual residence must be exercised in a voluntary and dignified manner,

Aware that intensified international, regional and national measures are required to ensure the full realization of the right of refugees and internally displaced persons to return to their homes and places of habitual residence and are indispensable elements of reintegration, reconstruction and reconciliation,

1. *Reaffirms* the right of all refugees, as defined in relevant international legal instruments, and internally displaced persons to return to their homes and places of habitual residence in their country and/or place of origin, should they so wish;

2. *Reaffirms* also the universal applicability of the right to adequate housing, the right to freedom of movement and the right to privacy and respect for the home, and the particular importance of these rights for returning refugees and internally displaced persons wishing to return to their homes and places of habitual residence;

3. *Confirms* that the adoption or application of laws by States which are designed to or result in the loss or removal of tenancy, use, ownership or other rights connected with housing or property, the active retraction of the right to reside within a particular place, or laws of abandonment employed against refugees or internally displaced persons pose serious impediments to the return and reintegration of refugees and internally displaced persons and to reconstruction and reconciliation;

---

[128] 26 August 1998.

4. *Urges* all States to ensure the free and fair exercise of the right to return to one's home and place of habitual residence by all refugees and internally displaced persons and to develop effective and expeditious legal, administrative and other procedures to ensure the free and fair exercise of this right, including fair and effective mechanisms designed to resolve outstanding housing and property problems;

5. *Invites* the United Nations High Commissioner for Human Rights, in consultation with the United Nations High Commissioner for Refugees, within her mandate, to facilitate the full implementation of the present resolution;

6. *Invites* the United Nations High Commissioner for Refugees, in consultation with the United Nations High Commissioner for Human Rights, to develop policy guidelines to promote and facilitate the right of all refugees and, if appropriate to her mandate, internally displaced persons, to return freely, safely and voluntarily to their homes and places of habitual residence;

7. *Decides* to consider the issue of return to place of residence and housing for refugees and internally displaced persons at its fifty-first session, under the agenda item entitled "Freedom of movement" to determine how most effectively to continue its consideration of these issues.

8.7. The Return of Refugees' or Displaced Persons' Property – Working Paper Submitted by Mr. Paulo Sérgio Pinheiro (2002)[129]

INTRODUCTION

1. The Commission on Human Rights, in its resolutions 1996/25, 1997/22 and 1998/28, called upon the Sub-Commission and its members further to enhance cooperation with mechanisms of the Commission and, within their competence, with all relevant bodies, including human rights treaty bodies. In its resolution 1999/81, the Commission welcomed the Sub-Commission's efforts to enhance such cooperation and in its resolution 2002/66 it reaffirmed that the Sub-Commission could best assist the Commission by providing it with independent expert studies carried out by its members.

[129] UN doc. E/CN.4/Sub.2/2002/17.

2. At the seventh meeting of persons chairing the human rights treaty bodies, in 1996, the chairpersons of the treaty-monitoring bodies recommended that the treaty bodies should take a more active role in supporting, suggesting topics for and cooperating in the preparation of studies by the Sub-Commission.[1]

3. The Committee on the Elimination of Racial Discrimination (CERD) discussed this issue during its fiftieth session in 1997,[2] and decided to propose to the Sub-Commission nine topics for the preparation of studies, including "the return of refugees' or displaced persons' property".[3] CERD observed that: "The flight of hundreds of thousands of refugees or displaced persons who leave their homes and properties empty, as a result of an armed conflict, frequently results in such property being occupied by non-authorized people. Such is at present the case in the Great Lakes region, Bosnia and Herzegovina, Cyprus and elsewhere. After their return to their homes of origin all such refugees and displaced persons have the right to have restored to them property of which they were deprived in the course of the conflict and to be compensated for any such property that cannot be restored. Furthermore, any commitments or statements relating to such property made under duress should be null and void. The magnitude of this problem is such that it requires a study on the basis of international law and existing international instruments in the field of human rights."[4]

4. Mr. Michael Banton, then Chairperson of CERD, in a letter dated 19 March 1997,[5] communicated these proposals to the Chairperson of the forty-eighth session of the Sub-Commission and requested that he present them to the Sub-Commission during its forty-ninth session.

5. At its forty-ninth session, the Sub-Commission, in resolution 1997/5, expressed its gratitude to CERD for recommending future Sub-Commission studies that could usefully contribute to the work of CERD. Furthermore, the Sub-Commission, in its decision 1997/112, decided to devote special attention to subjects proposed by treaty bodies when choosing new subjects for study. The Sub-Commission has also responded to the request of CERD by undertaking working papers, as well as subsequent comprehensive studies authorized by the Commission on Human Rights and the Economic and Social Council, with regard to two of the

other topics proposed by CERD: affirmative action, and the rights of non-citizens.

6. In its resolution 1999/47, the Commission on Human Rights encouraged the Sub-Commission to continue its work on the matter of housing and property restitution in the context of return of refugees and internally displaced persons.

7. At its fifty-third session, the Sub-Commission, in decision 2001/122, entrusted Mr. Paulo Sérgio Pinheiro with the preparation of a working paper on the return of refugees' or displaced persons' property, to be submitted to the Sub-Commission in order to enable it to take a decision at its fifty-fourth session on the feasibility of a comprehensive study on that subject.

8. This working paper is hereby submitted in accordance with Sub-Commission decision 2001/122.

I. TERMINOLOGY

9. For the purpose of this working paper, the phrase "housing and property" refers to housing and real property, including land. This definition is used for two key reasons. First, housing and real property restitution in the context of the right to return of refugees and other displaced persons has deservedly received a great deal of attention from the international community, more so than other types of property restitution. This attention is due in large part to the unique role that housing and real property restitution play in securing the voluntary, safe and dignified return of refugees and other displaced persons to their homes and places of original residence.

10. Second, housing rights are enshrined in international law to a far greater degree and encompass far more, substantively speaking, than are more general property rights.[6] Accordingly, the main focus of this working paper is on issues related to housing and real property restitution.

11. The term "restitution" refers to an equitable remedy, or a form of restorative justice, by which persons who suffer loss or injury are returned as far as possible to their original pre-loss or pre-injury position. The remedy includes, for example, the return of arbitrarily or illegally confiscated housing or property. Again, housing and property restitution is increasingly viewed as a right of displaced

persons and refugees under international human rights law, and as the key means of returning situations involving displacement to their original state.

12. The term "compensation" refers to a legal remedy by which a person receives monetary payment for harm suffered, for example resulting from the impossibility of restoring the person's property or house.

II. PRELIMINARY COMMENTS

13. The topic of this working paper is one of great importance, as it is increasingly being recognized that, for many refugees and other displaced persons, dispossession of their homes lies at the root of their displacement, and therefore one of the prime concerns for those returning or attempting to return to their countries of origin is the resolution of property and housing issues before and subsequent to return.

14. Additionally, ensuring the restitution of housing and property temporarily lost owing to displacement has also become an increasingly prominent component of efforts to protect human rights, restore the rule of law and prevent future conflict in countries currently undergoing post-conflict reconstruction.

15. The conditions under which people come to lose their homes and properties differ across cases, but often involve arbitrary displacement, protracted civil conflict, ethnic cleansing, uncompensated expropriation or discriminatory confiscation. Ensuring housing and property restitution and, thereby, the right to return in safety and in dignity, is essential in order not to allow the results of such conditions to remain in place, as well as to protect the human rights of the victims of such situations.

III. DURABLE SOLUTIONS TO DISPLACEMENT

16. The Office of the United Nations High Commissioner for Refugees (UNHCR) has identified three key durable solutions to the problems faced by refugees: (i) integration into countries of asylum; (ii) resettlement in third countries; and (iii) voluntary repatriation.[7] Housing and property restitution are often essential in order to facilitate the durable solution of repatriation, a solution often

preferred by many refugees and other displaced persons.

17. With respect to voluntary repatriation, this solution has its origins in General Assembly resolution of 14 December 1950, in which the Assembly adopted the UNHCR Statute and called upon Governments to cooperate with the High Commissioner for Refugees in the performance of his [or her] functions by, inter alia, assisting the High Commissioner in his [or her] efforts to promote the voluntary repatriation of refugees. Since then, various Executive Committee conclusions have further elaborated the role and policy perspectives of UNHCR with respect to voluntary repatriation.

18. For example, in EXCOM Conclusion No. 18 (XXXI) of 1980, the Executive Committee "called upon governments of countries of origin to provide formal guarantees for the safety of returning refugees and stressed the importance of such guarantees being fully respected and of returning refugees not being penalized for having left their country of origin for reasons giving rise to refugee situations".[8]

19. Similarly, in EXCOM Conclusion No. 40 (XXXVI) of 1985, the Executive Committee reaffirmed "the basic rights of persons to return voluntarily to the country of origin" and affirmed "the need for [repatriation] to be carried out under conditions of absolute safety, preferably to the place of residence of the refugee in his [or her] country of origin".[9]

20. The UNHCR Handbook on Voluntary Repatriation provides additional guidance on these issues. The Handbook stresses, for instance, that the mandate of UNHCR includes promoting "the creation of conditions that are conducive to voluntary return in safety and with dignity" and promoting "the voluntary repatriation of refugees once conditions are conducive to return".[10] In addition, it states that the recovery and restitution to returnees of their land or other immovable and movable property which they may have lost or left behind are to be included in any tripartite agreement or any declaration of amnesties and guarantees.[11]

21. UNHCR just recently stated that experience has shown that voluntary repatriation operations are likely to be less successful if housing and property issues are left too long unattended, particularly if refugees are not able to recover their houses and property in the country of origin.[12] This statement,

together with the aforementioned conclusions and guidelines acknowledges that, in many attempts at voluntary repatriation, return is neither successful nor durable if the underlying housing and property issues are not addressed.

IV. THE RIGHT TO RETURN TO ONE'S HOME AND THE ROLE OF HOUSING AND PROPERTY RESTITUTION

A. The Right to Return to One's Home

22. The right of return is now understood to encompass not merely returning to one's country, but to one's home as well. Indeed, the right of refugees and displaced persons to return to their homes is recognized by the international community as a free-standing, autonomous right in and of itself.[13] In 1980, the General Assembly, in its resolution 35/124 on international intervention to avert new flows of refugees, reaffirmed "the right of refugees to return to their homes in their homelands". This understanding is important in order to protect effectively the right to return of refugees and displaced persons and in order to ameliorate situations leading to instability and displacement.

23. The United Nations has also consistently reaffirmed this principle when addressing specific cases of displacement. For example, the Security Council, in its resolution 820 (1993) concerning Bosnia and Herzegovina, adopted on 17 April 1993, reaffirmed that "all displaced persons have the right to return in peace to their former homes and should be assisted to do so".

24. Similar language by the Security Council reaffirming the right to return to one's home can be found in resolutions addressing displacement in numerous countries and regions, including Abkhazia and the Republic of Georgia,[14] Azerbaijan,[15] Bosnia and Herzogovina,[16] Cambodia,[17] Croatia,[18] Cyprus,[19] Kosovo,[20] Kuwait,[21] Namibia[22] and Tajikistan.[23]

25. Other United Nations bodies have also reaffirmed the right to return to one's home. For instance, in addition to resolution 35/124 mentioned above, the General Assembly has reaffirmed or recognized the right to return to one's home in resolutions concerning Algeria,[24] Cyprus,[25] Palestine/Israel[26] and Rwanda.[27]

26. Likewise, the Sub-Commission reaffirmed "the right of all refugees ... and internally displaced persons to return to their homes and places of habitual residence in their country and/or place of origin, should they so wish" with the adoption, without a vote, of resolution 1998/26, entitled "Housing and property restitution in the context of the return of refugees and internally displaced persons".

27. CERD reaffirmed this principle in its General Recommendation XXII on article 5 and refugees and displaced persons, in which it states: "all ... refugees and displaced persons have the right freely to return to their homes of origin under conditions of safety".[28]

28. Finally, the international community, meeting in Durban, South Africa in August and September 2001 for the World Conference against Racism, Racial Discrimination, Xenophobia and Related Intolerance, unequivocally declared its universal recognition of "the right of refugees to return voluntarily to their homes and properties in dignity and safety, and urge[d] all States to facilitate such return".[29]

B. Housing and Property Restitution

29. Housing and property restitution must be seen as a necessary component of the implementation of the right to return to one's home. Indeed, within the context of international human rights law, the right to housing and property restitution is recognized as an essential element of the right to return for refugees and displaced persons.[30]

30. For example, as mentioned above, the Security Council in resolution 820 (1993) stated that "all displaced persons have the right to return in peace to their former homes and should be assisted to do so". The Durban Declaration reaffirms "the right of refugees to return voluntarily to their homes and properties in dignity and safety, and urge[s] all States to facilitate such return".[31] It is important to point out that the international community has thus affirmed that States should assist or facilitate the right to return to one's home. Assistance or facilitation implies, inter alia, the provision of housing and property restitution as a remedy for those displaced from their homes and lands.

31. The Commission on Human Rights has also addressed restitution as an essential remedy. Forced displacement is often precipitated by forced eviction, or in any event can be characterized as resulting in de facto forced eviction. The Commission has clearly stated that the practice of forced eviction "constitutes a gross violation of human rights".[32]

32. The Commission on Human Rights has examined the remedy of restitution in the context of such violations of human rights. In several resolutions concerning restitution, compensation and rehabilitation for victims of grave violations of human rights, the Commission has consistently referred to the "right to restitution ... for victims of grave violations of human rights".[33] It can therefore be construed that restitution as a remedy for actual or de facto forced eviction resulting from forced displacement is itself a free-standing, autonomous right.

33. Several international legal instruments recognize or include the principle of housing and property restitution. For instance, provisions of humanitarian law are applicable with respect to housing and property restitution. The Geneva Convention relative to the Protection of Civilian Persons in Time of War, of 1949, for example, provides in article 49 that: "Persons ... evacuated shall be transferred back to their homes as soon as hostilities in the area in question have ceased."

34. Likewise, the Rome Statute of the International Criminal Court authorizes restitution as a remedy for violations occurring under its jurisdiction. Article 75, paragraph 1, of the Rome Statute states: "The Court shall establish principles relating to reparations to, or in respect of, victims, including restitution, compensation and rehabilitation."

35. Other instruments recognize restitution as a remedy. For instance, the draft articles on the responsibility of States for internationally wrongful acts, adopted by the International Law Commission and transmitted to the United Nations General Assembly in 2001,[34] recognize restitution as a proper remedy for certain violations of international law.

36. Article 35 of the draft articles on State responsibility states: "Full reparation for the injury caused by the internationally wrongful act shall take the form of restitution, compensation and satisfaction, either singly or in combination."

37. Article 36 states further that: "A State responsible for an internationally wrongful act is under

an obligation to make restitution, that is, to re-establish the situation which existed before the wrongful act was committed."

38. The Sub-Commission has also addressed this subject, issuing one of the strongest statements regarding housing and property restitution in its resolution 1998/26 of 26 August 1998, in which it urged: "all States to ensure the free and fair exercise of the right to return to one's home and place of habitual residence by all refugees and internally displaced persons and to develop effective and expeditious legal, administrative and other procedures to ensure the free and fair exercise of this right, including fair and effective mechanisms designed to resolve outstanding housing and property problems."

39. CERD has recognized the necessity of restitution, of both housing and other property, as a remedy for displacement. In its General Recommendation XXII on article 5 and refugees and displaced persons, CERD stated: "All . . . refugees and displaced persons have, after their return to their homes of origin, the right to have restored to them property of which they were deprived in the course of the conflict and to be compensated appropriately for any such property that cannot be restored to them."[35]

40. The right to housing and property restitution has also been recognized and utilized in several agreements designed to end conflict, including those dealing with the return of displaced persons in post-conflict situations in Bosnia and Herzegovina,[36] Cambodia,[37] Guatemala,[38] Kosovo,[39] Mozambique[40] and Rwanda.[41]

41. Additionally, the right to housing restitution has been recognized at the national level, either constitutionally or through national legislation, in several countries, including Bosnia and Herzegovina,[42] Bulgaria,[43] the Czech Republic,[44] Estonia,[45] Germany,[46] Rwanda,[47] Slovenia,[48] South Africa[49] and Tajikistan.[50] This recognition illustrates how housing and property mechanisms can be created and implemented for specific situations.

V. Issues Requiring Further Study

42. It is clear from the above that the principle of housing and property restitution has been enshrined in international and national law, reaffirmed by the international community and recognized by independent United Nations expert bodies. Yet, housing and property restitution all too often is not a reality for millions of persons wishing to return to their homes in safety and dignity. This unfortunate reality illustrates that much more is needed with respect to the implementation of standards designed to facilitate the right to return to one's home. This disjunction between existing standards and the reality on the ground requires comprehensive examination in order to understand why those standards have not been adequately implemented and how best to implement them.

43. Several impediments to the right to return exist, and provide concrete examples of the problems resulting in inadequate implementation of housing and property restitution. While many are beyond the scope of this working paper, some can be addressed preliminarily within this context and others can at least be initially identified as impediments. A more comprehensive examination is required in order to identify all impediments to return. Analysing the particular manner by which each of these impediments manifests itself and developing effective measures to overcome them are crucial elements of any strategy to promote housing and property restitution, and thereby facilitate the right to return to one's home.

44. One of the key impediments to housing restitution, and thus the right to return, is the absence of effective and accessible judicial remedies, which severely limits the utility of pursuing judicially-based solutions as a means of restoring rights to housing and property. This is particularly the case in post-conflict situations and severely limits the utility of pursuing judicially-based solutions as a means of restoring rights to housing and property.

45. One interim solution to this impediment is the establishment of ad hoc independent housing and property commissions designed to promote the right to housing and property restitution. The Commission on Real Property Claims in Bosnia and Herzegovina[51] and the Housing and Property Directorate in Kosovo[52] provide examples of how the lack of independent local judicial systems can be overcome.

46. Secondary occupation of displaced persons' homes is another impediment to return. Indeed, the problem of secondary occupation continues to severely hamper return efforts in Bosnia and

Herzegovina, Croatia, Kosovo, Georgia, Azerbaijan, Armenia, Rwanda, Bhutan and elsewhere.[53]

47. In many cases, secondary occupation is enforced, encouraged and/or facilitated by the forces that caused the initial displacement, and the secondary occupiers themselves may have had little or no choice in relocating to the housing in question. In other circumstances, the empty housing may have been utilized for legitimate humanitarian purposes, for example housing other displaced persons. It is, thus, often innocent persons, acting in good faith, who occupy homes belonging to refugees or other displaced persons.

48. Reversing this particular obstacle to restitution has proven very difficult unless adequate measures are taken to ensure that current occupants will be protected against homelessness or unreasonable relocation. Secondary occupation thus creates challenges to housing restitution that require a coherent policy response, based on human rights and other legal principles which clearly recognize the pre-eminence of the right to housing and property restitution of legitimate title holders. A thorough examination and analysis of existing and potential policies designed to address secondary occupation should thus be part of a comprehensive study of housing and property restitution for refugees and displaced persons.

49. Abandonment laws pose yet another impediment to the right to return. Such laws and policies, by which persons who vacate their housing for a certain period are deemed to have voluntarily relinquished their housing and property rights, have often been employed against refugees and displaced persons. The cases arising out of the former Republic of Yugoslavia provide some examples.

50. Abandonment laws are often used to punish displaced persons for fleeing and may also be used to facilitate and entrench policies of ethnic cleansing or demographic manipulation. They are also responsible for much of the lack of confidence displaced persons may feel with respect to their ability realistically to return home in safety.

51. Such laws not only impede the right to return, but often violate the principles of non-discrimination and equality, as they usually apply to or are enforced against specific racial, ethnic, religious or other groups.

52. Similarly, failing to rectify discriminatory, arbitrary or otherwise unjust application of law in countries of return contributes to preventing successful measures of restitution and even to future instability and conflict. In Georgia, for example, the legacy of discriminatory application of the 1983 Housing Code against Ossetians who fled their homes during the 1990–1992 conflict prevented large-scale return for several years. Likewise, the application in Kosovo of the Law on Changes and Supplements to the Limitations on Real Estate Transactions, as well as the persistent discrimination directed against the Albanian population of Kosovo, resulted in the arbitrary annulment of housing and occupancy rights, thus complicating the restitution process.

53. Yet another impediment is created by the practice of intentionally destroying property registration and other official records giving proof of ownership or occupancy rights, which often accompanies forced displacement, particularly in the context of ethnic cleansing. The existence of such records, combined with rights to access them, facilitates the return process by enhancing successful housing restitution.

54. Additionally, potential returnees have alleged that they were forced to conclude sale or rental contracts under duress at the time of flight, and are thus unable to return to their homes. Such claims may or may not be true and proving them is often difficult. Mechanisms need to be developed in order to determine to the maximum possible extent which assertions of duress are true and which are false.

55. The impediments to return identified above require comprehensive examination. Likewise, there is a need to identify additional impediments to return, to analyse the particular manner in which individual impediments manifest themselves and to develop effective measures to overcome them.

56. Finally, the issue of compensation in lieu of restitution requires detailed examination. Some initial comments, however, can be made with respect to this issue.

57. The overwhelming consensus regarding the remedies of restitution and compensation is that compensation should not be seen as an alternative to restitution and should only be used when restitution is not factually possible or when the injured party knowingly and voluntarily accepts compensation in lieu of restitution. For example, an injured party should receive compensation to remedy the wrongful dispossession of housing only

if that particular housing no longer exists or if the injured party knowingly and voluntarily decides it is in her or his interest not to return to her or his home.

58. In its General Recommendation XXIII on indigenous peoples, CERD affirmed such a formulation in the context of indigenous land and resources, calling upon States parties to the Convention: "[T]o recognize and protect the rights of indigenous peoples to own, develop, control and use their communal lands, territories and resources and, where they have been deprived of their lands and territories traditionally owned or otherwise inhabited or used without their free and informed consent, to take steps to return those lands and territories. Only when this is for factual reasons not possible, the right to restitution should be substituted by the rights to just, fair and prompt compensation."[54]

59. CERD thereby affirmed that restitution must be impracticable for factual, rather than simply legal or political, reasons. This requirement is important as many claims for restitution are wrongfully, even unlawfully, denied on the basis of legal regimes imposed upon the indigenous peoples by the occupying power. The "factually impracticable" requirement shifts the balance of the analysis away from legal or political obfuscation to the concrete question of whether lands can, in fact, be returned.[55] A lack of legal or political will cannot, therefore, be an excuse to favour compensation over restitution.

VI. CONCLUSIONS

60. The right of return encompasses not merely returning to one's country, but to one's home and lands as well. Furthermore, the right to return to one's home and lands is a necessary element to facilitate the right to return and, indeed, is a freestanding, autonomous right.

61. The international community has correctly recognized housing restitution to be an essential element of the right to return to one's home of refugees and displaced persons and as a necessary component of any lasting solution involving the voluntary, safe, dignified and durable repatriation of refugees and displaced persons. Indeed, housing restitution is an indispensable component of any strategy aimed at promoting, protecting and implementing the right to return.

62. In most circumstances, the conditions for safe and dignified return will not and cannot be met without adequate safeguards and mechanisms designed to protect and fulfil the right to return to one's home in safety and dignity.

63. Such safeguards and mechanisms should include effective and expeditious legal, administrative and other procedures to ensure the free and fair exercise of the right to return to one's home, including fair and effective mechanisms designed to resolve outstanding housing and property problems and thereby facilitate housing and property restitution.

64. The problems associated with housing and property restitution for displaced persons wishing to return to their homes are emerging as some of the key dilemmas facing policy- and law-makers in countries of return, and for which there is only limited legislative and precedent-creating guidance. While considerable progress has been made in terms of institutional development in support of restitution, the actual implementation of housing and property restitution has lagged far behind.

65. The success of repatriation programmes can be maximized when housing-based impediments to return are clearly identified through consistent, principled and pre-emptive strategies aimed at overcoming these all-too-common barriers to restitution. Treating housing and property restitution as a fundamental core element of any repatriation process, as well as exhibiting the will and devoting the necessary resources to securing this right, will greatly strengthen the likelihood of return becoming a process which promotes and realizes the housing rights of returnees, thus ensuring that return is safe, dignified and durable.

66. The adoption or application by States of laws which are designed to facilitate, or otherwise result in, the loss or removal of tenancy, use, ownership or other rights connected with housing or property; the active retraction of the right to reside in a particular place; or laws of abandonment employed against refugees or other displaced persons pose serious impediments to the return and reintegration of refugees and displaced persons, as well as to reconstruction and reconciliation.

67. International law recognizes that the remedy of compensation should only be used when restitution is impossible in fact, or when the injured party

knowingly and voluntarily accepts compensation in lieu of restitution.

VII. RECOMMENDATION

68. The Sub-Commission should request, through the Commission on Human Rights, that the Economic and Social Council authorize the Sub-Commission to undertake a comprehensive study on housing and property restitution in the context of the return of refugees and displaced persons.

ENDNOTES

1. A/51/482 (11 October 1996), para. 53.

2. See CERD/C/SR.1189 (8 March 1997).

3. For the complete list of topics proposed to the Sub-Commission, see E/CN.4/Sub.2/1997/31, annex.

4. Ibid.

5. Ibid.

6. Housing rights are enshrined in numerous instruments. For instance, the Universal Declaration of Human Rights (art. 25) and the International Covenant on Economic, Social and Cultural Rights (art. 11.1) both guarantee the right to adequate housing. Additionally, the International Covenant on Civil and Political Rights protects persons from arbitrary or unlawful interference with their home (art. 17.1); the International Convention on the Elimination of All Forms of Racial Discrimination prohibits discrimination on account of race, colour, or national or ethnic origin with respect to the right to housing (art. 5(e)(iii)); the Convention on the Elimination of All Forms of Discrimination against Women obliges States parties to "condemn discrimination against women in all its forms" and, specifically, to eliminate discrimination against women in rural areas in order to ensure that such women enjoy adequate living conditions, particularly in relation to housing (arts. 2 and 14.2 (h)); the Convention on the Rights of the Child obliges States parties to provide, in cases of need, material assistance and support programmes to families and children, particularly with regard to housing (art. 27.3); and the International Convention on the Protection of the Rights of All Migrant Workers and Members of Their Families provides that "[m]igrant workers shall enjoy equality of treatment with nationals of the State of employment in relation to ... (d) [a]ccess to housing, including social housing schemes, and protection against exploitation in respect to rents" (art. 43.1(d)). Other international instruments guaranteeing housing rights include various International Labour Organization conventions, humanitarian law instruments and the Convention relating to the Status of Refugees.

7. See also UNHCR EXCOM Conclusion No. 56 (XL)-1989, "Durable solutions and refugee protection" (13 October 1989).

8. UNHCR EXCOM Conclusion No. 18 (XXXI)-1980, "Voluntary repatriation", para. 48 (3) (f), United Nations document A/AC.96/588 (16 October 1980).

9. UNHCR EXCOM Conclusion No. 40 (XXXVI)-1985, "Voluntary repatriation", paras. (a) and (b) (18 October 1985).

10. UNHCR, Handbook on Voluntary Repatriation, Geneva, UNHCR (1996).

11. See, ibid., annexes 5 and 6.

12. See UNHCR Global Consultations on International Protection, "Voluntary repatriation", EC/GC/02/5 (25 April 2002), para. 23.

13. See, e.g., Security Council resolutions 1287 (2000) (reaffirming the right of all refugees and displaced persons ... to return to their homes in secure conditions), 1244 (1999) (reaffirming the right of all refugees and displaced persons to return to their homes in safety), 1199 (1998) (reaffirming the right of all refugees and displaced persons to return to their homes in safety), 1036 (1996) (reaffirming the right of all refugees and displaced persons ... to return to their homes in secure conditions), 971 (1995) (reaffirming the right of all refugees and displaced persons ... to return to their homes in secure conditions), 876 (1993) (affirming the right of refugees and displaced persons to return to their homes), 820 (1993) (reaffirming ... that all displaced persons have the right to return in peace to their former homes and should be assisted in doing so); General Assembly resolutions 51/126 (reaffirming the right of all persons displaced ... to return to their homes or former places of residence), 35/124 (reaffirming the right of refugees to return to their homes in their homelands); Sub-Commission on the Prevention of Discrimination and Protection of Minorities resolutions 1998/26 (reaffirming the right of all refugees ... and internally displaced persons to return to their homes and places of habitual residence in their country and/or place of origin), 1994/24 (affirming the right of refugees and displaced persons to return, in safety and dignity, to their country and/or within it, to their place of origin or choice); Committee on the Elimination of Racial Discrimination, General Recommendation XXII on refugees and displaced persons, (forty-ninth session) (A/51/18) (reaffirming that all ... refugees and displaced persons have the right freely to return to their homes of origin under conditions of safety).

14. See Security Council resolutions 1287 (2000), 1036 (1996), 971 (1995) and 876 (1993).

15. See Security Council resolution 853 (1993).

16. See Security Council resolution 752 (1992).

17. See Security Council resolution 745 (1992).

18. See Security Council resolution 1009 (1995).

19. See Security Council resolution 361 (1974).

20. See Security Council resolutions 1244 (1999) and 1199 (1998).

21. See Security Council resolution 687 (1991).

22. See Security Council resolution 385 (1976).

23. See Security Council resolution 999 (1995).

24. General Assembly resolution 1672 (XVI).

25. General Assembly resolution 3212 (XXIX).

26. General Assembly resolutions 51/126 and 194 (III).

27. General Assembly resolution 51/114.

28. Committee on the Elimination of Racial Discrimination, General Recommendation XXII on article 5 and refugees and displaced persons (forty-ninth session), A/51/18 (1996).

29. World Conference against Racism, Racial Discrimination, Xenophobia and Related Intolerance, Declaration, para. 65.

30. See Scott Leckie, "Housing and property issues for refugees and internally displaced persons in the context of return: key considerations for UNHCR policy and practice", in Refugee Survey Quarterly, vol. 19, No. 3, Geneva, UNHCR (2000).

31. World Conference against Racism, Racial Discrimination, Xenophobia and Related Intolerance, Declaration, para. 65.

32. See Commission on Human Rights resolution 1993/77, para. 1.

33. See, e.g., Commission on Human Rights resolutions 2000/41 and 1999/33. Although resolution 1993/77 uses the term "gross" violation while resolution 1999/33 and 2000/41 use "grave" violation, the two terms are in practice synonymous. The draft "Basic principles and guidelines on the right to a remedy and reparation for victims of violations of international human rights and humanitarian law, to which resolutions 1999/33 and 2000/41 refer, apply to "gross violations of international human rights".

34. General Assembly resolution 56/83, annex.

35. Committee on the Elimination of Racial Discrimination, General Recommendation XXII on article 5 and refugees and displaced persons (forty-ninth session), A/51/18 (1996), annex VIII.C, para. 2 (d).

36. See General Framework Agreement for Peace in Bosnia and Herzegovina, Annex 7, Agreement on Refugees and Displaced Persons.

37. See Agreements on a Comprehensive Political Settlement of the Cambodia Conflict (1991).

38. See Agreement on Identity and Rights of Indigenous Peoples (Guatemala Peace Accords) (31 March 1995); Agreement on Resettlement of the Population Groups Uprooted by the Armed Conflict (17 June 1994).

39. See United Nations Interim Administration in Kosovo (UNMIK) Regulation No. 1999/23 (on the establishment of the Housing and Property Directorate and the Housing and Property Claims Commission) (15 November 1999).

40. See General Peace Agreement (4 October 1992), Protocol III, Section IV; Tripartite Agreement between the Government of the Republic of Mozambique, the Government of Zimbabwe and UNHCR for the Voluntary Repatriation of Mozambican Refugees from Zimbabwe (1993).

41. See Arusha Peace Agreement (August 1993).

42. See Law on the Cessation of the Application of the Law on Temporarily Abandoned Real Property Owned by Citizens (3 April 1998) (Federation of Bosnia and Herzegovina); Law on the Cessation of the Application of the Law on Abandoned Apartments (1998) (Federation of Bosnia and Herzegovina); Law on the Taking Over of the Law on Housing Relations (Federation of Bosnia and Herzegovina); Law Amending the Law on the Sale of Apartments with Occupancy Rights (6 December 1997) (Federation of Bosnia and Herzegovina); Law on the Cessation of the Application of the Law on the Use of Abandoned Property (2 December 1998) (Republika Srpska), in their amended forms.

43. See Restitution on Ownership of Nationalized Real Property Act of 1992.

44. See Law No. 116/1994 Coll.; Law No. 87/1991 Coll.

45. See Law on the Fundamentals of Ownership Reform of 1991, as amended in 1993; Land Reform Act of 1991, as amended in 1993.

46. See Federal Restitution Law of 1957; German Act Regulating Unresolved Property of 1990.

47. See Ministerial Order No. 01/96 of 23 September 1996 Regarding the Temporary Management of Land Property.

48. See Denationalization Law (1991, as amended 1998).

49. See Constitution of the Republic of South Africa, art. 25 (1996); Restitution of Land Rights Act 22 of 1994.

50. See Special Law on the Return of Illegally Occupied Houses; Law of the Republic of Tajikistan on Forced Migrants (20 July 1994); Resolution No. 542 of 22 August 1995 on Additional Measures Facilitating the Return of Refugees-Citizens of the Republic of Tajikistan and Forced Migrants to the Places of Permanent Residence and Their Social and Legal Protection.

51. See Annex 7, Chapter II of the General Framework Agreement for Peace in Bosnia and Herzegovina (14 December 1995).

52. See UNMIK Regulation No. 1999/23 (on the establishing of the Housing and Property Directorate and the Housing and Property Claims Commission) (15 November 1999).

53. UNHCR, UNHCR's Operational Experience with Internally Displaced Persons: A Preliminary Review, p. 9,

Geneva, UNHCR, Division of International Protection (1994).

54. Committee on the Elimination of Racial Discrimination, General Recommendation XXIII on the rights of indigenous peoples (fifty-first session), A/52/18, annex V, para. 5 (1997).

55. Bret Thiele, "Enforcing the right to restitution: legal strategies for indigenous peoples and the role of international law", in *Housing and Property Restitution: A Comparative Study* (Scott Leckie, ed.), New York, Transnational Publishers (2002).

8.8. Resolution 2002/7 – Housing and Property Restitution in the Context of Refugees and Other Displaced Persons (2002)[130]

The Sub-Commission on the Promotion and Protection of Human Rights,

Guided by the principles embodied in the Charter of the United Nations, the Universal Declaration of Human Rights, the International Covenants on Human Rights, the 1951 Convention relating to the Status of Refugees and its 1967 Protocol, and other relevant international instruments on human rights and humanitarian law,

Recalling Commission on Human Rights resolutions 1996/25 of 19 April 1996, 1997/22 of 11 April 1997 and 1998/26 of 17 April 1998 and resolution 1998/28 of 17 April 1998, in which the Commission called upon the Sub-Commission and its members to further enhance cooperation with mechanisms of the Commission and, within their competence, with all relevant bodies, including human rights treaty bodies; Commission resolution 1999/81 of 28 April 1999, in which the Commission welcomed the Sub-Commission's efforts to enhance such cooperation; and Commission resolution 2002/66 of 25 April 2002, in which it reaffirmed that the Sub-Commission could best assist the Commission by providing it with independent expert studies carried out by its members or alternates,

Recalling also Commission on Human Rights resolution 1999/47 of 27 April 1999, in which the Commission encouraged the Sub-Commission to continue its work on the matter of housing and property restitution in the context of the return of refugees and internally displaced persons,

[130] 14 August 2002.

Recalling further that the Committee on the Elimination of Racial Discrimination, at it fiftieth session, decided to propose to the Sub-Commission nine topics for the preparation of studies, including on the return of refugees' or displaced persons' property,

Welcoming the developing cooperation between the Committee on the Elimination of Racial Discrimination and the Sub-Commission on this and other topics of mutual interest,

Recalling Sub-Commission decision 2001/122 of 16 August 2001 on the return of refugees' or displaced persons' property,

1. *Takes note* of the working paper submitted by Mr. Paulo Sérgio Pinheiro on the return of refugees' or displaced persons' property (E/CN.4/Sub.2/2002/17) and endorses the conclusions and recommendation contained therein;

2. *Reaffirms* its resolution 1998/26 of 26 August 1998 on housing and property restitution in the context of the return of refugees and internally displaced persons;

3. *Urges* all States to ensure the free and fair exercise of the right to return to one's home and place of habitual residence by all refugees and internally displaced persons and to develop effective and expeditious legal, administrative and other procedures to ensure the free and fair exercise of this right, including fair and effective mechanisms designed to resolve outstanding housing and property problems;

4. *Reiterates* that the adoption or application of laws by States which are designed to or result in the loss or removal of tenancy, use, ownership or other rights connected with housing or property, the retraction of the right to reside in a particular place, or laws of abandonment employed against refugees or internally displaced persons pose serious impediments to the return and reintegration of refugees and internally displaced persons and to reconstruction and reconciliation;

5. *Affirms* that the remedy of compensation should only be used when the remedy of restitution is not possible or when the injured party knowingly and voluntarily accepts compensation in lieu of restitution;

6. *Decides* to appoint Mr. Paulo Sérgio Pinheiro as Special Rapporteur with the task of preparing a comprehensive study on housing and property

restitution in the context of the return of refugees and internally displaced persons based on his working paper as well as on the comments made and the discussions that took place at the fifty-fourth session of the Sub-Commission and the fifty-eighth session of the Commission;

7. *Requests* the Special Rapporteur to seek the advice and cooperation of the Committee on the Elimination of Racial Discrimination in carrying out his mandate;

8. *Also requests* the Special Rapporteur to submit a preliminary report to the Sub-Commission at its fifty-fifth session, a progress report at its fifty-sixth session and a final report at its fifty-seventh session;

[. . .]

8.9. Resolution 2002/30 – The Right to Return of Refugees and Internally Displaced Persons (2002)[131]

The Sub-Commission on the Promotion and Protection of Human Rights,

Recalling Sub-Commission resolutions 1994/24 of 26 August 1994 and 1998/26 of 26 August 1998, and Commission resolutions 1999/47 of 27 April 1999, 2000/53 of 25 April 2000 and 2001/54 of 24 April 2001,

Conscious that serious human rights violations and breaches of international humanitarian law are among the reasons why people flee their homes or places of habitual residence and become refugees or internally displaced persons,

Noting that millions of refugees and displaced persons remain in need of solutions and that voluntary return remains the durable solution sought by the largest number of them,

Concerned that the lack of progress with respect to voluntary repatriation reflects the fact that basic requirements for return, that is, physical, legal and material safety and the restoration of national protection, are not yet in place,

Recognizing that the right of refugees and internally displaced persons to return freely to their original homes or places of habitual residence in safety and dignity coupled with their right to adequate housing and property restitution or, should this

not be possible, just compensation or another form of just reparation, form indispensable elements of national reintegration, reconstruction and reconciliation, and that the recognition of such rights, as well as judicial or other mechanisms to ensure the implementation of such rights, should be included in peace agreements ending armed conflicts,

Recognizing also the right of all returnees to the free exercise of their right to freedom of movement and to choose their residence, including the right to re-establish residence in their original homes or places of habitual residence, including issuance of relevant documentation, their right to privacy and respect for the home, their right to reside peacefully in the security of their own home and their right to enjoy access to all necessary social and economic services, in an environment free of any form of discrimination,

Noting that the right to freedom of movement and the right to adequate housing and property restitution include the right of protection for returning refugees and internally displaced persons against being compelled to return to their original homes or places of habitual residence and that the right to return to their original homes or places of habitual residence must be exercised in a voluntary, safe and dignified manner,

Observing that, in the present resolution, "those displaced" and "displaced persons" refer to both refugees and internally displaced persons, unless otherwise indicated, and that nothing in the present resolution affects any disputes with regard to title to territory,

1. *Confirms* that all those displaced have the right to return voluntarily in safety and dignity, as established in international human rights law;

2. *Also confirms* that all displaced persons have a right to return to their original homes or places of habitual residence or to settle voluntarily elsewhere; where authorities send displaced persons to a place other than their habitual residence, this does not affect their right to return to their place of habitual residence, nor their right to restitution or compensation or both;

3. *Reaffirms* that all those displaced have the right to adequate housing and property restitution or, should this not be possible, appropriate compensation or another form of just reparation, and the particular importance of these rights for displaced

[131] 5 August 2002.

persons wishing to return to their original homes or places of habitual residence;

4. *Urges* all parties to peace agreements and voluntary repatriation agreements to include implementation of the right to return in safety and dignity, as well as housing and property restitution rights, consistent with the requirements of international law, in all such agreements;

5. *Confirms* that the exercise of the right to return is voluntary and not conditional upon permission or approval; if documentation of any sort is necessary, returnees are entitled to such documentation as of right and free of cost;

6. *Reminds* States of the right of all displaced persons to participate in the return and restitution process and in the development of the procedures and mechanisms put in place to protect these rights;

7. *Urges* all States to guarantee the free and fair exercise of the right to return to one's home or place of habitual residence by all displaced persons and to establish an enabling framework to enable return to take place in conditions of physical, legal and material safety and to restore full national protection of returning displaced persons; in this context, States are urged to take measures to ensure the physical safety of returnees; to remove legal and administrative barriers to return and to provide other legal guarantees for returnees; and to ensure non-discriminatory access to means of survival and basic services;

8. *Confirms* that the obligation of the State to assist the right of return includes an obligation, without which the right to return cannot be fulfilled, to make good any damage for which the authorities are responsible, including the obligation to restore the infrastructure, including water, sanitation, electricity, gas, roads and land, where it has been damaged or destroyed; in particular, States shall not charge returning displaced persons with the costs for services consumed by those who were temporarily accommodated in the displaced persons' homes;

9. *Reaffirms* the obligation of States to repeal any laws and regulations which are inconsistent with international legal standards, in particular the right to return and the right to adequate housing and property, and in this respect urges States to put in place effective and impartial mechanisms designed to resolve outstanding housing and property problems;

10. *Reminds* States of the need to ensure, in implementing the right to return, that measures are taken to address the special needs of women and children, including effective and equitable access to means of survival and basic services, including education, and the effective implementation of the right of women to full equality with respect to housing and property restitution, in particular in terms of access, control, ownership, possessory and inheritance rights;

11. *Confirms* that where displaced persons voluntarily settle elsewhere, this does not affect their right to return to their home or place of habitual residence, nor their right to housing and property restitution or, should this not be possible, just compensation or other form of just reparation;

12. *Recognizes* that displaced persons may choose voluntarily to exchange their property rights over their original homes or places of habitual residence for the same or similar rights over another property or undertake other possible transactions, on condition that such decisions are knowingly and voluntarily taken;

13. *Also recognizes* that property restitution processes are only effective if the rights of occupants of displaced persons' houses, who themselves are equally affected by displacement and in need of accommodation, are protected, and urges States to provide adequate alternative accommodation; where secondary occupants have no place to return to, States are encouraged to provide affordable social housing;

14. *Urges* States where secondary occupants are in possession of the homes of displaced persons as a result of criminal action to enforce their own laws and to ensure that displaced persons have the possibility to return in safety;

15. *Encourages* States to seek, through appropriate means, to cooperate with the Office of the United Nations High Commissioner for Refugees with regard to matters concerning refugees and, where appropriate, to internally displaced persons and with all other humanitarian organizations and other appropriate actors, in the exercise of their respective mandates, and to ensure rapid and unimpeded access to displaced persons in order to

assist in their voluntary return or voluntary relocation and reintegration;

[. . .]

8.10. Housing and Property Restitution in the Context of the Return of Refugees and Internally Displaced Persons – Preliminary Report of the Special Rapporteur, Paulo Sérgio Pinheiro (2003)[132]

INTRODUCTION

1. At its fifty-fourth session, the Sub-Commission
on the Promotion and Protection of Human Rights,
in its resolution 2002/7, decided to entrust Paulo
Sérgio Pinheiro with the task of preparing a comprehensive study on housing and property restitution in the context of the return of refugees
and internally displaced persons based on his
working paper (E/CN.4/Sub.2/2002/17) as well as
on the comments made and the discussions that
took place at the fifty-fourth session of the Sub-
Commission and the fifty-eighth session of the
Commission on Human Rights. At its fifty-ninth
session, in its decision 2003/109, the Commission
endorsed the decision of the Sub-Commission.

2. This preliminary report is hereby submitted
in accordance with Sub-Commission resolution
2002/7 and Commission decision 2003/109.

3. The Special Rapporteur would like to thank the
Centre on Housing Rights and Evictions (COHRE)
for its assistance with the preparation of this report.

I. TERMINOLOGY

4. For the purpose of this working paper, the
phrase "housing and property" refers to housing
and real property, including land. This definition
is used for two key reasons. First, housing and real
property restitution in the context of the right to
return of refugees and other displaced persons has
deservedly received a great deal of attention by
the international community, more so than other
types of property restitution. This attention is due
in large part to the unique role that housing and
real property restitution play in securing the voluntary, safe and dignified return of refugees and

other displaced persons to their homes and places
of original residence.

5. Second, housing rights are enshrined in international human rights and humanitarian law to a
far greater degree and encompass far more under
international law, substantively speaking, than do
property rights more generally.[1] The right to adequate housing is enshrined in several international
human rights instruments.[2] Indeed, housing rights
are not a new development within the human rights
field, but rather have long been regarded as essential to ensure the well-being and dignity of the
human person.[3] Accordingly, the main focus of this
working paper is on issues relating to housing and
real property restitution, including, in this case, the
restitution of land.

6. The practice of "forced evictions",[4] namely the
permanent or temporary removal against their will
of individuals, families and/or communities from
the homes and/or land which they occupy, without
the provision of, and access to, appropriate forms
of legal or other protection, is a phenomenon also
reflected in this report. Forced evictions are a particular type of displacement which are most often
characterized or accompanied by: (i) a relation to
specific decisions, legislation or policies of States or
the failure of States to intervene to halt evictions by
non-State actors; (ii) an element of force or coercion; and (iii) are often planned, formulated and
announced prior to being carried out. The Commission on Human Rights has affirmed "that the
practice of forced eviction constitutes a gross violation of human rights, in particular the right to
adequate housing".[5]

7. The "Basic Principles and Guidelines on the
Right to a Remedy and Reparation for Victims of Violations of International Human Rights
and Humanitarian Law" (E/CN.4/2000/62, annex)
(hereinafter "The Basic Principles and Guidelines")
note that victims of violations of international
human rights and humanitarian law, such as victims of forced eviction, have a right to a remedy.
The right to a remedy includes, inter alia, reparation for harm suffered.

8. Restitution is a particular form of reparation.
The term "restitution" refers to an equitable remedy, or a form of restorative justice, by which persons who suffer loss or injury are returned as far
as possible to their original pre-loss or pre-injury
position (i.e. status quo ante). Restitution includes:

---

[132] UN Doc. E/CN.4/Sub.2/2003/11.

restoration of liberty, legal rights, social status, family life and citizenship; return to one's place of residence; and restoration of employment and return of property (ibid.).

9. In this study, restitution refers specifically to the return of arbitrarily or illegally confiscated housing or property to the original owner(s) or rightholders. While there can be no dispute that housing and property restitution is a right of displaced persons and refugees under international human rights law, essential to the realization of the right to return, it must likewise be recognized as integral to the larger goals of peace-building and post-conflict resolution, essential for the creation of durable remedies to situations of displacement and conflict.

10. Compensation is a specific form of reparation. The term "compensation" refers to a legal remedy by which a person receives monetary payment for harm suffered. When appropriate, compensation may be given in lieu of restitution, for example, when it is either in fact impossible or impracticable to restore the person's property or house. Monetary compensation should, however, be seen as a last resort, and when used as a measure of restorative justice must be adequate, fair and just.

11. While the mandate given to the Special Rapporteur refers to "refugees and internationally displaced persons", it should be noted that the issues, norms and standards regarding housing and property restitution pertain to similarly situated persons as well. The phrase "refugees and internally displaced persons" unfortunately overlooks those persons displaced across borders, for example due to conflict or disaster, who may not meet the legal definition of a refugee under international law. Because such populations have the rights to housing and property restitution as do refugees and IDPs, this report utilizes the language "refugees and other displaced persons".

II. Past Situations Involving Housing and Property Restitution

12. Throughout the world, housing and property restitution programmes have represented a dramatic advance in the actual implementation of human rights norms. Literally hundreds of thousands of persons have been successfully returned to their original position after having been arbi-

trarily deprived of housing, land and other property. The development of the work of various United Nations organs in the area of housing and property restitution also represents a unique convergence between international human rights law, international humanitarian law and local-level implementation. This bridge between macro-level standards and micro-level implementation programmes holds great promise not only for the promotion, but also the realization, of human rights.

13. This preliminary study presents an overview of selected housing and property restitution programmes which were instituted in several countries as a result of internal conflict and mass displacement. The comparative aspect of this review has three main advantages: (i) it provides a foundation on which to distil general findings and observations regarding the effectiveness of housing and property restitution programmes; (ii) it provides insights into the common problems and obstacles faced by these programmes when implemented; and (iii) it helps establish a basis for future policymaking in the area of housing and property restitution. By identifying best practices, and identifying some of the more common obstacles to restitution, this study hopes to clarify some of the more difficult practical issues surrounding housing and property restitution.

A. Croatia

14. Croatia's declaration of independence in June 1991 saw the beginning of a major military offensive by rebel Serb forces. With the support of the Yugoslav People's Army (JNA), the Serb forces gained control over parts of Western Slavonia and Eastern Slavonia and eventually declared the unified territory to be a single State, the "Republika Srpska Krajina". Armed conflict in Eastern Slavonia in 1991 led to the expulsion of over 80,000 ethnic Croats from the region.

15. Once the JNA withdrew in 1992, a peace plan was agreed upon under the auspices of the United Nations, and United Nations peacekeepers deployed in the areas under Serb control (the United Nations Protection Force, or UNPROFOR) were charged both with the protection of Serb civilians and with facilitating the return of displaced Croats.[6]

16. In early 1995, the Government of Croatia indicated that it was unwilling to permit further

extensions of the UNPROFOR mandate in Croatia.[7] A mission with a more limited mandate and reduced troop strength was therefore authorized in February 1995 by the Security Council, with the consent of the Government. Its deployment was effectively ended in May 1995, however, when the Croatian army launched an offensive against Serb-held territory in Western Slavonia (known as "Operation Flash"), recapturing the territory. A similar action in sectors North and South (known as "Operation Storm") in August 1995 recaptured the remaining areas outside Eastern Slavonia. According to international human rights organizations, the two operations caused the flight of more than 200,000 Serbs to Eastern Slavonia, Bosnia and elsewhere in Croatia, the single largest population displacement during the conflict in the former Yugoslavia.

In the case of Operation Storm, the exodus was accompanied by the killing of Serb civilians and widespread forced eviction and the destruction of Serb housing.[8]

17. As a means of maintaining the displacement of persons of Serbian descent, the Government of Croatia adopted abandonment legislation favouring persons of Croat ethnic origin. Pursuant to the Law on Renting Apartments in the Liberated Areas and the Law on Temporary Taking Over and Administration of Specified Property (LTTP), Croats who fled their homes during the fighting in the early 1990s were considered to have justified reasons for doing so, while the flight of other ethnic groups, including the Serbs, was characterized as "voluntary", thus effectively denying them the remedy of restitution.[9] This legislation also applied to Croats, but it was in fact not applied in areas where Croats left following Serb aggression.

18. Furthermore, under the Croatian restitution programme, only owners of private property, and Croatian citizens of Croatian ethnicity, were entitled to benefit from measures of restitution. These restrictions, particularly in a country with a history of social housing, served to restrict severely the scope of restitution, thus compromising the ability of the restitution process to contribute to post-conflict peace-building in any meaningful way. The national housing commissions which were established to deal with the complicated process of restitution, and upon which a successful return programme hinged, unfortunately failed to function properly. In fact, in many cases, these housing commissions appear to have actually prevented the return of property to members of non-Croatian groups.

19. In December 2001, the Government presented an action plan for the repossession of property affected by LTTP by the end of 2002. As of today, a substantial number of properties remain occupied because, even though legislative reforms took place, the provision of alternative accommodation for the tenants before repossession can take place has been retained, a stand that negatively affects Serb owners.

20. The slow and restricted return of displaced Serbs to their homes and habitual residences in Croatia severely compromises the restitution process. Of the estimated 300,000 Croatian Serbs displaced during the conflict, only 80,000 have returned to their pre-war places of residence.[10] The Croatian case reveals the importance of integrating appropriate restitution laws within the legal structure of the State in a manner which is non-discriminatory. This case also highlights the importance of having capable institutions ready to facilitate return and restitution in a prompt manner which is consistent with human rights norms and standards, including those related to non-discrimination.

B. Bosnia and Herzegovina

21. Between 1992 and 1995, approximately half of Bosnia and Herzegovina's population was displaced. In total, some 2.2 million persons were forced to leave their homes. Approximately 1 million persons fled across borders, approximately half of whom fled to other republics of the former Yugoslavia, while approximately 1 million others became internally displaced. During the conflict, the different parties passed abandonment laws, a necessary response to the humanitarian crisis resulting from the conflict. The application of these laws was, however, discriminatory. In addition, the authorities used the "six-month vacancy" rule under the Law on Housing Relations to strip refugees and displaced persons of their occupancy rights.

22. Legislation adopted by the Entity authorities after the signing of the general framework agreement for peace in Bosnia and Herzegovina (Dayton Peace Accords) covered property restitution,

but in very restrictive terms. The Republika Srpska 1996 Law on Use of Abandoned Property included provisions regarding return of property, but they were impossible to fulfil. In the Federation of Bosnia and Herzegovina, a law was passed requiring persons to reclaim and reoccupy their socially owned apartments by January 1996. If persons failed to do so, their apartments could be declared "permanently abandoned" and allocated to other persons on a permanent basis. These laws served to block the return of tens of thousands of refugees and displaced persons to their pre-conflict homes.

23. In summary, many refugees and displaced persons were forced to transfer legal title of their original properties to municipal authorities or allocation right-holders, and many others lost documents during the course of their flight. As occurred very often during the conflict, those who fled their original homes but who did not flee across borders many times took up residence in another's abandoned house or flat. Such persons are known as "secondary occupiers".

24. Therefore, one of the formidable challenges of housing and property restitution in the context of the conflict in Bosnia and Herzegovina was to establish a fair and efficient property restitution framework in compliance with international and regional standards and to determine the rightful owners or right-holders of disputed properties.

25. Annex 7 to the Dayton Peace Accords, the agreement on refugees and displaced persons, established principles which are of fundamental importance to this discussion insofar as these principles delineate rights to housing and property restitution. As a notable contribution, this framework also recognized the rights of all displaced persons to housing and property restitution. Article 1 (1) of annex 7 states:

"All [r]efugees and displaced persons have the right freely to return to their homes of origin. They shall have the right to have restored to them property of which they were deprived in the course of hostilities since 1991 and to be compensated for any property that cannot be restored to them . . ."

26. International pressure, drawing on the Dayton Peace Accords and international and regional human rights treaties, eventually persuaded the Entity authorities to repeal the abandonment

laws in 1998, although the legislation passed still had flaws. Consequently, the High Representative imposed amendments to the property laws in both Entities to ensure that throughout Bosnia and Herzegovina a fair and consistent legal framework existed which would allow for the full implementation of annex 7. These efforts were complemented by the Property Law Implementation Plan (PLIP). PLIP developed from collaborative relationships between the Office of the High Representative in Bosnia and Herzegovina (OHR), the Office of the United Nations High Commissioner for Refugees (UNHCR), the Organization for Security and Cooperation in Europe (OSCE), the United Nations Mission in Bosnia and Herzegovina (UNMIBH) and the national Commission on Real Property Claims (CRPC). While property law implementation is a fundamental first step to restitution, these agencies have acknowledged that it is only one among many of the elements underpinning sustainable return.[11] Full implementation of annex 7 requires not only that people can return to their homes, but that they can do so safely with equal expectations of employment, education and social services.

27. CRPC, also created by the Dayton Peace Accords, was given the difficult task of processing the tens of thousands of contentious property restitution claims which eventually came forward. While CRPC worked to ensure the most orderly return process, property restitution remained fraught with difficulties at all stages.

28. One of the foremost difficulties encountered by CRPC was local resistance to implementing its decisions, especially when these decisions involved the eviction of secondary occupiers in order to facilitate minority return. Lack of adequate enforcement mechanisms compromised the effectiveness of the restitution programme and undercut the authority of CRPC. Lengthy delays in claim-processing procedures, lack of adequate enforcement mechanisms and an excessively limited mandate all served to erode the practical effectiveness and legitimacy of CRPC.

29. While the road to housing and property restitution in Bosnia and Herzegovina has been slow and arduous, there have been notable successes. In March 2003, the PLIP agencies (OHR, UNHCR, OSCE, CRPC) announced that the property law implementation reached 78 per cent throughout Bosnia and Herzegovina, and the return process

continues.[12] This important success underscores the importance of political will and strong organizations, at both national and international levels, which are necessary components of any effective restitution programme. Much can be learned from this experience regarding how best to implement housing and property restitution programmes in sensitive, and potentially unstable, post-conflict situations.

C. Rwanda

30. Rwanda faced similar problems associated with the return of refugees who fled as far back as 1959, many of whom returned to Rwanda in the mid-1990s. The genocide perpetrated against members of the Tutsi minority as well as against moderate Hutus left deep scars on the country, and brought to the forefront the irrefutable responsibility of the international community in preventing such violence. A considerable proportion of returning refugees to Rwanda, however, have not been able to return to their homes of origin because their houses were either destroyed during the genocide, or because their homes were subsequently occupied by others in the intervening period due to government relocation programmes.

31. While the Arusha Agreement and the accompanying Protocol on the repatriation of refugees and the resettlement of displaced persons[13] have proven difficult and slow to implement, they do provide important housing and land restitution rights to Rwandan refugees, provided they had not been out of the country for longer than 10 years. Those who had lived in exile for longer were, however, authorized to receive alternative lands and other assistance allowing them to resettle within the country. Nonetheless, the 10-year rule provides yet another example of how unjust policies often serve to deny certain persons their right to restitution, in this case through the imposition of arbitrary and discriminatory time limitations.

32. Like many countries struggling to implement restitution processes, the issue of secondary occupation has proven to be a volatile issue in Rwanda. National authorities attempted to ameliorate the conflicts surrounding secondary occupations by entrusting "abandoned land" to the municipalities, who were in turn empowered to administer and manage these lands. While secondary occupants were allowed to occupy temporarily abandoned lands, so long as they made a written request to do so, the original inhabitants maintained the right to immediate restitution should they return home. If an original inhabitant returned to find her or his home occupied by a secondary occupant, the secondary occupant was then given two months to vacate the premises voluntarily. If the secondary occupant was unable to find alternative accommodation within that time period, the Government was entrusted with finding her/him another home or providing building materials.

33. The Government of Rwanda established a ministerial committee to deal with property and land issues, designed to restrict the illegal occupation of homes, lands and properties. Yet, in practice, these restitution measures proved difficult to enforce and implement. Intimidation of lawful owners by some secondary occupants and the deliberate arrest of some returning refugees served to complicate matters further. On a positive note, however, restrictive Rwandan laws and traditions regarding inheritance by women created particular problems for returnee women who were seeking to regain access to their homes and land and whose husbands had died, disappeared, or remained behind in exile. This obstacle was removed through the 1999 Law on Matrimonial Regimes and Succession which now allows women to inherit the property of their husbands, while previously property had traditionally passed to the husband's heirs.

D. Georgia

34. Georgia has also dealt with extremely complex housing and property disputes related to the 1990–1992 conflict in South Ossetia. As a result of the conflict, housing and property disputes obstructed the safe and lasting return of over 53,000 refugees and IDPs.

35. Much of the housing originally registered to Georgian refugees and IDPs, particularly within urban areas, continued to be occupied by secondary occupants who were unwilling to vacate these premises voluntarily. Secondary occupation was often judicially sanctioned through biased application of a "six-month vacancy" rule under the 1983 Housing Code. This rule stipulated that a tenant could lose his or her right to reside in a given flat if they were absent for longer than six months without a "valid reason". On applying this rule, the courts often found that fleeing to escape

the conflict was not a valid reason to vacate one's home.

36. UNHCR, however, took the view that any application of this rule based upon any form of racial, ethnic or national origin or other forms of discrimination would be classified as both unreasonable and disproportionate, and thus a violation of international law.

37. In order to resolve these problems and promote voluntary repatriation, UNHCR supported a multifaceted strategy, emphasizing that both the rights of refugees and IDPs and the rights of secondary occupants must be ensured throughout all phases of the restitution process. The Government of Georgia was also instrumental to this process, and was urged by UNHCR to provide the legal framework required for large-scale return and to build a solid basis for national reconciliation.

E. Guatemala

38. In 1994, after a decades-long civil war which devastated Guatemala, the Government of Guatemala and the forces of the Unidad Revolucionaria Nacional Guatemalteca agreed through the Agreement on Resettlement of the Population Groups Uprooted by the Armed Conflict, signed in Oslo on 17 June 1994, to undertake measures to facilitate the return of persons who had fled the war-torn country. The Agreement was guided by the following principles:

"1. Uprooted population groups have the right to reside and live freely in Guatemalan territory. Accordingly, the Government of the Republic undertakes to ensure that conditions exist which permit and guarantee the voluntary return of uprooted persons to their places of origin or to the place of their choice, in conditions of dignity and security.

"2. Full respect for the human rights of the uprooted population shall be an essential condition for the resettlement of this population.

"3. Uprooted population groups deserve special attention, in view of the consequences they have suffered from being uprooted, through the implementation of a comprehensive, exceptional strategy which ensures, in the shortest possible time, their relocation in conditions of security and dignity and their free and full integration into the social, economic and political life of the country.

"4. Uprooted population groups shall participate in decision-making concerning the design, implementation and supervision of the comprehensive resettlement strategy and its specific projects. This participatory principle shall extend to population groups residing in resettlement areas in all aspects concerning them.

"5. A comprehensive strategy will be possible only within the perspective of a sustained, sustainable and equitable development of the resettlement areas for the benefit of all the population groups and individuals residing in them in the framework of a national development plan.

"6. The implementation of the strategy shall not be discriminatory and shall promote the reconciliation of the interests of the resettled population groups and the population groups already living in the resettlement areas."

39. In October 1992, the Guatemalan Government and the representatives of the Guatemalan refugees in Mexico had signed an agreement, witnessed by UNHCR, reiterating constitutional and other basic rights and creating a mechanism for landless refugees to acquire land, thus setting the stage for the organized collective returns. Further, the case of Guatemala highlights the importance of having both a strong normative framework in which to pursue restitution programmes, as well as the positive role that international institutions and refugees can play in legitimizing and/or facilitating this process.

40. UNHCR was also involved in programmes involving documentation enabling returning refugees to purchase, transfer or obtain title to land. Of the 20,000 returnees who repatriated collectively, approximately half recovered their original land or received alternative land in direct compensation for lost original land, while the other half bought new land under a land-buying programme. Another major achievement was the recognition of the individual title of returnee women to land held under cooperative agreements.

41. Despite these notable successes, however, the restitution process in Guatemala was hampered by a lack of legal titles to homes and property, the loss of documents during the conflict, destruction of property records, and the policy on the part of the Government to redistribute land and issue new deeds, leading to a complex layer of competing

claims. All of these factors contributed to the difficulties of return experienced in Guatemala.

F. Additional Cases

42. The United Nations, addressing the crisis in Kosovo, again recognized the remedy of housing restitution as essential to implementing the right to return to one's home. In 1999, the United Nations Mission in Kosovo (UNMIK) set up a Housing and Property Directorate and a Housing and Property Commission mandated to deal with the issue of housing restitution for returning refugees and other displaced persons.[14]

43. Similar mechanisms are now being considered by the United Nations for situations of displacement in East Timor, Georgia and Albania.

44. These and other case studies demonstrate that policy approaches to housing restitution premised on the human right to adequate housing may hold the greatest promise for ensuring that the process of voluntary repatriation protects human rights, strengthens the rule of law and provides the basis for economic and social stability. These are essential elements for any successful programme of reconstruction and reconciliation.

III. Common Obstacles to Housing and Property Restitution

A. Secondary Occupation

45. As the above examples indicate, secondary occupation is a common phenomenon in situations of displacement. It is also a reality which often complicates the process of return for refugees and other displaced persons. Secondary occupation may at times occur when the perpetrators of human rights abuses forcibly evict residents and subsequently loot property and move into the abandoned homes themselves. Yet, more often, secondary occupiers are themselves displaced persons. They themselves may have fled conflict, leaving behind their own homes and communities. In many cases, secondary occupation is enforced, encouraged, and/or facilitated by the forces that caused the initial displacement, and the secondary occupiers themselves may have had little or no choice in relocating to the housing in question.

46. Secondary occupation is an obstacle to return, and consequently to housing and property restitution, because it results in several practical difficulties. First, secondary occupation raises complex questions with regard to legal ownership and often necessitates judicial consideration in order to establish legal property rights and original residency. This problem may be further exacerbated by the loss of legal documents during flight, or by the destruction of legal documents which establish property ownership, discussed below. From a purely logistical perspective, documenting and verifying property ownership in these cases may be tedious, ineffective and slow. This is especially the case where domestic institutions do not have the capacity and resources to deal with the heavy caseloads resulting from widespread secondary occupation.

47. Furthermore, even in cases where property ownership can be established, the removal of secondary occupiers raises several difficulties. First, the legal eviction of secondary occupiers in order to facilitate return may unfortunately have the result of inciting local resistance to these evictions and may further deepen ethnic or other social divisions, as was the case in Bosnia and Herzegovina.

48. Adequately addressing the phenomenon of secondary occupation has proven extremely delicate. Such a common obstacle to return necessitates the formulation of a universally acceptable policy response based upon human rights principles in order to minimize social unrest and maximize effectiveness. For example, in all cases, adequate measures must be taken to ensure that secondary occupiers are protected against homelessness, unreasonable relocation and other violations of their human rights, including the right to adequate housing. Furthermore, due process guarantees, and access to fair and impartial legal institutions, must be assured for all parties. Institutional strength and political will are inevitably crucial factors, and restitution programmes may succeed or fail solely on the strength and capacity of existing institutions.

Commissions, courts and other legal mechanisms which may be entrusted with considering and ruling upon these complex restitution issues must have the enforcement authority necessary to put their decisions into practice.

B. Property Destruction

49. Because the destruction of property effectively precludes the possibility of restitution, the only

adequate alternative is compensation, be it financial or in lieu. Compensation must be granted with the same intention as restitution, however, so that victims are returned as far as possible to their original pre-loss or pre-injury position (i.e. status quo ante).

50. Even in situations where compensation is the only possible remedy, due process guarantees, and access to fair and impartial legal institutions, must be assured for all parties. The need to verify property ownership and economic value again highlights the importance of having functioning and effective institutions ready to oversee and administer complex return programmes.

C. Loss or Destruction of Housing and Property Records

51. As many of the above cases illustrate, the loss and destruction of housing and property records and documentation is a problem which significantly complicates the restitution process. The difficulties incurred by the loss of personal documents, however, may be partially offset if official government housing and property cadastres are kept intact. If no official documentation is available, the ability to implement restitution programmes effectively is substantially hindered, necessitating a formal investigation and verification procedures.

52. In cases where the documentation of property ownership is a formidable obstacle to return, formal investigations and property ownership verification procedures require that the overseeing institutions have the resources (including professional training, personnel and finances) needed in order to carry out their work effectively in a timely and efficient manner. Without the political will to meet these basic organizational needs, the restitution process is virtually doomed to failure from the outset.

D. Ineffectual Institutions

53. Effective and competent institutions are the cornerstone of successful restitution programmes. Judicial mechanisms are especially important here and the absence of effective and accessible judicial remedies severely limits the utility of pursuing legally based solutions as a means of protecting rights to housing and property and thereby facilitating their restoration. This is particularly the case

in post-conflict situations where internal political divisions render domestic institutions incapable of effectively administering restitution programmes, either due to institutional bias, or due to a lack of capacity and resources.

54. One interim solution to this impediment is the establishment of ad hoc independent housing and property commissions designed to promote and protect the right to housing and property restitution. Yet, these institutions must also have external support in order to meet their heavy caseloads and to overcome the many formidable challenges encountered during the restitution process.

E. Discriminatory Restitution Programmes

55. As with the application of discriminatory abandonment laws, Governments may design and implement restitution programmes which favour certain groups, all the while barring others from returning to their own homes. Discriminatory restitution programmes further entrench social divisions and animosities, and are counter to post-conflict resolution, peace-building, as well as to fundamental human rights principles and international legal obligations.

56. Discriminatory restitution programmes may also manifest themselves in unanticipated ways, especially in situations where the status quo ante itself discriminated against particular groups. In such cases, it may not be sufficient to simply restore the pre-displacement housing situation, and additional measures may be needed to ensure that housing rights are realized by all sectors of the population without discrimination.

IV. THE ROLE OF THE INTERNATIONAL COMMUNITY IN FACILITATING RETURN

A. Peace-Building, Peacekeeping and Conflict Resolution

57. While housing and property restitution is necessary to post-conflict resolution and peace-building, restitution programmes cannot be properly implemented under conditions which are overly volatile and unstable. In all cases of housing and property restitution, the safe and dignified return of affected persons must be the foremost consideration.

58. The international community, as represented by the United Nations, has an important role to play

in ensuring the success of housing and property restitution programmes simply by adequately fulfilling its peace-keeping role. Peacekeeping allows for the stabilization of conflict situations, paving the way for housing and property restitution programmes to be implemented and, perhaps even more importantly, enforced.

59. It is also important to mention that while housing and property restitution is best seen as a remedy, or as a particular kind of reparation, for past human rights abuses, there is much to be said for the prevention of these violations. Indeed, housing and property restitution programmes are often developed in the wake of widespread forced evictions and other violations of human rights, during which masses of people are forced to leave behind their homes and communities. The international community's peace-keeping role is also critical in the effort to stop these violations by preventing the spread of conflict and abuse and by holding Governments accountable for their actions.

B. Development of Restitution Programmes

60. The United Nations has a leading role to play in the development of housing and property restitution policies and programmes. While these programmes would no doubt be implemented in different countries and would address varying situations, it is important to develop a universal standard approach to the restitution issue so as to (i) anticipate and overcome common obstacles to return; (ii) establish an acceptable standard response consistent with international human rights laws and standards; and (iii) build the capacity of international organizations in responding to conflict situations.

61. In addition, the United Nations is perhaps best situated to address both the theoretical and practical concerns relating to housing and property restitution within the context of return. First, the human rights bodies of the United Nations, including expert bodies such as the Sub-Commission, could provide much needed insight into the human rights implications of various approaches to restitution, leading to the crafting of restitution policies consistent with human rights laws and standards. Second, institutions such as UNHCR have practical experience in restitution which would be an invaluable contribution to the design of a universal approach to housing and property restitution which would successfully address some of the

major problems and obstacles encountered during the process.

C. Oversight of Restitution Programmes

62. The international community, and the United Nations in particular, has an important role to play in overseeing the successful implementation of restitution programmes. This question should be seen as part of human rights monitoring more generally, an essential function of multiple United Nations bodies.

63. The international community also has a responsibility to act in ways which protect and promote the right to housing and property restitution as well as the right to return. Normative development and the strengthening of international standards in this regard could significantly improve the living situation of countless refuges and other displaced and vulnerable persons throughout the world.

64. Similarly, the careful monitoring of conflict situations and the adequate and prompt response to mass displacements and refugee flows would do much to facilitate any restitution process implemented later on, simply by narrowing and minimizing the scope of the human tragedy at the onset.

D. Implementation of Restitution Programmes

65. While the United Nations and other international agencies may be called upon to assist or to implement restitution programmes under specific circumstances, it is by no means a requirement in all post-conflict situations. Rather, domestic institutions and mechanisms may be designed and put in place to address and administer restitution processes. Such institutions should, however, have the support and guidance of the international community, and the international community should carefully monitor the progress of such programmes especially with regard to the common obstacles to return as identified above.

V. Conclusions

66. As this study illustrates, housing and property restitution for refugees and other displaced persons has been a remedy used in many post-conflict situations. While success with respect to the implementation of this remedy has been varied, much of this variation results from the failure to have a comprehensive approach, governed by

international human rights law, to address such situations. When properly implemented, housing and property restitution programmes are indispensable to post-conflict resolution and to creating a durable peace, as they are essential components of the right to reparations for past human rights violations as well as the right to return.

67. Not all situations requiring housing and property restitution as a remedy arise out of conflict situations. For instance, ethnic cleansing may involve one-sided violence against certain ethnic groups without the existence of an ongoing violent conflict. Nonetheless, in these cases, housing and property restitution remains a just and essential strategy to remedy the harms suffered by victims.

68. While each specific situation of displacement is unique, commonalities can be identified regarding obstacles to the effective implementation of housing and property restitution mechanisms. Such commonalities include the loss or destruction of housing and property records and documentation, secondary occupation, property destruction, the existence of ineffectual institutions, and the adoption of discriminatory restitution programmes and policies.

69. The international community, as manifest in the organs and agencies of the United Nations, has an important role to play in facilitating housing and property restitution for refugees and other displaced persons by contributing to the development of universally acceptable standards, based on human rights principles, which can be applied to different situations.

70. The success and effectiveness of housing and property restitution programmes also demands that the international community fulfil its peacekeeping obligations, so as to maintain stable domestic situations wherein appropriate restitution programmes may be successfully implemented and enforced. The international community should carefully monitor the progress of such programmes, especially with regard to the common obstacles to return identified above.

VI. Recommendations

A. Development of a Model Restitution Policy

71. That restitution programmes have been implemented in varying situations with varying results

is at least partly attributable to the lack of a comprehensive and universal approach to restitution policy, informed by international human rights law. Many of these disparate approaches to housing and property restitution have been marred by conceptually flawed strategies, biased policies and ineffectual institutions which have not had the internal and external supports necessary to complete their mandates.

72. Therefore, it would be desirable to draft a model policy on housing and property restitution, specifically within the context of the right to return for refugees and other displaced persons, which would help address and alleviate these problems. This model policy could serve as the foundation for implementing housing and property restitution programmes in different situations, addressing many of the common obstacles to return in a manner consistent with international human rights and humanitarian law.

73. The intended audience of such a model policy should be the institutions and commissions established at the national level to implement housing and property restitution programmes. The model policy should provide such entities with much-needed guidance regarding how best to design a policy which best fits their particular needs by providing them with a statement of universal principles on which they can build.

74. While the responsibility for the implementation of such a model policy would fall on the shoulders of institutions, the benefit would extend primarily to those persons who have been victims of human rights violations, as they would ultimately be the targets of housing and property restitution programmes.

75. While the model policy should be drafted with a view to the practical implementation of restitution programmes, it is not in itself meant to provide the technical basis on which to design and support such initiatives. Rather, the model policy shall be framed primarily as a statement of fundamental rights and shall address specifically, inter alia, the following themes:

(a) The underlying principles on which all housing and property restitution programmes must be based, inter alia, the principles of non-discrimination and equality of all parties and the principle of safe and dignified return;

(b) The right of displaced people to participate in decision-making concerning the design, implementation and supervision of restitution programmes;

(c) The rights of secondary occupiers to adequate housing and to reasonable relocation;

(d) The rights of all parties to petition and access independent and unbiased tribunals for the consideration of their case, including the right to an adequate appeals procedure;

(e) The right to adequate compensation in cases where housing and property restitution is not possible due to the destruction of housing; and

(f) The right to housing and property restitution as a key component of post-conflict resolution and peace-building.

B. Development of International Guidelines on Housing and Property Restitution

76. Because the model policy outlined above would not provide the technical basis on which to design and implement housing and property restitution programmes, it would also be of tremendous importance to develop a supplemental document which would provide specific guidelines for the practical implementation of such programmes.

77. As we have seen, the restitution of housing and property to those displaced can only take place if political will is present and results in the development and implementation of relevant institutions, laws and other protections. As such, the development of concrete international guidelines on housing and property restitution, based on international human rights laws and standards, would be a crucial step towards the development of a universal approach to the problem. Such a contribution would lend itself to the practical implementation of housing and property restitution programmes by offering specific policy recommendations and protocols for how best to overcome common obstacles.

78. While such guidelines would inevitably complement and even overlap with the model policy, the guidelines would go into considerably more detail with regard to all aspects of the restitution question. As such, the guidelines would make a very valuable contribution to this field by explicitly addressing what would in effect be the synthe-

sis of the legal, theoretical and institutional frameworks necessary to ensure the success of housing and property restitution programmes.

79. It is therefore suggested that, as a parallel measure to the model policy, specific guidelines on the question of housing and property restitution should be developed. It is suggested that such a document be organized so as to address the following:

(a) Principles: specific international human rights norms and standards underlying the right to housing and property restitution for refugees and other displaced persons, including:

(i) The right to return;

(ii) The right not to be forcibly evicted;

(iii) The right to adequate housing;

(iv) The right to non-discrimination;

(v) The right to equality; and

(vi) The right to a remedy for human rights violations;

(b) Guidelines: specific approaches to the design, implementation and enforcement of housing and property restitution programmes, including:

(i) Acceptable and effective responses to many of the common obstacles to housing and property restitution programmes, including secondary occupation, loss or destruction of property records and the destruction of property;

(ii) Specific criteria to assess the circumstances under which compensation may be granted in lieu of restitution, as well as criteria addressing what constitutes just and fair compensation; and

(iii) Institutional guidelines regarding institutional organization, staff training and caseloads, investigation and complaints procedures, verification of property ownership, and decision-making, enforcement and appeals mechanisms.

C. Final Recommendations

80. For all of the reasons outlined in this preliminary study, it is suggested that the Sub-Commission, based on the work of the Special Rapporteur, develop "Universal Principles and Guidelines for Housing and Property Restitution for Refugees and Other Displaced Persons" as well as a "Model Policy

on Housing and Property Restitution for Refugees and Other Displaced Persons", in consultation with all relevant agencies and organs of the United Nations, Governments and NGOs.[15]

81. The Sub-Commission should also reiterate its condemnation of the practice of forced evictions, and recommend to the Commission on Human Rights that it adopt a resolution on forced evictions during its sixtieth session in 2004 with a particular emphasis on issues such as government obligations and the discriminatory effect of forced evictions.

ENDNOTES

1. Housing rights are enshrined in numerous instruments. For instance, the Universal Declaration of Human Rights (art. 25) and the International Covenant on Economic, Social and Cultural Rights (art. 11(1)) both guarantee the right to adequate housing. Additionally, the International Covenant on Civil and Political Rights (art. 17(1)) protects persons from arbitrary or unlawful interference with their home; the International Convention on the Elimination of All Forms of Racial Discrimination (art. 5(e)(iii)) prohibits discrimination on account of race, colour, or national or ethnic origin with respect to the right to housing; the Convention on the Elimination of All Forms of Discrimination against Women (arts. 2 and 14(2)(h)) obliges States parties to "condemn discrimination against women in all its forms" and, specifically, to eliminate discrimination against women in rural areas in order to ensure that such women enjoy adequate living conditions, particularly in relation to housing; the Convention on the Rights of the Child (art. 27(3)) obliges States parties to provide, in cases of need, material assistance and support programmes to families and children, particularly with regard to housing; and the International Convention on the Protection of the Rights of All Migrant Workers and Members of Their Families (art. 43(1)(d)) provides that "[m]igrant workers shall enjoy equality of treatment with nationals of the State of employment in relation to ... (d) [a]ccess to housing, including social housing schemes, and protection against exploitation in respect of rents". Other international instruments guaranteeing housing rights include various International Labour Organization conventions and humanitarian law instruments, as well as the Convention relating to the Status of Refugees.

2. For example, the right to adequate housing is recognized and implicit in the following international human rights instruments: article 25 of the Universal Declaration of Human Rights; article 11(1) of the International Covenant on Economic, Social and Cultural Rights; article 5(e)(iii) of the International Convention on the Elimination of All Forms of Racial Discrimination; article 14(2)(h) of the Convention on the Elimination of All Forms of Discrimination against Women; article 27(3) of the Conven-

tion on the Rights of the Child; and article 21 of the Convention relating to the Status of Refugees.

3. See, for example, the work of the Special Rapporteur on adequate housing, Mr. Miloon Kothari, at www.unhchr.ch/housing.

4. See General Comment No. 7 of the United Nations Committee on Economic, Social and Cultural Rights on Forced Eviction (E/C.12/1997/4).

5. Commission on Human Rights resolution 1993/77 of 10 March 1993.

6. Human Rights Watch, Croatia, Second Class Citizens: The Serbs of Croatia, New York City: HRW, March 1999.

7. Readers may also be interested in the activities of the United Nations Transitional Administration for Eastern Slavonia, Baranja and Western Sirmium (UNTAES) in the process of housing and property restitution. Please see for more details: http://www.un.org/Depts/dpko/dpko/co_mission/untaes.htm.

8. Ibid.

9. Under the 1995 Law on Temporary Taking Over and Administration of Specified Property, more than 18,500 private residential properties belonging almost exclusively to Croatian Serbs were taken over by the Government and assigned to Bosnian and domestic Croats, including internally displaced persons and Bosnian refugees of Croatian ethnicity (settlers).

10. Organization for Security and Cooperation in Europe (OSCE), OSCE Mission to Croatia, "Return and Integration: Displaced Populations", 2003.

11. The Office of the High Representative in Bosnia and Herzegovina (OHR), "Property Law Implementation is Just One Element of Annex VII", press release, 27 February 2003.

12. UNHCR, OHR, OSCE and CRPC, "Statistics – Implementation of the Property Laws in Bosnia and Herzegovina", 31 March 2003.

13. The Arusha Peace Agreement was signed on 4 August 1993. For a detailed explanation of the efforts the United Nations to implement the Agreement, see the second progress report of the Secretary-General on the United Nations Assistance Mission for Rwanda (S/1994/360); see also General Assembly resolution 49/23 (1994) which recognized that the Arusha Peace Agreement provided an appropriate framework for national reconciliation in Rwanda.

14. See UNMIK Regulation No. 1999/23 (1999).

15. The Sub-Commission may, for example, take into account the recommendations to Governments on discrimination and housing proposed by the Special Rapporteur on adequate housing in his report to the fifty-eighth session of the Commission on Human Rights.

8.11. Housing and Property Restitution in the Context of the Return of Refugees and Internally Displaced Persons – Progress Report of the Special Rapporteur, Paulo Sérgio Pinheiro (2004)[133]

INTRODUCTION

1. This commentary on the Draft Principles on Housing and Property Restitution for Refugees and Displaced Persons (hereinafter "Draft Principles") is meant to provide an overview of the international human rights and humanitarian legal standards which serve to support the Draft Principles. The commentary is organized in parallel to the Draft Principles.

2. As with the Draft Principles, it is hoped that over the course of the next year, the scope of consultation can be further expanded in order to invite the participation of all relevant agencies and organs of the United Nations, Governments and non-governmental organizations in the development of the commentary. In particular, the Special Rapporteur would like to suggest that a high-level international meeting be convened in early 2005 to discuss the Draft Principles. It is hoped that the draft commentary, along with the Draft Principles, will be disseminated as widely as possible in order to facilitate the consultation process before the Special Rapporteur submits his final report in 2005.

3. While the mandate given to the Special Rapporteur refers to "refugees and internally displaced persons", it should be noted that the issues, norms and standards regarding housing and property restitution also pertain to persons in similar situations. The phrase "refugees and internally displaced persons" unfortunately overlooks those persons displaced across borders, for example following a conflict or disaster, who may not meet the legal definition of a refugee under international law. Because such populations have the right to housing and property restitution, as refugees and internally displaced persons do, the Draft Principles incorporates the language "refugees and displaced persons".

4. For the purpose of the Draft Principles, "housing and property" refers to housing and real property, including land and other forms of immovable property.

COMMENTARY TO SECTION I OF THE DRAFT PRINCIPLES ON THE RIGHT TO HOUSING AND PROPERTY RESTITUTION

5. Section I outlines overarching principles which shall be applied to all of the rights spelt out in the Draft Principles. In paragraph 1.1, and throughout the text, the term "restitution" refers to an equitable remedy, or a form of restorative justice, by which persons who suffer loss or injury are returned as far as possible to their original pre-loss or pre-injury position. The recognition of the right to housing and property restitution for refugees and other displaced persons is based on the standards articulated throughout the Draft Principles, inter alia, the right to safe and dignified return and the right to a remedy for violations of international human rights and humanitarian law.

6. The right to non-discrimination and equality are protected in virtually every major international human rights instrument, including article 2 of the Universal Declaration of Human Rights, articles 2 and 3 of the International Covenant on Economic, Social and Cultural Rights,[1] and articles 2 and 3 of the International Covenant on Civil and Political Rights.[2] Discrimination is also prohibited under the International Convention on the Elimination of All Forms of Racial Discrimination[3] and the Convention on the Elimination of All Forms of Discrimination against Women,[4] as well as under article 2 of the Convention on the Rights of the Child.[5] Discrimination is similarly prohibited under article II of the American Declaration on the Rights and Duties of Man,[6] article 1 of the American Convention on Human Rights: "Pact of San José, Costa Rica",[7] article 2 of the African Charter on Human and Peoples' Rights,[8] and article 14 of the Convention for the Protection of Human Rights and Fundamental Freedoms (European Convention on Human Rights).[9]

7. The right to equality between men and women is guaranteed in article 3 of the International Covenant on Civil and Political Rights[10] and in article 3 of the International Covenant on Economic, Social and Cultural Rights.[11] In cases where the status quo ante discriminated on the basis of social status, for example on the basis of gender, additional measures may be needed to ensure that

---

[133] E/CN.4/Sub.2/2004/22/Add.1.

housing rights are realized by all sectors of the population without discrimination.

8. In general comment No. 28 on the equality of rights of men and women, the Human Rights Committee states that "The State party must not only adopt measures of protection, but also positive measures in all areas so as to achieve the effective and equal empowerment of women", and further notes that "Articles 2 and 3 mandate States parties to take all steps necessary, including the prohibition of discrimination on the ground of sex, to put an end to discriminatory actions, both in the public and the private sector, which impair the equal enjoyment of rights." General comment No. 28 also notes that "The right of everyone . . . to be recognized everywhere as a person before the law is particularly pertinent for women, who often see it curtailed by reason of sex or marital status. This right implies . . . the capacity of women to own property. . . . "

COMMENTARY TO SECTION II OF THE DRAFT PRINCIPLES ON PROTECTION FROM DISPLACEMENT

9. Section II of the Draft Principles articulates several rights which are relevant to all points of the displacement cycle, and are of particular significance in terms of protecting people from forced displacement in the first place. As such, the Draft Principles address not only the issue of providing a remedy (i.e. restitution) to those persons already displaced, but also seek to avert the crisis of forced displacement itself. The rights articulated in section II include the right to be free from forced eviction, the right to privacy and respect for the home, the right to be free from the arbitrary deprivation of one's property, the right to non-discrimination and equality, the right to adequate housing, and the right to freedom of movement and freedom to choose his or her residence.

10. "Forced eviction" is the permanent or temporary removal against their will of individuals, families and/or communities from the homes and/or land which they occupy, without the provision of, and access to, appropriate forms of legal or other protection. Forced evictions are a particular type of displacement which are most often characterized by a relation to specific decisions, legislation or policies of States or the failure of States to intervene to halt evictions by non-State actors and an

element of force or coercion, and which are often planned, formulated and announced prior to being carried out. The right to be free from forced eviction is implicit in the right to adequate housing, as well as in the right to privacy and respect for the home.

11. In its general comment No. 7, the Committee on Economic, Social and Cultural Rights stated that "forced evictions are prima facie incompatible with the requirements of the Covenant" and can only be justified in the most exceptional circumstances, and in accordance with the relevant principles of international law.[12] The Committee further considered that the procedural protections which should be applied in relation to forced evictions include: (a) an opportunity for genuine consultation with those affected; (b) adequate and reasonable notice for all affected persons prior to the scheduled date of eviction; (c) information on the proposed evictions, and, where applicable, on the alternative purpose for which the land or housing is to be used, to be made available in reasonable time to all those affected; (d) especially where groups of people are involved, government officials or their representatives to be present during an eviction; (e) all persons carrying out the eviction to be properly identified; (f) evictions not to take place in particularly bad weather or at night unless the affected persons consent otherwise; (g) provision of legal remedies; and (h) provision, where possible, of legal aid to persons who are in need of it to seek redress from the courts.

12. The Geneva Convention relative to the Protection of Civilian Persons in Time of War states, in article 33, that "No protected person may be punished for an offence he or she has not personally committed. Collective penalties and likewise all measures of intimidation or of terrorism are prohibited" and that "Reprisals against protected persons and their property are prohibited."[13] Article 53 stipulates that "Any destruction by the Occupying Power of real or personal property belonging individually or collectively to private persons, or to the State, or to other public authorities, or to social or cooperative organizations, is prohibited, except where such destruction is rendered absolutely necessary by military operations." Article 14 of the Protocol Additional to the Geneva Conventions of 12 August 1949, and Relating to the Protection of Victims of Non-International Armed Conflicts (Protocol II)[14] states that "Starvation of civilians as a method of combat is prohibited. It is therefore prohibited to attack, destroy, remove or render useless, for that

purpose, objects indispensable to the survival of the civilian population, such as foodstuffs, agricultural areas for the production of foodstuffs, crops, livestock, drinking water installations and supplies and irrigation works."

13. Article 16 of the Convention against Torture and Other Cruel, Inhuman or Degrading Treatment or Punishment[15] states that "Each State Party shall undertake to prevent in any territory under its jurisdiction other acts of cruel, inhuman or degrading treatment or punishment which do not amount to torture as defined in article 1, when such acts are committed by or at the instigation of or with the consent or acquiescence of a public official or other person acting in an official capacity."

14. In applying article 16, the Committee against Torture has interpreted the Convention to protect persons from forced evictions. In *Hajrizi v. Yugoslavia*, for example, the Committee held that the forced eviction and destruction of a Roma settlement in Serbia and Montenegro violated the Convention, even though the eviction was not perpetrated by public officials. The case concerned the forced eviction and destruction of the Bozova Glavica settlement in the city of Danilovgrad by private residents who lived nearby.[16] Furthermore, in its concluding observations on the third periodic report of Israel (A/57/44, paras. 47-53), the Committee held that Israel's policies of demolishing housing may amount to cruel, inhuman or degrading treatment or punishment, in violation of article 16 of the Convention.

15. The Commission on Human Rights, in its resolution 1993/77, has also affirmed "that the practice of forced eviction constitutes a gross violation of human rights, in particular the right to adequate housing". Similarly, the Sub-Commission, in its resolution 1998/9, reaffirmed that "every woman, man and child has the right to a secure place to live in peace and dignity, which includes the right not to be evicted arbitrarily or on a discriminatory basis from one's home, land or community". In the same resolution, the Sub-Commission further reaffirmed that "the practice of forced eviction constitutes a gross violation of a broad range of human rights, in particular the right to adequate housing, the right to remain, the right to freedom of movement, the right to privacy, the right to property, the right to an adequate standard of living, the right to security of the home, the right to security of the person, the right to security of tenure and the right to equality of treatment".

16. Article 12 of the Universal Declaration of Human Rights states that "No one shall be subjected to arbitrary interference with his privacy, family, home or correspondence, nor to attacks upon his honour and reputation. Everyone has the right to the protection of the law against such interference or attacks."

17. Article 17 of the International Covenant on Civil and Political Rights states: "No one shall be subjected to arbitrary or unlawful interference with his privacy, family, home or correspondence, nor to unlawful attacks on his honour and reputation," and that "Everyone has the right to the protection of the law against such interference or attacks." Similarly, article 16, paragraph 1, of the Convention on the Rights of the Child states that "No child shall be subjected to arbitrary or unlawful interference with his or her privacy, family, home or correspondence, nor to unlawful attacks on his or her honour and reputation."

18. In its general comment No. 16 on the right to privacy, the Human Rights Committee stated that "[the right of every person to be protected against arbitrary or unlawful interference with his privacy, family, home or correspondence as well as against unlawful attacks on his honour and reputation] is required to be guaranteed against all such interferences and attacks whether they emanate from State authorities or from natural or legal persons. The obligations imposed by this article require the State to adopt legislative and other measures to give effect to the prohibition against such interferences and attacks as well as to the protection of this right".

19. Article IX of the American Declaration of the Rights and Duties of Man also states that "Every person has the right to the inviolability of his home." This right is also codified in the American Convention on Human Rights, which states, in article 11 that "No one may be the object of arbitrary or abusive interference with his private life, his family, his home, or his correspondence, or of unlawful attacks on his honour or reputation", and in article 8 of the European Convention on Human Rights: "Everyone has the right to respect for his private and family life, his home and his correspondence."

20. "Property", within the context of the Draft Principles, refers primarily to real and immovable

property, and in particular, but not exclusively, to housing and land. Article 17 of the Universal Declaration of Human Rights stipulates that "Everyone has the right to own property alone as well as in association with others. No one shall be arbitrarily deprived of his property." Article XXIII of the American Declaration of the Rights and Duties of Man states that "Every person has a right to own such private property as meets the essential needs of decent living and helps to maintain the dignity of the individual and of the home." Article 21 of the American Convention on Human Rights states that "Everyone has the right to the use and enjoyment of his property. The law may subordinate such use and enjoyment to the interest of society" and provides that "No one shall be deprived of his property except upon payment of just compensation, for reasons of public utility or social interest, and in the cases and according to the forms established by law." Similarly, article 14 of the African Charter on Human and Peoples' Rights states that "The right to property shall be guaranteed. It may only be encroached upon in the interest of public need or in the general interest of the community and in accordance with the provisions of appropriate laws." Article 1 of the Protocol to the Convention for the Protection of Human Rights and Fundamental Freedoms states: "Every natural or legal person is entitled to the peaceful enjoyment of his possessions. No one shall be deprived of his possessions except in the public interest and subject to the conditions provided for by law and by the general principles of international law. The preceding provisions shall not, however, in any way impair the right of a State to enforce such laws as it deems necessary to control the use of property in accordance with the general interest or to secure the payment of taxes or other contributions or penalties." ILO Convention No. 169 concerning Indigenous and Tribal Peoples in Independent Countries[17] provides that "The rights of ownership and possession of the peoples concerned over the lands which they traditionally occupy shall be recognized" (art.13). Article 16, paragraph 3, further stipulates that "Whenever possible, these peoples shall have the right to return to their traditional lands, as soon as the grounds for relocation cease to exist."

21. The right to adequate housing is enshrined in several international human rights instruments. The Universal Declaration of Human Rights stipulates that "Everyone has the right to a standard of living adequate for the health and well-being of himself and of his family, including food, clothing, housing and medical care and necessary social services, and the right to security in the event of unemployment, sickness, disability, widowhood, old age or other lack of livelihood in circumstances beyond his control" (art. 25).

22. The leading statement of international law relating to housing rights can be found in the International Covenant on Economic, Social and Cultural Rights, which states, in article 11, paragraph 1, that "The State parties to the present Covenant recognize the right of everyone to an adequate standard of living for himself and for his family, including adequate food, clothing and housing, and to the continuous improvement of living conditions." Housing rights are also enshrined and protected within other international human rights instruments, including the International Convention on the Elimination of All Forms of Racial Discrimination,[18] the Convention on the Elimination of All Forms of Discrimination against Women,[19] the Convention on the Rights of the Child,[20] the Convention relating to the Status of Refugees,[21] and the International Convention on the Protection of the Rights of All Migrant Workers and Members of Their Families.[22]

23. The right to adequate housing has been defined by the Committee on Economic, Social and Cultural Rights in its general comment No. 4. The Committee notes that the approach to the right to adequate housing should be holistic, encompassing the right to live somewhere in security, peace and dignity. In this regard, the Committee identified seven key criteria which comprise the right to adequate housing – legal security of tenure; availability of services, materials, facilities and infrastructure; affordability; habitability; accessibility; location and cultural adequacy.

24. The right to freedom of movement and residence is recognized in article 13, paragraph 1, of the Universal Declaration of Human Rights, which states that "Everyone has the right to freedom of movement and residence within the borders of each State." This right is also protected under article 12, paragraph 1, of the International Covenant on Civil and Political Rights,[23] as well as under article VIII of the American Declaration of the Rights and Duties of Man,[24] article 22, paragraph 1, of the American Convention on Human Rights,[25] and

article 12, paragraph 1, of the African Charter on Human and Peoples' Rights.[26]

25. General comment No. 27 of the Human Rights Committee on freedom of movement notes that "Everyone lawfully within the territory of a State enjoys, within that territory, the right to move freely and to choose his or her place of residence." The Committee further notes that "The right to move freely relates to the whole territory of a State, including all parts of federal States. According to article 12, paragraph 1, persons are entitled to move from one place to another and to establish themselves in a place of their choice. The enjoyment of this right must not be made dependent on any particular purpose or reason for the person wanting to move or to stay in a place [. . .]. Subject to the provisions of article 12, paragraph 3, the right to reside in a place of one's choice within the territory includes protection against all forms of forced internal displacement. It also precludes preventing the entry or stay of persons in a defined part of the territory."

COMMENTARY TO SECTION III OF THE DRAFT PRINCIPLES ON PROTECTING THE RIGHTS OF REFUGEES AND DISPLACED PERSONS

26. Section III of the Draft Principles addresses the rights of displaced persons, in particular, with respect to the right to safe and dignified return and the right to a remedy for human rights violations. Safe return encompasses the physical, legal and material aspects of safety. The right to housing and property restitution is seen as fundamentally connected to the realization of these human rights.

27. The right to return is guaranteed in article 13, paragraph 2, of the Universal Declaration of Human Rights,[27] article 12, paragraph 4, of the International Covenant on Civil and Political Rights,[28] articles 45, 127, 132, 134 and 135 of the Geneva Convention relative to the Protection of Civilian Persons in Time of War,[29] and article 12, paragraph 2, of the African Charter on Human and Peoples' Rights.[30]

28. General comment No. 27 of the Human Rights Committee on freedom of movement also notes that "The right to return is of the utmost importance for refugees seeking voluntary repatriation. It also implies prohibition of enforced population transfers or mass expulsions to other countries."[31]

29. The right to return is increasingly seen as encompassing not merely returning to one's coun-try, but to one's home as well. Indeed, the right of refugees and displaced persons to return to their homes is recognized by the international community as a free-standing, autonomous right in and of itself. In its resolution 35/124 on international intervention to avert new flows of refugees, the General Assembly reaffirmed "the right of refugees to return to their homes in their homelands". This understanding is important in order to protect effectively the right to return of refugees and displaced persons and to improve situations leading to instability and displacement.[32]

30. The United Nations has also consistently reaffirmed this principle when addressing specific cases of displacement. For example, the Security Council, in its resolution 820 (1993) on Bosnia and Herzegovina reaffirmed that "all displaced persons have the right to return in peace to their former homes and should be assisted to do so". Similar language can be found in other resolutions of the Security Council, addressing displacement in numerous countries and regions, such as Georgia including Abkhazid,[33] Azerbaijan (853 (1993)), Bosnia and Herzegovina (752 (1992)), Cambodia (745 (1992)), Croatia (1009 (1995)), Cyprus (361 (1974)), Kosovo (1244 (1999), 1199 (1998)), Kuwait (687 (1991)), Namibia (385 (1976)) and Tajikistan (999 (1995)).

31. Other United Nations bodies have also reaffirmed the right to return to one's home. In addition to resolution 35/124 mentioned above, the General Assembly has, for instance, reaffirmed or recognized the right to return to one's home in resolutions 1672 (XVI) on Algeria, 3212 (XXIX) on Cyprus, 194 (111) on Palestine, 51/126 on persons displaced as a result of the June 1967 and subsequent hostilities and 51/114 on Rwanda. In resolution 1998/26, adopted without a vote, the Sub-Commission reaffirmed "the right of all refugees [. . .] and internally displaced persons to return to their homes and places of habitual residence in their country and/or place of origin, should they so wish".

32. The Committee on the Elimination of Racial Discrimination also reaffirmed this principle in its general recommendation XXII: "all . . . refugees and displaced persons have the right freely to return to their homes of origin under conditions of safety". Similarly, in the Declaration adopted by the World Conference against Racism, Racial Discrimination, Xenophobia and Related Intolerance in Durban

in September 2001, the international community unequivocally declared its universal recognition: "We recognize the right of refugees to return voluntarily to their homes and properties in dignity and safety, and urge all States to facilitate such return" (para. 65).

33. The forced return of refugees and other displaced persons is, prima facie, incompatible with international human rights standards, as forced repatriation violates the principle of non-refoulement. Article 33, paragraph 1, of the Convention relating to the Status of Refugees provides that "No Contracting State shall expel or return ("refouler") a refugee in any manner whatsoever to the frontiers of territories where his life or freedom would be threatened on account of his race, religion, nationality, membership of a particular social group or political opinion." Similarly, Principle 15 of the Guiding Principles on Internal Displacement provides that "Internally displaced persons have . . . [t]he right to be protected against forcible return to or resettlement in any place where their life, safety, liberty and/or health would be at risk" (E/CN.4/1998/53, Add.2).

34. The right to a remedy for human rights violations has perhaps been best articulated in the Draft Basic Principles and Guidelines on the Right to a Remedy and Reparation for Victims of Violations of International Human Rights and Humanitarian Law (E/CN.4/2000/62), which is itself based on well-established principles of international human rights and humanitarian law.

Section II of the Draft Basic Principles and Guidelines provides that "The obligation to respect, ensure respect for and enforce international human rights and humanitarian law includes, inter alia, a State's duty to: (a) Take appropriate legal and administrative measures to prevent violations; (b) Investigate violations and, where appropriate, take action against the violator in accordance with domestic and international law; (c) Provide victims with equal and effective access to justice irrespective of who may be the ultimate bearer of responsibility for the violation; (d) Afford appropriate remedies to victims; and (e) Provide for or facilitate reparation to victims."

35. The Commission on Human Rights, in its resolution 2000/41, also reaffirmed that "pursuant to internationally proclaimed human rights principles, victims of grave violations of human rights should receive, in appropriate cases, restitution, compensation and rehabilitation", and called upon "the international community to give due attention to the right to restitution, compensation and rehabilitation for victims of grave violations of human rights".

36. The Draft Basic Principles and Guidelines on the Right to a Remedy and Reparation for Victims of Violations of International Human Rights and Humanitarian Law also stipulate, in paragraph 15, that "Reparation should be proportional to the gravity of the violations and the harm suffered", and, in paragraph 22, that "Restitution should, whenever possible, restore the victim to the original situation before the violations of international human rights or humanitarian law occurred. Restitution includes: restoration of liberty, legal rights, social status, family life and citizenship; return to one's place of residence; and restoration of employment and return of property."

COMMENTARY TO SECTION IV OF THE DRAFT PRINCIPLES ON ENSURING THE RIGHT TO HOUSING AND PROPERTY RESTITUTION

37. Section IV of the Draft Principles provides specific guidance regarding how best to ensure the right to housing and property restitution in practice. The principles articulated in this section are based, in part, on the findings of the preliminary report (E/CN.4/Sub.2/2003/11), which analysed some of the common obstacles to restitution programmes, including secondary occupation, property destruction, loss or destruction of property, ineffectual institutions and discriminatory restitution programmes. As such, the principles articulated in this section reflect some of the best practices which have been devised at the level of policy to address these common obstacles.

38. The right to adequate consultation and representation in decision-making has been articulated by the Committee on Economic, Social and Cultural Rights within the context of forced evictions. In its general comment No. 7, the Committee observed that affected communities should have a right to "an opportunity for genuine consultation". Similarly, Principle 28, paragraph 2, of the Guiding Principles on Internal Displacement stipulates that "Special efforts should be made to ensure the full participation of internally displaced persons in the

planning and management of their return or resettlement and reintegration."

39. The provisions of the Draft Principles regarding housing and property records and documentation are meant in part to facilitate, from a logistical point of view, restitution processes through the establishment of property registration systems. In certain cases, alternative mechanisms may need to be established in order to create or recreate a system for the registration of property. One effective way to do this would be by integrating housing and property restitution protections in registration procedures for refugees and displaced persons. Many States have registration systems for the provision of humanitarian aid to the displaced, and many States include, in their registration processes, a mechanism for the collection of demographic data on the displaced population. It would seem quite feasible to widen the data collection component of these registration processes to include information regarding the housing and property situation of refugees and displaced persons at the time they fled their homes – address, length of residency, estimated value, tenure status, ownership records and any other relevant personal information related to residency, ownership, possession or use and loss of property rights.

40. Because displacement often occurs in situations of armed conflict, including of ethnic cleansing, the Draft Principles stipulate that "States shall not recognize as valid any illegal property transaction, including any transfer that was made under duress, in exchange for exit permission or documents, or which was otherwise coerced or forced." Similar language was used in Security Council resolution 820 (1993) on the situation in Bosnia and Herzegovina.[34] This provision is consistent with basic tenets of contract law which stipulate that contracts entered into under duress or physical compulsion are void. Similarly, if a party's assent to a contract is induced by a threat from another party that leaves the victim no reasonable alternative, the contract is voidable by the victim.

41. Ensuring the rights of tenants and other non-owners is very important in situations of repatriation, resettlement and restitution, as in many cases only the minority of the affected displaced population will have actually owned their housing. Tenants and other non-owners do have rights of possession, including security of tenure, which pro-

tect them from forced eviction and displacement. The rights articulated in the Draft Principles apply equally to tenants and other non-owners as they do to persons who own their housing.

42. Ensuring the rights of secondary occupants is also a critical concern, as secondary occupation is itself a common phenomenon in situations of displacement. Secondary occupation is also a reality which often complicates the process of return for refugees and other displaced persons. Secondary occupation may at times occur when the perpetrators of human rights abuses forcibly evict residents and subsequently loot property and move into the abandoned homes themselves. Yet, most often, secondary occupiers are themselves displaced persons. Adequately addressing the phenomenon of secondary occupation has proven extremely delicate in practice. In all cases, however, secondary occupants must be protected against forced evictions and must benefit from the procedural protections outlined in general comment No. 7 of the Committee on Economic, Social and Cultural Rights. Similarly, secondary occupants have a right to adequate housing under international human rights laws and standards, and States should adopt adequate measures to ensure that secondary occupiers are protected against homelessness, unreasonable relocation and other violations of their human rights. Due process guarantees, and access to fair and impartial legal institutions, must be assured for all parties.

43. The term "compensation" refers to a legal remedy by which a person receives monetary payment for harm suffered, for example resulting from the impossibility of restoring the person's property or house. Compensation should not be seen as an alternative to restitution and should only be used when restitution is not factually possible or when the injured party knowingly and voluntarily accepts compensation in lieu of restitution. For example, an injured party should receive compensation to remedy the wrongful dispossession of housing only if that particular housing no longer exists or if the injured party knowingly and voluntarily decides it is in his or her interest not to return to his or her home. The Draft Principles do acknowledge, however, that in some cases, a combination of compensation and restitution may be the most appropriate remedy and form of restorative justice. There is flexibility in this regard. Nonetheless, in all cases it is the injured party who should be able to knowingly

and voluntarily decide whether to accept restitution, compensation, or a combination thereof.

44. In its general recommendation XXIII on the rights of indigenous peoples, the Committee on the Elimination of Racial Discrimination affirmed such a formulation in the context of indigenous land and resources, calling upon States parties "to recognize and protect the rights of indigenous peoples to own, develop, control and use their communal lands, territories and resources and, where they have been deprived of their lands and territories traditionally owned or otherwise inhabited or used without their free and informed consent, to take steps to return those lands and territories. Only when this is for factual reasons not possible, the right to restitution should be substituted by the right to just, fair and prompt compensation".

45. Similarly, Principle 29, paragraph 2, of the Guiding Principles on Internal Displacement provide that "Competent authorities have the duty and responsibility to assist returned and/or resettled internally displaced persons to recover, to the extent possible, their property and possessions which they left behind or were dispossessed of upon their displacement. *When recovery of such property and possessions is not possible, competent authorities shall provide or assist these persons in obtaining appropriate compensation or another form of just reparation*" (emphasis added).

COMMENTARY TO SECTION V OF THE DRAFT PRINCIPLES ON STRENGTHENING RESTITUTION PROCEDURES, INSTITUTIONS, MECHANISMS AND LEGAL FRAMEWORKS

46. The provision that procedures, institutions, mechanisms, and legal frameworks related to the right to restitution shall be fully consistent and compatible with international human rights and humanitarian law and standards is important to ensure that principles of international human rights and humanitarian law are adequately reflected at the level of national policy-making as concerns restitution. Doing so will ultimately serve to protect all persons from future violations of human rights.

47. Effective and competent national institutions are the cornerstone of successful restitution programmes. The provisions contained in Section V on restitution procedures, institutions, mechanisms

and legal frameworks are meant to provide practical guidelines for the establishment and support of institutions at national level and other institutions responsible for implementing restitution policies. Whenever possible, it is important that these institutions be directly established within peace settlement and voluntary repatriation agreements, so as to ensure that restitution is seen as an integral component of post-conflict and peacebuilding strategies.

48. It should be noted, in the commentary, that judicial mechanisms are especially important and that the absence of effective and accessible judicial remedies severely compromises the restitution process. This is particularly the case in post-conflict situations where internal political divisions render domestic institutions incapable of effectively administering restitution programmes, either due to institutional bias, or due to a lack of capacity and resources.

49. The Draft Principles also provide for the accessibility of restitution claims procedures, with the understanding that institutions not only must be effective in their work to implement restitution policies, they must also be accessible to those constituencies which they are meant to benefit. As such, claims procedures must be physically, linguistically and financially accessible, and special measures should be taken to ensure that especially vulnerable groups or persons are able to benefit from such institutions in an equitable and just manner.

50. The legal recognition of the right to housing and property restitution for refugees and other displaced persons is indispensable to the adequate implementation of restitution programmes and policies and their adequate enforcement. Legal protections should be clearly articulated in an internally consistent manner, and legal protections should be consistent with international human rights and humanitarian principles. In order to establish an adequate legal regime for the protection of the rights articulated in these Draft Principles, States will need to pursue a range of legislative measures, including the adoption, amendment, reform, or repeal of relevant laws.

51. The prohibition of arbitrary and discriminatory laws builds upon the right to non-discrimination recognized in Section I of the Draft Principles. As pointed out in the preliminary report, one of the

common obstacles to the successful implementation of restitution programmes has been the establishment of policies which favour certain groups while barring others from returning to their own homes, as has been the case with the application of discriminatory abandonment laws. Discriminatory restitution programmes further entrench social divisions and animosities, and are counter to post-conflict resolution, peace-building, as well as to fundamental human rights principles and international legal obligations. As such, it is essential for States to bring their national legislation into compliance with non-discrimination standards. It also deserves mention that the privatization of refugees' properties during their stay abroad can seriously complicate the exercise of property restitution rights. Efforts should be made to ensure that privatization does not result in the loss of property restitution rights of refugees.

52. The provision of legal aid and the additional provisions concerning enforcement are critical for the effective implementation of restitution policies and programmes. The provision of legal aid again increases the accessibility of restitution claims procedures, and ensures that persons are not deterred from benefiting from such procedures because of barriers associated with understanding and navigating the law. Similarly, the adequate enforcement of judgements related to restitution is essential to the effective implementation of restitution policies and programmes, and are especially important in situations where persons have been displaced due to violence.

COMMENTARY TO SECTION VI OF THE DRAFT PRINCIPLES ON THE ROLE OF THE INTERNATIONAL COMMUNITY AND OF INTERNATIONAL ORGANIZATIONS

53. Section VI of the Draft Principles outlines the role of the international community and of international organizations in facilitating restitution processes. In this regard, the Draft Principles note that the international community has a responsibility to act in ways which promote and protect the right to housing and property restitution, as well as the right to return.

54. The bodies and agencies of the United Nations system, in particular, have an important role to play in overseeing the successful implementation of restitution programmes. This role should be seen more generally, as part of the United Nations human rights monitoring activities. Most notably, the human rights treaty monitoring bodies and the Charter-based human rights bodies, including the Commission on Human Rights and the Sub-Commission, should monitor the implementation of restitution programmes within States in order to ensure that they comply with international standards. The Office of the United Nations High Commissioner for Refugees (UNHCR) also has a critical role to play in this regard, especially considering the central role that this body plays in the implementation of repatriation programmes.

55. The provisions articulated within Section VI on the role of international organizations in peacemaking and international peacekeeping recognize that while housing and property restitution is necessary to post-conflict resolution and peacebuilding, restitution programmes cannot be properly implemented under conditions which are overly volatile and unstable. As such, peacekeeping allows for the stabilization of conflict situations, paving the way for housing and property restitution programmes to be implemented and, perhaps even more importantly, enforced. The United Nations plays a unique role in this regard.

56. In many cases, the United Nations is also often called upon to negotiate and broker peace agreements between warring factions. As such, the Draft Principles stipulate that the international organizations, including the United Nations, should ensure that peace settlement and voluntary repatriation agreements which are brokered contain provisions related to the establishment of national institutions, procedures and mechanisms for the facilitation of the restitution process.

COMMENTARY TO SECTION VII OF THE DRAFT PRINCIPLES ON INTERPRETATION

57. The interpretation of the Draft Principles includes a saving clause which prohibits any interpretation of the universal principles which limits, alters or otherwise prejudices the provisions of any international human rights or international humanitarian legal instrument or rights consistent with such standards as recognized under national law. Finally, the Draft Principles also recognizes that the present commentary, because it provides the legal and normative underpinnings for the Draft

Principles, shall be regarded as their main author-itative interpretation.

ENDNOTES

1. United Nations, *Treaty Series*, vol. 993, p. 3.

2. *Ibid.*, vol. 999, p. 171.

3. Ibid., vol. 660, p. 195.

4. Ibid., vol. 1249, p. 13.

5. General Assembly resolution 44/25, annex.

6. Basic Documents Pertaining to Human Rights in the Inter-American System (OEA/Ser.L.V/II.82 6, rev.1).

7. United Nations, *Treaty Series*, vol. 1144, p. 123.

8. Ibid., vol. 1520, p. 243.

9. *Ibid.*, vol. 213, p. 221.

10. Article 3 stipulates "The States Parties to the present Covenant undertake to ensure the equal right of men and women to the enjoyment of all civil and political rights set forth in the present Covenant."

11. Article 3 stipulates "The States Parties to the present Covenant undertake to ensure the equal right of men and women to the enjoyment of all economic, social and cultural rights set forth in the present Covenant."

12. See also Fact Sheet No. 25, Forced Evictions and Human Rights.

13. United Nations, *Treaty Series*, vol. 75, p. 287.

14. Ibid., vol. 1125, p. 609.

15. General Assembly resolution 39/46, annex.

16. Communication No. 161/2000 (CAT/C/29/D/161/2000).

17. United Nations, *Treaty Series*, vol. 1650, p. 383.

18. Article 5 states: "In compliance with the fundamental obligations laid down in article 2 of this Convention, States Parties undertake to prohibit and eliminate racial discrimination in all of its forms and to guarantee the right of everyone, without distinction as to race, colour, or national or ethnic origin, to equality before the law, notably in the enjoyment of the following rights [. . .] the right to housing."

19. Article 14, paragraph 2 of the Convention stipulates that "State Parties shall take all appropriate measures to eliminate discrimination against women in rural areas in order to ensure, on a basis of equality of men and women, that they participate in and benefit from rural development and, in particular, shall ensure to such women the right [. . .] (h) to enjoy adequate living conditions, particularly in relation to housing, sanitation, electricity and water supply, transport and communications."

20. Article 27, paragraph 3, of the Convention stipulates: "State Parties, in accordance with national conditions and within their means, shall take appropriate measure to assist parents and others responsible for the child to implement this right and shall in the case of need provide material assistance and support programmes, particularly with regards to nutrition, clothing and housing."

21. United Nations, *Treaty Series*, vol. 189, p. 137. Article 21 of the Convention specifically addresses the issue of housing: "As regards housing, the Contracting States, insofar as the matter is regulated by laws or regulations or is subject to the control of public authorities, shall accord to refugees lawfully staying in their territory treatment as favourable as possible and, in any event, not less favourable than that accorded to aliens generally in the same circumstances."

22. General Assembly resolution 45/158, annex.

23. Article 12, paragraph 1, states that "Everyone lawfully within the territory of a State shall, within that territory, have the right to liberty of movement and freedom to choose his residence."

24. Article VIII states that "Every person has the right to fix his residence within the territory of the State of which he is a national, to move about freely within such territory, and not to leave it except by his own will."

25. Article 22, paragraph 1, states that "Every person lawfully in the territory of a State Party has the right to move about in it, and to reside in it subject to the provisions of the law."

26. Article 12, paragraph 1, states that "Every individual shall have the right to freedom of movement and residence within the borders of a State provided he abides by the law."

27. "Everyone has the right to leave any country, including his own, and to return to his country."

28. "No one shall be arbitrarily deprived of the right to enter his own country."

29. Article 45 states, inter alia "Protected persons shall not be transferred to a Power which is not a party to the Convention. This provision shall in no way constitute an obstacle to the repatriation of protected persons, or to their return to their country of residence after the cessation of hostilities." Article 127 states, inter alia "When making decisions regarding the transfer of internees, the Detaining Power shall take their interests into account and, in particular, shall not do anything to increase the difficulties of repatriating them or returning them to their own homes." Article 132 states, inter alia "The Parties to the conflict shall, moreover, endeavour during the course of hostilities, to conclude agreements for the release, the repatriation, the return to places of residence or the accommodation in a neutral country of certain classes of internees, in particular children, pregnant women and mothers with infants and young children, wounded and sick, and internees who have been detained for a long time." Article 134 states "The High Contracting Parties shall endeavour, upon the close of hostilities or occupation, to ensure the return of all internees to their last

place of residence, or to facilitate their repatriation." Article 135 states, inter alia "The Detaining Power shall bear the expense of returning released internees to the places where they were residing when interned, or, if it took them into custody while they were in transit or on the high seas, the cost of completing their journey or of their return to their point of departure."

30. "Every individual shall have the right to leave any country including his own, and to return to his country. This right may only be subject to restrictions, provided for by law for the protection of national security, law and order, public health or morality."

31. The Committee goes on to observe "In no case may a person be arbitrarily deprived of the right to enter his or her own country. The reference to the concept of arbitrariness in this context is intended to emphasize that it applies to all State action, legislative, administrative and judicial; it guarantees that even interference provided for by law should be in accordance with the provisions, aims and objectives of the Covenant and should be, in any event, reasonable in the particular circumstances. The Committee considers that there are few, if any, circumstances in which deprivation of the right to enter one's own country could be reasonable. A State party must not, by stripping a person of nationality or by expelling an individual to a third country, arbitrarily prevent this person from returning to his or her own country."

32. See, for example, Security Council resolutions 1287 (2000), 1244 (1999), 1199 (1998), 1036 (1996), 971 (1995), 876 (1993) and 820 (1993); General Assembly resolutions 35/124 and 51/126; resolutions 1994/24 and 1998/26 of the Sub-Commission; and general recommendation XXII on article 5 of the Convention on refugees and displaced persons of the Committee on the Elimination of Racial Discrimination.

33. See Security Council resolutions 1287 (2000), 1036 (1996), 971 (1995) and 876 (1993).

34. In operative paragraph 7, the Security Council reaffirmed "its endorsement of the principles that all statements or commitments made under duress, particularly those relating to land and property, are wholly null and void and that all displaced persons have the right to return in peace to their former homes and should be assisted to do so".

8.12. Resolution 2004/2 – Housing and Property Restitution (2004)[134]

The Sub-Commission on the Promotion and Protection of Human Rights,

Guided by the principles embodied in the Charter of the United Nations, the Universal Declaration of Human Rights, the International Covenants on Human Rights, the 1951 Convention relating to the Status of Refugees and its 1967 Protocol, and other relevant international instruments on human rights and humanitarian law,

Recalling its resolution 1998/26 of 26 August 1998 on housing and property restitution in the context of the return of refugees and internally displaced persons, its decision 2001/122 of 16 August 2001 on the return of refugees' or displaced persons' property, its resolution 2002/30 of 15 August 2002 on the right to return of refugees and internally displaced persons, its resolution 2002/7 of 14 August 2002 on housing and property restitution in the context of refugees and other displaced persons, its resolution 2003/17 of 13 August 2003 on prohibition of forced evictions and its resolution 2003/18 of 13 August 2003 on housing and property restitution,

Recalling also Commission on Human Rights decision 2003/109 of 24 April 2003 on housing and property restitution in the context of the return of refugees and internally displaced persons, and taking note of Commission resolution 2004/28 of 16 April 2004 on prohibition of forced evictions,

Reaffirming the right of all refugees and displaced persons to return freely to their countries and to have restored to them housing and property of which they were deprived during the course of displacement, or to be compensated for any property that cannot be restored to them,

1. *Urges* all States to ensure the free and fair exercise of the right to return to one's home and place of habitual residence by all refugees and displaced persons and to develop effective and expeditious legal, administrative and other procedures to ensure the free and fair exercise of this right, including fair and effective mechanisms designed to resolve outstanding housing and property problems;

2. *Reiterates* that the adoption or application of laws by States that are designed to or result in the loss or removal of tenancy, use, ownership or other rights connected with housing or property, the retraction of the right to reside in a particular place, or laws of abandonment employed against refugees or internally displaced persons pose serious impediments to the return and reintegration of refugees and internally displaced persons and to reconstruction and reconciliation;

3. *Affirms* that the remedy of compensation should only be used when the remedy of restitution is not

[134] 9 August 2004.

possible or when the injured party knowingly and voluntarily accepts compensation in lieu of restitution;

[. . .]

8.13. Housing and Property Restitution in the Context of the Return of Refugees and Internally Displaced Persons – Final Report of the Special Rapporteur, Paulo Sérgio Pinheiro (2005)[135]

Summary

At its fifty-sixth session the Sub-Commission on the Promotion and Protection of Human Rights, in its resolution 2004/2, welcomed the progress report of the Special Rapporteur and requested the Office of the United Nations High Commissioner for Human Rights to circulate the draft principles on housing and property restitution for refugees and displaced persons contained therein widely among non-governmental organizations, Governments, specialized agencies and other interested parties for comment, and requested the Special Rapporteur to take those comments into account in the preparation of his final report to be considered by the Sub-Commission at its fifty-seventh session.

This final report submitted by the Special Rapporteur reflects the results of this intensive consultation process and presents the Principles on housing and property restitution for refugees and displaced persons in their final version. The addendum to this report contains explanatory notes on the principles. The explanatory notes identify the provisions of international human rights, refugee and humanitarian law and related standards which serve as the foundation on which the principles themselves are built.

Introduction

1. At its fifty-sixth session, the Sub-Commission on the Promotion and Protection of Human Rights, in its resolution 2004/2, welcomed the progress report of the Special Rapporteur on housing and property restitution in the context of the return of refugees and internally displaced persons, which contained draft principles on housing and property restitution for refugees and displaced per-

sons (E/CN.4/Sub.2/2004/22) (hereinafter "Draft Principles"), as well as a supplementary draft commentary on the draft principles themselves (E/CN.4/Sub.2/2004/22/Add.1).

2. In resolution 2004/2 the Sub-Commission requested the Office of the United Nations High Commissioner for Human Rights to circulate the Draft Principles widely among non-governmental organizations, Governments, specialized agencies and other interested parties for comment, and requested the Special Rapporteur to take those comments into account in the preparation of his final report to be considered by the Sub-Commission at its fifty-seventh session. In addition, over the last year, the Special Rapporteur has similarly solicited comments from various agencies and experts, in order to invite a wide range of views, comments and input on the Draft Principles.

3. Since the Sub-Commission's fifty-sixth session, the Special Rapporteur has received many thoughtful and detailed written comments on the Draft Principles from non-governmental organizations, Governments, specialized agencies and other interested parties. The Special Rapporteur was extremely gratified by the careful and kind attention focused on the Draft Principles by so many interested parties, and wishes to gratefully acknowledge each contribution offered towards the development of this important work.

4. In order to further facilitate dialogue on the Draft Principles, an Expert Consultation on the Draft Principles on Housing and Property Restitution was held at Brown University in Providence, Rhode Island, United States of America, on 21 and 22 April 2005. The Expert Consultation allowed the Special Rapporteur to discuss the development of the Draft Principles in partnership with a broad range of international experts. The participants at the Expert Consultation brought to the forum a diverse and impressive range of expertise, including proficiency in the areas of refugee assistance and refugee law, internally displaced persons, restitution programme development and implementation, conflict and post-conflict situations, peace-building and peace negotiations, international housing rights, gender equality in situations of displacement and, of course, commendable expertise in the areas of international humanitarian law, and international human rights law.[1]

5. The Expert Consultation was coordinated jointly by the Watson Institute for International Studies at

---

[135] E/CN.4/Sub.2/2005/17.

Brown University and the Centre on Housing Rights and Evictions (COHRE), with the generous support of the Office of the United Nations High Commissioner for Refugees (UNHCR) and the Norwegian Refugee Council (NRC). The Special Rapporteur would like also to take this opportunity to gratefully acknowledge each of these agencies for its very kind and generous support.

6. The Expert Consultation invited participants to comment on the substantive and technical content of the Draft Principles, thereby ensuring that the final articulation of the Principles themselves address, as clearly and concisely as possible, real-world obstacles which may be experienced during the implementation of restitution programmes. As such, the Principles incorporate a forward-looking and holistic approach to housing, land and property restitution under international law. This approach is at the same time rooted in the lessons learned by experts in the field, and the "best practices" which have emerged in previous post-conflict situations wherein restitution has been seen as a key component of restorative justice. As such, the Principles incorporate some of the most useful provisions from various pre-existing national restitution policies and programmes, including those developed for Bosnia and Herzegovina, Burundi, Cambodia, Cyprus, Guatemala, Kosovo, South Africa and Rwanda.

7. Without doubt, this rigorous review process has improved the quality, depth and relevance of the Draft Principles. This final report submitted by the Special Rapporteur reflects the results of this intensive consultation process and presents the Principles on Housing and Property Restitution for Refugees and Displaced Persons in their final version. The addendum to this report presents explanatory notes on the Principles. The explanatory notes identify the provisions of international human rights, refugee and humanitarian law and related standards which serve as the very foundation on which the Principles themselves are built.

8. It must be noted that the Principles continue to reflect widely accepted principles of international human rights, refugee and humanitarian law and related standards, including those enshrined in the Universal Declaration of Human Rights; the International Covenant on Economic, Social and Cultural Rights; the International Covenant on Civil and Political Rights; the Convention on the

Elimination of All Forms of Discrimination against Women; the International Convention on the Elimination of All Forms of Racial Discrimination; the Convention on the Rights of the Child; the 1951 Convention relating to the Status of Refugees; the Geneva Convention relative to the Protection of Civilian Persons in Time of War and the Second Protocol Additional to the Geneva Conventions relating to the Protection of Victims of Non-International Armed Conflicts. The Principles also reflect other relevant international human rights and related standards, in particular, the Guiding Principles on Internal Displacement, the Basic Principles and Guidelines on the Right to a Remedy and Reparation for Victims of Violations of International Human Rights and Humanitarian Law,[2] and relevant UNHCR Executive Committee Conclusions.

9. At a later stage, it will be possible, and extremely worthwhile, to elaborate a more expansive and comprehensive commentary on the Principles which would encompass all of the relevant international law, as well as other applicable standards, which may be helpful in the interpretation of these Principles. The elaboration of such an exhaustive text is, however, beyond the current scope of this study. Rather, the development of a comprehensive commentary can, and should, be considered a project for future development. Certainly, this approach has been utilized in previous cases where human rights standards have been articulated and adopted by human rights bodies such as the Sub-Commission. It is hoped that the creation of a comprehensive commentary will be one of the many ways in which the Principles on housing and property restitution for refugees and displaced persons will continue to live on.

ENDNOTES

1. The Participants in the Expert Consultation were Ingunn-Sofie Aursnes, Paul Bentall, George Bisharat, Widney Brown, Pierre Buyoya, Roberta Cohen, Mayra Gómez, Agnes Hurwitz, Lisa Jones, Isabel G. Lavadenz Paccieri, Scott Leckie, Dan Lewis, Karolina Lindholm-Billing, Gert Ludekin, Carolyn Makinson, John Packer and Rhodri Williams.

2. The Commission recommended to the General Assembly that it adopt the Basic Principles and Guidelines as contained in the annex to Commission resolution 2005/35.

Note to readers: The full text of the 'Pinheiro Principles on Housing and Property Restitution for

Refugees and Displaced Persons' can be found in section 1.15 above.

8.14. Resolution 2005/21 – Housing and Property Restitution for Refugees and Displaced Persons (2005)[136]

The Sub-Commission on the Promotion and Protection of Human Rights,

Guided by the principles embodied in the Charter of the United Nations, the Universal Declaration of Human Rights, the International Covenants on Human Rights, the 1951 Convention relating to the Status of Refugees and its 1967 Protocol, and other relevant international instruments on human rights and humanitarian law,

Recalling its resolution 1998/26 of 26 August 1998 on housing and property restitution in the context of the return of refugees and internally displaced persons, its decision 2001/122 of August 2001 on the return of refugees' or displaced persons' property, its resolution 2002/30 of 15 August 2002 on the right to return of refugees and internally displaced persons, its resolution 2002/7 of 14 August 2002 on housing and property restitution in the context of refugees and other displaced persons, its resolution 2003/17 of 13 August 2003 on prohibition of forced evictions, its resolution 2003/18 of 13 August 2003 on housing and property restitution, and its resolution 2004/2 of 9 August 2004 on housing and property restitution,

Recalling also Commission on Human Rights decision 2003/109 of 24 April 2003 on housing and property restitution in the context of the return of refugees and internally displaced persons and resolution 2004/28 of 16 April 2004 on prohibition of forced evictions,

Convinced that the right to housing, land and property restitution is essential to the resolution of conflict and to post-conflict peacebuilding, safe and sustainable return and the establishment of the rule of law, and that careful monitoring of restitution programmes by international organizations and affected States is indispensable to ensuring their effective implementation,

1. *Urges* States to ensure the right of all refugees and displaced persons to return and have restored to them any housing, land and/or property of which they were arbitrarily or unlawfully deprived, and to develop effective and expeditious legal, administrative and other procedures to ensure the free and fair exercise of this right, including fair and effective mechanisms designed to implement this right;

2. *Reiterates* that States should neither adopt nor apply laws that prejudice the restitution process, in particular through arbitrary, discriminatory, or otherwise unjust abandonment laws or statutes of limitations;

3. *Affirms* that all refugees and displaced persons have the right to full and effective compensation as an integral component of the restitution process;

4. *Welcomes* the final report of the Special Rapporteur, Paulo Sérgio Pinheiro, on housing and property restitution in the context of the return of refugees and internally displaced persons (E/CN.4/Sub.2/2005/17), containing the Principles on Housing and Property Restitution for Refugees and Displaced Persons as well as the explanatory notes on the Principles (E/CN.4/Sub.2/2005/17/Add.1);

5. *Endorses* the Principles on Housing and Property Restitution for Refugees and Displaced Persons and encourages their application and implementation by States, intergovernmental organizations and other relevant actors;

6. *Requests* Mr. Pinheiro to compile and update the study on housing and property restitution for refugees and internally displaced persons so that it can be published in one volume as part of Human Rights Study Series, in all the official languages of the United Nations.

[. . .]

9. UN HUMAN RIGHTS TREATY BODIES

9.1. Committee on Economic, Social and Cultural Rights

9.1.1. General Comment 4 – The Right to Adequate Housing (1991)[137]

1. Pursuant to article 11 (1) of the Covenant, States parties "recognize the right of everyone to an adequate standard of living for himself and his family,

---

[136] 11 August 2005.

[137] U.N. Doc. E/1992/23. Footnotes omitted.

including adequate food, clothing and housing, and to the continuous improvement of living conditions". The human right to adequate housing, which is thus derived from the right to an adequate standard of living, is of central importance for the enjoyment of all economic, social and cultural rights.

2. The Committee has been able to accumulate a large amount of information pertaining to this right. Since 1979, the Committee and its predecessors have examined 75 reports dealing with the right to adequate housing. The Committee has also devoted a day of general discussion to the issue at each of its third (see E/1989/22, para. 312) and fourth sessions (E/1990/23, paras. 281–285). In addition, the Committee has taken careful note of information generated by the International Year of Shelter for the Homeless (1987) including the Global Strategy for Shelter to the Year 2000 adopted by the General Assembly in its resolution 42/191 of 11 December 1987. The Committee has also reviewed relevant reports and other documentation of the Commission on Human Rights and the Sub-Commission on Prevention of Discrimination and Protection of Minorities.

3. Although a wide variety of international instruments address the different dimensions of the right to adequate housing article 11 (1) of the Covenant is the most comprehensive and perhaps the most important of the relevant provisions.

4. Despite the fact that the international community has frequently reaffirmed the importance of full respect for the right to adequate housing, there remains a disturbingly large gap between the standards set in article 11 (1) of the Covenant and the situation prevailing in many parts of the world. While the problems are often particularly acute in some developing countries which confront major resource and other constraints, the Committee observes that significant problems of homelessness and inadequate housing also exist in some of the most economically developed societies. The United Nations estimates that there are over 100 million persons homeless worldwide and over 1 billion inadequately housed. There is no indication that this number is decreasing. It seems clear that no State party is free of significant problems of one kind or another in relation to the right to housing.

5. In some instances, the reports of States parties examined by the Committee have acknowl-

edged and described difficulties in ensuring the right to adequate housing. For the most part, however, the information provided has been insufficient to enable the Committee to obtain an adequate picture of the situation prevailing in the State concerned. This General Comment thus aims to identify some of the principal issues which the Committee considers to be important in relation to this right.

6. The right to adequate housing applies to everyone. While the reference to "himself and his family" reflects assumptions as to gender roles and economic activity patterns commonly accepted in 1966 when the Covenant was adopted, the phrase cannot be read today as implying any limitations upon the applicability of the right to individuals or to female-headed households or other such groups. Thus, the concept of "family" must be understood in a wide sense. Further, individuals, as well as families, are entitled to adequate housing regardless of age, economic status, group or other affiliation or status and other such factors. In particular, enjoyment of this right must, in accordance with article 2(2) of the Covenant, not be subject to any form of discrimination.

7. In the Committee's view, the right to housing should not be interpreted in a narrow or restrictive sense which equates it with, for example, the shelter provided by merely having a roof over one's head or views shelter exclusively as a commodity. Rather it should be seen as the right to live somewhere in security, peace and dignity. This is appropriate for at least two reasons. In the first place, the right to housing is integrally linked to other human rights and to the fundamental principles upon which the Covenant is premised. This "the inherent dignity of the human person" from which the rights in the Covenant are said to derive requires that the term "housing" be interpreted so as to take account of a variety of other considerations, most importantly that the right to housing should be ensured to all persons irrespective of income or access to economic resources. Secondly, the reference in article 11(1) must be read as referring not just to housing but to adequate housing. As both the Commission on Human Settlements and the Global Strategy for Shelter to the Year 2000 have stated: "Adequate shelter means... adequate privacy, adequate space, adequate security, adequate lighting and ventilation, adequate basic infrastructure and adequate location with regard to work and basic facilities – all at a reasonable cost".

8. Thus the concept of adequacy is particularly significant in relation to the right to housing since it serves to underline a number of factors which must be taken into account in determining whether particular forms of shelter can be considered to constitute "adequate housing" for the purposes of the Covenant. While adequacy is determined in part by social, economic, cultural, climatic, ecological and other factors, the Committee believes that it is nevertheless possible to identify certain aspects of the right that must be taken into account for this purpose in any particular context. They include the following:

(a) *Legal security of tenure.* Tenure takes a variety of forms, including rental (public and private) accommodation, cooperative housing, lease, owner-occupation, emergency housing and informal settlements, including occupation of land or property. Notwithstanding the type of tenure, all persons should possess a degree of security of tenure which guarantees legal protection against forced eviction, harassment and other threats. States parties should consequently take immediate measures aimed at conferring legal security of tenure upon those persons and households currently lacking such protection, in genuine consultation with affected persons and groups;

(b) *Availability of services, materials, facilities and infrastructure.* An adequate house must contain certain facilities essential for health, security, comfort and nutrition. All beneficiaries of the right to adequate housing should have sustainable access to natural and common resources, safe drinking water, energy for cooking, heating and lighting, sanitation and washing facilities, means of food storage, refuse disposal, site drainage and emergency services;

(c) *Affordability.* Personal or household financial costs associated with housing should be at such a level that the attainment and satisfaction of other basic needs are not threatened or compromised. Steps should be taken by States parties to ensure that the percentage of housing-related costs is, in general, commensurate with income levels. States parties should establish housing subsidies for those unable to obtain affordable housing, as well as forms and levels of housing finance which adequately reflect housing needs. In accordance with the principle of affordability, tenants should be protected by appropriate means against unreasonable rent levels or rent increases. In societies where natural materials constitute the chief sources of building materials for housing, steps should be taken by States parties to ensure the availability of such materials;

(d) *Habitability.* Adequate housing must be habitable, in terms of providing the inhabitants with adequate space and protecting them from cold, damp, heat, rain, wind or other threats to health, structural hazards, and disease vectors. The physical safety of occupants must be guaranteed as well. The Committee encourages States parties to comprehensively apply the Health Principles of Housing prepared by WHO which view housing as the environmental factor most frequently associated with conditions for disease in epidemiological analyses; i.e. inadequate and deficient housing and living conditions are invariably associated with higher mortality and morbidity rates;

(e) *Accessibility.* Adequate housing must be accessible to those entitled to it. Disadvantaged groups must be accorded full and sustainable access to adequate housing resources. Thus, such disadvantaged groups as the elderly, children, the physically disabled, the terminally ill, HIV-positive individuals, persons with persistent medical problems, the mentally ill, victims of natural disasters, people living in disaster-prone areas and other groups should be ensured some degree of priority consideration in the housing sphere. Both housing law and policy should take fully into account the special housing needs of these groups. Within many States parties increasing access to land by landless or impoverished segments of the society should constitute a central policy goal. Discernible governmental obligations need to be developed aiming to substantiate the right of all to a secure place to live in peace and dignity, including access to land as an entitlement;

(f) *Location.* Adequate housing must be in a location which allows access to employment options, health-care services, schools, child-care centres and other social facilities. This is true both in large cities and in rural areas where the temporal and financial costs of getting to and from the place of work can place excessive demands upon the budgets of poor households. Similarly, housing should not be built on polluted sites nor in immediate proximity to pollution sources that threaten the right to health of the inhabitants;

(g) *Cultural adequacy.* The way housing is constructed, the building materials used and the policies supporting these must appropriately enable the expression of cultural identity and diversity of housing. Activities geared towards development or modernization in the housing sphere should ensure that the cultural dimensions of housing are not sacrificed, and that, inter alia, modern technological facilities, as appropriate are also ensured.

9. As noted above, the right to adequate housing cannot be viewed in isolation from other human rights contained in the two International Covenants and other applicable international instruments. Reference has already been made in this regard to the concept of human dignity and the principle of non-discrimination. In addition, the full enjoyment of other rights – such as the right to freedom of expression, the right to freedom of association (such as for tenants and other community-based groups), the right to freedom of residence and the right to participate in public decision-making – is indispensable if the right to adequate housing is to be realized and maintained by all groups in society. Similarly, the right not to be subjected to arbitrary or unlawful interference with one's privacy, family, home or correspondence constitutes a very important dimension in defining the right to adequate housing.

10. Regardless of the state of development of any country, there are certain steps which must be taken immediately. As recognized in the Global Strategy for Shelter and in other international analyses, many of the measures required to promote the right to housing would only require the abstention by the Government from certain practices and a commitment to facilitating "self-help" by affected groups. To the extent that any such steps are considered to be beyond the maximum resources available to a State party, it is appropriate that a request be made as soon as possible for international cooperation in accordance with articles 11 (1), 22 and 23 of the Covenant, and that the Committee be informed thereof.

11. States parties must give due priority to those social groups living in unfavourable conditions by giving them particular consideration. Policies and legislation should correspondingly not be designed to benefit already advantaged social groups at the expense of others. The Committee is aware that external factors can affect the right to a contin-uous improvement of living conditions, and that in many States parties overall living conditions declined during the 1980s. However, as noted by the Committee in its General Comment 2 (1990) (E/1990/23, annex III), despite externally caused problems, the obligations under the Covenant continue to apply and are perhaps even more pertinent during times of economic contraction. It would thus appear to the Committee that a general decline in living and housing conditions, directly attributable to policy and legislative decisions by States parties, and in the absence of accompanying compensatory measures, would be inconsistent with the obligations under the Covenant.

12. While the most appropriate means of achieving the full realization of the right to adequate housing will inevitably vary significantly from one State party to another, the Covenant clearly requires that each State party take whatever steps are necessary for that purpose. This will almost invariably require the adoption of a national housing strategy which, as stated in paragraph 32 of the Global Strategy for Shelter, "defines the objectives for the development of shelter conditions, identifies the resources available to meet these goals and the most cost-effective way of using them and sets out the responsibilities and time-frame for the implementation of the necessary measures". Both for reasons of relevance and effectiveness, as well as in order to ensure respect for other human rights, such a strategy should reflect extensive genuine consultation with, and participation by, all of those affected, including the homeless, the inadequately housed and their representatives. Furthermore, steps should be taken to ensure coordination between ministries and regional and local authorities in order to reconcile related policies (economics, agriculture, environment, energy, etc.) with the obligations under article 11 of the Covenant.

13. Effective monitoring of the situation with respect to housing is another obligation of immediate effect. For a State party to satisfy its obligations under article 11 (1) it must demonstrate, inter alia, that it has taken whatever steps are necessary, either alone or on the basis of international cooperation, to ascertain the full extent of homelessness and inadequate housing within its jurisdiction. In this regard, the revised general guidelines regarding the form and contents of reports adopted by the Committee (E/C.12/1991/1) emphasize the need to "provide detailed information about those groups

within . . . society that are vulnerable and disadvantaged with regard to housing". They include, in particular, homeless persons and families, those inadequately housed and without ready access to basic amenities, those living in "illegal" settlements, those subject to forced evictions and low-income groups.

14. Measures designed to satisfy a State party's obligations in respect of the right to adequate housing may reflect whatever mix of public and private sector measures considered appropriate. While in some States public financing of housing might most usefully be spent on direct construction of new housing, in most cases, experience has shown the inability of Governments to fully satisfy housing deficits with publicly built housing. The promotion by States parties of "enabling strategies", combined with a full commitment to obligations under the right to adequate housing, should thus be encouraged. In essence, the obligation is to demonstrate that, in aggregate, the measures being taken are sufficient to realize the right for every individual in the shortest possible time in accordance with the maximum of available resources.

15. Many of the measures that will be required will involve resource allocations and policy initiatives of a general kind. Nevertheless, the role of formal legislative and administrative measures should not be underestimated in this context. The Global Strategy for Shelter (paras. 66–67) has drawn attention to the types of measures that might be taken in this regard and to their importance.

16. In some States, the right to adequate housing is constitutionally entrenched. In such cases the Committee is particularly interested in learning of the legal and practical significance of such an approach. Details of specific cases and of other ways in which entrenchment has proved helpful should thus be provided.

17. The Committee views many component elements of the right to adequate housing as being at least consistent with the provision of domestic legal remedies. Depending on the legal system, such areas might include, but are not limited to: (a) legal appeals aimed at preventing planned evictions or demolitions through the issuance of court-ordered injunctions; (b) legal procedures seeking compensation following an illegal eviction; (c) complaints against illegal actions carried out or supported by landlords (whether public or private) in relation to rent levels, dwelling maintenance, and racial or other forms of discrimination; (d) allegations of any form of discrimination in the allocation and availability of access to housing; and (e) complaints against landlords concerning unhealthy or inadequate housing conditions. In some legal systems it would also be appropriate to explore the possibility of facilitating class action suits in situations involving significantly increased levels of homelessness.

18. In this regard, the Committee considers that instances of forced eviction are prima facie incompatible with the requirements of the Covenant and can only be justified in the most exceptional circumstances, and in accordance with the relevant principles of international law.

19. Finally, article 11 (1) concludes with the obligation of States parties to recognize "the essential importance of international cooperation based on free consent". Traditionally, less than 5 per cent of all international assistance has been directed towards housing or human settlements, and often the manner by which such funding is provided does little to address the housing needs of disadvantaged groups. States parties, both recipients and providers, should ensure that a substantial proportion of financing is devoted to creating conditions leading to a higher number of persons being adequately housed. International financial institutions promoting measures of structural adjustment should ensure that such measures do not compromise the enjoyment of the right to adequate housing. States parties should, when contemplating international financial cooperation, seek to indicate areas relevant to the right to adequate housing where external financing would have the most effect. Such requests should take full account of the needs and views of the affected groups.

9.1.2. General Comment 7 – Forced Evictions and the Right to Adequate Housing (1997)[138]

1. In its General Comment No.4 (1991), the committee observed that all persons should possess a degree of security of tenure which guarantees legal protection against forced eviction, harassment and other threats. It concluded that forced evictions are prima facie incompatible with the requirements of the Covenant. Having considered a significant

---

[138] U.N. Doc. E/1998/22. Footnotes omitted.

number of reports of forced evictions in recent years, including instances in which it has determined that the obligations of States Parties were being violated, the Committee is now in a position to seek to provide further clarification as to the implications of such practices in terms of the obligations contained in the Covenant.

2. The International community has long recognised that the issue of forced evictions is a serious one. In 1976 the Vancouver Declaration on Human Settlements noted that "major clearance operations should take place only when conservation and rehabilitation are not feasible and relocation measures are made". In the 1988 Global Strategy for Shelter to the Year 2000, the General Assembly recognized the "fundamental obligation (of Governments) to protect and improve houses and neighbourhoods, rather than damage or destroy them". Agenda 21 stated that "people should be protected by law against unfair eviction from their homes or land". In the Habitat Agenda Governments committed themselves to "protecting all people from, and providing legal protection and redress for, forced evictions that are contrary to the law, taking human rights into consideration; [and] when evictions are unavoidable, ensuring, as appropriate, that alternative suitable solutions are provided". The Commission on Human Rights has also indicated that "forced evictions are a gross violation of human rights". However, although these statements are important, they leave open one of the most critical issues, namely that of determining the circumstances under which forced evictions are permissible and of spelling out the types of protection required to ensure respect for the relevant provisions of the Covenant.

3. The use of the term "forced evictions" is, in some respects, problematic. This expression seeks to convey a sense of arbitrariness and of illegality. To many observers, however, the reference to "forced evictions" is a tautology, while others have criticized the expression "illegal evictions" on the ground that it assumes that the relevant law provides adequate protection to the right to housing and conforms with the Covenant, which is by no means always the case. Similarly, it has been suggested that the term "unfair evictions" is even more subjective by virtue of its failure to refer to any legal framework at all. The international community, especially in the context of the Commission on Human Rights, has opted to refer to "forced evic-

tions" primarily since all suggested alternatives also suffer from many such defects.

4. The term "forced evictions" as used throughout this General Comment is defined as the permanent or temporary removal against their will of individuals, families and/or communities from the homes and/or land which they occupy, without the provision of, and access to, appropriate forms of legal or other protection. The prohibition on forced evictions does not, however, apply to evictions carried out by force in accordance with the law and in conformity with the provisions of the International Human Rights Covenants.

5. The practice of forced evictions is widespread and affects persons in both developed and developing countries. Owing to the interrelation and interdependency which exist among all human rights, forced evictions frequently violate other human rights. Thus, while manifestly breaching the rights enshrined in the Covenant, the practice of forced evictions may also result in violations of civil and political rights, such as the right to life, the right to security of the person, the right to non-interference with privacy, family and home and the right to the peaceful enjoyment of possessions.

6. Although the practice of forced evictions might appear to arise primarily in heavily populated urban areas, it also takes place in relation to forced population transfers, internal displacement, forced relocations in the context of armed conflict, mass exoduses and refugee movements. In all of these contexts, the right to adequate housing and not to be subject to forced evictions may be violated through a wide range of acts or omissions attributable to States Parties. Even in situations where it may be necessary to impose limitations on such a right, full compliance with Article 4 of the Covenant is required so that any limitations imposed must be "determined by law only in so far as this may be compatible with the nature of these rights [i.e. economic, social and cultural] and solely for the purpose of promoting the general welfare in a democratic society."

7. Many instances of forced evictions are associated with violence, such as evictions resulting from international armed conflicts, internal strife and communal or ethnic violence.

8. Other instances of forced evictions occur in the name of development. They might be carried out

in connection with conflict over land rights, development and infrastructure projects, such as the construction of dams or other large-scale energy projects, with land acquisition measures associated with urban renewal, housing renovation, city beautification programmes, the clearing of land for agricultural purposes, unbridled speculation in land, or the holding of major sporting events like the Olympic Games.

9. In essence, the obligations of States Parties to the Covenant in relation to forced evictions are based on Article 11(1), read in conjunction with other relevant provisions. In particular, Article 2(1) obliges States to use "all appropriate means" to promote the right to adequate housing. However, in view of the nature of the practice of forced evictions, the reference to Article 2(1) to progressive achievement based on the availability of resources will rarely be relevant. The State itself must refrain from forced evictions and ensure that the law is enforced against its agents or third parties who carry out forced evictions (as defined in para. 3 above). Moreover, this approach is reinforced by Article 17(1) of the International Covenant on Civil and Political Rights which complements the right not to be forcefully evicted without adequate protection. That provision recognises, inter alia, the right to be protected against "arbitrary or unlawful interference" with one's home. It is to be noted that the State's obligation to ensure respect for that right is not qualified by considerations relating to its available resources.

10. Article 2(1) of the Covenant requires States Parties to use "all appropriate means", including the adoption of legislative measures, to promote all the rights protected under the Covenant. Although the Committee has indicated in its General Comment No. 3 (1991) that such measures may not be indispensable in relation to all rights, it is clear that legislation against forced evictions is an essential basis upon which to build a system of effective protection. Such legislation should include measures which (a) provide the greatest possible security of tenure to occupiers of houses and land, (b) conform to the Covenant and (c) are designed to control strictly the circumstances under which evictions may be carried out. The legislation must also apply in relation to all agents acting under the authority of the State or who are accountable to it. Moreover, in view of the increasing trend in some States towards their government greatly reducing their responsibilities in the housing sector, States Par-

ties must ensure that legislative and other measures are adequate to prevent and, if appropriate, punish forced evictions carried out, without appropriate safeguards, by private persons or bodies. States parties should therefore review relevant legislation and policies to ensure that these are compatible with the obligations arising from the right to adequate housing and to repeal or amend any legislation or policies that are inconsistent with the requirements of the Covenant.

11. Women, children, youth, older persons, indigenous people, ethnic and other minorities, and other vulnerable individuals and groups all suffer disproportionately from the practice of forced evictions. Women in all groups are especially vulnerable given the extent to statutory and other forms of discrimination which often apply in relation to property rights (including home ownership) or rights of access to property or accommodation and their particular vulnerability to acts of violence and sexual abuse when they are rendered homeless. The non-discrimination provisions of Articles 2(2) and 3 of the Covenant impose an additional obligation upon governments to ensure that, where evictions do occur, appropriate measures are taken to ensure that no forms of discrimination are involved.

12. Where some evictions may be justifiable, such as in the case of the persistent non-payment of rent or of damage to rented property without any reasonable cause, it is incumbent upon the relevant authorities to ensure that those evictions are carried out in a manner warranted by a law which is compatible with the Covenant and that all the legal recourses and remedies are available to those affected.

13. Forced evictions and house demolitions as a punitive measure are also inconsistent with the norms of the Covenant. Likewise, the Committee takes note of the obligations enshrined within the 1949 Geneva Conventions and 1977 Protocols which relate to prohibitions on the displacement of the civilian population and the destruction of private property as these relate to the practice of forced evictions.

14. States Parties shall ensure, prior to carrying out any evictions, and particularly those involving large groups, that all feasible alternatives are explored in consultation with affected persons, with a view to avoiding, or at least minimizing, the need to use force. Legal remedies or procedures should

be provided to those who are affected by eviction orders. States Parties shall also see to it that all individuals concerned have a right to adequate compensation for any property, both personal and real, which is affected. In this respect, it is pertinent to recall article 2(3) of the International Covenant on Civil and Political Rights which requires States Parties to ensure "an effective remedy" for persons whose rights have been violated and the obligation upon the "competent authorities (to) enforce such remedies when granted".

15. In cases where eviction is considered to be justified, it should be carried out in strict compliance with the relevant provisions of international human rights law and in accordance with general principles of reasonableness and proportionality. In this regard it is especially pertinent to recall General Comment 16 by the Human Rights Committee, relating to Article 17 of the International Covenant on Civil and Political Rights, which states that interference with a person's home can only take place "in cases envisaged by the law". The Committee observed that the law "should be in accordance with the provisions, aims and objectives of the Covenant and should be, in any event, reasonable in the particular circumstances". The Committee also indicated that "relevant legislation must specify in details the precise circumstances in which such interferences may be permitted".

16. Appropriate procedural protection and due process are essential aspects of all human rights but it is especially pertinent in relation to a matter such as forced evictions which directly invokes a large number of the rights recognised in both International Human Rights Covenants. The Committee considers that the procedural protections which should be applied in relation to forced evictions include: (a) an opportunity for genuine consultation with those affected; (b) adequate and reasonable notice for all affected persons prior to the scheduled date of eviction; (c) information on the proposed evictions and where applicable, on the alternative purpose for which the land or housing is to be used, to be made available in reasonable time to all those affected; (d) especially where groups of people are involved, government officials or their representatives to be present during an eviction; (e) all persons carrying out the eviction to be properly identified; (f) evictions not to take place in particularly bad weather or at night unless the affected persons consent otherwise; (g) provision of legal remedies; and (h) provision, where possible, of legal aid to persons who are in need of it to seek redress from the courts.

17. Evictions should not result in rendering individuals homeless or vulnerable to the violation of other human rights. Where those affected are unable to provide for themselves, the State Party must take all appropriate measures, to the maximum of its available resources, to ensure that adequate alternative housing, resettlement or access to productive land, as the case may be, is available.

18. The Committee is aware that various development projects financed by international agencies within the territories of State Parties have resulted in forced evictions. In this regard, the Committee recalls its General Comment No. 2 (1990) which states, inter alia, that "international agencies should scrupulously avoid involvement in projects which, for example . . . promote or reinforce discrimination against individuals or groups contrary to the provisions of the Covenant, or involve large-scale evictions or displacement of person without the provision of all appropriate protection and compensation. Every effort should be made, at each phase of a development project, to ensure that the rights contained in the Covenant are duly taken into account".

19. Some institutions, such as the World Bank and the Organisation for Economic Co-operation and Development (OECD) have adopted guidelines on relocation and/or resettlement with a view to limiting the scale and human suffering associated with the practice of forced eviction. Such practices often accompany large-scale development projects, such as dam-building and other major energy projects. Full respect for such guidelines, in so far as they reflect the obligations contained in the Covenant, on the part of both the agencies themselves and by States Parties to the Covenant is essential. The committee recalls in this respect that statement in the Vienna Declaration and Programme of Action to the effect that: "while development facilitates the enjoyment of al human rights, the lack of development may not be invoked to justify the abridgement of internationally recognised human rights" (para. 10).

20. In accordance with the guidelines adopted by the Committee for reporting, State Parties are requested to provide various types of information pertaining directly to the practice of forced

evictions. This includes information relating to (a) the "number of persons evicted within the last five years and the number of persons currently lacking legal protection against arbitrary eviction or any other kind of eviction"; (b) "legislation concerning the rights of tenants to security of tenure, to protection from eviction" and (c) "legislation prohibiting any form of eviction".

21. Information is also sought as to "measures taken during, inter alia, urban renewal programmes, redevelopment projects, site upgrading, preparation for international events (Olympics and other sporting competitions, exhibitions, conferences, etc.), 'beautiful city' campaigns, etc. which guarantee protection from eviction or guarantee rehousing based on mutual consent, by any persons living on or near to affected sites". Despite these provisions, few States Parties have included the requisite information in their reports to the Committee. The Committee, therefore, wishes to emphasise in this regard the importance it attaches to the receipt of such information.

22. Some States Parties have indicated that information of this nature is not available. The Committee recalls that effective monitoring of the right to adequate housing, either by the Government concerned or by the Committee, is not possible in the absence of the collection of appropriate data and would request all States Parties to ensure that the necessary data is collected and is reflected in the reports submitted by them under the Covenant.

9.2. Committee on the Elimination of Racial Discrimination

9.2.1. General Recommendation 22 – Article 5 and Refugees and Displaced Persons (1996)[139]

The Committee on the Elimination of Racial Discrimination,

Conscious of the fact that foreign military, non-military and/or ethnic conflicts have resulted in massive flows of refugees and the displacement of persons on the basis of ethnic criteria in many parts of the world,

Considering that the Universal Declaration of Human Rights and the Convention on the Elimina-

tion of All Forms of Racial Discrimination proclaim that all human beings are born free and equal in dignity and rights and that everyone is entitled to all the rights and freedoms set out therein, without distinction of any kind, in particular as to race, colour, descent or national or ethnic origin,

Recalling the 1951 Convention and the 1967 Protocol relating to the status of refugees as the main source of the international system for the protection of refugees in general,

1. *Draws the attention* of States parties to article 5 of the International Convention on the Elimination of All Forms of Racial Discrimination as well as Committee's General Recommendation XX (48) on article 5, and reiterates that the Convention obliges States parties to prohibit and eliminate racial discrimination in the enjoyment of civil, political, economic, social and cultural rights and freedoms;

2. *Emphasizes* in this respect that:

(a) All such refugees and displaced persons have the right freely to return to their homes of origin under conditions of safety;

(b) States parties are obliged to ensure that the return of such refugees and displaced persons is voluntary and to observe the principle of non-refoulement and non-expulsion of refugees;

(c) All such refugees and displaced persons have, after their return to their homes of origin, the right to have restored to them property of which they were deprived in the course of the conflict and to be compensated appropriately for any such property that cannot be restored to them. Any commitments or statements relating to such property made under duress are null and void;

(d) All such refugees and displaced persons have, after their return to their homes of origin, the right to participate fully and equally in public affairs at all levels and to have equal access to public services and to receive rehabilitation assistance.

9.2.2. General Recommendation 23 – Rights of Indigenous Peoples (1997)[140]

1. In the practice of the Committee on the Elimination of Racial Discrimination, in particular in the

---

[139] U.N. Doc. A/51/18.

[140] U.N. Doc. A/52/18.

examination of reports of States parties under arti-cle 9 of the International Convention on the Elim-ination of All Forms of Racial Discrimination, the situation of indigenous peoples has always been a matter of close attention and concern. In this respect, the Committee has consistently affirmed that discrimination against indigenous peoples falls under the scope of the Convention and that all appropriate means must be taken to combat and eliminate such discrimination.

2. The Committee, noting that the General Assem-bly proclaimed the International Decade of the World's Indigenous Peoples commencing on 10 December 1994, reaffirms that the provisions of the International Convention on the Elimination of All Forms of Racial Discrimination apply to indigenous peoples.

3. The Committee is conscious of the fact that in many regions of the world indigenous peoples have been, and are still being, discriminated against and deprived of their human rights and fundamental freedoms and in particular that they have lost their land and resources to colonists, commercial com-panies and State enterprises. Consequently, the preservation of their culture and their historical identity has been and still is jeopardized.

4. The Committee calls in particular upon States parties to:

(a) Recognize and respect indigenous distinct cul-ture, history, language and way of life as an enrich-ment of the State's cultural identity and to promote its preservation;

(b) Ensure that members of indigenous peoples are free and equal in dignity and rights and free from any discrimination, in particular that based on indigenous origin or identity;

(c) Provide indigenous peoples with conditions allowing for a sustainable economic and social development compatible with their cultural char-acteristics;

(d) Ensure that members of indigenous peoples have equal rights in respect of effective participa-tion in public life and that no decisions directly relating to their rights and interests are taken with-out their informed consent;

(e) Ensure that indigenous communities can exer-cise their rights to practise and revitalize their cul-tural traditions and customs and to preserve and to practise their languages.

5. The Committee especially calls upon States par-ties to recognize and protect the rights of indige-nous peoples to own, develop, control and use their communal lands, territories and resources and, where they have been deprived of their lands and territories traditionally owned or otherwise inhabited or used without their free and informed consent, to take steps to return those lands and ter-ritories. Only when this is for factual reasons not possible, the right to restitution should be substi-tuted by the right to just, fair and prompt compen-sation. Such compensation should as far as possible take the form of lands and territories.

6. The Committee further calls upon States par-ties with indigenous peoples in their territories to include in their periodic reports full information on the situation of such peoples, taking into account all relevant provisions of the Convention.

9.3. Human Rights Committee

9.3.1. General Comment 16 – The Right to Respect of Privacy, Family, Home and Correspondence, and Protection of Honour and Reputation (Art. 17) (1988)[141]

1. Article 17 provides for the right of every per-son to be protected against arbitrary or unlawful interference with his privacy, family, home or cor-respondence as well as against unlawful attacks on his honour and reputation. In the view of the Committee this right is required to be guaranteed against all such interferences and attacks whether they emanate from State authorities or from nat-ural or legal persons. The obligations imposed by this article require the State to adopt legislative and other measures to give effect to the prohibition against such interferences and attacks as well as to the protection of this right.

2. In this connection, the Committee wishes to point out that in the reports of States parties to the Covenant the necessary attention is not being given to information concerning the manner in which respect for this right is guaranteed by leg-islative, administrative or judicial authorities, and

[141] Human Rights Committee, 32nd Session (1988).

in general by the competent organs established in the State. In particular, insufficient attention is paid to the fact that article 17 of the Covenant deals with protection against both unlawful and arbitrary interference. That means that it is precisely in State legislation above all that provision must be made for the protection of the right set forth in that article. At present the reports either say nothing about such legislation or provide insufficient information on the subject.

3. The term "unlawful" means that no interference can take place except in cases envisaged by the law. Interference authorized by States can only take place on the basis of law, which itself must comply with the provisions, aims and objectives of the Covenant.

4. The expression "arbitrary interference" is also relevant to the protection of the right provided for in article 17. In the Committee's view the expression "arbitrary interference" can also extend to interference provided for under the law. The introduction of the concept of arbitrariness is intended to guarantee that even interference provided for by law should be in accordance with the provisions, aims and objectives of the Covenant and should be, in any event, reasonable in the particular circumstances.

5. Regarding the term "family", the objectives of the Covenant require that for purposes of article 17 this term be given a broad interpretation to include all those comprising the family as understood in the society of the State party concerned. The term "home" in English, "manzel" in Arabic, "zhùzhái" in Chinese, "domicile" in French, "zhilische" in Russian and "domicilio" in Spanish, as used in article 17 of the Covenant, is to be understood to indicate the place where a person resides or carries out his usual occupation. In this connection, the Committee invites States to indicate in their reports the meaning given in their society to the terms "family" and "home".

6. The Committee considers that the reports should include information on the authorities and organs set up within the legal system of the State which are competent to authorize interference allowed by the law. It is also indispensable to have information on the authorities which are entitled to exercise control over such interference with strict regard for the law, and to know in what manner and through which organs persons concerned may complain of a violation of the right provided for in article 17 of the Covenant. States should in their reports make clear the extent to which actual practice conforms to the law. State party reports should also contain information on complaints lodged in respect of arbitrary or unlawful interference, and the number of any findings in that regard, as well as the remedies provided in such cases.

7. As all persons live in society, the protection of privacy is necessarily relative. However, the competent public authorities should only be able to call for such information relating to an individual's private life the knowledge of which is essential in the interests of society as understood under the Covenant. Accordingly, the Committee recommends that States should indicate in their reports the laws and regulations that govern authorized interferences with private life.

8. Even with regard to interferences that conform to the Covenant, relevant legislation must specify in detail the precise circumstances in which such interferences may be permitted. A decision to make use of such authorized interference must be made only by the authority designated under the law, and on a case-by-case basis. Compliance with article 17 requires that the integrity and confidentiality of correspondence should be guaranteed *de jure* and de facto. Correspondence should be delivered to the addressee without interception and without being opened or otherwise read. Surveillance, whether electronic or otherwise, interceptions of telephonic, telegraphic and other forms of communication, wire-tapping and recording of conversations should be prohibited. Searches of a person's home should be restricted to a search for necessary evidence and should not be allowed to amount to harassment. So far as personal and body search is concerned, effective measures should ensure that such searches are carried out in a manner consistent with the dignity of the person who is being searched. Persons being subjected to body search by State officials, or medical personnel acting at the request of the State, should only be examined by persons of the same sex.

9. States parties are under a duty themselves not to engage in interferences inconsistent with article 17 of the Covenant and to provide the legislative framework prohibiting such acts by natural or legal persons.

10. The gathering and holding of personal information on computers, data banks and other devices, whether by public authorities or private individuals

or bodies, must be regulated by law. Effective measures have to be taken by States to ensure that information concerning a person's private life does not reach the hands of persons who are not authorized by law to receive, process and use it, and is never used for purposes incompatible with the Covenant. In order to have the most effective protection of his private life, every individual should have the right to ascertain in an intelligible form, whether, and if so, what personal data is stored in automatic data files, and for what purposes. Every individual should also be able to ascertain which public authorities or private individuals or bodies control or may control their files. If such files contain incorrect personal data or have been collected or processed contrary to the provisions of the law, every individual should have the right to request rectification or elimination.

11. Article 17 affords protection to personal honour and reputation and States are under an obligation to provide adequate legislation to that end. Provision must also be made for everyone effectively to be able to protect himself against any unlawful attacks that do occur and to have an effective remedy against those responsible. States parties should indicate in their reports to what extent the honour or reputation of individuals is protected by law and how this protection is achieved according to their legal system.

9.3.2. General Comment 27 – Freedom of Movement (1999)[142]

1. Liberty of movement is an indispensable condition for the free development of a person. It interacts with several other rights enshrined in the Covenant, as is often shown in the Committee's practice in considering reports from States parties and communications from individuals. Moreover, the Committee in its general comment No. 15 ("The position of aliens under the Covenant", 1986) referred to the special link between articles 12 and 13.

2. The permissible limitations which may be imposed on the rights protected under article 12 must not nullify the principle of liberty of movement, and are governed by the requirement of necessity provided for in article 12, paragraph 3, and by the need

for consistency with the other rights recognized in the Covenant.

3. States parties should provide the Committee in their reports with the relevant domestic legal rules and administrative and judicial practices relating to the rights protected by article 12, taking into account the issues discussed in the present general comment. They must also include information on remedies available if these rights are restricted.

Liberty of Movement and Freedom to Choose Residence (Para. 1)

4. Everyone lawfully within the territory of a State enjoys, within that territory, the right to move freely and to choose his or her place of residence. In principle, citizens of a State are always lawfully within the territory of that State. The question whether an alien is "lawfully" within the territory of a State is a matter governed by domestic law, which may subject the entry of an alien to the territory of a State to restrictions, provided they are in compliance with the State's international obligations. In that connection, the Committee has held that an alien who entered the State illegally, but whose status has been regularized, must be considered to be lawfully within the territory for the purposes of article 12. Once a person is lawfully within a State, any restrictions on his or her rights guaranteed by article 12, paragraphs 1 and 2, as well as any treatment different from that accorded to nationals, have to be justified under the rules provided for by article 12, paragraph 3. It is, therefore, important that States parties indicate in their reports the circumstances in which they treat aliens differently from their nationals in this regard and how they justify this difference in treatment.

5. The right to move freely relates to the whole territory of a State, including all parts of federal States. According to article 12, paragraph 1, persons are entitled to move from one place to another and to establish themselves in a place of their choice. The enjoyment of this right must not be made dependent on any particular purpose or reason for the person wanting to move or to stay in a place. Any restrictions must be in conformity with paragraph 3.

6. The State party must ensure that the rights guaranteed in article 12 are protected not only from public but also from private interference. In the case of women, this obligation to protect is

---

[142] UN Doc. CCPR/C/21/Rev.1/Add.9. Footnotes omitted.

particularly pertinent. For example, it is incompatible with article 12, paragraph 1, that the right of a woman to move freely and to choose her residence be made subject, by law or practice, to the decision of another person, including a relative.

7. Subject to the provisions of article 12, paragraph 3, the right to reside in a place of one's choice within the territory includes protection against all forms of forced internal displacement. It also precludes preventing the entry or stay of persons in a defined part of the territory. Lawful detention, however, affects more specifically the right to personal liberty and is covered by article 9 of the Covenant. In some circumstances, articles 12 and 9 may come into play together.

Freedom to Leave Any Country, Including One's Own (Para. 2)

8. Freedom to leave the territory of a State may not be made dependent on any specific purpose or on the period of time the individual chooses to stay outside the country. Thus travelling abroad is covered, as well as departure for permanent emigration. Likewise, the right of the individual to determine the State of destination is part of the legal guarantee. As the scope of article 12, paragraph 2, is not restricted to persons lawfully within the territory of a State, an alien being legally expelled from the country is likewise entitled to elect the State of destination, subject to the agreement of that State.

9. In order to enable the individual to enjoy the rights guaranteed by article 12, paragraph 2, obligations are imposed both on the State of residence and on the State of nationality. Since international travel usually requires appropriate documents, in particular a passport, the right to leave a country must include the right to obtain the necessary travel documents. The issuing of passports is normally incumbent on the State of nationality of the individual. The refusal by a State to issue a passport or prolong its validity for a national residing abroad may deprive this person of the right to leave the country of residence and to travel elsewhere. It is no justification for the State to claim that its national would be able to return to its territory without a passport.

10. The practice of States often shows that legal rules and administrative measures adversely affect the right to leave, in particular, a person's own country. It is therefore of the utmost importance

that States parties report on all legal and practical restrictions on the right to leave which they apply both to nationals and to foreigners, in order to enable the Committee to assess the conformity of these rules and practices with article 12, paragraph 3. States parties should also include information in their reports on measures that impose sanctions on international carriers which bring to their territory persons without required documents, where those measures affect the right to leave another country.

Restrictions (Para. 3)

11. Article 12, paragraph 3, provides for exceptional circumstances in which rights under paragraphs 1 and 2 may be restricted. This provision authorizes the State to restrict these rights only to protect national security, public order (*ordre public*), public health or morals and the rights and freedoms of others. To be permissible, restrictions must be provided by law, must be necessary in a democratic society for the protection of these purposes and must be consistent with all other rights recognized in the Covenant (see para. 18 below).

12. The law itself has to establish the conditions under which the rights may be limited. State reports should therefore specify the legal norms upon which restrictions are founded. Restrictions which are not provided for in the law or are not in conformity with the requirements of article 12, paragraph 3, would violate the rights guaranteed by paragraphs 1 and 2.

13. In adopting laws providing for restrictions permitted by article 12, paragraph 3, States should always be guided by the principle that the restrictions must not impair the essence of the right (cf. art. 5, para. 1); the relation between right and restriction, between norm and exception, must not be reversed. The laws authorizing the application of restrictions should use precise criteria and may not confer unfettered discretion on those charged with their execution.

14. Article 12, paragraph 3, clearly indicates that it is not sufficient that the restrictions serve the permissible purposes; they must also be necessary to protect them. Restrictive measures must conform to the principle of proportionality; they must be appropriate to achieve their protective function; they must be the least intrusive instrument amongst those which might achieve the desired

result; and they must be proportionate to the interest to be protected.

15. The principle of proportionality has to be respected not only in the law that frames the restrictions, but also by the administrative and judicial authorities in applying the law. States should ensure that any proceedings relating to the exercise or restriction of these rights are expeditious and that reasons for the application of restrictive measures are provided.

16. States have often failed to show that the application of their laws restricting the rights enshrined in article 12, paragraphs 1 and 2, are in conformity with all requirements referred to in article 12, paragraph 3. The application of restrictions in any individual case must be based on clear legal grounds and meet the test of necessity and the requirements of proportionality. These conditions would not be met, for example, if an individual were prevented from leaving a country merely on the ground that he or she is the holder of "State secrets", or if an individual were prevented from travelling internally without a specific permit. On the other hand, the conditions could be met by restrictions on access to military zones on national security grounds, or limitations on the freedom to settle in areas inhabited by indigenous or minorities communities.

17. A major source of concern is the manifold legal and bureaucratic barriers unnecessarily affecting the full enjoyment of the rights of the individuals to move freely, to leave a country, including their own, and to take up residence. Regarding the right to movement within a country, the Committee has criticized provisions requiring individuals to apply for permission to change their residence or to seek the approval of the local authorities of the place of destination, as well as delays in processing such written applications. States' practice presents an even richer array of obstacles making it more difficult to leave the country, in particular for their own nationals. These rules and practices include, *inter alia*, lack of access for applicants to the competent authorities and lack of information regarding requirements; the requirement to apply for special forms through which the proper application documents for the issuance of a passport can be obtained; the need for supportive statements from employers or family members; exact description of the travel route; issuance of passports only on payment of high fees substantially exceeding the cost of the service rendered by the administration; unreasonable delays in the issuance of travel documents; restrictions on family members travelling together; requirement of a repatriation deposit or a return ticket; requirement of an invitation from the State of destination or from people living there; harassment of applicants, for example by physical intimidation, arrest, loss of employment or expulsion of their children from school or university; refusal to issue a passport because the applicant is said to harm the good name of the country. In the light of these practices, States parties should make sure that all restrictions imposed by them are in full compliance with article 12, paragraph 3.

18. The application of the restrictions permissible under article 12, paragraph 3, needs to be consistent with the other rights guaranteed in the Covenant and with the fundamental principles of equality and non-discrimination. Thus, it would be a clear violation of the Covenant if the rights enshrined in article 12, paragraphs 1 and 2, were restricted by making distinctions of any kind, such as on the basis of race, colour, sex, language, religion, political or other opinion, national or social origin, property, birth or other status. In examining State reports, the Committee has on several occasions found that measures preventing women from moving freely or from leaving the country by requiring them to have the consent or the escort of a male person constitute a violation of article 12.

The Right to Enter One's Own Country (Para. 4)

19. The right of a person to enter his or her own country recognizes the special relationship of a person to that country. The right has various facets. It implies the right to remain in one's own country. It includes not only the right to return after having left one's own country; it may also entitle a person to come to the country for the first time if he or she was born outside the country (for example, if that country is the person's State of nationality). The right to return is of the utmost importance for refugees seeking voluntary repatriation. It also implies prohibition of enforced population transfers or mass expulsions to other countries.

20. The wording of article 12, paragraph 4, does not distinguish between nationals and aliens ("no one"). Thus, the persons entitled to exercise this right can be identified only by interpreting the meaning of the phrase "his own country". The scope of "his own country" is broader than the concept

"country of his nationality". It is not limited to nationality in a formal sense, that is, nationality acquired at birth or by conferral; it embraces, at the very least, an individual who, because of his or her special ties to or claims in relation to a given country, cannot be considered to be a mere alien. This would be the case, for example, of nationals of a country who have there been stripped of their nationality in violation of international law, and of individuals whose country of nationality has been incorporated in or transferred to another national entity, whose nationality is being denied them. The language of article 12, paragraph 4, moreover, permits a broader interpretation that might embrace other categories of long-term residents, including but not limited to stateless persons arbitrarily deprived of the right to acquire the nationality of the country of such residence. Since other factors may in certain circumstances result in the establishment of close and enduring connections between a person and a country, States parties should include in their reports information on the rights of permanent residents to return to their country of residence.

21. In no case may a person be arbitrarily deprived of the right to enter his or her own country. The reference to the concept of arbitrariness in this context is intended to emphasize that it applies to all State action, legislative, administrative and judicial; it guarantees that even interference provided for by law should be in accordance with the provisions, aims and objectives of the Covenant and should be, in any event, reasonable in the particular circumstances. The Committee considers that there are few, if any, circumstances in which deprivation of the right to enter one's own country could be reasonable. A State party must not, by stripping a person of nationality or by expelling an individual to a third country, arbitrarily prevent this person from returning to his or her own country.

---

10. ADDITIONAL STANDARDS

10.1. The Cairo Declaration of Principles of International Law on Compensation to Refugees (1993)[143]

At its Sixty-Fifth Conference in Cairo, April 20–26, 1992, the International Law Association approved

[143] Footnotes omitted.

by consensus the Declaration of Principles of International Law on Compensation to Refugees. Prepared by the International Committee on the Legal Status of Refugees, these principles build upon earlier drafts that were debated at the Sixty-Third Conference in Warsaw in 1988, and were approved "in principle" at the Sixty-Fourth Conference in Queensland, Australia, in 1990.

The declaration was a follow-up to the Declaration of Principles of International Law on Mass Expulsion, approved by the International Law Association at its Sixty-Second Conference in Seoul in 1986. The final draft benefited greatly from the contribution of Professor Louis B. Sohn who, although not a member of the committee, gave generously of his time and advice.

The aftermath of the Persian Gulf war has seen renewed interest in compensation. Thus, the declaration is of particular interest to all those concerned with averting new flows of refugees by fixing responsibility for persons who have been driven to become refugees on their countries of origin.

The declaration reads as follows.

THE INTERNATIONAL LAW ASSOCIATION,

Recalling that the General Assembly in Resolution 41/70 of 3 December 1986 unanimously endorsed the Report of the Group of Governmental Experts on International Co-operation to Avert New Flows of Refugees (UN Doc. A/41/324), which calls upon Member States to respect as their "obligations," *inter alia*, "the rights of refugees to be facilitated in returning voluntarily and safely to their homes in their homelands and to receive adequate compensation therefrom, where so established, in cases of those who do not wish to return" (paragraph 66(f));

Recalling further that the General Assembly in Resolution 194(III) of 11 December 1948, which has since been reaffirmed every year, resolved that:

[T]he refugees wishing to return to their homes and live at peace with their neighbours should be permitted to do so at the earliest practical date, and that compensation should be paid for the property of those choosing not to return and for loss or damage to property which, under principles of international law or in equity, should be made good by the Governments or authorities responsible; . . . (paragraph 11);

Noting, however, that neither the 1986 nor the 1948 resolution identifies or elaborates upon specific principles of international law governing compensation to refugees;

Recognizing the need to provide such elaboration with a view both to rendering justice to refugees and to averting new flows of refugees;

Bearing in mind the significant contribution of the International Law Association in adopting by consensus at its 62nd Conference in Seoul, 24th–30th August 1986, the complementary Declaration of Principles of International Law on Mass Expulsion;

Declares the need for adopting the following principles, in the interest of the progressive development and codification of international law, in order to facilitate compensation, as appropriate, to persons who have been forced to leave their homes in their homelands and are unable to return to them.

Principle 1

The responsibility for caring for the world's refugees rests ultimately upon the countries that directly or indirectly force their own citizens to flee and/or remain abroad as refugees. The discharge of such responsibility by countries of asylum, international organizations (e.g., UNHCR, UNRWA, IOM) and donors (both governmental and non-governmental), pending the return of refugees, their settlement in place, or their resettlement in third countries, shall not relieve the countries of origin of their basic responsibility, including that of paying adequate compensation to refugees.

Principle 2

Since refugees are forced directly or indirectly out of their homes in their homelands, they are deprived of the full and effective enjoyment of all articles in the Universal Declaration of Human Rights that presuppose a person's ability to live in the place chosen as home. Accordingly, the State that turns a person into a refugee commits an internationally wrongful act, which creates the obligation to make good the wrong done.

Principle 3

The act of generating refugees in some situations should be considered genocide if it is committed "with intent to destroy, in whole or in part, a national, ethnical, racial or religious group, as such..."

Principle 4

A State is obligated to compensate its own nationals forced to leave their homes to the same extent as it is obligated by international law to compensate an alien.

Principle 5

A State that has committed an "internationally wrongful act" through the generation of refugees shall be required, as appropriate:

(a) to discontinue the act;

(b) to apply remedies provided under the municipal law;

(c) to restore the situation to that which existed prior to the act;

(d) to pay compensation in the event of the impossibility of the restoration of the pre-existing situation; and

(e) to provide appropriate guarantees against the repetition or recurrence of the act.

Principle 6

In implementing the right of refugees to compensation, States shall, directly or through the United Nations and intergovernmental organizations, tie the granting of economic or developmental assistance to countries of origin to their fulfillment of this right.

Principle 7

The United Nations may, in the discharge of its role as guardian of the interests of refugees, claim and administer compensation funds for refugees.

Principle 8

The possibility that refugees or UNHCR may one day successfully claim compensation from the country of origin should not serve as a pretext for withholding humanitarian assistance to refugees or refusing to join in international burden-sharing meant to meet the needs of refugees or otherwise to provide durable solutions, including mediation to facilitate voluntary repatriation in dignity and security, thereby removing or reducing the necessity to pay compensation.

10.2. The Practice of Forced Evictions: Comprehensive Human Rights Guidelines on Development-Based Displacement (1997)[144]

PREAMBLE

Recalling the human rights standards established pursuant to the International Bill of Human Rights,

Whereas many international treaties, resolutions, decisions, general comments, judgments and other texts have recognized and reaffirmed that forced evictions constitute violations of a wide range of internationally recognized human rights,

Recalling Economic and Social Council decision 1996/290, Commission on Human Rights Resolution 1993/77, and Sub-Commission on Prevention of Discrimination and Protection of Minorities resolution 1996/27,

Reaffirming that under international law every State has the obligation to respect and ensure respect for human rights and humanitarian law, including obligations to prevent violations, to investigate violations, to take appropriate action against violators, and to afford remedies and reparation to victims,

Reaffirming that development is a comprehensive economic, social, cultural and political process, which aims at the constant improvement of the well-being of the entire population and of all individuals on the basis of their active, free and meaningful participation in development and in the fair distribution of benefits resulting therefrom,

Whereas the Vienna Declaration and Plan of Action stipulated that while development facilitates the enjoyment of all human rights, the lack of development may not be invoked to justify the abridgment of internationally recognized human rights,

Recognizing the widespread nature of the practice of forced evictions and that when forced evictions are carried out this can occur in a variety of contexts including but not limited to conflicts over land rights, development and infrastructure projects,

[144] UN Doc. E/CN.4/Sub.2/1997/7.

such as the construction of dams or other large-scale energy projects, land acquisition measures associated with urban renewal, housing renovation, city beautification programmes, the clearing of land for agricultural purposes or macro-urban projects, unbridled speculation in land, and the holding of major international events such as the Olympic Games,

Conscious that forced evictions intensify social conflict and inequality and invariably affect the poorest, most socially, economically, and vulnerable sectors of society, specifically women, children, and indigenous peoples,

Conscious also of guidelines developed by international financial and other institutions on involuntary displacement and resettlement,

Resolved to protect human rights and prevent violations due to the practice of forced evictions,

SECTION ONE – BACKGROUND ISSUES

Scope and Nature of the Guidelines

1. The present Guidelines address the human rights implications of the practice of forced evictions associated with development-based displacement in urban and rural areas. The Guidelines reflect and are consistent with international human rights law and international humanitarian law and should be subject to the widest possible application.

2. Having due regard to all relevant definitions of the practice of forced evictions under international human rights provisions and instruments, the present Guidelines apply to instances of forced evictions in which there are acts and/or omissions involving the coerced and involuntary removal of individuals, groups and communities from their homes and/or lands and common property resources they occupy or are dependent upon, thus eliminating or limiting the possibility of an individual, group or community residing or working in a particular dwelling, residence or place.

3. While there are many similarities between the practice of forced evictions and internal displacement, population transfer, mass expulsions, mass exodus, ethnic cleansing and other practices involving the coerced and involuntary movement of people from their homes, lands and

communities, forced evictions constitute a distinct practice under international law. Persons, groups and communities subjected to or threatened with forced evictions form, therefore, a distinct group under international human rights law.

4. Forced evictions constitute prima facie violations of a wide range of internationally recognized human rights and can only be carried out under exceptional circumstances and in full accordance with the present Guidelines and relevant provisions of international human rights law.

SECTION TWO – GENERAL OBLIGATIONS

5. While forced evictions can be carried out, sanctioned, demanded, proposed, initiated or tolerated by a variety of distinct actors, responsibility for forced evictions under international law, ultimately, is held by States. This does not, however, relieve other entities from obligations in this regard, in particular occupying powers, international financial and other institutions or organizations, transnational corporations and individual third parties, including public and private landlords or land owners.

6. States should apply appropriate civil or criminal penalties against any person or entity, within its jurisdiction, whether public or private, who carries out any forced evictions, not in full conformity with applicable law and the present Guidelines.

7. States should object, through the appropriate international legal mechanisms, to the carrying out of forced evictions in other States when such forced evictions are not in full conformity with the present Guidelines and relevant provisions of international human rights law.

8. States should ensure that international organizations in which they are represented refrain from sponsoring or implementing any project, programme or policy which may involve the carrying out of forced evictions not in full conformity with international law and the present Guidelines.

SECTION THREE – SPECIFIC PREVENTATIVE OBLIGATIONS

The Obligation of Maximum Effective Protection

9. States should secure by all appropriate means, including the provision of security of tenure, the maximum degree of effective protection against the practice of forced evictions for all persons under their jurisdiction. In this regard, special consideration should be given to the rights of indigenous peoples, children and women, particularly female-headed households and other vulnerable groups. These obligations are of an immediate nature and are not qualified by resource-related considerations.

10. States should refrain from introducing any deliberately retrogressive measures with respect to de jure or de facto protection against forced evictions.

11. States should ensure that adequate and effective legal or other appropriate remedies are available to any persons claiming that his/her right of protection against forced evictions has been violated or is under threat of violation.

12. States should ensure that eviction impact assessments are carried out prior to the initiation of any project which could result in development-based displacement, with a view to fully securing the human rights of all potentially affected persons, groups and communities.

The Obligation to Prevent Homelessness

13. States should ensure that no persons, groups or communities are rendered homeless or are exposed to the violation of any other human rights as a consequence of a forced eviction.

The Obligation to Adopt Appropriate Measures of Law and Policy

14. States should carry out comprehensive reviews of relevant national legislation with a view to ensuring the compatibility of such legislation with the norms contained in the present Guidelines and other relevant international human rights provisions. In this regard, special measures shall be taken to ensure that no forms of discrimination, statutory or otherwise, are applied in relation to property rights, housing rights and access to resources.

15. States should adopt appropriate legislation and policies to ensure the protection of individuals, groups and communities from forced eviction, having due regard to their best interests. States are

encouraged to adopt constitutional provisions in this regard.

The Obligation to Explore All Possible Alternatives

16. States should fully explore all possible alternatives to any act involving forced eviction. In this regard, all affected persons, including women, children and indigenous peoples shall have the right to all relevant information and the right to full participation and consultation throughout the entire process and to propose any alternatives. In the event that agreement cannot be reached on the proposed alternative by the affected persons, groups and communities and the entity proposing the forced eviction in question, an independent body, such as a court of law, tribunal, or ombudsman may be called upon.

The Obligation to Expropriate Only as a Last Resort

17. States should refrain, to the maximum possible extent, from compulsorily acquiring housing or land, unless such acts are legitimate and necessary and designed to facilitate the enjoyment of human rights through, for instance, measures of land reform or redistribution. If, as a last resort, States consider themselves compelled to undertake proceedings of expropriation or compulsory acquisition, such action shall be: (a) determined and envisaged by law and norms regarding forced eviction, in so far as these are consistent internationally recognized human rights; (b) solely for the purpose of protecting the general welfare in a democratic society; (c) reasonable and proportional and (d) in accordance with the present Guidelines.

SECTION FOUR – THE RIGHTS OF ALL PERSONS

Integrity of the Home

18. All persons have the right to adequate housing which includes, inter alia, the integrity of the home and access to and protection of common property resources. The home and its occupants shall be protected against any acts of violence, threats of violence or other forms of harassment, in particular as they relate to women and children. The home and its occupants shall further be protected against any arbitrary or unlawful interference with privacy or respect of the home.

Assurances of Security of Tenure

19. All persons have a right to security of tenure which provides sufficient legal protection from forced eviction from one's home or land.

20. The present Guidelines shall apply to all persons, groups and communities irrespective of their tenure status.

SECTION FIVE – LEGAL REMEDIES

21. All persons threatened with forced eviction, notwithstanding the rationale or legal basis there of, have the right to:

(a) a fair hearing before a competent, impartial and independent court or tribunal

(b) legal counsel, and where necessary, sufficient legal aid

(c) effective remedies

22. States should adopt legislative measures prohibiting any forced evictions without a court order. The court shall consider all relevant circumstances of affected persons, groups and communities and any decision be in full accordance with principles of equality and justice and internationally recognized human rights.

23. All persons have a right to appeal any judicial or other decisions affecting their rights as established pursuant to the present Guidelines, to the highest national judicial authority.

Compensation

24. All persons subjected to any forced eviction not in full accordance with the present Guidelines, should have a right to compensation for any losses of land, personal, real or other property or goods, including rights or interests in property not recognized in national legislation, incurred in connection with a forced eviction. Compensation should include land and access to common property resources and should not be restricted to cash payments.

Restitution and Return

25. All persons, groups and communities subjected to forced evictions have the right to, but shall not be forced to return to their homes, lands or places of origin.

Resettlements

26. In full cognizance of the contents of the present Guidelines there may be instances in which, in the public interest, or where the safety, health or enjoyment of human rights so demands, particular persons, groups and communities may be subject to resettlement. Such resettlement must occur in a just and equitable manner and in full accordance with law of general application.

27. All persons, groups and communities have the right to suitable resettlement which includes the right to alternative land or housing, which is safe, secure, accessible, affordable and habitable.

28. In determining the compatibility of resettlement with the present Guidelines, States should ensure that in the context of any case of resettlement the following criteria are adhered to:

(a) No resettlement shall take place until such a time that a full resettlement policy consistent with the present Guidelines and internationally recognized human rights is in place.

(b) Resettlement must ensure equal rights to women, children and indigenous populations and other vulnerable groups including the right to property ownership and access to resources. Resettlement policies should include programmes designed for women with respect to education, health, family welfare and employment opportunities.

(c) The actor proposing and/or carrying out the resettlement shall be required by law to pay for any costs associated therewith, including all resettlement costs.

(d) No affected persons, groups or communities, shall suffer detriment as far as their human rights are concerned nor shall their right to the continuous improvement of living conditions be subject to infringement. This applies equally to host communities at resettlement sites, and affected persons, groups and communities subjected to forced eviction.

(e) That affected persons, groups and communities provide their full and informed consent as regards the relocation site. The State shall provide all necessary amenities and services and economic opportunities.

(f) Sufficient information shall be provided to affected persons, groups and communities concerning all State projects as well as to the planning and implementation processes relating to the resettlement concerned, including information concerning the purpose to which the eviction dwelling or site is to be put and the persons, groups or communities who will benefit from the evicted site. Particular attention must be given to ensure that indigenous peoples, ethnic minorities, the landless, women and children are represented and included in this process.

(g) The entire resettlement process should be carried out in full consultation and participation with the affected persons, groups and communities. States should take into account in particular all alternate plans proposed by the affected persons, groups and communities.

(h) If after a full and fair public hearing, it is found that thee is a need to proceed with the resettlement, then the affected persons, groups and communities shall be given at least ninety (90) days notice prior to the date of the resettlement; and

(i) Local government officials and neutral observers, properly identified, shall be present during the resettlement so as to ensure that no force, violence or intimidation is involved.

Section Six – Monitoring

29. The United Nations High Commissioner for Human Rights and other United Nations human rights institutions should seek by all possible means to secure full compliance with the present Guidelines.

Section Seven – Savings

Savings Clause

30. The provisions contained within the present Guidelines are without prejudice to the provisions of any other international instrument or national law which ensures the enjoyment of all human rights as they relate to the practice of forced evictions.

PART TWO

Housing and Property Restitution Standards – Regional

1. AFRICA

1.1. OAU Convention Governing the Specific Aspects of Refugee Problems in Africa (1974)[145]

[. . .]

Article 5 – Voluntary Repatriation

1. The essentially voluntary character of repatriation shall be respected in all cases and no refugee shall be repatriated against his will.

2. The country of asylum, in collaboration with the country of origin, shall make adequate arrangements for the safe return of refugees who request repatriation.

3. The country of origin, on receiving back refugees, shall facilitate their resettlement and grant them the full rights and privileges of nationals of the country, and subject them to the same obligations.

4. Refugees who voluntarily return to their country shall in no way be penalized for having left it for any of the reasons giving rise to refugee situations. Whenever necessary, an appeal shall be made through national information media and through the Administrative Secretary-General of the OAU, inviting refugees to return home and giving assurance that the new circumstances prevailing in their country of origin will enable them to return without risk and to take up a normal and peaceful life without fear of being disturbed or punished, and that the text of such appeal should be given to refugees and clearly explained to them by their country of asylum.

5. Refugees who freely decide to return to their homeland, as a result of such assurances or on their own initiative, shall be given every possible assistance by the country of asylum, the country of origin, voluntary agencies and international and intergovernmental organizations, to facilitate their return.

[. . .]

2. AMERICAS

2.1. American Convention on Human Rights (1969)[146]

[. . .]

Article 21 – Right to Property

1. Everyone has the right to the use and enjoyment of his property. The law may subordinate such use and enjoyment to the interest of society.

2. No one shall be deprived of his property except upon payment of just compensation, for reasons of public utility or social interest, and in the cases and according to the forms established by law.

3. Usury and any other form of exploitation of man by man shall be prohibited by law.

[. . .]

Article 25 – Right to Judicial Protection

1. Everyone has the right to simple and prompt recourse, or any other effective recourse, to a competent court or tribunal for protection against acts that violate his fundamental rights recognized by the constitution or laws of the state concerned or by this Convention, even though such violation may have been committed by persons acting in the course of their official duties.

---

[145] Adopted at Addis Ababa on 10 September 1969 and entered into force on 20 June 1974 in accordance with Article XI.

[146] Adopted on 22 November 1969 and entered into force on 18 July 1978 in accordance with Article 74.

2. The States Parties undertake:

(a) to ensure that any person claiming such remedy shall have his rights determined by the competent authority provided for by the legal system of the state;

(b) to develop the possibilities of judicial remedy; and

(c) to ensure that the competent authorities shall enforce such remedies when granted.

[. . .]

2.2. Cartagena Declaration on Refugees (1984)[147]

Having acknowledged with appreciation the commitments with regard to refugees included in the Contadora Act on Peace and Co-operation in Central America, the bases of which the Colloquium fully shares and which are reproduced below:

[. . .]

(f) "To ensure that any repatriation of refugees is voluntary, and is declared to be so on an individual basis, and is carried out with the co-operation of UNHCR."

(g) "To ensure the establishment of tripartite commissions, composed of representatives of the State of origin, of the receiving State and of UNHCR with a view to facilitating the repatriation of refugees."

[. . .]

(n) "To ensure that, once agreement has been reached on the bases for voluntary and individual repatriation, with full guarantees for the refugees, the receiving countries permit official delegations of the country of origin, accompanied by representatives of UNHCR and the receiving country, to visit the refugee camps."

[. . .]

(o) "To ensure that the receiving countries facilitate, in co-ordination with UNHCR, the departure procedure for refugees in instances of voluntary and individual repatriation."

[. . .]

---

147 Annual Report of the Inter-American Commission on Human Rights, OAS Doc. OEA/Ser.L/V/II.66/doc.10, rev.1, at 190–93 (1984–85), 22 November 1984.

The Colloquium adopted the following conclusions:

[. . .]

5. To reiterate the importance and meaning of the principle of non-refoulement (including the prohibition of rejection at the frontier) as a cornerstone of the international protection of refugees. This principle is imperative in regard to refugees and in the present state of international law should be acknowledged and observed as a rule of jus cogens.

[. . .]

12. To reiterate the voluntary and individual character of repatriation of refugees and the need for it to be carried out under conditions of absolute safety, preferably to the place of residence of the refugee in his country of origin.

[. . .]

The Cartagena Colloquium therefore Recommends:

[. . .]

That the conclusions reached by the Colloquium (III) should receive adequate attention in the search for solutions to the grave problems raised by the present massive flows of refugees in Central America, Mexico and Panama.

[. . .]

---

3. EUROPE

3.1. European Convention for the Protection of Human Rights and Fundamental Freedoms (1950)[148]

[. . .]

Article 8 – Right to Respect for Private and Family Life

1. Everyone has the right to respect for his private and family life, his home and his correspondence.

---

148 Adopted at Rome on 4 November 1950 and entered into force 3 September 1953, in accordance with Article 66. Protocol One was adopted on 20 March 1952 and entered into force on 18 May 1954.

2. There shall be no interference by a public authority with the exercise of this right except such as is in accordance with the law and is necessary in a democratic society in the interests of national security, public safety or the economic well-being of the country, for the prevention of disorder or crime, for the protection of health or morals, or for the protection of the rights and freedoms of others.

[. . .]

Article 13 – Right to an Effective Remedy

Everyone whose rights and freedoms as set forth in this Convention are violated shall have an effective remedy before a national authority notwithstanding that the violation has been committed by persons acting in an official capacity.

[. . .]

Article 1, Protocol One – Protection of Property (1952)

Every natural person has a right to the peaceful enjoyment of his possessions. No one shall be deprived of his possessions except in the public interest and subject to the conditions provided for by law and by the general principles of international law.

The preceding provisions shall not, however, in any way impair the right of a State to enforce such laws as it deems necessary to control the use of property in accordance with the general interest or to secure the payment of taxes or other contributions or penalties.

---

4. MIDDLE EAST

4.1. The Cairo Declaration on Human Rights in Islam (1990)[149]

[. . .]

Article 3

[. . .]

(b) It is prohibited to cut down trees, to destroy crops or livestock, to destroy the enemy's civilian

---

[149] U.N. Doc. A/CONF.157/PC/62/Add.18 (1993) [English translation].

buildings and installations by shelling, blasting or any other means.

[. . .]

Article 12

Every man shall have the right, within the framework of the Shari'ah, to free movement and to select his place of residence whether within or outside his country and if persecuted, is entitled to seek asylum in another country. The country of refuge shall be obliged to provide protection to the asylum-seeker until his safety has been attained, unless asylum is motivated by committing an act regarded by the Shari'ah as a crime.

[. . .]

Article 15

(a) Everyone shall have the right to own property acquired in a legitimate way, and shall be entitled to the rights of ownership without prejudice to oneself, others or the society in general. Expropriation is not permissible except for requirements of public interest and upon payment of prompt and fair compensation.

(b) Confiscation and seizure of property is prohibited except for a necessity dictated by law.

[. . .]

Article 18

(a) Everyone shall have the right to live in security for himself, his religion, his dependents, his honour and his property.

(b) Everyone shall have the right to privacy in the conduct of his private affairs, in his home, among his family, with regard to his property and his relationships. It is not permitted to spy on him, to place him under surveillance or to besmirch his good name. The State shall protect him from arbitrary interference.

(c) A private residence is inviolable in all cases. It will not be entered without permission from its inhabitants or in any unlawful manner, nor shall it be demolished or confiscated and its dwellers evicted.

[. . .]

4.2. Declaration on the Protection of Refugees and Displaced Persons in the Arab World (1992)[150]

1. Noting with deep regret the suffering which the Arab World has endured from large-scale flows of refugees and displaced persons, and also noting with deep concern the continuing outflow of refugees and displaced persons in the Arab World and the human tragedy encountered by them,

2. Recalling the humanitarian principles deeply rooted in Islamic Arab traditions and values and the principles and rules of Moslem law (Islamic Sharia), particularly the principles of social solidarity and asylum, which are reflected in the universally recognized principles of international humanitarian law,

3. Recognizing the imperative need for a humanitarian approach in solving the problems of refugees and displaced persons, without prejudice to the political rights of the Palestinian people,

4. Emphasizing the need for the effective implementation of paragraph 11 of General Assembly Resolution 194 (111) of 11 December 1948, calling for the right of return or compensation for Palestinian refugees,

5. Considering that the required solution is the full implementation of the Resolutions of the Security Council and of the United Nations, including Resolutions 181 of 1947 and Resolution 3236 of 1973, which guarantee the right of the Palestinian people to establish its independent State on its national territory,

6. Deeply concerned that Palestinians are not receiving effective protection either from the competent international organizations or from the competent authorities of some Arab countries,

7. Recognizing that the refugees' and displaced persons' problems must be addressed in all their aspects, in particular those relating to their causes, means of prevention and appropriate solutions,

8. Recalling that the United Nations Charter and the international human rights instruments affirm

the principle that human beings shall enjoy fundamental rights and freedoms without discrimination of whatever nature,

9. Considering that Asylum and Refugee Law constitute an integral part of Human Rights Law, respect for which should be fully ensured in the Arab World,

10. Recognizing that the United Nations Convention of 28 July 1951 and the Protocol of 31 January 1967 constitute the basic universal instruments governing the status of refugees,

11. Recalling the importance or regional legal instruments such as the 1969 OAU Convention governing the Specific Aspects of Refugee Problems in Africa and the 1984 Cartagena Declaration on Refugees,

12. Recognizing that the fundamental principles of human rights, international humanitarian law and international refugee law represent a common standard to be attained by all peoples and nations; that they should provide constant guidance to all individuals and organs of society; and that competent national authorities should ensure respect for these principles and should endeavour to promote them by means of education and dissemination,

13. Recalling the historic role of Islam and its contribution to humanity, and the fact that universal respect for human rights and fundamental freedoms for all constitute an integral part of Arab values and of the principles and rules of Moslem law (Islamic Sharia),

14. Noting with appreciation the humanitarian role of the Office of the United Nations High Commissioner for Refugees in providing protection and assistance to refugees and displaced persons,

15. Recalling with particular gratitude the efforts of the International Institute of Humanitarian Law for the developing of refugee law in the Arab World and for organizing the four Arab Seminars held for this purpose in San Remo (1984), Tunis (1989), Amman (1991) and Cairo (1992), and,

16. Recalling with appreciation the efforts or the International Committee or the Red Cross in protecting refugees and displaced persons in armed conflict situations,

Adopts the following Declaration:

---

[150] The Group of Arab Experts, meeting in Cairo, Arab Republic of Egypt, from 16 to 19 November 1992 at the Fourth Arab Seminar on "Asylum and Refugee Law in the Arab World," organized by the International Institute of Humanitarian Law in collaboration with the Faculty of Law of Cairo University, under the sponsorship of the United Nations High Commissioner for Refugees.

Article 1

Reaffirms the fundamental right of every person to the free movement within his own country, or to leave it for another country and to return to his country of origin;

Article 2

Reaffirms the importance of the principle prohibiting the return or the expulsion of a refugee to a country where his life or his freedom will be in danger and considers this principle as an imperative rule of the international public law;

Article 3

Considers that the granting or asylum should not as such be regarded as an unfriendly act vis-a-vis any other State;

Article 4

Hopes that Arab States which have not yet acceded to the 1951 Convention and the 1967 Protocol relating to the status of refugees will do so;

Article 5

In situations which may not be covered by the 1951 Convention, the 1967 Protocol, or any other relevant instrument in force or United Nations General Assembly resolutions, refugees, asylum seekers and displaced persons shall nevertheless be protected by:

(a) the humanitarian principles of asylum in Islamic law and Arab values,

(b) the basic human rights rules, established by international and regional organisations,

(c) other relevant principles or international law;

Article 6

Recommends that, pending the elaboration of an Arab Convention relating to refugees, Arab States adopt a broad concept of "refugee" and "displaced person" as well as a minimum standard for their treatment, guided by the provisions of the United Nations instruments relating to human rights and refugees as well as relevant regional instruments;

Article 7

Calls the League of Arab States to reinforce its efforts with a view to adopting an Arab Convention relating to refugees. These efforts will hopefully be brought to fruition within a reasonable period of time;

Article 8

Calls upon Arab States to provide the Secretariat of the League with relevant information and statistical data, in particular concerning:

(a) the condition of refugees and displaced persons in their territories,

(b) the extent of their implementation of international instruments relating to the protection of refugees,

(c) national laws, regulations and decrees in force, relating to refugees and displaced persons;

This will help the League of Arab States in taking an active role in the protection or refugees and displaced persons in cooperation with the competent international organizations;

Article 9

(a) Strongly emphasizes the need to ensure international protection for Palestinian refugees by competent international organizations and, in particular, by the United Nations, without in any way prejudicing the inalienable national rights of the Palestinian people, especially their right to repatriation and self-determination,

(b) Requests the competent organs of the United Nations to extend with due speed the necessary protection to the Palestinian people, in application of Security Council Resolution 681 of 20 December 1990,

(c) Requests the Arab States to apply in its entirety the Protocol relating to the Treatment of Palestinians in Arab States, adopted at Casablanca on 11 September 1965;

Article 10

Emphasizes the need to provide special protection to women and children, as the largest category of refugees and displaced persons, and the most to suffer, as well as the importance of efforts to reunite the families of refugees and displaced persons;

Article 11

Calls for the necessary attention which should be given to the dissemination of refugee law and to the development of the public awareness thereof in the Arab World; and for the establishment of an Arab Institute of International Humanitarian Law, in cooperation with the United Nations High Commissioner for Refugees, the International

Committee of the Red Cross and the League of Arab States.

4.3. Arab Charter on Human Rights (1994)[151]

PART II

[. . .]

---

[151] Adopted by the League of Arab States, Council of the League of Arab States, Cairo, on 15 September 1994; full text translated from Arabic.

Article 22

No citizen shall be expelled from his country or prevented from returning thereto.

[. . .]

Article 25

Every citizen has a guaranteed right to own private property. No citizen shall under any circumstances be divested of all or any part of his property in an arbitrary or unlawful manner.

[. . .]

PART THREE

Housing and Property Restitution Laws and Standards – National

1. AFGHANISTAN

1.1. Decree on Dignified Return of Refugees (2001)

The Afghan Administration,

Confident that the Bonn Agreement on Afghanistan dated 14.09.1380 (5 December 2001) has laid down the foundation for lasting peace, stability and social and economic progress in Afghanistan, safeguards the right and freedom of all returnees, observes the freedom of returnees to establish residence, to participate in the process of reconstruction, consolidation of peace, democracy and social development, AIA guarantees their safe and dignified return, expresses its gratitude and thankfulness to the countries that have given them refuge in the very difficult and hard days Afghanistan experienced, and expects that in conformity with the principle of voluntary repatriation, Afghans will be given the opportunity to decide freely to return to their country, and declares the following:

Article 1

Returning Afghan nationals, who were compelled to leave the country and found refuge in Iran, Pakistan and other countries of the world, will be warmly welcomed without any form of intimidation or discrimination.

Article 2

Returnees shall not be subject to harassment, intimidation, discrimination or persecution for reasons of race, religion, nationality and membership of a particular social group, political opinion or gender, and will be protected by the State.

Article 3

All returnees, irrespective of their political affiliations, are exempted form prosecution for all (with the exception of individual criminal accusations) criminal offenses committed up to 01.10.1380 (22 December 2001), prior to, or in exile against the international and external security of the country, according to enacted laws.

Article 4

The provisions of Article 3 of this decree will not apply to those returnees who have committed acts constituting a crime against peace or humanity, or a war crime, as defined in international instruments, or to acts contrary to the purpose and principles of the United Nations.

Article 5

The recovery of movable and immovable properties such as land, houses, markets, shops, sarai, apartments and etc. will be effected through relevant legal organs.

Article 6

All returnees will be guaranteed the same human rights and fundamental freedoms enjoyed by other citizens.

Article 7

The implementation of the provisions of this decree is the responsibility of the Ministry of Repatriation; law and order organs are obliged to assist the Ministry of Repatriation in this task.

Article 8

UNHCR and other relevant international agencies will be allowed to monitor the treatment of returnees to ensure these meet recognised humanitarian law and human rights standards, and to ensure that commitments contained in this decree are implemented.

Article 9

This decree is valid as of 1.10.1380 (22 December 2001) and will be printed in the Official Gazette.

1.2. Decree 89 of the Head of the Transitional Islamic State of Afghanistan, Regarding the Creation of a Special Property Disputes Resolution Court (2003)

Article 1

Based on the grave necessity for looking after returned refugees in Afghanistan and addressing their complaints, as well as to hasten the process of resolving property disputes, a Special Property Disputes Resolution Court (the "Court") shall be created within the framework of the Supreme Court on the terms contained herein.

Article 2

1. The Court will consist of two levels (primary and appellate).

2. The Court at the primary level will be divided into two courts, with one focused on cases involving real estate located in Kabul Province and one focused on cases involving real estate locate in provinces other than Kabul Province. Both of these courts are located in Kabul.

3. The Court focusing on disputes involving real estate in the provinces may, with the permission of the Chief Justice of the Supreme Court, travel to the provinces to hear certain of these cases in accordance with the provisions of this decree.

4. The Court at the appellate level (the "Mahkamae Nehayee") may review cases heard at the primary level involving real estate located in either the provinces outside of Kabul Province or within Kabul Province.

Article 3

1. For the purposes of ensuring justice, decisions or judgments of the Court's appellate level (Mahkamae Nehayee) can be reviewed, according to the provisions of Article 482 of the Civil Procedure Law, published under Official Gazette No. 772, dated 31 Asad 1369.

2. Revising and rehearing of decisions or judgments of the Court's appellate court shall be based on a proposal of the Supreme Court High Council in accordance with Paragraph (1) of this Article and an order of the President to send the decision or judgment to a Revision Committee.

Article 4

1. The Chairman and judges of the Court's primary and appellate courts shall be appointed on the recommendation of the Chief Justice of the Supreme Court Chairman and with the approval of the President.

2. The Chairman and judges of the Court's appellate court, which constitutes three persons, shall be from among the members of the Supreme Court and appointed through President.

3. The revision Committee consists of three persons from among Supreme Court members who are appointed by the President.

Article 5

Property or real estate in this decree includes land, residential areas, apartments, shops, Mendavi (market) and other immovable properties.

Article 6

Property disputes covered under this decree include and are limited to those which took place in the absence of the owners from the date 7th Saur 1357 (27 April 1987).

Article 7

1. The Court's primary court (both for cases in Kabul Province and for cases outside Kabul Province) is obligated to decide on all filed cases within two months from the date of being filed.

2. The Court's appellate court (Mahkamae Nehayee) is obliged to decide on all field cases within one month of the date of being filed with it.

3. The two-month deadline in Paragraph (1) of this Article may be extended by up to ten days in special and exceptional situations (i.e. complicated cases).

4. The Revision Committee shall review submitted cases within a one-month period after receiving the President's verdict regarding such submitted cases.

Article 8

Proof of forgery of property documents submitted under this decree, and the annulment thereof, is the authority of the Court. When property documents submitted under this decree are determined to be forged, for the purpose of justice the matter may be referred to the relevant authorities.

Article 9

1. Possession of property based on forged documents is illegal and the ownership of such property shall belong to the entitled person as based on the final decision of the Court. The costs of producing any new deeds or any other related expenditures may be charged to the forger in accordance with the provisions of law.

2. When illegally possessed or occupied property is, based on the final judgment of this Court, returned to its actual owner, compensation from the date of such illegal possession or occupation until the date of this Court's order for the actual owner to recover such property, shall be given from the illegal possessor or occupier to the actual owner.

Article 10

Cases of property disputes result from the direct application of natural persons and entities, and such cases may be referred to the Court, through relevant government authorities.

Article 11

This Decree is not applicable when one side in the dispute is a government administration. Such cases are reviewed in accordance with relevant laws and with the authority of the relevant court.

Article 12

Judgments and decisions of the Court's appellate court are generally obligatory and enforceable, with both parties and relevant authorities obliged to ensure their implementation.

Article 13

The Revision Committee is obliged to timely review claims prescribed under Article Seven hereof and report on the implementation of decisions made to the Office of the President.

Article 14

1. The Minister of Interior is specifically obliged to implement the final judgments and decisions of the Court, whether at the primary, appellate or highest level.

2. Other relevant governmental authorities are obliged to implement this Decree and to cooperate with the Court.

[. . .]

2. ALBANIA

2.1. Law No. 9235 on Restitution and Compensation of Property (2004)[152]

In reliance on articles 41, 78, 83 point 1 and 181 of the Constitution, by the proposal of a group of deputies,

THE ASSEMBLY OF THE REPUBLIC OF ALBANIA DECIDED:

CHAPTER I – GENERAL PROVISIONS

Article 1 – Object of the Law

The object of this law is:

a. the just regulation, according to the criteria of article 41 of the Constitution, of the issues of property rights that have arisen from expropriation, nationalisation or confiscation;

b. restitution, and when according to this law restitution of property is not possible, compensation;

c. the procedures for accomplishing restitution and compensation of property and the administrative bodies charged with its completion.

Article 2 – Right to Property

Every expropriated subject enjoys the right to request the right of ownership, in compliance with this law, if the property was taken by the state according to legal acts, sub-legal acts, criminal court decisions or in any other unjust form since 29.11.1944, and the restitution or compensation of the property.

Article 3 – Definitions

For the implementation of this law, the following terms have these meanings:

1. "Compensation" – means just remuneration, according to the market value of the property at the

---

[152] 29 July 2004. Footnotes omitted.

moment this remuneration is recognised, which is done in accordance with this law;

2. "Property" – means an immovable item as defined in the Civil Code;

3. "Expropriated subject" – means natural or juridical persons or their heirs whose property is nationalized, expropriated, confiscated or taken in any other unjust manner by the state;

4. "Alienation" – means the transfer of ownership or other real rights from one natural or juridical person to another as provided in the Civil Code;

5. "Building site" – means land that is located inside the border line of cities and inhabited zones at the moment this law enters into force. When the inhabited zone does not have a border line, the building site will be considered the surface area occupied by the construction built on it and the functional yard. The surface of this yard is calculated as three times the surface of the construction, but not more that 500 square meters.

Article 4 – Exclusions to this Law

Provisions of this law are not applicable:
a. for property gained as result of implementation of Law nr. 108, dated 29.08.1945 "On Agrarian Reform", with subsequent changes;

b. for expropriations made against a just compensation and used for a public interest;

c. for property donated to the state for which official documents exist.

Article 5 – Movable Property

The restitution and compensation of movable property will be done with a separate law.

CHAPTER II – RECOGNITION OF THE RIGHT TO OWNERSHIP AND RESTITUTION OF PROPERTY

Article 6 – Recognition of the Right to Ownership and Restitution of Property

1. Ownership to property is recognized and immovable property is restituted without limitation to the expropriated subjects, except for agricultural land, which is restituted or compensated up to 60 ha and when it is defined differently in this law.

2. The expropriated subjects, whose property was flooded as a result of the construction of the hydro-

power stations, are treated according to the provisions of this law, except for cases when they have benefited by the law "On expropriations in the public interest".

3. Expropriated subjects who have been compensated in accordance with the laws in force have the right to benefit from this law only for the part of property that has not been restituted or compensated.

Article 7 – Property Not Subject to Restitution

1. Immovable property is not restituted that serves a public interest and that:

a. is used to fulfill obligations of the Albanian state that are a result of treaties and conventions to which our state is a party;

b. has investments or is used for the realisation of projects on a territorial or local scale in the field of transportation of any kind, of energy, of telecommunications, of water works of any kind or other investments in the public interest set in accordance with the law "On expropriations in the public interest";

c. serves for the preservation of the environment, health, culture and public education or pre-school education;

ç. serves the national defense and that is non-transferable;

d. is special cultural and historical property as defined according to the legislation in force;

dh. is occupied according to the legal acts set forth in Annex 1 of this law, except for the cases when, according to these laws, the state is the owner and the immovable property does not serve the public interest.

2. In cases when it is proposed that immovable properties included in point 1 of this article be alienated, they pass to the expropriated subjects.

3. The properties defined in point 1 of this article are compensated according to the specifications set forth in this law.

Article 8 – Building Sites

1. When a building site has been alienated to third parties and there are no permanent legal buildings on it, it is restituted to the expropriated subjects, whereas the state will return to the third parties

the value of the purchase multiplied by the price increase index.

2. When on the building site of an expropriated subject, the state or third parties have made buildings or investments in conformity with legislation in force, they are valued according to the market value at the moment the right of ownership is recognized to the expropriated subject, and the following takes place when:

a. the value of the investment is up to 150% of the value of the building site, the property is restituted to the expropriated subject, after the latter pays for the investment made.

b. the value of the investment is more than 150% of the value of the building site, the state or third parties retain ownership and the expropriated subject receives compensation according to this law.

3. In cases when constructions have been erected on building sites before 10.8.1991, for which there is no registration of ownership of the site, the person who owns the building is obliged to pay the initial value of the site in accordance with art. 10 of law nr. 7652, dated 23.12.1992 "On privatization of state housing" multiplied by the price increase index.

4. In cases when legal constructions have been erected on a building site which is rented out or given in concession by the state, the owner of the building pays the value of the site upon which the building is erected according to the market value.

Article 9 – Housing

1. Houses that are owned by the expropriated subjects shall be freed by the lessees within a period of three years. The lessees continue to pay rent defined by the Council of Ministers up to two years from the date of entry into force of this law. The Council of Ministers must secure housing for the lessees, who enjoy the status of the homeless, through low rent houses, low interest rate loans or houses for which the rent is compensated by the state.

2. In cases when houses have been erected in violation of the legislation in force, their residents have the right to purchase the building site during the process of legalization defined in a special law. The valuation of the building site will be done in accor-dance with the market value at the moment the legalization of the housing is done.

Article 10 – Property No Longer Used for a Public Purpose

When an expropriation was done in the public interest and the State Committee for Restitution and Compensation of Property verifies that the immovable property is no longer used for this purpose, it is restituted to the expropriated subject while the expropriated subject, in case s/he received remuneration, returns to the state the remuneration received.

CHAPTER III – COMPENSATION OF PROPERTY

Article 11 – Forms of Compensation

1. For property defined in this law, for which physical restitution is impossible, the state compensates the expropriated subjects with one or more of the following forms:

a. With other immovable property of the same type of equal value in state ownership;

b. With other immovable property of any type of equal value in state ownership;

c. With shares in companies with state capital or where the state is co-owner with a value equal to the immovable property;

ç. With the value of objects that are subject to the process of privatisation;

d. With money.

2. The expropriated subject submits a written request, addressed to the Local Commission for Restitution and Compensation of Property, for the form of compensation to be given. Within 30 days from receipt of the request, the commission, through a reasoned decision, decides to accept or reject the request when the fulfillment of the request is objectively not possible. In this case it offers the expropriated subject another form of compensation, according to the definitions set forth in point 1 of this article. The expropriated subject has the right to submit an appeal to the State Committee for Restitution and Compensation of Property within 30 days from the notification of the decision of the commission for the form of compensation to be given, and in case s/he is not satisfied with the solution, the expropriated subject has the right to appeal to the court within 30 days from

the receipt of the written response from the State Committee for Restitution and Compensation of Property.

3. The remuneration given for compensation purposes is not subject to any fees, taxes or other financial obligations.

Article 12 – Location of Physical Compensation

Physical compensation according to article 11 is done within the same administrative territorial unit (within the village, commune, municipality, district, region), and where this is impossible, in the nearest administrative-territorial unit based on a decision of the State Committee for Restitution and Compensation of Property. For purposes of physical compensation state property in tourist zones will be also used. The areas defined for compensation are announced publicly in the Official Journal, stating their categories (type) as well as their value.

Article 13 – Valuation of Property

1. For the valuation of property that will be compensated, the Local Commission for Restitution and Compensation of Property establishes an expert group. The commission appoints as experts experienced and specially qualified persons in the fields of law, economics and engineering that is related to the process of restitution and compensation of property.

2. The value of the property that is compensated according to this law is calculated based on the market value in accordance with the methodology proposed by the State Committee for Restitution and Compensation of Property and approved by a decision of the Assembly.

3. In carrying out its activities, no member of the state bodies for the process of restitution and compensation of property or of the expert group shall be subject to any conflict of interest defined in the Code of Administrative Procedure.

Article 14 – Right of First Refusal (Right of First Purchase)

1. For immovable property occupied by state objects, expropriated subjects have the right of first refusal for these objects when they are privatised.

2. The expropriated subjects shall have the right to waive their right of first refusal and receive compensation based on article 11 of this law.

CHAPTER IV – STATE BODIES FOR THE PROCESS OF RESTITUTION AND COMPENSATION OF PROPERTY

Article 15 – State Committee for Restitution and Compensation of Property

1. The State Committee for Restitution and Compensation of Property is created for the implementation of this law. The State Committee is made up of 5 members who are appointed and dismissed by the Assembly. Two members are proposed by the parliamentary majority and two members are proposed by the parliamentary opposition. One member is proposed by the Council of Ministers to the President of the Republic, who sends the proposal for approval to the Assembly through a decree. The member sent by the President and approved by the Assembly shall be the Chairperson of the State Committee for Restitution and Compensation of Property.

2. A member of the State Committee for Restitution and Compensation of Property can be any Albanian citizen who:

a. has a bachelors degree as a lawyer, economist, agronomist or in the engineering field related to the process of restitution and compensation of property;

b. has a minimum of 7 years of work experience in the profession;

c. enjoys a good reputation and professional capabilities in their field;

ç. is not a member of a steering body of any political party;

d. has not been found guilty of committing a crime by a final court decision;

dh. has not had a disciplinary measure taken against him consisting of his/her dismissal.

e. has full capacity to act;

ë. does not have a conflict of interest with the position as a member of this Committee.

3. Membership in the State Committee for Restitution and Compensation of Property is incompatible with any other state or political activity.

4. The salary for the members of the State Committee for Restitution and Compensation of Property

is equal to the salary of a deputy minister, while that of the chairperson is 10% higher than the salary of the other members.

5. The member of the State Committee for Restitution and Compensation of Property is dismissed with a decision of the Assembly of Albania, when:

a. he/she has not been found guilty by final court decision for committing a criminal offence by a final court decision and/or prohibited or suspended from exercising his/her duty as public servant;

b. he/she is physically and mentally incapable of fulfilling his/her duties certified by a medical record or by a court decision;

c. he/she misses four or more meetings in a row of the State Committee for Restitution and Compensation of Property without reasonable motives;

ç. it is proved that he/she has gained unmerited profits linked to the exercising of his/her competencies;

d. he/she violates the article of this law.

No member of the State Committee for Restitution and Compensation of Property can be dismissed for other reasons and procedures that are not mentioned in this item, except for the case when he/she resigns.

Article 16 – Competencies of the State Committee for Restitution and Compensation of Property

1. The State Committee for Restitution and Compensation of Property has the following competencies:

a. examines and makes decisions for appeals against the decisions of the Local Commissions for Restitution and Compensation of Property, except for the case provided in article 19 of this law;

b. makes decisions to unify the practices for the process of restitution and compensation of property, on the basis of and for the implementation of the law;

c. nominates and dismisses the chairpersons and members of the Local Commissions for Restitution and Compensation of Property;

ç. directs and monitors the implementation of this law by the Local Commissions for Restitution and Compensation of Property;

d. proposes to the Council of Ministers for approval the draft-budget, organizational structure, organizational chart and salary for the administration of the State Committee for Restitution and Compensation of Property and the Local Commissions for Restitution and Compensation of Property and their administration;

dh. collects and analyzes data for the process of restitution and compensation of property and reports to the Assembly at least once per year or as many times as the Assembly requires and also informs the Council of Ministers upon its request;

e. approves the Regulation for the Organization and Functioning for the State Committee itself and for the Local Commissions for Restitution and Compensation of Property;

ë. defines the necessary documentation based on which the recognition, restitution and compensation of property will be done;

f. defines, in co-operation with the Ministry of Finance, the fees for services that will be paid by the expropriated subjects for the process of restitution and compensation of property;

g. defines the methods for co-operation between Local Commissions when the property that is to be recognized, restituted or compensated is located in two or more Local Commission jurisdictions;

gj. defines the manner for replacement of experts or members of the Local Commissions in cases when they are subject to legal restrictions for the exercise of their duty.

2. The State Committee for Restitution and Compensation of Property verifies the decisions of the Commissions for Restitution and Compensation of Property made according to Law nr. 7698, dated 15.4.1993 "On restitution and compensation of property to the former owners". The request for verification of the issued decisions must be substantiated and presented by local government bodies or expropriated subjects within 6 months from the entry into force of this law. The commission has the right to abrogate the administrative decision or to request the abrogation of this decision through the judicial process.

3. The State Committee for Restitution and Compensation of Property abrogates the decision of the Local Commissions when:

a. the Local Commission for Restitution and Compensation of Property has violated the provisions that regulate its jurisdiction and competencies;

b. the decision is based on incomplete documentation and verification;

c. The necessary documentation based on which the recognition, restitution or compensation of property should have been done.

4. The procedure for restitution and compensation of property is drafted by then State Committee for Restitution and Compensation of Property and shall include:

a. the legal status of the property that will be used for physical compensation for the expropriated subjects.

b. the recognition of the right of ownership for the expropriated subject;

c. the approval of preliminary studies for restitution and compensation of property at the regional level by the State Committee for Restitution and Compensation of Property, based on the proposal of the Local Commissions.

ç. the publication of the approved decisions on restitution and compensation of property at the regional level in the Official Journal.

Article 17 – Local Commissions for Restitution and Compensation of Property

1. Local Commissions for Restitution and Compensation of Property are created and function at the regional level. The territorial competencies of each Commission stretch throughout the territory covered by the respective regions.

2. Local Commissions for Restitution and Compensation of Property are made up of 5 members who are appointed by the State Committee for Restitution and Compensation of Property based on the competition criteria defined in the law "On civil service".

3. A member of the Local Commission for Restitution and Compensation of Property can be any Albanian citizen who:

a. has a bachelors degree as a lawyer, economist, agronomist, pedolog or in the engineering field related to the process of restitution and compensation of property;

b. has not been found guilty for committing a crime by a final court decision;

c. has a minimum of 5 years of work experience in the profession;

ç. has not had a disciplinary measure taken against him consisting of his/her dismissal.

d. has full capacity to act.

dh. has no conflict of interest with the position as a member of the Local Commission.

4. Membership in the Local Committee for Restitution and Compensation of Property is incompatible with any other state or political activity.

Article 18 – Competencies of the Local Commissions for Restitution and Compensation of Property

1. Local Commissions for Restitution and Compensation of Property have the following competencies:

a. verify the truth of documents submitted by expropriated subjects and compare them with legal acts, sub-legal acts and criminal court decisions, according to article 2 of this law, that have served as the basis for the expropriation, nationalization, confiscation of property, or the taking of property by the state;

b. verify and calculate the financial obligations of the state for the expropriated subjects or third parties as defined in this law;

c. nominate experts who help the Commission with technical issues during the process of recognition, restitution and compensation of property;

ç. confirm the ownership right of expropriated subjects, issuing the respective documentation for the recognition, the size and method of restitution or compensation according to the model set forth by the State Committee for Restitution and Compensation of Property;

d. order institutions that administer state or public property to submit documents or data which they consider necessary;

dh. define cases which do not benefit from this law, in accordance with the law and on the basis of documentation.

2. Decisions by the Local Commissions for Restitution and Compensation of Property shall be in writing, made during its meetings, reasoned and include other requirements foreseen in the Code of Administrative Procedure.

3. While defining property restitution or compensation, the Local Commissions shall base their work on a written certificate from the Immovable Property Registration Office regarding the legal status of the immovable property that will be restituted or the legal status of the property with which the expropriated subject will be compensated. The request to the Immovable Property Registration Office is addressed by the chairperson of the Local Commission in writing and before the Commission makes a decision. The Immovable Property Registration Office shall issue a written response within 5 working days from submission of the request and its written response shall be deposited in the respective file.

4. If at the end of the term for appeal, according to this law, no appeal has been filed, the Commissions shall send an original copy of their decisions for the recognition, restitution or compensation of property to the Immovable Property Registration Office.

Article 19 – Time Limits

1. Expropriated subjects have the right to submit any new requests to gain the rights foreseen in this law within 1 year from the date of entry into force of this law.

2. Local Commissions for Restitution and Compensation of Property first recognize the right of ownership and restitute the property within 45 days from submission of the request. The decision for recognition or restitution of property is made public. After the expiration of this deadline, the Local Commissions compensate within 45 days the property which cannot be restituted according to this law. In cases when, within this term, it is impossible for Local Commissions to decide with a reasoned decision they can postpone the time period but only for a period not more than 30 days.

3. In cases when the Local Commissions do not issue a decision within the period defined in point 2 of this article, the State Committee for Restitution and Compensation of Property reaches the decision within 30 days upon the termination of the time period defined in point 2 of this article.

4. If no appeal is presented against the decision issued by the Local Commission or the State Committee for Restitution and Compensation of Property within the terms provided in this law, this decision constitutes an executive title. The bailiff offices are in charge of its execution according to the regulations provided in the Code of Civil Procedure.

Article 20 – The Right to Appeal

1. Expropriated subjects are entitled to appeal to the State Committee for Restitution and Compensation of Property against a decision of the Local Commission, within the limits and manners provided in the Code of Administrative Procedure.

2. The State Committee for Restitution and Compensation of Property shall issue a decision on the appeal within 30 days from the moment the complaint is filed, leaving it in force or returning the case for review to the Local Commission for Restitution and Compensation of Property.

Chapter V – Final Dispositions

Article 21 – Establishment and Functioning of Commissions

1. The subjects defined in article 15 propose the candidates for members of the State Committee for Restitution and Compensation of Property to the Assembly within 30 days from entry into force of this law. The Assembly appoints the members of the State Committee within 30 days after the names of all candidates have been submitted.

2. The State Committee for Restitution and Compensation of Property, within 30 days from its appointment, appoints the members of the Local Commissions for Restitution and Compensation of Property. Within 60 days from the date this law enters into force, the Council of Ministers takes measures and secures the budget and office space for the State Committee and Local Commissions for Restitution and Compensation of Property.

3. Expropriated subjects present their requests for the recognition, restitution or compensation of property 90 days after the entry into force of this law.

Article 22 – Previous Decisions

1. When the files submitted to the Local Commissions for Restitution and Compensation of Property, created according to Law nr. 7698, dated 15.4.1993 "On restitution and compensation of property to the former owners", contain the necessary documentation for verification of the property to be gained from this law, the expropriated subject submits only a written request for recognition, restitution or compensation of the remaining part of the immovable property. Decisions that were issued based on Law nr. 7699, dated 21.04.1993 "On compensation in value or with sites to ex-owners of agricultural land, pastures, meadows, forestry land and forests" which have not been implemented, are considered valid as to the recognition of the right of ownership, and the Local Commission defines whether restitution of the immovable property is possible or else its compensation.

2. The process of restitution and compensation of property re-starts in the manner, form and conditions set forth in this law.

Article 23 – Fund of Compensation

1. The Property Compensation Fund is created for the implementation of financial compensation. This fund consists of budgetary incomes, incomes created by this law and incomes from different donors.

2. Starting from 2005 and for a subsequent period of ten years, the Assembly, at the proposal of the Council of Ministers, defines a Compensation Fund administered by the State Committee for Restitution and Compensation of Property for monetary compensation to expropriated subjects. For the period from the recognition of the right of ownership to receiving compensation in cash, the expropriated subject is also entitled to receive the bank interest rate calculated according to the annual average rate issued by the Bank of Albania.

3. Based on the decision of the Local Commissions for Restitution and Compensation of Property or by a court decision, and by its own order, the State Committee for Restitution and Compensation of Property divides the Compensation Fund proportionally.

Article 24 – Termination of the Process

The process of recognition, restitution and compensation of immovable property ends on 31.12.2006, except for the completion of payments for compensation, which shall end within the term defined in article 23 of this law.

Article 25 – Use of State Documents

For the implementation of this law, within 30 days from the submission of a request, state institutions shall make available copies of all documentation in their possession to the expropriated subjects and to the state commissions, for a fee.

Article 26 – Keeping Documentation

Documentation for the process of recognition, restitution and compensation of property is kept according to the legislation on archives. Upon the termination of the process, according to article 24, this documentation is submitted to the Central State Archive.

Article 27 – Auditing

An economic and financial audit of the activity of the State Commission for Restitution and Compensation of Property and of the Local Commissions is conducted by the High State Auditor at least once every six months. Audit results are always made public.

Article 28 – Transitory Provision

Until the process of restitution and compensation of property is finished the bodies responsible for public administration are prohibited from entering into possession or ownership contracts with third parties for land which is in state ownership.

Article 29 – Sub-legal Acts

The Council of Ministers shall issue the necessary sub-legal acts for the implementation of this law within 90 days from the entry into force of this law.

Article 30 – Abrogation

Law nr. 7698, dated 15.04.1993 "On restitution and compensation of property to the former owners", with subsequent amendments, Law nr. 7699, dated 21.04.1993 "On compensation in value of former owners of agricultural land, pastures, meadows, forestry land and forests", Decree nr. 1254, dated 19.10.1995 "On compensation of the former owners of agricultural land and non-agricultural land and occupied building sites, with sites in tourist lands and in the inhabited zones", article 10 of Law nr. 8030, dated 15.11.1995 "On the state contribution for unsheltered households", and letter ç of article 7 and article 13 of the Law nr. 7665, dated 21.11993 "On development of zones that have priority in the development of tourism" and any other provision which is in violation with this law, are abrogated.

Article 31 – Entrance in Force

This law enters in force 15 days after being published in the Official Journal.

---

3. ARMENIA

3.1. On the Legal and Socio-economic Guarantees for the Persons Who Had Been Forcibly Displaced from the Republic of Azerbaijan in 1988–1992 and Have Acquired the Citizenship of the Republic of Armenia (2000)

This law establishes the legal and socio-economic guarantees for the purpose of implementation of rights and protection of interests of the persons who had been forcibly displaced from the Republic of Azerbaijan in 1988–1992 and have acquired the citizenship of the Republic of Armenia.

Article 1. The Scope of the Law

The law is effective in relation to the persons who had been forcibly displaced from the Republic of Azerbaijan in 1988–1992 and have acquired the citizenship of the Republic of Armenia.

Article 2. The Right to Shelter

The Government of the Republic of Armenia shall define the procedure of providing housing to the forcibly displaced persons who have acquired citizenship of the Republic of Armenia.

Article 3. Recognition of the FDPs as Tenants of Occupied Housing

Forcibly displaced persons who have acquired the citizenship of the Republic of Armenia and who for more than 3 years have been residing in housing, which belongs to the State Housing Resources shall be recognised as tenants of that housing, if other persons have no tenancy or other rights to these housing.

Article 4. Privatisation of the Dormitories

Dwelling space at dormitories, which belong to the state, budget-funded organisations, is privatised in favour of the forcibly displaced persons, who for more than 3 years have been residing in those dormitories and have acquired the citizenship of the Republic of Armenia.

The order of privatisation and the list of dormitories shall be established by the Government of the Republic of Armenia.

Article 5. Privileges Established for Persons Residing in Temporary Dwellings

Forcibly displaced persons who have acquired the citizenship of the Republic of Armenia and have been residing in temporary dwellings (hotels, dormitories, rest houses, sanatoriums etc.) shall be exempted from the established payment for housing, except for the electricity and public utilities. The loss accumulated during their stay at temporary dwellings shall be compensated from the state budget of the Republic of Armenia in accordance with regulations established by the Government of the Republic of Armenia.

Article 6. Compensation for the Property Left in Azerbaijan

Should the issue of compensation for the property left by the forcibly displaced persons in the Republic of Azerbaijan be solved, those FDPs who have acquired the citizenship of the Republic of Armenia shall also be compensated the cost of the property left.

Article 7. Entry into Force of the Law

This law shall enter into force from the moment of publication.

---

4. AZERBAIJAN

4.1. Law on the Social Protection of Internally Displaced Persons and Persons with Equal Status (1999)

Article 1 – Purpose of the Present Law

The present Law outlines measures on the social protection of internally displaced persons and persons equated with them in the Azerbaijan Republic and associated duties of the state bodies.

Article 2 – Internally Displaced Persons and Persons Equated With Them

For the purposes of this Law, persons forced to leave their place of permanent residence in the territory of the Azerbaijan Republic, moved to another place within the country as a result of external military aggression, the capture of certain territories or presence in such territories under regular bombardment are considered internally displaced persons.

Persons who left their places of permanent residence in the territory of the Republic of Armenia as a result of ethnic cleaning conducted in Armenia and other countries, and who arrived in and are not permanent residents of the Azerbaijan Republic, are equated with internally displaced persons.

Article 3 – Scope of This Law

This law applies to persons who have been an IDP since January 1, 1988 until the effective date of the present Law and who have come to the Azerbaijan Republic due to the reasons stipulated in part 2 of Article 2 of this Law.

The measures on social protection stipulated by this Law are valid within 3 years from the date of creation of conditions for the return of IDPs to their former places of residence and from the date of the creation of conditions for permanent residence or for return by persons equated with them to their former places of residence.

The acquisition of separate living space by persons equated with IDPs according to housing legislation and civil–legal acts is considered as their permanent accommodation.

Article 4 – Measures on Social Protection of Internally Displaced Persons and Persons Equated With Them

In regard to Internally Displaced Persons and persons, equated with them (hereinafter referred to as "IDP"), the following measures of social protection are applied:

* provision of temporary dwelling;
* provision of employment;
* social maintenance;
* medical provision;
* provision of education rights;
* privileges on usage of transport and public-municipal utilities;
* taxation privileges.

Additional social protection measures can be determined for IDPs by the legislation of the Azerbaijan Republic.

Article 5 – Provision of the IDPs With Living Space

Accommodation of IDPs is carried out by the appropriate executive authorities. Accommodation, administrative and subsidiary buildings, as well as other buildings which are habitable or can be made habitable can be used for accommodation. If the accommodation of IDPs in such buildings is not possible due to the high density of such residences in certain settlements, they will be accommodated in camps, specifically organized for the IDPs. The camps should meet the requirements necessary for residence.

IDPs can independently find temporary residence as long as the rights and lawful interests of other persons are not violated. In such cases the appropriate executive authorities should ensure resettlement of the IDPs in the other living space within the same district.

Article 6 – Allocation of Land Plots for IDPs, Granting of Loans and Rendering Technical Assistance

For agricultural cultivation IDPs are provided with the temporary land plots of state and municipal land, granted with preferential loans, as well as technical and other assistance as stipulated by the state program.

Regulations and conditions for the allocation of the land plots, granting loans and rendering assistance is determined by the appropriate executive authority.

[. . .]

5. BOSNIA-HERZEGOVINA

5.1. Law on the Cessation of Application of the Law on the Use of Abandoned Property (Republika Srpska) (1996)

I. General Provisions

Article 1

The Law on Use of Abandoned Property (Official Gazette of RS, Nos. 3/96 and 21/96) shall cease to be in force, as well as the regulations passed thereunder and other regulations regulating the issues of abandoned property and apartments passed between 30 April 1991 and the entry into force of this Law.

Article 2

All administrative, judicial, and any other decisions enacted on the basis of the regulations referred to in Article 1 of this Law in which rights of temporary occupancy have been created shall remain effective until cancelled in accordance with this Law.

All administrative, judicial, and any other decisions enacted on the basis of the regulations referred to in Article 1 of this Law in which new occupancy rights have been created shall be treated as acts granting rights of temporary occupancy until cancelled in accordance with this Law.

All administrative, judicial and any other acts and any other disposals of real estate and apartments, enacted on the basis of the regulations referred to in Article 1 of this Law shall cease to be effective after a claim has been filed by the authorised claimant.

II. Return of Property to Private Owners, Possessors or Users

Article 3

The owner, possessor or user of the real property who abandoned the property shall have the right to repossess the real property with all the rights which s/he had before 30 April 1991 or before the real property became abandoned.

Article 4

For the purpose of this Law, the owner, possessor or user shall be understood to mean the person who was the owner, possessor or user of the real property under the applicable legislation at the time when the real property became abandoned.

Article 5

A user to whom the real property was allocated for temporary use pursuant to the Law on the Use of Abandoned Property (hereinafter referred as: the temporary user) may continue to use the real property under the conditions and in the manner as provided by the Law on the Use of Abandoned Property until a decision referred to in Article 11 of this Law has been issued.

Article 6

If the temporary user who is required to vacate the property pursuant to the provisions of this Law cannot or does not wish to return to the apartment in which s/he lived before 30 April 1991 and who has not been provided with another apartment meeting the conditions of appropriate accommodation, the responsible body of the Ministry of Refugees and Displaced Persons on the territory of which s/he had his/her last domicile or residence shall provide him/her with appropriate accommodation within the deadline set in the decision ordering him/her to move out.

If the temporary user referred to in Paragraph 1 of this Article presents evidence that s/he submitted a claim for repossession of his/her property, s/he may not be evicted by force until s/he is enabled to return or freely dispose of his/her property, in line with Annex 7 of the General Framework Peace Agreement for Bosnia and Herzegovina or until an alternative accommodation has been provided in another way within one year.

If the request of the temporary user and free disposal of his/her property has been resolved, in no event shall failure of the responsible body to meet its obligations under paragraph 1 of this Article operate to delay the ability of the owner, possessor or user to enter into possession of his/her property.

The body responsible for the provision of accommodation shall not be obliged to provide an accommodation to a person using the apartment without valid legal basis.

Article 7

The owner, possessor or user of abandoned real property, or his/her authorised representative, shall have the right to file a claim at any time for the repossession or disposal in another way of his/her abandoned property.

The right of the owner to file a claim shall not become obsolete.

Article 8

A claim under Article 7 of this Law may be filed by the owner, possessor or user of abandoned real property with the responsible body of the Minister of Refugees and Displaced Persons in the municipality on the territory of which the real property is located.

Claims may be made in writing signed by the claimant or an authorised representative, or orally by the claimant or an authorised representative. Claims made in writing may be submitted in person, by mail or by any other person. No power of attorney is required for another person to submit a claim signed by the claimant.

A claim should include:

- information on the owner, possessor or user;
- all necessary information on the real property;
- any evidence possessed by the claimant indicating that the claimant is the owner, possessor or user of the real property;
- the date when the claimant intends to repossess the real property.

The responsible body shall accept claims regardless of whether or not supporting documentation is supplied by the claimant. In the event that the claimant cannot provide the necessary supporting documentation, the responsible body shall check the records of the relevant court or administrative body and any other available documentation to confirm the rights of the claimant.

The responsible body shall accept any identification document issued by the state of Bosnia and Herzegovina or any administrative body in either Entity, and any other document which shows the claimant's identity, and shall use any options provided in the Law on General Administrative Proceedings in the identification process.

The claimant shall be fully released from taxation, as well as from other expenses of the proceedings as provided in Articles 113 through 119 of the Law on General Administrative Proceedings ("The SFRY Official Gazette", No. 47/86, "The RS Official Gazette", No. 1/94, Special Issue 10/95).

Article 9

The responsible body of the Ministry of Refugees and Displaced Persons shall be obliged to issue a decision to the claimant within 30 days from the date of receipt of the claim for repossession of real property.

Article 10

The proceedings to return the real property to the owner, possessor or user shall be carried out in accordance with the provisions of the Law on General Administrative Proceedings, unless this Law provides otherwise. The procedure until the issuance of the decision shall be carried out as an expedited procedure.

Article 11

The decision on return of the real property to the owner, possessor or user shall contain the following:

- information on the owner, possessor or user to whom the real property is returned,
- information on the real property subject to return,
- the time limit within which the real property will be returned or put at disposal of the owner, possessor or user,
- a decision whether the temporary user is entitled to appropriate accommodation,
- a decision terminating the right of the temporary user to use the real property as of the date of the intended return of the claimant,
- the time limit for the temporary user to vacate the property, or for handing over of the land.

The decision under Paragraph 1 of this Article may not set a time limit for the temporary user to vacate the property shorter than 90 days from the date of the issuance of the decision, nor longer than the date of the intended return of the owner, possessor or user, but the day of the intended return may not be earlier than 90 days from the date of submitting the claim.

The claimant may reoccupy property that is not in possession of a temporary user immediately on receipt of the decision.

In exceptional circumstances, the deadline referred to above may be extended by up to one year if the body responsible for providing another accommodation in accordance with Article 6 of this Law provides detailed documentation regarding the lack of available accommodation to the Ministry of Refugees and Displaced Persons.

In case of the return of arable land into possession, the time limit for its handing over may be extended, as an exception, until the harvest is collected.

Article 12

The responsible body of the Ministry of Refugees and Displaced Persons shall submit its decision to the claimant requesting the repossession of the property.

Article 13

The party to whom the decision under Article 11 of this Law is referred may at any time initiate proceedings before the Commission for Real Property Claims of Displaced Persons and Refugees (Annex 7 to the General Framework Agreement of Peace in Bosnia and Herzegovina, hereinafter referred to as the Commission).

In case that the proceedings under Paragraph 1 of this Article have been initiated, all other proceedings carried out before the competent bodies, including the procedure to enforce the decision referred to in Article 11 of this Law, shall be stayed pending the final decision of the Commission.

A decision of the Commission shall be final and binding.

In the light of specifying the rights and obligations of the party referred to in Paragraph 1 of this Article, the decision of the Commission shall have the same legal force as the decision of any other responsible body issued in accordance with this Law.

A decision of the Commission shall be enforced by the competent bodies of the Republika Srpska.

III. Return of Apartments to the Holders of Occupancy Right

Article 14

The occupancy right holder of an abandoned apartment shall have the right to return to the apartment in accordance with Annex 7 of the General Framework Agreement for Peace in Bosnia and Herzegovina.

Persons who have left their apartments after 30 April 1991, are presumed to be refugees and displaced persons under Annex 7, unless it is established that they left their apartments for reasons wholly unrelated to the conflict.

Article 15

The occupancy right holder referred to in Article 14 of this Law shall be entitled to file a claim for repossession of the apartment.

A claim for repossession of the apartment shall be filed with the responsible body of the Ministry of Refugees and Displaced Persons in the municipality in which the apartment is located.

A claim for repossession of the apartment should include:

- information on the claimant;
- information on the apartment;
- evidence that the claimant is the occupancy right holder or a member of the latter's family household;
- the date when the claimant intends to reoccupy the apartment, but not later than one year from the date of submitting the claim;
- information on the residence of the occupancy right holder and members of his/her household at the time when the claim is submitted.

If the temporary user of the apartment presents evidence that s/he submitted a claim for return of his/her occupancy right, s/he shall not be evicted by force from the apartment allocated to him/her for temporary use until s/he is enabled to freely dispose of his/her apartment, or until an appropriate accommodation has been provided in another way within one year.

The responsible body shall accept all claims with or without the appropriate documents enclosed by the claimant. In cases when the claimant is not able to provide the necessary relevant documents, the responsible body shall verify the evidence, as well as other available documents, with the allocation right holder, the appropriate court or administrative body in order to have the rights of the claimant confirmed.

The responsible body shall accept any identification document issued by the state of Bosnia and Herzegovina or any legal body in either Entity, as well as any other document confirming the identity of the claimant.

The claimant shall be fully exempted from taxation as well as from other expenses of the proceedings, as provided in Articles 113 through 119 of the Law on General Administrative Proceedings.

Article 16

A claim for repossession of the apartment may be filed within 6 months from the date of entry into force of this Law.

If the occupancy right holder does not file a claim within the time limit referred to in the previous paragraph, his/her occupancy right shall be cancelled.

Article 17

The responsible body of the Ministry of Refugees and Displaced Persons shall decide on the claim for the repossession of the apartment by the occupancy right holder within 30 days from the date of receipt of the claim.

The allocation right holder shall refer the case to the responsible municipal or city administrative body within 30 days from the issuance of the decision referred to in the Article above which relates to the apartment occupied by the new occupancy right holder based on an act issued by the allocation right holder, i.e. contract (hereinafter: the current user). The responsible municipal or city administrative body shall then pass a decision on the allocation of another apartment to the current user or occupancy right holder within a deadline which cannot be longer than the deadlines referred to in Article 18 of this Law.

If the responsible municipal body has decided to allocate another apartment to the occupancy right holder, this Decision shall have to be passed in accordance with the criteria which must be harmonised with Article 1 Annex 7 of the General Framework Agreement in line with the European Convention on Human Rights and with other regulations of the Republika Srpska.

Article 18

The decision on repossession of the apartment by the occupancy right holder shall contain:

- a decision confirming that the claimant is the occupancy right holder;

- a decision on repossession of the apartment by the occupancy right holder if there is a tempo-

rary user in the apartment, or if the apartment is vacant or occupied without legal basis;

- a decision on termination of the right of temporary use of the apartment if there is a temporary user of the apartment;

- a time limit for vacating the apartment by a temporary user or another person in possession of the apartment;

- a decision concerning whether the temporary user is entitled to accommodation in accordance with the ZOSO.

The time limit for vacating the apartment referred to in Paragraph 1(4) of this Article may not be shorter than 90 days from the date of the issuance of the decision, nor longer than the day of the intended return of the holder of the occupancy right, but the day of the intended return may not be earlier than 90 days from the date of submitting the claim.

The occupancy right holder may reoccupy an apartment that is vacant immediately on receipt of the decision, unless the apartment is in possession of a temporary user in accordance with this Law. In exceptional circumstances, the deadline referred to in Paragraph 2 of this Article may be extended by up to one year if the body responsible for providing alternative accommodation on the territory of which the temporary user of the apartment had the last domicile or residence provides detailed documentation regarding the lack of available housing for provision of appropriate accommodation the Ministry for Refugees and Displaced Persons.

In each individual case, the requirements of the European Convention on Human Rights and its Protocols must be met, and the occupancy right holder shall be notified of the decision to extend the deadline and the basis for the decision 30 days before the deadline has expired.

Article 19

The responsible body shall deliver the decision referred to in Article 18 of this Law within 8 days from the date of issuance of the decision to:

- the occupancy right holder;

- the user of the apartment;

- the allocation right holder.

Article 20

The proceedings to return the apartment to the occupancy right holder shall be carried out in accordance with the provisions of the Law on General Administrative Proceedings, unless this Law provides otherwise.

Article 21

The occupancy right to the apartment shall cease in case the occupancy right holder fails to reoccupy the apartment without a justified cause, within one year from the day when the decision becomes final.

The reason for which the occupancy right holder failed to commence to use the apartment shall be deemed justified:

- if the occupancy right holder has initiated an enforcement procedure, while the other party continues to occupy that apartment;

- if the occupancy right holder is unable to return to the municipality where the apartment is located for the reason of his/her justified fear of persecution;

- if the occupancy right holder has been drafted into the army;

- if the occupancy right holder is admitted to medical care;

- if the occupancy right holder is in the old peoples' home, disabled peoples' home, pensioners' home, etc.;

- if the occupancy right holder is serving a prison sentence during the period of imprisonment sentence;

- if a certain security measure is being taken against the occupancy right holder;

- if the occupancy right holder and members of her/his family household temporarily reside in a different place within the country or abroad for the reasons mentioned in Paragraph 1 of Article 48 of the ZOSO; or

- if an apartment is the subject of the claim submitted to the Commission for the Real Property Claims of the Displaced Persons and Refugees.

The occupancy right holder's right to use the apartment shall not cease in the cases referred to in the previous paragraph.

Article 22

Upon the cancellation of the occupancy right under Articles 16 and 21 of this Law, the allocation right holder may allocate the apartment for use to the temporary user or another person in accordance with the provisions of the ZOSO.

If the temporary user has been issued a decision by the Ministry of Refugees and Displaced Persons, s/he shall stay in possession of such an apartment until he is provided with another appropriate accommodation.

Article 23

The party referred to in the decision under Article 18 of this Law may initiate at any time proceedings before the Commission for Real Property Claims of Displaced Persons and Refugees (Annex 7 to the General Framework Agreement for Peace in Bosnia and Herzegovina, hereafter: the Commission).

In case that such proceedings have been initiated, all other proceedings carried out before the competent bodies, including the procedure to enforce the decision, shall be stayed pending the final decision of the Commission.

A decision of the Commission shall be final and binding.

In the light of specifying the rights and obligations of the party referred to in Paragraph 1 of this Article, the decision of the Commission shall have the same legal force as the decision of any other responsible body issued in accordance with this Law. A decision of the Commission shall be enforced by the competent body of Republika Srpska.

IV. SPECIAL PROVISIONS

Article 24

The repossession of abandoned real property or the apartment by the owner, user or occupancy right holder shall be witnessed by an official and interested parties.

A report shall be made on the return of the real property or apartment and on the reinstatement of the owner or user into possession of the property or apartment. The report shall contain a detailed description of the real property under the process of return.

Article 25

The provisions of this Law shall also apply to the abandoned real property the ownership of which has been acquired after 30 April 1991 under any title on sale of real property (contracts on exchange, purchase, gift, etc.).

Article 26

The provisions of this Law regulating the manner of repossession of the real property or apartment by the owner, possessor or user shall also apply regarding repossession of the real property allocated to temporary users on the basis of rationalisation (excess housing space).

Article 27

A decision on repossession of real property may be appealed with the Ministry of Refugees and Displaced Persons within 15 days from the date of the receipt of the decision.

Article 28

The conditions for and the manner of the purchase of an apartment for the occupancy right holders to whom the apartments have been returned in accordance with this Law shall be regulated by a separate law.

Article 29

The Minister of Refugees and Displaced Persons shall pass an instruction on the application of Articles 8 through 11 and Articles 15 through 18 of this Law within 30 days from the date of the entry into force of this Law.

Article 30

This Law shall enter into force on the 8th day after its publication in the Official Gazette of the Republika Srpska.

5.2. PIC Sintra Declaration (1997)[153]

Conditionality for Refugee Return

Refugees and displaced persons have the right to return to their pre-war homes in a peaceful, orderly and phased manner. Unless and until there is a process under way to enable them to do so, there will

be continued instability in Bosnia. Although all the authorities have agreed, as part of the Peace Agreement, to support these returns, none have abided by it in practice. International economic aid is conditional upon compliance with, and implementation of, the Peace Agreement.

In particular, assistance for housing and local infrastructure should be dependent on the acceptance of return. The international community is prepared to provide resources to those areas which welcome the return of refugees and displaced persons and co-operate actively in integrating them into local communities. Priority will be given to those municipalities receptive to minority returns and UNHCR's "Open Cities" project. The Reconstruction and Refugee Task Force, chaired by the Office of the High Representative, is asked to intensify its coordinating role in this respect.

The Steering Board is concerned that Serb refugees must be permitted to return to Drvar. Bosniac authorities need to take concrete steps to facilitate full return to Sarajevo, and Bosniacs and Croats must be able to return to their homes in Brcko, Banja Luka and numerous other cities. All returnees must be allowed to live free of harassment.

Of particular importance is the obligation of both the Federation and Republika Srpska to amend existing property laws. The current laws place insurmountable legal barriers in the path of return, effectively blocking hundreds of thousands of pre-war occupants from returning to their homes.

The Steering Board calls for the Federation and Republika Srpska to amend their property laws in order to make the full implementation of Annex 7 of the Peace Agreement possible. International support for housing reconstruction should be conditional upon fulfilment of these obligations.

In order to facilitate the return of refugees and displaced persons to that part of the original Brcko municipality now in Republika Srpska, as well as to safeguard the interests of displaced persons presently in the area, repair of existing housing and infrastructure as well the construction of new housing is essential. The Steering Board urged this to be taken into account at the Donors' Conference.

The Steering Board strongly censured the Federation for its failure to co-operate in the Brcko process, particularly for having blocked economic assistance to Brcko, hindering the return of refugees

---

[153] Office of the High Representative Peace Implementation Council, Friday, 30 May 1997.

through its failure to accept agreed procedures, and withholding its support for the electoral process.

5.3. Office of the High Commissioner, Federation Forum, Chairman's Conclusions (1997)[154]

On 20 August 1997, the Federation leadership met at a session of the Federation Forum in Sarajevo to discuss ways and means to further strengthen and implement the Federation. The meeting was co-chaired by Chief of US Mission, Robert M. Beecroft, and the Senior Deputy High Representative, Ambassador Gerd Wagner.

The following was agreed:

RETURN, HUMAN RIGHTS AND PROPERTY LEGISLATION

Participants welcomed the ongoing process of return of refugees and displaced persons in the Central Bosnia Canton, in particular in Jajce, as decided in the Federation meeting of 5 August chaired by OHR. They reaffirmed their commitment to formulate and adopt by 25 August a program for the return of all refugees and displaced persons in the Central Bosnia Canton. This plan will be reaffirmed at the JCC Working Group Meeting chaired by UNHCR on 25 August. In this context, another Federation meeting reconvening the participants of the 5 August meeting will be on 27 August. Participants called on the international community to provide assistance to the returnees.

Participants condemned the recent assaults on returnees in Bugojno and Stolac on 16 August, and emphasized that such incidents will not undermine their efforts to foster the return process. They called on the municipal authorities and the police to investigate such incidents thoroughly, publicly release their findings by September 1 and prosecute the perpetrators.

Participants affirmed their regret over the violent demonstrations by and manipulations of vulnerable displaced persons for the purpose of preventing Serb return to Vogosca. Participants agreed to call on municipal authorities and police to conduct a thorough investigation into the events leading up to demonstrations against returns to Vogosca. The findings of this investigation will be released by

1 September. Based on the findings of the investigation, we expect all responsible authorities to exercise the full power of their offices to prevent future violent demonstrations from occurring.

The President and the Vice-President of the Federation personally committed themselves to make every effort to resolve problems with which returnees are confronted. For this purpose, they will jointly and regularly visit municipalities which are experiencing difficulties with return, to promote the return of refugees and displaced persons throughout the Federation and to remind municipal officials, also with disciplinary measures, of their obligations under Annex 7 of the Peace Agreement.

The Federation Ombudsmen reminded the Forum of their reports on issues related to the exercise of return.

Participants welcomed that in accordance with the agreement of 5 August, the Federation Ombudsmen have been provided with premises in Travnik and will start their work in this city on 25 August.

On 10 July 1996, Federation authorities stated their commitment to urgent revision of existing property laws to comply with the Peace Agreement and eliminate obstacles to return. At Sintra, the PIC Steering Board reiterated that this as yet unmet demand must be fulfilled, and stated that "international support for housing reconstruction should be conditional upon the fulfillment of these obligations". On 6 August 1997 in Split, President Izetbegovic responded by making a concrete commitment that property legislation in the Federation will meet these obligations by 30 September 1997.

Participants will fulfil this commitment by ensuring that the Federation Parliament considers and adopts the three draft laws prepared by the OHR on this subject, which include:

- The Law on the Cessation of the Application of the Law on Abandoned Apartments;

- The Law Regulating the Application of the Law on Temporary Abandoned Real Property Owned by Citizens; and

- The Law on Amendments to the Law on Housing Relations.

The Participants will also ensure that local authorities comply with the new laws once adopted, and

---

[154] 20 August 1997.

that all returnees are able to return to their pre-war homes as guaranteed by Annex 7 of the Peace Agreement.

5.4. Law on Implementation of the Decisions of the Commission for Real Property Claims of Displaced Persons and Refugees (Republika Srpska) (1999)

Article 1

This Law shall regulate the administrative enforcement, by way of return into possession, on the territory of the Republika Srpska, of decisions of the Commission for Real Property Claims of Displaced Persons and Refugees (hereinafter referred to as the "Commission"), created under Annex 7 of the General Framework Agreement for Peace in Bosnia and Herzegovina.

Article 2

Decisions of the Commission are final and binding from the day of their adoption.

Decisions of the Commission confirm the rights to real properties of the person(s) named in the decision, and require the responsible enforcement organs to take measures as set out in this Law.

Decisions of the Commission also carry the force of legal evidence that may be used in administrative, judicial or other legal proceedings.

Article 3

The enforcement of a decision of the Commission shall be conducted administratively, if the persons referred to in Article 4, Paragraphs 1 or 2 (requestor for enforcement) request so.

The responsible body of the Ministry of Refugees and Displaced Persons in the municipality where the property is located shall enforce decisions of the Commission relating to real property owned by citizens or to apartments for which there is an occupancy right upon the request of a requestor for enforcement.

Article 4

The following persons are entitled to file a request for enforcement of a decision of the Commission relating to real property owned by citizens:

- the right holder specified in the decision of the Commission

- the heirs of the right holder specified in the decision of the Commission.

The following persons are entitled to file a request for enforcement of a decision of the Commission relating to an apartment for which there is an occupancy right:

- the occupancy right holder referred to in a decision of the Commission

- the persons who, in compliance with the Law on Housing Relations, are considered to be the members of the family household of the occupancy right holder referred to in the decision of the Commission, as of the date specified in the dispositive of the Commission decision.

Other persons, including those to whom these rights were transferred after the date specified in the dispositive of the Commission decision, are entitled to submit the decision of the Commission in administrative or court proceedings as legal evidence, in accordance with Article 2, paragraph 3 of this Law.

Article 5

The right to file a request for enforcement of a decision of the Commission confirming a right to private property is not subject to any statute of limitation.

The request for enforcement of a decision of the Commission confirming occupancy rights must be submitted within one year from the date when the Commission decision was issued, or for decisions issued before this Law entered into force, within one year from the entry into force of this Law.

Article 6

The request for enforcement of a Commission decision relating to real property owned by citizens shall include two certified photocopies of the decision of the Commission. The request for enforcement of a Commission decision relating to occupancy rights shall include three certified copies of the decision of the Commission.

Article 7

The administrative organ responsible for enforcement of a Commission decision is obliged to issue a conclusion on the permission of enforcement, within a period of 30 days from the date when the request for enforcement was submitted.

The administrative organ which is responsible for enforcement of decisions of the Commission shall not require any confirmation of the enforceability of the decision from the Commission or from any other body.

The administrative organ which is responsible for enforcement of a decision of the Commission shall obtain all necessary information about the identity of the enforcee (as defined in Article 9 of this Law), together with details of the legal basis, if any, on which the enforcee is inhabiting the property or apartment.

The conclusion referred to in paragraph 1 of this Article shall contain:

- a decision on repossession of the property or apartment by the right holder or other requestor for enforcement;

- a decision terminating the right of the temporary user (where there is one) to use the property or apartment;

- a time limit for the enforcee to vacate the property;

- a decision on whether the enforcee is entitled to accommodation in accordance with applicable laws;

- a requirement that the premises shall be vacated of all persons and possessions, other than those belonging to the person authorised to return into possession.

The time limit for vacating the property shall be the minimum time limit applicable under the Law on Cessation of the Application of the Law on the Use of Abandoned Property. No extension of this time limit shall be permitted.

In case a requestor for enforcement has commenced proceedings for enforcement of a decision issued by the responsible administrative organ in relation to the same property or apartment under the Law on Cessation of the Application of the Law on the Use of Abandoned Property, and this person subsequently submits the decision of the Commission for enforcement, the responsible administrative organ shall join the proceedings for enforcement of both decisions.

The date on which the person commenced enforcement proceedings for the first decision shall be considered, for the purposes of this Law, the date of submission of the request for enforcement.

Article 8

The administrative organ which is responsible for enforcement of a decision of the Commission is obliged to deliver one certified copy of the decision of the Commission together with the conclusion on permission of enforcement, within 5 days from the date of the issuance of the conclusion on permission of enforcement, to any person who is in possession of the property or apartment referred to in the decision and, in case of occupancy rights, also to the allocation right holder of the apartment.

Article 9

The enforcement of a decision of the Commission shall be conducted against the person who is in possession of the property or apartment designated in the decision, with or without legal basis ('enforcee').

The enforcement shall also be conducted against any third person using the property or apartment, even in the case where an enforcee from paragraph 1 of this Article voluntarily vacated the property or apartment at issue.

The enforcement of a decision shall be conducted regardless of whether the property or apartment referred to in the decision was declared abandoned or not and irrespective of any other decisions or regulations relating to its legal status.

The administrative body competent for enforcement shall suspend the commenced enforcement if it is established that the enforcee has voluntarily complied with the decision of the Commission.

Article 10

The right holder referred to in the Commission decision and/or any other person who held a legal interest in the property or apartment at issue on the date referred to in the dispositive of the Commission decision, is entitled to submit a request for reconsideration to the Commission, in accordance with Commission regulations.

A person with a legal interest in the property or apartment at issue which was acquired after the date referred to in the dispositive of the Commission decision, may lodge an appeal against the conclusion on permission of enforcement issued by the competent administrative organ, only as permitted by the provisions of this Law. The appeal procedure mentioned in this paragraph may not refute the regularity of the Commission decision. The regularity of the Commission decision may be reviewed only through the reconsideration procedures referred to in Article 11 of this Law.

Article 11

On receipt of a request for reconsideration, the Commission may notify the competent administrative organs responsible for the enforcement of the Commission decision of the pending request for reconsideration.

Once notified of the pending request for reconsideration by the Commission, the competent administrative organ shall suspend the enforcement of the Commission decision, until such time as it receives notification from the Commission of the outcome of the reconsideration.

In reference to the previous paragraph, the competent administrative organ shall not suspend the enforcement of the Commission decision, unless it has received official notification of the request for reconsideration from the Commission.

After examining the request for reconsideration, the Commission may:

a) refuse to admit the request as being inadmissible, not submitted within due time or as submitted by an unauthorised person;

b) reject the request as being unfounded;

c) accept the request, revoke its previous decision and issue a new decision.

The decision of the Commission refusing or rejecting the reconsideration request shall be delivered to the person who requested the reconsideration. The decision of the Commission accepting the reconsideration request and revoking its previous decision shall be delivered to the person who requested the reconsideration and all other persons who received the original decision, and to the administrative organ responsible for enforcement.

Article 12

The appeal against the conclusion on permission of enforcement of the decision of the Commission, referred to in paragraph 2 of Article 10 of the Law, must be lodged before the competent administrative body that issued the conclusion on permission of enforcement, within 8 days from the date of delivery of the conclusion on permission of enforcement.

The responsible administrative body shall direct the appellant to initiate proceedings before the competent court within 30 days, to prove that the right holder named in the Commission's decision voluntarily and lawfully transferred his/her rights to the appellant since the date referred to in the dispositive of the Commission's decision.

Enforcement proceedings before the responsible administrative organ shall not be suspended pending the court's decision.

As an exception to the previous paragraph, the competent court may make a specific order to suspend the enforcement proceedings before the responsible administrative organ if a verified contract on the transfer of rights was made after 14 December 1995.

Article 13

The competent court shall determine whether the transfer of rights to the appellant was conducted voluntarily and in accordance with the law.

If the transfer of rights was conducted between 1 April 1992 and 14 December 1995, and its validity is disputed by the respondent, the burden of proof shall lie on the party claiming to have acquired rights to the property under the transaction to establish that the transaction was conducted voluntarily and in accordance with the law.

If the validity of the transfer has been determined in previous proceedings which took place prior to the entry into force of this Law, the decision taken in the previous proceedings shall be null and void.

The court may make whatever orders are necessary to give effect to its decision, including orders setting aside legal transactions, orders for making or erasing entries in the appropriate public books/registers, and orders lifting any order for suspension of the administrative proceedings.

The relevant parties to the appeal shall notify the competent administrative body of the court's decision.

The responsible administrative body shall resume enforcement proceedings as required, or discontinue proceedings in accordance with the court's decisions.

[. . .]

5.5. Law on Implementation of the Decisions of the Commission for Real Property Claims of Displaced Persons and Refugees (Federation BiH) (1999)

Article 1

This Law shall regulate the administrative enforcement, by way of return into possession, on the territory of the Federation of Bosnia and Herzegovina, of decisions of the Commission for Real Property Claims of Displaced Persons and Refugees (hereinafter referred to as the "Commission"), created under Annex 7 of the General Framework Agreement for Peace in Bosnia and Herzegovina.

Article 2

Decisions of the Commission are final and binding from the day of their adoption.

Decisions of the Commission confirm the rights to real properties of the person(s) named in the decision, and require the responsible enforcement organs to take measures as set out in this Law.

Decisions of the Commission also carry the force of legal evidence that may be used in administrative, judicial or other legal proceedings.

Article 3

The enforcement of a decision of the Commission shall be conducted administratively, if the persons referred to in Article 4, Paragraphs 1 or 2 (requestor for enforcement) request so.

The administrative body responsible for property legal affairs in the municipality where the property is located shall enforce decisions of the Commission relating to real property owned by citizens upon the request of persons referred to in Article 4, Paragraph 1 of this Law.

The administrative body responsible for housing affairs in the municipality where the apartment is located shall enforce decisions of the Commission relating to an apartment for which there is an occupancy right upon the request of the persons referred to in Article 4, Paragraph 2 of this Law.

Article 4

The following persons are entitled to file a request for enforcement of a decision of the Commission relating to real property owned by citizens:

- the right holder specified in the decision of the Commission
- the heirs of the right holder specified in the decision of the Commission.

The following persons are entitled to file a request for enforcement of a decision of the Commission relating to an apartment for which there is an occupancy right:

- the occupancy right holder referred to in a decision of the Commission
- the persons who, in compliance with the Law on Housing Relations, are considered to be the members of the family household of the occupancy right holder referred to in the decision of the Commission, as of the date specified in the dispositive of the Commission decision.

Other persons, including those to whom these rights were transferred after the date specified in the dispositive of the Commission decision, are entitled to submit the decision of the Commission in administrative or court proceedings as legal evidence, in accordance with Article 2, paragraph 3 of this Law.

Article 5

The right to file a request for enforcement of a decision of the Commission confirming a right to private property is not subject to any statute of limitation.

The request for enforcement of a decision of the Commission confirming occupancy rights must be submitted within one year from the date when the Commission decision was issued, or for decisions issued before this Law entered into force, within one year from the entry into force of this Law.

Article 6

The request for enforcement of a Commission decision relating to real property owned by citizens shall include two certified photocopies of the decision of the Commission. The request for enforcement of a Commission decision relating to occupancy rights shall include three certified copies of the decision of the Commission.

Article 7

The administrative organ responsible for enforcement of a Commission decision is obliged to issue a conclusion on the permission of enforcement, within a period of 30 days from the date when the request for enforcement was submitted.

The administrative organ which is responsible for enforcement of decisions of the Commission shall not require any confirmation of the enforceability of the decision from the Commission or from any other body.

The administrative organ which is responsible for enforcement of a decision of the Commission shall obtain all necessary information about the identity of the enforcee (as defined in Article 9 of this Law), together with details of the legal basis, if any, on which the enforcee is inhabiting the property or apartment.

The conclusion referred to in paragraph 1 of this Article shall contain:

- in the case of property or apartments that have been declared abandoned, a decision terminating the municipal administration of the property;

- a decision on repossession of the property or apartment by the right holder or other requestor for enforcement;

- a decision terminating the right of the temporary user (where there is one) to use the property or apartment;

- a time limit for the enforcee to vacate the property;

- a decision on whether the enforcee is entitled to accommodation in accordance with applicable laws;

- a requirement that the premises shall be vacated of all persons and possessions, other than those belonging to the person authorised to return into possession.

The time limit for vacating the property shall be the minimum time limit applicable under the Law on Cessation of the Application of the Law on Temporarily Abandoned Real Property Owned by Citizens and the Law on Cessation of the Application of the Law on Abandoned Apartments. No extension of this time limit shall be permitted.

In case a requestor for enforcement has commenced proceedings for enforcement of a decision issued by the responsible administrative organ in relation to the same property or apartment under the Law on Cessation of the Application of the Law on Temporarily Abandoned Real Property owned by Citizens or under the Law on Cessation of the Application of the Law on Abandoned Apartments, and this person subsequently submits the decision of the Commission for enforcement, the responsible administrative organ shall join the proceedings for enforcement of both decisions. The date on which the person commenced enforcement proceedings for the first decision shall be considered, for the purposes of this Law, the date of submission of the request for enforcement.

Article 8

The administrative organ which is responsible for enforcement of a decision of the Commission is obliged to deliver one certified copy of the decision of the Commission together with the conclusion on permission of enforcement, within 5 days from the date of the issuance of the conclusion on permission of enforcement, to any person who is in possession of the property or apartment referred to in the decision and, in case of occupancy rights, also to the allocation right holder of the apartment.

Article 9

The enforcement of a decision of the Commission shall be conducted against the person who is in possession of the property or apartment designated in the decision, with or without legal basis ('enforcee').

The enforcement shall also be conducted against any third person using the property or apartment, even in the case where an enforcee from paragraph 1 of this Article voluntarily vacated the property or apartment at issue.

The enforcement of a decision shall be conducted regardless of whether the property or apartment referred to in the decision was declared abandoned or not and irrespective of any other decisions or regulations relating to its legal status.

The administrative body competent for enforcement shall suspend the commenced enforcement if it is established that the enforcee has voluntarily complied with the decision of the Commission.

Article 10

The right holder referred to in the Commission decision and/or any other person who held a legal interest in the property or apartment at issue on the date referred to in the dispositive of the Commission decision, is entitled to submit a request for reconsideration to the Commission, in accordance with Commission regulations.

A person with a legal interest in the property or apartment at issue which was acquired after the date referred to in the dispositive of the Commission decision, may lodge an appeal against the conclusion on permission of enforcement issued by the competent administrative organ, only as permitted by the provisions of this Law. The appeal procedure mentioned in this paragraph may not refute the regularity of the Commission decision. The regularity of the Commission decision may be reviewed only through the reconsideration procedures referred to in Article 11 of this Law.

Article 11

On receipt of a request for reconsideration, the Commission may notify the competent administrative organs responsible for the enforcement of the Commission decision of the pending request for reconsideration. Once notified of the pending request for reconsideration by the Commission, the competent administrative organ shall suspend the enforcement of the Commission decision, until such time as it receives notification from the Commission of the outcome of the reconsideration.

In reference to the previous paragraph, the competent administrative organ shall not suspend the enforcement of the Commission decision, unless it has received official notification of the request for reconsideration from the Commission.

After examining the request for reconsideration, the Commission may:

a) refuse to admit the request as being inadmissible, not submitted within due time or as submitted by an unauthorised person;

b) reject the request as being unfounded;

c) accept the request, revoke its previous decision and issue a new decision.

The decision of the Commission refusing or rejecting the reconsideration request shall be delivered to the person who requested the reconsideration. The decision of the Commission accepting the reconsideration request and revoking its previous decision shall be delivered to the person who requested the reconsideration and all other persons who received the original decision, and to the administrative organ responsible for enforcement.

Article 12

The appeal against the conclusion on permission of enforcement of the decision of the Commission, referred to in paragraph 2 of Article 10 of the Law, must be lodged before the competent administrative body that issued the conclusion on permission of enforcement, within 8 days from the date of delivery of the conclusion on permission of enforcement.

The responsible administrative body shall direct the appellant to initiate proceedings before the competent court within 30 days, to prove that the right holder named in the Commission's decision voluntarily and lawfully transferred his/her rights to the appellant since the date referred to in the dispositive of the Commission's decision.

Enforcement proceedings before the responsible administrative organ shall not be suspended pending the court's decision.

As an exception to the previous paragraph, the competent court may make a specific order to suspend the enforcement proceedings before the responsible administrative organ if a verified contract on the transfer of rights was made after 14 December 1995.

Article 13

The competent court shall determine whether the transfer of rights to the appellant was conducted voluntarily and in accordance with the law.

If the transfer of rights was conducted between 1 April 1992 and 14 December 1995, and its validity is disputed by the respondent, the burden of proof shall lie on the party claiming to have acquired rights to the property under the transaction to establish that the transaction was conducted voluntarily and in accordance with the law.

If the validity of the transfer has been determined in previous proceedings which took place prior to the entry into force of this Law, the decision taken in the previous proceedings shall be null and void.

The court may make whatever orders are necessary to give effect to its decision, including orders setting aside legal transactions, orders for making or erasing entries in the appropriate public books/registers, and orders lifting any order for suspension of the administrative proceedings.

The relevant parties to the appeal shall notify the competent administrative body of the court's decision.

The responsible administrative body shall resume enforcement proceedings as required, or discontinue proceedings (obustavi) in accordance with the court's decisions.

[. . .]

5.6. Property Law Implementation Plan (PLIP) Inter-Agency Framework Document (2000)

I. INTRODUCTION

Annex 7 of the Dayton Peace Agreement enshrines the right of all the citizens of Bosnia and Herzegovina, displaced during the war, to return to their homes. This most fundamental provision of the Peace Agreement can only be met if the property issue is fully solved. The Property Law Implementation Plan (PLIP) was conceived as a plan to ensure that those property rights are recognised and enforceable for every individual in the country, without regard to political considerations.

During the war in Bosnia and Herzegovina, more than 2.3 million people were displaced from their homes. Each of the wartime regimes allocated abandoned properties and established complex legal and administrative barriers to return, designed to make the separation of the population irreversible. Four years of international efforts have now achieved a legal framework that recognises property rights as they stood at the beginning of the conflict, and establishes a legal and administrative claims process for the repossession of property.

This reversal has been possible only because of a sustained, co-operative effort by the international community in Bosnia. History's lesson that unresolved property disputes remain as a source of tension for decades has made the return of property an essential part of the peace-building and reconciliation process in Bosnia. This has been a complex, laborious and expensive process, but one that after four and a half years of effort is finally yielding significant results throughout the country.

Returns and property repossession are taking place in every municipality and region, both rural and urban. At the end of July, of 231,000 claims for property (both socially-owned and private), some 15% have resulted in a family regaining possession of their home. Therefore, a process has been established, whereby the claimants have now a real prospect of success. The right to property repossession is now recognised in Entity laws, and the international organisations involved in Annex 7 issues have turned to the long task of implementation across 140 municipalities.

The Property Law Implementation Plan (PLIP) has developed from collaborative relationships between OHR, UNHCR, OSCE, UNMIBH and CRPC. It was conceived in October 1999 as a means of gathering the whole range of property-related activities of the different agencies into a coherent, goal-oriented strategy for securing implementation of the new laws. The PLIP is a specialist operation designed to ensure that all citizens of Bosnia and Herzegovina who were dispossessed of their property in the course of the conflict can repossess it. This is the most complex legal component of the implementation of Annex 7, and accordingly requires dedicated resources and thorough management.

This document outlines the PLIP approach, details the measures and mechanisms required to complete the task, and describes the essential elements of the management structure. At the heart of this approach is the bedrock principle that the same pressures, demands and expectations must be applied to all of the officials and municipalities of BiH. This standardisation in itself will serve to undermine the narrow collectivism and nationalist exclusion that has prevailed in Bosnia and Herzegovina.

The PLIP methodology is working. The components, rationale and managerial structures that enable international organisations to act collaboratively and to speak with a single voice are in place. From this point onwards, the path to the final completion of the task is through constant reiteration and ruthless perseverance. Unless there are exceptional reasons for change, this methodology should continue to be pursued along the lines outlined in this paper.

The PLIP methodology is consciously designed to institutionalise the process of reclaiming property, through administrative reform and the promotion of non-discriminatory practices. This ensures that not only can the problem of property rights be resolved in a finite time period, but also that the very process itself serves as a catalyst for creating, in the local language, the *pravna drzava* – a law-governed state.

II. Objective

The objective of the PLIP is to ensure that all outstanding claims by refugees and displaced persons to repossess their properties are resolved. It aims to do this by building domestic legal processes which apply the laws neutrally, processing property claims as efficiently as possible until all claimants are able to exercise their rights under Annex 7. By treating repossession of property as a question of rule of law, the PLIP promotes respect for civil rights over political interests and opens enormous possibilities for the overall return of DPs and refugees.

In 1996, the international community in BiH initiated a sustained campaign to repeal wartime laws on abandoned property, and create a legal framework for property repossession. The campaign met with intense resistance, and required all of the political leverage of the international community over an extended period of time to achieve results. In April 1998, the first legal framework for property repossession was adopted in Federation legislation, followed in December 1998 by like legislation in Republika Srpska. A further intensive campaign, involving the use of the High Representative's Bonn powers, was required in order to strengthen and harmonise the laws. In their current form, the laws have been in place since October 1999.

Implementation of the laws is the responsibility of administrative authorities in 140 municipalities across the country. At the outset, the new laws met with obstruction or inaction in most parts of the country, and international agencies working in the field became closely involved in implementation issues. From a difficult beginning, implementation is now making slow but steady progress through-out the country. As of 31 July 2000, 231,000 claims had been made for repossession of private and socially owned property. Of these, some 36% had received confirmation of their property rights, and 15% could repossess their property.

There is considerable regional variation. In some parts of the country, more than 50% of the claimants have recovered their property. In other places, the process has just recently begun. However, crucially, the process is now working in most Municipalities. The citizens of BiH are receiving the message that the rule of law in property rights has been established, and where necessary is being enforced. As a result, the rate of people voluntarily vacating property that does not belong to them is increasing. It is now possible to foresee the time when all refugees and displaced persons will have been given the opportunity to exercise their property rights; this however requires that the international community continues to devote close attention to the process.

There are three main obstacles to the full implementation of the property laws, which are addressed by the PLIP.

a) **Political obstacles:** The most important obstacle to the overall return and successful reintegration of refugees and displaced persons is still of a political nature. Nationalistic politicians throughout Bosnia and Herzegovina want to keep the three communities separate, in order to safeguard their power base and in certain municipalities also to consolidate their economic interests. Political resistance manifests itself in hostility to reintegration, and in unwillingness to implement the property laws. Experience has shown that political problems are overwhelmingly generated by political elites, rather than emerging from genuine inter-group hostility. Much of the PLIP is therefore directed at separating the question of civil rights from the post-war political problems of the country.

b) **Institutional problems:** A second obstacle to the strict implementation of the property laws is the weak institutional capacity of the responsible authorities. The implementation of Annex 7 has required the creation or strengthening of local administrative authorities in 140 municipalities. The PLIP contains various elements designed to build their capacity to process claims in an efficient and legally sound manner.

c) **Housing problems:** There continue to be shortages of housing in much of Bosnia and Herzegovina, which need to be addressed in order to create the space for return. The PLIP contains a plan to deal with this problem by addressing double/multiple occupancy and other forms of mismanagement of existing housing space, and by promoting a normalised housing policy and property market.

The PLIP harnesses all of the resources available to the international community in Bosnia to achieve this objective. This includes the principal organisations involved in property law implementation (OHR, OSCE, UNHCR, UNMIBH and CRPC), the main sectors of peace implementation (political, economic, judicial and human rights), and the available tools of influence. The PLIP is the mechanism through which international agencies develop common policy frameworks, perform comprehensive monitoring of progress in the field, and develop consistent strategies for overcoming problems.

III. Methodology

The PLIP approach is designed to be applicable throughout Bosnia and Herzegovina. This represents an evolution from earlier return strategies, which focussed on selected return locations mainly in rural areas (target areas; destroyed villages; empty space) or modalities of return (political declarations; reciprocal agreements; return quotas). This was necessary at the time in order to initiate the process of return.

The PLIP varies from these earlier policies by promoting the neutral application of the law across the board, rather than the notion of 'minority return' to rural areas. By insisting that no deviation is permitted from the strict requirements of the law, it ensures that equal standards, procedures and international pressure are applied throughout the country. This approach offers two concrete benefits:

a) **De-politicisation of the property issue:** The more that repossession is treated as a legal process of deciding and implementing individual return claims, the more it can be insulated from undesirable political influences.

b) **Institutionalisation of the property return process:** The PLIP aims to create legal-administrative structures that deal with property claims in a standardised and professional manner. While support and pressure from the international community is required now to make these systems fully operational, institutionalisation of the process ensures that it will continue to function in the future, even as international involvement is eventually phased out.

The PLIP approach also prevents local authorities from disguising ethno-political interests as humanitarian and social considerations. The law spells out in detail the rights and obligations of different parties. The PLIP aims to show to the people of BiH and its Government(s) that following the law strictly is the only way to ensure fair outcomes.

The PLIP is designed to overcome one of the most immediate obstacles to refugee return: access to contested property. It does not address return to destroyed properties in rural areas. Neither does it address the issues required for the creation of sustainable returnee communities, such as subsequent creation of effective and non-discriminatory social structures, especially in the areas of education, health care, employment and basic social welfare.

The PLIP seeks solely to ensure that pre-war owners or occupancy rights holders can repossess their homes of origin. This in turn will enable them to make a free choice whether or not to return. The full and complete resolution of property claims will prove to be the cornerstone of a sustainable and lasting peace in Bosnia and Herzegovina.

IV. Operational Mechanisms

A. Political Intervention Strategies

To date, local authorities have gone to considerable lengths to prevent, hinder, disrupt and delay return. The successful implementation of the PLIP will alter the political dynamics in many parts of the country. For this reason, a series of measures are necessary to ensure the smooth progress of implementation, and to discourage and remove resistance to the process.

The PLIP contains a range of different operational mechanisms that can be used to address political obstacles as they arise. All operational policy decisions concerning the return of property and related questions are made through the PLIP. It is vital that the international community sends out a strong and consistent political message. A number of operational elements of the PLIP are designed to ensure that the international community speaks with one voice.

1. Monitoring of the Implementation of the Property Laws

The PLIP uses OSCE, UNHCR and OHR field networks to conduct a monitoring and supervision operation, which aims to ensure that domestic mechanisms for resolving property claims operate consistently throughout the country. Monitoring serves a dual function. On the one hand, it is designed to detect whenever the process is not functioning satisfactorily, as a trigger for the use of an intervention strategy. At the same time, it provides a means whereby the message of the PLIP is constantly reiterated to the responsible authorities, promoting a process of cultural change. Through regular contacts between administrative authorities and international field officers, the PLIP promotes standardised and law-based approaches that gradually eliminate partisan politics. Over time, this begins to break down institutional discrimination, in favour of the neutral application of the law.

To keep the repossession process moving requires close monitoring at each of the key steps in the property repossession process, particularly:

- the issuance of decisions on property claims, including determination of whether the current occupant of the claimed property is entitled to alternative accommodation;
- the administrative appeals process;
- ensuring (if needed through enforced eviction) that the current occupant vacates the property.

The Focal Point Scheme (FoPs – see section V, par. 3 below) is central to monitoring activities. The Focal Points maintain close contacts with local administrative authorities, and collect monthly statistics on implementation. Through their work in the field, including investigation of complaints by individual claimants, they are able to double-check official information and identify cases in which the process is not functioning, or is being abused.

The individual Focal Points are members of a range of different local co-ordination structures set up by OSCE, UNHCR, and OHR (such as Local RRTFs, Human Rights Working Groups, Double Occupancy Commissions and other *ad hoc* arrangements). Together, these local representatives of the

international agencies are expected to develop consensus on joint objectives and effective deployment of their limited resources.

In this context, the Focal Points are well placed to enhance the monitoring capacity of the entire international field presence, distributing information and facilitating communication with the PLIP Cell.

2. Encouraging Enforcement of the Law by the Police

Local police are an essential element in the property repossession process. If current occupants refuse to voluntarily vacate the premises, local police are required by law to support the eviction process, if necessary through forcible eviction. They are also obliged to bring criminal charges against those who use force to try to prevent an eviction, or who strip properties before vacating them.

To date, the police have not uniformly supported the property repossession process. Accordingly, it is essential that the actions of the police be also closely monitored. The IPTF Commissioner has issued clear instructions to the Ministries of Interior of both entities as to their duties in connection with evictions. They are required to be present at every forcible eviction, and to actively ensure that the eviction is implemented.

The IPTF monitors each forcible eviction in the country, and maintains pressure on the police to fulfil their legal obligations. The role of PLIP local structures is to ensure that IPTF officers are fully informed as to the rationale and mechanisms behind the PLIP and the property repossession process. Through a close working relationship between IPTF officers and PLIP personnel, a coherent monitoring and intervention regime is being achieved.

A policy of zero tolerance should be adopted towards the refusal of police to perform their functions at evictions. Experience has shown that where consistent and strict standards are set, local police are insulated from political pressures, and become more willing to perform their responsibilities. The IPTF Police Non-Compliance mechanism should continue to be used to ensure that the refusal of police to carry out their responsibilities results in automatic de-authorisation and dismissal. Since the IPTF Commissioner's instruction, the performance of local police has improved considerably, and there have been fewer occasions of evictions postponed because of police inaction.

However, a new and disturbing trend has emerged in the increasing levels of return-related violence, such as explosions, attacks on returnees and the burning of houses. To date, these recent incidents have demonstrated the local police's unwillingness to respond to crises in a timely manner. UNMIBH's monitoring of these scenes of unrest has revealed cases of the local police standing by and witnessing house burnings, the establishment of barricades and the intimidation of returnee communities. To deter such incidents, the police must be encouraged to take preventive action and bring criminal charges against those responsible.

Concurrently it is vitally important that the UNMIBH/IPTF led minority police recruitment and re-deployment processes must be holistically and effectively supported with financial means. Specifically integration measures must be taken to ensure that returning minority police have their housing requirements met and are adequately supported. This in turn would lead to more effective police coverage of return related issues.

3. Demanding Respect for Property by Public Officials

i) Police housing

As a key part of the law enforcement process, police officers must be above criticism concerning their own housing situation. UNMIBH has issued a ruling that all police officers must vacate property belonging to others if they wish to remain employed as law enforcement officials. The housing situation of every police officer should be checked as a precondition to provisional authorisation by IPTF. According to the IPTF *Policy on Registration, Provisional Authorisation and Certification*, police officers who are double or illegal occupants face removal from their post if they do not vacate the property within one month from the issuance of IPTF/UN identification cards.

Since this policy entered into force, around 275 police officers have voluntarily vacated property they had illegally occupied, and one has been removed from the police for failure to do so. Nevertheless, hundreds of police officers in both Entities remain in inappropriate housing situations and there have been incidents in which local policemen required to vacate such accommodations have

done so in an inappropriate or illegal manner. Every effort must be made to ensure that local police throughout Bosnia bring their housing situation fully within the law.

ii) Elected officials and housing

In a similar vein, the Provisional Election Commission (PEC) adopted a regulation for the municipal elections in April 2000 providing that persons who occupy housing belonging to others are not eligible to stand for election to public office. The rule has since been extended to cover the November general elections. This is designed to target public officials who personally obstruct implementation of the property laws through their own personal housing situations. Any public official must vacate claimed property in accordance with the deadlines specified in the law, or face removal by the PEC. Following an extensive investigation of political candidates, 63 candidates and officials have been removed (52 candidates and 11 councillors). The PEC regulations have further led to the parties screening their lists to ensure that none of their candidates are in violation of the ruling and, in numerous cases, to the vacation of contested property by candidates/officials in order to avoid removal. The development of this indigenous regulatory process is a significant step forward. Officials who are themselves in compliance with the law have no vested interest in allowing its continued violation by others.

iii) Judges, prosecutors, and housing

Both Entities have recently established commissions to define and enforce standards of professional behaviour for judges and prosecutors. In this context, the PLIP agencies support serious attention to the issue of judges and prosecutors in inappropriate housing situations (who can all be considered multiple occupants by virtue of their salaries). Information on the housing situations of all judges and prosecutors throughout BiH should be collected from the field and forwarded to the commissions.

4. Setting a Good Example

The international community must insist that its employees bring their housing situations into full conformity with the property laws. Such measures are not merely symbolic – the IC employs thousands of Bosnians, usually at salaries high enough to make those of them in inappropriate housing situations multiple occupants solely based on their means. The member-agencies of PLIP take their responsibility very seriously and are committed to undertake measures to ensure staff compliance.

5. Monitoring Responsible Authorities and Dismissals

The PLIP structure has developed a standardised system for reporting failure to implement the property law by local officials charged with this task. Field officers keep running files on implementation issues in every single municipality. Where there is a clear abuse of the process, or systematic refusal to implement the law, the field officers file non-compliance reports. These reports are passed through the regional structure to the PLIP Cell, which develops the appropriate intervention strategy in response. In the most egregious cases, a recommendation to the High Representative will be made to dismiss the responsible official.

6. Principals' Visits

Over the past years, the Principals were closely involved in overcoming the obstacles to the return and property repossession process. At various times, the PLIP has co-ordinated intervention policies, whereby a sudden increase in the political profile of the return issue is used to boost the implementation process.

The PLIP recommends that this technique be regularised through a series of high-profile visits by principals to different locations around the country. This would ensure that continuing, steady political pressure is provided throughout the country.

7. Joint Letters

The PLIP is a mechanism for developing a common stance of the international community towards political problems in the return process. On a number of occasions, the PLIP has co-ordinated joint letters from the Principals in order to place combined pressure on state and entity authorities, and to express the international community's common expectations in the property law implementation process. This has proved to be an effective way of resolving problems, and should be continued.

The same policy can be followed down the command structure, at regional and even local level, in responding to problems that occur in the field.

8. UNMIBH Special Advisor Programme

In June 2000, UNMIBH launched a special project in Srpsko Gorazde after repeated reports that the local office of the Ministry of Refugees and Displaced Persons (OMI) was refusing to implement the property legislation. An IPTF monitor from the Human Rights Office was appointed as Special Advisor to the OMI, supported by a Language Assistant from UNHCR Gorazde. Over a 60-day period, he monitored, advised and reported weekly on the activities of the housing office. The presence of the Special Advisor created a feeling of security both for those claiming their property, and for the housing officials who were subject to pressure from applicants and local citizens. During this period, he achieved breakthroughs on the issuance and implementation of decisions in priority cases, helped to create an electronic database of claims, and promoted a system whereby claims would be resolved in chronological order of receipt.

This special operation provides a good example of an operational model that can be used to achieve breakthroughs in particularly difficult areas. The particular form of intervention used in each case must be tailored to the nature of the problem being addressed, and the resources available.

9. Sarajevo Housing Committee

Pursuant to the February 1998 Sarajevo Declaration, a Sarajevo Housing Committee (SHC) was established to act as a supervisory and joint planning body for the implementation of the property laws in Sarajevo Canton. SHC also provides a forum where the international community and the responsible officials can identify and discuss policy issues and practical problems in the implementation process. The Committee is comprised of officials from the Cantonal government and representatives of international organisations, under the chair of a highly experienced international staff member managing the UNHCR funded SHC project office.

The SHC represents perhaps the most successful model of a co-operative initiative between the international community and local authorities, and has produced consistently good results in Sarajevo Canton. The model has recently been transferred to Banja Luka, with the creation of the Property Implementation Monitoring Team (PIMT), where many of the lessons from Sarajevo are being applied.

B. Capacity Building

In order to create local structures capable of taking ownership of the process, institutional capacity building should be considered a priority. The PLIP contains various elements directed towards strengthening local structures.

1. Training of Personnel

The property laws require local housing authorities and Cantonal and Entity Ministries to undertake complex new tasks. Generally, these institutions are lacking both skilled, professional staff, and the resources or expertise to manage their own training needs. As a result, for some years international organisations, including OHR, CRPC, OSCE, UNHCR and the UNHCR-funded Legal Aid Centres, have been engaged in a co-operative programme to offer training seminars to the responsible authorities, familiarising them with the law and their responsibilities.

2. Budgetary Support

In 2000, US budgetary support to the government of Republika Srpska was tightly conditioned on staffing and procurement commitments by the Ministry of Refugees and Displaced Persons (MRDP) and the Finance Ministry. This support provided a significant boost to the resources available for the administrative property claims process. It also ensured that those resources were targeted specifically at the areas of greatest need. Although it suffered a number of delays, this form of influence over the bureaucratic process has proved to be highly effective. As a result, the institutional capacity of the MRDP has improved considerably over the past year.

3. Legislative Reform

The property laws will be kept under constant review, and further steps towards reform and harmonisation may be necessary. The PLIP Cell is ideally place to provide ongoing co-ordination, oversight and expert recommendations regarding legislative efforts in order to ensure their maximum impact on the implementation of Annex 7. Legislation that impinges on repossession can be more firmly linked to the goals of Annex 7 through the involvement of PLIP.

4. State and Entity Supervisory Mechanisms

One new concept to which serious consideration must be given is the possibility of creating Entity- and/or State-level supervisory mechanisms over property law implementation, capable of intervening wherever the local systems are not functioning effectively. Within the Dayton constitutional structure, the State has authority to secure the implementation of Annex 7 (Article III, par. 5(a) of the BiH Constitution). The State is ultimately also answerable for the implementation of European standards on human rights. This gives it the authority to act to ensure that the entities and local government authorities are upholding their constitutional and international obligations.

5. Judicial Reform, Domestic Remedies and Prosecution for Non-Compliance

The Judicial Reform Programme, implemented jointly by a number of international organisations in BiH, is one of the most extensive and important state-building programmes. There are various linkages between judicial reform and property law implementation. In particular, the PLIP endeavours to encourage the development of domestic remedies, which must be used in preference to international intervention wherever the administrative claims process does not function effectively. Accordingly, there is scope for co-operation between the Judicial Reform Programme and the PLIP in developing and promoting judicial review of the administration.

It is the policy of the PLIP to utilise domestic remedies wherever possible, before using international instruments of intervention. Both Entity criminal codes contain various criminal penalties for administrative officials who blatantly refuse to perform their duties, or who deliberately obstruct the return of refugees and displaced persons to their homes. OSCE has been promoting the use of these judicial mechanisms to address obstacles to property law implementation through a policy of encouraging investigation and prosecution. Several such prosecutions of officials for obstruction are currently either at the investigative stage or in procedure. Strengthening domestic judicial review mechanisms is a useful institution-building initiative, and only where this fails to produce results should punitive action by the international community be considered.

C. Housing Space

In many places around the country, there continue to be genuine shortages of housing space. Under the property laws, administrative authorities are required to assess whether the current occupants of a claimed property have a genuine need for housing, and if so, to find accommodation for them. However, if the authorities fail to identify alternative housing for the temporary occupants of claimed properties, this does not give them a legal basis for refusing to allow the repossession process to go ahead.

The alleged lack of interim accommodation has proved one of the most difficult problems facing the implementation of the property laws. It is important for both humanitarian and political reasons to avoid as far as possible the eviction of vulnerable families without making alternative arrangements for them. However, this provides a pretext for non-implementation of the law. If local authorities are not committed to implementing the law, they make no genuine effort to identify available housing stocks, and then use humanitarian arguments as an excuse for inaction. It is important that alternative accommodation be temporary, and of a basic standard, in order to encourage individuals to find their own solutions to their housing problems.

The PLIP is strict on following the letter of the law in the issuance and enforcement of eviction orders. PLIP deals with humanitarian issues arising in the field by stressing the obligation of the local authorities to identify temporary shelter, and to come up with new solutions to housing problems. In order to prevent abuse of the humanitarian provisions of the law, the right to property and the right to return cannot be made conditional on finding alternative accommodation for the current occupants of claimed properties.

1. Multiple Occupancy

In order to free housing space, the PLIP is developing systems to detect and eliminate multiple occupancy (also commonly referred to as "double occupancy") and the misuse of housing. Multiple occupancy occurs whenever a single household occupies more than one housing space and a refugee or displaced person has claimed one of the properties. This phenomenon is still widespread throughout the country, and typically arises in one of three situations:

i) where the household acquired more than one residential property during the conflict, either illegally or through misuse of the humanitarian provisions of the war-time abandoned property regimes;

ii) where the family's original home has been reconstructed, but the family does not vacate their temporary accommodation;

iii) where it becomes possible for the family to return to their vacant pre-war home under the property claims process, but they decide not to vacate their temporary accommodation.

Much of the legislative reform campaign has focused on tightening the rules against multiple occupancy, and making sure that humanitarian provisions in the law are only available to those who genuinely need them.

The international agencies involved in the PLIP have established a variety of different local systems to detect the first category of multiple occupancy ("i." above), including 'property commissions' and 'double occupancy commissions' run jointly with local authorities, and investigative mechanisms such as 'hot-lines'.

The second category ("ii." above, known as "reconstruction-related multiple occupancy") has been addressed in different ways, including the use of 'tri-partite contracts' through which the beneficiaries agree to vacate their temporary housing as soon as their original home becomes habitable. One successful monitoring scheme is the Housing Verification Mission, established jointly by the US Government Bureau of Population, Refugees and Migration (BPRM) and the European Commission Humanitarian Office (ECHO). It uses field teams consisting of 55 national staff to investigate the occupancy rates of property reconstructed with international donor funds, as well as to check whether the beneficiaries of the reconstruction have vacated their temporary accommodation. This information is used to compile a central database on housing units and their occupancy rates, which is then made available to the RRTF and to the responsible authorities to take action. Schemes following the model of the Housing Verification Mission should be developed within entity and cantonal structures, to make sure that each reconstructed property frees housing space for further returns.

The third category of multiple occupancy ("iii." above) will become more of an issue as the rate of return under the property law increases. There will be a growing need for systems to make sure that successful repossession of property does not increase the rate of multiple occupancy. This involves making sure that those who recover their property are immediately obliged to vacate any property they may have acquired illegally or through a temporary permit. The exchange of information and active co-operation between the municipality of origin and the municipality of displacement will be required to effectuate this process.

Institutionally, this represents a serious challenge for BiH, with its dispersed constitutional structure. For the time being, there are no centralised authorities capable of overseeing the process, and no operational horizontal links between municipalities. The PLIP organisations themselves are therefore taking on the responsibility of passing information and arranging co-operation between municipalities.

In addition, according to Entity legislation, displaced persons will lose their status and entitlement to temporary accommodation if they have the possibility of returning in safety and dignity to their former place of residence. The status of all displaced persons in BiH will be reviewed on the basis of a UNHCR sponsored re-registration exercise that started on 25 July 2000. The PLIP will benefit from the information resulting from this re-registration by identifying inter-entity multiple occupancy.

Each of these systems is designed with a view to creating a cycle of returns. Each time a property claim is successful, or a destroyed house is reconstructed, it should also lead to secondary returns. The more space is created, the more the process will gather momentum. If the systems can be made to function efficiently, this will be the best way of implementing the law without creating humanitarian problems.

2. Housing Reconstruction

In addition to the major international efforts for reconstruction, closer relations between donors and the responsible governmental bodies have been useful, helping them to develop transparent and responsible procedures. There is already evidence that some of the wealthier municipalities are beginning to channel funds from local budgets into small and precisely targeted repair works. This is a sign of ownership, and suggests that international donors may be able to maximise the return on their investments by helping to encourage these efforts and build local capacity.

3. Property Market Development

The CRPC and OHR have each conducted independent studies on the future of the real estate market in Bosnia and Herzegovina. At present, private property is being bought and sold throughout the country. However, the property market lacks safeguards to protect consumers, such as a clear legal framework, a system of licensing for professional real estate agents, and market information mechanisms. In the absence of such safeguards, there are risks that displaced persons will be exploited by unscrupulous middlemen, or pressured into taking decisions about their property without full knowledge of the situation.

As the demographics of the country settle over the coming years, influenced by economic as well as social factors, the volume of property transactions will remain high. One of the objectives of the PLIP is to ensure that those who choose not to return have an opportunity to sell or rent it under fair circumstances set out by law.

A number of initiatives will be necessary in the coming period. First, the system of property registration is an urgent need of repair and modernisation. CRPC has made a number of recommendations for how the property book and cadaster systems can be modernised to meet the needs of a private market. This will clarify and strengthen legal property title, essential to economic development. Improving the registration system will require both legislative reform and considerable technical assistance and international investment. Because this is necessarily a long-term project, it is important that work begin as soon as possible. A priority should therefore be to identify the international agencies that will drive this process forward.

Second, the process of privatisation of socially owned apartments must be completed successfully in both entities, with close supervision from the PLIP agencies to ensure that it works in a non-discriminatory fashion. Privatisation will free up a large section of the market. However, privatisation must be accompanied by the development of housing policy. In neither entity has the government have so far looked beyond the population displacement dimension to consider the economics of the housing sector. It is unclear how housing stocks are to be maintained in the post-privatisation environment, and whether BiH is to retain some form of social housing sector for low-income families. Development of housing policy, and the accompanying legislative reform, should be a priority in the coming period. The role of PLIP in this process should be to ensure that these vital reforms are carried out in a manner consonant with the goals of Annex 7.

V. PLIP Managerial Structures

1. The PLIP Cell

The PLIP Cell, comprised of experienced personnel from OHR, OSCE, UNHCR, UNMIBH and CRPC, meets once a week, and is responsible for the day to day management of the PLIP as well as the following duties:

- Providing clear overall operational policy direction, including policy guidelines and standardised procedures;

- Analysing and acting upon information collected from the field concerning the property claims process;

- Reporting to the respective organisations to ensure that they are informed of progress and areas of concern;

- Recommending courses of action for Principals to intervene to resolve problems;

- Co-ordinating intervention strategies.

- Providing co-ordination, oversight and expert recommendations regarding legislative efforts pertaining to Annex 7.

2. The Secretariat

The PLIP Cell is supported by a Secretariat, run by one long-term employee. This ensures continuity and the provision of a corporate memory for the PLIP operation. The Secretariat is responsible for preparing meetings through liaison with the field and the respective member organisations, and the production of an agenda for each meeting. The Secretariat produces minutes of decisions made in the PLIP cell meetings, which are communicated by the respective organisations to their field structures. This represents the Secretariat's essential function: ensuring an effective and fruitful operational relationship between the field and the PLIP Cell.

3. The Focal Point Scheme (FoP)

The Focal Point Scheme (FoP) is the field-level infrastructure of the PLIP organisation, covering every municipality in the country. The FoPs consist of personnel from OSCE and UNHCR and, to a lesser extent, OHR. They are responsible for ensuring that the same practices are exacted from all municipalities throughout the country. In addition to this, the FoPs solicit, check, correct, and transmit statistical data on property law implementation from the housing authorities. The Focal Point Scheme is managed by the PLIP Cell. The key tasks of the FoPs are:

- Providing complete, consolidated and accurate statistics on a monthly basis (see below);

- Keeping records of repossessions and reinstatements, in order to follow up on the consequential creation of double occupancy;

- Transmitting data and information to the housing offices;

- Acting as the information conduit for cases of multiple occupancy and other necessary information;

- Monitoring the conduct and practice of housing office staff;

- Recommending, in co-ordination with regional operational structures, courses of action for intervention according to PLIP criteria;

- Providing guidance to the housing offices on working practices, and advising where legitimate concerns arise;

- Co-operating with the rest of the international field presence to ensure the maximum net impact on the property law implementation process.

For resource planning purposes, it is important that the appropriate human and operational assets are allocated to the FoPs. FoPs must be staffed with responsible individuals. In turn, the PLIP Cell must ensure that FoPs are given full support, and have access to the decision-making process. As mentioned above, the PLIP operation is designed to remain lean and effective. Accordingly, it is essential that the FoPs are able to address issues readily to the Cell, and that the Cell is responsive to demands from the field.

VI. PLIP MANAGERIAL TOOLS

1. Statistics

Statistics on implementation of the property laws are produced by the local authorities, and checked and delivered to OSCE and UNHCR through the Focal Point Scheme. The statistical team in Sarajevo, comprising members of OSCE, UNHCR and OHR, are responsible for the provision of consolidated statistics to the PLIP Cell. The PLIP Cell then analyses and clears them for publication and intervention.

2. Public Information and Awareness

In order to ensure that the principles and rationale behind the PLIP are widely understood and absorbed, it is essential to articulate them over the heads of nationalist leaders and straight to the general public. Effective public relations offers a multiplier effect, supporting and consolidating all other aspects of the process.

The repossession of property must not be manipulated by self-interested politicians, or subject to self-defined notions of justice along the lines of: 'If I cannot repossess my apartment, they cannot repossess theirs'. The message of the PLIP is that property rights are individual, not reciprocal. They are neither negotiable, nor subject to ethnic or political considerations. The articulation of these principles provides the PLIP with its most powerful rhetoric, neutralising arguments that promote collective interests over individual rights.

Public service information needs to address the regional or local level, through local radio and TV, printed material or public meetings, and also a national audience. In order to change public attitudes and expectation towards property rights, consistent coverage of all levels is essential. The ongoing "Respect" (*Postovanje*) has exemplified how a successful public information campaign can support the PLIP process.

Because there is such a widespread need among the general public for information about property repossession, it is further recommended that a joint web site be established relating to all issues concerning the PLIP. The site should include statistics, monthly reports, media coverage and any other matters that serve to inform the public of the process. Given the deliberate lack of transparency among municipal authorities, it is important that administrative processes are de-mystified. The web page can also be used as a source of information by other interested parties.

5.7. A New Strategic Direction: Proposed Ways Ahead for Property Law Implementation in a Time of Decreasing IC [International Community] Resources (2002)

OVERVIEW

This paper sets out a new policy direction for the Property Law Implementation Plan (PLIP) building on the PLIP Inter-Agency Framework Document of October 2000 and focusing on the following elements:

Operationalizing chronological processing of claims and insisting on adherence to the letter and spirit of the property laws, as amended by the High Representative on 4 December 2001, save for subsequent HR decisions identifying specific categories of claimants who will be processed in an expedited manner. Creating legal certainty, fairness and transparency for both claimants and temporary occupants by requiring that decisions be issued and enforced in accordance with the laws. Protecting housing officials from political pressure and corruption by eliminating their discretion over order of case processing.

Immediate issuance and enforcement of decisions, according to the laws, for verified multiple occupants, without further investigation by the housing authorities.

Intensified monitoring engagement with municipal housing authorities, including all appropriate forms of support, regular consultation and sanctions where necessary.

Public information work to ensure that the property laws and the policies for their implementation are clarified for all affected parties and all sectors of the IC. Development of united IC position to counter obstruction at all levels.

Increasing consultation with domestic institutions on both interventions on individual cases and formulation and implementation of policy.

1. Background

The right of displaced persons and refugees to repossess and return to their pre-war property has long been one of the central concerns of the international community (IC) in Bosnia and Herzegovina and is guaranteed in Annex 7 of the Dayton Peace Agreement (GFAP). This is based on the recognition that the failure to return properties to their rightful owners represents a violation of the right to property *inter alia* under Article 1 of Protocol 1 to the *European Convention on Human Rights* (ECHR). Return of property is essential to the creation of durable solutions for refugees and displaced persons. This can take the form of either actual return to the property or sale of the property in order to finance one's own local integration elsewhere, through purchase or rental of a home that does not belong to someone else.

The centrality of property repossession to the goals set out in the GFAP is reflected by the priority given to the interagency Property Law Implementation Plan (PLIP). Ultimately, the viability of Bosnia and Herzegovina (BiH) as a stable, secure and independent state and the IC's plans for responsible disengagement both hinge on creating the conditions for full completion of the PLIP by end 2003.

However, despite considerable progress in property law implementation over the past three years, the current situation leaves considerable room for improvement and consolidation. The rate at which refugees and displaced persons are able to repossess property remains limited on average at 2% per month countrywide. Without exponential increases in this rate, full implementation of the Property Laws may be delayed from completion in many municipalities even as IC disengagement accelerates.

These concerns are heightened by the fact that the Bosnian political spectrum remains apathetic or openly hostile to a resolution of the problem. The estimated 110,000 families (according to the PLIP statistics at end July 2002) still waiting to repossess their homes are also becoming disillusioned, as reflected by the legally dubious but increasingly common practice of selling off property claims before they have been realised. These trends not only extinguish the possibility of return in individual cases, but also cast doubt on the sustainability of hard-won progress in overall returns made to date.

The current trend in the implementation of the property laws – based on the strategies the IC has adopted so far – risks leaving thousands of property claimants still without the prospect of having their property returned to them by the time the IC has substantially withdrawn. This paper sets out concrete steps that must be taken to address this situation.

2. Evolution of PLIP Policy

In its attempts to guarantee property rights and support return, the IC has proved adept at matching its tactics to changing conditions on the ground. First came the push for adoption of Entity laws on administrative property repossession in 1998, and their initial harmonisation through High Representative amendments in 1999. Early implementation efforts overcame local authorities' initial resistance, at first to taking, and later to deciding, claims.

The current phase of implementation has focused on enforcement by drawing the authorities' attention to cases of "double" or "multiple occupancy." The fact that multiple occupants are defined by their ability to otherwise meet their own housing needs (by dint of income, access to housing elsewhere, etc.) renders them "easy cases," whose eviction carries little political cost for the authorities.

As a result, the IC has been able to kick-start real enforcement of the property laws by encouraging the housing authorities to focus their resources on confirming and acting on allegations of multiple occupancy. Very often the IC field presence has been relied on to provide data confirming multiple occupancy status to be acted on by the authorities. In light of the ongoing reduction of IC resources, this pattern is no longer sustainable.

The initial focus on multiple occupancy saw implementation rates rise to 15% in the summer of 2000 and over 30% one year later, reaching an implementation rate of 57% at end July 2002. However, the cost of this strategy has been borne fully by those claimants whose property is occupied by "hard cases," i.e. temporary occupants who *cannot* otherwise meet their own housing needs and are therefore entitled to look to the authorities for alternative accommodation (AA). Where the authorities fail to provide AA within legal deadlines, they are required to evict the temporary occupant, unless, in accordance with the conditions prescribed by the property laws, they have conclusively proven to OHR's satisfaction the non-availability of AA. This requirement for eviction in accordance with the legal deadlines is the most widely breached provision of the property laws leaving the owners of properties occupied by 'hard cases' indefinitely dispossessed. Temporary occupants with the right to AA are effectively given an open-ended right to live in other people's claimed property in open violation of the law.

In effect, the current strategy risks creating the appearance of tacit IC approval of two illegal practices – the failure to provide AA (despite numerous available low-cost options) and the related failure to nevertheless return properties occupied by "hard cases" to their rightful owners. Compounding this problem, the freedom to pick and choose alleged multiple occupant cases for prioritised processing has left housing authorities with broad discretion over the order of processing all cases, inviting both bribery and pressure not to act against politically protected groups.

These concerns have given rise to the third phase of the PLIP, described in this paper. The "New Strategic Direction" (NSD) reflects a new emphasis on chronological processing of all cases, other than the exceptions provided by law. This policy must be supported by the provision of sufficient alternative accommodation to ensure smooth processing of "hard cases" as they arise within the chronology, and allowing the rightful owners to repossess their property without further delay.

Crucial preliminary steps have already been taken. Most importantly, the amendments imposed on 4 December 2001 to the property laws have made chronological processing an explicit legal obligation binding on housing authorities in both Entities, save for the exceptions defined in subsequent HR decisions. The PLIP agencies have also intensified their campaign of pressuring authorities at all levels to provide sufficient budgetary funds for AA and ensure their efficient use. Chronological processing is now virtually universally understood and accepted in principle and is being applied in

practice in an increasing number of municipalities. The time has come for ad hoc efforts to promote chronology based on adequate alternative accommodation to give way to a clear and systematic IC policy in line with recent amendments to the property laws as promulgated by the HR.

3. Elements of the New Strategic Direction

The new strategic direction set out in this paper focuses on the resolution of each claim in chronological order in compliance with the amended property laws and related decisions by the HR. The requirement that housing authorities provide alternative accommodation to those temporary occupants entitled to it can no longer be ignored. Neither, however, can the requirement that failure in this regard may not delay the reinstatement of the rightful owner to their pre-war home, unless the authorities have in accordance with the conditions prescribed by the property laws conclusively proven to OHR's satisfaction the non-availability of AA.

In order to bring this about, the IC must fully commit itself to the following basic principles. In most cases, the PLIP agencies have already taken significant steps in this direction. These must now become the PLIP's central policy tenets and be followed up rigorously and consistently.

3.1. Broadening Consensus and Strengthening Ownership

The New Strategic Direction, like all prior PLIP strategies, relies on a uniform IC approach in which the highest levels of each organisation routinely support the efforts of their respective field staff. Now, however, the prospect of international disengagement makes it more pressing than ever that domestic administrative and human rights bodies be actively included in the implementation of the strategy. Given that the ongoing property problem affects the work of such institutions, they have an inherent interest in resolving them. It is now incumbent upon PLIP to convince these institutions that the strategies adopted by the IC, to the extent consonant with their own mandates, are the best means of resolving outstanding property issues. To the extent such bodies take ownership of the PLIP process over the long run, they will allow the IC to disengage secure in the knowledge that they leave behind institutions capable of bringing the process to a close.

3.1.1. Human Rights Institutions

The PLIP Cell has made increasing efforts to bring domestic human rights institutions directly into its implementation efforts. Contacts have been made with BiH Ministry of Human Rights and Refugees (MHRR), the BiH and Entity Ombudsmen, and the BiH Human Rights Chamber (HRC). The Entity Ombudsmen and UNHCR-administered Legal Aid Information Centres (LAICs) have attended OSCE's January 2002 workshops on the recent property law amendments. The NSD should be distributed and explained to these institutions, which should be invited to participate in its implementation.

3.1.2. Local Authorities

The process of negotiating the 5 December 2001 inter-municipality information-exchange instruction with the competent Ministries as well as consulting with them in the drafting of the December 4, 2001 property amendments has improved the resulting legal instruments and points the way forward in legislative drafting and implementation issues. The State Commission on Refugees and Displaced Persons chaired by MHRR has become a particularly useful forum for such discussions.

3.1.3. Databases

OHR-RRTF has spearheaded efforts to ensure that databases developed in furtherance of return and the PLIP be transferred to domestic institutions in a manner that guarantees their continued application for property law implementation and return purposes. CRPC is beginning to identify issues related to the transfer of the numerous databases it disposes over to national bodies in this context.

3.2. Monitoring Chronology in the Field: From Casework to Consultation

Until now, implementation of the property laws has been largely subject to the discretion of local authorities. Decision-making has been conducted with little regard to principles of administrative fairness. Political interference, corruption and, often, pure arbitrariness have dictated which claims are processed and when. Temporary users have believed that – and behaved as if – they were entitled, as of right, to remain in other persons' property

indefinitely. Owners and occupancy right-holders have had no clear expectation as to when, if ever, their property would be returned. In response, the IC has all too often focused on ad hoc interventions in individual cases. While this undoubtedly benefited individual claimants, it hurt the process by undermining the principle of chronology.

The High Representative's 4 December 2001 Decisions make it clear that, almost four years after the property laws were passed, this situation is no longer tolerable. They explicitly set out the chronology requirement that has always been implicit in the law: claims for the return of property should be processed and implemented in the order in which they were received by the authorities. This will prevent manipulation of the order of claims processing for political and other purposes and ensure that claimants and temporary users have a clear expectation as to where determination of their rights stands.

Chronological processing in accordance with the law will lead to more efficient use of housing authority resources. Under the current system, housing officials throw virtually all of their interviewing and field research capacity into investigating cases of *alleged* multiple occupancy. These resources should now be redirected to processing the chronological list of all claims. Temporary occupants should be prioritised as multiple occupants when their status is verified by evidence strong enough that no confirmation by the housing authorities is justified. Examples include municipal reports indicating repossession-related multiple occupancy transmitted under the BiH-wide *Information Exchange Program*, as well as verified reports of reconstruction-related multiple occupancy delivered by the RRTF *Housing Verification and Monitoring Unit* (HVM). Claimants should be encouraged to bring forward any evidence of this nature available to themselves, such as official proof that the occupant of their property has repossessed and sold their own pre-war property.

Beyond verified multiple occupants and other categories exempted from chronology under the property laws, the claims of minority returnee police officers are prioritised in accordance with an April 2002 HR decision. Residents of collective and transit centres who registered their intent to return may also repossess their property on an expedited basis. This will take place based on a plan mandated by an August 2002 HR decision and will be co-ordinated by UNHCR, under which collective centre spaces occupied by this category of claimants are offered to the occupants of their property, rendering them multiple occupants. This plan allows expedited repossession without disrupting chronological processing. Given the small number of beneficiaries and their impact on return movements, these exceptions to chronology are justified in terms of the goals of Annex 7 of the GFAP.

The chronological principle will greatly facilitate a new model of PLIP Focal Point (FoP) monitoring. Instead of acting as ad hoc advocates for individual claimants, the FoPs should work closely with the housing authorities on improving the overall processing system. UNHCR has for the past two years already referred individual property cases to its network of Legal Aid Centres (LAICs) and OSCE has taken steps to do likewise. This should allow the FoPs to focus on collaborative monitoring of the local authorities in a systematic manner rather than monitoring individual cases.

PLIP FoPs have encouraged municipal efforts to translate broad acceptance of the chronological processing principle into practice. This trend will take on speed as increasing numbers of municipal chronological databases created by OSCE and CRPC Data Entry Clerks come on line. As chronology takes hold, monitoring will be facilitated by the resulting clear expectations of the housing authorities: As soon as a chronological list is in place, the first claim registered *must* be processed before the second and so on. Discretion on the part of the housing authorities to respond to bribes or political pressure will be eliminated. Meanwhile, the transparency afforded by the new system should be highlighted for affected parties in any way possible. Devices such as publicly available lists showing where all cases stand will show claimants that the process will end and encourage temporary occupants to voluntarily vacate occupied property and begin planning their next steps.

3.3. Adapting Existing PLIP Tactics to Chronology

Many of the initiatives already introduced by PLIP will complement chronological processing, enhancing the efficiency of the housing authorities' work. Such programs include:

3.3.1. Capacity-Building

Assistance by PLIP agencies such as OSCE's program of inserting short-term Data Entry Clerks into municipal housing offices to create chronological databases, and CRPC's pilot project for the comparison of municipal claims data with CRPC claims data can both improve housing authority performance and enhance IC monitoring. Trainings such as those conducted by OSCE in Fall 2001 on information exchange, in Spring 2002 on the property law amendments, and in Summer 2002 on revalidation issues, and those provided by UNHCR to its network of LAICs, are also helpful, especially when they bring together housing authorities who share axes of return.

3.3.2. Work with Donors

Alternative accommodation projects might be funded in municipalities that have already demonstrably done all they can to provide AA themselves. More reconstruction funds should be channelled to the needs of "PLIP Beneficiaries", i.e. displaced persons from destroyed villages who are occupying property in town. This type of reconstruction is known to increase public acceptance of the PLIP and can be the starting point for long chains of repossession via the BiH-wide Information Exchange Program. In some cases the material needs limiting housing authorities' ability to function (i.e. lack of computers) should be addressed.

3.3.3. Public Information Campaigns (PICs)

Interagency PICs, such as those which introduced the 4 December 2001 property amendments play a crucial role in ensuring that the rights of all parties affected by the PLIP process, as well as the proper role of housing officials, is understood. In some cases, such as recent OSCE posters setting out legal penalties for threatening housing officials, they can provide direct support. In others, such as UNHCR sponsored radio talk shows with LAICs professionals answering PLIP related queries from the public, they increase awareness of the laws and its entitlements. Wherever possible, local public information events should be arranged, allowing local authorities themselves to explain the law and forestalling social tensions often associated with PLIP.

In the past, interagency PICs have fallen into two broad categories. First, they have proven to be an excellent tool for delivering important new information to people directly affected by the property laws. Previous campaigns informing refugees and displaced persons of deadlines for claiming socially owned apartments as well as the campaign on the 4 December 2001 amendments to the property laws typify this category. Second, PICs have been used to change the perceptions of those affected by the property laws and counter systematic misinformation by local authorities. The summer 2000 "Postovanje/Respect" PIC and fall 2000 "Dosta Je/Its Enough" PICs have, for instance, been widely credited with dispelling the myth that temporary occupants were entitled to remain in other people's property indefinitely. Both types of PIC should continue to be used wherever appropriate in support of accelerated PLI.

3.4. Ensuring Adequate Alternative Accommodation

Alternative Accommodation is a key element of the new strategic direction. Authorities that have begun to take their obligation to provide AA seriously have often found that it increases the efficiency of the PLIP process exponentially. The basic standards for AA reflect its humanitarian nature, and temporary occupants often turn it down, revealing that they do, in fact, have better accommodation options elsewhere. This underlines the need for authorities to not only budget for AA but also to ensure that these funds are used with maximum efficiency. Expensive relocation projects in the guise of AA must be treated as what they are – obstruction – until such time as all available economically efficient means of providing AA have been harnessed to the resolution of local PLI issues.

Experience has shown that while it is relatively easy to identify buildings that could be used for AA, negotiations about their actual use become mired in inter-ministry arguments with negligible results. The IC should step back from micro-managing this process and reiterate strongly and publicly the responsibilities of the authorities to provide AA. Concerted pressure must remain on all levels of authority in BiH for the provision of appropriate units of AA, proportionate to the needs of each community. It must be emphasised that failure to provide AA has empirically been linked to obstruction, not scarcity. The property laws include provisions allowing evictions to be put on hold in municipalities that demonstrate complete lack of AA to OHR's satisfaction, but not one municipality has made a credible attempt to meet this burden.

Tools for ensuring provision of adequate budgetary funds are in place. In December 2001, the PLIP Cell sent a letter on responsibility for budgeting and providing AA to the competent Entity Ministers, all Entity Ombudsmen, and all Cantonal Prime Ministers. The PLIP Cell followed up by compiling information on planned and executed AA budgets for every municipality in BiH as well as specific projects. The High Representative's decision of 24 January 2002 requiring the competent ministers of both Entities to report quarterly to MHRR on the use of funds budgeted for return will complement these efforts.

The 4 December 2001 amendments to the property laws strengthen the hand of local authorities and the IC in ensuring AA is provided. Municipalities will now effectively be able to pool resources locally to account for uneven distributions of available AA and people who need it. Higher level authorities and ministries stand under a greater obligation to provide resources for AA. In addition, a process has been set up for returning to service the thousands of unclaimed socially owned apartments that should have been the single greatest source of AA but have instead been mired in illegal and corrupt transactions. Specifically, the amendments require the formation of long overdue "revalidation commissions" to oversee this process. In the course of the spring and summer of 2002, all necessary regulations were issued and revalidation commissions began to be set up. OSCE has provided trainings on revalidation to both IC monitors and newly constituted revalidation commissions.

The amendments also provide important new tools in ensuring that AA is only provided to those who need it. The conditions for entitlement have been tightened and an increased burden will be put on temporary occupants to show that they meet them. In doing so, they must now both show that they genuinely having no other housing options and demonstrate having taken all possible steps to help themselves by seeking repossession or reconstruction of their own pre-war property.

Finally, the amendments provide that prior decisions entitling temporary occupants to AA must immediately be revised and enforced when the holder is no longer entitled to AA. Thus, the category of persons to be evicted with no right to AA will become significantly larger. Given this reality, the most effective and judicious way to move forward with the current backlog of cases will be systematic chronological order.

3.5. Resolve in the Face of Obstruction

An encouraging number of communities are facing up to the challenge of putting property law implementation behind them. Responsible authorities that show genuine dedication to meeting their legal obligations should be encouraged with strong IC support as set out in section 3.3, above.

However, far too many housing authorities and political leaders remain set against PLIP because it threatens their financial and political interests. In implementing the new strategic direction, the IC must be prepared to face their arguments, and, ultimately, not to back down in the face of obstruction. Consistent and visible high-level support will be essential from all involved international organisations. The rest of the IC, including all international agency staff and Embassies will need to be informed of this approach and requested to give it public support.

Complaints against chronological implementation can be predicted at all levels. Housing authorities can be expected to balk at evicting temporary occupants without alternative accommodation, despite the fact that many such occupants have already enjoyed years of illegal shelter from eviction, blocking the return of pre-war owners. More plausibly, they will cite insufficient resources, political pressure not to implement the law, and interference and threats from individuals and groups opposed to property law implementation.

Political leaders such as Mayors, Cantonal Governors and Ministers often speciously refer to the failure of other political institutions to fully implement the property laws in explaining their own failures to take minimum steps. More concretely, they complain about the political and financial cost of evicting persons before they are able to return (i.e. having to provide AA for them pending repossession of their own property). This results in the periodic re-emergence of the completely impracticable idea that all displaced people should pick one day for mass collective movement to their pre-war homes.

Within political institutions, lack of coherent budgetary co-ordination typically leaves various levels of government pointing fingers at each other when none of them have provided sufficient funds for AA. As a result, political leaders often end up trying to push the costs of PLIP onto the pre-war municipalities of people displaced in their community or onto the international community. Pressure from interest groups opposed to PLIP is still a problem at all levels.

Particular resistance to the new strategic direction can be expected from interest groups representing war veterans or war victims as well politically connected persons with a stake in preventing PLI. Such groups are likely to continue harassing housing authorities, organising demonstrations against evictions and politicising the issue in the press. In some cases, the backlash may direct itself against PLIP Focal Points and international agencies associated with PLIP.

Field experience has repeatedly shown that political forces often orchestrate local obstruction to new initiatives to see if the IC will back down. *In each case*, a show of concerted IC purpose will be necessary to ensure consistent application of PLIP policy countrywide. It will be essential for the IC to be fully prepared to present a firm and united response to any pressure. This should include the following elements:

3.5.1. *Clear Message*

IC public information campaigns must stress that the authorities are legally obliged to implement the property laws in a transparent and consistent manner. They must also underline that interference in the work of the housing authorities is a criminal offence. The Principals of all PLIP agencies should undertake TV appearances and visits to key municipalities to reiterate the authorities' responsibility to implement the laws as amended, and subsequent HR decisions, and explain how the consistent implementation of the laws will accelerate PLIP, while reiterating the authorities' responsibility to provide AA.

3.5.2. *Sanctions*

PLIP Focal Points should report to their respective Regional or Head Offices any persons who interfere with the work of the housing offices as well as seek prosecution or administrative sanctions against local authorities who fail to carry out their duties. Where necessary as a last resort, OHR should swiftly remove persistent obstructers.

3.5.3. Focus on Evictions

The requirement of chronology and intensified monitoring under the New Strategic Direction will significantly constrain the discretion of housing authorities, minimising their ability to obstruct PLIP. It can therefore be predicted that the next phase of obstruction will focus on the eviction process, in which the housing authorities must rely on local police support, often in the face of public opposition. Close co-operation with the Ministries of Interior, as well as international agencies overseeing the police (IPTF and UNCA through their mandate, then the EUPM) will be necessary to ensure prompt and appropriate police support for the housing authorities to carry out scheduled evictions. However, sustained high-level support will also be necessary, as the highest-level Entity politicians have not shied away from personal interventions to postpone evictions.

4. Action Plan and Timeline

In practice, the New Strategic Direction will require co-ordinated Focal Point action and consistent Regional and Head Office support. The expectations of the International Community must be made crystal clear to the housing authorities and local politicians.

With immediate effect, the IC should emphasize publicly that all housing offices should begin chronological processing according to the letter and spirit of the law – including evicting persons with 90-day decisions in chronological order regardless of the availability of AA, unless the authorities have, in accordance with the conditions laid down by the laws, proven conclusively to OHR's satisfaction that there is a lack of AA. To this end, the IC should offer its assistance in accomplishing the following tasks:

Taking immediate steps to mobilise all locally available alternative accommodation.

Development of a full chronological list of claims, ideally in the form of municipal claims databases.

Reviewing procedures to ensure that requests for enforcement of CRPC decisions have been properly registered and implemented in accordance with the law.

Eliminating any backlog of cases. Scheduling and implementing evictions in all cases of multiple occupancy, and other cases that are an exception to chronology as specified in law, and requiring no further confirmation.

Systematically reviewing the legal status of occupants of unclaimed socially owned apartments, and putting all apartments thus made available to use as alternative accommodation, as set out in law.

As soon as these basic steps have been taken, the housing authorities should begin to systematically review all remaining claims in the order in which they were received. Evictions should immediately be scheduled and implemented in all cases of expired decisions, including where the claimant is entitled to AA. Decisions are to be issued in the case of all claims not yet decided.

Decisions should be issued outside of the chronological order and enforced immediately in all cases of verified multiple occupancy and other exceptions to chronology as set out by the HR's decisions. This procedure should be carried out on an ongoing basis without any further hearings or checks.

Throughout this process, the IC should support the New Strategic Direction by all means available to it, including:

Public information work to inform the public, local authorities and all members of the IC of the New Strategic Direction in the PLIP and expected acceleration in the repossession process.

Reporting any cases of political pressure, threats, attacks or offers of bribes to relevant prosecutors and IC monitors.

Monitoring to ensure that housing authorities schedule and execute evictions even in the absence of AA and do not postpone evictions under any circumstances except those set out in the law.

[. . .]

5.8. PLIP Municipal Guidelines for Substantial Completion of Property Law Implementation (2003)

Property Law Implementation is considered substantially completed in any municipality in which:

1. All pending claims made for property under the property laws, including requests for enforcement

of CRPC decisions, have been resolved, in the sense that a decision has been issued and all subsequent steps required by law have been taken.

2. All repossession information received from other municipalities has been acted on in accordance with the property laws and the *Instruction on Exchange of Information Related to the Sealing and Repossession of Property.*

3. All *ad acta* cases regarding claimed property in that municipality, including those for uncontested properties, have been reported to other municipalities and to PLIP Focal Points in accordance with the *Instruction on Exchange of Information Related to the Sealing and Repossession of Property.*

4. All reconstruction beneficiary information received from the Housing Verification and Monitoring Unit (HVM) has been acted on in accordance with the property laws and the PLIP *Legal Guidelines.*

5. A report has been made of (1) the number of unclaimed real properties and apartments in the municipality; (2) the number, location, current status and capacity of alternative accommodation resources; (3) the number of temporary users who remain entitled to alternative accommodation and the specific resources used to provide it to them; and (4) the number and procedural posture of appeals against administrative determinations under the property laws pending before any competent administrative or judicial body, as well as lawsuits filed in accordance with legal provisions regulating preliminary issues.

6. Sufficient administrative capacity has been specifically dedicated, on an ongoing basis and in accordance with law, to fully process (1) any future municipal claims made for private property; (2) any future requests for enforcement of CRPC decisions on private or socially-owned property; (3) any claims originally made to CRPC that may be received from CRPC in accordance with legal provisions regulating the transfer of CRPC's capacities to domestic bodies; (4) any final orders received from competent administrative or judicial appeals bodies; preparations for such processing should be based on a realistic assessment of the numbers of cases described under points (1) to (4), above, that are likely to arise in that municipality.

7. Sufficient administrative capacity has been specifically dedicated, on an ongoing basis and in accordance with law, to conduct regular, systematic checks of the continuing legal entitlement of alternative accommodation beneficiaries. Decisions are to be issued, in accordance with the property laws, related regulations, and any contractual arrangements between the competent authority and interested parties, terminating the right to alternative accommodation (AA) of any AA beneficiary who:

(1) vacated abandoned property without moving into AA offered to them;

(2) explicitly refused AA offered to them;

(3) vacated an allocated AA unit voluntarily;

(4) did not seek further instalments of lump sum or rental AA provided to them;

(5) lost their right to AA during a revision process;

(6) lost their right to AA based on information received from HVM or other municipalities;

(7) were placed on a waiting list for AA and did not turn up when notified it was available; or

(8) is found in any other way to fail to meet the criteria for AA in accordance with law.

The provisions of the laws on administrative procedure regarding providing adequate notice to the subject of such a decision should be respected wherever necessary.

8. All case-files and documentation regarding property claimants should be archived in a manner compatible with applicable data protection standards.

5.9. Law on the Cessation of the Application of the Law on Temporary Abandoned Real Property Owned by Citizens (Federation BiH) (2003)

I. GENERAL PROVISIONS

Article 1

From the day of the entry into force of this law, the *Law on Temporary Abandoned Real Property Owned by Citizens* (Official Gazette RBiH 11/93, 13/94 – hereinafter: the Law) and regulations regulating the issue of temporary abandoned property owned by citizens in the period between 30 April 1991 and the entry into force of this law, shall cease to applied on the territory of the Federation of Bosnia and Herzegovina (hereinafter: the Federation).

Article 2

From the day of the entry into force of this Law, the bodies and authorities of the Federation and other bodies in the Federation (hereinafter: the competent authorities) shall refrain from undertaking any new actions by which real property owned by citizens is declared abandoned or placed under municipal administration.

The competent authorities referred to in Paragraph 1 of this Article shall decide about the rights of owners to repossess their real property which has been declared temporarily or permanently abandoned and the rights of temporary occupants of the abandoned real property.

Article 3

Real property declared abandoned and placed under municipal administration on the basis of the *Law on Temporary Abandoned Real Property Owned by Citizens* shall remain under municipal administration until the return of the real property to the owner pursuant to the provisions of this Law.

Article 4

Owner of the real property declared abandoned shall have the right to file a claim for the return of the real property at any time.

Exceptionally, claims for repossession of real property may also be made by persons who were in unconditional possession of the real property at the time it was declared abandoned.

Article 5

For the purpose of this Law, the owner shall be understood to mean a person who, according to the legislation in force, was the owner of the real property at the moment when that property was declared abandoned.

The owner of the real property may authorize another person to submit the claim for the return of the real property.

Article 6

The user to whom the real property has been allocated for temporary use on the basis of the *Law* on Temporary Abandoned Real Property Owned by Citizens (hereinafter: the temporary user), shall continue to use the real property under the conditions and in the manner which were prescribed by the *Law on Temporary Abandoned Real Property Owned by Citizens*, until the issuance of a decision under Article 12 of this Law.

Article 7

A temporary user who has been ordered to vacate the property pursuant to the provisions of this Law and who is entitled to alternative accommodation pursuant to this Law, shall be provided with accommodation within the same canton by the competent service of the municipality on the territory of which s/he enjoyed the latest residence within the deadline set by the decision under Article 12 of this Law for his/her vacation of the property. The temporary user shall be obliged to move out of the property within the deadline set in Article 12 of this Law.

In case that the administrative authority of the territory of which the temporary user has his/her latest residence is unable to provide alternative accommodation, other competent bodies including other municipal organs, state-owned companies or firms, and cantonal and Federation authorities shall be obliged to make available facilities which are at their disposal for the purposes of providing alternative accommodation under this Law.

As an exception, if the temporary user's 30 April 1991 house or apartment is uninhabitable or occupied, on the written request of the temporary user and pending the reconstruction or vacation of the 30 April 1991 house or apartment, the authority responsible for providing temporary accommodation shall be the competent authority responsible for housing affairs in the municipality where the 30 April 1991 house or apartment is located.

The authorities responsible to provide alternative accommodation shall not be obliged to provide alternative accommodation to persons occupying the property without a valid legal title and shall be obliged to evict such persons, ex officio, immediately or at the latest within 15 days.

In all cases in which the current occupant remains in the property, all moveable property of the owner found in the property must be returned to him/her upon his/her request.

In no event shall the failure of the municipality to meet its obligations under Paragraph 1 of this Article operate to delay the ability of the owner to reclaim his property.

Article 8

For the purposes of this Law, the standard of alternative accommodation provided shall be one or more rooms which provide shelter to the user from adverse weather conditions and protects his or her furniture from damage, with a minimum of 5 square meters/person. Such accommodation may be in the form of business facilities or a co-tenancy.

Article 9

Parties in proceedings instituted at the owner's request for repossession of the real property shall be the owner of the real property and the temporary occupant at the time the request was submitted.

II. RETURN OF REAL PROPERTY TO THE OWNER

Article 10

The owner of private property has the right to claim at any time from the competent authorities the repossession of his/her property that has been declared abandoned or allocated for temporary use.

Article 11

A claim for repossession of a property under Article 10 of this Law shall be filed by the owner to the competent municipal, city or cantonal administrative body competent for property – law affairs.

The claim shall be submitted in writing, signed by the owner or orally, in person by the owner or an authorized representative. A claim should include:

1. all necessary information on the property;

2. any evidence in possession of the claimant that the claimant is the owner;

3. the date when the owner intends to reoccupy the property.

The claim for repossession of property referred to in Paragraph 1 of this Article shall not be subject to the statute of limitations.

Article 12

Upon the receipt of the owner's claim for the return of the property, the competent body shall issue a decision on the return of the property to the owner within a period of 30 days from the date of the receipt of the claim. The claim shall be solved in the chronological order in which it was received, unless specified otherwise in law.

The decision referred to in paragraph 1 of this Article by which the owner's claim is accepted shall contain:

- a decision terminating the municipal administration of the property as of the date of the intended return;

- a decision on repossession of the property by the owner;

- a decision terminating the right of the temporary user;

- a time limit for vacating the property by the temporary user or the person using the property without a valid legal title, or the time limit for returning the land;

- a decision whether the temporary user is entitled to alternative accommodation in accordance with this Law;

- an explicit warning that the current user will be subject to prosecution under the Criminal Code if s/he removes objects from, or otherwise damages, the property; and

- an explicit warning to a current user who is a multiple occupant that s/he is subject to the fines set out in Article 17c, Paragraph 3 of this Law.

Article 12a

The deadline for vacating the property, referred to in Article 12, Paragraph 2, Point 4 of this Law shall be 15 days from the date of delivery of the decision and the decision on entitlement to accommodation under Article 12, Paragraph 2, Point 5 of this Law shall be negative, unless the current user is a temporary user as defined in Article 6 of this Law and:

The temporary user is not a multiple occupant, as defined in Articles 16 and 16a of this Law; and:

The temporary user left his/her apartment or residential private property in the territory of Bosnia & Herzegovina between 30 April 1991 and 4 April 1998; and:

In the case that the apartment or residential private property s/he left is occupied, s/he or a member of his/her 1991 family household has applied to the competent administrative authority, court or the Commission for Real Property Claims of Displaced Persons and Refugees (hereinafter, CRPC) for repossession of that apartment within all deadlines prescribed by law, or for repossession of that residential private property within 60 days of this provision coming into force and is awaiting a decision on that claim; or

In the case that a decision on a claim for repossession or CRPC certificate has been issued with respect to the apartment or residential private property s/he left, s/he or a member of his/her 1991 family household has requested enforcement of that decision or CRPC certificate within 60 days of this provision coming into force or within 60 days of being legally entitled to seek enforcement, whichever is later; or

In the case that the apartment or residential private property s/he left is damaged or destroyed, s/he or a member of his/her 1991 family household has applied for return and reconstruction or is awaiting reconstruction assistance.

In case the current user fulfills the criteria set out in Paragraph 1 of this Article, the deadline for vacating the apartment shall be not more than 90 days from the date of the delivery of the decision. If a temporary user ceases to fulfill the conditions in this paragraph and a decision setting out a 90-day deadline to vacate has already been issued, the competent authority *ex officio* shall immediately issue a new decision specifying a deadline to vacate 15 days from the date of its delivery and then a conclusion on enforcement.

In exceptional circumstances, the deadline referred to in Paragraph 2 of this Article may be extended to up to one year if the municipality responsible for providing alternative accommodation in accordance with Article 7, Paragraph 1 of this Law provides detailed documentation regarding its efforts to secure alternative accommodation to the Federation Ministry of Urban Planning and Environment, and upon a finding by the Ministry, that there exists a documented absence of available housing in the municipality, which shall be agreed upon by the Office of the High Representative.

The current user shall be required to demonstrate that s/he meets the conditions for entitlement to alternative accommodation under this Law; including providing claim or decision numbers for the repossession of the current user's 1991 home. If the current user cannot demonstrate that s/he meets these conditions, the competent authority shall proceed in accordance with the *Law on Administrative Procedures* (Official Gazette of FBiH, No. 2/98) in order to determine relevant facts.

In case of the return of arable land, the time limit referred to in Article 12, Paragraph 2, Point 4 of this Law may be extended until the harvest is completed.

Article 13

The competent authority must notify the owner of the property and the temporary user of the property.

Any appeal against the decision must be submitted to the cantonal administrative body competent for the property law affairs within 15 days from the date of receipt of the decision.

An appeal shall not suspend the execution of the decision. In the event of an appeal, the competent authority shall retain copies of documents or take any other steps as necessary to ensure that the decision can be executed, notwithstanding the initiation of an appeal. If an appeal against a positive decision is not determined within the time period specified in the *Law on Administrative Procedures*, the decision of the first instance body, and therefore the claimant's legal right to the real property, shall be deemed to be confirmed.

In case the cantonal ministry competent for housing affairs annuls the first instance decision, the annulment shall be considered partial under Article 236, paragraph 3 of the *Law on Administrative Procedures*, in the sense that the annulment shall be related only to the decision on the rights of the current occupant unless there are grounds to annul the decision on the right of the claimant. If the competent authority again confirms the property right of the claimant, the deadline set for vacating the property pursuant to Article 12, paragraph 2, point 4 of this Law shall run from the date of delivery of the original decision that was partially annulled.

Article 14

A party affected by a decision made under Article 12 may at any time file a claim to the CRPC.

In the event that a proceeding from Paragraph 1 of this Article is initiated, all other proceedings before the competent authorities, including the enforcement of decision referred to in Article 12 of this Law, shall be stayed pending the final decision of the CRPC, but only in cases where the responsible body has rejected the request of the claimant on formal or material grounds, and where suspension has been requested by the CRPC.

A decision of the CRPC is final and binding.

Regarding the rights and obligations of a party referred to in Paragraph 1 of this Article, the decision of the CRPC shall have the same legal force as a decision of any other competent authority made in accordance with this Law.

Article 15

The return of the property to the owner shall be witnessed by an official of the competent office of the municipality referred to in Article 11, paragraph 1 of this Law.

The return of the property and the entering into possession by the owner shall be recorded in the minutes including, among other things, a detailed description of the current state of the premises and the movable property therein.

If minutes are unavailable from the time when the property was abandoned, the competent authority shall conduct an inspection of the property at the time the decision is made pursuant to Article 12 of this Law. The authorities *are obliged*, pursuant to their duties under the Criminal Code, to seek the prosecution of a current user who illegally removes property or fixtures from the property, or who wilfully causes damage to the property, when s/he vacates the property either voluntarily or by eviction. The competent authority shall include a notice or warning to a current user about the aforesaid criminal sanctions for such action pursuant to Article 12, paragraph 2, point 6 of this Law.

The competent authority shall record such information in the minutes, and distribute the information recorded therein, as well as other information regarding repossessed or vacant and sealed property, as is defined by instruction of the Federation Ministry of Urban Planning and Environment. Information distributed and received in this manner is to be stored, processed, distributed and used only in a manner consistent with and necessary to the purpose of promoting property law implementation in accordance with the General Framework Agreement for Peace.

Article 16

If the person occupying the property fails to voluntarily comply with the decision ordering him/her to vacate the property, the competent authority shall employ compulsory enforcement, in accordance with the law.

The enforcement shall be carried out at the request of the owner.

Exceptionally, the competent administrative body shall, ex officio, or upon the request of a person who has a legal interest in the procedure, pass a decision to vacate the real property immediately in cases where the current user is a multiple occupant. The affected person has the right to file an appeal against the decision, but the appeal does not suspend the eviction.

A multiple occupant includes, among others, a current user who uses a real property and who:

holds an occupancy right to or is using more than one apartment; or

has a house or is using an apartment in cases where the house or apartment is sufficiently intact, or can be made so with minimal repairs, to provide for basic living conditions (protection against weather; access to water and electricity; a heating source; basic privacy; and security of belongings); or

is in possession of the house or apartment in which s/he lived on 30 April 1991 (hereinafter "1991 home"); or where a member of his/her family household is in possession of his/her 1991 home; in cases where his/her 1991 home is sufficiently intact, or can be made so with minimal repairs, to provide for basic living conditions; or

has already been provided with alternative accommodation by a responsible body; or has a member of his/her family household who has accommodation anywhere on the territory of the Federation of Bosnia and Herzegovina or in the same city or municipality as the 1991 home anywhere else in the territory of Bosnia and Herzegovina, insofar as the accommodation accords with the minimum standard specified in Article 8 of this Law; or

has a legal right to return into possession of his/her 1991 home; and his/her 1991 home is sufficiently intact, or can be made so with minimal repairs, to provide for basic living conditions, as explained in this paragraph; and it is possible for him/her to return into possession of his/her 1991 home; or

whose accommodation needs are otherwise met, as defined in Article 16a of this Law. In cases where a claim has been filed under this Law for a real property which is vacated by a multiple occupant, and no decision has been issued at the date of vacation, the competent body shall immediately issue a decision on the claim.

For the purposes of this Article, "family household" shall mean all members of the family household as of 30 April 1991; or, if they were not members of the family household as of 30 April 1991, any spouse, parents, children; or other persons registered together with a temporary user.

Article 16a

A temporary user whose accommodation needs are otherwise met shall include, among others:

a temporary user who voluntarily sold the real property in which s/he lived on 30 April 1991; or

a temporary user who voluntarily exchanged the real property or apartment in which s/he lived on 30 April 1991 and who is in possession of the apartment or real property or has transferred it to a third party; or

a temporary user who refuses alternative accommodation offered in writing by the competent authority, or refuses assistance in the reconstruction of his/her residence of 30 April 1991. The competent authority shall inform the temporary user of the consequence of refusing alternative accommodation or reconstruction assistance; or

a temporary user who resides in the same municipality as s/he did in 1991, unless s/he can provide evidence as to why he or she cannot return to his or her 1991 home; or

a temporary user who was a sub-tenant in 1991; or

a temporary user who has sufficient disposable income, including assets, to provide for his/her own accommodation. Sufficient disposable income shall be defined as one-fourth of the applicable breadbasket, as calculated by the competent statistical institute, per current family household member, plus 200 KM; or

a temporary user, in a case where the owner provides him/her with a different accommodation as a tenant within the same canton, unless the temporary user agrees in writing to another municipality elsewhere, for at least six months. The standard of accommodation shall be that set out in Article 8 of this Law; or

a temporary user who left his/her apartment or residential private property in the territory of Bosnia & Herzegovina between 30 April 1991 and 4 April 1998 and there was a claim for repossession of that apartment or residential private property filed, if the claim for repossession is subsequently withdrawn; or

a temporary user who has been allocated any state-owned, including formerly socially-owned, land since 6 April 1992, more than 150 days from the date the allocation issued pursuant to a waiver granted by the Office of the High Representative, unless s/he cancels the allocation within 60 days of the date of the confirmation or of the date this provision comes into force, whichever date is the later; or

a temporary user who, unless a waiver application is pending before the Office of the High Representative, has been allocated any state-owned, including formerly socially-owned, land since 6 April 1992, unless s/he cancels the allocation within 60 days of the date this provision comes into force; or

a temporary user who has received housing credits, building materials, or any other form of housing construction/purchase assistance, more than 150 days from the date of receipt of the assistance or the date of receipt of the first instalment of the assistance, unless s/he cancels the assistance within 60 days of receipt of the assistance, or the first instalment of the assistance, or within 60 days of the date this provision comes into force, whichever date is the later.

For the purposes of Points 9 to 11 of Paragraph 1 of this Article, the competent authority shall inform the temporary user of the consequences of not cancelling the land allocation or housing construction/purchase assistance, whichever is applicable.

For the purposes of this Article, the term 'temporary user' shall include all members of the family household as defined in Article 16 paragraph 6 of this Law.

Article 17

The proceedings for the repossession of real property by the owner as determined in this law and proceedings of the compulsory enforcement referred to in Article 16 of this law shall be carried out in accordance with the *Law on Administrative Procedure*.

Article 17a

The provisions of this Law shall also apply to real property owned by citizens which was not declared abandoned in accordance with the regulations referred to in Article 1 of this Law, if the owner abandoned the real property before 4 April 1998.

All binding court decisions which order the return of real property to the possession of the owner shall be enforced by the court.

Pending proceedings on the return of real property to the possession of the owner will continue, while new claims for the return of property shall be submitted to the responsible organ under Article 11 of this Law.

Article 17b

The provisions of this Law shall also apply to the abandoned real property, the ownership of which has been acquired after 30 April 1991 based on any legal transfer of real property rights (contracts on exchange, sale, gift etc.).

In case of a dispute as to the lawfulness of the transferred real property right, the competent body shall refer the matter to the competent court according to the provisions of the *Law on Administrative Procedures* regulating preliminary issues, in order to rule on the allegation. Notwithstanding the provisions of the *Law on Civil Procedures* (FBH O.G. 42/98), the burden of proof shall lie upon the party claiming to have acquired rights to the real property through the transaction to establish that the transaction was conducted voluntarily and in accor-

dance with the law. Where one of the transferred properties is located in the territory of another republic of the former SFRY, the burden of proof shall lie upon the party claiming that the transfer of property was not conducted voluntarily and in accordance with the law to demonstrate that the status of the parties prior to the transfer of property shall be restored.

Exceptionally, in case of a dispute as to the validity of the transferred real property right in which the competent authority issued a decision on repossession prior to December 29, 2001 that has not yet been enforced, the competent authority shall *ex officio* suspend enforcement proceedings pending a final judicial decision on the matter, under the condition that an interested party provides evidence that they have initiated proceedings before the competent court.

Article 17c

The competent administrative body shall be fined 1000 to 5000 KM for the following minor offences:

if it does not order the vacation of the real property within 15 days in accordance with Article 12, Paragraph 2, Point 4 of the Law;

if it fails to process an eviction request because one of the parties filed an appeal against the prior decision, as set out in Article 13, Paragraph 3 of the Law;

if it fails to hand over the real property in accordance with Article 15 of the Law;

if it is required to take action against a multiple occupant, as set out in Article 16, Paragraph 3, or if it fails to issue a decision according to Article 16, Paragraph 6 of the Law;

The responsible person in the competent administrative body shall also be fined 200 to 1000 KM for violation of Paragraph 1 of this Article.

In addition to the above, a person who is a multiple occupant as defined: in Article 16, paragraph 4, Points 1, 2 or 7 of this Law and who fails to comply with the deadline to vacate the real property specified in a decision issued pursuant to Article 12 of this Law shall be fined 500 to 5000 KM;

in Article 16, Paragraph 4, Points 3 to 6 of the Law and who fails to comply with the deadline to vacate the real property specified in a decision issued pursuant to Article 12 of this Law shall be fined 250 to 1000 KM.

Article 17d

A person whose right of temporary use was terminated under Article 12, Paragraph 2, Point 3 of this Law, who spent his/her personal funds on necessary expenses for the real property, shall be entitled to recover those funds under the *Law on Obligations* (Official Gazette RBiH 2/92, 13/93 and 13/94). Proceedings under the Law on Obligations may be commenced from the date when the previous owner regains possession of the real property.

Where the court has awarded compensation to the person referred to in Paragraph 1, the owner may recover that sum from the competent authority under the *Law on Obligations.*

The competent authority shall be liable for all damage to the property from the time it was abandoned by the owner either until the time it is returned to the owner or a member of his/her 1991 household pursuant to this Law, or until the time that the property is vacated and sealed and notification has been delivered to the owner in accordance with the provisions of this Law and the Law on Administrative Procedure.

Article 18

This law shall enter into force on the day following its publication in the "Official Gazette" of the Federation of Bosnia and Herzegovina.

5.10. Law on the Cessation of the Application of the Law on Abandoned Apartments (Federation BiH) (2003)

I. General Provisions

Article 1

The Law on Abandoned Apartments ("Official Gazette of RBH" no. 6/92, 8/92, 16/92, 13/94, 36/94, 9/95 and 33/95), Decree on Use of Abandoned Apartments (Official Gazette HZHB 13/93) and the regulations passed thereunder, as well as other regulations regulating the issue of abandoned apartments passed between 30 April 1991 and the entry into force of this Law which are being applied on the territory of the Federation of Bosnia and Herzegovina (hereinafter: the Federation) shall cease to be applied on the day of the entry into force of this law.

Following the entry into force of this Law, the authorities of the Federation and other bodies in the Federation shall refrain from undertaking any new actions by which apartments will be declared abandoned or occupancy rights cancelled until after the occupancy right holder has been reinstated in his/her apartment in accordance with this Law.

The competent bodies referred to in Paragraph 2 of this Article shall decide about the rights of occupancy right holders to repossess their apartments which have been declared temporarily or permanently abandoned and the rights of temporary occupants of the abandoned apartment.

Article 2

All administrative, judicial and any other decisions enacted on the basis of the regulations referred to in Paragraph 1 of Article 1 of this Law terminating occupancy rights shall be null and void.

All administrative, judicial and any other decisions enacted on the basis of the regulations referred to in Paragraph 1 of Article 1 of this Law in which rights of temporary occupancy have been created shall remain effective until cancelled in accordance with this Law. Persons who moved into apartments on the basis of acts which have expired shall be considered to be temporary users. Article 3, Paragraph 3 of this Law shall not apply to such persons.

Any occupancy right or contract on use made between 1 April 1992 and 7 February 1998 is cancelled. A person who occupies an apartment on the basis of an occupancy right which is cancelled under this Article shall be considered a temporary user for the purposes of this Law.

A temporary user referred to in the previous paragraph who does not have other accommodation available to her/him has the right to a new contract on use to, or an extension of temporary use of, the apartment, in accordance with the provisions of this Law, when the occupancy right of the former occupant is cancelled under Article 5 of this Law or a claim of the former occupant to repossess the apartment is rejected by the competent authority in accordance with this Law.

An occupancy right holder to an apartment as at 1 April 1992, who agreed to the cancellation of her/his occupancy right and who subsequently received another occupancy right which is cancelled under this Article, is entitled to make a claim for repossession of her/his former apartment in accordance with this Law.

Article 2a

The provisions of this Law shall also apply to contracts on exchange of apartments, where the exchange took place between 1 April 1992 and 7 February 1998 in accordance with the Law on Housing Relations (FBH OG 11/98, 38/98, 12/99, 19/99) (hereinafter "ZOSO").

In the event that each party to the contract on exchange filed a claim for repossession before the expiry of the deadline set out in Article 5, the competent authority shall process the claims according to this Law. Notwithstanding, the competent authority in each municipality shall deem the exchange valid, if both parties give a statement reconfirming the contract on exchange, and shall revalidate the contracts on use pursuant to Article 18c paragraph 2, point 4 of this law.

In the event that neither party to the contract on exchange filed a claim for repossession before the expiry of the deadline set out in Article 5, the competent authority in each municipality shall revalidate the contracts on use pursuant to Article 18c paragraph 2 point 4 of this Law.

In the event that only one party to the contract on exchange filed a claim for repossession before the expiry of the deadline set out in Article 5, the competent authority shall inform in writing the corresponding competent authority in the municipality where the exchanged apartment is located of the claim. The receiving competent authority shall then deem a claim to have been filed, before the expiry of the deadline set out in Article 5, for the exchanged apartment within its jurisdiction and process the claim according to the Law.

In case of a dispute as to the validity of the contract on exchange, the competent authority shall suspend proceedings and shall refer the parties to the competent court according to the provision of the Law on Administrative Procedures (FBH OG 2/98)

regulating preliminary issues, in order to rule on the allegation.

Notwithstanding the provisions of the Law on Civil Procedures (FBH O.G. 42/98), the burden of proof shall lie upon the party claiming to have acquired rights to the apartment through the contract on exchange to establish that the transaction was conducted voluntarily and in accordance with the law. Where one of the exchanged apartments is located in the territory of another republic of the former SFRY, the burden of proof shall lie upon the party claiming that the contract on exchange was not conducted voluntarily and in accordance with the law to demonstrate that the status of the parties prior to the exchange shall be restored.

Exceptionally, in case of a dispute as to the validity of the contract on exchange in which the competent authority issued a decision on repossession prior to December 29, 2001 that has not yet been enforced, the competent authority shall ex officio suspend enforcement proceedings pending a final judicial decision on the matter, under the condition that an interested party provides evidence that they have initiated proceedings before the competent court.

Article 3

The occupancy right holder of an apartment declared abandoned or a member of his/her household as defined in Article 6 of the ZOSO (hereinafter the "occupancy right holder") shall have the right to return in accordance with Annex 7 of the General Framework Agreement for Peace in Bosnia and Herzegovina.

Paragraph 1 of this Article shall be applied only to those occupancy right holders who have the right to return to their homes of origin under Annex 7, Article 1 of the General Framework Agreement for Peace in Bosnia and Herzegovina. Persons who have left their apartments between 30 April 1991 and 4 April 1998 shall be considered to be refugees and displaced persons under Annex 7 of the General Framework Agreement for Peace in Bosnia and Herzegovina.

Holder of occupancy right in the apartment which is inhabited by a person using the apartment without legal basis or which is vacant as of the date this Law enters into force shall be able, without any restrictions, to repossess the apartment in which he has an occupancy right. Persons using the apartment without legal basis shall, ex officio, be evicted immediately or at the latest within 15 days and the competent authority shall not be obliged to provide alternative accommodation to such persons.

A temporary user of an apartment who is required to vacate the apartment pursuant to the provisions of this Law and to whom Article 7A and Article 11 or Article 11A of this Law apply shall be obliged to move out from the apartment that he/she has been using within 15 days of the date of delivery of the Decision from Article 6 of the Law confirming the right of an occupancy right holder to the relevant apartment.

A temporary user of an apartment who is required to vacate the apartment pursuant to the provisions of this Law and who is entitled to alternative accommodation pursuant to this Law, shall be provided with accommodation within the same canton by the administrative authority on the territory of which she/he had his/her latest residence. The temporary user shall be obliged to move out of the apartment within the deadline set in Article 7 of this Law.

The standard of alternative accommodation provided shall be one or more rooms which provide shelter to the user from adverse weather conditions and protects his or her furniture from damage, with a minimum of 5 square meters/person. Such accommodation may be in the form of business facilities or a co-tenancy.

In case that the administrative authority of the territory of which the temporary user has his/her latest residence is unable to provide alternative accommodation, other competent bodies including other municipal organs, state-owned companies or firms, and cantonal and Federation authorities shall be obliged to make available facilities which are at their disposal for the purposes of providing alternative accommodation under this Law.

As an exception, if the temporary user's 30 April 1991 house or apartment is uninhabitable or occupied, on the written request of the temporary user and pending the reconstruction or vacation of the 30 April 1991 house or apartment, the authority responsible for providing temporary accommodation shall be the competent authority responsible for housing affairs in the municipality where the 30 April 1991 house or apartment is located.

In all cases in which the current occupant remains in the apartment, all moveable property of the occupancy right holder found in the apartment must be returned to him/her upon his/her request.

In no event shall the failure of the competent bodies to meet their obligations under this Article operate to delay the ability of an occupancy right holder to enter into possession of the apartment.

Article 3a

As an exception to Article 3, paragraph 1 and 2 of the Law, regarding apartments declared abandoned on the territory of the Federation of Bosnia and Herzegovina, at the disposal of the Federation Ministry of Defense, the occupancy right holder shall not be considered a refugee nor have a right to repossess the apartment in the Federation of Bosnia and Herzegovina if after May 19, 1992 s/he remained in service as a military or civilian personnel of any armed forces outside the territory of Bosnia and Herzegovina, unless s/he had residence approved to him or her in the capacity of a refugee, or other equivalent protective status, in a country outside the former SFRY before 14 December 1995.

An occupancy right holder from paragraph 1 of this Article will not be considered a refugee or have a right to repossess the apartment in the Federation of Bosnia and Herzegovina, if s/he has acquired another occupancy right or other equivalent right from the same housing fund of former JNA or newly-established funds of armed forces of states created on the territory of former SFRY.

II. THE PROCEDURE FOR REPOSSESSION OF AN APARTMENT AND THE RIGHTS OF THE OCCUPANCY RIGHT HOLDER

Article 4

The occupancy right holder as defined in Article 3, Paragraph 1 of this Law shall be entitled to claim the repossession of an apartment.

A claim for repossession of an apartment shall be presented to the municipal administrative authority competent for housing affairs, unless otherwise determined by cantonal law.

The claim shall be submitted in writing signed by the occupancy right holder or orally, in person by the occupancy right holder or an authorised representative.

A claim should include:

1. information on the apartment;

2. any evidence that the claimant is the holder of an occupancy right or a member of the latter's household;

3. the date when the occupancy right holder intends to reoccupy the apartment, but not later than one year from the date of submitting the claim; and

4. information on the place of residence of the occupancy right holder and the members of the occupancy right holder's household at the time the claim is filed.

Article 5

A claim for repossession of the apartment must be filed within fifteen months from the date of the entry into force of this Law.

Exceptionally, the deadline for submission of claims for repossession of apartments under Article 2, paragraph 5 and Article 18b paragraph 1 of this Law, and Article 83a, paragraph 4 of the Law on Amendments to the Law on Taking Over of the Law on Housing Relations (Official Gazette of FBiH, No. 19/99) shall be 4 October 1999.

If the occupancy right holder does not file a claim to the competent administrative authority, to a competent court, or to the Commission for Real Property Claims of Displaced Persons and Refugees (hereinafter "CRPC"), within the appropriate time limit, or a request for enforcement of a decision of the CRPC within the deadline specified in the Law on Implementation of the Decisions of the CRPC (FBH OG 43/99, 51/00), the occupancy right is cancelled.

Article 6

Upon the receipt of a claim for return of the apartment to the occupancy right holder, the competent authority shall decide on the claim by a decision within 30 days from the date of receipt of the claim. The claim shall be solved in the chronological order in which it was received, unless specified otherwise in law.

The competent authority shall not reject a claim on the basis of provisions of the ZOSO, other than for failing to fall within the definition of member of household set out in Article 6 of the ZOSO. The competent authority also shall not reject a claim

on the basis of a foreign citizenship acquired by the claimant since 30 April 1991.

Article 7

The decision referred to in the preceding Article by which the claim of the occupancy right holder is accepted, shall contain:

1. a decision confirming that the claimant is the holder of the occupancy right as defined in Article 3, paragraph 1 of this Law;

2. a decision on repossession of the apartment by the occupancy right holder if there is a temporary user in the apartment, or if the apartment is vacant or occupied without legal basis;

3. in cases where there is a current user, a decision on whether the current user is using the apartment without a legal basis ("illegal user") or is a legal temporary user;

4. a decision on termination of the right of temporary use of the apartment, if there is a temporary user in the apartment;

5. a time limit for vacating the apartment by a temporary user or another person occupying the apartment;

6. a decision concerning whether the temporary user is entitled to accommodation in accordance with this Law;

7. an explicit warning that the current user will be subject to prosecution under the Criminal Code if s/he removes objects from, or otherwise damages, the apartment; and

8. an explicit warning to a current user who is a multiple occupant that s/he is subject to the fines set out in Article 18f, Paragraph 3 of this Law.

Article 7a

The deadline for vacating the apartment, referred to in Article 7, Paragraph 1, Point 5 of this Law shall be 15 days from the date of delivery of the decision and the decision on entitlement to accommodation under Article 7, Paragraph 1, Point 6 of this Law shall be negative, unless the current user is a temporary user as defined in Article 2, paragraph 3 of this Law and:

1. The temporary user is not a multiple occupant, as defined in Articles 11 and 11a of this Law; and:

2. The temporary user left his/her apartment or residential private property in the territory of

Bosnia & Herzegovina between 30 April 1991 and 4 April 1998; and:

(a) In the case that the apartment or residential private property s/he left is occupied, s/he or a member of his/her 1991 family household has applied to the competent administrative authority, court or CRPC for repossession of that apartment within all deadlines prescribed by law, or for repossession of that residential private property within 60 days of this provision coming into force and is awaiting a decision on that claim; or

(b) In the case that a decision on a claim for repossession or CRPC certificate has been issued with respect to the apartment or residential private property s/he left, s/he or a member of his/her 1991 family household has requested enforcement of that decision or CRPC certificate within 60 days of this provision coming into force or from the day of being legally entitled to seek enforcement, whichever is later; or

(c) In the case that the apartment or residential private property s/he left is damaged or destroyed, s/he or a member of his/her 1991 family household has applied for return and reconstruction or is awaiting reconstruction assistance.

In case the current user fulfills the criteria set out in Paragraph 1 of this Article, the deadline for vacating the apartment shall be not more than 90 days from the date of the delivery of the decision. If a temporary user ceases to fulfill the conditions in this paragraph and a decision setting out a 90-day deadline to vacate has already been issued, the competent authority ex officio shall immediately issue a new decision specifying a deadline to vacate 15 days from the date of its delivery and then a conclusion on enforcement.

In exceptional circumstances, the deadline referred to in Paragraph 2 of this Article may be extended to up to one year if the municipality or the allocation right holder responsible for providing alternative accommodation in accordance with Article 3 of this Law provides detailed documentation regarding its efforts to secure alternative accommodation to the cantonal administrative authority competent for housing affairs, and the cantonal authority finds that there is a documented absence of available housing which shall be agreed upon by the Office of the High Representative. In each individual case, the requirements of the European Convention on Human Rights and its Protocols must be met, and the occupancy right holder must be notified of the decision to extend the deadline and the basis for the decision 30 days before the deadline has expired.

The current user shall be required to demonstrate that s/he meets the conditions for entitlement to alternative accommodation under this Law; including providing claim or decision numbers for the repossession of the current user's 1991 home. If the current user cannot demonstrate that s/he meets these conditions, the competent authority shall proceed in accordance with the Law on Administrative Procedures in order to determine relevant facts.

Article 8

The competent administrative authority shall deliver the decision within 5 days from the date of issuance of the decision to:

1. the occupancy right holder;

2. the occupant of the apartment;

3. the allocation right holder.

Any appeal against a decision must be submitted by the claimant or current user to the cantonal ministry competent for housing affairs within 15 days from the date of receipt of the decision. Any appeal shall not suspend the execution of the decision.

In the event of an appeal, the competent authority shall retain copies of documents or take any other steps as necessary to ensure that the decision can be executed, notwithstanding the initiation of an appeal. If an appeal against a positive decision is not determined within the time period specified in the Law on Administrative Procedures, the decision of the first instance body, and therefore the claimant's occupancy right to the apartment, shall be deemed to be confirmed.

In case the cantonal ministry competent for housing affairs annuls the first instance decision, the annulment shall be considered partial under Article 236, paragraph 3 of the Law on Administrative Procedures, such that the annulment shall be related only to the decision on the rights of the current occupant unless there are grounds to annul the decision on the right of the claimant. If the competent authority again confirms the occupancy right of the claimant, the deadline set for vacating the apartment pursuant to Article 7, paragraph 1, point 5 of this Law shall run from the date of delivery of the original decision that was partially annulled.

Article 9

The handing over of the apartment to the occupancy right holder shall be witnessed by an official of the competent authority.

The handing over of the apartment and its contents shall be recorded in the minutes including, among other things, a detailed description of the current state of the apartment and its contents.

If minutes are unavailable from the time when the apartment was abandoned, the competent authority shall conduct an inspection of the apartment at the time the decision is made pursuant to Article 6 of this Law. The authorities are obliged, pursuant to their duties under the Criminal Code, to seek the prosecution of a current user who illegally removes property or fixtures from the apartment, or who wilfully causes damage to the apartment, when s/he vacates the apartment either voluntarily or by eviction. The competent authority shall include a notice or warning to a current user about the aforesaid criminal sanctions for such action pursuant to Article 7, Paragraph 1, Point 7 of this Law.

The competent authority shall record such information in the minutes, and distribute the information recorded therein, as well as other information regarding repossessed or vacant and sealed apartments, as is defined by instruction of the Federation Ministry of Urban Planning and Environment. Information distributed and received in this manner is to be stored, processed, distributed and used only in a manner consistent with and necessary to the purpose of promoting property law implementation in accordance with the General Framework Agreement for Peace.

Article 10

Proceedings in the cases initiated by the claims referred to in Article 4 of this Law shall be considered urgent.

Article 11

If the person occupying the apartment fails to voluntarily comply with a decision ordering him/her to vacate the apartment, the competent adminis-

trative authority shall employ compulsory enforcement in accordance with law.

The enforcement shall be carried out at the request of the occupancy right holder.

Exceptionally, the competent administrative authority shall, ex officio, or upon the request of a person who has a legal interest in the procedure, pass a decision to vacate the apartment immediately in cases where the current user is a multiple occupant. The affected person has the right to file an appeal against the decision, but the appeal does not suspend the eviction.

A multiple occupant includes, among others, a current user who uses an apartment and who:

1. holds an occupancy right to or is using more than one apartment; or

2. has a family house or a apartment, in cases where the house or apartment is sufficiently intact, or can be made so with minimal repairs, to provide for basic living conditions (basic protection against weather; access to water and electricity; a heating source; basic privacy and security of belongings); or

3. is in possession of the house or apartment in which s/he lived on 30 April 1991 (hereinafter: "1991 home"); or where a member of his/her family household is in possession of his/her 1991 home; in cases where his/her 1991 home is sufficiently intact, or can be made so with minimal repairs, to provide for basic living conditions; or

4. has already been provided with alternative accommodation by a competent authority; or

5. has a member of his/her family household who has accommodation anywhere on the territory of the Federation of Bosnia and Herzegovina or in the same city or municipality as the 1991 home anywhere else in the territory of Bosnia and Herzegovina, insofar as the accommodation accords with the minimum standard specified in Article 3, paragraph 6 of this Law; or

6. has a legal right to return into possession of his/her 1991 home; and his/her 1991 home is sufficiently intact, or can be made so with minimal repairs, to provide for basic living conditions, as explained in this paragraph; and it is possible for him/her to return into possession of his/her 1991 home; or

7. whose accommodation needs are otherwise met, as defined in Article 11a of this Law.

In cases where a claim has been filed under this Law for an apartment which is vacated by a multiple occupant, and no decision has been issued at the date of vacation, the competent authority shall immediately issue a decision on the claim.

For the purposes of this Article, "family household" shall mean all members of the family household as of 30 April 1991; or, if they were not members of the family household as of 30 April 1991, any spouse, parents, children; or other persons registered together with a temporary user.

Article 11a

A temporary user whose accommodation needs are otherwise met shall include, among others:

1. a temporary user who voluntarily sold the real property in which s/he lived on 30 April 1991; or

2. a temporary user who voluntarily exchanged the real property or apartment in which s/he lived on 30 April 1991 and who is in possession of the apartment or real property or has transferred it to a third party; or

3. a temporary user who refuses alternative accommodation offered in writing by the competent authority, or refuses assistance in the reconstruction of his/her residence of 30 April 1991. The competent authority shall inform the temporary user of the consequence of refusing alternative accommodation or reconstruction assistance; or

4. a temporary user who resides in the same municipality as s/he did in 1991, unless s/he can provide evidence as to why he or she cannot return to his or her 1991 home; or

5. a temporary user who was a sub-tenant in 1991; or

6. a temporary user who has sufficient disposable income, including assets, to provide for his/her own accommodation. Sufficient disposable income shall be defined as one-fourth of the applicable breadbasket, as calculated by the competent statistical institute, per current family household member, plus 200 KM; or

7. a temporary user, in a case where the occupancy right holder provides him/her with a different accommodation as a tenant within the same canton, unless the temporary user agrees in writing to another municipality elsewhere, for at least six months. The standard of accommodation shall be that set out in Article 3, Paragraph 6 of this Law; or

8. a temporary user who left his/her apartment or residential private property in the territory of Bosnia and Herzegovina between 30 April 1991 and 4 April 1998 and there was a claim for repossession of that apartment or residential private property filed, if the claim for repossession is subsequently withdrawn; or

9. a temporary user who has been allocated any state-owned, including formerly socially-owned, land since 6 April 1992, more than 150 days from the date the allocation issued pursuant to a waiver granted by the Office of the High Representative, unless s/he cancels the allocation within 60 days of the date of the confirmation or of the date this provision comes into force, whichever date is the later; or

10. a temporary user who, unless a waiver application is pending before the Office of the High Representative, has been allocated any state-owned, including formerly socially-owned, land since 6 April 1992, unless s/he cancels the allocation within 60 days of the date this provision comes into force; or

11. a temporary user who has received housing credits, building materials, or any other form of housing construction/purchase assistance, more than 150 days from the date of receipt of the assistance or the date of receipt of the first instalment of the assistance, unless s/he cancels the assistance within 60 days of receipt of the assistance, or the first instalment of the assistance, or within 60 days of the date this provision comes into force, whichever date is the later.

For the purposes of points 9 to 11 of paragraph 1 of this Article, the competent authority shall inform the temporary user of the consequences of not cancelling the land allocation or housing construction/purchase assistance, whichever is applicable.

For the purposes of this Article, the term 'temporary user' shall include all members of the family household as defined in Article 11 paragraph 6 of this Law.

Article 12

The competent authority may temporarily allocate for use as alternative accommodation by a temporary user entitled under this Law an apartment in cases where a decision has been issued under Article 6 and delivered to the occupancy right holder in accordance with law, and where:

1. the current user voluntarily vacates the apartment within the deadline stated in the Decision and the occupancy right holder, a member of his/her 1991 household, or an authorised proxy fails to collect the keys of the apartment within 30 days from the day on which s/he receives written notification from the competent authority that the apartment is vacant; or

2. the current user vacated the apartment following compulsory enforcement and the occupancy right holder, a member of his/her 1991 household, or an authorised proxy fails to collect the keys of the vacated apartment within 30 days from the day on which s/he receives written notification from the competent authority that the apartment is vacant.

In case the current user does not vacate the apartment within the deadline stated in the Decision and the occupancy right holder fails to initiate enforcement proceedings within 30 days after expiration of the deadline for the current user to vacate, the competent authority shall ex officio evict the current user if s/he is not entitled to alternative accommodation pursuant to this Law. The competent authority may then temporarily allocate the apartment for use by the current user, if they are entitled to alternative accommodation under this Law, or to another temporary user entitled to alternative accommodation under this Law or the Law on Cessation of the Application of the Law on Temporarily Abandoned Real Property Owned by Citizens (FBH OG 11/98, 29/98, 27/99, 43/99), as amended.

The competent authority shall set out fully for the claimant, in any decision on enforcement or notification that the apartment is vacant and sealed, her/his obligation to collect the keys or face the possibility of the use of the apartment for alternative accommodation pursuant to this Article.

Only once the occupancy right holder, a member of his/her 1991 household, or an authorised proxy collects the keys, shall the provisions of the ZOSO, with the exception of Article 44, Paragraph 1(6), Articles 47 and Article 49, apply to the occupancy right.

Article 12a

The competent authority must allocate the apartment referred to in Article 12 in accordance with Article 18d, and with the standard set out in Article 3, paragraph 6, of this Law to the temporary use of a person who is:

1. entitled to alternative accommodation in accordance with Article 7a, 11, and 11a of the Law; and

2. currently a temporary user of an apartment or real property; and

3. required to vacate that apartment or real property following a decision on a claim for repossession under this Law or the Law on Cessation of Application of the Law on Temporary Abandoned Real Property Owned by Citizens, or a request for enforcement of a decision of the CRPC.

The temporary permit shall not be extended if the occupancy right holder, a member of his/her 1991 household or an authorized proxy requests to collect the keys. The competent authority shall immediately evict the temporary user at the end of the current 6-month period and hand the keys over to the occupancy right holder, a member of his/her 1991 household or an authorized proxy.

If a cancellation procedure has been initiated before the court, and has not yet resulted in a final decision, the procedure shall be suspended. The competent authority shall send notice to the claimant that s/he, a member of his/her 1991 family household or an authorized proxy may collect the keys and repossess the apartment.

If the occupancy right holder, a member of his/her 1991 household or an authorised proxy does not request to collect the keys before the expiry of the deadline specified in Article 18d of this Law, the disposal of the apartment shall be regulated pursuant to Article 13 of this Law.

Article 13

Upon the cancellation of an occupancy right under Article 5, including an occupancy right for which a claim for repossession was rejected or withdrawn, the allocation right holder may regain control over the apartment only once the deadline specified in Article 18d of this Law for the administration by the administrative authority in charge of housing issues of such apartments has expired.

The return of apartments under the administration of the administrative authority in charge of housing issues to the allocation right holder upon the expiry of the deadline specified in Article 18d of this Law shall be regulated by an instruction of the Federation Ministry for Urban Planning and Environment.

Any allocation or other use of an apartment in contravention of Paragraph 1 of this Article and Article 18d of this Law is null and void.

III. CLAIMS TO THE COMMISSION FOR REAL PROPERTY CLAIMS OF DISPLACED PERSONS AND REFUGEES

Article 14

A party affected by a decision made under Article 7 may at any time file a claim with the CRPC. In the event that such a claim is filed, all proceedings, including execution of decisions or orders, shall be stayed pending the final decision of the CRPC but only in cases where the competent authority has rejected the request of the claimant on formal or material grounds, and where suspension has been requested by the CRPC.

A decision of the CRPC is final and binding.

Following a decision of the CRPC, the rights and obligations of the party referred to in Paragraph 1 of this Article shall be the same as if the decision of the CRPC was a decision of the competent authorities made in accordance with this law.

IV. PURCHASE OF APARTMENTS WHICH HAVE BEEN DECLARED ABANDONED

Article 15 – Repealed

V. FINAL PROVISIONS

Article 16

Contracts on the use of apartments declared abandoned in accordance with the regulations referred to in Article 1, paragraph 1 of this Law, as well as other decisions on allocation of apartment for use issued after 7 February 1998 are null and void.

Provision referred to in Paragraph 1 of this Article shall also apply to contracts on the use of apartment if they were concluded before 7 February 1998 but their beneficiary did not move into the apartment.

Any person who uses an apartment on the basis of a decision or contract referred to in Paragraph 1 of this Article shall be considered to occupy the apartment without legal basis.

Article 17

The Federation Minister of Urban Planning and Environment shall pass an instruction on the application of Article 4 of this Law within 30 days from the date of the entry into force of this Law.

Article 18

The procedure for the return of apartments to the possession of the occupancy right holders determined by this law shall be carried out in accordance with the Law on Administrative Procedures, unless otherwise stipulated by this law.

Article 18a

A person whose occupancy right was cancelled under Article 2 of this Law, who spent his/her personal funds on necessary expenses for the apartment, shall be entitled to recover those funds under the Law on Obligations (Official Gazette SFRJ, 29/78 and 39/85, Official Gazette RBiH 2/92, 13/93 and 13/94).

Proceedings under the Law on Obligations may be commenced from the date when the previous occupancy right holder regains possession of the apartment.

Where the court has awarded compensation to the person referred to in Paragraph 1, the occupancy right holder may recover that sum from the competent authority or allocation right holder under the Law on Obligations.

The competent authority shall be liable for all damage to the apartment from the time it was abandoned by the occupancy right holder until the time it is returned to the occupancy right holder or a member of his/her 1991 household pursuant to this law. Any repairs carried out by the occupancy right holder or a member of his/her 1991 household to restore the apartment to the state it was in prior to its abandonment shall be deemed "funds with which the holder of occupancy rights removed war damage" for the purposes of the Law on Sale of Apartments with Occupancy Right (FBH OG 27/97, 11/98, 22/99, 27/99, 7/00, and 32/01).

Article 18b

The provisions of this Law shall also apply to the apartments that have not been declared abandoned in terms of Article 1 of this Law, including damaged and destroyed apartments, provided that the occupancy right holder lost possession of the apartment in question before 4 April 1998.

All final judicial decisions ordering repossession of the apartment by the occupancy right holder shall be executed by the court. The initiated judicial proceedings for repossession of the apartment shall continue, while new claims shall be filed with the administrative authority in charge of the housing issues.

Article 18c

Where the temporary user has the right to a new contract on use of apartment under Article 2 Paragraph 4 of this Law, the administrative authority in charge of housing issues shall be authorised to conclude the contract on use of apartment in accordance with the ZOSO.

The temporary user shall have the right to a new contract on use of the apartment under Article 2 Paragraph 4 of this Law if s/he obtained the occupancy right in any of the following circumstances:

1. through transfer of the occupancy right to him/her as a spouse or as a member of the family household following the death of the previous occupancy right holder, in accordance with the ZOSO; or

2. through transfer following his/her divorce from the previous occupancy right holder; or

3. s/he was the first occupancy right holder of the apartment following its construction; or

4. through a valid contract on exchange of apartments, in accordance with the ZOSO and Article 2a of this Law.

In no case shall the temporary user have the right to a new contract on use of the apartment under Article 2, Paragraph 4 of this Law if s/he is a multiple occupant as defined in Article 11, Paragraph 4, Points 1 to 6 or Article 11a, Paragraph 1, Points 1, 2, 8, 9, 10, or 11 of this Law or if s/he is not entitled to alternative accommodation under Article 7a, paragraph 1, Points (2) (a) or (b) of this Law.

As an exception to Article 11, Paragraph 7 and Article 11a, Paragraph 3 of this Law, the criteria set out in the previous Paragraph of this Article shall apply only with regard to the temporary user and his or her family household as of 30 April 1991 for the purposes of this Article.

Any revalidation of a contract on use or allocation concluded in contravention of this Article shall be void.

The procedure by which the temporary user's right to revalidate a contract on use of the apartment is determined shall be regulated by instruction of the Federation Ministry for Urban Planning and Environment to be issued within 30 days of this Law coming into force. The competent public defender shall supervise the procedure and control the conformity of revalidations of contracts on use and allocations, as well as purchases of apartments based on such revalidations or allocations, with this Article, pursuant to his/her duties as set out in the Law and by instruction.

Article 18d

An apartment from Article 13 of this Law shall be administered by the administrative authority in charge of housing issues and used for the purpose of temporary use until all claims for the repossession of private property, made within 90 days of this provision coming into force, and for socially-owned property, made as defined in Article 5 of this Law, in that municipality are resolved. Upon expiration of this period, the apartment shall, after six months, be returned to the control of the allocation right holder pursuant to Article 13 of this Law. This paragraph shall apply to all apartments, whether or not they were declared abandoned.

The right to a temporary use of apartment in terms of the previous Paragraph shall be given to a person referred to in Article 3 Paragraph 5 of this Law or in Article 7, Paragraph 1 of the Law on Cessation of Application of the Law on Temporary Abandoned Real Property Owned by Citizens, in accordance with the standard set out in Article 3, paragraph 6 of this Law.

A temporary permit granted under this Article shall be given for a period of not longer than six months. A temporary user may apply for an extension of the temporary permit, for a period of not longer than six months, to expire at the latest by the deadline specified in Paragraph 1 of this Article.

In deciding on the claim for extension of the temporary permit, the competent authority must determine in a procedure whether the temporary user continues to be entitled to alternative accommodation pursuant to this Law. The competent authority can either issue a new temporary permit or indicate on the previous permit that the permit has been extended for another six months, including the expiration date of the permit. If the competent authority decides that the temporary user is not entitled to alternative accommodation, it shall order the temporary user to vacate the apartment within 15 days.

If the temporary user at any time ceases to meet the conditions for entitlement to alternative accommodation in accordance with the Law, the competent authority shall ex officio issue a decision cancelling the temporary permit and ordering the temporary user to vacate the apartment within 15 days.

Exceptionally, in respect of apartments at the disposal of the Federation Ministry of Defence, where an occupancy right to an apartment is cancelled in accordance with Article 5 or Article 12, or where the claim is finally rejected in accordance with this Law, the competent body of the Federation Ministry of Defence may issue a new contract on use to a temporary user of an apartment in cases where s/he is required to vacate the apartment under this Law to enable the return of a pre-war occupancy right holder or purchaser of the apartment, provided that his/her housing needs are not otherwise met.

Article 18e

As an exception to Article 5 of the Law, the occupancy right holder may file a claim for repossession of a destroyed or damaged apartment within six months of this Law entering into force.

Article 18f

The competent administrative authority shall be fined 1000 to 5000 KM for the following minor offences:

1. if it does not take into account the presumption that persons who have left their apartments between 30 April 1991 and 4 April 1998 shall be considered to be refugees and displaced persons under Annex 7 of the General Framework Agreement for Peace in Bosnia and Herzegovina, as set out in Article 3, paragraphs 1 and 2 of the Law;

2. if it does not order the vacating of the apartment within 15 days in accordance with Article 3, paragraphs 3 and 4 of the Law;

3. if it fails to process an eviction request because one of the parties filed an appeal against the prior Decision, as set out in Article 8, paragraph 3 of the Law;

4. if it fails to hand over the apartment in accordance with Article 9 of the Law;

5. if it is required to take action against a multiple occupant, as set out in Article 11, paragraph 3, or if it fails to issue a decision according to Article 11, paragraph 6, of the Law.

The responsible person in the competent administrative authority shall be fined 200 to 1000 KM for a violation of paragraph 1 of this Article.

In addition to the above, a person who is a multiple occupant, as defined:

1. in Article 11, paragraph 4, Items 1, 2 or 7 of the Law and who fails to comply with the deadline to vacate specified in a decision issued pursuant to Article 6 of this Law shall be fined 500 to 5000 KM;

2. in Article 11, paragraph 4, Items 3 to 6 of the Law and who fails to comply with the deadline to vacate specified in a decision issued pursuant to Article 6 of this Law shall be fined 250 to 1000 KM.

Penalty proceedings according to paragraphs 1 to 3 of this Article shall be carried out in accordance with the Federation Law on Minor Offences Violating Federation Regulations (FBH OG 9/96). The local competency shall be determined pursuant to the aforementioned law.

Article 19

This law shall enter into force on the day following its publication in the "Official Gazette of the Federation of Bosnia and Herzegovina".

5.11. Law on the Cessation of Application of the Law on the Use of Abandoned Property (Republika Srpska) (2003)

I. GENERAL PROVISIONS

Article 1

The Law on Use of Abandoned Property (Official Gazette of RS, Nos. 3/96, 21/96 and 31/99) shall cease to be in force, as well as the regulations passed thereunder and other regulations regulating the issues of abandoned property and apartments passed between 30 April 1991 and the entry into force of this Law.

The provisions of this Law shall apply to all real property, including privately-owned business premises, privately-owned houses and privately-owned apartments, and apartments with occupancy right ('apartments') which were vacated since 30 April 1991, whether or not the real property or apartment was declared abandoned: provided that the owner, possessor or user lost possession of the real property or the occupancy right holder lost possession of the apartment before 19 December 1998.

For the purpose of this Law, temporary user shall be understood to mean the person who is using real property or an apartment with a valid legal basis; an illegal user shall be understood to mean the person who is using the real property or an apartment without a valid legal basis. If a provision refers to both categories of users, the term current user is used.

Article 1a

For the purposes of this Law, the standard of alternative accommodation provided to temporary users entitled to it under this Law shall be one or more rooms which provide shelter to the user from adverse weather conditions and protects his or her furniture from damage, with a minimum of 5 square metres/person. Such accommodation may be in the form of business facilities or a co-tenancy.

Article 2

All administrative, judicial, and any other decisions enacted on the basis of the regulations referred to in Article 1 of this Law in which rights of temporary occupancy have been created shall remain effective until cancelled in accordance with this Law.

Any occupancy right or contract on use made between 1 April 1992 and 19 December 1998 is cancelled. A person who occupies an apartment on the basis of an occupancy right which is cancelled under this Article shall be considered a temporary user for the purposes of this Law.

A temporary user referred to in the previous paragraph who does not have other accommodation available to him/her has the right to a new contract on use to, or an extension of temporary use of, the apartment, in accordance with the provisions of this Law, if the occupancy right of the former occupant is cancelled under Article 16 of this Law or if a claim of the former occupant to repossess the apartment is rejected by the competent authority in accordance with this Law.

An occupancy right holder to an apartment as at 1 April 1992, who agreed to the cancellation of his/her occupancy right and who subsequently received another occupancy right which is cancelled under this Article, is entitled to make a claim for repossession of his/her former apartment in accordance with this Law.

Article 2a

The provisions of this Law shall also apply to contracts on exchange of apartments, where the exchange took place between 1 April 1992 and 19 December 1998 in accordance with the Law on Housing Relations (RS OG 19/93, 22/93, 12/99 and 31/99) (hereinafter "ZOSO").

In the event that each party to the contract on exchange filed a claim for repossession before the expiry of the deadline set out in Article 16, the competent authority shall process the claims according to this Law.

Notwithstanding, the competent authority in each municipality shall deem the exchange valid, if both parties give a statement reconfirming the contract on exchange, and shall revalidate the contracts on use pursuant to Article 27 paragraph 2, point 4 of this Law.

In the event that neither party to the contract on exchange filed a claim for repossession before the expiry of the deadline set out in Article 16, the competent authority in each municipality shall revalidate the contracts on use pursuant to Article 27 paragraph 2, point 4 of this Law.

In the event that only one party to the contract on exchange filed a claim for repossession before the expiry of the deadline set out in Article 16, the competent authority shall inform in writing the corresponding competent authority in the municipality where the exchanged apartment is located of the claim. The receiving competent authority shall then deem a claim to have been filed, before the expiry of the deadline set out in Article 16, for the exchanged apartment within its jurisdiction and process the claim according to the law.

In case of a dispute as to the validity of the contract on exchange, the competent authority shall suspend proceedings and shall refer the parties to the competent court according to the provision of the Law on General Administrative Procedures (SFRJ OG 47/86; taken over by Article 12 of the Constitutional Law on Implementation of the Constitution of the Republika Srpska, RS Official Gazette, No. 21/92) regulating preliminary issues, in order to rule on the allegation. Notwithstanding the provisions of the Law on Civil Procedures (SFRJ OG 4/77; taken over by Article 12 of the Constitutional Law on Implementation of the Constitution of the Republika Srpska, RS Official Gazette, No. 21/92), the burden of proof shall lie upon the party claiming to have acquired rights to the apartment through the contract on exchange to establish that the transaction was conducted voluntarily and in accordance with the law. Where one of the exchanged apartments is located in the territory of another republic of the former SFRY, the burden of proof shall lie upon the party claiming that the contract on exchange was not conducted voluntarily and in accordance with the law to demonstrate that the status of the parties prior to the exchange shall be restored.

Exceptionally, in case of a dispute as to the validity of the contract on exchange in which the competent authority issued a decision on repossession prior to December 29, 2001 that has not yet been enforced, the competent authority shall ex officio suspend enforcement proceedings pending a final judicial decision on the matter, under the condition that an interested party provides evidence that they have initiated proceedings before the competent court.

II. Return of Property to Private Owners, Possessors or Users

Article 3

The owner, possessor or user of the real property who abandoned the property shall have the right to repossess the real property with all the rights which s/he had before 30 April 1991 or before the real property became abandoned.

Article 4

For the purpose of this Law, the owner, possessor or user shall be understood to mean the person who was the owner, possessor or user of the real property

under the applicable legislation at the time when the real property became abandoned or at the time when the owner, possessor or user first lost possession of the real property, in cases where the real property was not declared as abandoned.

Article 5

A user to whom the real property was allocated for temporary use pursuant to the Law on the Use of Abandoned Property (hereinafter referred as: the temporary user) may continue to use the real property under the conditions and in the manner as provided by the Law on the Use of Abandoned Property until a decision referred to in Article 11 of this Law has been issued.

Article 6

If a temporary user is required to vacate the real property pursuant to the provisions of this Law, the competent authority of the Ministry of Refugees and Displaced Persons shall determine within the deadline of 30 days for making the decision under Articles 9 and 11 of this Law whether s/he is entitled to alternative accommodation in accordance with Article 34 of this Law. In case that the temporary user is entitled to alternative accommodation, the competent authority shall provide alternative accommodation within the time limit in which the temporary user is required to vacate the property under Article 11 of this Law.

In no event shall failure of the competent authority to meet its obligations under paragraph 1 of this Article operate to delay the ability of the owner, possessor or user to enter into possession of his/her property.

Article 7

The owner, possessor or user of abandoned real property, as referred to in Article 4, or his/her authorised representative, shall have the right to file a claim at any time for the repossession or disposal in another way of his/her abandoned property.

The right of the owner to file a claim shall not become obsolete.

All past final and binding court decisions which order the return of real property to the possession of the owner, possessor or user shall be enforced by the competent court. Any initiated court proceedings concerning the return of real property to the possession of the owner, possessor or user will continue unless withdrawn by the owner, possessor or user, while new claims for the repossession of property shall be submitted under Article 8 of this Law.

Article 8

A claim under Article 7 of this Law may be filed by the owner, possessor or user of abandoned real property with the competent authority of the Ministry of Refugees and Displaced Persons in the municipality on the territory of which the real property is located.

An owner, possessor or user shall be entitled to file a claim for repossession of real property, including privately-owned business premises, privately-owned houses and privately-owned apartments, including any real property which is or was at any time used partly or wholly for business purposes. The competent authority of the Ministry of Refugees and Displaced Persons shall be competent to receive and decide the claim in accordance with this Law.

Claims may be made in writing signed by the claimant or an authorised representative, or orally by the claimant or an authorised representative. Claims made in writing may be submitted in person, by mail or by any other person. No power of attorney is required for another person to submit a claim signed by the claimant.

A claim should include:

1. information on the owner, possessor or user;

2. all necessary information on the real property;

3. any evidence possessed by the claimant indicating that the claimant is the owner, possessor or user of the real property;

4. the date when the claimant intends to repossess the real property.

The competent authority shall accept claims regardless of whether or not supporting documentation is supplied by the claimant. In the event that the claimant cannot provide the necessary supporting documentation, the competent authority shall check the records of the relevant court or administrative body and any other available documentation to confirm the rights of the claimant.

The competent authority shall accept any identification document issued by the state of Bosnia and Herzegovina or any administrative body in either Entity, and any other document which shows the claimant's identity, and shall use any options provided in the Law on General Administrative Procedures (SFRY Official Gazette, No 47/86; taken over by Article 12 of the Constitutional Law on Implementation of the Constitution of the Republika Srpska, RS Official Gazette, No. 21/92) in the identification process.

The claimant shall be fully released from taxation, as well as from other expenses of the proceedings as provided in Articles 113 through 119 of the Law on General Administrative Procedures.

Article 9

The competent authority of the Ministry of Refugees and Displaced Persons shall be obliged to issue a decision to the claimant within 30 days from the date of receipt of the claim for repossession of real property. The claim shall be solved (rjesen) in the chronological order in which it was received, unless specified otherwise in law.

Article 10

The proceedings to return the real property to the owner, possessor or user shall be carried out in accordance with the provisions of the Law on General Administrative Procedures, unless this Law provides otherwise. The procedure until the issuance of the decision shall be carried out as an expedited procedure.

Article 11

The decision on return of the real property to the owner, possessor or user shall contain the following:

1. information on the owner, possessor or user to whom the real property is returned;

2. information on the real property subject to return;

3. the time limit within which the real property will be returned or put at disposal of the owner, possessor or user;

4. in cases where there is a current user, a decision on whether the current user is using the real

property without legal basis ('illegal user') or is a legal temporary user;

5. a decision whether the temporary user is entitled to alternative accommodation under this Law;

6. a decision terminating the right of the temporary user;

7. the time limit for the current user to vacate the property, or for handing over of the land;

8. an explicit warning that the current user will be subject to prosecution under the Criminal Code if he or she removes objects from, or otherwise damages, the property, and;

9. an explicit warning to a current user who is a multiple occupant that he or she is subject to the fines set out in Article 37, Paragraph 3 of this Law.

Article 11a

The deadline for vacating the property, referred to in Article 11, Paragraph 1, Point 7 of this Law shall be 15 days from the date of delivery of the decision and the decision on entitlement to accommodation under Article 11, Paragraph 1, Point 5 of this Law shall be negative, unless the current user is a temporary user as defined in Article 1, Paragraph 3 of this Law and:

1. The temporary user is not a multiple occupant, as defined in Articles 24a and 24b of this Law; and:

2. The temporary user left his/her apartment or residential private property in the territory of Bosnia & Herzegovina between 30 April 1991 and 19 December 1998; and:

(a) In the case that the apartment or residential private property s/he left is occupied, s/he or a member of his/her 1991 family household has applied to the competent administrative authority, court or the Commission for Real Property Claims of Displaced Persons and Refugees (hereinafter, CRPC) for repossession of that apartment within all deadlines prescribed by law, or for repossession of that residential private property within 60 days of this provision coming into force and is awaiting a decision on that claim; or;

(b) In the case that a decision on a claim for repossession or CRPC certificate has been issued with respect to the apartment or residential private property s/he left, s/he or a member of his/her 1991 family household has requested enforcement

of that decision or CRPC certificate within 60 days of this provision coming into force or within 60 days of being legally entitled to seek enforcement, whichever is later; or

(c) In the case that the apartment or residential private property s/he left is damaged or destroyed, s/he or a member of his/her 1991 family household has applied for return and reconstruction or is awaiting reconstruction assistance.

In case the current user fulfills the criteria set out in Paragraph 1 of this Article, the deadline for vacating the apartment shall be not more than 90 days from the date of the delivery of the decision. If a temporary user ceases to fulfill the conditions in this paragraph and a decision setting out a 90-day deadline to vacate has already been issued, the competent authority ex officio shall immediately issue a new decision specifying a deadline to vacate 15 days from the date of its delivery and then a conclusion on enforcement.

In exceptional circumstances, the deadline referred to above may be extended by up to one year if the body responsible for providing another accommodation in accordance with this Law provides detailed documentation regarding the lack of available accommodation to the Ministry of Refugees and Displaced Persons, which shall be agreed upon by the Office of the High Representative. In each individual case, the requirements of the European Convention on Human Rights and its Protocols must be met, and the owner, possessor or user shall be notified of the decision to extend the deadline and the basis for the decision 30 days before the deadline has expired.

The current user shall be required to demonstrate that s/he meets the conditions for entitlement to alternative accommodation under this Law; including providing claim or decision numbers for the repossession of the current user's 1991 home. If the current user cannot demonstrate that s/he meets these conditions, the competent authority shall proceed in accordance with the Law on General Administrative Procedures in order to determine relevant facts.

The owner, possessor or user may immediately reoccupy real property that is vacant.

In case of the return of arable land into possession, the time limit for its handing over may be extended, as an exception, until the harvest is collected.

Article 12

The competent authority of the Ministry of Refugees and Displaced Persons shall submit its decision to the claimant requesting the repossession of the property and the current user of the property.

Any appeal against a decision may be submitted to the responsible second instance body in accordance with the Law on General Administrative Procedures within 15 days of receipt of the decision. Any appeal shall not suspend the execution of the decision.

In the event of an appeal, the competent authority shall retain copies of documents or take any other steps as necessary to ensure that the decision can be executed, notwithstanding the initiation of an appeal. If an appeal against a positive decision is not determined within the time period specified in the Law on General Administrative Procedures, the decision of the first instance body, and therefore the claimant's legal right to the real property, shall be deemed to be confirmed.

In case the responsible second instance body annuls the first instance decision, the annulment shall be considered partial under Article 239, paragraph 3 of the Law on General Administrative Procedures, in the sense that the annulment shall be related only to the decision on the rights of the current occupant unless there are grounds to annul the decision on the right of the claimant. If the competent authority again confirms the property right of the claimant, the deadline set for vacating the property pursuant to Article 11, paragraph 1, point 7 of this Law shall run from the date of delivery of the original decision that was partially annulled.

Article 13

The owner, possessor or user of real property as referred to in Article 3 of this Law may at any time initiate proceedings before the CRPC.

In case that the proceedings under Paragraph 1 of this Article have been initiated, all other proceedings carried out before the competent bodies, including the procedure to enforce the decision referred to in Article 11 of this Law, shall be stayed pending the final decision of the CRPC, but only in cases where the competent authority has rejected the request of the claimant on formal or material grounds, and where suspension is requested by the CRPC.

A decision of the CRPC shall be final and binding.

In the light of specifying the rights and obligations of the party referred to in Paragraph 1 of this Article, the decision of the CRPC shall have the same legal force as the decision of any other competent authority issued in accordance with this Law.

A decision of the CRPC shall be enforced by the competent bodies of the Republika Srpska.

III. Return of Apartments to the Holders of Occupancy Right

Article 14

The occupancy right holder of an abandoned apartment or a member of his or her family household as defined in Article 6 of the ZOSO (hereinafter the "occupancy right holder") shall have the right to return to the apartment in accordance with Annex 7 of the General Framework Agreement for Peace in Bosnia and Herzegovina. The provisions of this Law shall apply to all apartments vacated between 30 April 1991 and 19 December 1998, whether or not the apartment was registered as abandoned, and regardless of whether the apartment was used for business purposes after 30 April 1991.

A person who left his/her apartment between 30 April 1991 and 19 December 1998 shall be presumed to be a refugee or displaced person under Annex 7 of the General Framework Agreement for Peace in Bosnia and Herzegovina with a right to return to that apartment irrespective of the circumstances under which s/he left the apartment.

Exceptionally from the previous paragraph, an occupancy right holder on apartment owned by the RS Ministry of Defence, and who remained in the professional military service of any armed forces outside of the territory of Bosnia and Herzegovina after 14 December 1995, shall not be considered a refugee neither and has a right to repossess apartment in Republika Srpska.

An occupancy right holder on apartment mentioned in the previous paragraph neither is considered a refugee nor has a right to repossess apartment in Republika Srpska, if he obtained a new occupancy right or a corresponding right from the same housing fund of former JNA or newly established funds of the armed forces of states created on the territory of former SFRY."

All past final and binding court decisions which order the return of an apartment to the occupancy right holder as defined in this Law shall be enforced by the competent court. Any initiated court proceedings concerning the return of an apartment to the occupancy right holder will continue unless withdrawn by the occupancy right holder, while new claims for the repossession of occupancy rights shall be submitted to the competent authority under Article 15 of this Law.

Article 15

The occupancy right holder as defined in Article 14, Paragraph 1, of this Law shall be entitled to file a claim for repossession of the apartment.

A claim for repossession of the apartment shall be filed with the competent authority of the Ministry of Refugees and Displaced Persons in the municipality in which the apartment is located.

A claim for repossession of the apartment should include:

1. information on the claimant;

2. information on the apartment;

3. evidence that the claimant is the occupancy right holder or a member of the latter's family household;

4. the date when the claimant intends to reoccupy the apartment, but not later than one year from the date of submitting the claim;

5. information on the residence of the occupancy right holder and members of his/her household at the time when the claim is submitted.

The competent authority shall accept all claims with or without the appropriate documents enclosed by the claimant. In cases when the claimant is not able to provide the necessary relevant documents, the competent authority shall verify the evidence, as well as other available documents, with the allocation right holder, the appropriate court or administrative body in order to have the rights of the claimant confirmed.

The competent authority shall accept any identification document issued by the state of Bosnia and Herzegovina or any legal body in either Entity, as well as any other document confirming the identity of the claimant.

The claimant shall be fully exempted from taxation as well as from other expenses of the proceedings, as provided in Articles 113 through 119 of the Law on General Administrative Procedures.

Article 16

A claim for repossession of the apartment may be filed within 16 months from the date of entry into force of this Law.

If the occupancy right holder does not file a claim to the competent administrative authority, to a competent court, or to the CRPC within the appropriate time limit, or a request for enforcement of a decision of the CRPC within the deadline specified in the Law on Implementation of the Decisions of the CRPC (Official Gazette of the Republika Srpska, Nos. 31/99, 2/00, 39/00 and 65/01) his/her occupancy right shall be cancelled.

Article 17

The competent authority of the Ministry of Refugees and Displaced Persons shall decide on the claim for the repossession of the apartment by the occupancy right holder within 30 days from the date of receipt of the claim. The claim shall be solved (rjesen) in the chronological order in which it was received, unless specified otherwise in law.

The competent authority shall not reject a claim on the basis of provisions of the ZOSO, other than for failing to fall within the definition of member of household set out in Article 6 of the ZOSO. The competent authority also shall not reject a claim on the basis of a foreign citizenship acquired by the claimant since 30 April 1991.

Article 18

The decision on repossession of the apartment by the occupancy right holder shall contain:

1. a decision confirming that the claimant is the occupancy right holder;

2. a decision on repossession of the apartment by the occupancy right holder if there is a temporary user in the apartment, or if the apartment is vacant or occupied without legal basis;

3. in cases where there is a current user, a decision on whether the current user is using the real

property without legal basis ('illegal user') or is a legal temporary user;

4. a decision on termination of the right of temporary use of the apartment if there is a temporary user of the apartment;

5. a time limit for vacating the apartment by a current user or another person in possession of the apartment;

6. a decision concerning whether the temporary user is entitled to alternative accommodation in accordance with this law;

7. an explicit warning that the current user will be subject to prosecution under the Criminal Code if he or she removes objects from, or otherwise damages, the apartment; and

8. an explicit warning to a current user who is a multiple occupant that he or she is subject to the fines set out in Article 37, Paragraph 3 of this Law.

Article 18a

The deadline for vacating the apartment, referred to in Article 18, Paragraph 1, Point 5 of this Law shall be 15 days from the date of delivery of the decision and the decision on entitlement to accommodation under Article 18, Paragraph 1, Point 6 of this Law shall be negative, unless the current user is a temporary user as defined in Article 1, paragraph 3 of this Law and:

1. The temporary user is not a multiple occupant, as defined in Articles 24a and 24b of this Law; and:

2. The temporary user left his/her apartment or residential private property in the territory of Bosnia & Herzegovina between 30 April 1991 and 19 December 1998; and:

(a) In the case that the apartment or residential private property s/he left is occupied, s/he or a member of his/her 1991 family household has applied to the competent administrative authority, court or CRPC for repossession of that apartment within all deadlines prescribed by law, or for repossession of that residential private property within 60 days of this provision coming into force and is awaiting a decision on that claim; or

(b) In the case that a decision on a claim for repossession or CRPC certificate has been issued with respect to the apartment or residential private property s/he left, s/he or a member of his/her 1991 family household has requested enforcement of that decision or CRPC certificate within 60 days of this provision coming into force or from the day of being legally entitled to seek enforcement, whichever is later; or

(c) In the case that the apartment or residential private property s/he left is damaged or destroyed, s/he or a member of his/her 1991 family household has applied for return and reconstruction or is awaiting reconstruction assistance.

In case the current user fulfills the criteria set out in Paragraph 1 of this Article, the deadline for vacating the apartment shall be not more than 90 days from the date of the delivery of the decision. If a temporary user ceases to fulfill the conditions in this paragraph and a decision setting out a 90-day deadline to vacate has already been issued, the competent authority ex officio shall immediately issue a new decision specifying a deadline to vacate 15 days from the date of its delivery and then a conclusion on enforcement.

In exceptional circumstances, the deadline referred to in Paragraph 2 of this Article may be extended by up to one year if the body responsible for providing alternative accommodation on the territory of which the temporary user of the apartment had the last domicile or residence provides detailed documentation regarding the lack of available housing for provision of appropriate accommodation from the Ministry for Refugees and Displaced Persons; which shall be agreed upon by the Office of the High Representative. In each individual case, the requirements of the European Convention on Human Rights and its Protocols must be met, and the occupancy right holder shall be notified of the decision to extend the deadline and the basis for the decision 30 days before the deadline has expired.

The current user shall be required to demonstrate that s/he meets the conditions for entitlement to alternative accommodation under this Law; including providing claim or decision numbers for the repossession of the current user's 1991 home. If the current user cannot demonstrate that s/he meets these conditions, the competent authority shall proceed in accordance with the Law on General Administrative Procedures in order to determine relevant facts.

The occupancy right holder may immediately re-occupy an apartment that is vacant.

In no event shall failure of the competent authority to meet its obligations to provide alternative accommodation operate to delay the ability of the occupancy right holder to enter into possession of the apartment.

Article 19

The competent authority shall deliver the decision referred to in Article 18 of this Law within 8 days from the date of issuance of the decision to:

1. the occupancy right holder;

2. the user of the apartment;

3. the allocation right holder.

Any appeal against a decision may be submitted to the responsible second instance body in accordance with the Law on General Administrative Procedures within 15 days of receipt of the decision. Any appeal shall not suspend the execution of the decision.

In the event of an appeal, the competent authority shall retain copies of documents or take any other steps as necessary to ensure that the decision can be executed, notwithstanding the initiation of an appeal. If an appeal against a positive decision is not determined within the time period specified in the Law on General Administrative Procedures, the decision of the first instance body, and therefore the claimant's occupancy right to the apartment, shall be deemed to be confirmed.

In case the responsible second instance body annuls the first instance decision, the annulment shall be considered partial under Article 239, paragraph 3 of the Law on General Administrative Procedures. If the competent authority again confirms the occupancy right of the claimant, the deadline set for vacating the apartment pursuant to Article 18, paragraph 1, point 5 of this Law shall run from the date of delivery of the original decision that was partially annulled.

Article 20

The proceedings to return the apartment to the occupancy right holder shall be carried out in accordance with the provisions of the Law on General Administrative Procedures, unless this Law provides otherwise.

Article 21

The competent authority may temporarily allocate for use as alternative accommodation by a temporary user entitled under this Law an apartment in cases where a decision has been issued under Article 17 of this Law and delivered to the occupancy right holder in accordance with law, and where:

1. the current user voluntarily vacates the apartment within the deadline stated in the Decision and the occupancy right holder, a member of his/her 1991 household, or an authorised proxy fails to collect the keys of the apartment within 30 days from the day on which s/he receives written notification from the competent authority that the apartment is vacant; or

2. the current user vacated the apartment following compulsory enforcement and the occupancy right holder, a member of his/her 1991 household, or an authorised proxy fails to collect the keys of the vacated apartment within 30 days from the day on which s/he receives written notification from the competent authority that the apartment is vacant.

In case the current user does not vacate the apartment within the deadline stated in the Decision and the occupancy right holder fails to initiate enforcement proceedings within 30 days after expiration of the deadline for the current user to vacate, the competent authority shall ex officio evict the current user if s/he is not entitled to alternative accommodation pursuant to this Law.

The competent authority may then temporarily allocate the apartment for use by the current user, if they are entitled to alternative accommodation under this Law, or to another temporary user entitled to alternative accommodation under this Law. The competent authority shall set out fully for the claimant, in any decision on enforcement or notification that the apartment is vacant and sealed, her/his obligation to collect the keys or face the possibility of the use of the apartment for alternative accommodation pursuant to this Article.

Only once the occupancy right holder, a member of his/her 1991 household, or an authorised proxy collects the keys, shall the provisions of the ZOSO, with the exceptions of Articles 44, Paragraph 1(6), Article 47 and Article 49, apply to the occupancy right.

Article 21a

The competent authority must allocate the apartment referred to in Article 21 of this Law in accordance with Article 31 of this Law, and with the standard set out in Article 1a of this Law to the temporary use of a person who is:

1. entitled to alternative accommodation in accordance with Article 34 of this Law; and

2. currently a temporary user of an apartment or real property; and

3. required to vacate that apartment or real property following a decision on a claim for repossession under this Law, or a request for enforcement of a decision of the CRPC.

The temporary permit shall not be extended if the occupancy right holder, a member of his/her 1991 household or an authorised proxy requests to collect the keys. The competent authority shall immediately evict the temporary user at the end of the current 6-month period and hand the keys over to the occupancy right holder, a member of his/her 1991 household or an authorised proxy.

If a cancellation procedure has been initiated before the court, and has not yet resulted in a final decision, the procedure shall be suspended. The competent authority shall send notice to the claimant that s/he, a member of his/her 1991 family household or an authorised proxy may collect the keys and repossess the apartment.

If the occupancy right holder, a member of his/her 1991 household or an authorised proxy does not request to collect the keys before the expiry of the deadline specified in Article 31 of this Law, the disposal of the apartment shall be regulated pursuant to Article 22 of this Law.

Article 22

Upon the cancellation of the occupancy right under Article 16 of this Law, including an occupancy right for which a claim for repossession was rejected or withdrawn, the allocation right holder may regain control over the apartment only once the deadline specified in Article 31 of this Law for the administration by the competent authority of such apartments has expired.

The return of apartments under the administration of the Ministry for Refugees and Displaced Persons to the allocation right holder upon the expiry of the deadline specified in Article 31 of this Law, shall be regulated by an instruction.

Any allocation or other use of an apartment in contravention of Paragraph 1 of this Article and Article 31 of this Law is null and void.

Article 23

The occupancy right holder as referred to in Article 14 and Article 15, paragraph 1 of this Law may initiate at any time proceedings before the CRPC.

In case that such proceedings have been initiated, all other proceedings carried out before the competent bodies, including the procedure to enforce the decision, shall be stayed pending the final decision of the CRPC, but only in cases where the competent authority has rejected the request of the claimant on formal or material grounds, and where suspension is requested by the CRPC.

A decision of the CRPC shall be final and binding.

In the light of specifying the rights and obligations of the party referred to in Paragraph 1 of this Article, the decision of the CRPC shall have the same legal force as the decision of any other competent authority issued in accordance with this Law.

A decision of the CRPC shall be enforced by the competent body of Republika Srpska.

IV – Special Provisions

Article 24

The repossession of abandoned real property or the apartment by the owner, user or occupancy right holder shall be witnessed by an official of the competent authority and interested parties.

A report shall be made on the return of the real property or apartment and on the reinstatement of the owner or user into possession of the property or apartment. The report shall contain, among other things, a detailed description of the current state of the apartment and its contents.

If minutes are unavailable from the time when the real property or apartment was abandoned, the competent authority shall conduct an inspection of the real property or apartment at the time the decision is made pursuant to Article 9 or 17 of this Law. The authorities are obliged, pursuant to their duties under the Criminal Code, to seek the prosecution of a current user who illegally removes property or fixtures from the real property or apartment, or who wilfully causes damage to the real property or apartment, when s/he vacates the real property or apartment either voluntarily or by eviction. The competent authority shall include a notice or warning to a current user about the aforesaid criminal sanctions for such action pursuant to Article 11, Paragraph 1, Point 8 or Article 18, Paragraph 1, Point 7 of this Law.

The competent authority shall record such information in the minutes, and distribute the information recorded therein, as well as other information regarding repossessed or vacant and sealed apartments, as is defined by instruction of the Ministry of Refugees and Displaced Persons. Information distributed and received in this manner is to be stored, processed, distributed and used only in a manner consistent with and necessary to the purpose of promoting property law implementation in accordance with the General Framework Agreement for Peace.

Article 24a

If the person occupying the real property or apartment fails to voluntarily comply with the decision ordering him/her to vacate the real property or apartment, the competent authority shall employ compulsory enforcement, in accordance with the law.

The enforcement shall be carried out at the request of the owner, possessor or user for real property, or occupancy right holder for an apartment and/or a member of his family household.

Exceptionally, the competent authority shall ex officio or upon the request of a person who has a legal interest in the procedure pass a decision to vacate a real property or apartment immediately in cases where the current user is a multiple occupant. The affected person has the right to file an appeal against the decision, but the appeal does not suspend the eviction.

A multiple occupant includes, among others, a current user who uses a real property or an apartment and who:

1. holds an occupancy right to or is using more than one apartment; or

2. has a family house or apartment, in cases where the family house or apartment is sufficiently intact, or can be made so with minimal repairs, to provide for basic living conditions (basic protection against

weather; access to water and electricity; a heating source; basic privacy; and security of belongings); or

3. is in possession of the house or apartment in which s/he lived on 30 April 1991 ('1991 home'); or where a member of his/her family household is in possession of his/her 1991 home; in cases where his/her 1991 home is sufficiently intact, or can be made so with minimal repairs, to provide for basic living conditions; or

4. has already been provided with alternative accommodation by a competent authority; or

5. has a member of his/her family household who has accommodation anywhere on the territory of the Republika Srpska or in the same city or municipality as the 1991 home anywhere else in the territory of Bosnia and Herzegovina, insofar as the accommodation accords with the minimum standard specified in Article 1a of this Law; or

6. has a legal right to return into possession of his/her 1991 home; and his/her 1991 home is sufficiently intact, or can be made so with minimal repairs, to provide for basic living conditions, as explained in this paragraph; and it is possible for him/her to return into possession of his/her 1991 home; or

7. whose accommodation needs are otherwise met, as defined in Article 24b of this Law.

In cases where a claim has been filed under this Law for a real property or apartment which is vacated by a multiple occupant, and no decision has been issued at the date of vacation, the competent body shall immediately issue a decision on the claim.

For the purposes of this Article, "family household" shall mean all members of the family household as of 30 April 1991; or, if they were not members of the family household as of 30 April 1991, any spouse, parents, children; or other persons registered together with a temporary user.

Article 24b

A temporary user whose accommodation needs are otherwise met shall include, among others:

1. a temporary user who voluntarily sold the real property in which s/he lived on 30 April 1991; or

2. a temporary user who voluntarily exchanged the real property or apartment in which s/he lived on 30 April 1991 and who is in possession of the

apartment or real property or has transferred it to a third party; or

3. a temporary user who refuses alternative accommodation offered in writing by the competent authority, or refuses assistance in the reconstruction of his/her residence of 30 April 1991. The competent authority shall inform the temporary user of the consequence of refusing alternative accommodation or reconstruction assistance; or

4. a temporary user who resides in the same municipality as s/he did in 1991, unless s/he can provide evidence as to why he or she cannot return to his or her 1991 home; or

5. a temporary user who was a sub-tenant in 1991; or

6. a temporary user who has sufficient disposable income, including assets, to provide for his/her own accommodation. Sufficient disposable income shall be defined as one-fourth of the applicable breadbasket, as calculated by the competent statistical institute, per current family household member, plus 200 KM; or

7. a temporary user, in a case where the owner or occupancy right holder provides him/her with a different accommodation as a tenant within the same municipality, unless the temporary user agrees in writing to another municipality elsewhere, for at least six months. The standard of accommodation shall be that set out in Article 1a of this Law; or

8. a temporary user who left his/her apartment or residential private property in the territory of Bosnia and Herzegovina between 30 April 1991 and 19 December 1998 and there was a claim for repossession of that apartment or residential private property filed, if the claim for repossession is subsequently withdrawn; or

9. a temporary user who has been allocated any state-owned, including formerly socially-owned, land since 6 April 1992, more than 150 days from the date the allocation issued pursuant to a waiver granted by the Office of the High Representative, unless s/he cancels the allocation within 60 days of the date of the confirmation or of the date this provision comes into force, whichever date is the later; or

10. a temporary user who, unless a waiver application is pending before the Office of the High Rep-

resentative, has been allocated any state-owned, including formerly socially-owned, land since 6 April 1992, unless s/he cancels the allocation within 60 days of the date this provision comes into force; or

11. a temporary user who has received housing credits, building materials, or any other form of housing construction/purchase assistance, more than 150 days from the date of receipt of the assistance or the date of receipt of the first instalment of the assistance, unless s/he cancels the assistance within 60 days of receipt of the assistance, or the first instalment of the assistance, or within 60 days of the date this provision comes into force, whichever date is the later.

For the purposes of points 9 to 11 of paragraph 1 of this Article, the competent authority shall inform the temporary user of the consequences of not cancelling the land allocation or housing construction/purchase assistance, whichever is applicable.

For the purposes of this Article, the term 'temporary user' shall include all members of the family household as defined in Article 24a paragraph 6 of this Law.

Article 25

The provisions of this Law shall also apply to the abandoned real property, the ownership of which has been acquired after 30 April 1991 under any title on sale of real property (contracts on exchange, purchase, gift, etc.).

In case of a dispute as the lawfulness of the transferred real property right, the competent authority shall suspend proceedings and refer the parties to the competent court according to the provision of the Law on General Administrative Procedures regulating preliminary issues, in order to rule on the allegation. Notwithstanding the provisions of the Law on Civil Procedures, the burden of proof shall lie upon the party claiming to have acquired rights to the real property through the transaction to establish that the transaction was conducted voluntarily and in accordance with the law. Where one of the transferred properties is located in the territory of another republic of the former SFRY, the burden of proof shall lie upon the party claiming that the transfer of property was not conducted voluntarily and in accordance with the law to demonstrate that the status of the parties prior to the transfer of property shall be restored.

Exceptionally, in case of a dispute as to the validity of the transferred real property right in which the competent authority issued a decision on repossession prior to December 29, 2001 that has not yet been enforced, the competent authority shall ex officio suspend enforcement proceedings pending a final judicial decision on the matter, under the condition that an interested party provides evidence that they have initiated proceedings before the competent court.

Article 26

The provisions of this Law regulating the manner of repossession of the real property or apartment by the owner, possessor or user shall also apply regarding repossession of the real property allocated to temporary users on the basis of rationalization (excess housing space).

A claim may also be filed under this Law for real property and apartments which were re-allocated pursuant to provisions, laws, instruments and decrees adopted or applied after 30 April 1991 which regulated the rational use of space, including but not limited to all of the laws and regulations referred to in Article 1 of this Law, and including among others Article 17 of the Law on the Use of Abandoned Property (RS Official Gazette, Nos. 3/96, 21/96); the Decree on the Accommodation of Refugees (RS Official Gazette, No. 19/95); the Decree on the Accommodation of Refugees and other Persons in the Territory of the Republika Srpska (RS Official Gazette, No. 27/93); and the Law on Amendments to the Law on Housing Relations (RS Official Gazette, Nos. 19/93, 22/93). Claims may also be filed by occupancy right holders whose occupancy rights were cancelled under the Law on Housing Relations (Law on Housing Relations, SRBH Official Gazette, Nos. 13/74, 23/76, 34/83, 12/87, 36/89; RS Official Gazette, No. 12/99).

Article 27

Where the temporary user has the right to a new contract on use of apartment under Article 2 Paragraph 3 of this Law, the Ministry for Refugees and Displaced Persons shall be authorised to conclude the contract on use of apartment in accordance with the ZOSO.

The temporary user shall have the right to a new contract on use of the apartment under Article 2

Paragraph 3 of this Law if s/he obtained the occupancy right in any of the following circumstances:

1. through transfer of the occupancy right to him/her as a spouse or as a member of the family household following the death of the previous occupancy right holder, in accordance with the ZOSO; or

2. through transfer following his/her divorce from the previous occupancy right holder; or

3. s/he was the first occupancy right holder of the apartment following its construction; or

4. through a valid contract on exchange of apartments, in accordance with the ZOSO and Article 2a of this Law.

In no case shall the temporary user have the right to a new contract on use of the apartment under Article 2, Paragraph 3 of this Law if s/he is a multiple occupant as defined in Article 24a, Paragraph 4, Points 1 to 6 or Article 24b, Paragraph 1, Points 1, 2, 9, 10, 11, or 12 of this Law or if s/he is not entitled to alternative accommodation under Article 11a, Paragraph 1, Points (2) (a) or (b) or Article 18a, Paragraph 1, Points (2) (a) or (b) of this Law.

As an exception to Article 24a, Paragraph 7 and Article 24b, Paragraph 3 of this Law, the criteria set out in the previous Paragraph of this Article shall apply only with regard to the temporary user and his or her family household as of 30 April 1991 for the purposes of this Article.

Any revalidation of a contract on use or allocation concluded in contravention of this shall be void.

The procedure by which the temporary user's right to revalidate a contract on use of the apartment is determined shall be regulated by instruction. The competent public defender shall supervise the procedure and control the conformity of revalidations of contracts on use and allocations, as well as purchases of apartments based on such revalidations or allocations, with this Article, pursuant to his/her duties as set out in the Law and by instruction.

Article 27a

A person whose right of temporary occupancy or occupancy right was cancelled under Article 2 of this Law, who spent his/her personal funds on necessary expenses for the real property or apartment, shall be entitled to recover those under the Law on Obligations (Official Gazette of the SFRY, Nos. 29/78 and 39/85; Official Gazette of the Republika Srpska, Nos. 17/93 and 3/96). Proceedings under the Law on Obligations may be commenced from the date when the previous owner or occupancy right holder regains possession of the real property or apartment.

Where the court has awarded compensation to the person referred to in paragraph 1, the owner or occupancy right holder may recover that sum from the competent authority or, in the case of an apartment, the allocation right holder under the Law on Obligations.

The competent authority shall be liable for all damage to the real property or apartment from the time it was abandoned by the owner or occupancy right holder until the time it is returned to the owner or occupancy right holder or a member of his/her 1991 household pursuant to this Law, or, in the case of real property, until the time that the property is vacated and sealed and notification has been delivered to the owner in accordance with the provisions of this Law and the Law on General Administrative Procedures. In the case of an apartment, any repairs carried out by the occupancy right holder or a member of his/her 1991 household to restore the apartment to the state it was in prior to its abandonment shall be deemed "funds with which the holder of occupancy rights removed war damage" for the purposes of the Law on Privatization of State Owned Apartments (RS OG 11/00, 18/00, 35/01 and 47/02).

Article 28

The conditions for and the manner of the purchase of an apartment for the occupancy right holders to whom the apartments have been returned in accordance with this Law shall be regulated by a separate law.

Article 29

The Minister of Refugees and Displaced Persons shall pass an instruction on the application of Articles 8 through 11 and Articles 15 through 18 of this Law within 30 days from the date of the entry into force of this Law.

Article 30

All proceedings commenced under the Law on the Use of Abandoned Property (RS Official Gazette,

Nos. 3/96, 21/96) before the Law was repealed shall be terminated ex lege, regardless of the stage of the proceedings, with the exception of repossession claims to apartments which shall be processed in accordance with this Law.

Article 31

An apartment from Article 22 of this Law shall be administered by the Ministry for Refugees and Displaced Persons and used for the purpose of temporary use until all claims for the repossession of private property, made within 90 days of this provision coming into force, and for socially-owned property, made as defined in Article 16 of this Law, in that municipality are resolved. Upon expiration of this period, the apartment shall, after six months, be returned to the control of the allocation right holder pursuant to Article 22 of this Law. This paragraph shall apply to all apartments, whether or not they were declared abandoned.

The right to a temporary use of an apartment in terms of the previous paragraph shall be given to a person referred to in Article 35 of this Law, in accordance with the standard of Article 1a of this Law.

A temporary permit granted under this Article shall be given for a period of not longer than six months. The temporary occupant referred to in Paragraph 3 of this Article may request extension of the time limit for the use of apartment, to expire at the latest by the deadline specified in Paragraph 1.

In deciding on the claim for extension of the temporary permit, the competent authority must determine in a procedure whether the temporary user continues to be entitled to alternative accommodation pursuant to this Law. The competent authority can either issue a new temporary permit or indicate on the previous permit that the permit has been extended for another six months, including the expiration date of the permit. If the competent authority decides that the temporary user is not entitled to alternative accommodation, it shall order the temporary user to vacate the apartment within 15 days.

If the temporary user at any time ceases to meet the conditions for entitlement to alternative accommodation in accordance with the Law, the competent authority shall ex officio issue a decision cancelling the temporary permit and ordering the temporary user to vacate the apartment within 15 days.

Article 32

A claim must also be filed under this Law for an apartment, which was damaged or destroyed, provided that the occupancy right holder of the apartment lost possession of the claimed apartment before 19 December 1998. If a claimed apartment is reconstructed, the claimant shall return into possession of the apartment without limitation or restriction.

As an exception to Article 16 of the Law, the occupancy right holder may file a claim for repossession of a destroyed or damaged apartment within six months of this Law coming into effect.

V. – ENTITLEMENTS TO ALTERNATIVE ACCOMMODATION

Article 33

A person using a real property or an apartment without legal basis shall be evicted, at the latest within 15 days of the day of issuance of the decision, and the owner, possessor or user of the real property or the occupancy right holder of the apartment and/or any member of his/her household shall be entitled to repossess the real property or apartment without any restriction or limitation. The body responsible for providing alternative accommodation shall not be obliged to provide alternative accommodation under this Law to an illegal user.

The competent authority shall ex officio pass a decision to vacate a real property or apartment immediately, and at the latest within 15 days of the issuance of the decision, in cases where the current user is an illegal occupant. The affected person has the right to file an appeal against the decision, but the appeal does not suspend the eviction.

In a case of eviction an illegal user of a real property or apartment, relevant laws on displaced persons and refugees shall be applied to determine if s/he is entitled to accommodation. If the person is not entitled to accommodation under a law on displaced persons and refugees, the competent authority for social protection in the municipality where the real property or apartment is located shall determine whether such a person is entitled to any form of assistance. The failure of the competent authority to determine the entitlement of a

temporary user or other user of a real property or an apartment or provide accommodation or assistance shall not delay eviction.

Article 34

When a temporary user is required to vacate a real property or an apartment in accordance with the Law, the competent authority of the Ministry for Refugees and Displaced Persons shall determine whether the temporary user has the right to alternative accommodation under this Law.

In determining whether a temporary user is entitled to alternative accommodation, the competent authority shall determine in the procedure and within the deadlines for making a decision under Articles 9 and 11, and Articles 17 and 18 of this Law:

1. where the temporary user lived on 30 April 1991;

2. in what capacity the temporary user occupied the apartment or real property where s/he lived on 30 April 1991;

3. whether it is possible to live in the apartment or real property;

4. whether the temporary user or a member of his/her family household from 30 April 1991 currently possesses that apartment or real property;

5. whether s/he voluntarily exchanged or sold the apartment in question or real estate in his/her possession;

6. or any other relevant facts which show that the temporary user's housing needs are otherwise met.

In accordance with the previous paragraph, multiple occupants, as defined in Articles 24a and 24b of this Law, and temporary users who must vacate within 15 days from the date of the delivery of a decision under Article 11a or Article 18a of this Law, among others, shall not be entitled to alternative accommodation.

Article 35

A temporary user of a real property or an apartment who is required to vacate the real property or an apartment and is entitled to alternative accommodation in accordance with this Law shall be provided with alternative accommodation in accordance with this Law by the competent authority on the territory of which she/he had his/her latest residence. The temporary user shall be obliged to vacate the real property within the deadline set under Article 11 of this Law; or vacate the apartment within the deadline set under Article 18 of this Law.

A temporary user of a real property or an apartment who is required to vacate the real property or an apartment and is entitled to alternative accommodation in accordance with this Law shall be provided with alternative accommodation on the territory of the Republika Srpska in accordance with this Law by the competent authority on the territory of which she/he had his/her latest residence.

The temporary user shall be obliged to vacate the real property within the deadline set under Article 11 of this Law; or vacate the apartment within the deadline set under Article 18 of this Law.

Article 36

In case that the Ministry for Refugees and Displaced Persons is unable to provide alternative accommodation, other responsible bodies including the Ministry for Urban Planning, the Ministry for Social Welfare, the Ministry of Defence, companies, firms and Municipalities shall be obliged to make available accommodation which is at their disposal for the purposes of providing alternative accommodation under this Law.

VI. – PENALTY PROVISIONS

Article 37

The competent body shall be fined 1000 to 5000 KM for the following minor offences:

1. if it violates Article 1 of this Law and continues to apply the Law on Use of Abandoned Property;

2. if it fails to accept claims as set out in Article 8, or Article 15 of this Law;

3. if it fails to take into account the presumption that persons who have left their apartments between 30 April 1991 and 19 December 1998 shall be considered to be refugees and displaced persons under Annex 7 of the General Framework Agreement for Peace in Bosnia and Herzegovina, as set out in Article 14, paragraphs 1 and 2 of this Law;

4. if it fails to order in the Decision (Article 11, Paragraph 1 or Article 18, Paragraph 1 of the Law) the vacating of the real property or apartment within 15 days in accordance with Article 33 , paragraph 1 and Article 35 , paragraph 1 of the Law;

5. if it fails to allow immediate repossession by an owner, possessor, or user of a vacant real property, as set out in Article 11, paragraph 2, or Article 18, paragraph 3 of the Law;

6. if it fails to process an eviction request according to this Law and the Law on General Administrative Procedures;

7. if it fails to hand over the real property or apartment in accordance with Article 24 of the Law;

8. if it fails to take the required action against a multiple occupant, as set out in Article 24a, paragraph 3, or if it fails to issue a decision according to Article 24a, paragraph 5 of the Law.

The responsible person in the competent authority shall also be fined 200 to 1000 KM for a violation of paragraph 1 of this Article.

In addition to the above, a person who is a multiple occupant, as defined:

1. in Article 24a, paragraph 4, Items 1, 2, 3, or 7 of the Law and who fails to comply with the deadline to vacate the real property or apartment specified in the decision shall be fined 500 to 5000 KM;

2. in Article 24a, paragraph 4, Items 4 to 6 of the Law and who fails to comply with the deadline to vacate the real property or apartment specified in the decision shall be fined 250 to 1000 KM.

Penalty proceedings according to paragraphs 1 to 3 of this Article shall be carried out in accordance with the Law on Minor Offences. The local competency of the Court shall be determined according to the location of the seat of the competent body which violated the provisions of this Article or the seat of the competent body where the responsible person is carrying out his/her official duties, or the permanent residence of the multiple occupant.

Article 38

This Law shall enter into force on the 8th day after its publication in the Official Gazette of the Republika Srpska.

5.12. Law on Implementation of the Decisions of the Commission for Real Property Claims of Displaced Persons and Refugees (Federation of BiH) (2003)

Article 1

This Law shall regulate the administrative enforcement, by way of return into possession, on the territory of the Federation of Bosnia and Herzegovina, of decisions of the Commission for Real Property Claims of Displaced Persons and Refugees (hereinafter referred to as the "Commission"), created under Annex 7 of the General Framework Agreement for Peace in Bosnia and Herzegovina.

Article 2

Decisions of the Commission are final and binding from the day of their adoption.

Decisions of the Commission confirm the rights to real properties of the person(s) named in the decision, and require the responsible enforcement organs to take measures as set out in this Law.

Decisions of the Commission also carry the force of legal evidence that may be used in administrative, judicial or other legal proceedings.

Article 3

The enforcement of a decision of the Commission shall be conducted administratively, if the persons referred to in Article 4, Paragraphs 1 or 2 (requestor for enforcement) request so.

The administrative body responsible for property legal affairs in the municipality where the property is located shall enforce decisions of the Commission relating to real property owned by citizens upon the request of persons referred to in Article 4, Paragraph 1 of this Law.

The administrative body responsible for housing affairs in the municipality where the apartment is located shall enforce decisions of the Commission relating to an apartment for which there is an occupancy right upon the request of the persons referred to in Article 4, Paragraph 2 of this Law.

Article 4

The following persons are entitled to file a request for enforcement of a decision of the Commission relating to real property owned by citizens:

the right holder specified in the decision of the Commission;

the heirs of the right holder specified in the decision of the Commission.

The following persons are entitled to file a request for enforcement of a decision of the Commission relating to an apartment for which there is an occupancy right:

the occupancy right holder referred to in a decision of the Commission;

the persons who, in compliance with the Law on Housing Relations, are considered to be the members of the family household of the occupancy right holder referred to in the decision of the Commission, as of the date specified in the dispositive of the Commission decision.

If a request for enforcement of the Commission's decision is submitted by a person not named in the preamble of the decision the administrative body shall decide whether s/he can be considered as a member of the family household of the occupancy right holder identified in the decision.

Other persons, including those to whom these rights were transferred after the date specified in the dispositive of the Commission decision, are entitled to submit the decision of the Commission in administrative or court proceedings as legal evidence, in accordance with Article 2, paragraph 3 of this Law.

Article 5

The right to file a request for enforcement of a decision of the Commission confirming a right to private property is not subject to any statute of limitation.

The request for enforcement of a decision of the Commission confirming occupancy rights must be submitted within eighteen months from the date when the Commission decision was issued.

Article 6

The request for enforcement of a Commission decision relating to real property owned by citizens shall include two certified photocopies of the decision of the Commission. The request for enforcement of a Commission decision relating to occupancy rights shall include three certified copies of the decision of the Commission.

Article 7

The administrative organ responsible for enforcement of a Commission decision is obliged to issue a conclusion on the permission of enforcement, within a period of 30 days from the date when the request for enforcement was submitted.

The administrative organ which is responsible for enforcement of decisions of the Commission shall not require any confirmation of the enforceability of the decision from the Commission or from any other body.

The administrative organ which is responsible for enforcement of a decision of the Commission shall obtain all necessary information about the identity of the enforcee (as defined in Article 9 of this Law), together with details of the legal basis, if any, on which the enforcee is inhabiting the property or apartment.

The conclusion referred to in paragraph 1 of this Article shall contain:

in the case of property or apartments that have been declared abandoned, a decision terminating the municipal administration of the property;

a decision on repossession of the property or apartment by the right holder or other requestor for enforcement;

a decision terminating the right of the temporary user (where there is one) to use the property or apartment;

a time limit for the enforcee to vacate the property;

a decision on whether the enforcee is entitled to accommodation in accordance with applicable laws;

a requirement that the premises shall be vacated of all persons and possessions, other than those belonging to the person authorised to return into possession.

The time limit for vacating the property shall be the minimum time limit applicable under the Law on Cessation of the Application of the Law on Temporarily Abandoned Real Property Owned by Citizens and the Law on Cessation of the Application of the Law on Abandoned Apartments. No extension of this time limit shall be permitted.

If the requestor for enforcement has submitted a claim for repossession at the responsible administrative body in relation to the same property or apartment in accordance with the Law on Cessation of the Application of the Law on Abandoned Apartments or the Law on Cessation of the Application of the Law on Temporary Abandoned Real Property Owned by the Citizens and the requestor for enforcement subsequently submits a decision of the Commission for enforcement, the responsible administrative body shall join the proceedings for enforcement of both decisions and issue a conclusion on the permission of enforcement in accordance with this Article.

In case a person claims a legal interest in the property or apartment at issue which was acquired after the date referred to in the operative part of the Commission decision and can show a valid contract on exchange or transfer of rights, the competent administrative organ shall suspend proceedings and shall refer the parties to the competent court according to the provisions of the Law on Administrative Procedures (Official Gazette of the Federation of Bosnia and Herzegovina, No. 2/98) regulating preliminary issues, in order to rule on the allegation.

Exceptionally, in the case where a person claims a legal interest in the property or apartment at issue which was acquired after the date referred to in the operative part of the Commission decision, in which the competent administrative organ issued a conclusion on permission of enforcement prior to the date of entry into force of this Law and that has not yet been enforced, the competent administrative organ shall ex officio suspend enforcement proceedings pending a final judicial decision on the matter, under the condition that an interested party provides evidence that he/she has initiated proceedings before the competent court and can show a valid contract on exchange or transfer of rights.

Article 8

The administrative organ which is responsible for enforcement of a decision of the Commission is obliged to deliver one certified copy of the decision of the Commission together with the conclusion on permission of enforcement, within 5 days from the date of the issuance of the conclusion on permission of enforcement, to any person who is in possession of the property or apartment referred to in the decision and, in case of occupancy rights, also to the allocation right holder of the apartment.

Article 9

The enforcement of a decision of the Commission shall be conducted against the person who is in possession of the property or apartment designated in the decision, with or without legal basis ('enforcee').

The enforcement shall also be conducted against any third person using the property or apartment, even in the case where an enforcee from paragraph 1 of this Article voluntarily vacated the property or apartment at issue.

The enforcement of a decision shall be conducted regardless of whether the property or apartment referred to in the decision was declared abandoned or not and irrespective of any other decisions or regulations relating to its legal status.

The administrative body competent for enforcement shall suspend the commenced enforcement if it is established that the enforcee has voluntarily complied with the decision of the Commission.

Article 10

The right holder referred to in the Commission decision and/or any other person who held a legal interest in the property or apartment at issue on the date referred to in the dispositive of the Commission decision, is entitled to submit a request for reconsideration to the Commission, in accordance with Commission regulations. The regularity of the Commission decision may be reviewed only through the reconsideration procedure referred to in Article 11 of this Law.

Article 11

On receipt of a request for reconsideration, the Commission may notify the competent administrative body responsible for the enforcement of the Commission decision of the pending request for reconsideration.

The competent administrative body shall not suspend the enforcement of the Commission decision, unless it has received official notification from the Commission specifically requesting suspension pending the outcome of the reconsideration.

After examining the request for reconsideration, the Commission may:

reject the request as being inadmissible, not submitted within due time or as submitted by an unauthorised person;

reject the request as being unfounded; or

accept the request, revoke its previous decision and issue a new decision.

The decision of the Commission accepting the reconsideration request and revoking its previous decision or refusing to admit or rejecting the reconsideration request shall be delivered to the person who requested the reconsideration and all other persons who received the original decision, and to the administrative body responsible for enforcement.

Article 12

The appeal against the conclusion on the permission of enforcement of the decision of the Commission shall be submitted to the responsible second instance body in accordance with the Law on Administrative Procedure by the administrative body that issued the conclusion on the permission of enforcement, within 8 days from the date of delivery of the conclusion on the permission of enforcement.

The grounds for the appeal shall be limited to the following:

the decision of the Commission upon which the conclusion on the permission of enforcement was based has not been issued at all or is revoked by the Commission in its reconsideration proceedings;

whether the enforcee is entitled to alternative accommodation or the time limit provided for the enforcee to vacate the property is in accordance with the applicable laws; or other reasons for appeals against conclusions on the permission of enforcement which are in accordance with the Law on Administrative Procedure.

Article 13

The competent court shall determine whether the transfer of rights to the appellant was conducted voluntarily and in accordance with the law.

If the transfer of rights was conducted between 1 April 1992 and 14 December 1995, and its validity is disputed by the respondent, the burden of proof shall lie on the party claiming to have acquired rights to the property under the transaction to establish that the transaction was conducted voluntarily and in accordance with the law. Where one of the transferred properties is located in the territory of another republic of the former SFRY, the burden of proof shall lie upon the party claiming that the transfer of property was not conducted voluntarily and in accordance with the Law to demonstrate that the status of the parties prior to the transfer of property shall be restored.

If the validity of the transfer has been determined in previous proceedings which took place prior to the entry into force of this Law, the decision taken in the previous proceedings shall be null and void.

The court may make whatever orders are necessary to give effect to its decision, including orders setting aside legal transactions, orders for making or erasing entries in the appropriate public books/registers, and orders lifting any order for suspension of the administrative proceedings.

The relevant parties to the appeal shall notify the competent administrative body of the court's decision.

The responsible administrative body shall resume enforcement proceedings as required, or discontinue proceedings (obustavi) in accordance with the court's decisions.

[. . .]

5.13. Law on Implementation of the Decisions of the Commission for Real Property Claims of Displaced Persons and Refugees (Republika Srpska) (2003)

Article 1

This Law shall regulate the administrative enforcement, by way of return into possession, on the territory of the Republika Srpska, of decisions of the Commission for Real Property Claims of Displaced Persons and Refugees (hereinafter referred to as the "Commission"), created under Annex 7 of the General Framework Agreement for Peace in Bosnia and Herzegovina.

Article 2

Decisions of the Commission are final and binding from the day of their adoption.

Decisions of the Commission confirm the rights to real properties of the person(s) named in the decision, and require the responsible enforcement organs to take measures as set out in this Law.

Decisions of the Commission also carry the force of legal evidence that may be used in administrative, judicial or other legal proceedings.

Article 3

The enforcement of a decision of the Commission shall be conducted administratively, if the persons referred to in Article 4, Paragraphs 1 or 2 (requestor for enforcement) request so.

The responsible body of the Ministry of Refugees and Displaced Persons in the municipality where the property is located shall enforce decisions of the Commission relating to real property owned by citizens or to apartments for which there is an occupancy right upon the request of a requestor for enforcement.

Article 4

The following persons are entitled to file a request for enforcement of a decision of the Commission relating to real property owned by citizens:

the right holder specified in the decision of the Commission.

The following persons are entitled to file a request for enforcement of a decision of the Commission relating to an apartment for which there is an occupancy right:

- the heirs of the right holder specified in the decision of the Commission;

- the occupancy right holder referred to in a decision of the Commission;

- the persons who, in compliance with the Law on Housing Relations, are considered to be the members of the family household of the occupancy right holder referred to in the decision of the Commission, as of the date specified in the dispositive of the Commission decision.

If a request for enforcement of the Commission's decision is submitted by a person not named in the preamble of the decision the administrative body shall decide whether s/he can be considered as a member of the family household of the occupancy right holder identified in the decision.

Other persons, including those to whom these rights were transferred after the date specified in the dispositive of the Commission decision, are entitled to submit the decision of the Commission in administrative or court proceedings as legal evidence, in accordance with Article 2, paragraph 3 of this Law.

Article 5

The right to file a request for enforcement of a decision of the Commission confirming a right to private property is not subject to any statute of limitation.

The request for enforcement of a decision of the Commission confirming occupancy rights must be submitted within eighteen months from the date when the Commission decision was issued.

Article 6

The request for enforcement of a Commission decision relating to real property owned by citizens shall include two certified photocopies of the decision of the Commission. The request for enforcement of a Commission decision relating to occupancy rights shall include three certified copies of the decision of the Commission.

Article 7

The administrative organ responsible for enforcement of a Commission decision is obliged to issue a conclusion on the permission of enforcement, within a period of 30 days from the date when the request for enforcement was submitted.

The administrative organ which is responsible for enforcement of decisions of the Commission shall not require any confirmation of the enforceability of the decision from the Commission or from any other body.

The administrative organ which is responsible for enforcement of a decision of the Commission shall obtain all necessary information about the identity of the enforcee (as defined in Article 9 of this Law), together with details of the legal basis, if any, on which the enforcee is inhabiting the property or apartment.

The conclusion referred to in paragraph 1 of this Article shall contain:

- a decision on repossession of the property or apartment by the right holder or other requestor for enforcement;

- a decision terminating the right of the temporary user (where there is one) to use the property or apartment;

- a time limit for the enforcee to vacate the property;

- a decision on whether the enforcee is entitled to accommodation in accordance with applicable laws;

- a requirement that the premises shall be vacated of all persons and possessions, other than those belonging to the person authorised to return into possession.

The time limit for vacating the property shall be the minimum time limit applicable under the Law on Cessation of the Application of the Law on the Use of Abandoned Property. No extension of this time limit shall be permitted.

If the requestor for enforcement has submitted a claim for repossession at the responsible administrative organ in relation to the same property or apartment in accordance with the Law on Cessation of the Application of the Law on the Use of Abandoned Property and the requestor for enforcement subsequently submits a decision of the Commission for enforcement, the responsible administrative body shall join the proceedings for enforcement of both decisions and issue a conclusion on the permission of enforcement in accordance with this Article.

In case a person claims a legal interest in the property or apartment at issue which was acquired after the date referred to in the operative part of the Commission decision and can show a valid contract on exchange or transfer of rights, the competent administrative organ shall suspend proceedings and shall refer the parties to the competent court according to the provisions of the Law on General Administrative Procedures (Official Gazette of the Republika Srpska, No. 13/02) regulating preliminary issues, in order to rule on the allegation.

Exceptionally, in the case where a person claims a legal interest in the property or apartment at issue which was acquired after the date referred to in the operative part of the Commission decision, in which the competent administrative organ issued a conclusion on permission of enforcement prior to the date of entry into force of this Law and that has not yet been enforced, the competent administrative organ shall ex officio suspend enforcement proceedings pending a final judicial decision on the matter, under the condition that an interested party provides evidence that he/she has initiated proceedings before the competent court and can show a valid contract on exchange or transfer of rights.

Article 8

The administrative organ which is responsible for enforcement of a decision of the Commission is obliged to deliver one certified copy of the decision of the Commission together with the conclusion on permission of enforcement, within 5 days from the date of the issuance of the conclusion on permission of enforcement, to any person who is in possession of the property or apartment referred to in the decision and, in case of occupancy rights, also to the allocation right holder of the apartment.

Article 9

The enforcement of a decision of the Commission shall be conducted against the person who is in possession of the property or apartment designated in the decision, with or without legal basis ('enforcee').

The enforcement shall also be conducted against any third person using the property or apartment, even in the case where an enforcee from paragraph 1 of this Article voluntarily vacated the property or apartment at issue.

The enforcement of a decision shall be conducted regardless of whether the property or apartment referred to in the decision was declared abandoned or not and irrespective of any other decisions or regulations relating to its legal status.

The administrative body competent for enforcement shall suspend the commenced enforcement if it is established that the enforcee has voluntarily complied with the decision of the Commission.

Article 10

The right holder referred to in the Commission decision and/or any other person who held a legal interest in the property or apartment at issue on the date referred to in the dispositive of the Commission decision, is entitled to submit a request for reconsideration to the Commission, in accordance with Commission regulations. The regularity of the Commission decision may be reviewed only through the reconsideration procedure referred to in Article 11 of this Law.

Article 11

On receipt of a request for reconsideration, the Commission may notify the competent administrative body responsible for the enforcement of the Commission decision of the pending request for reconsideration.

The competent administrative body shall not suspend the enforcement of the Commission decision, unless it has received official notification from the Commission specifically requesting suspension pending the outcome of the reconsideration.

After examining the request for reconsideration, the Commission may:

- reject the request as being inadmissible, not submitted within due time or as submitted by an unauthorised person;
- reject the request as being unfounded; or
- accept the request, revoke its previous decision and issue a new decision.

The decision of the Commission accepting the reconsideration request and revoking its previous decision or refusing to admit or rejecting the reconsideration request shall be delivered to the person who requested the reconsideration and all other persons who received the original decision, and to the administrative body responsible for enforcement.

Article 12

The appeal against the conclusion on the permission of enforcement of the decision of the Commission shall be submitted to the responsible second instance body in accordance with the Law on General Administrative Proceedings by the administrative body that issued the conclusion on the permission of enforcement, within 8 days from the date of delivery of the conclusion on the permission of enforcement.

The grounds for the appeal shall be limited to the following:

- the decision of the Commission upon which the conclusion on the permission of enforcement was based has not been issued at all or is revoked by the Commission in its reconsideration proceedings;

- whether the enforcee is entitled to alternative accommodation or the time limit provided for the enforcee to vacate the property is in accordance with the applicable laws; or

- other reasons for appeals against conclusions on the permission of enforcement which are in accordance with the Law on General Administrative Proceedings.

Article 13

The competent court shall determine whether the transfer of rights to the appellant was conducted voluntarily and in accordance with the law.

If the transfer of rights was conducted between 1 April 1992 and 14 December 1995, and its validity is disputed by the respondent, the burden of proof shall lie on the party claiming to have acquired rights to the property under the transaction to establish that the transaction was conducted voluntarily and in accordance with the law. Where one of the transferred properties is located in the territory of another republic of the former SFRY, the burden of proof shall lie upon the party claiming that the transfer of property was not conducted voluntarily and in accordance with the Law to demonstrate that the status of the parties prior to the transfer of property shall be restored.

If the validity of the transfer has been determined in previous proceedings which took place prior to the entry into force of this Law, the decision taken in the previous proceedings shall be null and void.

The court may make whatever orders are necessary to give effect to its decision, including orders setting aside legal transactions, orders for making or erasing entries in the appropriate public books/registers, and orders lifting any order for suspension of the administrative proceedings.

The relevant parties to the appeal shall notify the competent administrative body of the court's decision.

The responsible administrative body shall resume enforcement proceedings as required, or discontinue proceedings in accordance with the court's decisions.

[. . .]

5.14. Commission for Real Property Claims of Displaced Persons and Refugees – Book of Regulations on Confirmation of Occupancy Rights of Displaced Persons and Refugees (2003)

[. . .]

I. GENERAL PROVISIONS

Article 1

This Book of Regulations, with the aim of confirming occupancy rights of displaced persons and refugees through the Commission for Real Property Claims of Displaced Persons and Refugees (in following text: 'the Commission'), shall regulate the criteria based on which claims shall be considered and decisions on confirmation of occupancy rights of displaced persons and refugees shall be made. In addition, this Book of Regulations shall regulate the procedure for submitting claims for confirmation of occupancy rights, the decision-making procedure on these claims, the determination, contents and form of decisions confirming occupancy rights, the distribution and delivery of decisions, the moment from which the decisions of the Commission become final and binding, and the procedure for reconsideration of issued decisions confirming occupancy rights, the application of decisions, and other issues of importance to the decision-making process on confirmation of occupancy rights of displaced persons and refugees.

Article 2

Confirmation of occupancy rights of displaced persons and refugees, for the purposes of this Book of Regulations, means confirming occupancy rights to apartments to the persons who held this right on 1 April 1992.

Article 3

For the purposes of this Book of Regulations, persons who abandoned their apartments in the period between April 30, 1991 and April 4, 1998 and who are not in possession of these apartments are considered to be displaced persons and refugees.

The refugee or displaced person status of a person who submits a claim for return of an occupancy right to the Commission is presumed.

II. Criteria Based on Which Claims Shall Be Considered and Decisions Shall Be Made on Confirmation of Occupancy Rights of Displaced Persons and Refugees

Article 4

The Commission shall consider and deliver decisions on confirmation of occupancy rights of displaced persons and refugees on the basis of claims which are submitted in the appropriate form by holders of occupancy rights or other eligible persons, and which are submitted in due time within the deadlines determined by this Book of Regulations, by the Law on the Cessation of the Application of the Law on Abandoned Apartments and by the Law on the Cessation of the Application of the Law on Using the Abandoned Property and on the basis of relevant evidence relating to occupancy rights as provided in this Book of Regulations.

Article 5

The Commission shall make a decision on a claim if:

a) it is determined that the claim was filed by an eligible person; and

b) the claim satisfies one of the conditions stated in Article 7 of this Book of Regulations;

and

c) the claim was filed in due time; and

d) there is evidence based on which the Commission may deliver a decision on confirming the occupancy right to the person who was holder of an occupancy right on 1 April 1992; or

e) the Commission was unable to obtain relevant evidence confirming the claimed occupancy right of an eligible person, although measures to obtain such evidence were undertaken.

Article 6

It shall be regarded that a claim for confirmation of an occupancy right was submitted by an eligible person if the claim was submitted by:

a) a person who was the holder of an occupancy right to a certain apartment on 1 April 1992; or

b) a person who, in accordance with the Law on Housing Relations which was in effect in BiH on 1 April 1992, is regarded as member of the family household of the occupancy right holder to a certain apartment on 1 April 1992; or

c) a person authorised to submit a claim for confirmation of an occupancy right on behalf of the holder of an occupancy right to a certain apartment on 1 April 1992 or on behalf of a member of his/her family household.

Article 7

It shall be regarded that a claim to the Commission for confirmation of an occupancy right was justified:

a) if it was not possible for an eligible person to submit a claim to the competent first instance body, although serious intentions were held and concrete measures to submit the claim were undertaken; or

b) if the claimant was not served with a decision made by the competent body on his/her claim, within a period of 45 days after the date of submission of the claim to the competent body; or

c) if the claimant received a negative decision of the competent body upon his/her claim for repossession of his/her apartment, or if a third person filed an appeal against a positive decision which the claimant received; or

d) if the claim was submitted to the Commission prior to the coming into effect of this Book of Regulations; or

e) if the claim was submitted prior to the commencement of the relevant law referred to in Article 4 of this Book of Regulations in the Entity in which the apartment is located.

Article 8

As an exception to Article 7 of this Book of Regulations, the Commission shall accept as justified, claims submitted by claimants who did not submit or attempted to submit in due time a claim to the competent administrative body, if they claimed to the Commission prior to expiry of the deadline for submitting a claim to the administrative body.

If the claim was submitted to the Commission in due time, but after expiry of the deadline for submitting a claim to the competent administrative body and without any evidence that the claimant submitted or made an attempt to submit a claim to the competent administrative body, the Commission shall assume, unless the evidence in the claim file proves otherwise, that the claimant attempted to submit a claim to the competent administrative body in due time. The claim shall be accepted as justified, without any additional checks.

Article 9

It shall be regarded that a claim for confirmation of an occupancy right was submitted in due time if:

a) it was submitted to the Commission within the deadlines stipulated by the relevant laws referred to in Article 4 of this Book of Regulations; or

b) it was submitted to the Commission no later than 60 days beginning with the last day on which, under the provisions of the relevant laws referred to in Article 4 of this Book of Regulations, a claim for repossession of an apartment could have been submitted to a first-instance body; or

c) the claim was submitted to the Commission prior to the coming into effect of this Book of Regulations; or

d) the claim was submitted prior to the commencement of a relevant law referred to in Article 4 of this Book of Regulations in the Entity in which the apartment is located.

Article 10

It shall be regarded that the relevant evidence for making a decision on confirmation of an occupancy right is available if the Commission determines that the claim was based on one of the following basic types of evidence for confirmation of an occupancy right:

a) Contract on apartment usage; or

b) Contract on apartment exchange; or

c) Court decision confirming the occupancy right (with the clause of validity); or

d) Decision of a competent administrative body replacing the contract on apartment usage with the clause of validity; or

e) Excerpt from official records of holders of occupancy rights which indicates the holder of the occupancy right on 1 April 1992.

If the Commission is in possession of any one of the basic types of evidence from the previous paragraph, a decision on confirmation of an occupancy right can be proposed and adopted without further discussion.

Article 11

In the event that the Commission is not in possession of any of the basic types of evidence stated in Article 10, the Commission can confirm an occupancy right based on other types of supporting evidence, such as:

a) Decision on apartment usage (decision on allocation of apartment);

b) Decision on apartment rent;

c) Apartment rent slip;

d) Decision by which an apartment is declared abandoned;

e) Decision by which an apartment is allocated to another person for his/her temporary usage;

f) Certificate of place of residence at claimed apartment;

g) Utility bills; or

h) Other appropriate evidence.

When considering claims for confirmation of occupancy rights for which only the supporting types of evidence referred to in the previous paragraph are available, the Commission shall make a decision having regard to all of the available evidence and taking into consideration the connections between and quality of the different types of evidence.

Article 12

The provisions of this Book of Regulations shall apply to all apartments regardless of whether the apartment was declared abandoned or not.

III. SUBMISSION OF CLAIMS FOR CONFIRMATION OF OCCUPANCY RIGHTS

Article 13

Claims for confirmation of occupancy rights shall be submitted in the form stipulated by the Commission.

Article 14

Claims may be submitted by eligible persons as defined in Article 6 of this Book of Regulations.

Claims shall be submitted to the Regional Offices of the Commission in BiH and abroad, or to other organizations authorized to collect claims on the Commission's behalf.

Article 15

Together with the claim for confirmation of an occupancy right, the claimant shall present originals or verified photocopies of documentation which can confirm his/her identity, as follows:

a) a personal ID card or any other document based on which the identity of the claimant can positively be confirmed – if the claim is submitted by a person who seeks confirmation of an occupancy right; or

b) a personal ID card or any other document based on which the identity of the claimant can positively be confirmed, and corresponding documents which may prove that the claimant is a member of the family household of the person who was the holder of an occupancy right on 1 April 1992 – if the claim is submitted by a member of the family household of the occupancy right holder; or

c) if the claim is submitted by an authorised representative on behalf of a person who was an occupancy right holder, or was a member of the family household of an occupancy right holder, on 1 April 1992 – a verified power of attorney and personal ID card or any other document based on which the identity of the authorised representative can positively be confirmed.

Article 16

If the claim falls within Article 7, Item a)–d), the claimant shall present, in addition to any of the forms of evidence stated in Article 15, originals or verified photocopies of:

a) receipt or photocopy of the claim for repossession of the apartment filed with the competent first-instance body, from which it appears that the claim was filed within the deadlines stipulated by relevant laws and not less than 45 days before submission of the claim to the Commission; or

b) a decision of the competent first-instance body on a claim for repossession of the claimed apartment; or

c) receipt or photocopy of an appeal, filed in due time against the decision of the first-instance body on the claim for repossession of the apartment; or

d) decision of the second-instance body on the appeal brought against the decision of the first-instance body on the claim for repossession of the apartment; or

e) receipt of registered mail, from which it could be concluded that the sent item was a claim for repossession of an apartment to the competent first-instance body. The receipt must be dated no later than the last day on which, under the relevant laws referred to in Article 4 of this Book of Regulations a claim for repossession of an apartment could have been submitted to a first-instance body; and not less than 45 days before submission of the claim to the Commission; or

f) receipt of registered mail, from which it could be concluded that the claimant attempted to send a claim for repossession of an apartment to the competent first-instance body. If the postal authorities have refused to issue such a receipt, the claimant may submit a signed statement describing his/her attempt. A receipt or statement submitted under this paragraph must be dated no later than the last day on which a claim for repossession of an apartment could have been submitted to a first-instance body in accordance with the relevant laws referred to in Article 4 of this Book of Regulations.

Article 17

If the evidence required by Article 15 is not presented with the claim, the Commission shall not register the claim.

If the evidence required by Article 16 is not presented with the claim, the Commission may reject the claim as inadmissible (*odbaciti*), refuse (*odbiti*) the claim, or conclude that the claim should be supplemented with the required evidence.

Article 18

In addition, a claimant may present originals or verified photocopies of basic forms of evidence or supporting evidence of an occupancy right.

If a claimant is not in possession of any basic forms of evidence or supporting evidence of an occupancy right, the Commission shall register the claim and undertake activities to obtain such evidence.

Article 19

The Commission shall strike out a claim or a part of claim if it establishes that:

- the claimant repossessed the claimed apartment, or
- the claimant submitted the claim for the same apartment to the relevant administrative body, or
- the claimant lost interest for pursuing the claim since he/she failed to respond to a written invitation to remove deficiencies in the claim, or the written invitation has not been delivered to him/her since he/she failed to inform the Commission about a change of address, or
- it has decided all primary properties within a claim and the remaining part of the claim relates to secondary properties within the same political municipality.

The Commission shall make an individual Report on Strike Out for each claim affected stating applicable reasons for strike out.

The Report on Strike Out shall not be delivered to the claimant.

The Commission shall notify claimants on the categories of claims that have been struck out through a public information campaign.

IV. Procedure for Decision Making on Claims for Confirmation of Occupancy Rights

Article 20

Claims for confirmation of occupancy rights shall be registered with attached evidence on the basis of which it shall be possible to determine whether the claims have been submitted in the proper form, whether they were submitted by eligible persons and whether they were submitted in due time and in accordance with other requirements.

Claims that are not submitted by eligible persons shall be rejected as inadmissible (*odbaciti*).

The Commission shall decide on the requirements stated in paragraph 2 of this Article.

Article 21

If the claimant is unable or unwilling to present any evidence of an occupancy right, the Commission shall nevertheless register and consider the claim.

Article 22

If a claim is registered which does not fulfill the requirements stated in this Book of Regulations, it shall be rejected as inadmissible (*odbacen*) or refused by the Commission (*odbiti*).

Article 23

Claims for confirmation of occupancy rights shall be delivered to the Executive Office (Legal Department), together with photocopies of the presented evidence.

Article 24

The Legal Department shall review the delivered claims and assess the evidence on the basis of which draft decisions are prepared.

The Legal Department is responsible for preparing draft decisions on the submitted claims.

Article 25

The Legal Department prepares draft decisions by which the claim may be:

a) adopted; or

b) rejected as inadmissible; or

c) refused.

Article 26

A Legal Working Group of the Commission shall regularly review the draft decisions to ensure that they are consistent with this Book of Regulations.

After reviewing draft decisions, a Legal Working Group of the Commission shall establish decision proposals and present them to the Commission for consideration and adoption.

Article 27

The Commission decides on the proposed decisions at its plenary sessions.

Decisions on confirmation of occupancy rights shall be adopted in accordance with the procedures prescribed by the Commission from time to time.

Article 28

The Commission shall have the power to make the following decisions on claims for confirmation of occupancy rights:

a) a decision by which the claim shall be refused (*odbija*) because the Commission was not in possession of relevant evidence to confirm the occupancy right, or

b) a decision by which the claim shall be rejected as inadmissible (*odbacuje*) because the claim was submitted by an ineligible person, or because the claim was not submitted in due time, or otherwise did not meet the requirements for submission as stated in this Book of Regulations or if it is established that the claimant does not have the status of a refugee or displaced person in accordance with Article 3 of this Book of Regulations; or

c) a decision that confirms the occupancy right.

Article 29

When considering the claim for confirmation of an occupancy right, the Commission may decide that the claimant shall be invited to supplement the claim with further evidence.

V. CONFIRMATION OF ENTITLEMENT TO REPOSSESS AN APARTMENT TO WHICH OCCUPANCY RIGHT HAS NOT BEEN ACQUIRED

Article 30

The Commission shall confirm that a person who occupied a claimed apartment before 1 April 1992, on the basis of an allocation decision, but without a contract on use of the apartment or another act that, under the Law on Housing Relations in force in Bosnia and Herzegovina on 1 April 1992, constitutes legal grounds for occupying the apartment, shall be entitled to repossess the claimed apartment.

The Commission shall confirm the same entitlement to members of the family household of the person referred to in paragraph 1 of this Article,

who acquired that status in accordance with the Law on Housing Relations, in force in Bosnia and Herzegovina on 1 April 1992.

Article 31

The Commission shall confirm that a person in possession of a claimed apartment on 1 April 1992, without any legal basis under the Law on Housing Relations, is entitled to repossess provided that the following criteria are met:

a) the claimant was in possession of the claimed apartment on 1 April 1992; and

b) the claimant was using the claimed apartment continuously for no less than 8 years until 1 April 1992; and

c) no procedure for eviction of the claimant from the claimed apartment was initiated at the competent housing body or court before 1 April 1992.

The claimant is obliged to supply evidence to the Commission relating to the facts stipulated in (a) and (b) of the previous paragraph.

The Commission will assume that no procedure for eviction of the claimant from the claimed apartment was initiated at the competent housing body or court before 1 April 1992.

Article 32

To any matters not regulated by Articles 30 and 31, the Commission shall apply provisions of the Book of Regulations that are not contrary to those Articles.

VI. DECISION MAKING UPON CLAIMS FOR APARTMENTS FROM THE HOUSING FUND OF THE FORMER JNA

Article 33

The Commission shall, in accordance with the provisions of this Book of Regulations, confirm the right to repossess an apartment to each person who lodged a claim for an apartment from the housing fund of former JNA and who was the occupancy right holder of that apartment on 1 April 1992, except if it was established that such occupancy right holder:

a) Remained in armed forces of another country after 14 December 1995, or

b) Acquired an apartment from the housing fund of former JNA or newly formed funds of the armed forces established in the territory of former SFRY after 1 April 92.

In the case referred to in a) of the previous paragraph of this Article, the Commission shall reject the claim as inadmissible due to lack of jurisdiction, while in the case referred to in b) of the previous paragraph of this Article, the Commission shall refuse the claim for repossession of apartment.

VII. Final and Binding Nature of the Decisions on Confirmation of Occupancy Rights

Article 34

The decision of the Commission on confirmation of occupancy right shall be final and binding (*obavezuje*) for the persons affected by those decisions. This includes the competent administrative bodies responsible for execution of decisions on repossession of apartments with occupancy rights in accordance with the relevant laws referred to in Article 4 of this Book of Regulations.

It shall be regarded that decisions upon claims for confirmation of occupancy right are final and binding for:

a) the claimant, as of the date when he/she received the decision, in accordance with this Book of Regulations;

b) the municipal body which is competent for execution of the decision confirming occupancy rights, as of the date of filing the claim for repossession of the apartment, as filed by an eligible person within the deadlines stipulated by the law.

Article 35

Upon adoption of a decision of the Commission which confirms the occupancy right of a certain person to a certain apartment:

a) the person whose occupancy right was confirmed or the members of his/her family household may, upon presentation of the Commission's decision, enter into possession of the apartment in accordance with Article 1 of Annex 7 of the General Framework Agreement for Peace in Bosnia and Herzegovina.

b) in addition to the occupancy right holder, the right to initiate reconsideration of the decision of the Commission shall be open to the current user of the apartment, the allocation right holder, or a member of the family household of the persons whose occupancy right was confirmed.

VIII. Composition and Form of Decisions on Confirmation of Occupancy Rights

Article 36

The decision of the Commission by which it is decided upon confirmation of occupancy right shall include:

a) the place, date, and number of the decision;

b) the date of submission of the claim;

c) the legal basis for delivery of the decision;

d) the name and family name of the person to whom the decision relates;

e) the address of the apartment for which the claim for confirmation of an occupancy right was filed;

f) the dispositive of the decision (confirmation of occupancy right, rejection of the claim as inadmissible (*odbacuje*) or refusal (*odbija*) of the claim);

g) the deadline for submission of request for enforcement of the decision; and

h) the legal effects of the decision, including the right to initiate the procedure for reconsideration.

Article 37

Decisions on claims for confirmation of occupancy rights shall be printed on specially manufactured paper with the "Commission for Real Property Claims of Displaced Persons and Refugees" heading written in English language with a serial number and raised seal on paper size A4.

Article 38

The Executive Office shall maintain special documentation relating to submitted claims, evidence for confirmation of occupancy rights and decisions. The composition, the form and the security measures shall be determined by the Executive Officer of the Commission.

Article 39

A decision on a claim for confirmation of occupancy rights adopted by the Commission may be used exclusively for the purposes stated in the decision.

IX. PREPARATION OF DECISIONS ON CONFIRMATION OF OCCUPANCY RIGHTS: DELIVERY AND RECEPTION

Article 40

After decisions are adopted by the Commission, the Legal Department, with the assistance of other departments of the Executive Office, shall:

a) prepare the text of the adopted decisions on the claims for confirmation of the occupancy right for the purpose of printing the decisions;

b) prepare the text of the resolutions relating to incomplete claims;

c) return the printed decisions and resolutions on incomplete claims to the offices to which they were submitted, in order to deliver the decisions to the claimant or to act upon the resolutions on incomplete claims.

Article 41

The offices where the claims were collected shall deliver the decisions on confirmation of occupancy rights to the relevant claimants.

As an exception to paragraph 1 of this Article, the decision may be delivered by another CRPC Regional Office chosen by the claimant.

The decisions issued upon claims collected in a CRPC Regional Office which has been closed down shall be delivered by the Central Regional Office in Sarajevo, or another CRPC Regional Office chosen by the claimant.

The decisions must be delivered to the claimant within the shortest possible period of time. The decision of the Commission should be delivered to the claimant or his authorized representative within 30 days from the day of its adoption.

If it was not possible to deliver the decision in a timely manner, it shall be considered that it has been delivered to the claimant – after expiry of 8 days after posting the decision on the bulletin board of the relevant regional office.

It shall be regarded that the decision could not be delivered in a timely manner if the Regional Office has undertaken all necessary measures to deliver it within 30 days after its adoption (through telephone or mail invitation sent to the claimant or other appropriate means).

X. RECONSIDERATION OF DECISIONS ON CONFIRMATION OF OCCUPANCY RIGHTS

Article 42

The person to whom the decision on confirmation of the occupancy right applies, as well as the current user of the apartment and the allocation right holder, under the condition that they deliver new evidence or information of the new evidence which the Commission has not considered when the Decision was made and which could materially affect the decision, shall have the right to submit the request for reconsideration of the decision.

The person to whom the decision on confirmation of the occupancy right applies may submit a request for reconsideration within 60 days from the day when the decision was received, whereas the current user and allocation right holder may do so within 60 days from the day when they receive a verified copy of the decision, which the competent administrative body is obliged to deliver to them together with the conclusion on permission of enforcement of the decision of the Commission.

The persons referred to in paragraph 1 of this Article shall not have the right to submit a request for reconsideration of a decision issued as the outcome of the reconsideration procedure initiated by the same person.

Article 43

The Commission may *ex officio* initiate the reconsideration procedure at any time if it deems it justified.

Article 44

The persons to whom the decision on confirmation of the occupancy right applies, the current user or the allocation right holder may submit the reconsideration request on the standard form to any CRPC Regional Office or directly, in the form of a letter, to the Legal Department, Executive Office.

The procedure for reconsideration of a decision on confirmation of an occupancy right shall be identical to the prescribed procedure for the preparation and adoption of a decision upon a claim for confirmation of an occupancy right.

As an exception to paragraph 2 of this Article, the Commission may notify the claimant of the pending request for reconsideration.

Article 45

The decision of the Commission issued upon a request for reconsideration shall be delivered to the requestor and all other persons who received the original decision, as well as to the administrative body responsible for enforcement.

XI. EXECUTION OF THE DECISION UPON THE CLAIM FOR CONFIRMATION OF AN OCCUPANCY RIGHT

Article 46

The decisions of the Commission upon claims for confirmation of occupancy rights shall be executed by competent administrative bodies in the Federation of BiH and the Republika Srpska in accordance with the relevant laws referred to in Article 4 of the Book of Regulations, and other relevant laws in force.

Article 47

The enforcement of the decision of the Commission confirming the occupancy right, along with the presentation of the decision of the Commission, can be requested of competent bodies by those persons whose occupancy rights have been confirmed, as well as persons who, in accordance with the Law on Housing Relations which was in force in BiH on 1 April 1992, are considered members of the family household of the occupancy right holder.

XII. TRANSITIONAL AND FINAL PROVISIONS

Article 48

In order to ensure the application of this Book of Regulations, instructions governing the work of the departments and other units of the Commission are needed, as well as other acts on the internal organi-

sation of the Commission, the Executive Office, the Legal Department, the Operations Department and other units within the Executive and other Commission offices in BiH and abroad; financial plans and other acts and plans of the Commission relating to finances, organisation, and management. Such instructions, acts and plans shall be passed after this Book of Regulation comes into force.

The Executive Officer shall be responsible to the Commission for execution of the tasks mentioned in the previous paragraph.

Article 49

In the course of preparing and making decisions upon claims for confirmation of occupancy rights, the Commission shall apply the provisions of the "Book of the Regulations on the Conditions and Decision-Making Procedure for Claims for Return of Real Property of Displaced Persons and Refugees", insofar they are not inconsistent with the provisions of this Book of Regulations.

Article 50

This Consolidated version of this Book of Regulations contains the provisions of the Consolidated Version of the Book of Regulations issued on 8 October 2002, including amendments adopted on 9 July 2003 and 3 September 2003, and shall take effect as of 29 November 2003.

5.15. Commission for Real Property Claims of Displaced Persons and Refugees – Book of Regulations on the Conditions and Decision Making Procedure for Claims for Return of Real Property of Displaced Persons and Refugees (2003)

[. . .]

I. GENERAL PROVISIONS

Article 1

This Book of Regulations regulates the conditions and decision making on claims for the return of real property of displaced persons and refugees and other persons with a legal interest in order to confirm rights to real property which is not in their possession.

Article 2

This Book of Regulations governs the terms and the procedure for:

a) the submission and registration of claims;

b) the selection of evidence relevant for decision making;

c) the decision making on claims;

d) the legal effectiveness, delivery and publication of decisions;

e) the correction and reconsideration of decisions;

f) the enforcement of decisions and the supervision of enforcement; and

g) other issues relevant for decision making on claims for return, or for compensation in lieu of return of real property.

Article 3

All documents on the organizational structure of the Executive Office of the Commission ("the Executive Office") and other offices of the Commission in Bosnia and Herzegovina and abroad, financial plans and other documents and plans of the Commission related to the financing, organization and management of the Commission offices will be adjusted in accordance with this Book of Regulations.

Article 4

The components of the Book of Regulations are:

a) the claim form for submission of claims for return of real property;

b) decisions on the organization of the Executive office and other offices of the Commission in BiH and abroad; and

c) the forms of decisions on claims for real property.

Article 5

The Executive Officer of the Commission is responsible for the implementation of the Book of Regulations.

II. Submission and Reception of Claims

A) Information on Claim Submission

Article 6

Claimants will be informed through the Executive Office and other offices of the Commission of how to register claims and to complete the claim form.

Article 7

Potential claimants will receive information in the Commission offices orally or through written instructions, by media, by distribution of pamphlets, by direct participation of the Commissioners, the Executive Officer and other authorized persons in radio and TV programs or at meetings with representatives of potential claimants and in other appropriate ways.

B) Submission of Claims

Article 8

A claim for return of real property ("a claim") is submitted by persons who, in accordance with this Book of Regulations, have a right to submit a claim, or by their representatives.

Article 9

A claim is submitted on the form provided.

Article 10

Persons authorized to submit a claim are:

a) displaced persons;

b) refugees; and

c) other natural persons with a legal interest in the claimed real property.

Socially or state owned real property may not be the subject of the claim except in the case of city construction land.

Article 11

It is presumed that persons who submit claims are not in possession of the claimed real property.

Article 12

Displaced persons and refugees are not required to prove their status at the time of registering a claim. The status of these persons is presumed.

Article 13

It is considered that the claimant has legal interest to submit the claim if he or she is in a family or civil law relationship with the person who was the right holder to the claimed real properties as of 01.04.1992.

The types and degrees of family relationship referred to in the previous paragraph as well as the evidence establishing the family and civil law relationship shall be specified by a special instruction.

The Commission shall presume for all persons who submitted a private property claim to CRPC, to have a legal interest for submitting a claim, unless the claim clearly indicates that legal interest does not exist.

Article 14

Claims may be submitted by authorized representatives of the persons mentioned under Article 10 of this Book of Regulations.

Article 15

An authorised representative must present a valid power of attorney when submitting a claim.

Article 16

A valid power of attorney is one given by a person who is entitled to submit a claim and which is verified by the authorized bodies of the Entities, or diplomatic/consular offices of Bosnia and Herzegovina, or by the authorized bodies of the countries where a claimant has temporary or permanent residence.

Article 17

The claimant should attach any available evidence proving his or her rights to the claimed real property.

Article 18

A claim may also be submitted when the claimant does not present any evidence, because it is not available to him.

Article 19

Evidence on the claimant's identity and power of attorney for the claim submission are to be presented as original documents.

Evidence on rights to real property may be presented as original documents or verified copies.

An authorized staff member at the Commission office will examine the documents, make copies and attach the copies to the claim form.

C) Registration of Claims

Article 20

Registration of claims is conducted in the offices of the Commission, established within the territory of Bosnia and Herzegovina or abroad.

Article 21

Claims registration may occasionally be conducted outside the offices, in a manner approved by the Executive Officer.

Article 22

The Commission may entrust claims registration abroad to an international or nongovernmental organization under terms agreed between the Commission and the organization.

Article 23

The scope, work organization, location and order of the establishment of these offices will be specified by special resolution of the Commission.

Article 24

Claims registration is conducted by authorized staff members of the Commission within working hours determined by the Executive Officer.

Article 25

Before claims registration takes place, an authorized staff member is obliged to inform the potential claimant as to how to submit a claim, about evidence and other information relevant for submitting a claim. The authorized staff member is also obliged to ensure that the potential claimant has expressed his free will regarding the disposal of the claimed real property.

Article 26

Incomplete claims shall not be registered.

In case an incomplete claim has been registered, it shall be supplemented or refused.

The claim is considered to be incomplete if it does not contain:

- data on the claimant;
- data on the claimed real property;
- signature;
- valid power of attorney.

Provisions related to supplementing or refusing the claim, as well as requirements for a claim to be considered complete, shall be specified in a special instruction.

Article 27

The Head of the Office and the staff members responsible for claims registration shall ensure that claims are registered correctly.

Article 28

After the claim is received, an authorised staff member of the office enters the data registered on the claim form in the appropriate computer software. After two copies are printed, the claimant signs both copies and retains one for himself.

Any deficiency in the evidence concerning the claimant's identity or the identification of the real property must be corrected by the claimant.

Article 29

The registered claim is retained in the file of the claimant opened in the office where the claim was submitted.

Article 30

The claimant's file should include:

a) the signed printed form of the submitted claim;

b) a power of attorney, in the case when the claim is submitted through the authorized representative;

c) copies of all evidence.

Article 31

The claimant may amend the claim, supplement the claim with further evidence or withdraw the claim or part of the claim at any time until the decision is adopted.

The withdrawal of a claim shall be explicit, in written form and signed by the claimant.

In the above mentioned cases, the Regional Office must inform the Executive Office without delay.

Article 32

In case the claimant dies before issuance of a decision, the proceedings may be suspended or resumed upon request of an heir.

Persons identified as heirs of the first succession order may request suspension or resumption of the proceedings before the probate hearing takes place.

Article 33

The Commission shall strike out a claim or a part of claim if it establishes that:

- the claimant repossessed the claimed property or the claimed property has been reconstructed, or
- the claimant submitted the claim for the same property to the relevant administrative body, or
- the claimant lost interest for pursuing the claim since he/she failed to respond to a written invitation to remove deficiencies in the claim, or the written invitation has not been delivered to him/her since he/she failed to inform the Commission about a change of address, or
- it has decided all primary properties within a claim and the remaining part of the claim relates to secondary properties within the same political municipality and
- it has no available evidence prescribed by this Book of Regulations for confirmation of a right.

The Commission shall make an individual Report on Strike Out for each claim affected, stating applicable reasons for strike out.

The Report on Strike Out shall not be delivered to the claimant.

The Commission shall notify claimants on the categories of claims that have been struck out through a public information campaign.

III. Procedure for Collection and Verification of Evidence Relevant for Deciding Claims for Return of Real Property

Article 34

Evidence relevant for deciding claims for return of real property should be presented to the Commission by claimants if available to them.

Article 35

If no relevant evidence is available to a claimant or if the evidence presented by the claimant is of doubtful credibility, the Commission will initiate evidence collection or evidence verification procedures.

Article 36

The Commission may conduct evidence collection or evidence verification through the Executive Office, its regional offices or through an international or nongovernmental organization.

The Commission will adopt a special decision to conduct the collection or verification of evidence through a particular international or nongovernmental organization.

The decision under the previous paragraph will contain all the essential elements of a contract on agency or a contract on donation.

Article 37

If the Commission decides to conduct evidence collection and verification directly, it will be conducted through the Executive Office or, upon instruction by the Executive Office, through the regional office responsible for the area where the claimed real property is located, as well as through the office responsible for the area where there are bodies or services holding records on real property, whether concerning ownership or lawful possession.

The office registering a claim will co-operate with the offices mentioned in the previous paragraph.

Article 38

Evidence will be collected and verified at the offices of bodies and services where the records on real property, owners and possessors are kept (first instance courts, municipal administrative bodies and all other bodies and services whose records may be used as evidence).

Article 39

Evidence may be collected and verified in other suitable ways, subject to approval by the Commission.

Article 40

These offices will co-operate through the Executive Office.

Article 41

Other offices cannot undertake any activities concerning collection and verification of evidence without obtaining the approval of the Executive Office.

Article 42

The Executive Office may order other offices to conduct collection and verification of evidence, if it is considered necessary.

Article 43

The Commission will consider all types of evidence with the aim of establishing the state of facts.

IV. Deciding Claims for Return of Real Property (Ownership Right, Lawful Possession, Annulment of Contracts on Transfer of Real Property)

A) Evidence

Article 44

The types of evidence for confirming an ownership right are:

(1) property book extracts confirming an ownership right to the claimed real property, with the situation as of 01.04.1992; or

(2) real property cadaster extracts confirming an ownership right to the claimed real property with the situation as of 01.04.1992 for cadaster municipalities where the real property cadaster came into effect prior to 01.04.1992 by the decision of the competent authority;

(3) real property cadaster extracts confirming ownership to the claimed real property, issued after 01.04.1992, for areas where the real property

cadaster has not entered into force or where it entered into force after 01.04.1992, provided that the competent authority has confirmed that the recorded status is identical to the status as of 01.04.1992.

For municipalities where the Property Book is not in existence, the types of evidence for confirming an ownership right are:

(1) property book extracts issued before 01.04.1992; or

(2) court decisions allowing the presentation of documents with the aim of acquiring ownership over the claimed real property; or

(3) legally valid contracts of sale or legally valid gift contracts of the claimed real property concluded prior to 01.04.1992, if the person who acquired rights to the claimed real property is found to be registered in the cadastral records valid for 01.04.1992; or

(4) legally valid contract on transfer of real property from social ownership concluded before 01.04.1992. if the buyer of the claimed real property is found to be registered in the cadastral records valid for 01.04.1992; or

(5) inheritance decisions, made prior to 01.04.1992, which include the clause of validity; or

(6) court decisions on ownership rights to the claimed real property, made prior to 01.04.1992, which include the clause of validity; or

(7) valid decisions made before 01.04.1992 in administrative procedures on the basis of which agrarian based ownership (usurpation, redistribution of land, redistribution of fields and others) is acquired.

Article 45

The types of evidence for confirming lawful possession are:

(1) cadastral records (transcript of the possession document) for the claimed real property which indicate the state of facts on 01.04.1992;

In cases where the evidence referred to in the previous paragraph is not available, lawful possession may be confirmed on the basis of the following:

(2) building permits issued prior to 01.04.1992; or

(3) usage permits issued prior to 01.04.1992; or

(4) urbanistic agreement issued prior to 01.04.1992 for reconstruction, additional building and other works on objects that already exist as well as for legalisation of objects which were built without a building permit; or

(5) contracts on current maintenance of joint premises concluded prior to 01.04.1992 in the building where, according to the statement of the claimant, there is ownership by floors of an apartment; or

(6) decisions on presentation of real property and determining right to the real property, issued prior to 01.04.1992, for cadastral municipalities for which the real property cadaster did not come into effect prior to 01.04.1992; or

(7) court decisions on inheritance prior to 01.04.1992, with the clause of validity; or

(8) other court decisions establishing the right to real property prior to 01.04.1992, with the clause of validity; or

(9) decisions made prior to 01.04.1992 in administrative procedures on the basis of which agrarian based ownership (usurpation, redistribution of land, redistribution of fields and others) is acquired; or

(10) decisions of administrative organs related to the claimed real property, made before 01.04.1992; or

(11) property book extracts issued before 01.04.1992, confirming the right of use of the claimed city construction land; or

(12) legally valid contracts on sale or legally valid contracts on gift of the claimed real property concluded prior to 01.04.1992; or

(13) legally valid contract on transfer of the claimed real property from social ownership, concluded prior to 01.04.1992; or

(14) records on payment of tax on transfer of real property, income tax from real property, or tax on real property itself and other taxes; or

(15) copies of possession lists related to the claimed real property issued prior to 01.04.1992; or

(16) copies of cadastral plans with complete data on the real properties and their users issued prior to 01.04.1992; or

(17) real property cadaster extracts confirming the right to use city construction land, issued after 01.04.1992, for areas where the real property cadaster has not entered into force or where it entered into force after 01.04.1992, provided that the competent authority has confirmed that the recorded status is identical to the status as of 01.04.1992; or

(18) copy of possession list referring to the claimed real property issued after 01.04.1992 which, in combination with other evidence, confirms that the claimant was lawful possessor of the claimed real property on 01.04.1992. In the event that the types of evidence listed in items 1 to 18 of this Article are not available, lawful possession may be confirmed on the basis of the following data of the New Survey in municipalities where the RPC/Land Cadastre, created on the basis of such New Survey, has not entered into force:

a) the alphabetical list of possessors, and

b) the aerial photo of the area verified by the competent body.

Evidence referred to in paragraph 3 of this Article may be attached to the claim file or may be replaced by a report of an authorized person created on the basis of a review of such evidence.

In the event that the types of evidence listed in items 1 to 18 of this Article are not available, lawful possession may be confirmed on the basis of the following data of the New Survey in municipalities where the RPC/Land Cadastre, created on the basis of such New Survey, has not entered into force:

a) inventory list,

b) the alphabetical list of possessors, and

c) the aerial photo of the area verified by the competent body.

Evidence referred to in items b) and c) may be attached to the claim file or may be replaced by a report of unauthorized person created on the basis of a review of such evidence.

Article 46

A contract is considered legally valid, for the purpose of Articles 44 and 45 of this Book of Regulations, if it has been concluded in written form and if the signatures of contractors have been verified at the competent court.

As an exception, the verification of signatures of contractors at the competent court is not a condition for the validity of the contract on transfer of real property from social ownership.

Article 47

In individual cases, the Commission will evaluate the validity of any other evidence which is not included in Articles 44, 45, and 46.

The Commission shall establish a separate procedure for claims which do not contain the evidence stipulated in Articles 44 and 45 of this Book of Regulations, or for claims which contain evidence which is not sufficient for the confirmation of rights.

Article 48

If the attached evidence contains a deficiency which prevents the Commission from rendering a decision and only the claimant is authorized to initiate the appropriate procedure for remedying the deficiency, the claimant will be informed through the Regional Office of the need to remedy the deficiency.

Article 49

Where a claimant has presented evidence containing formal or other deficiencies which renders the evidence unacceptable for the confirmation of an ownership right or right to lawful possession, the Executive Office may:

a) have regard to other evidence referring to the same real property; or

b) try to obtain further evidence in accordance with Articles 36 and 37; or

c) invite the claimant, through the Regional Office, to supplement the claim with valid evidence or to provide precise information as to the availability or location of the required evidence.

Article 50

The evidence listed in Articles 44, 45 and 46 of this Book of Regulations may be accepted from any authority in Bosnia and Herzegovina or the Entities:

a) which was competent to issue such a document at the time when it was issued; or

b) which keeps relevant records on real properties and other data which it was competent to issue prior to 01.04.1992.

Article 51

When no evidence proving a right to the claimed real property is submitted with the claim, and the Commission obtains evidence on lawful possession or ownership, the decision may be rendered on the basis of such evidence.

B) Decision Making Procedure

Article 52

The Regional Offices will forward all claims to the Executive Office with photocopies of all evidence.

Article 53

The Executive Office – Legal Department is competent for the preparation of draft decisions upon the claims submitted.

A Legal Working Group of the Commission shall consider the prepared draft decisions and confirms the decision proposals.

The procedure for preparation of draft decisions shall be regulated by a special instruction issued by the Executive Director upon the proposal of directors of departments that participate in the preparation of draft decisions.

Article 54

The Executive Office reviews the claims through its expert staff, and assesses the evidence which is the basis of the draft decision.

Article 55

After reviewing the claim, the Executive Office prepares the draft decision.

Article 56

The Executive Office may propose to the Commission a decision by which the claim is:

a) refused as inadmissible; or

b) adopted; or

c) rejected.

Article 57

A Legal Working Group of the Commission will regularly review draft decisions to ensure that they are in accordance with this Book of Regulations.

After reviewing draft decisions, the Legal Working Group confirms decision proposals and presents them to the Commission for consideration and decision making.

Article 58

The Commission decides on the decision proposals in plenary session.

The Commission will make decisions on claims for return of real property based on the proposal of the Executive Office.

Article 59

While considering decision proposals, the Commission may:

a) completely accept the decision proposals; or

b) partly change or amend the decision proposals; or

c) send the proposal back for supplementing.

Article 60

In principle, the Commission shall decide upon the claim as a whole. If only evidence for a part of the claimed real property is available to the Commission, the Commission may decide only upon that part.

In the case referred to in the previous paragraph, the Commission shall issue a new decision for the real properties for which it subsequently obtains evidence.

Article 61

Every individual decision contains:

a) the title of the Commission

b) the date and place of adoption

c) the introduction

d) the date of submission of the claim

e) the dispositive

f) the legal remedy

g) the signatures of the authorized persons.

Article 62

The Chairperson and one other authorized person will sign individual decisions.

Article 63

Individual decisions adopted by the Commission confirming a right to the claimed real property, shall be issued in the form of a Certificate. Each Certificate shall have a serial number and shall be verified with a dry stamp.

Article 64

Individual Decisions of the Commission shall:

a) confirm rights on behalf of the person who is found to be registered as right holder to the claimed real property on 01.04.1992;

b) enable the right holder, his or her heirs and other persons to whom that right was transferred after 01.04.1992 in accordance with the Law on Inheritance or a legal business concluded by free will of the participants, to enter into possession of the designated real properties upon the presentation of the decision, within 60 days from the day when the request is submitted to the competent authority;

c) oblige the competent judicial and municipal administrative bodies to bring the persons referred to in paragraph b) of this Article, at their request, into possession of the designated real properties upon the presentation of the decision, within 60 days from the day when the request is submitted, and to make the relevant changes in real property records;

d) enable the persons referred to in paragraph b) of this Article to transfer their rights to the claimed real properties to other natural and legal persons, in accordance with the law, and Article XII of Annex 7 of the Dayton Peace Agreement;

e) enable the claimant or other individual with legal interest in the designated real property to file a reconsideration request within 60 days from the day they learn of the new evidence which may materially affect the decision.

V. SPECIAL PROCEDURE FOR DECIDING CLAIMS FOR RETURN OF REAL PROPERTY, CONFIRMING AN OWNERSHIP RIGHT TO REAL PROPERTY, AND ACQUIRING THE RIGHT TO JUST COMPENSATION IN LIEU OF RETURN TO PROPERTY

Article 65

Just compensation may be awarded, when the means become available, to the person who chooses that option instead of repossession of the property, if the Commission establishes that he/she is the legitimate owner of that property.

Article 66

The Commission shall establish fixed fees which shall be the basis for valuation of the real properties for which the just compensation is claimed.

VI. DECISION MAKING UPON CLAIMS FOR APARTMENTS FROM THE HOUSING FUND OF THE FORMER JNA

Article 67

The Commission shall, in accordance with the provisions of this Book of Regulations, confirm the right to repossess an apartment to each person who lodged a claim for an apartment from the housing fund of former JNA and who was the owner or lawful possessor of that apartment on 1 April 1992, except if such person remained in armed forces of another country after 14 December 1995.

In the exception referred to in the previous paragraph of this Article, the Commission shall reject the claim as inadmissible due to lack of jurisdiction.

VII. LEGAL EFFECTIVENESS, DELIVERY AND PUBLICATION OF INDIVIDUAL DECISIONS ON RETURN OF REAL PROPERTY

Legal Effectiveness

Article 68

Individual decisions on claims for return of real property, or for just compensation in lieu of return, will become final and binding as of the day they are adopted.

Delivery

Article 69

Individual decisions on claims for return of real property made by the Commission will be delivered through the Regional Offices to the claimant in person, and if the claimant has an authorized representative, the decision will be delivered to the representative.

If it is not possible to deliver individual decision to the claimant, a verified copy of the certificate shall be delivered upon his or her request to every person who is able to prove his/her legal interest as provided by this Book of Regulations.

In the case described in the previous paragraph, the original certificate shall be kept in the Executive Office.

Article 70

If the claimant changes residential address after submitting the claim, he or she is obliged to notify the Office where the claim was submitted.

If the claimant does not inform the office about the change of the address, the delivery of the decision will be performed through the main notice board of the office.

Article 71

In the case referred to in paragraph 2 of the previous Article, it is considered that the delivery is conducted when eight days pass after the decision has been placed on the main notice board.

Publication

Article 72

Summaries of individual decisions of the Commission may be published in the Official Gazette of Bosnia and Herzegovina and in the Official Gazettes of the Federation of Bosnia and Herzegovina and Republika Srpska, as well as listed on our website, www.crpc.org.ba. The failure to publish the decision shall not affect its final and binding nature.

Article 73

The summary of an individual decision shall contain:

a) number of the decision;

b) property description; and

c) information on the holder of the right to the real property.

VIII. Correction of Errors in Decisions

Article 74

The Commission shall correct any errors in names and numbers and any other obvious mistakes in the decision certificate, as well as discrepancies between a transcript of the certificate and the original certificate.

Article 75

The Commission may make the correction referred to in Article 74 at the request of the claimant, or of its own initiative.

Article 76

In order to correct such errors, the Commission shall issue a separate decision on correction.

IX. Reconsideration of Decisions

A) Principle

Article 77

The Commission may reconsider a decision if the claimant or any other person with a legal interest in the real property designated in the original decision, within 60 days of learning of new evidence which could materially affect the decision, presents such evidence to the Commission, or gives indications of the new evidence.

B) Submission of Requests for Reconsideration

Article 78

A request for reconsideration may be submitted on the appropriate forms as designated by the Commission or in another written form that meets the requirements of Article 77.

Article 79

The request for reconsideration contains:

(i) the identification of the original decision, including its number and date;

(ii) the reasons for submitting a request for reconsideration;

(iii) the new evidence or indications of new evidence which may materially affect the decision;

(iv) the date on which the requestor learned of the decision or of the new evidence;

(v) the signature of the requestor.

Article 80

The following person ("requestor") can submit a request:

a) the claimant;

b) any other person with a legal interest in the real property designated in the decision.

The persons referred to in paragraph 1 of this Article shall not have the right to submit a request for reconsideration of a decision issued as the outcome of the reconsideration procedure initiated by the same person.

Article 81

The requestor shall provide the Commission with all new evidence available to him.

Article 82

The Commission may *ex officio* initiate the reconsideration procedure at any time if it deems it justified.

C) Decision Making Procedure

Article 83

The Commission shall consider the request for reconsideration, together with any further submissions or evidence provided.

Article 84

If appropriate, the Commission may invite any party to provide further submissions or additional information in writing, or undertake further investigations as it sees fit.

Article 85

The Commission will examine the request for reconsideration and any other available material as soon as practicable.

Article 86

After examining the request for reconsideration, the Commission may:

a) refuse to admit the request as being inadmissible, not submitted within due time or as submitted by an unauthorised person;

b) reject the request as being unfounded;

c) accept the request, revoke its previous decision and issue a new certificate.

D) Notification

Article 87

The decision of the Commission issued in the reconsideration proceedings shall be delivered to the requestor and all other persons who received the original decision, as well as to the administrative body responsible for enforcement.

Article 88

The Commission's determination to revoke a previous decision certificate may be published in the Official Gazette of Bosnia and Herzegovina, the Federation of Bosnia and Herzegovina and the Republika Srpska.

The failure to publish the decision shall not affect its final and binding nature.

X. Decision Enforcement

Article 89

The competent authorities of the municipality where the claimed real property is located are responsible for the enforcement of decisions, as well as the Commission offices when enforcing the Commission decisions on compensation, in lieu of return of the real property.

Article 90

The Executive Office is obliged to arrange to monitor the enforcement of the decisions, and to inform the Commission by special report.

Article 91

In order to assist with the monitoring of enforcement, summaries of decisions will be distributed by the Executive Office every 30 days to:

a) The Office of the High Representative;

b) UNHCR;

c) OSCE;

d) The Office of Ombudsman;

e) The Human Rights Chamber.

XI. Transitional and Closing Provisions

Article 92

Any procedural matters not regulated by this Book of Regulations will be regulated by the provision of the Law on Civil Procedure.

Article 93

This Consolidated Book of Regulations, drafted in Bosnian, Croatian, Serbian and English, becomes effective on 29 November 2003, and may be published in the Official Gazette of Bosnia and Herzegovina and the Official Gazettes of the Entities.

Article 94

CRPC reserves the right to give authentic interpretation of the provisions of this Book of Regulations.

Article 95

The Provisions of Article 44, 45 and 46 of this Book of Regulations will be applied from January 1, 1997. The provisions of Article 13 will be applied to all claims registered since 1 July 1998.

Article 96

All normative and other documents which are a constitutive part of this Book of Regulations shall be coordinated with this Book of Regulations within 30 days from the day the Book of Regulations has become effective.

Article 97

The Consolidated Book of Regulations on the Conditions and Decision-Making Procedure for Claims for Return of Real Property of Displaced Persons and Refugees which was adopted on 8 October 2002, shall become ineffective by the entry into force of this Book of Regulations.

Article 98

This Consolidated version of the Book of Regulations incorporates The Consolidated Version of the Book of Regulations on the Conditions and Decision-Making Procedure for Claims for Return of Real Property of Displaced Persons and Refugees which was adopted on 8 October 2002, as well as amendments adopted on 16 April 2003, 9 July 2003 and 3 September 2003.

6. BULGARIA

6.1. Restitution of Nationalised Real Property Act (1992)

Article 1

(1) This Act restores ownership of real property expropriated under the Expropriation of Large Urban Housing Property Act (SG No. 87/1948; amnd, No. 91/1948) which is now owned by the State, municipal and public organisations, or by their companies, or by sole proprietorships under Article 61 of the Trade Act, and exists in the same physical dimensions as when it was expropriated.

(2) Transactions in real property, such as have been executed in violation of the resolution, enacted by the Grand National Assembly on 6 December 1990 (SG, No. 101/1990), on the partial lifting of the ban on the disposal of State and municipal property, are hereby declared null and void, and ownership of such property shall be restored.

Article 2

(1) This Act also restores the ownership of property expropriated under: the Government Tobacco Monopoly Act (SG, No. 96/1947; amnd, Nos 93 & 234/1948, Izv., Nos 41/1951 & 39/1952); the Government Oil Products Monopoly Act (SG, No. 55/1948; rpld, No. 39/1991); the Spirits and Alcoholic Beverages Monopoly Act (SG, No. 178/1947; amnd, Nos 93 & 234 /1948 & 36/1949); the Nationalisation of Private Industrial and Mining Enterprises Act (SG, No. 302/1947; amnd, No. 176/1949); the Cinematography Act (SG, No. 78/1948; amnd, Izv., Nos 95/1953, 65/1959 & SG, No. 85/1974); the Book Printing Act (SG, No. 52/1949; amnd & suppl., Izv., No 19/1951); and the Decree on the Expropriation of Foods Warehouses (Izv., No. 13/1952).

(2) Ownership of property under the preceding paragraph shall be restored, provided that, on the date that this Act takes effect, such property is owned by the State, municipal and public organisations, or by their companies, or by sole proprietorships under Article 61 of the Trade Act, and provided also that such property exists in the same physical dimensions as when it was expropriated.

Article 3

(1) Ownership of property under Articles 1 and 2 shall be restored to the persons who were therefrom expropriated or to such persons' heirs by law.

(2) Ownership shall be restored to corporate persons expropriated under any of the Acts mentioned in Article 2. Where such corporate persons do not exist on the date that this Act shall take effect, ownership shall be restored to the partners or members thereof, or, as the case may be, to such physical persons who were partners or members thereof at the time of dissolution, and to such partners or members, according to their respective title, or their heirs by law.

(3) Where conditions are not present for the restitution of property under Articles 1 and 2, the former owners, or their heirs by law, shall be compensated under a procedure laid down in a separate enactment.

Article 4

(1) The ownership of property under Articles 1 and 2 shall be restored, provided that the former owners thereof did not receive an equivalent monetary compensation or an equivalent real property in compensation. Bonds received shall not be deemed a form of compensation.

(2) Persons shall not be deemed compensated whose accounts were debited for liabilities to the State, banks and State enterprises pursuant to the Decree on the Liabilities of Former Owners of Expropriated Property and Nationalised Enterprises (Izv., No. 60/1955).

(3) The former owners of property, expropriated pursuant to Article 8 of the Expropriation of Large Urban Housing Property Act or pursuant to Article 7 of the Nationalisation of Private Industrial and Mining Enterprises Act, who received homes in, or by way of, compensation, may request restitution. The request shall be addressed to the Minister of Finance not later than six months after the date that this Act shall take effect, and the Minister of Finance shall give a ruling thereon within thirty days of receipt. If no ruling is given within the latter period, the request shall be deemed tacitly rejected. A rejection shall be subject to appeal within a period of fourteen days before the Supreme Court who shall decide the matter. In the absence of other specific provisions, those of the Administrative Procedure Act shall apply.

(4) As the ruling pursuant to the preceding paragraph takes effect, real property granted in, or by way of, compensation shall pass to the State or the local municipality and shall be taken pursuant to Article 16 of the Property Act. The said property may not be taken earlier than six months after the ruling on restitution, and, in the cases under Article 6, paragraph (2) below, not earlier than after the statutory three-year period.

Article 5

The heirs of persons whose ownership is restored pursuant to Articles 1 and 2 shall be exempt from inheritance tax.

Article 6

(1) Existing leases of any real property under Articles 1 and 2 shall be deemed concluded without any specific duration.

(2) Any physical person who, under any administrative procedure, possesses of a home which is subject to restitution under this Act, shall retain his tenancy rights under the Rental Relationships Act for a period of three years as of the date that this Act takes effect. As of the date that ownership of such a property changes hands, such a person shall pay rent to the new owner. The lease may not be revoked before the expiry of the said three-year period, save in cases under Article 36, paragraph (1), items 1–4 and 11 of the Rental Relationships Act.

(3) The provisions of the preceding paragraph shall also apply where the property is in tenant use by a child-care institution, school, or health-care establishment.

Article 7

(Amended SG Nos. 28/1992; 51/1996) The former owners of property under Articles 1 and 2, or the heirs thereof, who have not received indemnification, may claim restitution where the property has been acquired by a third party in violation of statutes, or by resort to any official or political capacity, or through the misuse of power. Claims may be lodged within one year of the date that this Act takes effect.

The procedure under such cases shall be payment-free.

Article 8

(1) Former owners and the heirs thereof may not claim foregone benefits and yields from the property.

(2) Any reasonable expenses, related to the property, incurred by the tenant, where the latter is a physical person, may be claimed under the standard procedure.

Article 9

Persons whose property is subject to restitution under this Act, may obtain title documents of verification of circumstances if they are able to prove that, at the date of expropriation, they themselves, or their testator, held title to the subject property.

The statutory fee shall not be collected for the verification of circumstances.

Article 10

The ownership of shops, workshops, warehouses, and studios sold during the period from 30 March 1973 to 16 March 1990 under any procedure other than the procedure laid down in the Decree No. 60/1975 of the Council of Ministers on the Purchase of Shops, Workshops, Warehouses, and Studios (SG, No. 39/1975), shall be restored pursuant to the Restitution of Some Shops, Workshops, Warehouses, and Studios Act (SG, No. 105/1991).

SUPPLEMENTARY PROVISIONS

Section 1. Local Councils shall take appropriate measures to provide with priority, and within the statutory period, for the housing needs of tenants under Article 6 paragraph (2).

Section 2. (Amended SG No. 51/1996)

(1) Persons sentenced pursuant to Articles 6 and 7 to vacate the respective lodgings, shall be provided with priority by the municipal councils with lodgings in compliance with Section 11 of the Municipal Property Act (SG, No. 44/1996). This right shall not apply to sentenced persons, if they or members of their families own a housing or villa fit for permanent occupancy.

(2) Whereas of the date of removal of persons under paragraph (1) from the housing premises occupied thereby the municipal councils could not provide them with housings, and therefore they had to rent lodgings on free rent, the difference to the price of the free rent shall be on the account of the municipality. This right shall not apply to persons who have income and property sufficient to afford housing on free rent.

Section 3. (Amended SG No. 51/1996) The State shall restore to persons sentenced under Article 7 the monies paid thereby for the respective housing, taking in consideration the market price as of the time of execution of the decision. The amount to be reimbursed and procedure for payment shall be specified by Regulation of the Council of Ministers. After receipt of the amount such persons shall vacate the housing they have been admitted to pursuant to Section 2, paragraph (1), and in cases under Section 2, paragraph (2), the municipalities shall discontinue payment of the difference to free rent.

Section 4. (Repealed SG No. 61/1996)

CONCLUDING PROVISION

Section 5. (1) Within one month of the date that this Act takes effect, the Council of Ministers shall issue a decree whereby ownership of real property expropriated under acts of the Council of Ministers during the 1947–1962 period shall be restored, save such acts as were issued pursuant to Article 101 of the Property Act.

(2) Within the same period, the Council of Ministers shall submit to the National Assembly a bill to repeal the Decrees under which individual property has been confiscated for the State.

[. . .]

6.2. Decree No. 60 on Applying Article 1, Paragraph 2 of the Restitution of Nationalised Real Property Act (1992)

THE COUNCIL OF MINISTERS HAS DECREED:

Section 1

(1) Repeals all decrees, ordnances and decisions of the Council of Ministers by virtue of which real property has been nationalized under the acts listed in Art. 1 and 2 of the Restitution of Nationalised Real Property Act (SG, No 15/1992) from 1947 through 1962.

(2) in cases when one and the same act settles other legal relationships as well, that part referring to nationalized real property shall be repealed.

Section 2

Repeals the following acts of the Council of Ministers:

1. Regulation No 4 of 1948 on Nationalising Real Property under Art. 8 of the State Sanitary and Pharmaceutical Enterprise Act (SG, No 125/1948);

2. Decree No 10 of 1948 on Nationalising All Assets and Debits of the Dental Cooperative Consumer Society and Those of Its Branches in Favour of the State Sanitary Pharmaceutical Enterprise (SG. No 165/1948).

Section 3

(1) The restitution of property nationalized under repealed acts of the Council of Ministers shall be conducted under the conditions and in the manner specified by the Restitution of Nationalized Real Property Act.

(2) Following the deletion of the real property in the registration books under Art. 88, para 4 of the Regulation on State Property (SG, No. 79/1975; amended, Nos. 24/1978, 52/1979, 7 and 78/1980, 70 and 77/1983, 36/1984, 37/1985, 19/1988, 71/1989, 34 and 72/1990, 75/1991 and 26/1992) the municipal councils shall send to the respective notary offices letters confirming the fact of the deletion and indicating the names of the owners. All necessary entries in the registers shall be made on the grounds of the above documents.

[. . .]

---

7. COLOMBIA

7.1. Decree No. 2007 (2001)

THE MINISTRY OF AGRICULTURE
AND RURAL DEVELOPMENT

Partially regulated by Articles 7, 17 and 19 of Law 387 from 1997. This decree pertains to the appropriate assistance to the population displaced by violence who seek to voluntarily return to their place of origin or to resettle in another place, and to measures to prevent future displacement.

The President of the Republic of Colombia, by virtue of the powers conferred on him by Article 189 Number 11 of the Political Constitution, **decrees:**

Article 1

In light of the imminent risk of displacement or of forced displacement in a given area and the limitations on the transfer of property or real estate titles,

With the goal of protecting the population from arbitrary acts against their lives, integrity and property, under circumstances which may lead or have in fact led to forced displacement,

The Municipal, Regional or Departmental Committee for Care of Populations Displaced by Violence (*Comité Municipal, Distrital o Departamental de Atención Integral a la Población Desplazada por la Violencia*), shall declare and substantiate the imminent risk of displacement or the fact of a displacement underway due to violence, in a given area within its jurisdiction. Such a declaration shall require:

1. Identification of property owners, landholders, tenants and occupants residing within the displacement zone, establishing to the greatest extent possible how long each person has been associated with the specific piece of real estate. To that end, the respective City Mayors, Rural District Attorneys (*procuradores judiciales agrarios*), Section Chiefs of the Agustín Codazzi Geographic Institute (IGAC for its Spanish acronym), Public Registrars (*Registradores de Instrumentos Públicos*) and Regional Managers of the Colombian Land Reform Institute (INCORA for its Spanish acronym), will, within 8 calendar days of when the declaration of imminent risk of displacement is made, present a report on the existing properties at the time of the declaration, specifying the ownership and basic characteristics of the properties. This report shall be based on the existing records of the Technical Farm Management Units (UMATAS for its Spanish acronym), the Office of Land Titles (*Oficina de Catastro*), the Office of Public Records, the INCORA or other similar entities. Once this report has been endorsed by the committee, it shall constitute sufficient proof of the possession, tenancy or occupancy of displaced persons. Additionally, and without affecting the above, the Social Solidarity Network can ask the appropriate Municipal and Regional Mayors to present a report on

the forms of land tenure and the basic characteristics of the rural areas before the declaration of imminent risk of displacement or forced displacement is made. A copy of such report shall be sent to INCORA and to the appropriate Rural District Attorneys.

2. Inform the appropriate Office of Public Records of the declaration of imminent risk of displacement or forced displacement. This information should include the names of the landholders or occupants in the area who might be affected by the displacement, as well as a request that the office not endorse any title transfers while the declaration is in effect, unless previously authorized under the special requirements established by Article 4 of the present decree.

3. Request that INCORA halt all title transfers in the zone of imminent risk of displacement or forced displacement that are sought by individuals other than those listed as occupants in the Committee's report as listed above in Number 1.

Paragraph 1. Once the committee has established that the acts which led to the declaration of imminent risk of displacement or forced displacement have ceased, it shall create an Act lifting the prohibition on transfers of property titles, which should be recorded and officiated by the respective Office of Public Records and INCORA.

Paragraph 2. The High Office of Notaries and Records (*La Superintendencia de Notariado y Registro*) will see that the Public Registrars ensure the fulfillment of the requirements laid out in Article 4 of the present decree, before recording the transfer of property or real estate in zones of imminent risk of displacement or forced displacement. Every six months, the Offices of Public Records shall inform the Social Solidarity Network of what has occurred during that time.

Paragraph 3. In its Regional Action Plan – RAP (PAZ in Spanish) – the Committee shall include strategies for the coordinated application of different programs that contribute to the economic stabilization and consolidation of the beneficiaries of land reform. To that end, the Committee and the Social Solidarity Network shall have previously and jointly prepared a diagnostic tool, which shall involve the participation of the population at risk of displacement or actually displaced.

Article 2

INCORA, the Rural District Attorneys, and the Public Registrars shall be invited to participate in any meetings of the Departmental, District or Municipal Committees for Care of the Displaced Population that involve topics, programs or procedures that fall within their mandate.

Article 3

Special Procedures and Programs for Efficient Attention to the Risks of Displacement:

In fulfillment of Article 19 of Law 387 from 1997, INCORA shall initiate special programs and procedures for property transfers, awards and conferral of land titles in the zones of eventual expulsion within 30 days from the date when the Committee informs them that a declaration of imminent risk of displacement or forced displacement is in effect in an area. This shall serve as a preventative strategy. To that end, it shall also consider the report on property owners, landholders, tenants and occupants endorsed by the respective Committee for Care of the Displaced Population.

Article 4

Special Requirements for the Transfer of Real Estate:

The owners of property located within the zones that are declared to be under imminent risk of displacement or forced displacement as a result of violence, who wish to transfer the rights of ownership of said property before the declaration is lifted must obtain authorization from the Municipal, District or Departmental Committee for Care of the Populations Displaced by Violence, or they can transfer the property to INCORA, in accordance with the procedures specified in section 4, Number 1 of Article 1 of Law 387 from 1997. In the case of the latter, they do not need authorization from the Committee.

The Public Registrars can only record the transfer if it is carried out under INCORA or, alternately, once the Committee has given its authorization. Such authorization should be included in the contract or title transfer.

Article 5

Temporary Socioeconomic Stabilization:

The following programs shall be adopted in order to guarantee appropriate attention to members of the displaced population who wish to continue working in the field of farming or livestock:

1. Transitional Properties. In towns that receive an influx of people displaced by violence, INCORA shall designate properties appropriate for provisional cultivation to groups of displaced households. These landholders will be required to undertake productive activities that can generate subsistence earnings in the short and intermediate term, while they evaluate the possibility of returning to their place of origin or of permanent resettlement elsewhere. The entities which make up the National System of Aid to the Displaced Population, particularly the Ministry of Agriculture and Rural Development, the Fund for Rural Investment and Financing (DRI for its Spanish acronym), Farm Bank and others, shall also develop programs of food security, income generation, community organizing and communal living in these transitional areas.

2. Temporary Settlements on Confiscated Properties or those Provisionally Assigned by INCORA.

Under the processes of ownership expiration described in Law 333 of 1996, properties that have been permanently or temporarily turned over to INCORA may be provisionally handed over to the population displaced by violence.

Paragraph. The aforementioned programs shall be offered to displaced people in conjunction with humanitarian aid so as to guarantee a continual solution until the stage of return or relocation. As such, these programs shall apply only temporarily, not to exceed three years time. On such properties, the displaced people may only undertake transitional activities related to farming and livestock.

Article 6

Socioeconomic Consolidation and Stabilization:

When displaced people opt for rural relocation, INCORA shall assume ownership of the properties abandoned as a result of violence. The value of such properties shall be included in the total or partial payment of the Family Farm Unit (FFU, or UAF in Spanish), under Article 38 Law 160/94, which shall be determined according to the following conditions:

1. When the abandoned property constitutes a Family Farm Unit, the INCORA shall assume possession of the abandoned unit and confer upon the

displaced another FFU located in an area that offers conditions for relocation.

2. If the displaced person possesses more than one Farm Family Unit, INCORA shall provide one FFU title exchange and may or may not carry out the process for land acquisition for the remaining properties, based on the procedures and criteria established under Law 160 of 1994 and regulations therein.

3. If the displaced person possesses less than one Family Farm Unit, INCORA shall take possession of the land and confer a Family Farm Unit in exchange. In accordance with the previous numeral, the value of the land transferred by the displaced person shall be used towards payment of the FFU that he or she receives. If the value of the FFU is less than 70% of the value of the abandoned land, the displaced shall receive a subsidy towards the purchase of other lands, equal to the remaining value of the land, in accordance with the conditions specified in Law 160 of 1994.

If the value of the land received by INCORA is less than the value of the FFU and the land subsidies, the awardee shall pay the difference according to the procedures specified in Article 18 of Decree 182 of 1998.

Paragraph 1. Those displaced people who are not landowners or landholders shall have access to the transitional socioeconomic stabilization programs established under this Decree and under Law 160 of 1994.

Paragraph 2. Properties that INCORA receives from the displaced that are smaller than a single Farm Family Unit shall be designated for the elderly or for single mothers, with the goal of establishing Special Farm Family Units or HOUSE PLOTS (*CASAS PARCELA*), which shall be used for building housing and cultivating subsistence crops, with the participation of the Ministry of Agriculture and Rural Development, which shall assign funds through the Farm Bank.

Article 7

Time Period Qualifications for Uncultivated Land:

In the event that a displaced person returns to uncultivated land located in the displacement zone, he or she will automatically be credited with the time of displacement, to be duly recognized by the competent authorities, as well as the actual period of occupation and cultivation of such land.

Paragraph 1. When a displaced person cannot return to uncultivated land located in the zone of imminent risk of displacement or forced displacement, and that person meets all the necessary requirements for qualification, he or she shall have priority in the INCORA land title programs for populations displaced by violence.

Article 8

Land Acquisition and Adjudication:

The acquisition of properties by INCORA under the situations reviewed in this decree, will be based on the results of a project that is jointly designed and carried out by INCORA, the National Learning Service (SENA), UMATAS, and other governmental and nongovernmental organizations, along with the prospective land recipients, in accordance with the Regional Action Plans – RAP (defined in Article 6, Decree 951 of May 24, 2001.) Before acquiring lands, those people who are expecting land subsidies should be alerted of the properties that are being offered with a possibility to buy. Such properties shall be preferentially awarded to the Community Fund (*Empresa Comunitaria*) or other duly recognized collective organizations of the displaced which collaborate with the State's activities as described in the paragraph of Article 18 of Law 387 of 1997. Any such transactions shall be subject to the internal procedures established by INCORA for that purpose.

[. . .]

---

8. ESTONIA

8.1. Republic of Estonia Principles of Ownership Reform Act (1991)[155]

I. General Provisions

Section 1 – Purposes of Act

The Principles of Ownership Reform Act determines the purpose, content, object and subjects of and the procedure for ownership reform, and is the

[155] 13 June 1990.

basis for other legislation necessary for ownership reform.

Section 2 – Purpose of Ownership Reform

(1) The purpose of ownership reform is to restructure ownership relations in order to ensure the inviolability of property and free enterprise, to undo the injustices caused by violation of the right of ownership and to create the preconditions for the transfer to a market economy.

(2) Return of property to or compensation of former owners or their legal successors for property in the course of ownership reform shall not prejudice the interests protected by law of other persons or cause new injustices.

Section 3 – Content and Object of Ownership Reform

(1) In the course of ownership reform, the following unlawfully expropriated property shall be returned or compensated for:

1) property which was nationalised pursuant to legislation which has been declared unlawful by the Republic of Estonia Supreme Council Resolution of 19 December 1990 "Concerning Restoration of Continuity of Right of Ownership" (RT 1990, 22, 280) (denationalisation);

2) property which was communised during collectivisation (decollectivisation);

3) property which was expropriated through unlawful repression or by any other method which violated the rights of the owner.

(2) In the course of ownership reform, the following changes shall be made in the form of ownership of property:

1) property in state ownership shall be transferred without charge into municipal ownership (municipalisation of property);

2) property in state ownership or property transferred into municipal ownership shall be transferred for or without charge into private ownership (privatisation of property);

3) property which was formerly transferred by the state without charge to co-operative, state co-operative or non-profit organisations shall be

returned to the Republic of Estonia (re-nationalisation of property).

(3) Property is returned, compensated for or transferred under the conditions and pursuant to the procedures provided for in this Act and other legislation of the Republic of Estonia.

Section 4 – Entitled Subjects of Ownership Reform

Entitled subjects of ownership reform are persons, including the state, who by law are entitled to claim return of or compensation for property or who are entitled to claim or apply for transfer of property for a charge or without charge.

Section 5 – Obligated Subjects of Ownership Reform

(1) Obligated subjects of ownership reform are the state and other persons who by law are obligated to return or compensate for property or to transfer property for a charge or without charge to entitled subjects of ownership reform. (29.01.97 entered into force 02.03.97 – RT I 1997, 13, 210)

(2) Ownership reform is ensured by the Government of the Republic, which shall appoint ministers responsible for different areas of ownership reform. In carrying out ownership reform, local governments perform acts prescribed by law and by the Government of the Republic pursuant to law. (29.01.97 entered into force 02.03.97 – RT I 1997, 13, 210)

II. RETURN OF AND COMPENSATION FOR UNLAWFULLY EXPROPRIATED PROPERTY

Section 6 – Definition of Unlawful Expropriation of Property

(1) Unlawful expropriation of property means the taking away of property from the owner against the owner's will or placement of the owner in a situation where, due to a real danger of repression, the person is forced to give up or abandon property if the legislation on the basis of which the property was expropriated is declared unlawful or if the property was expropriated on the basis of an unlawful decision or due to the arbitrary action of officials.

(2) In this Act, nationalisation, collectivisation and expropriation of property in the course of unlawful repression, including mass repression, and by other methods as set out in subsection (1) of this section during the period between 16 June 1940 and 1 June 1981 are deemed to be unlawful expropriation of property.

(3) In this Act, unlawful repression means either judicial or extra-judicial repression (death penalty, imprisonment, exilement or deportation) pursuant to unlawful decisions or decisions which were later declared unlawful.

(4) In this Act, a real danger of repression means a danger of either judicial or extra-judicial repression (death penalty, imprisonment, exilement or deportation).

(5) Unlawfully expropriated property is returned or compensated for on equal bases regardless of the method of unlawful expropriation provided for in subsection (2) of this section, except in the cases provided for in subsection 13 (3) and SECTION 14 of this Act.

Section 7 – Former Owners of Unlawfully Expropriated Property as Entitled Subjects of Ownership Reform

(1) The following persons are entitled to claim return of or compensation for unlawfully expropriated property:

1) natural persons whose property was nationalised or communised in the course of collectivisation and persons whose property was unlawfully expropriated in the course of unlawful repression and who have been rehabilitated if, on the date of entry into force of this Act, such natural persons reside permanently in the territory of the Republic of Estonia which at present is under the jurisdiction of the Republic of Estonia, or if they were citizens of the Republic of Estonia on 16 June 1940;

2) natural persons whose property was unlawfully expropriated pursuant to an unlawful decision or due to the arbitrary action of officials or who, due to a real danger of repression, were forced to give up or abandon their property if, on the date of entry into force of this Act, such natural persons reside permanently in the territory of the Republic of Estonia which at present is under the jurisdiction of the Republic of Estonia, or if they were citizens of the

Republic of Estonia on 16 June 1940 and the existence of the unlawful decision or arbitrary action of officials or real danger of repression has been proved in court;

3) natural persons who within the meaning and under the conditions provided for in SECTION 8 of this Act are successors of the persons specified in clauses 1) and 2) of this subsection;

4) organisations within the meaning and under the conditions provided for in SECTION 9 of this Act;

5) a local government with regard to unlawfully expropriated municipal property which was in the ownership of the local government on 16 June 1940 and is located in the current administrative territory of the local government applying for return thereof; if the unlawfully expropriated property which was in the ownership of the local government is located in the administrative territory of another local government, the property shall be returned to the local government with the consent of the local government council of the location of the property; (29.01.97 entered into force 02.03.97 – RT I 1997, 13, 210)

6) the Republic of Estonia with regard to property which was in the ownership of the Republic of Estonia on 16 June 1940;

7) successors provided for in SECTION 8 of persons who are citizens of Estonia or who reside permanently in the territory under the jurisdiction of the Republic of Estonia at the time of entry into force of this Act with regard to unlawfully expropriated property which was in the ownership of citizens of foreign states and stateless persons; (29.01.97 entered into force 02.03.97 – RT I 1997, 13, 210)

8) persons to whom the right of claim has been assigned or who have succeeded thereto pursuant to SECTION 16 of this Act. (29.01.97 entered into force 02.03.97 – RT I 1997, 13, 210)

(2) Applications for return of or compensation for unlawfully expropriated property which was in the ownership of foreign states, legal persons and citizens of foreign states and stateless persons, except for persons specified in clauses (1) 1)–4) and 7) of this section, and which was located in the Republic of Estonia are resolved by an agreement between the Republic of Estonia and the corresponding state. (29.01.97 entered into force 02.03.97 – RT I 1997, 13, 210)

(3) Applications for return of or compensation for unlawfully expropriated property which was in the ownership of persons who left Estonia on the basis of agreements entered into with the German state and which was located in the Republic of Estonia are resolved by an international agreement. (29.01.97 entered into force 02.03.97 – RT I 1997, 13, 210)

(4) A person who entered into a contract with an owner of property before 16 June 1940 to acquire the property and performed the obligations assumed by him or her under the contract for acquisition of the property and whose right of ownership was not formalised for reasons independent of the parties is entitled to claim return of the unlawfully expropriated property. Successors within the meaning and under the conditions provided for in SECTION 8 of this Act of such persons have the same right. The burden of proof of his or her rights rests with the person or his or her successors. If another person applies for return of or compensation for the same property, the dispute is resolved by a court. (29.01.97 entered into force 02.03.97 – RT I 1997, 13, 210)

Section 8 – Successors as Entitled Subjects of Ownership Reform

(1) If a former owner of unlawfully expropriated property is deceased and has made a will, testate successors are entitled subjects of ownership reform to the extent specified in the will.

(2) The will of a former owner must comply with the requirements of law at the time the will was made and must have been made before the unlawful expropriation of the property specified in the will or after the entry into force of this Act.

(3) If a former owner of unlawfully expropriated property is deceased and there is no will or it fails to comply with the requirements of subsection (2) of this section, or if the will does not include all of the unlawfully expropriated property, or if the testate successor (successors) is (are) deceased, the following persons are entitled subjects of ownership reform with regard to the unlawfully expropriated property in whole or to the extent of the property which is not specified in the will: (13.04.94 entered into force 15.05.94 – RT I 1994, 33, 507)

1) parents, spouse and children of the former owner in equal shares;

2) grandchildren and other descendants of the former owner if their parent is dead (regardless of the date of death) in equal shares; however, they are only entitled to claim return of or compensation for the property to which their parent would have been entitled. (29.01.97 entered into force 02.03.97 – RT I 1997, 13, 210)

(4) Adoptive parents and adopted children have equal rights with persons specified in subsections (1) and (3) of this section upon return of or compensation for unlawfully expropriated property.

(5) Only persons specified in this section are deemed to be successors of unlawfully expropriated property. If a successor of a former owner is deceased, the right to claim his or her share of the estate shall not transfer to his or her successors except for the persons specified in clause (3) 2) of this section.

(6) If the filiation of a parent or grandparent of a person who applies for declaration as an entitled subject of the ownership reform on the basis of subsection (3) or (4) of this section from the father who was the former owner of unlawfully expropriated property has not been ascertained earlier, such person may apply for the court to establish the filiation on the bases provided for in the Family Law Act (RT I 1994, 75, 1326; 1996, 40, 773; 49, 953; 1997, 28, 422; 35, 538; 2000, 50, 317; 2001, 16, 69; 53, 307; 2002, 53, 336).(08.10.97 entered into force 06.11.97 – RT I 1997, 74, 1230)

Section 9 – Organisations as Entitled Subjects of Ownership Reform

(1) Non-profit organisations and religious societies which operated in the Republic of Estonia until 16 June 1940 are entitled subjects of ownership reform if the activities specified in their articles of association did not discontinue. (02.06.93 entered into force 21.06.93 – RT I 1993, 35, 546)

(2) The right of an organisation specified in subsection (1) of this section to be an entitled subject of ownership reform shall be established by a court, and disputes between several organisations are resolved by a court.

(3) For the purposes of this Act, a non-profit organisation means an organisation whose activities were not aimed at distribution of revenue between members. (29.01.97 entered into force 02.03.97 – RT I 1997, 13, 210)

(4) Legal persons in public law may be declared entitled subjects only by an Act. Property is returned to such persons on the bases provided by this Act and pursuant to the procedure established by the Government of the Republic. They are not compensated for the property which is not returned. (29.01.97 entered into force 02.03.97 – RT I 1997, 13, 210)

Section 10 – Procedure for Declaration of Organisation as Entitled Subject of Ownership Reform

(1) After receipt of the application of an organisation specified in subsection 9 (1) of this Act for declaration of the organisation as an entitled subject of ownership reform, a court shall publish a corresponding announcement in a national newspaper within ten days.

(2) All persons who have objections to a filed application shall notify the court thereof within three months after the date of publication of the announcement.

(3) The court shall summon all persons specified in subsections (1) and (2) of this section to the hearing of the matter.

(4) An application specified in subsection (1) of this section shall be filed with a court according to the location of the organisation on 16 June 1940.

Section 11 – Unlawfully Expropriated Property as Object of Ownership Reform

(1) Objects of ownership reform are unlawfully expropriated land with inseparably attached natural objects, structures, ships entered in the register of ships, agricultural inventory, machinery in production buildings, stocks and share certificates, without considering incumbent loans. (29.01.97 entered into force 02.03.97 – RT I 1997, 13, 210)

The bases for determination of the value of property which is an object of ownership reform shall be established by law. (02.06.93 entered into force 21.06.93 – RT I 1993, 35, 545)

(3) Stocks and share certificates are objects of ownership reform if such stocks and share certificates were registered pursuant to SECTION 6 and 7 of the Securities Circulation Regulation Act of 18 July 1940 (RT 1940, 69, 678) or were filed and entered in an appropriate list pursuant to SECTION 12 of

the Organisation of Nationalisation Act of 1 August 1940 (RT 1940, 89, 870). (29.01.97 entered into force 02.03.97 – RT I 1997, 13, 210)

(4) For the purpose of this Act, agricultural inventory means machines, equipment, tools and animals used for agricultural purposes. (29.01.97 entered into force 02.03.97 – RT I 1997, 13, 210)

(5) For the purposes of this Act, machinery in production buildings means machines, equipment and tools used for production. (29.01.97 entered into force 02.03.97 – RT I 1997, 13, 210)

Section 12 – Return of Unlawfully Expropriated Property

(1) Persons who own unlawfully expropriated property which is an object of ownership reform are required to return it to the entitled subjects unless otherwise provided by this Act. Legal persons in private law, except for state commercial undertakings, public limited companies all the stocks of which are held by a local government, private limited companies the only share of which is held by a local government, and obligated subjects of agricultural reform and re-nationalisation, who by law acquired property subject to return on the basis of a contract of purchase and sale shall be compensated by the state for the sum paid to purchase the property. The compensation procedure shall be established by the Government of the Republic. Based on the provisions provided for in subsection (10) of this section, legal persons in private law who are compensated by the state for the sum paid to purchase property are entitled, pursuant to SECTION 27 and 28 of the Law of Property Act (RT I 1993, 39, 590; 1999, 44, 509; 2001, 34, 185; 52, 303; 93, 565; 2002, 47, 297; 53, 336), to claim compensation for expenses made on the property from entitled subjects to whom the property was returned. (29.01.97 entered into force 02.03.97 – RT I 1997, 13, 210)

(2) If several persons are entitled to claim property subject to return, the property shall be returned in whole if it is claimed by at least one person, in which case the person to whom the property is returned shall compensate other persons for their share pursuant to the procedure provided by law. If several entitled subjects claim return of property, the property shall be returned into their common ownership according to their shares. If property to be returned was in common ownership, the property corresponding to shares in common ownership is returned into common ownership of the entitled subjects according to their shares. Upon partial return of property, it is returned as a legal share. (29.01.97 entered into force 02.03.97 – RT I 1997, 13, 210)

(3) Unlawfully expropriated property as an object of ownership reform is not subject to return if:

1) entitled subjects of ownership reform do not claim return of the property but wish to be compensated therefore;

2) the property is not preserved in its former distinct condition as provided for in subsection (8) of this section; (02.06.93 entered into force 21.06.93 – RT I 1993, 35, 545)

3) the property is in the ownership of a natural person in good faith; above all, an acquirer in good faith shall not be a person who participated in extrajudicial repression of the owner of the property or unlawful expropriation of the property of the person; (29.01.97 entered into force 02.03.97 – RT I 1997, 13, 210)

4) the property is a structure in the ownership of the state, legal persons or municipalities which is in the possession of natural persons or legal persons pursuant to a commercial lease contract or residential lease contract, and the entitled subject does not agree to take over the rights and obligations arising from the contract; (29.01.97 entered into force 02.03.97 – RT I 1997, 13, 210)

5) on the proposal of a government agency or a local government council, the Government of the Republic decides to refuse to return military objects, law enforcement sites, cultural objects, social assets or objects under state protection, and administrative buildings in the possession of the state or local government; (29.01.97 entered into force 02.03.97 – RT I 1997, 13, 210)

6) (Repealed – 28.60.94 entered into force 25.07. 94 – RT I 1994, 51, 859)

7) on the proposal of a local government, the county governor decides that separation of the unlawfully expropriated property renders the purposeful use of the remaining property technologically impossible or that in the case of return of an economically affiliated outbuilding, the normal use of the building would be impeded; (29.01.97 entered into force 02.03.97 – RT I 1997, 13, 210)

8) the property is located on land which is not returned pursuant to clause 31 (1) 2) of the Republic of Estonia Land Reform Act (RT 1991, 34, 426; RT I 2001, 52, 304; 93, 565; 2002, 11, 59; 47, 297; 298). (29.01.97 entered into force 02.03.97 – RT I 1997, 13, 210)

(4) (Repealed – 29.01.97 entered into force 02.03.97 – RT I 1997, 13, 210)

(5) Return of property shall be decided and organised by rural municipality governments or city governments unless otherwise provided by law. (29.01.97 entered into force 02.03.97 – RT I 1997, 13, 210)

(6) Prior to the return of property, the Government of the Republic or a local government council may, by a resolution, require that the entitled subject enter into a contract for the use of the property for the current designated purpose with a term of five years as a prerequisite for return of the property. The person to whom property is returned is required to perform the protection regime established for the property. Unless the protection regime arises from law or a protection obligation notice, the performance of such obligation is ensured by a contract entered into by the competent state agency or local government agency and the entitled subject. Property shall not be returned if an entitled subject refuses to enter into a contract for designated use or a contract to ensure performance of the protection regime. (29.01.97 entered into force 02.03.97 – RT I 1997, 13, 210)

(7) During a proceeding for the return of property, the person who has been declared an entitled subject is required to perform acts necessary for the proceeding within the term and pursuant to the procedure established by the Government of the Republic. If, without good reason, an entitled subject fails to perform the necessary acts within the term notified to the entitled subject in writing, the person is deemed to have renounced the claim and the return proceeding is terminated. If after a decision on return of property is made, the entitled subject fails, without good reason, to accept the property within the term notified to the entitled subject in writing, the return proceeding is terminated and the return decision is annulled. In such cases, property compensation proceedings are not commenced. (29.01.97 entered into force 02.03.97 – RT I 1997, 13, 210)

(8) Property is deemed to have retained its former distinct condition if the form, value and size of the property has not changed significantly taking into account that:

1) a structure is deemed to have retained its former distinct condition if, due to major repairs, alterations or additions, the value of the structure has not increased by more than one quarter of the total value of the structure; (31.05.2000 entered into force 26.06.2000 – RT I 2000, 47, 288)

2) a structure is deemed not to have retained its former distinct condition if, due to major repairs, alterations or additions, the value of the structure has increased by at least three-quarters of its total value; (31.05.2000 entered into force 26.06.2000 – RT I 2000, 47, 288)

3) a ship is deemed to have retained its former distinct condition even if, during major repairs or alterations, the purpose of the ship has been changed and power installations, navigation equipment, electrical equipment and communications equipment have been exchanged or new ones have been installed;

4) agricultural inventory and machinery in production buildings are deemed to have retained their former distinct condition even if they are not in good technical condition or are used for other purposes;

5) a residential building is deemed not to have retained its former distinct condition if the executive body of a local government establishes that the residential building became restricted in habitability or came into danger of collapse after unlawful expropriation and that it was lawfully made habitable again by a natural person at his or her own expense who themselves or whose spouse, ascendants or descendants live in it on the basis of a residential lease contract at the time a decision on the return of the property is made and who have filed an application for privatisation of the residential building. (22.03.94 entered into force 16.04.94 – RT I 1994, 24, 395; 29.01.97 entered into force 02.03.97 – RT I 1997, 13, 210)

[. . .]

(9) If the value of a structure has increased significantly due to major repairs, alterations or additions and the basis provided for in clauses (8) 1) and 2) of this section for return or refusal to return the structure as a whole does not exist, the legal

share corresponding to the retained value of the structure shall be returned. If dwellings have been added to the structure, a share corresponding to the retained value of the structure is returned in the case provided for in clause (8) 1) of this section. Such restriction does not apply to dwellings which were converted from non-residential premises. (29.01.97 entered into force 02.03.97 – RT I 1997, 13, 210)

(10) In assessments of objects specified in subsection (8) of this section, repairs and renovations made after the entry into force of the Republic of Estonia Principles of Ownership Reform Act are not taken into account. Assessment of the value of a structure is based on the value at the time of the assessment, taking into account wear and tear. In the assessment of the value of a structure, new parts which are subject to demolition due to non-compliance with the building code and the requirements of SECTION 43 of the Planning and Building Act (RT I 1995, 59, 1006; 1996, 36, 738; 49, 953; 1999, 27, 380; 29, 398; 399; 95, 843; 2000, 54, 348; 2001, 42, 234; 50, 283; 65, 377; 2002, 47, 297; 53, 336) are not assessed. If, upon refusal to return a structure on the bases provided for in subsection (8) of this section, outbuildings are not returned as well, the assessment of the preservation of the former distinct condition of the structure shall be based on the condition of the structure and its outbuildings in the aggregate. (29.01.97 entered into force 02.03.97 – RT I 1997, 13, 210)

(11) The procedure and methods for assessment of the preservation of the former distinct condition of structures shall be established by the Government of the Republic. (29.01.97 entered into force 02.03.97 – RT I 1997, 13, 210)

Section 12.1 – Validity of Residential Lease Contract in Respect of Returned Residential Building

(1) A residential lease contract in force at the time of return of a residential building is deemed to be valid for three years after the transfer of the right of ownership in the residential building to the entitled subject unless the tenant and the owner agree otherwise upon return of the residential building. If a residential lease contract with the tenant has not been entered into in writing, the obligated subject of ownership reform shall enter into such contract with the tenant before the transfer of the residential building to be returned.

(2) (Repealed – 05.06.2002 entered into force 01.07.2002 – RT I 2002, 53, 336)

(3) Upon expiry of the term of a residential lease contract specified in subsection (1) of this section, the contract is extended for five years. A lessor may contest the extension of a residential lease contract only in the cases provided for in this section. In the case of a dispute, such extension is decided by a court. If a tenant is granted another dwelling pursuant to SECTION 45 of the Republic of Estonia Dwelling Act, the residential lease contract extends to the dwelling.

(4) A lessor may contest the extension of a residential lease contract only if:

1) the tenant has repeatedly failed to perform his or her contractual obligations or has repeatedly violated other terms and conditions of the contract and the lessor has performed the lessor's principal obligations;

2) the leased dwelling is needed for the lessor or his or her family members to live in on the condition that the lessor or his or her family members have not been granted the use of an equivalent dwelling in the territory of the local government or they have not transferred it after return of the residential building or they have not exchanged the right of use of the dwelling with the tenant after return of the residential building;

3) the leased dwelling came into danger of collapse before the return or for reasons independent of the lessor;

4) the leased dwelling is excluded from the category of dwellings because of natural wear and tear.

(5) Upon eviction of a tenant on the bases provided for in clause (4) 2), 3) or 4) of this section, the local government shall grant the tenant the use of a dwelling which is located in the same district, is in a state of repair equal to the dwelling used earlier and the size and number of rooms of the which are in accordance with socially justified standards. In such case, local governments use the options provided for in the Privatisation of Dwellings Act (RT I 1993, 23, 411; 2000, 99, 638; 2001, 93, 565; 2002, 47, 297; 53, 336) and the Use of Privatisation Proceeds Act (RT I 1996, 26, 529; 1997, 13, 210; 28, 424; 1998,

97, 1521; 1999, 23, 352; 356; 54, 583; 95, 841; 2000, 92, 600).

(6) (Repealed – 05.06.2002 entered into force 01.07.2002 – RT I 2002, 53, 336)

(7) Tenants and persons living with tenants are required to vacate a dwelling which is in their use upon receipt of a new dwelling pursuant to subsection (5) of this section. (05.06.2002 entered into force 01.07.2002 – RT I 2002, 53, 336)

(8) If a tenant has lawfully done major repairs or made alterations to the dwelling, the owner of the dwelling shall compensate the tenant upon refusal to extend the residential lease contract for necessary expenses as defined in the Law of Property Act made during major repairs or alterations. Tenants may remove improvements without causing damage if the lessor of the dwelling does not agree to compensate for the improvements.

(9) Tenants living in a returned residential building are entitled to receive a new dwelling pursuant to the procedure provided by the Privatisation of Dwellings Act or are entitled to apply for a loan or grant from the state or local government for resettlement or for purchase of a dwelling pursuant to the Use of Privatisation Proceeds Act.

(10) Tenants have a joint right of pre-emption in the transfer of a returned residential building and of a corresponding registered immovable or a part thereof. Upon transfer of a physical share which is not subject to commercial restrictions, a tenant of the physical share has the right of pre-emption. The right of pre-emption does not apply upon transfer to a spouse, descendants, parents, sisters and brothers and their descendants. Otherwise, the provisions of the Law of Property Act apply to the right of pre-emption. (31.05.2000 entered into force 26.06.2000 – RT I 2000, 47, 288)

(11) The provisions of this section extend to lease relations concerning a dwelling in which a tenant who is party to such relations resides on the date on which the residential building is returned. Upon expiry of the term of a residential lease contract which was extended pursuant to this section, the residential lease contract may be extended pursuant to SECTION 32 or 33 of the Republic of Estonia Dwelling Act. In the case specified in this section, provisions of the Law of Obligations Act concerning residential lease contracts do not apply to the extension of the residential lease contract.

(05.06.2002 entered into force 01.07.2002 – RT I 2002, 53, 336)

(12) Local governments are required to notify tenants of decisions to return property to entitled subjects prior to the return of residential buildings. (29.01.97 entered into force 02.03.97 – RT I 1997, 13, 210)

Section 13 – Compensation for Unlawfully Expropriated Property

(1) If unlawfully expropriated property as an object of ownership reform has been destroyed, is not returned pursuant to SECTION 12 of this Act or if such property comprises shares or share certificates, the state shall compensate for the property to the extent and pursuant to the procedure provided by law. Natural persons, legal persons and local governments who own unlawfully expropriated property which is not returned in the cases provided for in SECTION 12 of this Act or in whose ownership the property was destroyed or from whose ownership the property was removed by any other method are not required to pay compensation except for the cases provided for in SECTION 14 of this Act. (02.06.93 entered into force 21.06.93 – RT I 1999, 545, 577; 29.01.97 entered into force 02.03.97 – RT I 1997, 13, 210; 17.02.99 entered into force 19.03.99 – RT I 2000, 23, 354)

(2) Persons specified in clauses 7 (1) 1)–4) of this Act are compensated for the value of property unless otherwise provided by this Act. (29.01.97 entered into force 02.03.97 – RT I 1997, 13, 210)

(3) Unlawfully repressed and rehabilitated persons are compensated to the extent determined by law for unlawfully expropriated property which is not an object of ownership reform pursuant to subsection 11 (1) of this Act. (02.06.93 entered into force 21.06.93 – RT I 1993, 35, 545)

(4) Unreceived revenue shall not be compensated for. The state shall not compensate for unlawfully expropriated property which is destroyed unless otherwise provided by law. (29.01.97 entered into force 02.03.97 – RT I 1997, 13, 210)

(5) (Repealed – 02.06.93 entered into force 21.06. 93 – RT I 1993, 35, 545)

(6) (Repealed – 02.06.93 entered into force 21.06. 93 – RT I 1993, 35, 545)

(7) During a property compensation proceeding, a person who has been declared an entitled subject is required to perform acts necessary for the proceeding within the terms and pursuant to the procedure established by the Government of the Republic. If, without good reason, an entitled subject fails to perform the necessary acts within the term notified to the entitled subject in writing, the person is deemed to have renounced the claim and the compensation proceeding shall be terminated. If within six months after a compensation decision is made the entitled subject fails, without good reason, to submit an application for transfer of the compensation to a privatisation voucher account, the compensation proceeding shall be terminated and the compensation decision shall be annulled. (29.01.97 entered into force 02.03.97 – RT I 13, 210, 12; 14.01.98 entered into force 16.02.98 – RT I 1997, 1998, 1314)

Section 14 – Return of or Compensation for Communised Property

(1) Property which was communised in the establishment of collective farms is returned or compensated for on equal bases with other unlawfully expropriated property unless otherwise provided by this Act or other laws of the Republic of Estonia. (2) (Repealed – 02.06.93 entered into force 21.06.93 – RT I 1993, 35, 545)

(3) If communised property is not returned pursuant to this Act or is destroyed, it shall be compensated for pursuant to the procedure provided by law:

1) by the collective farm during the foundation of which the property was communised; in the case of reorganisation of a collective farm, by the collective farm into whose ownership the communised property was transferred;

2) by another legal person which was founded upon reorganisation or liquidation of a collective farm if the legal person is the legal successor of the collective farm or has been transferred all or part of the property of the collective farm;

3) by the state if the collective farm founded upon communisation of property has been reorganised into an enterprise based on state ownership; if a legal successor to the collective farm does not exist or cannot be determined, or if the collective farm or

its legal successor does not have necessary assets for the compensation. (29.01.97 entered into force 02.03.97 – RT I 1997, 13, 210)

(4) Communised property which has been returned or compensated for by a collective farm by the time of entry into force of this Act shall be set off against compensation specified in subsection (3) of this section.

(5) If an entitled subject is a farmer, he or she has the preferential right with respect to other persons to receive compensation in kind.

(6) Pursuant to a corresponding Act of the Republic of Estonia, communised property may be returned earlier than provided for in subsection 17 (2) of this Act.

Section 15 – Exceptions for Return of and Compensation for Nationalised Land

This Act applies upon return of and compensation for nationalised land and natural objects inseparably attached thereto, unless otherwise provided by the Republic of Estonia Land Reform Act (RT 1991, 34, 426; RT I 2001, 52, 304; 93, 565; 2002, 11, 59; 47, 297; 298). (02.06.93 entered into force 21.06.93 – RT I 1993, 35, 545; 29.01.97 entered into force 02.03. 97 – RT I 1997, 13, 210)

Section 16 – Filing and Registration of Applications for Return of or Compensation for Unlawfully Expropriated Property

(1) Entitled subjects of ownership reform are entitled to file applications for return of or compensation for unlawfully expropriated property until 17 January 1992. Documents that the applicants have concerning the ownership, form and value of property shall be appended to such applications. (18.12.91 – RT 1991, 45, 565)

(2) The procedure for filing and review of applications and the procedure for filing and assessment of evidence shall be established by the Government of the Republic. County or city committees for return of and compensation for unlawfully expropriated property (hereinafter local committees) established by county governors or the city governments of Tallinn, Tartu, Pärnu, Narva, Kohtla-Järve, Sillamäe or Narva-Jõesuu decide on declaring applicants entitled subjects. (29.01.97 entered

into force 02.03.97 – RT I 13, 210, 96; 15.12.99 entered into force 01.01.2000 – RT I 1997, 1999, 1314)

(3) A register of entitled subjects and property to be returned or compensated for is prepared on the basis of filed applications and decisions on return of or compensation for property. The procedure for preparation of the register shall be established by the Government of the Republic. (02.06.93 entered into force 21.06.93 – RT I 1993, 35, 545)

(4) Entitled subjects have the right to change the claim indicated in their application within one month after receipt of the decision to declare the person an entitled subject. If the property subject to return is a residential building and the land adjacent thereto or the land used by the owner of a structure, which upon privatisation of land with the right of pre-emption is not deemed to be included in the land necessary for servicing the structure, the entitled subject has the right to change an application for return into an application for compensation until a decision concerning the return is made. (09.02.94 entered into force 05.03.94 – RT I 1994, 2000, 210; 29.01.97 entered into force 02.03.97 – RT I 1997, 13, 47)

(5) If by 31 December 1997 applicants have not filed evidence concerning the circumstances which they are required to prove pursuant to the procedure established by the Government of the Republic, they shall file evidence within the term and pursuant to the procedure established by the Government of the Republic. If an applicant fails to file evidence without good reason within the term notified to the entitled person in writing, the local committee shall terminate the processing of the application. (29.01.97 entered into force 02.03.97 – RT I 1997, 13, 210)

(6) Received documents are assessed in the aggregate. If circumstances which are subject to proof cannot be substantiated by evidence filed and collected, and the local committee finds that it is not possible to obtain additional evidence, the local committee shall deny the application. (29.01.97 entered into force 02.03.97 – RT I 1997, 13, 210)

(7) Until the entry into force of a court order in a matter regarding a decision to declare a person an entitled subject, the processing of the application shall not be terminated and the application shall not be denied. (29.01.97 entered into force 02.03. 97 – RT I 1997, 13, 210)

Section 16.1 – Succession of Right of Claim and Assignment of Right of Claim for Return of Property

(1) The right of claim is inheritable pursuant to the procedure provided by civil law. The provisions of Estonian law apply to succession of the right of claim regardless of the place of the opening of succession. If no decision has been made on return of or compensation for property, a decision to declare a person an entitled person is the basis for issue of a certificate of succession of the right of claim. In such case, the property is returned to the successor or the successor is compensated therefore.

(2) Until a decision on return of property is made, an entitled subject may assign the right of claim for return of the property to his or her spouse, descendants, sisters and brothers and their descendants or to other entitled subjects with regard to the same property or land under the structure. The provisions of civil law apply to assignment of the right of claim unless otherwise provided by this Act. Assignment of the right of claim is binding on the organiser of the return of property if the agreement concerning assignment of the right of claim or a notarised copy thereof is filed with the organiser. (14.11.2001 entered into force 01.02.2002 – RT I 2001, 93, 565)

(3) A person may assign the right of claim for an object in full only. If the right of claim belongs to several entitled subjects, each person may assign their share of the right of claim in full. An agreement concerning assignment of the right of claim shall be notarised. (29.01.97 entered into force 02.03.97 – RT I 1997, 13, 210)

Section 17 – Procedure for Return of and Compensation for Unlawfully Expropriated Property

(1) In order to compensate for unlawfully expropriated property, compensation vouchers are issued to entitled subjects of ownership reform. After the end of issue of compensation vouchers, property shall be compensated for in other manners provided by law. Such vouchers shall not be issued upon compensation for communised property by

collective farms or other legal persons in the cases provided for in clauses 14 (3) 1) and 2) of this Act. (02.06.93 entered into force 21.06.93 – RT I 1993, 545, 577; 29.01.97 entered into force 02.03.97 – RT I 1997, 13, 210; 14.06.2000 entered into force 10.07.2000 – RT I 2000, 51, 324)

(2) Unlawfully expropriated property is returned pursuant to the procedure established by the Government of the Republic. The value of property is not determined upon return of property unless otherwise provided by law. (09.02.94 entered into force 05.03.94 – RT I 1994, 13, 231; 29.01.97 entered into force 02.03.97 – RT I 1997, 13, 210)

(3) Unlawfully expropriated property is compensated for by exchange of the vouchers specified in subsection (1) of this section for stocks or other property subject to privatisation, or by other methods. (4) (Repealed – 02.06.93 entered into force 21.06.93 – RT I 1993, 35, 545)

(5) A person who is an entitled subject of ownership reform is not entitled to claim return of unlawfully expropriated property or claim compensation for the portion of property which has already been returned or compensated for, except if it is established that the property has been returned to an unauthorised person or unauthorised person has been compensated for the property without legal basis. (31.05.2000 entered into force 26.06.2000 – RT I 2000, 47, 288)

(6) Unlawfully expropriated property which is an object of ownership reform is returned to persons whose property was expropriated due to repression or who were forced to give up or abandon property due to a real danger of repression, arbitrary action or pursuant to the unlawful decisions of officials or such persons are compensated therefore after filing a rehabilitation certificate or a court order certifying the unlawfulness of the expropriation. In order to receive a court order or a rehabilitation certificate, such persons shall take recourse to a court or the corresponding state authority within one month after the executive body of the local government has presented the person with a requirement arising from law to prove the method of expropriation of property specified in this section. (18.12.91 – RT 1991, 45, 565)

(7) A simplified procedure for rehabilitation and for proving the unlawfulness of expropriation of property may be established by law. (02.06.93 entered into force 21.06.93 – RT I 1993, 35, 545)

(8) Entitled subjects and associations representing entitled subjects are entitled to receive information from the organiser of the return of property concerning the return process, to file additional documents and records, and to demand application of measures to ensure preservation of the property. (29.01.97 entered into force 02.03.97 – RT I 1997, 13, 210)

(9) Supervision over return of property shall be exercised pursuant to the procedure provided by the Government of the Republic by county governors, who have the right to apply the measures provided for in the Government of the Republic Act (RT I 1995, 94, 1628; 1996, 49, 953; 88, 1560; 1997, 29, 447; 40, 622; 52, 833; 73, 1200; 81, 1361; 1362; 87, 1468; 1998, 28, 356; 36/37, 552; 40, 614; 71, 1201; 107, 1762; 111, 1833; 1999, 10, 155; 16, 271; 274; 27, 391; 29, 398; 401; 58, 608; 95, 843; 845; 2000, 49, 302; 51, 319; 320; 54, 352; 58, 378; 95, 613; 102, 677; 2001, 7, 16; 24, 133; 52, 303; 53, 305; 59, 358; 94, 578; 100, 646; 102, 677; 2002, 13, 79). The Minister of Finance has the right to request that county governors commence supervision proceedings. (29.01.97 entered into force 02.03.97 – RT I 1997, 13, 210)

Section 18 – Transactions with Unlawfully Expropriated Property and Liability for Ensuring Preservation Thereof

(1) Until a decision is made on return of unlawfully expropriated property which is an object of ownership reform (including resolution of an extrajudicial dispute or dispute in court), state agencies, local government agencies, other legal persons and natural persons who own or possess the property are prohibited from transferring such property or encumbering it with a real right unless otherwise provided by this Act. Transactions in violation of this prohibition are void. Such property may be transferred to the state or local governments, or to other persons with the notarised consent of the entitled subjects. Until a decision on return of unlawfully expropriated property is made, the current possessors of the property have the right to subject it to a commercial lease or grant possession of the property by any other method only without specifying the term, except if the entitled subject agrees to a relationship with a specified term.

The provisions of SECTION 12 of this Act do not apply to residential lease contracts without a term. Termination of contracts without a term is subject to three months' advance notice. (29.01.97 entered into force 02.03.97 – RT I 1997, 13, 210; 14.11.2001 entered into force 01.02.2002 – RT I 2001, 93, 565)

(2) The owners and possessors of property specified in subsection (1) of this section are required to ensure preservation of the property. If this requirement is not complied with, they are required to compensate for damage.

(3) Until a decision is made on return of land, regeneration cutting on unlawfully expropriated land is prohibited. Entitled subjects for the return of land have the right to carry out improvement cutting and cut boundary lines without charge; entitled subjects for privatisation of land are entitled to cut boundary lines without charge and, after an order of the local government on privatisation of land with the right of pre-emption is issued, to carry out improvement cutting pursuant to the procedure established by the Government of the Republic. Upon waiving the return or privatisation of land, entitled subjects are required to pay for cutting pursuant to the usual value of standing crop. Compensation collected for damages caused by illegal cutting on unlawfully expropriated land and the money received from sale of illegally cut timber sold by a state agency, from which expenses related to the sale of the timber are deducted, shall be deposited and, after the land is entered in the land register, paid pursuant to the procedure established by the Government of the Republic to the person to whom the land is returned or to an heir thereof. If illegal cutting is carried out with the participation or consent of such persons, they do not have the right to the aforementioned amounts and such amounts shall not be deposited. (14.10.99 entered into force 14.11.99 – RT I 1999, 82, 751)

(4) Until a decision is made on return of unlawfully expropriated property, structures to be returned may be demolished or altered only at the request of a county governor with the permission of the Government of the Republic, or with the notarised consent of the entitled subjects. Demolished buildings shall be compensated for. (29.01.97 entered into force 02.03.97 – RT I 1997, 13, 210; 14.11.

2001 entered into force 01.02.2002 – RT I 2001, 93, 565)

Section 19 – Resolution of Disputes Concerning Return of or Compensation for Unlawfully Expropriated Property

(1) Disputes arising from return of or compensation for unlawfully expropriated property are resolved extra-judicially or by a court proceeding. The term for recourse to an administrative court concerning a decision made in the course of return of or compensation for unlawfully expropriated property is two months as of the date on which the person became aware of a decision which violates his or her rights. Limitation periods established by other acts apply to civil disputes. (16.11. 98 entered into force 10.12.98 – RT I 1998, 103, 1697)

(2) Extra-judicially, county committees resolve appeals against decisions made in proceedings for return and compensation of property. A county committee may also act as a conciliation committee. (29.01.97 entered into force 02.03.97 – RT I 13, 210, 96; 15.12.99 entered into force 01.01.2000 – RT I 1997, 1999, 1314)

(3) If a party files an appeal with a court and concurrently one of the parties takes recourse to the county committee for resolution thereof, the court shall refuse to accept the appeal or hear it. The period for recourse to the county committee is one month after the date on which the person became or should have become aware of the violation of his or her rights. Recourse to county committees is exempt from state fees. If an appeal is filed, county committees may discontinue the processing of the application for return of or compensation for property. (29.01.97 entered into force 02.03.97 – RT I 1997, 13, 210)

(4) Complaints filed in writing with county committees shall be heard within two months after receipt of such complaints. At the request of an applicant or a county committee, the complaint shall be heard in the presence of the persons concerned or their representatives. The members of county committees are subject to removal if there is reason to believe that they are personally interested in the ultimate determination of the matter or if other circumstances cast suspicion upon their impartiality. A county committee has the right to

demand delivery of all documents relevant to a matter. (29.01.97 entered into force 02.03.97 – RT I 1997, 13, 210)

(5) In a meeting of a county committee, the explanations of the persons concerned shall be heard, and documents and other evidence shall be examined and assessed. Minutes shall be taken of meetings of county committees. A county committee shall make its decision on the day on which the matter is heard. Decisions of county committees are made by majority vote. Upon an equal division of votes, the vote of the chairman of the county committee governs. The decision shall be signed by the chairman and secretary of the county committee. Copies of a decision shall be personally delivered or delivered to the persons concerned by post within five working days after the decision is made. (29.01.97 entered into force 02.03.97 – RT I 1997, 13, 210)

(6) If the persons concerned do not agree with a decision of a county committee, the persons concerned may take recourse to a court within two months after the date of receipt of a copy of the decision of the county committee. A decision of a county committee enters into force after expiry of the period for recourse to a court if no person concerned files a claim with a court. A decision which has entered into force is binding on the persons concerned. (29.01.97 entered into force 02.03.97 – RT I 1997, 13, 210; 16.11.98 entered into force 10.12.98 – RT I 1998, 103, 1697)

(6) (Repealed – 15.12.1999 entered into force 01.01.2000 – RT I 1999, 96, 847)

(7) A more specific procedure for extra-judicial resolution of appeals shall be established by the Government of the Republic. (29.01.97 entered into force 02.03.97 – RT I 1997, 13, 210).

[. . .]

---

9. GEORGIA

9.1. Law of the Republic of Georgia Concerning Internally Displaced People (1996)

[. . .]

Article 7. State Guarantees for Rehabilitation of Displaced Persons at Their Places of Permanent Residence

If a displaced person after the elimination of the reasons mentioned in Article 1 of this law returns to his place of permanent residence:

a) The relevant organs of executive bodies and local administration, among them the Ministry of Refugees and Accommodation will provide the implementation of their constitutional rights, will take measures to create necessary social-economic living conditions for the safety at their places of permanent residence; to return to displaced persons, their legal heritage, the personal assets, among them house and the land in the present condition; the compensation of the damage, after estimation of its amount, will be made by the local administrative bodies according to the established by the government law, also to give the guarantee to a person for the return to the damaged house after the reparation.

b) The National Bank of Georgia will determine the law for giving out the loans.

[. . .]

9.2. Law of Georgia on Property Restitution and Compensation on the Territory of Georgia for the Victims of Conflict in Former South Ossetia District (2006, Draft)

The Georgian State

recognizing the human rights and freedoms enshrined in the Constitution of Georgia and international law,

namely, the right of every person to property and adequate standards of living regardless of his/her race, skin colour, sex, language, ethnic or social origin, religion, belief, political or other views,

realizing the consequences of the 1990–1992 Conflict in the Former South Ossetia Autonomous District, which resulted in gross violation of rights and freedoms of a significant part of the population Georgia and forced them to leave their own houses,

takes over the responsibility to rehabilitate the rights of the victims of the conflict in 1990–1992 and afterwards and to bring them in conformity with the standards recognized by international law.

CHAPTER I

General Provisions

Article 1. The Purpose of the Law

The purpose of the present Law is restitution of property, provision of adequate (substitute) immovable property or compensation of property damage to natural persons who suffered damage on the territory of Georgia as a result of the Conflict in the Former South Ossetia Autonomous District.

Article 2. Notions and Definitions

The notions used in the present Law for its purposes shall have the following definitions:

a) conflict – the armed conflict in the Former South Ossetia District and/or the conflict on the ethnic basis between the Georgian and Ossetian population on the territory of Georgia in the period of 1990–1992 and afterwards.

b) right to residence – right to usage or ownership of the original residence.

c) original residence – residence of a forced migrant, where he/she had the right to reside at the moment of leaving the latter;

d) original resident – individual, who had the right to reside in the original residence;

e) forced migrant – individual, displaced within or beyond the territory of Georgia as a result of the conflict;

f) bona fide and mala fide owners – individuals, defined in the articles 159 and 164 of the Civil Code of Georgia;

g) relative – individuals, defined in the article 31 part II of the Civil Procedural Code of Georgia

h) family member – spouse, children, parents, adoptive parents, adopted children, grandparents, grandchildren, siblings;

i) reconstruction – modification of immovable property, as a result of which the size and market value of the property was significantly changed;

j) residence – immovable property designed for housing;

k) state property – property, more than 50% of which is owned by the state or local self-administration body;

l) other immovable property – land parcel and immovable property firmly fixed to it not designed for housing;

m) property restitution – returning of residence or other immovable property, lost within the territory of Georgia as a result of the conflict to the rightful owners;

n) secondary resident – individual presently residing (bona fide or mala fide) in the original residence of a forced migrant.

Article 3. Principles of the Law

The present Law shall be based upon the following principles:

a) justice and equality;

b) lawfulness;

c) respect for human dignity and protection and provision of the universally recognized rights and freedoms;

d) the right of an individual to get comprehensive information from the state agencies on the issues related to him/her;

e) the right of an individual to be provided with effective legal remedies;

f) accountability and responsibility of the government to the citizens and people present on its territory;

g) ensuring the right of the forced migrants to free and voluntary return.

Article 4. Scope of the Application

The present Law shall apply:

a) to the original residents, who as a result of the conflict were or are not able to return to their original residence due to lack of safety or adequate (substitute) residence;

b) to the secondary residents, who are bona or mala fide owners of the place of residence or other immovable property belonging to the original resident;

c) to the original residents, who received a substitute residence and/or monetary compensation with the help of state bodies or international or national organizations, and if the value of their original residence exceeds the compensation received or the value of the substitute residence;

1. The present Law shall recognize the right of forced migrants and other individuals to submit for the Commission's review all decisions made on the basis of Article 69 of the Housing Code of 1983 pursuant to which they lost their right to reside in the period during and following the conflict.

Article 5. Right to Property Restitution and Compensation

1. The present Law recognizes the right of all forced migrants and other individuals to return to their original residence and be provided with immovable property, to receive adequate (substitute) residence of the same value if their residence and other immovable property is demolished, or if this is not possible, to get compensation of the property damage.

2. Also, the present Law recognizes the right of the secondary bona fide resident to own adequate (substitute), safe and reasonable residential and immovable property.

CHAPTER II

The Commission on Restitution and Compensation

Article 6. Status of the Commission

1. For the purpose of implementing the goals envisaged by the present Law, a Commission on Restitution and Compensation (hereinafter the Commission) shall be established for the period of 9 years. In case of achieving the goals of the Commission ahead of schedule, the Commission shall make decision on early termination of its authority, and if the Commission fails to fully resolve the disputes within the term of authority, it shall make decision on prolonging of the authority of the Commission for a certain period of time.

2. The Commission shall be a legal entity of public law, which shall not be under the oversight of any state controlling agency.

Article 7. The Goals of the Commission

The goal of the Commission shall be:

a) restoration of the property;

b) provision of the adequate (substitute) residence;

c) compensation of property damage

for the individuals, who suffered damage on the territory of Georgia as a result of the conflict.

Article 8. Publicity of the Activities of the Commission

1. The meetings of the Commission on Restitution and Compensation and its committees are public. The Commission and its Committees are obliged to hold closed meetings, if this is requested at least by one of the parties in accordance with the legislation of Georgia.

2. The information obtained in the process of working of the Commission and its committees shall be public, except when confidentiality of specific information is required by the present Law, legislation of Georgia or if this is necessary for the effective performance of the functions of the Commission.

3. Any member of the Commission or staff working for the Bureau of the Commission shall be obliged to keep confidential the information determined by the legislation of Georgia, that has come to his/her knowledge due to his/her position or in the course of performing the activities, and also facilitate provision of confidentiality of such information.

4. Any individual shall be obliged in accordance with the legislation of Georgia not to disclose the confidential information, that has come to his/her knowledge in the course of supporting the activities of the Commission, as a result of being present at a meeting of the Commission or its committees or in any other way. A representative of the Commission shall forewarn the individual about this.

5. In case of disclosure of confidential information by the Commission or its committees accordingly the Commission or the committee shall be liable to compensate moral and/or material damages, caused by it.

Article 9. The Rule for Establishment of the Commission and its Composition

1. The Commission shall consist of 18 members, who shall be appointed for a term of 9 years by international organization.

2. The Commission shall be composed of representatives of the Georgian and Ossetian sides of

the conflict, and international organization(s), on a parity basis.

3. International organizations within the limits of their quota nominate 6 members of the Commission, who further appoint members of the Commission out of representatives of Georgian and Ossetian parties on the open competition basis.

4. International organization, a political party, non-commercial legal entity of private law or a group of at least 50 citizens are eligible to nominate candidates from the Georgian and Ossetian sides of the conflict.

5. A member of the Commission may be a capable individual, with higher education degree and at least 5 years of working experience. He/she must have the recognition and trust of the public. At least one third of the members of the Commission must have higher legal education.

6. Any person can take part in the competition, provided that he/she complies with the requirements, set for the members of the commission by the present law. The term for submitting the competition documents is at most 45 days after the competition is announced.

7. If within the term set by the present law at least 2 candidates are not presented for each vacancy, the competition will be prolonged for the period, within which there will be at least 2 candidates presented per vacancy. Within 2 days after expiry of the term of presenting of the candidates the list of the candidates will be published.

8. Within 30 days after expiry of the deadline for submitting the candidates for the Commission on Restitution and Compensation, the members appointed under the quota of international organizations will appoint the members nominated under the quota of the Georgian and Ossetian sides.

9. The terms and procedures for appointment of members under the quota of international organizations as well as for execution of their authority, the rule and conditions of holding the competition shall be determined by the resolution of the Government of Georgia in accordance with the memorandum endorsed with the international organizations participating to the process of formation of this Commission.

Article 10. Structure of the Commission

1. The Commission shall have a Chair and two deputy Chairs, who shall be elected by the Commission from its own members by the majority of votes.

2. The Chair and the Deputy Chairs of the Commission shall each represent the candidates nominated by the different parties.

3. The Chair and the Deputy Chairs of the Commission shall rotate every three years. A person already nominated by one side shall not be eligible for a second term as Chairperson.

4. Within the commission 3 committees will be established.

Article 11. Conflict of Interest Rule

1. A person cannot be a member of the Commission if he/she, at the same time:

a) has another wage-earning employment, save for teaching, scientific and artistic work;

b) is a member of a political party;

c) has directly participated in the armed clashes during the conflict or openly called for violence, ethnic discrimination and enmity.

2. The same requirement is applicable to the staff of the bureau, save for supporting/technical personnel.

3. A member of the Commission or staff of the bureau, except for supporting/technical personnel, who appears to have a direct or indirect economic interest with a person whose case is under examination by the Commission, shall notify of this interest in writing and refrain from taking part in the examination of the case and decision-making.

4. A member of the Commission or staff of the bureau, except supporting/technical personnel, who is a family member of the person defined by the sub-clause c) of the clause 1 of the present article or participated to the court hearing of the case during the conflict period or worked in a governmental body or held state position, who was directly connected to the arguable property, shall notify of this fact in writing and refrain from taking part in the examination of the case and making decision.

5. The conflict of interests, described in the sub-clause "a" of the clause one of the present article

is not applicable to a member of the Commission nominated under the quota of an international organization, if he/she is paid for working in the commission by the international organization appointing him/her.

6. The conflict of interests, described in the subclause "b" of the clause one of the present article is not applicable to a member of the Commission nominated under the quota of an international organization.

Article 12. Termination of the Authority of a Member of the Commission before Expiry of the Term

1. The Authority of a member of the Commission shall be terminated before the expiry of his/her term in service on the following basis:

a) his/her personal application;

b) failure to accomplish the duties for more than three months or for a period of 20 working days without acceptable reason;

c) gross violations of the duties and responsibilities;

d) appointment to a position or activity incompatible with the status of member of the Commission;

e) court ruling determining him/her as incapable or as a person with limited capacity;

f) conviction in effect;

g) death.

2. The issue of early termination of the authority of a member of the Commission in cases stipulated in the sub-clauses b–d of the first clause of the present law shall be determined by a vote of at least 2/3 of the full complement of the Commission, and in other cases the Commission will take into consideration existence of the ground for termination of authority. At this moment the authority of the member of the commission is terminated.

3. Filling of the vacancy for a member of the Commission is carried out through the rules set in the Article 10 of the present law on the parity basis between the parties, but within 1 month after the vacancy was announced.

Article 13. Chair of the Commission

1. The chair of the Commission shall:

a) chair the meetings of the Commission;

b) creates the committees of the Commission;

c) undersign the decisions of the Commission;

d) is responsible for management of the resources of the accounts of the Commission;

e) on the competition basis nominates the secretary of the Commission and other staff, except the supporting/technical personnel;

f) accomplish other authorities, prescribed by the charter of the Commission.

2. By order of the Chair one of the deputies of the chair shall act as a chair in the absence of the latter or failure thereof to perform his/her duties.

Article 14. Bureau of the Commission

1. The authority of the Bureau of the Commission involves:

a) organizational and technical provision of the activities of the Commission;

b) helping persons involved in preparing their complaints properly;

c) as per the task of the Commission and the committees carry out other obligations.

2. Structure of the bureau and the rules of performance are determined in the charter of the Commission.

3. The Secretary of the Commission:

a) draws up the minutes of the meetings of the Commission and other documents;

b) supervises implementation of the decisions of the Commission. Notifies the Commission of failure to implement its decisions within the set schedule;

c) is a director of the bureau of the Commission and is responsible for the daily activities of the bureau;

d) nominates and dismisses supporting/technical personnel of the Commission;

e) carries out other functions, defined by the Commission.

4. The Secretary of the Commission must have experience of working in management field of at least 5 years.

5. The Secretary of the Commission is appointed by the Chair of the Commission.

Article 15. Guarantees of Independence and Impartiality of the Commission

1. The Commission, its members and employees, in the performance of their duties and rights, shall be impartial and independent from any political or financial interests and comply to the Constitution and the legislation of Georgia only. Any exercise of influence or interference into their activities is inadmissible and shall be punished in accordance with applicable legislation, and the decision made under such influence and interference shall be considered as null.

2. The members of the Commission act within the frame of their authority in accordance with the present law, the principles and norms of the international law and their inner belief.

3. Obstructing the activities of the Commission shall be punished in accordance with applicable legislation.

Article 16. Decision-Making Procedures

1. The meeting of the Commission shall be authorized, when at least 12 of its members are present at the meeting. The Commission is authorized regarding appealed decisions, if at least 8 of its members are present at the meeting. If one of the parties does not participate to the working process of the Commission, the meeting of the Commission shall be authorized, when at least 10 of its members are present at the meeting, and the Commission is authorized regarding appealed decisions in this case, if at least 7 of its members are present at the meeting.

2. The meeting of the Committee shall be authorized, when at least 4 of its members are present at the meeting. If one of the parties does not participate to the working process of the Committee, the meeting of the Committee shall be authorized, when at least 3 of its members are present at the meeting.

3. The Committee shall make decisions by majority of the votes of the members present at the meeting.

In case of division of the votes the decisive vote shall be the vote of the Chairperson of the Committee.

4. The Commission shall make decisions by majority of the votes of the members present at the meeting. In case of division of the votes the decision shall not be made.

Article 17. Legal Acts of the Commission and the Committees

1. The Commission and the Committees in accordance with the rule set by the legislation within the limits of their own authority shall adopt the following legal acts: Decision of the Commission, Decision of the Committee and Order of the chair of the Commission.

2. A decision of the Commission and the Committee and the Order of the Chair of the Commission are individual administrative legal acts, which shall be adopted within the limits of the authority granted to them by the legislation.

3. Legal acts of the Commission and the Committee shall be adopted at their meetings.

4. The Commission adopts the charter of the Commission.

5. The Chair of the Commission shall issue orders on specific cases, defined by the present law and under the charter of the Commission.

Article 18. Functions and Authorities of the Commission

1. The authority, rule of activities and structure of the Commission shall be defined by the present Law and the Charter of the Commission.

2. In accordance with the rules set by the legislation, the Commission shall be authorized to:

a) By its own initiative or upon request of a party request and receive from any natural or legal person or state agency any information connected to the application to be examined by the Commission;

b) by the initiative of one of the parties, without the independent count, involve the third party into the case. Such a decision shall be made by it taking into account the considerations of the parties;

c) twice a year prepare reports to be presented to the Parliament, the Government and the President of Georgia;

d) the complaints related to the decision of the Commission, submitted by authorized persons in connection with newly found and newly revealed circumstances;

e) examine the complaints in essence, related to the decision of the Committees, submitted by authorized persons in connection with newly found and newly revealed circumstances and violation of the procedures set by the present law.

3. For the purpose of effective accomplishment of its own functions, the Commission shall be authorized:

a) to execute administrative authorities;

b) when necessary, to act as a mediator in dispute resolution and facilitate conciliation.

4. Any body, authority or a private person is obliged to provide the Commission at its request with the necessary information or a document, help it due to its competence in carrying out certain activities. Relevant bodies and authorities are obliged to provide the requested information immediately, but within at most 10 days.

5. The Commission is obliged to immediately submit the case to the relevant bodies, if it finds any signs of criminal in connection with the case under review.

6. The decisions made by the Commission and the Committees shall be mandatory for execution within the whole territory of Georgia.

7. For effective exercise of its activities and goals set by the present law the members of the Commission by the task of the Chair of the Commission or the Committees shall be authorized:

a) collect evidences, observe on site and request from administrative bodies and natural persons any information or document, record, give them a task to collect and process information, among them according to the rule set by the legislation, immediately get acquainted with or request the materials of investigation of criminal cases both completed and under investigation;

b) by the order of the judge, without preliminary notice enter, observe and study any territory;

c) receive explanations from any person, invite him/her to the meeting of the Commission or the Committee and ask them to give explanations;

d) request certain information from a state body of Georgia or any other country, also receive explanation from a citizen of a different state, or a person in the territory of a different state with preliminary agreement with the state, and according to the rules and conditions stipulated in the international agreements of Georgia.

8. The Commission and the Committees examine the cases in accordance with the rule set by the Civil Procedural legislation of Georgia, except otherwise stipulated by the present law.

Article 19. Committees of the Commission

1. For the Commission to exercise effectively its functions, timely examine and decide on the applications, restitute the property, which was illegally or unjustly forfeited during the conflict, provide adequate (substitute) residence and compensation of property damage, the Committees are established.

2. The committees are led by the Chair of the committee, who is elected by the Commission.

3. The Committees are established by the Chair of the Commission from the members of the Commission on the parity basis with 6 members in each Committee.

Article 20. Authorities of the Committee

1. For the purpose of effective accomplishment of its own functions, the Committee shall be authorized to the following:

a) to receive and process the applications on property restitution and return of other immovable property from an authorized person;

b) for the purpose of comprehensive, thorough and objective examine of cases, a Committee shall collect full information related to the case;

c) on the basis of the application or by its own initiative collect the evidences of property damage suffered by the applicant;

d) by its own initiative or upon a request of a party request and receive from any legal or private person or state agency information related to the application received by the Committee for examination;

e) by the initiative of one of the parties without the independent motion involve the third party into the case. Such a decision shall be made by it taking into account the considerations of the parties;

f) to receive and process the applications from citizens;

g) to generalize the collected information and materials and analyze them;

h) make decisions on particular cases;

i) to exercise other authorities prescribed by the present Law and the charter of the Commission.

Article 21. Responsibility for Impeding the Activities of the Commission and Committee

1. The Commission and the Committee shall be authorized to fine any natural or legal person, who:

a) violates the requirements of the present Law;

b) does not carry out a decision of the Commission and a Committee or an order of the Chair of the Commission;

c) does not submit the information documents requested in a legal form;

d) discloses ahead of time the expected results of the investigation or performs such action, which puts at risk or impedes the objective and comprehensive examination of the case;

e) hinders the execution of the authorities assigned by the present Law to an agency or its official;

f) fails to appear at the meeting of the Commission or a Committee without the acceptable reason or deliberately misguides or provides false information to the Commission or the Committee, or refuses to submit the documentation available to hand, which is necessary for examination or hearing of the case.

2. The amount of the fine shall be determined in accordance with Georgian legislation.

3. The decision on fining a person must be made at an open meeting of the Commission. The person, whose case is under review, must be given a reasonable term for the opportunity to express his/her opinion.

4. The person fined must be notified about the possible fining and the grounds for it. The Commission and the Committee is liable to explain to him/her the charges against him/her.

Article 22. Reporting and Recommendations

1. The Commission shall submit to the Parliament, Government and the President of Georgia periodic reports twice a year.

2. The reports must include description of the materials collected by the Commission as well as report on activities and financial report and on recommendations for measures necessary for political, administrative and other activities necessary for achieving the goals set for the Commission.

3. The Commission shall submit to the Parliament, Government and President of Georgia information on specific or general issues, if:

a) the issue involves public interest;

b) the issue requires immediate attention or involvement of the Parliament, President or Government;

c) there is a request from the President, Government or at least of 1/3 of the members of the Parliament.

4. After submitting the report to the President, Parliament and Government, the Commission shall publish the report through existing electronic and/or printed media; it shall also ensure public accessibility of the report.

5. After publishing the report, the Commission shall monitor and facilitate implementation of the recommendations made by the Commission.

Article 23. Location of the Commission

1. The Commission shall be located in Tbilisi.

2. According to the circumstances of specific case the Commission is entitled to gather in a different place.

Chapter III

Examination of Restitution and Compensation Cases

Article 24. The Right to Apply to the Commission

1. Forced migrants and other individuals, who suffered property damage as a result of the conflict, may apply to the Commission, with no regard to their citizenship.

2. In the cases defined in the present Law, forced migrants and other persons shall apply to the Commission within 7 years from the moment when the Commission started to execute its authorities.

Article 25. Application

1. An application must include the following:

a) name and surname of the applicant;

b) information about the events, which resulted in property damage;

c) request about return of the original residence or owned immovable property.

2. Evidences, which the applicant has on hand, should be attached to the application.

Article 26. Initiation of Proceedings

1. The Commission shall initiate proceedings when there is an application by the victim or his/her successor or representative.

2. The application shall be immediately forwarded to one of the committees. The committee shall make a decision on admitting or rejecting the application within 15 days.

3. The committee shall be authorized to reject an application if:

a) the claim is manifestly ill-founded;

b) a claim does not fall within the Commission's competence;

c) the term for submission of applications set by the present law has expired;

d) the decision by the Commission or the court related to the arguable property already exists.

4. The Commission shall be authorized to reject an appeal if:

a) the claim is manifestly ill-founded;

b) in case of appealing against the decision of the Commission there are no newly revealed or found circumstances;

c) in case of appealing against the decision of the Commission there are no facts of violation of the procedures defined by the present Law;

d) the term for submission of applications set by the present law has expired;

e) the decision of the court related to the arguable property already exists.

Article 27. Case Proceeding

1. The Commission and the Committees shall proceed with oral hearings or through formal administrative proceeding, except in cases provided by the General Administrative Code of Georgia and the present Law and in cases when the resolution of the disputed issues does not require inquiry procedures.

2. Proceedings in the Commission and the Committees are performed in the state language of Georgia. Taking into consideration the interests of the parties as working languages for the Commission and the Committees can also be used Ossetian and one international language, if this is decided by the Commission in accordance with the rules set by the charter of the Commission. Participation of an interpreter to case proceeding shall be provided.

3. The Commission and a Committee shall make and publish a final decision within 6 months from the moment of admitting the application for proceeding.

4. In case of existence of special circumstances, if the facts indicated in the application require examination, which may be related to complicated administrative procedures, the term for making a final decision shall not exceed 9 months.

5. The Commission and the committee shall make the following decisions within the limits of their competence:

a) on satisfying the application entirely;

b) on satisfying the application partially;

c) on rejecting the application.

6. The decision must be justified.

7. The decision on satisfying of the application must define the grounds, conditions and rules for returning to the original residence, provision of adequate (substitute) residence and compensation of property damage.

8. The decision of the Commission and the committee comes into force as from the moment of public announcement made at the meeting.

9. The Commission and the Committee issue an act of execution for the decisions made by them and come into force.

10. In case of necessity the Ministry of Refugees and Accommodations may be requested by the Committee or the Commission to ensure the implementation of the decisions adopted by the Committee or the Commission.

Article 28. Appealing Against Decision

1. The decision of the Commission in case of violation of the procedures set by the present law can be appealed against in the Supreme Court of Georgia, and in connection with newly revealed circumstances – in the Commission. The decisions of the Committees for reviewing in essence, in case of violation of the procedures set by the present law or in connection with some newly revealed circumstances can be appealed against in the Commission.

2. The term of appealing against the decision made by the Committee is one month from the day of adopting the decision. Execution of the decision will be suspended within this term.

3. In relation with revealing and finding new circumstances application on appealing against the decision can be submitted within 90 days after revealing and finding new circumstances.

4. In case of violation of the procedures set by the present law, the term for appealing against the decision is 3 months after making the decision.

5. In case of appeal execution of the decision of the committee shall not be terminated as a rule. However, the commission has the authority to suspend execution of the decision with mediation of a party.

6. In relation to the decision appealed against the Commission makes a decision through the rules set for case proceeding. At this time the members of the Committee, who made the decision appealed against can not participate to the work of the Commission.

Chapter IV

Rules for Property Restitution and Payment of Compensation

Article 29. General Norms of Property Restitution and Compensation

1. Original residence and other immovable property attached to it shall be immediately returned to its lawful owner, if the property:

a) is owned by the state/self-administration;

b) is owned by a mala fide owner.

2. If the original residence or other immovable property is owned by a bona fide owner, this property can be returned to the original resident only after the bona fide owner receives adequate (substitute) immovable property or, if he/she so wishes, monetary compensation.

3. In case if the property is destroyed, removed or reconstructed, the original resident shall receive other adequate (substitute) immovable property of similar value.

4. The original resident shall receive as adequate (substitute) immovable property the property, which by the moment of handing over has similar market value and is located in the same location as the forfeited property. With the consent of the original resident it shall be possible to hand him/her over immovable property of other type.

5. If the immovable property requires rehabilitation or reconstruction works the estimated cost of such works must be compensated.

6. By the decision of the Commission payment of monetary compensation can be proceeded only in case if returning of the original residence or the immovable property attached to it to the person or handing over of adequate (substitute) immovable property is not possible.

Article 30. Property, That Is Not Subject to Returning

1. Property shall not be subject to returning if by the time the application for restitution is made, it:

a) is located within the area in which handing over of property to legal or physical persons is forbidden by the legislation of Georgia;

b) is unsuitable for further usage due to depreciation or other circumstances, when the danger of its falling down exists or it is hazardous in terms of health and life and it can not be refurbished, or it impedes traffic safety, which makes it impossible to use this property for its purposes.

2. In this case the original owner shall be given adequate (substitute) immovable property, and if this is not possible, he/she shall receive property compensation.

Article 31. Calculation of the Value of the Property

1. The immovable property to be restituted and adequate (substitute) immovable property shall be evaluated in accordance with its market value by the moment of the restitution of the property. The property to be restituted shall be evaluated with the same criteria, also in the case of monetary compensation.

2. If there is difference between the value of the original property and other immovable property and the property to be restituted on the basis of the decision of the Commission or adequate (substitute) immovable property, this difference shall be covered from the fund of the Commission except for the value, which results from natural depreciation of the property.

Article 32. Payment of the Compensation

1. Monetary compensation shall be paid by either as a whole or in stages, but no longer than within 1 year of the Commission's decision.

2. In the case when the person entitled in accordance with the present Law to receive property chooses Georgia as his/her permanent place of residence he/she shall be given both one-time and monthly aid.

3. One-time aid for the beneficiary of the property and his/her family members shall amount to 1500 GEL per person.

4. Monthly aid shall be paid during 6 months and its amount shall be determined by the Commission based on the minimum consumer basket.

CHAPTER V

Financing of the Commission: Social Protection of the Members of the Commission

Article 33. Financing of the Commission

1. Financial provision of the activities of the Commission and a Committee and execution of their decisions shall be supported from the Financial Fund of the Commission.

2. The rules of establishment of the Fund of the Commission shall be defined by the present Law and the Charter of the Commission.

3. The sources for supplying the Fund of the Commission shall be the State Budget, grants and char-

ity contributions made by governments of other states, inter-governmental and non-governmental organizations or private persons, as well as disputable property handed over by the government or mala fide owners.

4. The Commission shall have a bank account where the resources of the Fund of the Commission shall be allocated.

5. The Commission shall submit its draft budget to the government according to the rule and term set by the legislation of Georgia.

Article 34. Salaries and Social Security of the Members of the Commission

1. The salaries and material benefits of the members of the Commission shall not be less than the salaries and material benefits of members of the Appeal Court of Georgia. It shall be inadmissible to reduce the salary of the members of the Commission during the whole period of his/her term of service.

2. For the members nominated under the quota of international organizations it is possible that other additional remuneration is used, amount and rules of payment of which is determined by the Charter of the Commission.

Article 35. Control of the Finances of the Commission

1. The Commission shall be obliged to:

a) keep the accounting records and other documents related to the activities of the Commission;

b) prepare quarterly accounting, which includes information about monthly expenses;

c) provide comprehensive information about the information systems of Commission management based on budgetary control;

d) ensure lawful management of funds by the Commission.

2. The Chamber of Control shall perform the annual audit of the budgetary fund management by the Commission, while the management of other resources of the Commission shall be audited by a highly reputable independent auditor appointed by the Commission. Accounting of the Commission and conclusions of the auditors shall be submitted to the Parliament of Georgia, President of

Georgia and other sponsors of the Fund of the Commission.

CHAPTER VI

Transitional Provisions

Article 36. Measures to Be Taken by the Commission

1. Formation of the Commission shall be conducted within 5 months after the present Law comes into force.

2. Before election of the Chairman, the first meeting of the Commission shall be chaired by the oldest member of the Commission. At the same meeting the Chairman and the Secretary of the Commission shall be elected in accordance with the procedures established by the Law.

3. The first Chairs of the Commission and the Committees shall be the persons elected under the quota of international organizations.

4. The Commission adopts its charter within 2 months after formation.

5. The Commission shall start to receive applications 9 months after the present Law comes into force.

[. . .]

10. GERMANY

10.1. Joint Declaration by the Governments of the Federal Republic of Germany and the German Democratic Republic on the Settlement of Unresolved Property Issues (1990)[156]

The division of Germany, the resulting population movement from East to West and the divergent legal systems in the two German states have given rise to numerous property law problems which affect many citizens in the German Democratic Republic and the Federal Republic of Germany.

In resolving the property issues ahead, the two Governments agree that various interests are to be balanced in a socially compatible manner. Legal certainty and legal clarity as well as the right of ownership are principles by which the Governments

[156] 15 June 1990.

of the German Democratic Republic and the Federal Republic of Germany shall be guided in resolving the property issues ahead. Only in this way can enduring legal peace be guaranteed in a future Germany.

The two German Governments agree on the following fundamental values:

1. The expropriations carried out on the basis of occupation legislation or sovereign acts of the occupying powers (1945 to 1949) can no longer be revoked. The Governments of the Soviet Union and the German Democratic Republic see no means of revising the measures taken at that time. The Government of the Federal Republic of Germany takes note of this in view of historical developments. It is of the opinion that a final decision on any state compensation must remain a matter for a future all-German parliament.

2. Trusteeships and similar measures imposing restraints on the alienation of real estate, commercial enterprises and other property will be revoked. Those citizens whose property had been administered by the state because they escaped from the GDR or for some other reason will regain the power of disposal over their property.

3. Expropriated real estate is in principle to be returned to the former owners or their heirs, having regard to the type of case specified in subparagraphs (a) and (b) below.

(a) It is not possible to restore rights of ownership over land and buildings whose use or purpose has been altered, in particular by being dedicated to public purposes, used for housing developments, for commercial purposes or incorporated into new business units.

Compensation will be paid in these cases, insofar as it has not already been made pursuant to the laws and regulations applicable to citizens of the German Democratic Republic.

(b) Insofar as citizens of the German Democratic Republic have in good faith acquired ownership or rights of user *in rem* over real estate, socially compatible indemnification is to be made to the former owner by substituting real estate of a comparable value or by paying compensation.

The same applies, mutatis mutandis, for real estate the ownership of which was transferred to third parties by the state trustees. The details still need to be settled.

(c) Former owners or their heirs entitled to the return of property may choose to receive compensation instead.

The question of compensation for additions and improvements will be regulated separately.

4. The provisions of paragraph (3) above shall apply mutatis mutandis to residential real estate formerly administered by the beneficiaries themselves or on their behalf which had been nationalized for reasons of economic necessity.

5. Tenant protection and existing rights of use enjoyed by citizens of the German Democratic Republic over real estate falling under this Declaration will be guaranteed as before and will be subject to the applicable legislation of the German Democratic Republic.

6. The existing restraints on alienation on administered enterprises will be revoked; the owner will acquire the assets of his/her enterprise.

The Act of 7 March 1990 on the Establishment and Activities of Private Companies and on Holdings in Companies applies to enterprises and holdings that were nationalized in 1972. Section 19(2) fourth sentence of the Act will be interpreted in such a way that any public holdings are to be sold to the private companies in question upon request; the decision to sell does not therefore lie within the discretion of the competent agency.

7. As regards companies and holdings that were confiscated and nationalized between 1949 and 1972, the company as a whole or shares in it will be transferred to the former owner, taking into consideration the performance of the enterprise, insofar as he or she does not wish to claim compensation. Details still need to be clarified.

8. If assets – including rights of use – have been acquired on the basis of unfair practices (e.g. by abuse of power, corruption, duress or deception on the part of the acquiring party), the acquisition of title does not merit protection and is to be voided. In cases of acquisition in good faith paragraph 3 (b) above shall apply.

9. Insofar as property has been seized in connection with criminal proceedings in violation of the rule of law, the German Democratic Republic will create the statutory basis required to correct such seizures in proceedings that conform with the principles of justice.

10. Equity interests in pre-currency-reform balance commutation loans owned by citizens of the Federal Republic of Germany, as well as interest on such loans, will be serviced in the second half of 1990 – i.e. after currency conversion.

11. Insofar as exchange restrictions still apply to monetary transactions, these shall lapse upon the entry into force of Monetary, Economic and Social Union.

12. The property of legal entities under public law that exist or existed within the territory of the GDR which was administered in trust by governmental agencies of the Federal Republic of Germany on the basis of the Legal Entity Liquidation Act will be transferred to the beneficiaries or their successors.

13. On the liquidation procedure:

(a) The German Democratic Republic will put in place the necessary legislation and procedural arrangements without delay.

(b) It will publicize where and within what period the citizens concerned can register their claims. The application period will not exceed six months.

(c) A legally distinct compensation fund separate from the government budget will be set up in the German Democratic Republic to meet compensation claims.

(d) The German Democratic Republic will ensure that prior to the end of the period referred to in sub-paragraph (b) above, no real estate or buildings will be sold with respect to which the former rights of ownership are unclarified, unless agreement has been reached by all those involved that a return of the property is out of the question or will not be requested. Any alienation of real estate and buildings with respect to which the former rights of ownership are unclarified that nevertheless occurred after 18 October 1989 will be reviewed.

14. The two Governments will charge their experts with the clarification of further details.

---

11. IRAQ

11.1. Coalition Provisional Authority Order Number 6 – Eviction of Persons Illegally Occupying Public Buildings (2003)

Pursuant to my authority as Administrator of the Coalition Provisional Authority (CPA), and the laws and usages of war, and consistent with relevant U.N. Security Council resolutions, including Resolution 1483 (2003),

Recognizing that the assets and property of the Iraqi Ba'ath Party constitute State assets,

Affirming the CPA's commitment to counter the threat to security and civil order posed by the illegal occupation of public property and improper disposition of that property,

Acting on behalf, and for the benefit, of the Iraqi people,

I hereby promulgate the following:

SECTION 1 – EVICTION

1. The CPA now exercises control over all public property and all property formerly owned by the Ba'ath Party within Iraq. Any individual or groups determined to be in illegal occupation of such public property shall be evicted.

2. The determination of illegal occupancy for purposes of this Order shall be made by the Commander of Coalition Forces or his designee.

SECTION 2 – INVENTORY

The CPA Facility Manager shall prepare and maintain an inventory describing the location and contents of all public property and property formerly owned by the Ba'ath Party within Iraq.

SECTION 3 – RIGHT OF APPEAL

Individuals or groups who are evicted from public property, or property formerly owned by the Ba'ath Party within Iraq, may appeal their eviction by submitting, to the Administrator or his designee, written evidence showing a valid right of occupancy, such as evidence of purchase for full value, or that the property did not properly fall within Section 1 of this Order.

11.2. Coalition Provisional Authority Regulation Number 4 – Establishment of the Iraqi Property Reconciliation Facility (2004)

Pursuant to my authority as Administrator of the Coalition Provisional Authority (CPA) and the laws

and usages of war, and consistent with relevant U.N. Security Council resolutions, including Resolution 1483 (2003),

Recognizing that large numbers of people from different ethnic and religious backgrounds in Iraq have been uprooted and forced to move from their properties to serve political objectives of the Ba'athist regime,

Recognizing that as a result of these Ba'athist policies, many individuals have conflicting claims to the same real property, resulting in instability and occasional violence,

Recognizing that pending the establishment of a means of finally resolving property related claims by a future Iraqi government, certain of these claims may be amenable to voluntary reconciliation immediately, thereby avoiding further instability and violence,

I hereby promulgate the following:

SECTION 1 – ESTABLISHMENT

1) There shall be established an Iraqi Property Reconciliation Facility (IPRF) that shall commence operation at a time to be fixed by the Administrator, for the purpose of collecting real property claims and promptly resolving such claims on a voluntary basis in a fair and judicious manner.

2) The IPRF shall operate under the authority of the Administrator and shall terminate operation at such time as the Administrator shall determine.

3) The Administrator may authorize the establishment of an IPRF Fund to be used in connection with the operations of the IPRF.

SECTION 2 – DELEGATION OF AUTHORITY

The Administrator may delegate any of the authorities hereunder, including by designating an international organization to implement IPRF.

SECTION 3 – COMPOSITION

1) The IPRF central office shall be located in Baghdad, and it shall administer the IPRF and coordinate with other entities as necessary to accomplish the objectives of the IPRF.

2) The IPRF shall also have several regional offices located throughout Iraq. Each office will be staffed

with one or more international staff and five or more Iraqis who are representative of the geographical area covered by that office.

3) The Administrator, or his delegate in consultation with the Administrator, will select the individuals who will serve in the regional offices and the Executive Secretariat.

SECTION 4 – POWERS AND FUNCTIONS

1) The head of the central office shall:

a) provide advice to and coordinate with the regional offices to ensure consistent procedures and policies among the regional offices;

b) report to the Administrator with respect to all aspects of the IPRF; and

c) perform such other functions delegated by the Administrator.

2) The regional IPRF offices shall:

a) provide information to the Iraqi public about the IPRF, its regional offices and the services provided by such offices;

b) receive claims from individuals with property disputes;

c) provide a voluntary dispute resolution and reconciliation facility that individuals may use to resolve their disputes; and

d) perform such other functions delegated by the Administrator.

SECTION 5 – REGULATION

The IPRF shall be bound by and operate in accordance with any Regulations, Orders or Memoranda issued by the Administrator.

11.3. Coalition Provisional Authority Regulation Number 12 – Iraqi Property Claims Commission (2004)

Pursuant to my authority as Administrator of the Coalition Provisional Authority (CPA), and under the laws and usages of war, and consistent with relevant U.N. Security Council resolutions, including Resolutions 1483 and 1511 (2003) and 1546 (2004),

Noting that the Statute of the Establishment of the Iraq Property Claims Commission, which was promulgated pursuant to Coalition Provisional Authority Regulation 8, Delegation of Authority Regarding an Iraq Property Claims Commission, (CPA/REG/14 January 2004/8), did not provide adequate mechanisms for the appointment, management, and operation of the Iraq Property Claims Commission,

Recognizing that the Statute of the Establishment of the Iraq Property Claims Commission requires amendment to ensure that the Iraq Property Claims Commission can function properly,

Acknowledging that an initial set of Instructions for Operation are needed to implement the Statute of the Establishment of the Iraq Property Claims Commission so that claimants, court officials, and administrators can understand better the claims process of the Iraq Property Claims Commission, and

Desiring to amend the Statute of the Establishment of the Iraq Property Claims Commission and to promulgate the Instructions for Operation of the Iraq Property Claims Commission,

I hereby promulgate the following:

SECTION 1 – AMENDED IRAQ PROPERTY CLAIMS COMMISSION STATUTE

The Statute of the Establishment of the Iraq Property Claims Commission, which became effective on January 15, 2004 pursuant to Coalition Provisional Authority Regulation 8, Delegation of Authority Regarding an Iraq Property Claims Commission, (CPA/REG/14 January 2004/8), is hereby amended and restated in full in the form attached hereto as Annex A.

SECTION 2 – PROMULGATION OF INSTRUCTIONS FOR OPERATION

The Instructions for Operation of the Iraq Property Claims Commission which are attached hereto as Annex B shall implement the Statute of the Establishment of the Iraq Property Claims Commission and shall apply to all claims filed before the Iraq Property Claims Commission.

Annex A – Establishment of the Iraq Property Claims Commission (As Amended and Restated)

Section One – Establishment

Article One

This Statute hereby establishes the Iraq Property Claims Commission (the "IPCC"), which shall resolve real property claims in a fair and judicious manner.

The IPCC shall encourage the voluntary resolution of claims.

Section Two – Organization

Article Two

The IPCC shall consist of the following structures established by the Iraqi Interim Government:

A. An Appellate Division, composed of judges and established as a separate chamber of the Iraqi Court of Cassation;

B. Regional Commissions established in each governorate in Iraq, and a maximum of three regional commissions in the Kurdistan Regional Government area. The Appellate Division may then establish more than one Regional Commission in a governorate; and

C. A National Secretariat which shall be responsible for overseeing all operational and management activities of the IPCC.

Article Three

A. The Appellate Division of the IPCC shall be composed of five judges, one of whom shall be nominated by the judicial authority in the Kurdistan Regional Government, who have experience in adjudicating property disputes. They may be retired or serving judges and are to be appointed by the Council of Judges.

B. Each Regional Commission shall be composed of (i) a judge, appointed by the Council of Judges, who shall preside as chairman, (ii) the Director of the Office of Real Estate Registry in the Governorate, or his representative, and (iii) the Director of State Property of such Governorate, or his representative. The Regional Commission may also request the assistance of persons who are experts on the subject of any claim.

C. The National Secretariat shall be composed of (i) a Head of the National Secretariat who shall serve as the highest official of the National Secretariat, (ii) operational managers, auditors, data managers, legal advisers, public relations personnel, and any other staff necessary to ensure the orderly functioning of the National Secretariat, (iii) Regional Secretariats situated in each Governorate with all necessary staff to ensure the IPCC's orderly functioning, including Regional Commission Clerk's offices, which shall provide operational and legal support as necessary to each Regional Commission, and (iv) an Appellate Secretariat with the necessary staff to ensure the Appellate Division's orderly functioning, including an Appellate Division Clerk's office which shall provide operational and legal support as necessary to the Appellate Division.

Article Four

The Iraqi Interim Government shall ensure that the IPCC has the necessary funds to discharge its administrative duties and that the Regional Commissions and Regional Secretariats are provided with appropriate premises from which to operate in the capital of the relevant Governorate or Kurdistan Regional Government area or at any such locations as shall be deemed expedient by the IPCC.

Section Three – Procedures

Article Five

A. The IPCC shall designate the form of documents for submission of claims and for administrative purposes.

B. The process of adjudicating claims filed with the IPCC shall commence with the claimant(s), or his representative filing a claim in the proper form at any IPCC office, including any properly designated IPCC office outside Iraq.

Article Six

A. Following receipt of a properly completed claim form, the Regional Secretariat shall open a claim file and record the claim in the intake register in the order received.

B. After receipt of a properly completed claim form, the relevant Regional Secretariat shall serve notice of the claim on any interested parties, including natural or juridical persons, in accordance with the Guidelines issued by the National Secretariat and Instructions for Operation approved (if before June 30, 2004) by the Administrator or (if after June 30, 2004) the Iraqi Interim Government.

C. The Regional Secretariat shall serve notice of the claim on the General Directorate of Real Estate Registration, and the General Directorate of Real Estate Registration shall cause the official title record to be endorsed with the date and reference number of the claim.

D. The Regional Secretariat shall verify the claim administratively, and authenticate the identity of the parties.

E. The Regional Commission Clerk's Office shall then review each claim file, and, prior to submitting the file to the Regional Commission, prepare for the Regional Commission a case report which summarizes the factual background of the case, the legal issues involved, the parties' arguments, and the Clerk's Office's recommendation, made by a legal advisor, as to how the case should be decided.

F. The Regional Commission may request the assistance of other governmental and non-governmental parties for purposes of valuation of interests and other related matters.

G. The Regional Commission shall issue its decision with respect to the claim, but the Regional Secretariat shall be responsible for notifying the claimants and any known interested parties of the Regional Commission's decision.

Article Seven

A. Any appeal of a decision of the Regional Commission must be filed within sixty days from the date of the decision.

B. Orders issued by the Regional Commission shall be final and binding unless appealed within sixty days.

C. A decision of the Regional Commission will not be enforceable until the requisite period for filing an appeal has passed and no appeal has been lodged.

D. A decision made by the Appellate Division is final and binding in respect of any IPCC related matter.

E. The final order of the Regional Commission or Appellate Division, as appropriate, shall be issued to all relevant parties and the appropriate competent authorities for enforcement.

F. If the property in question is occupied, possessed or used by the nonprevailing party, and such party has no other property, then the nonprevailing party would be granted a prescribed period of time to surrender possession of the premises.

The Regional Secretariat shall also inform the displaced person(s) of the availability of any services for assistance.

Section Four – General Principles
Article Eight

The IPCC shall comply with, but not be limited to, the application of the following examples when resolving real property claims:

A. Any properties that were confiscated or seized, or on which liens or other encumbrances were placed by the former governments of Iraq (not in the ordinary course of commercial business), but with title remaining in the name of the original owner shall be returned to the original owner, freed and discharged from any such liens or other encumbrances.

B. Any properties that were confiscated or seized and whose title was transferred to the former governments of Iraq, or an agent thereof, and which were not sold to a third party, shall be returned to the original owner.

C. Any properties confiscated by the former governments of Iraq that were used as mosques, other places of worship, religious schools, charities or were associated with such uses shall be returned to the appropriate *waqfs* (religious endowments) connected to such uses or to the appropriate holders of title to such properties prior to their confiscation.

D. Any properties whose title is in the name of senior members of the former governments of Iraq shall be returned to the rightful owners, if it is established that such properties were improperly acquired.

E. If a property was confiscated and subsequently sold to a buyer (the "First Buyer"), and (i) title remains in the name of the First Buyer and (ii) no improvements were made to the property, then title to the property will be transferred back to the original owner, and the First Buyer would not be entitled to compensation from the original owner.

F. If the property was an unimproved property (that is, a property not built upon) when confiscated or otherwise seized, and then subsequently sold to the First Buyer, and the First Buyer has improved the property by building upon it, then the original owner would be entitled to either (i) having title transferred to him, provided that he pays the First Buyer the value of the improvements or (ii) being paid appropriate compensation for the property (as an unimproved property).

G. If the property was sold to the First Buyer, who subsequently acquired an adjoining property from the state, then title to both the original property and the adjoining property shall be transferred to the original owner, provided that such original owner pay the First Buyer the amount that such First Buyer paid for the adjoining property.

H. If the property has a building on it and then was sold to the First Buyer, who subsequently demolished the original building and built a new building on it, then the original owner of the property may (i) request that title be transferred to him, after paying for the new building, less the value of the old demolished building, or (ii) may request that the First Buyer acquire the property, including the demolished building (less any amounts paid by the First Buyer to the former governments of Iraq).

I. If the property was subsequently sold by the First Buyer to other buyers, then the original owner could either (i) request that title be transferred to him, or (ii) request compensation for the value of the property. If the original owner chooses option (i) above, then the final buyer would be entitled to compensation for the value of the property.

J. If the property was charged as security to a lender for a loan to the First Buyer, then title to the property would be freed and discharged from any such charge, and the lender would then have a right of action against the First Buyer to recover any outstanding balance due under the loan.

K. If the property was unimproved and a building was built on it by the First Buyer, and the property was charged to a lender as security for a loan, then any amounts due to the First Buyer by the original owner (pursuant to Paragraph F above) would be paid by the original owner direct to the lender to fully or partially satisfy the loan.

L. If the property was confiscated and sold in a public auction and was purchased by either the original owner or his heirs, then they will be entitled to compensation from the state in an amount equivalent to the purchase price.

M. If the property is currently being used for a public or charitable purpose, the property shall continue to be used for that purpose, and the Government or current owner, user or possessor shall provide the original owner, user or possessor with compensation.

N. Any other relevant situation in line with these provisions.

Section Five – Other Matters

Article Nine

This Statute governs claims:

A. (1) Arising between July 17, 1968 and April 9, 2003, inclusive; (2) Involving immovable property, assets affixed to immovable property, easements or servitudes ("real property"), or an interest in real property; (3) That was confiscated, seized, expropriated, forcibly acquired for less than full value, or otherwise taken, by the former governments of Iraq for reasons other than land reform or lawfully used eminent domain. Any taking that was due to the owner's or possessor's opposition to the former governments of Iraq, or their ethnicity, religion, or sect, or for purposes of ethnic cleansing, shall meet this standard; or

B. (1) Arising between March 18, 2003 and June 30, 2005, inclusive; (2) Involving real property, or an interest in real property; (3) That was confiscated, seized, expropriated, forcibly taken for less than full value, or otherwise acquired and/or reacquired:

i. as a result of the owner's or possessor's ethnicity, religion, or sect, or for purposes of ethnic cleansing, or;

ii. by individuals who had been previously dispossessed of their property as a result of the former Ba'athist governments' policy of property confiscation.

Article Ten

A. Newly introduced inhabitants of residential property in areas that were subject to ethnic cleansing by the former governments of Iraq prior to April 9, 2003 may be (i) resettled, (ii) may receive compensation from the state, (iii) may receive new property from the state near their residence in the governorate or area from which they came, or

(iv) may receive compensation for the cost of moving to such area.

B. The Ministry of Displacement and Migration shall be responsible for administering this policy.

Article Eleven

A. Claims must be filed in the proper form and properly completed by June 30, 2005. Any claims filed with the IPCC after such date will not be accepted.

B. Any claims with respect to properties within the jurisdiction of this Statute but filed subsequently to June 30, 2005 may be referred to the Iraqi Courts, which shall apply the principles included in this Statute. This provision is not available to any claimant who has already filed a claim with respect to the same property with the IPCC.

C. The IPCC is to have exclusive jurisdiction over all claims involving immovable property, assets affixed to immovable property, easements or servitudes on property or land or other interests in real property brought in accordance with Articles 9A and 9B. Any such cases pending must be transferred by the relevant court to the jurisdiction of the IPCC.

Article Twelve

The terms of this Statute shall take precedence over any provisions in resolutions or orders or laws that are inconsistent.

Article Thirteen

The National Secretariat shall issue Guidelines which will set forth the procedures to be followed by the IPCC.

The National Secretariat may issue interpretative memoranda which set forth the manner in which it shall construe the Instructions for Operation.

Article Fourteen

The Iraqi Interim Government means the Government appointed on June 1, 2004, and assuming sovereignty on July 1, 2004. The authority of the Iraqi Interim Government for the purposes of this Statute will transfer to the successor governments of Iraq.

Article Fifteen

Transfers of real property pursuant to this Statute shall not be subject to income tax, a tax on a transfer of real property, or any other tax or duty.

Article Sixteen

This Statute will become effective on 1 July 2004.

ANNEX B – IRAQ PROPERTY CLAIMS COMMISSION

INSTRUCTIONS FOR OPERATION

Section One – General Provisions

Article 1

These Instructions implement the Statute of the Establishment of the Iraq Property Claims Commission (As Amended and Restated) (the "Statute") and apply to all claims filed before the Iraq Property Claims Commission (IPCC).

Unless otherwise stated, references to Articles are Articles in these Instructions.

Article 2

Together with the Statute, these Instructions govern:

a. The composition of the IPCC;

b. The submission of claims before the IPCC;

c. The reception of claims by the IPCC;

d. The process for deciding claims;

e. The legal effectiveness of IPCC decisions.

Section Two – Composition of the IPCC

Article 3

In accordance with Article 2 and Article 3 of the Statute, the IPCC shall consist of a National Secretariat, an Appellate Division and one or more Regional Commissions in each governorate or Kurdistan Regional Government area.

NATIONAL SECRETARIAT

Article 4

a. A National Secretariat for property claims shall be established. The initial Head of the National Secretariat shall be appointed by the Administrator after consultation with the Iraqi Interim Government for a term of two years which may be renewed once at the discretion of the Prime Minister of Iraq. The initial Head of the National Secretariat shall then take action to manage the work of the National

Secretariat by setting up an office, including but not limited to, the following staff:

i. Operational managers to oversee IPCC operations, to coordinate among the different branches of the IPCC, and, where appropriate, to issue user manuals and operating guidelines to direct certain functions of the IPCC;

ii. Auditors to inspect IPCC operations for fraud, waste or mismanagement;

iii. Data managers to enter into the national database of claims the information on forms submitted to the IPCC, and to review the national database for cases with similar and recurrent factual patterns;

iv. Legal advisers to ensure consistent application of IPCC rules, to oversee orders of compensation, and, where appropriate, to request that the Appellate Division issue an advisory opinion addressing an unresolved issue of law or fact;

v. Public relations personnel to advertise the existence of the IPCC, the location of IPCC offices, the rules of procedure of the IPCC, and other issues it deems appropriate;

vi. Appellate Division Secretariat and Regional Secretariats in accordance with Article 3(C) of the Statute and Article 8, Article 9, Article 16, and Article 17; and

vii. Any other staff necessary to ensure an orderly functioning of the National Secretariat in accordance with the responsibilities outlined in these Instructions.

b. All subsequent appointments to the office of Head of the National Secretariat shall be for four years, without term limits, and made in accordance with the following procedure:

The Council of Judges shall recommend three candidates to be considered for appointment as Head of the National Secretariat. The Iraqi Interim Government or successor Government of Iraq shall then appoint one of these candidates as Head of the National Secretariat.

Article 5

The National Secretariat shall:

a. Ensure consistent implementation of, and compliance with, the Statute, these Instructions, any

legal determinations made by the Appellate Division, and any IPCC Guidelines issued by the National Secretariat;

b. Audit IPCC offices;

c. Establish a national database of claims, and enter into that database the information received from the Regional Secretariats, IPCC offices or from persons living outside Iraq.

d. Review the national database for cases with similar and recurrent factual patterns and common legal issues, and notify the Regional Commissions or Appellate Division, as necessary, of such cases for coordinated treatment.

e. Coordinate among the different branches of the IPCC, and between the IPCC and the Ministry of Housing, the Ministry of Justice, the Council of Judges, the Ministry of Displacement and Migration, and the Ministry of Finance, and any other resource as necessary;

f. Issue user manuals and operating guidelines;

g. Manage IPCC public relations and communications;

h. Oversee orders of compensation and the implementation of orders requiring persons to surrender possession of their property;

i. Support the Appellate Division and Regional Commissions; and

j. Accomplish other tasks assigned to it herein or in future IPCC Instructions.

APPELLATE DIVISION

Article 6

The Appellate Division shall be an independent review body within the IPCC located in Baghdad and established as a separate chamber of the Iraqi Court of Cassation. It shall hear appeals of decisions made by the Regional Commissions.

Article 7

a. In accordance with Article 3(A) of the Statute, the Appellate Division shall be comprised of five retired or serving judges who have experience in adjudicating property disputes, to be appointed by the Council of Judges. The judges of the Appellate Division shall represent a cross section of the Iraqi population. Each Judge shall have a deputy who must be approved by the Council of Judges.

b. To the extent that the Council of Judges appoints to the Appellate Division any serving judges, such judges shall be transferred to the IPCC to serve on a full-time basis.

c. Each judge of the Appellate Division shall act as Chief Judge in turn, in an order of appointment to be determined by the Council of Judges. Each appointment shall have a maximum duration of two years.

Article 8

In accordance with Article 3(C) of the Statute, an Appellate Division Secretariat shall be established for the Appellate Division to assist in the IPCC's administration. The Appellate Division Secretariat shall report to, and take guidance and instructions from, the National Secretariat. To establish the Appellate Division Secretariat, the National Secretariat shall appoint a Head of the Appellate Division Secretariat, who shall then take action to establish a support service for the Appellate Division by setting up an office, including but not limited to, the following staff:

a. Receptionists to ensure the orderly flow of people through the office, and to answer basic questions relating to the IPCC.

b. Persons tasked with notifying the Regional Commissions and Regional Secretariats of Appellate Division decisions, as required by these Instructions.

c. Persons trained in: (i) distributing and receiving claim, response and appeal forms, and (ii) entering such forms into a computer and sending the electronic data to the National Secretariat for data processing.

d. Docket managers to oversee case files and issue final orders.

e. Any other staff necessary to ensure the orderly functioning of the Appellate Secretariat, in accordance with the responsibilities outlined in these Instructions.

Article 9

In accordance with Article 3(C) of the Statute, an Appellate Division Clerk's Office shall be established in the Appellate Division Secretariat and provide operational and legal support as necessary to the Appellate Division. The Appellate Division Clerk's Office shall report to, and take guidance and instructions from the Appellate Division Secretariat and (as necessary) the National Secretariat.

To establish the Appellate Division Clerk's Office, the Head of the Appellate Division Secretariat (in consultation with the Head of the National Secretariat) shall provide the Chief Judge of the Appellate Division with a list of ten candidates qualified to serve as the Head of the Appellate Division Clerk's Office.

The Chief Judge of the Appellate Division (in consultation with all other Appellate Division Judges) shall then appoint one candidate from the list of ten candidates provided by the Appellate Division Secretariat as the Head of the Appellate Division Clerk's Office. The Head of the Appellate Division Clerk's Office shall then set up an office in the Appellate Division Secretariat which shall be composed of legal advisors who shall review case files and prepare for the Appellate Division a case report which summarizes:

(i) the factual background of the case;

(ii) the legal issues involved;

(iii) the parties' arguments; and

(iv) the Clerk's Office's recommendation, made by a legal adviser, as to how the case should be decided.

Article 10

In accordance with Article 2(B) of the Statute, the Appellate Division may determine that a governorate or Kurdistan Regional Government area would benefit from more than one Regional Commission, and, if it does, shall establish the territorial boundaries of each Regional Commission within a governorate or government area. The Appellate Division also may determine that a Regional Commission should operate in more than one governorate.

Article 11

Upon request of the National Secretariat or a Regional Commission, the Appellate Division may issue an advisory opinion on any unresolved question of law or common issue of fact to establish the rule to be applied uniformly to subsequent similar cases.

Article 12

The term of office of the judges of the Appellate Division shall expire after five years and may be renewed upon decision by the Council of Judges, except that the term of office shall terminate upon completion of all claims before the Appellate Division.

Article 13

The standards under which a judge of the Appellate Division shall disqualify himself or herself from considering a claim are the same as the standards under which a Regional Commissioner shall disqualify himself or herself. Where a judge of the Appellate Division is not available to consider a claim, whether because they disqualify themselves or otherwise, their deputy may sit on the Appellate Division and act with the full powers of the unavailable judge.

REGIONAL COMMISSIONS

Article 14

a. In accordance with Article 2(B) of the Statute, each Regional Commission shall serve a different governorate or Kurdistan Regional Government area and shall be located in the capital city of the governorate or Kurdistan Regional Government area in which it serves, unless the Appellate Division otherwise determines in accordance with Article 10.

b. Notwithstanding Paragraph (a) of this Article, a Regional Commission may sit in any part of the territory over which it has jurisdiction if the Chairman of the Regional Commission or the National Secretariat determines, in their discretion, that the circumstances so warrant.

Article 15

In accordance with Article 3(B) of the Statute, each Regional Commission shall be comprised of (i) a judge appointed by the Council of Judges, who shall serve as the Chairperson; (ii) the Director of the Office of Real Estate Registry in the Governorate in which the Commission sits, or their representative; and (iii) the Director of State Property of such Governorate, or their representative.

Article 16

In accordance with Article 3(C) of the Statute, a Regional Secretariat shall be established for each Regional Commission to assist in the IPCC's administration.

The Regional Secretariat shall report to, and take guidance and instruction from, the National Secretariat. To establish the Regional Secretariat, the National Secretariat shall appoint a Head of the Regional Secretariat, who shall then take action to establish a support service for the Regional Commission by setting up any necessary offices, including but not limited to, the following staff:

a. Receptionists to ensure the orderly flow of people through the office, and to answer basic questions relating to the IPCC.

b. Persons tasked with notifying interested parties, as required by these Instructions.

c. Persons trained in: (i) distributing and receiving claim, response and appeal forms, and (ii) entering such forms into a computer and sending the electronic data to the National Secretariat for data processing.

d. Docket managers to oversee case files and issue final orders.

e. Mediators and staff to assist in the voluntary resolution of claims.

f. Any other staff necessary to ensure the orderly functioning of the Regional Secretariat, in accordance with the responsibilities outlined in these Instructions.

Article 17

In accordance with Article 3(C) of the Statute, a Regional Commission Clerk's Office shall be established in each Regional Secretariat and provide operational and legal support as necessary to the Regional Commission. The Regional Commission's Clerk's Office shall report to, and take guidance and instructions from the Regional Secretariat and (as necessary) the National Secretariat.

To establish the Regional Commission Clerk's Office, the Head of the Regional Secretariat shall provide the Chairperson of the Regional Commission with a list of ten candidates qualified to serve as Head of the Regional Commission Clerk's Office. The Chairperson of the Regional Commission (in consultation with all other members of the Regional Commission) shall then appoint one candidate from the list of ten candidates provided by the Head of the Regional Secretariat as the Head of the Regional Commission Clerk's Office. The Head of the Regional Commission Clerk's Office shall then set up an office in the Regional Secretariat which shall be composed of legal advisers who shall (in accordance with Article 6(E) of the Statute) review case files and prepare for the Regional Commission a case report which summarizes:

(i) the factual background of the case;

(ii) the legal issues involved;

(iii) the parties' arguments; and

(iv) the Clerk's Office's recommendation, made by a legal adviser, as to how the case should be decided.

Article 18

Members of a Regional Secretariat may be required by these Instructions, by the Chairperson of the appropriate Regional Commission or by the National Secretariat to travel to any part of the territory over which the Regional Commission has jurisdiction in order to facilitate the intake or processing of claims.

Article 19

The commissioners' term of office shall expire after three years and may be renewed upon decision by the relevant appointing authority, except that the term of office shall terminate upon completion of the Regional Commission's consideration of the claims before it.

Article 20

a. A Regional Commissioner shall disqualify himself or herself from considering any claim in which their impartiality might reasonably be questioned.

b. The impartiality of a Commissioner might reasonably be questioned, *inter alia*, if:

i. The Commissioner is a relative of one of the parties;

ii. The Commissioner or their spouse, child, parent, son-in-law or daughter-in-law has an ongoing dispute with one of the parties;

iii. The Commissioner has been a legal advisor for one of the parties, business partner of any kind, held an interest in a company, or been a board member of a company in which one of the parties has a controlling interest;

iv. The Commissioner or their relative has given advice or an opinion on the particular case before it reached the Regional Commission; or

v. The Commissioner has any other interest (financial or otherwise) in the claim.

c. For the purposes of these Instructions, "relative" is defined as "a relation through parentage, marriage or adoption up to the fourth degree".

d. Where a Commissioner is not available to consider a claim, whether because they disqualify themselves or otherwise, their position shall be filled by an ad hoc appointment by the appointing authorities, so that the appointing authority which appointed the disqualified Commissioner shall appoint the ad hoc replacement.

Submission and Reception of Claims

A. Information on Claim Submission

Article 21

The National Secretariat shall carry out national and international information programs, and Regional Secretariats shall carry out such programs within the territories of their respective Regional Commissions, to ensure that potential claimants receive notice of, and instructions on submitting a claim to the IPCC. Such programs shall employ notices to be published widely (i.e., both inside and outside Iraq, as appropriate, and via a number of different media) and repeatedly in order to reach all potential claimants.

B. Submission of Claims

Article 22

Any person, natural or juridical, or their heirs, may submit a claim to the IPCC so long as the claim:

A. (1) Arose between July 17, 1968 and April 9, 2003, inclusive; (2) Involves immovable property, assets affixed to immovable property, easements or servitudes ("real property"), or an interest in real property; (3) That was confiscated, seized, expropriated, forcibly acquired for less than full value, or otherwise taken, by the former governments of Iraq for reasons other than land reform or lawfully used eminent domain. Any taking that was due to the owner's or possessor's opposition to the former governments of Iraq, or their ethnicity, religion, or sect, or for purposes of ethnic cleansing, shall meet this standard; or

B. (1) Arose between March 18, 2003 and June 30, 2005, inclusive; (2) Involves real property, or an interest in real property; (3) That was confiscated, seized, expropriated, forcibly taken for less than full value, or otherwise acquired and/or reacquired:

i. as a result of the owner's or possessor's ethnicity, religion, or sect, or for purposes of ethnic cleansing, or;

ii. by individuals who had been previously dispossessed of their property as a result of the former Ba'athist governments' policy of property confiscation.

For purposes of the IPCC's jurisdiction, actions or inactions attributable to the former governments of Iraq include, but are not limited to:

1. The actions or inactions of any State organ in Iraq, whether of the central government or of a territorial unit of the State, and whether the organ exercised legislative, executive, judicial or any other functions within the former governments;

2. The actions or inactions of a Ba'ath party member, or of a relative of a senior official of the Government or party, operating with apparent authority, or under color of authority, or with the implicit or explicit license of the former governments. Claims for damages only are not within the jurisdiction of the IPCC.

Article 23

A claimant who brings a claim in bad faith and with knowledge that such claim is fraudulent will be deemed to commit a criminal offence under the Iraqi Penal Code.

Article 24

A claimant who, after issuance of these Instructions, wilfully returns to currently occupied property and takes measures to force the current occupiers to vacate that property will be deemed to commit a criminal offence under the Iraqi Penal Code.

Article 25

a. Claims shall be submitted in person, in the prescribed form, at any IPCC office as required under Article 5 of the Statute.

b. Claims submitted by persons located outside Iraq will be governed by a separate set of Instructions.

c. Claims will be deemed to be filed once the claim has been accepted by the Regional Secretariat acting through any IPCC office and the applicant has been issued an acknowledgement bearing the claim reference number.

Article 26

Where security conditions or geographical conditions so warrant, the Regional Secretariat may dispatch a mobile team, consisting of members of the Regional Secretariat, to an area with a concentrated population of potential claimants, to facilitate the intake and processing of claims.

Article 27

a. Where a representative acts on behalf of a claimant, the representative must prove their representation. The IPCC shall prescribe the form of evidence of representation, and the signature of the claimant authorizing representation on that form shall be considered sufficient evidence of representation unless there is reason to believe that such signature was wrongfully obtained.

b. Where property rights are communally held, and the person in whose name the property is registered cannot be found, other members of the community may file a claim on behalf of the entire community if such members offer proof of the registered person's absence and proof of membership in the community.

Article 28

The claimant, or their representative, shall attach to the claim form any available evidence, including any testimonial evidence, proving their rights to the claimed property.

a. Written testimony shall be sworn and notarized, in accordance with Iraqi law.

b. For documentary evidence, the claimant, or their representative, shall submit a certified copy. Wherever possible, the IPCC shall review and certify, as true and correct, any original documents pertaining to the claim, but the IPCC will not accept custody of any original documents.

Article 29

The claimant, or their representative, may withdraw the claim or part of the claim at any time until a decision is issued.

a. A withdrawal shall be explicit, in the prescribed form, signed by the claimant and filed in the manner specified for claims in Article 25.

b. Upon receipt of notification of a withdrawal, the Regional Commission may accept the withdrawal, with or without prejudice, and the Regional Secretariat shall record in the national database that the claim has been withdrawn.

C. Processing of Claims (In-Country Claimants)

Article 30

Upon receipt of a claim in the proper form, the Regional Secretariat shall review the form in the claimant's presence, or in the presence of their representative, to ensure that all obligatory information is provided. Where the claim form is missing obligatory information, the Regional Secretariat shall advise the claimant, or their representative, of what must be done to provide the missing information and shall return the claim form to the claimant, or to their representative, without processing it.

Article 31

Once the Regional Secretariat has reviewed the claim form and advised the claimant, or their representative, of any missing obligatory information, it is the responsibility of the claimant to complete the form within the filing period. The claim will not be accepted for processing by the Commission until all obligatory information is provided.

Article 32

Immediately upon receipt of a properly completed claim form, and, in the claimant's presence, or in the presence of their representative, the Regional Secretariat shall:

a. Assign the claim a unique claim number;

b. Affix a pre-printed label with the unique claim number to the claim form;

c. Provide the claimant with confirmation of receipt in the prescribed form showing the unique claim number for future reference.

Article 33

After assigning a unique claim number to the claim, the Regional Secretariat shall serve notice of the claim on all identifiable interested parties, in accordance with Article 6(B) of the Statute.

a. The Regional Secretariat shall serve notice of the claim on interested parties by:

i. Physically posting notice for a minimum of one month on the subject property, at the office of the Regional Commission and in any local or electronic venues that may attract an interested party's attention; and

ii. Communicating the notice in writing to any identifiable interested parties, unless impracticable.

b. Upon serving or posting notice (whichever is later), the Regional Secretariat shall record the date of notice.

c. The notice shall provide sufficient details to enable any interested party to file a response to the claim. Further information relating to the claim may be provided by the Regional Commission, if the Head of the Regional Secretariat determines that such information is necessary for the proper filing of a response.

Article 34

The Regional Secretariat shall identify interested parties by reviewing the national database for any other claims relating to the subject property, searching the appropriate property registry for current and previous owners, identifying any current users or occupiers of the property, and taking any other steps it deems appropriate.

Article 35

Absent good cause, interested parties shall have forty-five days from the date on which notice is served or posted (whichever is later) to submit a response to the claim. A response shall be submitted in the prescribed form and shall be submitted in the manner specified for a claim form in Article 25.

Article 36

For any form received by the Regional Secretariat, the Regional Secretariat shall enter the data from the form into the computer, and transmit the electronic version of the form data to the National Secretariat for data processing. The Regional Secretariat shall also send the original version of the form to the National Secretariat for filing in the national repository.

Article 37

Upon receiving the data from the Regional Secretariat, the National Secretariat shall transfer that data into the national database. Upon receiving the original paper copy, the National Secretariat shall file it at a national repository.

D. Processing of Claims (of Out-of-Country Claimants)

Article 38

The National Secretariat shall process the claims of out-of-country claimants in the same way that the Regional Secretariats process the claims of in-country claimants, except as provided herein or in future IPCC Instructions.

Article 39

The appropriate Regional Secretariat remains responsible for notifying all identifiable interested parties of a claim, and the Regional Commission with jurisdiction over the area in which the property is located shall decide the claim.

PROCESS FOR DECIDING CLAIMS

Article 40

The Regional Secretariat or the National Secretariat may, at any time, consolidate claims that arise out of the same sequence of events or that are otherwise intertwined, in the interest of expediting the resolution of all claims.

A. Principles

Article 41

The IPCC shall comply with, but not be limited to, the application of principles set forth in Article 8 of the Statute.

B. Settlement

Article 42

The Regional Secretariat shall encourage the voluntary resolution of claims, and may arrange mediation or otherwise facilitate the amicable settlement of issues among the claimant(s) and any identifiable interested parties. The National Secretariat will provide guidance on the procedures to be followed.

Article 43

Where all parties resolve a claim voluntarily, the claim shall be removed from the Regional Commission's docket in one of the following ways:

a. The claimant may withdraw their claim, pursuant to Article 29; or

b. The parties may notify, in the prescribed form, the Regional Secretariat of the settlement.

c. Where the parties notify the Regional Secretariat of the settlement under Paragraph (b) above, the Regional Secretariat shall convey that form to the Regional Commission. The Regional Commission shall then approve or, in extraordinary circumstances, disapprove the terms of voluntary resolution.

Article 44

Where the Regional Commission approves the terms of voluntary resolution, such approval shall be final and binding between the parties to that resolution, not subject to appeal, and of the same force and effect as a Final Order.

a. If the settlement is not submitted to the Commission because the claim is withdrawn by the claimant, or the Commission disapproves the settlement, the voluntary resolution will have only the legal effect that it would have had under Iraqi law in the absence of the Statute and these Instructions.

b. Where the Commission disapproves the terms of settlement, the claim shall be adjudicated in accordance with these Instructions, unless the claimant chooses to withdraw the claim.

C. Adjudication

Article 45

Where the parties do not pursue amicable settlement or fail to resolve the claim voluntarily, the

Regional Commission Clerk's Office shall review the case file and prepare for the Regional Commission a case report which summarizes:

(i) the factual background of the case;

(ii) the legal issues involved;

(iii) the parties' arguments; and

(iv) the Clerk's Office's recommendation, made by a legal adviser, as to how the case should be decided.

Article 46

If, in analyzing the evidence, the Regional Secretariat determines that the evidence submitted is insufficient or of doubtful reliability, the Regional Secretariat may initiate evidence collection and/or verification procedures.

Article 47

Upon receiving the case file and the case report from the Regional Secretariat, the Regional Commission may, in its discretion, hold a hearing to develop the factual record.

Article 48

a. In accordance with Article 6(F) of the Statute, the Regional Commission may request the assistance of other governmental and non-governmental parties for purposes of valuation of interests and other matters relating to the issues in dispute.

b. Where the Regional Commission requests the assistance of other governmental parties, such parties shall provide the requested assistance.

Article 49

The Regional Commission shall decide the claim and the appropriate remedy by majority vote with three members present.

Article 50

In making a decision, the Regional Commission shall look to the previous decisions of other regional commissions for guidance and shall accept the previous decisions of the Appellate Division as conclusive on any resolved issue of law or fact.

Article 51

The Regional Commission shall issue a decision that:

a. identifies the parties' names;

b. identifies the property at issue;

c. determines the parties' respective rights to the subject property, including ownership rights, rights of possession, and rights of use;

d. provides the legal basis for that determination;

e. sets forth such legal remedy as the Regional Commission deems appropriate; and

f. if applicable, identifies for the parties the availability of any governmental services or assistance.

Article 52

In accordance with Article 6(G) of the Statute, the Regional Secretariat shall notify the parties, or their representatives, of the Commission's decision by delivering to them a copy of that decision, if such delivery is practicable, and by posting notice of the decision both at the office of the Regional Commission and in any local or electronic venues that may attract the parties' attention.

Article 53

Decisions of the Regional Commissions shall be final and binding on the parties, unless appealed within sixty days from the date of decision, except that the Commissions may correct any clerical or technical errors in any earlier decisions.

D. Appeals

Article 54

Any party may appeal a decision of a Regional Commission on the grounds of new evidence or manifest error.

Article 55

To appeal a decision of the Regional Commission, a party shall file, within sixty days from the date of the Regional Commission's decision, an appeal in the prescribed form. Such form shall be filed in the manner specified for claims in Article 25.

Article 56

Upon receipt of an appeal, the Regional Secretariat shall:

a. Stay issuance of a Final Order; and

b. Enter the form into a computer and send the electronic version of it to the National Secretariat for data processing.

c. Forward the appeal form and the case file to the Appellate Division Secretariat.

Article 57

The Appellate Division Secretariat shall:

a. Notify the Regional Secretariat of its receipt of the Appeal;

b. Review the case file and the decision being appealed;

c. Transfer the case file and the decision being appealed to the Appellate Division Clerk's Office who shall prepare for the Appellate Division a case report setting forth:

(i) the decision below;

(ii) the ground for appeal;

(iii) a summary of the parties' arguments; and

(iv) the Appellate Division Clerk's Office's recommendation, made by a legal adviser, as to whether to consider the appeal and how to resolve it.

Article 58

All decisions by the Appellate Division shall be made by a majority vote and with five members present. In the event that a Judge is unavailable, their deputy may sit on the Appellate Division and act with the full powers of the unavailable judge.

Article 59

The Appellate Division may not reconsider its decision, but it may correct any clerical or technical errors of any earlier decision.

Article 60

The Appellate Division Secretariat shall notify the appropriate Regional Commission and Regional Secretariat of the Appellate Division's decision. The Regional Secretariats shall be responsible for notifying the parties, or their representatives, of the Appellate Division's decision in accordance with the provisions of Article 52.

LEGAL EFFECTIVENESS OF IPCC DECISIONS

Article 61

Upon issuance of a decision by the Appellate Division, or, where no appeal is made, fifteen days after expiration of the sixty day period for appeal, the Regional Secretariat shall issue to the parties and to the appropriate Office of Property Registration a Final Order confirming that the decision is final and binding. The Final Order shall identify the name(s) of the rights holders, the subject property, and the remedy, if applicable. In addition, each Final Order shall have a unique serial number and shall be verified with an official stamp.

Article 62

In accordance with Article 7(E) of the Statute, Final Orders are directly enforceable by the competent authorities of the district where the subject property is located.

Article 63

Final Orders may be reopened only if a person:

a. Files a claim or response before the IPCC within the filing period;

b. Has a claim to the subject property under Article 22; and

c. Demonstrates that they did not know, and could not reasonably be expected to know, of the previous claim with respect to that property.

Article 64

In accordance with Article 7(F) of the Statute, Final Orders requiring the current occupants to surrender possession of the property may be enforced after sixty days if the occupants do not vacate the premises voluntarily. All other Final Orders may be implemented immediately.

Article 65

Where a Final Order results in a previous occupier, possessor or user of property surrendering possession of the premises, the Regional Secretariat shall inform that person of any services available for assistance, and of any policy of the Ministry of Displacement and Migration to resettle or compensate such persons, in accordance with Article 7(F) and Article 10(B) of the Statute.

Article 66

These Instructions may be revised or supplemented by the Iraqi Interim Government. Additional details regarding the claims process may also be found in Guidelines, interpretive memoranda, and literature prepared by the National Secretariat.

Article 67

The National Secretariat may issue interpretative memoranda which set forth the manner in which it shall construe the Instructions.

[. . .]

11.4. Statute of the Commission for the Resolution of Real Property Disputes (2006)[157]

Order No. (2)

In the name of the People

The Presidency Council

By virtue of what was approved by the National Assembly in accordance with the provisions of paragraphs A and B of article thirty three of the Law of Administration for the State of Iraq for the Transitional Period, and pursuant to the provisions of article thirty seven of the Law of the Administration for the State of Iraq.

The Presidency Council decided by a majority vote in its session held on January 9, 2006 to issue the following law.

We have issued the following Statute:

NUMBER (2) of the year 2006

STATUTE
OF THE COMMISSION FOR THE RESOLUTION
OF REAL PROPERTY DISPUTES

SECTION I
PRELIMINARY PROVISIONS

Article 1

I   The Commission for the Resolution of Real Property Disputes replaces the Iraq Property Claims Commission established pursuant to the Coalition Provisional Authority Regulation number 12 of the year 2004.

II   The Commission for the Resolution of Real Property Disputes is related to the Council of Ministers and it is presided by an official who

has the level of a Minister, holding at least a first university degree in law.

III   The administrative and judicial structure of the Commission shall be formulated by a regulation.

IV   The office of the province of Kurdistan shall be one of the administrative formations of the Commission and the offices in the governorates of the province shall be related to it.

Article 2

The meaning of the terms mentioned below is as indicated hereunder:

I   The Commission: the Commission for the Resolution of Real Property Disputes.

II   The Appellate Commission: the commission competent to review the objections and the appeals relating to the decisions and judgments issued by the Judicial Committees.

III   The Judicial Committee: the committee competent to review and resolve the real property claims.

IV   The branches of the Commission: the branches of the Commission that are established pursuant to this Statute in the governorates, counties and districts.

V   The properties: and they include the tangible rights (primary rights *in rem*) set forth in paragraph (1) of article 68 of the applicable Iraqi civil code number 40 of the year 1959.

Article 3

I   The Ministry of Finance shall pay the compensation amounts that the government is liable to pay pursuant to the decisions issued in accordance with the provisions of this Statute.

II   The government shall ensure that the Commission has all the necessary funds and amounts to facilitate discharging of its administrative duties and to ensure the appropriate premises for the Commission and its branches for the purpose of performance of their function.

SECTION II
APPLICABILITY OF THE STATUTE

Article 4

The provisions of this Statute are applicable to the claims for properties that fall within the

---

[157] *Note:* This Statute contains provisions replacing the terms of CPA Regulation Number 12 as contained in Section 11.3 of this book. Although technically repealed, Section 11.3 was retained to give the reader a point of comparison between the new Statute and the Regulation adopted by the Occupying Power.

jurisdiction of the Statute during the period from 17 July 1968 to 9 April 2003 and that includes the following:

I   The properties that were confiscated and seized for political, ethnic reasons or on the basis of religion or religious doctrine or any other events resulting from the policies of the previous regime of ethnic, sectarian and nationalist displacement.

II The properties that were seized without consideration or appropriated with manifest injustice or in violation of the legal practices adopted for property acquisition. Exception is made to the properties that were seized pursuant to the law of agricultural reform, the cases of in kind compensation and appropriation for purposes of public use and which were actually utilized for public use.

III The State real properties that were allocated to the factions of the previous regime without consideration or for a symbolic amount.

Article 5

I   The Commission shall have jurisdiction on the claims that fall within the provisions of this Statute.

II All the Iraqi courts must transfer the claims that fall within the jurisdiction of this statute to the Judicial Committees of the Commission until the end of the filing period.

III The Judicial Committees in the Commission have precedence over all the Iraqi courts with respect to the mandate of such Committees on the claims that fall within the jurisdiction of this statute.

SECTION III

FORMAL PROCEDURES

Article 6

The Judicial Committees shall take the following procedures when reviewing the claims brought before them:

I   Annul the decisions of confiscation, seizure and allocation which took place in violation of the adopted legal norms on any property which title deed is still registered in the name of its original owner in the records of the real estate registration.

II   Restitute the ownership of the properties that were confiscated or seized and that are still registered in the name of the State, to its original owner.

III Restitute the ownership of the mosques, places of worship, religious schools, places of worship (husseiniyat), hospices and charities associations that were confiscated or seized with manifest injustice, to its original owners.

IV   If it is established that some senior members of the former regime or its factions and those who took advantage of their powers, acquired a property in an illegal manner, such property shall be returned to its original owner pursuant to the provisions of this Statute.

V   If the confiscated or seized property was sold to an individual (natural or juristic) and no adjuncts or improvements were made, the original owner has one of the following two options:

a) Return the title to the property back to his name, and in this case, the current owner shall be compensated the equivalent value of the property at the time the claim is lodged. The party that sold the property after confiscation or seizure shall be liable to pay the compensation.

b) Compensation for the value of the property, and the party that (first) sold the property after confiscation or seizure shall be liable to pay compensation for the value of the property at the time the claim is lodged.

VI   If a property was confiscated or seized and subsequently adjuncts or improved were made to it, the original owner has one of the following two options:

a) Return the title of the property back to his name and pay to the current owner the value of the existing adjuncts or improvements valued at the time the claim is lodged. In this case, the party that (first) sold the property after confiscation or seizure shall be liable to compensate the current owner for the equivalent value of the property at the time the claim is lodged less the value of such adjuncts or improvements.

b) Accept compensation equivalent to the value of the property at the time the claim was lodged less the value of the adjuncts or improvements made. In this case, the party who (first) sold the property after confiscation or seizure is liable to pay compensation.

VII If a property was sold after it was confiscated or seized and subsequently an adjoining property was added to it and both properties were combined, then the original owner has the following options:

a) Have the original and adjoining property registered back in his name, if it is impossible to separate both properties, provided that such original owner compensates the current owner the equivalent value of such adjoining property valued at the time the claim is lodged. The party that (first) sold the property after confiscation or seizure shall be liable to compensate the current owner for the value of the original property at the time the claim is lodged.

b) Have the ownership of the confiscated or seized property, without the adjoining property, if this is possible, restituted to his name; have the ownership of the confiscated or seized property registered back in his name and the title to the adjoining property shall remain in the name of the current owner. The party that (first) sold the property after confiscation or seizure shall be liable to compensate for the value of the original property at the time the claim is lodged.

c) Request compensation if the value of the adjoining property is higher than that of the confiscated or seized property and it is not possible to separate them without damage or high costs.

VIII If the confiscated or seized property was charged with a loan or a mortgage registered in the real property records, the property shall be returned to the original owner free from any such charge or loan after payment of the mortgage value by the party who seized the property or sold it. Such party can claim the value of the settled mortgage from the mortgagor provided the mortgage was certified before 09/04/2003.

IX If the confiscated property was sold in a public auction and was thereafter purchased by its original owner or his heirs or one of his heirs, such owner or heirs are entitled to claim from the party who sold the property, an amount equivalent to the purchase price at the time the claim is lodged provided that the title to such property be re-registered in the name of all the heirs if it was purchased by one of them.

X If the confiscated or seized property was utilized for public use or charitable purposes, the government or the party who (first) sold the property shall be liable to compensate the original owner for the value of the property, at the time the claim is lodged provided the property continues to be used for the purposes mentioned.

XI If the confiscated or seized property was given to another party without consideration or for a symbolic amount, such property shall be registered back in the name of its original owner and the provision of item VI of this article shall apply in case of adjuncts or improvements.

XII If the property was built prior to confiscation or seizure and then it was sold and subsequently demolished and a new building was built on it, the original owner has one of the following two options:

a) The transfer of the ownership of the property to his name after he pays for the value of the constructions that were built less the value of the construction that was demolished. The party that sold the property shall be liable to compensate the current owner for the value of the property before its demolition valued at the time the claim is lodged.

b) Compensation for the value of the property in its condition at the time of confiscation and with its equivalent value at the time the claim is lodged and the party that sold the property shall be liable to pay such compensation.

XIII a) If the confiscated or seized property was an empty plot not built upon and subsequently constructions were made on such plot and the value of these constructions is higher than that of the plot, the title to the property shall remain in the name of the current owner and the party that (first) sold the plot shall compensate the original owner for its value at the time the claim is lodged.

b) However, if the value of the plot is higher than that of the constructions, the property, land and building, shall be returned to the original owner who shall be liable to compensate the current owner for the value of the constructions as they exist at the time the claim is lodged. The party that (first) sold the plot shall compensate the current owner for value of such plot, to be valued at the time the claim is lodged.

XIV 1 – If the property was confiscated in violation of the legal practices or with manifest injustice or was not utilized for public use, then the original owner has the following two options which are:

a) Return the ownership of the property to his name and in this case, he shall be liable to pay the consideration of the appropriation that he received valued in gold and with the equivalent of gold in Iraqi dinar at the time the claim is lodged.

b) Get compensated for the difference between the consideration of the appropriation that he received from the appropriation claim and the actual value of the property at the time of appropriation, valued in gold and with the equivalent of gold in Iraqi dinar at the time the claim is lodged before the Commission.

2 – If the property was appropriated in violation of the legal practices or with manifest injustice and was utilized for public use, then the original owner is compensated pursuant to the provisions of paragraph (b) 1 of item 14 of this article.

SECTION IV

THE FUNCTIONS OF THE COMMISSION
AND ITS BRANCHES

Article 7

I   The Commission shall prepare the claim form of the property claims.

II   The party concerned (either natural or juristic person) or his/her legal representative shall submit the claim to any of the branches of the Commission provided that it is forwarded to the competent branch of the Commission according to the location of the property.

III The claim must meet all the conditions required in the claim form.

IV   The branch of the Commission shall request from the relevant Real Property Registration Department a detailed report about the transactions made on the property at issue.

V   The branch of the Commission shall carefully examine the claim form and the report of the Real Property Registration Department to ensure that all the conditions required are met. The claim is then recorded in the claims' ledger, a file is opened for the claim, it is assigned a unique number and the claimant will be given a filing receipt.

VI   The claim and its data shall be entered in the computer, and then an electronic copy of such data is sent to the central computer section in the headquarters of the Commission.

VII The branch of the Commission shall notify the respondent of the subject of the claim to allow him to respond within a period of 15 days starting from the day that follows the day he is notified or considered as notified according to the response form prepared by the Commission.

VIII The competent branch of the Commission shall enter the notification sheet of the respondent and the response form in the computer.

IX   The claim file shall be transferred to the competent Judicial Committee for consideration in accordance with the Statute.

X   The notifications shall be served pursuant to the applicable Civil Procedures Law.

XI   When the decision of the Judicial Committee is issued, the claim file shall be forwarded to the computer section for data entry of the necessary data.

Article 8

a) The Commission shall encourage reconciliation and amicable resolution of the property disputes between parties of the claim in accordance with a form prepared for this purpose to the extent that they do not contravene with the law, the public order and the public morals.

b) The Judicial Committee shall certify the agreement of amicable resolution between the parties in the claim and its decision shall be subject to cassation.

SECTION V
THE JUDICIAL COMMITTEE

Article 9

The judicial Committee shall be composed of:

1. A judge appointed by the Supreme Council of Judges, who acts as the chairman of the Committee.
2. The Director of the Real Property Registration Department or the person who represents him.
3. A legal officer nominated by the chairman of the Commission from Commission's staff and who has legal experience or practice as a lawyer for a minimum period of ten years.

Article 10

The Judicial Committee shall consider the claims brought before it, after holding a pleading session at least once. The Committee is entitled to conduct a site visit to the property within its jurisdiction to listen to the statements necessary for the resolution of the claim.

Article 11

The Judicial Committee shall consider the claim in the event the parties are not present, after verification of the accuracy of the notifications and it is entitled to issue the appropriate decision to resolve the claim in light of the documents and attachments that are presented. The claim shall not be deferred and cancelled in case one of the parties was present.

Article 12

I   If the claimant is present and the respondent is absent, even though he was notified, the Committee issues a decision *in absentia*. The respondent is then entitled to object to the decision within a period of (ten days) starting from the day following the day he is notified of the decision or considered as notified.

II If a decision *in absentia* is not appealed within the deadline specified under (I) above, or an appeal was made but does not state the reasons for the appeal, the Judicial Committee shall reject the appeal as formally deficient, otherwise the Committee shall consider the appeal pursuant to the Statute by upholding the decision, revoking it or amending it as the case may be.

Article 13

The Judicial Committee shall hold its session to consider the claim and the chairman of the Committee shall issue his decision resolving the claim pursuant to the Statute. The two other commissioners or one of the two is entitled to record his dissenting opinion on a separate sheet in the event he has as an opposing opinion.

Article 14

The decisions issued by the Judicial Commission are final and binding, unless they are appealed before the Appellate Division within a period of 30 days starting from the day following the day the decision is notified or the day it is considered notified.

Article 15

The chairman of the Judicial Committee shall place a sign on the property at dispute indicating that it should not be subject to any legal transaction by notifying the competent Real Estate Registration Department when a claim is submitted.

Article 16

The heir shall represent the rest of the heirs if he submits a claim in his name requesting the return of the ownership of the property.

SECTION VI
THE APPELLATE COMMISSION

Article 17

The Appellate Commission shall be composed of seven judges who have legal practice in the Cassation Court. They are nominated by the Higher Judicial Council either from active or retired judges, one is nominated as chairman and another one is his deputy provided that two of them are nominated by the government of Kurdistan province. This Commission shall be independent in its jurisdiction from the Cassation Court. Two alternate members are also nominated to replace any member of the Commission who may be absent or unavailable for any reason and in case of absence of the chairman of the Commission, he shall be replaced by his deputy.

Article 18

The Appellate Commission shall take its decision by a majority vote.

Article 19

The Appellate Commission shall be competent to consider the following requests:

a) The appeals relating to decisions and judgments issued by the Judicial Committees.
b) The transfer of a claim from one committee to the other.
c) Disqualification of the Chairman of the Judicial Committee.
d) Rejection of judges.
e) Providing advisory opinions.

Article 20

The chairman of the Appellate Commission shall examine the request for disqualification by a member of the Appellate Commission from considering the claim. Where the chairman of the Appellate Commission disqualifies himself, the chairman of the Higher Judicial Council shall be competent to examine such request.

Article 21

The Appellate Commission issues decisions either to uphold the appealed decision or judgment, to amend it or to substitute it. Such decision of amendment or substitution is binding in case it is upheld.

Article 22

When the decision of the Appellate Commission is issued, the branch of the Commission shall transfer the claim file to the computer section for data entry of the necessary data.

Article 23

The judgments issued by the Judicial Committees can be objected by reconsidering the trial or by the objection of another party pursuant to the provisions set forth in the procedural law.

SECTION VII
ENFORCEMENT OF THE DECISIONS AND JUDGMENTS

Article 24

I The final judgments and decisions are executed in the Execution and Real Estate Registration Departments according to the competence of each department pursuant to the provisions of the law.

II The occupant of the property is given a period that does not exceed 90 days, starting from the date notification of the execution is served, to vacate and deliver the property free from any hindrance.

SECTION VIII
THE FINAL PROVISIONS

Article 25

The real property claims shall be adjudicated pursuant to the provisions of this Statute, and the provisions of Procedural Civil Law number 83 of the year 1969, as amended and Evidence Law number 107 for the year 1979, as amended shall govern matters not provided for in the Statute.

Article 26

The transfer of real property on which a final decision is issued pursuant to this Statute shall not be subject to income tax, or tax on transfer of real property, or any other tax or duties.

Article 27

Any provision that is inconsistent with this Statute shall not be applicable.

Article 28

I The claimant or his legal representative may withdraw a claim or part of the claim at any time until the Judicial Committee issues its decision.

II The decision of the Judicial Committee approving the withdrawal of the claim shall be final and not subject to any objection.

III The withdrawal of the claim shall be pursuant to a form prepared for this purpose.

Article 29

Any person who files a claim in bad faith and using fraudulent means shall be punished pursuant to the applicable Penal Code.

Article 30

The individuals who reside outside the country may submit their claims pursuant to the provisions of this Statute to the branches of the Commission which shall be opened for this purpose or through the Iraqi diplomatic missions.

Article 31

The courts shall refrain from considering the claims falling within the jurisdiction of this Statute and shall forward such claims to the Judicial Committees of the Commission during the period of validity of this Statute.

Article 32

The Head of the Commissions occupies the highest position in the Commission; he shall supervise all the activities of the Commission and its branches; he has the authority to create or cancel any staffing positions, as the work of the Commission requires.

Article 33

The Head of the Secretariat may issue regulations to facilitate the implementation of this Statute.

Article 34

The provisions of this statute shall apply to the compensation decisions issued by the Judicial Committees before enforcement of this statute as follows:

a)   The decisions that do not specify the party who is responsible for the payment of compensation or that do not specify the amount of compensation or that gave the right to one of the parties to refer to the civil courts to request compensation.
b)   The decisions involving valuation of the compensation amounts at the time of confiscation and appropriation or seizure and not at the time the claim is lodged.
c)   The decisions issued rejecting the claims for compensation pursuant to the annulled Regulation number 12 of the year 2004.

Article 35

The provisions of the Civil Service Law number 24 of the year 1960 and the Employees Law number 25 of the year 1960 the Law of Discipline of the Employees of the State and the socialist sector number 14 of the year 1991 and the Civil Retirement Law number 33 of the year 1966, apply to the employees of the Commission.

Article 36

All the decisions of the dissolved revolution command council and the consequences resulting from them that contradict the provisions of this law shall be cancelled.

Article 37

Commissions shall be established in the Commission for the Resolution of Real Property Disputes to consider claims for properties that fall within the jurisdiction of this Statute during the period from 14 July 1958 to 16 July 1968. The work of such committees shall be regulated by an annex to this Statute.

Article 38

The Appellate Commission shall refer to the experts of the Islamic law (Al Sharia'a) and follow their opinions upon the request of either parties of the claim.

Article 39

The Regulation number 12 of the year 2004 issued by the Coalition Provisional Authority shall be annulled.

Article 40

The order number 22 of the year 2004 issued by the Council of Ministers shall be annulled.

Article 41

This statute shall apply from the date of its publication in the Official Gazette.

---

12. KOSOVO

12.1. UNMIK Regulation 1999/10 on the Repeal of Discriminatory Legislation Affecting Housing and Rights in Property (1999)

The Special Representative of the Secretary-General, Pursuant to the authority given to him under United Nations Security Council Resolution 1244 (1999) of 10 June 1999, Taking into account United Nations Interim Administration Mission in Kosovo (UNMIK) Regulation No. 1999/1 of 25 July 1999 on the Authority of the Interim Administration in Kosovo, For the purpose of repealing certain legislation that are discriminatory in nature and that are contrary to international human rights standards, Hereby promulgates the following:

SECTION 1 – REPEAL OF CERTAIN LEGISLATION

The following laws, which do not comply with the standards referred to in section 2 of UNMIK regulation No. 1999/1 are repealed in Kosovo:

- The Law on Changes and Supplements on the Limitation of Real Estate Transactions (Official Gazette of Republic of Serbia, 22/91 of 18 April 1991);

- The Law on the Conditions, Ways and Procedures of Granting Farming Land to Citizens Who Wish to Work and Live in the Territory of the Autonomous Province of Kosovo and Metohija (Official Gazette of Republic of Serbia, 43/91 of 20 July 1991).

[. . .]

12.2. UNMIK Regulation 1999/23 on the Establishment of the Housing and Property Directorate and the Housing and Property Claims Commission (1999)

The Special Representative of the Secretary-General, Pursuant to the authority given to him under United Nations Security Council Resolution 1244 (1999) of 10 June 1999, Taking into account United Nations Interim Administration Mission in Kosovo (UNMIK) Regulation No. 1999/1 of 25 July 1999 on the Authority of the Interim Administration in Kosovo, For the purpose of achieving efficient and effective resolution of claims concerning residential property, Hereby promulgates the following:

SECTION 1 – HOUSING AND PROPERTY DIRECTORATE

1.1 The Housing and Property Directorate (the "Directorate") shall provide overall direction on property rights in Kosovo until the Special Representative of the Secretary-General determines that local governmental institutions are able to carry out the functions entrusted to the Directorate. In particular, the Directorate shall:

- Conduct an inventory of abandoned private, state and socially owned housing;

- Supervise the utilization or rental of such abandoned property on a temporary basis for humanitarian purposes; rental monies of abandoned private and socially owned property shall be recorded in a separate account in trust for the rightful owner, subject to deduction of relevant expenses;

- Provide guidance to UNMIK, including CIVPOL and UNHCR, as well as KFOR on specific issues related to property rights; and

- Conduct research leading to recommended policies and legislation concerning property rights.

1.2 As an exception to the jurisdiction of the local courts, the Directorate shall receive and register the following categories of claims concerning residential property including associated property:

- Claims by natural persons whose ownership, possession or occupancy rights to residential real property have been revoked subsequent to 23 March 1989 on the basis of legislation which is discriminatory in its application or intent;

- Claims by natural persons who entered into informal transactions of residential real property on the basis of the free will of the parties subsequent to 23 March 1989;

- Claims by natural persons who were the owners, possessors or occupancy right holders of residential real property prior to 24 March 1999 and who do not now enjoy possession of the property, and where the property has not voluntarily been transferred.

The Directorate shall refer these claims to the Housing and Property Claims Commission for resolution or, if appropriate, seek to mediate such disputes and, if not successful, refer them to the Housing and Property Claims Commission for resolution.

SECTION 2 – HOUSING AND PROPERTY CLAIMS COMMISSION

2.1 The Housing and Property Claims Commission (the "Commission") is an independent organ of the Directorate which shall settle private non-commercial disputes concerning residential property referred to it by the Directorate until the Special Representative of the Secretary-General determines that local courts are able to carry out the functions entrusted to the Commission.

2.2   The Commission shall initially be composed of one Panel of two international and one local members, all of whom shall be experts in the field of housing and property law and competent to hold judicial office. The Special Representative of the Secretary-General shall appoint the members of the Panel and shall designate one member as the chairperson. The Special Representative of the Secretary-General may establish additional Panels of the Commission in consultation with the Commission.

2.3   Before taking office, the members of the Commission shall make in writing the following solemn declaration:

> "I solemnly declare that I will perform my duties and exercise my power as a member of the Housing and Property Claims Commission honourably, faithfully, impartially and conscientiously."

The declarations shall be put in the archives of the Commission.

2.4   The Commission shall be entitled to free access to any and all records in Kosovo relevant to the settlement of a dispute submitted to it.

2.5   As an exception to the jurisdiction of local courts, the Commission shall have exclusive jurisdiction to settle the categories of claims listed in section 1.2 of the present regulation. Nevertheless, the Commission may refer specific separate parts of such claims to the local courts or administrative organs, if the adjudication of those separate parts does not raise the issues listed in section 1.2. Pending investigation or resolution of a claim, the Commission may issue provisional measures of protection.

2.6   The Special Representative of the Secretary-General shall establish by regulation the Rules of Procedure and Evidence of the Commission, upon the recommendation of the Commission. Such rules shall guarantee fair and impartial proceedings in accordance with internationally recognized human rights standards. In particular, such rules shall include provisions on reconsideration of decisions of the Commission.

2.7   Final decisions of the Commission are binding and enforceable, and are not subject to review by any other judicial or administrative authority in Kosovo.

Section 3 – Executive Director and Staff

The Special Representative of the Secretary-General shall appoint an Executive Director of the Directorate after consultation with the Executive Director of the United Nations Centre for Human Settlements (UNCHS) (Habitat). The Executive Director shall appoint the staff of the Directorate, which shall comprise local experts, and shall allocate staff to the Commission who shall be under the exclusive control of the Commission.

Section 4 – Applicable Law

The provisions of the applicable laws relating to property rights shall apply subject to the provisions of the present regulation.

[. . .]

12.3. UNMIK Regulations 2000/60 on Residential Property Claims and the Rules of Procedure and Evidence of the Housing and Property Directorate and the Housing and Property Claims Commission (2000)

The Special Representative of the Secretary-General,

Pursuant to the authority given to him under United Nations Security Council resolution 1244 (1999) of 10 June 1999,

Taking into account United Nations Interim Administration Mission in Kosovo (UNMIK) Regulation No. 1999/1 of 25 July 1999, as amended, on the Authority of the Interim Administration in Kosovo,

Recalling UNMIK Regulation No. 1999/23 of 15 November 2000 on the Establishment of the Housing and Property Directorate and the Housing and Property Claims Commission,

For the purpose of further elaborating the law relating to residential property in Kosovo, and establishing the Rules of Procedure and Evidence of the Housing and Property Directorate and the Housing and Property Claims Commission, Hereby promulgates the following:

SECTION 1 – DEFINITIONS

For the purposes of the present regulation:

'Abandoned housing' means any property, which the owner or lawful possessor and the members of his/her family household have permanently or temporarily, other than for an occasional absence, ceased to use and which is either vacant or illegally occupied.

'Allocation right holder' means the holder of the right of disposal of a socially owned apartment in accordance with the law that was applicable at the time.

'Associated property' means land and buildings owned or used by the claimant, which form a unit with a residential property.

'Commission' means the Housing and Property Claims Commission established under UNMIK Regulation No. 1999/23.

'Directorate' means the Housing and Property Directorate established under UNMIK Regulation No. 1999/23.

'Discrimination' means any distinction on grounds such as language, religion, political or other opinion, national or ethnic origin, or association with a national community, which has the purpose or effect of nullifying or impairing the recognition, enjoyment or exercise, on an equal footing, of a property right.

'Informal transaction' means any real property transaction, which was unlawful under the provisions of the Law on Special Conditions Applicable to Real Estate Transactions (Official Gazette SRS 30/89, as amended by the laws published in Official Gazette SRS 42/89 and 22/91) or other discriminatory law, and which would otherwise have been a lawful transaction.

'Occupancy right' means a right of use of a socially owned apartment under a contract on use of the apartment made under the Law on Housing Relations or the Law on Housing. It does not include the right to use apartments for official purposes ('service apartments') or apartments used as temporary accommodation, or leases of socially owned apartments.

'Property' means any residential house or apartment, any socially owned apartment, and any associated property.

'Property right' means any right of ownership of, lawful possession of, right of use of or occupancy right to, property.

CHAPTER I – SUBSTANTIVE PROVISIONS

Section 2 – General Principles

2.1 Any property right which was validly acquired according to the law applicable at the time of its acquisition remains valid notwithstanding the change in the applicable law in Kosovo, except where the present regulation provides otherwise.

2.2 Any person whose property right was lost between 23 March 1989 and 24 March 1999 as a result of discrimination has a right to restitution in accordance with the present regulation. Restitution may take the form of restoration of the property right (hereafter "restitution in kind") or compensation.

2.3 Any property transaction which took place between 23 March 1989 and 13 October 1999, which was unlawful under the provisions of the Law on Special Conditions Applicable to Real Estate Transactions (Official Gazette SRS 30/89, as amended by the laws published in Official Gazette SRS 42/89 and 22/91) or other discriminatory law, and which would otherwise have been a lawful transaction, is valid.

2.4 Any person who acquired the ownership of a property through an informal transaction based on the free will of the parties between 23 March 1989 and 13 October 1999 is entitled to an order from the Directorate or Commission for the registration of his/her ownership in the appropriate public record. Such an order does not affect any obligation to pay any tax or charge in connection with the property or the property transaction.

2.5 Any refugee or displaced person with a right to property has a right to return to the property, or to dispose of it in accordance with the law, subject to the present regulation.

2.6 Any person with a property right on 24 March 1999, who has lost possession of that property and has not voluntarily disposed of the property right, is entitled to an order from the Commission for repossession of the property. The Commission shall not receive claims for compensation for damage to or destruction of property.

Section 3 – Restitution of Property Lost as a Result of Discrimination

3.1 No claim for restitution of residential property lost between 23 March 1989 and 24 March 1999 as a result of discrimination may be made to any court or tribunal in Kosovo except in accordance with UNMIK Regulation No. 1999/23 and the present regulation.

3.2 Claim under section 1.2 (a), (b) or (c) of UNMIK Regulation No. 1999/23 must be submitted to the Directorate before 1 December 2001. The deadline for submission of claims may be extended by announcement of the Special Representative of the Secretary-General, who may:

- decline to extend the deadline for a category of claims or for purposes of section 5.2; and

- provide different deadlines for different categories of claims or for purposes of section 5.2.

3.3 Where a claimant is found by the Commission to be entitled to restitution, the Commission shall award restitution in kind unless the ownership of the property has been acquired by a natural person through a valid voluntary transaction for value before the date this regulation entered into force.

Section 4 – Restitution of Occupancy Rights to Socially Owned Apartments Lost as a Result of Discrimination

4.1 This section applies to any occupancy right to a socially-owned apartment which was cancelled as a result of discrimination.

4.2 As an exception to section 3.3, in relation to a socially owned apartment which was subsequently purchased from the allocation right holder by the current owner under the Law on Housing (hereafter "First Owner"), the following rules shall apply:

- the claimant has a right to the ownership of the apartment upon payment to the Directorate of:

(i) the purchase price for the apartment contained in the contract of sale concluded by the First Owner; or

(ii) the price at which the claimant would have been entitled to purchase the apartment under the Law on Housing but for the discrimination (whichever is determined by the Directorate to be less), plus a percentage of the current market value of the apartment, as determined by the Directorate, and the cost of any improvements made to the apartment by the First Owner.

- to exercise the right to restitution in kind, the claimant must pay the sum referred to in section 4.2(a) to the Directorate within 120 days of the Commission's decision on the right to restitution. Upon the claimant's application, the Directorate may extend the deadline by up to 120 days if not extending it would result in undue hardship to the claimant. Upon payment of this sum, the Commission shall issue a decision awarding ownership of the apartment to the claimant; and

- money paid under section 4.2(b) will be held by the Directorate in a trust fund.

A First Owner who loses the ownership of an apartment under this section will upon request be compensated by the Directorate from the trust fund for the amount s/he paid for the purchase of the apartment, a percentage of the current market value of the apartment, as determined by the Directorate, as well as for the cost of any improvements s/he made to the apartment. Any outstanding obligations of the First Owner under the Law on Housing are cancelled.

4.3 Except as provided in the previous section, no person whose rights are affected by a decision of the Commission awarding restitution in kind shall be entitled to any form of compensation.

4.4 Any claimant found by the Commission to have a right to restitution of a socially owned apartment, but who is not awarded restitution in kind in accordance with section 4.2, shall be issued a certificate by the Directorate stating the current market value of the apartment in its current condition, minus the amount which the claimant would have been required to pay for the purchase of the apartment under the Law on Housing. The Directorate shall establish formulae for determining these amounts and the amounts referred to in sections 4.2 (a) and (c).

4.5 Any person with a certificate under section 4.4 shall be entitled to fair compensation proportionate to the amount stated in the certificate, to be paid from such funds as may be allocated in the Kosovo Consolidated Budget or any fund set up for this purpose under the present regulation. The method of calculation and payment of such compensation shall be established in subsequent legislation.

Section 5 – Restrictions on Disposal of Apartments Pending Restitution Claims

5.1 This section applies to any person who purchased an apartment from the allocation right holder in accordance with the Law on Housing, where neither that person nor a member of that person's family household was the occupancy right holder of the apartment before 23 March 1989.

5.2 Until the deadline referred to in section 3.2 of the present regulation, or until the resolution of any claim for the apartment made under the present regulation, whichever is the later, a person to whom this section applies shall be considered a lawful possessor of the apartment. During this period, the person may not transfer the apartment to any other person, except when the transfer is part of an amicable settlement of the claim through the agreement of the parties in accordance with section 10.1 of the present regulation. Any contract relating to a sale, exchange or gift made in contravention of this section shall be null and void.

Section 6 – Allocation and Use of Socially Owned Apartments

With regard to the exclusive jurisdiction entrusted to the Directorate over the matters set out in section 1.2 of UNMIK Regulation No. 1999/23, the following provisions shall apply:

Article 3 of the Law on Housing Relations is suspended by the present regulation;

notwithstanding the provisions of any other law, no occupancy right to a socially owned apartment may be terminated without:

(i) the consent of the occupancy right holder or the Housing and Property Directorate; or an order of the Commission, as provided for in the present regulation; and

(ii) notwithstanding Article 24 of the Law on Housing Relations, leases of socially owned apartments are permitted.

CHAPTER II – RULES OF THE HOUSING AND PROPERTY DIRECTORATE

Section 7 – Registration of Claims

7.1 The Directorate shall register claims under section 1.2 of UNMIK Regulation No. 1999/23 at offices established for this purpose in Kosovo and in such other locations as it sees fit.

7.2 A claim may be made by a person referred to in section 1.2 of UNMIK Regulation No. 1999/23, or, where that person is unable to make a claim, by a member of the family household of that person. For the purposes of the present regulation, the members of the family household of a property right holder are determined in accordance with Article 9 of the Law on Housing Relations.

7.3 A claimant or a party to the claim may be represented by an authorized person with a valid and duly executed power of attorney. In exceptional cases, where the provision of a power of attorney is problematic the Directorate may certify an alternative document authorizing representation of a claimant.

Section 8 – Content of Claims

8.1 The claim shall be made in a form determined by the Directorate providing all necessary particulars of the claim, signed by the claimant or the authorized person in the presence of a responsible officer of the Directorate (hereafter "Claim Form").

8.2 The claimant must submit with the Claim Form the originals or certified copies of any documents relevant to the claim which are in his/her possession, or which s/he can reasonably obtain from a public record. The Directorate is authorized to certify copies.

8.3 For claims under section 1.2(c) of Regulation 1999/23, the claimant may, in addition to any other order, seek an order:

restoring possession of the property for the purposes of returning to the property or disposing of it in accordance with the law; and

placing the property under the administration of the Directorate until such time as the claimant elects to return to the property or dispose of it.

Section 9 – The Rights of Parties to the Claim

After receipt of a claim, the Directorate will notify the current occupant of the claimed property if any, and shall make reasonable efforts to notify other persons with a legal interest in the property. In appropriate cases, such reasonable efforts shall take the form of an announcement in an official publication of the Directorate.

The parties to the claim shall be

- the claimant and any current occupant of the claimed property; and

- any other natural person with a legal interest, who informs the Directorate of their intention to participate in the proceedings within 30 days of being notified of the claim by the Directorate in accordance with section 9.1. A person with a legal interest in the claim, who did not receive notification of a claim, may be admitted as a party at any point in the proceedings, provided the claim has not been finally adjudicated.

9.3   The current or former allocation right holder to a claimed apartment may make submissions or present evidence in connection with the claim. Anyone who makes submissions in their capacity as a representative of the current or former allocation right holder shall prove to the satisfaction of the Directorate their identity, and a connection to the allocation right holder. However, in no event is the Directorate or the Commission obliged to decide upon any legal question concerning the identity of the allocation right holder or the right to represent the allocation right holder.

9.4   In the notice of intention to participate referred to in section 9.2, the current occupant and any other natural person with a legal interest shall notify the Directorate of an address for delivery of documents. The Directorate shall deliver copies of the Claim Form to each party.

9.5   Within 30 days of receiving a copy of the Claim Form, the receiving party may respond to the claim in a form determined by the Directorate (hereafter

"Reply to Claim"). Subject to section 21.1, each party must submit originals or certified copies of any documents relevant to the claim which are in his/her possession, or which s/he can reasonably obtain from a public record.

9.6   In the Reply to Claim, the current occupant may request that his/her housing needs be taken into consideration by the Directorate, and, if so, shall provide to the Directorate all information relevant to an assessment of his/her housing needs.

9.7   The Directorate shall deliver copies of the Reply to Claim to the other parties. In appropriate cases, the Directorate may provide the parties with summaries in the language of their choice of any document presented by another party. Any party may respond to any matter raised in the Reply to Claim within 30 days.

9.8   The Directorate may decline to disclose any information submitted to it by a party to the claim, including the identity of any party or witness, where necessary for the security of any person.

9.9   A Claim Form and a Reply to Claim may be submitted in Albanian, English or Serbian.

9.10   In the interests of the efficient and fair resolution of claims, the Directorate may, in specific cases, extend any deadline or dispense with any procedural rule in this Chapter, where there is good reason to do so and this would not materially prejudice the rights of any party. However, the failure of any party without proper justification to participate in the proceedings or comply with any rule shall not delay the resolution of the claim.

Section 10 – Resolution of Claims

10.1   The Directorate shall endeavour to settle claims amicably through the agreement of the parties. The Directorate shall inform the parties of their rights and obligations under the present regulation, and may take whatever steps it sees fit to facilitate settlements or to assist the parties to resolve their housing needs. The Directorate may develop standardised settlement agreements for use by the parties, and may certify settlement agreements.

10.2   The Directorate may investigate a claim, and obtain evidence relevant to a claim from any record held by a public body, corporate or natural person. The Directorate is entitled to free access without charge to any records in Kosovo relevant to the settlement of a claim or for any other verification purposes.

10.3 The Directorate may, by written decision, reject a claim if it manifestly falls outside the Commission's jurisdiction. A claim may be rejected at any stage of the proceedings before the Directorate.

10.4 The Directorate shall refer to the Commission any claim which cannot be settled amicably or in respect of which the claimant disputes the Directorate's rejection in terms of section 10.3. The Directorate may prepare summaries of submissions and evidence, translations of evidence, and recommendations for the consideration of the Commission.

10.5 The Directorate may at any time in the proceedings, either on the request of the claimant or on its own initiative, recommend that the Commission issues provisional measures of protection or any other directive or order necessary to secure the orderly and expeditious resolution of the claim.

Section 11 – Uncontested Claims to Register Informal Transactions

11.1 For claims under section 1.2(b) of UNMIK Regulation No. 1999/23, the Directorate may issue an order for registration of the claimant's informal transaction in the appropriate public record if:

- the claim is uncontested; and

- the Directorate is satisfied that there is sufficient evidence that the claimant acquired the property right through an informal transaction between 23 March 1989 and 13 October 1999.

11.2 An order of the Directorate under this section is not a binding decision on property rights, and does not affect the right of any person to make a further claim to the Directorate under section 1.2 of UNMIK Regulation No. 1999/23. Such further claim must be made within 30 days of learning of the Directorate's order but not later than one (1) year from the date of the Directorate's order. The Directorate must publish orders made in terms of this section.

Section 12 – Properties under the Administration of the Directorate

12.1 The Directorate is authorized to administer abandoned housing for the purpose of providing for the housing needs of displaced persons and refugees.

12.2 The Directorate may make an order placing a property under its administration in any of the following circumstances:

- by agreement of the parties in settlement of a claim;

- on the request of the claimant, following a decision by the Commission confirming the property right of the claimant;

- following eviction of the current occupant, if the claimant fails to repossess the property within 14 days of being notified of the execution of the eviction;

- where no claim has been submitted for the property, and the property is either vacant, or the current occupant of the property does not assert any property right to the property; or

- where no claim has been submitted for the property, on the request of the owner or occupancy right holder of the property.

12.3 For as long as a property is under the administration of the Directorate (hereafter "property under administration"), the rights of possession of the owner or occupancy right holder are suspended in the public interest.

12.4 The Directorate may grant temporary permits to occupy property under its administration, subject to such terms and conditions as it sees fit. Temporary permits shall be granted for a limited period of time, but may be renewed upon application.

12.5 The Directorate shall establish criteria for the allocation of properties under administration on a temporary humanitarian basis.

12.6 The Directorate may issue an eviction order in relation to a property under administration at any time in any of the following circumstances:

where the current occupant does not qualify for a temporary permit;

where a temporary permit has expired; or

where the holder of a temporary permit ceases to qualify for accommodation on humanitarian grounds or does not comply with the terms and conditions of the temporary permit.

12.7   The owner or occupancy right holder of a property under administration may give notice to the Directorate of his/her intention to return into possession of the property. Following a request from the owner or occupancy right holder, the Directorate will deliver an eviction order requiring the current occupant to vacate the property within 90 days, and if the current occupant does not voluntarily vacate the property, the Directorate will issue a warrant authorizing execution of the eviction order. The administration of the property by the Directorate terminates upon repossession of the property by the owner or occupancy right holder.

12.8   The Directorate shall make reasonable efforts to minimize the risk of damage to any property under its administration. The Directorate shall bear no responsibility for any damage to property under administration or loss of or damage to its contents.

Section 13 – Execution of Decisions and Eviction Orders

13.1   The Directorate shall deliver a certified copy of a Commission decision and any order to each party at the address given in terms of section 9.4. The decision and any order are effective from the date of delivery to the last party, unless the decision or order provides otherwise.

The Directorate shall deliver an eviction order issued by the Commission to the current occupant of the claimed property. The Directorate may, at its discretion, delay execution of the eviction order for up to 6 months, pending resolution of the housing needs of the current occupant, or under circumstances that the Directorate deems fit. The Directorate shall inform the current occupant and the claimant of the reason for the delay.

Save for an eviction order in section 12.7 or an order by the Commission providing otherwise, an eviction order issued by the Commission, or in the case of property under its administration, by the Directorate, is executable 30 days after delivery. The eviction order may be executed against any person occupying the property at the time of the eviction.

An eviction shall be executed by the responsible officer of the Directorate, with the support of the law enforcement authorities. The said officer and authorities must be in possession of a warrant signed by:

- the Registrar, in the case of an order of the Commission; or

- a senior official of the Directorate, in the case of an order made by it, authorizing execution of the eviction order.

13.5   During the execution of an eviction order, any person who fails to obey an instruction of the responsible officer to leave the premises may be removed by the law enforcement authorities. In the event that movable property is also removed, the Directorate shall make reasonable efforts to minimize the risk of damage to or loss of such property. The Directorate shall bear no responsibility for any damage to or loss of removed property.

13.6   The Directorate shall notify the claimant of the scheduled date of the eviction. Following the execution of an eviction, if the claimant or temporary occupant is not present to take immediate possession of the property, the responsible officer shall seal the property, and notify the claimant. Any person who, without lawful excuse, enters a property by breaking a seal may be subject to removal from the property by the law enforcement authorities.

Section 14 – Reconsideration Requests of Commission Decisions

14.1   Any party to a claim may submit to the Directorate a request to the Commission for the reconsideration of a Commission decision within 30 days of being notified of the decision:

- upon the presentation of legally relevant evidence, which was not considered by the Commission in deciding the claim; or

- on the ground that there was a material error in the application of the present regulation.

14.2   Any interested person who was not a party to the claim, and who can show good cause why s/he did not participate as a party to the claim, may request reconsideration of a Commission decision within 30 days of learning of the Commission's decision but not later than one (1) year from the date of the Commission's decision.

14.3   The execution of a pending eviction order shall be stayed from the time of lodging of the reconsideration request until the Commission has decided on the reconsideration request, unless the Commission determines otherwise.

Section 15 – Cooperation and Delegation

15.1 In the performance of any of its functions under the present regulation, the Directorate may co-operate with and receive information from any intergovernmental, governmental or non-governmental entity.

15.2 The Directorate may delegate any of its functions to the responsible municipal service in one or more municipalities in Kosovo, subject to such supervision arrangements as it considers appropriate.

Section 16 – Additional Rules

The Directorate may adopt additional rules for carrying out its functions provided that they are consistent with the present regulation.

Chapter III – Rules of Procedure of the Housing and Property Claims Commission

Section 17 – General Rules of the Commission

17.1 The Commission shall sit in plenary session or in such Panels as are established under section 2.2 of UNMIK Regulation No. 1999/23. In the present regulation, once two or more Panels have been created, the terms "Commission" and "Chairperson" shall mean "Commission" and "Chairperson of the Commission" in relation to plenary sessions, and "Panel" and "Chairperson of the Panel" in relation to claims considered in Panels.

The Chairperson of the Commission shall be designated by the Special Representative of the Secretary-General from among members of the Commission. If the Chairperson of the Commission resigns, is removed or is not re-appointed, the longest-serving Panel Chairperson shall be the Acting Chairperson of the Commission pending the designation of the Chairperson by the Special Representative of the Secretary-General. For Panels established subsequent to the first Panel, the Chairperson shall be designated by the Chairperson of the Commission after consultation with the members of the Panel.

Members of the Commission shall be appointed by the Special Representative of the Secretary-General for an initial term of one year. They may be re-appointed for one or more additional terms.

A member of the Commission may be removed from office by the Special Representative of the Secretary-General on the recommendation of a majority of the members of the Commission for failure to meet the qualifications for office or for persistent and unjustified refusal to perform the duties of office.

A member of the Commission who intends to resign shall:

- provide at least one month's written notice to the Registrar and the chairperson of the plenary Commission;

- continue to perform all his/her functions until the end of the notice period subject to section 17.5 (c); and

- continue to serve after the end of the notice period for the limited purpose of finalizing any claim or group of claims which is still pending before that member's Panel.

17.6 Without prejudice to any other law or regulation dealing with immunity, members of the Commission and staff members of the Commission and Directorate shall be immune from any criminal or civil proceedings for any acts carried out within the scope of their official duties.

17.7 The Registrar in consultation with the Chairperson of the Commission shall determine the number and date of its sessions.

17.8 The seat of the Commission shall be in Pristina. The Commission may decide to hold sessions elsewhere if it thinks fit. In appropriate cases, deliberations of the Commission may take place through electronic means.

17.9 The Chairperson of the Commission shall direct the work of the Commission and preside at its sessions.

17.10 The Commission shall elect a Vice-Chairperson who shall perform the functions of the Chairperson in the absence of the Chairperson.

17.11 Members of the Commission unable to participate in a session shall give written notice to the Registrar and the Chairperson at least two weeks before the session. The notice must provide the reasons for the inability to participate.

17.12 Members of the Commission serve only in their personal capacity. They shall not take part in any proceedings on a claim in which they have a personal interest, or if they have been consulted by or are associated with a party to the claim, or if they have been involved in any legal proceedings on the claim other than the proceedings before the Directorate and Commission, or if there are any other circumstances which may affect their impartiality. In case of any doubt concerning this paragraph, or in any other circumstance which might affect the impartiality of members in deciding a claim, the Chairperson shall decide or, in the event that the Chairperson's impartiality could be affected, the Vice-Chairperson shall decide.

17.13   The Registrar of the Commission shall be appointed by the Executive Director of the Directorate in consultation with the Chairperson. The Registrar and staff members of the Commission will provide administrative, technical and legal support to the Commission.

17.14   The Registrar, in consultation with the Chairperson of the plenary Commission, shall determine the order in which claims will be considered by the Commission, and shall allocate claims between the Panels, taking into account the desirability of developing a consistent practice.

17.15   The official languages of the Commission shall be Albanian, English and Serbian. The Chairperson may permit any member or person appearing before the Commission to speak in any other language.

17.16   Interpreters employed by the Directorate or the Commission in connection with Commission proceedings shall make the following declaration:

"I solemnly declare that I will perform my duties as interpreter faithfully, impartially and conscientiously, and with full respect for the duty of confidentiality."

Section 18 – Plenary Sessions of the Commission

18.1   The Commission shall decide, in plenary session, on additional rules of procedure and evidence in accordance with section 26, and on such issues that may be referred to it in accordance with section 20.4.

18.2   Until such time as more than one Panel is established, the quorum for plenary sessions of the Commission shall be two members. Decisions shall be made in accordance with section 20.3.

18.3   Following the establishment of two or more Panels, the quorum for plenary sessions shall be a majority of the members of all Panels. Decisions shall normally be taken by consensus. If a consensus cannot be reached, a decision shall be taken by majority vote. In the event of a tied vote, the Chairperson of the Commission shall have the casting vote in addition to the vote to which each member is entitled.

Section 19 – Proceedings of the Commission

19.1   The Commission shall, subject to sections 19.2 and 19.3, decide claims on the basis of written submissions, including documentary evidence.

19.2   No party may give oral evidence or argument before the Commission unless invited to do so by the Commission. An oral hearing shall take place in public, with due notice to the parties, unless the Chairperson determines otherwise for reasons of the security of the parties or other special circumstance. Proceedings in an oral hearing shall be conducted under the direction of the Chairperson.

19.3   The Commission may consider written or oral submissions from any intergovernmental, governmental or non-governmental entity or expert witness on any matter relevant to a claim.

19.4   The Commission may appoint any one of its members to carry out any of its functions, including attending the hearing of oral evidence at any place, and to report back to the Commission.

19.5   The Commission may:

- consider claims raising common legal and evidentiary issues together;

- delegate to the Registrar and the staff members of the Directorate assigned to service the Commission certain claims review and evidentiary review functions, subject to the supervision of the Commission;

- use computer databases, programs and other electronic tools in order to expedite its decision-making; and

- take any other measures it considers appropriate to expedite its decision-making.

19.6   The Commission may, in specific cases, proceed notwithstanding non-compliance with any procedural rule by any Party or by the Directorate in the interests of the efficient administration of justice, where there is good reason to do so and this would not materially prejudice the rights of any party.

19.7   Prior to deciding a claim, the Commission may issue any interim order consistent with the present regulation, which it considers necessary for an orderly and expeditious resolution of the claim.

19.8   All proceedings before the Directorate and the Claims Commission, including the completion and submission of claim and reply to claim forms, are considered to be administrative proceedings for the purposes of section 176 of the Penal Law of Kosovo (Official Gazette of the SAPK no 20/77, 25/84 and 44/84) concerning false testimony.

Section 20 – Panels

20.1   Subject to sections 17.11, 17.12, 20.2 and 25.1, claims shall be adjudicated by a Panel.

20.2   The quorum for meetings of a Panel shall be two members.

20.3   Decisions of a Panel shall normally be taken by consensus. If all members of a Panel are present and a consensus cannot be reached, a decision shall be taken by majority vote. If two members of a Panel are present and a consensus cannot be reached, the Chairperson of the Panel shall defer consideration of the claim to the next session of the Panel.

20.4   A Panel or the Chairperson of a Panel may refer specific issues relating to a claim to the plenary session of the Commission for guidance. Decisions of a Panel to refer specific issues to the plenary session of the Commission shall be made in accordance with section 20.2 and 20.3.

20.5   In deciding on a claim or on whether to refer specific issues relating to a claim to the plenary session of the Commission, members of a Panel may not abstain.

20.6   The Chairperson of the Commission may temporarily designate a member of a Panel to serve on a different Panel where s/he deems it necessary for the proper functioning of the Commission.

Section 21 – Evidence

21.1   The Commission may be guided but is not bound by the rules of evidence applied in local courts in Kosovo. The Commission may consider any reliable evidence, which it considers relevant to the claim, including evidence presented by the Directorate concerning the reliability of any public record.

21.2   The Commission may require the Directorate to obtain more information from a party, or to conduct additional investigations.

Section 22 – Decisions of the Commission

22.1   The Commission may refer issues arising in connection with a claim, which are not within its jurisdiction to a competent local court or administrative board or tribunal.

22.2   A panel shall be bound by the principles established in:

- its own decisions and the decisions of another Panel, unless compelling reasons exist for deviating from those principles; and

- the decisions of the plenary Commission.

22.3   The Commission shall not award any remedies other than those provided for in the present regulation.

22.4   No party may recover any costs from any other party in connection with proceedings before the Directorate or Commission.

22.5   The Commission may limit its decision to rights of possession of the claimed property where that would provide an effective remedy for the claim.

22.6   Where a claim is made by a family member of the property right holder in accordance with section 6.2, the Commission may decide any property right in the name of the property right holder, and make an order for possession in favour of the claimant. Such a decision shall not determine or affect any legal issue between the claimant and the property right holder or any other person not a party to the claim. Following the Commission's decision, local courts in Kosovo retain jurisdiction to adjudicate any legal issue not decided by the Commission.

22.7   In its decision, the Commission may:

- decide such property rights as are necessary to resolve the claim;

- make an order for possession of the property in favour of any party;

- order the registration of any property right in the appropriate public record;

- where necessary, to resolve a claim, vary the terms of any contract made for the purpose of avoiding a discriminatory law, so as to reflect the actual intention of the parties to the contract;

- cancel any lease agreement in respect of a property which is subject to an order in terms of the present regulation and make ancillary orders to give effect to the cancellation;

- refuse a claim; and

- make any other decision or order necessary to give effect to the present regulation.

22.8   A decision shall contain:

- the date of adoption;

- the names of the parties and their representatives;

- the relief sought;

- the reasons for the decision, including the material facts and property rights found by the Commission; and

- the orders of the Commission.

22.9   Decisions shall be signed by the Chairperson, provided that if the number of claims decided in a session is high, the Chairperson may sign a cover decision approving all individual decisions identified in the cover decision. The individual decisions shall be certified by the Registrar. A copy of an original document signed by the Chairperson which has been sent to the Registrar by facsimile transmission of the original is sufficient authority for any actions taken pursuant to the document.

22.10   The Registrar shall publish the decisions of the Commission, or summaries of the decisions.

22.11   The Registrar is authorized to correct any textual errors in a Commission decision, which do not materially affect the rights of any party, if the Chairperson of the Commission agrees.

Section 23 – Summary Procedure

Any claim under section 1.2(c) of UNMIK Regulation No. 1999/23, which is uncontested, may be considered by the Commission under a summary procedure.

In a summary procedure, the Commission may make an order for recovery of possession of the property if satisfied that there is evidence that the claimant was in uncontested possession of the property prior to 24 March 1999.

A summary decision shall contain:

a. the date of adoption;

b. the names of the parties and their representatives; and

c. the operative provisions of the decision.

23.4   Section 23 does not prevent the Commission from deciding any other uncontested claim summarily.

Section 24 – Provisional Measures

24.1   Upon the recommendation of the Directorate, whether at the request of the claimant or otherwise, the Commission may issue provisional measures of protection where it appears likely that, if provisional measures were not issued, a party would suffer harm, which cannot subsequently be remedied.

24.2   In exceptional circumstances, on the recommendation of the responsible law enforcement agencies and where necessary to control a continuing threat to public security, provisional measures may include the eviction of the current occupant of the claimed property, where the Commission is satisfied that there is evidence of prior uncontested occupation of the property by the claimant. An eviction order issued under this section may be executed by the responsible law enforcement authorities without notice.

Section 25 – Reconsideration of Decisions

25.1   Following the establishment of two or more Panels of the Commission, any reconsideration of a matter shall be conducted by a different Panel than the one that decided the claim, unless the Chairperson of the Panel appointed to conduct the reconsideration, in consultation with the Chairperson of the Commission, determines that it should be conducted in plenary session.

25.2   In the reconsideration of a decision, the Commission or a Panel established by it shall consider all evidence and representations submitted with respect to the original claim and any new evidence and representations with respect to the reconsideration request. The Commission or Panel concerned shall either reject the reconsideration request, or issue a new decision on the claim.

Section 26 – Additional Rules

The Commission may adopt additional rules for carrying out its functions provided that they are consistent with the present regulation.

CHAPTER IV – GENERAL PROVISIONS

Section 27 – Implementation

The Special Representative of the Secretary-General may issue administrative directions for the implementation of the present regulation.

Section 28 – Applicable Law

The present regulation shall supersede any provision in the applicable law that is inconsistent with it.

[. . .]

13. ROMANIA

13.1. Law No. 112 Regulating the Legal Status of Certain Residential Property (1995)

SECTION 1

Individuals who formerly owned residential property which passed lawfully into the ownership of the State or of another artificial person after 6 March 1945 and which was still in the possession of the State or another artificial person on 22 December 1989 shall be entitled to benefit, by way of reparation, from the measures in this Act.

The provisions of this Act shall apply equally to the successors in title of such former owners, subject to existing statutory provisions.

SECTION 2

The persons referred to in section 1 shall be entitled to restitution in the form of the restoration to them of the ownership of flats in which they currently live as tenants or which are vacant. In respect of other flats, those persons shall receive compensation as provided in section 12.

[. . .]

SECTION 13

The amount of compensation to be awarded to former owners or their successors in title in respect of flats which have not been returned to them, or the sale price of such flats, as the case may be, shall be determined in accordance with Decree no. 93/1977, legislative Decree no. 61/1990 and Law no. 85/1992. The value of the appurtenant land shall be determined according to the criteria (Document 2665 of 28 February 1992) for identifying and valuing land held by State-owned commercial companies. . . . The values so determined shall be converted to present-day levels by means of multipliers which may not be lower than the rate of increase in the national average salary over the relevant period.

Neither the total value of a flat which is returned nor the total amount of compensation due for a flat which is not returned and for the appurtenant land may exceed the cumulative total of the national average salary for each year over the period of twenty years expiring on the date on which the compensation is assessed.

Where a flat whose value, calculated according to the rules laid down in the first paragraph of this section, exceeds the total referred to in the second paragraph is returned, pursuant to section 2, to its former owner, his heirs or living relatives to the second degree of consanguinity, those persons cannot be obliged to pay the difference.

The amount of compensation due at present-day levels under the above provisions shall be calculated on the day of payment, on the basis of the national average salary for the last month of the previous quarter.

For the purpose of implementing this Act, an extra-budgetary fund shall be established, on which the Ministry of Finance may draw and into which shall be paid:

(a) the proceeds of the sale of non-returned flats, including payments in full, deposits, monthly instalments and interest (less commission of 1% of the value of each flat); and

(b) the proceeds of government bonds issued for the purpose of financing the fund, as provided in Law no. 91/1993 on public borrowing.

The above fund may be drawn on for the following purposes, in order of priority:

(a) to pay the compensation due under the provisions of this Act to owners or their successors in title;

(b) to redeem the bonds issued and cover the expenses entailed by their issue; and

(c) to build housing to be allocated in the first instance to tenants in the situation referred to in section 5(3).

[. . .]

14. RWANDA

14.1. Ministerial Order No. 01 – Regarding the Temporary Management of Land Property (1996)

CHAPTER ONE – PRELIMINARY PROVISIONS

Article 1

The Commune is bestowed with full authority to ensure on behalf of the government the management of all the land property in rural areas of their jurisdiction that have been abandoned by their owners.

Article 2

Within the framework of the present order, portions of land in rural areas are those that are not located in boundary limits of towns as determined by the decree of April 20, 1979. The present order concerns land property that is not registered in official documents and has been abandoned by its owners. It does not concern all the land in rural areas which has been registered (in cadastre) or any other land that is normally counted in Government property and has never been allocated (leftovers, swamps, military fields, research fields, etc.).

Article 3

Shall be considered as abandoned property:

1. Any land whose owner died without leaving behind his legitimate wife or children;

2. Any land whose owner, his legitimate wife and children are out of the country.

[. . .]

CHAPTER FIVE – MODALITIES FOR THE LAND OWNER TO BE REINSTATED IN HIS RIGHTS

Article 23

The land owner, his legitimate wife and children have the full right to have their property returned upon their repatriation.

They shall submit their request to the Bourgmestre where the property is located.

The Bourgmestre shall immediately inform the temporary occupant in writing.

The Secretary to the Commission mentioned in Article 4 of the present Order [Communal Commission] writes the request in an ad hoc register and acknowledges in writing that he received the request.

The ad hoc register shall mention:

1. The identification of the land owner requesting to be reinstated;

2. The date on which the request was handed in to the Secretary of the Commission;

3. Summarized reasons or proofs on which the owner bases his request;

4. The date on which the Commission made the decision, including a summary of the contents of the decision.

Article 24

Requests to be reinstated in ownership rights are examined by the relevant commission within fifteen days from the time the request has reached the Commune Office.

The Commission's decision is communicated to those concerned within seven days after the decision has been made. A copy of the decision is handed to the people concerned.

Article 25

If either party is not satisfied with the Commission's decision, he shall submit his appeal to the Prefet of Prefecture within 8 days after being informed of the decision.

In the event of the Commune Commission's refusal to make a decision within fifteen days after it has received the request, the applicant has seven days to appeal to the Prefet against the refusal to decide.

The Prefet shall make a decision on the appeal not later than one month from the time the appeal was registered at the Prefecture. If, after one month, no decision has been made by the Prefet or if his decision does not satisfy the person appealing, the latter may submit the case to the judicial authority.

Article 26

A register book shall be held in the Prefet's Secretariat for recording all the appeals regarding decisions made by the Communal Commission responsible for the abandoned land property.

1. The identity of the person appealing;

2. The date on which the appeal was received;

3. A summary of reasons/proofs on which the person bases his appeal;

4. The date on which the appealing person was informed of the decision made by the Commission;

5. The date of the Prefet's decision on the appeal as well as its contents.

[. . .]

15. SOUTH AFRICA

15.1. Restitution of Land Rights Act 22 (1994)[158]

Whereas the Constitution of the Republic of South Africa, 1996 (Act. No. 108 of 1996) provides for restitution of property or equitable redress to a person or community dispossessed of property after 19 June 1913 as a result of past racially discriminatory law or practices;

[. . .]

SECTION 1 – DEFINITIONS

In this Act, unless the context indicate otherwise –

[. . .]

'Restitution of a right in land' means:

[158] As amended in 1999.

(a) the restoration of a right in land; or

(b) equitable redress.

'Restoration of a right in land' means the return of a right in land dispossessed after 19 June 1913 as a result of past racially discriminatory laws or practices;

'Right in land' means any right in land whether registered or unregistered, and may include the interest of a labour tenant and sharecropper, a customary law interest, the interest of a beneficiary under a trust arrangement and beneficial occupation for a continuous period of not less than 10 years prior to the dispossession in question;

[. . .]

SECTION 2 – ENFORCEMENT OF CLAIM FOR RESTITUTION

1. A person shall be entitled to restitution of a right in land if –

(a) he or she is a person dispossessed of a right in land after 19 June 1913 as a result of past racially discriminatory laws or practices; or

(b) it is a deceased estate dispossessed of a right in land after 19 June 1913 as a result of past racially discriminatory laws or practices; or

(c) he or she is the direct descendant of a person referred to in paragraph (a) who has died without lodging a claim and has no ascendant who-

(i) is a direct descendant of a person referred to in paragraph (a); and

(ii) has lodged a claim for the restitution of a right in land; or

(d) it is a community or part of a community dispossessed of a right in land after 19 June 1913 as a result of past racially discriminatory laws or practices; and

(e) the claim for such restitution is lodged not later than 31 December 1998.

[. . .]

SECTION 3 – CLAIMS AGAINST NOMINEES

Subject to the provisions of this Act a person shall be entitled to claim title in land if such claimant or his, her or its antecedent –

(a) was prevented from obtaining or retaining title to the claimed land because of a law which would have been inconsistent with the prohibition of racial discrimination contained in section 9(3) of the Constitution had that subsection been in operation at the relevant time; and

(b) proves that the registered owner of the land holds title as a result of a transaction between such registered owner or his, her or its antecedents and the claimant or his, her or its antecedents, in terms of which such registered owner or his, her or its antecedents held the land on behalf of he claimant or his, her or its antecedents.

Chapter II – Commission on Restitution of Land Rights

Section 4 – Establishment of Commission on Restitution of Land Rights

(1) There is hereby established a commission to be known as the Commission on Restitution of Land Rights.

[. . .]

Section 10 – Lodgement of Claims

(1) Any person or the representative of any community who is of the opinion that he or she or the community which he or she represents is entitled to claim restitution of a right in land as contemplated in section 121 of the Constitution, may lodge such claim, which shall include a description of the land in question, and the nature of the right being claimed, on the form prescribed for this purpose by the Chief Land Claims Commissioner under section 16.

[. . .]

Section 22 – Land Claims Court

(1) There shall be a court of law to be known as the Land Claims Court which, in addition to the powers contemplated in section 123 of the Constitution, shall have the power –

(a) to determine restitution of any right in land in accordance with this Act;

(b) to determine compensation in terms of this Act;

(c) in respect of a claim in terms of section 3, to determine the person entitled to ownership;

(d) to determine all other matters which require to be determined in terms of sections 121, 122 and 123 of the Constitution.

(2) The Court shall have jurisdiction throughout the Republic and shall have all the ancillary powers necessary or reasonably incidental to the performance of its functions, including the power to grant interlocutory orders and interdicts.

[. . .]

Section 33 – Factors to Be Taken in Account by Court

In considering its decision in any particular matter, excluding the review of a decision in terms of section 15, the Court shall, in addition to the matters referred to in section 121, 122 and 123 of the Constitution, have regard to the following factors:

(a) The desirability of providing for restitution of rights in land or compensation to people who were dispossessed of their rights in land as a result of or in pursuance of racially based discriminatory laws;

(b) the desirability of remedying past violations of human rights;

(c) the requirements of equity and justice;

(d) the desirability of avoiding major social disruption;

(e) any provision which already exists, in respect of the land in question in any matter, for that land to be dealt with in a manner which is designed to achieve the goals contemplated in section 8(3)(a) of the Constitution;

(f) any other factor which the Court may consider relevant and consistent with the spirit and objects of the Constitution and in particular the provisions of section 8 of the Constitution.

[. . .]

15.2. South Africa Constitution (1996)

[. . .]

SECTION 25 – PROPERTY

(1) No one may be deprived of property except in terms of law of general application, and no law may permit arbitrary deprivation of property.

(2) Property may be expropriated only in terms of law of general application –

(a) for a public purpose or in the public interest; and

(b) subject to compensation, the amount of which and the time and manner of payment of which have either been agreed to by those affected or decided or approved by a court.

(3) The amount of the compensation and the time and manner of payment must be just and equitable, reflecting an equitable balance between the public interest and the interests of those affected, having regard to all relevant circumstances, including –

(a) the current use of the property;

(b) the history of the acquisition and use of the property;

(c) the market value of the property;

(d) the extent of direct state investment and subsidy in the acquisition and beneficial capital improvement of the property; and

(e) the purpose of the expropriation.

(4) For the purposes of this section –

(a) the public interest includes the nation's commitment to land reform, and to reforms to bring about equitable access to all South Africa's natural resources; and

(b) property is not limited to land.

(5) The state must take reasonable legislative and other measures, within its available resources, to foster conditions which enable citizens to gain access to land on an equitable basis.

(6) A person or community whose tenure of land is legally insecure as a result of past racially discriminatory laws or practices is entitled, to the extent provided by an Act of Parliament, either to tenure which is legally secure or to comparable redress.

(7) A person or community dispossessed of property after 19 June 1913 as a result of past racially

discriminatory laws or practices is entitled, to the extent provided by an Act of Parliament, either to restitution of that property or to equitable redress.

(8) No provision of this section may impede the state from taking legislative and other measures to achieve land, water and related reform, in order to redress the results of past racial discrimination, provided that any departure from the provisions of this section is in accordance with the provisions of section 36(1).

(9) Parliament must enact the legislation referred to in subsection (6).

[. . .]

---

16. TAJIKISTAN

16.1. The Law of the Republic of Tajikistan on Forced Migrants (1994)

[. . .]

Article 11 – Safeguarding Security of the Forced Migrants on Their Return to Places of Permanent Residence

Organs of State power and administration are obliged to safeguard the security of the forced migrants on their return to their places of permanent residences as well as observation of their rights and lawful interests.

Article 12 – The Rights of Forced Migrants upon Arrival in Their Places of Permanent Residence

A forced migrant, after return to his place of permanent residence, has the right to:

- repossess the personal and real estate left by him under the circumstances foreseen by the Article 1 of the present law;

- receive a lump sum allowance or other cash benefit, the sum of which is determined by the Council of Ministers of the Republic of Tajikistan;

- receive credit on preferential terms to reconstruct and build new houses and outbuildings to replace what has been destroyed;

Article 13 – The Fund of Assistance to Forced Migrants

To ensure favourable material conditions and compensation of expenses on accommodation at new permanent places of residence in the territory of the Republic of Tajikistan and at the places of previous residence the Fund of Assistance to Forced migrants hereby is established within the Central Refugee Department of the Ministry of Labour and Employment of Population of the Republic of Tajikistan.

The Fund shall be formed on the basis of receipts from the State Budget of the Republic of Tajikistan, other states and international organizations on the basis of agreements and other documents concluded by the Republic of Tajikistan, receipts from province, town and district budgets, voluntary donations on the part of domestic and foreign enterprises, public organisations and individual persons.

Article 14 – Sources of Compensation of Expenses of Reception and Accommodation of Forced Migrants

Expenses on the part of the local State power and administration organs connected with reception and accommodation of forced migrants on their territory shall be reimbursed from republican budget of the Republic of Tajikistan and the fund of Assistance within the Central Refugee Department of the Ministry of Labour and Employment of Population of the Republic of Tajikistan.

16.2. Resolution No. 542 – Additional Measures Facilitating the Return of Refugees-Citizens of the Republic of Tajikistan and Forced Migrants to the Places of Permanent Residence and Their Social and Legal Protection (1995)

With the aim of activating efforts on returning refugees-citizens of the Republic of Tajikistan and forced migrants to the places of permanent residence, strengthening their social and legal protection and in accordance with the statement of the government delegation of the Republic of Tajikistan on the results of the fourth round of inter-Tajik talks in Almaty, the Government of the Republic of Tajikistan resolves;

1. The ministries departments of the Republic of Tajikistan, heads of oblasts, cities and rayons of the Republic of Tajikistan shall intensify the work of the organized return of the refugees and forced migrants to the places of permanent residence and their social and legal protection.

2. With the aim of efficiently solving the questions arising in connection with the return of refugees – citizens of the Republic of Tajikistan and forced migrants to the places of permanent residence, their social and legal protection a government commission shall be set up in accordance with the supplement.

[. . .]

4. With the aim of facilitating the earliest social and economic adaptation of the refugees-citizens of the Republic of Tajikistan and forced migrants returned to the places of permanent residence, the Ministry of Internal Affairs of the Republic of Tajikistan, hukumats of oblasts, cities and rayons of the Republic of Tajikistan in common with the agencies of the Procurator's Office of the Republic of Tajikistan shall:

- immediately vacate illegally occupied dwellings owned or rented by the refugees-citizens of the Republic of Tajikistan and forced migrants in houses belonging to the State or communal housing fund and pass them to their rightful owners;

- in case of the destruction or loss of the State-owned dwelling, provide out of turn an available dwelling space at his whereabouts in conformity with the standards in force in the Republic. According to the wish of the victims, in return for the dwelling, allot them a land plot for the construction of a dwelling house or give them a right to join a building cooperative out of turn.

[. . .]

6. The State Committee of the Republic of Tajikistan on Contracts and Trade, the Board of Tajikmatlubot shall provide persons from among refugees-citizens of the Republic of Tajikistan and forced migrants and forced migrants building their own houses with main types of building materials in the first instance according to the claims of thukumats.

[. . .]

PART FOUR

Housing and Property Restitution Case Law

1. PERMANENT INTERNATIONAL COURT OF JUSTICE

1.1. *The Factory at Chórzow (Indemnity) Case* (1928)[159]

[. . .]

It is a principle of international law that the reparation of a wrong may consist in an indemnity corresponding to the damage which the nationals of the injured State have suffered as a result of the act which is contrary to international law. This is even the most usual form of reparation; it is the form selected by Germany in this case and the admissibility of it has not been disputed. The reparation due by one State to another does not however change its character by reason of the fact that it takes the form of an indemnity for the calculation of which the damage suffered by a private person is taken as the measure. The rules of law governing the reparation are the rules of international law in force between the two States concerned, and not the law governing relations between the State which has committed a wrongful act and the individual who has suffered damage. Rights or interests of an individual the violation of which rights causes damage are always in a different plane to rights belonging to a State, which rights may also be infringed by the same act. The damage suffered by an individual is never therefore identical in kind with that which will be suffered by a State; it can only afford a convenient scale for the calculation of the reparation due to the State.

[. . .]

The action of Poland which the Court has judged to be contrary to the Geneva Convention is not an

[159] PCIJ (ser. A) No. 17 (Judgment of Sept. 13 1928), p. 47. Footnotes omitted.

expropriation – to render which lawful only the payment of fair compensation would have been wanting; it is a seizure of property, rights and interests which could not be expropriated even against compensation, save under the exceptional conditions fixed by Article 7 of the said Convention. As the Court has expressly declared in Judgment No. 8, reparation is in this case the consequence not of the application of Articles 6 to 22 of the Geneva Convention, but of acts contrary to those articles. It follows that the compensation due to the German Government is not necessarily limited to the value of the undertaking at the moment of dispossession, plus interest to the day of payment. This limitation would only be admissible if the Polish Government had had the right to expropriate, and if its wrongful act consisted merely in not having paid to the two Companies the just price of what was expropriated; in the present case, such a limitation might result in placing Germany and the interests protected by the Geneva Convention, on behalf of which interests the German Government is acting, in a situation more unfavourable than that in which Germany and these interests would have been if Poland had respected the said Convention. Such a consequence would not only be unjust, but also and above all incompatible with the aim of Article 6 and following articles of the Convention – that is to say, the prohibition, in principle, of the liquidation of the property, rights and interests of German nationals and of companies controlled by German nationals in Upper Silesia – since it would be tantamount to rendering lawful liquidation and unlawful dispossession indistinguishable in so far as their financial results are concerned.

The essential principle contained in the actual notion of an illegal act – a principle which seems to be established by international practice and in particular by the decisions of arbitral tribunals – is that reparation must, as far as possible, wipe-out all the consequences of the illegal act and re-establish the situation which would, in all probability, have existed if that act had not been committed. Restitution in kind, or, if this is not possible, payment of a sum corresponding to the value which a restitution in kind would bear; the award, if need be, of damages for loss sustained which would not be covered by restitution in kind or payment in place of it – such are the principles which should serve to determine the amount of compensation due for an act contrary to international law.

This conclusion particularly applies as regards the Geneva Convention, the object of which is to provide for the maintenance of economic life in Upper Silesia on the basis of respect for the *status quo*. The dispossession of an industrial undertaking – the expropriation of which is prohibited by the Geneva Convention – then involves the obligation to restore the undertaking and, if this be not possible, to pay its value at the time of the indemnification, which value is designed to take the place of restitution which has become impossible. To this obligation, in virtue of the general principles of international law, must be added that of compensating loss sustained as the result of the seizure. The impossibility, on which the Parties are agreed, of restoring the Chorzów factory could therefore have no other effect but that of substituting payment of the value of the undertaking for restitution; it would not be in conformity either with the principles of law or with the wish of the Parties to infer from that agreement that, the question of compensation must henceforth be dealt with as though an expropriation properly so called was involved.

[. . .]

DISSENTING OPINION BY LORD FINLAY

I regret that I am unable to concur in the judgment that has just been delivered. I think that question II ought not to have been put to the experts and am further unable to agree with what is said in the judgment as to the principles governing the assessment of the indemnity.

[. . .]

The Party who has been dispossessed has a choice of remedies. He may claim restitution of the prop-

erty taken. This is what is meant by *restitutio in integrum*. He may on the other hand abandon any claim to restitution of the actual property and claim damages instead. The German Government abandoned its claim to restitution, possibly under the impression – which may have been correct – that the alterations were not of a nature which would harmonize with the use to which the German Government intended that the property should be put. If the German Government had obtained *restitutio in integrum*, it would have got the property itself and any enhanced value which it had reached would necessarily go to the German Government with the property. But since the claim to restitution is abandoned, the only claim is for damages for the wrongful act. A Party who has given up his right to *restitutio in integrum* is not entitled to claim damages on the footing that it is right that he should have the enhanced value, if any that he would have got if he had pressed his claim for restitution. The German Government having renounced restitution cannot make good a claim to recover an amount representing the value of the property which would have to be restored. It has given up restitution and elected to take damages and these damages must be assessed according to the general rule as at the time of the wrong.

There is no trace of anything from which it could be implied that on giving up the right to *restitutio in integrum*, Germany should be entitled in lieu thereof to get damages on a higher scale than that on which the damages for a wrongful taking would by law be assessed. If the Parties had intended this they would have said so. Germany and Poland merely agreed that the claim for restitution had been abandoned, and that left matters exactly as if that claim had never been put forward. To construe this transaction as involving an agreement that the damages should be assessed in any but the usual way is to make a new agreement for the Parties. What the Parties did was merely to abandon restitution with the consequence that Germany took the right to damages to be assessed in the usual way.

In my opinion, according to the general principle of international law, these damages should be assessed upon the basis of the value of the undertaking at the time of the seizure, that is the 3rd July, 1922, together with a fair rate of interest on that value from that date until the date of payment; and in addition any other damage directly consequent upon the seizure.

It may be that damages so assessed will amount to no more than the amount which the Polish Government would have had to pay if it had been able to expropriate the undertaking in conformity with the terms of the Geneva Convention; but this is immaterial. Germany has selected as the form of reparation for the wrong done to her at international law a pecuniary indemnity corresponding to the loss sustained by her nationals. It is immaterial whether the result of this selection is to put Germany and the German Companies in a better or worse position than that in which they would otherwise have been.

It is said that the general rule as to assessment of damages cannot here be applied and that some distinction must be made between the consequences of a wrongful expropriation and those of a lawful expropriation in accordance with the provisions of the Geneva Convention. The fact that Poland, had she expropriated in accordance with the Geneva Convention, would have been bound to pay an indemnity equal to the amount of the damages, if the damages are assessed according to the general rule of international law, does not affect the matter. The question is what was the loss inflicted on the two Companies by the seizure.

It is argued that it would not be equitable that the liability of a mere wrongdoer should be no greater than that of one who had expropriated the property in accordance with the terms of the Geneva Convention.

Expropriation in accordance with those terms was at the time impossible, in the absence of recognition by the Mixed Commission that this measure was indispensable for the maintenance of the working of the undertaking (Article 7). No special provision is made in the Convention as to what is to happen if the Government takes property in contravention of these provisions: that is left to the general law. It is now however argued that it is not equitable that the general law should apply in such a case, and an effort is made to modify it so as to prevent the Government which has so acted being financially in no worse position than one which has acted under the provisions of the Geneva Convention.

It seems to me that it is entirely beyond the province of the Court in effect to introduce provisions of this nature, in the absence of agreement in treaty or convention to that effect.

[. . .]

2. INTERNATIONAL COURT OF JUSTICE

2.1. *Advisory Opinion on the Legal Consequences of the Construction of a Wall in the Occupied Palestinian Territory* (2004)

[. . .]

148. The Court will now examine the legal consequences resulting from the violations of international law by Israel by distinguishing between, on the one hand, those arising for Israel and, on the other, those arising for other States and, where appropriate, for the United Nations. The Court will begin by examining the legal consequences of those violations for Israel.

149. The Court notes that Israel is first obliged to comply with the international obligations it has breached by the construction of the wall in the Occupied Palestinian Territory (see paragraphs 114–137 above). Consequently, Israel is bound to comply with its obligation to respect the right of the Palestinian people to self-determination and its obligations under international humanitarian law and international human rights law. Furthermore, it must ensure freedom of access to the Holy Places that came under its control following the 1967 War (see paragraph 129 above).

150. The Court observes that Israel also has an obligation to put an end to the violation of its international obligations flowing from the construction of the wall in the Occupied Palestinian Territory. The obligation of a State responsible for an internationally wrongful act to put an end to that act is well established in general international law, and the Court has on a number of occasions confirmed the existence of that obligation (*Military and Paramilitary Activities in and against Nicaragua (Nicaragua v. United States of America), Merits, Judgment, I.C.J. Reports 1986*, p. 149; *United States Diplomatic and Consular Staff in Tehran, Judgment, I.C.J. Reports*

1980, p. 44, para. 95; *Haya de la Torre, Judgment, I.C.J. Reports 1951*, p. 82).

151. Israel accordingly has the obligation to cease forthwith the works of construction of the wall being built by it in the Occupied Palestinian Territory, including in and around East Jerusalem. Moreover, in view of the Court's finding (see paragraph 143 above) that Israel's violations of its international obligations stem from the construction of the wall and from its associated régime, cessation of those violations entails the dismantling forthwith of those parts of that structure situated within the Occupied Palestinian Territory, including in and around East Jerusalem. All legislative and regulatory acts adopted with a view to its construction, and to the establishment of its associated régime, must forthwith be repealed or rendered ineffective, except in so far as such acts, by providing for compensation or other forms of reparation for the Palestinian population, may continue to be relevant for compliance by Israel with the obligations referred to in paragraph 153 below.

152. Moreover, given that the construction of the wall in the Occupied Palestinian Territory has, *inter alia*, entailed the requisition and destruction of homes, businesses and agricultural holdings, the Court finds further that Israel has the obligation to make reparation for the damage caused to all the natural or legal persons concerned. The Court would recall that the essential forms of reparation in customary law were laid down by the Permanent Court of International Justice in the following terms:

"The essential principle contained in the actual notion of an illegal act – a principle which seems to be established by international practice and in particular by the decisions of arbitral tribunals – is that reparation must, as far as possible, wipe out all the consequences of the illegal act and re-establish the situation which would, in all probability, have existed if that act had not been committed. Restitution in kind, or, if this is not possible, payment of a sum corresponding to the value which a restitution in kind would bear; the award, if need be, of damages for loss sustained which would not be covered by restitution in kind or payment in place of it – such are the principles which should serve to determine the amount of compensation due for an act contrary to

international law." (*Factory at Chorzów, Merits, Judgment No. 13, 1928, P.C.I.J., Series A, No. 17*, p. 47)

153. Israel is accordingly under an obligation to return the land, orchards, olive groves and other immovable property seized from any natural or legal person for purposes of construction of the wall in the Occupied Palestinian Territory. In the event that such restitution should prove to be materially impossible, Israel has an obligation to compensate the persons in question for the damage suffered. The Court considers that Israel also has an obligation to compensate, in accordance with the applicable rules of international law, all natural or legal persons having suffered any form of material damage as a result of the wall's construction.

[. . .]

3. HUMAN RIGHTS COMMITTEE

3.1. *Simunek, Hastings, Tuzilova and Prochazka v. The Czech Republic* (1995)

The Human Rights Committee, established under article 28 of the International Covenant on Civil and Political Rights,

Meeting on 19 July 1995,

Having concluded its consideration of communication No. 516/1992 submitted to the Human Rights Committee by Mrs. Alina Simunek, Mrs. Dagmar Hastings Tuzilova and Mr. Josef Prochazka under the Optional Protocol to the International Covenant on Civil and Political Rights,

Having taken into account all written information made available to it by the authors of the communication and the State party,

Adopts its Views under article 5, paragraph 4, of the Optional Protocol.

1. The authors of the communications are Alina Simunek, who acts on her behalf and on behalf of her husband, Jaroslav Simunek, Dagmar Tuzilova Hastings and Josef Prochazka, residents of Canada and Switzerland, respectively. They claim to be victims of violations of their human rights by the Czech Republic. The Covenant was ratified by Czechoslovakia on 23 December 1975. The Optional Protocol

entered into force for the Czech Republic on 12 June 1991 [The Czech and Slovak Federal Republic ratified the Optional Protocol in March 1991 but, on 31 December 1992, the Czech and Slovak Federal Republic ceased to exist. On 22 February 1993, the Czech Republic notified its succession to the Covenant and the Optional Protocol].

THE FACTS AS SUBMITTED BY THE AUTHORS

2.1   Alina Simunek, a Polish citizen born in 1960, and Jaroslav Simunek, a Czech citizen, currently reside in Ontario, Canada. They state that they were forced to leave Czechoslovakia in 1987, under pressure of the security forces of the communist regime. Under the legislation then applicable, their property was confiscated. After the fall of the Communist government on 17 November 1989, the Czech authorities published statements which indicated that expatriate Czech citizens would be rehabilitated in as far as any criminal conviction was concerned, and their property restituted.

2.2   In July 1990, Mr. and Mrs. Simunek returned to Czechoslovakia in order to submit a request for the return of their property, which had been confiscated by the District National Committee, a State organ, in Jablonece. It transpired, however, that between September 1989 and February 1990, all their property and personal effects had been evaluated and auctioned off by the District National Committee. Unsaleable items had been destroyed. On 13 February 1990, the authors' real estate was transferred to the Jablonece Sklarny factory, for which Jaroslav Simunek had been working for twenty years.

2.3   Upon lodging a complaint with the District National Committee, an arbitration hearing was convened between the authors, their witnesses and representatives of the factory on 18 July 1990. The latter's representatives denied that the transfer of the authors' property had been illegal. The authors thereupon petitioned the office of the district public prosecutor, requesting an investigation of the matter on the ground that the transfer of their property had been illegal, since it had been transferred in the absence of a court order or court proceedings to which the authors had been parties. On 17 September 1990, the Criminal Investigations Department of the National Police in Jablonece launched an investigation; its report of 29 November 1990 concluded that no violation of (then) applicable regu-

lations could be ascertained, and that the authors' claim should be dismissed, as the Government had not yet amended the former legislation.

2.4   On 2 February 1991, the Czech and Slovak Federal Government adopted Act 87/1991, which entered into force on 1 April 1991. It endorses the rehabilitation of Czech citizens who had left the country under communist pressure and lays down the conditions for restitution or compensation for loss of property. Under Section 3, subsection 1, of the Act, those who had their property turned into State ownership in the cases specified in Section 6 of the Act are entitled to restitution, but only if they are citizens of the Czech and Slovak Federal Republic *and* are permanent residents in its territory.

2.5   Under Section 5, subsection 1, of the Act, anyone currently in (illegal) possession of the property shall restitute it to the rightful owner, upon a written request from the latter, who must also prove his or her claim to the property and demonstrate how the property was turned over to the State. Under subsection 2, the request for restitution must be submitted to the individual in possession of the property, within six months of the entry into force of the Act. If the person in possession of the property does not comply with the request, the rightful owner may submit his or her claim to the competent tribunal, within one year of the date of entry into force of the Act (subsection 4).

2.6   With regard to the issue of exhaustion of domestic remedies, it appears that the authors have not submitted their claims for restitution to the local courts, as required under Section 5, subsection 4, of the Act. It transpires from their submissions that they consider this remedy ineffective, as they do not fulfil the requirements under Section 3, subsection 1. Alina Simunek adds that they have lodged complaints with the competent municipal, provincial and federal authorities, to no avail. She also notes that the latest correspondence is a letter from the Czech President's Office, dated 16 June 1992, in which the author is informed that the President's Office cannot intervene in the matter, and that only the tribunals are competent to pronounce on the matter. The author's subsequent letters remained without reply.

2.7   Dagmar Hastings Tuzilova, an American citizen by marriage and currently residing in Switzerland, emigrated from Czechoslovakia in 1968. On 21 May 1974, she was sentenced *in absentia* to a prison term as well as forfeiture of her property, on the ground that she had 'illegally emigrated' from Czechoslovakia. Her property, 5/18 shares of her family's estate in Pilsen, is currently held by the Administration of Houses in this city.

2.8 By decision of 4 October 1990 of the District Court of Pilsen, Dagmar Hastings Tuzilova was rehabilitated; the District Court's earlier decision, as well as all other decisions in the case, were declared null and void. All her subsequent applications to the competent authorities and a request to the Administration of Houses in Pilsen to negotiate the restitution of her property have, however, not produced any tangible result.

2.9 Apparently, the Administration of Housing agreed, in the spring of 1992, to transfer the 5/18 of the house back to her, on the condition that the State notary in Pilsen agreed to register this transaction. The State notary, however, has so far refused to register the transfer. At the beginning of 1993, the District Court of Pilsen confirmed the notary's action (Case No. 11 Co. 409/92). The author states that she was informed that she could appeal this decision, via the District Court in Pilsen, to the Supreme Court. She apparently filed an appeal with the Supreme Court on 7 May 1993, but no decision had been taken as of 20 January 1994.

2.10 On 16 March 1992, Dagmar Hastings Tuzilova filed a civil action against the Administration of Houses, pursuant to Section 5, subsection 4, of the Act. On 25 May 1992, the District Court of Pilsen dismissed the claim, on the ground that, as an American citizen residing in Switzerland, she was not entitled to restitution within the meaning of Section 3, subsection 1, of Act 87/1991. The author contends that any appeal against this decision would be ineffective.

2.11 Josef Prochazka is a Czech citizen born in 1920, who currently resides in Switzerland. He fled from Czechoslovakia in August 1968, together with his wife and two sons. In the former Czechoslovakia, he owned a house with two three-bedroom apartments and a garden, as well as another plot of land. Towards the beginning of 1969, he donated his property, in the appropriate form and with the consent of the authorities, to his father. By judgments of a district court of July and September 1971, he, his wife and sons were sentenced to prison terms on the grounds of "illegal emigration" from Czechoslovakia. In 1973, Josef Prochazka's father died; in his

will, which was recognized as valid by the authorities, the author's sons inherited the house and other real estate.

2.12 In 1974, the court decreed the confiscation of the author's property, because of his and his family's "illegal emigration", in spite of the fact that the authorities had, several years earlier, recognized as lawful the transfer of the property to the author's father. In December 1974, the house and garden were sold, according to the author at a ridiculously low price, to a high party official.

2.13 By decisions of 26 September 1990 and of 31 January 1991, respectively, the District Court of Ustí rehabilitated the author and his sons as far as their criminal conviction was concerned, with retroactive effect. This means that the court decisions of 1971 and 1974 (see paragraphs 2.11 and 2.12 above) were invalidated.

THE COMPLAINT

3.1 Alina and Jaroslav Simunek contend that the requirements of Act 87/1991 constitute unlawful discrimination, as it only applies to "pure Czechs living in the Czech and Slovak Federal Republic". Those who fled the country or were forced into exile by the ex-communist regime must take a permanent residence in Czechoslovakia to be eligible for restitution or compensation. Alina Simunek, who lived and worked in Czechoslovakia for eight years, would not be eligible at all for restitution, on account of her Polish citizenship. The authors claim that the Act in reality legalizes former Communist practices, as more than 80% of the confiscated property belongs to persons who do not meet these strict requirements.

3.2 Alina Simunek alleges that the conditions for restitution imposed by the Act constitute discrimination on the basis of political opinion and religion, without however substantiating her claim.

3.3 Dagmar Hastings Tuzilova claims that the requirements of Act 87/1991 constitute unlawful discrimination, contrary to article 26 of the Covenant.

3.4 Josef Prochazka also claims that he is a victim of the discriminatory provisions of Act 87/1991; he adds that as the court decided, with retroactive effect, that the confiscation of his property was null and void, the law should not be applied to him at all, as he never lost his legal title to his property, and because there can be no question of 'restitution' of the property.

THE COMMITTEE'S ADMISSIBILITY DECISION

4.1 On 26 October 1993, the communications were transmitted to the State party under rule 91 of the rules of procedure of the Human Rights Committee. No submission under rule 91 was received from the State party, despite a reminder addressed to it. The authors were equally requested to provide a number of clarifications; they complied with this request by letters of 25 November 1993 (Alina and Jaroslav Simunek), 3 December 1993 and 11/12 April 1994 (Josef Prochazka) and 19 January 1994 (Dagmar Hastings Tuzilova).

4.2 At its 51st session the Committee considered the admissibility of the communication. It noted with regret the State party's failure to provide information and observations on the question of the admissibility of the communication. Notwithstanding this absence of cooperation on the part of the State party, the Committee proceeded to ascertain whether the conditions of admissibility under the Optional Protocol had been met.

4.3 The Committee noted that the confiscation and sale of the property in question by the authorities of Czechoslovakia occurred in the 1970's and 1980's. Irrespective of the fact that all these events took place prior to the date of entry into force of the Optional Protocol for the Czech Republic, the Committee recalled that the right to property, as such, is not protected by the Covenant.

4.4 The Committee observed, however, that the authors complained about the discriminatory effect of the provisions of Act 87/1991, in the sense that they apply only to persons unlawfully stripped of their property under the former regime who now have a permanent residence in the Czech Republic and are Czech citizens. Thus the question before the Committee was whether the law could be deemed discriminatory within the meaning of article 26 of the Covenant.

4.5 The Committee observed that the State party's obligations under the Covenant applied as of the date of its entry into force. A different issue arose as to when the Committee's competence to consider complaints about alleged violations of the Covenant under the Optional Protocol was

engaged. In its jurisprudence under the Optional Protocol, the Committee has consistently held that it cannot consider alleged violations of the Covenant which occurred before the entry into force of the Optional Protocol for the State party, unless the violations complained of continue after the entry into force of the Optional Protocol. A continuing violation is to be interpreted as an affirmation, after the entry into force of the Optional Protocol, by act or by clear implication, of the previous violations of the State party.

4.6 While the authors in the present case have had their criminal convictions quashed by Czech tribunals, they still contend that Act No. 87/1991 discriminates against them, in that in the case of two of the applicants (Mr. and Mrs. Simunek; Mrs. Hastings Tuzilova), they cannot benefit from the law because they are not Czech citizens or have no residence in the Czech Republic, and that in the case of the third applicant (Mr. Prochazka), the law should not have been deemed applicable to his situation at all.

5. On 22 July 1994 the Human Rights Committee therefore **decided** that the communication was admissible in as much as it may raise issues under articles 14, paragraph 6, and 26 of the Covenant.

THE STATE PARTY'S EXPLANATIONS

6.1 In its submission, dated 12 December 1994, the State party argues that the legislation in question is not discriminatory. It draws the Committee's attention to the fact that according to article 11, Section 2, of the Charter of Fundamental Rights and Freedoms, which is part of the Constitution of the Czech Republic, " ... the law may specify that some things may be owned exclusively by citizens or by legal persons having their seat in the Czech Republic."

6.2 The State party affirms its commitment to the settlement of property claims by restitution of properties to persons injured during the period of 25 February 1948 to 1 January 1990. Although certain criteria had to be stipulated for the restitution of confiscated properties, the purpose of such requirements is not to violate human rights. The Czech Republic cannot and will not dictate to anybody where to live. Restitution of confiscated property is a very complicated and de facto unprecedented measure and therefore it cannot be expected to rectify all damages and to satisfy all the people injured by the Communist regime.

7.1 With respect to the communication submitted by Mrs. Alina Simunek the State party argues that the documents submitted by the author do not define the claims clearly enough. It appears from her submission that Mr. Jaroslav Simunek was probably kept in prison by the State Security Police. Nevertheless, it is not clear whether he was kept in custody or actually sentenced to imprisonment. As concerns the confiscation of the property of Mr. and Mrs. Simunek, the communication does not define the measure on the basis of which they were deprived of their ownership rights. In case Mr. Simunek was sentenced for a criminal offence mentioned in Section 2 or Section 4 of Law No. 119/1990 on judicial rehabilitation as amended by subsequent provisions, he could claim rehabilitation under the law or in review proceedings and, within three years of the entry into force of the court decision on his rehabilitation, apply to the Compensations Department of the Ministry of Justice of the Czech Republic for compensation pursuant to Section 23 of the above-mentioned Law. In case Mr. Simunek was unlawfully deprived of his personal liberty and his property was confiscated between 25 February 1948 and 1 January 1990 in connection with a criminal offence mentioned in Section 2 and Section 4 of the Law but the criminal proceedings against him were not initiated, he could apply for compensation on the basis of a court decision issued at the request of the injured party and substantiate his application with the documents which he had at his disposal or which his legal adviser obtained from the archives of the Ministry of the Interior of the Czech Republic.

7.2 As concerns the restitution of the forfeited or confiscated property, the State party concludes from the submission that Alina and Jaroslav Simunek do not comply with the requirements of Section 3 (1) of Law No. 87/1991 on extrajudicial rehabilitations, namely the requirements of citizenship of the Czech and Slovak Federal Republic and permanent residence on its territory. Consequently, they cannot be recognized as persons entitled to restitution. Remedy would be possible only in case at least one of them complied with both requirements and applied for restitution within 6 months from the entry into force of the law on extrajudicial rehabilitations (i.e. by the end of September 1991).

8.1 With respect to the communication of Mrs. Dagmar Hastings-Tuzilova the State party clarifies that Mrs. Dagmar Hastings-Tuzilova claims the restitution of the 5/18 shares of house No. 2214 at Cechova 61, Pilsen, forfeited on the basis of the ruling of the Pilsen District Court of 21 May 1974, by which she was sentenced for the criminal offence of illegal emigration according to Section 109 (2) of the Criminal Law. She was rehabilitated pursuant to Law No. 119/1990 on judicial rehabilitations by the ruling of the Pilsen District Court of 4 October 1990. She applied for restitution of her share of the estate in Pilsen pursuant to Law No. 87/1991 on extrajudicial rehabilitations. Mrs. Hastings-Tuzilova concluded an agreement on the restitution with the Administration of Houses in Pilsen, which the State Notary in Pilsen refused to register due to the fact that she did not comply with the conditions stipulated by Section 3 (1) of the law on extrajudicial rehabilitations.

8.2 Mrs. Hastings-Tuzilova, although rehabilitated pursuant to the law on judicial rehabilitations, cannot be considered entitled person as defined by Section 19 of the law on extrajudicial rehabilitations, because on the date of application she did not comply with the requirements of Section 3 (1) of the above-mentioned law, i.e. requirements of citizenship of the Czech and Slovak Federal Republic and permanent residence on its territory. Moreover, she failed to fulfil the requirements within the preclusive period stipulated by Section 5 (2) of the law on extrajudicial rehabilitations. Mrs. Hastings-Tuzilova acquired Czech citizenship and registered her permanent residence on 30 September 1992.

8.3 Section 20 (3) of the law on extrajudicial rehabilitations says that the statutory period for the submission of applications for restitution based on the sentence of forfeiture which was declared null and void after the entry into force of the law on extrajudicial rehabilitations starts on the day of the entry into force of the annulment. Nevertheless, this provision cannot be applied in the case of Mrs. Hastings-Tuzilova due to the fact that her judicial rehabilitation entered into force on 9 October 1990, i.e. before the entry into force of Law No. 87/1991 on extrajudicial rehabilitations (1 April 1991).

9.1 With respect to the communication of Mr. Josef Prochazka the State party argues that

Section 3 of Law No. 87/1991 on extrajudicial rehabilitations defines the entitled person, i.e. the person who could within the statutory period claim the restitution of property or compensation. Applicants who did not acquire citizenship of the Czech and Slovak Federal Republic and register their permanent residence on its territory before the end of the statutory period determined for the submission of applications (i.e. before 1 October 1991 for applicants for restitution and before 1 April 1992 for applicants for compensation) are not considered entitled persons.

9.2   From Mr. Prochazka's submission the State party concludes that the property devolved to the State on the basis of the ruling of the Usti and Labem District Court of 1974 which declared the 1969 deed of gift null and void for the reason that the donor left the territory of the former Czechoslovak Socialist Republic. Such cases are provided for in Section 6 (1) (f) of the law on extrajudicial rehabilitations which defined the entitled person as the transferee according to the invalidated deed, i.e. in this case the entitled person is the unnamed father of Mr. Prochazka. Consequently, the persons to whom the sentence of forfeiture invalidated under Law No. 119/1990 on judicial rehabilitations applies, cannot be regarded as entitled persons, as Mr. Prochazka incorrectly assumes.

9.3   With regard to the fact that the above-mentioned father of Mr. Prochazka died before the entry into force of the law on extrajudicial rehabilitations, the entitled persons are the testamentary heirs – Mr. Prochazka's sons Josef Prochazka and Jiri Prochazka, provided that they were citizens of the former Czech and Slovak Federal Republic and had permanent residence on its territory. The fact that they were rehabilitated pursuant to the law on judicial rehabilitations has no significance in this case. From Mr. Prochazka's submission the State party concludes that Josef Prochazka and Jiri Prochazka are Czech citizens but live in Switzerland and did not apply for permanent residence in the Czech Republic.

AUTHORS' COMMENTS ON THE STATE PARTY'S SUBMISSIONS

10.1   By letter of 21 February 1995, Alina and Jaroslav Simunek contend that the State party has not addressed the issues raised by their communication, namely the compatibility of Act No. 87/1991

with the non-discrimination requirement of article 26 of the Covenant. They claim that Czech hardliners are still in office and that they have no interest in the restitution of confiscated properties, because they themselves benefited from the confiscations. A proper restitution law should be based on democratic principles and not allow restrictions that would exclude former Czech citizens and Czech citizens living abroad.

10.2   By letter of 12 June 1995 Mr. Prochazka informed the Committee that by order of the District Court of 12 April 1995 the plot of land he inherited from his father will be returned to him (paragraph 2.11).

10.3   Mrs. Hastings Tuzilova had not submitted comments by the time of the consideration of the merits of this communication by the Committee.

EXAMINATION OF THE MERITS

11.1   The Human Rights Committee has considered the present communication in the light of all the information made available to it by the parties, as provided in article 5, paragraph 1, of the Optional Protocol.

11.2   This communication was declared admissible only insofar as it may raise issues under article 14, paragraph 6, and article 26 of the Covenant. With regard to article 14, paragraph 6, the Committee finds that the authors have not sufficiently substantiated their allegations and that the information before it does not sustain a finding of a violation.

11.3   As the Committee has already explained in its decision on admissibility (para. 4.3 above), the right to property, as such, is not protected under the Covenant. However, a confiscation of private property or the failure by a State party to pay compensation for such confiscation could still entail a breach of the Covenant if the relevant act or omission was based on discriminatory grounds in violation of article 26 of the Covenant.

11.4   The issue before the Committee is whether the application of Act 87/1991 to the authors entailed a violation of their rights to equality before the law and to the equal protection of the law. The authors claim that this Act, in effect, reaffirms the earlier discriminatory confiscations. The Committee observes that the confiscations themselves are not here at issue, but rather the denial of a remedy to the authors, whereas other claimants have recovered their properties or received compensation therefor.

11.5 In the instant cases, the authors have been affected by the exclusionary effect of the requirement in Act 87/1991 that claimants be Czech citizens and residents of the Czech Republic. The question before the Committee, therefore, is whether these preconditions to restitution or compensation are compatible with the non-discrimination requirement of article 26 of the Covenant. In this context the Committee reiterates its jurisprudence that not all differentiation in treatment can be deemed to be discriminatory under article 26 of the Covenant [Zwaan de Vries v. The Netherlands, Communication No. 182/1984, Views adopted on 9 April 1987, para. 13]. A differentiation which is compatible with the provisions of the Covenant and is based on reasonable grounds does not amount to prohibited discrimination within the meaning of article 26.

11.6 In examining whether the conditions for restitution or compensation are compatible with the Covenant, the Committee must consider all relevant factors, including the authors' original entitlement to the property in question and the nature of the confiscations. The State party itself acknowledges that the confiscations were discriminatory, and this is the reason why specific legislation was enacted to provide for a form of restitution. The Committee observes that such legislation must not discriminate among the victims of the prior confiscations, since all victims are entitled to redress without arbitrary distinctions. Bearing in mind that the authors' original entitlement to their respective properties was not predicated either on citizenship or residence, the Committee finds that the conditions of citizenship and residence in Act 87/1991 are unreasonable. In this connection the Committee notes that the State party has not advanced any grounds which would justify these restrictions. Moreover, it has been submitted that the authors and many others in their situation left Czechoslovakia because of their political opinions and that their property was confiscated either because of their political opinions or because of their emigration from the country. These victims of political persecution sought residence and citizenship in other countries. Taking into account that the State party itself is responsible for the departure

of the authors, it would be incompatible with the Covenant to require them permanently to return to the country as a prerequisite for the restitution of their property or for the payment of appropriate compensation.

11.7 The State party contends that there is no violation of the Covenant because the Czech and Slovak legislators had no discriminatory intent at the time of the adoption of Act 87/1991. The Committee is of the view, however, that the intent of the legislature is not alone dispositive in determining a breach of article 26 of the Covenant. A politically motivated differentiation is unlikely to be compatible with article 26. But an act which is not politically motivated may still contravene article 26 if its effects are discriminatory.

11.8 In the light of the above considerations, the Committee concludes that Act 87/1991 has had effects upon the authors that violate their rights under article 26 of the Covenant.

12.1 The Human Rights Committee, acting under article 5, paragraph 4, of the Optional Protocol, is of the view that the denial of restitution or compensation to the authors constitutes a violation of article 26 of the International Covenant on Civil and Political Rights.

12.2 In accordance with article 2, paragraph 3 (a), of the Covenant, the State party is under an obligation to provide the authors with an effective remedy, which may be compensation if the properties in question cannot be returned. To the extent that partial restitution of Mr. Prochazka's property appears to have been or may soon be effected (para. 10.2), the Committee welcomes this measure, which it deems to constitute partial compliance with these Views. The Committee further encourages the State party to review its relevant legislation to ensure that neither the law itself nor its application is discriminatory.

12.3 Bearing in mind that, by becoming a party to the Optional Protocol, the State party has recognized the competence of the Committee to determine whether there has been a violation of the Covenant or not and that, pursuant to article 2 of the Covenant, the State party has undertaken to ensure to all individuals within its territory and subject to its jurisdiction the rights recognized in the Covenant and to provide an effective and enforceable remedy in case a violation has been established, the Committee wishes to receive from the State party, within ninety days, information about the measures taken to give effect to the Committee's Views.

3.2. *Dr. Karel Des Fours Walderode v. The Czech Republic* (1996)

[...]

The Human Rights Committee, established under article 28 of the International Covenant on Civil and Political Rights,

Meeting on 30 October 2001,

Having concluded its consideration of communication No. 747/1997, submitted to the Human Rights Committee by the late Dr. Karel Des Fours Walderode and Dr. Johanna Kammerlander under the Optional Protocol to the International Covenant on Civil and Political Rights,

Having taken into account all written information made available to it by the author of the communication and by the State party,

Adopts the following:

VIEWS UNDER ARTICLE 5, PARAGRAPH 4, OF THE OPTIONAL PROTOCOL

1. The original author of the communication was Dr. Karel Des Fours Walderode, a citizen of the Czech Republic and Austria, residing in Prague, Czech Republic. He was represented by his spouse, Dr. Johanna Kammerlander, as counsel. He claimed to be a victim of violations of article 14, paragraph 1, and article 26 of the International Covenant on Civil and Political Rights by the Czech Republic. The Covenant was ratified by Czechoslovakia in December 1975, the Optional Protocol in March 1991. (1) The author passed away on 6 February 2000, and his surviving spouse maintains the communication before the Committee.

THE FACTS AS SUBMITTED

2.1 Dr. Des Fours Walderode was born a citizen of the Austrian-Hungarian empire on 4 May 1904 in Vienna, of French and German descent. His family had been established in Bohemia since the seventeenth century. At the end of the First World War in 1918, he was a resident of Bohemia, a kingdom in the former empire, and became a citizen of the newly created Czechoslovak State. In 1939, because of his German mother tongue, he automatically became a German citizen by virtue of Hitler's decree of 16 March 1939, establishing the Protectorate of Bohemia and Moravia. On 5 March 1941, the author's father died and he inherited the Hruby Rohozec estate.

2.2 At the end of the Second World War, on 6 August 1945, his estate was confiscated under Benes Decree 12/1945, pursuant to which the landed properties of German and Magyar private persons were confiscated without any compensation. However, on account of his proven loyalty to Czechoslovakia during the period of Nazi occupation, he retained his Czechoslovak citizenship, pursuant to paragraph 2 of Constitutional Decree 33/1945. Subsequently, after a Communist government came to power in 1948, he was forced to leave Czechoslovakia in 1949 for political and economic reasons. In 1991, after the "velvet revolution" of 1989, he again took up permanent residence in Prague. On 16 April 1991 the Czech Ministry of Interior informed him that he was still a Czech citizen. Nevertheless, Czech citizenship was again conferred on him by the Ministry on 20 August 1992, apparently after a document was found showing that he had lost his citizenship in 1949, when he left the country.

2.3 On 15 April 1992, Law 243/1992 came into force. The law provides for restitution of agricultural and forest property confiscated under Decree 12/1945. To be eligible for restitution, a claimant had to have Czech citizenship under Decree 33/1945 (or under Law 245/1948, 194/1949 or 34/1953), permanent residence in the Czech Republic, having been loyal to the Czechoslovak Republic during the period of German occupation, and to have Czech citizenship at the time of submitting a claim for restitution. The author filed a claim for restitution of the Hruby Rohozec estate within the prescribed time limit and on 24 November 1992 concluded a restitution contract with the then owners, which was approved by the Land Office on 10 March 1993 (PU-R 806/93). The appeal by the town of Turnov was rejected by the Central Land Office by decision 1391/93-50 of 30 July 1993. Consequently, on 29 September 1993 the author took possession of his lands.

2.4   The author alleges State interference with the judiciary and consistent pressure on administrative authorities and cites in substantiation from a letter dated 29 April 1993 by the then Czech Prime Minister Vaclav Klaus, addressed to party authorities in Semily and to the relevant Ministries, enclosing a legal opinion according to which the restitution of property confiscated before 25 February 1948 was "legal", but nevertheless "unacceptable". The author states that this political statement was subsequently used in court proceedings. The author further states that, because of increasing political pressure at the end of 1993 the Ministry of Interior reopened the issue of his citizenship. Furthermore, the former owners of the land were persuaded to withdraw their consent to the restitution to which they had previously agreed.

2.5   On 22 December 1994 the Public Prosecutor's Office in the Semily District filed an application with the District Court under paragraph 42 of Law 283/1993 to declare the Land Office's decision of 10 March 1993 null and void. On 29 December 1994, the District Court rejected this application. On appeal, the matter was referred back to the first instance.

2.6   On 7 August 1995, a "citizens' initiative" petitioned revision of the Semily Land Office's decision of 10 March 1993. On 17 October 1995, the Central Land Office examined the legality of the decision and rejected the request for revision. Nevertheless, on 2 November 1995 the author was informed by the Central Land Office that it would, after all, begin to revise the decision. On 23 November 1995, the Minister of Agriculture annulled the Semily Land Office decision of 10 March 1993, purportedly because of doubts as to whether the author fulfilled the requirement of permanent residence, and referred the matter back. On 22 January 1996, the author applied to the High Court in Prague against the Minister's decision.

2.7   On 9 February 1996, Law 243/1992 was amended. The condition of permanent residence was removed (following the judgement of the Constitutional Court of 12 December 1995, holding the residence requirement to be unconstitutional), but a new condition was added, of uninterrupted Czechoslovak/Czech citizenship from the end of the war until 1 January 1990. The author claims that this law specifically targeted him and submits evidence of the use of the term "Lex Walderode" by the

Czech media and public authorities. On 3 March 1996 the Semily Land Office applied the amended Law to his case to invalidate the restitution agreement of 24 November 1992, since Dr. Des Fours did not fulfil the new eligibility requirement of continuous citizenship. On 4 April 1996, the author lodged an appeal with the Prague City Court against the Land Office's decision.

2.8   As regards the exhaustion of domestic remedies, the late author contended that the proceedings were being deliberately drawn out because of his age and, moreover, that the negative outcome was predictable. He therefore requested the Committee to consider his communication admissible, because of the delay in the proceedings and the unlikelihood of the effectiveness of domestic remedies.

The Complaint

3.1   The late author and his surviving spouse claim that the restitution of the property in question was annulled for political and economic reasons and the legislation was amended to exclude him from the possibility of obtaining redress for the confiscation of his property. It is claimed that this constitutes a violation of article 26 of the Covenant, as well as of article 14, paragraph 1, because of political interference with the legal process (such as the Minister's decision of 23 November 1995). In this context, the author also refers to the long delays in the hearing of his case.

3.2   Further, he claims that the requirement of continuous citizenship for the restitution of property is in violation of article 26 of the Covenant and refers to the Committee's jurisprudence on this point. The author also claims that the restitution conditions applying to him are discriminatory in comparison with those applying to post-1948 confiscations.

[. . .]

The Author's Comments

5.1   In his comments, the author refers to his original communication and submits that the State party has basically failed to contradict any of his claims.

5.2   He emphasizes that he retained his Czech citizenship under Benes Decree No. 33/1945, and that thus all the requirements of the original Law 243/1992 had been fulfilled when the Land Office approved the return of his property. The author notes that the State party remains silent about amendment 30/1996, introducing a further condition of continuous Czech citizenship, which did not apply when his restitution contract was approved in 1993. According to the author, this amendment made it possible to expropriate him again.

5.3 According to the author, the application of further domestic remedies would be futile because of the political interests in his case. He moreover points to the delays in the handling of the case, whether intentional or not.

5.4 The author dismisses the State party's attempt to explain away the Minister's letter as a simple expression of opinion and maintains that the opinion of the Prime Minister was equated with an interpretation of the law, and submits that the political dimension of his restitution procedure is evident from the interaction of several components.

5.5 With regard to the petition received by the Ministry of Agriculture from local residents, the author points out that the decision of the Semily Land Office was handed down on 10 March 1993 and the petition against it was submitted on 7 August 1995, two years and five months later. The Minister of Agriculture's order quashing the Semily Land Office's earlier decision followed on 23 November 1995, three and half months after the petition. It becomes evident that the 30-day time limit stipulated in Law 85/1990 concerning the right of petition was not observed.

5.6 In a further submission, the author states that his complaint against the Minister's decision of 23 November 1995 was rejected by the High Court on 25 August 1997. The author claims that the reasons given by the court again illustrate the political nature of the process.

5.7 On 25 March 1998, the Prague City Court rejected the author's appeal against the refusal of the restitution of his property by the Land Office in 1996, since he no longer fulfilled the requirements added to the law in amendment 30/1996. On 24 July 1998, the author filed a complaint against this decision with the Czech Constitutional Court.

5.8 The author further submits that even if the Constitutional Court would find in his favour,

the decision would again be referred to the first instance (the Land Office), thus entailing considerable further delay and opening the door for more political intervention. According to the author, the whole procedure could easily take another five years. He considers this to be unjustifiably long, also in view of his age.

5.9 In this context, the author recalls the salient aspects of his case. The restitution contract which he concluded was approved by the Land Office on 10 March 1993, and the appeal against the approval was rejected by the Central Land Office on 30 July 1993, after which the restitution was effected in accordance with Law 243/1992. Only on 25 November 1995, that is more than two years after he had taken possession of his lands, did the Minister of Agriculture quash the Land Office's decision, on the ground that the Office had not sufficiently verified whether the author complied with the requirement of permanent residence. It appears from the Court judgements in the case, that at the time of the Minister's decision, it was expected that the Constitutional Court would declare this residence requirement unconstitutional (it subsequently did so, on 12 December 1995, less than a month after the Minister's decision). After a requirement of continued citizenship was added to Law 243/1992 by law 30/1996 of 9 February 1996, the Land Office then reviewed the legality of the restitution agreement in the author's case, and applying the new law declared the agreement invalid on 3 March 1996. The two court proceedings which the author then initiated, were delayed, as acknowledged by the State party, in one case because the Ministry was not in a position to furnish the papers needed by the Court, and in the other because of a backlog at the court in handling cases.

ADMISSIBILITY CONSIDERATIONS

6.1 Before considering any claims contained in a communication, the Human Rights Committee must, in accordance with article 87 of its rules of procedure, decide whether or not it is admissible under the Optional Protocol to the Covenant.

6.2 During its sixty-fifth session in March 1999, the Committee considered the admissibility of the communication. It noted the State party's objection to the admissibility of the communication on the ground that the author had failed to exhaust all domestic remedies available to him. The

Committee noted, however, that in August 1997, the High Court rejected the author's complaint against the Minister's decision, and on 25 March 1998, the City Court in Prague rejected his appeal against the Land Office's decision of 1996. The text of these decisions shows that no further appeal is possible. The effect is to preclude any further attempt by the author to validate and seek approval of the restitution agreement of 1992.

6.3 The author has since filed a constitutional complaint against the Prague City Court decision that the requirement of continued citizenship is legitimate. The Committee noted that in the instant case, the Constitutional Court had already examined the constitutionality of Law 243/1992. In the opinion of the Committee and having regard to the history of this case, a constitutional motion in the author's case would not offer him a reasonable chance of obtaining effective redress and therefore would not constitute an effective remedy which the author would have to exhaust for purposes of article 5, paragraph 2 (b), of the Optional Protocol.

6.4 In this context, the Committee also took note of the author's arguments that even if he were to win a constitutional appeal, the case would then be referred back, and the proceedings could take another five years to become finalized. In the circumstances, taking into account the delays which had already been incurred in the proceedings and which were attributable to the State party, the delays which would likely occur in future and the author's advanced age, the Committee also found that the application of domestic remedies had been unreasonably prolonged.

7. On 19 March 1999, the Committee held that the communication was admissible insofar as it might raise issues under articles 14, paragraph 1, and 26 of the Covenant.

CONSIDERATION OF THE MERITS

8.1 Pursuant to article 5, paragraph 1, of the Optional Protocol, the Committee proceeds to an examination of the merits, in the light of the information submitted by the parties. It notes that it has received sufficient information from the late author and his surviving spouse, and that no further information on the merits has been received from the State party subsequent to the transmittal of the Committee's admissibility decision, notwithstanding two reminders. The Committee recalls that a State party has an obligation under article 4, paragraph 2, of the Optional Protocol to cooperate with the Committee and to submit written explanations or statements clarifying the matter and the remedy, if any, that may have been granted.

8.2 The Committee has noted the author's claims that the State party has violated article 14, paragraph 1, of the Covenant because of alleged interference by the executive and legislative branches of government in the judicial process, in particular through the letter of the Prime Minister dated 29 April 1993, and because of the adoption of retroactive legislation aimed at depriving the author of rights already acquired by virtue of prior Czech legislation and decisions of the Semily Land Office. With regard to the adoption of retroactive legislation, the Committee observes that, whereas an allegation of arbitrariness and a consequent violation of article 26 is made in this respect, it is not clear how the enactment of law 30/1996 raises an issue under article 14, paragraph 1. As to the Prime Minister's letter, the Committee notes that it was part of the administrative file in respect of the author's property which was produced in Court, and that there is no indication whether and how this letter was actually used in the court proceedings. In the absence of any further information, the Committee takes the view that the mere existence of the letter in the case file is not sufficient to sustain a finding of a violation of article 14, paragraph 1, of the Covenant.

8.3 With regard to the author's allegation of a violation of article 26 of the Covenant, the Committee begins by noting that Law No. 243/1992 already contained a requirement of citizenship as one of the conditions for restitution of property and that the amending Law No. 30/1996 retroactively added a more stringent requirement of continued citizenship. The Committee notes further that the amending Law disqualified the author and any others in this situation, who might otherwise have qualified for restitution. This raises an issue of arbitrariness and, consequently, of a breach of the right to equality before the law, equal protection of the law and non-discrimination under article 26 of the Covenant.

8.4   The Committee recalls its Views in cases No. 516/1993 (Simunek et al.), 586/1994 (Joseph Adam) and 857/1999 (Blazek et al.) that a requirement in the law for citizenship as a necessary condition for restitution of property previously confiscated by the authorities makes an arbitrary, and, consequently a discriminatory distinction between individuals who are equally victims of prior state confiscations, and constitutes a violation of article 26 of the Covenant. This violation is further exacerbated by the retroactive operation of the impugned Law.

9.1   The Human Rights Committee, acting under article 5, paragraph 4, of the Optional Protocol, is of the view that article 26, in conjunction with article 2 of the Covenant, has been violated by the State party.

9.2   In accordance with article 2, paragraph 3 (a) of the Covenant, the State party is under an obligation to provide the late author's surviving spouse, Dr. Johanna Kammerlander, with an effective remedy, entailing in this case prompt restitution of the property in question or compensation therefor, and, in addition, appropriate compensation in respect of the fact that the author and his surviving spouse have been deprived of the enjoyment of their property since its restitution was revoked in 1995. The State party should review its legislation and administrative practices to ensure that all persons enjoy both equality before the law as well as the equal protection of the law.

9.3   The Committee recalls that the Czech Republic, by becoming a State party to the Optional Protocol, recognized the competence of the Committee to determine whether there has been a violation of the Covenant or not and that, pursuant to article 2 of the Covenant, the State party has undertaken to ensure to all individuals within its territory or subject to its jurisdiction the rights recognized in the Covenant and to provide an effective and enforceable remedy in case a violation has been established. Furthermore, the Committee urges the State party to put in place procedures to deal with Views under the Optional Protocol.

9.4   In this connection, the Committee wishes to receive from the State party, within 90 days following the transmittal of these Views to the State party, information about the measures taken to give effect to these Views. The State party is also requested to publish the Committee's Views.

3.3. *Josef Frank Adam v. The Czech Republic* (1996)

[...]

The Human Rights Committee, established under article 28 of the International Covenant on Civil and Political Rights,

Meeting on 23 July 1996,

Having concluded its consideration of communication No. 589/1994 submitted to the Human Rights Committee by Mr. Josef Frank Adam under the Optional Protocol to the International Covenant on Civil and Political Rights,

Having taken into account all written information made available to it by the author of the communication, his counsel and the State party,

Adopts the following:

VIEWS UNDER ARTICLE 5, PARAGRAPH 4, OF THE OPTIONAL PROTOCOL

1. The author of the communication, dated 14 March 1994, is Joseph Frank Adam, an Australian citizen, born in Australia of Czech parents, residing in Melbourne, Australia. He submits the communication on his own behalf and on that of his two brothers, John and Louis. He claims that they are victims of a violation of article 26 of the International Covenant on Civil and Political Rights by the Czech Republic. The Optional Protocol entered into force for the Czech Republic on 12 June 1991.

THE FACTS AS SUBMITTED BY THE AUTHORS

2.1   The author's father, Vlatislav Adam, was a Czech citizen, whose property and business were confiscated by the Czechoslovak Government in 1949. Mr. Adam fled the country and eventually moved to Australia, where his three sons, including the author of the communication, were born. In 1985, Vlatislav Adam died and, in his last will and testament, left his Czech property to his sons. Since then, the sons have been trying in vain to have their property returned to them.

2.2   In 1991, the Czech and Slovak Republic enacted a law, rehabilitating Czech citizens who had left the country under communist pressure and providing for restitution of their property or compensation for the loss thereof. On 6 December 1991, the author and his brothers, through Czech solicitors, submitted a claim for restitution of their property. Their claim was rejected on the grounds that they did not fulfil the then applicable dual requirement of Act 87/91 that applicants have Czech citizenship and be permanent residents in the Czech Republic.

2.3   Since the rejection of their claim, the author has on several occasions petitioned the Czech authorities, explaining his situation and seeking a solution, all to no avail. The authorities in their replies refer to the legislation in force and argue that the provisions of the law, limiting restitution and compensation to Czech citizens are necessary and apply uniformly to all potential claimants.

The Complaint

3.   The author claims that the application of the provision of the law, that property be returned or its loss be compensated only when claimants are Czech citizens, makes him and his brothers victims of discrimination under article 26 of the Covenant.

State Party's Observations and Author's Comments

4.1   On 23 August 1994 the communication was transmitted to the State party under rule 91 of the Committee's rules of procedure.

4.2   In its submission dated 17 October 1994 the State party states that the remedies in civil proceedings such as that applicable in the case of Mr. Adam are regulated by Act No. 99/1963, by the Code of Civil Procedure as amended, in particular by Act No. 519/1991 and Act No. 263/1992.

4.3   The State party quotes the texts of several sections of the law, without, however, explaining how the author should have availed himself of these provisions. It concludes that since 1 July 1993, Act No. 182/1993 on the Constitutional Court stipulates the citizens' right to appeal also to the Constitutional Court of the Czech Republic. Finally, Mr. Adam did not use the possibility to file a claim before the Constitutional Court.

5.1   By letter of 7 November 1994 the author informs the Committee that the State party is trying to circumvent his rights by placing his property and business on sale.

5.2   By letter of 5 February 1995 the author contests the relevance of the State party's general information and reiterates that his lawyers in Czechoslovakia have been trying to obtain his property since his father passed away in 1985. He submits that as long as Czech law requires claimants to be Czech citizens, there is no way that he can successfully claim his father's property in the Czech courts.

The Committee's Decision on Admissibility

6.1   Before considering any claims contained in a communication, the Human Rights Committee must, in accordance with rule 87 of its rules of procedure, decide whether or not it is admissible under the Optional Protocol to the Covenant.

6.2   The Committee observed ratione materiae that although the author's claims relate to property rights, which are not themselves protected in the Covenant, he also alleges that the confiscations under prior Czechoslovak governments were discriminatory and that the new legislation of the Czech Republic discriminates against persons who are not Czech citizens. Therefore, the facts of the communication appear to raise an issue under article 26 of the Covenant.

6.3   The Committee has also considered whether the violations alleged can be examined ratione temporis. It notes that although the confiscations took place before the entry into force of the Covenant and of the Optional Protocol for the Czech Republic, the new legislation that excludes claimants who are not Czech citizens has continuing consequences subsequent to the entry into force of the Optional Protocol for the Czech Republic, which could entail discrimination in violation of article 26 of the Covenant.

6.4   Article 5, paragraph 2 (a), of the Optional Protocol, precludes the Committee from considering a communication if the same matter is being examined under another procedure of international investigation or settlement. In this connection, the Committee has ascertained that the same matter is not being examined under another procedure of international investigation or settlement.

6.5   With respect to the requirement of exhaustion of domestic remedies, the Committee recalls that only such remedies have to be exhausted which are both available and effective. The applicable law on confiscated property does not allow for restoration or compensation to the author. Moreover, the Committee notes that the author has been trying to recover his property since his father passed away in 1985 and that the application of domestic remedies can be deemed, in the circumstances, unreasonably prolonged.

7. Based on these considerations the Human Rights Committee decided on 16 March 1995 that the communication was admissible inasmuch as it may raise issues under article 26 of the Covenant.

OBSERVATIONS FROM THE STATE PARTY

8.1 By note verbale of 10 November 1995 the State party reiterates its objections to the admissibility of the communication, in particular, that the author has not availed himself of all national legal remedies.

8.2 It argues that the author is an Australian citizen permanently resident in that country. As to the alleged confiscation of his father's property in 1949, the State party explains that the Decree of the President of the Republic No. 5/1945 did not represent the conveyance of the ownership title to the State but only restricted the owner in exercising his ownership right.

8.3 The author's father, Vlatislav Adam, was a citizen of Czechoslovakia and left the country for Australia, where the author was born. If indeed Mr. Vlatislav Adam willed his Czech property to his sons by virtue of his testament, it is not clear whether he owned any Czech property in 1985, and the author has not explained what steps, if any, he has taken to acquire the inheritance.

8.4 In 1991 the Czech and Slovak Federal Republic adopted a law (Act No. 87/1991 on Extrajudicial Rehabilitations) which rehabilitates Czech citizens who left the country under communist oppression and stipulates the restitution of their property and compensation for their loss. On 6 December 1991 the author and his brothers claimed the restitution of their property. Their claim was rejected because they were not persons entitled for the recovery of property pursuant to the Extrajudicial Rehabilitation Act, since they did not satisfy the then applicant conditions of citizenship of the Czech Republic and of permanent residence therein. The author failed to invoke remedies available against the decision denying him restitution. Moreover, the author

failed to observe the legal six-month term to claim his property, the statute of limitations having run on 1 October 1991. Nevertheless, Pursuant to Article 5, paragraph 4, of the Extrajudicial Rehabilitation Act, the author could have filed his claims in court until 1 April 1992, but he did not do so.

8.5 The author explains that his attorney felt that there were no effective remedies and that because of this they did not pursue their appeals. This subjective assessment is irrelevant to the objective existence of remedies. In particular, he could have lodged a complaint with the Constitutional Court.

8.6 Czech Constitutional Law, including the Charter of Fundamental Rights and Freedoms, protects the right to own property and guarantees inheritance. Expropriation is possible only in the public interest and on the basis of law, and is subject to compensation.

8.7 The Act on Extrajudicial Rehabilitation was amended in order to eliminate the requirement of permanent residence; this occurred pursuant to a finding of the Constitutional Court of the Czech Republic of 12 July 1994. Moreover, in cases where the real estate cannot be surrendered, financial compensation is available.

8.8 Articles 1 and 3 of the Charter stipulate equality in the enjoyment of rights and prohibits discrimination. The right to judicial protection is regulated in article 36 of the Charter. The Constitutional Court decides about the abrogation of laws or of their individual provisions, if they are in contradiction with a constitutional law or international treaty. A natural person or legal entity is entitled to file a constitutional complaint.

8.9 Besides the author's failure to invoke the relevant provisions of the Extrajudicial Rehabilitation Act in a timely fashion, he could also have lodged a claim to domestic judicial authorities based on the direct applicability of the International Covenant on Civil and Political Rights, with reference to article 10 of the Constitution, Article 36 of the Charter, articles 72 and 74 of the Constitutional Court Act, and article 3 of the Civil Procedure Code. If the author had availed himself of these procedures and if he had not been satisfied with the result, he could still have sought review of legal regulations pursuant to the Constitutional Court Act.

9.1 The State party also endeavors to explain the broader political and legal circumstances of the case and contends that the author's presentation of the facts is misleading. After the democratization process begun in November 1989, the Czech and Slovak Republic and subsequently the Czech Republic have made a considerable effort to remove some of the property injustices caused by the communist regime. The endeavor to return property as stipulated in the Rehabilitation Act was in part a voluntary and moral act of the Government and not a duty or legal obligation. "It is also necessary to point out the fact that it was not possible and, with regard to the protection of the justified interests of the citizens of the present Czech Republic, even undesirable, to remove all injuries caused by the past regime over a period of forty years."

9.2   The precondition of citizenship for restitution or compensation should not be interpreted as a violation of the prohibition of discrimination pursuant to article 26 of the Covenant. "The possibility of explicit restriction of acquiring the ownership of certain property by only some persons is contained in Article 11, paragraph 2 of the Charter. This article states that law may determine that certain property may only be owned by citizens or legal entities having their seat in the Czech and Slovak Federal Republic. In this respect the Charter speaks of citizens of the Czech and Slovak Federal Republic, and after January 1, 1993 of citizens of the Czech Republic."

9.3   The Czech Republic considers the restriction in exercising rights of ownership by imposing the condition of citizenship to be legitimate. In this connection it refers not only to Article 3, paragraph 1 of the Charter, containing the non-discrimination clause, but above all to the relevant clauses of international human rights treaties.

Author's Comments

10.1   As to the facts of the claim, the author explains that in January 1949 his father was ordered out of his business, which was confiscated. He had to hand over the books and the bank accounts and was not even able to take his own personal belongings. As to his departure from Czechoslovakia, he was not able to emigrate legally but had to cross the border illegally into West Germany, where he remained in a refugee camp for one year before being able to immigrate to Australia.

10.2   He disputes the State party's contention that he did not avail himself of domestic remedies. He reiterates that he himself and his attorneys in Prague have tried to assert the claim to inheritance since his father died, in 1985, without success. In December 1991 he and his brothers submitted their claim, which was rejected for lack of citizenship and permanent residence. Moreover, their claim was by virtue of inheritance. He further complains about unreasonably prolonged proceedings in the Czech Republic, in particular that regards to whereas their letters to the Czech Government reached the Czech authorities within a week, the replies took 3 to 4 months.

10.3   As to their Czech citizenship, they claim that the Consulate in Australia informed them that if both mother and father were Czech citizens, the children were automatically Czech citizens. However, the Czech Government subsequently denied this interpretation of the law.

Review of Admissibility

11.1   The State party has requested that the Committee revise its decision on admissibility on the grounds that the author has not exhausted domestic remedies. The Committee has taken into consideration all arguments presented by the State party and the explanations given by the author. In the circumstances of this case, considering that the authors are abroad and that his lawyers are in the Czech Republic, it would seem that the imposition of a strict statute of limitations for lodgings claims by persons abroad is unreasonable. In the author's case, the Committee has taken into account the circumstance that he has been trying to assert his inheritance claim since 1985, and that his Prague attorneys have been unsuccessful, ultimately not because of the statute of limitations, but because the Rehabilitation Act, as amended, stipulates that only citizens can claim restitution or compensation. Since the author, according to his last submission, which has not been disputed by the State party (para. 10.3) is not a Czech citizen, he cannot invoke the Rehabilitation Act in order to obtain the return of his father's property.

11.2   In the absence of legislation enabling the author to claim restitution, recourse to the Constitutional Court cannot be considered an available and effective remedy for purposes of article

5, paragraph 2(b), of the Optional Protocol. In the circumstances of this case, such a remedy must be considered as an extraordinary remedy, since the right being challenged is not a constitutional right to restitution as such, bearing in mind that the Czech and Slovak legislature considered the 1991 Rehabilitation Act to be an measure of moral rehabilitation rather than a legal obligation (paragraph 9.1). Moreover, the State has argued that it is compatible with the Czech Constitution and in keeping with Czech public policy to restrict the ownership of property to citizens.

11.3   Under these circumstances the Committee finds no reason to set aside its decision on admissibility of 16 March 1995.

EXAMINATION OF THE MERITS

12.1   The Human Rights Committee has considered the present communication in the light of all the information made available to it by the parties, as provided in article 5, paragraph 1, of the Optional Protocol.

12.2   This communication was declared admissible only insofar as it may raise issues under article 26 of the Covenant. As the Committee has already explained in its decision on admissibility (para. 6.2 above), the right to property, as such, is not protected under the Covenant. However, a confiscation of private property or the failure by a State party to pay compensation for such confiscation could still entail a breach of the Covenant if the relevant act or omission was based on discriminatory grounds in violation of article 26 of the Covenant.

12.3   The issue before the Committee is whether the application of Act 87/1991 to the author and his brothers entailed a violation of their right to equality before the law and to the equal protection of the law. The Committee observes that the confiscations themselves are not here at issue, but rather the denial of a restitution to the author and his brothers, whereas other claimants under the Act have recovered their properties or received compensation therefore.

12.4   In the instant case, the author has been affected by the exclusionary effect of the requirement in Act 87/1991 that claimants be Czech citizens. The question before the Committee, therefore, is whether the precondition to restitution or compensation is compatible with the non-discrimination requirement of article 26 of the Covenant. In this context the Committee reiterates its jurisprudence that not all differentiation in treatment can be deemed to be discriminatory under article 26 of the Covenant. A differentiation which is compatible with the provisions of the Covenant and is based on reasonable grounds does not amount to prohibited discrimination within the meaning of article 26.

12.5   In examining whether the conditions for restitution or compensation are compatible with the Covenant, the Committee must consider all relevant factors, including the original entitlement of the author's father to the property in question and the nature of the confiscation. The State party itself has acknowledged that the confiscations under the Communist governments were injurious and this is the reason why specific legislation was enacted to provide for a form of restitution. The Committee observes that such legislation must not discriminate among the victims of the prior confiscations, since all victims are entitled to redress without arbitrary distinctions. Bearing in mind that the author's original entitlement to his property by virtue of inheritance was not predicated on citizenship, the Committee finds that the condition of citizenship in Act 87/1991 is unreasonable.

12.6   In this context the Committee recalls its rationale in its Views on communication No. 516/1992 (Simunek et al. v. The Czech Republic), in which it considered that the authors in that case and many others in analogous situation had left Czechoslovakia because of their political opinions and had sought refuge from political persecution in other countries, where they eventually established permanent residence and obtained a new citizenship. Taking into account that the State party itself is responsible for the departure of the author's parents in 1949, it would be incompatible with the Covenant to require him and his brothers to obtain Czech citizenship as a prerequisite for the restitution of their property or, in the alternative, for the payment of appropriate compensation.

12.7   The State party contends that there is no violation of the Covenant because the Czech and Slovak legislators had no discriminatory intent at the time of the adoption of Act 87/1991. The Committee is of the view, however, that the intent of the legislature is not dispositive in determining a breach of article 26 of the Covenant, but rather the consequences of the enacted legislation. Whatever the motivation or intent of the legislature, a law may still contravene article 26 of the Covenant if its effects are discriminatory.

12.8   In the light of the above considerations, the Committee concludes that Act 87/1991 and the continued practice of non-restitution to non-citizens of the Czech Republic have had effects upon the author and his brothers that violate their rights under article 26 of the Covenant.

13.1   The Human Rights Committee, acting under article 5, paragraph 4, of the Optional Protocol, is of the view that the denial of restitution or compensation to the author and his brothers constitutes a violation of article 26 of the International Covenant on Civil and Political Rights.

13.2   In accordance with article 2, paragraph 3 (a), of the Covenant, the State party is under an obligation to provide the author and his brothers with an effective remedy, which may be compensation if the property in question cannot be returned. The Committee further encourages the State party to review its relevant legislation to ensure that neither the law itself nor its application is discriminatory.

13.3   Bearing in mind that, by becoming a party to the Optional Protocol, the State party has recognized the competence of the Committee to determine whether there has been a violation of the Covenant or not and that, pursuant to article 2 of the Covenant, the State party has undertaken to ensure to all individuals within its territory and subject to its jurisdiction the rights recognized in the Covenant and to provide an effective and enforceable remedy in case a violation has been established, the Committee wishes to receive from the State party, within ninety days, information about the measures taken to give effect to the Committee's Views.

3.4. *Ms. Eliska Fábryová v. The Czech Republic* (1997)

[. . .]

The Human Rights Committee, established under article 28 of the International Covenant on Civil and Political Rights,

Meeting on 30 October 2001,

Having concluded its consideration of communication No. 765/1997, submitted to the Human Rights Committee by Eliska Fábryová under the Optional Protocol to the International Covenant on Civil and Political Rights,

Having taken into account all written information made available to it by the author of the communication, and the State party,

Adopts the following:

VIEWS UNDER ARTICLE 5, PARAGRAPH 4, OF THE OPTIONAL PROTOCOL

1.   The author of the communication is Eliska Fábryová, née Fischmann, a Czech citizen, born on 6 May 1916. The author claims to be a victim of discrimination by the Czech Republic. The Optional Protocol entered into force for the Czech Republic on 12 June 1991.

THE FACTS AS SUBMITTED BY THE AUTHOR

2.1   The author's father Richard Fischmann owned an estate in Puklice in the district of Jihlava, Czechoslovakia. In 1930, at a national census, he and his family registered as Jews. In 1939, after the occupation by the Nazis, the estate was "aryanised" and a German sequestrator was appointed. Richard Fischmann died in 1942 in Auschwitz. The author is not represented by counsel.

2.2   The rest of the family was interned in concentration camps and only the author and her brother Viteslav returned. In 1945, the estate of Richard Fischmann was confiscated under Benes decree 12/1945 because the district committee decided that he was German as well as a traitor to the Czech Republic, the assumption that he was German being based on the assertion that he had lived "in a German way".

2.3   The author's appeal against the confiscation was dismissed. The decision of the district committee was upheld by a judgment of the highest administrative court in Bratislava on 3 December 1951.

2.4   After the end of communist rule in Czechoslovakia, the author lodged a complaint to the General procurator, on 18 December 1990, for denial of justice with regard to her claim for restitution.

Her complaint was dismissed on 21 August 1991 for being out of time, having been lodged more than five years after the confiscation. The author states that under Communist rule it was not possible to lodge a complaint within the time limit of five years as prescribed by law.

2.5   The author states that on 17 June 1992 she applied for restitution according to the law No. 243/1992 (4). Her application was dismissed on 14 October 1994 by the Land Office of Jihlava.

The Complaint

3.   The author claims to be a victim of discrimination as under the law No. 243/1992 she is not entitled to restitution of her father's property.

[. . .]

The Author's Comments

5.1   By a letter of 21 January 1998, the author rejected the State party's argument that her communication was inadmissible, since she had already appealed up to the Constitutional Court and no further appeal was available. However, the author confirmed that after her communication was registered for consideration by the Human Rights Committee, new proceedings were ordered.

5.2   In a further submission, the author forwarded a copy of a letter by the Ministry for Agriculture, dated 25 May 1998, in which she was informed that the decision of the Central Land Office of 9 October 1997 to quash the decision of the Land Office of 14 October 1994 had been served to other interested parties after the expiration term of three years of the latter decision, and that it therefore did not attain legal force.

5.3   The author claimed that the pattern of arbitrariness in her case constitutes a flagrant violation of human rights in denying her a remedy for the abuses committed against her and her family in the past.

[. . .]

Decision on Admissibility

7.   At its sixty-sixth session, on 9 July 1999, the Committee considered the admissibility of the communication. Having ascertained, pursuant to

article 5, paragraph 2 of the Optional Protocol, that the author had exhausted all available domestic remedies and that the same matter was not being examined under another procedure of international investigation or settlement, the Committee also noted that the State party reopened the author's case by a decision of the Central Land Office of 9 October 1997 and that, as a result of errors apparently committed by the State party's authorities, the decision to quash the original decision of the Land Office had never come into effect. In the circumstances, the Committee declared the communication admissible.

Observations by the Parties on the Merits

8.1   Despite having been invited to do so by the decision of the Committee of 9 July 1999 and by a reminder of 19 September 2000, the State party has not submitted any observations or comments on the merits of the case.

8.2   By letters of 25 January 2000, 29 August 2000 and 25 June 2001, the author brought to the attention of the Committee that despite the adoption by the State party's Parliament of new legislative measures governing the restitution of property confiscated as a result of the Holocaust (Act No. 212/2000), the authorities had not been willing to apply such a legislation and have never compensated her.

8.3   Despite having been transmitted the above information by a letter of 24 July 2001, the State party has not made any additional comments.

Issues and Proceeding before the Committee

9.1   The Human Rights Committee has considered the present communication in the light of all the information made available to it by the parties, as provided in article 5, paragraph 1 of the Optional Protocol. Moreover, in the absence of any submission from the State party following the Committee's decision on admissibility, the Committee relies on the detailed submissions made by the author so far as they raise issues concerning Law nr. 243/1992 as amended. The Committee recalls in this respect that a State party has an obligation under article 4, paragraph 2, of the Optional Protocol to cooperate with the Committee and to submit written explanations or statements clarifying the matter and the remedy, if any, that may have been granted. The complaint of the author raises issues under article 26 of the Covenant.

9.2 The Committee notes that the State Party concedes that under Law nr. 243/1992 individuals in a similar situation as that of the author qualify for restitution as a result of the subsequent interpretation given by the Constitutional Court (para. 4.4). The State Party further concedes that the decision of the Jihlava Land Office of 14 October 1994 was wrong and that the author should have had the opportunity to enter a fresh application before the Jihlava Land Office. The author's renewed attempt to obtain redress has, however, been frustrated by the State party itself which, through a letter of the Ministry of Agriculture of 25 May 1998, informed the author that the decision of the Jihlava Land Office of 14 October 1994 had become final on the ground that the decision of the Central Land Office reversing the decision of the Jihlava Land Office had been served out of time.

9.3 Given the above facts, the Committee concludes that, if the service of the decision of the Central Land Office reversing the decision of the Jihlava Land Office was made out of time, this was attributable to the administrative fault of the authorities. The result is that the author was deprived of treatment equal to that of persons having similar entitlement to the restitution of their previously confiscated property, in violation of her rights under article 26 of the Covenant.

10. The Human Rights Committee, acting under article 5, paragraph 4, of the Optional Protocol to the International Covenant on Civil and Political Rights, is therefore of the view that the facts before it disclose a violation of article 26 of the Covenant.

11. In accordance with article 2, paragraph 3 (a), of the Covenant, the State party is under an obligation to provide the author with an effective remedy, including an opportunity to file a new claim for restitution or compensation. The State party should review its legislation and administrative practices to ensure that all persons enjoy both equality before the law as well as the equal protection of the law.

12. The Committee recalls that the Czech Republic, by becoming a State party to the Optional Protocol,

recognized the competence of the Committee to determine whether there has been a violation of the Covenant or not and that, pursuant to article 2 of the Covenant, the State party has undertaken to ensure to all individuals within its territory or subject to its jurisdiction the rights recognized in the Covenant and to provide an effective and enforceable remedy in case a violation has been established.

13. The Committee wishes to receive from the State party, within 90 days following the transmittal of these Views to the State party, information about the measures taken to give effect to the Views.

3.5. *Robert Brok v. The Czech Republic* (2001)

[. . .]

The Human Rights Committee, established under article 28 of the International Covenant on Civil and Political Rights,

Meeting on 31 October 2001,

Having concluded its consideration of communication No. 774/1997, submitted to the Human Rights Committee by Mr. Robert Brok (deceased) and by his surviving spouse Dagmar Brokova under the Optional Protocol to the International Covenant on Civil and Political Rights,

Having taken into account all written information made available to it by the authors of the communication and by the State party,

Adopts the following:

Views under Article 5, Paragraph 4, of the Optional Protocol

1. The original author of the communication dated 23 December 1996, Robert Brok, was a Czech citizen, born in September 1916. When he passed away on 17 September 1997, his wife Dagmar Brokova maintained his communication. It is claimed that the Czech Republic has violated articles 6, 9, 14 (1), 26 and 27 of the Covenant. The Optional Protocol entered into force for the Czech Republic on 12 June 1991. The Czech and Slovak Federal Republic ratified the Optional Protocol in March 1991, but

on 31 December 1992 the Czech and Slovak Federal Republic ceased to exist. On 22 February 1993, the Czech Republic notified its succession to the Covenant and the Optional Protocol. The author is not represented by counsel.

THE FACTS AS SUBMITTED

2.1 Robert Brok's parents owned a house in the centre of Prague since 1927 (hereinafter called the property). During 1940 and 1941, the German authorities confiscated their property with retroactive effect to 16 March 1939, because the owners were Jewish. The property was then sold to the company Matador on 7 January 1942. The author himself was deported by the Nazis, and returned to Prague on 16 May 1945, after having been released from a concentration camp. He was subsequently hospitalized until October 1945.

2.2 After the end of the war, on 19 May 1945, President Benes' Decree No. 5/1945, followed up later by Act 128/1946, declared null and void all property transactions effected under pressure of the occupation regime on the basis of racial or political persecution. National administration was imposed on all enemy assets. This included the author's parents' property pursuant to a decision taken by the Ministry of Industry on 2 August 1945. However, in February 1946, the Ministry of Industry annulled that decision. It also annulled the prior property confiscation and transfers, and the author's parents were reinstated as the rightful owners, in accordance with Benes Decree No. 5/1945.

2.3 However, the company Matador, which had been nationalized on 27 October 1945, appealed against this decision. On 7 August 1946, the Land Court in Prague annulled the return of the property to the author's parents and declared Matador to be the rightful owner. On 31 January 1947, the Supreme Court confirmed this decision. The Court found that since the company with all its possessions had been nationalized in accordance with Benes Decree No. 100/1945 of 24 October 1945, and since national property was excluded from the application of Benes Decree No. 5/1945, the Ministry had wrongfully restored the author's parents as the rightful owners. The property thereby stayed in possession of Matador, and was later, in 1954, transferred to the state company Technomat.

2.4 Following the change to a democratic government at the adoption of restitution legislation, the author applied for restitution under Act No. 87/1991 as amended by Act No. 116/1994. The said law provides restitution or compensation to victims of illegal confiscation carried out for political reasons during the Communist regime (25 February 1948–1 January 1990). The law also matter provisions for restitution or compensation to victims of racial persecution during the Second World War, who have an entitlement by virtue of Decree No. 5/1945. The courts (District Court decision 26 C 49/95 of 20 November 1995 and Prague City Court decision 13 Co 34/94-29 of 28 February 1996), however, rejected the author's claim. The District Court states in its decision that the amended Act extends the right to restitution to persons who lost their property during the German occupation and who could not have their property restituted because of political persecution, or who went through legal procedures that violated their human rights subsequent to 25 February 1948, on condition that they comply with the terms set forth in Act No. 87/1991. However, the court was of the opinion that the author was not eligible for restitution, because the property was nationalized before 25 February 1948, the retroactive cut-off date for claims under Act No. 87/1991 Section 1, paragraph 1, and Section 6. This decision was confirmed by the Prague City Court.

2.5 Pursuant to section 72 of Act No. 182/1993, the author filed a complaint before the Constitutional court that his right to property had been violated. This provision allows an individual to file a complaint to the Constitutional Court if the public authority has violated the claimant's fundamental rights guaranteed by a constitutional law or by an international treaty in particular the right to property.

2.6 The Constitutional Court concluded that since the first and second instances had decided that the author was not the owner of the property, there were no property rights that could have been violated. In its decision, the Constitutional Court invoked the question of fair trial on its own motion and concluded that "the legal proceedings were conducted correctly and all the legal regulations have been safeguarded". Accordingly, the Constitutional Court rejected the author's constitutional complaint on 12 September 1996.

The Complaint

3.1   The author alleges that the court decisions in this case are vitiated by discrimination and that the courts' negative interpretation of the facts is manifestly arbitrary and contrary to the law.

3.2   The author's widow contends that the Act No. 87/1991, amended by Act No. 116/1994, is not applied to all Czech citizens equally. She deems it obvious that Robert Brok met all the conditions for restitution set forth in the law, but contends that the Czech courts were not willing to apply these same criteria to his case, in violation of articles 14 paragraph 1 and 26 of the Covenant.

3.3   The author's widow contends that the decision by the Supreme Court in 1947 was contrary to the law, in particular Benes Decree No. 5/1945 and Act No. 128/1946, which annul all property transfers after 29 September 1938 taken for reasons of national, racial or political persecution. She points out that at the time that Benes Decree No. 5/1945 was issued (10 May 1945), the company Matador had not yet been nationalized and that the exclusion of restitution therefore did not apply.

3.4   The author's widow states that the Act No. 87/1991 amended by Act No. 116/1994 Section 3, paragraph 2 contains an exception to the time limitations and enables the author as entitled through Benes Decree No. 5/1945 to claim restitution. According to the author's widow, the intention of this exception is to allow restitution of property that was confiscated before 25 February 1948 owing to racial persecution, and especially to allow restitution of Jewish property.

3.5   The author's widow further claims that since the initial expropriations happened as part of genocide, the property should be restored regardless of the positive law in the Czech Republic. The author points to other European countries where confiscated Jewish properties are restituted to the rightful owners or to Jewish organizations if the owners could not be identified. Article 6 of the Covenant refers to obligations that arise from genocide. In the authors' opinion, the provision should not be limited to obligations arising from complainants killed in genocide, but also to those, like Robert Brok, who survived genocide. The refusal to restitute property thereby constitutes violation of article 6, paragraph 3, of the Covenant.

3.6   The Czech Republic has, according to the author's widow, systematically refused to return Jewish properties. She claims that since the Nazi expropriation targeted the Jewish community as a whole, the Czech Republic's policy of non-restitution also affects the whole group. As a result and for the reason of lacking economical basis, the Jewish community has not had the same opportunity to maintain its cultural life as others, and the Czech Republic has thereby violated their right under article 27 of the Covenant.

[. . .]

Author's Comments to State Party's Submission

5.1   By letter of 29 January 2001, the author's widow contends that the State party has not addressed her arguments concerning the amendment to Act No. 87/1991 by Act No. 116/1994, which she considers crucial for the evaluation of the case.

5.2   She further states that the property would never have become subject to nationalization if it were not for the prior transfer of the assets to the German Reich which was on racial basis, and therefore the decisions allowing nationalization were discriminatory. The author's widow concedes that the communication concerns a property right, but explains that the core of the violation is the element of discrimination and the denial of equality in contravention of articles 6, 14, 26 and 27 of the Covenant.

5.3   The author's widow further contends that the claim complies with the ratione temporis condition, since the claim relates to the decisions made by the Czech courts in 1995 and 1996.

5.4   With regard to the State party's claim that the author's father could have claimed the property pursuant to Act No. 128/1946 until 31 December 1949, the author's widow contends that the author's father had good reason to fear political persecution from the Communist regime after 25 February 1948. Moreover, the violations of the Communist regime are not before the Committee, but rather the ratification and continuation of those violations by the arbitrary denial of redress following the adoption of restitution legislation in the 1990s. The author's submission was transmitted to the State party on 7 February 2001. The State party, however, has not responded to the author's comments.

EXAMINATION OF ADMISSIBILITY

6.1 Before considering any claims contained in a communication, the Human Rights Committee must in accordance with rule 87 of its rules of procedure, decide whether or not it is admissible under the Optional Protocol to the Covenant.

6.2 As required under article 5, paragraph 2 (a) of the Optional Protocol, the Committee has ascertained that the same matter is not being examined under another procedure of international investigation or settlement.

6.3 The Committee has noted the State party's objections to the admissibility and the author's comments thereon. It considers that the State party's allegations that the author has not met the ratione temporis condition for admissibility, is not relevant to the case, viewing that the author specifically noted that his claim relates to the decisions of the Czech courts in 1995 and 1996.

6.4 With regard to the State party's objections ratione materiae, the Committee notes that the author's communication does not invoke a violation of the right to property as such, but claims that he is denied a remedy in a discriminatory manner.

6.5 Furthermore, to the State party's objections that the communication is inadmissible for non-exhaustion of domestic remedies, the Committee notes that the facts raised in the present communication have been brought before the domestic courts of the State party in the several applications filed by the author, and have been considered by the State party's highest judicial authority. However, the issues relating to article 6, 9 and 27 appear not to have been raised before the domestic courts. The Committee considers that it is not precluded from considering the remaining claims in the communication by the requirement contained in article 5, paragraph 2 (b), of the Optional Protocol.

6.6 In its inadmissibility decisions on communications No. 669/1995 Malik v. the Czech Republic and 670/1995 Schlosser v. the Czech Republic, the Committee held that the author there had failed to substantiate, for purposes of admissibility, that Act No. 87/1991 was prima facie discriminatory within the meaning of article 26. The Committee observes that in this case the late author and his widow have made extensive submissions and arguments which are more fully substantiated, thus bringing the case over the threshold of admissibility so that the issues must be examined on the merits. Moreover, the instant case is distinguishable from the above cases in that the amendment of Act No. 87/1991 by Act No. 116/1994 provides for an extension for a claim of restitution for those entitled under Benes Decree No. 5/1945. The non-application of this extension to the author's case raises issues under article 26, which should be examined on the merits.

6.7 The Committee finds that the author has failed to substantiate for purposes of admissibility his claims under articles 14, paragraph 1 of the Covenant. Thus, this part of the claim is inadmissible under article 2 of the Optional Protocol.

EXAMINATION OF MERITS

7.1 The Human Rights Committee has considered the present communication in the light of all the information made available to it by the parties, as provided in article 5, paragraph 1, of the Optional Protocol.

7.2 The question before the Committee is whether the application of Act No. 87/1991, as amended by Act No. 116/1994, to the author's case entails a violation of his right to equality before the law and to the equal protection of the law.

7.3 These laws provide restitution or compensation to victims of illegal confiscation carried out for political reasons during the Communist regime. The law also provides for restitution or compensation to victims of racial persecution during the Second World War who had an entitlement under Benes Decree No. 5/1945. The Committee observes that legislation must not discriminate among the victims of the prior confiscation to which it applies, since all victims are entitled to redress without arbitrary distinctions.

7.4 The Committee notes that Act No. 87/1991 as amended by Act No. 116/1994 gave rise to a restitution claim of the author which was denied on the ground that the nationalization that took place in 1946/47 on the basis of Benes Decree No. 100/1945 falls outside the scope of laws of 1991 and 1994. Thus, the author was excluded from the benefit of the restitution law although the Czech nationalization in 1946/47 could only be carried out because the author's property was confiscated by the Nazi authorities during the time of German occupation.

In the Committee's view this discloses a discriminatory treatment of the author, compared to those individuals whose property was confiscated by Nazi authorities without being subjected, immediately after the war, to Czech nationalization and who, therefore, could benefit from the laws of 1991 and 1994. Irrespective of whether the arbitrariness in question was inherent in the law itself or whether it resulted from the application of the law by the courts of the State party, the Committee finds that the author was denied his right to equal protection of the law in violation of article 26 of the Covenant.

8. The Human Rights Committee, acting under article 5, paragraph 4, of the Optional Protocol, is of the view that the facts before it substantiate a violation of article 26 in conjunction with article 2 of the Covenant.

9. In accordance with article 2, paragraph 3 (a), of the Covenant, the State party is under an obligation to provide the author with an effective remedy. Such remedy should include restitution of the property or compensation, and appropriate compensation for the period during which the author and his widow were deprived of the property, starting on the date of the court decision of 20 November 1995 and ending on the date when the restitution has been completed. The State party should review its relevant legislation and administrative practices to ensure that neither the law nor its application entails discrimination in contravention of article 26 of the Covenant.

10. Bearing in mind that, by becoming a party to the Optional Protocol, the State party has recognized the competence of the Committee to determine whether there has been a violation of the Covenant or not and that, pursuant to article 2 of the Covenant, the State party has undertaken to ensure to all individuals within its territory and subject to its jurisdiction the rights recognized in the Covenant and to provide an effective remedy in case a violation has been established, the Committee wishes to receive from the State party, within 90 days, information about the measures taken to give effect to the Committee's Views.

3.6. *Miroslav Blazek, George A. Hartman and George Krizek v. The Czech Republic* (2001)

[. . .]

The Human Rights Committee, established under article 28 of the International Covenant on Civil and Political Rights,

Meeting on: 12 July 2001,

Having concluded its consideration of communication No. 857/1999 submitted to the Human Rights Committee by Messrs. Miroslav Blazek, George A. Hartman and George Krizek under the Optional Protocol to the International Covenant on Civil and Political Rights,

Having take into account all written information made available to it by the authors of the communication, and the State party,

Adopts the following:

Views under Article 5, Paragraph 4, of the Optional Protocol

1. The authors of the communications (dated 16 October 1997, 13 November 1997, and 29 November 1997 and subsequent correspondence) are Miroslav Blazek, George Hartman and George Krizek, natives of Czechoslovakia who emigrated to the United States after the Communist takeover in 1948, and who subsequently became naturalized United States citizens. They claim to be victims by the Czech Republic of violations of their Covenant rights, in particular of article 26. They are not represented by counsel.

The Facts as Submitted

2.1   The authors are naturalized United States citizens, who were born in Czechoslovakia and lost Czechoslovak citizenship by virtue of the 1928 Naturalization Treaty between the United States and Czechoslovakia, which precludes dual citizenship. They left Czechoslovakia after the Communist takeover in 1948. Their properties in Czechoslovakia were subsequently confiscated pursuant to confiscation regulations of 1948, 1955 and 1959.

2.2   Mr. Miroslav Blazek states that he is precluded from claiming his inheritance, including real property in Prague and agricultural property in Plananod-Luznici because he is not a Czech citizen. He submits copy of a letter from his lawyer in the Czech Republic, advising him that he could not file a claim in the present circumstances, since he does not fulfil the conditions of Czech citizenship required by the applicable law. However, his uncle, a French and Czech citizen, submitted a claim on his own behalf and on behalf of the author concerning jointly-owned property in Prague; the Government, however, severed the case and denied the author his share.

2.3   George A. Hartman, an architect by profession, was born in 1925 in the then Czechoslovak Republic and emigrated to the United States on 26 December 1948. He obtained political asylum in the United States and became a naturalized United States citizen on 2 April 1958, thus becoming ineligible for dual citizenship according to the 1928 Naturalization Treaty between the United States and Czechoslovakia. Until December 1948 he and his brother Jan (who subsequently became a French citizen while retaining Czech citizenship) had owned four apartment buildings in Prague and a country home in Zelizy.

2.4   By judgement of 1 July 1955 the Criminal Court in Klatovy found Mr. Hartman to have illegally left Czechoslovakia. He was sentenced in absentia and his property in Czechoslovakia was formally confiscated as a punishment for the illegal act of leaving the Czechoslovak Republic in 1948. Pursuant to law 119/1990, adopted after the demise of the Communist government, the author's criminal conviction for illegally leaving the country was invalidated.

2.5   By application of 17 October 1995 Mr. Hartman sought the restitution of his property, but his application was rejected because he did not fulfil the requirement of Czech citizenship. In order to qualify under the restitution law, Mr. Hartman continued to seek to obtain Czech citizenship for many years. Since 9 November 1999 he has dual Czech and United States citizenship. Notwithstanding his current Czech citizenship, he has not been able to obtain restitution because the statute of limitations for filing claims for restitution expired in 1992.

2.6   George Krizek states that his parents' property, including a wholesale business (bicycles) in Prague, a grain and dairy farm in a Prague suburb, and agricultural land in Sestajovice, was confiscated in 1948 without any compensation. After the death of his parents, he fled Czechoslovakia and emigrated to the United States, becoming a naturalized citizen in 1974. In April 1991 he claimed ownership of his property pursuant to Law No. 403/1990, but his claims were rejected by the Ministry of Agriculture. In 1992 the author again presented his claims under

laws 228 and 229/1991. However, he was informed that in order to be eligible for restitution, he would have to apply for Czech citizenship and take up permanent residence in the Czech Republic. Notwithstanding, he again filed a claim through his lawyer in Prague in 1994, without success.

2.7   By virtue of a 1994 judgement of the Czech Supreme Court, the requirement of permanent residence for restitution claims was removed, however the requirement of Czech citizenship remains in force.

The Complaint

3.1   The authors claim to be victims of violations of their Covenant rights by the Czech Republic in connection with the confiscation of their properties by the Communist authorities and the discriminatory failure of the democratic Governments of Czechoslovakia and of the Czech Republic to make restitution. They contend that the combined effect of Czech laws 119/1990 (of 23 April 1990) on Judicial Rehabilitation, 403/1990 (of 2 October 1990) on restitution of property, 87/1991 (of 21 February 1991, subsequently amended) on Extra-Judicial Rehabilitation, 229/1991 (of 21 May 1991) on Agricultural Land and 182/1993 (of 16 June 1993) on the creation of the Constitutional Court together with the position taken by the Czech Government on Czech citizenship discriminates against Czech émigrés who lost Czech citizenship and are now precluded from recovering their property.

3.2   The authors refer to the Committee's decision concerning communication No. 516/1992 (*Simunek v. The Czech Republic*) in which the Committee held that the denial of restitution or compensation to the authors of that communication because they were no longer Czech citizens constituted a violation of article 26 of the Covenant, bearing in mind that the State party itself had been responsible for the departure of its citizens, and that it would be incompatible with the Covenant to require them again to obtain Czech citizenship and permanently to return to the country as a prerequisite for the restitution of their property or for the payment of appropriate compensation.

3.3   The authors contend that, in order to frustrate the restitution claims of Czech émigrés to the United States, the Czech authorities used to invoke the 1928 United States Treaty with Czechoslovakia which required that anyone applying for the return of Czech citizenship. First renounce United States citizenship. Although the Treaty was abrogated in 1997, the subsequent acquisition of Czech citizenship does not, in the view of Czech authorities, entitle the authors to reapply for restitution, because the date for submission of claims has expired.

3.4   Reference is made to the case of two other American citizens who applied to the Czech courts for a ruling aimed at the deletion of the citizenship requirement from law 87/1991. The Czech Supreme Court, however, confirmed in its Judgement US 33/96 that the citizenship requirement was constitutional.

3.5   The authors further complain that the State party is deliberately denying them a remedy and that there has been a pattern of delay and inaction aimed at defeating their claims, in contravention of article 2 of the Covenant.

3.6   One of the authors, George A. Hartman, illustrates the alleged discrimination by referring to the case of his brother Jan Hartman, who is a Czech and French citizen, and who was able to obtain restitution for his half of the property in Prague confiscated in 1948 pursuant to judgement of 25 June 1991, whereas the author was denied compensation because at the time of filing his claim he was not a Czech citizen.

Exhaustion of Domestic Remedies

4.1   The authors claim that in their cases domestic remedies are non-existent, because they do not qualify under the restitution law. Moreover, the constitutionality of this law has already been tested by other claimants and affirmed by the Czech Constitutional Court. They refer, in particular, to the finding of the Constitutional Court in case US 33/96 (*Jan Dlouhy v. Czech Republic*, decision of 4 June 1997), confirming the constitutionality of the citizenship requirement in order to be an "eligible person" under the Rehabilitation Law No. 87/1991.

4.2   They complain that since 1989 they have devoted considerable amount of time and money in futile attempts to obtain restitution, both by engaging formal judicial procedures and by addressing petitions to government ministries and officials, including judges at the Constitutional Court, invoking *inter alia* the Czech Charter on Basic Rights and Freedoms.

Consideration of Admissibility and Examination of the Merits

5.1   Before considering any claims contained in a communication, the Human Rights Committee must, in accordance with rule 87 of its rules of procedure, decide whether or not it is admissible under the Optional Protocol to the Covenant.

5.2   The Committee has ascertained that the same matter is not and has not been submitted to any other instance of international investigation or settlement.

5.3   With regard to the requirement laid down in article 5, paragraph 2 (b), of the Optional Protocol that authors exhaust domestic remedies, the Committee notes that the State party has not contested the authors' argument that in their cases there are no available and effective domestic remedies, and in particular, that because of the preconditions of law 87/1991, they cannot claim restitution. In this context, the Committee notes that other claimants have unsuccessfully challenged the constitutionality of the law in question; that earlier views of the Committee in the cases of *Simunek* and *Adam* remain unimplemented; and that even following those complaints, the Constitutional Court has upheld the constitutionality of the Restitution Law. In the circumstances, the Committee finds that article 5, paragraph 2 (b), of the Optional Protocol does not preclude the Committee's consideration of the communications of Messrs. Blazek, Hartman and Krizek.

5.4   With regard to the author's claim that they have suffered unequal treatment by the State party in connection with the scheme of restitution and compensation put into effect after the Optional Protocol entered into force for the State party the Committee declares the communication admissible, insofar as it may raise issues under articles 2 and 26 of the Covenant.

5.5   Accordingly, the Committee proceeds to an examination of the merits of the case, in the light of the information before it, as required by article 5, paragraph 1, of the Optional Protocol. It notes that it has received sufficient information from the authors, but no submission whatever from the State party. In this connection, the Committee recalls that a State party has an obligation under article 4, paragraph 2, of the Optional Protocol to cooperate with the Committee and to submit written explanations or statements clarifying the matter and the remedy, if any, that may have been granted.

5.6   In the absence of any submission from the State party, the Committee must give due weight to the submissions made by the authors. The Committee has also reviewed its earlier Views in cases No. 516/1993, *Mrs. Alina Simunek et al.* and No. 586/1994, *Mr. Joseph Adam*. In determining whether the conditions for restitution or compensation are compatible with the Covenant, the Committee must consider all relevant factors, including the original entitlement of the authors to the properties in question. In the instant cases the authors have been affected by the exclusionary effect of the requirement in Act 87/1991 that claimants be Czech citizens. The question before the Committee is therefore whether the precondition of citizenship is compatible with article 26. In this context, the Committee reiterates its jurisprudence that not all differentiations in treatment can be deemed to be discriminatory under article 26. A differentiation which is compatible with the provisions of the Covenant and is based on reasonable grounds does not amount to prohibited discrimination within the meaning of article 26.

5.7   Whereas the criterion of citizenship is objective, the Committee must determine whether in the circumstances of these cases the application of the criterion to the authors would be reasonable.

5.8   The Committee recalls its Views in *Alina Simunek v. The Czech Republic* and *Joseph Adam v. The Czech Republic*, where it held that article 26 had been violated: "the authors in that case and many others in analogous situations had left Czechoslovakia because of their political opinions and had sought refuge from political persecution in other countries, where they eventually established permanent residence and obtained a new citizenship. Taking into account that the State party itself is responsible for [their] ... departure, it would be incompatible with the Covenant to require [them] ... to obtain Czech citizenship as a prerequisite for the restitution of their property, or, alternatively, for the payment of compensation" (CCPR/C/57/D/586/1994, para. 12.6). The Committee finds that the precedent established in the *Adam* case applies to the authors of this communication. The Committee would add that it cannot conceive that the distinction on grounds of citizenship can be considered reasonable in the light of the fact that the loss of Czech citizenship was a function of their presence in a State in which they were able to obtain refuge.

5.9   Further, with regard to time limits, whereas a statute of limitations may be objective and even reasonable in abstracto, the Committee cannot accept such a deadline for submitting restitution claims in the case of the authors, since under the explicit terms of the law they were excluded from the restitution scheme from the outset.

The Committee's Views

6. The Human Rights Committee, acting under article 5, paragraph 4, of the Optional Protocol to the International Covenant on Civil and Political Rights, is of the view that the facts before it disclose a violation of article 26, in relation to Messrs. Blazek, Hartman, and Krizek.

7. In accordance with article 2, paragraph 3 (a), of the Covenant, the State party is under an obligation to provide the authors with an effective remedy, including an opportunity to file a new claim for restitution or compensation. The Committee further encourages the State party to review its relevant legislation and administrative practices to ensure that neither the law nor its application entails discrimination in contravention of article 26 of the Covenant.

8. The Committee recalls, as it did in connection with its prior Views concerning the cases of *Alina Simunek* and *Joseph Adam*, that the Czech Republic, by becoming a State party to the Optional Protocol, recognized the competence of the Committee to determine whether there has been a violation of the Covenant or not and that, pursuant to article 2 of the Covenant, the State party has undertaken to ensure to all individuals within its territory or subject to its jurisdiction the rights recognized in the Covenant and to provide an effective and enforceable remedy in case a violation has been established.

9. In this connection, the Committee wishes to receive from the State party, within 90 days following the transmittal of these Views to the State party, information about the measures taken to give effect to the Views. The State party is also requested to translate into the Czech language and to publish the Committee's Views.

4. EUROPEAN COURT OF HUMAN RIGHTS

4.1. *Sporrong and Lönnroth v. Sweden* (1982)

[. . .]

I. THE CIRCUMSTANCES OF THE CASE

9. The two applications relate to the effects of long-term expropriation permits and prohibitions on construction on the Estate of the late Mr. Sporrong and on Mrs. Lönnroth, in their capacity as property owners.

A. The Sporrong Estate

10. The Sporrong Estate, which has legal personality, is composed of Mrs. M. Sporrong, Mr. C.-O. Sporrong and Mrs. B. Atmer, the joint heirs of the late Mr. E. Sporrong; they reside in or near Stockholm. They own a property, situated in the Lower Norrmalm district in central Stockholm and known as "Riddaren No. 8", on which stands a building dating from the 1860's. In the 1975 tax year the rateable value of the property was 600,000 Swedish crowns.

1. The Expropriation Permit

11. On 31 July 1956, acting pursuant to Article 44 of the Building Act 1947 (byggnadslagen – "the 1947 Act"), the Government granted the Stockholm City Council a zonal expropriation permit (expropriationstillstånd) covering 164 properties, including that owned by the Sporrong Estate. The City intended to build, over one of the main shopping streets in the centre of the capital, a viaduct leading to a major relief road. One of the viaduct's supports was to stand on the "Riddaren" site, the remainder of which was to be turned into a car park.

Under the Expropriation Act 1917 (expropriationslagen – "the 1917 Act"), the Government set at five years the time-limit within which the expropriation might be effected; before the end of that period the City Council had to summon the owners to appear before the Real Estate Court (fastighetdomstolen) for the fixing of compensation, failing which the permit would lapse.

12. In July 1961, at the request of the City, the Government extended this time-limit to 31 July 1964. Their decision affected 138 properties, including "Riddaren No. 8". At that time, the properties in question were not the subject of any city plan (stadsplan).

13. On 2 April 1964, the Government granted the City Council a further extension of the expropriation permit; this extension was applicable to 120 of the 164 properties originally concerned, including "Riddaren No. 8", and was valid until 31 July 1969. The City had prepared for Lower Norrmalm a general development plan, known as "City 62", which gave priority to street-widening for the benefit of private traffic and pedestrians.

Subsequently, "City 67", a revised general development plan for Lower Norrmalm and Östermalm (another district in the city centre), stressed the need to improve public transport by means of a better network of roads. Some of the sites involved were to be used for street-widening, but any final decision had to await a decision as to the utilisation of the orders. It was estimated that the revised plan, which was of the same type as "City 62", should be implemented before 1985.

14. In July 1969, the City Council requested a third extension of the expropriation permit as regards certain properties, including "Riddaren No. 8", pointing out that the reasons for expropriation given in the "City 62" and "City 67" plans were still valid. On 14 May 1971, the Government set 31 July 1979, that is to say ten years from the date of the request, as the time-limit for the institution of the judicial proceedings for the fixing of compensation.

In May 1975, the City Council put forward revised plans according to which the use of "Riddaren No. 8" was not to be modified and the existing building was not to be altered.

On 3 May 1979, the Government cancelled the expropriation permit at the Council's request (see paragraph 29 below).

15. The Sporrong Estate has never attempted to sell its property.

2. The Prohibition on Construction

16. On 11 June 1954, the Stockholm County Administrative Board (länsstyrelsen) had imposed a prohibition on construction (byggnadsförbud) on "Riddaren No. 8", on the ground that the proposed viaduct and relief road would affect the use of the property. The prohibition was subsequently extended by the Board to 1 July 1979.

17. In 1970, the Sporrong Estate obtained an exemption from the prohibition in order to widen the front door of the building. It never applied for any other exemptions.

18. The expropriation permit and the prohibition on construction affecting "Riddaren No. 8" were in force for total periods of twenty-three and twenty-five years respectively.

B. Mrs. Lönnroth

19. Mrs. I. M. Lönnroth lives in Stockholm, where she owns three-quarters of a property situated at "Barnhuset No. 6", in the Lower Norrmalm district; it is occupied by the two buildings erected in 1887–1888, one of which faces the street and the other the rear. In the 1975 tax year the rateable value of the applicant's share of the property was 862,500 Swedish crowns.

1. The Expropriation Permit

20. On 24 September 1971, the Government authorised the Stockholm City Council to expropriate 115 properties, including "Barnhuset No. 6", and set 31 December 1979, that is to say ten years from the date of the Council request, as the time-limit for the institution of the judicial proceedings for the fixing of compensation. They justified their decision by reference to the "City 67" plan which envisaged that a multi-storey car park would be erected on the site of the applicant's property.

21. However, work in this district was postponed and new plans were prepared for consideration. Believing her property to be in urgent need of repair, Mrs. Lönnroth requested the Government to withdraw the expropriation permit. The City Council replied that the existing plans did not allow any derogation to be made, and on 20 February 1975 the Government refused the request on the ground that the permit could not be revoked without the express consent of the City Council.

On 3 May 1979, the Government cancelled the permit at the Council's request (see paragraph 29 below).

22. Mrs. Lönnroth's financial situation obliged her to try to sell her property. She made seven attempts to do so between 1970 and 1975, but the prospective buyers withdrew after they had consulted the city authorities. In addition, she sometimes had difficulty in finding tenants.

2. The Prohibition on Construction

23. On 29 February 1968, the Stockholm County Administrative Board decided to impose a prohibition on construction on "Barnhuset No. 6", on the ground that the site was to be turned into a car park. The prohibition was subsequently extended by the Board to 1 July 1980.

24. In 1970, Mrs. Lönnroth was granted an exemption in order to make alterations to the third floor of her premises; she never sought any other exemptions.

She failed to obtain a loan when, in the early 1970's, one of the property's major mortgagees demanded that the façade be renovated.

25. To sum up, Mrs. Lönnroth's property was subject to an expropriation permit and a prohibition on construction for eight and twelve years respectively.

C. The Town-Planning Policy of the City of Stockholm

26. For several decades, spectacular changes have been taking place in the centre of Stockholm, comparable to those which have occurred in many cities which were reconstructed after being destroyed or severely damaged during the second world war.

27. Lower Norrmalm is a district where most of the capital's important administrative and commercial activities used to be concentrated. Around 1945, the view was taken that the district should be restructured so that those activities could be carried on satisfactorily. For instance, a proper network of roads was needed.

Furthermore, most of the buildings were decrepit and in a poor state of repair. A large-scale redevelopment scheme was necessary in order to provide suitable premises for offices and shops as well as to create a healthy and hygienic working environment. Zonal expropriation, introduced by an Act of 1953 which amended, inter alia, Article 44 of the 1947 Act, became the key instrument for implementing the City Council's plans. In less than ten years more than one hundred buildings were demolished. Some of the vacant sites thereby created were used to make new roads and others were integrated into larger and more functional complexes.

28. During the 1970's, town-planning policy in Stockholm evolved considerably. Far from being in favour of opening access roads to the centre, the city authorities were now trying to reduce the number of cars in the capital. This new policy was reflected in the "City 77" plan, which was adopted on 19 June 1978. It makes provision for urban renovation based above all on gradual rebuilding that takes account of the present urban fabric and it envisages the preservation and restoration of most of the existing buildings.

29. On 3 May 1979, the Government, granting a request submitted by the City Council in October 1978, cancelled, as regards about seventy properties including those of the applicants, the expropriation permits issued in 1956 and 1971. This was because it was by then considered unlikely that the City would need to acquire these properties in order to implement its new town-planning scheme.

30. Notwithstanding the difficulties occasioned by the existence of zonal expropriation permits, it has proved possible to sell sixty-six properties in Stockholm affected by such permits.

[. . .]

I. The Alleged Violation of Article 1 of Protocol No. 1 (P1-1)

56. The applicants complained of the length of the period during which the expropriation permits, accompanied by prohibitions on construction, affecting their properties had been in force. It amounted, in their view, to an unlawful infringement of their right to the peaceful enjoyment of their possessions, as guaranteed by Article 1 of Protocol No. 1 (P1-1), which reads as follows:

"Every natural or legal person is entitled to the peaceful enjoyment of his possessions. No one shall be deprived of his possessions except in the public interest and subject to the conditions provided for by law and by the general principles of international law.

The preceding provisions shall not, however, in any way impair the right of a State to enforce such laws as it deems necessary to control the use of property in accordance with the general interest or to secure the payment of taxes or other contributions or penalties."

57. In its Marckx judgment of 13 June 1979, the Court described as follows the object of this Article (P1-1):

"By recognising that everyone has the right to the peaceful enjoyment of his possessions, Article 1 (P1-1) is in substance guaranteeing the right of property. This is the clear impression left by the words 'possessions' and 'use of property' (in French: 'biens', 'propriété', 'usage des biens'); the 'travaux préparatoires', for their part, confirm this unequivocally: the drafters continually spoke of "'right of property' or 'right to property' to describe the subject-matter of the successive drafts which were the forerunners of the present Article 1 (P1-1)." (Series A no. 31, p. 27, par. 63)

It has to be determined whether the applicants can complain of an interference with this right and, if so, whether the interference was justified.

1. The Existence of an Interference with the Applicants' Right of Property

58. The applicants did not dispute that the expropriation permits and prohibitions on construction in question were lawful in themselves. On the other hand, they complained of the length of the time-limits granted to the City of Stockholm for the institution of the judicial proceedings for the fixing of compensation for expropriation (five years, extended for three, then for five and finally for ten years, in the case of the Sporrong Estate; ten years in the case of Mrs. Lönnroth; see paragraphs 11–14 and 20 above). They also complained of the fact that the expropriation permits and the prohibitions on construction had been maintained in force for a lengthy period (twenty-three and eight years for the permits; twenty-five and twelve years for the prohibitions; see paragraphs 18 and 25 above). They pointed to the adverse effects on their right of property allegedly occasioned by these measures when they were combined in such a way. They contended that they had lost the possibility of selling their properties at normal market prices. They added that they would have run too great a risk had they incurred expenditure on their properties and that if all the same they had had work carried out after obtaining a building permit, they would

have been obliged to undertake not to claim – in the event of expropriation – any indemnity for the resultant capital appreciation. They also alleged that they would have encountered difficulties in obtaining mortgages had they sought them. Finally, they recalled that any "new construction" on their own land was prohibited.

Though not claiming that they had been formally and definitively deprived of their possessions, the Sporrong Estate and Mrs. Lönnroth alleged that the permits and prohibitions at issue subjected the enjoyment and power to dispose of their properties to limitations that were excessive and did not give rise to any compensation. Their right of property had accordingly, so they contended, been deprived of its substance whilst the measures in question were in force.

59. The Government accepted that market forces might render it more difficult to sell or let a property that was subject to an expropriation permit and that the longer the permit remained in force the more serious this problem would become. They also recognised that prohibitions on construction restricted the normal exercise of the right of property. However, they asserted that such permits and prohibitions were an intrinsic feature of town planning and did not impair the right of owners to "the peaceful enjoyment of (their) possessions", within the meaning of Article 1 of Protocol No. 1 (P1-1).

60. The Court is unable to accept this argument.

Although the expropriation permits left intact in law the owners' right to use and dispose of their possessions, they nevertheless in practice significantly reduced the possibility of its exercise. They also affected the very substance of ownership in that they recognised before the event that any expropriation would be lawful and authorised the City of Stockholm to expropriate whenever it found it expedient to do so. The applicants' right of property thus became precarious and defeasible.

The prohibitions on construction, for their part, undoubtedly restricted the applicants' right to use their possessions.

The Court also considers that the permits and prohibitions should in principle be examined together, except to the extent that analysis of the case may require a distinction to be drawn between them. This is because, even though there was not necessarily a legal connection between the measures

(see paragraph 35 above) and even though they had different periods of validity, they were complementary and had the single objective of facilitating the development of the city in accordance with the successive plans prepared for this purpose.

There was therefore an interference with the applicants' right of property and, as the Commission rightly pointed out, the consequences of that interference were undoubtedly rendered more serious by the combined use, over a long period of time, of expropriation permits and prohibitions on construction.

2. The Justification for the Interference with the Applicants' Right of Property

61. It remains to be ascertained whether or not the interference found by the Court violated Article 1 (P1-1).

That Article (P1-1) comprises three distinct rules. The first rule, which is of a general nature, enounces the principle of peaceful enjoyment of property; it is set out in the first sentence of the first paragraph. The second rule covers deprivation of possessions and subjects it to certain conditions; it appears in the second sentence of the same paragraph. The third rule recognises that the States are entitled, amongst other things, to control the use of property in accordance with the general interest, by enforcing such laws as they deem necessary for the purpose; it is contained in the second paragraph.

The Court must determine, before considering whether the first rule was complied with, whether the last two are applicable.

(a) The applicability of the second sentence of the first paragraph

62. It should be recalled first of all that the Swedish authorities did not proceed to an expropriation of the applicants' properties. The applicants were therefore not formally "deprived of their possessions" at any time: they were entitled to use, sell, devise, donate or mortgage their properties.

63. In the absence of a formal expropriation, that is to say a transfer of ownership, the Court considers that it must look behind the appearances and investigate the realities of the situation complained of (see, mutatis mutandis, the Van Droogenbroeck judgment of 24 June 1982, Series A no. 50, p. 20, par. 38). Since the Convention is intended to guarantee

rights that are "practical and effective" (see the Airey judgment of 9 October 1979, Series A no. 32, p. 12, par. 24), it has to be ascertained whether that situation amounted to a de facto expropriation, as was argued by the applicants.

In the Court's opinion, all the effects complained of (see paragraph 58 above) stemmed from the reduction of the possibility of disposing of the properties concerned. Those effects were occasioned by limitations imposed on the right of property, which right had become precarious, and from the consequences of those limitations on the value of the premises. However, although the right in question lost some of its substance, it did not disappear. The effects of the measures involved are not such that they can be assimilated to a deprivation of possessions. The Court observes in this connection that the applicants could continue to utilise their possessions and that, although it became more difficult to sell properties in Stockholm affected by expropriation permits and prohibitions on construction, the possibility of selling subsisted; according to information supplied by the Government, several dozen sales were carried out (see paragraph 30 above).

There was therefore no room for the application of the second sentence of the first paragraph in the present case.

(b)   The applicability of the second paragraph

64. The prohibitions on construction clearly amounted to a control of "the use of [the applicants'] property", within the meaning of the second paragraph.

65. On the other hand, the expropriation permits were not intended to limit or control such use. Since they were an initial step in a procedure leading to deprivation of possessions, they did not fall within the ambit of the second paragraph. They must be examined under the first sentence of the first paragraph.

(c)   Compliance with the first sentence of the first paragraph as regards the expropriation permits

66. The applicants' complaints concerned in the first place the length of the time-limits granted to the City of Stockholm, which they regarded as contrary to both Swedish law and the Convention.

67. The 1917 Act did not contain any provisions either on the length of the time-limit during which the expropriating authority had to institute judicial proceedings for the fixing of compensation for expropriation, or on the extension of the validity of permits.

According to the Sporrong Estate and Mrs. Lönnroth, it had been the established practice since the entry into force of the Act for the normal time-limit for service of a summons to appear before the Real Estate Court to be one year. Since the time-limits in the present case were as long as five and ten years respectively, it was alleged that there was no legal basis for the original permits; the same was said to apply to the three extensions of the permit affecting the property of the Sporrong Estate.

The respondent State replied that the issue and the extension of the permits were in conformity with Swedish law: it argued that since the Government were entitled to fix the period of validity of the original permit, they were also empowered, in the absence of any provision to the contrary, to extend it.

68. The Court does not consider that it has to resolve this difference of opinion over the interpretation of Swedish law. Even if the permits complained of were not contrary to that law, their conformity therewith would not establish that they were compatible with the right guaranteed by Article 1 (P1-1).

69. The fact that the permits fell within the ambit neither of the second sentence of the first paragraph nor of the second paragraph does not mean that the interference with the said right violated the rule contained in the first sentence of the first paragraph.

For the purposes of the latter provision, the Court must determine whether a fair balance was struck between the demands of the general interest of the community and the requirements of the protection of the individual's fundamental rights (see, mutatis mutandis, the judgment of 23 July 1968 in the "Belgian Linguistic" case, Series A no. 6, p. 32, par. 5). The search for this balance is inherent in the whole of the Convention and is also reflected in the structure of Article 1 (P1-1).

The Agent of the Government recognised the need for such a balance. At the hearing on the morning of 23 February 1982, he pointed out that, under the

Expropriation Act, an expropriation permit must not be issued if the public purpose in question can be achieved in a different way; when this is being assessed, full weight must be given both to the interests of the individual and to the public interest.

The Court has not overlooked this concern on the part of the legislature. Moreover, it finds it natural that, in an area as complex and difficult as that of the development of large cities, the Contracting States should enjoy a wide margin of appreciation in order to implement their town-planning policy. Nevertheless, the Court cannot fail to exercise its power of review and must determine whether the requisite balance was maintained in a manner consonant with the applicants' right to "the peaceful enjoyment of [their] possessions", within the meaning of the first sentence of Article 1 (P1-1).

70. A feature of the law in force at the relevant time was its inflexibility. With the exception of the total withdrawal of the expropriation permits, which required the agreement of the municipality, the law provided no means by which the situation of the property owners involved could be modified at a later date. The Court notes in this connection that the permits granted to the City of Stockholm were granted for five years in the case of the Sporrong Estate – with an extension for three, then for five and finally for ten years – and for ten years in the case of Mrs. Lönnroth. In the events that happened, they remained in force for twenty-three years and eight years respectively. During the whole of this period, the applicants were left in complete uncertainty as to the fate of their properties and were not entitled to have any difficulties which they might have encountered taken into account by the Swedish Government. The Commission's report furnishes an example of such difficulties. Mrs. Lönnroth had requested the Government to withdraw the expropriation permit. The City Council replied that the existing plans did not authorise any derogation; the Government, for their part, refused the request on the ground that they could not revoke the permit without the Council's express consent (see paragraph 21 above).

The Courts have not overlooked the interest of the City of Stockholm in having the option of expropriating properties in order to implement its plans. However, it does not see why the Swedish legislation should have excluded the possibility of

re-assessing, at reasonable intervals during the lengthy periods for which each of the permits was granted and maintained in force, the interests of the City and the interests of the owners. In the instant case, the absence of such a possibility was all the less satisfactory in that the town-planning schemes underlying the expropriation permits and, at the same time, the intended use prescribed for the applicants' properties were modified on several occasions.

71. As is shown by the official statement of reasons accompanying the Bill in which the 1972 Act originated, the Swedish Government conceded that "in certain respects, the existing system is a source of disadvantages for the property owner":

> "Naturally, the mere issue of an expropriation permit often places him in a state of uncertainty. In practice, his opportunities for disposing of his property by selling it, assigning the use thereof or having premises erected thereon are considerably restricted. He may also have difficulty in deciding whether to incur expenditure on upkeep or modernisation. The disadvantages resulting from an expropriation permit are, of course, increased if the judicial proceedings are not set in motion for a long time." (Kungl. Maj:ts proposition nr. 109, 1972, p. 227)

The 1972 Act takes partial account of these problems. Admittedly, it does not provide for compensation to be granted to property owners who may have been prejudiced by reason of the length of the validity of the permit; however, it does enable them to obtain a reduction of the time-limit for service of the summons to appear before the Real Estate Court if they establish that the fact that the question of expropriation remains pending has caused significantly more serious prejudice (see paragraph 37 above). Since the Act was not applicable in the present case (see paragraph 39 above), it could not have been of assistance to the applicants in overcoming any difficulties which they might have encountered.

72. The Court also finds that the existence throughout this period of prohibitions on construction accentuated even further the prejudicial effects of the length of the validity of the permits. Full enjoyment of the applicants' right of property was impeded for a total period of twenty-five years in the case of the Sporrong Estate and of twelve years

in the case of Mrs. Lönnroth. In this connection, the Court notes that in 1967 the Parliamentary Ombudsman considered that the adverse effects on property owners that could result from extended prohibitions were irreconcilable with the position that should obtain in a State governed by the rule of law (see paragraph 42 above).

73. Being combined in this way, the two series of measures created a situation which upset the fair balance which should be struck between the protection of the right of property and the requirements of the general interest: the Sporrong Estate and Mrs. Lönnroth bore an individual and excessive burden which could have been tendered legitimate only if they had had the possibility of seeking a reduction of the time-limits or of claiming compensation. Yet at the relevant time Swedish law excluded these possibilities and it still excludes the second of them.

In the Court's view, it is not appropriate at this stage to determine whether the applicants were in fact prejudiced (see, mutatis mutandis, the above-mentioned Marckx judgment, Series A no. 31, p. 13, par. 27): it was in their legal situation itself that the requisite balance was no longer to be found.

74. The permits in question, whose consequences were aggravated by the prohibitions on construction, therefore violated Article 1 (P1-1), as regards both applicants.

[. . .]

4.2. *Lithgow and Others v. United Kingdom* (1986)

[. . .]

As to the Facts

9. The applicants in the present case had certain of their interests nationalised under the Aircraft and Shipbuilding Industries Act 1977 ("the 1977 Act"). Whilst not contesting the principle of the nationalisation as such, they claimed that the compensation which they received was grossly inadequate and discriminatory and alleged that they had been victims of breaches of Article 1 of Protocol No. 1 (P1-1) to the Convention, taken alone and in conjunction with Article 14 (art. 14+P1-1) of the Con-

vention. They also invoked Article 6 (art. 6) and – in one case – Article 13 (art. 13) of the Convention. Certain claims of violation of Articles 17 and 18 (art. 17, art. 18) of the Convention, which had been made before the Commission, were not pursued before the Court.

[. . .]

As to the Llaw

I. Article 1 of Protocol No. 1 (P1-1)

A. Introduction

105. The applicants did not contest the principle of the nationalisation as such. However, they alleged that, for various reasons, the compensation which they had received was grossly inadequate and that on that account they had been victims of a violation of Article 1 of Protocol No. 1 (P1-1), which reads as follows:

> "Every natural or legal person is entitled to the peaceful enjoyment of his possessions. No one shall be deprived of his possessions except in the public interest and subject to the conditions provided for by law and by the general principles of international law.
>
> The preceding provisions shall not, however, in any way impair the right of a State to enforce such laws as it deems necessary to control the use of property in accordance with the general interest or to secure the payment of taxes or other contributions or penalties."

The applicants' allegation was contested by the Government and rejected by a majority of the Commission.

106. The Court recalls that Article 1 (P1-1) in substance guarantees the right of property (see the Marckx judgment of 13 June 1979, Series A no. 31, pp. 27–28, para. 63). In its judgment of 23 September 1982 in the case of Sporrong and Lönnroth, the Court analysed Article 1 (P1-1) as comprising "three distinct rules": the first rule, set out in the first sentence of the first paragraph, is of a general nature and enunciates the principle of the peaceful enjoyment of property; the second rule, contained in the second sentence of the first paragraph, covers deprivation of possessions and subjects it to certain conditions; the third rule, stated in the second paragraph, is concerned, amongst other things, with the right of a State to control the use of property

(Series A no. 52, p. 24, para. 61). However, the Court made it clear in its James and Others judgment of 21 February 1986 that the three rules are not "distinct" in the sense of being unconnected: the second and third rules are concerned with particular instances of interference with the right to peaceful enjoyment of property and should therefore be construed in the light of the general principle enunciated in the first rule (Series A no. 98, p. 30, para. 37 in fine).

107. The applicants were clearly "deprived of (their) possessions", within the meaning of the second sentence of Article 1 (P1-1); indeed, this point was not disputed before the Court. It will therefore examine the scope of that sentence's requirements and then, in turn, whether they were satisfied.

B. Were the Applicants Deprived of Their Property "in the Public Interest" and "Subject to the Conditions Provided for by Law"?

108. The applicants contended that a taking of property for compensation which – as in the present case, so they alleged – was unfair because it represented only a fraction of the property's value at the date of taking could not be regarded as being "in the public interest", within the meaning of the second sentence of Article 1 of Protocol No. 1 (P1-1). They further contended that if – as here, in their view – the compensation was arbitrary because it bore no reasonable relationship to that value, the taking could not be regarded as having been effected "subject to the conditions provided for by law", within the meaning of the same sentence.

109. The Court is unable to accept the first of these contentions. The obligation to pay compensation derives from an implicit condition in Article 1 of Protocol No. 1 (P1-1) read as a whole (see paragraph 120 below) rather than from the "public interest" requirement itself. The latter requirement relates to the justification and the motives for the actual taking, issues which were not contested by the applicants.

110. As regards the phrase "subject to the conditions provided for by law", it requires in the first place the existence of and compliance with adequately accessible and sufficiently precise domestic legal provisions (see, amongst other authorities, the Malone judgment of 2 August 1984, Series A no. 82, pp. 31–33, paras. 66–68). Save as stated in paragraph 153 below, the applicants did not dispute that these requirements had been satisfied.

It is true that the word "law" in this context refers to more than domestic law (ibid., p. 32, para. 67). However, the applicants' contention in this respect (see paragraph 108 above) is, in the Court's view, so closely linked to the main issues in the present case, which are dealt with in paragraphs 123–175 below, that it would be superfluous also to examine this question under this phrase of Article 1 (P1-1).

C. "General Principles of International Law"

111. The applicants argued that the reference in the second sentence of Article 1 (P1-1) to "the general principles of international law" meant that the international law requirement of, so they asserted, prompt, adequate and effective compensation for the deprivation of property of foreigners also applied to nationals.

112. The Commission has consistently held that the principles in question are not applicable to a taking by a State of the property of its own nationals. The Government supported this opinion. The Court likewise agrees with it for the reasons which are already set out in its above-mentioned James and Others judgment (Series A no. 98, pp. 38–40, paras. 58–66) and are repeated here, mutatis mutandis.

113. In the first place, purely as a matter of general international law, the principles in question apply solely to non-nationals. They were specifically developed for the benefit of non-nationals. As such, these principles did not relate to the treatment accorded by States to their own nationals.

114. In support of their argument, the applicants relied first on the actual text of Article 1 (P1-1). In their submission, since the second sentence opened with the words "No one", it was impossible to construe that sentence as meaning that whereas everyone was entitled to the safeguards afforded by the phrases "in the public interest" and "subject to the conditions provided for by law", only non-nationals were entitled to the safeguards afforded by the phrase "subject to the conditions provided for . . . by the general principles of international law". They further pointed out that where the authors of the Convention intended to differentiate between nationals and non-nationals, they did so expressly, as was exemplified by Article 16 (art. 16).

Whilst there is some force in the applicants' argument as a matter of grammatical construction, there are convincing reasons for a different interpretation. Textually the Court finds it more natural to take the reference to the general principles of international law in Article 1 of Protocol No. 1 (P1-1) to mean that those principles are incorporated into that Article, but only as regards those acts to which they are normally applicable, that is to say acts of a State in relation to non-nationals. Moreover, the words of a treaty should be understood to have their ordinary meaning (see Article 31 of the 1969 Vienna Convention on the Law of Treaties), and to interpret the phrase in question as extending the general principles of international law beyond their normal sphere of applicability is less consistent with the ordinary meaning of the terms used, notwithstanding their context.

115. The applicants also referred to arguments to the effect that, on the Commission's interpretation, the reference in Article 1 (P1-1) to the general principles of international law would be redundant since non-nationals already enjoyed the protection thereof.

The Court does not share this view. The inclusion of the reference can be seen to serve at least two purposes. Firstly, it enables non-nationals to resort directly to the machinery of the Convention to enforce their rights on the basis of the relevant principles of international law, whereas otherwise they would have to seek recourse to diplomatic channels or to other available means of dispute settlement to do so. Secondly, the reference ensures that the position of non-nationals is safeguarded, in that it excludes any possible argument that the entry into force of Protocol No. 1 (P1) has led to a diminution of their rights. In this connection, it is also noteworthy that Article 1 (P1-1) expressly provides that deprivation of property must be effected "in the public interest": since such a requirement has always been included amongst the general principles of international law, this express provision would itself have been superfluous if Article 1 (P1-1) had had the effect of rendering those principles applicable to nationals as well as to non-nationals.

116. Finally, the applicants pointed out that to treat the general principles of international law as inapplicable to a taking by a State of the property of its own nationals would permit differentiation on the ground of nationality. This, they said, would be incompatible with two provisions that are incorporated in Protocol No. 1 (P1) by virtue of Article 5 thereof (P1-5): Article 1 (art. 1) of the Convention which obliges the Contracting States to secure to everyone within their jurisdiction the rights and freedoms guaranteed and Article 14 (art. 14) of the Convention which enshrines the principle of non-discrimination.

As to Article 1 (art. 1) of the Convention, it is true that under most provisions of the Convention and its Protocols nationals and non-nationals enjoy the same protection but this does not exclude exceptions as far as this may be indicated in a particular text (see, for example, Articles 5 para. 1 (f) and 16 (art. 5-1-f, art. 16) of the Convention, Articles 3 and 4 of Protocol No. 4 (P4-3, P4-4)).

As to Article 14 (art. 14) of the Convention, the Court has consistently held that differences of treatment do not constitute discrimination if they have an "objective and reasonable justification" (see, as the most recent authority, the Abdulaziz, Cabales and Balkandali judgment of 28 May 1985, Series A no. 94, pp. 35–36, para. 72).

Especially as regards a taking of property effected in the context of a social reform or an economic restructuring, there may well be good grounds for drawing a distinction between nationals and non-nationals as far as compensation is concerned. To begin with, non-nationals are more vulnerable to domestic legislation: unlike nationals, they will generally have played no part in the election or designation of its authors nor have been consulted on its adoption. Secondly, although a taking of property must always be effected in the public interest, different considerations may apply to nationals and non-nationals and there may well be legitimate reason for requiring nationals to bear a greater burden in the public interest than non-nationals (see paragraph 120 below).

117. Confronted with a text whose interpretation has given rise to such disagreement, the Court considers it proper to have recourse to the travaux préparatoires as a supplementary means of interpretation (see Article 32 of the Vienna Convention on the Law of Treaties).

Examination of the travaux préparatoires reveals that the express reference to a right to compensation contained in earlier drafts of Article 1 (P1-1) was excluded, notably in the face of opposition on the part of the United Kingdom and other

States. The mention of the general principles of international law was subsequently included and was the subject of several statements to the effect that they protected only foreigners. Thus, when the German Government stated that they could accept the text provided that it was explicitly recognised that those principles involved the obligation to pay compensation in the event of expropriation, the Swedish delegation pointed out that those principles only applied to relations between a State and non-nationals. And it was then agreed, at the request of the German and Belgian delegations, that "the general principles of international law, in their present connotation, entailed the obligation to pay compensation to non-nationals in cases of expropriation" (emphasis added).

Above all, in their Resolution (52) 1 of 19 March 1952 approving the text of the Protocol (P1) and opening it for signature, the Committee of Ministers expressly stated that, "as regards Article 1 (P1-1), the general principles of international law in their present connotation entail the obligation to pay compensation to non-nationals in cases of expropriation" (emphasis added). Having regard to the negotiating history as a whole, the Court considers that this Resolution must be taken as a clear indication that the reference to the general principles of international law was not intended to extend to nationals.

The travaux préparatoires accordingly do not support the interpretation for which the applicants contended.

118. Finally, it has not been demonstrated that, since the entry into force of Protocol No. 1 (P1), State practice has developed to the point where it can be said that the parties to that instrument regard the reference therein to the general principles of international law as being applicable to the treatment accorded by them to their own nationals. The evidence adduced points distinctly in the opposite direction.

119. For all these reasons, the Court concludes that the general principles of international law are not applicable to a taking by a State of the property of its own nationals.

D. Entitlement to Compensation

120. The question remains whether the availability and amount of compensation are material considerations under the second sentence of the first paragraph of Article 1 (P1-1), the text of the provision being silent on the point. The Commission, with whom both the Government and the applicants agreed, read Article 1 (P1-1) as in general impliedly requiring the payment of compensation as a necessary condition for the taking of property of anyone within the jurisdiction of a Contracting State.

Like the Commission, the Court observes that under the legal systems of the Contracting States, the taking of property in the public interest without payment of compensation is treated as justifiable only in exceptional circumstances not relevant for present purposes. As far as Article 1 (P1-1) is concerned, the protection of the right of property it affords would be largely illusory and ineffective in the absence of any equivalent principle.

In this connection, the Court recalls that not only must a measure depriving a person of his property pursue, on the facts as well as in principle, a legitimate aim "in the public interest", but there must also be a reasonable relationship of proportionality between the means employed and the aim sought to be realised. This latter requirement was expressed in other terms in the above-mentioned Sporrong and Lönnroth judgment by the notion of the "fair balance" that must be struck between the demands of the general interest of the community and the requirements of the protection of the individual's fundamental rights (Series A no. 52, p. 26, para. 69). The requisite balance will not be found if the person concerned has had to bear "an individual and excessive burden" (ibid., p. 28, para. 73). Although the Court was speaking in that judgment in the context of the general rule of peaceful enjoyment of property enunciated in the first sentence of the first paragraph, it pointed out that "the search for this balance is . . . reflected in the structure of Article 1 (P1-1)" as a whole (ibid., p. 26, para. 69).

Clearly, compensation terms are material to the assessment whether a fair balance has been struck between the various interests at stake and, notably, whether or not a disproportionate burden has been imposed on the person who has been deprived of his possessions.

E. Standard of Compensation

121. The Court further accepts the Commission's conclusion as to the standard of compensation: the taking of property without payment of an amount

reasonably related to its value would normally constitute a disproportionate interference which could not be considered justifiable under Article 1 (P1-1). Article 1 (P1-1) does not, however, guarantee a right to full compensation in all circumstances, since legitimate objectives of "public interest", such as pursued in measures of economic reform or measures designed to achieve greater social justice, may call for less than reimbursement of the full market value (see the above-mentioned James and Others judgment, Series A no. 98, p. 36, para. 54).

In this connection, the applicants contended that, as regards the standard of compensation, no distinction could be drawn between nationalisation and other takings of property by the State, such as the compulsory acquisition of land for public purposes.

The Court is unable to agree. Both the nature of the property taken and the circumstances of the taking in these two categories of cases give rise to different considerations which may legitimately be taken into account in determining a fair balance between the public interest and the private interests concerned. The valuation of major industrial enterprises for the purpose of nationalising a whole industry is in itself a far more complex operation than, for instance, the valuation of land compulsorily acquired and normally calls for specific legislation which can be applied across the board to all the undertakings involved. Accordingly, provided always that the aforesaid fair balance is preserved, the standard of compensation required in a nationalisation case may be different from that required in regard to other takings of property.

122. Whilst not disputing that the State enjoyed a margin of appreciation in deciding whether to deprive an owner of his property, the applicants submitted that the Commission had wrongly concluded from this premise that the State also had a wide discretion in laying down the terms and conditions on which property was to be taken.

The Court is unable to accept this submission. A decision to enact nationalisation legislation will commonly involve consideration of various issues on which opinions within a democratic society may reasonably differ widely. Because of their direct knowledge of their society and its needs and resources, the national authorities are in principle better placed than the international judge to appreciate what measures are appropriate in this area

and consequently the margin of appreciation available to them should be a wide one. It would, in the Court's view, be artificial in this respect to divorce the decision as to the compensation terms from the actual decision to nationalise, since the factors influencing the latter will of necessity also influence the former. Accordingly, the Court's power of review in the present case is limited to ascertaining whether the decisions regarding compensation fell outside the United Kingdom's wide margin of appreciation; it will respect the legislature's judgment in this connection unless that judgment was manifestly without reasonable foundation.

F. Did the Compensation Awarded to the Applicants Meet the Standard Identified by the Court?

1. Issues Common to All the Applicants

(a) Approach to the Case

123. The applicants criticised the Commission for having, in its report, looked solely at the compensation system, as such, established by the 1977 Act; in their view, it should rather have examined the consequences of applying that system, but had failed to do so.

The Government, on the other hand, submitted that if the valuation method laid down by the legislation were a proper one, then it would of necessity have produced compensation that was real and effective. For them, the value of nationalised property could only be determined by the application of a proper valuation method.

124. In proceedings originating in an individual application (Article 25) (art. 25) the Court has to confine itself, as far as possible, to an examination of the concrete case before it (see, amongst numerous authorities, the Ashingdane judgment of 28 May 1985, Series A no. 93, p. 25, para. 59). In the present case, the applicants' complaint is that the 1977 Act resulted in the payment of compensation which was not reasonably related to the value of their property when it was taken. This raises issues concerning both the terms and conditions of the legislation and its effects. The Court must therefore direct its attention in the first place to the contested legislation itself, and the effects of the legislation must be considered in the context of terms and conditions which Parliament had to determine in advance and which had to be of general application to the nationalised companies.

(b) The System Established by the 1977 Act

(i) Compensation Based on Share Values

125. Parliament decided to base compensation on the value of the shares in the nationalised companies. Since, under the 1977 Act, it was the shares themselves that passed into public ownership, this decision, which was not as such contested by the applicants, appears to the Court to be appropriate. There are, moreover, well-established techniques for valuing shares, notably in the field of taxation.

The principal alternative would have been to base compensation on the value of the underlying assets but, as the Government pointed out, this would have necessitated, by reason of the different accounting practices as regards book values, a costly and time-consuming revaluation of the assets concerned. Moreover, in valuing a business which is to continue to operate as a going concern earnings may often be a more important factor than assets. In any event the chosen method did enable account to be taken of asset values, in addition to the other relevant factors (see paragraph 36 above).

126. The Court thus concludes that Parliament's decision was not in principle inconsistent with the requirements of Article 1 (P1-1).

(ii) The Hypothetical Stock Exchange Quotation Method of Valuation

127. The 1977 Act provided that the "base value" for compensation purposes of securities listed on the London Stock Exchange was to be the average of their weekly quotations during the Reference Period. The "base value" of unquoted securities was, in general, to be the base value which they would have had if they had been listed on the Stock Exchange throughout the Reference Period (see paragraph 19 above). The applicants – whose complaints all related to shares in the latter category – contended that the prescribed method was a distorted and untrue basis for valuation.

128. Notwithstanding the complexities involved in treating, for valuation purposes, shares which were not quoted as if they were quoted, the Court notes that the chosen method had a distinct advantage. Being based on the impression which a Stock Exchange investor might be presumed to have formed about the company in question, it enabled account to be taken, in an objective manner, of all relevant factors such as historic and prospec-

tive earnings, asset-backing, dividend yield and the price of any comparable quoted shares (see paragraphs 36 and 97 above). It is also a method that had been used previously, notably in the United Kingdom Iron and Steel Acts 1949 and 1967.

As the applicants pointed out, it is true that, by resorting to the information assumed to be available to investors, the system involved having regard in the first place to material that had already been published, some of which could and did relate to periods prior to the valuation reference period. However, in practice assumptions were also made as to the other – and more up-to-date – information that would have been supplied to the stock market if the shares in question had been listed (see paragraph 97 above). Moreover, utilisation of the chosen method did not prevent account being taken, in the course of the compensation negotiations, of a company's prospective earnings after the end of the Reference Period.

129. The applicants suggested that a more appropriate method would have been to estimate the price which their shares would have fetched on a sale by private treaty between a willing seller and a willing buyer. However, the Court, like the Commission, observes that even in the valuations prepared on this basis and supplied to it by the applicants recourse was had to comparisons with analogous quoted shares, notably for such purposes as the selection of an appropriate price/earnings ratio.

Apart from the fact that compensation assessed by the hypothetical Stock Exchange quotation method contained no element representing the special value of a large or controlling shareholding – a matter dealt with by the Court in paragraphs 148–150 below–, the principal difference between the methods would appear to be that a purchaser by private treaty might be assumed to have more complete information about a company than a Stock Exchange investor (see paragraph 98 above). However, the Court does not consider that this difference is of such moment as to lead to the conclusion that the United Kingdom acted unreasonably and outside its margin of appreciation in opting for the hypothetical Stock Exchange quotation method. This is especially so if one bears in mind that a degree of artificiality would also have been involved in an assumption that there would have been a willing buyer for large shareholdings in a company engaged in the particular industries concerned.

130. The Court thus concludes that recourse to the method in question was not in principle contrary to Article 1 (P1-1).

(iii) The Reference Period

131. The compensation which the applicants received was based on the value of their shares during the reference period laid down by the 1977 Act, namely 1 September 1973 to 28 February 1974 (see paragraph 19 above). This period antedated by more than three years the formal transfer of the shares (see paragraph 18 above), whereas the applicants maintained that in order to be "reasonably related" to the value of the property taken, compensation had to be assessed by reference to the value at the time of taking.

In selecting the valuation reference period, the Government sought to take a period which was as recent as possible and was also not untypical, provided always that it was not one in which the value of the shares could have been distorted by the announcement of the nationalisation or of the compensation terms: experience showed that such an announcement was liable to affect the value of the property in question, with the result that an objective valuation, free of such influences, could only be effected if the valuation date or period preceded the announcement.

132. The Court notes in the first place that the Reference Period terminated on the date of the election of the Labour Government (see paragraphs 10 and 19 above). That was the date on which the prospect of nationalisation became a reality, even though, as the applicants pointed out, the precise identity of the undertakings that would pass into public ownership was not known for certain until the 1977 Act received the Royal Assent.

The applicants argued that the sole justification for selecting a reference period preceding vesting day was to exclude the artificial influence on the value of the property caused by the threat or fact of nationalisation. They asserted that in the present case the prospect of nationalisation had not affected the profits or assets of their companies and that any impact it might have had on the value of their shares could, under the hypothetical quotation method, have been left out of account.

The Court would point out that the possibility of distortion cannot be assessed after the event and with the benefit of hindsight. In its opinion, the Government did not act unreasonably in assuming, at the time when the legislation was in the process of preparation and adoption, that the nationalisation programme would have a distorting effect on the value of the shares to be acquired. Indeed, in the circumstances which prevailed, particularly the decline after February 1974 in the value of shares generally as evidenced by the Financial Times Industrial Ordinary Share Index (see paragraph 93 above), the selection of certain later valuation reference periods might not have been universally welcomed.

133. The Court also notes that there are a number of precedents for the utilisation of a valuation reference period antedating vesting date.

Thus, such a system was incorporated in previous United Kingdom nationalisation legislation to which the applicants referred and which they admitted did provide fair and just compensation. What is more, as the Government pointed out, in none of that legislation was proof of actual distortion of prices or values a condition precedent to the operation of the system.

134. The applicants also laid considerable stress on the references in international-law cases to valuation as at vesting date. The Court, however, does not find these references to be persuasive. Some of the cases cited did not raise issues comparable to those in the present case; moreover, in many international cases the date of the nationalisation announcement and the date of taking were, in fact, one and the same, with the result that there was no period during which a threat of impending nationalisation could have caused distortion. In any event, international practice does not show that only the vesting date can be taken as the basis for valuation.

135. For these reasons, the choice of the Reference Period was not, in the Court's view, in principle inconsistent with Article 1 (P1-1).

(iv) Conclusion Regarding the System Established by the 1977 Act

136. The Court thus concludes that, as regards the compensation system established by the 1977 Act, as such, none of its components can be regarded as in principle unacceptable in terms of Protocol No. 1 (P1).

*(c) The Effects of the System Established
by the 1977 Act*

(i) Introduction

137. The applicants have furnished to the Court copious material in support of their plea that there was a gross disproportionality between the compensation awarded and the actual value of their nationalised undertakings on Vesting Day. Whilst the Government have not in general commented on this material, they have indicated that they are not to be taken as having accepted it as correct (see paragraph 39 above).

The Court notes that the alleged disproportionality is basically attributable to three general effects of the system established by the 1977 Act; it will examine these effects in turn.

(ii) Absence of Allowance for Developments between 1974 and 1977 in the Companies Concerned

138. The applicants contended that they had not received fair compensation because, under the 1977 Act, the shares in the nationalised companies fell to be valued as at the Reference Period. They complained that the effect of this provision was to exclude any allowance for subsequent developments in the companies' fortunes up to Vesting Day and, in particular, for the growth that occurred in the undertakings with which the present case is concerned.

The Commission expressed the view that it was within the bounds of Article 1 of Protocol No. 1 (P1-1) for the British legislature to see the growth after the commencement of the nationalisation process as growth for which compensation would not necessarily be due.

139. This complaint calls for the following initial observations on the part of the Court.

(a) When a nationalisation measure is adopted, it is essential – and this the applicants accepted – that the compensation terms be fixed in advance. This is not only in the interests of legal certainty but also because it would clearly be impractical, especially where a large number of undertakings is involved, to leave compensation to be assessed and fixed subsequently on an ad hoc basis or on whatever basis the Government might at their discretion select in each individual case. The Court recognises the need to establish at the outset a common formula which, even if tempered with a degree of inbuilt flexibility, is applicable across the board to all the companies concerned.

(b) Compensation based on Reference Period values remained payable not only in respect of companies whose fortunes improved between then and Vesting Day but also in respect of companies whose fortunes declined. The public sector thus not only reaped the benefit of any appreciation but also bore the burden of any depreciation. It is true, as the applicants pointed out, that in the course of the legislative process certain companies might have been excluded from the nationalisation programme and that in fact Drypool Group Ltd., which had become insolvent, was so excluded (see paragraphs 14–15 above). However, this one case does not alter the fact that, as regards the companies which were actually nationalised, there was also a risk that remained at the end of the day with the public sector; indeed it appears probable that some of the nationalised companies, other than those with which the present proceedings are concerned, did decline in value between 1974 and 1977.

(c) Admittedly, such growth in the applicants' companies as may have occurred in the period in question may have been partly attributable to their efforts, notably in fulfilment of their statutory obligations to shareholders. However, it cannot be excluded that it was also partly attributable to a wide variety of factors some of which were outside the applicants' control, such as the very prospect of nationalisation and the provision of Government financial assistance to ensure the companies' continuing viability.

(d) Under the hypothetical Stock Exchange quotation method of valuation, future developments in the companies' fortunes were taken into account as one of the "relevant factors", to the extent that those developments could have been foreseen by a prudent investor in the Reference Period (see paragraph 97 above).

140. The applicants emphasised at the hearings before the Court that the duty to ensure fairness as regards the quantum of compensation was a continuing duty. Accordingly, a compensation formula which might have been fair when initially selected should be modified if, as here, it ceased to be so as a result of supervening developments.

141. The Court would observe that the long interval between the Reference Period and Vesting Day was solely the result of a very thorough democratic Parliamentary process during which criticisms substantially identical to those made by the applicants in the present proceedings were exhaustively discussed (see paragraphs 13 and 16 above). In particular, the possibility of amending the statutory compensation formula to take account of intervening developments was fully debated and rejected.

142. Whilst these historical facts are not of themselves decisive, the Court notes that the discussions at the time highlight the following difficulties which would have been involved in modifying the proposed system.

(a) Any amendment would have undermined the legal certainty created by the initial choice of compensation formula.

(b) The announcement of the compensation terms had created certain public expectations, on the basis of which share dealings had taken place.

(c) Between 1974 and 1977 the Financial Times Industrial Ordinary Share Index fluctuated; at times – and in particular between the end of the Reference Period and March 1975 (when the compensation terms were first announced) – it stood below the figure obtaining at the end of the Reference Period (see paragraph 93 above). The selection of a different date or period might therefore have been disadvantageous for former owners; indeed, retention of the reference period initially chosen served to protect them against any adverse effects of a decline in stock market prices.

(d) The Court has already observed that the United Kingdom Government did not act unreasonably in selecting, with a view to ensuring that the valuation of the applicants' shares be effected free of any distorting influences, a valuation reference period that preceded the announcement of the nationalisation (see paragraph 132 above). Since the risk of distortion continued to exist until the shares passed into public ownership, to have opted, by way of modification of the original terms, for a later reference period would have left room for those influences to take effect.

143. In coming to its conclusion on this aspect of the case, the Court attaches particular importance to the considerations that nationalisation is a measure of a general economic nature in regard to which the State must be allowed a wide margin of appreciation (see paragraph 122 above) and that it requires the adoption of legislation laying down a common compensation formula (see paragraph 139 above). Moreover, the system established by the 1977 Act has been found not to be in principle unacceptable in terms of Protocol No. 1 (P1) (see paragraph 136 above). In view of these factors and also of the aggregate of the other considerations set out in paragraphs 139 and 141–142 above, the Court is of the opinion that there are sufficiently cogent reasons to regard the decision to adopt provisions making no allowance for intervening developments in the companies concerned as one which the United Kingdom was reasonably entitled to take in the exercise of its margin of appreciation.

(iii) Absence of Allowance for Inflation

144. The applicants referred to the facts that the 1977 Act tied the amount of compensation to Reference Period values and that compensation was not paid until some years later. Seen in combination, these facts, it was argued, meant that they had not received fair compensation since no account had been taken of the fall in the value of money between 1974 and the date of payment, a period of high inflation (see paragraph 92 above).

145. As regards the facts underlying this complaint, the Court observes that compensation bore interest – at a rate reasonably close to the average Bank of England minimum lending rate – as from Vesting Day (see paragraphs 21 (a) and 94 above), thus providing some shelter against inflation during the period from then until the date of payment. Furthermore, after Vesting Day, all the applicants received payments on account of compensation and did not have to wait until its amount had been finally determined (see paragraphs 45, 53, 64, 69, 75, 82 and 91 above).

Again, as regards the period between the Reference Period and Vesting Day, the applicants were not deprived of income from their investments since they remained entitled to dividends on the acquired securities in respect of that period. It is true that the safeguarding provisions contained in the 1977 Act imposed restrictions in this connection but, broadly speaking, they did no more than limit the amount of such dividends to the amount paid in respect of the period immediately preceding the Reference Period (see paragraph 23 above). Moreover, a higher rate was payable with the authority of the Secretary of State for Industry.

146. The information supplied to the Court reveals that in the interval between the Reference Period and Vesting Day share prices did not increase to the same extent as the Retail Price Index (see paragraphs 92–93 above). Accordingly, to have adjusted compensation by reference to that Index would have provided the applicants with an advantage not available to other investors in securities.

The Commission pointed out that the most that could have been demanded would have been that compensation be linked to the general level of share prices. It is true that between the Reference Period and the respective Vesting Days there was, according to the Financial Times Industrial Ordinary Share Index, a certain increase in share values generally (see paragraph 93 above). However, matters of this kind cannot be judged with hindsight: by effectively freezing the value of the nationalised shares at the Reference Period figure, the 1977 Act not only excluded account being taken of any increase in the share price index but also protected the applicants against any adverse effects of subsequent fluctuations in that index.

147. The Court thus considers that, in the circumstances prevailing, the decision to adopt provisions that excluded any allowance for inflation was one which the United Kingdom was reasonably entitled to take within its margin of appreciation.

(iv) Absence of an Element Representing the Special Value of a Large or Controlling Shareholding

148. The applicants referred to the facts that, under the 1977 Act, their shares were valued by the hypothetical Stock Exchange quotation method and that Stock Exchange prices represented merely what would be paid for a small parcel of shares (see paragraph 98 above). Taken in combination, these facts, it was argued, meant that they had not received fair compensation since the amounts paid to them included no element representing the special value attaching to their large – and in most of the cases controlling – shareholdings in the companies concerned.

149. As the Government rightly pointed out, a nationalisation measure cannot be assimilated to a takeover bid: the nationalising State is proceeding by compulsion and not by inducement. Accordingly, there is, in the Court's view, no warrant for holding that the applicants' compensation should have been aligned on the price that might have been offered in such a bid.

It is true that in a sale by private treaty between a willing seller and a willing buyer the price paid for the applicants' securities might have included an element representing the special value attributable to the size of their shareholdings. However, to have assessed compensation on this basis would have involved assuming that a buyer could be found for the large blocks of shares in question, an assumption which, in the case of these particular industries, would have been at least questionable.

Finally, the Court does not consider that the United Kingdom was obliged under Article 1 of Protocol No. 1 (P1-1) to treat the former owners differently according to the class or size of their shareholdings in the nationalised undertakings: it did not act unreasonably in taking the view that compensation would be more fairly allocated if all the owners were treated alike.

150. In these circumstances, the Court considers that the decision to adopt provisions that excluded from the compensation an element representing the special value of the applicants' large or controlling shareholdings was one which the United Kingdom was reasonably entitled to take within its margin of appreciation.

(v) Conclusion Regarding the Effects of the System Established by the 1977 Act

151. In the light of the foregoing, the Court concludes, as regards the issues common to all the applicants, that the effects produced by the system established by the 1977 Act were not incompatible with Article 1 of Protocol No. 1 P1-1).

In reaching this conclusion, the Court has also had regard to certain aspects of the method of payment of compensation which were advantageous to the former owners: thus, interest, at a reasonable rate, accrued on compensation as from Vesting Day, payments on account were made as early as practicable and the balance was paid as soon as the final amount had been determined (see paragraphs 20–21 and 45, 53, 64, 69, 75, 82 and 91 above).

2. Issues Specific to Individual Applicants

152. In addition to the common issues dealt with above, certain of the applicants alleged that, by reason of factors specific to their individual cases, their award of compensation failed to meet the

requirements of Article 1 of Protocol No. 1 (P1-1). Their complaints, which were contested by the Government and rejected by the Commission, will be considered in turn.

(a) Alleged Disparity between Compensation and Reference Period Values (Kincaid and Yarrow Shipbuilders Cases)

153. By way of alternative plea, Sir William Lithgow and Yarrow PLC asserted that the compensation they received did not represent even the value as at the Reference Period of their shares in Kincaid and Yarrow Shipbuilders, respectively.

154. The Court notes that this complaint amounts in essence to a submission that the 1977 Act was misapplied.

It has, however, to be pointed out that the sums offered by the Department of Industry at the close of the negotiations were agreed to by the respective Stockholders' Representatives, as an acceptable valuation within the confines of the statutory formula. Furthermore, the Arbitration Tribunal could have been seized in both cases of a claim by the Representative that the former owners were entitled under that formula to more than was being offered. Admittedly, such a course might not have been open to Sir William Lithgow himself, although this point is disputed (see paragraph 30 above). However, the other Kincaid shareholders raised no objection (see paragraph 44 above) and he was in any event bound – and, for the reasons developed in paragraphs 193–197 below, legitimately so – by the collective system established by the 1977 Act.

155. In these circumstances, the Court sees no reason to doubt that the results of the agreements were reasonable valuations, within the confines of the statutory formula. It accordingly rejects this complaint.

(b) Incidence of Capital Gains Tax (Kincaid Case)

156. Sir William Lithgow complained of the fact that although the Treasury Stock which he received by way of compensation was not subject to tax on receipt, disposal or redemption thereof rendered him liable to capital gains tax (see paragraphs 21 (b) and 45 above). In his view, his compensation was thus not "effective", in that it did not enable him to purchase equivalent replacement assets.

157. This complaint does not appear to the Court to be well-founded. As the Commission pointed out, the applicant would also have been potentially liable to such tax had he disposed before 1977 of his original shareholding in Kincaid. It cannot be regarded as unreasonable that the same applied on the redemption or earlier disposal of the Compensation Stock which he received in exchange for his shares.

(c) Use of an Earnings-Based Method of Valuation (Kincaid Case)

158. Sir William Lithgow complained of the fact that the compensation paid for his ordinary shares in Kincaid had been assessed by reference to its earnings rather than to its assets, and by reference to historic rather than prospective earnings. This, he said, had deprived him of the value attributable to these other factors.

159. The Court does not consider that recourse to the earnings-based method, as such, can be regarded as inappropriate in terms of Article 1 of Protocol No. 1 (P1-1). It is a route that is commonly used, especially in the context of the stock market, in valuing companies which, like Kincaid, are profitable. Moreover, neither Kincaid's prospective earnings nor its assets were actually disregarded: Messrs. Whinney Murray & Co. took the company's prospects into account in preparing their suggested valuation (see paragraph 43 above) and they reviewed that valuation against, inter alia, the criterion of asset-backing.

Above all, the Court notes that the 1977 Act provided that the "base value" of unlisted securities was to be determined having regard to "all relevant factors" (see paragraph 19 above). It did not prescribe any particular route to be used for that purpose, this being a matter for negotiation or, in default, for decision by the Arbitration Tribunal. It was therefore open to the Kincaid Stockholders' Representative – whether or not to Sir William Lithgow himself (see paragraph 154 above) – to argue in the course of the compensation negotiations that greater weight should be attached to the company's assets or prospective earnings and, if he failed to obtain satisfaction, to refer the matter to arbitration. However, the Stockholders' Representative did not do so, having, after consulting the shareholders, accepted the Government's offer (see paragraph 44 above).

160. This complaint has therefore to be rejected.

(d) Use of the Parent-Company-Related Method of Valuation (Yarrow Shipbuilders Case)

161. Yarrow complained of the fact that the compensation paid for its shares in its subsidiary Yarrow Shipbuilders had been assessed, solely so it said, by reference to the stock market price of its own (Yarrow's) shares in the Reference Period. It referred to the restrictions, which were already operative during the Reference Period, imposed by the terms of the Ministry of Defence loan on the payment of dividends by the subsidiary to the parent (see paragraph 70 above). As a result of those restrictions, Yarrow was deprived of income with which to pay dividends to its own shareholders and the price of its shares was therefore depressed. A valuation of Yarrow Shipbuilders based on that price therefore failed to reflect its profitability and prospects, factors which at the time were unknown to the stock market. The effect of this valuation method was that the compensation comprised no allowance for profits totalling £9,400,000 which Yarrow Shipbuilders had been obliged to retain as a result of the dividend restrictions (see paragraph 71 (a) above).

162. The Court does not consider that in the present case recourse to the method complained of was unacceptable in terms of Article 1 of Protocol No. 1 (P1-1). As the Commission rightly observed, it is reasonable, when valuing a subsidiary whose activities, like those of Yarrow Shipbuilders, represent a substantial part of the total activities of the parent (see paragraph 70 above), to have regard to the price of the latter's shares.

Furthermore, it has to be recalled that the 1977 Act did not prescribe any specific route for arriving at the "base value" of unlisted securities: as the Commission pointed out, the stock market price of a parent company's shares was but one of the "relevant factors" to be taken into account (see paragraph 19 above). Accordingly, the Yarrow Shipbuilders Stockholders' Representative could have argued in the negotiations that too much weight was being attached to this factor and too little to the subsidiary's earnings, prospects and retained profits. Indeed, the Court notes that in the Parliamentary debates it was stated on behalf of the Government that the effects of the Ministry of Defence loan terms on the valuation of the nationalised concern would be covered by the phrase "all rel-

evant factors" (Official Report, 16 March 1976, cols. 1789–1792, 25 October 1976, cols. 198–199, and 5 November 1976, cols. 1659–1664). Again, if the Stockholders' Representative failed to obtain satisfaction on this point in the negotiations, he could have referred the matter to arbitration. However, he did not do so, having, after consulting Yarrow, accepted the Government's offer (see paragraph 74 above).

Finally, as to the effects of this valuation method, it appears to the Court that the Government, in addition to relying on the stock market price of Yarrow's shares, must have made some allowance for the earnings, prospects and retained profits of the subsidiary itself: the compensation of £6,000,000 finally paid did actually exceed the total capitalisation of Yarrow during the Reference Period, which was not more than £4,800,000 (see paragraphs 71 (c) and 74 above). That full allowance may not have been made for these items is, in the Court's view, justified by the fact that Yarrow Shipbuilders was particularly dependent on Government financial assistance, in the form either of the Ministry of Defence loan itself or of shipbuilding grants (see paragraph 71 (a) above).

163. The Court is thus unable to accept this complaint.

(e) Operation of the Safeguarding Provisions (BAC Case)

164. English Electric and Vickers complained of the fact that, under the safeguarding provisions contained in the 1977 Act, a sum of £19,700,000 in respect of certain lawfully-paid dividends had been deducted from the "base value" of their shares in BAC (see paragraphs 22–24 and 61–62 above). They alleged that this deduction was unfair and had, notably, deprived them of much of the income from the shares for the years 1973 to 1976.

165. The Court notes that the dividends in question were paid pursuant to resolutions all of which were passed after 28 February 1974, the date from which the relevant safeguarding provisions took effect. The deduction would not have been made if the dividends had been approved by the Secretary of State for Industry (see paragraph 22 above). However, it appears that, with minor exceptions, no such approval was sought until the matter was raised by the BAC Stockholders' Representative

during the course of the compensation negotiations (see paragraph 62 above).

Furthermore, there is nothing to suggest that the deduction was not in accordance with the terms of the 1977 Act: the Stockholders' Representative could otherwise have referred the matter to the Arbitration Tribunal (see paragraph 27 above), but he did not do so.

Finally, the Court would observe that the safeguarding provisions were not unreasonable per se: it was clearly necessary to prevent any dissipation of the nationalised undertakings' assets between the end of the Reference Period and Vesting Day (see paragraph 22 above). Neither does the Court consider that, when seen in terms of income yield, the result of applying those provisions can be regarded as unreasonable in terms of Article 1 of Protocol No. 1 (P1-1). The broad effect was that the amount of post-Reference Period dividends was, subject to the discretionary powers of the Secretary of State, limited to the amount paid in the immediately preceding period (see paragraph 23 above). Ensuring continuity of dividend levels in this way is consonant with the notion that any growth in the fortunes of a nationalised company after the Reference Period should accrue to the benefit of the public sector just as that sector bore the risk of any decline (see paragraph 139 (b) above).

166. For these reasons, the Court concludes that this complaint has to be rejected.

(f) Alleged Excessive Delay in Paying Compensation and Alleged Insufficiency of Payments on Account (Vickers Shipbuilding Case)

167. Vickers complained of excessive delay in the payment of compensation and of insufficiency of the payments on account, matters which were said to have retarded the implementation of major restructuring plans.

168. The Court notes from the Parliamentary debates (see paragraphs 12–16 above) the controversial nature of the 1977 Act. Until it received the Royal Assent on 17 March 1977, there was no certainty as to the form it would take and it would therefore have been virtually impossible to commence the compensation negotiations before that date. The Vickers Shipbuilding negotiations were concluded on 26 September 1980 and the final payment of compensation was made shortly thereafter,

so that, reckoning from Vesting Day (1 July 1977), the period to be taken into account for the purposes of this complaint is some three and a quarter years (see paragraphs 76 and 81–82 above).

Formal negotiations in this case were not opened until June 1978; however, the interval between the Royal Assent and that date is accounted for by the preparation not only of Messrs. Whinney Murray & Co.'s valuation report but also of financial data treating the component parts of Vickers Shipbuilding as a single enterprise (see paragraphs 33 and 79–80 above). These were complex matters. Again, the period between September 1979 and September 1980 is accounted for by the fact that the Vickers Shipbuilding Stockholders' Representative had instituted proceedings before the Arbitration Tribunal (see paragraph 81 above). In these circumstances and having regard to the size of the nationalised undertaking, the Court does not find that the overall period – of which some fifteen months were devoted to negotiations – was unreasonable.

169. As regards the payments on account, it has to be recalled that they were made unconditionally (see paragraph 20 above) and thus necessarily had to be limited in amount. Moreover, by November 1978 (some five months after the opening of formal negotiations) Vickers had received £8,450,000 on account – that is, more than half of the total compensation of £14,450,000 finally agreed – and a further payment on account, of £3,150,000, was made in March 1980, whilst the arbitration proceedings were pending (see paragraph 82 above). Above all, the totality of the compensation bore interest as from Vesting Day (see paragraph 21 (a) above) and this, bearing in mind the dates of the payments on account, must have mitigated the effects of the inevitable delay in making the final payment.

170. The Court is accordingly unable to accept these complaints.

(g) Alleged Particular Inappropriateness of the Reference Period in the Brooke Marine Case

171. The former owners of Brooke Marine alleged that the compensation provisions in the 1977 Act were particularly inappropriate in their case because during the Reference Period, but not at Vesting Day, the value of their shares in that company was adversely affected by the existence of certain unfavourable contracts and of options to

convert debenture stock into shares (see paragraph 89 above).

172. The Court agrees with the Commission that this complaint cannot be sustained. Firstly, it is necessary, in a nationalisation measure, to establish a common formula that is applicable across the board (see paragraph 139 (a) above) and the fact that, for each individual company, the most favourable valuation date is not chosen cannot be regarded as contrary to Article 1 of Protocol No. 1 (P1-1) (see, mutatis mutandis, the above-mentioned James and Others judgment, Series A no. 98, pp. 41–42, para. 68). Secondly, this particular complaint amounts in substance to a claim that valuation should have been effected as at Vesting Day, whereas the Court has already held that the utilisation for this purpose of an earlier period was neither in principle nor by reason of its effects incompatible with the said Article (see paragraphs 136 and 151 above).

(h) Disparity between Compensation Paid and Cash in Hand (Kincaid, Vosper Thornycroft, BAC, Hall Russell and Brooke Marine)

173. Sir William Lithgow and the former owners of Vosper Thornycroft, BAC, Hall Russell and Brooke Marine contrasted the amount of compensation which they had received with the amount of cash which the company concerned had in hand on Vesting Day (see paragraphs 41 (b), 47 (b), 55 (b), 66 (b) and 84 (b) above).

174. The Court is not persuaded that this factor establishes that the appropriate standard of compensation had not been met. The amount of cash in hand at Vesting Day is not a determining factor where the value of the shares which are to pass into public ownership has effectively been frozen at the start of the nationalisation process. In any event, a company's current asset position has to be determined by reference not only to cash in hand but also to such items as its liabilities and advance payments received on contracts (see paragraph 38 above).

G. Conclusion on Article 1 of Protocol No. 1 (P1-1)

175. In the light of the foregoing, the Court concludes that no violation of Article 1 of Protocol No. 1 (P1-1) has been established in the present case.

The Court is unable to accept the applicants' contention that since the Government had recognised that "the terms of compensation imposed by the 1977 Act were grossly unfair to some of the companies" (see paragraph 17 above), it was no longer open to them to argue that fair compensation had been paid. The statement in question was made as an expression of opinion in a political context and is not conclusive for the Court in making its appreciation of the case.

[. . .]

4.3. *Papamichalopoulos and Others v. Greece* (1993)

[. . .]

I. THE PARTICULAR CIRCUMSTANCES OF THE CASE

6. The applicants, who are all of Greek nationality, are the owners or co-owners of land in the area of Agia Marina Loimikou, near Marathon, Attica. On 16 March 1963 the Greek Office of Tourism gave its consent for the construction of a hotel complex on the site. At the applicants' request, an American firm of architects drew up plans.

A. The Actions for Recovery of the Land

7. By a Law of 20 August 1967 (anagastikos nomos no. 109 – "Law no. 109/1967"), which was passed some months after the dictatorship was established, the Greek State transferred an area of 1,165,000 sq. m near Agia Marina beach to the Navy Fund (Tamio Ethnikou Stolou).

Ten of the applicants, who owned part of this land (approximately 165,000 sq. m), applied to State Counsel at the Athens Court of First Instance (Isageleas Protodikon), requesting him to take interim measures and "restore the original position".

On 30 July 1968 State Counsel made three orders granting the applications, as the land in question was not public forest but consisted of agricultural land cultivated by the owners. One of the three orders, however, was revoked by State Counsel at the Athens Court of Appeal on the ground of "lack of urgency", following an application by the Navy Fund.

On 12 April 1969 the Minister of Agriculture informed Navy headquarters that part of the land transferred was not available for disposal and that it was necessary to take steps to "restore the rightful position".

8. Far from restoring the land to its owners, however, the Navy proceeded to construct a naval base and a holiday resort for officers. A royal decree of 12 November 1969 (published in the Official Gazette of 15 December 1969) designated the entire Agia Marina Loimikou region as a "naval fortress".

9. After the fall of the dictatorship in 1974, Mr Petros Papamichalopoulos, the father of the applicants Ioannis and Pantelis Papamichalopoulos, commenced proceedings in the Athens Court of First Instance to establish his title to three parcels of land. In a judgment (no. 3031/1976) given on 28 February 1976 the court held that in 1964 the plaintiff had indeed acquired title to 2,500 sq. m of land by a notarially recorded deed; that the land in question was not public forest but consisted of parcels which had been cultivated and occupied bona fide by various individuals successively since 1890; and that the Navy Fund was therefore obliged to return it.

10. The Athens Court of Appeal upheld this decision on 31 December 1976 (in judgment no. 8011/1976). It considered that the State had not transferred ownership of the land in question in 1967 since it had no title and the presumption of ownership applied only to forests, not to agricultural land.

11. An appeal on points of law by the Navy Fund was dismissed by the Court of Cassation (Arios Pagos) on 14 June 1978 (in judgment no. 775/1978), on the ground that Mr Petros Papamichalopoulos's ascendants had acquired title to their land by prescription and in accordance with the Romano-Byzantine law applicable at the time (1860).

12. On 17 July 1978 Mr Petros Papamichalopoulos sent a bailiff to serve the above-mentioned judgments on the Navy Fund with a view to their enforcement. On 28 September, accompanied by a bailiff, he went to the entrance of the naval base and sought enforcement of the court decisions, but the commanding officer of the base refused to admit them on the grounds that he had been ordered not to and that they required authorisation from Navy headquarters, which was refused. An application to State Counsel at the Court of Cassation was also unsuccessful.

13. In August 1977 Mr Karayannis and the other applicants brought two actions in the Athens Court of First Instance to establish their title to the land in issue. The State intervened in the proceedings in support of the Navy Fund.

In two interlocutory decisions of 1979 (nos. 11903 and 11904/1979) the court ordered further inquiries into the facts. It also held it necessary to commission several experts to examine the title documents in the applicants' and the Navy Fund's possession and file an opinion within five months on whether the land belonged to the plaintiffs or was part of the public forest transferred by Law no. 109/1967. However, the proceedings remained pending.

B. The Attempt to Obtain Land of Equal Value in Exchange

14. On 22 July 1980 the Minister of Defence informed the applicants that the construction of the naval base prevented return of the land in question, but that proceedings were under way with a view to a grant of other plots of land to replace those occupied by the Navy Fund.

15. On 16 October 1980 the Minister of Agriculture requested the Prefect of East Attica to transfer to the applicants land of equal value situated in that region. He stated that even though the court decisions delivered so far related to only some of the private individuals who had been dispossessed in 1967, future or pending actions brought by other owners would certainly have the same outcome.

Notwithstanding a decree of 19 June 1981 regulating building development within the "Ramnoudos" archaeological site in the Loimiko valley (in which the disputed land was situated), the Navy Fund carried on with the construction of a hotel complex within the perimeter of the naval base.

16. By a joint decision of 9 September 1981 the Minister for Economic Affairs and the Ministers of Agriculture and Defence set up a committee of experts to choose certain of the pieces of land offered in exchange by the Ministry of Agriculture and value them; among these was a plot at Dionysos

in Attica (see paragraph 27 below). The committee expressed its findings in a report of 14 January 1982.

17. In section 10 (see paragraph 29 below) of Law no. 1341/1983, published in the Official Gazette of 30 March 1983, it was expressly acknowledged that private individuals who were claiming title to land occupied by the Navy Fund were entitled to apply for other land in exchange, using the procedure laid down in Article 263 of the Rural Code (see paragraph 30 below); for this purpose it provided for a procedure for verifying title to the land in accordance with Article 246 of that code.

The explanatory memorandum on the Law contained the following:

"[S]ection [10] provides for the possibility of settling the case of the properties included in the area ... transferred to the Navy Fund under Law no. 109/1967.

This is an area of approximately 165,000 sq. m. It is claimed by a number of private individuals. Some of these have brought actions in the civil courts and obtained from the Court of Cassation a final decision in which they are acknowledged to be the owners. Having regard to the fact that the other [pending] cases are likely to have the same outcome and that paying compensation would be a solution disadvantageous to the authorities, an enactment must be passed enabling [the remaining private individuals] to replace their properties by others, which belong to the State and are available, subject to prior verification of the owners' title. ... "

18. Under this Law the applicants applied to the Athens second Expropriation Board (Epitropi apallotrioseon), composed of the President of the Athens Court of First Instance and civil-service experts. In decision no. 17/1983 of 19 September 1983 the Board acknowledged their ownership of an area of 104,018 sq. m. It stated the following:

"... it appears from the hearings, written submissions, oral statements and documents in the case file that the applicants ... occupied bona fide in continuous and regular fashion from time immemorial until 1967 an area of approximately [160,000 sq. m] situate at Agia Marina Loimikou ...; that the aforesaid area had for a long time been used

for agriculture, as shown by several items of evidence ... "

19. On 8 December 1983 the Navy Fund appealed to the Athens Court of First Instance against this decision. The Greek State joined it by intervening in the proceedings on 25 January 1984.

In a judgment of 31 May 1984 (no. 1890) the Court of First Instance declared the appeal inadmissible; in the court's opinion, only the State and the parties concerned had standing to appeal against the decision in question, and not third parties such as the Navy Fund.

20. On 29 December 1986 the Athens Court of Appeal upheld this decision.

21. The Minister for Economic Affairs lodged an appeal on points of law, which was declared inadmissible by the Court of Cassation on 8 January 1988 (in judgment no. 5/1988) on the following grounds:

"... Law no. 1341/1983 gave third parties ... who claim ownership of the tract contained within the larger area transferred to the Navy Fund the possibility of applying for the claimed land to be exchanged for another plot of equal value. ... Such exchanges will be effected in accordance with the procedure laid down in paragraphs 3, 4 and 5 of Article 263 of the Rural Code, that is to say by a decision of the Minister of Agriculture, after administrative proceedings before a tripartite board and in accordance with Article 263 of the Rural Code. ... In order to ensure that these exchanges are effected quickly and simply, the legislature has given interested parties the possibility of using the simple, quick procedure provided for in Article 246 of the Rural Code in order to have their [title] acknowledged. In adopting the aforementioned provision of section 10 of Law no. 1341/1983, it did not intend to provide, in accordance with Article 246 of the Rural Code, a solution for the dispute which might arise if the Navy Fund claimed against third parties the ownership of the area transferred by Law no. 109/1967. For that purpose the Navy Fund will have to use the procedure of ordinary law. This is apparent not only from the wording and the grammatical interpretation of the aforementioned provision ... but also from the purpose that the legislature sought to achieve ...

... In granting the right to have their title ... acknowledged only to the 'private individuals' (natural and legal persons) that own [these] areas of land ..., the legislature did not introduce any unjustified discrimination against the Navy Fund and did not deprive it of judicial protection, as it is still open to it, under ordinary-law procedure, to secure recognition of its title, which will not, however, enable it to receive other areas of land as this was not the legislature's intention ... "

On 24 June 1988 (in judgment no. 1149/1988) the Court of Cassation dismissed, on the same grounds, an appeal on points of law that had been brought by the Navy Fund.

22. On 25 July 1984 a further decree extended the geographical boundaries of the "naval fortress".

Pursuant to section 10 of Law no. 1341/1983, the Prefect of East Attica informed the Minister of Agriculture and the applicants on 11 September 1985 that some of the parcels of land offered in exchange were subject to special rules of ownership, while others had already been developed, and others again were protected by the legislation on forests.

In November 1987 the Minister of Agriculture suggested to the applicants that they should accept land in the prefecture of Pieria, 450 km from Agia Marina; it asked the Prefect of Pieria to look for land for this purpose. In view of the authorities' silence, three Members of Parliament in November 1988 put questions in Parliament to the Ministers of Defence and Agriculture asking what action had been taken in the matter. In a letter of 25 October 1990 the Pieria Agricultural Department admitted that it had been unable to find suitable land.

C. The Actions for Damages

23. On 2 December 1979 the applicants had brought two actions in the Athens Court of First Instance against the Navy Fund and the Greek State, represented by the Ministry of Finance, for damages for the loss of use of their property. In two judgments of 21 June 1985 the court adjourned the cases on the ground that verification of the applicants' title to the land had not been completed except in the case of Mr Petros Papamichalopoulos.

24. Earlier, the Navy Fund had asked the Association of Court Experts to produce a valuation of the property in issue. The designated expert obtained from the third applicant, Mr Karayannis, the opinion of all the owners in question on the documents which the Navy Fund had communicated to him. On 20 June 1986 Mr Karayannis asked the Navy Fund for information about the nature of the documents made available to the expert. On 10 March 1987 the Fund refused to provide any on the ground that the matter was of the nature of an internal procedure and this ruled out any intervention by third parties.

25. Several other actions for damages brought over a period up to 1991 were adjourned by the Athens Court of First Instance or else have not yet been heard.

D. Facts Subsequent to the Commission's Decision on the Admissibility of the Application

26. On 29 October 1991 the Ministry of Economic Affairs wrote to the State Lands Authority (Ktimatiki Etairia tou Demosiou) asking them to find land which might be used for the proposed exchange; it also drew their attention to the State's obligation to pay the applicants exorbitant sums of money if the exchange did not take place. In its answer the State Lands Authority again stated that there was no land available.

27. By decision no. 131 of the Cabinet, published in the Official Gazette of 17 October 1991, the administrative board of the Defence Fund had transferred to the Ministry of Economic Affairs ownership of 470,000 sq. m of land belonging to the disused Dounis military camp at Dionysos, Attica, in the vicinity of the land in issue (see paragraph 16 above). This land, which was intended for sale, was included in the land register and given the name "Semeli estate". On 31 May 1992 the State Lands Authority placed advertisements in the press.

On 21 July 1992 the applicants' lawyer wrote to the State Lands Authority, asking whether it would be possible to allocate the new estate to his clients; on the following day he sent an identical letter to all the relevant ministers, the President of the Legal Council of State and the Director of the Navy Fund. The applicants have not yet received any response, apart from a copy of a letter from the Ministry of Economic Affairs department responsible for public property to the State Lands Authority asking the latter to take action under its powers and notify the writer and the other public authorities dealing with the case.

[. . .]

II. Alleged Violation of Article 1 of Protocol No. 1 (P1-1)

37. In the applicants' submission, the unlawful occupation of their land by the Navy Fund since 1967 contravened Article 1 of Protocol No. 1 (P1-1), which provides:

> "Every natural or legal person is entitled to the peaceful enjoyment of his possessions. No one shall be deprived of his possessions except in the public interest and subject to the conditions provided for by law and by the general principles of international law.
>
> The preceding provisions shall not, however, in any way impair the right of a State to enforce such laws as it deems necessary to control the use of property in accordance with the general interest or to secure the payment of taxes or other contributions or penalties."

The Government rejected this submission but the Commission accepted it.

38. The Government disputed that the applicants – other than the heirs of Mr Petros Papamichalopoulos – had the status of owners, since this had not been acknowledged in any judicial decision and the proceedings brought by the applicants in 1977 had still not ended (see paragraph 13 above). The Government held the applicants responsible for the delay, attributing it to their refusal to facilitate the preparation of the expert opinion commissioned in 1979 (see paragraph 13 above).

39. The Court does not share this view.

As early as 1968 State Counsel at the Athens Court of First Instance allowed the applications made by some of the applicants for interim measures (see paragraph 7 above). Furthermore, the Minister of Agriculture, in his letter of 12 April 1969, asked Navy headquarters to take steps to "restore the rightful position". Lastly, the authorities' conduct during 1980 (see paragraphs 14–15 above) and especially the passing of Law no. 1341/1983 (see paragraph 17 above), together with the decision of the Athens second Expropriation Board (see para-

graph 18 above), tell in favour of the applicants' submission.

For the purposes of the present dispute, the applicants must therefore be regarded as the owners of the land in issue.

40. The breach claimed by the applicants began in 1967 with the passing of Law no. 109/1967 (see paragraph 7 above). At that time Greece had already ratified the Convention and Protocol No. 1 (P1), on 28 March 1953; they had already come into force in respect of Greece, on 3 September 1953 and 18 May 1954 respectively. Greece denounced them on 12 December 1969 with effect from 13 June 1970 (under Article 65 para. 1 of the Convention) (art. 65-1) but was not thereby released from its obligations under them "in respect of any act which, being capable of constituting a violation of such obligations, [might] have been performed by it" earlier (see Article 65 para. 2) (art. 65-2); it ratified them again on 28 November 1974 after the collapse of the military dictatorship established by the coup d'état of April 1967.

Admittedly, Greece did not recognise the Commission's competence to receive "individual" petitions (under Article 25) (art. 25) until 20 November 1985 and then only in relation to acts, decisions, facts or events subsequent to that date (Yearbook of the European Convention, volume 28, p. 10), but the Government did not in this instance raise any preliminary objection in this regard and the question does not call for consideration by the Court of its own motion. The Court notes merely that the applicants' complaints relate to a continuing situation, which still obtains at the present time.

41. The occupation of the land in issue by the Navy Fund represented a clear interference with the applicants' exercise of their right to the peaceful enjoyment of their possessions. The interference was not for the purpose of controlling the use of property within the meaning of the second paragraph of Article 1 of Protocol No. 1 (P1-1). Moreover, the applicants were never formally expropriated: Law no. 109/1967 did not transfer ownership of the land in question to the Navy Fund.

42. Since the Convention is intended to safeguard rights that are "practical and effective", it has to be ascertained whether the situation complained of amounted nevertheless to a de facto expropriation, as was argued by the applicants (see, among other authorities, the Sporrong and Lönnroth v. Sweden

judgment of 23 September 1982, Series A no. 52, p. 24, para. 63).

43. It must be remembered that in 1967, under a Law enacted by the military government of the time, the Navy Fund took possession of a large area of land which included the applicants' land; it established a naval base there and a holiday resort for officers and their families.

From that date the applicants were unable either to make use of their property or to sell, bequeath, mortgage or make a gift of it; Mr Petros Papamichalopoulos, the only one who obtained a final court decision ordering the Navy to return his property to him, was even refused access to it (see paragraphs 11–12 above).

44. The Court notes, however, that as early as 1969 the authorities had drawn the Navy's attention to the fact that part of the land was not available for disposal (see paragraph 7 above). After democracy had been restored, they sought means of making good the damage caused to the applicants. Thus in 1980 they recommended, if not returning the land, at least exchanging it for other land of equal value (see paragraphs 15–16 above). This initiative led to the enacting of Law no. 1341/1983, which was designed to settle as quickly as possible – in the very terms of the Court of Cassation's judgment of 8 January 1988 – the problem created in 1967 (see paragraph 21 above). The Athens second Expropriation Board having recognised them all in 1983 as having title (see paragraphs 18–21 above), the applicants thereafter awaited allocation of the promised land. However, neither the land in Attica nor the land in Pieria was able to be used for the proposed scheme (see paragraph 22 above); in 1992 the applicants attempted to secure part of the "Semeli estate" but again without success (see paragraph 27 above).

45. The Court considers that the loss of all ability to dispose of the land in issue, taken together with the failure of the attempts made so far to remedy the situation complained of, entailed sufficiently serious consequences for the applicants de facto to have been expropriated in a manner incompatible with their right to the peaceful enjoyment of their possessions.

46. In conclusion, there has been and there continues to be a breach of Article 1 of Protocol No. 1 (P1-1).

[. . .]

4.4. *Loizidou v. Turkey* (1996) and *Damages* (1998)

[. . .]

As to the Facts

Particular Circumstances of the Case

11. The applicant, a Cypriot national, grew up in Kyrenia in northern Cyprus. In 1972 she married and moved with her husband to Nicosia.

12. She claims to be the owner of plots of land nos. 4609, 4610, 4618, 4619, 4748, 4884, 5002, 5004, 5386 and 5390 in Kyrenia in northern Cyprus and she alleges that prior to the Turkish occupation of northern Cyprus on 20 July 1974, work had commenced on plot no. 5390 for the construction of flats, one of which was intended as a home for her family. Her ownership of the properties is attested by certificates of registration issued by the Cypriot Lands and Surveys Department at the moment of acquisition.

She states that she has been prevented in the past, and is still prevented, by Turkish forces from returning to Kyrenia and "peacefully enjoying" her property.

13. On 19 March 1989 the applicant participated in a march organised by a women's group ("Women Walk Home" movement) in the village of Lymbia near the Turkish village of Akincilar in the occupied area of northern Cyprus. The aim of the march was to assert the right of Greek Cypriot refugees to return to their homes.

Leading a group of fifty marchers she advanced up a hill towards the Church of the Holy Cross in the Turkish-occupied part of Cyprus passing the United Nations' guard post on the way. When they reached the churchyard they were surrounded by Turkish soldiers and prevented from moving any further.

14. She was eventually detained by members of the Turkish Cypriot police force and brought by ambulance to Nicosia. She was released around midnight, having been detained for more than ten hours.

15. In his report of 31 May 1989 (Security Council document S/20663) on the United Nations Operation in Cyprus (for the period 1 December 1988–31

May 1989) the Secretary-General of the United Nations described the demonstration of 19 March 1989 as follows (at paragraph 11):

> "In March 1989, considerable tension occurred over the well-publicized plans of a Greek Cypriot women's group to organize a large demonstration with the announced intention of crossing the Turkish forces cease-fire line. In this connection it is relevant to recall that, following violent demonstrations in the United Nations buffer-zone in November 1988, the Government of Cyprus had given assurances that it would in future do whatever was necessary to ensure respect for the buffer-zone ... Accordingly, UNFICYP asked the Government to take effective action to prevent any demonstrators from entering the buffer-zone, bearing in mind that such entry would lead to a situation that might be difficult to control. The demonstration took place on 19 March 1989. An estimated 2,000 women crossed the buffer-zone at Lymbia and some managed to cross the Turkish forces' line. A smaller group crossed that line at Akhna. At Lymbia, a large number of Turkish Cypriot women arrived shortly after the Greek Cypriots and mounted a counter demonstration, remaining however on their side of the line. Unarmed Turkish soldiers opposed the demonstrators and, thanks largely to the manner in which they and the Turkish Cypriot police dealt with the situation, the demonstration passed without serious incident. Altogether, 54 demonstrators were arrested by Turkish Cypriot police in the two locations; they were released to UNFICYP later the same day."

A. Turkish Military Presence in Northern Cyprus

16. Turkish armed forces of more than 30,000 personnel are stationed throughout the whole of the occupied area of northern Cyprus, which is constantly patrolled and has checkpoints on all main lines of communication. The army's headquarters are in Kyrenia. The 28th Infantry Division is based in Asha (Assia) with its sector covering Famagusta to the Mia Milia suburb of Nicosia and with about 14,500 personnel. The 39th Infantry Division, with about 15,500 personnel, is based at Myrtou village, and its sector ranges from Yerolakkos village to Lefka. TOURDYK (Turkish Forces in Cyprus under the Treaty of Guarantee) is stationed at Orta Keuy

village near Nicosia, with a sector running from Nicosia International Airport to the Pedhieos River. A Turkish naval command and outpost are based at Famagusta and Kyrenia respectively. Turkish airforce personnel are based at Lefkoniko, Krini and other airfields. The Turkish airforce is stationed on the Turkish mainland at Adana.

17. The Turkish forces and all civilians entering military areas are subject to Turkish military courts, as stipulated so far as concerns "TRNC citizens" by the Prohibited Military Areas Decree of 1979 (section 9) and Article 156 of the Constitution of the "TRNC".

B. Article 159 (1) (b) of the "TRNC" Constitution

18. Article 159 (1) (b) of the 7 May 1985 Constitution of the "Turkish Republic of Northern Cyprus" (the "TRNC") provides, where relevant, as follows:

> "All immovable properties, buildings and installations which were found abandoned on 13 February 1975 when the Turkish Federated State of Cyprus was proclaimed or which were considered by law as abandoned or owner-less after the above-mentioned date, or which should have been in the possession or control of the public even though their ownership had not yet been determined ... and ... situated within the boundaries of the TRNC on 15 November 1983, shall be the property of the TRNC notwithstanding the fact that they are not so registered in the books of the Land Registry Office; and the Land Registry Office shall be amended accordingly."

C. The International Response to the Establishment of the "TRNC"

19. On 18 November 1983, in response to the proclamation of the establishment of the "TRNC", the United Nations Security Council adopted Resolution 541 (1983) which provides, where relevant, as follows:

> "The Security Council ...
>
> 1. Deplores the declaration of the Turkish Cypriot authorities of the purported secession of part of the Republic of Cyprus;

2. Considers the declaration...as legally invalid and calls for its withdrawal . . .

6. Calls upon all States to respect the sovereignty, independence, territorial integrity and non-alignment of the Republic of Cyprus;

7. Calls upon all States not to recognise any Cypriot State other than the Republic of Cyprus . . ."

20. Resolution 550 (1984), adopted on 11 May 1984 in response to the exchange of "ambassadors" between Turkey and the "TRNC" stated, inter alia:

"The Security Council . . .

1. Reaffirms its Resolution 541 (1983) and calls for its urgent and effective implementation;

2. Condemns all secessionist actions, including the purported exchange of ambassadors between Turkey and the Turkish Cypriot leadership, declares them illegal and invalid and calls for their immediate withdrawal;

3. Reiterates the call upon all States not to recognise the purported State of the "Turkish Republic of Northern Cyprus" set up by secessionist acts and calls upon them not to facilitate or in any way assist the aforesaid secessionist entity;

4. Calls upon all States to respect the sovereignty, independence, territorial integrity, unity and non-alignment of the Republic of Cyprus . . . "

21. In November 1983, the Committee of Ministers of the Council of Europe decided that it continued to regard the Government of the Republic of Cyprus as the sole legitimate Government of Cyprus and called for the respect of the sovereignty, independence, territorial integrity and unity of the Republic of Cyprus.

22. On 16 November 1983 the European Communities issued the following statement:

"The ten Member States of the European Community are deeply concerned by the declaration purporting to establish a 'Turkish Republic of Northern Cyprus' as an independent State. They reject this declaration, which is in disregard of successive resolutions of the United Nations. The Ten reiterate their unconditional support for the independence, sovereignty, territorial integrity and

unity of the Republic of Cyprus. They continue to regard the Government of President Kyprianou as the sole legitimate Government of the Republic of Cyprus. They call upon all interested parties not to recognize this act, which creates a very serious situation in the area."

23. The Commonwealth Heads of Government, meeting in New Delhi from 23 to 29 November 1983, issued a press communiqué stating, inter alia, as follows:

"[The] Heads of Government condemned the declaration by the Turkish Cypriot authorities issued on 15 November 1983 to create a secessionist state in northern Cyprus, in the area under foreign occupation. Fully endorsing Security Council Resolution 541, they denounced the declaration as legally invalid and reiterated the call for its non-recognition and immediate withdrawal. They further called upon all States not to facilitate or in any way assist the illegal secessionist entity. They regarded this illegal act as a challenge to the international community and demanded the implementation of the relevant UN Resolutions on Cyprus."

D. The Turkish Declaration of 22 January 1990 under Article 46 of the Convention Art. 46

24. On 22 January 1990, the Turkish Minister for Foreign Affairs deposited the following declaration with the Secretary General of the Council of Europe pursuant to Article 46 of the Convention (art. 46):

"On behalf of the Government of the Republic of Turkey and acting in accordance with Article 46 (art. 46) of the European Convention for the Protection of Human Rights and Fundamental Freedoms, I hereby declare as follows:

The Government of the Republic of Turkey acting in accordance with Article 46 (art. 46) of the European Convention for the Protection of Human Rights and Fundamental Freedoms, hereby recognises as compulsory ipso facto and without special agreement the jurisdiction of the European Court of Human Rights in all matters concerning the interpretation and application of the Convention which relate to the exercise of jurisdiction within the meaning of Article 1 of the Convention (art. 1), performed within the boundaries of the national territory of the Republic of Turkey, and provided further that such matters have previously been examined by the Commission within the power conferred upon it by Turkey.

This Declaration is made on condition of reciprocity, including reciprocity of obligations assumed under the Convention. It is valid for a period of 3 years as from the date of its deposit and extends to matters raised in respect of facts, including judgments which are based on such facts which have occurred subsequent to the date of deposit of the present Declaration."

25. The above declaration was renewed for a period of three years as from 22 January 1993 in substantially the same terms.

Proceedings before the Commission

26. Mrs Loizidou lodged her application (no. 15318/89) on 22 July 1989. She complained that her arrest and detention involved violations of Articles 3, 5 and 8 of the Convention (art. 3, art. 5, art. 8). She further complained that the refusal of access to her property constituted a continuing violation of Article 8 of the Convention (art. 8) and Article 1 of Protocol No. 1 (P1-1).

27. On 4 March 1991 the Commission declared the applicant's complaints admissible in so far as they raised issues under Articles 3, 5 and 8 (art. 3, art. 5, art. 8) in respect of her arrest and detention and Article 8 and Article 1 of Protocol No. 1 (art. 8, P1-1) concerning continuing violations of her right of access to property alleged to have occurred subsequent to 29 January 1987. Her complaint under the latter two provisions (art. 8, P1-1) of a continuing violation of her property rights before 29 January 1987 was declared inadmissible.

In its report of 8 July 1993 (Article 31) (art. 31), it expressed the opinion that there had been no violation of Article 3 (art. 3) (unanimously); Article 8 (art. 8) as regards the applicant's private life (eleven votes to two); Article 5 para. 1 (art. 5-1) (nine votes to four); Article 8 (art. 8) as regards the applicant's home (nine votes to four) and Article 1 of Protocol No. 1 (P1-1) (eight votes to five). The full text of the Commission's opinion and of the three separate opinions contained in the report is reproduced

as an annex to the Loizidou v. Turkey judgment of 23 March 1995 (preliminary objections), Series A no. 310.

Final Submissions to the Court

28. In her memorial, the applicant requested the Court to decide and declare:

1. that the respondent State is responsible for the continuing violations of Article 1 of Protocol No. 1 (P1-1);

2. that the respondent State is responsible for the continuing violations of Article 8 (art. 8);

3. that the respondent State is under a duty to provide just satisfaction in accordance with the provisions of Article 50 of the Convention (art. 50); and

4. that the respondent State is under a duty to permit the applicant to exercise her rights, in accordance with the findings of violations of the Protocol and Convention, freely in the future.

29. The Cypriot Government submitted that:

1. the Court has jurisdiction ratione temporis to deal with the applicant's case because Turkey's declaration under Article 46 of the Convention (art. 46) did not clearly exclude competence in respect of violations examined by the Commission after the Turkish declaration of 22 January 1990. Turkey is thus liable for the continuing violations complained of by the applicant in the period since 28 January 1987;

2. in any event Turkey is liable for those violations continuing in the period since 22 January 1990 and which have been examined by the Commission;

3. there is a permanent state of affairs, still continuing, in the Turkish-occupied area, which is in violation of the applicant's rights under Article 8 of the Convention (art. 8) and Article 1 of Protocol No. 1 (P1-1).

30. In their memorial, the Turkish Government made the following submissions:

1. the applicant was irreversibly deprived of her property situated in northern Cyprus by an act of the "Government of the Turkish Republic of Northern Cyprus", on 7 May 1985, at the latest;

2. the act referred to under (1) above does not constitute an act of "jurisdiction" by Turkey within the meaning of Article 1 of the Convention (art. 1);

3. Turkey has not violated the rights of the applicant under Article 8 of the Convention (art. 8).

[. . .]

II. ALLEGED VIOLATION OF ARTICLE 1 OF PROTOCOL NO. 1 (P1-1)

48. The applicant contended that the continuous denial of access to her property in northern Cyprus and the ensuing loss of all control over it are imputable to the Turkish Government and constitute a violation of Article 1 of Protocol No. 1 (P1-1), which reads as follows:

> "Every natural or legal person is entitled to the peaceful enjoyment of his possessions. No one shall be deprived of his possessions except in the public interest and subject to the conditions provided for by law and by the general principles of international law.
>
> The preceding provisions (P1-1) shall not, however, in any way impair the right of a State to enforce such laws as it deems necessary to control the use of property in accordance with the general interest or to secure the payment of taxes or other contributions or penalties."

A. The Imputability Issue

49. The applicant insisted, in line with her submissions concerning the preliminary objection ratione materiae (Loizidou judgment (preliminary objections) cited above at paragraph 32, pp. 22–23, paras. 57–58), that the present case was exceptional in that the authorities alleged to have interfered with the right to the peaceful enjoyment of possessions are not those of the sole legitimate Government of the territory in which the property is situated. That particularity entailed that, in order to determine whether Turkey is responsible for the alleged violation of her rights under Article 1 of Protocol No. 1 (P1-1) with respect to her possessions in northern Cyprus, the Court should take into account the principles of State responsibility under international law. In this context Mrs Loizidou repeated her criticism that the Commission had focused too much on the direct involvement of Turkish officials in the impugned continuous

denial of access. Whilst evidence of direct involvement of Turkish officials in violations of the Convention is relevant, it is not a legal condition of responsibility under public international law.

She went on to contend that the concept of State responsibility rested on a realistic notion of accountability. A State was responsible in respect of events in the area for which it is internationally responsible, even if the conduct or events were outside its actual control. Thus, even acts of officials which are ultra vires may generate State responsibility.

According to international law, in the applicant's submission, the State which is recognised as accountable in respect of a particular territory remained accountable even if the territory is administered by a local administration. This was the legal position whether the local administration is illegal, in that it is the consequence of an illegal use of force, or whether it is lawful, as in the case of a protected State or other dependency. A State cannot by delegation avoid responsibility for breaches of its duties under international law, especially not for breaches of its duties under the Convention which, as illustrated by the wording of Article 1 of the Convention (art. 1), involve a guarantee to secure Convention rights.

Mrs Loizidou maintained that the creation of the "TRNC" was legally invalid and no State, except Turkey, or international organisation has recognised it. Since the Republic of Cyprus obviously cannot be held accountable for the part of the island occupied by Turkey, it must be Turkey which is so accountable. Otherwise the northern part of Cyprus would constitute a vacuum as regards responsibility for violations of human rights, the acceptance of which would be contrary to the principle of effectiveness which underlies the Convention. In any case there is overwhelming evidence that Turkey has effective overall control over events in the occupied area. She added that the fact that the Court, at the preliminary objections phase of the present case, had found Turkey to have jurisdiction created a strong presumption of Turkish responsibility for violations occurring in the occupied area.

50. According to the Cypriot Government, Turkey is in effective military and political control of northern Cyprus. It cannot escape from its duties under international law by pretending to hand over

the administration of northern Cyprus to an unlawful "puppet" regime.

51. The Turkish Government denied that they had jurisdiction in northern Cyprus within the meaning of Article 1 of the Convention (art. 1). In the first place they recalled the earlier case-law of the Commission which limited the jurisdiction of Turkey "to the border area and not to the whole of northern Cyprus under the control of the Turkish Cypriot authorities" (see the Commission's decisions on the admissibility of applications nos. 6780/74, 6950/75 and 8007/77, cited in paragraph 42 above). In the second place, the presumption of control and responsibility argued for by the applicants was rebuttable.

In this respect it was highly significant that the Commission in the Chrysostomos and Papachrysostomou v. Turkey report of 8 July 1993 found that the applicants' arrest, detention and trial in northern Cyprus were not "acts" imputable to Turkey. Moreover, the Commission found no indication of control exercised by the Turkish authorities over the prison administration or the administration of justice by Turkish Cypriot authorities in the applicant's case (cited above at paragraph 32).

In addition, the Turkish Government contended that the question of jurisdiction in Article 1 of the Convention (art. 1) is not identical with the question of State responsibility under international law. Article 1 (art. 1) was not couched in terms of State responsibility. In their submission this provision (art. 1) required proof that the act complained of was actually committed by an authority of the defendant State or occurred under its direct control and that this authority at the time of the alleged violation exercised effective jurisdiction over the applicant.

Furthermore they argued that seen from this angle, Turkey had not in this case exercised effective control and jurisdiction over the applicant since at the critical date of 22 January 1990 the authorities of the Turkish Cypriot community, constitutionally organised within the "TRNC" and in no way exercising jurisdiction on behalf of Turkey, were in control of the property rights of the applicant.

In this context they again emphasised that the "TRNC" is a democratic and constitutional State which is politically independent of all other sovereign States including Turkey. The administration in northern Cyprus has been set up by the Turkish Cypriot people in the exercise of its right to self-determination and not by Turkey. Moreover, the Turkish forces in northern Cyprus are there for the protection of the Turkish Cypriots and with the consent of the ruling authority of the "TRNC". Neither the Turkish forces nor the Turkish Government in any way exercise governmental authority in northern Cyprus. Furthermore, in assessing the independence of the "TRNC" it must also be borne in mind that there are political parties as well as democratic elections in northern Cyprus and that the Constitution was drafted by a constituent assembly and adopted by way of referendum.

52. As regards the question of imputability, the Court recalls in the first place that in its above-mentioned Loizidou judgment (preliminary objections) (pp. 23–24, para. 62) it stressed that under its established case-law the concept of "jurisdiction" under Article 1 of the Convention (art. 1) is not restricted to the national territory of the Contracting States. Accordingly, the responsibility of Contracting States can be involved by acts and omissions of their authorities which produce effects outside their own territory. Of particular significance to the present case the Court held, in conformity with the relevant principles of international law governing State responsibility, that the responsibility of a Contracting Party could also arise when as a consequence of military action – whether lawful or unlawful – it exercises effective control of an area outside its national territory. The obligation to secure, in such an area, the rights and freedoms set out in the Convention, derives from the fact of such control whether it be exercised directly, through its armed forces, or through a subordinate local administration (see the above-mentioned Loizidou judgment (preliminary objections), ibid.).

53. In the second place, the Court emphasises that it will concentrate on the issues raised in the present case, without, however, losing sight of the general context.

54. It is important for the Court's assessment of the imputability issue that the Turkish Government have acknowledged that the applicant's loss of control of her property stems from the occupation of the northern part of Cyprus by Turkish troops and the establishment there of the "TRNC" (see the above-mentioned preliminary objections judgment, p. 24, para. 63). Furthermore, it has not been

disputed that the applicant has on several occasions been prevented by Turkish troops from gaining access to her property (see paragraphs 12–13 above).

However, throughout the proceedings the Turkish Government have denied State responsibility for the matters complained of, maintaining that its armed forces are acting exclusively in conjunction with and on behalf of the allegedly independent and autonomous "TRNC" authorities.

55. The Court recalls that under the scheme of the Convention the establishment and verification of the facts is primarily a matter for the Commission (Articles 28 para. 1 and 31) (art. 28-1, art. 31). It is not, however, bound by the Commission's findings of fact and remains free to make its own appreciation in the light of all the material before it (see, inter alia, the Cruz Varas and Others v. Sweden judgment of 20 March 1991, Series A no. 201, p. 29, para. 74, the Klaas v. Germany judgment of 22 September 1993, Series A no. 269, p. 17, para. 29, and the McCann and Others v. the United Kingdom judgment of 27 September 1995, Series A no. 324, p. 50, para. 168).

56. The Commission found that the applicant has been and continues to be denied access to the northern part of Cyprus as a result of the presence of Turkish forces in Cyprus which exercise an overall control in the border area (see the report of the Commission of 8 July 1993, p. 16, paras. 93–95). The limited ambit of this finding of "control" must be seen in the light of the Commission's characterisation of the applicant's complaint as essentially concerning freedom of movement across the buffer-zone (see paragraphs 59 and 61 below). The Court, however, must assess the evidence with a view to determining the issue whether the continuous denial of access to her property and the ensuing loss of all control over it is imputable to Turkey.

It is not necessary to determine whether, as the applicant and the Government of Cyprus have suggested, Turkey actually exercises detailed control over the policies and actions of the authorities of the "TRNC". It is obvious from the large number of troops engaged in active duties in northern Cyprus (see paragraph 16 above) that her army exercises effective overall control over that part of the island. Such control, according to the relevant test and in the circumstances of the case, entails her responsibility for the policies and actions of the "TRNC" (see paragraph 52 above). Those affected by such policies or actions therefore come within the "jurisdiction" of Turkey for the purposes of Article 1 of the Convention (art. 1). Her obligation to secure to the applicant the rights and freedoms set out in the Convention therefore extends to the northern part of Cyprus.

In view of this conclusion the Court need not pronounce itself on the arguments which have been adduced by those appearing before it concerning the alleged lawfulness or unlawfulness under international law of Turkey's military intervention in the island in 1974 since, as noted above, the establishment of State responsibility under the Convention does not require such an enquiry (see paragraph 52 above). It suffices to recall in this context its finding that the international community considers that the Republic of Cyprus is the sole legitimate Government of the island and has consistently refused to accept the legitimacy of the "TRNC" as a State within the meaning of international law (see paragraph 44 above).

57. It follows from the above considerations that the continuous denial of the applicant's access to her property in northern Cyprus and the ensuing loss of all control over the property is a matter which falls within Turkey's "jurisdiction" within the meaning of Article 1 (art. 1) and is thus imputable to Turkey.

B. Interference with Property Rights

58. The applicant and the Cypriot Government emphasised that, contrary to the Commission's interpretation, the complaint is not limited to access to property but is much wider and concerns a factual situation: because of the continuous denial of access the applicant had effectively lost all control over, as well as all possibilities to use, to sell, to bequeath, to mortgage, to develop and to enjoy her land. This situation, they contended, could be assimilated to a de facto expropriation within the meaning of the Court's case-law. They denied that there had been a formal expropriation, but added that if and in so far as there had been attempts at formal expropriation the relevant enactments should be disregarded as being incompatible with international law.

59. For the Turkish Government and the Commission the case only concerns access to property, and the right to the peaceful enjoyment of possessions

does not include as a corollary a right to freedom of movement.

The Turkish Government further submitted that if the applicant was held to have absolute freedom of access to her property, irrespective of the de facto political situation on the island, this would undermine the intercommunal talks, which were the only appropriate way of resolving this problem.

60. The Court first observes from the Commission's decision on admissibility that the applicant's complaint under Article 1 of Protocol No. 1 (P1-1) was not limited to the question of physical access to her property. Her complaint, as set out in the application form to the Commission, was that Turkey, by refusing her access to property "has gradually, over the last sixteen years, affected the right of the applicant as a property owner and in particular her right to a peaceful enjoyment of her possessions, thus constituting a continuing violation of Article 1 (P1-1)" (see the report of the Commission of 8 July 1993, p. 21, and the decision of admissibility in Chrysostomos, Papachrysostomou and Loizidou v. Turkey, DR 68, p. 228). Moreover it is this complaint as formulated above that is addressed by the applicants and the Turkish Government in both their written and oral submissions.

61. Seen in the above light, the Court cannot accept the characterisation of the applicant's complaint as being limited to the right to freedom of movement. Article 1 of Protocol No. 1 (P1-1) is thus applicable.

62. With respect to the question whether Article 1 (P1-1) is violated, the Court first recalls its finding that the applicant, for purposes of this Article (P1-1), must be regarded to have remained the legal owner of the land (see paragraphs 39–47 above).

63. However, as a consequence of the fact that the applicant has been refused access to the land since 1974, she has effectively lost all control over, as well as all possibilities to use and enjoy, her property. The continuous denial of access must therefore be regarded as an interference with her rights under Article 1 of Protocol No. 1(P1-1). Such an interference cannot, in the exceptional circumstances of the present case to which the applicant and the Cypriot Government have referred (see paragraphs 49-50 above), be regarded as either a deprivation of property or a control of use within the meaning of the first and second paragraphs of Article 1 of Protocol No. 1 (P1-1-1, P1-1-2). However, it clearly falls within the meaning of the first sentence of that provision (P1-1) as an interference with the peaceful enjoyment of possessions. In this respect the Court observes that hindrance can amount to a violation of the Convention just like a legal impediment (see, mutatis mutandis, the Airey v. Ireland judgment of 9 October 1979, Series A no. 32, p. 14, para. 25).

64. Apart from a passing reference to the doctrine of necessity as a justification for the acts of the "TRNC" and to the fact that property rights were the subject of intercommunal talks, the Turkish Government have not sought to make submissions justifying the above interference with the applicant's property rights which is imputable to Turkey.

It has not, however, been explained how the need to rehouse displaced Turkish Cypriot refugees in the years following the Turkish intervention in the island in 1974 could justify the complete negation of the applicant's property rights in the form of a total and continuous denial of access and a purported expropriation without compensation.

Nor can the fact that property rights were the subject of intercommunal talks involving both communities in Cyprus provide a justification for this situation under the Convention.

In such circumstances, the Court concludes that there has been and continues to be a breach of Article 1 of Protocol No. 1 (P1-1).

III. ALLEGED VIOLATION OF ARTICLE 8 OF THE CONVENTION (ART. 8)

65. The applicant also alleged an unjustified interference with the right to respect for her home in violation of Article 8 of the Convention (art. 8), paragraph 1 of which (art. 8-1) provides, inter alia, that:

"Everyone has the right to respect for ... his home ... "

In this respect she underlined that she had grown up in Kyrenia where her family had lived for generations and where her father and grandfather had been respected medical practitioners. She conceded that after her marriage in 1972 she had moved to Nicosia and had made her home there ever since. However, she had planned to live in one of the flats whose construction had begun at the time of the Turkish occupation of northern Cyprus in 1974 (see paragraph 12 above). As a result, it had been impossible to complete the work and subsequent events had prevented her from returning to live in what she considered as her home town.

66. The Court observes that the applicant did not have her home on the land in question. In its opinion it would strain the meaning of the notion "home" in Article 8 (art. 8) to extend it to comprise property on which it is planned to build a house for residential purposes. Nor can that term be interpreted to cover an area of a State where one has grown up and where the family has its roots but where one no longer lives.

Accordingly, there has been no interference with the applicant's rights under Article (art. 8).

[. . .]

Damages (1998)

[. . .]

As to the law

19. Article 50 provides as follows:

> "If the Court finds that a decision or a measure taken by a legal authority or any other authority of a High Contracting Party is completely or partially in conflict with the obligations arising from the . . . Convention, and if the internal law of the said Party allows only partial reparation to be made for the consequences of this decision or measure, the decision of the Court shall, if necessary, afford just satisfaction to the injured party."

20. The applicant and the Cypriot Government submitted that an award of compensation should be made in the present case in the light of the Court's finding of a violation of her property rights. In the course of the hearing before the Court the applicant withdrew a claim which had been made in her memorial for the restoration of her rights.

The Turkish Government, on the other hand, submitted that there was no entitlement to just satisfaction.

I. Entitlement to Just Satisfaction

21. In the submission of the Turkish Government they cannot be held liable in international law for the acts of the "Turkish Republic of Northern Cyprus". There is no legal basis for holding Turkey liable as it is well settled in international law that the first condition that has to be satisfied for a State to incur liability is that the unlawful act or conduct is attributable to the State on whose behalf the perpetrator of the unlawful act or conduct was acting.

Regard should be had to the fact that the Commission has accepted, even in cases where the allegedly unlawful act resulted directly from the actions of a national authority, that a national authority cannot incur liability where jurisdiction in the relevant sphere has been transferred to an international organisation (see M. and Co. v. Germany, Decisions and Reports 64, p. 138).

Any power that Turkey has in Cyprus is derived from the Zürich and London Agreements of 1959 and the treaties signed in 1960, which remain in force. Subsequent agreements or texts (such as the Geneva Declaration of 30 August 1974, the "ten-point" agreement of 1979 or the Set of Ideas of 1992) have not conferred any new responsibilities on Turkey. The activity complained of, in other words the alleged unlawful act, must result directly from an act attributable to the State, whether it be an administrative act, an act of the military authorities, of the legislature or of the judiciary. There is no case where a third-party State has been held liable for the acts of another State – whether or not such State is recognised – which exercises effective authority through constitutionally established organs.

It would therefore be incompatible with principles of international law to award compensation against Turkey.

In addition, the Turkish Government stressed that the question of property rights and reciprocal compensation is the very crux of the conflict in Cyprus. These issues can only be settled through negotiations and on the basis of already agreed principles of bi-zonality and bi-communality. Inevitably the principle of bi-zonality will involve an exchange of Turkish Cypriot properties in the south with Greek Cypriot properties in the north, and, if need be, the payment of compensation for any difference. An award under Article 50 would undermine the negotiations between the two communities and would spoil the efforts to reach a settlement on the basis of agreed principles and criteria.

In conclusion, it was submitted that compensation was not "necessary" under the terms of Article 50.

Moreover the claim should be disallowed on the basis that this provision requires that the "decision" or "measure" involved be that of a "High Contracting Party". For the reasons given above that was not the situation in the present case.

22. The applicant pointed out that the Court's principal judgment on the merits had established that there was a continuous breach of Article 1 of Protocol No. 1 which was imputable to Turkey. In accordance with the principle *ubi jus ibi remedium* it was necessary to make an award to ensure that the applicant was not left without a remedy.

23. The Cypriot Government emphasised that Article 50 proceedings do not constitute an appeal from the Court's judgments on the preliminary objections and the merits. It was not open to those appearing before the Court to seek to relitigate issues upon which the Court had already decided. Article 50 was applicable in the present case since no reparation had been made by the Turkish Government in respect of the violation of the applicant's property rights.

24. The Delegate of the Commission also maintained that the applicant should receive just satisfaction. The fact that political efforts were being made to resolve the "Cyprus problem" was not a valid reason for refusing to make an award.

25. The Court recalls its finding in paragraph 57 of its principal judgment on the merits in the present case "that the continuous denial of the applicant's access to her property in northern Cyprus and the ensuing loss of all control over the property is a matter which falls within Turkey's 'jurisdiction' within the meaning of Article 1 and is thus imputable to Turkey" (the principal judgment, *Reports of Judgments and Decisions* 1996-VI, p. 2236).

The Court also found that the applicant must be regarded to have remained the legal owner of the land for the purposes of Article 1 of Protocol No. 1 and that "as a consequence of the fact that [she] has been refused access to the land since 1974, she has effectively lost all control over, as well as all possibilities to use and enjoy her property" (ibid., p. 2237, § 63). It concluded that the continuous denial of access to her property was an unjustified interference with her property rights in breach of Article 1 of Protocol No. 1 (ibid., pp. 2237–38, § 64).

26. In view of the above the Court is of the opinion that the question of Turkey's responsibility under the Convention in respect of the matters complained of is *res judicata*. It considers that it should make an award under Article 50. It is not persuaded by the argument that in doing so it would undermine political discussions concerning the Cyprus problem any more than it was by the same argument at the merits stage as regards finding a violation of Article 1 of Protocol No. 1 (ibid., pp. 2236–38, §§ 59 and 64).

That being the case the Court finds that the applicant is entitled under Article 50 to a measure of just satisfaction by way of compensation for the violation of her property rights.

II. PECUNIARY DAMAGE

27. The applicant stressed that she did not claim compensation for any purported expropriation of her property. In the light of the Court's finding that she is still the legal owner of the property no issue of expropriation arises. Her claim is thus confined to the loss of use of the land and the consequent lost opportunity to develop or lease it. With reference to a valuation report assessing the value of her property and the return that could be expected from it, she claimed 621,900 Cypriot pounds (CYP) by way of pecuniary damage concerning the period between 22 January 1990, the date of the acceptance by Turkey of the compulsory jurisdiction of the Court, and the end of 1997 (see paragraph 4 above).

The method employed in the valuation report involved calculating the market price of the property as at 1974 and increasing it by 12% per year to calculate the value that the property would have had if the northern part of Cyprus had not been occupied by the Turkish army. It was emphasised that the property was situated in an area of Kyrenia which in 1974 had been undergoing intensive residential and tourist development. The occupation of the properties had deprived the owner of her right to lease and thus resulted in a substantial loss of rent.

The sum claimed by way of pecuniary damage represented the aggregate of ground rents that could have been collected during the period 1990–97 calculated as 6% of the estimated market value of the property for each of the years in question.

28. The Cypriot Government supported the applicant's claim. In particular they contended that Turkey's continued unlawful occupation of part of the Republic of Cyprus should not be used as a

reason to reduce the amount awarded by way of pecuniary damage. To do so would be to permit a wrongdoer to benefit from his wrongdoing since the violation of the Convention found in the present case arose as a consequence of the unlawful invasion and occupation of part of the island by Turkey.

29. The Turkish Government maintained that the claim for damage should not be entertained by the Court for the reasons set out above (see paragraph 21). They did not offer any comments on the amount claimed by the applicant under this head.

30. The Delegate of the Commission submitted that the valuer's opinion on the development potential of the land which had been prepared on the applicant's behalf did not provide a realistic basis for the assessment of the pecuniary damage (see paragraph 4 above). The historical events in Cyprus affected not only the applicant individually but numerous other people in a similar situation. They could not therefore be completely disregarded. The applicant was entitled to be fully compensated for loss of access to and control of her property but not for the diminished value of that property due to the general political situation. In his view CYP 100,000 would be a more appropriate award.

31. The Court recalls that the applicant is still the legal owner of nine plots of land and one apartment (see paragraph 13 above) and that its finding of a violation of Article 1 of Protocol No. 1 was based on the fact that, as a consequence of being denied access to her land since 1974, she had effectively lost all control as well as all possibilities to use and enjoy her property (see the principal judgment cited above, pp. 2237–38, §§ 60–64). She is therefore entitled to a measure of compensation in respect of losses directly related to this violation of her rights as from the date of Turkey's acceptance of the compulsory jurisdiction of the Court, namely 22 January 1990, until the present time.

32. Although the Turkish Government have limited their submissions to contesting the applicant's right to compensation and have thus not sought to challenge the applicant's approach to the calculation of her economic loss, the Court does not for this reason alone accept without question the estimates provided by the applicant.

33. In this regard the Court considers as reasonable the general approach to assessing the loss suffered by the applicant with reference to the annual ground rent, calculated as a percentage of the market value of the property, that could have been earned on the properties during the relevant period.

However, the applicant's valuation inevitably involves a significant degree of speculation due to the absence of real data with which to make a comparison and makes insufficient allowance for the volatility of the property market and its susceptibility to influences both domestic and international. Her method of assessment presupposes that property prices in the Kyrenia area would have risen consistently by 12% each year from 1974 until 1997 and that the applicant would have actually sought to or have been able to rent her plots of land at 6% of this enhanced value. Even making allowances for the undoubted development potential of the area in which the land is situated, the presumption that the property market would have continued to flourish with sustained growth over a period of twenty-three years is open to question. The Court accordingly cannot accept these percentage increases as a realistic basis for calculating the applicant's loss.

34. Taking into account the above-mentioned uncertainties, inherent in any attempt to quantify the real losses incurred by the applicant, and making an assessment on an equitable basis, the Court decides to award CYP 300,000 under this head.

III. Non-Pecuniary Damage

35. The applicant also claimed CYP 621,900 in respect of non-pecuniary damage. She contended that various aggravating factors directly concerning her should be taken into account in the Court's assessment. These encompassed distress and feelings of frustration in face of the prolonged deprivation of her rights as well as feelings of helplessness connected to the presence of the Turkish army in northern Cyprus and her unsuccessful efforts to have the property returned to her. It also had to be borne in mind that the applicant had grown up in Kyrenia where her family had lived for generations and was now a displaced person in her own country. The fact that the Turkish Government had not sought to provide any justification for the interference with her property rights was a further aggravating factor to be taken into account.

In the applicant's submission there were also factors related to considerations of the public interest and the public order of Europe. In addition to the obligation to compensate there was in the present situation a need for a large award of non-pecuniary damages to act as an inducement to observe the legal standards set out in the Convention. The slowness and depressing effects of the procedural pathways open to the applicant, the dilatory attitude of the respondent Government and the various unfounded objections raised by them throughout the procedure also had to be taken into account.

A further aggravating factor related to the consistent policy of Turkey and her agents in the occupied area to exercise control over, and to exclude, the Greek Cypriot owners of property on a discriminatory basis. Such policies amounted to racial discrimination, were a source of distress to the applicant and constituted an affront to international standards of human rights.

36. The Cypriot Government supported the applicant's claims under this head. They considered that the sense of helplessness and frustration was deeply felt by the applicant in relation to denial of access and that there was a strong family relationship with regard to the property in question which forms part of the family heritage. The ethnic discrimination practised against Greek Cypriots was also a relevant consideration and must have had an impact upon the feelings of the applicant.

37. The Turkish Government offered no observations under this head.

38. The Delegate of the Commission considered that an award should be made but was unable to accept some of the "aggravating circumstances" invoked by the applicant, in particular her arguments that she had been deprived of her home – the Article 8 complaint having been dismissed by the Court – and that she had been discriminated against as a Greek Cypriot – no complaint under Article 14 having been raised in the original application. He further considered that no punitive element should be imported into the application of Article 50 since the "public policy" considerations adduced by the applicant concerned the global situation of displaced Greek Cypriots and thus went far beyond the perimeters of the individual case. He considered that CYP 20,000 would be an appropriate award.

39. The Court is of the opinion that an award should be made under this head in respect of the anguish and feelings of helplessness and frustration which the applicant must have experienced over the years in not being able to use her property as she saw fit.

40. However, like the Delegate of the Commission, the Court would stress that the present case concerns an individual complaint related to the applicant's personal circumstances and not the general situation of the property rights of Greek Cypriots in northern Cyprus. In this connection it recalls that in its principal judgment it held that "[it] need not pronounce itself on the arguments which have been adduced by those appearing before it concerning the alleged lawfulness or unlawfulness under international law of Turkey's military intervention in the island in 1974" (cited above, p. 2236, § 56). It also rejected the applicant's allegations that there had been a violation of the right to respect for her home (ibid., p. 2238, §§ 65–66) and made no finding concerning the question of racial discrimination which had not formed part of the applicant's complaint under the Convention.

Making an equitable assessment, the Court awards CYP 20,000 under this head.

[. . .]

4.5. *Zubani v. Italy* (1996)

[. . .]

As to the Facts

I. Circumstances of the Case

21. The applicants, three sisters and a brother, own a farmhouse and adjoining land, which they use for agricultural purposes.

22. On 21 August 1979, as part of the implementation of the general development plan adopted pursuant to Law no. 167/62, the Municipality of Brescia ("the Municipality") issued an order, under an expedited procedure, for the possession of the applicants' land, which was located in a zone intended for the construction of low-cost and social housing ("*edilizia economica e popolare*").

23. On 16 July 1980 the Municipality took physical possession of the land, aided by the police. On 6 October 1981 the Lombardy Regional Council issued an expropriation order.

24. From the outset the applicants challenged the lawfulness of the measures taken by the authorities;

they brought several actions in the administrative courts and in the ordinary civil courts.

A. Action for Possession in the Ordinary Civil Courts

25. On 1 October 1980 they applied to the Brescia Magistrate's Court (*pretore*) seeking the restitution of their land on the ground that the order for possession under the expedited procedure of 21 August 1979 had been executed after the expiry of the statutory time-limit (three months).

By an interim decision of 10 January 1981, the Magistrate's Court found for the applicants. The Municipality did not comply with the decision.

On 16 March 1983 the Magistrate's Court reversed its earlier interim decision because in the meantime the expropriation order of 6 October 1981 (see paragraph 9 above) had legalised the occupation of the land. It ruled nevertheless that the taking of possession of the land on 16 July 1980 had been unlawful and amounted to an act of theft. It ordered the Municipality to pay compensation for the damage sustained by the applicants on this account.

26. The Municipality contested its liability to pay compensation and, on 13 June 1983, appealed to the Brescia District Court, which, on 18 December 1985, upheld the impugned decision. The text of the judgment was deposited in the registry on 13 June 1986.

27. In the meantime, on 16 April 1981, the two cooperatives responsible for carrying out the building work (see paragraph 18 below) had brought an action against the applicants seeking compensation for the damage deriving from the delay to the property development scheme caused by the proceedings brought by the applicants.

B. Proceedings on the Merits in the Administrative Courts

28. By a writ served on 12 November 1979, the applicants instituted proceedings in the Lombardy Regional Administrative Court ("the RAC") seeking judicial review of the expedited order for possession of 21 August 1979.

On 22 July 1980 they filed a new action contesting the occupation of the land and on 6 January 1982, in the same court, they challenged the expropriation order of 6 October 1981.

29. Following the joinder of these different proceedings, the RAC quashed, on 15 June 1984, the various administrative measures – including the expropriation order –, but found that it lacked jurisdiction to rule on the lawfulness of the taking of possession of the applicants' land on 16 July 1980; it took the view that this question was a matter for the ordinary courts. The text of its decision was deposited in the registry on 30 July 1984.

30. The Municipality appealed to the *Consiglio di Stato*, which, in a judgment of 21 November 1985, deposited in the registry on 17 January 1986, upheld the RAC's decision.

C. Enforcement Proceedings

1 In the Administrative Courts

31. As the Municipality failed to comply with the latter decision, the applicants instituted proceedings in the *Consiglio di Stato*.

32. On 10 June 1986 the *Consiglio di Stato* found that it lacked jurisdiction and remitted the case to the Lombardy RAC.

On 16 July 1986 the applicants applied to the RAC, which, on 24 October 1986, found partly in their favour, holding in substance that the annulment by the *Consiglio di Stato* of the contested expropriation measures had the effect of imposing a duty on the Municipality to return immediately the part of the land that it had occupied on which no buildings had been erected, namely 12,000 square metres. It accordingly ordered that the land in question be returned to the applicants within thirty days. In respect of the remaining parcels of land, on which residential accommodation had been built in the meantime, the RAC held that it had no jurisdiction to order enforcement, because even before the annulment of the expropriation, the Municipality had transferred the land in question to two building cooperatives. As a result physical possession of the property had passed to the members of the two cooperatives. As the latter were private citizens, neither the Municipality nor the RAC was empowered to make any order whatsoever in regard to enforcement. It referred the applicants to the ordinary courts.

This decision was deposited in the registry on 31 October 1986; it was not complied with.

2 In the Ordinary Courts

33. On 29 July 1986 the applicants served notice on the Municipality calling on it to comply with the decision of the Lombardy RAC of 15 June 1984, upheld by the *Consiglio di Stato* on 21 November 1985.

34. By a writ served on 5 August 1986, the Municipality brought proceedings against the applicants in the Brescia District Court seeking a declaration that the applicants' notice to comply was invalid or inoperative because the judgment in question did not constitute a proper basis for initiating enforcement proceedings.

The applicants filed a cross-action seeking, in addition to the restitution of their land, an order from the District Court for the demolition of the buildings constructed on part of it and the erection of a fence. They also claimed compensation for the damage sustained.

35. At the hearing on 26 March 1987 judgment was reserved. On 2 April 1987 the District Court declared the notice served on the Municipality invalid on the ground that although the RAC judgment had quashed the measures adopted in connection with the expropriation, it was not automatically enforceable. At the same time the court partly allowed the applicants' cross-action in so far as it related to compensation for damage and the restitution of the land.

36. By a writ served on 12 June 1987, the Municipality appealed.

On 19 October 1988 judgment was reserved. On 9 November 1988 the Brescia Court of Appeal partly set aside the impugned decision pursuant to Law no. 458 of 27 October 1988 ("the 1988 Law" – the so-called "*Legge Zubani*"). This law, which came into force on 3 November 1988, gave legislative force to a principle laid down by the Court of Cassation (in plenary session) in its judgment no. 1464 of 16 February 1983, namely that property on which public work had been carried out making it impossible to restore it to its owner was to be the subject of compulsory transfer to the public authorities. In such circumstances the person concerned was entitled to full compensation.

Thus the appeal court dismissed the applicants' claim for the restitution of the land. However, it confirmed their right to compensation for the damage sustained. The text of its judgment was deposited in the registry on 15 November 1988.

39. At a date that has not been specified, the applicants appealed on points of law, challenging, among other things, the retrospective application of the 1988 Law. On 18 September 1989 the Court of Cassation adjourned the hearing to a later date.

37. In a judgment of 6 November 1989, deposited in the registry on 3 April 1990, the Court of Cassation dismissed the appeal on the ground that the appeal court had correctly applied the 1988 Law in the case before it because the applicants had not yet obtained a final decision ordering the Municipality to return the land which had been built on.

38. In addition, on 15 November 1989, in connection with the proceedings instituted by the cooperatives in 1981 (see paragraph 13 above) the Brescia District Court raised, on the applicants' motion, an objection based on the unconstitutional nature of section 3 of the 1988 Law. This objection was dismissed by the Constitutional Court on 12 July 1990 (judgment no. 384 – see paragraph 35 below).

On 28 November the District Court dismissed the plaintiffs' claims and held that the Municipality should compensate the applicants for the damage sustained, but that this issue should be the subject of separate proceedings.

39. On 4 and 5 March 1993 the applicants issued a writ against the cooperatives and the Municipality in the District Court for a decision fixing the amount to be reimbursed to them.

40. On 26 April 1995 the District Court, finding that the Municipality alone was liable for the occupation and the resulting damage, awarded the applicants 599,605,830 Italian lire less the 100,000,000 lire (reassessed at 139,650,600 to take account of monetary depreciation) paid by the defendant as an advance in 1988. They were also awarded 22,300,000 lire for lawyers' fees and expenses. The judgment was deposited in the registry on 2 August 1995. It was declared enforceable on 11 October and was served on the Municipality on 13 October.

41. On 29 September 1995 the Brescia Municipal Council decided that the sums in question should be paid to the applicants. The first sum plus statutory interest up to the probable date of payment (31 October 1995) totalled 1,015,255,000 lire.

42. On 20 October 1995 the applicants served a notice to comply on the Municipality, which, on the following 29 November paid them 751,164,000 lire.

43. On 17 January 1996, they issued a writ under Article 543 of the Code of Civil Procedure requiring the Municipality and its bank to appear on 26 March 1996 before the enforcement judge so that he could order the attachment of funds belonging to the Municipality with a view to securing payment of the outstanding amount. On 18 January 1996 a bailiff attached 250,000,000 lire.

[...]

II. Alleged Violation of Article 1 of Protocol No. 1

44. The applicants complained that their right to peaceful enjoyment of their possessions had been breached by the authorities' unlawful occupation of their land. They relied on Article 1 of Protocol No. 1, which provides:

> "Every natural or legal person is entitled to the peaceful enjoyment of his possessions. No one shall be deprived of his possessions except in the public interest and subject to the conditions provided for by law and by the general principles of international law.
>
> The preceding provisions shall not, however, in any way impair the right of a State to enforce such laws as it deems necessary to control the use of property in accordance with the general interest or to secure the payment of taxes or other contributions or penalties."

45. The Court observes that in the view of both the Government and the Commission the interference in issue was a deprivation of property within the meaning of the second sentence of Article 1, was provided for in section 3 of the 1988 Law (see paragraph 32 above) and pursued a public-interest aim, namely the construction of housing for a category of disadvantaged persons.

46. The only outstanding issue is therefore whether a fair balance was struck between the demands of the general interest of the community and the requirements of the individual's fundamental rights (see, among other authorities, the Sporrong and Lönnroth v. Sweden judgment of 23 September 1982, Series A no. 52, p. 26, § 69).

47. The Government maintained that, in enacting the 1988 Law, the Italian legislature had struck an appropriate balance between the relevant interests by making the provision that the "victims" of unlawful expropriation should be entitled to full compensation. Indeed the applicants' objection that section 3 of the Law was unconstitutional had been dismissed on 12 July 1990 on that ground (see paragraphs 25 and 35 above). The Commission's argument that the authorities would be encouraged to commit abuses if they knew in advance that any unlawful act would be legalised retrospectively was based on a rather superficial understanding of the expropriation procedures. An official responsible for an unlawful administrative act could be called upon to reimburse the State for the damage that his conduct had caused.

The Government also drew attention to the size of the amount awarded to the applicants in relation to the total surface occupied by the buildings erected by the cooperatives (1,015,255,000 lire for only 8,670 square metres). Moreover, the applicants had not claimed compensation for the loss of their land until May 1993.

In conclusion, the Government submitted that the Italian State had not overstepped the margin of appreciation left to it under the second paragraph of Article 1 of Protocol No. 1.

48. The applicants complained of the theft of which they had been the victims on 16 July 1980 and the Municipality's refusal to comply with the decisions of the administrative and the civil courts ordering it either to return the disputed land or to pay compensation. They also criticised the Municipality's attempt to apply to the dispute between them, a dispute that had lasted more than sixteen years, Law no. 549 of 28 December 1995 ("the 1995 Law"), which authorised a 40% reduction of the compensation awarded for unlawful expropriations. The legislature's action in this respect was in blatant conflict with the spirit of the 1988 Law and the interpretation of section 3 given by the Constitutional Court in 1990.

49. The Court shares the view of the Delegate of the Commission that the legislature might reasonably choose to give preference to the interests of the community in cases of unlawful expropriation or occupation of land. Full compensation for the damage sustained by the proprietors concerned constitutes sufficient reparation as the authorities

are required to pay an additional sum corresponding to monetary depreciation since the day of the unlawful action. Nevertheless the Law in question did not enter into force until 1988, when the litigation concerning the applicants' property had already lasted eight years (see paragraph 11 above) and although the Municipality had initially, on 29 September 1995, agreed to pay to the persons concerned the sums awarded by the Brescia District Court, it now appears reluctant to pay the whole amount. Furthermore, and even though this is not a circumstance that is directly material, the minutes of the session of Brescia Municipal Council held on that date indicate that the proposal to ask the Audit Court to determine the administrative responsibility for the loss incurred for the municipal budget was rejected by twenty-four votes to six, with one abstention.

As regards finally the remaining argument of the respondent Government, the Court considers that the size of the sum awarded by the Brescia District Court cannot be decisive in this case in view of the length of the proceedings instituted by the Zubanis.

The Court confines itself to noting that, although the sum of 1,015,255,000 lire may appear enormous in relation to the surface area actually occupied by the buildings, an additional factor to be borne in mind was that a new road was laid through the applicant's property – 21,960 square metres which they used to raise livestock – and this rendered access to the plots returned to them difficult.

50. Having regard to all these considerations, the Court finds that a "fair balance" between protecting the right of property and "the demands of the general interest" has not been struck. Accordingly, there has been a violation of Article 1 of Protocol No. 1.

[. . .]

4.6. *Akdivar and Others v. Turkey* (1996) and *Damages* (1998)

[. . .]

As to the Facts

12. The facts are based on the Commission's findings of fact as set out and developed in its report of 26 October 1995.

I. Particular Circumstances of the Case

A. The Situation in the South-East of Turkey

13. Since approximately 1985, serious disturbances have raged in the South-East of Turkey between the security forces and the members of the PKK (Workers' Party of Kurdistan). This confrontation has so far, according to the Government, claimed the lives of 4,036 civilians and 3,884 members of the security forces. It appears from information submitted by the applicants and by the amicus curiae that a large number of villages, estimated at more than 1,000, have been destroyed and evacuated during this conflict (see paragraph 7 above).

14. Since 1987, ten of the eleven provinces of southeastern Turkey have been subjected to emergency rule which was in force at the time of the facts complained of.

B. Destruction of the Applicants' Houses

15. The applicants (see paragraph 1 above), Turkish nationals, were residents in the village of Kelekçi in the Dicle district of the province of Diyarbakir. The village of Kelekçi and the surrounding areas have been the centre of intense PKK terrorist activity. It is undisputed that the PKK launched serious attacks on Kelekçi on 17 or 18 July 1992, and the neighbouring village of Bogazköy on 1 November 1992. As a result of the first attack, three Kelekçi villagers were killed and three others wounded. The second attack on 1 November 1992 was directed at the Bogazköy gendarme station, which was destroyed, with one gendarme being killed and eight others injured. Thereafter security forces were reinforced in the area and extensive searches were carried out for terrorists. The applicants alleged that on 10 November 1992 State security forces launched an attack on the village of Kelekçi, burnt nine houses, including their homes, and forced the immediate evacuation of the entire village.

16. The Government categorically denied these allegations, contending that the houses had been set on fire by the PKK. Initially they stated that the village had merely been searched and that no damage had been caused. Subsequently, it was maintained that no soldiers had entered Kelekçi on 10 November 1992, and, if they had been in the vicinity, they had stopped on the outskirts of the village to take a rest.

17. On 6 April 1993 houses in Kelekçi were set on fire and the village was almost completely destroyed. It is disputed, however, whether this destruction was caused by terrorists or by security forces.

18. The Commission established that nine houses, including those of the applicants, were destroyed or seriously damaged by fire not long after the attack on the Bogazköy gendarme station on 1 November 1992. Although noting that there was some uncertainty as to the exact date when the nine houses were burnt, it accepted the applicants' claims that this occurred on 10 November 1992.

C. Commission's Findings Concerning Investigations at the Domestic Level

19. The Commission found that no proper investigation was carried out at the domestic level regarding the destruction of the nine houses at Kelekçi on 10 November 1992 either immediately after the event or thereafter. Apparently, a gendarmerie report of 29 November 1993 dealt with events at Kelekçi. However, the Commission concluded that this report and other "incident reports" which had been submitted to the Chief Public Prosecutor at the Diyarbakir State Security Court, in so far as they concerned the destruction of the nine houses, did not result in any investigation of the facts and involved no attempt to establish responsibility for the destruction.

20. It was also established by the Commission that, although the applicants had lost their homes, no one gave proper advice to them or, apparently, to the other displaced Kelekçi villagers, on how to obtain compensation for the loss of their homes or other forms of assistance. Petitions were made by the mayor of the village and statements were given to several State officials. However, no authority took up the applicants' problems or referred them to the competent body.

21. There was also evidence before the Commission that, after the case had been brought to it, certain of the applicants, or persons who were believed to be applicants such as Hüseyin Akdivar and Ahmet Çiçek (see paragraphs 48–50 below), had been questioned by the State authorities about their applications to the Commission. The Commission had been provided with a filmed interview

with these two persons, during which they were asked about the case in Strasbourg.

22. As regards the events on 10 November 1992 (see paragraph 15 above), the Commission noted that the investigation reports and the recorded statements by villagers which had been submitted to it by the respondent Government were dated September 1994, i.e. almost two years after the destruction of the nine houses. In these statements they placed the blame on the PKK for setting fire to the houses. At that time, a number of villagers had been heard by the authorities about events at Kelekçi. It was observed that this inquiry had taken place at a time when the village had been further damaged on 6 April 1993, and after the Commission had communicated the applicants' complaints to the Government for observations and decided to hold an oral hearing in the case.

It was further noted that the investigation reports of September 1994 were based on an exploratory mission undertaken by helicopter on 21 September 1994. During this mission, the investigating team did not land at Kelekçi but only observed the village during low-level flights. The report stated that all the houses at Kelekçi had collapsed and that there were no inhabitants in the village.

23. As to the events of 6 April 1993, the Commission found that a team of gendarmes had heard various villagers in April 1993. However, in their recorded statements no reference was made by the villagers to the incident of 10 November 1992. The statements were examined by the Commission in order to determine whether they should affect the Commission's findings on questions of fact in respect of the incident complained of. In its report of 26 October 1995 it concluded as follows:

"197. In this respect, it is striking that the various statements by the villagers are drafted in a stereotyped form and have on the whole the same contents (see paragraphs 54, 56, 57, 59, 61, 65, 66, 68, 71, 73 and 75). Most of them describe the events of 6 April 1993 in an almost identical manner. In the recorded statements the villagers refer to the fact that the terrorists had made a previous attack on the village during which three persons had been killed and three others injured, this general formula being used even in the statements of the applicants Ahmet Çiçek and Abdurrahman Aktas whose close relatives, including the latter's father, had been killed on that occasion. The statements also contain a declaration about the villagers' respect for the State and their willingness to help the State. All in all, the recorded statements give the impression of having been drafted in a uniform manner by the gendarmes rather than reflecting spontaneous declarations by the villagers. This may also explain why some of these statements are in complete contradiction to what the same persons have stated on other occasions (see Ahmet Çiçek's statements referred to in paragraphs 61 and 89–90 above, Abdurrahman Aktas's statements referred to in paragraphs 54 and 98 above, and Abdullah Karabulut's statements referred to in paragraphs 66, 67 and 111 above). Thus it seems highly doubtful whether the recorded statements to the gendarmes can be said to reflect the information that the villagers intended to convey in regard to the events at issue."

24. The Commission concluded that it attached no particular weight to the statements of the villagers in April 1993. It further noted the inadequacy of any real investigations at the domestic level which could be of assistance in elucidating the events on 10 November 1992. It concluded that the absence of any such investigations was in itself a disturbing element in regard to a serious matter such as the destruction of the homes of a considerable number of persons.

D. Commission's Evaluation of the Evidence

25. In the absence of any relevant investigations at the domestic level, the Commission based its finding on the evidence which had been given orally by various persons or submitted in writing in the course of the proceedings before it.

26. The Commission concluded that there was no evidence of any conspiracy between the villagers to accuse the State of the burning of the houses in order to obtain compensation or for any other purpose.

It also noted that, while there was evidence that the security forces were in the village, none of the witnesses stated that any stranger had been seen at Kelekçi on 10 November 1992. It was unlikely that terrorists would have set fire to nine houses in the village without anyone having noted their presence. Nor was there any other evidence showing that terrorists had been at Kelekçi on that day.

27. Following an assessment of the evidence, the Commission found it convincingly shown that security forces – presumably under the strain of intense terrorist activity in the area – were responsible for the burning of the nine Kelekçi houses on 10 November 1992. However, it had not been shown that the applicants were forcibly expelled from Kelekçi, but the loss of their homes caused them to abandon the village and move elsewhere.

[. . .]

E. Alleged Violation of Article 8 of the Convention (Art. 8) and Article 1 of Protocol No. 1 (P1-1)

83. Article 8 of the Convention (art. 8) provides as follows:

"1. Everyone has the right to respect for his private and family life, his home and his correspondence.
2. There shall be no interference by a public authority with the exercise of this right except such as is in accordance with the law and is necessary in a democratic society in the interests of national security, public safety or the economic well-being of the country, for the prevention of disorder or crime, for the protection of health or morals, or for the protection of the rights and freedoms of others."

84. Article 1 of Protocol No. 1 (P1-1) provides:

"Every natural or legal person is entitled to the peaceful enjoyment of his possessions. No one shall be deprived of his possessions except in the public interest and subject to the conditions provided for by law and by the general principles of international law.
    The preceding provisions shall not, however, in any way impair the right of a State to enforce such laws as it deems necessary to control the use of property in accordance with the general interest or to secure the payment of taxes or other contributions or penalties."

85. The applicants submitted that in the light of all the evidence they had adduced, they have convincingly established that they were victims of a governmental policy of forced eviction which constitutes a practice in violation of Article 8 (art. 8). In addition, they maintained that the burning

of their houses amounted to a very serious violation of their rights under Article 1 of Protocol No. 1 (P1-1).

86. The Government submitted that it had not been shown that there had been any interference by the Turkish authorities with the applicants' rights under these provisions (art. 8, P1-1). Moreover, the Commission had found that it had not been proved that the applicants had been deliberately removed from the village.

87. The Commission maintained that there had been a breach of both of these provisions (art. 8, P1-1).

88. The Court is of the opinion that there can be no doubt that the deliberate burning of the applicants' homes and their contents constitutes at the same time a serious interference with the right to respect for their family lives and homes and with the peaceful enjoyment of their possessions. No justification for these interferences having been proffered by the respondent Government – which have confined their response to denying involvement of the security forces in the incident –, the Court must conclude that there has been a violation of both Article 8 of the Convention (art. 8) and Article 1 of Protocol No. 1 (P1-1).

It does not consider that the evidence established by the Commission enables it to reach any conclusion concerning the allegation of the existence of an administrative practice in breach of these provisions (art. 8, P1-1).

[. . .]

Damages (1998)

[. . .]

II. Pecuniary Damage

50. The applicants claimed pecuniary damage in respect of the loss of houses, cultivated land, household property and livestock. They also claimed that an award should be made in respect of the cost of alternative accommodation. The Government submitted a valuation report prepared by a commission of experts which contested the amounts claimed by the applicants in various respects (see paragraph 6 above).

A. Houses

51. The experts nominated by the Government found that, according to the records kept by the Dicle municipality, only three houses were listed, namely those of Ahmet Akdivar (100 sq. m), Ali Akdivar (60 sq. m) and Zülfükar Çiçek (300 sq. m). They considered that a base rate per square metre of 3,482,400 Turkish liras (TRL) should be used to assess compensation.

52. The applicants maintained that in the rural area where they lived there was no tradition of registering property, which passed from generation to generation and was acquired by prescriptive use. They claimed compensation for the houses of Ahmet Akdivar (200 sq. m), Ali Akdivar (200 sq. m), Zülfükar Çiçek (600 sq. m), Abdurrahman Akdivar (250 sq. m), Abdurrahman Aktaş (300 sq. m), Mehmet Karabulut (200 sq. m) and Ahmet Çiçek (500 sq. m). They accepted that the base rate per square metre proposed by the experts be used in the calculation of the value of the houses. However, they disagreed with the experts' indication of the size of the listed houses.

53. The Court recalls its finding that the applicants' houses were burnt down by the security forces (see the principal judgment, *Reports* 1996-IV, p. 1214, § 81). Bearing in mind the rural area in which the events took place and that the experts were unable to visit the applicants' village (see paragraph 6 above), it does not regard it as conclusive that no record exists in respect of the houses of four of the applicants.

It considers that an award should be made in respect of the houses for which a record exists based on the surface area noted by the experts at the base rate per square metre proposed by them.

54. The Court also considers it appropriate to make an award in respect of the remaining houses. However, due to the absence of evidence which substantiates the size of these properties any calculation must inevitably involve a degree of speculation. It will base its award on fifty percent of the surface area claimed by the applicants at the base rate.

55. Accordingly, the Court makes the following awards under this head:

(a) TRL 348,240,000   (Ahmet Akdivar);
(b) TRL 208,944,000   (Ali Akdivar);
(c) TRL 1,044,720,000   (Zülfükar Çiçek);
(d) TRL 435,300,000   (Abdurrahman
                    Akdivar);
(e) TRL 522,360,000   (Abdurrahman Aktaş);
(f) TRL 348,240,000   (Mehmet Karabulut);
(g) TRL 870,600,000   (Ahmet Çiçek).

B. Cultivated and Arable Land

56. The applicants claim compensation in respect of both the loss of cultivated and arable land and the loss of income in respect of the following holdings:

Ahmet Akdivar (2 acres of orchards, 3 acres of vineyards, 10 acres of arable land and 2 acres of oak groves);

Ali Akdivar (8 acres of orchards, 2 acres of vineyards, 20 acres of arable land and 3 acres of oak groves);

Zülfükar Çiçek (96 acres of orchards, 70 acres of vineyards, 30 acres of arable land and 5 acres of oak groves);

Abdurrahman Akdivar (24 acres of orchards, 12 acres of vineyards, 3 acres of arable land and 20 acres of oak groves);

Abdurrahman Aktaş (10 acres of orchards, 12 acres of vineyards and 20 acres of oak groves);

Mehmet Karabulut (36 acres of orchards, 14 acres of vineyards, 15 acres of arable land and 2 acres of oak groves);

Ahmet Çiçek (48 acres of orchards, 48 acres of vineyards and 20 acres of oak groves).

They accept the experts' estimates as regards the yearly loss of income per acre.

57. The Government's experts note that only the first three applicants have registered land (3 acres, 2,500 sq. m and 3 acres respectively). However, they submitted the following figures as an estimate of loss of income per acre per year multiplied by the acreage claimed by the applicants: TRL 6,710,000 in respect of vineyards, TRL 7,020,000 for orchards, TRL 2,875,000 for arable land and TRL 13,500,000 for oak groves.

58. The Court notes that there was no finding of expropriation of property in the principal judg-

ment and that the applicants still remain the owners of their land.

Accordingly, it makes no award in respect of loss of land.

59. On the other hand, as a result of the destruction of their houses the applicants were obliged to leave their village and were no longer able to exploit their land.

In consequence, they are entitled to claim for loss of income.

60. The Court recalls that the applicants accept the estimate provided by the experts in respect of loss of income per acre per year. Bearing in mind the absence of independent evidence concerning the size of the individual holdings and having regard to equitable considerations, it considers that the amount awarded should cover five years' loss of income and should be based on these figures in respect of the acreage claimed by the applicants.

61. Accordingly, the Court awards under this head:

(a) TRL 449,600,000   (Ahmet Akdivar);
(b) TRL 837,900,000   (Ali Akdivar);
(c) TRL 6,486,850,000   (Zülfükar Çiçek);
(d) TRL 2,638,125,000   (Abdurrahman Akdivar);
(e) TRL 2,103,600,000   (Abdurrahman Aktaş);
(f) TRL 2,083,925,000   (Mehmet Karabulut);
(g) TRL 4,645,200,000   (Ahmet Çiçek).

C. Household Property

62. The Government experts also submitted figures for loss of household property. They based their estimates on the price in September 1997 of certain household items in the shops in Diyarbakır.

63. The applicants' claims were somewhat higher.

64. The Court considers that the amounts proposed by the experts are reasonable.

It thus makes the following awards:

(a) TRL 263,050,000   (Ahmet Akdivar);
(b) TRL 233,300,000   (Ali Akdivar);
(c) TRL 279,050,000   (Zülfükar Çiçek);
(d) TRL 298,650,000   (Abdurrahman Akdivar);
(e) TRL 313,750,000   (Abdurrahman Aktaş);
(f) TRL 243,650,000   (Mehmet Karabulut);
(g) TRL 300,450,000   (Ahmet Çiçek).

D. Livestock and Feed

65. The experts pointed out that none of the applicants had livestock registered in their names in the records of the District Agricultural Directorate. However, they submitted an estimate in respect of each applicant's claim with reference to prices for livestock which were significantly lower than those advanced by the applicants.

66. Although it lacks independent evidence of the applicants' claims, the Court also considers that an award should be made under this head on the basis of the estimated prices provided by the experts. It accepts, however, the applicants' figures as regards feed and the number of livestock involved whether registered or unregistered.

It thus makes the following award:

(a) TRL 460,000,000 in respect of 6 cattle, 20 sheep and winter-feed (Ahmet Akdivar);

(b) TRL 552,500,000 in respect of 7 cattle, 25 sheep and winter-feed (Ali Akdivar);

(c) TRL 1,035,500,000 in respect of 17 cattle, 60 sheep and winter-feed (Zülfükar Çiçek);

(d) TRL 880,000,000 in respect of 10 cattle, 40 sheep and winter-feed (Abdurrahman Akdivar);

(e) TRL 882,500,000 in respect of 12 cattle, 35 sheep and winter-feed (Abdurrahman Aktaş);

(f) TRL 605,000,000 in respect of 8 cattle, 30 sheep and winter-feed (Mehmet Karabulut);

(g) TRL 1,112,500,000 in respect of 15 cattle, 45 sheep and winter-feed (Ahmet Çiçek).

E. Cost of Alternative Accommodation in Diyarbakır

67. The applicants claimed that an award should be made in respect of the cost of rented accommodation in Diyarbakır following their relocation there in November 1992 after the destruction of their houses. This point was not addressed in the experts' report.

68. The Court considers that an award should also be made in this respect since the expenses incurred are directly linked to the violation found by it in the principal judgment.

It finds that the amounts claimed by the applicants (TRL 2,000,000 per month – TRL 2,250,000 in the case of Abdurrahman Akdivar) in respect of the period November 1992–January 1998 to be

reasonable. No claim was made for Zülfükar Çiçek who lives with Ahmet Çiçek.

It makes the following award in respect of a period of sixty-two months:

(a) TRL 124,000,000   (Ahmet Akdivar);
(b) TRL 124,000,000   (Ali Akdivar);
(c) TRL 139,500,000   (Abdurrahman Akdivar);
(d) TRL 124,000,000   (Abdurrahman Aktaş);
(e) TRL 124,000,000   (Mehmet Karabulut);
(f) TRL 124,000,000   (Ahmet Çiçek).

F. Summary

69. The total amounts awarded per applicant in respect of pecuniary damage are set out below. Having regard to the high rate of inflation in Turkey these amounts have been converted into pounds sterling in order to preserve their value at the rate applicable when the commission of experts made its estimates, i.e. 17 September 1997. At that date one pound sterling (GBP) was worth TRL 271,530 (the purchase price according to the exchange rates operated by the Turkish Central Bank).

(a) TRL 1,644,890,000 – GBP   6,057.85
                                         (Ahmet Akdivar);
(b) TRL 1,956,644,000 – GBP   7,205.99
                                         (Ali Akdivar);
(c) TRL 8,846,120,000 – GBP   32,578.79
                                         (ZülfükarÇiçek);
(d) TRL 4,391,575,000 – GBP   16,173.44
                                         (Abdurrahman
                                         Akdivar);
(e) TRL 3,946,210,000 – GBP   14,533.23
                                         (Abdurrahman
                                         Aktaş);
(f) TRL 3,404,815,000 – GBP   12,539.36
                                         (Mehmet
                                         Karabulut); and
(g) TRL 7,052,750,000 – GBP   25,974.10
                                         (Ahmet Çiçek).

III. Non-Pecuniary Damage

70. The applicants submitted that they should each be awarded GBP 20,000 in respect of non-pecuniary damage. They also claimed GBP 5,000 each for punitive damages in respect of the violation of their Convention rights.

71. The Government contended that, if an award for non-pecuniary damage was to be made, it should take into account the economic circumstances prevailing in Turkey. They pointed out in

this respect that the monthly minimum wage of an adult worker is approximately GBP 53.

72. The Court considers that an award should be made under this head bearing in mind the seriousness of the violations which it has found in respect of Article 8 of the Convention, Article 1 of Protocol No. 1 and Article 25 § 1 of the Convention (see the principal judgment, *Reports* 1996 IV, p. 1215, § 88, and p. 1219, § 106).

It awards the applicants GBP 8,000 each.

73. It rejects the claim for punitive damages.

IV. Costs and Expenses

A. Article 50 Proceedings

74. The applicants claim GBP 8,140 by way of costs and expenses in respect of the Article 50 proceedings.

75. The Government made no comment on this claim.

76. The Court observes that the Article 50 proceedings in the present case concerned complex questions and involved three sets of detailed observations by the applicants' legal representatives. It considers that the costs and expenses were actually and necessarily incurred and reasonable as to quantum and should be awarded in full together with any value-added tax that may be chargeable.

B. Compliance with Order for Costs in the Principal Judgment

77. The applicants complained that notwithstanding the order in the principal judgment for costs to be paid in pounds sterling, the respondent Government had paid only part of the costs owed, in equal divisions, into bank accounts opened by the authorities on behalf of each of the applicants. The sums were paid in Turkish liras some four months after the delivery of the principal judgment, on 13 January 1997. As a result the applicants state that there was a shortfall of GBP 5,681.89 as of 13 January 1997, which sum has accumulated 8% interest since.

They requested that this sum, adjusted by the interest accrued, be awarded by the Court in the present proceedings.

78. The Government did not comment on this point.

79. The Court points out that by Article 53 of the Convention the High Contracting Parties undertake to abide by the decision of the Court in any case to which they are parties. Furthermore, Article 54 provides that:

> "The judgment of the Court shall be transmitted to the Committee of Ministers which shall supervise its execution."

It considers that the issue of a shortfall in the payment of costs ordered in the principal judgment is a matter which concerns the proper execution of a judgment of the Court by the respondent State. Accordingly, it is a question which falls to be decided by the Committee of Ministers of the Council of Europe.

V. Request for Restoration of Rights

80. The applicants further submitted that the Court should confirm, as a necessary implication of an award of just satisfaction, that the Government should (1) bear the costs of necessary repairs in Kelekçi to enable the applicants to continue their way of life there; and (2) remove any obstacle preventing the applicants from returning to their village.

In their view such confirmation was necessary to prevent future and continuing violations of the Convention, in particular the *de facto* expropriation of their property.

81. The Government maintained that the restoration of rights is not feasible due to the emergency conditions prevailing in the region. However, resettlement will take place when the local inhabitants feel themselves to be safe from terrorist atrocities.

82. The Court recalls that a judgment in which it finds a breach imposes on the respondent State a legal obligation to put an end to such breach and make reparation for its consequences in such a way as to restore as far as possible the situation existing before the breach (*restitutio in integrum*). However, if *restitutio in integrum* is in practice impossible the respondent States are free to choose the means whereby they will comply with a judgment in which the Court has found a breach, and the Court will not make consequential orders or declaratory statements in this regard. It falls to the Committee of Ministers acting under Article 54 of the Convention to supervise compliance in this respect (see the Papamichalopoulos and Others v. Greece judgment of 30 October 1995 (*Article 50*), Series A no. 330-B, pp. 58–59, § 34, and, as regards

consequential orders, *inter alia* the Tolstoy Miloslavsky v. the United Kingdom judgment of 13 July 1995, Series A no. 316-B, p. 82, §§ 69–72).

VI. Default Interest

83. According to the information available to the Court, the statutory rate of interest applicable in the United Kingdom at the date of adoption of the present judgment is 8% per annum.

[. . .]

4.7. *Guillemin v. France* (1997)

[. . .]

I. CIRCUMSTANCES OF THE CASE

6. In a decision of 7 October 1982 the Prefect of the département of Essonne made a declaration that it was in the public interest to acquire by compulsory purchase land needed for the development of a residential area in the town of Saint-Michel-sur-Orge, known as the Fontaine de l'Orme project. The land included a plot belonging to the applicant on which stood a building used as a secondary residence by a member of her family.

A. The Expropriation Proceedings

7. On 10 September 1982 the mayor of Saint-Michel-sur-Orge had applied to the Essonne expropriations judge, who on 6 December 1982 made an expropriation order transferring the applicant's land to the municipality and setting the amount of compensation to be paid to her. On 28 March 1983 the applicant appealed against the order.

8. On 28 July 1983 the Evry New Town Development Corporation (EPEVRY), which was responsible for carrying out the scheme, informed Mrs Guillemin that she should have vacated the land by 14 July 1983. In the same month the town council demolished the fence, the buildings, the infrastructure for the supply of services, the vegetable garden and the orchard on the land.

9. On 14 October 1983, on the appeal by the expropriated applicant, the Expropriations Division of the Paris Court of Appeal increased the amount of the expropriation compensation to 221,858 French francs (FRF), which is currently held in deposit at the Bank for Official Deposits (Essonne Treasury).

B. Setting Aside of the Public-Interest Declaration

10. On 19 November 1982 Mrs Guillemin had brought proceedings in the Versailles Administrative Court. On 24 October 1985 the court set aside the public-interest declaration on the grounds that it was ultra vires. It held that the declaration should have been made in a decree after consultation of the Conseil d'Etat and not in a prefectoral decision (see paragraph 23 below). The inspector appointed to conduct the inquiry prior to the declaration in question had recommended that the scheme should not include existing houses that had sufficient land to make a garden for family use, as was the case with the applicant's property.

11. The town council appealed on 26 December 1985 and lodged a pleading on 28 April 1986.

In a judgment of 13 March 1989 the Conseil d'Etat upheld the Administrative Court's judgment. It refused Mrs Guillemin's application for formal note to be taken that the town council had automatically abandoned the proceedings as it had failed to file a supplementary pleading in time, and also refused her claim for compensation, which had been submitted for the first time on appeal.

C. Setting Aside of the Expropriation Measures

12. The applicant lodged two appeals on points of law with the Court of Cassation, the first against the expropriation order of 6 December 1982 and the second against the judgment of the Paris Court of Appeal of 14 October 1983.

In two judgments of 4 January 1990 the Court of Cassation (Third Civil Division) set aside the expropriation order providing for the transfer of ownership and "in consequence" set aside the judgment of the Paris Court of Appeal, which had ruled on the expropriation compensation. These judgments were served on the town council on 22 May 1990.

D. The Applications for Compensation

1. The application to the expropriating town council

13. On 20 June 1990 Mrs Guillemin applied unsuccessfully to the town council, seeking either restoration of her rights or compensation in the amount of FRF 4,194,655.65.

2. In the courts

14. On 10 November and 17 December 1990 Mrs Guillemin applied to Evry State Counsel. On 11 March 1991 he decided to take no action.

15. On 23 December 1991 the applicant challenged the town council's simplied decision to refuse her application in the Versailles Administrative Court. Her claim for restoration of her rights was accompanied by an application for compensation for non-pecuniary damage and loss of enjoyment of her property, which she assessed at FRF 1,971,795.

16. On 13 January 1992 she brought proceedings in the Evry tribunal de grande instance against the mayor of Saint-Michel-sur-Orge and EPEVRY, seeking an order for demolition of the buildings erected on her land by the town council, with periodic penalties in the event of failure to comply, and damages.

In joint submissions the defendants argued that it was not possible to return the property. It had been sold to EPEVRY with a view to a housing development and the individual building plots had in turn been sold to various different purchasers and had now been built on and were occupied.

17. On 1 February 1993 the Evry tribunal de grande instance deferred judgment until the Versailles Administrative Court ruled and listed the case for the hearing that was to be held on 10 June 1993 by the judge in charge of preparing the case for trial.

18. The Administrative Court held a hearing on 10 May 1994 and gave judgment on 24 May 1994.

It held that the claim for return of the land was inadmissible on the ground that "it [was] not for the administrative courts to issue orders to the authorities" and ruled as follows on the claim for compensation:

> "It is clear from the preparation of the case for trial that the expropriation . . . in the public interest [on] 7 October 1982 was carried out unlawfully. The dispossession of [Mrs Guillemin] was accordingly an illegal expropriation of private property. It is for the ordinary courts alone, which protect private property, to deal with [her] claim for compensation for the loss [she allegedly] sustained as a result of the dispossession or of any direct consequences of it."

19. In the meantime, on 3 March 1994, Mrs Guillemin's application had been struck off the list of the Evry tribunal de grande instance. It was entered in the list again on 25 November 1994. On 5 January 1995 the applicant filed fresh submissions seeking compensation.

20. In a judgment of 23 October 1995 the Evry tribunal de grande instance noted that Mrs Guillemin had implicitly abandoned her application for the buildings on her land to be demolished and held that she was entitled to compensation from the expropriating town council. It deferred judgment on the compensation claim, ordered an expert report on the value of the expropriated plot of land as at December 1982 and on the loss arising from her being deprived of her land and the price of it since then, and ruled that the town council should pay an advance on the costs of the expert report.

21. The expert received the file on 27 November 1995. He summoned the parties to an inspection of the site on 12 March 1996 and filed his report on 29 July 1996. He assessed the total value at FRF 1,602,805, which he broke down as follows: FRF 462,139 for the value of the property, covering the sum needed to purchase a similar property, FRF 746,338 for the interest on the principal sum from 14 July 1983 to 30 September 1996 and FRF 394,328 compensation for loss of the enjoyment of the property over the same period. For this last item he adopted a rate of return of 6.50% on the value of the property, excluding the sum needed to purchase a similar property.

22. The proceedings are at present pending in the Evry tribunal de grande instance.

[. . .]

II. Alleged Violation of Article 1 of Protocol No. 1 (P1-1)

46. Mrs Guillemin submitted that the unlawful expropriation of her property had infringed Article 1 of Protocol No. 1 (P1-1), which provides:

> "Every natural or legal person is entitled to the peaceful enjoyment of his possessions. No one shall be deprived of his possessions except in the public interest and subject to the conditions provided for by law and by the general principles of international law.
>
> The preceding provisions (P1-1) shall not, however, in any way impair the right of a State to enforce such laws as it deems necessary to control the use of property in accordance with the general interest or to secure the

payment of taxes or other contributions or penalties."

A. Government's Preliminary Objections

47. The Government maintained, firstly, that Mrs Guillemin could not claim to be a "victim" within the meaning of Article 25 of the Convention (art. 25) as the domestic courts had recognised the principle of compensation and therefore made good the consequences of the violation of her right to the peaceful enjoyment of her possessions. Secondly, the applicant had not exhausted domestic remedies as her action for compensation was still pending in the Evry tribunal de grande instance, which on 23 October 1995 had upheld the principle of her entitlement to compensation and would give her full compensation for the loss sustained.

48. The applicant replied that the satisfaction in principle that had been obtained from the Conseil d'Etat, the Court of Cassation and the Evry tribunal de grande instance had not led to the payment of any compensation, even partial, and that she was still the victim of a breach. It was clear from the length of the proceedings she had already instituted that domestic remedies were not effective. The objection that she was not a victim had not been raised before the Commission and was therefore out of time.

49. The Delegate of the Commission agreed with the applicant. Fourteen years after the irreparable loss of her property Mrs Guillemin could not be satisfied with promises, and there was nothing to show that the proceedings still pending in a court of first instance would not lead to an appeal to the Court of Appeal and even, on points of law, to the Court of Cassation.

50. The Court does not share the Government's opinion.

As to the objection that the applicant is not a victim, the Court is of the view, firstly, that the Government were not out of time in raising this objection for the first time before the Court. The judgment in which the Evry tribunal de grande instance held that the applicant was entitled to compensation from the expropriating town council was delivered on 23 October 1995 (see paragraph 20 above), that is to say after the end of the proceedings before the Commission. The Court considers, however, that the domestic courts' acknowledgment of the applicant's right to compensation does not mean

that she ceases to be a victim. The position might have been different if, for instance, the national authorities had afforded effective redress for the alleged violation (see, mutatis mutandis, the Eckle v. Germany judgment of 15 July 1982, Series A no. 51, pp. 30–31, para. 66, and the Inze v. Austria judgment of 28 October 1987, Series A no. 126, p. 16, para. 32). This is not so in the case of Mrs Guillemin, who remains dispossessed of her property without any compensation after its unlawful expropriation by the administrative authorities. The applicant has consequently not ceased to be a "victim" within the meaning of Article 25 of the Convention (art. 25).

Secondly, the Court notes that the applicant has had recourse to all the domestic remedies available to her. It accepts the Commission's opinion in its decision on admissibility, namely that as the proceedings to which she was a party had been so slow, it was unnecessary at that time for Mrs Guillemin to institute further proceedings in order to comply with the requirements of Article 26 of the Convention (art. 26). Nor, in the particular circumstances of the case, can she be criticised for not awaiting the outcome of the proceedings pending in the Evry tribunal de grande instance. In conclusion, the requirement of Article 26 (art. 26) that domestic remedies must be exhausted has been satisfied.

51. The Government's objections must consequently be dismissed.

B. Merits of the Complaint

52. It was common ground that Mrs Guillemin had been deprived of her possessions within the meaning of the second sentence of Article 1 of Protocol No. 1 (P1-1) and that the expropriation of her property had not been carried out in the manner laid down in domestic law.

53. The Government maintained that the actions to have public-interest declarations and expropriation orders set aside and to secure compensation for unlawful expropriation constituted sufficient, adequate remedies within the meaning of the Court's case-law to guarantee the protection of the applicant's right to the peaceful enjoyment of her possessions. Moreover, she had won her three actions and would receive compensation once the expert had filed his report. She could not therefore rely on any violation.

54. The Court notes that in 1982 the French authorities unlawfully expropriated the applicant's

property to develop an extensive residential area. By erecting new buildings, later sold individually, the expropriating town council and the corporation in charge of the scheme permanently deprived the applicant of the chance of regaining possession of her land. Her only course was to seek compensation.

Compensation for the loss sustained by the applicant can only constitute adequate reparation where it also takes into account the damage arising from the length of the deprivation. It must moreover be paid within a reasonable time.

55. On 20 June 1990 Mrs Guillemin made an initial application to the town council for compensation, but it was implicitly refused (see paragraph 13 above). No proposal for a friendly settlement was made to her subsequently. The court proceedings for compensation have lasted five years so far (see paragraphs 15–22 above), have already exceeded a reasonable time (see paragraphs 43–45 above) and are continuing (see paragraph 22 above). Compensation has not to date begun to be paid, although it could have been agreed on even after the expropriation order had been issued (see paragraph 24 above).

56. The Court considers that the potentially large sum that may be awarded at the end of the pending proceedings does not offset the previously noted failure to pay compensation and cannot be decisive in view of the length of all the proceedings already instituted by the applicant (see, mutatis mutandis, the Zubani v. Italy judgment of 7 August 1996, Reports 1996-IV, p. 1078, para. 49).

57. Having regard to all these considerations, the Court finds that there has been a violation of Article 1 of Protocol No. 1 (P1-1).

[. . .]

4.8. *Brumărescu v. Romania* (1999)

[. . .]

I. THE CIRCUMSTANCES OF THE CASE

11. In 1930 the applicant's parents had a house built in Bucharest. From 1939 onwards they let the ground floor to the Mirescu brothers, the uncles of the third party intervening in the case, Mr Mircea Dan Mirescu.

12. In 1950 the State took possession of the applicant's parents' house in Bucharest, allegedly under Decree no. 92/1950 on nationalisation. The applicant's parents were never informed of the grounds or legal basis for that deprivation of property. They were, however, allowed to continue to live in one of the flats in the house as tenants of the State.

13. In 1973, pursuant to Law no. 4/1973, the State sold the Mirescu brothers the flat which they had hitherto occupied as tenants. The intervener, Mr Mircea Dan Mirescu, and his sister, A.M.M., inherited the flat in 1988. After his sister's death in 1997 the intervener was left as the sole successor in title to the flat.

[. . .]

A. Action for Recovery of Possession

14. In 1993 the applicant, as the beneficiary of his parents' estate, brought an action in the Bucharest Court of First Instance ("the Court of First Instance") seeking a declaration that the nationalisation was null and void on the ground that Decree no. 92/1950 provided that the property of employees could not be nationalised and his parents had been employed at the time of the nationalisation of their house. It is not clear from the documents before the Court whether the applicant informed the Court of First Instance of the sale by the State to the Mirescu brothers in 1973.

15. In a judgment of 9 December 1993 the Court of First Instance held that the nationalisation of the applicant's parents' house under Decree no. 92/1950 had been a mistake, as his parents had belonged to a category of persons whose property the decree exempted from nationalisation. The court went on to hold that the State had obtained possession by duress and so could not rely on prescription to establish title. It also ruled that the State could not have acquired title to the house under Decree no. 218/1960 or Decree no. 712/1966 since those instruments had been contrary to the Constitutions of 1952 and 1965 respectively. The court therefore ordered the administrative authorities – namely the mayor of Bucharest and a State-owned company, C., which managed State-owned housing – to return the house to the applicant.

16. No appeal was lodged and the judgment became final and irreversible since it could no longer be challenged by way of an ordinary appeal.

17. On 31 March 1994 the mayor of Bucharest ordered the house to be returned to the applicant and on 27 May 1994 the C. company complied.

18. As of that date the applicant ceased to pay rent on the flat he was occupying in the house.

19. The applicant began paying land tax on the house on 14 April 1994 and continued doing so until a date in 1996 (see paragraph 25 below).

20. On an unknown date the Procurator-General of Romania, acting at the instance of Mr Mircea Dan Mirescu, lodged an application (*recurs în anulare*) with the Supreme Court of Justice to have the judgment of 9 December 1993 quashed on the grounds that the Court of First Instance had exceeded its jurisdiction in examining the lawfulness of the application of Decree no. 92/1950.

21. The hearing before the Supreme Court of Justice was set down for 22 February 1995. Mr Mircea Dan Mirescu was not invited to take part in the proceedings. On the day of the hearing, the applicant requested an adjournment as his lawyer was absent through illness.

22. The Supreme Court of Justice refused that request and proceeded to hear oral argument, after which it reserved judgment until 1 March 1995, the applicant being ordered to file written submissions before that date.

23. In those submissions, the applicant requested the Supreme Court of Justice to dismiss the Procurator-General's application. He argued, first, that Decree no. 92/1950 had been incompatible with the 1948 Constitution, both in that it had been published only in part and in that it had breached the principle that no expropriation should be effected save in the public interest and after payment of fair compensation. Secondly, he submitted that, since his parents had been employees at the time of the nationalisation, the decision to nationalise their house had contravened the terms of the decree, which provided that dwellings belonging to employees could not be nationalised. Lastly, the applicant relied on Article 21 of the Romanian Constitution of 1991, which guarantees unrestricted access to the courts.

24. On 1 March 1995 the Supreme Court of Justice quashed the judgment of 9 December 1993 and dismissed the applicant's claim. It held that property could be acquired by way of legislation, noted that the State had taken the house on the very day on which Decree no. 92/1950 on nationalisation had come into force and reiterated that the manner in which that decree had been applied could not be reviewed by the courts. Accordingly, the Bucharest Court of First Instance could not have found that the applicant was the rightful owner of the house without distorting the provisions of the decree, thus exceeding its powers and encroaching on those of the legislature. The Supreme Court of Justice confirmed that former owners were entitled to bring actions for recovery of possession but held that the applicant in the case before it had not established his title, whereas the State had demonstrated title under the nationalisation decree. In any event, provision as to redress for any wrongful seizure of property by the State would have to be made in new legislation.

25. Thereupon, the tax authorities informed the applicant that the house would be reclassified as State property with effect from 2 April 1996.

B. Developments after the Adoption of the Commission's Report: Proceedings for Restitution

26. On an unspecified date the applicant lodged an application for restitution with the administrative board established to deal with applications lodged in Bucharest pursuant to Law no. 112/1995 ("the Administrative Board"). He submitted that he had been dispossessed of his house in 1950 in breach of Decree no. 92/1950 on nationalisation; that the Bucharest Court of First Instance had held that that deprivation of property had been unlawful in a final judgment of 9 December 1993; and that he was therefore entitled to be reinstated as the owner of the whole house.

27. In a report drawn up in November 1997 the valuation board established under Law no. 112/1995 valued the applicant's house at 274,621,286 Romanian lei (ROL), of which the flat occupied by the applicant accounted for ROL 98,221,701.

28. On 24 March 1998 the Administrative Board vested ownership of the flat rented by the applicant in him and awarded him financial compensation

for the rest of the house. Having regard to section 12 of Law no. 112/1995, which put a ceiling on compensation, and to the ceiling applicable in November 1997 – ROL 225,718,800 – the Board awarded him ROL 147,497,099.

29. On 14 May 1998 the applicant challenged that decision in the Bucharest Court of First Instance, attacking the Board's refusal to return the whole house to him and pointing out that no grounds for that refusal had been given. He argued that in his case, where there had been an unlawful deprivation of property, Law no. 112/1995 – which concerned lawful expropriations – did not apply. Accordingly, his only means of protecting his right of property was an action for recovery of possession. However, since he had already brought such an action, and since the Court of First Instance, in a final judgment of 9 December 1993, had held him to be the owner of the house, he believed himself to be debarred from bringing a fresh action for recovery of possession. Consequently, he sought a declaration that he was the owner of the whole house and stated that he was not seeking compensation under Law no. 112/1995.

30. That application was dismissed on 21 April 1999. The applicant appealed and the proceedings are currently pending in the Bucharest County Court.

[. . .]

III. Alleged Violation of Article 1 of Protocol No. 1

66. The applicant complained that the Supreme Court of Justice's judgment of 1 March 1995 had had the effect of infringing his right to peaceful enjoyment of his possessions as secured by Article 1 of Protocol No. 1, which provides:

"Every natural or legal person is entitled to the peaceful enjoyment of his possessions. No one shall be deprived of his possessions except in the public interest and subject to the conditions provided for by law and by the general principles of international law.

The preceding provisions shall not, however, in any way impair the right of a State to enforce such laws as it deems necessary to control the use of property in accordance with the general

interest or to secure the payment of taxes or other contributions or penalties."

A. Whether There Was a Possession

67. The Government accepted that the recognition by a court of the applicant's title on 9 December 1993 represented a "possession" for the purposes of Article 1 of Protocol No. 1. However, at the hearing on 17 June 1999 the Government raised for the first time the argument that the judgment of 9 December 1993 had not concerned the ground floor, which had been sold by the State in 1973.

68. In the applicant's submission, the State could not lawfully have sold property that did not belong to it. Moreover, the tenants of the ground-floor flat could not have purchased it without acting in bad faith since they were perfectly aware that the applicant's parents had been dispossessed unlawfully.

The intervener submitted that any possession of the applicant's could not include the flat on the ground floor of the house since that flat had been purchased by his uncles in 1973 and he had inherited it. He stated that the purchase had been in accordance with the law as it stood in 1973.

69. The Court takes note of the fact that the applicant's title to the flat on the ground floor of the house is disputed by the intervener. It points out, however, that the proceedings before it, brought by the applicant against the Romanian State, can only affect the rights and obligations of those parties. The Court also notes that the intervener was not a party to any of the domestic proceedings at issue in the present case, the sole parties to those proceedings having been the applicant and the Government.

70. The Court considers that the applicant had a "possession" for the purposes of Article 1 of Protocol No. 1. The Court of First Instance, in its judgment of 9 December 1993, established that the house in question had been nationalised in breach of Decree no. 92/1950 on nationalisation and held, with retrospective effect, that the applicant, as his parents' successor in title, was the lawful owner of that house. The Court also notes that that finding as to the applicant's right was irrevocable. Furthermore, the applicant had peaceful enjoyment of his possession, as its rightful owner, from 9 December

1993 to 1 March 1995. He also paid real-property taxes on it.

B. Whether There Was Interference

71. In the applicant's submission, the consequence of the quashing of the judgment of 9 December 1993 was to make it absolutely impossible for him to assert his right of property, something which amounted to interference with his right to peaceful enjoyment of his possessions.

72. The Government submitted that the Supreme Court of Justice's judgment, while not determining the issue of the applicant's title, had created short-lived uncertainty as to it, and thus constituted temporary interference with the applicant's right to peaceful enjoyment of his possessions.

73. The Commission observed that the applicant's title had been recognised in a final judgment, with the result that he could have legitimately expected to have peaceful enjoyment of his right. The quashing of the judgment of 9 December 1993 amounted to interference with the applicant's right of property.

74. The Court acknowledges that the Supreme Court of Justice did not intend to rule on the applicant's claim to a property right. However, the Court considers that there has been an interference with the applicant's right of property as guaranteed by Article 1 of Protocol No. 1, in that the Supreme Court of Justice's judgment of 1 March 1995 quashed the final judgment of 9 December 1993, vesting the house in the applicant, even though the judgment had been executed.

C. Whether the Interference Was Justified

75. It remains to be ascertained whether or not the interference found by the Court violated Article 1 of Protocol No. 1. This necessitates determining whether, as the Government submit, the interference in question fell under the first sentence of the first paragraph of Article 1 on the grounds that the judgment of the Supreme Court of Justice amounted neither to a formal deprivation of the applicant's possessions nor to a control of their use or whether, as the Commission found, the case concerns a deprivation of property covered by the second sentence of the first paragraph of that Article.

76. The Court recalls that in determining whether there has been a deprivation of possessions within the second "rule", it is necessary not only to consider whether there has been a formal taking or expropriation of property but to look behind the appearances and investigate the realities of the situation complained of. Since the Convention is intended to guarantee rights that are "practical and effective", it has to be ascertained whether the situation amounted to a *de facto* expropriation (see the Sporrong and Lönnroth v. Sweden judgment of 23 September 1982, Series A no. 52, pp. 24–25, § 63, and the Vasilescu judgment cited above, p. 1078, § 51).

77. The Court notes that, in the present case, the judgment of the Court of First Instance, ordering the administrative authorities to return the house to the applicant, became final and irrevocable and that, in compliance with the judgment, the mayor of Bucharest ordered the house to be returned to the applicant, an order which was given effect by the C. company in May 1994. The Court further notes that, as of that date, the applicant ceased to pay rent on the flat he was occupying in the house and that from April 1994 until April 1996 the applicant paid land tax on the house. The Court observes that the effect of the judgment of the Supreme Court of Justice was to deprive the applicant of all the fruits of the final judgment in his favour by holding that the State had demonstrated its title to the house under the nationalisation decree. Following that decision, the applicant was informed that the house would again be classified as State property with effect from April 1996. In consequence of the judgment of the Supreme Court of Justice, the applicant was accordingly deprived of the rights of ownership of the house which had been vested in him by virtue of the final judgment in his favour. In particular, he was no longer able to sell, devise, donate or otherwise dispose of the property. In these circumstances, the Court finds that the effect of the judgment of the Supreme Court of Justice was to deprive the applicant of his possessions within the meaning of the second sentence of the first paragraph of Article 1 of Protocol No. 1.

78. A taking of property within this second rule can only be justified if it is shown, *inter alia*, to be "in the public interest" and "subject to the conditions provided for by law". Moreover, any interference with the property must also satisfy the requirement of proportionality. As the Court has repeatedly stated, a fair balance must be struck between the demands of the general interest of the community and the requirements of the protection of the individual's

fundamental rights, the search for such a fair balance being inherent in the whole of the Convention. The Court further recalls that the requisite balance will not be struck where the person concerned bears an individual and excessive burden (see the Sporrong and Lönnroth judgment cited above, pp. 26–28, §§ 69–74).

79. The Court, like the Commission, observes that no justification has been offered for the situation brought about by the judgment of the Supreme Court of Justice. In particular, neither the Supreme Court of Justice itself nor the Government have sought to justify the deprivation of property on substantive grounds as being "in the public interest". The Court further notes that the applicant has now been deprived of the ownership of the property for more than four years without being paid compensation reflecting its true value, and that his efforts to recover ownership have to date proved unsuccessful.

80. In these circumstances, even assuming that the taking could be shown to serve some public interest, the Court finds that a fair balance was upset and that the applicant bore and continues to bear an individual and excessive burden. There has accordingly been and continues to be a violation of Article 1 of Protocol No. 1.

[. . .]

4.9. *Bilgin v. Turkey* (2000)

[. . .]

I. THE CIRCUMSTANCES OF THE CASE

9. The applicant, Mr İhsan Bilgin, is a Turkish citizen who was born in 1960 and is at present living in Batman (Turkey). At the time of the events giving rise to his application, he was living in Yukarıgören, a hamlet attached to the village of Güzderesi in the Province of Diyarbakır (south-east Turkey). The application concerns the applicant's allegations that his house and other possessions in Yukarıgören were destroyed by security forces.

A. The Facts

10. The facts concerning the destruction of the applicant's possessions are disputed between the parties.

11. The facts as presented by the applicant are set out in paragraphs 14 to 17 below. In his memorial to the Court, the applicant relied on the facts as established by the Commission in its report adopted on 21 October 1999. The facts as presented by the Government are set out in paragraphs 18 to 20 below.

12. A description of the material submitted to the Commission is found in paragraphs 21 to 26 below. A description of the proceedings before the domestic authorities regarding the destruction of the applicant's possessions is set out in paragraphs 39 to 61 below.

13. The Commission, in order to establish the facts disputed between the parties, conducted an investigation in accordance with former Article 28 § 1 (a) of the Convention. To this end, the Commission examined documents submitted by both the applicant and the respondent Government in support of their respective assertions and appointed three delegates to take the evidence of witnesses at a hearing conducted in Ankara on 13 and 14 March 1997. The Commission's evaluation of the evidence and its findings are summarised in paragraphs 66 to 70 below.

1. Facts as Presented by the Applicant

14. On 28 September 1993 a large number of gendarmes arrived in Yukarıgören, a hamlet attached to the village of Güzderesi. They were probably looking for Faysal Alpan, who lived there and who was suspected of PKK related activities. The gendarmes ordered him and the other inhabitants of Yukarıgören to remove the harvested tobacco leaves from their houses and to pile them up in front of the houses. The gendarmes then set fire to the tobacco. On that day the gendarmes apprehended 11 or 12 persons in Güzderesi, including the two sons of Hüsnü Eraslan and a son of Mehmet Salih Eraslan, and placed them in detention.

15. Although the applicant had no precise recollection whether this occurred on the same day or two weeks later, the gendarmes further damaged and broke the furnishings, windows and various household goods in his house. The applicant took photographs of the burned mound of tobacco and the damage caused to his possessions in his house.

16. In the late summer or fall of 1994, on a day when the applicant was in Batman, the gendarmes returned to Yukarıgören. The applicant's family was

the only household to have remained in the hamlet, all other inhabitants having moved away in the meantime. After the gendarmes had gathered the applicant's family and a visiting guest at the water tower in the hamlet, the gendarmes set fire to the houses in the hamlet. The applicant returned to Yukarıgören in the morning of the following day. After the burning of his house, the applicant and his family left Yukarıgören.

17. The burning of the harvested tobacco and the destruction of the applicant's house and other possessions was conducted by the gendarmes under the orders and responsibility of the Commander of the Çatakköprü gendarmerie station and the Commander of the Silvan District gendarmerie station. The gendarmes of both units were engaged in a series of raids and operations in 1993 and 1994 in both Yukarıgören and Güzderesi culminating in the burning down of Yukarıgören. The purpose of this series of attacks was to force its inhabitants, including the applicant, to leave.

2. Facts as Presented by the Government

18. The Government stated that at the relevant time there were many PKK activities in the region and the area was regularly patrolled by gendarmes for military, administrative, judicial and civil purposes.

19. According to the military authorities no operation had been conducted in or around Güzderesi at the material time.

20. The Government further stated that, as the applicant had not filed an official complaint with the domestic authorities, a preliminary investigation was opened and conducted once the application had been brought to the notice of the Turkish Government. The case was transferred to the Provincial Administrative Council for a decision whether or not to prosecute those allegedly responsible, i.e. İbrahim Aktürk (Commander of the Silvan District gendarmerie station), Hakan Temel (Commander of a commando unit of the Silvan District gendarmerie station) and Hüdaverdi Tunç (Commander of the Çatakköprü gendarmerie station). In its decision of 4 June 1998, the Provincial Administrative Council found that there was insufficient evidence in support of the allegations made against İbrahim Aktürk, Hakan Temel and Hüdaverdi Tunç.

[. . .]

III. ALLEGED VIOLATIONS OF ARTICLE 8 OF THE CONVENTION AND ARTICLE 1 OF PROTOCOL NO. 1

105. The applicant complained that the deliberate destruction of his home and possessions by the security forces, thus forcing him from his home and lose his livelihood, constituted violations both of Article 8 of the Convention, which reads:

"1. Everyone has the right to respect for his private and family life, his home and his correspondence.

2. There shall be no interference by a public authority with the exercise of this right except such as is in accordance with the law and is necessary in a democratic society in the interests of national security, public safety or the economic well-being of the country, for the prevention of disorder or crime, for the protection of health or morals, or for the protection of the rights and freedoms of others."

and of Article 1 of Protocol No. 1, which provides:

"Every natural or legal person is entitled to the peaceful enjoyment of his possessions. No one shall be deprived of his possessions except in the public interest and subject to the conditions provided for by law and by the general principles of international law.

    The preceding provisions shall not, however, in any way impair the right of a State to enforce such laws as it deems necessary to control the use of property in accordance with the general interest or to secure the payment of taxes or other contributions or penalties."

106. The Government denied that there had been a violation of these provisions on the same grounds as those advanced in connection with Article 3 of the Convention.

107. The Commission considered that there had been a breach of Article 8 of the Convention and Article 1 of Protocol No. 1.

108. The Court has found it established that the applicant's home and possessions were destroyed by the security forces, thus depriving the applicant of his livelihood and forcing him and his family to leave Yukarıgören (see § 96 above). There can be no doubt that these acts constituted grave and unjustified interferences with the applicant's rights

to respect for his private and family life and home, and to the peaceful enjoyment of his possessions.

109. Accordingly, there have been violations of Article 8 of the Convention and Article 1 of Protocol No. 1.

[. . .]

4.10. *Zwierzyński v. Poland* (2001)

[. . .]

I. The Circumstances of the Case

7. In 1937 the applicant's father purchased from S. a property located in Łomża.

8. In 1950 the Białystok Regional Office (*Urząd Wojewódzki*) asked the Land Registry Division of Łomża Municipal Court (*Sąd Grodzki*) to insert a notice in the register stating that an expropriation procedure had begun in respect of the property, the registered owner of which was Mr B. Zwierzyński, the applicant's father. On 26 June 1950 the Municipal Court decided to file the application with the Land Registry Division and notify the interested parties.

On 24 July 1952 the Białystok Regional Executive of the National Council (*Prezydium Wojewódzkiej Rady Narodowej*) expropriated B. Zwierzyński's property in the public interest in accordance with the decree of 7 April 1948. Compensation was awarded to the former owner by a decision of 10 July 1961, upheld on 10 February 1962. The payment in compensation was credited to the State deposit account but neither the former owner nor his heirs claimed it.

9. On 2 December 1980 the Minister for Economic Affairs (*Minister Gospodarki*) dismissed an application by the applicant's father for the expropriation decision to be set aside.

10. On 10 August 1990, after B. Zwierzyński's death, the applicant's mother lodged an application to set aside the decision of 2 December 1980. On 18 July 1991 the Minister for Economic Affairs declared the entirety of the proceedings since the 1952 expropriation decision null and void on account of a manifest mistake in law. In 1945 the owner had entered into a leasing contract with the State authorities and so it could not legitimately be stated that the land

and the building had been occupied unilaterally by the administrative authorities. Consequently, the situation did not fall within the scope of the 1948 expropriation decree.

11. The Łomża regional police authority (*Komenda Wojewódzka Policji*), which currently occupies the premises, appealed against the Minister's decision to the Supreme Administrative Court (*Naczelny Sąd Administracyjny*) in Warsaw.

12. On 19 December 1992 that court set aside the decision and remitted the case to the Minister for reconsideration.

13. In a decision of 24 July 1992, upheld by the Supreme Administrative Court on 23 November 1993, the Minister reiterated his finding that the proceedings since 1952 were null and void.

14. On 21 June 1994 the Olsztyn District Court decided that the applicant and his sister should each inherit half of their deceased parents' estate.

15. The tax authorities asked the applicant to pay inheritance tax. The applicant asked for the deadline for payment to be extended because negotiations with a view to the sale or rent of the building were under way with the regional police authority, which was occupying the premises. On 4 November 1994, having received confirmation from the regional police authority that negotiations were indeed taking place, the Chairman of Olsztyn Municipal Council extended the deadline. On 20 June 1995 the Olsztyn Tax Office (*Urząd Skarbowy*) extended the deadline to a date which has not been specified.

16. On 12 September 1994 the Land Registry Division of the District Court (*Sąd Rejonowy Wydział Ksiąg Wieczystych*) entered the property in the Land Register, identifying the applicant and his sister as the owners. However, they have never obtained its return.

17. The negotiations on the sale of the property foundered and, moreover, the occupier never paid the rent fixed by the owners. Since 1995 the applicant has been paying property tax.

18. On 28 September 1992 the Treasury (*Skarb Państwa*), assisted by the Łomża District Office Director (*Kierownik Urzędu Rejonowego*), acting on behalf of the regional police authority (the current occupier), brought an action before the civil courts asserting acquisition of title to the property

through adverse possession (*stwierdzenie nabycia własności nieruchomosci przez zasiedzenie*). On 25 November 1992 the Łomża District Court stayed the proceedings at the request of the Łomża District Office Director, taking the view that the outcome of the administrative proceedings pending before the Supreme Administrative Court on the application to set aside the 1952 expropriation decision would have a decisive impact on the action for acquisition of title to the property through adverse possession. On 18 January 1995 it lifted the stay at the Director's request.

19. On 6 October 1995 the District Court granted the Treasury's application, taking the view that the public authority had occupied the premises in good faith for the period of twenty years required under Article 172 of the Civil Code. The decision was upheld on 1 February 1996 by the Łomża Regional Court (*Sąd Wojewódzki*).

20. On 3 October 1996 the Minister of Justice lodged an appeal on points of law with the Supreme Court (*Sąd Najwyższy*) on the applicant's behalf. He submitted that in the light of the Supreme Court's case-law, there could be no possession in good faith where an expropriation decision had been set aside. Consequently, in view of the decision of 1993 setting aside the expropriation decision of 1952, the applicant had retrospectively recovered title to the property for the entire period during which the premises had been occupied by the State.

21. On 29 October 1996 the Supreme Court set aside the lower courts' decisions and remitted the case to the District Court for reconsideration. It pointed out that it had had to rule on the same question on a number of occasions. It had consistently held that if the Treasury's right to dispose of a property "like a property owner" was based on an administrative decision which was subsequently set aside with retrospective effect on account of a manifest mistake of law, the period of occupation could not be taken into account when calculating the period of possession giving title to property through adverse possession for the purposes of Article 172 of the Civil Code.

22. The case was remitted to the Łomża District Court. On 11 February 1997 the District Office Director, who is a representative of the State, applied for the proceedings to be stayed on the ground that the District Office had asked the Minister of Justice to lodge an appeal on points of law

against the decision of 21 June 1994 in which the Olsztyn District Court had ruled that the applicant and his sister should each inherit half of their parents' estate.

23. On 24 February 1997 the Land Registry Division of the Łomża District Court informed the applicant that the Treasury had been listed in the register as the owner of the property. It specified, however, that it had added of its own motion a notice referring to the proceedings brought for the acquisition of title to the property through adverse possession in order to protect the applicant's and his sister's claims.

24. On 2 April 1997 the Minister of Justice lodged the requested appeal with the Supreme Court and on 24 June 1997 the Łomża District Court stayed the proceedings.

25. On 9 September 1997 the Supreme Court granted the appeal on points of law, set aside the decision of 21 June 1994 and remitted the case to the District Court. It pointed out that the first issue to be decided was whether the heirs' parents were indeed the owners of the property in question. When the property had been purchased by the applicant's parents, the law had required that a notarial deed be drawn up for the purchase to be valid. In the absence of such a deed, and where no one had been in possession of the property long enough to acquire title to it by adverse possession, the assets of the estate were deemed to comprise only the possession (*posiadanie*) of the property, not the title to it.

The Supreme Court also noted that the appeal had been lodged after the expiry of the time-limit (six months after the disputed decision) set by Article 421 § 2 of the Code of Civil Procedure, but considered that questions relating to property law required special protection and that it would have been detrimental to the Republic of Poland's interests to dismiss the application for being out of time because to do so would have infringed a right which was actually vested in another person.

26. On 8 July 1998 the Olsztyn District Court, to which the case had been remitted, ruled that the applicant's parents' estate should be shared equally between the applicant and his sister. The assets of the estate comprised the disputed property. The decision was identical in substance to the one of 21 June 1994.

27. On 23 September 1998 the Łomża District Court lifted the stay ordered on 24 June 1997 on the proceedings for acquisition of title to the property through adverse possession.

28. On 17 September 1998 the applicant lodged an application with the Land Registry Division of the Łomża District Court to have the entry in the register rectified so that he was listed as the owner. The ground for his application was that on 8 July 1998 the Olsztyn District Court had named him and his sister as the inheritors of their parents' property. On 6 November 1998 the District Court asked the applicant to produce a decision proving that the entry in the register was not consistent with the legal status of the property, failing which his application would be dismissed. On 14 January 1999 the applicant complained about that requirement to the Łomża Regional Court, but without success. On 3 February 1999 the Land Registry Division of the District Court rejected his application to have the entry in the register rectified.

29. In December 1998 the applicant was summoned to the Olsztyn District Court, which had decided the matter of the division of the estate. He was told that the heirs of S., who had sold the property in issue to the applicant's father in 1937, had brought an action to have the proceedings concerning the division of the estate reopened. They said that they had been informed of the outcome of the proceedings by the regional police authority's legal adviser and argued that they had rights over the property. On 14 December 1998 the District Court to which the Treasury had applied for acquisition of title to the property through adverse possession suspended its consideration of that case pending the outcome of the action to reopen the proceedings concerning the division of the estate.

30. After hearings held on 28 January, 9 March, 26 April and 13 May 1999, the Olsztyn District Court rejected the application by S.'s heirs. Its decision was upheld on appeal by the Olsztyn Regional Court on 27 October 1999. On 17 December 1999 S.'s heirs lodged an appeal on points of law with the Supreme Court.

31. On 17 October 2000 the Supreme Court allowed the appeal and remitted the case to the Olsztyn Regional Court for reconsideration. It observed that the Regional Court should have satisfied itself not only that the appellant had *locus standi*, which it had done, but also that the decision taken by the

District Court on 8 July 1998 at the end of the proceedings which S. had applied to have reopened had related to his rights.

32. The case is still pending before the Olsztyn Regional Court.

[. . .]

II. Alleged Violation of Article 1 of Protocol No. 1

57. The applicant complained of an infringement of his right to the peaceful enjoyment of his possessions within the meaning of Article 1 of Protocol No. 1, which provides:

> "Every natural or legal person is entitled to the peaceful enjoyment of his possessions. No one shall be deprived of his possessions except in the public interest and subject to the conditions provided for by law and by the general principles of international law.
>
> The preceding provisions shall not, however, in any way impair the right of a State to enforce such laws as it deems necessary to control the use of property in accordance with the general interest or to secure the payment of taxes or other contributions or penalties."

This provision comprises three distinct rules. The first, which is expressed in the first sentence of the first paragraph and is of a general nature, lays down the principle of peaceful enjoyment of property. The second rule, in the second sentence of the same paragraph, covers deprivation of possessions and subjects it to certain conditions. The third, contained in the second paragraph, recognises that the Contracting States are entitled, amongst other things, to control the use of property in accordance with the general interest. These rules are not "distinct" in the sense of being unconnected: the second and third rules, which are concerned with particular instances of interference with the right to peaceful enjoyment of property, are to be construed in the light of the general principle laid down in the first rule.

58. The Court observes moreover that it has jurisdiction as regards Article 1 of Protocol No. 1 only for facts occurring after 10 October 1994, the date on which Poland ratified the Protocol. In its assessment, it will, however, take account of events occurring prior to that date.

A. Whether There Was a "Possession"

59. The Government refused to accept that the applicant was the owner of the property. In their opinion, the fact that the case concerning the application for acquisition of title to the property through adverse possession was still pending before the Polish courts called the legal status of the property into question. The Government also expressed doubts as to whether the applicant's father could legitimately be regarded as the owner, firstly since the land register of the time of the sale of the property in 1937 had been destroyed during the Second World War, and secondly because there was lingering uncertainty about the circumstances in which the sale of the property and its purchase by the applicant's father had taken place in the period between 1937 and 1939.

60. The Government submitted moreover that Article 1 of Protocol No. 1 was not applicable in the instant case. They pointed out that, at the time of the expropriation in 1952, the State had been exercising its sovereign prerogatives ("*imperium*"). Since the setting aside of the expropriation decision in 1992 the State had acted only as one of the parties in a civil law relationship ("*dominium*"). The Government submitted that although the administrative decision quashing the expropriation had re-established the status of the property in 1952 it had not given the applicant title to the property. At no time had the applicant and his sister proved that they were the sole inheritors with any claim over the object in dispute.

61. Referring to the Court's case-law on the subject, the Government observed that Article 1 of Protocol No. 1 applies only to a person's existing possessions, that the applicant must be able to prove that he has a legitimate expectation of exercising his property rights and that the Convention does not guarantee the right to become the owner of a property (see the following judgments: *Marckx v. Belgium*, 13 June 1979, Series A no. 31; *Stran Greek Refineries and Stratis Andreadis v. Greece*, 9 December 1994, Series A no. 301-B; and *Brumărescu v. Romania* [GC], no. 28342/95, ECHR 1999-VII).

62. The applicant claimed to be the owner of the property. He derived his title from the decision of the Land Registry Division of the Municipal Court on 26 June 1950 (see paragraph 8 above), in which his father, B. Zwierzyński, was clearly identified as the owner of the property. He pointed out that only an owner could be expropriated and that the expropriation decision had identified his father as the owner of the expropriated property and awarded compensation to him. According to the applicant, the setting aside of the expropriation decision with retrospective effect had re-established the situation prior to 1952.

The applicant also pointed out that on 8 July 1998 the Łomża District Court had recognised his status as heir, particularly as regards the property in issue, thus enabling him to take over his father's property rights.

63. The Court points out that the concept of "possessions" in Article 1 of Protocol No. 1 has an autonomous meaning (see *Beyeler v. Italy* [GC], no. 33202/96, § 100, ECHR 2000-I). Consequently, the issue that needs to be examined is whether the circumstances of the case, considered as a whole, conferred on the applicant a substantive interest protected by Article 1 of Protocol No. 1, having regard to the relevant points of law and of fact.

64. The Municipal Court decision of 26 June 1950 (see paragraph 8 above) proves conclusively that the applicant's father was considered by the authorities of the time as the owner of the property in issue. The Court agrees with the applicant's argument that only an owner could be expropriated. It also notes that the decision of the Supreme Administrative Court of 23 November 1993 restored the applicant's father's title to the property with retrospective effect (see paragraph 13 above). As regards the applicant himself, the Court observes that on 21 June 1994 the Olsztyn District Court recognised him as the owner of the property when dividing up his parents' estate (see paragraph 14 above), and that that decision was upheld by the Olsztyn District Court on 8 July 1998 (see paragraph 26 above) despite the regional police authority's attempts to call his right into question (see paragraphs 22–25 above). The Court further notes that when conducting the negotiations for the sale or rent of the property (see paragraph 17 above), after the applicant had been listed in the Land Register (see paragraph 16 above) and while the application for acquisition of title to the property through adverse possession was pending, the authorities treated the applicant as the owner of the property. It observes that the proceedings brought subsequently do not cast any doubt on the applicant's status as

the owner of property within the meaning of the Convention.

65. Lastly, the Court notes that the applicant regularly pays the rates and property taxes in respect of the disputed property (see paragraphs 15 and 17 above).

66. This being so, it considers that the applicant had a "possession" within the meaning of the Convention.

B. Whether There Was Interference

67. The Court considers that there has been a clear interference with the applicant's right to peaceful enjoyment of his possessions in that the regional police authority continues to occupy the premises despite the fact that an administrative decision retrospectively restored the title to the property to the applicant's father, whose estate the applicant inherited, and on account of the actions brought directly or implicitly by the current occupier.

It must therefore determine whether the interference complained of is justified under Article 1 of Protocol No. 1.

C. Whether the Interference Was Justified

68. The Court must begin by establishing whether the interference in question amounted to a formal deprivation of the disputed property, a measure encompassed within the power to control the use of property granted to the States by the second paragraph of Article 1 of Protocol No. 1, or a deprivation of property covered by the second sentence of the first paragraph of that Article.

69. The Court points out that in determining whether there has been a deprivation of possessions, it is necessary not only to consider whether there has been a formal taking or expropriation of property but to look behind the appearances and investigate the realities of the situation complained of. Since the Convention is intended to guarantee rights that are "practical and effective", it has to be ascertained whether the situation amounted to a *de facto* expropriation (see *Sporrong and Lönnroth v. Sweden*, judgment of 23 September 1982, Series A no. 52, pp. 24–25, § 63, and *Brumărescu*, cited above, § 76).

70. The Court notes that the effect of the Supreme Administrative Court's judgment of 23 November 1993 was retrospectively to restore the title to the property to the applicant's father, whose estate was inherited by the applicant following the decision of 8 July 1998 in which his status as heir was conclusively recognised. Since the Supreme Administrative Court's decision, the State authorities have done all they can to delay the restitution of the property (see paragraph 54 above). All the proceedings instituted directly or indirectly by them have resulted in infringements of the applicant's right to peaceful enjoyment of his possessions within the meaning of the second sentence of the first paragraph of Article 1 of Protocol No. 1.

71. A deprivation of possessions within the meaning of this sentence can only be justified if it is shown to be "in the public interest" and "subject to the conditions provided for by law". Moreover, any interference with the property must also satisfy the requirement of proportionality (see *Brumărescu*, cited above). The Court reiterates that an interference must strike a "fair balance" between the demands of the general interest of the community and the requirements of the protection of the individual's fundamental rights (see *Pressos Compania Naviera S.A. and Others v. Belgium*, judgment of 20 November 1995, Series A no. 332, p. 23, § 38). The requisite balance will be upset if the person concerned bears an individual and excessive burden (see *Sporrong and Lönnroth*, cited above, pp. 26–28).

72. The Court can find no justification for the situation in which the public authorities have placed the applicant. It cannot discern in the present case any genuine "public interest" that would justify a deprivation of possessions.

73. The Court points out that where an issue in the general interest is at stake it is incumbent on the public authorities to act in an appropriate manner and with the utmost consistency (see *Beyeler*, cited above). Moreover, as the guardian of public order, the State has a moral obligation to lead by example and a duty to ensure that the bodies it has charged with the protection of public order follow that example.

74. In the instant case, the Court considers that the "fair balance" referred to above has been upset and that the applicant has borne and continues to bear an individual and excessive burden.

It finds therefore that there has been a violation of Article 1 of Protocol No. 1.

[. . .]

4.11. *Cyprus v. Turkey* (2001)

The Circumstances of the Case

A. General Context

13. The complaints raised in this application arise out of the Turkish military operations in northern Cyprus in July and August 1974 and the continuing division of the territory of Cyprus. At the time of the Court's consideration of the merits of the Loizidou v. Turkey case in 1996, the Turkish military presence at the material time was described in the following terms (Loizidou v. Turkey judgment of 18 December 1996 (*merits*), *Reports of Judgments and Decisions* 1996-VI, p. 2223, §§ 16–17):

"16. Turkish armed forces of more than 30,000 personnel are stationed throughout the whole of the occupied area of northern Cyprus, which is constantly patrolled and has checkpoints on all main lines of communication. The army's headquarters are in Kyrenia. The 28th Infantry Division is based in Asha (Assia) with its sector covering Famagusta to the Mia Milia suburb of Nicosia and with about 14,500 personnel. The 39th Infantry Division, with about 15,500 personnel, is based at Myrtou village, and its sector ranges from Yerolakkos village to Lefka. TOURDYK (Turkish Forces in Cyprus under the Treaty of Guarantee) is stationed at Orta Keuy village near Nicosia, with a sector running from Nicosia International Airport to the Pedhieos River. A Turkish naval command and outpost are based at Famagusta and Kyrenia respectively. Turkish airforce personnel are based at Lefkoniko, Krini and other airfields. The Turkish airforce is stationed on the Turkish mainland at Adana.

17. The Turkish forces and all civilians entering military areas are subject to Turkish military courts, as stipulated so far as concerns 'TRNC citizens' by the Prohibited Military Areas Decree of 1979 (section 9) and Article 156 of the Constitution of the 'TRNC'."

14. A major development in the continuing division of Cyprus occurred in November 1983 with the proclamation of the "Turkish Republic of Northern Cyprus" (the "TRNC") and the subsequent enactment of the "TRNC Constitution" on 7 May 1985.

This development was condemned by the international community. On 18 November 1983 the United Nations Security Council adopted Resolution 541 (1983) declaring the proclamation of the establishment of the "TRNC" legally invalid and calling upon all States not to recognise any Cypriot State other than the Republic of Cyprus. A similar call was made by the Security Council on 11 May 1984 in its Resolution 550 (1984). In November 1983 the Committee of Ministers of the Council of Europe decided that it continued to regard the government of the Republic of Cyprus as the sole legitimate government of Cyprus and called for respect of the sovereignty, independence, territorial integrity and unity of the Republic of Cyprus.

15. According to the respondent Government, the "TRNC" is a democratic and constitutional State which is politically independent of all other sovereign States including Turkey, and the administration in northern Cyprus has been set up by the Turkish-Cypriot people in the exercise of its right to self-determination and not by Turkey. Notwithstanding this view, it is only the Cypriot government which is recognised internationally as the government of the Republic of Cyprus in the context of diplomatic and treaty relations and the working of international organisations.

16. United Nations peacekeeping forces ("UNFICYP") maintain a buffer-zone. A number of political initiatives have been taken at the level of the United Nations aimed at settling the Cyprus problem on the basis of institutional arrangements acceptable to both sides. To this end, inter-communal talks have been sponsored by the Secretary-General of the United Nations acting under the direction of the Security Council. In this connection, the respondent Government maintain that the Turkish-Cypriot authorities in northern Cyprus have pursued the talks on the basis of what they consider to be already agreed principles of bizonality and bi-communality within the framework of a federal constitution. Support for this basis of negotiation is found in the UN Secretary-General's Set of Ideas of 15 July 1992 and the UN Security Council resolutions of 26 August 1992 and

25 November 1992 confirming that a federal solution sought by both sides will be "bi-communal" and "bi-zonal".

Furthermore, and of relevance to the instant application, in 1981 the United Nations Committee on Missing Persons ("CMP") was set up to "look into cases of persons reported missing in the inter-communal fighting as well as in the events of July 1974 and afterwards" and "to draw up comprehensive lists of missing persons of both communities, specifying as appropriate whether they are still alive or dead, and in the latter case approximate times of death". The CMP has not yet completed its investigations.

B. The Previous Inter-State Applications

17. The events of July and August 1974 and their aftermath gave rise to three previous applications by the applicant Government against the respondent State under former Article 24 of the Convention. The first (no. 6780/74) and second (no. 6950/75) applications were joined by the Commission and led to the adoption on 10 July 1976 of a report under former Article 31 of the Convention ("the 1976 report") in which the Commission expressed the opinion that the respondent State had violated Articles 2, 3, 5, 8, 13 and 14 of the Convention and Article 1 of Protocol No. 1. On 20 January 1979 the Committee of Ministers of the Council of Europe in turn adopted, with reference to an earlier decision of 21 October 1977, Resolution DH (79) 1 in which it expressed, *inter alia*, the conviction that "the enduring protection of human rights in Cyprus can only be brought about through the re-establishment of peace and confidence between the two communities; and that inter-communal talks constitute the appropriate framework for reaching a solution of the dispute". In its resolution the Committee of Ministers strongly urged the parties to resume the talks under the auspices of the Secretary-General of the United Nations in order to agree upon solutions on all aspects of the dispute (see paragraph 16 above). The Committee of Ministers viewed this decision as completing its consideration of the case.

The third application (no. 8007/77) lodged by the applicant Government was the subject of a further report under former Article 31 adopted by the Commission on 4 October 1983 ("the 1983 report"). In that report the Commission expressed the opin-

ion that the respondent State was in breach of its obligations under Articles 5 and 8 of the Convention and Article 1 of Protocol No. 1. On 2 April 1992 the Committee of Ministers adopted Resolution DH (92) 12 in respect of the Commission's 1983 report. In its resolution the Committee of Ministers limited itself to a decision to make the 1983 report public and stated that its consideration of the case was thereby completed.

C. The Instant Application

18. The instant application is the first to have been referred to the Court. The applicant Government requested the Court in their memorial to "decide and declare that the respondent State is responsible for continuing violations and other violations of Articles 1, 2, 3, 4, 5, 6, 8, 9, 10, 11, 13, 14, 17 and 18 of the Convention and of Articles 1 and 2 of Protocol No. 1".

These allegations were invoked with reference to four broad categories of complaints: alleged violations of the rights of Greek-Cypriot missing persons and their relatives; alleged violations of the home and property rights of displaced persons; alleged violations of the rights of enclaved Greek Cypriots in northern Cyprus; alleged violations of the rights of Turkish Cypriots and the Gypsy community in northern Cyprus.

D. The Commission's Findings of Fact in the Instant Application

19. The Court considers it appropriate at this stage to summarise the Commission's findings of fact in respect of the various violations of the Convention alleged by the applicant Government as well as the essential arguments advanced by both parties and the documentary and other evidence relied on by the Commission.

1. Alleged Violations of the Rights of Greek-Cypriot Missing Persons and Their Relatives

20. The applicant Government essentially claimed in their application that about 1,491 Greek Cypriots were still missing twenty years after the cessation of hostilities. These persons were last seen alive in Turkish custody and their fate has never been accounted for by the respondent State.

21. The respondent Government maintained in reply that there was no proof that any of the missing persons were still alive or were being kept in custody. In their principal submission, the issues raised by the applicant Government should continue to be pursued within the framework of the United Nations Committee on Missing Persons (see paragraph 16 above) rather than under the Convention.

22. The Commission proceeded on the understanding that its task was not to establish what actually happened to the Greek-Cypriot persons who went missing following the Turkish military operations conducted in northern Cyprus in July and August 1974. Rather, it saw its task as one of determining whether or not the alleged failure of the respondent State to clarify the facts surrounding the disappearances constituted a continuing violation of the Convention.

23. To that end, the Commission had particular regard to its earlier findings in its 1976 and 1983 reports. It recalled that in its 1976 report it had stated that it was widely accepted that a considerable number of Cypriots were still missing as a result of armed conflict in Cyprus and that a number of persons declared to be missing were identified as Greek Cypriots taken prisoner by the Turkish army. This finding, in the Commission's opinion at the time, created a presumption of Turkish responsibility for the fate of persons shown to be in Turkish custody. While noting that killings of Greek-Cypriot civilians had occurred on a large scale, the Commission also considered at the time of its 1976 report that it was unable to ascertain whether, and under what circumstances, Greek-Cypriot prisoners declared to be missing had been deprived of their life.

24. In the present case, the Commission further recalled that in its 1983 report it found it established that there were sufficient indications in an indefinite number of cases that missing Greek Cypriots had been in Turkish custody in 1974 and that this finding once again created a presumption of Turkish responsibility for the fate of these persons.

25. The Commission found that the evidence submitted to it in the instant case confirmed its earlier findings that certain of the missing persons were last seen in Turkish or Turkish-Cypriot custody. In this connection, the Commission had regard to the following: a statement of Mr Denktaş, "President of the TRNC", broadcast on 1 March 1996, in which he admitted that forty-two Greek-Cypriot prisoners were handed over to Turkish-Cypriot fighters who killed them and that in order to prevent further such killings prisoners were subsequently transferred to Turkey; the broadcast statement of Professor Yalçin Küçük, a former Turkish officer who had served in the Turkish army at the time and participated in the 1974 military operation in Cyprus, in which he suggested that the Turkish army had engaged in widespread killings of, *inter alia*, civilians in so-called cleaning-up operations; the Dillon Report submitted to the United States Congress in May 1998 indicating, *inter alia*, that Turkish and Turkish-Cypriot soldiers rounded up Greek-Cypriot civilians in the village of Asha on 18 August 1974 and took away males over the age of 15, most of whom were reportedly killed by Turkish-Cypriot fighters; the written statements of witnesses tending to corroborate the Commission's earlier findings that many persons now missing were taken into custody by Turkish soldiers or Turkish-Cypriot paramilitaries.

26. The Commission concluded that, notwithstanding evidence of the killing of Greek-Cypriot prisoners and civilians, there was no proof that any of the missing persons were killed in circumstances for which the respondent State could be held responsible; nor did the Commission find any evidence to the effect that any of the persons taken into custody were still being detained or kept in servitude by the respondent State. On the other hand, the Commission found it established that the facts surrounding the fate of the missing persons had not been clarified by the authorities and brought to the notice of the victims' relatives.

27. The Commission further concluded that its examination of the applicant Government's complaints in the instant application was not precluded by the ongoing work of the CMP. It noted in this connection that the scope of the investigation being conducted by the CMP was limited to determining whether or not any of the missing persons on its list were dead or alive; nor was the CMP empowered to make findings either on the cause of death or on the issue of responsibility for any deaths so established. Furthermore, the territorial jurisdiction of the CMP was limited to the island of Cyprus, thus excluding investigations in Turkey where some of the disappearances were claimed to have occurred. The Commission also observed that persons who

might be responsible for violations of the Convention were promised impunity and that it was doubtful whether the CMP's investigation could extend to actions by the Turkish army or Turkish officials on Cypriot territory.

2. Alleged Violations of the Rights of the Displaced Persons to Respect for Their Home and Property

28. The Commission established the facts under this heading against the background of the applicant Government's principal submission that over 211,000 displaced Greek Cypriots and their children continued to be prevented as a matter of policy from returning to their homes in northern Cyprus and from having access to their property there for any purpose. The applicant Government submitted that the presence of the Turkish army together with "TRNC"-imposed border restrictions ensured that the return of displaced persons was rendered physically impossible and, as a corollary, that their cross-border family visits were gravely impeded. What started as a gradual and continuing process of illegality over the years had now resulted in the transfer of the property left behind by the displaced persons to the "TRNC" authorities without payment of compensation and its re-assignment, together with "title deeds", to State bodies, Turkish Cypriots and settlers from Turkey.

29. The respondent Government maintained before the Commission that the question of the Varosha district of Famagusta along with the issues of freedom of movement, freedom of settlement and the right of property could only be resolved within the framework of the inter-communal talks (see paragraph 16 above) and on the basis of the principles agreed on by both sides for the conduct of the talks. Until an overall solution to the Cyprus question, acceptable to both sides, was found, and having regard to security considerations, there could be no question of a right of the displaced persons to return. The respondent Government further submitted that the regulation of property abandoned by displaced persons, as with restrictions on cross-border movement, fell within the exclusive jurisdiction of the "TRNC" authorities.

30. The Commission found that it was common knowledge that with the exception of a few hundred Maronites living in the Kormakiti area and Greek Cypriots living in the Karpas peninsula, the whole Greek-Cypriot population which before 1974 resided in the northern part of Cyprus had left that area, the large majority of these people now living in southern Cyprus. The reality of this situation was not contested by the respondent Government.

31. The Commission noted with reference to its earlier findings in its 1976 and 1983 reports that there was no essential change in the situation obtaining at the time of the introduction of the instant application. Accordingly, and this was not disputed either by the respondent Government, displaced Greek Cypriots had no possibility of returning to their homes in northern Cyprus and were physically prevented from crossing into the northern part on account of the fact that it was sealed off by the Turkish army. The arrangements introduced by the "TRNC" authorities in 1998 to allow Greek Cypriots and Maronites to cross into northern Cyprus for the purposes of family visits or, as regards Greek Cypriots, visits to the Apostolos Andreas Monastery, did not affect this conclusion.

32. Nor did the respondent Government dispute the fact that Greek-Cypriot owners of property in northern Cyprus continued to be prevented from having access to, controlling, using and enjoying their property. As to the fate of that property, the Commission found it established that up until 1989 there was an administrative practice of the Turkish-Cypriot authorities to leave the official Land Register unaffected and to register separately the "abandoned" property and its allocation. The beneficiaries of allocations were issued with "possessory certificates" but not "deeds of title" to the properties concerned. However, as from June 1989 the practice changed and thereafter "title deeds" were issued and the relevant entries concerning the change of ownership were made in the Land Register. The Commission found it established that, at least since June 1989, the Turkish-Cypriot authorities no longer recognised any ownership rights of Greek Cypriots in respect of their properties in northern Cyprus. The Commission found confirmation for this finding in the provisions of "Article 159 § 1 (b) of the TRNC Constitution" of 7 May 1985 and "Law no. 52/1995" purporting to give effect to that provision.

33. Although the respondent Government pointed out in their submissions to the Commission that the issue of the right of displaced Greek Cypriots to return to their homes was a matter

to be determined within the framework of the inter-communal talks sponsored by the Secretary-General of the United Nations (see paragraph 16 above), the Commission found that there had been no significant progress in recent years in the discussion of issues such as freedom of settlement, payment of compensation to Greek Cypriots for the interference with their property rights, or restitution of Greek-Cypriot property in the Varosha district.

3. Alleged Violations Arising out of the Living Conditions of Greek Cypriots in Northern Cyprus

34. The applicant Government adduced evidence in support of their complaint that the dwindling number of Greek Cypriots living in the Karpas peninsula of northern Cyprus were subjected to continuing oppressive treatment which amounted to a complete denial of their rights and a negation of their human dignity. In addition to the harassment and intimidation which they suffered at the hands of Turkish settlers, and which has gone unpunished, the enclaved Greek Cypriots laboured under restrictions which violated many of the substantive rights contained in the Convention. The continuous daily interferences with their rights could not be redressed at the local level on account of the absence of effective remedies before the "TRNC" courts. Similar but less extensive restrictions applied to the Maronite population living in the Kormakiti area of northern Cyprus.

35. The respondent Government maintained before the Commission that effective judicial remedies were available to all Greek Cypriots living in northern Cyprus. However, they claimed that the applicant Government actively discouraged them from taking proceedings in the "TRNC". The respondent Government further submitted that the evidence before the Commission did not provide any basis of fact for the allegations made.

36. The Commission established the facts under this heading with reference to materials submitted by both Governments. These materials included, *inter alia*, written statements of persons affected by the restrictions alleged by the applicant Government; press reports dealing with the situation in northern Cyprus; case-law of the "TRNC" courts on the availability of remedies in the "TRNC"; "TRNC legislation" and decisions of the "TRNC Council of Ministers" on entry and exit arrange-

ments at the Ledra Palace check-point. The Commission also had regard to United Nations documents concerning the living conditions of enclaved Greek Cypriots and especially to the UN Secretary-General's progress reports of 10 December 1995 and 9 March 1998 on the humanitarian review carried out by UNFICYP in 1994-95 concerning the living conditions of Karpas Greek Cypriots, the so-called "Karpas Brief".

37. Furthermore, the Commission's delegates heard the evidence of fourteen witnesses on the situation of Greek Cypriots and Maronites living in northern Cyprus. These witnesses comprised two persons who were closely associated with the preparation of the "Karpas Brief" as well as persons proposed by both Governments. The delegates also visited, on 23 and 24 February 1998, a number of localities in northern Cyprus, including Greek-Cypriot villages in the Karpas area, and heard statements from officials and other persons encountered during the visits.

38. The Commission considered the above-mentioned "Karpas Brief" an accurate description of the situation of the enclaved Greek-Cypriot and Maronite populations at about the time of the introduction of the instant application and that the proposals for remedial action recommended by UNFICYP following the humanitarian review reflected the real needs of these groups in the face of administrative practices which actually existed at the material time. Although the Commission noted that there had been a considerable improvement in the overall situation of the enclaved populations, as evidenced by the UN Secretary-General's progress reports on the "Karpas Brief" recommendations, there still remained a number of severe restrictions. These restrictions were not laid down in any "TRNC legislation" and were in the nature of administrative practices.

39. The Commission further found that there existed a functioning court system in the "TRNC" which was in principle accessible to Greek Cypriots living in northern Cyprus. It appeared that at least in cases of trespass to property or personal injury there had been some successful actions brought by Greek-Cypriot litigants before the civil and criminal courts. However, in view of the scarcity of cases brought by Greek Cypriots, the Commission was led to conclude that the effectiveness of the judicial

system for resident Greek Cypriots had not really been tested.

40. In a further conclusion, the Commission found that there was no evidence of continuing wrongful allocation of properties of resident Greek Cypriots to other persons during the period under consideration. However, the Commission did find it established that there was a continuing practice of the "TRNC" authorities to allocate to Turkish-Cypriots or immigrants the property of Greek Cypriots who had died or left northern Cyprus.

41. In the absence of legal proceedings before the "TRNC" courts, the Commission noted that it had not been tested whether or not Greek Cypriots or Maronites living in northern Cyprus were in fact considered as citizens enjoying the protection of the "TRNC Constitution". It did however find it established that, in so far as the groups at issue complained of administrative practices such as restrictions on their freedom of movement or on family visits which were based on decisions of the "TRNC Council of Ministers", any legal challenge to these restrictions would be futile given that such decisions were not open to review by the courts.

42. Although the Commission found no evidence of cases of actual detention of members of the enclaved population, it was satisfied that there was clear evidence that restrictions on movement and family visits continued to be applied to Greek Cypriots and Maronites notwithstanding recent improvements. It further observed that an exit visa was still necessary for transfers to medical facilities in the south, although no fees were levied in urgent cases. There was no evidence to confirm the allegation that the processing of applications for movement was delayed in certain cases with the result that the health or life of patients was endangered; nor was there any indication of a deliberate practice of delaying the processing of such applications.

43. The Commission found it established that there were restrictions on the freedom of movement of Greek-Cypriot and Maronite schoolchildren attending schools in the south. Until the entry into force of the decision of the "TRNC Council of Ministers" of 11 February 1998, they were not allowed to return permanently to the north after having attained the age of 16 in the case of males and 18 in the case of females. The age-limit of 16 years was still maintained for Greek-Cypriot male

students. Up to the age-limit, certain restrictions applied to the visits of students to their parents in the north, which were gradually relaxed. However, even today such visits are subject to a visa requirement and a reduced "entry fee".

44. As to educational facilities, the Commission held that, although there was a system of primary-school education for the children of Greek Cypriots living in northern Cyprus, there were no secondary schools for them. The vast majority of schoolchildren went to the south for their secondary education and the restriction on the return of Greek-Cypriot and Maronite schoolchildren to the north after the completion of their studies had led to the separation of many families. Furthermore, school textbooks for use in the Greek-Cypriot primary school were subjected to a "vetting" procedure in the context of confidence-building measures suggested by UNFICYP. The procedure was cumbersome and a relatively high number of school-books were being objected to by the Turkish-Cypriot administration.

45. Aside from school-books, the Commission found no evidence of any restrictions being applied during the period under consideration to the importation, circulation or possession of other types of books; nor was there evidence of restrictions on the circulation of newspapers published in southern Cyprus. However, there was no regular distribution system for the Greek-Cypriot press in the Karpas area and no direct post and telecommunications links between the north and south of the island. It was further noted that the enclaved population was able to receive Greek-Cypriot radio and television.

46. The Commission did not find any conclusive evidence that letters destined for Greek Cypriots were opened by the "TRNC" police or that their telephones were tapped.

47. As to alleged restrictions on religious worship, the Commission found that the main problem for Greek Cypriots in this connection stemmed from the fact that there was only one priest for the whole Karpas area and that the Turkish-Cypriot authorities were not favourable to the appointment of additional priests from the south. The Commission delegates were unable to confirm during their visit to the Karpas area whether access to the Apostolos Andreas Monastery was free at any time for Karpas Greek Cypriots. It appeared to be the case that on

high religious holidays (which occur three times a year) visits to the monastery are also allowed to Greek Cypriots from the south.

48. Concerning alleged restrictions on the freedom of association of the enclaved population, the Commission observed that the relevant "TRNC" law on associations only covered the creation of associations by Turkish Cypriots.

4. Alleged Violations in Respect of the Rights of Turkish Cypriots and the Turkish-Cypriot Gypsy Community in Northern Cyprus

49. The applicant Government contended before the Commission that Turkish Cypriots living in northern Cyprus, especially political dissidents and the Gypsy community, were the victims of an administrative practice of violation of their Convention rights. They adduced evidence in support of their claim that these groups were victims of arbitrary arrest and detention, police misconduct, discrimination and ill-treatment and interferences in various forms with other Convention rights such as, *inter alia*, fair trial, private and family life, expression, association, property and education.

50. The respondent Government essentially maintained that the above allegations were unsubstantiated on the evidence and pointed to the availability of effective remedies in the "TRNC" to aggrieved persons.

51. The Commission's investigation into the applicant Government's allegations was based mainly on the oral evidence of thirteen witnesses who testified before the Commission's delegates on the situation of Turkish Cypriots and the Gypsy community living in northern Cyprus. The witnesses were proposed by both parties. Their evidence was taken by the delegates in Strasbourg, Cyprus and London between November 1997 and April 1998.

52. The Commission found that there existed rivalry and social conflict between the original Turkish Cypriots and immigrants from Turkey who continued to arrive in considerable numbers. Some of the original Turkish Cypriots and their political groups and media resented the "TRNC" policy of full integration for the settlers.

53. Furthermore, while there was a significant incidence of emigration from the "TRNC" for economic reasons, it could not be excluded that there were also cases of Turkish Cypriots having fled the

"TRNC" out of fear of political persecution. The Commission considered that there was no reason to doubt the correctness of witnesses' assertions that in a few cases complaints of harassment or discrimination by private groups of or against political opponents were not followed up by the "TRNC" police. However, it concluded that it was not established beyond reasonable doubt that there was in fact a consistent administrative practice of the "TRNC" authorities, including the courts, of refusing protection to political opponents of the ruling parties. In so far as it was alleged by the applicant Government that the authorities themselves were involved in the harassment of political opponents, the Commission did not have sufficient details concerning the incidents complained of (for example, the dispersing of demonstrations, short-term arrests) which would allow it to form an opinion as to the justification or otherwise of the impugned acts. The Commission noted that, in any event, it did not appear that the remedy of habeas corpus had been invoked by persons claiming to be victims of arbitrary arrest or detention.

54. Regarding the alleged discrimination against and arbitrary treatment of members of the Turkish-Cypriot Gypsy community, the Commission found that judicial remedies had apparently not been used in respect of particularly grave incidents such as the pulling down of shacks near Morphou and the refusal of airline companies to transport Gypsies to the United Kingdom without a visa.

55. In a further conclusion, the Commission observed that there was no evidence before it of Turkish-Cypriot civilians having been subjected to the jurisdiction of military courts during the period under consideration. Furthermore, and with respect to the evidence before it, the Commission considered that it had not been established that, during the period under consideration, there was an official prohibition on the circulation of Greek-language newspapers in northern Cyprus or that the creation of bi-communal associations was prevented. In respect of the alleged refusal of the "TRNC" authorities to allow Turkish Cypriots to return to their properties in southern Cyprus, the Commission observed that no concrete instances were referred to it of any persons who had wished to do so during the period under consideration.

[. . .]

IV. Alleged Violations of the Rights of Displaced Persons to Respect for Their Home and Property

A. As to the Facts Established by the Commission

162. The applicant Government endorsed the facts as found by the Commission (see paragraphs 30–33 above). In respect of those findings they requested the Court to conclude that the facts disclosed violations of Articles 8 and 13 of the Convention and Article 1 of Protocol No. 1 as well as of Article 14 of the Convention taken in conjunction with these provisions. They further submitted that the facts at issue gave rise to violations of Articles 3, 17 and 18 of the Convention.

163. The Court considers that there are no exceptional circumstances which would lead it to take a different view of the facts established by the Commission (see paragraphs 30–33 above). It notes in this regard that the Commission was able to draw on the findings contained in its 1976 and 1983 reports and took into account the impact of "legislative" and other texts in force in the "TRNC" on the enjoyment of the rights invoked by the applicant Government. It further notes that the respondent Government did not contest the accuracy of several allegations of fact made by the applicant Government in the proceedings before the Commission (see paragraph 29 above).

164. The Court will accordingly examine the merits of the applicant Government's complaints with reference to the facts established by the Commission.

B. As to the Merits of the Applicant Government's Complaints

1. Article 8 of the Convention

165. The applicant Government maintained that it was an unchallengeable proposition that it was the respondent State's actions which had prevented the displaced Greek Cypriots from returning to their homes, in violation of Article 8 of the Convention which provides:

"1. Everyone has the right to respect for his private and family life, his home and his correspondence.

2. There shall be no interference by a public authority with the exercise of this right except such as is in accordance with the law and is necessary in a democratic society in the interests of national security, public safety or the economic well-being of the country, for the prevention of disorder or crime, for the protection of health or morals, or for the protection of the rights and freedoms of others."

166. The applicant Government declared that the policy of the respondent State, aimed at the division of Cyprus along racial lines, affected 211,000 displaced Greek Cypriots and their children as well as a number of Maronites, Armenians, Latins and individual citizens of the Republic of Cyprus who had exercised the option under the Constitution to be members of the Greek-Cypriot community. They submitted that the continuing refusal of the "TRNC" authorities to allow the displaced persons to return to the north violated not only the right to respect for their homes but also the right to respect for their family life. In this latter connection, the applicant Government observed that the impugned policy resulted in the separation of families.

167. In a further submission, the applicant Government requested the Court to find that the facts also disclosed a policy of deliberate destruction and manipulation of the human, cultural and natural environment and conditions of life in northern Cyprus. The applicant Government contended that this policy was based on the implantation of massive numbers of settlers from Turkey with the intention and the consequence of eliminating Greek presence and culture in northern Cyprus. In the view of the applicant Government, the notions of "home" and "private life" were broad enough to subsume the concept of sustaining existing cultural relationships within a subsisting cultural environment. Having regard to the destructive changes being wrought to that environment by the respondent State, it could only be concluded that the rights of the displaced persons to respect for their private life and home were being violated in this sense also.

168. The Commission observed in the first place that the issue of whether the persons concerned by the impugned measures could have been expected to use local remedies to seek redress for their grievances did not have to be examined. In the Commission's opinion, the refusal of the "TRNC"

authorities to allow the displaced persons to return to their homes reflected an acknowledged official policy and, accordingly, an administrative practice. In these circumstances there was no Convention requirement to exhaust domestic remedies.

169. As to the merits of the complaints concerning the plight of the displaced persons, the Commission found, with reference to its conclusions in its 1976 and 1983 reports and the findings of fact in the instant case (see paragraphs 30–33 above), that these persons, without exception, continued to be prevented from returning to or even visiting their previous homes in northern Cyprus. In the Commission's opinion, the facts disclosed a continuing violation of Article 8 in this respect, irrespective of the respondent Government's appeal to the public-safety considerations set out in the second paragraph of Article 8. As to the respondent Government's view that the claim of Greek-Cypriot displaced persons to return to the north and to settle in their homes had to be solved in the overall context of the inter-communal talks, the Commission considered that these negotiations, which were still very far from reaching any tangible result on the precise matter at hand, could not be invoked to justify the continuing maintenance of measures contrary to the Convention.

170. Having regard to its Article 8 finding as well as to its conclusions on the applicant Government's complaint under Article 1 of Protocol No. 1 (see paragraph 183 below), the Commission considered that it was not necessary to examine the applicant Government's further allegations concerning the manipulation of the demographic and cultural environment of the displaced persons' homes.

171. The Court notes that in the proceedings before the Commission the respondent Government did not dispute the applicant Government's assertion that it was not possible for displaced Greek Cypriots to return to their homes in the north. It was their contention that this situation would remain unchanged pending agreement on an overall political solution to the Cypriot question. In these circumstances the Court, like the Commission, considers that the issue of whether the aggrieved persons could have been expected to avail themselves of domestic remedies in the "TRNC" does not arise.

172. The Court observes that the official policy of the "TRNC" authorities to deny the right of

the displaced persons to return to their homes is reinforced by the very tight restrictions operated by the same authorities on visits to the north by Greek Cypriots living in the south. Accordingly, not only are displaced persons unable to apply to the authorities to reoccupy the homes which they left behind, they are physically prevented from even visiting them.

173. The Court further notes that the situation impugned by the applicant Government has obtained since the events of 1974 in northern Cyprus. It would appear that it has never been reflected in "legislation" and is enforced as a matter of policy in furtherance of a bi-zonal arrangement designed, it is claimed, to minimise the risk of conflict which the intermingling of the Greek and Turkish-Cypriot communities in the north might engender. That bi-zonal arrangement is being pursued within the framework of the inter-communal talks sponsored by the United Nations Secretary-General (see paragraph 16 above).

174. The Court would make the following observations in this connection: firstly, the complete denial of the right of displaced persons to respect for their homes has no basis in law within the meaning of Article 8 § 2 of the Convention (see paragraph 173 above); secondly, the inter-communal talks cannot be invoked in order to legitimate a violation of the Convention; thirdly, the violation at issue has endured as a matter of policy since 1974 and must be considered continuing.

175. In view of these considerations, the Court concludes that there has been a continuing violation of Article 8 of the Convention by reason of the refusal to allow the return of any Greek-Cypriot displaced persons to their homes in northern Cyprus.

176. As to the applicant Government's further allegation concerning the alleged manipulation of the demographic and cultural environment of the displaced persons' homes, the Court, like the Commission, considers that it is not necessary to examine this complaint in view of its above finding of a continuing violation of Article 8 of the Convention.

177. Furthermore, the Court considers it appropriate to examine the applicant Government's submissions on the issue of family separation (see paragraph 166 above) in the context of their allegations in respect of the living conditions of the Karpas Greek Cypriots.

2. Article 1 of Protocol No. 1

178. The applicant Government maintained that the respondent State's continuing refusal to permit the return of the displaced persons to northern Cyprus not only prevented them from having access to their property there but also prevented them from using, selling, bequeathing, mortgaging, developing and enjoying it. In their submission, there were continuing violations of all the component aspects of the right to peaceful enjoyment of possessions guaranteed by Article 1 of Protocol No. 1, which states:

"Every natural or legal person is entitled to the peaceful enjoyment of his possessions. No one shall be deprived of his possessions except in the public interest and subject to the conditions provided for by law and by the general principles of international law.

The preceding provisions shall not, however, in any way impair the right of a State to enforce such laws as it deems necessary to control the use of property in accordance with the general interest or to secure the payment of taxes or other contributions or penalties."

179. The applicant Government contended that the respondent State had adopted a systematic and continuing policy of interference with the immovable property of the displaced persons. They stated, *inter alia*, that the properties in question, of which the displaced persons were unlawfully dispossessed following their eviction from the north, were transferred into Turkish possession. Steps were then taken to "legalise" the illegal appropriation of the properties and their allocation to "State" bodies, Turkish Cypriots and settlers from the Turkish mainland. This was effected by means such as the assignment of "title deeds" to their new possessors. No compensation had ever been awarded to the victims of these interferences. Furthermore, specific measures had been taken to develop and exploit commercially land belonging to displaced persons, Church-owned land had been transferred to the Muslim religious trust, and agricultural produce from Greek-Cypriot land was now being exported accompanied by Turkish certificates.

180. In the applicant Government's submission, the continuing violation of property rights clearly engaged the responsibility of the respondent State under the Convention in view of the conclusions reached by the Court in its Loizidou judgment (*merits*). Quite apart from that consideration, the applicant Government pointed out that, in so far as the respondent State sought to justify the interferences with the displaced persons' property rights by invoking the derogation contained in Article 1 of Protocol No. 1, the "legal" measures relied on had necessarily to be considered invalid since they emanated from an illegal secessionist entity and could not for that reason be considered to comply with the qualitative requirements inherent in the notion of "provided for by law".

181. The Commission observed that the applicant Government's complaints were essentially directed at the "legislation" and the acknowledged administrative practice of the "TRNC" authorities. On that account, the persons aggrieved were not required to take any domestic remedies, it being noted by the Commission that, in any event, it did not appear that any remedies were available to displaced Greek Cypriots deprived of their property in northern Cyprus.

182. As to the merits, the Commission considered that the nature of the alleged interferences with the property rights of displaced Greek Cypriots was in essence the same as the interference of which Mrs Loizidou had complained in her application. Although that application concerned one particular instance of the general administrative practice to which the complaints in the present case relate, the Court's reasoning at paragraphs 63 and 64 of its Loizidou judgment (*merits*) (pp. 2237–38) must also apply to the administrative practice as such.

183. The Commission, essentially for the reasons set out by the Court in the above-mentioned judgment, concluded that during the period under consideration there had been a continuing violation of Article 1 of Protocol No. 1 by virtue of the fact that Greek-Cypriot owners of property in northern Cyprus were being denied access to and control, use and enjoyment of their property as well as any compensation for the interference with their property rights.

184. The Court agrees with the Commission's analysis. It observes that the Commission found it established on the evidence that at least since June 1989 the "TRNC" authorities no longer recognised any ownership rights of Greek Cypriots in respect of their properties in northern Cyprus (see

paragraph 32 above). This purported deprivation of the property at issue was embodied in a constitutional provision, "Article 159 of the TRNC Constitution", and given practical effect in "Law no. 52/1995". It would appear that the legality of the interference with the displaced persons' property is unassailable before the "TRNC" courts. Accordingly, there is no requirement for the persons concerned to use domestic remedies to secure redress for their complaints.

185. The Court would further observe that the essence of the applicant Government's complaints is not that there has been a formal and unlawful expropriation of the property of the displaced persons but that these persons, because of the continuing denial of access to their property, have lost all control over, as well as possibilities to enjoy, their land. As the Court has noted previously (see paragraphs 172–73 above), the physical exclusion of Greek-Cypriot persons from the territory of northern Cyprus is enforced as a matter of "TRNC" policy or practice. The exhaustion requirement does not accordingly apply in these circumstances.

186. The Court recalls its finding in the Loizidou judgment (*merits*) that that particular applicant could not be deemed to have lost title to her property by operation of "Article 159 of the TRNC Constitution", a provision which it held to be invalid for the purposes of the Convention (p. 2231, § 44). This conclusion is unaffected by the operation of "Law no. 52/1995". It adds that, although the latter was not invoked before the Court in the Loizidou case, it cannot be attributed any more legal validity than its parent "Article 159" which it purports to implement.

187. The Court is persuaded that both its reasoning and its conclusion in the Loizidou judgment (*merits*) apply with equal force to displaced Greek Cypriots who, like Mrs Loizidou, are unable to have access to their property in northern Cyprus by reason of the restrictions placed by the "TRNC" authorities on their physical access to that property. The continuing and total denial of access to their property is a clear interference with the right of the displaced Greek Cypriots to the peaceful enjoyment of possessions within the meaning of the first sentence of Article 1 of Protocol No. 1. It further notes that, as regards the purported expropriation, no compensation has been paid to the displaced persons in respect of the interferences which they

have suffered and continue to suffer in respect of their property rights.

188. The Court notes that the respondent Government, in the proceedings before the Commission, sought to justify the interference with reference to the inter-communal talks and to the need to rehouse displaced Turkish-Cypriot refugees. However, similar pleas were advanced by the respondent Government in the Loizidou case and were rejected in the judgment on the merits (pp. 2237–38, § 64). The Court sees no reason in the instant case to reconsider those justifications.

189. For the above reasons the Court concludes that there has been a continuing violation of Article 1 of Protocol No. 1 by virtue of the fact that Greek-Cypriot owners of property in northern Cyprus are being denied access to and control, use and enjoyment of their property as well as any compensation for the interference with their property rights.

[. . .]

4.12. *Dulaş v. Turkey* (2001)

[. . .]

I. THE CIRCUMSTANCES OF THE CASE

7. The facts of the case, particularly concerning events on or about 8 November 1993 when the gendarmes carried out an operation at Çitlibahçe, were disputed by the parties. The Commission, pursuant to former Article 28 § 1 (a) of the Convention, conducted an investigation with the assistance of the parties.

The Commission heard witnesses in Ankara on 7 February 1997. These included the applicant; Avni Dulaş, her son; and Emin Bulen, a villager. The Commission also had regard to the oral evidence given by witnesses on 3 and 4 July 1996 in the case of Çakıcı (see *Çakıcı v. Turkey* [GC], no. 23657/94, ECHR 1999-IV), which concerned the same operation. This included the testimony of İzzet Çakıcı, whose brother had disappeared after being taken into custody by the gendarmes; Remziye Çakıcı, a villager and spouse of the disappeared person; Fevzi Okatan, previously muhtar of the village; Ertan Altınoluk, the gendarme commander of the operation; and Mehmet Bitgin, a villager.

8. The Commission's findings of fact are set out in its report of 6 September 1999 and summarised below (Section A). The applicant accepts the Commission's findings of fact. The Government's submissions concerning the facts are summarised below (Section B).

A. The Commission's Findings of Fact

9. Çitlibahçe was in a district in which terrorist activity was intense in 1993. The PKK used to come to the village, holding meetings and taking food by force. The security forces made regular visits and operations were not uncommon. They told the villagers not to give food to the PKK.

10. The applicant, Avni Dulaş and Remziye Çakıcı all recalled an incident in July 1993 when villagers were forced by the security forces to pull up their tobacco crops. Although there was some disparity amongst the witnesses as to how this was done, the witnesses' accounts were similar in stating that the tobacco crops were destroyed by order of the security forces. The gendarme commander who gave evidence before the Delegates denied that this occurred but recalled that he had destroyed hemp crops. The Commission did not make any finding in regard of this aspect as it was not the subject-matter of any specific complaint.

11. Shortly before 8 November 1993, PKK terrorists went to the village of Dadaş in the Hazro district and took away five teachers, the imam and the imam's brother. All, save one of the teachers, were shot. The imam's brother, though wounded, survived.

12. Following the discovery of the bodies of the teachers, the gendarmes at Hazro gathered information from their contacts and sources as to what had happened and who had been involved. They had descriptions of the villagers in the area who had been assisting the PKK in holding the group of teachers. On 8 November 1993, an operation, under the command of Lieutenant Altınoluk, was carried out by the Hazro gendarmes in Çitlibahçe, while gendarmes from Lice went to Bağlan nearby.

13. Concerning what happened during the operation at Çitlibahçe, the Commission's Delegates had earlier found Lieutenant Altınoluk to be an evasive witness, with a volubly unhelpful response to questioning. They found a lack of sincerity in the way in which he drowned simple questions in long and complicated explanations, which were often contradictory and inconsistent. On the other hand, the Delegates had found that the villagers, Remziye Çakıcı, Fevzi Okatan and Mehmet Bitgin, who gave eyewitness accounts, were on the whole consistent and credible and that they were convincing in their demeanour and their response to questions. Their evidence was found to support the testimony of the witnesses heard in this case. In this regard, the Commission's Delegates found the applicant to be a convincing witness, an elderly, simple and unsophisticated lady who was on the whole credible. Her oral testimony was largely consistent with the statement given by her to the Human Rights Association shortly after the incident. While there were some inconsistencies in her accounts, the Commission considered that they could be attributed to the applicant's advanced years and the passage of time since the events in question. Her evidence accorded in essentials with that of her son Avni Dulaş and the villager Emin Bilen.

14. The Commission found that the Hazro gendarmes included Çitlibahçe in the operation since they intended to look for and take into custody Ahmet Çakıcı, who, as a person already under suspicion of involvement in PKK activities, would be likely to have information about the kidnap group that passed through the village.

15. When the gendarmes arrived at the village, early in the morning, they left their vehicles outside and entered. They gathered the men together in one place and the women in another. Ahmet Çakıcı had hidden. A search was carried out by the gendarmes, who also started setting fire to houses. Ahmet Çakıcı was found and taken into custody. He was last seen by the witnesses being taken by village guards and soldiers to the vehicles.

16. The applicant had gone into her house when she saw all the soldiers but had been forced to leave by the soldiers. They set fire to her house, which had seven rooms and was made of timber. The family stored provisions, crops and wheat inside and these, along with the furniture and other household goods, were destroyed. About fifty houses in the village were burned down. She stated that once they had caught Ahmet Çakıcı the gendarmes left. After the departure of the gendarmes, the village was left in ruins and villagers were forced to leave.

17. Having regard to the evidence as a whole, the Commission accepted the evidence of the

applicant as regards its principal elements. It did not find the matters referred to by the Government as being indicative of bad faith or as materially undermining the credibility and reliability of the applicant and her witnesses, which its Delegates assessed in generally positive terms. While the Commission took note of the applicant's age, its Delegates had not found any indication of mental infirmity that would cast doubt on her ability to give evidence.

18. The Commission found in conclusion that the applicant's property, furniture and possessions were deliberately burnt and destroyed during an operation by security forces in the village of Çitlibahçe on 8 November 1993. This led to the evacuation of the village. The possessions burned included a fridge, television, kitchen utensils, household goods, and produce (including tobacco, wheat, barley, lentils, and winter provisions).

19. The applicant and other villagers went to Diyarbakır after the operation. Accompanied by her son and three or four other villagers, the applicant went to the Human Rights Association. She made a statement and thumbprinted it.

20. Sometime later, the applicant was summoned to a police station. In his evidence to the Delegates, her son, Avni Dulaş remembered that she had been summoned to the public prosecutor's office in about the summer of 1995. He accompanied her there. She had been asked to make a statement. The public prosecutor read out of a file, stating that she had complained to Europe about Turkey. He told the Delegates that he thought the prosecutor was trying to put pressure on his mother.

[. . .]

IV. Alleged Violation of Article 8 of the Convention and Article 1 of Protocol No. 1

57. The applicant complained of the destruction of her home and property, invoking Article 8 of the Convention and Article 1 of Protocol No. 1, which provide:

Article 8:

"1. Everyone has the right to respect for his private and family life, his home and his correspondence.

2. There shall be no interference by a public authority with the exercise of this right except such as is in accordance with the law and is necessary in a democratic society in the interests of national security, public safety or the economic well-being of the country, for the prevention of disorder or crime, for the protection of health or morals, or for the protection of the rights and freedoms of others."

Article 1 of Protocol No. 1:

"Every natural or legal person is entitled to the peaceful enjoyment of his possessions. No one shall be deprived of his possessions except in the public interest and subject to the conditions provided for by law and by the general principles of international law.

The preceding provisions shall not, however, in any way impair the right of a State to enforce such laws as it deems necessary to control the use of property in accordance with the general interest or to secure the payment of taxes or other contributions or penalties."

58. The applicant submitted that the destruction of her home, property and possessions represented a serious violation of her right to respect for private and family life, her right to respect for home and her right to peaceful enjoyment of property. Further, the expulsion from her home and the fact that she cannot return to her village represented a serious interference with her lifestyle and a continuing violation of her right to peaceful enjoyment of her possessions. She contended that the expulsion from her village constituted separate and additional violations of both Articles above.

59. The Government submitted the applicant's allegations had no factual foundation and that there was no substantiation of her claims that the security forces had burned and destroyed her house and goods.

60. The Court has found it established that the applicant's house and property were deliberately destroyed by the security forces, obliging her to leave her village. There is no doubt that these acts, in addition to giving rise to a violation of Article 3, constituted particularly grave and unjustified interferences with the applicant's right to respect for her private life, family life and home and with her peaceful enjoyment of her possessions (see also the

Mentes and Others v. Turkey judgment, cited above, p. 2711, § 73; the Selçuk and Asker v. Turkey judgment, cited above, p. 911, § 86).

61. The Court, accordingly, finds violations of Article 8 of the Convention and Article 1 of Protocol No. 1.

[. . .]

4.13. *Orhan v. Turkey* (2002)

[. . .]

V. ALLEGED VIOLATION OF ARTICLE 8 AND ARTICLE 1 OF PROTOCOL NO. 1 TO THE CONVENTION IN RESPECT OF THE APPLICANT AND THE ORHANS

376. The applicant further complained under Article 8 and Article 1 of Protocol No. 1 that the destruction of his and the Orhans' home, property and possessions represented a serious violation of their right to respect for their private and family lives and their homes and of their right to peaceful enjoyment of their possessions. He also argued that his expulsion from his home, village and community represented a separate and serious violation of his rights under these provisions. The Government disputed that there was any such military operation in Deveboyu as alleged or at all.

377. Article 8 reads as follows:

"1. Everyone has the right to respect for his private and family life, his home and his correspondence.

2. There shall be no interference by a public authority with the exercise of this right except such as is in accordance with the law and is necessary in a democratic society in the interests of national security, public safety or the economic well-being of the country, for the prevention of disorder or crime, for the protection of health or morals, or for the protection of the rights and freedoms of others."

378. Article 1 of Protocol No. 1 reads as follows:

"Every natural or legal person is entitled to the peaceful enjoyment of his possessions. No one shall be deprived of his possessions except in the public interest and subject to the condi-

tions provided for by law and by the general principles of international law.

The preceding provisions shall not, however, in any way impair the right of a State to enforce such laws as it deems necessary to control the use of property in accordance with the general interest or to secure the payment of taxes or other contributions or penalties."

379. The Court has found it established that the homes and certain possessions of the applicant and of the Orhans were deliberately destroyed by the security forces. The applicant's house continued to be Cezayir Orhan's home in Deveboyu. In addition, the village had to be evacuated after the harvest. There is no doubt that these acts constituted particularly grave and unjustified interferences with the applicant's and the Orhans' right to respect for their private and family lives and homes. Such acts also amounted to serious and unjustified interferences with the peaceful enjoyment by the applicant, by Hasan Orhan and by Selim Orhan of their property and possessions. No evidence has been offered as regards the property or possessions of Cezayir Orhan in Deveboyu (the above-cited judgments of Akdivar and Others, § 88, Menteş and Others, § 73, *Dulaş*, § 60, and Selçuk and Asker, § 86). The Court does not find it necessary to consider whether the forced evacuation of the village is sufficient, of itself, to constitute a violation of these Articles.

380. Accordingly, the Court finds a violation of Article 8 and of Article 1 of Protocol No. 1 in respect of the applicant, Selim Orhan and Hasan Orhan and of Article 8 only in respect of Cezayir Orhan.

[. . .]

4.14. *Zvolský and Zvolská v. The Czech Republic* (2003)

[. . .]

I. THE CIRCUMSTANCES OF THE CASE

9. On 20 June 1967 the applicants executed a deed of sale and gift (*kupní a darovací smlouva*) under which M.R., as vendor, agreed to sell them a farmhouse in Srch and to transfer the adjoining agricultural land to them without consideration. At the time, the system for transferring agricultural

holdings was by a sale of the house and gift of the adjoining land that was farmed by a socialist cooperative. The approval of the cooperative and the agreement of the competent national committee were required before the deed of sale and gift could be executed. Purchasers of land were required to give an undertaking that they would work for the cooperative.

According to the applicants, M.R. wished to secure his release from his obligation to work for the socialist cooperative and could only do so by transferring the land. It was he who had proposed the arrangement, as he wanted to sort out his domestic affairs. Under the statutory provisions then in force, the applicants were obliged, as a condition for purchasing the house, to give an undertaking to work for the cooperative as a replacement for M.R. They paid him 30,000 Czechoslovak korunas on top of the purchase price of the house, as compensation for the value of the transferred land.

10. In 1991 M.R. signed a declaration that he had transferred the land of his own free will. In the applicants' submission, that declaration constituted a rider to the deed confirming M.R.'s consent.

11. However on 1 July 1993 M.R. brought a civil action against the applicants seeking, *inter alia*, rescission under section 8(3) of the Land Act (Law no. 229/1991) of the part of the agreement that concerned the transfer of the agricultural land.

12. In a judgment of 30 September 1994, the Pardubice District Court (*okresní soud*) found in favour of M.R., holding, *inter alia*:

"[The applicants] have invited the Court to dismiss M.R.'s actions on the ground that he transferred his land of his own free will to sort out his domestic affairs and that in consideration [for that transfer] they had assumed his obligation to work for the agricultural cooperative. . . .

Section 8(3) of the Land Act (Law no. 229/1991) provides that if a landowner has donated land to a private individual under duress or transferred it without consideration under a contract for the sale of an adjoining building and at the date this Act entered into force the land was still in that person's possession, the court shall, on application by a person with standing, either (a) order rescission of that part of the sale agreement by which the

land was donated or transferred without consideration, or (b) order the current owner to reimburse the price of the land. . . .

The Court . . . finds that the aforementioned conditions were satisfied in the present case and therefore finds in favour of [M.R.]. It has been established that [M.R.] is the person with standing within the meaning of Law no. 229/1991, that is to say the person who gave [the applicants] – the obligees within the meaning of that Act – the agricultural land in connection with the sale of the building. . . . It has also been established that [the applicants] are currently in possession of the land. Consequently, the Court . . . rescinds the section of the deed of sale and gift executed by the parties on 20 June 1967 that provides for the transfer of ownership of the land in question without consideration. . . . It does not consider that the 'minuted rider to the deed' dated 6 April 1991 constitutes a valid rider to the deed of sale and gift. The statement in which [M.R.] expressly confirmed that he had sold his immovable property voluntarily and at the agreed price has no . . . value in law, as it was made before the amendment to the legislation on land law that enabled him to seek restitution was passed. In fact, [M.R.] denies that he intended to sell the land [to the applicants] and the intentions of both parties are set out in the notary's minutes. . . . The Court finds that the [applicants'] argument that a decision in favour of [M.R.] would entail a violation of Article 11 of the Charter of Fundamental Rights and Freedoms is unfounded, as the latter was obliged to transfer ownership of the agricultural land used by the agricultural cooperative without consideration."

13. In a judgment of 29 February 1996, the Hradec Králové Regional Court (*krajský soud*) upheld the District Court's judgment rescinding the relevant part of the deed of sale and gift. It found that M.R. had given, and thus *de facto* transferred without consideration, the agricultural land to the applicants as part of the agreement for the sale of the adjoining house. The Regional Court also noted that the terms "donate" and "transfer without consideration" were identical. At the same time, it dismissed an application by the applicants for leave to appeal on points of law (*dovolání*), holding that the request for a ruling on the construction of the words "transfer without consideration" in section 8(4) of

the Land Act did not raise a question of crucial legal importance (*rozhodnutí po právní stránce zásadního významu*).

14. Article 239 § 2 of the Code of Civil Procedure provides that leave to appeal on points of law will be granted if the court hearing the appeal on points of law (*dovolací soud*) considers that the impugned decision gives rise to a question of crucial legal importance. In reliance on that provision, the applicants appealed to the Supreme Court on 14 June 1996, alleging that the ordinary courts had construed the Land Act erroneously by confusing two incompatible concepts: "donations" and "transfers without consideration".

15. In a judgment of 29 July 1997, the Supreme Court (*Nejvyšší soud*) refused the applicants leave to appeal on points of law, holding that the Regional Court's judgment did not give rise to a question of crucial legal importance. It noted that it had considered the question of the definition of the terms "donations" and "transfers without consideration" in a number of previous decisions in which it had construed the Act as not requiring duress to have been used if the agricultural land had been transferred without consideration. The Supreme Court's judgment was served on the applicants at the earliest on 11 September 1997.

16. On 12 November 1997 the applicants lodged a constitutional appeal (*ústavní stížnost*) in which they alleged that the domestic courts' decisions had violated the constitutional guarantees embodied in Articles 1, 11 §§ 1 and 3 of the Charter of Fundamental Rights and Freedoms (*Listina základních práv a svobod*), namely equality of rights for citizens and protection of property. They also sought an order abrogating section 8(4) of the Land Act.

17. On 4 August 1998 the Constitutional Court (*Ústavní soud*) declared their appeal inadmissible as being out of time. It held, *inter alia*:

"The Constitutional Court considers that litigants are not entitled to bring proceedings in the Supreme Court that do not qualify for leave under the statutory rules or to make an application in such proceedings for an order quashing decisions of the ordinary courts, unless a refusal to hear [the appeal on points of law] would constitute a denial of justice and, consequently, a breach of the right to a fair trial.

The [Supreme Court's] judgment does not constitute a decision on the final statutory remedy for the protection of rights . . . The constitutional appeal could only be brought against the appeal court's decision, which became enforceable on 15 May 1996. Since it was not lodged until 17 November 1997, it fails to satisfy the condition set out in section 72(2) of the Constitutional Court Act. For this reason, the Constitutional Court has no alternative but to declare the appeal inadmissible, as it was lodged after the expiry of the statutory time-limit."

[. . .]

A. The Parties' Submissions

58. The Government accepted that the State had interfered with the applicants' right of property, but argued that the requirements of Article 1 of Protocol No. 1 had been complied with. They called, firstly, for a distinction to be drawn between the notions of "restitution", which entailed remedying an unlawful transfer or breach of property rights by restoring the original legal position with retrospective effect, and "expropriation", which referred to the compulsory deprivation of a right of property on statutory grounds in the public interest with prospective effect in exchange for compensation.

59. They pointed out that in the present case the domestic courts had relied on section 8(4) of the Land Act in their decisions. The aim of that Act was to "provide owners of agricultural and forestry land some redress for certain breaches of their rights of property between 1948 and 1989 and to restore so far as possible the former proprietary interests in that land". In the Government's submission, that meant that although the restitution of agricultural land pursuant to section 8(4) of the Land Act interfered with rights of property, it pursued a legitimate aim under the Czech Constitution. They referred to the Constitutional Court's findings that landowners' freedom of contract had been unduly restricted under the communist regime in that, in order to be able to sell their houses, landowners were obliged to transfer the adjoining agricultural and forestry land to the purchaser without consideration, on pain of nullity. Such transfers could be regarded as unlawful acts of compulsory expropriation without compensation that now required remedying; as a

result, the courts were entitled to order the restitution of the land concerned. In the light of those observations, the Government submitted that the obligation imposed on the applicants to return the property they had obtained free of charge was legitimate and in the general interest.

Further, since the order for rescission did not apply to the deed of sale and gift in its entirety, but only to the transfer of land without consideration, the interference was reasonably proportionate to the legitimate aim pursued. Lastly, since the applicants had obtained the land free of charge, they were not entitled to claim any compensation.

60. The applicants said that section 8(4)(a) of the Land Act empowered the court to rescind part of a contract if the landowner had given the land to a private individual under duress or had transferred the land without consideration under a contract for the sale of an adjoining building.

That showed that the existence of duress was relevant only under the first limb, the question of vitiated consent not being pertinent to the second. As a result, any transfer of land made without consideration under a contract for the sale of a building entitled the former owner to seek either rescission of part of the contract or financial compensation. The applicants accepted that such a solution was right and proper in cases in which the transfer had been made against the owner's will. However, they argued that it should only be used on condition that the true content of the deed was established in each case. The courts should avoid applying the rule to voluntary transfers, and seek to establish in every case whether there was evidence of consent or duress, or of a payment of compensation to the former owner, notwithstanding the contractual stipulation for the transfer to be made without consideration.

61. As regards the circumstances in which they had entered into the agreement with the former owner, the applicants said that at the time he wished to be released from his obligation to work for the agricultural cooperative, something he could only achieve by transferring ownership. He had thus been acting in his own interests when he agreed to transfer the land to the applicants. Under the statutory provisions applicable at the material time, the vendor was obliged to enter into a contract for the sale of the farmhouse and to transfer the adjoining agricultural land without consideration, while

the purchaser was required to give an undertaking to work for the cooperative. In the instant case, the applicants had also paid the former owner 30,000 Czechoslovak korunas on top of the purchase price as compensation for the value of the land, as indeed had been confirmed by the former owner in the domestic proceedings. In 1997 he had also made a declaration stating that he had assigned his rights of property, including his rights of property in the agricultural land farmed by the cooperative, of his own free will.

62. The applicants thus submitted that the transfer had not, in fact, been made gratuitously, as they had paid financial consideration to the former owner and given an undertaking to work for the cooperative as his replacement, thus forgoing the chance to follow their own chosen career. Since they had performed their obligations, they considered that they had been adversely affected by the rescission of the deed of gift and that section 8(4) of the Land Act was unjust and contravened Article 1 of Protocol No. 1.

B. The Court's Assessment

63. The Court reiterates that Article 1 of Protocol No. 1 guarantees in substance the right of property and comprises three distinct rules. The first, which is expressed in the first sentence of the first paragraph and is of a general nature, lays down the principle of peaceful enjoyment of property. The second rule, in the second sentence of the same paragraph, covers deprivation of possessions and subjects it to certain conditions. The third, contained in the second paragraph, recognises that the Contracting States are entitled, amongst other things, to control the use of property in accordance with the general interest. The Court has to ensure that the last two rules are applicable before determining whether the first one has been complied with. The three rules are not, however, "distinct" in the sense of being unconnected. The second and third rules are concerned with particular instances of interference with the right to peaceful enjoyment of property; accordingly, they must be construed in the light of the general principle laid down in the first rule (see *Iatridis v. Greece* [GC], no. 31107/96, § 55, ECHR 1999-II, and *Elia S.r.l. v. Italy*, no. 37710/97, § 51, ECHR 2001-IX).

64. In the instant case, the Court notes that it is common ground that the applicants' right to the peaceful enjoyment of their possessions has been

interfered with. It must therefore go on to consider whether or not that interference was in breach of Article 1 of Protocol No. 1.

1. Interference Prescribed by Law

65. The Court notes that Article 1 of Protocol No. 1 requires that any interference by a public authority with the peaceful enjoyment of possessions should be lawful. Moreover, the rule of law, one of the fundamental principles of a democratic society, is inherent in all the Articles of the Convention (see *Amuur v. France*, judgment of 25 June 1996, *Reports* 1996-III, pp. 850–51, § 50).

The law upon which the interference is based should be in accordance with the internal law of the Contracting State, including the relevant provisions of the Constitution. It is in the first place for the domestic authorities to interpret and apply the domestic law and to decide on issues of constitutionality.

66. In the present case, the statutory basis for the interference complained of was the Land Act. The Court finds that there is no reason to doubt that the deprivation was in accordance with law, as required by Article 1 of Protocol No. 1.

2. In the Public Interest

67. As to whether the deprivation of property in issue pursued a legitimate aim, in other words whether there was a "public interest" within the meaning of the second rule set out in Article 1 of Protocol No. 1, the Court notes that because of their direct knowledge of their society and its needs, the national authorities are in principle better placed to appreciate what is "in the public interest". Under the system of protection established by the Convention, it is thus for the national authorities to make the initial assessment of the existence of a problem of public concern warranting measures of deprivation of property. Here, as in other fields to which the safeguards of the Convention extend, the national authorities enjoy a certain margin of appreciation (see *Malama v. Greece*, no. 43622/98, § 46, ECHR 2001-II).

Furthermore, the notion of "public interest" is necessarily extensive. In particular, the decision to enact laws expropriating property will commonly involve consideration of political, economic and social issues. The Court finds it natural that the margin of appreciation available to the legislature in

implementing social and economic policies should be a wide one and will respect the legislature's judgment as to what is "in the public interest" unless that judgment is manifestly without reasonable foundation. This necessarily applies, and perhaps to a greater extent, in the event of changes to a country's political system (see, *mutatis mutandis, The former King of Greece and Others v. Greece* [GC], no. 25701/94, § 87, ECHR 2000-XII).

68. In the present case, the Court notes that the aim pursued by the Land Act is to redress infringements of property rights that occurred under the communist regime and accepts that the Czech State may have considered it necessary to resolve this problem, which it considered damaging to its democratic regime. The general purpose of the Act cannot be regarded as illegitimate, as it is indeed "in the public interest".

3. Proportionality of the Interference

69. The Court notes that it is well-established case-law that the second paragraph of Article 1 of Protocol No. 1 must be construed in the light of the principle laid down in the first sentence of the Article. Consequently, an interference with the right to the peaceful enjoyment of possessions must achieve a "fair balance" between the demands of the general interest of the community and the requirements of the protection of the individual's fundamental rights. In particular, there must be a reasonable relationship of proportionality between the means employed and the aim sought to be realised by any measure depriving a person of his possessions (see, among other authorities, *Pressos Compania Naviera S.A. and Others v. Belgium*, judgment of 20 November 1995, Series A no. 332, p. 23, § 38, and *Malama*, cited above, § 48). In determining whether this requirement is met, the Court recognises that the State enjoys a wide margin of appreciation with regard both to choosing how the measures are to be implemented and to ascertaining whether the consequences of implementation are justified in the general interest for the purpose of achieving the object of the law in question (see *Chassagnou and Others v. France* [GC], nos. 25088/94, 28331/95 and 28443/95, § 75, ECHR 1999-III). Nevertheless, the Court cannot fail to exercise its power of review which requires it to determine whether the requisite balance was maintained in a manner consonant with the applicants' right to the peaceful enjoyment of their possessions, within the

meaning of the first sentence of Article 1 of Protocol No. 1.

70. Under the Court's case-law, compensation terms under the relevant legislation are material to the assessment whether the contested measure respects the requisite fair balance and, notably, whether it imposes a disproportionate burden on the applicants. A total lack of compensation can be considered justifiable under Article 1 only in exceptional circumstances (see *The Holy Monasteries v. Greece*, judgment of 9 December 1994, Series A no. 301-A, p. 35, § 71, and *Malama*, cited above, § 48).

71. In the instant case, the Court observes that the Land Act does not afford any means of obtaining compensation in the event of rescission of the deed of gift. As it has already been established that the interference in issue satisfied the requirement of lawfulness and was not arbitrary, the lack of compensation does not make the taking of the applicants' property *eo ipso* wrongful (see, *mutatis mutandis, The former King of Greece and Others*, cited above, § 90). It remains therefore to be examined whether in the context of a lawful expropriation the applicants had to bear a disproportionate and excessive burden.

72. The Court considers that the legislature's decision to deal with infringements of property rights under the communist regime globally, with the occasional distinction, where necessary for analytical purposes, is reasonable. It is conscious of the legislature's concern to afford some redress for the infringements and accepts that the exceptional circumstances – the manner in which land was generally acquired at the time – justify the lack of compensation. However, it fails to comprehend why the Czech legislation precluded any possibility of re-examination of individual cases involving transfers of land in special circumstances. It considers that in a case such as the present one the courts should seek clearly to establish whether the land was transferred against the former owner's will – which, in the light of his declaration, does not appear to have been the position – and whether, in view of the consideration provided, the transfer genuinely infringed his rights of property.

73. The Court finds that the fact that the domestic courts were able to rescind the deed of gift without taking into consideration the compensation paid at the time by the current owners or the former owner's declaration that he had fully consented to

the arrangement created a situation in which the fair balance required between the protection of private property and the demands of the general interest was upset, to the applicants' detriment.

74. In conclusion, notwithstanding the fact that the aim pursued by the Land Act on its enactment in 1991 was legitimate, the Court finds that the obligation imposed on the applicants to return, without compensation, the land they had acquired in good faith under a deed of gift that was freely entered into in exchange for equivalent consideration amounts to a disproportionate burden that cannot be justified under the second paragraph of Article 1 of Protocol No. 1.

There has, therefore, been a violation of Article 1 of Protocol No. 1.

[. . .]

4.15. *Jasiūnienė v. Lithuania* (2003)

[. . .]

I. The Circumstances of the Case

8. The applicant was born in 1923 and lives in Palanga.

9. Before the Second World War the applicant's mother occupied a dwelling house ("the house") on a plot of land measuring 1,422 square metres ("the plot") in the centre of the tourist resort of Palanga on the Baltic Sea coast. Following the Soviet occupation of Lithuania in 1940, the land was nationalised and the house was demolished in the 1960s.

10. By a decision of 25 September 1992 the Palanga City Council, by reference to the Restitution of Property Act, decided to "restore the property rights" of the applicant and her sister in regard to their late mother's land. No form of restitution was specified in the decision.

11. The decision of 25 September 1992 was not implemented as no land was returned and no compensation was offered. In January 1995 the applicant brought a court action against the local authority, claiming that the plot should have been returned to her and her sister.

12. On 15 December 1995 the Palanga City District Court dismissed the applicant's action. By reference

to Article 5 of the Restitution of Property Act (see § 22 below), the court held that the applicant was not entitled to recover the plot, but that she should have been offered an alternative parcel in compensation as required by the law.

13. The applicant appealed, stating that the plot had to be returned to her.

14. On 3 April 1996 the Klaipėda Regional Court quashed the judgment of the District Court. The Regional Court found that the decision of the Palanga City Council of 25 September 1992 did not comply with Article 19 of the Restitution of Property Act as the local authority had not decided whether land or money and, in either case, which land or what amount of money should have been offered to the applicant as a compensation. The Regional Court held that the local authority had to resolve these questions. The court required the administration of Klaipėda County to "adopt, by 30 June 1996, a decision on the request by Stasė Jasiūnienė to restore her property rights in regard to the plot of land (*iki 1996 m. birželio 30 d. priimti sprendimą pagal Stasės Jasiūnienės prašymą dėl nuosavybės teisės į žemės sklypą atstatymo)*".

15. However, no such decision was taken as the applicant refused an alternative parcel of land in another area of Palanga. The applicant's sister accepted an alternative parcel.

16. On 13 August 1996 the applicant obtained an execution warrant for the judgment of 3 April 1996. She put the matter in the hands of bailiffs who were unable to execute the warrant against the county administration. The executive authorities took no further decision as the applicant had again refused an alternative parcel of land.

17. By a letter of 15 December 1997, the Klaipėda County Governor stated that the applicant had misinterpreted the judgment of 3 April 1996. In the Governor's opinion, the Regional Court had only required the county administration to adopt a decision in accordance with the Restitution of Property Act. As the applicant had no buildings or other property on the plot, she was not entitled to its return. The Governor requested the applicant to approach planners at the Palanga City Council to choose an alternative parcel. He warned her that a different parcel would be allotted without her consent in order to comply with the judgment of 3 April 1996.

18. On 31 December 1997 the applicant wrote to the Prime Minister, stating that she had been entitled to the plot, that the alternative parcels offered by the local authority were located in the outskirts of Palanga, and that their value was thus not equivalent to the plot in the centre of town.

19. In a letter of 11 February 1998, the Director of the Land Authority of the Ministry for Agriculture and Forestry stated that on 25 September 1992 the Palanga City Council had decided to restore the applicant's property rights notwithstanding the fact that there had been a lack of relevant documentation proving her late mother's ownership of the plot. Moreover, the Director stated that from the decision of 25 September 1992 it was "unclear in respect of which owner or land the property rights were restored[;] the form of the restitution of property was also unclear . . .". The Director requested the Klaipėda County Governor to re-examine the lawfulness of the decision of 25 September 1992.

20. Until 1999 the applicant was proposed and refused three offers by the Klaipėda County Governor for alternative parcels of land in various areas of Palanga.

21. By a letter of 30 August 1999, the executive authorities informed the applicant that she had not proved her mother's ownership of the original plot in accordance with the governmental instructions of 13 July 1998, i.e. she had not submitted the original papers confirming the purchase of the plot by her mother, or a court decision proving ownership. The executive authorities held that they could not proceed with a decision on compensation until the applicant presented these papers.

[. . .]

II. ALLEGED VIOLATION OF ARTICLE 1 OF PROTOCOL NO. 1, TAKEN ALONE AND IN CONJUNCTION WITH ARTICLE 14 OF THE CONVENTION

33. The applicant also complained under Article 1 of Protocol No. 1, taken alone and in conjunction with Article 14 of the Convention.

Article 1 of Protocol No. 1 provides as follows:

"Every natural or legal person is entitled to the peaceful enjoyment of his possessions. No one shall be deprived of his possessions except in the public interest and subject to the conditions provided for by law and by the general principles of international law.

The preceding provisions shall not, however, in any way impair the right of a State to enforce such laws as it deems necessary to control the use of property in accordance with the general interest or to secure the payment of taxes or other contributions or penalties."

Article 14 of the Convention states:

"The enjoyment of the rights and freedoms set forth in [the] Convention shall be secured without discrimination on any ground such as sex, race, colour, language, religion, political or other opinion, national or social origin, association with a national minority, property, birth or other status."

34. Under these provisions the applicant complained about the nationalisation of the plot and the destruction of her late mother's house. She also complained that the plot was not returned to her in kind following the re-establishment of Lithuanian State, and that the court judgment of 3 April 1996 was not executed.

35. The Government stated that the nationalisation of the plot and the destruction of the house had been carried out by the Soviet authorities before 24 May 1996, i.e. the date of entry into force of Protocol No. 1 with respect to Lithuania, and that the Court had no competence *ratione temporis* to examine this part of the application.

The Government further stated that the applicant had not proved her entitlement to benefit from the domestic legislation on restitution of property rights in regard to the plot as the applicant had not shown that her mother had owned the plot (also see § 25 above). According to the Government, the applicant thus had no "possessions" with regard to her claims to return the plot in kind or to be compensated therefore under the domestic legislation on restitution of property rights.

36. The applicant argued that the nationalisation and destruction of her late mother's property were flagrant and continuous breaches of her property rights. She also claimed that the decision of 25 September 1992 and the judgment of 3 April 1996 restored her property rights and entitled her to the return of the plot or proper compensation. However, the plot was not returned to her, and no com-

pensation was afforded in breach of Article 1 of Protocol No. 1. According to the applicant, the violation of her property rights occurred only because her late mother's land was on a valuable location in the centre of the resort. Accordingly, the State allegedly discriminated against her in breach of Article 14 of the Convention.

37. The Court considers that in this part of the application the applicant complained about three different episodes. Firstly, she complained about the nationalisation of the plot and the destruction of her late mother's house by the Soviet authorities in the 1960s. Secondly, she complained about her current inability to recover the plot in kind. Lastly, she complained about the authorities failure to execute the court judgment of 3 April 1996. The Court will examine each of these complaints separately.

1. Nationalisation of the Plot and the Destruction of the House

38. To the extent that the applicant complained about the nationalisation of the plot and the destruction of her late mother's house by the Soviet authorities in the 1960s, the Court points out that is has no competence *ratione temporis* to examine this part of the application as it relates to events prior to 20 June 1995, that is the date of the entry into force of the Convention with regard to Lithuania, and 24 May 1996, i.e. the date of the entry into force of Protocol No. 1 with regard to Lithuania. It follows that this part of the application is incompatible with the provisions of the Convention and its Protocols.

39. There has therefore been no breach of Article 1 of Protocol No. 1, taken alone or in conjunction with Article 14 of the Convention, in this respect.

2. The Applicant's Inability to Recover the Plot in Kind

40. To the extent that the applicant complained about her inability to recover the plot in kind following the re-establishment of the Lithuanian State, the Court recalls that the Convention does not guarantee, as such, the right to restitution of property. "Possessions" within the meaning of Article 1 of Protocol No. 1 can be either "existing possessions" or assets, including claims, in respect of which an applicant can argue that he has at least a "legitimate expectation" that they will be realised. The hope that a long-extinguished property right may

be revived cannot be regarded as a "possession" within the meaning of Article 1 of Protocol No. 1; nor can a conditional claim which has lapsed as a result of the failure to fulfil the condition (see, as a recent authority, the *Polacek and Polackova v. the Czech Republic* decision [GC], no. 38645/97, 10 July 2002, § 62).

41. On the basis of the judgment of 3 April 1996 it is clear that the applicant had no "legitimate expectation" to recover the plot in accordance with the applicable domestic legislation, and the authorities were only required to take appropriate measures to afford her compensation in land or money provided for by the law on restitution of property rights (see §§ 24–32 above, also see § 44 below). It follows that the applicant has no "possessions" in regard to her claim to recover the plot in kind, and this complaint is incompatible *ratione materiae* with the provisions of Article 1 of Protocol No. 1 within the meaning of Article 35 § 3 of the Convention.

42. Having regard to the fact that Article 14 of the Convention is not autonomous and to the conclusion that Article 1 of Protocol No. 1 is not applicable, the Court considers that Article 14 cannot apply with respect to this complaint (see, *mutatis mutandis*, the *Polacek and Polackova* decision cited above, §§ 61–70).

43. Consequently, there has been no violation of Article 1 of Protocol No. 1, taken alone or in conjunction with Article 14 of the Convention, with respect to this part of the application.

3. The Authorities' Failure to Execute the Judgment of 3 April 1996

44. To the extent that the applicant complained about the authorities' failure to execute the judgment of 3 April 1996, the Court reiterates that a "claim" can constitute a "possession" within the meaning of Article 1 of Protocol No. 1 to the Convention if it is sufficiently established to be enforceable (see § 40 above, also see the *Burdov* judgment cited above, § 40). The Court has already found in connection with the applicant's complaint under Article 6 of the Convention that the judgment of 3 April 1996 had placed on the authorities an obligation to afford the applicant compensation in land or money in connection with the plot in accordance with the domestic legislation on restitution of property rights (see §§ 28–30 above). The Court considers therefore that the judgment, which was never

revoked, provided the applicant with an enforceable claim to constitute a "possession" within the meaning of Article 1 of Protocol No. 1.

45. However, the judgment was not executed, and at least from 2 June 1999 the non-execution could be attributed solely to the authorities (also see § 29 above). It follows that the impossibility for the applicant to obtain the execution of the judgment constituted an interference with her right to peaceful enjoyment of possessions, as set out in the first sentence of the first paragraph of Article 1 of Protocol No. 1 (see the aforementioned *Burdov* judgment, § 40).

46. By failing to comply with the judgment the national authorities prevented the applicant from obtaining the compensation she could reasonably have expected to receive, given in particular that the applicant's sister had been afforded such compensation in regard to the plot. The Government have advanced no plausible justification for this interference acceptable from the point of view of Article 1 of Protocol No. 1 (also see §§ 28–30 above).

47. In sum, there has also been a violation of Article 1 of Protocol No. 1 in this regard.

[...]

4.16. *Pincová and Pinc v. The Czech Republic* (2003)

[...]

I. THE CIRCUMSTANCES OF THE CASE

9. On 29 December 1967 the first applicant and her husband purchased a forester's house with a barn and cowshed which they had been renting since 1953. The sale price – 14,703 Czechoslovak korunas (CSK) – was fixed by a surveyor appointed by the landlord, a State enterprise which was also the couple's employer and which had acquired the house without compensating the former owners, who had been dispossessed of their property in 1948 pursuant to Law no. 142/1947 on revision of the First Land Reform (*zákon o revizi první pozemkové reformy*).

10. On 30 June 1968 the first applicant and her husband paid the vendor CSK 2,030 under the terms of

an agreement giving them the right to make personal use of the land attached to the house.

11. On 23 December 1992, after the entry into force of Law no. 229/1991 (*zákon o půdě* – "the Land Act"), the son of the persons to whom the forester's house had belonged until its confiscation in 1948 instituted proceedings in the Příbram District Court (*okresní soud*) seeking recovery of the property by virtue of section 8(1) of the Land Act. He alleged that the acquisition of the house by the first applicant and her husband had been vitiated by a breach of the regulations in force at the time and that they had enjoyed an unlawful advantage in that the price they had been required to pay had been lower than the property's real value. He argued that the valuation of the house had been neither objective nor compatible with the legislation then in force.

12. In their defence, filed with the District Court on 12 February 1993, the applicants submitted that the purchase price had been properly calculated in accordance with the provisions applicable at the material time, and pointed out that the contract of sale had been adjudged valid by the Příbram branch of the State notary service (*státní notářství*), which had registered it.

13. On 7 February 1994 the District Court commissioned an expert opinion to establish whether the 1967 valuation had complied with the regulations then in force. The expert's report was filed with the court on 30 March 1994. In it the expert stated that after studying the file and the 1967 valuation he had found that "this valuation was not entirely compatible with the legislation in force at the time" and that he had "in addition noted instances of underestimation of area". He had therefore decided to "carry out a complete revaluation, applying the legislation formerly applicable and taking as [his] basis the state of affairs as described in the course of the proceedings" in order to be able to compare the two valuations and quantify the difference between them. The expert report assessed (a) the inhabitable parts of the property and (b) the non-inhabitable parts, namely the barn and cowshed. With regard to the latter, the expert reported:

"... the small barn and the adjoining cowshed were classified as 'small constructions', as they served only for the use of the occupier, not for any agricultural activity. That led

to an essential difference between the valuation produced ... in 1967 and the present one. My valuation is justified by a written instruction of 1965 relating to Article 7, which provides: 'The purchase price may also be applied to small constructions used for animal husbandry, provided that this activity does not go beyond the personal needs of the owner and the members of his family.' The barn is currently used as a toolshed.... My classification of the two buildings complied with Annex 5 to Decree no. 73/1964.... I took the barn and cowshed to be possessions in personal ownership, as they were not used for agricultural activities but only for the needs of the owner. If they had been private property the legislation then in force would not have permitted their transfer. Public establishments could sell to individuals only buildings classifiable as properties in personal ownership.... The difference in price for these two buildings, in relation to the 1967 valuation, is nearly CSK 4,600 ... "

14. The applicants pointed out that the expert's valuation of the inhabitable parts of the premises was practically identical to the 1967 valuation, the difference of CSK 4,600 being solely due to the valuation of the barn and cowshed. They challenged the valuation procedure because it had been based on Decree no. 73/1964, which did not specify the prices applicable in practice to buildings belonging to socialist organisations, and whose Article 7 § 2, they argued, excluded its application to their case. They further submitted that the price difference that had been noted was due in large part to a different assessment of the depreciation to be taken into account for the two buildings in question.

15. After the death of the first applicant's husband, her son, the second applicant, became the co-owner of the forester's house.

16. In a judgment of 12 September 1994 the District Court allowed the application by the son of the former owners and decided to transfer title to the disputed property to him, ruling as follows:

"After assessing the evidence, particularly the depositions of the parties and the witnesses, the contract of sale registered by the Příbram State notary service on 3 February 1969, the agreement of 30 June 1968 conferring the right to make personal use of the land, ..., the valuation of the house ... made on 20 December 1967 ..., the expert report of 15 December 1992, drawn up in accordance with instructions from [the first applicant] and admitted by the court in evidence, ..., and the expert report on the price of the buildings, drawn up by the court-appointed expert ..., the Court notes that ... the Land Act (Law no. 229/1991) applies, since the dispute concerns transfer of title to buildings intended for forestry production, within the meaning of section 1(1)(c) of the Land Act ...

The claimant ... is entitled to claim restitution under the restitution legislation ... The members of the defendants' family were not leading figures of the former communist regime but simple forestry workers who moved into the house as employees of the enterprise. They agreed to buy it when their employer gave them the opportunity to do so because they had no alternative accommodation. As for the purchase price, they accepted the amount fixed by [the surveyor], which they had no reason to challenge.

Nevertheless, it is incontestable that whereas the purchase price of the house should have been fixed at CSK 19,477, it cost them only CSK 14,703. Consequently, the conditions of section 8(1) of the Land Act are satisfied in the instant case because, in 1967, the defendants acquired the property at a price lower than the true value. The difference amounted to a quarter of the true value."

17. On 11 October 1994 the applicants appealed against the above judgment to the Prague Regional Court (*krajský soud*). They submitted that at the time when the proposal that they should purchase the house had been made to them they were under threat of eviction. They pointed out that both the surveyor's report and the contract of sale had been drawn up by the vendor, and that the transaction had been effected in accordance with the legislation then in force – indeed the Příbram State notary service had verified the purchase price before registering the contract. They alleged that the court expert's report did not constitute sufficient proof that the purchase price had been lower than the price required by the regulations at that time. They accordingly asked the Regional Court to order a new expert report.

18. On 4 January 1995 the Prague Regional Court upheld the first-instance judgment, ruling as follows:

"It emerges from the [1994] expert report ... that the valuation made [in 1967] did not comply with the rules in force at the time. ... The barn and the cowshed should have been valued as buildings in personal ownership, since they were not used for agricultural purposes but had been placed at the disposal of the owners of the house. ... According to Regulation 10/1964 of the Ministry of Economic Affairs ... only buildings in personal ownership could be sold to citizens by a socialist organisation. If the regulation then in force and Decree no. 73/1964 had been applied, the purchase price would have been fixed at CSK 19,477.

Consequently, the Regional Court upholds the District Court's finding that the question of the transfer of title must be considered under Law no. 229/1991. ... It has been established that the purchase price was determined by the vendor without the benefit of any expert report ... and that it was lower than the price required by the rules on prices then in force, which is apparent from the [court] expert's report.

As to the appellants' objection that the contract of sale was registered by the State notary service ... which deemed the barn and cowshed to be buildings in private ownership, it should be noted that this classification was the result of a legal opinion which is not a binding precedent for adjudication of the case. ... Moreover, regard being had to the fact that the claimant has already obtained the restitution of 50 hectares of woodland, it is desirable, in accordance with Law no. 229/1991 ..., for the forester's house to be used for its original purpose."

19. On 17 March 1995 the applicants appealed to the Constitutional Court (*Ústavní soud*), submitting that they had purchased the house in accordance with the rules then in force and without any unlawful advantage. They also relied on Article 399 § 2 of the Civil Code, under which a contract of sale could be declared void only when the purchase price was too high. They argued that the Regional Court had deprived them of their property and that accordingly their right to protection of their property under Article 11 § 1 of the Charter of

Fundamental Rights and Freedoms (*Listina základních práv a svobod*) had been infringed. They further complained that they had been deprived of fair and appropriate compensation, contending that although by virtue of section 8(3) of the Land Act a natural person was entitled to reimbursement of the purchase price and the costs reasonably incurred for the upkeep of the property, the sum of 14,703 Czech korunas (CZK) for the purchase price and reimbursement of their costs could never make good the loss of the house. They had been deprived of their title to the property on account of the difference noted between two prices calculated according to two different methods. Moreover, in the judicial proceedings they had not been on an equal footing with the other party, particularly in view of the possibility the claimant enjoyed of consulting the relevant documents. In that connection they relied on Article 37 of the Charter.

20. The applicants also asked the Constitutional Court to stay execution of the Regional Court's judgment and declare null and void part of section 8(1) of the Land Act. They argued that in so far as the provision in question permitted restitution in the event of "the purchase of immovable property at a price lower than the price required by the regulations on prices then in force", thus threatening title acquired in accordance with the legislation applicable at the time of purchase, it gave former owners the possibility of challenging the valuation of properties made at the time of their transfer. They asserted that section 8(1) of the Land Act thus caused them prejudice identical to that caused between 1948 and 1989, which the Act was supposed to attenuate. They submitted that it was inadmissible to make natural persons who had acquired property in good faith and in accordance with the legislation applicable at the material time bear responsibility for unlawful decisions or incorrect procedures adopted by the State.

21. On 24 April 1995 the applicants asked the District Court to stay execution of the Prague Regional Court's judgment, to exempt them from payment of the costs of the proceedings and to reopen the case. In the latter application they based their arguments on an opinion on the question of methodology delivered by the author of an exegesis of the relevant legislation published by the Czech Prices Authority (*Český cenový úřad*), which in their submission proved unequivocally that the court expert

had made a mistake. They also submitted to the District Court documents from the State archives capable of proving what use the disputed property had been put to in the past.

22. On 21 April 1995 people living in the municipality of Hříměždice and other villages sent a petition to the President of the Republic and to Parliament expressing their belief that the human rights guaranteed by the Constitution had been infringed in the applicants' case. They pointed out that the son of the former owners had recovered possession of a large estate (40 hectares of woodland and 100 hectares of other land), whereas the applicants had lost nearly all their possessions, although they had acquired them in good faith.

23. On 20 June 1995, in response to the petition, an MP sent a written question to the Deputy Prime Minister, the Minister of Agriculture and the Director of the Legislation and Public Administration Office, saying that he wondered whether section 8(1) of the Land Act, which provided for the possibility of restitution in the event of "the purchase of immovable property at a price lower than the price required by the regulations on prices then in force", was not contrary to the principle of legal certainty, in so far as it made it possible to transfer the responsibility for unlawful acts by the State to individuals who had acted in good faith. He also considered problematical, from the point of view of equality between litigants, legal provisions such as section 21(a) of the Land Act, which guaranteed persons who could claim restitution the right to various forms of assistance or exemption from costs in the judicial proceedings.

24. The Deputy Prime Minister replied on 7 July 1995. He said the doubts expressed were unfounded and pointed out that the Land Act had been framed in such a way as to pose, in addition to the general conditions, three additional tests each designed to exclude the purchasers' good faith. The fact that the Land Act referred to the legislation in force at the time of purchase could not be considered to impair legal certainty on account of some retrospective effect.

25. On 23 August 1995 the District Court examined at a public hearing the applicants' application for the proceedings to be reopened. Despite a new expert report submitted by them and drawn up on their own initiative, it refused the application, noting, *inter alia*, that in the original proceedings

neither party had called as a witness the expert appointed by the court and that it was only on appeal that the applicants had asked for the expert evidence to be reviewed. Consequently, the statutory conditions for a retrial had not been met in the instant case.

26. On 27 September 1995 the applicants appealed against the above decision, asserting that they had submitted evidence which it would have been objectively impossible for them to present during the original proceedings. On 26 February 1996 the Prague Regional Court upheld the decision of 23 August 1995, holding that there were no facts, decisions or evidence which it would have been impossible for the defendants to rely on in the initial proceedings. However, it gave leave for an appeal on points of law against its ruling.

27. On 11 April 1996, therefore, the applicants appealed on a point of law to the Supreme Court (*Nejvyšší soud*). They argued that in the proceedings on their appeal against the judgment which had transferred title they had proposed in vain the commissioning of a second expert report and that the Regional Court's attitude had prompted them to have a new expert report drawn up on their own initiative.

28. On 13 January 1997 the Constitutional Court dismissed the applicants' constitutional appeal as manifestly ill-founded, ruling as follows:

"The alleged violation of Article 11 § 1 of the Charter of Fundamental Rights and Freedoms must be examined not just from the appellants' point of view but also from that of the person claiming restitution.... The Court refers in that connection to its judgment published under file no. 131/1994 ..., in which it noted that the purpose of restitution was to attenuate infringements of the rights of real-property owners by making reparation for the unlawful act committed at the time of the transfer of the property and by giving priority to the restitution of properties in their original condition. Consequently, the Court cannot find a violation of Article 11 § 1 unless the statutory conditions for restitution are satisfied....

The annulment sought by the applicants, of part of section 8(1) of the Land Act (Law no. 229/1991), would have limited the right to restitution and would have harmed the

interests of a large number of restitution claimants.... The laws on restitution must establish the conditions for redressing wrongs, it being understood that it is for the national courts to examine all the circumstances in the light of the purport and general object of those laws.

The reporting judge has established, in the light of all the documents submitted, that the ordinary courts correctly applied the law to the case in allowing the claim for restitution and in deciding that title should be transferred to the claimant ..., as the appellant and her husband had bought the house at a price lower than the price resulting from application of the rules on prices then in force.

As regards violation of Article 37 of the Charter, which enshrines the principle of equality between litigants, the Court notes that during the judicial proceedings the courts scrupulously examined both the evidence adduced by the person claiming restitution and the evidence adduced by the defendants....

Having regard to the circumstances of the case, the reporting judge did not deem it necessary to stay execution of the Regional Court's judgment, bearing in mind the fact that if the appellants were to be evicted they would be allocated alternative accommodation."

29. On 24 March 1997 the applicants submitted further grounds for their appeal on points of law (*dovolání*), observing that all the courts dealing with their case, including the Constitutional Court, had proceeded on the assumption that the report of the court-appointed expert was correct, whereas, among other defects, it had been established on the basis of a directive from the Ministry of Economic Affairs which had no legal validity, and that Decree no. 73/1964 was not applicable to the case. They also drew attention to the fact that, according to the second expert report drawn up at their request, the purchase price they had paid in 1967 was not lower but higher than the price required by the legislation in force at the time of the sale.

30. On 28 April 1997 the Supreme Court declared the applicants' appeal on points of law inadmissible, pointing out that it could have been admitted in the initial proceedings but could not be in proceedings brought by means of an application for a retrial.

31. The applicants were reimbursed by the Ministry of Agriculture the purchase price they had

paid in 1967 and the sum they had paid for the right to make personal use of the land. They thus received altogether CZK 16,733. On the other hand, reimbursement of the costs they had reasonably incurred for the upkeep of the house was put off on account of a disagreement between the applicants and the State over the applicable rate. According to the applicants, the State had announced that it was prepared to pay them CZK 156,646 but had never made the slightest payment, in spite of their request that it do so. The amount must therefore be fixed by the District Court, the applicants having brought an action against the Ministry of Agriculture in April 2000 seeking payment in the sum of CZK 364,430.

32. According to the information supplied by the parties, the new owner of the property has not to date offered the applicants alternative accommodation and they still live in the house. They contended that the new owner had refused to sign a tenancy agreement with them in order to regularise the situation but had brought an action in the District Court seeking payment of arrears of rent in the sum of CZK 28,072 (corresponding to more than CZK 900 per month), plus default interest. Apparently this action led on 31 March 2000 to an order to pay being made against them. When they appealed, two hearings were seemingly held on 27 April and 26 June 2000, and the owner, it would appear, is now seeking a still higher sum, corresponding to a rent of CZK 1,200 per month. The applicants observe that the proceedings they brought in April 2000 in order to determine how much they should be reimbursed for the costs they incurred for the upkeep of the property are still pending. They therefore consider that their position *vis-à-vis* the public authorities is less favourable than that of the new owner.

[. . .]

I. Alleged Violation of Article 1 of Protocol No. 1

42. The applicants complained that they had been deprived of possessions they had acquired in good faith and in accordance with domestic legislation, alleging that they had not received adequate compensation. They relied on Article 1 of Protocol No. 1, which provides:

"Every natural or legal person is entitled to the peaceful enjoyment of his possessions. No one shall be deprived of his possessions except in

the public interest and subject to the conditions provided for by law and by the general principles of international law.

The preceding provisions shall not, however, in any way impair the right of a State to enforce such laws as it deems necessary to control the use of property in accordance with the general interest or to secure the payment of taxes or other contributions or penalties."

43. According to the Court's case-law, Article 1 of Protocol No. 1 comprises three distinct rules. The first, which is expressed in the first sentence of the first paragraph and is of a general nature, lays down the principle of peaceful enjoyment of property. The second rule, in the second sentence of the same paragraph, covers deprivation of possessions and subjects it to certain conditions. The third, contained in the second paragraph, recognises that the Contracting States are entitled, amongst other things, to control the use of property in accordance with the general interest. These rules are not "distinct" in the sense of being unconnected: the second and third rules, which are concerned with particular instances of interference with the right to peaceful enjoyment of property, are to be construed in the light of the principle laid down in the first rule.

44. In the present case it is not disputed that the applicants suffered an interference with their right of property which amounted to a "deprivation" of possessions within the meaning of the second sentence of the first paragraph of Article 1 of Protocol No. 1. The Court must therefore examine the justification for that interference in the light of the requirements of Article 1 of Protocol No. 1.

45. It reiterates that the first and most important requirement of Article 1 of Protocol No. 1 is that any interference by a public authority with the peaceful enjoyment of possessions should be lawful: the second sentence of the first paragraph authorises a deprivation of possessions only "subject to the conditions provided for by law" and the second paragraph recognises that the States have the right to control the use of property by enforcing "laws". Moreover, the rule of law, one of the fundamental principles of a democratic society, is inherent in all the Articles of the Convention (see *Amuur v. France*, judgment of 25 June 1996, *Reports of Judgments and Decisions* 1996-III, pp. 850–51, § 50; *The former King of Greece and Others v. Greece* [GC], no. 25701/94,

§ 79, ECHR 2000-XII; and *Malama v. Greece*, no. 43622/98, § 43, ECHR 2001-II).

46. In the present case it is not in dispute between the parties that the deprivation of the applicants' possessions was based on the Land Act (Law no. 229/1991), which made it possible for persons who satisfied the relevant conditions to recover certain types of property and therefore authorised the dispossession of the persons in possession of the property concerned. The Court notes that the requirement of lawfulness was met.

47. The Court must now ascertain whether this deprivation of possessions pursued a legitimate aim, that is, whether there was a "public interest" within the meaning of the second rule set forth in Article 1 of Protocol No. 1. It considers in that connection that, because of their direct knowledge of their society and its needs, the national authorities are in principle better placed than the international judge to appreciate what is "in the public interest". Under the system of protection established by the Convention, it is thus for the national authorities to make the initial assessment of the existence of a problem of public concern warranting measures of deprivation of property. They accordingly enjoy in this sphere a certain margin of appreciation, as in other areas to which the Convention guarantees extend.

48. Furthermore, the notion of "public interest" is necessarily extensive. In particular, the decision to enact laws expropriating property will commonly involve consideration of political, economic and social issues. The Court, finding it natural that the margin of appreciation available to the legislature in implementing social and economic policies should be a wide one, will respect the legislature's judgment as to what is "in the public interest" unless that judgment be manifestly without reasonable foundation (see *James and Others v. the United Kingdom*, judgment of 21 February 1986, Series A no. 98, p. 32, § 46, and *Malama*, cited above, § 46).

49. In the instant case the Government asserted that the objective of the Land Act was to "attenuate the consequences of certain infringements of property rights suffered by the owners of real property used in agriculture and forestry between 1948 and 1989". The legal instrument chosen to attain that objective was "restitution"; the system was aimed at providing reparation for the unlawful act committed at the time of the property's transfer and gave priority to the restitution of properties in their original state.

Restitution was intended to provide redress for the illegality of a transfer of title, or other unlawful interference with the right of property, by the handover of the property in its original legal condition, with retrospective effects. Restitution was therefore not an enforced deprivation of property, but an obligation to reconstitute the original legal situation.

50. The applicants did not dispute that the Land Act's objective was as represented by the Government, but submitted that it was still necessary to respect the essential principles of fairness, which should govern both substantive law and its application. Those principles had not been respected in the instant case, since although the State had attenuated the effects of the earlier infringements of property rights it had done nothing to lessen those of the new interference committed to their detriment.

51. The Court notes that the aim pursued by the Land Act is to attenuate the effects of the infringements of property rights that occurred under the communist regime and understands why the Czech State should have considered it necessary to resolve this problem, which it considered damaging to its democratic regime. The general purpose of the Act cannot therefore be regarded as illegitimate, as it is indeed "in the public interest" (see, *mutatis mutandis, Zvolský and Zvolská v. the Czech Republic* (dec.), no. 46129/99, 11 December 2001).

52. The Court observes that any measure which interferes with the right to peaceful enjoyment of possessions must strike a fair balance between the demands of the general interest of the community and the requirements of the protection of the individual's fundamental rights (see, among other authorities, *Sporrong and Lönnroth v. Sweden*, judgment of 23 September 1982, Series A no. 52, p. 26, § 69). The concern to achieve this balance is reflected in the structure of Article 1 of Protocol No. 1 as a whole, including therefore the second sentence, which is to be read in the light of the general principle enunciated in the first sentence. In particular, there must be a reasonable relationship of proportionality between the means employed and the aim sought to be realised by any measure depriving a person of his possessions

(see *Pressos Compania Naviera S.A. and Others v. Belgium*, judgment of 20 November 1995, Series A no. 332, p. 23, § 38, and *The former King of Greece and Others*, cited above, § 89). Thus the balance to be maintained between the demands of the general interest of the community and the requirements of fundamental rights is upset if the person concerned has had to bear a "disproportionate burden" (see, among many other authorities, *The Holy Monasteries v. Greece*, judgment of 9 December 1994, Series A no. 301-A, pp. 34–35, §§ 70–71).

53. Consequently, the Court has held that the person deprived of his property must in principle obtain compensation "reasonably related to its value", even though "legitimate objectives of 'public interest' may call for less than reimbursement of the full market value" (ibid.). It follows that the balance mentioned above is generally achieved where the compensation paid to the person whose property has been taken is reasonably related to its "market" value, as determined at the time of the expropriation.

54. In the present case, the Government asserted that the Land Act maintained a reasonably proportionate relationship between the means employed and the aim pursued, since it required, in addition to the illegal transfer of the property concerned to the State, a further element of illegality vitiating the transfer of the same property from the State to a natural person. At the same time, it entitled the latter to reimbursement of the purchase price and the costs reasonably incurred for the upkeep of the property.

In addition, the law prohibited the eviction of the former owner from the returned property before appropriate alternative accommodation had been made available to him. The Government pointed out, however, that although an offer of alternative accommodation from the new owner was not excluded *a priori*, there was no requirement under Czech law for him or her to make such an offer. In that respect, therefore, the evicted person could not press any claim through the courts. Further, regard being had to the general provisions of the Civil Code, persons obliged to return a property (like the applicants) were not required to vacate it until alternative accommodation had been allocated to them.

55. The Government accordingly considered that the burden to be borne by natural persons required to return a property was not excessive and that the means employed were not disproportionate in relation to the interest to be protected.

56. The applicants submitted that it was unfair that the only compensation they could secure was reimbursement of the price they had paid for the purchase in the 1960s, which represented approximately one fiftieth of the present market value, and the costs they had reasonably incurred for the upkeep of the property, the amount under the latter head being fixed according to the tariff in force on 24 June 1991. They also considered unfair the obligation they were under to move out and rent alternative accommodation, or pay rent in order to be able to occupy the building they had looked after for most of their lives. They complained that they had been deprived of their title to the house, which they had allegedly acquired in breach of the rules in force at the time, but also of their title to the land, which they had acquired in accordance with those rules.

57. The applicants therefore submitted that the requirement of proportionality between the means employed and the aim pursued had not been satisfied in their case. They considered that they had had to bear an individual and excessive burden, aggravated by the long periods of mental distress which the first applicant, who was nearly 80 years of age, and the original applicant, who had been afflicted by illness, had had to endure.

They further asserted that neither the first applicant nor her late husband knew when they bought the house in 1967 that it had not previously belonged to the State, which had acquired it by confiscation. In that context they pointed out that in 1967 only persons who could show that they had a legitimate interest were permitted to consult the land register. Taking into account the fact that they were forestry workers, it would be unreasonable to criticise them for not making any effort to ascertain, at a time when everything was in principle owned by the State, whether or not the house had belonged at some time in the past to a different owner.

58. The Court accepts that the general objective of the restitution laws, namely to attenuate the consequences of certain infringements of property rights caused by the communist regime, is a legitimate aim and a means of safeguarding the lawfulness of legal transactions and protecting the country's socio-economic development. However, it considers it necessary to ensure that the attenuation of

those old injuries does not create disproportionate new wrongs. To that end, the legislation should make it possible to take into account the particular circumstances of each case, so that persons who acquired their possessions in good faith are not made to bear the burden of responsibility which is rightfully that of the State which once confiscated those possessions.

59. In the present case the Court accepts the applicants' argument that they had acquired their possessions in good faith, without knowing that they had previously been confiscated and without being able to influence the terms of the transaction or the purchase price. Moreover, it seems that the Czech courts' finding that the applicants had acquired the property at a price lower than that required by the regulations was due above all to a different valuation of the barn and cowshed, that is, of the non-inhabitable parts of the building.

60. On the question of the burden borne by the applicants in the case, the Court considers that it is not required to decide on what basis the domestic courts should have assessed the amount of compensation payable; it cannot take the place of the Czech authorities in determining the year that should have been taken into consideration for the valuation of the house and for the assessment of the costs reasonably incurred for its upkeep (see, *mutatis mutandis*, *Malama*, cited above, § 51).

61. However, the Court cannot fail to observe that the purchase price paid in 1967, which was given back to the applicants, could not be reasonably related to its value thirty years later.

In addition, the house in question was for the applicants the only housing available. At the time of the restitution decision, in 1995, they had lived there for forty-two years, and twenty-eight of those as its owners.

62. It should also be noted that the applicants are in an uncertain, and indeed difficult, social situation. With the reimbursed purchase price they are unable to buy somewhere else to live. It is true that to date they have not been compelled to leave the house and that, according to Article 712 of the Civil Code, they must be offered alternative accommodation. Nevertheless, the Government themselves accept that it is impossible to assert that right in the courts. Moreover, the new owner of the property seems to be taking advantage of his position of strength *vis-à-vis* the applicants, whom he has asked to pay a monthly rent even though they have no tenancy agreement. As the applicants refused to pay rent in those circumstances, the new owner has brought proceedings which are still pending.

63. The Court accordingly notes that the "compensation" awarded to the applicants did not take account of their personal and social situation and that they were not awarded any sum for the non-pecuniary damage they sustained as a result of being deprived of their only property. In addition, they have still not obtained reimbursement of the costs reasonably incurred for the upkeep of the house, even though a period of seven and a half years has elapsed since 23 January 1995, the day when the judgment of the Prague Regional Court confirming the transfer of title to the son of the former owners became final.

64. The applicants have thus had to bear an individual and excessive burden which has upset the fair balance that should be maintained between the demands of the general interest on the one hand and protection of the right to the peaceful enjoyment of possessions on the other. There has therefore been a violation of Article 1 of Protocol No. 1.

[. . .]

4.17. *Wittek v. Germany* (2003)

[. . .]

I. THE CIRCUMSTANCES OF THE CASE

9. The first applicant was born in 1958 and the second applicant in 1948; they both live in Bad Münder (Germany).

A. Background to the Case

10. Under a purchase agreement dated 26 May 1986, the applicants purchased a dwelling house in Leipzig, on the territory of the German Democratic Republic (GDR) for 56,000 East German marks. The house was built on land belonging to the State (*volkseigenes Grundstück*) over which the applicants obtained a usufruct (*dingliches Nutzungsrecht*) under Articles 287 et seq. of the Civil Code (*Zivilgesetzbuch*) of the GDR.

11. On 26 October 1989 the applicants made an official request for permission to leave the GDR, as they believed that they had been discriminated against on political grounds in their work.

The applicants say that they were informed by the District Internal Affairs Department (*Abteilung innere Angelegenheiten des Stadtbezirks*) in Leipzig that to obtain permission to leave the GDR permanently they would have to transfer (*veräussern*) their property by sale or gift.

12. On 8 December 1989 the applicants purported to transfer the property to a couple, Mr and Mrs Böllmann, by a notarial deed of gift in which the dwelling house was stated to be worth 120,000 East German marks. In reality, Mr and Mrs Böllmann paid the applicants 55,000 German marks (DEM) into a Swiss bank account.

13. The applicants say that the true value of their house and land would today be approximately DEM 600,000.

14. That figure is disputed by the Government, who say that the applicants had possessed only a usufruct over the land.

15. Following German reunification, the applicants attempted to recover their house and their usufruct over the land, firstly from the purchasers and subsequently in proceedings in the civil and administrative courts of the Federal Republic of Germany (FRG).

B. Proceedings in the Civil Courts

16. On 21 March 1991 the applicants applied to the Leipzig Court of First Instance (*Kreisgericht*) for an order for restitution of their house and rectification of the entry in the land register (*Grundbuch*).

17. The Leipzig Court of First Instance rejected that application on 26 June 1991.

18. In a judgment of 5 March 1992, the Leipzig District Court (*Bezirksgericht*) dismissed an appeal by the applicants, holding that they had no right to restitution. It pointed out that no transfer of property had in fact taken place, as both the gift and the sale in the GDR were null and void. However, the applicants were not entitled to rely on that nullity, as they had opted for that form of contract in full knowledge of the facts and the purchasers had

not taken advantage of any coercion (*Zwangslage*) to which the applicants may have been subject at the time. The application for restitution accordingly failed under the principle of good faith and fair dealing (*Treu und Glauben*).

19. In a judgment of 19 November 1993, the Federal Court of Justice (*Bundesgerichtshof*) dismissed a further appeal by the applicants. In common with the ordinary courts, it found that both the gift and the sale were null and void. However, it reiterated that in cases such as this, in which the applicants had made a sham gift in order to attenuate the effects of being forced to sell their property on leaving the GDR, the applicable legislation was the Resolution of Outstanding Property Issues Act – the Property Act – of 23 September 1990 (*Gesetz zur Regelung offener Vermögensfragen – Vermögensgesetz*; see "Relevant domestic law and practice" below), whose interpretation was a matter for the administrative, not the civil, courts.

C. Proceedings in the Administrative Courts

20. The applicants then lodged an administrative appeal with the Leipzig City Council requesting the restitution of their property. They relied on the Property Act.

21. In a decision of 2 June 1994, the Leipzig City Council turned down their request on the grounds that the conditions set out in section 1(3) of the Property Act (see "Relevant domestic law and practice" below) were not satisfied, as the applicants had not shown that they had acted under duress (*Nötigung*). Duress linked to a departure from the GDR could only have existed prior to the opening of the border on 9 November 1989. Thereafter, it was clear that all restrictions on leaving the GDR had been lifted.

22. The applicants appealed against that decision to the Regional Office for the Resolution of Outstanding Property Issues (*Landesamt zur Regelung offener Vermögensfragen*) of the Land of Saxony, which dismissed their appeal, again on the grounds that the applicants had not acted under duress following the opening of the border on 9 November 1989, and in particular following the Resolution of Property Issues Order (*Anordnung zur Regelung von Vermögensfragen* – see "Relevant domestic law

and practice" below) of 11 November 1989 and its publication on 23 November 1989.

23. In a judgment of 21 December 1995, the Leipzig Administrative Court (*Verwaltungsgericht*) found against the applicants following a hearing.

It found that they were not entitled to restitution (*Rücküber-tragungsanspruch*) in the absence of any unfair dealings (*unlautere Machenschaften*) within the meaning of section 1(3) of the Property Act. The border had been opened on 9 November 1989, with the result that all citizens of the GDR had been free to leave the country, while the Resolution of Property Issues Order of 11 November 1989 stipulated that they were no longer required to transfer their property prior to their departure. However, the deed of transfer was only executed on 8 December 1989. It added that there had not been any deception (*Täuschung*) within the meaning of section 1(3) of the Property Act.

The Administrative Court also found that even if the previous position had remained unchanged, the conditions set out in section 1(3) of Property Act would not in any event have been satisfied, as the applicants did not own the land but merely had a usufruct over it. Under GDR legislation – the State-Owned Land (Grants of Usufructs) Act of 14 December 1970 (*Gesetz über die Verleihung von Nutzungsrechten an einem volkseigenen Grundstück*) – persons entitled to a usufruct were required to use the land themselves. Even if the applicants had moved house within the GDR, the land would have reverted to the State and the applicants' only entitlement would have been to compensation. The applicants had been aware of that situation, which is why they had sought to transfer their property.

24. By two decisions of 2 September and 22 October 1996, the Federal Administrative Court (*Bundesverwaltungsgericht*) declined to examine an application for review by the applicants.

It referred to its leading judgment of 29 February 1996 in which it had stated that instances of unfair dealings between 23 November 1989 (the date of publication of the Resolution of Property Issues Order in the Official Gazette (*Gesetzblatt*) of the GDR) and 31 January 1990 (when the Travel Order (*Reiseverordnung*) of the GDR dated 30 November 1988 was revoked) would be rare. The Leipzig

Administrative Court had conducted a thorough review of the facts of the case and concluded that there had been no duress or deception within the meaning of section 1(3) of the Property Act.

The Federal Administrative Court also referred to its leading judgment of 29 August 1996, in which it stated that there would not be unfair dealing within the meaning of section 1(3) of the Property Act in cases in which the obligation to transfer property had arisen under the State-Owned Land (Grants of Usufructs) Act of 14 December 1970 of the GDR.

D. Proceedings in the Federal Constitutional Court

25. In two decisions of 22 January 1997, the Federal Constitutional Court (*Bundesverfassungsgericht*) declined to hear constitutional appeals by the applicants against either the civil courts' or the administrative courts' decisions.

It referred, *inter alia*, to its leading judgment of 8 October 1996 in which it had held that it was not unconstitutional for civil rights to be supplanted (*verdrängt*) by the provisions of the Property Act in cases involving the departure of GDR citizens for the FRG. Accordingly, the Federal Court of Justice's interpretation in the instant case was consistent with that authority.

II. RELEVANT DOMESTIC LAW AND PRACTICE

A. The Resolution of Property Issues Order (GDR)

26. Article 1 § 1 of the Resolution of Property Issues Order of 11 November 1989, which came into force on 14 November and was published on 23 November 1989, laid down that citizens of the GDR wishing to leave the GDR to settle permanently in another State or in West Berlin were required to "take necessary measures to ensure the conservation and proper administration of their property in the GDR" ("haben die notwendigen Massnahmen für die ordnungsgemässe Sicherung und Verwaltung Ihres in der Deutschen Demokratischen Republik zurückgelassenen Vermögens zu treffen"). Article 3 revoked with immediate effect GDR Orders nos. 1 and 2 of 1 December 1953 and 20 August 1958 on the Use of the Property of People who left the GDR

after 10 June 1953, and the Works Directive (Arbeitsanweisung) of 5 December 1953 of the same name, which at the time required GDR citizens wishing to leave the GDR to transfer their property before their departure.

B. The Joint Statement of the FRG and the GDR on the Resolution of Outstanding Property Issues

27. During the reunification process in 1990, the two German governments began negotiations on the many property issues arising and subsequently issued the Joint Statement of the Federal Republic of Germany and the German Democratic Republic on the Resolution of Outstanding Property Issues (*Gemeinsame Erklärung der Bundesrepublik Deutschland und der Deutschen Demokratischen Republik zur Regelung offener Vermögensfragen*), which became an integral part of the German Unification Treaty (*Einigungsvertrag*) of 31 August 1990. The negotiations covered both the questions of restitution of property that had been expropriated in the GDR to its owners and the transfer of property by citizens of the GDR on leaving the country.

In the statement, the two governments said that in seeking solutions to the contentious property issues, they needed to find a socially acceptable balance (*sozial verträglicher Ausgleich*) between the competing interests, while taking into account the need for legal certainty and clarity and to protect the right of property.

C. The Resolution of Outstanding Property Issues Act (FRG)

28. The Resolution of Outstanding Property Issues Act of 23 September 1990, also known as the Property Act, entered into force on 29 September 1990 and was also a part of the German Unification Treaty. Under the terms of the Treaty, the Property Act was to continue to subsist in the reunified Germany after the reunification of the two German States on 3 October 1990. The aim of the Act was to resolve disputes over property in the territory of the GDR in a way that was socially acceptable, in order to achieve permanent legal order in Germany.

29. Section 1(3) of the Property Act provides:

"This Act shall also apply to rights in or over immovable property and usufructary rights

acquired by unfair dealings, such as abuse of power, corruption, duress or deception by the purchaser, the State authorities or third parties."

30. The Property Act established the principle of a right to restitution for citizens of the GDR who had been forced to transfer their property in order to leave the country legally, save where restitution was precluded, as for instance if the purchasers had acted in good faith (*redlicher Erwerb*) (section 4(2) of the Act). In such cases, the former owners had a right to compensation under the Resolution of Outstanding Property Issues (Compensation) Act of 27 September 1994 (*Gesetz über die Entschädigung nach dem Gesetz zur Regelung offener Vermögensfragen*).

31. However, the rule set out in section 4(2) of the Property Act does not apply in principle if the transfer was made after the transitional date of 18 October 1989 (when Mr Erich Honecker, President of the Council of State (*Staatsratsvorsitzender*) of the GDR, resigned) and without the parties' agreement (however, see below for the decisions of the Federal Court of Justice on this point).

32. The legislature deliberately chose to give the administrative courts jurisdiction for the interpretation of the Property Act in litigation concerning the transfer of property by citizens wishing to leave the GDR, in order to avoid direct confrontation between former owners and new owners in the civil courts. To that end, it set up offices for the resolution of outstanding property issues which were responsible for deciding the disputes by carrying out investigations of their own motion (*Amtsermittlungsgrundsatz*), while also having regard to the general interest.

D. The Case-Law of the Federal Court of Justice

33. In a leading judgment of 3 April 1992 (Fifth Civil Division, no. 83/91), the Federal Court of Justice held that a sale agreement could not be challenged in the civil courts when the dispute concerned property which citizens of the GDR had been forced to transfer. For such cases, the Property Act had established an exclusive right to restitution under public law (*öffentlich-rechtlicher Rückübertragungsanspruch*).

34. In two other leading judgments of 16 April and 7 May 1993 (Fifth Civil Division, nos. 87/92 and

99/92), it extended that principle to cases in which, as here, the former owners had executed a sham deed of gift in order to attenuate the effect of being required to transfer their property before leaving the GDR.

35. In two further leading judgments of 14 January and 12 May 2000 (Fifth Civil Division, nos. 439/98 and 47/99), the Federal Court of Justice held that the Property Act could apply to legal transactions entered into after the transitional date of 18 October 1989 if the factors vitiating consent would have resulted in the transfer being null and void in the light of the new situation obtaining in the GDR, both on the facts and in law.

Complaint

36. The applicants submitted that the German courts' refusal to order the restitution of their property situated on the territory of the GDR had infringed their right of property, as guaranteed by Article 1 of Protocol No. 1.

The Law

I. ALLEGED VIOLATION OF ARTICLE 1 OF PROTOCOL NO. 1

37. The applicants submitted that the German courts' refusal to order the restitution of their property situated on the territory of the GDR had infringed their right of property, as guaranteed by Article 1 of Protocol No. 1, which provides:

> "Every natural or legal person is entitled to the peaceful enjoyment of his possessions. No one shall be deprived of his possessions except in the public interest and subject to the conditions provided for by law and by the general principles of international law.
>
> The preceding provisions shall not, however, in any way impair the right of a State to enforce such laws as it deems necessary to control the use of property in accordance with the general interest or to secure the payment of taxes or other contributions or penalties."

A. The Parties' Submissions

1. The Government

38. The Government said that even if there had been an interference in the present case, it had been

provided for by the Property Act, was in the public interest and struck a fair balance between the competing interests. They stressed the special nature of German reunification and the fact that the Property Act sought to ensure legal order by protecting purchasers' rights too, provided they had acted in good faith. The legislature had chosen to give jurisdiction to hear disputes over the restitution of property which people had been forced to transfer on leaving the GDR to the administrative courts and it was they who were competent to decide questions of construction of the Property Act. Their interpretation in the instant case had not been arbitrary. Moreover, under the case-law of the Federal Court of Justice, the Property Act could also apply to legal transactions entered into after the transitional date of 18 October 1989. Lastly, the applicants had received fair compensation, as they had been paid a consideration of 55,000 German marks (DEM) for the property.

2. The Applicants

39. The applicants submitted that the transfer made under pressure from the GDR authorities was null and void and that they had only lost their title to the house with the Federal Court of Justice's decision of 19 November 1993, that being the true act of expropriation for practical purposes. Above all, they contested the interpretation of the Property Act by the Federal Court of Justice, the Federal Administrative Court and the Federal Constitutional Court, whose decisions were, in their submission, inconsistent. Initially, the Federal Court of Justice had found that the transfer agreement was null and void, but held that their civil rights had been supplanted by the provisions of the Property Act, which were applicable in their case. Subsequently, the Federal Administrative Court had ruled that the conditions under which the Property Act would be applicable were not satisfied. Lastly, neither court had taken into account the fact that the transfer agreement had been entered into after the transitional date of 18 October 1989. The Property Act ceased to be applicable after that date and the need to protect bona fide purchasers had to yield to the right of former owners to restitution.

B. The Court's Assessment

40. The Court notes at the outset that it has jurisdiction in the present case, since, even though the Property Act of 23 September 1990 was passed in

the GDR on 29 September 1990, it continued to be applicable in the reunified Germany after 3 October 1990.

41. The Court reiterates that Article 1 of Protocol No. 1, which guarantees in substance the right of property, comprises three distinct rules (see *James and Others v. the United Kingdom*, judgment of 21 February 1986, Series A no. 98, pp. 29–30, § 37). The first, which is expressed in the first sentence of the first paragraph and is of a general nature, lays down the principle of peaceful enjoyment of property. The second rule, in the second sentence of the same paragraph, covers deprivation of possessions and subjects it to certain conditions. The third, contained in the second paragraph, recognises that the Contracting States are entitled, amongst other things, to control the use of property in accordance with the general interest. The second and third rules, which are concerned with particular instances of interference with the right to peaceful enjoyment of property, must be construed in the light of the general principle laid down in the first rule (see, among other authorities, *Iatridis v. Greece* [GC], no. 31107/96, § 55, ECHR 1999-II).

1. Whether there Was Interference

42. Under the Court's case-law, the notion "possessions" in Article 1 of Protocol No. 1 has an autonomous meaning which is not limited to ownership of physical goods: certain other rights and interests constituting assets can also be regarded as "property rights", and thus as "possessions", for the purposes of this provision (see, among other authorities, *Gasus Dosier- und Fördertechnik GmbH v. the Netherlands*, judgment of 23 February 1995, Series A no. 306-B, p. 46, § 53, and *Iatridis*, cited above, § 54).

43. The Court notes that in the present case the applicants had a right of property in their dwelling house, coupled with a usufruct over the land belonging to the State on which it stood in accordance with the relevant GDR legislation, the State-Owned Land (Grants of Usufructs) Act of 14 December 1970.

44. Accordingly, it considers that the present dispute should be examined under the first sentence of Article 1 of Protocol No. 1 (see, *mutatis mutandis, Českomoravská myslivecká jednota v. the Czech Republic* (dec.), no. 33091/96, 23 March 1999, and

Teuschler v. Germany (dec.), no. 47636/99, 4 October 2001).

45. In the present case, the Federal Court of Justice found that the transfer of the land by the applicants during the subsistence of the GDR was null and void. However, the applicants were subsequently unable to establish a right to restitution in either the civil or the administrative courts.

46. Consequently, there has been an interference with the applicants' right to the peaceful enjoyment of their possessions.

2. Whether the Interference Was Justified

47. As to whether the interference was prescribed by law, the Court notes that it was based on the provisions of the Property Act, which are precise and accessible to all. In addition, the Federal Court of Justice, the Federal Administrative Court and the Federal Constitutional Court have established rules governing the application of that Act to disputes over the deprivation of property in the GDR.

48. In the instant case, in a judgment of 19 November 1993, the Federal Court of Justice dismissed the applicants' claim for restitution by applying a rule that was well-established in both its own and the Federal Constitutional Court's case-law that an agreement for sale could not be challenged in the civil courts if the dispute was over the restitution of property which citizens of the GDR had been forced to transfer before leaving the country. In such cases, the applicable legislation was the Property Act and its interpretation was a matter for the administrative, not the civil, courts. Subsequently, when the administrative courts applied the Act to the facts of the present case, they held that the conditions set out in section 1(3) of the Property Act (see "Relevant domestic law and practice" above) were not satisfied.

49. The Court considers that that was not an arbitrary interpretation and reiterates in that connection that it is primarily for the national authorities, notably the courts, to interpret and apply domestic law (see *Brualla Gómez de la Torre v. Spain*, judgment of 19 December 1997, *Reports of Judgments and Decisions* 1997-VIII, p. 2955, § 31, and *Glässner v. Germany* (dec.), no. 46362/99, ECHR 2001-VII).

50. As regards the purpose of the interference, the Court finds that the Property Act, which was intended to resolve property disputes following

German reunification by seeking to establish a socially acceptable balance between the competing interests, indisputably pursued an aim that was in the public interest (see *Teuschler*, decision cited above).

51. It also considers that it was legitimate for the legislature to treat all disputes over the restitution of property which citizens of the GDR were forced to transfer before their departure in a uniform manner under the Property Act and to leave the interpretation of that Act to the administrative courts.

52. Lastly, the Court has to consider whether the interference was proportionate.

53. Under the Court's case-law, an interference with the peaceful enjoyment of possessions must strike a fair balance between the demands of the general interest of the community and the requirements of the protection of the individual's fundamental rights (see, among other authorities, *Sporrong and Lönnroth v. Sweden*, judgment of 23 September 1982, Series A no. 52, p. 26, § 69). The concern to achieve this balance is reflected in the structure of Article 1 as a whole. In particular, there must be a reasonable relationship of proportionality between the means employed and the aim sought to be realised by any measure depriving a person of his possessions (see *Pressos Compania Naviera S.A. and Others v. Belgium*, judgment of 20 November 1995, Series A no. 332, p. 23, § 38, and *Yagtzilar and Others v. Greece*, no. 41727/98, § 40, ECHR 2001-XII).

54. The Court must examine in particular whether the contested measure strikes the requisite fair balance and whether it imposes a disproportionate burden on the applicants.

55. In the present case, the Court notes that, in its judgment of 21 December 1995, the Leipzig Administrative Court conducted a thorough review of the facts of the case and the applicants' arguments before finding that, in the absence of duress or deception, there had been no unfair dealing within the meaning of section 1(3) of the Property Act.

56. The applicants executed the deed transferring their property on 8 December 1989, almost a month after the border opened on 9 November 1989 – by which time citizens of the GDR were free to leave the country – and after the publication of the Resolution of Property Issues Order on 23 November

1989, which released citizens of the GDR from the obligation to transfer their property before leaving.

57. In the Court's view, that analysis was sound, even though the period between the opening of the border between the two German States on 9 November 1989 and formal German reunification on 3 October 1990 was a time of considerable uncertainty, particularly from a legal standpoint.

58. Independently of that aspect, the applicants' only interest in the land under GDR law was a usufruct under the State-Owned Land (Grants of Usufructs) Act, so they would have been unable to retain the property even if they had moved house within the GDR.

59. There is a further factor which the Court finds decisive: the applicants purchased the house on 26 May 1986 for 56,000 East German marks. When they made the sham gift of the property on 8 December 1989, they were paid DEM 55,000 by the purchasers, which, at the exchange rate of 1 to 4 applicable at the time to transactions between private individuals, was equivalent to 220,000 East German marks.

60. Accordingly, even allowing for subsequent increases in value of the property, the applicants cannot be regarded as having borne "a disproportionate burden".

61. Having regard to all of the above considerations and in particular to the exceptional circumstances of German reunification, the Court considers that the respondent State has not overstepped its margin of appreciation and, in view of the legitimate aim pursued, has succeeded in achieving a "fair balance" between the applicants' interests and the general interest of German society.

62. There has therefore been no violation of Article 1 of Protocol No. 1.

[. . .]

4.18. *Jantner v. Slovakia* (2003)

[. . .]

I. The Circumstances of the Case

8. The applicant left Czechoslovakia for Germany in 1968. After his judicial rehabilitation in 1990 he

started living partly in Czechoslovakia and partly in Germany. According to the applicant, he spent the major part of the year 1992 in Czechoslovakia. On 25 September 1992 he registered his permanent residence at his friend's address in Krompachy. He remained registered at this address until 22 June 1994.

9. On 28 September 1992 the applicant lodged a claim for restitution of his father's and uncle's property under the Land Ownership Act of 1991.

10. On 15 May 1996 the Spišská Nová Ves Land Office dismissed the applicant's claim on the ground that at the relevant time he had not permanently resided within the territory of the former Czech and Slovak Federal Republic as required by Section 4(1) of the Land Ownership Act.

11. The Land Office established that a registered letter sent on 8 April 1993 could not be delivered as at that time nobody had lived at the applicant's address in Krompachy. The Land Office had before it also a certificate in which the competent German authority confirmed that the applicant had registered his main abode (*Hauptwohnung*) in Wendelstein since 1973. The accompanying letter by the Slovakian vice-consul to Munich explained that, unlike in Slovakia, no distinction was made between permanent and temporary residence in Germany. The letter further stated that under German law the main abode was the place of residence preponderantly used by the person concerned in Germany, and that there was no obligation under German law to terminate its registration when a person spent the major part of a year abroad. The vice-consul expressed the view that in case that the applicant's stay in Slovakia exceeded 183 days a year, his residence there could, theoretically, be regarded as permanent within the meaning of the Citizens' Residence Registration Act of 1982.

12. In its decision the Land Office referred also to a police report according to which the applicant had not effectively established his permanent residence in Krompachy. The Land Office concluded, with reference to Section 3(2) and (5) and Section 4(1) of the Citizens' Residence Registration Act of 1982 and to the relevant case-law and administrative practice, that the applicant did not meet the permanent residence requirement.

13. On 19 June 1996 the applicant requested the Košice Regional Court to review the Land Office's decision. He alleged that since the beginning of 1992 he had resided at various places in Slovakia and submitted witness statements to this effect. The applicant further explained that several times a year he went to Germany where he was undergoing cancer therapy.

14. On 29 November 1996 the Košice Regional Court upheld the administrative decision challenged by the applicant. It noted that by the date of expiry of the deadline for lodging his claim on 31 December 1992 the applicant had not permanently resided within the former Czech and Slovak Federal Republic as required by Section 4(1) of the Land Ownership Act.

15. The Regional Court recalled, in particular, that under Section 4(1) of the Citizens' Residence Registration Act of 1982 citizens cannot permanently reside at more than one address at the same time. As the applicant failed to terminate the registration of his main abode in Germany prior to the registration of his permanent residence in Krompachy, his stay in the then Czechoslovakia was to be regarded as temporary. Reference was made to the relevant case-law and to the practice of the Ministry of the Interior.

16. The Regional Court further held that the applicant had submitted no evidence indicating that his abode in Krompachy met the requirements of a permanent residence within the meaning of Section 3(2) of the Citizens' Residence Registration Act. Moreover, a police report before the court indicated that the applicant's registration in Krompachy had been of a formal nature.

17. On 30 July 1999 the Supreme Court refused to re-examine the case as there was no remedy available against the Regional Court's judgment of 29 November 1996.

[. . .]

I. Alleged Violation of Article 1 of Protocol No. 1

23. The applicant complained that the permanent residence requirement laid down in Section 4(1) of the Land Ownership Act and the refusal to grant his claim for restitution of property for his alleged failure to comply with that requirement infringed

his property rights. He relied on Article 1 of Protocol No. 1 which provides as follows:

> "Every natural or legal person is entitled to the peaceful enjoyment of his possessions. No one shall be deprived of his possessions except in the public interest and subject to the conditions provided for by law and by the general principles of international law.
>
> The preceding provisions shall not, however, in any way impair the right of a State to enforce such laws as it deems necessary to control the use of property in accordance with the general interest or to secure the payment of taxes or other contributions or penalties."

24. The Government argued that the applicant had failed to meet the permanent residence requirement laid down in the Land Ownership Act of 1991 and that his claim cannot, therefore, be regarded as a "possession" within the meaning of Article 1 of Protocol No. 1. In particular, the applicant did not terminate the registration of his main abode in Germany prior to registering in Slovakia which was a prerequisite for considering his residence in Slovakia as permanent. In the Government's view, the information available indicates that the applicant did not register in Slovakia with a genuine intention to permanently reside there as required by the practice of the national authorities.

25. The applicant contended that he was entitled to have the property restored as he met the requirements of the relevant law and that the dismissal of his action amounted to a violation of his right to peacefully enjoy his possessions guaranteed by Article 1 of Protocol No. 1.

26. He maintained, in particular, that he had had his permanent residence registered in Slovakia at the moment when he had filed the claim for restitution of property as required by the law. He explained that at that time he had lived together with his friend in the latter's house in Krompachy and that they had later moved to the latter's flat in Košice as the house was not suitable for living in winter time. The applicant unregistered his permanent residence in Krompachy on 22 June 1994. As from 1993, he actually lived in Piešťany in a house under reconstruction and paid social security contributions under the Slovakian scheme as required in cases when a person had permanent residence in

Slovakia. He argued that such payments had not been required by the law in 1992.

27. The Court recalls that the Convention institutions have consistently held that "possessions" within the meaning of Article 1 of Protocol No. 1 can be either "existing possessions" or assets, including claims, in respect of which an applicant can argue that he has at least a "legitimate expectation" that they will be realised. On the other hand, the hope that a long-extinguished property right may be revived cannot be regarded as a "possession" within the meaning of Article 1 of Protocol No. 1; nor can a conditional claim which has lapsed as a result of the failure to fulfil the condition (see the recapitulation of the relevant principles in *Malhous v. the Czech Republic* (dec.) [GC], no. 33071/96, 13 December 2000, ECHR 2000-XII and *Gratzinger and Gratzingerova v. the Czech Republic* (dec.) [GC], no. 39794/98, § 69, to be published in ECHR 2002, with further references).

28. In the present case the applicant's action did not concern his "existing possessions" and the applicant did not have the status of an owner but was merely a claimant, like the applicants in the case of Gratzinger and Gratzingerova v. the Czech Republic cited above.

29. It therefore remains to be determined whether the applicant had a "legitimate expectation" that a current, enforceable claim would be determined in his favour. In this respect the Court notes that Section 4(1) of the Land Ownership Act of 1991 entitled the applicant to claim the restitution of his relatives' property provided that, *inter alia*, he met the requirement of permanent residence within the then Czech and Slovak Federal Republic.

30. As to the applicant's argument that the domestic authorities decided on his action erroneously, the Court notes that in its judgment of 29 November 1996 the Košice Regional Court recalled that under Section 4(1) of the Citizens' Residence Registration Act of 1982 citizens cannot permanently reside at more than one address at the same time. As the applicant failed to terminate the registration of his main abode in Germany prior to the registration of his permanent residence in Krompachy, his stay in the then Czechoslovakia was to be regarded as temporary. Reference was made to the relevant case-law and to the practice of the Ministry of the Interior.

31. In addition, the evidence available indicated that the applicant's stay at his friends' address in Krompachy had lacked the attributes of permanent residence within the meaning of Section 3(2) of the Citizens' Residence Registration Act, and that his registration at that address had been formal. The Regional Court concluded that by the date of expiry of the deadline for lodging his claim on 31 December 1992 the applicant had not resided permanently within the former Czech and Slovak Federal Republic as required by Section 4(1) of the Land Ownership Act.

32. Having regard to the information before it and considering that it has only limited power to deal with alleged errors of fact or law committed by the national courts (see *García Ruiz v. Spain* [G.C.] no. 30544/96, § 28, ECHR 1999-I and *Kopp v. Switzerland*, judgment of 25 March 1998, *Reports of Judgments and Decisions* 1988-II, p. 540, § 59), the Court considers that it cannot substitute its view for that of the Košice Regional Court on the applicant's compliance with the permanent residence requirement laid down in Section 4(1) of the Land Ownership Act of 1991.

33. Thus under the relevant law, as applied and interpreted by domestic authorities, the applicant neither had a right nor a claim amounting to a legitimate expectation in the sense of the Court's case-law to obtain restitution of the property in question and therefore no "possession" within the meaning of Article 1 of Protocol No. 1.

34. The Court further recalls that Article 1 of Protocol No. 1 does not guarantee the right to acquire property (see e.g. *Van der Mussele v. Belgium*, judgment of 23 November 1983, Series A no. 70, § 48). It also cannot be interpreted as imposing any restrictions on the Contracting States' freedom to choose conditions under which they accept to restore property which had been transferred to them before they ratified the Convention.

35. Consequently, neither the decisions complained of by the applicant nor the application of the Land Ownership Act of 1991 in his case amounted to an interference with his right to the peaceful enjoyment of his possessions.

36. There has therefore been no violation of Article 1 of Protocol No. 1.

[. . .]

4.19. *Valová, Slezák and Slezák v. Slovakia* (2004)

[. . .]

I. The Circumstances of the Case

8. On 10 February 1992 the Topol'čany Land Office *(Pozemkový úrad)* delivered two decisions granting the applicants' claims for restitution of real property under the Land Ownership Act. The defendants appealed.

9. On 16 December 1993 the Nitra branch office of the Bratislava Regional Court *(Krajský súd Bratislava, pobočka v Nitre)* quashed these decisions on the ground that at the moment of the expropriation the land in question had been formally owned by a private company established by the members of the applicants' family. However, the Land Ownership Act provided exclusively for restitution of property taken away from individuals. The Regional Court therefore sent the case back to the administrative authority. Prior to deciding on the case the Regional Court held a hearing with reference to Section 250q of the Code of Civil Procedure.

10. In the meantime, on 13 November 1992, the applicants and another member of their family concluded an agreement with the Western Slovakia Forest Administration. Under the agreement the Western Slovakia Forest Administration undertook to restore, in accordance with the Land Ownership Act, different real property expropriated from the applicants' family. On 26 November 1992 the Topol'čany Land Office approved the agreement pursuant to Section 9 of the Land Ownership Act. Its decision became final on 18 December 1992.

11. On 17 June 1994 the Topol'čany Land Office decided to reopen the proceedings leading to its decision of 26 November 1992 pursuant to Section 62 (1) (a) and (b) of the Administrative Proceedings Act of 1967. The decision referred to the above finding of the Nitra branch office of the Bratislava Regional Court of 16 December 1993 according to which the land taken away from the applicants' relatives could not be restored under the Land Ownership Act as it had been formally owned by a legal person.

12. On 4 July 1997 the applicants appealed through the intermediary of their lawyer. They argued that

no relevant new facts had been established and that the decision to reopen the proceedings was not justified by the public interest. The applicants concluded that there existed no legal entitlement for having the proceedings reopened.

13. On 22 May 1995 the Ministry of Agriculture upheld the Land Office's decision of 17 June 1994. The decision stated that no reasons for quashing or modifying the Land Office's decision had been found.

14. The applicants sought a judicial review of the decision of the Ministry of Agriculture. On 29 September 1995 the Supreme Court *(Najvyšší súd)* discontinued the proceedings for lack of jurisdiction to review administrative decisions of a procedural nature. Reference was made to Article 248 (2) (e) of the Code of Civil Procedure.

15. By a decision of 8 June 1995 the Topol'čany Land Office disapproved the agreement concluded on 13 November 1992 on the ground that the property in question had been taken away from a legal person and that under the Land Ownership Act only property originally owned by individuals could be restored.

16. The applicants appealed and argued that there existed no reason for reopening the proceedings and that the land had been taken away from the members of their family.

17. On 30 January 1998 the Nitra Regional Court upheld the Land Office's decision of 8 June 1995. The judgment stated that the only point to be determined was a question of law, namely whether the plaintiffs were entitled, within the meaning of Section 4 of the Land Ownership Act, to acquire the property. The court noted that in the judgment of 16 December 1993 it had found that the property had been taken away from a private company of which the applicants' predecessors had been members and which had been a legal person. The Regional Court concluded that the applicants lacked standing to claim restitution under the Land Ownership Act.

18. The Regional Court further noted that a decision on reopening of proceedings before an administrative authority could not be reviewed by a court. It decided on the case without a hearing with reference to Article 250f of the Code of Civil Procedure.

[. . .]

I. Alleged Violation of Article 1 of Protocol No. 1

40. The applicants alleged that their property rights had been violated as a result of the decision to reopen the original proceedings and the subsequent disapproval of the agreement on restitution of property concluded on 13 November 1992. They relied on Article 1 of Protocol No. 1 which provides as follows:

"Every natural or legal person is entitled to the peaceful enjoyment of his possessions. No one shall be deprived of his possessions except in the public interest and subject to the conditions provided for by law and by the general principles of international law.

The preceding provisions shall not, however, in any way impair the right of a State to enforce such laws as it deems necessary to control the use of property in accordance with the general interest or to secure the payment of taxes or other contributions or penalties."

41. The Government admitted that by the decision of the Topol'čany Land Office of 8 July 1995 the applicants had been deprived of property which they had earlier acquired by virtue of the same authority's decision of 26 November 1992. They argued that both the decision of 8 July 1995 and the decision to reopen the proceedings had been in accordance with the relevant provisions of the Land Ownership Act and the Administrative Proceedings Act respectively. The interference was in the public interest as it was aimed at bringing an earlier decision concerning the applicants' restitution claim into conformity with the subsequent finding of a court which was pertinent for the assessment of that claim. The interference complained of was not disproportionate in the particular circumstances of the case.

42. As regards the lawfulness of the decision to reopen the proceedings in particular, the Government argued that neither in their appeal against the Topol'čany Land Office's decision of 17 June 1994 nor in their submissions to the Nitra Regional Court had the applicants explicitly mentioned their argument according to which Section 62 (3) of the Administrative Proceedings Act excluded the possibility of reopening the proceedings in their case.

43. The Government recalled that under the domestic practice administrative courts were bound by the submissions of parties. In their view, the alleged failure by the administrative authority to comply with Section 62 (3) of the Administrative Proceedings Act cannot as such affect the validity of the decision in question. They concluded that the court dealing with the case was therefore not required to examine of its own initiative whether the procedure had been flawed as a result of the disregard by the administrative authority of Section 62 (3) of the Administrative Proceedings Act. The Government concluded that the applicants' rights under Article 1 of Protocol No. 1 had not been violated.

44. The applicants maintained that they had been deprived of their property as a result of the decision to reopen the proceedings in which the agreement on its restitution had been approved. The interference was contrary to the relevant law, namely Section 62 (3) of the Administrative Proceedings Act. They argued, in particular, that the above provision prevented the administrative authority from reopening the proceedings as the decision in question had entitled them to exercise civil rights. Furthermore, it was not established that they had acquired the property in bad faith. In their view, the administrative authorities should have satisfied themselves of their own initiative whether or not the conditions laid down in Section 62 (3) of the Administrative Proceedings Act were met.

45. The applicants also contended that the interference with their property rights was not in the general interest and that it was disproportionate.

46. The Court notes that on 26 November 1992 the Topol'čany Land Office approved the decision on restitution of the property in question to the applicants. The Land Office's decision became final on 18 December 1992. The applicants became owners of that property and exercised property rights in respect of it. Subsequently the competent administrative authority decided to reopen the proceedings leading to the decision of 26 November 1992 and disapproved the restitution agreement. As a result, the applicants lost their title to the property. The Court therefore finds, and it was not disputed between the parties, that the interference complained of amounted to a deprivation of possessions within the meaning of the second sentence of the first paragraph of Article 1 of Protocol No. 1.

A taking of property within this "second rule" can only be justified if it is shown, *inter alia*, to be "in the public interest" and "subject to the conditions provided for by law" (see, e.g., *Brumarescu v. Romania* [GC], no. 28432/95, § 78, ECHR 1999-VII).

47. The Court shares the Government's view that in the present case the deprivation of property was in the public interest as it was aimed at bringing an earlier decision concerning the applicants' restitution claim into conformity with the subsequent finding of a court which was pertinent for the assessment of that claim.

48. As regards compliance with "the conditions provided for by law", the only point in dispute was whether the reopening of the original proceedings, which brought about the decision to disapprove the restitution agreement, had been permissible in the particular circumstances of the case. The information available indicates that Section 62 (3) of the Administrative Proceedings Act of 1967 was pertinent in this respect. In accordance with this provision, administrative proceedings cannot be reopened when the decision in question entitled a party, *inter alia*, to exercise civil rights provided that the party concerned acquired the rights in question in good faith.

49. The Court considers irrelevant the Government's argument that the applicants failed to expressly raise their objection concerning the alleged unlawfulness of the decision to reopen the proceedings before an administrative court and that the court dealing with their case was not required to examine of its own initiative whether the procedure had been flawed in that respect. In fact, the applicants challenged the decision to reopen the proceedings both before the Supreme Court and the Nitra Regional Court which found that under Article 248 (2) (e) of the Code of Civil Procedure such decisions fell outside the scope of judicial review (see paragraphs 14 and 18 above).

50. It is true that in their appeal against the Topol'čany Land Office's decision of 17 June 1994 the applicants challenged the decision to reopen the proceedings in general terms only in that they claimed that there existed no legal entitlement to have the proceedings reopened. However, the information before the Court indicates that, unlike in proceedings before administrative courts governed by Part 5 of the Code of Civil Procedure, administrative authorities proceeding pursuant to

the relevant provisions of the Administrative Proceedings Act of 1967 are not bound by the submissions of the parties when dealing with a case.

51. The Court notes, in particular, that under the Administrative Proceedings Act of 1967 administrative authorities are required to proceed in accordance with the law, to examine each case thoroughly and to use all means available with a view to resolving it in the correct manner. Facts on which their decisions are based must be reliably established in an exact and comprehensive manner, and in doing so they are not bound by the submissions of the parties. Appellate administrative authorities are required to review the administrative decisions appealed against as a whole. If need be, the appellate authorities are obliged to take further action and eliminate shortcomings in the earlier procedure which they have established (see paragraphs 23–27 above).

52. In the Court's view, the approach outlined in the Administrative Proceedings Act of 1967, supported by the information available, would also best meet the requirements of the Convention. Re-opening of proceedings being an exceptional measure affecting the binding nature of a decision which has become final, the Court would find it natural, from the point of view of legal certainty, that it is up to the authorities concerned to establish the existence of circumstances justifying the taking of such an exceptional step.

53. Thus both the Topol'čany Land Office which decided the case at first instance and the Ministry of Agriculture which acted as appellate authority were required to ensure that the decision to reopen the proceedings was in conformity with the relevant law. As the original decision to approve the restitution agreement entitled the applicants to exercise civil rights within the meaning of Section 62 (3) of the Administrative Proceedings Act of 1967, those authorities should have satisfied themselves that the applicants had not acquired the rights in question in good faith which was a prerequisite for reopening the proceedings in their case. However, it does not appear from their respective decisions that the Topol'čany Land Office and the Ministry of Agriculture considered this issue.

54. The Court has before it no information which would *prima facie* indicate that the applicants acted in bad faith when acquiring the property in question. In these circumstances, and notwithstanding the fact that it has only limited power in matters relating to supervision of interpretation and application of national law by authorities of the Contracting States (see *Prince Hans-Adam II of Liechtenstein v. Germany* [GC], no. 42527/98, §§ 49–50, ECHR 2001-VIII and *Beyeler v. Italy*, [GC], no. 33202/96, § 108, ECHR 2000-I), it comes to the conclusion that the decision to reopen the original restitution proceedings cannot be regarded as having been "subject to the conditions provided for by law". Accordingly, there has been a violation of Article 1 of Protocol No. 1.

[. . .]

4.20. *Broniowski v. Poland* (2004)

[. . .]

I. The Circumstances of the Case

9. The applicant is a Polish national who was born in 1944 and lives in Wieliczka, Małopolska Province, in Poland.

A. Historical Background

10. The eastern provinces of pre-war Poland were (and in dated usage still are) called "Borderlands" ("*Kresy*"). They included large areas of present-day Belarus and Ukraine and territories around Vilnius in what is now Lithuania.

Later, when after the Second World War Poland's eastern border was fixed along the Bug River (whose central course formed part of the Curzon line), the "Borderlands" acquired the name of "territories beyond the Bug River" ("*ziemie zabużańskie*").

Those regions had been invaded by the USSR in September 1939.

11. Following agreements concluded between the Polish Committee of National Liberation (*Polski Komitet Wyzwolenia Narodowego*) and the former Soviet Socialist Republics of Ukraine (on 9 September 1944), Belarus (on 9 September 1944) and Lithuania (on 22 September 1944) ("the Republican Agreements" – "*umowy republikańskie*"), the Polish State took upon itself the obligation to compensate persons who were "repatriated" from the

"territories beyond the Bug River" and had to abandon their property there. Such property is commonly referred to as "property beyond the Bug River" ("*mienie zabużańskie*").

12. The Polish government estimated that from 1944 to 1953 some 1,240,000 persons were "repatriated" under the provisions of the Republican Agreements. At the oral hearing, the parties agreed that the vast majority of repatriated persons had been compensated for loss of property caused by their repatriation.

In that connection, the Government also stated that, on account of the delimitation of the Polish-Soviet State border – and despite the fact that Poland was "compensated" by the Allies with former German lands east of the Oder-Neisse line – Poland suffered a loss of territory amounting to 19.78%.

B. The Circumstances of the Case

13. The facts of the case, as submitted by the parties, may be summarised as follows.

1. Facts before 10 October 1994

14. After the Second World War, the applicant's grandmother was repatriated from Lwów (now Lviv in Ukraine).

On 19 August 1947 the State Repatriation Office (Państwowy Urząd Repatriacyjny) in Cracow issued a certificate attesting that she had owned a piece of real property in Lwów and that the property in question consisted of approximately 400 sq. m of land and a house with a surface area of 260 sq. m.

15. On 11 June 1968 the Cracow District Court (*Sąd Rejonowy*) gave a decision declaring that the applicant's mother had inherited the whole of her late mother's property.

16. On an unknown later date the applicant's mother asked the mayor of Wieliczka to enable her to purchase the so-called right of "perpetual use" (*prawo użytkowania wieczystego*) of land owned by the State Treasury (see also paragraph 66 below).

17. In September 1980 an expert from the Cracow Mayor's Office made a report assessing the value of the property abandoned by the applicant's grandmother in Lwów. The actual value was estimated at 1,949,560 old Polish zlotys (PLZ) but, for the

purposes of compensation due from the State, the value was fixed at PLZ 532,260.

18. On 25 March 1981 the mayor of Wieliczka issued a decision enabling the applicant's mother to purchase the right of perpetual use of a plot of 467 sq. m situated in Wieliczka. The fee for the right of perpetual use was PLZ 392 per year and the duration was set at a minimum of forty and a maximum of ninety-nine years. The total fee for use, which amounted to PLZ 38,808 (PLZ 392 × 99 years) was offset against the compensation calculated by the expert in September 1980.

In June 2002 an expert commissioned by the government established that the value of this transaction corresponded to 2% of the compensation to which the applicant's family was entitled (see also paragraph 35 below).

19. The applicant's mother died on 3 November 1989. On 29 December 1989 the Cracow District Court gave a decision declaring that the applicant had inherited the whole of his late mother's property.

20. In 1992, on a date that has not been specified, the applicant sold the property that his mother had received from the State in 1981.

21. On 15 September 1992 the applicant asked the Cracow District Office (*Urząd Rejonowy*) to grant him the remainder of the compensation for the property abandoned by his grandmother in Lwów. He stressed that the value of the compensatory property received by his late mother had been significantly lower than the value of the original property.

22. In a letter of 16 June 1993, the town planning division of the Cracow District Office informed the applicant that his claim had been entered in the relevant register under no. R/74/92. The relevant part of that letter read as follows:

"We would like to inform you that at present there is no possibility of satisfying your claim.... Section 81 of the Land Administration and Expropriation Act of 29 April 1985 [*Ustawa o gospodarce gruntami i wywłaszczaniu nieruchomości*] became, for all practical purposes, a dead letter with the enactment of the Local Self-Government Act of 10 May 1990. [The enactment of that Act] resulted in land being transferred from the

[Cracow branch of the] State Treasury to the Cracow Municipality. Consequently, the Head of the Cracow District Office who, under the applicable rules, is responsible for granting compensation, has no possibility of satisfying the claims submitted. It is expected that new legislation will envisage another form of compensation. We should accordingly inform you that your claim will be dealt with after a new statute has determined how to proceed with claims submitted by repatriated persons."

23. On 14 June 1994 the Cracow Governor's Office (*Urząd Wojewódzki*) informed the applicant that the State Treasury had no land for the purposes of granting compensation for property abandoned in the territories beyond the Bug River.

24. On 12 August 1994 the applicant filed a complaint with the Supreme Administrative Court (*Naczelny Sąd Administracyjny*), alleging inactivity on the part of the government in that it had failed to introduce in Parliament legislation dealing with claims submitted by repatriated persons. He also asked for compensation in the form of State Treasury bonds.

2. Facts after 10 October 1994

(a) Events that Took Place up to 19 December 2002, the Date on which the Court Declared the Application Admissible

25. On 12 October 1994 the Supreme Administrative Court rejected the applicant's complaint. It found no indication of inactivity on the part of the State authorities because "the contrary transpired from the fact that the applicant had received replies from the Cracow District Office and the Cracow Governor's Office".

26. On 31 August 1999, in connection with the entry into force of the Cabinet's Ordinance of 13 January 1998 (see also paragraphs 51–52 below), the Cracow District Office transmitted the applicant's request of 15 September 1992 for the remainder of the compensation, and the relevant case file, to the mayor (*Starosta*) of Wieliczka. Meanwhile, following a reform of the local administrative authorities, the former Cracow Province (*Województwo Krakowskie*) – in which the Wieliczka district is situated – had been enlarged and renamed "Małopolska Province" (*Województwo Małopolskie*).

27. On 11 April 2002 the mayor of Wieliczka organised a competitive bid for property situated in Chorągwica being sold by the State Treasury. The bid was entered by seventeen persons, all of whom were repatriated persons or their heirs. The applicant did not participate in the auction.

28. On 5 July 2002 the Ombudsman (*Rzecznik Praw Obywatelskich*), acting on behalf of repatriated persons, made an application under Article 191 of the Constitution, read in conjunction with Article 188, to the Constitutional Court (*Trybunał Konstytucyjny*), asking for legal provisions that restricted the possibility of satisfying their entitlements to be declared unconstitutional (see also paragraphs 50, 55, 60 and 70–71 below).

(b) Events that Took Place on and after 19 December 2002

29. On 19 December 2002 the Constitutional Court heard, and granted, the Ombudsman's application (see also paragraphs 79–87 below). The Constitutional Court's judgment took effect on 8 January 2003.

30. On 8 January 2003 the Military Property Agency issued a communiqué, which was put on its official website and which read, in so far as relevant, as follows:

"The Constitutional Court, in its judgment of 19 December 2002, declared that the provisions relating to the realisation of the Bug River claims by, *inter alia*, the Military Property Agency were unconstitutional.

However, the implementation of the court's judgment requires that the Land Administration Act 1997, the Law of 30 May 1996 on the administration of certain portions of the State Treasury's property and the Military Property Agency, as well as the Law of 25 May 2001 on the reconstruction, technical modernisation and financing of the Polish army in the years 2001–06, be amended.

It is also necessary to amend the Law of 15 February 1995 on income tax from legal persons, in respect of the proceeds received by the agency upon satisfying the Bug River claims.

In the circumstances, the Military Property Agency will be able to organise auctions for the sale of immovable property after the amendments to the existing legislation have been made.

Auctions will be advertised in the press ... and on the [agency's] website."

According to information made available on the agency's website, in 2002 it had in its possession two categories of property. The first was immovable property no longer used for any military purposes, which was normally sold at auctions. It comprised 13,800 hectares of land and 4,500 buildings with a total surface area of 1,770,000 sq. m. This property included military airports, testing grounds, rifle ranges, hospitals, barracks, offices, recreation and sports centres, buildings designated for social and cultural activities and various other buildings (fuelling stations, workshops, warehouses, etc.). The second category was property that was only temporarily not used by the army. It comprised 650 hectares of land and buildings with a total surface area of 100,000 sq. m.

31. On 8 January 2003 the State Treasury's Agricultural Property Agency (*Agencja Własności Rolnej Skarbu Państwa*), a body which at that time administered the State Treasury's Agricultural Property Resources (*Zasoby Własności Rolnej Skarbu Państwa*) (see also paragraph 91 below), issued a similar communiqué, which was put on its official website and which read as follows:

"On 8 January 2003 the Constitutional Court's judgment of 19 December 2002 concerning the constitutionality of the provisions governing compensation for the Bug River property came into force.

As a consequence of the Court's judgment, it is necessary to amend the provisions relating to the land administration. The judgment does not by itself create a new legal regime and cannot constitute a basis for offsetting the value of the property abandoned outside the State's border against the price of the State Treasury's agricultural property. The principles, conditions and procedure in that respect should therefore be determined. Such actions have already been taken by the Office for Dwellings and Town Development and the Ministry for the Treasury.

In the circumstances, this agency will desist from organising auctions for the sale of immovable property held among its resources, except for small plots of agricultural property.

The agency's decision is inspired by the need to ensure that the Bug River claimants have their claims satisfied on conditions that are equal for all claimants."

32. By the end of 2003 neither of the above-mentioned agencies had resumed auctions. On the date of adoption of this judgment, the Military Property Agency website still contained the – unchanged – communiqué of 8 January 2003 on the suspension of auctions.

On 2 February 2004, two days after the entry into force of new legislation on the Bug River claims (see paragraphs 114–19 below), the Agricultural Property Agency (*Agencja Nieruchomości Rolnych*), a body which had in the meantime replaced the State Treasury's Agricultural Property Agency (see also paragraph 91 below) removed the communiqué of 8 January 2003 from its website and added an announcement entitled "Information for the Bug River people" ("*Informacja dla zabużan*"), providing a detailed explanation of the operation of the new statute.

33. Meanwhile, in the spring and summer of 2003, during the process of preparing a bill designed to settle the "Bug River claims" ("*roszczenia zabużańskie*"; hereafter "the Government Bill" – see also paragraphs 111–13 below), the government estimated the number of claimants and the value of the claims. According to the government, there were 4,120 registered claims, of which 3,910 were verified and regarded as meeting the statutory conditions. The registered claims were valued at three billion new Polish zlotys (PLN). There were also 82,740 unverified claims pending registration, of which 74,470 were likely to be registered. The anticipated value of the unverified claims was PLN 10.45 billion. The anticipated total number of entitled persons was 78,380. As the parliamentary debate over the Government Bill – a debate which was widely discussed throughout the Polish media – progressed, the number of Bug River claims started to grow, since many new claims were being registered.

34. The statistical reports prepared by the government, in particular the Ministry for the Treasury (*Ministerstwo Skarbu Państwa*) and the Ministry for Infrastructure (*Ministerstwo Infrastruktury*), have to date not addressed the question of how many

of the Bug River claimants have ever obtained any compensation and, if so, whether it was full or partial, and how many of them have not yet received anything at all.

The idea of keeping a register of Bug River claims emerged in the course of the preparation of the Government Bill, and such a register is to be kept in the future. Nevertheless, the need to collect the relevant data had already been perceived by the Minister for Infrastructure in July 2002, when he replied to a question by J.D., a member of parliament, concerning, in the MP's words, "the final discharge of the Polish State's obligations towards persons who, after the Second World War, had abandoned their immovable property beyond the eastern border". In his reply, the Minister stated, *inter alia*:

"In reply to the question relating to the number of unsatisfied claims, it has to be said that it was estimated by the Cabinet's Office [*Urząd Rady Ministrów*] at the beginning of the 1990s that there were about 90,000 [such claims]. At present it is very difficult to make such an estimation. . . . In practice, every legal successor [of a Bug River claimant] could, and can, obtain a certificate – at present, a decision – [confirming the right to] a share in the abandoned property. What should be the criteria according to which the number of satisfied and unsatisfied claims is to be estimated? Should it be the number of applications made, including [several] applications by legal successors regarding one property abandoned by one owner (testator), or should it be the number of properties abandoned beyond the State's borders?

It is also difficult to estimate the number of persons whose entitlement has been satisfied, especially as the entitlement can be enforced throughout the country and it often happens that it is satisfied partially in different provinces until it has been fully settled. This situation creates conditions in which the entitled persons may abuse their rights – a fact of which governors and mayors have notified us. They accordingly suggest that a register . . . of the certificates issued confirming the entitlement to . . . compensatory property be kept. At present, however, there is no single, comprehensive system for the registration of

certificates and decisions entitling claimants to [compensatory property].

Accordingly, the answer to the deputy's question as to the form in which the [Bug River claims] are to be satisfied and as to the possible legal solutions depends on reliable information on the number of unsatisfied claims. If it emerged that the number was significant and that not all claims could be satisfied under the applicable laws, other legislative solutions would have to be found – which, however, would be particularly difficult in view of the economic and financial problems of the State."

35. On 12 June 2003 the Government produced a valuation report prepared by an expert valuer commissioned by them. That report had been drawn up on 14 June 2002. The value of the property that the applicant's grandmother had had to abandon was estimated at PLN 390,000. The expert stated that the applicant's family had so far received 2% of the compensation due.

36. On 28 October 2003 the mayor of Wieliczka organised a competitive bid for property situated in Chorągwica and Niepołomice, in the Małopolska Province, that was being sold by the State Treasury. The reserve prices were PLN 150,000 and PLN 48,000 respectively. The bid was entered by several Bug River claimants. The first property was sold for PLN 900,000, the second for PLN 425,000. The applicant did not participate in those auctions.

37. On 30 January 2004, by virtue of the Law of 12 December 2003 on offsetting the value of property abandoned beyond the present borders of the Polish State against the price of State property or the fee for the right of perpetual use (*Ustawa o zaliczaniu na poczet ceny sprzedaży albo opłat z tytułu użytkowania wieczystego nieruchomości Skarbu Państwa wartości nieruchomości pozostawionych poza obecnymi granicami Państwa Polskiego* – "the December 2003 Act"), the State's obligations towards persons who, like the applicant, have obtained some compensatory property under the previous statutes are considered to have been discharged (see also paragraph 116 below).

38. On 30 January 2004 fifty-one members of parliament from the opposition party, "Civic Platform" (*Platforma Obywatelska*), applied to the Constitutional Court, challenging a number of the

provisions of the December 2003 Act (see also paragraph 120 below).

[. . .]

I. ALLEGED VIOLATION OF ARTICLE 1 OF PROTOCOL NO. 1

121. The applicant alleged a breach of Article 1 of Protocol No. 1 in that his entitlement to compensation for property abandoned in the territories beyond the Bug River, the so-called "right to credit", had not been satisfied.

Article 1 of Protocol No. 1 provides:

> "Every natural or legal person is entitled to the peaceful enjoyment of his possessions. No one shall be deprived of his possessions except in the public interest and subject to the conditions provided for by law and by the general principles of international law.
>
> The preceding provisions shall not, however, in any way impair the right of a State to enforce such laws as it deems necessary to control the use of property in accordance with the general interest or to secure the payment of taxes or other contributions or penalties."

A. Scope of the Case

122. Determining the scope of its jurisdiction *ratione temporis* in the decision on the admissibility of the application, the Court found that the applicant's grievance did not concern a single specific measure or decision taken before, or even after, 10 October 1994, the date of ratification of Protocol No. 1 by Poland. The crux of the applicant's Convention claim lay in the State's failure to satisfy his entitlement to compensatory property, which had been continuously vested in him under Polish law.

Noting that that entitlement had been conferred on him on the date of ratification and subsisted both on 12 March 1996, the date on which he had lodged his application with the Commission, and on 19 December 2002, the date of the decision on admissibility, the Court held that it had temporal jurisdiction to entertain the application. It also held that it could have regard to the facts prior to ratification inasmuch as they could be considered to have created a situation extending beyond that date or might be relevant for the understanding of facts occurring after that date (see *Broniowski v.*

Poland (dec.) [GC], no. 31443/96, §§ 74–77, ECHR 2002-X).

123. However, the date from which the Court has jurisdiction *ratione temporis* not only marks the beginning of the period throughout which, up to the present day, acts or omissions of the Polish State will be assessed by the Court from the point of view of their compliance with the Convention, but is also relevant for the determination of the actual content and scope of the applicant's legal interest guaranteed by Polish law to be considered under Article 1 of Protocol No. 1.

124. While the historical background of the case, including the post-war delimitations of State borders, the resultant migration of persons affected by those events and the Republican Agreements, in which the applicant's entitlement to compensation originated (see paragraphs 10–12, 39–41, 67 and 81 above), is certainly important for the understanding of the complex legal and factual situation obtaining today, the Court will not consider any legal, moral, social, financial or other obligations of the Polish State arising from the fact that owners of property beyond the Bug River were dispossessed and forced to migrate by the Soviet Union after the Second World War. In particular, it will not deal with the issue whether Poland's obligation under the Republican Agreements to return to those persons the value of the property abandoned in the former Soviet republics might have any bearing on the scope of the applicant's right under domestic legislation and under the Convention and whether Poland honoured the obligations it had taken upon itself by virtue of those Agreements.

125. The sole issue before the Court is whether Article 1 of Protocol No. 1 was violated by reason of the Polish State's acts and omissions in relation to the implementation of the applicant's entitlement to compensatory property, which was vested in him by Polish legislation on the date of the Protocol's entry into force and which subsisted on 12 March 1996, the date on which he lodged his application with the Commission.

B. Applicability of Article 1 of Protocol No. 1

1. The Parties' Submissions

(a) The Applicant

126. The applicant, as he had already done in the proceedings concerning the admissibility of the

application, maintained that his entitlement constituted a property right which Poland had originally recognised in taking upon itself the obligation to compensate repatriated persons under Article 3 § 6 of the relevant Republican Agreement. That obligation had later been incorporated into domestic law, which vested in him, as the heir of his repatriated grandmother, a specific right to offset the value of the property abandoned by his family beyond the Bug River against the price, or the fee for perpetual use, of immovable property purchased from the State. That right, he added, was explicitly recognised by the Polish courts as a property right and had recently been defined by the Constitutional Court as the "right to credit". It indisputably fell within the concept of "possessions" for the purposes of Article 1 of Protocol No. 1.

(b) The Government

127. Referring to the Court's decision on the admissibility of the application and to its finding that Article 1 of Protocol No. 1 was applicable, the Government maintained that under domestic legislation the applicant was "merely a claimant" with the possibility of asking for compensatory property. He had made an application to that effect but, as he had not submitted an expert report determining the present market value of the abandoned property, the authorities could not issue the necessary additional documents enabling him to participate in auctions for the sale of State property.

128. In that respect, the Government compared Mr Broniowski's situation to that of the applicant in the case of *Jantner v. Slovakia* (no. 39050/97, §§ 27 et seq., 4 March 2003) and submitted that his entitlement constituted – like that of Mr Jantner – a conditional claim which, by reason of the applicant's non-compliance with the procedural requirements for his application, had lapsed as a result of the failure to fulfil a condition.

2. The Court's Assessment

129. The concept of "possessions" in the first part of Article 1 of Protocol No. 1 has an autonomous meaning which is not limited to the ownership of material goods and is independent from the formal classification in domestic law. In the same way as material goods, certain other rights and interests constituting assets can also be regarded as "property rights", and thus as "possessions" for the purposes of this provision. In each case the issue that

needs to be examined is whether the circumstances of the case, considered as a whole, conferred on the applicant title to a substantive interest protected by Article 1 of Protocol No. 1 (see *Iatridis v. Greece* [GC], no. 31107/96, § 54, ECHR 1999-II, and *Beyeler v. Italy* [GC], no. 33202/96, § 100, ECHR 2000-I).

130. When declaring the application admissible, the Court rejected the Government's arguments as to the inapplicability of Article 1 of Protocol No. 1. It found that the applicant had a proprietary interest eligible for protection under that Article. It further noted that the applicant's entitlement had continuously had a legal basis in domestic legislation which had subsisted after 10 October 1994 and that it was defined by the Polish Supreme Court as, *inter alia*, a "debt chargeable to the State Treasury" which had "a pecuniary and inheritable character" (see *Broniowski*, decision cited above, §§ 97–101).

131. Subsequently, when ruling in December 2002 on the application brought by the Ombudsman (see paragraph 28 above), the Constitutional Court described the applicant's entitlement as the "right to credit", having a "special nature as an independent property right", which "should be recognised as enjoying the constitutionally guaranteed protection of property rights" and which was a "special property right of a public-law nature". While the Constitutional Court accepted that the materialisation of that right depended on action by an entitled person, it rejected the idea that the right did not exist until its realisation through a successful bid at an auction for the sale of State property. In sum, the Constitutional Court had no doubts that the right to credit was subject to protection under Article 1 of Protocol No. 1 (see paragraphs 80–87, especially at paragraph 83, above).

In the judgment of 21 November 2003 that followed the above ruling, the Polish Supreme Court considered that the right to credit was a "particular proprietary right" of a "pecuniary value", which was "inheritable and transferable in a specific manner" and whose substance consisted in "the possibility of having a certain pecuniary obligation satisfied through the use of the so-called 'Bug River money'" (see paragraph 109 above).

The Court subscribes to the analysis, in Convention terms, made by the highest Polish judicial authorities of the entitlement which was conferred on the applicant by Polish legislation. It finds nothing in the Government's present arguments to change the conclusion that, as has already been established in the decision on admissibility, the applicant's right to credit constitutes a "possession" within the meaning of Article 1 of Protocol No. 1.

132. As regards the content and scope of the right in question, the Court has already observed that that issue must be seen from the perspective of what "possessions" the applicant had on the date of the Protocol's entry into force and, critically, on the date on which he submitted his complaint to the Convention institutions (see paragraph 125 above).

In fact, on both those dates (10 October 1994 and 12 March 1996) the applicant's situation was essentially the same. At the relevant time the right to credit was laid down in section 81 of the Land Administration Act 1985, which provided that persons repatriated from beyond the Bug River, or their heirs, could, on an application lodged with the relevant authority, offset the value of their abandoned property against the price, or against the fee for perpetual use, of a building plot and any houses or buildings situated on it which were being sold by the State (see paragraph 46 above).

The procedure for enforcing the right was set out in the 1985 Ordinance, which provided, in paragraph 3, that if the value of the Bug River property exceeded the price of the compensatory property that had been sold by the State – which was the case as far as the applicant was concerned – the outstanding amount could be offset against the price of an industrial or commercial plot of State land and specific categories of buildings or establishments situated thereon (see paragraphs 18–21 and 47 above).

133. Accordingly, for the purposes of Article 1 of Protocol No. 1, the applicant's "possessions" comprised the entitlement to obtain, further to the application he had made already on 15 September 1992, compensatory property of the kind listed in paragraph 3 of the 1985 Ordinance (see paragraphs 18 *in fine* and 21 above). While that right was created in a somewhat inchoate form, as its materialisation was to be effected by an administrative decision allocating State property to him, section 81 clearly constituted a legal basis for the State's obligation to implement it.

C. Compliance with Article 1 of Protocol No. 1

1. Applicable Rule of Article 1 of Protocol No. 1

134. Article 1 of Protocol No. 1 comprises three distinct rules: the first rule, set out in the first sentence of the first paragraph, is of a general nature and enunciates the principle of the peaceful enjoyment of property; the second rule, contained in the second sentence of the first paragraph, covers deprivation of possessions and subjects it to certain conditions; the third rule, stated in the second paragraph, recognises that the Contracting States are entitled, *inter alia*, to control the use of property in accordance with the general interest. The three rules are not, however, distinct in the sense of being unconnected. The second and third rules are concerned with particular instances of interference with the right to peaceful enjoyment of property and should therefore be construed in the light of the general principle enunciated in the first rule (see, among other authorities, *James and Others v. the United Kingdom*, judgment of 21 February 1986, Series A no. 98, pp. 29–30, § 37, which reiterates in part the principles laid down by the Court in *Sporrong and Lönnroth v. Sweden*, judgment of 23 September 1982, Series A no. 52, p. 24, § 61; see also *Iatridis*, cited above, § 55, and *Beyeler*, cited above, § 98).

135. The parties did not take clear positions on the question under which rule of Article 1 of Protocol No. 1 the case should be examined. While neither of them argued that the situation complained of had resulted from measures designed to "control the use of property" within the meaning of the second paragraph, the applicant alleged that there had been a general failure by the State to satisfy his right, and the Government maintained that neither any failure to respect that right nor any interference with it could be attributed to the authorities (see also paragraphs 137–42 below).

136. Having regard to the complexity of the legal and factual issues involved in the present case, the Court considers that the alleged violation of the right of property cannot be classified in a precise category. In any event, the situation mentioned in the second sentence of the first paragraph is only a particular instance of interference with the right to peaceful enjoyment of property as guaranteed by the general rule laid down in the first sentence (see *Beyeler*, cited above, § 106). The case should

therefore more appropriately be examined in the light of that general rule.

2. Nature of the Alleged Violation

(a) The Parties' Submissions

(i) The Applicant

137. The applicant considered that the State's continuous failure to satisfy his entitlement – a failure that, in his view, by itself amounted to an interference with his property rights – had been caused by a series of acts and omissions on the part of the authorities.

According to the applicant, the situation complained of originated in the State's failure to fulfil its legislative duty to regulate in a proper and timely manner the question of the Bug River claims and to create conditions for the full implementation of the claimants' rights. Throughout the period falling within the Court's temporal jurisdiction, the State had not only constantly failed to react to, and to resolve through legislative measures, the problem of the insufficient amount of State property designated for the purposes of satisfying those claims – a shortage which resulted from the 1990 "communalisation" of State land – but had also enacted laws that had successively all but removed the possibility of obtaining property from among its land resources.

138. What was more, the applicant added, the State authorities had made the realisation of his entitlement impossible in practice. It had been their common and widespread policy not to put State land up for sale and to prevent the entitled persons from bidding for State property at auctions.

139. The final act had taken place on 30 January 2004, the date of entry into force of the December 2003 Act, by virtue of which all the State's obligations towards the applicant, and all other Bug River claimants who had ever obtained any compensatory property under the previous legislation, had been deemed to have been discharged.

(ii) The Government

140. The Government did not accept that there had been an interference with the applicant's right to the peaceful enjoyment of his possessions because, as they had stated at the oral hearing and maintained in their further written pleadings, he had no

"possessions" for the purposes of Article 1 of Protocol No. 1.

141. As regards the State's alleged failure to fulfil its positive obligations under Article 1 of Protocol No. 1 by reason of its legislative omissions, the Government stressed that, since 1944–47, the time of the first and main wave of repatriation of Polish citizens from beyond the Bug River, the State had continued to legislate on the matter. Owing to those earlier laws, the vast majority of repatriated persons had obtained compensatory property, in particular in the western part of Poland, which before the war had belonged to Germany.

142. Subsequent laws governing land administration, especially those applicable throughout the period falling within the Court's temporal jurisdiction, had set out extensive rules governing the realisation of the remaining Bug River claims. Furthermore, the State had made constant efforts to enact specific legislation dealing with various restitution claims, including the applicant's entitlement. It was true that the first such attempt had been futile, as the Restitution Bill 1999 had been rejected by Parliament. However, the work on the Bug River legislation had continued and, recently, Parliament had passed the December 2003 Act, which comprehensively regulated the whole set of issues concerning the Bug River claims.

In sum, the Government considered that it could not be said that the issue before the Court involved the Polish State's failure to fulfil its positive obligation to secure to the applicant the peaceful enjoyment of his possessions.

(b) The Court's Assessment

143. The essential object of Article 1 of Protocol No. 1 is to protect a person against unjustified interference by the State with the peaceful enjoyment of his or her possessions.

However, by virtue of Article 1 of the Convention, each Contracting Party "shall secure to everyone within [its] jurisdiction the rights and freedoms defined in [the] Convention". The discharge of this general duty may entail positive obligations inherent in ensuring the effective exercise of the rights guaranteed by the Convention. In the context of Article 1 of Protocol No. 1, those positive obligations may require the State to take the measures necessary to protect the right of property (see *Sovtransavto Holding v. Ukraine*, no. 48553/99, § 96, ECHR 2002-VII, with further references, and, *mutatis mutandis, Keegan v. Ireland*, judgment of 26 May 1994, Series A no. 290, p. 19, § 49, and *Kroon and Others v. the Netherlands*, judgment of 27 October 1994, Series A no. 297-C, p. 56, § 31).

144. However, the boundaries between the State's positive and negative obligations under Article 1 of Protocol No. 1 do not lend themselves to precise definition. The applicable principles are nonetheless similar. Whether the case is analysed in terms of a positive duty of the State or in terms of an interference by a public authority which needs to be justified, the criteria to be applied do not differ in substance. In both contexts regard must be had to the fair balance to be struck between the competing interests of the individual and of the community as a whole. It also holds true that the aims mentioned in that provision may be of some relevance in assessing whether a balance between the demands of the public interest involved and the applicant's fundamental right of property has been struck. In both contexts the State enjoys a certain margin of appreciation in determining the steps to be taken to ensure compliance with the Convention (see, *mutatis mutandis, Keegan*, cited above, p.19, § 49, and *Hatton and Others v. the United Kingdom* [GC], no. 36022/97, §§ 98 et seq., ECHR 2003-VIII).

145. In the present case, the applicant's submission under Article 1 of Protocol No. 1 is that the Polish State, having conferred on him an entitlement to compensatory property, subsequently made it impossible for him – by obstruction and inaction, both legislative and administrative, and by extra-legal practices – to benefit from that entitlement and that, ultimately, by virtue of the recent legislation, it extinguished his legal interest (see paragraphs 137–39 above).

The mutual interrelation of the alleged omissions on the part of the State and of accompanying acts that might be regarded as an "interference" with the applicant's property right makes it difficult to classify them in a single precise category. As shown by the course of the events described above, culminating in the enactment of the December 2003 legislation, the facts of "commission" and "omission" were closely intertwined (see paragraphs 30–31; 48–49; 56–57; 59–61; 63–65; 69–70; 84–86; 96–98; 102; 110; and 114–19 above).

Also, the legal and practical consequences of those facts and the State's conduct were variously assessed by the national courts; for instance, the Constitutional Court considered that the laws restricting the Bug River claimants' access to State property had resulted in *de facto* expropriation (see paragraph 84 above). Some civil courts considered that the State was liable for damage sustained by the Bug River claimants on account of both the fact that it had imposed unjustified restrictions on the exercise of the right to credit and the fact that it had failed to fulfil its positive obligations to protect property rights and duly to publish the Republican Agreements (see paragraphs 98 and 102 above). The Supreme Court held that the State's practices did not amount to a deprivation of property, but had nevertheless unduly restricted the right in question (see paragraph 110 above).

146. The facts of the case may well be examined in terms of a hindrance to the effective exercise of the right protected by Article 1 of Protocol No. 1 or in terms of a failure to secure the implementation of that right. Having regard to the particular circumstances of the present case, the Court considers it unnecessary to categorise strictly its examination of the case as being under the head of the State's positive obligations or under the head of the State's negative duty to refrain from an unjustified interference with the peaceful enjoyment of property.

The Court will determine whether the conduct of the Polish State – regardless of whether that conduct may be characterised as an interference or as a failure to act, or a combination of both – was justifiable in the light of the applicable principles set out below.

3. General Principles

(a) Principle of Lawfulness

147. The first and most important requirement of Article 1 of Protocol No. 1 is that any interference by a public authority with the peaceful enjoyment of possessions should be lawful: the second sentence of the first paragraph authorises a deprivation of possessions only "subject to the conditions provided for by law" and the second paragraph recognises that States have the right to control the use of property by enforcing "laws". Moreover, the rule of law, one of the fundamental principles of a democratic society, is inherent in all the Articles of the Convention (see *The former King of Greece*

and Others v. Greece [GC], no. 25701/94, § 79, ECHR 2000-XII, with further references, and *Iatridis*, cited above, § 58).

The principle of lawfulness also presupposes that the applicable provisions of domestic law are sufficiently accessible, precise and foreseeable in their application (see *Beyeler*, cited above, §§ 109–10).

(b) Principle of a Legitimate Aim in the Public Interest

148. Any interference with the enjoyment of a right or freedom recognised by the Convention must pursue a legitimate aim. By the same token, in cases involving a positive duty, there must be a legitimate justification for the State's inaction. The principle of a "fair balance" inherent in Article 1 of Protocol No. 1 itself presupposes the existence of a general interest of the community. Moreover, it should be reiterated that the various rules incorporated in Article 1 are not distinct, in the sense of being unconnected, and that the second and third rules are concerned only with particular instances of interference with the right to the peaceful enjoyment of property. One of the effects of this is that the existence of a "public interest" required under the second sentence, or the "general interest" referred to in the second paragraph, are in fact corollaries of the principle set forth in the first sentence, so that an interference with the exercise of the right to the peaceful enjoyment of possessions within the meaning of the first sentence of Article 1 must also pursue an aim in the public interest (see *Beyeler*, cited above, § 111).

149. Because of their direct knowledge of their society and its needs, the national authorities are in principle better placed than the international judge to appreciate what is "in the public interest". Under the system of protection established by the Convention, it is thus for the national authorities to make the initial assessment as to the existence of a problem of public concern warranting measures to be applied in the sphere of the exercise of the right of property, including deprivation and restitution of property. Here, as in other fields to which the safeguards of the Convention extend, the national authorities accordingly enjoy a certain margin of appreciation.

Furthermore, the notion of "public interest" is necessarily extensive. In particular, the decision to enact laws expropriating property or affording pub-

licly funded compensation for expropriated property will commonly involve consideration of political, economic and social issues. The Court has declared that, finding it natural that the margin of appreciation available to the legislature in implementing social and economic policies should be a wide one, it will respect the legislature's judgment as to what is "in the public interest" unless that judgment is manifestly without reasonable foundation (see *James and Others*, cited above, p. 32, § 46, and *The former King of Greece and Others*, cited above, § 87). This logic applies to such fundamental changes of a country's system as the transition from a totalitarian regime to a democratic form of government and the reform of the State's political, legal and economic structure, phenomena which inevitably involve the enactment of large-scale economic and social legislation.

(c) Principle of a "Fair Balance"

150. Both an interference with the peaceful enjoyment of possessions and an abstention from action must strike a fair balance between the demands of the general interest of the community and the requirements of the protection of the individual's fundamental rights (see, among other authorities, *Sporrong and Lönnroth*, cited above, p. 26, § 69).

The concern to achieve this balance is reflected in the structure of Article 1 of Protocol No. 1 as a whole. In particular, there must be a reasonable relationship of proportionality between the means employed and the aim sought to be realised by any measures applied by the State, including measures depriving a person of his of her possessions. In each case involving the alleged violation of that Article the Court must, therefore, ascertain whether by reason of the State's action or inaction the person concerned had to bear a disproportionate and excessive burden (see *Sporrong and Lönnroth*, p. 28, § 73, and *The former King of Greece and Others*, §§ 89–90, both cited above, with further references).

151. In assessing compliance with Article 1 of Protocol No. 1, the Court must make an overall examination of the various interests in issue, bearing in mind that the Convention is intended to safeguard rights that are "practical and effective". It must look behind appearances and investigate the realities of the situation complained of. That assessment may involve not only the relevant compensation

terms – if the situation is akin to the taking of property – but also the conduct of the parties, including the means employed by the State and their implementation. In that context, it should be stressed that uncertainty – be it legislative, administrative or arising from practices applied by the authorities – is a factor to be taken into account in assessing the State's conduct. Indeed, where an issue in the general interest is at stake, it is incumbent on the public authorities to act in good time, in an appropriate and consistent manner (see *Vasilescu v. Romania*, judgment of 22 May 1998, *Reports of Judgments and Decisions* 1998-III, p. 1078, § 51; *Beyeler*, cited above, §§ 110 *in fine*, 114 and 120 *in fine*; and *Sovtransavto Holding*, cited above, §§ 97–98).

4. Application of the Above Principles to the Present Case

(a) Whether the Polish Authorities Respected the Principle of Lawfulness

(i) The Applicant

152. The applicant maintained that the State's failure to satisfy his property entitlement was inherently incompatible with its general legal duty to enforce rights recognised by law and, in particular, to create conditions for their implementation.

As regards the successive restrictions on the exercise of his right, he admitted that they had been introduced through a number of statutes, in particular the Land Administration Act 1997 and the 2001 Amendment. He stressed, however, that those laws had been incompatible with the Constitution and, in consequence, with the legal order as a whole. Despite that fact and the clear message emerging from the Constitutional Court's judgment that obstacles to the realisation of the Bug River claims should be removed in law and in practice, the State had continued to enact unconstitutional laws and to tolerate practices contrary to that judgment, such as the suspension of auctions for the sale of State property by the Military Property Agency and the State Treasury's Agricultural Property Agency. As the applicant expressed it, the final, crowning achievement of the State had been to enact the December 2003 Act, legislation running counter to the Constitutional Court's judgment and extinguishing his right to compensation.

It could not, therefore, be said that the authorities had observed the principle of lawfulness.

(ii) The Government

153. The Government saw no issue of "unlawfulness" as regards the State's conduct since, as they had already submitted (see paragraph 140 above), there had, in their view, been no interference with the applicant's right to the peaceful enjoyment of his possessions.

(iii) The Court's Assessment

154. The Court notes that, as the applicant conceded, the restrictions on his right were indeed introduced through several statutes (see paragraphs 49, 59 and 114–19 above). It is true that the legal provisions, which up to the entry into force of the Constitutional Court's judgment had prevented him from materialising his entitlement, were found to be incompatible with the rule of law and the principle of protection of property rights (see paragraphs 84–86 above). It is also true that some Polish civil courts and, most notably, the Supreme Court, regarded the situation obtaining after the entry into force of the Constitutional Court's judgment, in particular the authorities' practices, to be unacceptable and contrary to the rule of law. The Cracow Regional Court called it, *inter alia*, a "state of lawlessness" (see paragraphs 98 and 110 above).

However, in the Court's opinion, those findings and the consequences they entail from the point of view of compliance with Article 1 of Protocol No. 1 are material considerations to be taken into account in determining whether the Polish authorities, in applying various impugned measures or in refraining from action, struck a fair balance between the interests involved. The Court will therefore proceed on the assumption that, in so far as the acts and omissions of the Polish State constituted interferences or restrictions on the exercise of the applicant's right to the peaceful enjoyment of his possessions, they were "provided for by law" within the meaning of Article 1 of Protocol No. 1.

(b) Whether the Polish Authorities Pursued a "Legitimate Aim"

(i) The Applicant

155. The applicant considered that no public interest could possibly justify the State's persistent failure to resolve the problem of the Bug River claims, which had been recognised by Polish law for nearly sixty years. He stressed that under the Republican Agreements the State had taken upon itself the

obligation to return to the Bug River owners, without any conditions or financial or other limitations, the value of the property they had had to abandon. While it might be acceptable that the implementation of that obligation should, on account of the general interest of the community, be achieved over a period of time, nothing could explain the adoption of legislative policy that for several decades had completely disregarded the obligations towards the Bug River claimants.

(ii) The Government

156. The Government replied that the State had done everything possible to satisfy the Bug River claimants and stressed, once again, that most of them had obtained compensatory property. However, in the 1990s the demands of the country's political and economic transformation had made it necessary to reintroduce local self-government and to change the ownership relations between the State and municipalities. That, in turn, had resulted in most of the State's land being transferred to the latter, within whose powers the administration of land within their administrative territories had been placed. The crucial importance of that reform had been indisputable, although it had very considerably reduced the possibility of satisfying the Bug River claims.

157. In the Government's view, the State had not, as the applicant alleged, disregarded the rights of the Bug River claimants. The authorities had made many efforts to resolve their problems and it should not be overlooked that, in that context, they had been faced with very difficult legal and moral issues. Thus, they had been required to deal with a variety of restitution and compensation claims that had originated in past events occurring under the totalitarian regime, and they had had to act in a manner ensuring that the rights of all those wronged by that regime were given equal consideration.

(iii) The Court's Assessment

158. The aims pursued by the State in relation to the enactment of the statutes that impeded the realisation of the applicant's entitlement were, as evidenced by the relevant court judgments, to reintroduce local self-government, to restructure the agricultural system and to generate financial means for the modernisation of military institutions (see paragraphs 85 and 98 above). The Court does not doubt that during the political, economic

and social transition undergone by Poland in recent years, it was necessary for the authorities to resolve such issues. It accordingly accepts that it was legitimate for the respondent State to take measures designed to achieve those aims, in the general interest of the community.

(c) Whether the Polish authorities struck a fair balance between the general interest of the community and the applicant's right to the peaceful enjoyment of his possessions

(i) Background to the Bug River Claims

(α) The Parties' Submissions

159. The applicant accepted that the loss of property by his family had been caused by historical and political events and that, in reality, it had not been the Polish State that had expropriated his family or had forced them to migrate from their homeland. However, it had been the Polish State's undertaking under the relevant international agreements to compensate his family. That obligation had been incorporated into domestic legislation since 1946 and, as far as he was concerned, had never been discharged in its entirety.

160. The Government stressed that the migration of the Polish population from the territories beyond the Bug River had resulted from territorial changes following the Second World War. They had been decided by the "Big Three" at the Tehran, Yalta and Potsdam conferences, initially without the consent of the legitimate, exiled Polish government in London, on whom they had later been imposed. As a result of those changes Poland, which before the war had comprised 388,600 sq. km, had lost 19.78% of its original territory.

Furthermore, under the Republican Agreements concluded by the Polish communist authorities, in 1944–45 Poland had had to accommodate some 1,240,000 Polish nationals repatriated from beyond the new border and to provide them with the necessary housing and financial assistance. Despite that fact, under the terms of the 1952 Pact, Poland had had to pay the Soviet Union 76 million roubles (calculated under the gold standard) for the evacuation. Thus, it had been forced to pay heavily for the so-called "repatriation" of its own nationals and, often, for their lives, since most of those who had remained in the Soviet Union had been either resettled in Kazakhstan or other parts of that country or had lost their lives in the course of the widespread Stalinist persecutions.

161. The "fair balance" in the present case should, in the Government's view, be seen from this perspective and in the light of the fact that, apart from the difficult financial situation of the State, which had been impoverished by years of totalitarian rule, the authorities had consistently tried to satisfy the Bug River claims.

(β) The Court's Assessment

162. The Court recognises that, given the particular historical and political background of the case, as well as the importance of the various social, legal and economic considerations that the authorities had to take into account in resolving the problem of the Bug River claims, the Polish State had to deal with an exceptionally difficult situation, involving complex, large-scale policy decisions. The vast number of persons involved – nearly 80,000 – and the very substantial value of their claims (see paragraph 33 above) are certainly factors that must be taken into account in ascertaining whether the requisite "fair balance" was struck.

Also in that context, it should be noted that the Polish State chose, by adopting both the 1985 and 1997 Land Administration Acts, to reaffirm its obligation to compensate the Bug River claimants and to maintain and to incorporate into domestic law obligations it had taken upon itself by virtue of international treaties entered into prior to its ratification of the Convention and the Protocol (see paragraphs 46, 48 and 81 above). It did so irrespective of the fact that it faced various significant social and economic constraints resulting from the transformation of the country's entire system, and was undoubtedly confronted with a difficult choice as to which pecuniary and moral obligations could be fulfilled towards persons who had suffered injustice under the totalitarian regime.

163. The Court accepts that these factors should be taken into account in determining the scope of the margin of appreciation to be allowed to the respondent State.

(ii) *Conduct of the Authorities*

(α) The Parties' Submissions

164. The applicant once again repeated that the State's conduct constituted a mixture of acts and omissions which had ultimately led to the destruction of his right of property as a result of the enactment of the December 2003 Act, whereby the State had – unilaterally and arbitrarily – written off its obligation to satisfy his entitlement. That final act had for all practical purposes been tantamount to an expropriation without the payment of compensation.

Turning to the earlier events, the applicant maintained that the State, while having been fully aware that the so-called "communalisation" under the 1990 Act had made the implementation of the Bug River claims nearly impossible, had decided, instead of resolving the problem of the shortage of State land, to introduce laws that had limited even more severely the pool of land set aside for settling those claims.

165. In that connection, he stressed that the Constitutional Court had explicitly held that both the applicable legislation and the practices applied by the authorities in respect of the Bug River claimants had been in flagrant violation of fundamental constitutional principles, including the principle of proportionality.

Following the entry into force of the Constitutional Court's judgment, the applicant added, the State, instead of creating conditions for the execution of that judgment, had only made efforts to hinder the satisfaction of his entitlement. Precisely on the date on which the judgment had come into force, the authorities, under the pretext that its implementation had required the adoption of a number of statutes, had suspended virtually all auctions for the sale of State property, in order to avoid settling the Bug River claims.

166. The Government disagreed. They maintained that all the alleged restrictions on the applicant's right had been strictly necessary and had been prompted by important considerations of general State policy, with the implementation of a programme of social and economic reform. They stressed that in cases like the present one, involving the assessment of complicated political, economic and social questions, on which opinions within a democratic society might legitimately vary, the Contracting States should be allowed a broad margin of appreciation in the choice of the measures designed to achieve the aims pursued by reforms.

167. The Government further submitted that the Constitutional Court's judgment had removed a number of obstacles to the realisation of the applicant's entitlement since the cluster of legal provisions that had previously hindered the proper operation of the compensation machinery had been repealed.

The Government did not address the applicant's argument that the authorities, by suspending the auctions, had not implemented that judgment in practice. Instead, they referred to the new legislation, emphasising that it had been specifically designed to deal with the Bug River claims, and that it would comprehensively resolve all the complex matters concerning the rights of the Bug River repatriates.

(β) The Court's Assessment

The period up to 19 December 2002

168. At the beginning of the period under consideration, the applicant had, as already noted above, the entitlement to obtain, further to the application he had made to that effect, compensatory property corresponding to the remainder of the property lost by his family. Even though that right was created in an inchoate form, as its materialisation was to be effected by an administrative decision allocating State property to him, section 81 of the Land Administration Act 1985 clearly constituted a legal basis for the State's obligation to implement it (see paragraphs 46–47 and 133 above).

Yet the situation obtaining both before and at the relevant time made the implementation very difficult, if not impossible, because, in the aftermath of the re-establishment of local self-government in Poland, the State Treasury scarcely had any land at its disposal. The shortage of land was officially acknowledged. In that context, as well as in connection with the suspension of the possibility of obtaining State agricultural property under the 1993 Amendment, the authorities made public promises – confirmed by statutes, for instance section 17 of the 1993 Amendment – to enact specific legislation dealing with forms of compensation for loss of property and the rules for the restitution of property to the Bug River claimants. They further envisaged legislation designed specifically for a variety of restitution and compensation claims, including the applicant's entitlement (see paragraphs 22–23, 44, 53–54, 56 and 62–65 above).

169. Between 1994 and 1998 certain portions of State property could still have been set aside for the settlement of Bug River claims since, pursuant to the 1994 and the 1996 Acts, property taken over by the State Treasury from the army of the Russian Federation and property administered by the Military Property Agency were – at least in law – available for those purposes (see paragraphs 56–59 above).

Be that as it may, that fact does not seem to have had any discernible positive impact on the realisation of the applicant's entitlement since, as established by the Cracow Regional Court, between 1991 and 1998 the authorities of the district in which his claim was registered at that time organised only twenty-two auctions for the sale of State property (see paragraph 97 above).

170. Further events, starting on 1 January 1998, the date of entry into force of the Land Administration Act 1997, had a decisive impact on the applicant's situation. By that date the authorities had not yet enacted the promised restitutive legislation; in fact, the relevant bill was later ultimately rejected by Parliament (see paragraph 62–65 above).

Nevertheless, in section 212 of the Land Administration Act 1997, the State explicitly confirmed the applicant's right and its obligation to implement it in a manner similar to that specified in the previous laws. That section reiterated, in practically identical terms, the provision for compensation laid down in the Land Administration Act 1985. Admittedly, the renewed validation of the State's obligation was not accompanied by the creation of conditions for its implementation. On the contrary, it imposed a further restriction on the applicant's entitlement. By virtue of section 213, the possibility of obtaining compensatory property from among the State's agricultural land, a possibility which up to that time had only been suspended pending the introduction of new restitution laws, was eliminated. Furthermore, under the 1998 Ordinance, the acquisition of compensatory property could be enforced solely through participation in a competitive bid organised by the relevant public authority (see paragraphs 48–52 and 54 above).

171. As emerges from the material before the Court, it was a matter of common knowledge that the authorities desisted from organising auctions for the Bug River claimants, subjected their participation in auctions to various conditions or, as

shown by the practices of the Military Property Agency, openly denied them the opportunity to seek to enforce their entitlement through the bidding procedure (see paragraphs 61, 84, 97 and 110 above). The practices of that agency, which were described in detail in its own official instruction and which, in the Court's opinion, constituted a purposeful attempt to circumvent the rules governing the procedure for the implementation of the applicant's entitlement, in reality prepared the ground for the next restrictive statute. The 2001 Amendment, which came into force on 1 January 2002, eliminated the possibility for the applicant to seek compensation from among the State's military property resources (see paragraphs 58–59 above).

172. Bearing in mind that, by that time, the only State property resources available to the Bug River claimants were those previously administered by the army of the Russian Federation and that, as the Government admitted, those resources were practically exhausted (see paragraphs 49, 56–57 and 59 above), the Court considers that the authorities gradually all but wiped out the applicant's right from the domestic legal order and that his right, even though still theoretically existing, was rendered illusory.

173. That finding is in accordance with the assessment of the State's conduct by the Polish courts, including the highest judicial authorities (see paragraphs 84–86 and 110 above).

The Constitutional Court, referring to the State's conduct, had no doubt whatsoever that the combination of the restrictions imposed on the right to credit had resulted in a paradoxical situation in which that right could not be realised in practice, and that those restrictions were not justified in a democratic State governed by the rule of law. In that context, it also found that that conduct of the authorities was incompatible with the constitutional principle of maintaining citizens' confidence in the State and the law made by it, ensuing from the rule of law.

That court considered that the right to credit was becoming an "empty obligation" and that the limitations excluding substantial portions of property from the compensation procedure in fact "paralys[ed] the possibility for beneficiaries to derive any economic advantage" from their rights. It also held that the right to credit was formulated in such a way that it "could not be materialised in the existing legal environment, so that it ha[d] become illusory and a mere sham" (see paragraphs 80–86 above).

The Court sees no cause to depart from the Constitutional Court's findings, which were based on its direct knowledge of the national circumstances.

The period after 19 December 2002

174. The Government contended that the Constitutional Court's ruling of 19 December 2002 on the constitutional application brought by the Ombudsman had removed a number of obstacles to the realisation of the applicant's entitlement (see paragraph 167 above). In the Court's view, that might have been the case had the authorities complied with that judgment.

It is true that, on 14 January 2003, the legislation was amended so as to enable the Bug River claimants to bid at auctions for the sale of privatised State enterprises (see paragraph 88 above). It is also true that, pursuant to the January 2003 and the August 2003 Ordinances, the Bug River claimants were exempted from the payment of a security before an auction for the sale of State Treasury and municipal property, and that the offsetting of the value of their entitlement against the price of property sold at such auctions could no longer be excluded (see paragraphs 90 and 92 above).

However, having regard to the other events that followed the Constitutional Court's judgment, the Court does not consider that those changes to legislation, although they were generally in the applicant's favour, materially improved his situation.

175. To begin with, on the date of entry into force of that judgment, the State Treasury's Agricultural Property Agency and the Military Property Agency issued official communiqués, disseminated via the Internet. Both communiqués were worded similarly and announced that the agencies had suspended all auctions for the sale of State property because, allegedly, they could not be held before numerous amendments to the legislation had been introduced (see paragraphs 30–32 above). This policy resulted in the effective suspension of the execution of the judgment because the provisions restoring State agricultural and military property to the pool of property available to the Bug River people could not be implemented in practice. It was strongly condemned by the judicial authorities, most notably the Supreme Court, which deemed

such acts to amount to constitutional torts. However, neither the executive nor the legislative power reacted to the agencies' conduct (see paragraphs 30–32, 98, 102 and 110 above).

In the Court's opinion, such conduct by State agencies, which involves a deliberate attempt to prevent the implementation of a final and enforceable judgment and which is, in addition, tolerated, if not tacitly approved, by the executive and legislative branch of the State, cannot be explained in terms of any legitimate public interest or the interests of the community as a whole. On the contrary, it is capable of undermining the credibility and authority of the judiciary and of jeopardising its effectiveness, factors which are of the utmost importance from the point of view of the fundamental principles underlying the Convention and which, in the context of the present case, must prevail over any conceivable considerations of economic or social policy that might have been behind the Polish State's failure to rectify the policy of the agencies concerned.

That assessment appears to have been shared by the Polish Supreme Court which, in its judgment of 21 November 2003, found that the authorities had made the right to credit unenforceable in practice and held, *inter alia*, that "such actions cannot be accepted in a democratic State governed by the rule of law and applying the principles of social justice . . . " (see paragraph 110 above).

176. The culminating event, however, took place on 30 January 2004, the date of entry into force of the December 2003 Act, a law whose constitutionality was challenged before the Constitutional Court by a group of members of parliament on that very date (see paragraphs 37–38 and 120 above).

By virtue of that Act, the Polish State deemed discharged all obligations which might have arisen in relation to the implementation of the applicant's right to credit, because his family had already obtained partial compensation under the previous legislation (see paragraphs 35, 37 and 114–19 above).

The Court would reiterate that compensation terms under the relevant legislation may be material to the assessment whether the contested measure respects the requisite fair balance and, notably, whether it imposes a disproportionate burden on applicants. The taking of property without payment of an amount reasonably related to its value

will normally constitute a disproportionate interference, and a total lack of compensation can be considered justifiable under Article 1 of Protocol No. 1 only in exceptional circumstances (see *The former King of Greece and Others*, cited above, § 89, with further references).

The Court considers, however, that the terms under which the State's obligation towards the applicant was written off are one more material factor to be taken into account in assessing as a whole the State's compliance with Article 1 of Protocol No. 1. For that reason, it finds it more appropriate to draw its conclusion as to the effects of the recent legislation on the applicant's previously existing entitlement after having determined whether his conduct, in the particular circumstances of the present case, had a bearing on the effective implementation of his right to credit.

(iii)   Conduct of the Applicant

(α) The Parties' Submissions

177. The Government, as they had done at the admissibility stage, pleaded that the applicant had failed to exhaust the domestic remedies available to him, as required by Article 35 § 1 of the Convention, and that his conduct had not been consistent with the diligence required of a claimant.

They stressed that domestic law implied that a person seeking to satisfy a claim for compensation for Bug River property should display an active attitude. Yet the applicant, throughout the entire period under consideration, had not made a single attempt to participate in auctions for the sale of State property. The Government admitted that the bidding procedure could not by itself be regarded as an effective remedy under Article 35 § 1 of the Convention, but they nevertheless considered that it had constituted a condition *sine qua non* for the implementation of the applicant's entitlement.

178. In the Government's submission, the applicant, by his own inaction, namely his failure to comply with the statutory requirements for his application for compensatory property, had deliberately excluded any possibility for him to participate in auctions. They contended that the fact that he had not submitted to the authorities an updated expert report determining the current market value of the abandoned property had prevented them from

issuing a decision confirming his entitlement, as required by the 1998 Ordinance.

Lastly, the Government pointed out that even recently, between April 2002 and October 2003, the mayor of Wieliczka, the applicant's place of residence, had organised three auctions and that, had the applicant observed the procedural requirements for his application, nothing would have prevented him from bidding for, and possibly acquiring, the properties concerned, situated in Chorągwica and Niepołomice, close to his home.

179. The applicant submitted that the allegation that his conduct had not been diligent should be assessed in the light of all the relevant circumstances. First of all, the authorities had not given any real effect to the previous legislation, however defective and restrictive. The minimal number of auctions organised in the Cracow District in the 1990s and the large number of claimants, with similar yet unsatisfied claims, demonstrated that, as established by the Cracow Regional Court, it had been almost impossible for him to enforce his right to credit. The same conclusion, in respect of the situation subsisting within the entire country, had been reached by the Constitutional Court.

He further referred to the findings of the Constitutional Court and the Cracow Regional Court that it had been a common phenomenon for the Bug River claimants, given the chronic shortage of land, to have lost a significant proportion of their claim by "pushing up" the prices of property sold at auctions to a level considerably exceeding its market value. The same applied to the auctions mentioned by the Government, at which the land in question had been sold for sums several times in excess of the reserve prices and, also, significantly exceeding the value of his entitlement, as stated in the valuation report supplied to the Court by the Government.

(β) The Court's Assessment

180. The question of the effectiveness of the procedure for the implementation of the applicant's entitlement was examined in depth by the national courts which, as the Court has noted, had the advantage of possessing direct knowledge of the situation (see paragraphs 172–73 above).

Assessing the general situation up to 19 December 2002, the Constitutional Court observed that "all

laws restricting the Bug River claimants' access to acquisition by means of bids for certain categories of State Treasury's property [had] a direct impact on the possibility of realising the right to credit". It went on to find that "the lack of opportunity to benefit from this right, within the framework set out by the legislature, show[ed] that an illusory legal institution [had] been created". It held that, in consequence, the existing compensation machinery had become a "fictional instrument of compensation" (see paragraphs 82–86 above).

As regards the situation in the district in which the applicant's claim was registered at the relevant time, the Cracow Regional Court, on the basis of evidence before it, established – and that finding has not been contested by the Government – that during the eight years up to 1998 the authorities had organised only twenty-two auctions and that, on the whole, only twenty persons out of the 300 who had an entitlement, had had their right to credit satisfied (see paragraphs 97 and 169 above).

Furthermore, it has already been established that on 8 January 2003, after the entry into force of the Constitutional Court's judgment, the authorities, in an attempt to hinder the implementation of that judgment, suspended nearly all auctions for the sale of State property (see paragraphs 174–75 above). The Cracow Regional Court and, subsequently, the Supreme Court held that the State's conduct amounted to a constitutional tort and the possibility of realising the right to credit was considered to have been illusory (see paragraphs 98, 102 and 110).

181. In the circumstances and bearing in mind the risk inherent in the auction bidding procedure, the Court considers that, by reason of the State's own obstructive action and inaction, that procedure could not be regarded as an "effective" or "adequate" means for realising the applicant's entitlement to compensation vested in him under Polish legislation. It cannot be said that the applicant was responsible for, or culpably contributed to, the state of affairs of which he is complaining. Rather, as the Court finds on the evidence before it, the hindrance to the peaceful enjoyment of his possessions is solely attributable to the respondent State (see also paragraphs 168–76 above).

That being so, the Government's plea of inadmissibility on the ground of non-exhaustion of domestic remedies, which was reserved in the decision on admissibility (see *Broniowski*, decision cited above, §§ 86–87), should be dismissed.

(iv) Conclusion as to "Fair Balance"

182. The Court accepts that in situations such as the one in the present case, involving a wide-reaching but controversial legislative scheme with significant economic impact for the country as a whole, the national authorities must have considerable discretion in selecting not only the measures to secure respect for property rights or to regulate ownership relations within the country, but also the appropriate time for their implementation. The choice of measures may necessarily involve decisions restricting compensation for the taking or restitution of property to a level below its market value. Thus, Article 1 of Protocol No. 1 does not guarantee a right to full compensation in all circumstances (see *James and Others*, cited above, p. 36, § 54).

Balancing the rights at stake, as well as the gains and losses of the different persons affected by the process of transforming the State's economy and legal system, is an exceptionally difficult exercise. In such circumstances, in the nature of things, a wide margin of appreciation should be accorded to the respondent State.

Nevertheless, the Court would reiterate that that margin, however considerable, is not unlimited, and that the exercise of the State's discretion, even in the context of the most complex reform of the State, cannot entail consequences at variance with Convention standards (see paragraphs 149–51 above).

183. Whilst the Court accepts that the radical reform of the country's political and economic system, as well as the state of the country's finances, may justify stringent limitations on compensation for the Bug River claimants, the Polish State has not been able to adduce satisfactory grounds justifying, in terms of Article 1 of Protocol No. 1, the extent to which it has continuously failed over many years to implement an entitlement conferred on the applicant, as on thousands of other Bug River claimants, by Polish legislation.

184. The rule of law underlying the Convention and the principle of lawfulness in Article 1 of Protocol No. 1 require States not only to respect and apply, in a foreseeable and consistent manner, the laws they have enacted, but also, as a corollary of this duty, to ensure the legal and practical conditions for their implementation (see also paragraph 147 above). In the context of the present case, it was incumbent on the Polish authorities to remove the existing incompatibility between the letter of the law and the State-operated practice which hindered the effective exercise of the applicant's right of property. Those principles also required the Polish State to fulfil in good time, in an appropriate and consistent manner, the legislative promises it had made in respect of the settlement of the Bug River claims. This was a matter of important public and general interest (see paragraph 150 above). As rightly pointed out by the Polish Constitutional Court (see paragraph 82 above), the imperative of maintaining citizens' legitimate confidence in the State and the law made by it, inherent in the rule of law, required the authorities to eliminate the dysfunctional provisions from the legal system and to rectify the extra-legal practices.

185. In the present case, as ascertained by the Polish courts and confirmed by the Court's analysis of the respondent State's conduct, the authorities, by imposing successive limitations on the exercise of the applicant's right to credit, and by applying the practices that made it unenforceable and unusable in practice, rendered that right illusory and destroyed its very essence.

The state of uncertainty in which the applicant found himself as a result of the repeated delays and obstruction continuing over a period of many years, for which the national authorities were responsible, was in itself incompatible with the obligation arising under Article 1 of Protocol No. 1 to secure the peaceful enjoyment of possessions, notably with the duty to act in good time, in an appropriate and consistent manner where an issue of general interest is at stake (see paragraph 151 above).

186. Furthermore, the applicant's situation was compounded by the fact that what had become a practically unenforceable entitlement was legally extinguished by the December 2003 legislation, pursuant to which the applicant lost his hitherto existing entitlement to compensation. Moreover, this legislation operated a difference of treatment between Bug River claimants in so far as those

who had never received any compensation were awarded an amount which, although subject to a ceiling of PLN 50,000, was a specified proportion (15%) of their entitlement, whereas claimants in the applicant's position, who had already been awarded a much lower percentage, received no additional amount (see paragraphs 115 and 118–19 above).

As stated above (see paragraphs 134 and 182), under Article 1 of Protocol No. 1 the State is entitled to expropriate property – including any compensatory entitlement granted by legislation – and to reduce, even substantially, levels of compensation under legislative schemes. This applies particularly to situations in which the compensatory entitlement does not arise from any previous taking of individual property by the respondent State, but is designed to mitigate the effects of a taking or loss of property not attributable to that State. What Article 1 of Protocol No. 1 requires is that the amount of compensation granted for property taken by the State be "reasonably related" to its value (see paragraph 176 above). It is not for the Court to say in the abstract what would be a "reasonable" level of compensation in the present case. However, given that – as acknowledged by the Government (see paragraph 35 above) – the applicant's family had received a mere 2% of the compensation due under the legislation as applicable before the entry into force of the Protocol in respect of Poland, the Court finds no cogent reason why such an insignificant amount should *per se* deprive him of the possibility of obtaining at least a proportion of his entitlement on an equal basis with other Bug River claimants.

(d) General Conclusion

187. Having regard to all the foregoing factors and in particular to the impact on the applicant over many years of the Bug River legislative scheme as operated in practice, the Court concludes that, as an individual, he had to bear a disproportionate and excessive burden which cannot be justified in terms of the legitimate general community interest pursued by the authorities.

There has therefore been a violation of Article 1 of Protocol No. 1 in the applicant's case.

[. . .]

4.21. *Doğan and Others v. Turkey* (2004)

[. . .]

I. The Circumstances of the Case

8. The facts as submitted by the parties may be summarised as follows.

A. General Background

9. Until October 1994 the applicants all lived in Boydaş, a village of Hozat district in Tunceli province, in the then state-of-emergency region of Turkey.

10. The applicants Abdullah Doğan, Ali Rıza Doğan, Ahmet Doğan, Kazım Balık, Müslüm Yılmaz and Yusuf Doğan (applications nos. 8803/02, 8805/02, 8806/02, 8811/02, 8815/02 and 8817/02 respectively) owned houses and land in Boydaş, whereas the other applicants cultivated land and lived in the houses owned by their fathers.

In particular, Cemal Doğan is the son of Ahmet Doğan (applications nos. 8804/02 and 8806/02 respectively).

Ali Murat Doğan, Hüseyin Doğan and Ali Rıza Doğan are the sons of Yusuf Doğan (applications nos. 8807/02, 8816/02, 8819/02 and 8817/02 respectively).

Hasan Yıldız (application no. 8808/02) cultivated the land owned by his father Nurettin Yıldız.

Hıdır and İhsan Balık are brothers (applications nos. 8809/02 and 8810/02 respectively). They used the property owned by their father Haydar Balık.

Mehmet Doğan is the son of Ali Rıza Doğan (applications nos. 8813/02 and 8805/02 respectively).

Hüseyin Doğan (application no. 8818/02) cultivated the land owned by his father Hasan Doğan.

11. Boydaş village may be described as an area of dispersed hamlets and houses spread over mountainous terrain, where there is insufficient land suitable for agriculture. For administrative purposes the village was regarded as being in the Hozat district. An extended patriarchal family system prevailed in the region, where there were no large landowners but generally small family farms. These usually took the form of livestock farms

(sheep, goats and bee-keeping) revolving around the grandfather or father and run by their married children. The applicants earned their living by farming, in particular stockbreeding, land cultivation, tree felling and the sale of timber, as did their fellow villagers.

12. In 1994, terrorist activity was a major concern in this area. Since the 1980s a violent conflict had been going on in the region between the security forces and sections of the Kurdish population in favour of Kurdish autonomy, in particular members of the PKK (*Workers' Party of Kurdistan*). This resulted in the displacement of many people from in and around Boydaş village either because of the difficulty of life in the remote mountainous area or because of the security situation.

13. The facts of the case, in particular the circumstances of the applicants' and the denial of access to their property in Boydaş village, are disputed.

B. The Applicants' Version of the Facts

14. In October 1994 the inhabitants of Boydaş were forcibly evicted from their village by security forces on account of the disturbances in the region. The security forces also destroyed the applicants' houses with a view to forcing them to leave the village. The applicants and their families thus moved to safer areas, namely to Elazığ and Istanbul where they currently live in poor conditions.

1. The Applicants' Complaints to the Authorities

15. Between 29 November 1994 and 15 August 2001 the applicants petitioned various administrative authorities, namely the offices of the Prime Minister, the Governor of the state-of-emergency region, the Tunceli Governor and the Hozat District Governor, complaining about the forced evacuation of their village by the security forces. They also requested permission to return to their village and to use their property.

2. The Authorities' Responses to the Applicants

16. Although the applicants' petitions were received by the authorities, no response was given to the applicants, except the letters in reply sent to Abdullah, Ahmet, Mehmet and Hüseyin Doğan, within the 60-day period prescribed by Law no. 2577.

17. By a letter of 5 May 2000, the District Governor of Hozat replied to Abdullah Doğan's petition dated 24 February 2000 and stated the following:

"The Project 'Return to the Village and Rehabilitation in Eastern and South-eastern Anatolia' is developed by the South-eastern Anatolia Project Regional Development Directorate (*GAP Bölge Kalkındırma İdaresi Başkanlığı*). It aims to facilitate the re-settlement of any inhabitants who unwillingly left their land due to various reasons, particularly terrorist incidents and who now intend to return to secure collective settlement units, since the number of terrorist incidents has decreased in the region. The Project also aims at creating sustainable living standards in the re-settlement areas.

In this context, your petition has been taken into consideration."

18. By letters of 10 October and 5 and 25 June 2001, the state-of-emergency office attached to the Tunceli Governor's office stated the following in response to the petitions submitted by Ahmet, Mehmet and Hüseyin Doğan:

"Return to Boydaş village is forbidden for security reasons. However, you can return and reside in Çaytaşı, Karaca, Karaçavuş, Kavuktepe and Türktaner villages.

Furthermore, your petition will be considered under the 'Return to the Village and Rehabilitation Project'."

C. The Government's Version of the Facts

19. Since the early 1980s the PKK terrorist organization waged a vicious and deadly campaign against the Turkish State with a view to separating a part of its territory and setting up a Kurdish State. The terrorist campaign carried out by the PKK focused on the south-east provinces of Turkey and aimed at destabilizing the region morally and economically as well as coercing the innocent population in the area to join the terrorist organisation. Those who refused to join the terrorist organisation were intimidated with random killings and village massacres. In this connection, between 1984 and 1995, 852 incidents occurred causing the death of 383 people and the wounding of 460.

20. This terrorist campaign resulted in a drastic movement of population from the area to more

secure cities and areas of the country. Thus, the inhabitants of the villages and hamlets in the region left their homes owing to the terrorist threat by the PKK.

21. However, a number of settlements might have been evacuated by the local authorities to ensure the safety of the population as a precaution. According to the official figures, the number of people internally displaced on account of the terrorism is around 380,000. This figure corresponds to the evacuation of 48,822 houses located in 853 villages and 2,183 hamlets.

22. The applicants were residents of Boydaş village. The official records indicate that the inhabitants of Boydaş evacuated the village because of the PKK intimidation. They were not forced to leave the village by the security forces.

[. . .]

E. Relevant International Materials

1. Humanitarian Situation of the Displaced Kurdish Population in Turkey, Report of the Committee on Migration, Refugees and Demography, adopted by Recommendation 1563 (2002) of the Parliamentary Assembly

55. Between 8 and 12 October 2001 Mr John Connor, the rapporteur of the Committee on Migration, Refugees and Demography, established by the Parliamentary Assembly of the Council of Europe, carried out a fact-finding visit to Turkey concerning the "humanitarian situation of the displaced Kurdish population in Turkey". Mr Connor prepared a report based on the information gathered from a number of sources, including his visit, official statements by the Turkish authorities and information received from local and international non-governmental organisations, as well as international governmental organisations.

56. In this report, Mr Connor drew attention to the controversy concerning the figures for displaced persons. The Turkish authorities' official figure for "evacuated persons" amounts to 378,000 originating from 3,165 villages at the end of 1999, whereas credible international estimates concerning the population displaced as a result of the conflict in south-east Turkey range between 400,000 and 1 million by December 2000. As to the cause of the movement of the population, the Turkish

authorities maintained that the movement was not caused by the violence in the region alone. They contended that economic factors also accounted for the "migration". The report, recognising the situation of internal displacement due to the conflict in the region, confirmed the Government's stand point. However, it pointed out that there was no doubt that there had been a major displacement and migration to towns affecting those caught in the crossfire of the conflict: on the one hand Turkish security forces had targeted villages suspected of supporting the PKK. On the other hand the PKK had assassinated inhabitants of the villages "collaborating" with the State authorities (i.e. belonging to the village guards system) or refusing to support the PKK. This vicious circle of violence had forced many people to flee their homes.

57. Mr Connor pointed to the failure of the Turkish Government to provide emergency assistance to people forcibly displaced in the south-east, including persons displaced directly as a result of the actions of the security forces. He further underlined the failure of the Government to provide a sanitary environment, housing, health care and employment to the internally displaced population.

58. As to the prospects for the future, Mr Connor observed that the respondent Government had started developing return and rehabilitation projects as early as 1994. However, the first returns had occurred in 1997, as the region had not been secure before the latter date. Despite obvious improvements, security remained the main concern conditioning mass return movements. On the one hand, the authorities felt reluctant to allow for a large influx of returnees fearing the return of PKK militants. For that reason, they scrutinize every application and did not authorize returns to certain areas. On the other hand, the displaced population was in most cases unable to return without state financial or subsistence assistance and sometimes reluctant because of fresh memory of the atrocities committed in the past. Nevertheless, the South Eastern Anatolia Project (GAP), which is a comprehensive development programme aimed at the ending of the disparities between this region and the rest of the country, financed a number of projects concerning the return and resettlement of displaced persons. Among them was the "town-villages project", which, through the construction of centralised villages, had allowed 4,000 displaced

persons to return to their region. According to the official figures, approximately 28,000 persons had returned to 200 villages up to July 2001. Even so, a number of human rights organisations were critical of the Government's efforts since the application forms for those who wished to return included a question concerning the reason for leaving the village. According to these organisations, displaced persons were not allowed to return unless they gave the actions of the PKK as a reason. Furthermore, there had been allegations that return was authorised only to the villages within the village guard system.

59. Mr Connor concluded with satisfaction that the humanitarian situation in the region had progressed in relation to the situation presented in the last report of the Committee on Migration, Refugees and Demography; although the aims of provision of full security for mass returns and taking measures for revitalisation of the economy were still to be achieved. He made recommendations to the Turkish Government concerning a number of issues, which constituted the basis for Recommendation 1563 (2002) of the Parliamentary Assembly of the Council of Europe.

2. Recommendation 1563 (2002) of the Parliamentary Assembly on the Humanitarian Situation of the Displaced Kurdish Population in Turkey

60. On 29 May 2002 the Parliamentary Assembly of the Council of Europe adopted Recommendation 1563 (2002) on the "humanitarian situation of the displaced Kurdish population in Turkey". The Parliamentary Assembly urged Turkey to take the following steps:

"a. lift the state of emergency in the four remaining provinces as quickly as possible, namely in Hakkari and Tunceli, Diyarbakır and Şırnak;

b. refrain from any further evacuations of villages;

c. ensure civilian control over military activity in the region and make security forces more accountable for their actions;

d. step up investigations into alleged human rights violations in the region;

e. properly implement the rulings of the European Court of Human Rights;

f. abolish the village guard system;

g. continue its efforts to promote both the economic and social development and the reconstruction of the south-eastern provinces;

h. involve representatives of the displaced population in the preparation of return programmes and projects;

i. speed up the process of returns;

j. allow for individual returns without prior permission;

k. not to precondition assistance to displaced persons with the obligation to enter the village guard system or the declaration on the cause of their flight;

l. present reconstruction projects to be financed by the Council of Europe's Development Bank in the framework of return programmes;

m. adopt measures to integrate those displaced persons who wish to settle in other parts of Turkey and provide them with compensation for damaged property;

n. grant full access to the region for international humanitarian organisations, and provide them with support from local authorities."

3. Report of the Representative of the Secretary-General on Internally Displaced Persons, Mr Francis Deng, the United Nations Economic and Social Council, Commission on Human Rights, 59th Session, 27 November 2002

61. Between 27 and 31 May 2002 the Representative of the Secretary-General of the United Nations on internally displaced persons, Mr Francis Deng, undertook a visit to Turkey, at the invitation of the Government of Turkey. He aimed to gain a first-hand understanding of the situation of the displaced and to engage in a dialogue with the Government, international agencies, non-governmental organisations and representatives of the donor countries. Following his visit the Representative prepared a report which was submitted to the Commission on Human Rights of the United Nations.

62. Mr Deng reported that the figures concerning the displaced population ranged widely between

378,000 and 4,5 million persons, predominantly of ethnic Kurds. Regarding the cause of the displacement in Turkey, the Representative contended that the situation of displacement had mainly resulted from armed clashes, violence and human rights violations in south-east Turkey. Like the rapporteur of the Council of Europe, he recognised the Government's claim that economic factors also accounted for the population movements.

63. Mr Deng stated that the majority of the displaced persons had moved into provincial cities, where they had reportedly lived in conditions of extreme poverty, with inadequate heating, sanitation, infrastructure, housing and education. He noted that the displaced persons had to seek employment in overcrowded cities and towns, where unemployment levels were described as "disastrous". Mr Deng observed that the Government officials were mainly concerned with explaining the initiatives that the authorities were taking regarding the return and resettlement of the displaced population. He further observed that there was a tendency not to refer to the current conditions of the displaced. He noted that the problems of the displaced were not specific to the displaced, but affected the population of south-east Turkey as a whole.

64. Regarding the return and resettlement initiatives, Mr Deng primarily reported the "Return to Village and Rehabilitation Project", which was announced by the Turkish Government in 1999. Citing the positive aspects of the project, such as the feasibility study conducted prior to the development of the project and the voluntary nature of any return and resettlement, Mr Deng expressed his concerns on a number of issues. He noted that the extent of the consultation with the displaced and the non-governmental organisations working on their behalf might be insufficient. He further reported the concerns regarding the plan of a new centralised settlement pattern, as opposed to the traditional pattern of one large settlement (village) surrounded by smaller settlements (hamlets). Mr Deng noted that, although establishing security in the region through promoting centralised settlement units was a legitimate policy, the authorities should consult the displaced themselves. Two other issues that were of concern for Mr Deng were the absence of basic data which would give an accurate picture of the displacement and the failure to implement the project.

65. As to return and resettlement initiatives other than the "Return to Village and Rehabilitation Project", Mr Deng noted that there had not been sufficient information as to their target groups and how exactly they related to one another.

66. Concerning the obstacles to return, Mr Deng referred to the practice of requiring persons to declare that they would not seek damages from the State. Mr Deng noted that Government officials denied the existence of a non-litigation clause in the application forms for those who wished to return. Furthermore, he had received information concerning the application forms, which included a question concerning the reason for leaving the village. According to the reports, only those persons who stated that they had been displaced as a result of "terror" were allowed to return. Mr Deng further noted that there had been allegations that return was authorised only to villages within the village guard system. He finally noted that anti-personnel mines posed a threat to those who wished to return to their villages in south-east Turkey.

67. The recommendations of the Representative of the Secretary-General of the United Nations on internally displaced persons were summarised as follows:

"a. The Government should clarify its policy on internal displacement, including return, resettlement and reintegration, make its policy widely known, create focal points of responsibility for the displaced at various levels of the government structures, and facilitate co-ordination and co-operation among government institutions and with non-governmental organisations, civil society and the international community.

b. The Government should enhance their efforts to address the current conditions of the displaced, which are reported to be poor, in co-operation with non-governmental organisations and United Nations agencies.

c. The Government should provide more comprehensive and reliable data on the number of persons displaced as a result of the actions of both the Kurdistan Workers' Party (PKK) and the security forces, on their current whereabouts, conditions and specific needs, and on their intentions with respect to return or resettlement.

d. The Government should facilitate broad consultation with the displaced and the non-governmental organisations and civil society organisations working with them. The Government should further consider producing a document that clearly outlines the objectives, scope and resource implications of the Return to Village and Rehabilitation Project. Finally the results of the feasibility study conducted should be made public and the Government should facilitate an open discussion with the displaced and non-governmental organisations on the findings of this study and the steps which should be taken to implement them.

e. The Government should examine areas of possible co-operation with the international community. In this connection, the Government might consider convening a meeting with international agencies, including the World Bank, and representatives of the potential partners to explore ways in which the international community could assist the Government in responding to the needs of the displaced.

f. The Government should ensure a non-discriminatory approach to return by investigating and preventing situations in which former village guards are allegedly given preference in the return process over those persons perceived as linked to PKK.

g. The Government should ensure that the role of the security forces, or *jandarma,* in the return process is primarily one of consultation on security matters. Displaced persons who have been granted permission by the authorities to return to their villages – the decision being based on the advice of the *jandarma* – should be allowed to do so without unjustified or unlawful interference by the *jandarma*.

h. The Government should take steps to abolish the village guard system and find alternative employment opportunities for existing guards. Until such time as the system is abolished, the process of disarming village guards should be expedited.

i. The Government should undertake mine clearance activities in the relevant areas of the south-east to which displaced persons are returning, so as to facilitate that process.

j. The Government should enhance their efforts to develop legislation providing compensation to those affected by the violence in the south-east, including those who were evacuated from their homes by the security forces."

[. . .]

II. Alleged Violation of Article 1 of Protocol No. 1

134. The applicants alleged that their forced eviction from their village by the security forces and the refusal of the authorities to allow them to return to their homes and land had amounted to a breach of Article 1 of Protocol No. 1, which provides:

> "Every natural or legal person is entitled to the peaceful enjoyment of his possessions. No one shall be deprived of his possessions except in the public interest and subject to the conditions provided for by law and by the general principles of international law.
>
> The preceding provisions shall not, however, in any way impair the right of a State to enforce such laws as it deems necessary to control the use of property in accordance with the general interest or to secure the payment of taxes or other contributions or penalties."

A. Whether There Was a "Possession"

135. The Government averred that the applicants Abdullah Doğan, Cemal Doğan, Ali Murat Doğan, Hıdır Balık, İhsan Balık, Kazım Balık, Mehmet Doğan, Hüseyin Doğan and Ali Rıza Doğan did not have "possessions" within the meaning of Article 1 of Protocol No. 1 since they had failed to submit title deeds attesting that they had owned property in Boydaş village. Consequently, these nine applicants could not claim to be victims of a violation of a property right that had not been established.

136. The Government submitted that for there to be an infringement of a property within the meaning of Article 1 of Protocol No. 1, an applicant must demonstrate that he had a title to that property. With reference to the Court's jurisprudence on the subject, they maintained that the description and identification of property rights were matters for

the national legal system and that it was incumbent on an applicant to establish the precise nature of the right under domestic law and his entitlement to enjoy it. The Government noted in this connection that under Turkish law all transactions related to immovable property and all proof concerning ownership had to be based on records of land registry. In cases where the immovable property, such as land, was not recorded at the registry, proof of ownership had to be established in accordance with the rules set out in the Civil Code. Further, where no land survey had been conducted, a decision of a judge was necessary to provide proof of ownership. Finally, the Government stressed that the statements of the mayor of Boydaş village (see paragraphs 23 and 24 above) had no evidential value as such unless they had been admitted as evidence by a national judge in a case which concerned the ownership of land or the ownership of movable property such as livestock.

137. The applicants disputed the Government's arguments and contended that, according to the Court's case-law, the concept of "possessions" comprised, in addition to all forms of corporeal moveable and immoveable property, "rights" and "interests" which do not physically exist and all forms of assets and financial as well as economic resources included in the persons' property. They noted that in the rural area where they lived the patriarchal family system prevailed, wherein adults married, built houses on their fathers' land and made use of their fathers' property as a natural requirement of the social system. In that connection, the applicants argued that "property rights" should not be regarded as exclusively covering property which was registered under a personal title, but should include all the economic resources jointly enjoyed by all the villagers. The applicants further asserted that they all had separate families and economic activities in the village even though they had used their fathers' property. Relying on the provisions of the Code of Civil Procedure, they also claimed that the statements given by the mayor of Boydaş village (see paragraphs 23 and 24 above) should be taken into account with a view to proving that they had been using their ascendants' registered and unregistered property in accordance with the local traditions and that they had been earning their living from stockbreeding and forestry.

138. The Court reiterates that Article 1 of Protocol No. 1 in substance guarantees the right of property

(see *Marckx v. Belgium*, judgment of 13 June 1979, Series A no. 31, pp. 27–28, § 63). However, the notion "possessions" (in French: *biens*) in Article 1 has an autonomous meaning which is certainly not limited to ownership of physical goods: certain other rights and interests constituting assets can also be regarded as "property rights", and thus as "possessions" for the purposes of this provision (see *Gasus Dosier- und Fördertechnik GmbH v. The Netherlands*, judgment of 23 February 1995, Series A no. 306-B, p. 46, § 53, and *Matos e Silva, Lda., and Others v. Portugal*, judgment of 16 September 1996, *Reports 1996*-IV, p. 1111, § 75).

139. The Court notes that it is not required to decide whether or not in the absence of title deeds the applicants have rights of property under domestic law. The question which arises under this head is whether the overall economic activities carried out by the applicants constituted "possessions" coming within the scope of the protection afforded by Article 1 of Protocol No. 1. In this regard, the Court notes that it is undisputed that the applicants all lived in Boydaş village until 1994. Although they did not have registered property, they either had their own houses constructed on the lands of their ascendants or lived in the houses owned by their fathers and cultivated the land belonging to the latter. The Court further notes that the applicants had unchallenged rights over the common lands in the village, such as the pasture, grazing and the forest land, and that they earned their living from stockbreeding and tree-felling. Accordingly, in the Court's opinion, all these economic resources and the revenue that the applicants derived from them may qualify as "possessions" for the purposes of Article 1.

B. Whether There Was an Interference

140. The applicants argued that it was not in doubt that there had been an interference with their right to peaceful enjoyment of their possessions. They were forcibly evicted from their homes and land by the security forces and restrictions were imposed by the authorities on their return to their village. As a result of continuous denial of access to the village they were effectively deprived of their revenue and forced to live in poor conditions in other regions of the country.

141. The Government denied that the applicants had been compelled to evacuate their village by the

security forces. They claimed that the applicants had left their village on account of the disturbances in the region and intimidation by the PKK. They admitted however that a number of settlements had been evacuated by the relevant authorities to ensure the safety of the population in the region. The Government further submitted that the applicants had no genuine interest in going back to their village since in its present state Boydaş village was not suitable for accommodation and offered very poor economic conditions to sustain life. Nevertheless, with reference to the Ministry of Interior Gendarmerie General Command's letter of 22 July 2003, the Government pointed out that there remained no obstacle to the applicants' return to Boydaş village (see paragraph 37 above).

142. In the present case, the Court is required to have regard to the situation which existed in the state of emergency region of Turkey at the time of the events complained of by the applicants, characterised by violent confrontations between the security forces and members of the PKK. It notes that this two-fold violence resulting from the acts of the two parties to the conflict forced many people to flee their homes (see paragraphs 56 and 62 above). Furthermore, and as admitted by the Government, the authorities have evicted the inhabitants of a number of settlements to ensure the safety of the population in the region (see paragraph 141 above). The Court has also found in numerous similar cases that security forces deliberately destroyed the homes and property of the respective applicants, depriving them of their livelihoods and forcing them to leave their villages in the state of emergency region of Turkey (see, among many others, *Akdivar and Others, Selçuk and Asker, Menteş and Others, Yöyler, İpek,* judgments cited above; *Bilgin v. Turkey,* no. 23819/94, 16 November 2000, and *Dulaş v. Turkey,* no. 25801/94, 30 January 2001).

143. Turning to the particular circumstances of the instant case, the Court observes that it is unable to determine the exact cause of the displacement of the applicants because of the lack of sufficient evidence in its possession and the lack of an independent investigation into the alleged events. On that account, for the purposes of the instant case it must confine its consideration to the examination of the applicants' complaints concerning the denial of access to their possessions since 1994. In this connection, the Court notes that despite the appli-

cants' persistent demands, the authorities refused any access to Boydaş village until 22 July 2003 on the ground of terrorist incidents in and around the village (see paragraphs 15, 17 and 18 above). These disputed measures deprived the applicants of all resources from which they derived their living. Moreover, they also affected the very substance of ownership in respect of six of the applicants in that they could not use and dispose of their property for almost nine years and ten months. The result of these contested measures has been that since October 1994 their right over the possessions has become precarious.

In conclusion, the denial of access to Boydaş village must be regarded as an interference with the applicants' right to the peaceful enjoyment of their possessions (see *Loizidou v. Turkey,* judgment of 18 December 1996, *Reports* 1996-VI, p. 2216, § 63).

C. Whether the Interference Was Justified

144. It remains to be determined whether or not this interference contravenes Article 1.

1. The Applicable Rule

145. The Court reiterates that Article 1 of Protocol No. 1 comprises three distinct rules. The first rule, which is set out in the first sentence of the first paragraph, is of a general nature and enunciates the principle of the peaceful enjoyment of property. The second rule, contained in the second sentence of the first paragraph, covers deprivation of possessions and subjects it to certain conditions. The third rule, stated in the second paragraph, recognises that the Contracting States are entitled, amongst other things, to control the use of property in accordance with the general interest, by enforcing such laws as they deem necessary for the purpose. However, the rules are not "distinct" in the sense of being unconnected. The second and third rules are concerned with particular instances of interference with the right to peaceful enjoyment of property and should therefore be construed in the light of the general principle enunciated in the first rule (see, *inter alia, James and Others v. the United Kingdom,* judgment of 21 February 1986, Series A no. 98, pp. 29–30, § 37, which partly reiterates the terms of the Court's reasoning in *Sporrong and Lönnroth v. Sweden,* judgment of 23 September 1982, Series A no. 52, p. 24, § 61; see also *The Holy Monasteries v. Greece,* judgment of 9 December 1994, Series A

no. 301-A, p. 31, § 56; *Iatridis v. Greece* [GC], no. 31107/96, § 55, ECHR 1999-II; *Beyeler v. Italy* [GC], no. 33202/96, § 106, ECHR 2000-I).

146. The Court notes that the parties did not comment on the rule applicable to the case. It points out that the measures in question did not involve a deprivation of property within the meaning of the second sentence of the first paragraph of Article 1 because the applicants have remained the legal owner or possessor of the lands in Boydaş. The measures did not amount to control of the use of property either since they did not pursue such an aim. The Court considers therefore that the situation of which the applicants complain fails to be dealt with under the first sentence of the first paragraph of Article 1 since the impugned measures undoubtedly restricted the applicants' rights to use and dispose of their possessions (*Cyprus v. Turkey* ([GC], no. 25781/94, § 187, ECHR 2001-IV).

2. Lawfulness and Purpose of the Interference

147. The applicants asserted that the impugned measures had a legal basis in domestic law in that the governor of the state-of-emergency region could order the permanent or temporary evacuation of villages and impose residence restrictions pursuant to Article 4 (h) of Decree no. 285 and Article 1 (b) of Decree no. 430 in force at the relevant time (see paragraph 82 above). They argued however that the state-of-emergency governor's office had employed illegal methods to depopulate the region rather than relying on the aforementioned provision. In their opinion, the motive behind this choice was to blame the illegal organisations, such as the PKK and the TİKKO (*Workers and Peasants' Independence Army of Turkey*), for village evacuations, to avoid the economic burden of re-housing the population and to grant impunity to the security forces for their illegal acts.

148. The Government disputed the applicants' assertions and maintained that the refusal of access to Boydaş village had aimed at protecting the lives of the applicants on account of the insecurity of the region. In their opinion, had the applicants been evicted from their village by the security forces as alleged, this must have been carried out in pursuance of the State's duty to fulfil its obligation under Article 2 of the Convention, which overrode its undertakings under Article 1 of Protocol No. 1.

149. Notwithstanding its doubts as to the lawfulness of the impugned interference, the Court notes the security motives invoked by the Government in this context and for the purposes of the present case would refrain from ruling that these aims cannot be regarded as legitimate "in accordance with the general interest" for the purposes of the second paragraph of Article 1. It thus leaves the question regarding the lawfulness of the interference open, as in the present case it is more essential to decide on the proportionality of the interference in question.

3. Proportionality of the Interference

150. The applicants maintained that, as a result of their displacement and denial of access to their possessions, they had been forced to live in very poor conditions due to the lack of employment, housing, health care and a sanitary environment. They contended that, in the absence of economic and social measures to remedy their living conditions, the interference complained of could not be described as proportionate to the aim pursued.

151. The Government claimed that they had taken all necessary measures with a view to tackling the problems of the internally displaced persons, including the applicants. They asserted that the "return to village and rehabilitation project" had been developed by the authorities to remedy the problems of those who had had to leave their homes on account of the terrorist incidents in the region (see paragraphs 45–48 above). The aim of this project was to ensure the voluntary return of the displaced population. Thus, its implementation had been subjected to the strict control of Parliament (see paragraphs 39–42 above). The Government had also obtained the support of several international agencies to assist in the successful implementation of this project (see paragraph 44 above). Despite budgetary restraints and serious economic difficulties, the Government had spent approximately sixty million euros within the context of this project. An important amount of this money had been used for improvement of the infrastructure in the region. The progress achieved so far had been positive and encouraging given the fact that 94,000 persons, which was approximately 25% of the total number of displaced persons, had already returned to their settlement units between June 2000 and December 2003.

152. The Government further referred to draft legislation for compensation of damage caused by terrorist violence or as a result of measures taken by the authorities against terrorism. They explained that, when enacted, this law would provide a remedy whereby the internally displaced persons could claim compensation for the damage they had sustained in the course of the struggle against terrorism. Against this background, the Government concluded that the measures taken by the authorities had been proportionate to the aims pursued.

153. For the purposes of the first sentence of the first paragraph, the Court must determine whether a fair balance was struck between the demands of the general interest of the community and the requirements of the protection of the individual's fundamental rights (see *Sporrong and Lönnroth*, cited above, § 69). The Court recognises that the interference complained of in the instant case did not lack a basis. As noted above, armed clashes, generalised violence and human rights violations, specifically within the context of the PKK insurgency, compelled the authorities to take extraordinary measures to maintain security in the state-of-emergency region. These measures involved, among others, the restriction of access to several villages, including Boydaş, as well as evacuation of some villages on the ground of the lack of security. However, it observes that in the circumstances of the case the refusal of access to Boydaş had serious and harmful effects that have hindered the applicants' right to enjoyment of their possessions for almost ten years, during which time they have been living in other areas of the country in conditions of extreme poverty, with inadequate heating, sanitation and infrastructure (see paragraphs 14, 57 and 63 above). Their situation was compounded by a lack of financial assets, having received no compensation for deprivation of their possessions, and the need to seek employment and shelter in overcrowded cities and towns, where unemployment levels and housing facilities have been described as disastrous (see paragraph 63 above).

154. While the Court acknowledges the Government's efforts to remedy the situation of the internally displaced persons generally, for the purposes of the present case it considers them inadequate and ineffective. In this connection, it points out that the return to village and rehabilitation project referred to by the Government has not been converted into practical steps to facilitate the return of the applicants to their village. According to the visual records of 29 December 2003, Boydaş village seems to be in ruins and without any infrastructure (see paragraph 38 above). Besides the failure of the authorities to facilitate return to Boydaş, the applicants have not been provided with alternative housing or employment. Furthermore, apart from the aid given to Mr Kazım Balık and Mr Müslüm Yılmaz by the Social Aid and Solidarity Fund, which in the Court's opinion is insufficient to live on, the applicants have not been supplied with any funding which would ensure an adequate standard of living or a sustainable return process. For the Court, however, the authorities have the primary duty and responsibility to establish conditions, as well as provide the means, which allow the applicants to return voluntarily, in safety and with dignity, to their homes or places of habitual residence, or to resettle voluntarily in another part of the country (see in this respect Principles 18 and 28 of the United Nations Guiding Principles on Internal Displacement, E/CN.4/1998/53/Add.2, dated 11 February 1998). Moreover, as regards the draft legislation on compensation for damage occurred as a result of the acts of terrorism or of measures taken against terrorism, the Court observes that this law is not yet in force and, accordingly, does not provide any remedy for the applicants' grievances under this heading.

155. Having regard to the foregoing, the Court considers that the applicants have had to bear an individual and excessive burden which has upset the fair balance which should be struck between the requirements of the general interest and the protection of the right to the peaceful enjoyment of one's possessions.

156. In view of these considerations, the Court dismisses the Government's preliminary objection with respect to nine of the applicants who have not presented title deeds and holds that there has been a violation of Article 1 of Protocol No. 1.

III. ALLEGED VIOLATION OF ARTICLE 8 OF THE CONVENTION

157. The applicants, referring to their expulsion from their village and their inability to return

thereto, maintained that there had been a breach of Article 8 of the Convention, which reads:

"1. Everyone has the right to respect for his private and family life, his home and his correspondence.

2. There shall be no interference by a public authority with the exercise of this right except such as is in accordance with the law and is necessary in a democratic society in the interests of national security, public safety or the economic well-being of the country, for the prevention of disorder or crime, for the protection of health or morals, or for the protection of the rights and freedoms of others."

158. The Government denied that there had been any violation of this provision, on the same grounds as those advanced in connection with Article 1 of Protocol No. 1.

159. The Court is of the opinion that there can be no doubt that the refusal of access to the applicants' homes and livelihood, in addition to giving rise to a violation of Article 1 of Protocol No. 1, constitutes at the same time a serious and unjustified interference with the right to respect for family lives and homes.

160. Accordingly, the Court concludes that there has been a violation of Article 8 of the Convention.

[. . .]

4.22. *Străin and Others v. Romania* (2005)

[. . .]

A. The Circumstances of the Case

4. The applicants were born in 1914, 1920, 1921 and 1945 respectively. The first lives in Timişoara, the second in Delémont (Switzerland) and the others in Arad.

5. The first two applicants and their deceased brother, Mircea Stoinescu, whose heirs are the other two applicants, were the owners of a house in Arad. In 1950 the State took possession of that house under Decree no. 92/1950 on nationalisation. The house was converted into four flats intended for rental.

6. On 27 September 1993 the first two applicants and Mircea Stoinescu brought an action for the recovery of possession of immovable property in the Arad Court of First Instance, against Arad Town Council and R., a State-owned company responsible for the management of property belonging to the State. After the death of Mircea Stoinescu, the action was pursued by his heirs, Mrs Felicia Stoinescu and Mrs Maria Tăucean. The applicants sought a declaration that they were the rightful owners of the house and appurtenant land that the State had, in their opinion, wrongfully seized in 1950. They claimed that, under Article 2 of Decree no. 92/1950, property belonging to persons in certain social categories was not subject to nationalisation, and that they fell within such a category. In their view, the nationalisation of the house in question had therefore been improper and unlawful.

7. In a judgment of 12 April 1994 the Arad Court of First Instance dismissed the applicants' action, refusing to rule on the merits on the ground that they could not obtain redress for the damage they had sustained until the enactment of special legislation introducing reparation measures. The judgment was upheld by the Arad County Court on 3 November 1995. The applicants appealed against that decision.

8. In 1996 the tenants of the flats making up the house applied to purchase them, relying on Law no. 112/1995. Arad Town Council informed the R. company that a dispute was pending concerning the title to the house and instructed it not to pursue the sale of the flats in question.

9. Consequently, the tenants of three flats had their purchase applications rejected, but not H.D. (a former football player and international celebrity) and his wife, to whom the R. company sold flat no. 3 on 18 December 1996.

10. On 25 February 1997 the Timişoara Court of Appeal upheld an appeal by the applicants and remitted the case to the Arad Court of First Instance for a decision on the merits.

11. On 12 May 1997 Mr and Mrs D. applied to intervene in the Court of First Instance proceedings on the ground that they had been the owners of flat no. 3 since its sale on 18 December 1996.

12. Further to the couple's application to intervene, the applicants requested the court to find that the sale of flat no. 3 was null and void. In their view, as

the nationalisation had been improper and unlawful, the State could not have been the rightful owner of the property and thus could not lawfully have sold any part of it. The applicants relied in particular on Article 966 of the Civil Code, whereby an undertaking entered into on an erroneous or unlawful basis could not produce any useful effect.

13. On 7 June 1997 the Arad Court of First Instance held that the nationalisation of the house had been unlawful and that the applicants were therefore the rightful owners. However, the court dismissed the request for the rescission of the contract of sale between the State and Mr and Mrs D., on the ground that the couple had made the purchase in good faith.

14. The applicants appealed against that judgment. On 28 November 1997 the Arad County Court allowed the appeal and remitted the case to the Court of First Instance for reconsideration.

15. In a judgment of 6 July 1998 the Arad Court of First Instance held that the nationalisation of the house had been unlawful, that the applicants were the rightful owners and that the contract of sale between the State and Mr and Mrs D. was null and void.

16. On 2 February 1999 the Arad County Court allowed an appeal by Mr and Mrs D. and dismissed the applicants' action, finding that the nationalisation had been lawful and that, consequently, the sale by the State of flat no. 3 was also lawful.

17. The applicants appealed to the Timişoara Court of Appeal, which gave its judgment on 30 June 1999. It partly allowed the applicants' appeal in so far as it found the nationalisation to have been unlawful and acknowledged that they had remained the rightful owners of the property. However, it dismissed the appeal as regards the rescission of the sale of flat no. 3, considering that the State had been presumed to be the owner of the property at the time of the sale, in spite of the dispute over the property that was pending in the courts. It moreover relied on the fact that Law no. 112/1995, which had formed the statutory basis for the sale of the property, did not provide for any penalty in respect of property sold when the title to it was in dispute before the courts. The Court of Appeal did not address the applicants' argument relating to the principle of unjust enrichment (see paragraph 27 below).

18. On 20 August 2001 the applicants again requested the Arad Court of First Instance to order the rescission of the sale of flat no. 3, contending that the purchasers had broken the law. Their action was dismissed on 13 December 2001 on the ground that the matter had become *res judicata*.

[. . .]

I. ALLEGED VIOLATION OF ARTICLE 1 OF PROTOCOL NO. 1

28. The applicants alleged that the sale of their flat to a third party, which had been validated by the judgment of the Timişoara Court of Appeal on 30 June 1999 and for which they had received no compensation, entailed a breach of Article 1 of Protocol No. 1, which provides:

> "Every natural or legal person is entitled to the peaceful enjoyment of his possessions. No one shall be deprived of his possessions except in the public interest and subject to the conditions provided for by law and by the general principles of international law.
>
> The preceding provisions shall not, however, in any way impair the right of a State to enforce such laws as it deems necessary to control the use of property in accordance with the general interest or to secure the payment of taxes or other contributions or penalties."

A. Admissibility

29. The Court observes that this complaint is not manifestly ill-founded within the meaning of Article 35 § 3 of the Convention. It moreover observes that no other ground for declaring it inadmissible has been established and therefore declares it admissible.

B. Merits

30. The Government submitted that the applicants did not have a possession within the meaning of Article 1 of Protocol No. 1 as their right of property had not been acknowledged by a final judicial decision prior to the sale of the property in question to third parties. In this connection, they relied on the precedents of *Malhous v. the Czech Republic* ((dec.), no. 33071/96, ECHR 2000-XII) and *Constandache v. Romania* ((dec.), no. 46312/99, 11 June 2002). They

contended that the property had been nationalised in accordance with Decree no. 92/1950 and had not therefore been part of the applicants' estate at the time when they had brought their action for recovery of possession in the Arad Court of First Instance on 27 September 1993. Moreover, the applicants had failed to have their title entered in the land register before the property was sold by the State. Under Legislative Decree no. 115/1938 on land registers, which had been applicable in Transylvania, such an omission amounted to an absence of valid title.

31. The Government considered that, in any event, the applicants had been entitled to claim compensation under Law no. 10/2001.

32. The applicants pointed out that in its final decision of 30 June 1999 the Timişoara Court of Appeal had acknowledged, with retrospective effect, that the nationalisation of their property had been unlawful and that they were therefore the rightful owners.

33. They submitted that the *Brumărescu* case-law (*Brumărescu v. Romania* [GC], no. 28342/95, § 65, ECHR 1999-VII) was relevant in the present case and that the courts could not refuse to rule on the compensation due to them for the deprivation of their possession without impairing their right to a hearing under Article 6 § 1 of the Convention.

34. The applicants claimed that the impugned deprivation had resulted from the sale by the State of flat no. 3, of which they claimed possession and in respect of which proceedings had been pending at the time of the sale. Under Law no. 112/1995, on the basis of which the sale had been agreed, the State was only entitled to sell property that it had acquired legally. As the proceedings brought by the applicants had resulted in a declaration that the nationalisation had been unlawful, their title to the flat had accordingly been acknowledged, with retrospective effect. Given that at the time of the sale the applicants had already brought an action against the State, asserting that the nationalisation had been unlawful, and that the existence of the proceedings was indicated in the land register, the sale could not have been lawful. As evidence of the unlawfulness of the sale, the applicants pointed out that the other flats in the house had not been sold to their tenants, precisely because an action was pending in the courts. Those flats had been returned to the applicants as a result of their

action for recovery of possession. It was only because of the influence of the tenant in flat no. 3, H.D., that the flat had unlawfully been sold to him.

Accordingly, the decision of 30 June 1999 in which the Court of Appeal had dismissed the claim for recovery of possession of the flat even though the applicants' title had been acknowledged amounted to an expropriation.

35. The applicants pointed out that, at the time they had lodged their application with the Court, Law no. 10/2001 had not yet been enacted. As that Law was not retrospective in its effect, any compensation they might have been entitled to claim would not have made good the loss they had sustained until such compensation was awarded to them. In any event, they contended that the compensation provided for by Law no. 10/2001 consisted in an award of shares in various State-owned companies, which fell far short of the property's value. Through an action for recovery of possession, by contrast, they would be entitled to the return of the property or in any event to reparation representing the actual value of the property.

36. In line with a number of previous findings, the Court reiterates that Article 1 of Protocol No. 1 comprises three distinct rules: "the first rule, set out in the first sentence of the first paragraph, is of a general nature and enunciates the principle of the peaceful enjoyment of property; the second rule, contained in the second sentence of the first paragraph, covers deprivation of possessions and subjects it to certain conditions; the third rule, stated in the second paragraph, recognises that the Contracting States are entitled, amongst other things, to control the use of property in accordance with the general interest. ... The three rules are not, however, 'distinct' in the sense of being unconnected. The second and third rules are concerned with particular instances of interference with the right to peaceful enjoyment of property and should therefore be construed in the light of the general principle enunciated in the first rule" (see, among other authorities, *James and Others v. the United Kingdom*, judgment of 21 February 1986, Series A no. 98, pp. 29–30, § 37, citing part of the Court's analysis in *Sporrong and Lönnroth v. Sweden*, judgment of 23 September 1982, Series A no. 52, p. 24, § 61; see also *The Holy Monasteries v. Greece*, judgment of 9 December 1994, Series A no. 301-A, p. 31, § 56,

and *Iatridis v. Greece* [GC], no. 31107/96, § 55, ECHR 1999-II).

1. Whether There Was a Possession

37. The Court notes that the parties disagreed as to whether the applicants had a property interest eligible for protection under Article 1 of Protocol No. 1. Accordingly, the Court must determine whether the applicants' legal position is such as to attract the application of Article 1.

38. It observes that the applicants brought an action for the recovery of possession of immovable property, requesting the court to declare the nationalisation of their property unlawful and to order its return to them. In its final judgment of 30 June 1999 the Timişoara Court of Appeal established that the property in question had been nationalised in breach of Decree no. 92/1950 on nationalisation, declared that the applicants had remained the lawful owners of the property and ordered the return of virtually the entire premises. The Court of Appeal admittedly refused to order the return of one flat. Nevertheless, the finding – with retrospective effect – that the applicants had title to the property, including flat no. 3, was irrevocable. Moreover, it has not been quashed or challenged to date. The Court therefore considers that the applicants had a "possession" within the meaning of Article 1 of Protocol No. 1.

2. Whether There Was Interference

39. The Court reiterates that the domestic courts found that the nationalisation of the property belonging to the applicants had been unlawful (see paragraphs 17 and 34 above). By selling one of the flats in the building to a third party before the question of the lawfulness of the nationalisation had been finally settled by the courts, the State deprived the applicants of any possibility of recovering possession (see *Guillemin v. France*, judgment of 21 February 1997, *Reports of Judgments and Decisions* 1997-I, p. 164, § 54). Subsequently, whilst finding the nationalisation unlawful and thus upholding the applicants' right of property, the Court of Appeal refused, since flat no. 3 had in the meantime been sold, to order its return to the applicants. By its refusal, it confirmed with final effect that the applicants were unable to recover the property in question.

40. In view of the foregoing, the Court considers that the applicants' inability to recover possession of their flat undoubtedly constitutes interference with their right to the peaceful enjoyment of their possession.

3. Whether the Interference Was Justified

41. It remains to be ascertained whether or not the interference found by the Court violated Article 1 of Protocol No. 1.

42. In determining whether there has been a deprivation of possessions within the second "rule", it is necessary not only to consider whether there has been a formal taking or expropriation of property but to look behind the appearances and investigate the realities of the situation complained of. Since the Convention is intended to guarantee rights that are "practical and effective", it has to be ascertained whether the situation amounted to a *de facto* expropriation (see *Sporrong and Lönnroth*, cited above, pp. 24–25, § 63; *Vasilescu v. Romania*, judgment of 22 May 1998, *Reports* 1998-III, p. 1078, § 51; and *Brumărescu*, cited above, § 76).

43. The Court notes that the situation arising from the combination of the sale of the flat and the 13 June 1999 judgment of the Timişoara Court of Appeal – which confirmed the applicants' title to the entire property whilst refusing to order the return of flat no. 3 – had the effect of depriving the applicants of the benefit of the judgment in so far as it established their title to the flat. They were no longer able to take possession of the property or sell, devise, donate or otherwise dispose of it. In these circumstances, the Court finds that the effect of the situation was to deprive the applicants of their possession within the meaning of the second sentence of the first paragraph of Article 1 of Protocol No. 1.

44. A taking of property within this second rule can only be justified if it is shown, *inter alia*, to be in the public interest and subject to the conditions provided for by law. Moreover, any interference with the enjoyment of the property must also satisfy the requirement of proportionality. As the Court has repeatedly stated, a fair balance must be struck between the demands of the general interest of the community and the requirements of the protection of the individual's fundamental rights, the search for such a fair balance being inherent in the Convention as a whole. The requisite balance will

not be struck where the person concerned bears an individual and excessive burden (see *Sporrong and Lönnroth*, cited above, pp. 26–28, §§ 69–74).

(a) "Provided for by Law"

45. The first and most important requirement of Article 1 of Protocol No. 1 is that any interference by a public authority with the peaceful enjoyment of possessions should be lawful (*Iatridis*, cited above, § 58). The principle of lawfulness also presupposes that the provisions of domestic law are sufficiently accessible, precise and foreseeable in their application (see *Hentrich v. France*, judgment of 22 September 1994, Series A no. 296-A, pp. 19–20, § 42, and *Lithgow and Others v. the United Kingdom*, judgment of 8 July 1986, Series A no. 102, p. 47, § 110). The Court's power to review compliance with domestic law is, however, limited (see *Håkansson and Sturesson v. Sweden*, judgment of 21 February 1990, Series A no. 171-A, p. 16, § 47).

46. The Court observes that Romanian law, as applicable at the material time, including the case-law, was lacking in clarity as regards the consequences of the recognition of a private individual's title to property which had passed into the ownership of the State but had been sold by the State to a third party.

47. It notes that at the material time there were two different situations in which private individuals would seek the return of residential property that the communist regime had taken from them and placed under State ownership:

(a) The situation where the State had a document of title (*cu titlu*). The statutory framework for this type of situation was laid down in Law no. 112/1995, which was a *lex specialis* in that it created an exception to the general law of the Civil Code (section 24 of the Law). The Law, which on 8 February 2001 was superseded by Law no. 10/2001, set up an administrative body responsible for examining applications for restitution. As a further exception to the general law, section 9 of Law no. 112/1995 allowed the State to sell residential property to its tenants who were occupying that property. Section 9 also provided that the property could only be sold to the tenants after a period of six months, during which time the former owners were entitled to apply for the return of the property or to claim compensation.

In the Court's view, the intention behind that provision was clearly to prevent the sale of property in respect of which an application for restitution had been lodged before the matter of restitution was settled. The Court notes, however, that section 9 did not contain any express or precise provision for cases where property was sold to tenants after the expiry of the six-month period but before an administrative decision on the application for restitution.

(b) The situation where the State had no document of title (*fără titlu*). Before the entry into force of Law no. 10/2001 that type of situation had been governed by the ordinary law, that is to say by the property-law provisions of the Civil Code, incorporating the case-law concerning actions for recovery of possession.

Accordingly, as Law no. 112/1995 only applied to property in respect of which the State had a document of title, the Court observes that no other domestic provision entitled the State to sell property that fell *de facto* under its ownership, that is to say for which it had no document of title, or property that was being disputed in the courts by a party claiming that no such document existed. Moreover, neither the applicants nor the Government claimed that there was any statutory basis at the material time for the sale to a private individual of property that had been confiscated or nationalised *de facto*.

48. In the present case, the Court notes that the action for recovery of possession lodged by the applicants in the domestic courts was founded on the Civil Code and its purpose was to obtain a ruling that the State had no statutory title to the property. It is accordingly of the view that the applicants could legitimately consider that their property did not fall within the scope of Law no. 112/1995, the *lex specialis*, and that the property could not therefore be put up for sale by the State as lessor. That was precisely the reasoning adopted by the Arad authorities when they refused to sell most of the flats in the applicants' house (see paragraphs 8 and 9 above).

Accordingly, the Court finds certain inconsistencies between, on the one hand, the refusal of the Arad local authorities – on the basis of domestic law – to sell the flats making up the property until such time as the lawfulness of the nationalisation had been determined by the courts and, on the other, the same authorities' decision to allow an exception by selling flat no. 3, and the Court of Appeal's decision of 20 June 1999 in which it declared the sale lawful whilst finding unlawful the deprivation of property sustained in 1950.

49. However, in view of the margin of appreciation enjoyed by the domestic authorities, and more particularly by the courts, in the interpretation and application of domestic law, the Court considers that it is not necessary to give a categorical answer to the question whether the sale by the State of the applicants' property was "provided for by law", or in other words whether the domestic law in such matters satisfied the requirements of foreseeability and precision, and whether or not that law was construed arbitrarily in the present case.

The Court is accordingly prepared to accept that the interference in question was "provided for by law". Its role is nevertheless to verify whether the consequences of the interpretation and application of the domestic law, even when statutory requirements were complied with, were compatible with the principles of the Convention. From that perspective, the element of uncertainty in the law and the wide discretion that the law confers on the authorities will have to be taken into account when examining whether the impugned measure strikes a fair balance.

(b) Aim of the Interference

50. As regards the aim of the interference, the Government did not put forward any justification. However, the Court is prepared to accept that in the present case the interference pursued a legitimate aim, namely the protection of the rights of others – the "others" here being the purchasers who were acting in good faith – taking into account the principle of legal certainty.

(c) Proportionality of the Interference

51. Interference with the peaceful enjoyment of possessions must strike a fair balance between the demands of the general interest of the community and the requirements of the protection of the individual's fundamental rights (see, among other authorities, *Sporrong and Lönnroth*, cited above, p. 26, § 69). The concern to achieve this balance is reflected in the structure of Article 1 (of Protocol No. 1) as a whole, including therefore in the second sentence which is to be read in the light of the prin-ciple enunciated in the first sentence. In particular, there must be a reasonable relationship of proportionality between the means employed and the aim sought to be realised by any measure depriving a person of his or her possessions (see *Pressos Compania Naviera S.A. and Others v. Belgium*, judgment of 20 November 1995, Series A no. 332, p. 23, § 38).

52. Compensation terms under the relevant domestic legislation are material to the assessment whether the contested measure respects the requisite fair balance and, notably, whether it imposes a disproportionate burden on the applicants. In this connection, the Court has previously held that the taking of property without payment of an amount reasonably related to its value will normally constitute a disproportionate interference and that a total lack of compensation can be considered justifiable under Article 1 of Protocol No. 1 only in exceptional circumstances (see *The Holy Monasteries*, cited above, p. 35, § 71; *Former King of Greece and Others v. Greece* [GC], no. 25701/94, § 89, ECHR 2000-XII; and *Broniowski v. Poland* [GC], no. 31443/96, § 176, ECHR 2004-V).

53. In any event, the Court reiterates that whilst a radical reform of a country's political and economic system, or the state of the country's finances, may justify stringent limitations on compensation, such circumstances cannot be relied on to the detriment of the fundamental principles underlying the Convention, such as the principles of lawfulness and the authority and effectiveness of the judiciary (see *Broniowski*, cited above, §§ 175, 183 and 184). *A fortiori*, a total lack of compensation cannot be considered justifiable, even in exceptional circumstances, where there is a breach of the fundamental principles enshrined in the Convention.

54. In the present case, the Court notes that no provision of domestic law gives a clear and authoritative indication of the consequences for an individual's right of property when his or her possession is sold by the State to a third party acting in good faith.

More precisely, domestic law does not provide any clear or precise answer to the question whether, or how, an owner thus deprived of his possession can obtain compensation.

Whilst an action for recovery of possession, according to legal theory, appears to render the State liable to pay full compensation, where it has sold the property and is unable to return it (see paragraph 26 above), the principle of unjust enrichment releases a vendor who has been enriched by the sale from any obligation to pay compensation when the enrichment is the result of a legal transaction (in the present case, a sale).

In addition, an action for tortious liability can only be brought where there has been negligence on the part of the person who caused the damage (see paragraph 27 above). In the present case, the conclusion of the Court of Appeal that the sale had been lawful, since the parties had been acting in good faith, thus rules out, in theory, any liability of the State for negligence.

55. To sum up, in cases similar to that of the applicants it is doubtful whether at the material time domestic law would have provided for any compensation. Moreover, the Government did not argue that the applicants had such a possibility under domestic law or that there was any case-law to show that a means of obtaining compensation existed under domestic law as it was construed or applied.

56. The Government contended, however, that Law no. 10/2001 afforded the applicants a right of compensation.

In this connection, the Court observes firstly that, at the time Law no. 10/2001 entered into force on 8 February 2001, the applicants had already been deprived of their possession without compensation since June 1999, having also lodged their application with the Court in November 1999.

Secondly, the Court notes that section 1 of Law no. 10/2001 affords a right of restitution or compensation to persons who were unlawfully deprived of their property between 6 March 1945 and 22 December 1989 (see paragraph 23 above). However, the Law contains no specific provision on entitlement to compensation where the unlawfulness of such deprivation had been recognised by a court before the legislation's entry into force, or where the deprivation originated in the sale of property after 22 December 1989, as in the present case.

However, even assuming that Law no. 10/2001 constitutes a statutory basis for a compensation claim, as the Government have argued, the Court observes that section 21 provides that subsequent legislation is to lay down the conditions, amounts and procedures applicable to such claims (see paragraph 23 above). No such law on compensation has been passed to date. Consequently, the Court considers that Law no. 10/2001 does not enable the applicants to obtain compensation for the deprivation in question.

57. It remains to be determined whether a total lack of compensation could be justified in the circumstances of the case.

58. Firstly, no exceptional circumstance was relied upon by the Government to justify the total lack of compensation.

Secondly, the State sold the property despite the fact that an action brought by the applicants, claiming to be the victims of an unlawful nationalisation, was pending against it and that it had recently refused to sell the other flats in the same building. In the Court's view, such an attitude on the part of the State cannot be explained in terms of any legitimate public interest, be it political, social or financial, or by the interests of the community at large. Not only did that attitude give rise to discrimination between the various tenants who wished to acquire their respective flats, it was also capable of undermining the effectiveness of the court which the applicants had requested to protect the title they claimed to have to the property in question.

59. Consequently, in view of the fact that the deprivation in question infringed the fundamental principles of non-discrimination and the rule of law which underlie the Convention, the total lack of compensation caused the applicants to bear a disproportionate and excessive burden in breach of their right to the peaceful enjoyment of their possessions, as guaranteed by Article 1 of Protocol No. 1.

Accordingly, there has been a violation of that Article in the present case.

[. . .]

4.23. *Xenides-Arestis v. Turkey* (2006)

[. . .]

THE FACTS

9. The applicant, Mrs Myra Xenides-Arestis, is a Cypriot national of Greek-Cypriot origin, who was born in 1945 and lives in Nicosia.

10. The applicant owns property in the area of Ayios Memnon (Esperidon Street), in the fenced-up area of Famagusta, that she acquired by way of a gift from her mother. In particular, she owns half a share in a plot of land (plot no. 142, sheet/plan 33/29) with buildings thereon, consisting of one shop, one flat and three houses. One of the houses was her home, where she lived with her husband and children, whereas the rest of the property was used by members of the family and/or rented out to third parties. Furthermore, the applicant partly owns a plot of land (plot no. 158, sheet/plan 33/29) with an orchard (her share being equivalent to 5/48). This was registered in her name on 31 January 1984. The rest of the property is owned by other members of her family.

11. In August 1974 she was forced by the Turkish military forces to leave Famagusta with her family and abandon their home, property and possessions. Since then she has been prevented from having access to, using and enjoying her home and property, which are under the occupation and the control of the Turkish military forces. According to the applicant, only the Turkish military forces have access to the fenced-up area of Famagusta.

12. On 23 April 2003 new measures were adopted by the authorities of the "Turkish Republic of Northern Cyprus" ("TRNC") regarding crossings from northern to southern Cyprus and vice versa through specified checkpoints. On 30 June 2003 the "Parliament of the TRNC" enacted "Law no. 49/2003" on compensation for immovable properties located within the boundaries of the "TRNC", which entered into force on the same day. On 30 July 2003, under Article 11 of this "Law", an "Immovable Property, Determination, Evaluation and Compensation Commission" was established in the "TRNC". The rules of the commission were published in the "TRNC Official Gazette" on 15 August 2003 and the commission was constituted by a decision of the "TRNC Council of Ministers" published in the aforementioned gazette on 18 August 2003.

13. On 24 April 2004 two separate referendums were held simultaneously in Cyprus on the Foundation Agreement–Settlement Plan ("Annan Plan") which had been finalised on 31 March 2004. Since the plan was approved in the Turkish-Cypriot referendum but not in the Greek-Cypriot referendum, the Foundation Agreement did not enter into force.

[. . .]

II. Alleged Violation of Article 8 of the Convention

16. The applicant complained of an unjustified interference with the right to respect for her home, in violation of Article 8 of the Convention, which reads as follows:

"1. Everyone has the right to respect for his private and family life, his home and his correspondence.

2. There shall be no interference by a public authority with the exercise of this right except such as is in accordance with the law and is necessary in a democratic society in the interests of national security, public safety or the economic well-being of the country, for the prevention of disorder or crime, for the protection of health or morals, or for the protection of the rights and freedoms of others."

4. The Parties' Submissions

(a) The Applicant

17. The applicant relied on the findings of the Court in its judgments in the cases of *Loizidou v. Turkey* ((preliminary objections), judgment of 23 March 1995, Series A no. 310), *Loizidou v. Turkey* ((merits), judgment of 18 December 1996, *Reports of Judgments and Decisions* 1996-VI), *Cyprus v. Turkey* ([GC], no. 25781/94, ECHR 2001-IV), *Demades v. Turkey* (no. 16219/90, § 46, 31 July 2003), and *Eugenia Michaelidou Developments Ltd and Michael Tymvios v. Turkey* (no. 16163/90, § 31, 31 July 2003). Furthermore, in her earlier observations on the admissibility of the application, she had distinguished her case from that of *Loizidou v. Turkey* (merits, cited above) in so far as Article 8 of the Convention was concerned, since her complaint related to an interference with her right to respect for the home in which she lived with her husband and children and of which she was the owner. This was irrespective of whether the area in which her home was situated was the same as that where she grew up and her family had its roots.

(b) The Government

18. The Government did not make any submissions under this head on their observations on the

merits of the case. In their earlier observations on the admissibility of the application, however, the Government had made limited submissions under this head. In particular, they disputed the applicant's complaint under Article 8 of the Convention, on the basis that the notion of "home" in Article 8 could not be interpreted to cover an area of the State where one had grown up and where the family had its roots but where one no longer lived (*Loizidou* (merits), cited above, p. 2238, § 66).

5. The Court's Assessment

19. At the outset, the Court observes that the present case differs from the *Loizidou* case (merits, cited above) since, unlike Mrs Loizidou, the applicant actually had her home in Famagusta.

20. Further, the Court notes that since 1974 the applicant has been unable to gain access to, use and enjoy her home. In connection with this the Court observes that, in its judgment in the case of *Cyprus v. Turkey* (cited above, §§ 172–175), it concluded that the complete denial of the right of Greek-Cypriot displaced persons to respect for their homes in northern Cyprus since 1974 constituted a continuing violation of Article 8 of the Convention. The Court reasoned as follows:

"172. The Court observes that the official policy of the 'TRNC' authorities to deny the right of the displaced persons to return to their homes is reinforced by the very tight restrictions operated by the same authorities on visits to the north by Greek Cypriots living in the south. Accordingly, not only are displaced persons unable to apply to the authorities to reoccupy the homes which they left behind, they are physically prevented from even visiting them.

173. The Court further notes that the situation impugned by the applicant Government has obtained since the events of 1974 in northern Cyprus. It would appear that it has never been reflected in 'legislation' and is enforced as a matter of policy in furtherance of a bi-zonal arrangement designed, it is claimed, to minimise the risk of conflict which the intermingling of the Greek and Turkish-Cypriot communities in the north might engender. That bi-zonal arrangement is being pursued within the framework of the inter-communal talks sponsored by the United Nations Secretary-General . . .

174. The Court would make the following observations in this connection: firstly, the complete denial of the right of displaced persons to respect for their homes has no basis in law within the meaning of Article 8 § 2 of the Convention . . . ; secondly, the inter-communal talks cannot be invoked in order to legitimate a violation of the Convention; thirdly, the violation at issue has endured as a matter of policy since 1974 and must be considered continuing.

175. In view of these considerations, the Court concludes that there has been a continuing violation of Article 8 of the Convention by reason of the refusal to allow the return of any Greek-Cypriot displaced persons to their homes in northern Cyprus."

21. In this connection the Court also reiterates its findings in the case of *Demades v. Turkey* (cited above, §§ 29–37).

22. The Court sees no reason in the instant case to depart from the above reasoning and findings. Accordingly, it concludes that there has been a continuing violation of Article 8 of the Convention by reason of the complete denial of the right of the applicant to respect for her home.

III. Alleged Violation of Article 1 of Protocol No. 1

23. The applicant contended that the continuous denial of access to her property in northern Cyprus and the ensuing loss of all control over it and all possibilities to use and enjoy it constituted a violation of Article 1 of Protocol No. 1, which reads as follows:

"Every natural or legal person is entitled to the peaceful enjoyment of his possessions. No one shall be deprived of his possessions except in the public interest and subject to the conditions provided for by law and by the general principles of international law.

The preceding provisions shall not, however, in any way impair the right of a State to enforce such laws as it deems necessary to control the use of property in accordance with the general interest or to secure the payment of taxes or other contributions or penalties."

6. The Parties' Submissions

(a) The Applicant

24. The applicant relied on the Court's judgments in the cases of *Loizidou* (preliminary objections, cited above), *Loizidou* (merits, cited above), *Cyprus v. Turkey* (cited above), *Demades* (cited above, § 46) and *Eugenia Michaelidou Developments Ltd and Michael Tymvios* (cited above, § 31).

(b) The Government

25. The Government limited their submissions under this head to contesting the applicant's ownership of the property in question (see paragraph 14 above) and the status of Famagusta (Varosha), where the properties in question were situated. With regard to the latter, the Government stated that the Greek-Cypriot authorities had been responsible for the evacuation of Varosha and for rejecting proposals for and attempts at resettlement of the area. In this connection, they referred to the inter-communal talks concerning this area, various proposals and excerpts of statements made in that context. They submitted that it was not possible for Turkey unilaterally to open this area for settlement on an individual basis without agreed administrative arrangements and the setting up of funds for development and infrastructural projects designed to assist in the process of readjustment. The Government also considered that the Court at this stage in the proceedings and in the absence of a comprehensive and final settlement of the property issue should not proceed to determine the title over the properties in question.

26. In their earlier observations on the admissibility of the application, the Government had contended that the applicant's complaint under Article 1 of Protocol No. 1 related in essence to freedom of movement, guaranteed under Article 2 of Protocol No. 4, which Turkey had not ratified. They therefore argued that the right to peaceful enjoyment of property and possessions did not include, as a corollary, the right to freedom of movement.

7. The Court's Assessment

27. At the outset, the Court observes that in its admissibility decision in the present case, in line with the cases of *Loizidou* (preliminary objections), *Loizidou* (merits) and *Cyprus v. Turkey* (all cited above), it dismissed the Government's objections as to Turkey's alleged lack of jurisdiction

and responsibility for the acts in respect of which complaint was made. It further rejected the Government's arguments concerning both freedom of movement and the effect which the Court's consideration of the applicant's claims could have on the inter-communal talks. It noted that no change had occurred since its adoption of the judgments in the above-mentioned cases which could justify a departure from its conclusions as to Turkey's jurisdiction. In this connection, the Court also pointed out, *inter alia*, that the Government continued to exercise overall military control over northern Cyprus and that the fact that the Greek Cypriots had rejected the Annan Plan did not have the legal consequence of bringing to an end the continuing violation of the displaced persons' rights.

28. The Court further reiterates that in accordance with its findings in the cases of *Loizidou* (preliminary objections), *Loizidou* (merits) and *Cyprus v. Turkey* (all cited above) the applicant must still be regarded as the legal owner of her land. In this connection it notes that it has dismissed the Government's arguments concerning the applicant's title to the relevant properties.

29. In the *Loizidou* case ((merits), cited above, pp. 2237–38, §§ 63–64) the Court reasoned as follows:

> "63. . . . as a consequence of the fact that the applicant has been refused access to the land since 1974, she has effectively lost all control over, as well as all possibilities to use and enjoy her property. The continuous denial of access must therefore be regarded as an interference with her rights under Article 1 of Protocol No. 1. Such an interference cannot, in the exceptional circumstances of the present case to which the applicant and the Cypriot Government have referred . . . , be regarded as either a deprivation of property or a control of use within the meaning of the first and second paragraphs of Article 1 of Protocol No. 1. However, it clearly falls within the meaning of the first sentence of that provision as an interference with the peaceful enjoyment of possessions. In this respect the Court observes that hindrance can amount to a violation of the Convention just like a legal impediment. . . .
>
> 64. Apart from a passing reference to the doctrine of necessity as a justification for the acts of the 'TRNC' and to the fact that property rights were the subject of inter-communal talks, the Turkish Government

have not sought to make submissions justifying the above interference with the applicant's property rights which is imputable to
Turkey.

It has not, however, been explained how
the need to rehouse displaced Turkish Cypriot
refugees in the years following the Turkish
intervention in the island in 1974 could justify
the complete negation of the applicant's property rights in the form of a total and continuous
denial of access and a purported expropriation
without compensation.

Nor can the fact that property rights were the
subject of intercommunal talks involving both
communities in Cyprus provide a justification
for this situation under the Convention.

In such circumstances, the Court concludes
that there has been and continues to be a
breach of Article 1 of Protocol No. 1."

30. In the case of *Cyprus v. Turkey* (cited above) the
Court confirmed the above conclusions:

"187. The Court is persuaded that both its reasoning and its conclusion in *Loizidou* (merits) apply with equal force to displaced Greek
Cypriots who, like Mrs Loizidou, are unable
to have access to their property in northern
Cyprus by reason of the restrictions placed
by the 'TRNC' authorities on their physical
access to that property. The continuing and
total denial of access to their property is a
clear interference with the right of the displaced Greek Cypriots to the peaceful enjoyment of possessions within the meaning of
the first sentence of Article 1 of Protocol No.
1. It further notes that, as regards the purported expropriation, no compensation has
been paid to the displaced persons in respect of
the interferences which they have suffered and
continue to suffer in respect of their property
rights.

[. . .]

189. For the above reasons, the Court concludes that there has been a continuing violation of Article 1 of Protocol No. 1 by virtue of
the fact that Greek-Cypriot owners of property
in northern Cyprus are being denied access to
and control, use and enjoyment of their property as well as any compensation for the interference with their property rights."

31. The Court in this connection reiterates its findings in the cases of *Demades* (cited above, §§ 43–46)
and *Eugenia Michaelidou Developments Ltd and
Michael Tymvios* (cited above, §§ 28–31).

32. In the light of the above the Court sees no reason
in the instant case to depart from the conclusions
which it reached in the above cases. Accordingly, it
concludes that there has been and continues to be
a violation of Article 1 of Protocol No. 1 by virtue of
the fact that the applicant is denied access to and
control, use and enjoyment of her property and any
compensation for the interference with her property rights.

IV. Alleged Violation of Article 14 of the Convention Taken in Conjunction with Article 8 of the Convention and Article 1 of Protocol No. 1

33. The applicant maintained that she was the victim of discrimination in relation to the enjoyment
of her rights in respect of her home and property,
contrary to Article 14 of the Convention, which
reads as follows:

"The enjoyment of the rights and freedoms
set forth in the Convention shall be secured
without discrimination on any ground such as
sex, race, colour, language, religion, political or
other opinion, national or social origin, association with a national minority, property, birth
or other status."

34. The Government did not make any submissions under this head.

35. The Court notes that in the above-mentioned
Cyprus v. Turkey case it found that, in the circumstances of that case, the Cypriot Government's
complaints under Article 14 amounted in effect to
the same complaints, albeit seen from a different
angle, as those considered in relation to Article 8
of the Convention and Article 1 of Protocol No. 1.
Since it had found violations of those provisions,
it considered that it was not necessary in that case
to examine whether there had been a violation of
Article 14 taken in conjunction with Article 8 of the
Convention and Article 1 of Protocol No. 1 by virtue
of the alleged discriminatory treatment of Greek
Cypriots not residing in northern Cyprus as regards
their rights to the peaceful enjoyment of their possessions (see *Cyprus v. Turkey*, cited above, § 199).

36. The Court sees no reason in this case to depart from that approach. Bearing in mind its conclusion on the complaints under Article 8 of the Convention and Article 1 of Protocol No. 1, it finds that it is not necessary to carry out a separate examination of the complaint under Article 14 in conjunction with these provisions.

[. . .]

4.24. *Blečić v. Croatia* (2006)

[. . .]

A. THE CIRCUMSTANCES OF THE CASE

7. The applicant was born in 1926 and lives in Zadar, Croatia.

8. In 1953 the applicant, together with her husband, acquired a specially protected tenancy (*stanarsko pravo*) of a flat in Zadar. After her husband's death in 1989 the applicant became the sole holder of the specially protected tenancy.

9. On 3 June 1991, Parliament enacted the Specially Protected Tenancies (Sale to Occupier) Act (*Zakon o prodaji stanova na kojima postoji stanarsko pravo*), which regulates the sale of publicly-owned flats previously let under specially protected tenancy.

10. On 26 July 1991 the applicant went to visit her daughter who lived in Rome. She intended to stay with her daughter for the summer. She locked the flat in Zadar and left all the furniture and personal belongings in it. She asked a neighbour to pay the bills in her absence and to take care of the flat. However, by the end of August 1991, the armed conflict escalated in Dalmatia, resulting in severe travel difficulties in that area, including the town of Zadar.

11. In October 1991 the Croatian authorities stopped paying the applicant's pension. The payments were resumed in April 1994. The applicant also lost the right to medical insurance. In these circumstances, the applicant decided to remain in Rome.

12. From 15 September 1991 the town of Zadar was exposed to constant shelling and the supply of electricity and water was disrupted for over one hundred days.

13. In November 1991 a certain M.F., with his wife and two children, broke into the applicant's flat in Zadar.

14. On 12 February 1992 the Zadar Municipality (*Općina Zadar*) brought a civil action against the applicant before the Zadar Municipal Court (*Općinski sud u Zadru*) for termination of her specially protected tenancy on the flat in question. The Municipality claimed that the applicant had been absent from the flat for more than six months without justified reason.

15. In her submissions to the court, the applicant explained that she had been forced to stay with her daughter in Rome from July 1991 until May 1992. She had not been able to return to Zadar since she had no means of subsistence and no medical insurance and was in poor health. Furthermore, during her stay in Rome, she had learned from the neighbour that M.F. had broken into her flat with his family. When she had enquired about her flat and her possessions in the flat, M.F. had threatened her over the telephone.

16. On 9 October 1992 the Zadar Municipal Court terminated the applicant's specially protected tenancy. The court established that the applicant had left Zadar on 26 July 1991 and had not returned until 15 May 1992. It stated that in the relevant period no order had been issued to the citizens of Zadar to evacuate the town owing to the escalation of the armed conflict but that it had been the personal decision of every citizen whether to leave the town or to stay. On that basis the court found that the applicant's absence was not justified by the war in Croatia.

17. Furthermore, the court did not accept the applicant's explanation that she had fallen ill during her stay in Rome and was not able to travel. It was established that the applicant had suffered from spinal arthrosclerosis and diffuse osteoporosis for a long time, which had not affected her ability to travel. Even though her left shoulder had been dislocated on 25 March 1992, she had been able to travel following the immobilisation of the injured joint. Furthermore, by 25 March 1992 she had already been absent from the flat for a period of more than six months.

18. The applicant's further explanation that she had stopped receiving her pension in October 1991 and thus had been left without any means of subsistence was not accepted by the court as a justified reason for not returning to Zadar. It took the view that the applicant's daughter could have sent her money. Therefore, the court concluded that the applicant's reasons for not having lived in the flat were not justified.

19. Following an appeal by the applicant against the judgment, it was quashed by the Zadar County Court (*Županijski sud u Zadru*) on 10 March 1993. The County Court found that the court of first instance had not taken into careful consideration the applicant's personal circumstances, namely her age and poor health, the fact that she had lost her pension and the fact that she had lived alone in Zadar without any close relatives. Furthermore, the applicant's decision to prolong her stay in Rome should have been carefully assessed against the background of objective circumstances, namely that Zadar had been exposed to daily shelling and had not had a regular supply of water or electricity in the material period, and that third persons had occupied the applicant's flat. The case was remitted to the first-instance court.

20. In the resumed proceedings, on 18 January 1994 the Zadar Municipal Court ruled again in favour of the municipality and terminated the applicant's specially protected tenancy. It observed that she had been absent from the flat for over six months without justified reason and repeated in substance the findings of the judgment of 9 October 1992.

21. The applicant appealed. On 19 October 1994 the County Court reversed the first-instance judgment and dismissed the municipality's claim. It found that the escalation of war and the applicant's personal circumstances, as described above (see paragraphs 11–13), justified her absence from the flat.

22. On 10 April 1995 the Zadar Municipality filed a request for revision on points of law (*revizija*) with the Supreme Court (*Vrhovni sud Republike Hrvatske*).

23. On 15 February 1996 the Supreme Court accepted the request for revision and reversed the County Court's judgment. It found that the reasons submitted by the applicant for her absence from the flat were not justified.

24. The relevant part of the Supreme Court's judgment reads as follows:

"In the period of the aggression against Croatia, living conditions were the same for all citizens of Zadar and, as rightly submitted by the plaintiff, it is neither possible nor legitimate to separate the defendant's case from the context of that aggression. Holding the contrary would mean assessing her case in a manner isolated from all the circumstances which marked that time and determined the conduct of each individual.

Contrary to the appellate court's opinion, this court, assessing in that context the defendant's decision not to return to Zadar during the aggression but to stay in Italy, considers the non-use of the flat unjustified. The factual findings made in the case reveal that, in view of her health condition and the available travel connections, the defendant was able to come to Zadar; her health would not have deteriorated because of her stay in Zadar; and she could have taken care of herself. The assumption that she would have had to make a considerable mental and physical effort in order to provide for her basic living needs (all the residents of Zadar who remained in the town, from the youngest to the oldest, were exposed to the same living conditions) does not justify her failure to return to Zadar and, accordingly, does not constitute a justified reason for the non-use of the flat."

25. On 8 November 1996 the applicant filed a constitutional complaint with the Constitutional Court (*Ustavni sud Republike Hrvatske*). She claimed that her rights to respect for her home and property had been violated and that she had been deprived of a fair trial.

26. On 8 November 1999 the Constitutional Court dismissed the applicant's complaint. It found that the Supreme Court had correctly applied the relevant legal provisions to the factual background established by the lower courts when holding that the applicant's absence from the flat for more than six months had been unjustified. The Constitutional Court concluded that the applicant's constitutional rights had not been violated.

[. . .]

I. ALLEGED VIOLATION OF ARTICLE 8 OF THE CONVENTION

33. The applicant complained that the Croatian courts' decisions to terminate her specially protected tenancy had amounted to a violation of her right to respect for her home, guaranteed under Article 8 of the Convention, which, in its relevant part, provides:

> "1. Everyone has the right to respect for . . . his home . . .
>
> 2. There shall be no interference by a public authority with the exercise of this right except such as is in accordance with the law and is necessary in a democratic society in the interests of . . . the economic well-being of the country, . . . or for the protection of the rights and freedoms of others."

A. The Parties' Submissions

1. The Government

34. The Government argued that the applicant, after the death of her husband in 1989, had not lived in the flat in Zadar continuously, but had spent more than five months annually visiting her daughter in Rome. In July 1991 the applicant had abandoned the flat completely and had not returned to Zadar until May 1992. Although she had meanwhile learnt that M.F. had occupied her flat in her absence, she had failed to notify the owner of the flat or to institute any proceedings to have him evicted. She had also failed to notify the owner of the fact that she had been in Rome and that she had not been able to return to Zadar owing to her illness and the war. In those circumstances, it could not be argued that the flat in question was the applicant's home for the purposes of Article 8 of the Convention.

35. The Government stated further that there had been no interference with the applicant's right to respect for her home since she had not been evicted; rather, she had voluntarily abandoned the flat.

36. Moreover, the Government submitted that, even if the Court were to find that there had been

interference, it had been prescribed by law, namely section 99 of the Housing Act.

37. In the Government's opinion, there had existed a legitimate aim for the termination of the applicant's specially protected tenancy. They explained that specially protected tenancies were mostly granted by various companies or municipalities to meet housing needs. The flats in question remained in the ownership of these companies or municipalities. Persons holding a specially protected tenancy paid a very low rent and were protected from arbitrary eviction. However, the purpose of such protected tenancies being to provide housing for workers, the owners were entitled to seek the termination of a tenancy before a court whenever the holder of a tenancy ceased to occupy the flat for a period of more than six months.

38. In the instant case, the applicant was not the owner of the flat but had only obtained a specially protected tenancy. By terminating the applicant's tenancy, the domestic authorities had pursued the legitimate aims of preserving the economic well-being of the country and protecting of the rights of others. By abandoning the flat, the applicant had shown that she no longer needed it, which had allowed the authorities to grant the flat to another person in need.

39. As to the proportionality of the measure in question, the Government emphasised that the domestic courts had assessed all the relevant facts of the applicant's case, namely her personal circumstances such as her health, age and reasons for leaving the flat, and the general living conditions in Zadar at the relevant time. The courts had found that, in spite of the attacks on Zadar, there had been no immediate need to leave the city at any time and observed that a number of displaced persons from the surrounding area had actually moved into the town. In sum, the termination of the applicant's tenancy could not be considered arbitrary.

2. The Applicant

40. The applicant stressed that she had always considered her flat in Zadar her home, to which she intended to return. She argued that she had not abandoned the flat but had only been visiting her daughter. During her absence, the war in Croatia had escalated and she had not been able to return. Afterwards she had fallen ill and had had to stay

in Rome. When she had returned in May 1992, she had not been able to enter the flat, which had been occupied by M.F., and had therefore been forced to go back to Rome. Her intention to return to her home in Zadar was supported by the fact that she had left all the furniture and her personal belongings there.

41. The applicant maintained that the courts' termination of her specially protected tenancy had amounted to a violation of her right to respect for her home.

42. Furthermore, the applicant asserted that there had been no need to terminate her tenancy. That measure, which had purportedly pursued the legitimate aim of providing a displaced person with accommodation, had not been justified, as this goal could have been achieved by allocating the flat to another person temporarily. The authorities had, by depriving her of the specially protected tenancy, left her with no home or place to live, and this situation had become permanent. Therefore, the measure had placed an excessive burden on her and had been disproportionate to the legitimate aim pursued.

43. The applicant also submitted the Norwegian Refugee Council's analysis of 586 individual cases of termination of specially protected tenancies in court proceedings in Croatia.

3. The Third Party

44. The OSCE argued that the applicant's specially protected tenancy could be appropriately viewed only in the overall context of actions by the judiciary and legislature that had resulted in the mass termination of such tenancies during and after the homeland war in Croatia. It submitted that, from 1991 onwards, 23,700 proceedings for the termination of specially protected tenancies had been initiated.

45. Most of these proceedings had been instituted against persons of Serbian origin, which had resulted in a significant decline in the minority population in Croatia. In the OSCE's view, the termination of specially protected tenancies had had a strong negative effect on minority return.

46. The OSCE further submitted a detailed analysis of the legal status accorded to specially protected tenancies in Bosnia and Herzegovina. They maintained that specially protected tenancies in the for-

mer Yugoslavia had constituted a strong form of tenure, which had allowed their holders to permanently use publicly-owned flats. Such flats had been generally built and disposed of by a State-owned enterprise or a public body entitled to allocate specially protected tenancies to persons they had employed. In order to provide the means for such a system, all citizens had paid an obligatory, income-scaled contribution to housing construction funds. Once obtained, a specially protected tenancy could be terminated only in accordance with the law and in court proceedings.

47. While providing displaced persons with housing could be regarded as a legitimate aim, the permanent termination of specially protected tenancy rights under wartime conditions could represent an excessive burden on the tenants. The need to provide housing for refugees and displaced persons should ultimately be balanced against the interests of the tenancy right-holders. The Croatian authorities could have declared their flats temporarily abandoned, allocating them to displaced persons for temporary use until the end of hostilities, and thereby easing the burden on the original holders of the tenancies.

The OSCE observed that the Court had examined certain situations involving displaced persons in, for example, the case of *Loizidou v. Turkey* (judgment of 18 December 1996, *Reports of Judgments and Decisions* 1996-VI), where it had found a violation of Article 1 of Protocol No. 1 in that the Turkish Government had not explained how the legitimate aim of providing housing to Turkish Cypriot refugees could justify the complete negation of the applicant's property rights in the form of total and continuous denial of access and a purported expropriation without compensation.

48. Addressing an argument of the domestic courts – according to which all Zadar residents were exposed to the same living conditions – the OSCE pointed out that while it was true that the entire population of areas involved in conflict suffered many of the same difficulties, such as shelling and loss of water and electricity, individuals of minority ethnicity additionally faced harassment, threats, and in many cases, forcible eviction from their homes and property. The conditions under which these persons left were illustrated by the fact that many had left their personal belongings in their flats. Under these circumstances, the OSCE found

it difficult to view absence from flats owing to war activities as voluntary in nature.

4. The Government's Comments on the Third-Party Intervention

49. The Government challenged in general the relevance of the third party's submissions, arguing that the present case did not raise any question regarding the return of refugees or displaced persons or minority return, as the applicant had never been a refugee or displaced person. They also submitted an overview of achievements in the process of the return of refugees and displaced persons in the Republic of Croatia, arguing that, despite many difficulties, this should be deemed successful.

50. As to the part of the third-party intervention that related to the legal nature of the specially protected tenancy, the Government, acknowledging similarity to a certain extent, pointed out the differences in the legal regulation of specially protected tenancies in Croatia and in Bosnia and Herzegovina. They emphasised that the third-party intervention on this point primarily dealt with the situation in Bosnia and Herzegovina and, therefore, was not directly relevant to the situation in Croatia. Following the dissolution of the former Yugoslavia, Croatia had become an independent state, which enacted its own legislation, and the development of its legal order had since been different. The mere fact that the problems relating to the war were similar did not mean that they necessarily required identical legal solutions in two different States. Interferences with the rights protected by the Convention had to be considered independently with regard to each Contracting State's legal order and social and political situation, and regard being had to its margin of appreciation.

B. The Court's Assessment

1. Whether the Flat in Question Was the Applicant's Home within the Meaning of Article 8 of the Convention

51. The Court notes that the applicant continuously lived in her flat in Zadar from 1953 until 26 July 1991, when she departed for Rome. On her departure, the applicant left all the furniture in the flat as well as her personal belongings. She did not rent the flat to any other person; she locked it and asked her neighbour to take care of it during her absence.

52. In these circumstances, the Court is satisfied that the applicant did not intend to abandon the flat; rather, she made appropriate arrangements for its maintenance, with a view to her return. The flat in question can therefore reasonably be regarded as her home, at the material time, for the purposes of Article 8 of the Convention.

2. Whether There Was Any Interference by a Public Authority with the Exercise of the Applicant's Right to Respect for Her Home

53. The Court notes that the Zadar Municipality sought before the Zadar Municipal Court the termination of the applicant's specially protected tenancy of the flat in question. The court allowed the claim and the first-instance judgment was upheld by the higher courts, resulting in the applicant having no home in Croatia.

54. Having established that the flat in question was the applicant's home for the purposes of Article 8 of the Convention, the Court finds that the termination of the applicant's specially protected tenancy by the domestic courts constituted an interference with her right to respect for her home.

3. Whether the Interference Was Justified

55. In order to determine whether the interference was justified under paragraph 2 of Article 8, the Court must examine in turn whether it was "in accordance with the law", whether it had an aim that was legitimate under that paragraph and whether it was "necessary in a democratic society" for the aforesaid aim (see *Gillow v. the United Kingdom*, judgment of 24 November 1986, Series A no. 124-C, p. 20, § 48).

a. In Accordance with the Law

56. It has not been disputed that the interference, which was based on section 99(1) of the Housing Act, was "in accordance with the law". The Court has no reason to hold otherwise.

b. Legitimate Aim

57. The Court notes that, according to the Government, specially protected tenancies were established on publicly-owned flats in the former Yugoslavia in order to satisfy the housing needs of citizens. The policy governing these tenancies secured quite favourable terms for the tenants, while requiring them actually to live in those flats.

Section 99(1) of the Housing Act was aimed at the prevention of any abuse of the tenancy right by allowing for its termination in cases where persons holding the right did not observe its purpose – in other words, did not occupy the flat granted to them. This has not been disputed by the applicant.

58. The Court considers that the legislation applied in the applicant's case pursued a legitimate aim, namely, the satisfaction of the housing needs of citizens, and that it was thus intended to promote the economic well-being of the country and the protection of the rights of others. The Court sees no reason to assume that it pursued any other purpose. It is not in dispute that, in pursuit of those aims, the Croatian legislature was entitled, by enacting section 99 of the Housing Act, to prescribe the termination of specially protected tenancies held by individuals who no longer lived in the publicly-owned flats allocated to them and the subsequent redistribution of such flats to those in need. The only point at issue is whether, in applying this provision in the applicant's case, the Croatian courts infringed her right to respect for her home in a disproportionate manner.

c. *Necessary in a Democratic Society*

59. In determining whether the impugned measure was "necessary in a democratic society", the Court has to consider whether, in the light of the case as a whole, the reasons adduced to justify this measure were relevant and sufficient for the purposes of paragraph 2 of Article 8 of the Convention (see *Hoppe v. Germany*, no. 28422/95, § 48, 5 December 2002). The notion of necessity implies a pressing social need; in particular, the measure employed must be proportionate to the legitimate aim pursued. In addition, the scope of the margin of appreciation enjoyed by the national authorities will depend not only on the nature of the aim of the restriction but also on the nature of the right involved.

60. In the instant case, satisfying housing needs must be balanced against the applicant's right to respect for her home, a right which is pertinent to her own personal security and well-being. The importance of such a right to the individual must be taken into account in determining the scope of the margin of appreciation allowed to the Government (see *Gillow v. the United Kingdom*, cited above, p. 22, § 55).

61. The Court also reiterates that, in accordance with Article 19 of the Convention, its only task is to ensure the observance of the obligations undertaken by the Parties to the Convention. In particular, it is not competent to deal with an application alleging that errors of law or fact have been committed by domestic courts, except where it considers that such errors might have involved a possible violation of any of the rights and freedoms set out in the Convention (see *Kaneva v. Bulgaria*, no. 26530/95, Commission decision of 27 February 1997). It follows that the Court's task is not to substitute itself for the domestic authorities in the exercise of their responsibilities regarding termination of the specially protected tenancies in Croatia, but rather to review, in the light of the Convention, the decisions taken by those authorities in the exercise of their margin of appreciation (see, *mutatis mutandis, Hokkanen v. Finland*, judgment of 23 September 1994, Series A no. 299-A, p. 20, § 55, and *Elsholz v. Germany*, no. 25735/94, ECHR 2000-VIII, p. 363, § 48).

62. Turning to the present case, there remains the question whether the manner in which the domestic courts exercised their discretion in the applicant's case corresponded to a pressing social need and, in particular, was proportionate to the legitimate aim pursued.

63. The Court notes that both the Municipal Court and the Supreme Court held that, in the circumstances of the case, there had been no justified reason for the applicant not to return to Zadar. Each of those courts reached this conclusion after having duly considered the factual and legal questions arising in the dispute and conducted a careful analysis of the arguments put forward by the applicant. The courts gave detailed reasons for their decisions.

In particular, both courts took account of the applicant's age and health problems and were satisfied that her physical condition would have enabled her to travel. Furthermore, they took the view that the escalation of the armed conflict could not be seen as a justified reason for leaving Zadar, since it affected every citizen of the town equally. Their conclusions were in evident compliance with the previously established case-law of the Supreme Court on that matter (see paragraphs 30–31 above).

The Court notes at this juncture that the final decision in the case, directly decisive for the applicant's rights under the Convention, was given by the Constitutional Court on 8 November 1999. That court deferred to the Supreme Court's findings, when ruling that the latter's decision did not constitute a violation of the applicant's constitutional rights.

64. The Court accepts that where State authorities reconcile the competing interests of different groups in society, they must inevitably draw a line marking where a particular interest prevails and another one yields, without knowing precisely its ideal location. Making a reasonable assessment as to where the line is most properly drawn, especially if that assessment involves balancing conflicting interests and allocating scarce resources on this basis, falls within the State's margin of appreciation.

65. State intervention in socio-economic matters such as housing is often necessary in securing social justice and public benefit. In this area, the margin of appreciation available to the State in implementing social and economic policies is necessarily a wide one. The domestic authorities' judgment as to what is necessary to achieve the objectives of those policies should be respected unless that judgment is manifestly without reasonable foundation. Although this principle was originally set forth in the context of complaints under Article 1 of Protocol No. 1 – in, for example, *James and Others v. the United Kingdom*, judgment of 21 February 1986, Series A no. 98, p. 32, § 46; and *Mellacher and Others v. Austria*, judgment of 19 December 1989, Series A no. 169, p. 25, § 45 – the Court, bearing in mind that the Convention and its Protocols must be interpreted as a whole, considers that the State enjoys an equally wide margin of appreciation as regards respect for the home in circumstances such as those prevailing in the present case, in the context of Article 8. Thus, the Court will accept the judgment of the domestic authorities as to what is necessary in a democratic society unless that judgment is manifestly without reasonable foundation, that is, unless the measure employed is manifestly disproportionate to the legitimate aim pursued.

This margin is afforded both to the domestic legislature ("in accordance with the law") and to the bodies, judicial amongst others, that are called upon to interpret and apply the laws in force (see, *mutatis mutandis*, *Handyside v. the United Kingdom*, judgment of 7 December 1976, Series A no. 24, p. 22, § 48).

66. In the light of the foregoing, the Court is satisfied that the contested decisions were based on reasons which were not only relevant but also sufficient for the purposes of paragraph 2 of Article 8. It cannot be argued that the Croatian courts' decisions were arbitrary or unreasonable, or that the solution they reached in seeking a fair balance between the demands of the general interest of the community and the requirement of protecting the applicant's right to respect for her home was manifestly disproportionate to the legitimate aim pursued. The Court considers that, when terminating the applicant's specially protected tenancy, the national authorities acted within the margin of appreciation afforded to them in such matters.

67. Turning to the applicant's and the third party's suggestion (see paragraphs 42 and 47 above) that the national authorities imposed an excessive burden on the applicant when terminating her tenancy right, rather than merely allocating the flat temporarily to another person, the Court finds that this suggestion amounts to reading a test of strict necessity into Article 8, an interpretation which the Court does not find warranted in the circumstances. The availability of alternative solutions does not in itself render the termination of a tenancy unjustified; it constitutes one factor, among others, that is relevant for determining whether the means chosen may be regarded as reasonable and suited to achieving the legitimate aim being pursued. Provided the interference remained within these bounds – which, in view of its above considerations (see paragraph 66 above), the Court is satisfied that it did – it is not for the Court to say whether the measure complained of represented the best solution for dealing with the problem or whether the State's discretion should have been exercised in another way (see, *mutatis mutandis, James and Others v. the United Kingdom*, op. cit., p. 35, § 51).

68. Furthermore, whilst Article 8 of the Convention contains no explicit procedural requirements, the decision-making process involved in measures of interference must be fair and such as to ensure due respect of the interests safeguarded by Article 8. The Court must therefore determine whether, having regard to the circumstances of the case and notably the importance of the decisions to be taken, the applicant has been involved in the decision-making process, seen as a whole, to a degree sufficient to provide her with the requisite protection of her interests (see *W. v. the United*

Kingdom, judgment of 8 July 1987, Series A no. 121, p. 29, § 64; *Elsholz v. Germany*, cited above, § 52; and *T.P. and K.M. v. the United Kingdom*, no. 28945/95, § 72, ECHR 2001-V).

69. The Court notes that in the first-instance proceedings the applicant, assisted by counsel, had the opportunity to present her arguments both orally and in writing. Although in the appellate proceedings the County Court and the Supreme Court based their decisions on the first-instance case-file, the applicant was given the opportunity to put forward in writing any views which in her opinion were decisive for the outcome of the proceedings. Consequently, a hearing before the appellate courts was not necessary.

70. In these circumstances the Court is satisfied that the procedural requirements implicit in Article 8 of the Convention were complied with and that the applicant was involved in the decision-making process to a degree sufficient to provide her with the requisite protection of her interests.

71. Accordingly, there has been no violation of Article 8 of the Convention.

II. Alleged Violation of Article 1 of Protocol No. 1 to the Convention

72. The applicant also complained that the loss of her specially protected tenancy had amounted to a breach of her right to the peaceful enjoyment of her possession. Additionally, she argued that her property rights had been violated because she had been deprived of the possibility of buying the flat in question (see paragraph 32 above). She relied on Article 1 of Protocol No. 1, which reads as follows:

"Every natural or legal person is entitled to the peaceful enjoyment of his possessions. No one shall be deprived of his possessions except in the public interest and subject to the conditions provided for by law and by the general principles of international law.

The preceding provisions shall not, however, in any way impair the right of a State to enforce such laws as it deems necessary to control the use of property in accordance with the general interest or to secure the payment of taxes or other contributions or penalties."

73. The Court does not find it necessary to decide whether or not a specially protected tenancy constitutes property or a possession within the meaning of Article 1 of Protocol No. 1 for the following reasons.

74. Even assuming that the termination of the applicant's tenancy involved a right to property, the Court considers that the interference in question was neither an expropriation nor a measure to control the use of property. Therefore, it falls to be dealt with under the first sentence of the first paragraph of Article 1 of Protocol No. 1.

75. Any interference with a right of property, irrespective of the rule it falls under, can only be justified if it serves a legitimate public (or general) interest. The termination of the applicant's tenancy, as the Court has already held (see paragraphs 57–58 above), pursued a legitimate social-policy aim.

76. Furthermore, for the requirements of Article 1 of Protocol No. 1 to be satisfied, an interference with the individual's rights under this provision must strike a fair balance between the demands of the general interest of the community and the requirements of the protection of the individual's fundamental rights (see, among other authorities, *Sporrong and Lönnroth v. Sweden*, judgment of 23 September 1982, Series A no. 52, p. 26, § 69; *Scollo v. Italy*, judgment of 28 September 1995, Series A no. 315-C, p. 53, § 32).

77. In this connection, the Court refers to its considerations relating to the alleged infringement of the applicant's right to respect for her home (see paragraphs 63–71 above), which are also applicable to her right to the peaceful enjoyment of her possessions.

78. The Court accordingly concludes that the termination of the tenancy and the resultant loss of a possible opportunity to purchase the flat in question did not amount to a violation of Article 1 of Protocol No. 1.

[. . .]

PART FIVE

Useful Resources on Housing and Property Restitution

1. GENERAL RESOURCES

- Aldrich, G. H., "What Constitutes a Compensable Taking of Property? The Decision of the Iran–United States Claims Tribunal," in *American Journal of International Law*, 88(4): 585–610 (Oct. 1994).

- Allen, T., "The United Nations and the Homecoming of Displaced Populations," in *International Review of the Red Cross*, No. 301. Geneva: ICRC (1994).

- Amerasinghe, C. F., "Issues of Compensation for the Taking of Alien Property in the Light of Recent Cases and Practice," in *International and Comparative Law Quarterly*, Vol. 41, No. 1: 22 (Jan. 1992).

- Amnesty International (AI), *Who's Living in My House? Obstacles to the Safe Return of Refugees and Internally Displaced People*, Report No. EUR/ID. Amnesty International Publications (1997).

- Aursnes, I. S., and Foley, C., "Property Restitution in Practice: The Experience of the Norwegian Refugee Council," in *Returning Home: Housing and Property Restitution Rights for Refugees and Displaced Persons – Volume 2* (Scott Leckie, ed.). New York: Transnational Publishers (2007).

- Bagshaw, S., "Property Restitution for Internally Displaced Persons: Developments in the Normative Framework," in *Returning Home: Housing and Property Restitution Rights of Refugees and Displaced Persons – Volume 1* (Scott Leckie, ed.). New York: Transnational Publishers (2003).

- ———, "Property Restitution and the Development of a Normative Framework for the Internally Displaced," in *Refugee Survey Quarterly*, Vol. 19, No. 3. Oxford: Oxford University Press (2000).

- Barkan, E., *The Guilt of Nations: Restitution and Negotiating Historical Injustices*. New York: W.W. Norton & Co. (2000).

- ———, "Payback Time: Restitution and the Moral Economy of Nations," in *Tikkun*, Vol. 11, No. 5 (1996).

- Bentwich, N., "International Aspects of Restitution and Compensation for Victims of the Nazis," in *British Year Book of International Law*. London (1955–56).

- Black, R., and Koser, K. (eds.), *The End of the Refugee Cycle? Refugee Repatriation & Reconstruction*. New York: Berghahn Books (1999).

- van Boven, T., *Final Report: Study Concerning the Right to Restitution, Compensation and Rehabilitation for Victims of Gross Violations of Human Rights and Fundamental Freedoms*, Sub-Commission on Human Rights, UN Doc. E/CN.4/Sub.2/1993/8.

- van Boven, T., Flinterman, C., Grünfeld, F., and Westendorp, I. (eds.), *Seminar on the Right to Restitution, Compensation and Rehabilitation for Victims of Gross Violations of Human Rights and Fundamental Freedoms*. Utrecht: University of Limburg and Netherlands Institute of Human Rights (1992).

- Brooks, R. L. (ed.), *When Sorry Isn't Enough: The Controversy over Apologies and Reparations for Human Injustice*. New York: New York University Press (1999).

- Centre on Housing Rights and Evictions (COHRE), *The Pinheiro Principles – United Nations Principles on Housing and Property*

Restitution for Refugees and Displaced Persons. Geneva COHRE: (2006).

- ———, *Sources No. 7: Legal Resources on Housing and Property Restitution for Refugees and IDPs.* Geneva: COHRE (2001).

- ———, *Sources No. 3: Forced Evictions and Human Rights: A Manual for Action.* Geneva: COHRE (1999).

- Deng, Francis M., *Protecting the Dispossessed: A Challenge for the International Community.* Washington, DC: The Brookings Institution (1993).

- Fosseldoorf, H., and Medson, C., *Refugees Repatriation: A Selected and Annotated Bibliography.* Copenhagen: Danish Refugee Council (1994).

- Gasarasi, C. P., "Development, Refugee Generation, Resettlement and Repatriation: A Conceptual Review," in *Refuge – Canada's Periodical on Refugees: Special Issue on Refugee Return,* Vol. 15:2, No. 1 (1997).

- Goodwin-Gill, G. S., "Refugee Identity and Protection's Fading Prospect," in *Refugee Rights and Realities: Evolving International Concepts and Regimes.* Cambridge: Cambridge University Press (1998).

- ———, "The Right to Leave, the Right to Return and the Question of a Right to Remain," in *Colloquium: The Problem of Refugees in the Light of Contemporary International Law Issues.* Geneva: UNHCR (August 1994).

- Hammon, L., "Examining the Discourse of Repatriation: Towards a More Proactive Theory of Return Migration," in *The End of the Refugee Cycle.* New York: Berghahn Books (1999).

- Helle, D., "Enhancing the Protection of Internally Displaced Persons," in *Rights Have No Borders: Worldwide Internal Displacement.* Geneva: Norwegian Refugee Council/Global IDP Survey (1998).

- Helsinki Committee for Human Rights in Serbia, *Refugees on Their Return.* Belgrade: Helsinki Committee for Human Rights in Serbia (1996).

- Henckaerts, J.-M., *Mass Expulsion in Modern International Law and Practice – International Studies in Human Rights, Vol. 41.* The Hague: Kluwer Law International (1995).

- International Committee of the Red Cross, *Going Home: A Guidebook for Refugees.* Sarajevo: ICRC Publication (1997).

- International Council on Human Rights Policy. *Negotiating Justice? Human Rights and Peace Agreements.* Geneva: ICHRP (2006).

- International Federation of the Red Cross and Red Crescent Societies (IFRC), *Dealing with Refugees, Displaced Persons, and Returnee Programmes – Why? What? How?* Geneva: IFRC (1994).

- Jackson-Preece, J., "Ethnic Cleansing as an Instrument of National-State Creation: Changing State Practices and Evolving Legal Norms," *Human Rights Quarterly,* Vol. 20, No. 4: 824 (1998).

- Kirgis, F., "Restitution as a Remedy in US Courts for Violations of International Law," *American Journal of International Law,* Vol. 95, No. 2: 343, (2001).

- Leckie, S. (ed.), *Returning Home: Housing and Property Restitution Rights for Refugees and Displaced Persons – Volume 2.* New York: Transnational Publishers, 2007.

- ———, *Housing, Land and Property Rights in Post-Conflict Societies: Proposals for a New United Nations Institutional Policy Framework.* UNHCR, 2005.

- ———, *Returning Home: Housing and Property Restitution Rights of Refugees and Displaced Persons.* New York: Transnational Publishers (2003).

- ———, "Housing and Property Issues for Refugees and Internally Displaced Persons in the Context of Return: Key Considerations for UNHCR Policy and Practice," *Refugee Survey Quarterly,* Vol. 19, No. 3:5 (August 2000).

- Lee, L., "The Right to Compensation: Refugees and Countries of Asylum," *The American Journal of International Law,* Vol. 80, No. 3:532 (1998).

- Norwegian Refugee Council, *ICLA Handbook, Return Facilitation, Information, Counselling and Legal Assistance.* NRC (2004).

- Pinheiro, P. S., "Housing and Property Restitution in the Context of the Return of Refugees and Internally Displaced Persons," *Final Report* of the Special Rapporteur on Housing and Property Restitution in the Context of the Return of Refugees and Internally Displaced Persons (UN Doc. E/CN.4/Sub.2/2005/17 and UN Doc. E/CN.4/Sub.2/2005/17/Add.1) (2005). [Note: This document contains the official UN text of the Principles on Housing and Property Restitution for Refugees and Displaced Persons, as approved Sub-Commission Resolution 2005/21 of 11 August 2005.]

- ———, "Housing and Property Restitution in the Context of the Return of Refugees and Internally Displaced Persons," Progress Report of the Special Rapportuer, Paulo Sergio Pinheiro. Addendum. Commentary on the Draft Principles on Housing and Property Restitution for Refugees and Displaced Persons (UN Doc. E/CN.4/Sub.2/2004/22/Add.1 [2004]).

- ———, "Housing and Property Restitution in the Context of the Return of Refugees and Internally Displaced Persons," Preliminary Report of the Special Rapporteur Mr. Paulo Sergio Pinheiro, Submitted in accordance with the Sub-Commission Resolution 2002/7 (UN Doc. E/CN.4/Sub.2/2003/11 [2003]).

- ———, "The Return of Refugees' or Displaced Persons' Property, Working Paper Submitted by Mr. Paulo Sergio Pinheiro Pursuant to Sub-Commission Decision 2001/122 (UN Doc. E/CN.4/Sub.2/2002/17 [2002]).

- Reilly, R., and Risser, G., "Return, Resettlement and Reintegration: Application of the Guiding Principles on Internal Displacement," Refugee Survey Quarterly, Vol. 19, No. 2: 170 (2000).

- Schachter, O., "What Price Expropriation? Compensation for Expropriation: The Case Law," American Journal of International Law, Vol. 79: 414 (1985).

- Shelton, D., Remedies in International Human Rights Law. Oxford: Oxford University Press (2000).

- Stavropoulou, M., "The Question of the Right Not to Be Displaced," in Proceedings of the 90th Annual Meeting of the American Society of International Law. Washington, DC: American Society of International Law (27–30 March 1996).

- Thiele, B., "Enforcing the Right to Restitution: Legal Strategies for Indigenous People and the Role of the International Community," in Returning Home: Housing and Property Restitution Rights of Refugees and Displaced Persons – Volume 1 (Scott Leckie, ed.). New York: Transnational Publishers (2003).

- ———, "Housing and Property Restitution in the Context of the Return of Refugees and Internally Displaced Persons: Developments at the United Nations," Netherlands Quarterly of Human Rights, Vol. 18: 283 (June 2000).

- Torpey, J. C., Politics and the Past: On Repairing Historical Injustices, World Social Change. Lanham, MD: Rowman and Littlefield (2003).

- USAID – Office of Conflict Management and Mitigation, Land and Conflict – A Toolkit for Intervention. Washington, DC: USAID (2004).

- Vasarhelyi, I., Restitution in International Law. Budapest: Hungarian Academy of Sciences (1964).

- Wichert, T. "Property Issues in Displacement and Conflict Resolution," Refuge – Canada's Periodical on Refugees: Special Issue on Refugee Return, Vol. 16, No. 6 (December 1997).

- Zayas, A. M. de, "The Legality of Mass Population Transfers: The German Experience 1945–48," East European Quarterly, Vol. XII, No. 1: 2 (1978).

- Zieck, M., UNHCR and Voluntary Repatriation of Refugees: A Legal Analysis. The Hague: Martinus Nijhoff Publishers (1997).

- Zweig, R. W., "Restitution of Property and Refugee Rehabilitation: Two Case Studies," Journal of Refugee Studies, Vol. 6, No. 1–4: 56–64 (1993).

2. COUNTRY/REGIONAL RESOURCES

Africa

- Amnesty International, Report: Rwanda and Burundi, The Return Home: Rumours and Realities. London: Amnesty International (1996).

- Bakewell, O., Refugee Repatriation in Africa: Towards a Theoretical Framework? Centre for Development Studies, University of Bath (1996).

- Bruyn de, et al., *International Precedents for the Restitution of Land Rights in South Africa*. New York: UNDP (1999).

- Budlender, G., "Restitution for Housing and Property Rights: Some Lessons from the South-African Experience," *Refugee Survey Quarterly*, Vol. 19, No. 3 (2000).

- Hanchinamani, B., "The Impact of Mozambique's Land Tenure Policy on Refugees and Internally Displaced Persons," *Human Rights Brief*, Vol. 7, No. 2 (Winter 2000).

- Jones, L., "Giving and Taking Away: The Difference Between Theory and Practice Regarding Property in Rwanda," in *Returning Home: Housing and Property Restitution Rights of Refugees and Displaced Persons – Volume 1* (Scott Leckie, ed.). New York: Transnational Publishers (2003).

- ———, "The Evolution of Property Use in Rwanda," *Refugee Survey Quarterly*, Vol. 19, No. 3 (2000).

- Klung, H., "Historical Claims and the Right to Restitution," in *Agricultural Land Reform in South Africa: Policies, Markets and Mechanisms* (von Zyl, J., ed.). Cape Town: Oxford University Press (1996).

- Naldi, G. J., "Reparations in the Practice of the African Commission on Human and People's Rights," *Leiden Journal of International Law*, Vol. 14, No. 3: 681 (2001).

- Roodt, M. J., "Land Restitution in South Africa," in *Returning Home: Housing and Property Restitution Rights of Refugees and Displaced Persons – Volume 1* (Scott Leckie, ed.). New York: Transnational Publishers (2003).

- Rwelamira, M. R., and Werle, G. (eds.), *Confronting Past Injustices: Approaches to Amnesty, Punishment, Reparation and Restitution in South Africa and Germany*. Cape Town: Butterworths (1996).

- Scollo-Lavizzari, C., *Restitution of Land Rights in an Administrative Law Environment: The German and South African Experience Compared*. Cape Town: University of Cape Town (1996).

- Shriver, D. W., "Apology and Restitution," *South African Outlook* (July–August 1992).

- South African Department of Land Affairs, *International Precedents for the Restitution of Land Rights in South Africa*. SADLA (August 1999).

- Unruh, J., "The Role of Land and Conflict Resolution in a Peace Process: Mozambique's Return to Agriculture," *Refuge*, Vol. 16, No. 1 (December 1997).

- Wilkinson, R., "Going Home: Mozambique Revisited," *Refugees*, Vol. 2, No. 112 (1998).

Asia and the Pacific

- Du Plessis, J., "Slow Start on a Long Journey: Land Restitution Issues in East Timor, 1999–2001," in *Returning Home: Housing and Property Restitution Rights of Refugees and Displaced Persons – Volume 1* (Scott Leckie, ed.). New York: Transnational Publishers (2003).

- Fitzpatrick, D., *Land Claims in East Timor*. Canberra: Asia Pacific Press (2002).

- Gazmere, R., and Dilip B., "Bhutanese Refugees: Rights to Nationality, Return and Property," *Forced Migration Review*, No. 7 (April 2000).

- Lang, T. J., "Refugees from Bhutan: Nationality, Statelessness and the Right to Return," *International Journal of Refugee Law*, Vol. 10, No. 1/2 (1998).

- Leckie, S., and du Plessis J., "Housing, Property and Land Rights in East Timor: Proposal for an Effective Dispute Resolution and Claim Verification Mechanism," *Refugee Survey Quarterly*, Vol. 19, No. 3: 5 (August 2000).

- Norwegian Refugee Council, *Afghanistan's Special Property Disputes Resolution* Court. Kabul: NRC (2005).

- ———, *A Guide to Property Law in Afghanistan*. Kabul: NRC and UNHCR Afghanistan (2005).

- ———, *Land and Property Disputes in Eastern Afghanistan*. Kabul: NRC (2004).

- Rodicio, A. G., "Restoration of Life: A New Theoretical Approach to Voluntary Repatriation Based on a Cambodian Experience of Return," *International Journal of Refugee Law*, Vol. 13, No. 1/2 (2001).

- UNHCR and The National Human Rights Commission, *Land, Housing and Property, Proposals to the Parties for Comprehensively Addressing*

Land, Housing and Property Rights in the Context of Refugee and IDP Return Within and to Sri Lanka. Colombo: UNHCR (2003).

Eastern Europe/CIS/Europe

- Balabkins, N., *West German Reparations to Israel*. New Brunswick, NJ: Rutgers University Press (1971).

- Bentwich, N. D. M., *International Aspects of Restitution and Compensation for Victims of the Nazis*. Oxford: Oxford University Press (1956).

- ———, *The United Restitution Organization, 1948–1968*, London (1968).

- Blacksell M., Born, K. M., and Bohlander, M., "Settlement of Property Claims in Former Eastern Germany," *Geographic Review*, Vol. 86, No. 2 (April 1996).

- Burduli, Z., and Dolidze, A., "Housing and Property Restitution in the Republic of Georgia," in *Returning Home: Housing and Property Restitution Rights of Refugees and Displaced Persons – Volume 1* (Scott Leckie, ed.). New York: Transnational Publishers (2003).

- Comisso, E., "Legacies of the Past or New Institutions? The Struggle over Restitution in Hungary," *Comparative Political Studies*, Vol. 28: 200 (1995).

- Denburg, S. A., "Reclaiming Their Past: A Survey of Jewish Efforts to Restitute European Property," *Boston College Third World Law Journal* Vol. XVIII, No. 2: 233 (1998).

- Dodson, A., and Heiskanen, V., "Housing and Property Restitution in Kosovo," in *Returning Home: Housing and Property Restitution Rights of Refugees and Displaced Persons – Volume 1* (Scott Leckie, ed.). New York: Transnational Publishers (2003).

- Druke, L., "Housing and Property Restitution for Returnees in Tajikistan in the 1990s," *Refugee Survey Quarterly*, Vol. 19, No. 3 (2000).

- Elinger, A. D., "Expropriation and Compensation: Claims to Property in East Germany in Light of German Unification," *Emory International Law Review*, 6: 215 (1992).

- Grimsted, P. K., "Displaced Archives and Restitution Problems on the Eastern Front in the Aftermath of the Second World War," *Contemporary European History*, Vol. 6: 27 (1997).

- Henry, M., *The Restitution of Jewish Property in Central and Eastern Europe*. New York: American Jewish Committee (1997).

- Hochstein, R., "Jewish Property Restitution in the Czech Republic," *Boston College International and Comparative Law Review*, Vol. 19, No. 423 (1995).

- Institute of Jewish Affairs, *Compensation to Victims of Nazi Persecution for Property Losses in Expulsion and Similar Areas*. New York (1957).

- Karasik, M., "Problems of Compensation and Restitution in Germany and Austria," *Law and Contemporary Problems*, Vol. 44 (1951).

- Kozminski, A. K., "Restitution of Private Property: Re-Privatization in Central and Eastern Europe," *Communist and Post-Communist Studies*, Vol. 30, No. 1: 95 (1997).

- OSI, *Forced Migration: Repatriation in Georgia*. New York: Open Society Institute (2000).

- ———, *Return to Tajikistan: Continued Regional and Ethnic Tension*. New York: Open Society Institute (1998).

- ———, *Tajikistan: Refugee Reintegration and Conflict Prevention*. New York: Open Society Institute (1998).

- Ott, A. F., and Desai, K., "Land Reform: Restitution and Valuation in the Republic of Estonia," *Assessment Journal* (September–October 1998).

- Pasachoff, N., and Robert, J. L., "German Restitution to Victims of Nazism," in *Jewish History in 100 Nutshells*. Northvale: Jason Aaronson (1996).

- Rundstedt, S. von, "The Restitution of Property After Communism: Germany, the Czech Republic and Poland," *Parker School Journal of East European Law*, Vol. 4 (1997).

- Schechtman, J. B., *Post-War Population Transfers in Europe: 1945–1955*. Liverpool, Charles Birchall and Sons (1962).

- Shingleton, A. B., Ahrens, V., and Ries, P., "Property Rights in Eastern Germany: An Overview of the Amended Property Law," *Georgia Journal of International and Comparative Law*, Vol. 21, No. 3: 345 (Fall 1991).

- Sieradza, K., *Jewish Restitution and Compensation Claims in Eastern Europe and the Former USSR*. London: Institute of Jewish Affairs (1994).

- ———, *Restitution of Jewish Property in the Czech Republic*. London: Institute of Jewish Affairs (1994).

- Southern, D. B., "Restitution or Compensation: The Land Question in East Germany," *International Comparative Law Quarterly*, Vol. 42: 690 (1993).

- Sugden, J., "Housing and Property Restitution in Turkey," in *Returning Home: Housing and Property Restitution Rights of Refugees and Displaced Persons – Volume 1* (Scott Leckie, ed.). New York: Transnational Publishers (2003).

- Wassgren, H., "Some Reflections on 'Restitutio in Iintegrum' Especially in the Practice of the European Court of Human Rights," *Finnish Yearbook of International Law*, Vol. 6: 575 (1991).

- Weinbaum, L., *Righting an Historic Wrong: Restitution of Jewish Property in Central and East Europe*. Jerusalem: Institute of the World Jewish Congress (1995).

- Youngblood, W. R., "Poland's Struggle for a Restitution Policy in the 1990s." *Emory International Law Review* (1995).

Former Yugoslavia

- Albert, S., "The Return of Refugees to Bosnia and Herzegovina: Peacebuilding with People," *International Peacekeeping*, Vol. 4, No. 3 (1997).

- Avdispahíc, M., *Occupancy Rights: Between International Law and National Law in Dayton Bosnia and Herzegovina*. University of Sarajevo (January 2000).

- Bagshaw, S., "Benchmarks or Deutschmarks? Determining the Criteria for the Repatriation of Refugees to Bosnia and Herzegovina," *International Journal of Refugee Law*, Vol. 99: 566 (1997).

- Bildt, C., *Peaceful Journey: The Struggle for Peace in Bosnia*. London: Weidenfeld and Nicolson (1996).

- Carlowitz, L. von, "Settling Property Issues in Complex Peace Operations: The CRPC in Bosnia and Herzegovina and the HPD/CC in Kosovo," *Leiden Journal of International Law*, Vol. 17: 599 (2004).

- ——— "Crossing the Boundary from the International to the Domestic Legal Realm: UNMIK Lawmaking and Property Rights in Kosovo," *Global Governance*, Vol. 10: 307 (2004).

- Commission for Real Property Claims of Displaced Persons and Refugees (CRPC), *End of Mandate Report (1996–2003)* (2003).

- ———, *Analysis of Property Claim Forms* (26 June 1997).

- ———, *Refugee Return: The Problem of Property Rights*. Sarajevo: Commission for Real Property Claims of Displaced Persons and Refugees (1996).

- Cox, M., *Return, Relocation and Property Rights: A Discussion Paper*. Sarajevo: Commission for Real Property Claims of Displaced Persons and Refugees and UNHCR (1997).

- Cox, M., and Garlick, M., "Musical Chairs: Property Repossessions and Return Strategies in Bosnia and Herzegovina," in *Returning Home: Housing and Property Restitution Rights of Refugees and Displaced Persons – Volume 1* (Scott Leckie, ed.). New York: Transnational Publishers (2003).

- Englebrecht, W., "Property Rights in Bosnia and Herzegovina: The Contributions of the Human Rights Ombudsperson and the Human Rights Chamber Towards Their Protection," in *Returning Home: Housing and Property Restitution Rights of Refugees and Displaced Persons – Volume 1* (Scott Leckie, ed.). New York: Transnational Publishers (2003).

- Garlick, M., "Protection for Property Rights: A Partial Solution? The Commission for Real Property Claims of Displaced Persons and Refugees (CRPC) in Bosnia and Herzegovina," *Refugee Survey Quarterly*, Vol. 19, No. 3: 66–67 (2000).

- Hastings, L., "Implementation of the Property Legislation in Bosnia Herzegovina," *Stanford Journal of International Law*, Vol. 37, No. 221 (2001).

- Houtte, H. van, "The Property Claims Commission in Bosnia-Herzegovina – A New Path to Restore Real Estate Rights in Post-War Societies," in *International Law: Theory and*

Practice: Essays in Honour of Eric Suy (Ken Wellends, ed.). The Hague: M. Nijhoff (2001).

- Hovey, G., "The Rehabilitation of Homes and Return of Minorities to Republika Srpska, Bosnia and Herzegovina," *Forced Migration Review*, No. 7 (April 2000).

- Jacquot, R., "Managing the Return of Refugees to Bosnia and Herzegovina," *Forced Migration Review*, No. 1: 24 (1998).

- Leckie, S., "Resolving Kosovo's Housing Crisis: Challenges for the UN Housing and Property Directorate," *Forced Migration Review: Land and Property Issues for Refugees and IDP's*, No. 7: 12 (April 2000).

- ———, "Kosovo's Next Challenge: Fixing the Housing Mess," *Human Rights Tribune*, Vol. 6, No. 4: 28 (December 1999).

- Madsen, L., "Homes of Origin: Return and Property Rights in Post-Dayton Bosnia and Herzegovina," *Refuge – Canada's Periodical on Refugees: Special Issue on Refugee Return*, Vol. 19, No. 3: 8 (December 2000).

- NRC Civil Rights Project, *Triumph of Form Over Substance: Judicial Termination of Occupancy Rights in the Republic of Croatia and Attempted Legal Remedies – Analysis of 586 Individual Cases*. Croatia: Norwegian Refugee Council (October 2002).

- Open Society Institute, *The Commission for Displaced Persons and Refugees: Options and Issues*. New York: Open Society Institute (1996).

- ———, *Property Law in Bosnia and Herzegovina*. New York: Open Society Institute (1996).

- ———, *Property Law in Republika Srpska*. New York: Open Society Institute (1997).

- Philpott, C., "Though the Dog Is Dead, the Pig Must Be Killed: Finishing with Property Restitution to Bosnia-Herzegovina's IDPs and Refugees," *Journal of Refugee Studies*, Vol. 18, No. 1 (2005).

- Phuong, C., "At the Heart of the Return Process: Solving Property Issues in Bosnia and Herzegovina," *Forced Migration Review*, No. 7 (2000).

- ———, "Freely to Return: Reversing Ethnic Cleansing in Bosnia-Herzegovina," *Journal of Refugee Studies*, Vol. 13, No. 2: 165 (2000).

- Prettitore, P., *The Right to Housing and Property Restitution in Bosnia and Herzegovina: A Case Study* (Working Paper No. 1). Bethlehem: Badil (2003).

- Rosand, E., "The Right to Compensation in Bosnia: An Unfulfilled Promise and a Challenge to International Law," *Cornell International Law Journal*, Vol. 33, 113, No. 1 (2000).

- ———, "The Right to Return under International Law Following Mass Dislocation: The Bosnia Precedent?" *Michigan Journal of International Law*, Vol. 35: 1091 (Summer 1998).

- Scheib, J. M., "Threshold of Lasting Peace: The Bosnian Property Commission, Multiethnic Bosnia and Foreign Policy," *Syracuse Journal of International Law and Commerce*, Vol. 24: 119 (1997).

- UN Centre on Human Settlements (Habitat), *Housing and Property in Kosovo: Rights, Law and Justice: Proposals for a Comprehensive Plan of Action for the Promotion and Protection of Housing and Property Rights in Kosovo* (30 August 1999).

- UNHCR/OHR and the CRPC, *Property and Housing Issues Affecting Repatriates and Displaced Persons in Bosnia and Herzegovina*. Geneva: UNHCR (1999).

- UNHCR Inspection and Evaluation Service, *Review of the UNHCR Housing Programme in Bosnia and Herzegovina*. Geneva: UNHCR (1998).

- ———, *A Regional Strategy for Sustainable Return of Those Displaced by the Conflict in the Former Yugoslavia*. Geneva: UNHCR (1998).

- ———, *Bosnia and Herzegovina Repatriation and Return Operation: 1998*. Geneva: UNHCR (1997).

- Wak-Woya, B., "Property Restitution in Post-War Croatia: Problems and Perspectives," *Refugee Survey Quarterly*, Vol. 19, No. 3 (2000).

- Waters, T. W., "The Naked Land: The Dayton Accords, Property Disputes, and Bosnia's Real Constitution," *Harvard International Law Journal*, Vol. 40 (1999).

- Williams, R., "Post-Conflict Property Restitution and Refugee Return in Bosnia and Herzegovina:

Implications for International Standard-Setting and Practice," *NYU Journal of International Law and Politics*, Vol. 37, No. 3: 441 (2006).

- Zayas, A. de, "The Right to One's Homeland, Ethnic-Cleansing and the International Criminal Tribunal in the Former Yugoslavia," *Criminal Law Forum*, Vol. 6, No. 2 (1995).

Middle East

- Aruri, N. (ed.), *Palestinian Refugees: The Right of Return*. London: Pluto Press (2001).

- Badil Resource Center for Palestinian Residency and Refugee Rights, *Internally Displaced Palestinians, International Protection and Durable Solutions – Badil Information and Discussion Brief, Issue No. 9*. Bethlehem: Badil (2002).

- ————, *Survey of Palestinian Refugees and Internally Displaced Persons 2002*. Bethlehem: Badil (2003).

- ————, *UNHCR, Palestinian Refugees and Durable Solutions – Badil Information and Discussion Brief, Issue No. 7*. Bethlehem: Badil (2002).

- Benvenisti, E., and Zamir, E., "Private Claims to Property Rights in the Future Israeli-Palestinian Settlement," *American Journal of International Law*, Vol. 89: 294 (1995).

- Boling, G., *The 1948 Palestinian Refugees and the Individual Right of Return: An International Law Analysis*. Bethlehem: BADIL (2001).

- Centre on Housing Rights and Evictions (COHRE), *Ruling Palestine: A History of the Legally Sanctioned Jewish-Israeli Seizure of Land and Housing in Palestine*. Geneva: COHRE (2005).

- Fischbach, M. R., *Records of Dispossession: Palestinian Refugee Property and the Arab-Israeli Conflict* (Institute for Palestine Studies Series). New York: Columbia University Press (2003).

- ————, "The United Nations and Palestinian Refugee Property Compensation," *Journal of Palestine Studies*, Vol. 31, No. 2, Issue 122 (Winter 2002).

- Hammarberg, T., *The Palestinian Refugees: After Five Decades of Betrayal – Time at Last?* (Study

Paper 16) Swedish Ministry of Foreign Affairs, Stockholm (2000).

- Howlett, S., "Palestinian Private Property Rights in Israel and the Occupied Territories," *Vanderbilt Journal of Transnational Law*, Vol. 34, No. 1: 117 (2001).

- Human Rights Watch (HRW), *Claims in Conflict: Reversing Ethnic Cleansing in Northern Iraq*, New York: Human Rights Watch (August 2004).

- Jiryis, S., "Settling Historical Land Claims," *Journal of Palestine Studies*, Vol. 27, No. 1: 40 (1997).

- Kalumiya, K., "Angola: A Model Repatriation Programme?" *Refugee Survey Quarterly*, Vol. 23, No. 3: 205 (2004).

- Khaled al-Aza'r, M., *Arab Protection for Palestinian Refugees* (Working Paper No. 8). Bethlehem: BADIL (2004).

- Kramer, T., "The Controversy of a Palestinian 'Right to Return' to Israel," *Arizona Journal of International and Comparative Law*, Vol. 18, No. 3: 979 (Fall 2001).

- Lapidoth, R., "The Right to Return in International Law, with Special Reference to the Palestinian Refugees," *Israel Yearbook on Human Rights*, 103 (1986).

- Lawand, K., "The Right to Return of Palestinians in International Law," *International Journal of Refugee Law*, Vol. 8, No. 4 (1996).

- Nabulsi, K., *Popular Sovereignty, Collective Rights, Participation and Crafting Durable Solutions for Palestinian Refugees* (Working Paper No. 4). Bethlehem: BADIL (2003).

- Parvathaneni, H., *UNRWA's Role in Protecting Palestine Refugees* (Working Paper No. 9). Bethlehem: BADIL (2004).

- Quigley, J., "Displaced Palestinians and a Right of Return," *Harvard International Law Journal*, Vol. 39, No. 1: 171 (Winter 1998).

- Radley, K. R., "The Palestinian Refugees: The Right to Return in International Law," *American Journal of International Law*, 586 (1978).

- Rempel, T., "Housing and Property Restitution: The Palestinian Refugee Case," in *Returning*

Home: Housing and Property Restitution Rights of Refugees and Displaced Persons – Volume 1 (Scott Leckie, ed.). New York: Transnational Publishers (2003).

- Wakim, W., "The "Internally Displaced": Seeking Return within One's Own Land," *Journal of Palestine Studies: A Quarterly on Palestinian Affairs and the Arab-Israeli Conflict*, Vol. 31, No. 1, Issue 121:32 (2001).

- Welchman, L., *The Role of International Law and Human Rights in Peacemaking and Crafting Durable Solutions for Refugees: Comparative Comment* (Working Paper No. 3). Bethlehem: BADIL (2003).

- Wühler, N., "The United Nations Compensation Commission: A New Contribution to the Process of International Claims Resolution," *Journal of International Economic Law*, 249 (1999).

North, Central, and South America

- Bailliet, C., "Property Restitution in Guatemala: A Transnational Dilemma," in *Returning Home: Housing and Property Restitution Rights of Refugees and Displaced Persons – Volume 1* (Scott Leckie, ed.). New York: Transnational Publishers (2003).

- Centre on Housing Rights and Evictions (COHRE), *Housing and Property Restitution for Displaced Persons in Colombia*. Geneva: COHRE (2004).

- Egan, B., "Somos de la Tierra: Land and the Guatemalan Refugee Return," in *Journeys of Fear: Refugee Return and National Transformation in Guatemala* (Liisa L. North and Alan B. Simmons, eds.). Montreal: McGill-Queen's University Press (1999).

- Ferch, M. L., "Indian Land Rights: An International Approach to Just Compensation," *Transnational Law & Contemporary Problems*, Vol. 2, No. 1: 301 (Spring 1992).

- Mahony, L., *Risking Return: NGOs in the Guatemalan Refugee Repatriation*. Uppsala: Life & Peace Institute (1999).

- Newton, N. J., "Compensation, Reparations, and Restitution: Indian Property Claims in the United States," *Georgia Law Review*, 28: 453 (1994).

- Painter, A. R., "Property Rights of Returning Displaced Persons: The Guatemalan Experience," *Harvard Human Rights Journal*, Vol. 9: 145–183 (Spring 1996).

3. USEFUL WEB SITES

- **Centre on Housing Rights and Evictions (COHRE)** – Housing and Property Restitution Programme (HPRP) – http://www.cohre.org

- **Displacement Solutions** – http://www.displacementsolutions.org

- **International Committee of the Red Cross** – http://www.icrc.org

- **Norwegian Refugee Council (NRC)** – http://www.nrc.no

- **Norwegian Refugee Council/Internal Displacement Monitoring Centre(IDMC)** – http://www.internal-displacement.org

- **Relief Web** – http://www.reliefweb.int

- **United Nations** – http://www.un.org

- **United Nations Habitat Programme** – http://www.unhabitat.org

- **United Nations High Commissioner for Refugees (UNHCR)** – http://www.unhcr.org

- **United Nations Office for the Coordination of Humanitarian Affairs(OCHA)** – http://www.ochaonline.un.org

- **United Nations Office of the High Commissioner for Human Rights** – http://www.ohchr.org

Index